Rizos Sakellariou   John Keane
John Gurd   Len Freeman (Eds.)

Euro-Par 2001
Parallel Processing

7th International Euro-Par Conference
Manchester, UK, August 28-31, 2001
Proceedings

 Springer

Series Editors

Gerhard Goos, Karlsruhe University, Germany
Juris Hartmanis, Cornell University, NY, USA
Jan van Leeuwen, Utrecht University, The Netherlands

Volume Editors

Rizos Sakellariou
John Gurd
Len Freeman
University of Manchester, Department of Computer Science
Oxford Road, Manchester M13 9PL, U.K.
E-mail: {rizos/john/lfreeman}@cs.man.ac.uk

John Keane
UMIST, Department of Computation
P.O. Box 88, Manchester M60 1QD, U.K.
E-mail: jak@co.umist.ac.uk

Cataloging-in-Publication Data applied for

Die Deutsche Bibliothek - CIP-Einheitsaufnahme

Parallel processing : proceedings / Euro-Par 2001, 7th International
Euro-Par Conference, Manchester, UK, August 28 - 31, 2001. Rizos Sakellariou
... (ed.). - Berlin ; Heidelberg ; New York ; Barcelona ; Hong Kong ; London ;
Milan ; Paris ; Singapore ; Tokyo : Springer, 2001
 (Lecture notes in computer science ; Vol. 2150)
 ISBN 3-540-42495-4

CR Subject Classification (1998): C.1-4, D.1-4, F.1-3, G.1-2, E.1, H.2

ISSN 0302-9743
ISBN 3-540-42495-4 Springer-Verlag Berlin Heidelberg New York

This work is subject to copyright. All rights are reserved, whether the whole or part of the material is concerned, specifically the rights of translation, reprinting, re-use of illustrations, recitation, broadcasting, reproduction on microfilms or in any other way, and storage in data banks. Duplication of this publication or parts thereof is permitted only under the provisions of the German Copyright Law of September 9, 1965, in its current version, and permission for use must always be obtained from Springer-Verlag. Violations are liable for prosecution under the German Copyright Law.

Springer-Verlag Berlin Heidelberg New York
a member of BertelsmannSpringer Science+Business Media GmbH

http://www.springer.de

© Springer-Verlag Berlin Heidelberg 2001
Printed in Germany

Typesetting: Camera-ready by author, data conversion by DA-TeX Gerd Blumenstein
Printed on acid-free paper   SPIN 10845494   06/3142   5 4 3 2 1 0

Lecture Notes in Computer Science 2150
Edited by G. Goos, J. Hartmanis and J. van Leeuwen

Springer
*Berlin
Heidelberg
New York
Barcelona
Hong Kong
London
Milan
Paris
Tokyo*

Preface

Euro-Par – the European Conference on Parallel Computing – is an international conference series dedicated to the promotion and advancement of all aspects of parallel computing. The major themes can be divided into the broad categories of hardware, software, algorithms, and applications for parallel computing. The objective of Euro-Par is to provide a forum within which to promote the development of parallel computing both as an industrial technique and an academic discipline, extending the frontiers of both the state of the art and the state of the practice. This is particularly important at a time when parallel computing is undergoing strong and sustained development and experiencing real industrial take up. The main audience for and participants in Euro-Par are seen as researchers in academic departments, government laboratories, and industrial organisations. Euro-Par aims to become the primary choice of such professionals for the presentation of new results in their specific areas. Euro-Par is also interested in applications that demonstrate the effectiveness of the main Euro-Par themes.

Euro-Par has its own Internet domain with a permanent web site where the history of the conference series is described: http://www.euro-par.org. The Euro-Par conference series is sponsored by the Association of Computer Machinery and the International Federation of Information Processing.

Euro-Par 2001

Euro-Par 2001 was organised by the University of Manchester and UMIST. Manchester has a long tradition in computing and currently hosts CSAR (Computer Services for Academic Research), a high performance computing service run on behalf of the UK Research Councils by a consortium of SGI, CSC, and the University of Manchester, offering access to world-class high-performance computing facilities.

The format of Euro-Par 2001 follows that of the previous five editions of the conference and consists of a number of topics each individually monitored by a committee of four members. There were originally 20 topics for this year's conference one of which was included for the first time: Parallel and Distributed Embedded Systems. The call for papers attracted 207 submissions of which 108 were accepted. Of the papers accepted, 69 were presented as regular and 39 as research notes. There were 830 reviews collected, an average of 4.01 reviews per paper. Submissions were received from 38 countries (based on the corresponding author's country), 25 of which were represented at the conference. The principal contributors by country were Spain and the UK with 29 submissions each, USA with 26, France with 21 and Germany with 20.

The programme of Euro-Par 2001 also featured invited talks from Jack Dongarra, Ian Foster, Dennis Gannon, Tony Hey, Martin Kersten, and Thomas Sterling. The conference's web site is http://europar.man.ac.uk/.

Acknowledgments

The organisation of an international event such as Euro-Par 2001 was a difficult and time-consuming task that could not have been accomplished without the help of numerous people. First, we are especially grateful to Christian Lengauer and Ron Perrott from the Steering Committee as well as last year's organisers, Thomas Ludwig and Roland Wismüller especially, who gave us the benefit of their experience in the 18 months leading to the conference. We are grateful also to the nearly 80 members of the programme committee, who contributed to form an excellent scientific programme. The programme committee meeting at Manchester in April was well attended and, thanks to the sound preparation by everyone and Christian Lengauer's guidance, resulted in a coherent, well-structured conference.

Locally, there were several people whose help was instrumental at various stages and to whom we owe special thanks. First, our colleagues in the Local Organisation Committee, John Brooke, Terry Hewitt, and Kaukab Jaffri, spent considerable time and effort to make the conference a success. Joanna Leng was involved at the initial preparation phase and was our liaison with last year's organisers. YingLiang Ma maintained the conference's web site. Christopher Rauh, from Munich, came to Manchester for a week and installed a new version of the legacy software for the submission and review of papers which provided the basis for a fully online reviewing system. Owen LeBlanc provided administration support for the computer systems used to host the conference's web site and the paper management software. Finally, Andrew Yates and Janet Adnams from the Manchester Conference Centre supported us with the handling of registration and local arrangements.

Manchester, June 2001

Rizos Sakellariou
John Keane
John Gurd
Len Freeman

Euro-Par Steering Committee

Chair
Christian Lengauer   University of Passau, Germany
Vice Chair
Luc Bougé   ENS Lyon, France
European Representatives
Marco Danelutto   University of Pisa, Italy
Michel Daydé   INP Toulouse, France
Péter Kacsuk   MTA SZTAKI, Hungary
Paul Kelly   Imperial College, UK
Thomas Ludwig   University of Heidelberg, Germany
Luc Moreau   University of Southampton, UK
Henk Sips   Technical University Delft, The Netherlands
Marian Vajtersic   Slovak Academy, Slovakia
Mateo Valero   Universitat Politècnica de Catalunya, Spain
Emilio Lopéz-Zapata   University of Málaga, Spain
Representative of the European Commission
Renato Campo   European Commission, Belgium
Non-European Representatives
Jack Dongarra   University of Tennessee at Knoxville, USA
Shinji Tomita   Kyoto University, Japan
Honorary Members
Ron Perrott   Queen's University Belfast, UK
Karl Dieter Reinartz   University of Erlangen-Nuremberg, Germany

Euro-Par 2001 Local Organisation

Euro-Par 2001 was jointly organised by the University of Manchester and UMIST.

Conference Chairs
John R. Gurd   W. Terry Hewitt
Committee
John M. Brooke   Len Freeman
Kaukab Jaffri   John A. Keane
Rizos Sakellariou

Euro-Par 2001 Programme Committee

Topic 01: Support Tools and Environments

Global Chair
Michael Gerndt   TU München, Germany
Local Chair
Omer F. Rana   University of Wales, Cardiff, UK
Vice Chairs
Marios Dikaiakos   University of Cyprus, Cyprus
Karen Karavanic   Portland State University, USA

Topic 02: Performance Evaluation and Prediction

Global Chair
Allen D. Malony   University of Oregon, USA
Local Chair
Graham Riley   University of Manchester, UK
Vice Chairs
Mark Bull   EPCC, University of Edinburgh, UK
Tomàs Margalef   Universitat Autònoma de Barcelona, Spain
Bernd Mohr   Forschungszentrum Jülich, Germany

Topic 03: Scheduling and Load Balancing

Global Chair
Yves Robert   École Normale Supérieure de Lyon, France
Local Chair
Rupert Ford   University of Manchester, UK
Vice Chairs
Ishfaq Ahmad   Hong Kong University of Science and Technology, Hong Kong
Henri Casanova   University of California, San Diego, USA

Topic 04: Compilers for High Performance

Global Chair
Jens Knoop   University of Dortmund, Germany
Local Chair
Michael F. P. O'Boyle   University of Edinburgh, UK
Vice Chairs
Manish Gupta   IBM T. J. Watson Research Center, USA
Keshav K. Pingali   Cornell University, USA

Topic 05: Parallel and Distributed Databases, Data Mining and Knowledge Discovery

Global Chair
Harald Kosch   University of Klagenfurt, Austria
Local Chair
Pedro R. Falcone Sampaio   University of Manchester, UK
Vice Chairs
Lionel Brunie   INSA, Lyon, France
Abdelkader Hameurlain   IRIT, Université Paul Sabatier, France

Topic 06: Complexity Theory and Algorithms

Global Chair
Gianfranco Bilardi   Università degli Studi di Padova, Italy
Local Chair
Kieran Herley   University College Cork, Ireland
Vice Chairs
Rainer Feldmann   University of Paderborn, Germany
Bruce Maggs   Carnegie Mellon University, USA

Topic 07: Applications on High-Performance Computers

Global Chair
Yoichi Muraoka — Waseda University, Japan

Local Chair
David Snelling — Fujitsu European Centre for Information Technology, UK

Vice Chairs
Randall Bramley — Indiana University, Bloomington, USA
Harry Wijshoff — Leiden University, The Netherlands

Topic 08: Parallel Computer Architecture

Global Chair
André Seznec — IRISA/INRIA-Rennes, France

Local Chair
Henk Muller — University of Bristol, UK

Vice Chairs
Fredrik Dahlgren — Ericsson Mobile Communications, Sweden
Roger Espasa — Universitat Politècnica de Catalunya, Spain

Topic 09: Distributed Systems and Algorithms

Global Chair
Bertil Folliot — Université Pierre et Marie Curie, France

Local Chair
Anne-Marie Kermarrec — Microsoft Research, UK

Vice Chairs
Giovanni Chiola — Università degli Studi di Genova, Italy
Peter Druschel — Rice University, USA

Topic 10: Parallel Programming: Models, Methods and Programming Languages

Global Chair
    Scott B. Baden   University of California, San Diego, USA

Local Chair
    Paul H. J. Kelly   Imperial College, London, UK

Vice Chairs
    Sergei Gorlatch   TU Berlin, Germany
    Calvin Lin   University of Texas, Austin, USA

Topic 11: Numerical Algorithms

Global Chair
    Henk van der Vorst   Utrecht University, The Netherlands

Local Chair
    Rob Bisseling   Utrecht University, The Netherlands

Vice Chairs
    Iain Duff   Rutherford Appleton Laboratory, UK
    Bernard Philippe   IRISA/INRIA-Rennes, France

Topic 12: Routing and Communication in Interconnection Networks

Global Chair
    Ramón Beivide   Universidad de Cantabria, Spain

Local Chair
    Chris Jesshope   University of Hull, UK

Vice Chairs
    Cruz Izu   University of Adelaide, Australia
    Antonio Robles   Universidad Politecnica de Valencia, Spain

Topic 13: Instruction-Level Parallelism and Architecture

Global Chair
    Guang R. Gao   University of Delaware, USA

Local Chair
    Rizos Sakellariou   University of Manchester, UK

Vice Chairs
    Eduard Ayguadé   Universitat Politècnica de Catalunya, Spain
    Christine Eisenbeis   INRIA-Rocquencourt, France

Topic 15: Architectures and Algorithms for Multimedia Applications

Global Chair
David De Roure — University of Southampton, UK

Vice Chairs
Stephan Fischer — Mobile Video Communication GmbH, Germany
Paul McKee — BT Laboratories, UK
Michael Vernick — Lucent Bell Labs, USA

Topic 16: Cluster Computing

Global Chair
Mark Baker — University of Portsmouth, UK

Local Chair
John Brooke — University of Manchester, UK

Vice Chairs
Rajkumar Buyya — Monash University, Australia
Ken Hawick — University of Wales, Bangor, UK

Topic 17: Metacomputing and Grid Computing

Global Chair
Alexander Reinefeld — Konrad-Zuse-Zentrum für Informationstechnik Berlin, Germany

Local Chair
Omer F. Rana — University of Wales, Cardiff, UK

Vice Chairs
Jarek Nabrzyski — Poznan Supercomputing and Networking Centre, Poland
David W. Walker — University of Wales, Cardiff, UK

Topic 18: Parallel I/O and Storage Technology

Global Chair
Peter Brezany   University of Vienna, Austria
Local Chair
Denis A. Nicole   University of Southampton, UK
Vice Chairs
Toni Cortes   Universitat Politècnica de Catalunya, Spain
Marianne Winslett   University of Illinois, Urbana-Champaign, USA

Topic 19: Problem Solving Environments

Global Chair
David W. Walker   University of Wales, Cardiff, UK
Local Chair
Ken Hawick   University of Wales, Bangor, UK
Vice Chairs
Efstratios Gallopoulos   University of Patras, Greece
Domenico Laforenza   CNUCE Institute, CNR-Pisa, Italy

Topic 20: Parallel and Distributed Embedded Systems

Global Chair
Stamatis Vassiliadis   TU Delft, The Netherlands
Local Chair
Sorin D. Cotofana   TU Delft, The Netherlands
Vice Chairs
Francky Catthoor   IMEC, Belgium
Mateo Valero   Universitat Politècnica de Catalunya, Spain

Euro-Par 2001 Referees

(not including members of the programme and organisation committees)

Abdallah, Haiscam
Addison, Cliff
Adve, Vikram
Agrawal, Gagan
Amaral, Jose Nelson
Amarsinghe, Saman
Amiranoff, Pierre
Ancona, Massimo
Anglano, Cosimo
Anterrieu, Eric
Apon, Amy
Arantes, Luciana
Arruabarrena, Agustin
Ashworth, Mike
Atnafu, Solomon
Ayani, Rassul
Badia, Rosa
Baiao, Fernanda
Balls, Greg
Bane, Michael
Basermann, Achim
Beaumont, Olivier
Beckmann, Olav
van den Berghe, Sven
Bernholdt, David
Berrendorf, Rudolf
Bettini, Lorenzo
Bischof, Holger
Bobbio, Andrea
Bodin, François
Boudet, Vincent
Bouganim, Luc
Boutros, Céline
Brent, Richard
Burtscher, Martin
Bylaska, Eric
Cahoon, Brendon
Cardone, Richard
Carpentieri, Bruno
Casanova, Marco Antonio
Chamberlain, Bradford
Chapin, Steve
Chatterjee, Sid
Choi, Sung-Eun
Chretienne, Philippe
Ciaccio, Giuseppe
Cilio, Andrea
Cohen, Albert
Cohen, Norman
Coppola, Massimo
Corbal, Jesus
Costa, Gerardo
Cox, Simon
Czumaj, Artur
Dail, Holly
Dal Zilio, Silvano
Darling, Gordon
Dehnert, Jim
Demsky, Brian
Dias da Cunha, Rudnei
Diaz de Cerio, Luis
Dijkstra, Marjolein
Dolbeau, Romain
Dongarra, Jack
Douglas, Craig
Dutheillet, Claude
Erhel, Jocelyne
Faerman, Marcio
Fagg, Graham
Farcy, Alexandre
Feautrier, Paul
Feitelson, Dror
Feo, John
Ferscha, Alois
Field, Tony
Fink, Stephen
Fischer, Markus
Fisler, Kathi
Fladenmuller, Anne
Fournet, Cedric
Fraigniaud, Pierre
Franceschinis, Giuliana

Franco, Daniel
Frayssé, Valérie
Freitag, Lori
Freitas, Alex
Froehlich, Antonio
Ganesh, Ayalvadi
Garcia, Jordi
Gatlin, Kang Su
Gaujal, Bruno
Geist, Al
Generowicz, Jacek
Genius, Daniela
Gentzsch, Wolfgang
Gerlach, Jens
Germain-Renaud, Cécile
Getta, Janusz
Giraud, Luc
Glendinning, Ian
Gonzalez, Antonio
Gonzalez, Manuel
Goossens, Bernard
Gottschling, Peter
Graham, Paul
Gray, Alex
Gregorio, Jose-Angel
Guerin-Lassous, Isabelle
Guivarch, Ronan
Guralnik, Valery
Gürsoy, Attila
Guyer, Samuel
Guyomarc'h, Frédéric
Haddad, Serge
Hajmahmoud, Yanal
Hammond, Kevin
Hascoet, Laurent
Heinrich, Mark
Henty, David
Herrmann, Christoph
Hidrobo, Francisco
Hill, Steve
Hogstedt, Karin
Hollingsworth, Jeff
Hoteit, Hussein
Hoy, Jeff
Hu, Ziang

Huang, Shing-Tsaan
Hur, Ibrahim
Hurfin, Michel
Huss-Lederman, Steven
Hyde, Daniel
Ilié, Jean-Michel
Inda, Marcia
Irigoin, François
Jalby, William
Jenkins, Kate
Jimenez, Daniel
Jin, Hai
Johnson, Chris
Johnson, David
Johnston, William
Jones, Richard
Juan, Toni
Juurlink, Ben
Karl, Wolfgang
Katz, Daniel
Kavoussanakis, Kostas
Kebbal, Djemai
Kerridge, John
Kessler, Christoph
Kielmann, Thilo
Kirkham, Chris
Kleist, Josva
Klepacki, David
Knijnenburg, Peter
Knobe, Kath
Knottenbelt, William
Kohn, Scott
Koster, Jacko
Kotsis, Gabriele
Krawczyk, Henryk
Krstic, Angela
Kshemkalyani, Ajay
Kuchen, Herbert
Kulkarni, Dattatraya
Kumar, Rishi
Kuzmanov, Georgi
Kwiatkowski, Jan
Lageweg, Casper
Langou, Julien
Lanteri, Stéphane

Larrea, Mikel
von Laszewski, Gregor
Lauwereins, Rudy
Le Fessant, Fabrice
Lechtchinsky, Roman
Leclerc, Tony
Lecussan, Bernard
Lee, Jonghyun
Lee, Kukjin
Lester, David
Lewis, E.
Lifka, David
Limousin, Claude
Loukopoulos, Thanasis
Lourenço, Joao
Lowenthal, David
Lu, Honghui
Lu, Paul
Luecke, Glenn
Luján, Mikel
Luksch, Peter
Luque, Emilio
Lysne, Olav
Ma, Xiaosong
Mancini, Luigi
Manning, Anna
Marcuello, Pedro
Marquez, Andres
Märtens, Holger
Martorell, Xavier
Martyna, Glenn
Mattoso, Marta
Mayes, Ken
McMullen, Donald F.
Megson, Graham
Mehofer, Eduard
Melon, Anne
Merzky, André
Meurant, Gerard
Michaud, Pierre
Miguel, Jose
Mihajlović, Milan
Miller, Crispin
Mitchell, Nick
Mohnen, Markus

Moreau, Luc
Moreira, Jose
Morin, Christine
Morrone, Christopher
Morvan, Franck
Motivala, Ashish
Mourlas, Costas
Mucci, Phil
Müller-Olm, Markus
Mussi, Philippe
Newhall, Tia
Newhouse, Steven
Nisbet, Andy
Nolte, Jorg
Obertelli, Graziano
O'Donnell, John
Ogston, Elizabeth
Oguz, Ceyda
Omnes, Thierry
Ong, Hong
Orduña, Juan Manuel
Ortega, Daniel
Ould-Khaoua, Mohamed
Padua, David
Paprzycki, Marcin
Parchment, Oz
Park, Seungjin
Pearce, David
Peh, Li-Shiuan
Pelagatti, Susanna
Peyre, Jean-François
Pham, Cong-Duc
Philippsen, Michael
Piccardi, Massimo
Piernas, Juan
Pinotti, Maria Cristina
Plateau, Brigitte
Poitrenaud, Denis
Priol, Thierry
Pucceli, Riccardo
Puente, Valentin
Quinlan, Dan
Rabhi, Fethi
Ramanujam, J.
Ramirez, Alex

Ranganathan, Parthasarathy
Rankin, Ricky
Rantakokko, Jarmo
Rastello, Fabrice
Rathmayer, Sabine
Rauchwerger, Lawrence
Reeber, Erik
Reggio, Gianna
Retalis, Simos
Ribaudo, Marina
Rioual, Jean-Christophe
Robinson, Guy
Rodrigues, Luis
Rodríguez, Casiano
Roman, Jean
Roos, Steven
Rownstron, Antony
Rubio, Angel
Rünger, Gudula
Rüthing, Oliver
Sahelices, Benjamin
Sampaio, Sandra
Sanchez, Jesus
Santonja, Vicente
Sazeides, Yiannakis
Schikuta, Erich
Schintke, Florian
Schreiber, Robert
Schulz, Martin
Scott, Stephen
Sebot, Julien
Seinturier, Lionel
Sellars, Malcolm
Sellmann, Meinolf
Senar, Miquel A.
Shapiro, Marc
Shende, Sameer
Shields, Matthew
Silva, Claudio
Silva, Joao Gabriel
Sivasubramaniam, Anand
Smith, Alison
Smith, Garry
Smith, Jim
Smith, Lorna

Sousa, Leonel
Sreedhar, Vugranam
van der Stappen, Frank
Stathis, Pyrrhos
Stéfani, Jean-Bernard
Stewart, Craig
van Straalen, Brian
Su, Alan
de Supinski, Bronis
Sura, Zehra
Suter, Frederic
Symvonis, Antonios
Takeda, Kenji
Takefusa, Atsuko
Talbi, El-Ghazali
Tang, Xinan
Tel, Gerard
Temam, Olivier
Tiskin, Alexandre
Tok, Teck
Torres, Jordi
Traff, Jesper Larsson
Trancoso, Pedro
Trefethen, Anne
Trystram, Denis
Tseng, Chau-Wen
Tseng, Yu-Chee
Tyrtyshnikov, Evgeni
Utard, Gil
Vajtersic, Marian
Vallejo, Fernando
Van Oudheusden, Karel
Vernick, Michael
Vetter, Jeffrey
Voemel, Christof
Walker, Paul
Wang, C. L.
Wanka, Rolf
Wasserman, Harvey
Watson, Ian
Weisz, Willy
Whalley, David
Wismueller, Roland
Wong, Stephan
Worley, Patrick

Wu, Haiping
Wu, Jie
Wu, Peng
Wylie, Brian
Yang, Hongbo
Yang, Tao
Yau, Hon
Yotov, Kamen
Yu, Shengke
Zegeling, Paul
Zhao, Rongcai
Zima, Hans

Table of Contents

Invited Talks

The Anatomy of the Grid: Enabling Scalable Virtual Organizations 1
Ian Foster

Software Component Technology for High Performance Parallel
and Grid Computing 5
Dennis Gannon

Macro- and Micro-parallelism in a DBMS 6
Martin Kersten, Stefan Manegold, Peter Boncz and Niels Nes

An Introduction to the Gilgamesh PIM Architecture 16
Thomas Sterling

High Performance Computing and Trends:
Connecting Computational Requirements with Computing Resources 33
Jack Dongarra

Topic 01

Support Tools and Environments 34
Michael Gerndt

Dynamic Performance Tuning Environment 36
*Anna Morajko, Eduardo César, Tomàs Margalef,
Joan Sorribes and Emilio Luque*

Self-Organizing Hierarchical Cluster Timestamps 46
Paul A.S. Ward and David J. Taylor

A Tool for Binding to Threads Processors 57
Magnus Broberg, Lars Lundberg and Håkan Grahn

VizzScheduler – A Framework for the Visualization
of Scheduling Algorithms 62
Welf Löwe and Alex Liebrich

A Distributed Object Infrastructure for Interaction and Steering 67
Rajeev Muralidhar and Manish Parashar

Checkpointing Facility on a Metasystem 75
Yudith Cardinale and Emilio Hernández

Optimising the MPI Library for the T3E 80
Stephen Booth

Topic 02

Performance Evaluation and Prediction 84
*Allen D. Malony, Graham D. Riley, Bernd Mohr, Mark Bull
and Tomàs Margalef*

Optimal Polling for Latency-Throughput Tradeoffs
in Queue-Based Network Interfaces for Clusters 86
Dmitry Ponomarev, Kanad Ghose and Eugeny Saksonov

Performance Prediction of Oblivious BSP Programs 96
*Jesús A. González, Coromoto León, Fabiana Piccoli, Marcela Printista,
José L. Roda, Casiano Rodríguez and Francisco de Sande*

Performance Prediction of Data-Dependent Task Parallel Programs 106
Hasyim Gautama and Arjan J. C. van Gemund

The Tuning Problem on Pipelines 117
*Luz Marina Moreno, Francisco Almeida,
Daniel González and Casiano Rodríguez*

The Hardware Performance Monitor Toolkit 122
Luiz A. DeRose

VIA Communication Performance on a Gigabit Ethernet Cluster 132
Mark Baker, Paul A. Farrell, Hong Ong and Stephen L. Scott

Performance Analysis of Intel's MMX and SSE: A Case Study 142
Alfred Strey and Martin Bange

Group-Based Performance Analysis
for Multithreaded SMP Cluster Applications 148
Holger Brunst, Wolfgang E. Nagel and Hans-Christian Hoppe

Topic 03

Scheduling and Load Balancing 154
Ishfaq Ahmad, Henri Casanova, Rupert Ford and Yves Robert

On Minimising the Processor Requirements of LogP Schedules 156
Cristina Boeres, Gerson N. da Cunha and Vinod E. F. Rebello

Exploiting Unused Time Slots
in List Scheduling Considering Communication Contention 166
Oliver Sinnen and Leonel Sousa

An Evaluation of Partitioners for Parallel SAMR Applications 171
Sumir Chandra and Manish Parashar

Load Balancing on Networks with Dynamically Changing Topology 175
Jacques M. Bahi and Jaafar Gaber

A Fuzzy Load Balancing Service for Network Computing Based on Jini ... 183
Lap-Sun Cheung and Yu-Kwong Kwok

Approximation Algorithms for Scheduling Independent Malleable Tasks ... 191
J. Błażewicz, M. Machowiak, G. Mounié and D. Trystram

The Way to Produce the Quasi-workload in a Cluster 198
Fumie Costen and John Brooke

Topic 04

Compilers for High Performance 204
Jens Knoop, Manish Gupta, Keshav K. Pingali and Michael F. P. O'Boyle

Handling Irreducible Loops: Optimized Node Splitting vs. DJ-Graphs 207
Sebastian Unger and Frank Mueller

Load Redundancy Elimination on Executable Code 221
Manel Fernández, Roger Espasa and Saumya Debray

Loop-Carried Code Placement 230
Peter Faber, Martin Griebl and Christian Lengauer

Using a Swap Instruction to Coalesce Loads and Stores 235
Apan Qasem, David Whalley, Xin Yuan and Robert van Engelen

Data-Parallel Compiler Support for Multipartitioning 241
Daniel Chavarría-Miranda, John Mellor-Crummey and Trushar Sarang

Cache Models for Iterative Compilation 254
Peter M. W. Knijnenburg, Toru Kisuki and Kyle Gallivan

Data Sequence Locality: A Generalization of Temporal Locality 262
Vincent Loechner, Benoît Meister and Philippe Clauss

Efficient Dependence Analysis for Java Arrays 273
Vivek Sarkar and Stephen Fink

Topic 05

Parallel and Distributed Databases, Data Mining
and Knowledge Discovery 278
*Harald Kosch, Pedro R. Falcone Sampaio, Abdelkader Hameurlain
and Lionel Brunie*

An Experimental Performance Evaluation of Join Algorithms
for Parallel Object Databases 280
*Sandra de F. Mendes Sampaio, Jim Smith,
Norman W. Paton and Paul Watson*

A Classification of Skew Effects in Parallel Database Systems 291
Holger Märtens

Improving Concurrency Control in Distributed Databases
with Predeclared Tables 301
Azzedine Boukerche and Terry Tuck

Parallel Tree Projection Algorithm for Sequence Mining 310
Valerie Guralnik, Nivea Garg and George Karypis

Parallel Pruning for K-Means Clustering
on Shared Memory Architectures 321
Attila Gürsoy and İlker Cengiz

Experiments in Parallel Clustering with DBSCAN 326
Domenica Arlia and Massimo Coppola

Topic 06

Complexity Theory and Algorithms 332
Gianfranco Bilardi, Rainer Feldmann, Kieran Herley and Bruce Maggs

Beyond External Computing:
Analysis of the Cycle Structure of Permutations 333
Jörg Keller and Jop F. Sibeyn

Heaps Are Better than Buckets:
Parallel Shortest Paths on Unbalanced Graphs 343
Ulrich Meyer

Efficient Synchronization of Asynchronous Processes 352
Sandeep Lodha, Punit Chandra, Ajay Kshemkalyani and Mayank Rawat

Topic 07

Applications on High-Performance Computers 358
Yoichi Muraoka, Randall Bramley, David F. Snelling and Harry Wijshoff

Scanning Biosequence Databases on a Hybrid Parallel Architecture 360
Bertil Schmidt, Heiko Schröder and Manfred Schimmler

A Parallel Computation of Power System Equations 371
Y. F. Fung, M.F. Ercan, T.K. Ho and W. L. Cheung

Level-3 Trigger for a Heavy Ion Experiment at LHC 375
*U. Frankenfeld, H. Helstrup, J. Lien, V. Lindenstruth, D. Röhrich,
M. Schulz, B. Skaali, T. Steinbeck, K. Ullaland, A. Vestbø and A. Wiebalck*

Experiences in Using MPI-IO on Top of GPFS
for the IFS Weather Forecast Code 380
Nicholas K. Allsopp, John F. Hague and Jean-Pierre Prost

Topic 08+13

Instruction-Level Parallelism and Computer Architecture 385
Eduard Ayguadé, Fredrik Dahlgren, Christine Eisenbeis, Roger Espasa, Guang R. Gao, Henk Muller, Rizos Sakellariou and André Seznec

Branch Prediction Using Profile Data 386
Alex Ramirez, Josep L. Larriba-Pey and Mateo Valero

An Efficient Indirect Branch Predictor 394
Yul Chu and M. R. Ito

The Behavior of *Efficient* Virtual Machine Interpreters
on Modern Architectures 403
M. Anton Ertl and David Gregg

Improving Conditional Branch Prediction
on Speculative Multithreading Architectures 413
Chitaka Iwama, Niko Demus Barli, Shuichi Sakai and Hidehiko Tanaka

Instruction Wake-Up in Wide Issue Superscalars 418
Soner Önder and Rajiv Gupta

Execution Latency Reduction via Variable Latency Pipeline
and Instruction Reuse 428
Toshinori Sato and Itsujiro Arita

Memory Bandwidth: The True Bottleneck
of SIMD Multimedia Performance on a Superscalar Processor 439
Julien Sebot and Nathalie Drach-Temam

Macro Extension for SIMD Processing 448
Patricio Bulić and Veselko Guštin

Performances of a Dynamic Threads Scheduler 452
Smail Niar and Mahamed Adda

Topic 09

Distributed Systems and Algorithms 457
*Bertil Folliot, Giovanni Chiola, Peter Druschel
and Anne-Marie Kermarrec*

Self-stabilizing Neighborhood Unique Naming under Unfair Scheduler 458
Maria Gradinariu and Colette Johnen

Event List Management in Distributed Simulation 466
Jörgen Dahl, Malolan Chetlur and Philip A. Wilsey

Performance Evaluation of Plausible Clocks 476
Francisco J. Torres-Rojas

Building TMR-Based Reliable Servers Despite Bounded Input Lifetimes ...482
Paul Ezhilchelvan, Jean-Michel Hélary and Michel Raynal

Fractional Weighted Reference Counting 486
Erik Klintskog, Anna Neiderud, Per Brand and Seif Haridi

Topic 10

Parallel Programming: Models, Methods and Programming Languages 491
Scott B. Baden, Paul H. J. Kelly, Sergei Gorlatch and Calvin Lin

Accordion Clocks: Logical Clocks for Data Race Detection 494
Mark Christiaens and Koen De Bosschere

Partial Evaluation of Concurrent Programs 504
Matthieu Martel and Marc Gengler

A Transparent Operating System Infrastructure
for Embedding Adaptability to Thread-Based Programming Models 514
*Ioannis E. Venetis, Dimitrios S. Nikolopoulos
and Theodore S. Papatheodorou*

Nepal – Nested Data Parallelism in Haskell 524
*Manuel M. T. Chakravarty, Gabriele Keller, Roman Lechtchinsky
and Wolf Pfannenstiel*

Introduction of Static Load Balancing
in Incremental Parallel Programming 535
Joy Goodman and John O'Donnell

A Component Framework for HPC Applications 540
*Nathalie Furmento, Anthony Mayer, Stephen McGough,
Steven Newhouse and John Darlington*

Towards Formally Refining BSP *Barriers*
into Explicit *Two – Sided* Communications 549
Alan Stewart, Maurice Clint, Joquim Gabarró and Maria J. Serna

Solving Bi-knapsack Problem Using Tiling Approach
for Dynamic Programming 560
Benamar Sidi Boulenouar

Topic 11

Numerical Algorithms 566
*Henk A. van der Vorst, Rob Bisseling, Iain S. Duff
and Bernard J. Philippe*

Parallel Implementation of a Block Algorithm
for Matrix 1-Norm Estimation 568
Sheung Hun Cheng and Nicholas J. Higham

Eigenvalue Spectrum Estimation and Photonic Crystals 578
*Ken S. Thomas, Simon J. Cox, Duan H. Beckett, Ben P. Hiett,
Jasek Generowicz and Geoffrey J. Daniell*

Polynomial Preconditioning for Specially Structured Linear Systems
of Equations 587
Y. Liang, J. Weston and M. Szularz

Parallel Application of a Novel Domain Decomposition Preconditioner
for the Stable Finite Element Solution
of Three-Dimensional Convection-Dominated PDEs 592
Peter K. Jimack and Sarfraz A. Nadeem

Performance of High-Accuracy PDE Solvers
on a Self-Optimizing NUMA Architecture 602
Sverker Holmgren and Dan Wallin

Topic 12

Routing and Communication in Interconnection Networks 611
Ramón Beivide, Chris Jesshope, Antonio Robles and Cruz Izu

An Analytical Model of Deterministic Routing
in the Presence of Hot-Spot Traffic 613
Samia Loucif and Mohamed Ould-Khaoua

Improving the Accuracy of Reliability Models
for Direct Interconnection Networks 621
Rosa Alcover, Vicente Chirivella and José Duato

On Deadlock Frequency during Dynamic Reconfiguration in NOWs 630
Lorenzo Fernández, José M. García and Rafael Casado

Analysis of Broadcast Communication in 2D Tori 639
A. Shahrabi, M. Ould-Khaoua and L. M. Mackenzie

Optimal Many-to-One Routing on the Mesh with Constant Queues 645
Andrea Pietracaprina and Geppino Pucci

Topic 15+20

Multimedia and Embedded Systems 651
Stamatis Vassiliadis, Francky Catthoor, Mateo Valero and Sorin Cotofana

A Software Architecture
for User Transparent Parallel Image Processing on MIMD Computers 653
Frank Seinstra, Dennis Koelma and Jan-Mark Geusebroek

A Case Study of Load Distribution
in Parallel View Frustum Culling and Collision Detection 663
Ulf Assarsson and Per Stenström

Parallelisable Zero-Tree Image Coding with Significance Maps 674
Rade Kutil

Performance of the Complex Streamed Instruction Set
on Image Processing Kernels 678
*Dmitri Tcheressiz, Ben Juurlink, Stamatis Vassiliadis
and Harry Wijshoff*

A Two Dimensional Vector Architecture for Multimedia 687
Ahmed El-Mahdy and Ian Watson

Multiprocessor Clustering for Embedded Systems 697
Vida Kianzad and Shuvra S. Bhattacharyya

Topic 16

Cluster Computing 702
Mark Baker, John Brooke, Ken Hawick and Rajkumar Buyya

Prioritizing Network Event Handling in Clusters of Workstations 704
Jørgen S. Hansen and Eric Jul

Fault Tolerance for Cluster Computing Based on Functional Tasks 712
Wolfgang Schreiner, Gabor Kusper and Karoly Bosa

PAPI Message Passing Library: Comparison of Performance
in User and Kernel Level Messaging 717
Eric Renault and Pierre David

Implementing Java on Clusters 722
Yariv Aridor, Michael Factor and Avi Teperman

Predictive Coscheduling Implementation
in a Non-dedicated Linux Cluster 732
Francesc Solsona, Francesc Giné, Porfidio Hernández and Emilio Luque

Self-Adjusting Scheduling of Master-Worker Applications
on Distributed Clusters 742
Elisa Heymann, Miquel A. Senar, Emilio Luque and Miron Livny

Smooth and Efficient Integration of High-Availability
in a Parallel Single Level Store System 752
Anne-Marie Kermarrec and Christine Morin

Optimal Scheduling of Aperiodic Jobs on Cluster 764
Ligang He, Hai Jin, Ying Chen and Zongfen Han

HMM: A Cluster Membership Service 773
*Francesc D. Muñoz-Escoí, Óscar Gomis,
Pablo Galdámez and José M. Bernabéu-Aubán*

Dynamic Processor Allocation
in Large Mesh-Connected Multicomputers 783
César A. F. De Rose and Hans-Ulrich Heiss

A New Communication Mechanism for Cluster Computing 793
Andres Ibañez, Valentin Puente, Jose Angel Gregorio and Ramón Beivide

Isolated Dynamic Clusters for Web Hosting 801
Michael Kalantar and Jun Fong

Topic 17

Metacomputing and Grid Computing 805
*Alexander Reinefeld, Omer F. Rana, Jarek Nabrzyski
and David W. Walker*

Cactus Application: Performance Predictions in Grid Environments 807
Matei Ripeanu, Adriana Iamnitchi and Ian Foster

Cactus Grid Computing: Review of Current Development 817
*Gabrielle Allen, Werner Benger, Thomas Dramlitsch, Tom Goodale,
Hans-Christian Hege, Gerd Lanfermann, André Merzky, Thomas Radke
and Edward Seidel*

UNICORE: A Grid Computing Environment 825
Dietmar W. Erwin and David F. Snelling

Portable Parallel CORBA Objects: An Approach to Combine Parallel
and Distributed Programming for Grid Computing 835
Alexandre Denis, Christian Pérez and Thierry Priol

CORBA *Lightweight Components*:
A Model for Distributed Component-Based Heterogeneous Computation .. 845
Diego Sevilla, José M. García and Antonio Gómez

Building Computational Communities from Federated Resources 855
Nathalie Furmento, Steven Newhouse and John Darlington

Scalable Causal Message Logging for Wide-Area Environments 864
Karan Bhatia, Keith Marzullo and Lorenzo Alvisi

From Cluster Monitoring to Grid Monitoring Based on GRM 874
Zoltán Balaton, Péter Kacsuk, Norbert Podhorszki and Ferenc Vajda

Use of Agent-Based Service Discovery
for Resource Management in Metacomputing Environment 882
Junwei Cao, Darren J. Kerbyson and Graham R. Nudd

Topic 18

Parallel I/O and Storage Technology 887
Peter Brezany, Marianne Winslett, Denis A. Nicole and Toni Cortes

Optimal Partitioning for Efficient I/O in Spatial Databases 889
Hakan Ferhatosmanoglu, Divyakant Agrawal and Amr El Abbadi

Improving Network Performance by Efficiently Dealing
with Short Control Messages in Fibre Channel SANs 901
Xavier Molero, Federico Silla, Vicente Santonja and José Duato

Improving MPI-I/O Performance on PVFS 911
Jonathan Ilroy, Cyrille Randriamaro and Gil Utard

Topic 19

Problem Solving Environments 916
*David W. Walker, Ken Hawick, Domenico Laforenza
and Efstratios Gallopoulos*

Remote Visualization of Distributed Electro-Magnetic Simulations 918
Erik Engquist

Solving Initial Value Problems with Parallel Maple Processes 926
Dana Petcu

Design of Problem-Solving Environment for Contingent Claim Valuation .. 935
F. Oliver Bunnin, Yike Guo and John Darlington

Author Index 939

The Anatomy of the Grid:
Enabling Scalable Virtual Organizations

Ian Foster

Mathematics and Computer Science Division, Argonne National Laboratory
Department of Computer Science, The University of Chicago
foster@{mcs.anl.gov,cs.uchicago.edu}
http://www.mcs.anl.gov/~foster

Extended Abstract

The term "the Grid" was coined in the mid-1990s to denote a proposed distributed computing infrastructure for advanced science and engineering [4]. Considerable progress has since been made on the construction of such an infrastructure (e.g., [1,6,7]) but the term "Grid" has also been conflated, at least in popular perception, to embrace everything from advanced networking to artificial intelligence. One might wonder whether the term has any real substance and meaning. Is there really a distinct "Grid problem" and hence a need for new "Grid technologies"? If so, what is the nature of these technologies, and what is their domain of applicability? While numerous groups have interest in Grid concepts and share, to a significant extent, a common vision of Grid architecture, we do not see consensus on the answers to these questions.

My purpose in this talk is to argue that the Grid concept is indeed motivated by a real and specific problem and that there is an emerging, well-defined Grid technology base that solves this problem. In the process, I develop a detailed architecture and roadmap for current and future Grid technologies. I also argue that while Grid technologies are currently distinct from other major technology trends, such as Internet, enterprise, distributed, and peer-to-peer computing, these other trends can benefit significantly from growing into the problem space addressed by Grid technologies.

The real and specific problem that underlies the Grid concept is *coordinated resource sharing and problem solving in dynamic, multi-institutional virtual organizations*. The sharing that we are concerned with is not primarily file exchange but rather direct access to computers, software, data, and other resources, as is required by a range of collaborative problem-solving and resource-brokering strategies emerging in industry, science, and engineering. This sharing is, necessarily, highly controlled, with resource providers and consumers defining clearly and carefully just what is shared, who is allowed to share, and the conditions under which sharing occurs. A set of individuals and/or institutions defined by such sharing rules form what we call a *virtual organization* (VO).

The following are examples of VOs: the application service providers, storage service providers, cycle providers, and consultants engaged by a car manufacturer to perform scenario evaluation during planning for a new factory; members of an industrial consortium bidding on a new aircraft; a crisis management team and the databases and simulation systems that they use to plan a response to an emergency situation; and members of a large, international, multiyear high-energy physics collaboration. Each represents an approach to computing and problem solving based on collaboration in computation- and data-rich environments.

As these examples show, VOs vary tremendously in their purpose, scope, size, duration, structure, community, and sociology. Nevertheless, careful study of underlying technology requirements leads us to identify a broad set of common concerns and requirements. In particular, we see a need for highly flexible sharing relationships, ranging from client-server to peer-to-peer and brokered; for complex and high levels of control over how shared resources are used, including fine-grained access control, delegation, and application of local and global policies; for sharing of varied resources, ranging from programs, files, and data to computers, sensors, and networks; and for diverse usage modes, ranging from single user to multi-user and from performance sensitive to cost-sensitive and hence embracing issues of quality of service, scheduling, co-allocation, and accounting.

Current distributed computing technologies do not address the concerns and requirements just listed. For example, current Internet technologies address communication and information exchange among computers but not the coordinated use of resources at multiple sites for computation. Business-to-business exchanges focus on information sharing (often via centralized servers). So do virtual enterprise technologies, although here sharing may eventually extend to applications and physical devices. Enterprise distributed computing technologies such as CORBA and Enterprise Java focus on enabling resource sharing within a single organization. Storage service providers (SSPs) and application service providers allow organizations to outsource storage and computing requirements to other parties, but only in constrained ways: for example, SSP resources are typically linked with a customer via a virtual private network. Emerging "Internet computing" companies seek to harness idle computers on an international scale [3] but, to date, support only centralized access to those resources. In summary, current technology either does not accommodate the range of resource types or does not provide the flexibility and control on sharing relationships needed to establish VOs.

It is here that Grid technologies enter the picture. Over the past five years, research and development efforts within the Grid community have produced protocols, services, and tools that address precisely the challenges that arise when we seek to build scalable VOs. These technologies include security solutions that support management of credentials and policies when computations span multiple institutions; resource management protocols and services that support secure remote access to computing and data resources and the co-allocation of multiple resources; information query protocols and services that provide configuration, monitoring, status information about resources, organizations, and services [2]; and data management services that locate and transport datasets between storage systems and applications.

Because of their focus on dynamic, cross-organizational sharing, Grid technologies complement rather than compete with existing distributed computing technologies. For example, enterprise distributed computing systems can use Grid technologies to achieve resource sharing across institutional boundaries; in the ASP/SSP space, Grid technologies can be used to establish dynamic markets for computing and storage resources, hence overcoming the limitations of current static configurations.

In my talk, I will expand upon each of these points in turn. My objectives are to (1) clarify the nature of VOs and Grid computing for those unfamiliar with the area; (2) contribute to the emergence of Grid computing as a discipline by establishing a standard vocabulary and defining an overall architectural framework; and (3) define clearly how Grid technologies relate to other technologies, explaining both why various emerging technologies are not yet the Grid and how these technologies can benefit from Grid technologies.

It is my belief that VOs have the potential to change dramatically the way we use computers to solve problems, much as the web has changed how we exchange information. As the examples presented here illustrate, the need to engage in collaborative processes is fundamental to many diverse disciplines and activities: it is not limited to science, engineering and business activities. It is because of this broad applicability of VO concepts that Grid technology is important.

Acknowledgments

This text is based on the introductory section of an article [5] that addresses these issues at length. I thank my co-authors, Carl Kesselman and Steven Tuecke, for their contributions, as well as numerous colleagues with whom we have discussed these ideas.

References

1. J. Beiriger, W. Johnson, H. Bivens, S. Humphreys, R. Rhea. Constructing the ASCI Grid. *Proc. 9th IEEE Symposium on High Performance Distributed Computing*, 2000, IEEE Press.
2. K. Czajkowski, S. Fitzgerald, I. Foster, C. Kesselman. Grid Information Services for Distributed Resource Sharing. *Proc. 10th IEEE Intl. Symp. on High Performance Distributed Computing*, IEEE Press, 2001. www.globus.org/research/papers/MDS-HPDC.pdf
3. I. Foster. Internet Computing and the Emerging Grid. *Nature Web Matters*, 2000. www.nature.com/nature/webmatters/grid/grid.html.
4. I. Foster, C. Kesselman (eds.). *The Grid: Blueprint for a New Computing Infrastructure*, Morgan Kaufmann, 1999.
5. I. Foster, C. Kesselman, S. Tuecke. The Anatomy of the Grid: Enabling Scalable Virtual Organizations. *Intl. Journal Supercomputer Applications*, 2001. www.globus.org/research/papers/anatomy.pdf.

6. W. Johnston, D. Gannon, W. Nitzberg. Grids as Production Computing Environments: The Engineering Aspects of NASA's Information Power Grid. *Proc. 8th IEEE Symposium on High Performance Distributed Computing*, 1999, IEEE Press.
7. R. Stevens, P. Woodward, T. DeFanti, C. Catlett. From the I-WAY to the National Technology Grid. *Communications of the ACM*, 40(11):50-61. 1997.

Software Component Technology for High Performance Parallel and Grid Computing

Dennis Gannon

Department of Computer Science, Indiana University

Abstract

A software component framework is one where an application designer programs by composing well understood and tested "components" rather than writing large volumes of not-very-reusable code. The software industry has been using component technology to build desktop applications for about ten years now. More recently this idea has been extended to application in distributed systems with frameworks like the Corba Component Model and Enterprise Java Beans. With the advent of Grid computing, high performance applications may be distributed over a wide area network of compute and data servers. Also "peer-to-peer" applications exploit vast amounts of parallelism exploiting the resources of thousands of servers.

In this talk we look at the problem of building a component technology for scientific applications. The common component architecture project seeks to build a framework that allows software components runing on a massively parallel computers to be linked together to form wide-area, high performance application services that may be accessed from desktop applications. This problem is far from being solved and the talk will describe progress to date and outline some of the difficult problems that remain to be solved.

Macro- and Micro-parallelism in a DBMS

Martin Kersten, Stefan Manegold, Peter Boncz, and Niels Nes

CWI
Kruislaan 413, 1098 SJ, Amsterdam, The Netherlands

Abstract. Large memories have become an affordable storage medium for databases involving hundreds of Gigabytes on multi-processor systems. In this short note, we review our research on building relational engines to exploit this major shift in hardware perspective. It illustrates that key design issues related to parallelism poses architectural problems at all levels of a system architecture and whose impact is not easily predictable. The sheer size/complexity of a relational DBMS and the sliding requirements of frontier applications are indicative that a substantial research agenda remains wide open.

1 Introduction

Database management systems have become a commodity system-software component to manage huge amounts of business data in a reliable and efficient manner. Its application space encompasses the whole spectrum of storage systems, ranging from databases fitting on a smart-card up to dealing with the petabyte archives produced in nuclear physics experiments. Likewise, it spans the complete space of responsiveness, from sub-second transaction management in telecom and financial sectors up to management of long-living transactions in aircraft construction.

This broad applicability and wide-spread use of a DBMSs make their design still an art, balancing end-user requirements with state-of-the-art software/hardware technology. The easy part is the functional requirement list. A new system should support an (object-)relational data model with its algebraic operators, transaction management and facilities to extend the system architecture with application-specific code.

The more difficult part is to predict the resources needed to manage the physical database itself and to predict hardware trends to satisfy these needs. For over two decades, commercial database systems have been designed from the assumption that a database is stored on disk with too little memory to keep a hot-set resident. Furthermore, they assume that the processing power offered by a single CPU is often insufficient to satisfy the application needs for cycles. Given manufacturing limitations to satisfy infinite memory and CPU power, a substantial effort has been devoted to realize parallel and distributed database technology.

1.1 Main-Memory Database Systems

Within the solution space for DBMS architectures we have focused our attention on systems with a sizable main-memory and deployment of parallel processing. The key assumptions underlying this part of the design space are that *the database hot-set can be economically held in main-memory, operating system technology will evolve and should be relied upon*, and *commodity hardware and parallel processing can be used to leverage the shortage of* CPU *power*. The two reference database architectures developed are: PRISMA and Monet.

PRISMA The PRISMA project (1986-1992) [3,22] was a large national project geared at advancing computer science technology in the area of language design, operating system design, database system design, and network technology. The central theme was to develop a parallel object-oriented programming language with supportive operating system on which a complete SQL-based DBMS should run. The hardware platform consisted of 100 Motorola microprocessors with a total of 1.5 GByte main-memory. A sizable amount for the era it was constructed and used. The processors were linked into a configurable network to facilitate experimentation with network topologies. Each processor pair shared a disk (50GB) for persistence.

Monet The Monet project (1993-) was set-up to explore in more detail the effect of main-memory database technology. Furthermore, it took an offbeat approach in the design of the DBMS internals. The relational database tables were broken down into binary tables only, the relational algebra took a *materialize all intermediates* approach, indexing and operator optimization became automatic, and resource competition, such as transaction management, was moved to the intermediate language. Monet has been in production both experimentally and commercially since 1995. It runs under a variety of operating systems, i.e. NT, Linux, Solaris, IRIX, AIX. The largest experimentation platform is a SGI Origin 2000 with 32 CPUs and 64GB of RAM.

1.2 Parallel Database Technology

Both systems illustrate extreme approaches in terms of software architectures addressing the key design issues of a DBMS:

- *Persistent storage*, for which conventionally disk-farms and RAID systems are being used to secure the database content. Their capabilities define the bandwidth and latency to be expected when access randomly data.
- *Communication infrastructure*, which provides the framework to offload work over multiple systems. The full range of system architectures can be considered, e.g. shared-everything, shared-nothing, shared-disk, SIMD, etc..
- *Physical layout*, which encompasses the data structures to organize the records in memory and on persistent store, as well as the index structures needed to achieve reasonable performance.
- *Execution paradigm*, which dictates the way relational algebra expressions are being evaluated. The predominant approach is to use an operator pipeline, which makes resource management of intermediate results relatively

easy at the expense of repeated context switches amongst the operators. The alternative approach is to materialize the result of every operator before proceeding to the next level in the algebraic expression. The advantage is a simplified parallelism technique at the expense of possibly substantial storage overhead.
- *Transaction management*, which involves all techniques to support concurrent access to the database and to safeguard operations against accidental loss.
- *Query optimizer*, which involves the intelligence layer to derive a optimal plan of execution for a given database query. Query optimizers commonly generate a large portion of the semantic-equivalent formulations of a database query and select a good plan by running a cost-metric over each plan.

For a more detailed introduction to these topics we refer to the excellent textbook such as by Valduriez and Oszu [18] and the plethora of research results accessible through the digital library http://www.informatik.uni-trier.de/~ley/db/index.html.

In the remainder of this note we illustrate the choices and the lessons learned from building and deployment of just two large-scale experimental systems.

2 Macro-parallelism

The PRISMA project [21] can be characterized as a system architecture geared at exploring opportunities for macro parallelism, i.e. the system used functional components and large storage fragments as the unit of distribution and parallel processing.

The relational tables were broken down into horizontal fragments using a hash-distribution over their primary keys. These fragments were distributed over the processor pool by the operating system, without any influence of the DBMS software. Each table fragment was controlled by a small-footprint relational algebra engine. SQL queries where translated into a distributed relational algebra expression, whose execution was handled by a distributed query scheduler. Likewise, a distributed concurrency manager was installed for transaction management.

The implementation language POOL (Parallel Object-oriented Language) [2,1] was developed by research groups at Philips Natlab and universities. Together they realized a language-specific operating system and compiler toolkit for this language, with the ambition that parallelism can be transparently handled at those levels. It was the (contractual) target language for the database designers. The language implementation did not provide any control over the object granularity (initially). Rather, every object -small and large- was mapped into a separate process, which communicates with its environment through message passing. It was the task of the network infrastructure to resolve locality and a distributed scheduler ensured load distribution. Typically a small POOL program led to several thousands of objects distributed over the processor pool.

From the perspective of the database designers this level of transparency and object granularity caused major problems. Traversing simple binary search trees to organize information in the database became excessively expensive, e.g. memory references were cast into inter-process communication. Furthermore, the query optimizer of a DBMS is able to construct a proper execution plan, based on size, CPU, and communicating cost estimates. The underlying platform made this hardly useful, because the placement of intermediate results as well as the location of the operator threads was decided by the operating system without knowledge about the global (optimal) plan of action. Halfway of the project this had to be rectified using an advisory scheme to ensure locality of objects on a single processor and to identify where expensive message passing could be replaced by memory references.

Despite the limitations and problems caused by the implementation platform, the PRISMA project demonstrated that main-memory distributed database techniques are effective to speed-up performance on large processor clusters. Parallelism techniques were geared towards macro-entities in terms of size and granules of execution. Novel relational-join algorithms were discovered [20,13] to achieve linear speed-up over >60 processors, schemes for dynamic query scheduling were developed [19], and progress was made in semantic query optimization and reliability.

3 Micro-parallelism

The most disappointing result of the PRISMA project was the in-surmounted problem to make macro-parallelism transparent at the system programming language interface. In addition, the software architecture of PRISMA/DB followed traditional lines, mimicking techniques nowadays common in commercial systems. As a result we started from scratch in 1993 with a new system architecture, nicknamed *Monet* [1].

The main design considerations underlying PRISMA/DB were carried over, i.e. the hot-set is memory resident, rely on the operating system, and move transaction decisions as high as possible in the application infrastructure. In addition, we envisioned a need to open up the kernel to accommodate better user-defined functions to support non-administrative applications. The most drastic steps where taken in the physical database design and the query execution paradigm. In combination with the coding style it lead to focusing on micro parallelism, i.e. dealing with critical instruction threads to extract the performance offered by a main-memory database on a multi-pipeline processor.

A long standing implementation approach is to physically cluster the fields of database records, to group those records into pages, and subsequently map them to segments (files or disk volumes). Instead, we took an orthogonal approach by breaking up relational tables into collections of binary tables. The underlying reason was that this way we simplified introduction of abstract data types, e.g.

---

[1] http://www.cwi.nl/~monet

polygons, to organize their storage without concern on the total record layout. Furthermore, both columns of a binary table could be easily extended with search accelerators. Such auxiliary structures were, however, constructed on the fly and basically never saved in persistent store.

Since the primary store for tables is main-memory, one doesn't have the luxury to permit sloppy programming without experiencing a major performance degradation. Sloppy programming in disk-based systems doesn't have that effect unless the system becomes CPU-bound. The consequence was that the database kernel algorithms were carefully engineered using code-expansion techniques to avoid type-analysis at the inner layers of the algorithms. For example, Monet version 4 contains about 55 implementations of the relational *select* operator, 149 for the unary operators, 355 for the relational *join* and *group* operations, and 72 for table aggregations.

The query execution paradigm was shifted towards concrete materialization of intermediates, thereby stepping away from the still predominant operator pipeline approach. The primary reason was to optimize the operators in isolation, i.e. each relational operator started out with just-in-time, cost-model based optimization decisions on the specific algorithm to use and beneficial search accelerators.

The primary interface to Monet became a textual-based Monet Interface Language [4]. This language is the target for both SQL-based and object-oriented front-ends [9,11]. The overhead incurred by textual interaction with those front-ends was negligible, an observation shared nowadays in the community with the broad deployment of XML-based interaction schemes.

With a mature database kernel emerging from our lab in 1996 we embarked upon a series of performance studies. The first studies were aimed to assess the main-memory based approach against the traditional database techniques and its scalability beyond the main-memory size. To illustrate, in [9] we demonstrated the achievable performance on the TPC-D benchmark, and [5] illustrates that the engine could beneficially be used to support an object-oriented front-end. A short side-track assessed its performance capabilities as an active DBMS kernel [14].

3.1 Architecture-Aware Optimization

Our recent studies showed that database systems — when designed and implemented "the traditional way" — do not lack CPU power [16,15]. Actually, current database system are not even able to fully exploit the massive CPU power that nowadays super-scalar CPUs provide with their ever-rising clock speeds and inherent micro-parallelism. Rather, when executing database code, CPUs are stalled most of the time waiting for data to be brought in from main memory. While memory bandwidth has been improving reasonably (though not as rapidly as I/O-bandwidth or especially CPU speed) over the recent past, memory latency has stagnated or even got worse. As opposed to scientific programs, database operators usually create a random memory access pattern such as pointer-chasing. Hence, the performance is limited by latency rather than by bandwidth, making memory access the major performance bottleneck.

Choosing for vertically decomposed tables in Monet, was already a first step to improve memory performance as this avoids moving "superfluous" data around. In [6], we demonstrate, how properly designed cache-conscious algorithms can eliminate the memory access bottleneck by reducing random memory access to the fastest level of the systems cache memory hierarchy. Once memory access is optimized (i.e., the number of data cache misses is minimized), the costs of sloppy programming become obvious. The penalties for instruction cache misses and branch mispredictions — formerly "hidden" behind memory access — now dominate the performance. Using code-expansion techniques in Monet, we managed to eliminate both instruction cache misses (by having small-footprint operators) and most branch mispredictions (by avoiding type-dependent branching and/or function calls in the innermost loops) [16]. While now being "almost" CPU bound, the code is still not able to fully exploit the CPU inherent parallelism, e.g. moving from a 4 to a 9 instruction pipeline architecture did not significantly improve performance. We believe that there are three reasons for this. First, algorithm-inherent conditionals still require branches and hence keep the code "unpredictable" for compilers and the CPU itself. Second, loop bodies are too small to provide enough "meat" for parallelism. And third, the work to be done per data item is usually too small to keep more than one execution pipeline busy while loading the next data from memory.

3.2 3-Tier Query Optimization

Since 1999 we have shifted our focus on the middle-tier layer of a DBMS, i.e. its query optimizer infrastructure. The state-of-the-art in query optimization is for over a decade dictated by cost-based optimizers [17]. However, these model all assume that every query basically runs in isolation on a given platform, the database is in a cold-state, and that CPU- and I/O- activity can be analytically described. Although ideal assumptions for a laboratory setup and a sound basis to construct analytical models, it is far from reality.

Database systems are mostly called from applications that determine a context of interest, where queries are semantically related. Likewise, ad-hoc interactive session typically show quite an overlap amongst queries as the user successively refines it to locate the information of interest. Aside from personal use of a database, it is more common that at any time there are tens to hundreds of users interacting with a database, causing quite some overlap in interest and, indirectly, sharing/caching of critical table fragments.

To avoid inaccurate predictions and better exploit opportunities offered by a large query stream, we developed a novel just-in-time optimization scheme. Our hypothesis is that the optimization process can be split into a three-tier framework without jeopardizing the effectiveness of the optimization process. Instead of exploring a single huge search space in one optimization phase per query, we employ three smaller optimizers — *Strategic*, *Tactical*, and *Operational*.

The *strategic* optimizer exploits the application logic and data model semantic (e.g. rule constraints) for finding a good plan. At this level, the cost of a plan is only based on factors that are independent from the state of the DBMS, like intermediate result size and sort order, thus making volume reduction the prime optimization target. The plan generated by the strategic optimizer only describes the partial order amongst the database operators. The *tactical* optimizer consumes the query streams and minimize the resource requirements at runtime by exploiting the overlap encountered. It rewrites the plans such that (within the limits of the available resources, e.g. memory) the total execution time of all plans are minimized. The *operational* optimization works at operator evaluation time. The decisions taken focus on algorithm selection, which is based on the properties of their parameters and the *actual* state of the database. This technique is heavily exploited in Monet [4] already and proven effective in concrete real-life products.

This architecture is currently being build into Monet Version 5 and is expected to lead to a drastic speed-up for database intensive applications.

4 Applications

Development of novel database technology is greatly speed-up using concrete and challenging application areas. In the context of the PRISMA project this aspect was largely neglected, i.e. we were looking for a 'pure' parallel SQL database solution. During the development of Monet we used three major application areas to steer functionality and to assess its performance: geographical information systems, data mining, and image processing.

4.1 Geographical Information Systems

The first challenge for the Monet architecture was to support geographical applications [7]. Therefore, we realized a geographical extension module to implement the Sequoia benchmark [12]. This benchmark, developed at University of Berkeley, focuses on three aspects: user-defined functions, query performance, and scalability.

Its implementation pushed the development of extensibility features, such as an easy to use API generator for C/C++ based extension modules. Moreover, it demonstrated that many of the algorithms prevalent in this area could effectively use the restricted storage model and algebraic structure.

The query performance obtained was an order of magnitude better than reported by the competition. The queries ran in fractions of seconds without the need to rely on parallel processing at all.

The scalability aspect of the benchmark (>1Gb) made full reliance on a database stored in main memory impossible. The approach taken in Monet to use memory-mapped files over binary tables turned out to be profitable. A surprise was that clustering data in main-memory still made a big difference, effectively killing the to date notion that access cost in main-memory can be considered uniform. A signal that cache-aware algorithms were needed even in a database management system.

4.2 Data Mining

The second challenge for the Monet architecture arose when it became the prime vehicle for data mining in a commercial setting. In 1995 we established the company Data Distilleries (www.datadistilleries.com), which developed and sold solutions for the analytical CRM space using Monet at its core.

The negative effect of this move for the Monet research team was that functionality and stability became somewhat dictated by the environment. In practical terms it meant that transaction processing features where put aside to focus on query-dominant environments. Moreover, the application interface language (MIL) was enhanced to simplify off-loading tasks to the database server. Finally, an extensive quality control system was set up to support overnight compilations and testing on all platforms supported.

On the positive side, early exposure to real end-user needs pushes the architecture to its limits. The database and query loads to be supported exploded in size, filling complete disk farms, and the functionality required for data mining called for extending the database kernel with efficient grouping and aggregation operations.

The effects of this engineering phase became visible in 1998, when we compared the behavior of Monet against Oracle. For this purpose we designed a benchmark reflecting the typical interaction between the data mining software and the database kernel. Subsequently we assessed the behavior of both systems in a memory-bound and disk-bound setting. For Monet it proved to provide the required supreme performance and also scaled beyond the main-memory limitations without additional tuning of the system (see [8]).

4.3 Image Processing

Given the good performance observed in both data mining and geographical information systems stressed our desire to find application domains that could both benefit from database technology and that posed real performance challenges. An area satisfying this criteria is image retrieval from multi-media databases.

In this context we are currently experimenting with indexing techniques based on traditional color-feature vectors scaled to handle over a million images. Moreover, we are looking for effective techniques that permit sub-image retrieval, an area often ignored in the image processing community. In [11,10] we have demonstrated that such indices can be readily supported in Monet without impairing the performance.

Furthermore, we have introduced the notion of *query articulation*, the process to aid querying an image database using image spots marked by the user as relevant for retrieval. Finding such spots in the image collection is supported by the sub-image indexing scheme. Adequate performance will be obtained with the 3-tier query optimizer, because many interactions lead to overlapping sub-queries.

5 Conclusions

In this short note we have covered fifteen years of research with a focus on database technology using large main-memories and parallelism at a macro and micro scale. The large body of expertise obtained [2] illustrate that to some extend we are confronted with a legacy problem. The commercial DBMS software architecture and its mapping to current hardware is far from optimal. Whether it is economical justified to replace them totally remains to be seen, but new markets may be conquered using database solutions currently available in laboratories only.

Recognition of this state of affairs provides a sufficient base to pursue system architecture research for DBMS and the applications it supports. The parallel research community can contribute to the evolution of database technology in many ways. To illustrate, just-in-time optimization and scheduling techniques at the high-end of the memory hierarchy should be improved. Likewise, cache-aware indexing schemes and relational operator algorithms may prove to form the basis for an order of magnitude performance improvement. But, the proof of the eating is in the pudding, being deployment of the solution in a concrete application setting with recognized benefit for the end-user.

References

1. P. America and J. J. M. M. Rutten. A Layered Semantics for a Parallel Object-Oriented Language. *Formal Aspects of Computing*, 4(4):376–408, 1992.
2. P. America and F. van der Linden. A Parallel Object-Oriented Language with Inheritance and Subtyping. In *Conference on Object-Oriented Programming Systems, Languages, and Applications / European Conference on Object-Oriented Programming (OOPSLA/ECOOP)*, pages 161–168, Ottawa, Canada, October 1990.
3. P. M. G. Apers, C. A. van den Berg, J. Flokstra, P. W. P. J. Grefen, M. L. Kersten, and A. N. Wilschut. PRISMA/DB: A Parallel Main Memory Relational DBMS. *IEEE Transactions on Knowledge and Data Engineering (TKDE)*, 4(6):541–554, December 1992.
4. P. A. Boncz and M. L. Kersten. MIL Primitives for Querying a Fragmented World. *The VLDB Journal*, 8(2):101–119, October 1999.
5. P. A. Boncz, F. Kwakkel, and M. L. Kersten. High Performance Support for OO Traversals in Monet. In *Proceedings of the British National Conference on Databases (BNCOD)*, volume 1094 of *Lecture Notes in Computer Science*, pages 152–169, Edinburgh, United Kingdom, July 1996.
6. P. A. Boncz, S. Manegold, and M. L. Kersten. Database Architecture Optimized for the New Bottleneck: Memory Access. In *Proceedings of the International Conference on Very Large Data Bases (VLDB)*, pages 54–65, Edinburgh, United Kingdom, September 1999.
7. P. A. Boncz, W. Quak, and M. L. Kersten. Monet and its Geographical Extensions: a Novel Approach to High-Performance GIS Processing. In *Proceedings of the International Conference on Extending Database Technology (EDBT)*, volume 1057 of *Lecture Notes in Computer Science*, pages 147–166, Avignon, France, June 1996.

---

[2] see http://www.cwi.nl/htbin/ins1/publications

8. P. A. Boncz, T. Rühl, and F. Kwakkel. The Drill Down Benchmark. In *Proceedings of the International Conference on Very Large Data Bases (VLDB)*, pages 628–632, New York, NY, USA, August 1998.
9. P. A. Boncz, A. N. Wilschut, and M. L. Kersten. Flattening an Object Algebra to Provide Performance. In *Proceedings of the IEEE International Conference on Data Engineering (ICDE)*, pages 568–577, Orlando, FL, USA, February 1998.
10. H. G. P. Bosch, A. P. de Vries, N. Nes, and M. L. Kersten. A case for Image Querying through Image Spots. In *Storage and Retrieval for Media Databases 2001*, volume 4315 of *Proceedings of SPIE*, pages 20–30, San Jose, CA, USA, January 2001.
11. H. G. P. Bosch, N. Nes, and M. L. Kersten. Navigating Through a Forest of Quad-Trees to Spot Images in a Database. Technical Report INS-R0007, CWI, Amsterdam, The Netherlands, February 2000.
12. J. Dozier, M. Stonebraker, and J. Frew. Sequoia 2000: A Next-Generation Information System for the Study of Global Change. In *Proceedings of the IEEE Symposium on Mass Storage Systems (MSS)*, pages 47–56, L'Annecy, France, June 1994.
13. M. A. W. Houtsma, A. N. Wilschut, and J. Flokstra. Implementation and Performance Evaluation of a Parallel Transitive Closure Algorithm on PRISMA/DB. In *Proceedings of the International Conference on Very Large Data Bases (VLDB)*, pages 206–217, Dublin, Ireland, August 1993.
14. M. L. Kersten. An Active Component for a Parallel Database Kernel. In *International Workshop on Rules in Database Systems (RIDS)*, number 985 in Lecture Notes in Computer Science, pages 277–291, Athens, Greece, September 1995.
15. S. Manegold, P. A. Boncz, and M. L. Kersten. Optimizing Database Architecture for the New Bottleneck: Memory Access. *The VLDB Journal*, 9(3):231–246, December 2000.
16. S. Manegold, P. A. Boncz, and M. L. Kersten. What happens during a Join? — Dissecting CPU and Memory Optimization Effects. In *Proceedings of the International Conference on Very Large Data Bases (VLDB)*, pages 339–350, Cairo, Egypt, September 2000.
17. S. Manegold, A. Pellenkoft, and M. L. Kersten. A Multi-Query Optimizer for Monet. In *Proceedings of the British National Conference on Databases (BNCOD)*, volume 1832 of *Lecture Notes in Computer Science*, pages 36–51, Exeter, United Kingdom, July 2000.
18. M. T. Ozsu and P. Valduriez. *Principles of Distributed Database Systems*. Prentice Hall, Englewood Cliffs, NJ, USA, 1991.
19. C. A. van den Berg. *Dynamic query processing in a parallel object-oriented database system*. PhD thesis, Universiteit van Amsterdam, Amsterdam, The Netherlands, 1994.
20. A. N. Wilschut, J. Flokstra, and P. M. G. Apers. Parallel Evaluation of Multi-Join Queries. In *Proceedings of the ACM SIGMOD International Conference on Management of Data (SIGMOD)*, pages 115–126, San Jose, CA, USA, May 1995.
21. A. N. Wilschut, J. Flokstra, and P. M. G. Apers. Parallelism in a Main-Memory DBMS: The performance of PRISMA/DB. In *Proceedings of the International Conference on Very Large Data Bases (VLDB)*, Vancouver, BC, Canada, 1995.
22. A. N. Wilschut, P. W. P. J. Grefen, P. M. G. Apers, and M. L. Kersten. Implementing PRISMA/DB in an OOPL. In *International Workshop on Database Machines (IWDM)*, pages 97–111, Deauville, France,, June 1989.

An Introduction to the Gilgamesh PIM Architecture

Thomas Sterling

Center for Advanced Computing Research, California Institute of Technology, and
High Performance Computing Group, NASA Jet Propulsion Laboratory

1 Introduction

Throughout the history of computer implementation, the technologies employed for logic to build ALUs and the technologies employed to realize high speed and high-density storage for main memory have been disparate, requiring different fabrication techniques. This was certainly true at the beginning of the era of electronic digital computers where logic was constructed from vacuum tubes and main memory was produced by wired arrays of magnetic cores. But it is also true with today's conventional computing systems. Yes, both logic and memory are now fabricated with semiconductors. But the fabrication processes are quite different as they are optimized for very different functionality. CMOS logic pushes speed of active components while DRAM storage maximizes density of passive capacitive bit cells. As a consequence of this technology disparity between the means of achieving distinct capabilities of memory and logic, computer architecture has been constrained by the separation of logical units and main memory units. The *von Neumann bottleneck* is the communication's channel choke point between CPUs and main memory resulting from the separation imposed by these distinct device types. Much of modern microprocessor architecture is driven by the resulting data transfer throughput and latency of access due to this separation as well as the very different clock speeds involved. More subtle but of equal importance are the limitations imposed on the diversity of possible structures that might be explored and achieved were it feasible to bridge this gap and intertwine memory and logic. An entire class of computer structure design space has been precluded because of this technological barrier. Content addressable memories, cellular automata, systolic arrays, neural networks, and adaptive computing structures have all been limited in their practicality and application because of the isolation of DRAM cells from CMOS logic. And without the means of embedding logic in memory, many other structures not yet conceived will never be investigated, let alone practically applied to real-world problems.

Several years ago, semiconductor device manufacturers developed a new generation of process and established fabrication lines that allowed for the first time the design and implementation of single chip components integrating CMOS logic with DRAM cells. The technology barrier between logic and memory was eliminated. For the initial processes, some compromises were necessary: device density and logic speeds were not as high as the best segregated technology wafers of the time. Gate switching rates were approximately a factor of 2 or more slower. But many other advantages were accrued by this breakthrough in manufacturing processes. Since then, second generation lines have been installed with the speed-density disparity shrinking significantly. Consequently, an entirely new digital component design space has been enabled. Two classes of structures made possible by the merger of logic and memory are System On a Chip (SOC) and Processing In Memory (PIM). SOC is a direct porting of classical system configurations including processor core, L1 and L2 caches, memory and I/O busses, and DRAM main memory on to a single chip, thus exploiting a number of advantages gained through these new fabrication processes. PIM extends the design space much farther by closely associating the logic with the memory interface to realize innovative structures never previously possible and thus exposing entirely new opportunities for computer architecture. It is concepts of this second class of computing organization that are the focus of the work conducted under the Gilgamesh (Billion Logic Gate Assemblies - Mesh) project and described in this paper.

The ability to co-locate and integrate CMOS logic and DRAM cell arrays on the same die provides the potential for an unprecedented degree of coupling between these two historically segregated digital devices. A number of advantages compared to conventional practices are implied by this new strategy to devising digital structures. To what degree they are exploited depends on the specific architecture devised and the operational execution model employed.

The Gilgamesh project is developing a new generation of PIM architecture, the MIND (Memory, Intelligent, Network Devices) chip. the nodes of the Gilgamesh system will be MIND chips. MIND is an advanced scalable processor in memory architecture for spaceborne and general robotic embedded applications that is described in sections 2.1 and 3.

Memory Bandwidth A memory access operation to a DRAM cell block acquires an entire row of 1K or more bits in a single cycle. Ordinarily, only a small number of the bits (in the worst case, only one) are used per access in conventional systems as one or a few are selected from the contents of the row buffer to be deposited at the memory chip's output pins. PIM positions logic directly adjacent to the row buffer exposing the entire contents of an acquired memory row. PIM also permits the partitioning of the chip's memory contents into multiple separate memory blocks, each operating independently. Although smaller in capacity than the entire chip's storage contents, each of these blocks has the same row length, thus increasing the internal peak memory bandwidth proportional to the number of memory blocks. Employing today's fabrication processes, a typical PIM chip could deliver a peak on-chip memory bandwidth on the order of 100 Gbps or more. A moderate scale array of MIND chips can exceed one Terabyte per second aggregate bandwidth.

Access Latency The close proximity of the PIM logic to the cell block memory row buffers permits short transit times of the acquired data to the processing

ALU. Unlike conventional system architectures, there need not be multiple levels of memory hierarchy comprising one or more caches between the processor and memory in combination with the cache control logic delays. Nor are there the multiple stages of communication required between each level with the resulting propagation delays. While delays may vary widely, the degree of improvement can be a factor of two or more. Additional delays incurred due to contention for shared communication channels are also avoided since such accesses are local to a specific chip and do not require system level resources.

Efficiency in the Presence of Low Locality Most modern memory systems supporting high-speed microprocessors employ a hierarchy of SRAM caches that rely on temporal and spatial locality of data access to operate efficiently. Temporal locality is the property of data usage that reflects the tendency for multiple references to the same word within a narrow time frame. While many classes of applications work well within this framework, a number of important types of algorithms exhibit low or no temporal locality in the short term, making poor use of cache resources and resulting in low processor efficiency. Examples of such cache unfriendly operations include the manipulation of irregular data structures, pointer chasing, parallel prefix, and gather scatter. PIM makes it possible to perform low temporal locality operations directly in the memory without experiencing the long transit times or cache disruption. Such data intensive functions can be performed in place without any data movement off chip and performed simultaneously across an array of PIM chips, yielding very high efficiency with respect to conventional systems undertaking equivalent tasks.

Low Gate Count Processors Within a multi-chip PIM structure, performance is dominated by effective memory bandwidth and not ALU utilization as is the case with conventional microprocessors. The design considerations for PIM processors can differ greatly from those of typical processors, emphasizing availability to servicing data from memory rather than high floating-point throughput. In contrast to current trends in processor design, PIM processors can be implemented with a relatively small gate count. Since they operate directly on data from their immediate memory, data caches are of less importance for PIM processors and may be eliminated entirely in some cases. Under certain conditions, execution control can be simplified as well. As a result, PIM processors may be implemented in a few hundred thousand devices rather than many millions. This provides simplicity of design for rapid development and high confidence as well as contributing to other features discussed below.

Low Power Consumption A major advantage of the PIM concept is its excellent power consumption efficiency. This is a consequence of several aspects of PIM structure and operation that distinguish it from conventional processor design practices. One important factor is reduced use of external chip input and output drivers. Data transfers through IC pins is a major source of power consumption for ordinary systems, especially for high speed I/O. Driving transmission lines and buses can consume a significant portion of a system's total power budget.

But PIM performs many of a system's operations on chip, avoiding the necessity of moving the data to the caches and registers of some remote processor and therefore eliminating the pin driver usage for those operations. Another improvement in power consumption is derived from the reduction in gate count for the processors. Historically, the trend has been reduced efficiency per transistor with respect to performance. As transistor count has increased, the concomitant performance gain has not been proportional and power consumption has exceeded a hundred watts for many processors. By reducing the number of devices per processor by an order of magnitude, the power consumption per operation performed is greatly reduced as well. The reduction or elimination of caches is one source of such improvement. Today, caches can cover as much as three quarters of a microprocessor chip's area and consume considerable power. PIM's low dependence on cache structures diminishes its power budget substantially. Redundant memory accesses are also a contributor to power consumption. Because conventional remote processors rarely acquire the data contents of an entire memory block row (some new memory chips are improving this aspect of system operation), multiple read access cycles to the same row are often required. PIM memory exposes all row data to their local processors, permitting a single access cycle to suffice and reducing the total power consumed to effect the equivalent data availability to processing logic.

High Availability PIM itself is not intrinsically fault tolerant. But PIM exhibits a number of properties that are conducive to realizing high availability architectures. The multi-nodal organization of a PIM chip provides a natural boundary of repetitive structure that can be exploited for reliability. Since each node is capable of carrying out a computation independently, it is able to take on work that was to be performed by a failed node on the same chip. The overall performance of the chip is reduced but its basic functionality is retained in the presence of faults. In this mode of operation, high availability is achieved through graceful degradation. Faults may be transient, such as single even upsets, or permanent, such as hard faults. PIM allows one node to diagnose another and, if the failure mode is ephemeral, to correct the error and bring the faulty node back online. If the failure is a hard fault, then the node in question can be isolated from the remaining chip units by the other nodes, permitting continued operation of the chip. Many other issues remain before true nonstop computation can be realized. But PIM clearly is beneficial to accomplishing this goal.

In spite of these attributes, Processor-in-Memory technology has been slow to migrate in to commercial computing products. With the exception of limited penetration in the stand-alone embedded computing market (e.g. Mitsubishi M32R/S) and research into data streaming accelerators (e.g. UC Berkeley IRAM), PIM's potential has gone largely untapped. There are multiple factors contributing to this lethargy in exploiting the potential opportunities. One of course, is that such usage is outside the scope of common system practices and therefore must compete with the inertia of an installed base of hardware and software products addressing similar user application base. But PIM architecture, while enticing, has proven inadequate to the promise and challenges of realizing effective general PIM-based computing. In spite of ten years or more of development, PIM has not significantly penetrated the high-end market. The reasons relate to the limited generality of extant chips, the challenge of integrating them within otherwise conventional systems, and the inadequacy of current programming methodologies as well as resource management techniques. The Gilgamesh project is developing the MIND architecture, an advanced PIM-based scalable building block that addresses many of these challenges to a significant degree.

2   Gilgamesh System Architecture Overview

The Gilgamesh architecture is developed in the context of the new structural and operational opportunities made possible by PIM technology. It is designed to support high performance computing both for spaceborne platforms and ground based supercomputers. The unique properties of PIM allows new structures and capabilities within memory devices previously impossible. Gilgamesh extends PIM computing from basic physical level to virtual level naming and addresses of both data and tasks. It provides hardware support for message driven (parcel) computation and multithreaded control of local execution. The architecture is developed to provide a basis for fault tolerance support and real time processing. It is intended to operate at low power compared to conventional systems while provide great scalability to meet many different system requirements.

2.1   Three Primary Levels

The Gilgamesh system architecture exhibits a hierarchical structure of functional elements and their interconnection. Different system implementations may vary dramatically in their actual structure depending on scale, functionality, and relationship to other elements of the global system in which they are embedded. Nonetheless, all Gilgamesh systems may be devised within a three-level framework as described below.

The basic building block of the Gilgamesh architecture is the MIND chip, which has been designed to overcome the logical and efficiency limitations of earlier PIM devices by incorporating several critical mechanisms not previously found in PIM. Message-driven computation employing light weight Parcels permits direct memory chip to memory chip interaction. A new scalable address mapping scheme permits the direct manipulation of virtually addressed objects in a distributed system. A multithreaded task switching and management capability provides overlapping use of parallel on-chip resources for high efficiency of memory and I/O channels.

System Level Organization   The top level of the Gilgamesh system architecture is defined in terms of the number of MIND modules employed, their interconnect topology and network components, and the external devices attached to it. In principle, a Gilgamesh may be as small as a single MIND chip or as large as a three-dimensional mesh incorporating thousands of such chips. At this top level, the integrated MIND modules may comprise a standalone system or they may be part of a larger system with external microprocessors, one or more levels of cache supporting these processors, and mass storage such as disks for persistent backing store. At this level, a Gilgamesh system may be a parallel embedded processor connected to sensors and controlling computers to further process their result data or it may be a general purpose computer connected to user I/O devices and external internet connect.

MIND Chip Level Subsystems The MIND module or chip has an internal structure that includes memory, processing, and communication functionality. It is capable of fully independent operation or to serve as a cooperating element in a highly parallel structure. The MIND module incorporates a number of processor/memory nodes that store the internal data and control the system operation. It also includes shared functional units such as floating point processing used by all of the nodes. The MIND chip has several external interfaces to support its integration as part of larger systems. The parcel interface supports interaction among the MIND modules making up a Gilgamesh architecture. An external master-slave interface allows the MIND module to be used under the control of external microprocessors so that the MIND module can control external I/O or mass storage devices. A streaming interface permits direct memory access of large blocks of data at high speed such as data from mass storage or image sensors. Separate signal lines permit rapid response to external conditions and the control of external actuators.

MIND Node Architecture The processor/memory node architecture has all the functionality required to perform core calculations and manage physical and logical resources. Each node comprises a memory block of a few Mbits of data organized in rows of 1 Kbits or more and accessed in a single memory cycle. The node processor architecture differs substantially from conventional microprocessors, emphasizing effective memory bandwidth instead of ALU throughput. The node ALU is as wide as the row buffer and can perform basic operations on all row buffer data simultaneously. A wide-register bank permits temporary storage of the contents of row buffer. A multithreaded scheduling controller supports the concurrent execution of multiple separate threads, simplifying management of resources and handling hazards. Each node interfaces with others on the chip as well as with external interfaces by means of a common shared internal communications channel.

2.2 Modes of System Integration

The MIND architecture and chip design are devised to address the requirements of a diversity of advanced system requirements. It may contribute to a wide range of operational contexts from simple single-chip embedded computing tasks to large hierarchical Petaflops-scale supercomputers and many configurations in between. MIND chips may perform as masters, slaves, or in peer-to-peer relationships. They may operate alone, within a homogeneous structure comprised uniquely of themselves, or in conjunction with a plethora of other component types including other technologies. They may be completely responsible for all aspects of a computation or provide specific optimal but narrow mechanisms contributing to the broader computing model supported and even guided by other elements as well. Depending on their role, the organization of the systems that they in part comprise may vary. MIND is of a sufficiently general nature that the number of ways in which it may be employed is larger than it is reasonable to describe exhaustively in this note. Some key classes of structure are briefly discussed to suggest the manner and means of their utility.

Single-Chip Embedded The simplest system employing the MIND component is a single chip structure in which all responsibilities of computation and external interface are supported by the one device. The chip interfaces permit independent input and output signals for sensors and actuators, a control bus for managing external slaved devices such as secondary storage and user interfaces, and a data streaming port for rapid transfer of bulk data such as that from real time image (CCD) sensors. Although a single chip, a MIND device still incorporates multiple processor-memory nodes to provide mutual fault diagnosis, high performance through parallel computing, bounded real-time response, and graceful degradation in the presence of faults.

Gilgamesh Scalability Approach Gilgamesh is a scalable system comprising multiple MIND chips interconnected to operate as a single tightly coupled parallel computer without additional processing support. The number of MIND chips within a Gilgamesh systems can range from a few (typically four to sixteen) that easily fit on a small to moderate board to extremely large systems of many thousands or even a million chips packaged possibly in a 3-D matrix. A cubic structure of MIND chips a meter on a side, including cooling could sustain Petaflops scale computation. The actual interconnect network and topology will differ depending on Gilgamesh system scale and time critical factors as well as power and reliability considerations. The array of MIND components shares a global virtual name space for program variables and tasks that are allocated at run time to the distributed physical memory and processing resources. The MIND chips interoperate through an active message protocol called *parcels* that supports everything from simple memory access requests to the remote invocation of entire programs with efficient light-weight transport, interpretation, and context switching mechanisms for effective handling of a range of parcel packet sizes. Individual processor-memory nodes can be activated or powered-down at run time to provide active power management and to configure around faults.

Smart Memory — Slaved MIND chips can be a critical component of larger systems, replacing the "dumb" memory of a conventional system with smart memories capable of performing operations within the memory chips themselves. Such systems still maintain the conventional structure involving one or more microprocessors responsible for conducting, coordinating, and managing the computation and overall system resources performing it. Such a structure may even employ a typical cache hierarchy for SMP or DSM operation, or support shared memory without cache coherence. The MIND chips replace some or all of the main memory in such structures, providing a memory system with logic for local operations.

In its most simple form, MIND employed as smart memory can be used directly in place of conventional DRAM (or advanced versions) parts. This does not mean they would plug into the same slot; pin compatibility is unlikely. But the general structure remains identical, even if the pin-outs are modified. All MIND chips are operated directly under the control of the host or main microprocessors of the system. In this slaved mode, the MIND components receive direct commands from their host microprocessors. These may be as simple as basic read-write requests to the memory itself or compound atomic operations such as *test-and-set*. But the set of operations that can be performed is much larger and in slaved mode a MIND chip array can perform a wide array of such instructions on streams of physical memory blocks. Performing scaling functions for numeric applications or associative operations for relational transaction processing are two such examples, each operation triggered by a command from the host microprocessor but performed in parallel by the many processor-memory nodes on the array of MIND chips. This data parallel operational mode can be extended to the execution of simple multi-instruction functions, invoked by the host processor(s) and performed on local data by each of the MIND nodes. In slaved systems, all MIND chips, like their dumb DRAM counterparts, are interconnected through the system memory channel.

Smart Memory — Peer to Peer There are many opportunities to derive performance benefit through the execution of data parallel instructions or functions on single data elements or contiguous blocks of physical memory by means of a master-slave relationship described above. This is the primary way by which the majority of PIM architectures are structured and their computations managed. However, more sophisticated functions require access to data that may be distributed across multiple nodes, not just local to a particular memory block. One important class of operations involves irregular data structures that incorporate virtual pointers that must be de-referenced by the MIND nodes themselves to identify data values stored on other nodes. In other cases, the result of a function performed on one node may require an intermediate solution to a computation performed on another node. Under such circumstances, more general computations than those accomplished in a slaved mode require a peer-to-peer relationship among all of the MIND nodes. This could be achieved through the common memory channel with provision made either for the host microprocessors to coordinate and conduct transactions between chips or for the MIND chips themselves to become master of the memory channel. However, traffic congestion due to contention for this shared communication resource would impose a bottleneck that could severely constrain throughput and scalability. Rather, where peer-to-peer inter-MIND chip operation and virtual memory references are to constitute a significant proportion of the system activity, a richer network infrastructure dedicated to communications between MIND chips is to be preferred, altering and extending the structure beyond that of conventional systems. The MIND architecture supports the use of an independent memory network and node-to-node direct cooperation for peer-to-peer functionality. The host microprocessors are still responsible for the overall control of the computation and broad coordination of the system resources. But at the finer grained details of the system operation, in a peer-to-peer functional relationship, the MIND nodes themselves interoperate on behalf of, but not in direct control by, their hosting microprocessors.

Smart Memory — Master through Percolation An innovative concept has emerged from the HTMT project that may revolutionize the relationship between processors and their main memory, enabled by the potential of advanced PIM architecture such as MIND. Traditionally, in addition to performing the actual computations related to an application for which the conventional register-register microprocessor architectures are optimized, the same microprocessors are also required to synchronize the tasks making up the computation and manage the movement of instruction, variable, and context data to high speed local memory, usually L1 and L2 caches. Because of latency and the classical memory bottleneck, load store operations are not very effective and can cause significant reduction of processor efficiency. PIM provides a new opportunity to improve significantly the efficiency and scalability of shared memory MPP systems and the MIND architecture is devised in part to implement the new paradigm. *Percolation* is a proposed methodology by which the control of physical and logical components of a computation are managed not by the main microprocessors that are ill suited to these responsibilities but by the main memory incorporating PIM MIND chips. Under the percolation model the small, inexpensive, and highly replicated MIND processors assume the task of managing all memory resources, accomplishing all memory intensive functions (such as parallel prefix, or associative update), and coordinating the execution of distributed parallel tasks. Most importantly, percolation provides the means of migrating all necessary data to the local high speed memory or cache of the main microprocessors and scheduling their use; thus relieving the hosts of all overhead and latency intensive activities. Through percolation, the smart memory can become the master and the main microprocessors become the slaves, potentially revolutionizing the architecture and operation of future generation high performance computers.

2.3 Interconnect

MIND modules are connected by a fabric of channels that permit parcel message packets to be passed between any pair of nodes within a Gilgamesh system. The topology of the Gilgamesh interconnect may differ depending on the system scale, usage, and requirements. The parcel transport layer hardware interface supports various network structures through a programmable routing table. Each MIND module contains multiple parcel interfaces. For example, there may be one parcel interface for each MIND node on the chip. Through the internal MIND module shared communication channel, incoming parcel messages can be rerouted to other parcel interfaces. The MIND chip can act as a routing switch of degree equal to the number of parcel interfaces on the chip. With four parcel interfaces on each chip, a small four chip system has complete interconnect. A sixteen chip hyper-cube interconnect can be implemented with the same chip type. Mesh and toroidal structures can be implement for larger organizations as well. For higher bi-section bandwidth and shorter latencies for larger systems, external networks comprising independent switches may be used to build more powerful networks. These can be particularly useful when MIND chips are used in conjunction with larger systems.

3 MIND Module Subsystems

The principal building block of the Gilgamesh systems, including the anticipated PIM enhanced main memory subsystems of future high performance computers, is the MIND chip or module. The MIND module is designed to serve both as a complete standalone computational element and as a component in a synergistic cooperation with other like modules. The subsystems comprising the MIND module are devised to support both its own internal functionality and its cooperative interrelationship with other such devices. This section provides a brief description and discussion about the chief critical subsystems making up a MIND module.

3.1 MIND Nodes

The MIND node is the principal execution unit of the MIND architecture. Multiple nodes are incorporated on a single MIND chip, the exact number dictated by fabrication technology, chip real estate, and design considerations including the number of gates per node processor. The node consists of the node memory block, the node wide-word multithreaded processor, and the connections to parcel message interface and the MIND chip internal bus. The MIND node memory is DRAM with the entire row buffer exposed to the node processor. The node processor ALU and data paths are structured to make the best usage of the high bandwidth direct access to the memory block. A wide register bank is integrated into the data path. Each wide-register is the width of the row buffer and allows temporary buffering of the contents of the row buffer. The ALU is also capable of working on all bits of the row buffer or wide register within one memory access cycle time. The node executes instruction streams called threads. A thread employs a wide-register as its primary state definition. A multithreaded sequencer manages multiple threads concurrently, allowing interleaved instructions from among the many active threads to share the same physical execution resources, actually simplifying handling of data and control hazards as well as providing rapid response to real time signals. Node memory is used to contain pages with virtual addresses and address translation is performed among the nodes through a distributed address mapping directory table.

3.2 Shared Function Units

While each node incorporates essentially all logic needed to undertake any general computation, the operational capability of the nodes can be extended by some additional units that are not necessarily justified for inclusion within each and every node. Not every possible functional unit may have sufficient usage to warrant replication on a single chip or may require too much die area for more than one such unit to be practical on a given chip. MIND provides the necessary logical and physical infrastructure to permit the addition of separate functional units that can be accessed by all of the MIND nodes as well as through the master-slave external interface. For the first design, three possible such units are under consideration for incorporation: floating point multiply, floating point addition, and permutation network. These can be pipelined, supporting multiple requests concurrently and have their own dedicated access arbitration controllers. Future designs may include additional shared functional units.

3.3 Internal Shared Communications

The majority of node operations employ local resources within the node, but some operational functionality is provided through subsystems on the MIND module but external to the specific node. The shared function units described above are examples as are the external interfaces to be described below. Another important class of resource to which every node must have access is the combined memory blocks of the other nodes on the same MIND module. To support the sharing of function units, control of external interfaces, and access to chip-wide memory blocks, an internal shared communication mechanism is incorporated as part of every MIND module. This channel may take any one of several possible forms but provides fast reliable access to all needed chip resources. It is anticipated that such shared communications within the module will employ a split transaction protocol to decouple the communication throughput from the natural operating speeds of the shared elements. Depending on the number of nodes within a module and their speeds, either multi-drop buses or point-to-point network topologies may be employed. But in either case, redundancy or graceful degradation of path between any two subunits within the module is required for fault tolerance. The internal shared communications medium will support its own access arbitration and error detection mechanisms.

3.4 Master-Slave External Interface

A Gilgamesh ensemble of MIND units may operate as an independent system or in cooperation, support, or control of external computing elements. The MIND chip architecture incorporates an external interface that services the necessary communications, command, and control functions for interoperability with external computing components (not including other MIND chips). One or a collection of MIND modules may be slaved and responsive to the commands of one or more external master microprocessors. This would be a comparable relationship to that of a primary microprocessor to its main memory chips except that the MIND chip surrogates can also perform in situ operations. The MIND modules may also perform as master by means of this external interface controlling external devices such as network ports and mass storage devices or real time sensors. In this mode, it may be used in conjunction with the streaming I/O interface described below.

3.5 Streaming I/O External Interface

The external streaming interface provides a direct high bandwidth connection between external remote devices and the MIND memory blocks. The interface will support full direct memory access rate of data transfer in or out of the chip. It can be used for such input devices as real time digital cameras or output stereoscopic projectors at full frame rate. Using this interface, MIND units can be used as post-sensor processors for digital signal processing tasks such as passive sonar or radar return data. It can be used for accepting large blocks of data from mass storage devices or can dump data into such devices as holographic storage.

3.6 Parcel Interface

Inter MIND chip communication is supported by the parcel packet transport layer. Each MIND chip includes multiple parcel interfaces to an external network providing access to all MIND chip nodes comprising a Gilgamesh system. Parcels have to be fast enough to perform basic memory operations at the same rate that conventional memory chips support memory accesses. Therefore, the interface has to be wide enough to accept the packets for these operations. However, parcels also have to support variable format packets for a wide array of more sophisticated remote operation invocation. Thus, a combination of parallel and serial acquisition of parcel packets is required of the interface. The parcel interface has to be capable of interpreting basic parcel operation types to perform the most simple instructions without demanding full operation of the thread scheduler. For example, a thread can read any state within the node and generate a new parcel containing that state to be returned to the calling MIND chip without employing any higher functionality of the MIND architecture.

3.7 Signals

External events from secondary storage devices, sensors, command interfaces (e.g. mouse, keyboard) and other asynchronous triggers can be communicated directly to the MIND module through a set of two-state signal pins. Such signal conditions, when detected, can cause an active thread to be immediately scheduled by the multithread controller or cause a new thread to be instantiated and executed. Signal pins can also be used to provide external voltage or current switching to external logic, power, or actuator devices to control their operation. The input and output signal pins are shared among all nodes of the MIND module and can be directly controlled by other MIND modules through the parcel interface or by a master microprocessor through the master-slave external interface.

4 MIND Node Architecture Overview

The node of a MIND chip provides the primary storage and operational resources of a Gilgamesh system. It manages the DRAM main memory providing both local and remote access to its stored data. It performs basic operations on multiple fields of data simultaneously. It initiates fine grain tasks, carries them out, and completes them, interleaving operations from separate but concurrent tasks to achieve high efficiency. The node assimilates messages and derives new tasks from them. The architecture of the node includes its principal elements, the data paths interconnecting them, and the control logic determining their behavior. This section describes these in some detail.

4.1 Memory Block

The node memory block has at its core (no pun intended) one or more conventional stacks of DRAM cells arranged by rows of individual single bit storage cells. Each row may typically contain on the order of 2048 such cells. The sense amps are connected to columns of corresponding cells across all of the rows. However, due to the extra fine pitch of the cells, it is not possible to lay metal output bus lines such that adjacent cells in a given row can be read out at the same time. As a result, groups of eight adjacent cells in a row share the same output bus line and use it in a time multiplexed manner. There are one eighth as many output bus lines as row cells, e.g., for 2048 cells per row, there are 256 output bus lines. Thus a row, once addressed, is read in a succession of eight 256-bit groups. The output of the row sense amps is fed directly to the row buffer, a row wide fast register that holds the contents of the row and is available to feed it back to the DRAM cells; this behavior is necessary because such a read is destructive. The contents of the row buffer, which represents all the data of the selected row, are then available for immediate processing.

Access to the memory block is managed by the memory controller. This simple hardware subsystem performs two primary functions related to the allocation and operation of the memory block. The memory controller arbitrates among the potential sources of memory requests. These include the MIND intra-chip communications bus, the parcel handler, and the thread coordinator. Access is prioritized with five levels of priority to support both essential accesses and optimal resource utilization. The priorities are: (1) basic; (2) preferred; (3) exception; (4) real time; (5) parcel diagnostics.

Most thread requests to memory are issued with the basic priority, which accounts for the majority of accesses. General accesses through the MIND intra-chip bus from other nodes are asserted with the *preferred* priority as are general memory access parcel requests. As these are shared and limited resources, responding quickly to these requests will free them earlier than would otherwise occur. Supervisor memory requests and interrupt handlers are supported at the *exception* priority level, which takes precedence over the general execution accesses. To support real time operation with bounded and predictable response time, a high priority is provided. The *real time* priority level is distinguished from those below it in that not only will it take precedence over requests at lower priority but it will preempt any current memory request that is being performed, unless the actual discharge phase is taking place. If so, that subcycle will be completed, its contents temporarily buffered and the real time request immediately initiated. The highest priority is *parcel diagnostics* that is used to force the memory controller to operate, even if there is a fault in part of the hardware. This is used when the node has failed and must be controlled externally. In this case, the memory controller is really disabled and the signals provided by the parcel handler.

The memory block itself performs some simple compound-atomic operations on the data stored. Thus the controller accepts as part of the request certain basic op codes to be employed by the wide ALU during such cycles. This allows parcels or other nodes on the MIND chip to perform atomic synchronization primitives without invoking threads and incurring the concomitant overhead in space and time.

4.2 Parcel Handler

The Parcel handler is responsible for the transfer of MIND active messages, or Parcels, between MIND modules. Each MIND node has a local parcel handler, although a parcel arriving at any node on a MIND chip can be redirected to any other node on the same MIND chip through the internal intra-chip communications channels. This permits the on-chip parcel handlers to perform as an intermediate router of parcels in a potentially large network of MIND chips.

The parcel carries multiple fields of information that influences its transport across the Gilgamesh system between source and final destination nodes, determines the actions to be performed at the destination MIND node, and specifies the way in which flow control is to be continued upon completion of the parcel task. The basic fields comprising a standard parcel include: (1) target physical node destination; (2) context id; (3) destination data or object name (virtual or physical); (4) action specifier; (5) operands (values or names); (6) continuation.

A separate address translation mechanism predicts the physical node on which a virtually named destination is anticipated to be and the parcel moves through one or more hops through the system network to this physical location. At this destination, the presence of the sought-after entity is verified. It is possible that the parcel will be redirected to a new physical destination at this point, creating a new physical address in the parcel's first field entry. Low level parcels may deal directly with the system's physical elements for low level diagnostics, initialization, and maintenance including reconfiguration. The context id field indicates domain of execution including physical, supervisor, or any one of a number application name spaces, for hardware supported security. This, in conjunction with the destination name field, fixes the logical (and possibly physical) data or object that the parcel is to effect. The action specifier dictates that effect. It can be a basic hardware operation performed by the parcel handler on the node. It can be a call to a object method, function, or system service routine that initiates a thread to be executed, or it can contain a sequence of instructions to be directly executed. The operands field is variable length and self-formatted, possibly containing a mix of different typed values and variable names to be de-referenced during the course of the action to be performed associated with the parcel. When the parcel action terminates, there are two ways to initiate a follow-on action.

4.3 Wide Register Bank

The MIND node processor employs a bank of registers, each of which is as wide as the row buffer and sense amps, perhaps a couple of thousand bits, which may be 2048 bits. Being able to repeatedly access an entire row multiple times after the first read cycle is of tremendous value when the cycle time difference exhibited is a ratio of an order of magnitude or more between memory and registers.

5 Execution Model and Mechanisms

The Gilgamesh MIND architecture supports a dynamic adaptive resource model of execution at the fine, medium, and coarse levels of granularity. Many of the attributes have been touched upon in earlier sections. The purpose of this brief closing section is to highlight the logical dynamic functionality enabled by the efficient hardware mechanisms of the MIND architecture that contributes to the determination of the allocation of tasks to execution resources, both within MIND nodes and shared across MIND nodes and chips. Although there are many ways to manage the node resources, Gilgamesh promotes a dynamic multilevel multithreaded methodology that establishes a new design space for both hardware and software.

The central premise is that unlike conventional multimode statically scheduled systems, the work goes where the data is, rather than always presuming a locus of work sites and designating data partitions local to them. Thus an action or task is to be performed on a dense data construct, possibly multi-field in structure, and an action-specifier is dispatched to the site of the data. This specifier can be tiny compared to the size of the data operated upon. Equally, the virtual data can be distributed by a number of different algorithms and the operation and efficiencies are still retained, whether static or dynamic. This message driven model of computation using parcel type of active messages exploits a simple multithreaded intra-node instruction issue mechanism. For persistent control state, medium grained objects can handle complex timing and control relationships. These points are expanded somewhat below.

5.1 Parcel Driven Computing

Parcel dynamic structures were described in some detail in section 4. The important idea is that parcels are an embodiment of a remote task call and a decoupled or split transaction method of creating remote flow control. One consequence of active messages including parcels is their intrinsic property of latency hiding. Once a node has launched a parcel, it can forget about it, using its own resources for other work. Until a remote node assimilates such a parcel, it dedicates no resources to it, doing so only when it has been completely received and interpreted by the node's parcel handler and then only when other tasks are not consuming these resources already. Thus a node can be imagined as a small computing engine that holds data and processes parcels directed to that data while directing result parcels to other data.

5.2 Virtual Memory

Unlike almost all other examples of experimental PIM architectures, Gilgamesh manages a distributed but shared virtual memory space such that all data is viewed by all nodes within the system and all address pointers can be translated, perhaps through a multistage procedure so that a parcel will reach the physical location that holds the logical page of data sought. Virtual paged data is used in this structure so that everything within the page is accessed via physical offset to the page header. The distributed address translation scheme creates a distributed page table, the entries of which are allocated to specific physical MIND chips. Actual virtual pages may be placed anywhere but are preferentially placed in the same chip or collection of chips in which the respective directory table entry resides. A new affinity model is offered that allows virtual pages to be realigned to manage locality without artificially changing the logical data structures themselves. A preparation stage of data realignment, like a kind of gather, will be possible and overlap the other computation and synchronization phases of execution management for latency hiding.

5.3 Multithreaded Control

The basic management of the node memory block was described with several requests for the memory block being asserted at the same time. The multithreaded control unit extends this class of resource management scheme to support other resources such as basis integer and floating point operation units, register to register transfers and perturbations, and others. Such asynchronous instruction issue controllers permit a number of active threads to exists simultaneously, each with a pending action type ready to be performed or waiting for its previously issued instruction to be completed. Although simple in concept, the tradeoffs for optimality are subtle. It turns out that overall performance increases with multithreaded systems if the processors are made small and many more nodes are used in order to maximize sustained memory bandwidth, which is the critical resource.

5.4 Object Based Computation

Gilgamesh uses an object-based programming model based on the notion of "macroservers". Macroservers are associated with a state space in which a set of lightweight threads executes asynchronously; the location and distribution of objects and data in PIM memory can be dynamically controlled. A detailed description of this computation model is outside the scope of this article.

6 Summary

This paper serves as an introduction to the Gilgamesh hardware architecture and that of its building block, the MIND chip. The goal of both architectures is to provide much better access to memory and to facilitate programming of vast arrays of nodes, while reducing power consumption and manufacturing cost.

High Performance Computing and Trends: Connecting Computational Requirements with Computing Resources

Jack Dongarra

University of Tennessee

Abstract

Today networking, distributed computing, and parallel computation research have matured to make it possible for distributed systems to support high-performance applications, but:

> Resources are dispersed,
> Connectivity is variable,
> Dedicated access is not possible.

In this talk we advocate the 'Computational Grids' to support 'large-scale' applications. These must provide transparent access to the complex mix of resources — computational, networking, and storage — that can be provided through aggregation of resources. The vision is of uniform, location independent, and transient access to the

> Computational,
> Catalogued data,
> Instrument system,
> Human collaborator,

resources of contemporary research activity in order to facilitate the solution of large-scale, complex, multi-institutional/multidisciplinary data and computational based problems. It envisages these resources being accessible through a Problem Solving Environment appropriate to the target community.

Topic 01
Support Tools and Environments

Michael Gerndt

Global Chair

Parallel computing is a key technology for many areas in science and industry. Outstanding examples are the ASCI and Blue Gene programs that target only very few but critical applications. A much broader spectrum of applications can be found on any of the machines of supercomputing centers all over the world.

Although programming parallel computers is a difficult and time consuming task, a lot of highly skilled programmers are engaged in this to make most efficient use of the expensive resources. Tools are crucial to facilitate their task. Not only classical tools, such as performance analysis and debugging tools, are required but also very specialized tools that are useful only on parallel computers.

Critical to the acceptance of those tools by the programmers is their integration into a programming environment and their availability across multiple platforms, thus reducing the learning effort. In addition, tools have to be integrated with the programming language and ideally with the high-level model of the application that the programmers has in mind before actually writing Fortran or C/C++ code.

The articles selected for presentation within this topic demonstrate the wide range of tools necessary to ease programming of parallel computers.

Four papers have been selected in the area of parallel programming environments. The tool described in *Dynamic Performance Tuning Environment* by Anna Morajko, Eduardo César, Tomàs Margalef, Joan Sorribes, and Emilio Luque supports automatic online performance analysis and tuning based on the knowledge of special design patterns.

A technique that underlies a lot of tools for parallel programming is the efficient recording of partial orderings of tasks during parallel execution. Paul Ward and David Taylor present a new technique in the paper on *Self-Organizing Hierarchical Cluster Timestamps*.

The paper on *A Tool for Binding Threads to Processors* by Magnus Broberg, Lars Lundberg, and Håkan Grahn; and the paper on *VizzScheduler - A Framework for the Visualization of Scheduling Algorithms* by Welf Löwe and Alex Liebrich present tools to compute and understand scheduling decisions.

The article by Rajeev Muralidhar and Manish Parashar on *A Distributed Object Infrastructure for Interaction and Steering* describes an application-level tool facilitating the development of interactive parallel applications.

Two papers have been selected for this topic that describe tools on system level. Checkpointing parallel applications is already a difficult and I/O intensive task on parallel machines. The paper on *Checkpointing Facility on a Metasystem* by Yudith Cardinale and Emilio Hernández presents a tool for a much more dynamic environment, a metacomputing system.

Crucial to any parallel program is an efficient implementation of communication abstractions. The paper on *Optimising the MPI Library for the T3E* by Stephen Booth gives a detailed overview of optimization techniques for MPI implementations based on remote memory access on the Cray T3E.

The broad spectrum of tools for parallel computers presented in this topic makes very clear that this area of research still gives a lot of opportunities for bright ideas and many talented students.

Dynamic Performance Tuning Environment [1]

Anna Morajko, Eduardo César, Tomàs Margalef, Joan Sorribes, and Emilio Luque

Computer Science Department. Universitat Autònoma de Barcelona
08193 Bellaterra, Spain
ania@aows10.uab.es;
{eduardo.cesar,tomas.margalef,joan.sorribes,emilio.luque}@uab.es

Abstract. Performance analysis and tuning of parallel/distributed applications are very difficult tasks for non-expert programmers. It is necessary to provide tools that automatically carry out these tasks. Many applications have a different behavior according to the input data set or even change their behavior dynamically during the execution. Therefore, it is necessary that the performance tuning can be done on the fly by modifying the application according to the particular conditions of the execution. A dynamic automatic performance tuning environment supported by dynamic instrumentation techniques is presented. The environment is completed by a pattern based application design tool that allows the user to concentrate on the design phase and facilitates on the fly overcoming of performance bottlenecks.

1 Introduction

Parallel and distributed processing are very promising approaches due to the high computation power offered to the users. However, designing and developing parallel/distributed applications are quite hard tasks because of the lack of tools that facilitate several aspects of parallel/distributed processing.

The programmer must take into account the low level implementation details of the parallel programming model being used. This fact implies that the programmer must be very careful to avoid dangerous situations such as deadlocks. When the first version of the application is completed, the programmer must consider the correct functioning of the application. It implies to go through a functional debugging phase to fix all bugs and ensure that the program provides the right functionality. The mentioned phases are also present in classical sequential programming, but the complexity of these tasks is significantly higher on parallel/distributed systems.

Once the program works correctly, the programmer must analyze the application performance. The decision of developing a parallel application is related to the performance requirements, and therefore the programmer must be aware of obtaining a satisfactory performance. This new task is not common in sequential programming because in most cases sequential programmers rely on compiler optimizations.

---

[1] This work was supported by the Comisión Interministerial de Ciencia y Tecnología (CICYT) under contract number TIC 98-0433.

This performance analysis is a hard task that requires using some performance analysis tools. The classical way to carry out performance analysis is to run the application using some monitoring tool that creates a trace file. This trace file includes all the events recorded during the execution of the application. The task of the programmer is to analyze these events looking for performance bottlenecks found during the execution in order to determine their causes and modify the program to improve the performance. There are several visualization tools that try to help the user by providing a set of different views of the program execution [1, 2]. The user can analyze the views searching for performance bottlenecks and this is much easier to do than reading plain trace files. The use of such visualization tools allows the user to detect the main performance bottlenecks quite easily, but the most difficult task is to relate the performance bottleneck to its causes. Therefore, these tools do not provide direct information that can guide the programmer in the performance improvement phase. Tuning a parallel/distributed application is a difficult task that requires great experience and deep knowledge about the program and the system itself.

There are some tools that go a step ahead providing not only visualization facilities, but offering some hints that try to guide the user in the decision that must be taken to improve the performance [3, 4]. The main feature of these tools is that they provide some automatic techniques that analyze the trace file and provide some hints to the non-expert user in the performance tuning phase.

However, the use of trace files and the fact that the analysis is done in a post-mortem phase imply some constraints in the applicability of the methodology:

1. The trace files can be really big. The execution of a real application that takes some hours usually creates enormous files that are difficult to manage and to analyze in order to find the performance bottlenecks.
2. The use of a single trace file to tune the application is not completely significant, specially when the application behavior depends on the input data set. In this case, the modifications done to overcome some bottleneck present in one run may be inadequate for the next run of the application. This could be solved by selecting a representative set of runs, but the provided suggestions would not be specific for a particular run.
3. Certain applications can change their behavior during their execution. In this case, the modification suggested by the post-mortem analysis cannot cover the dynamic behavior of the application.

In these conditions, the post-mortem methodology is not the best approach since the modifications that could be carried out from the suggestions provided by the performance analysis tool do not cover all the possible behaviors of the application. Therefore, the only feasible solution to provide real performance tuning facilities is to carry out the performance tuning on the fly.

Dynamic performance tuning is an important facility to be incorporated in a parallel/distributed programming environment. This approach is presented in section 2, showing the design of a dynamic performance tuning environment. Section 3 introduces a pattern based application design environment, that facilitates the program tuning on the fly. Section 4 shows an example of how an application is designed and tuned using our dynamic performance tuning environment. Finally, section 5 presents some conclusions of this work.

2   Dynamic Performance Tuning Environment

The main goal of our dynamic performance tuning environment is to improve performance by modifying the program during its execution without recompiling and rerunning it. This goal requires several steps: monitoring of the application, analyzing the performance behavior and modifying the running program to obtain better performance.

2.1   Dynamic Performance Tuning of Parallel/Distributed Applications

Since parallel applications consists of several intercommunicating processes executed on different machines, it is not enough to improve task performance separately without considering the global application view. To improve the performance of the entire application, we need to access global information about all associated tasks on all machines. The parallel application processes are executed physically on distinct machines and our performance tuning system must be able to control all of them. To achieve this goal, we need to distribute the modules of our dynamic tuning tool to machines where application processes are running. So, our dynamic performance tuning environment consists of several tools (see figure 1):

1. The monitoring tool (*monitor*) inserts the instrumentation in all the processes and collects the events produced during the execution of the application. However, our approach to dynamic analysis requires the global ordering of the events and thus we have to gather all events at a central location.
2. The analysis tool (*analyzer*) receives all the events generated in different processors during the execution, detects the performance bottlenecks, determines the causes and decides which modification should be done on the application program. The analysis may be time-consuming, and can significantly increase the application time execution if both – the analysis and the application - are running on the same machine. In order to reduce intrusion, the analysis should be executed on a dedicated and distinct machine. Obviously, during the analysis, *monitor* modules are collecting and providing new data to the *analyzer*. In some cases, the *analyzer* may need more information about program execution to determine the causes of a particular problem. Therefore, it can request the *monitor* to change the instrumentation dynamically. Consequently, the *monitor* must be able to modify program instrumentation – i.e., add more or remove redundant instrumentation – depending on its necessity to detect performance problems.
3. The automatic tuning tool (*tuner*) inserts modifications into the running application processes. When a problem has been detected and the solution has been given, *tuner* must apply modifications dynamically to the appropriate process or processes.

Using this dynamic methodology when a bottleneck is detected, the appropriate modifications are inserted into the address-space image of the running program. These changes will be invoked the next time the application reaches that point. The methodology can only be applied to problems that appear several times during the execution of the application. This fact could seem to be a constraint. However, it must be pointed out that the main performance problems of parallel/distributed application are those that appear many times during the execution of the application.

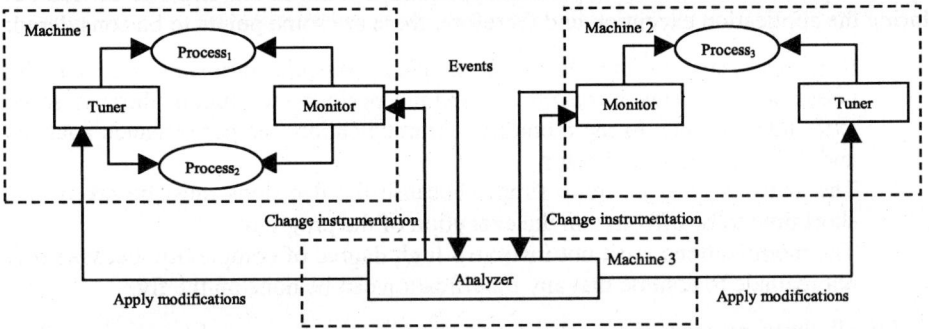

Fig. 1. Dynamic performance tuning

This dynamic tuning approach is a real challenge that requires the use of some dynamic instrumentation technique that allows the inclusion of some new code in a running program without recompiling or even rerunning it.

2.2 Dynamic Instrumentation

The Paradyn group developed a special API called DynInst API [5] that supports dynamic instrumentation.

DynInst is an API for runtime code patching. It provides a C++ class library for machine independent program instrumentation during application execution. DynInst API allows the users to attach to an already running process or start a new process, create a new piece of code and finally insert created code into the running process. The next time the instrumented program executes the block of code that has been modified, the new code is executed. Moreover, the program being modified is able to continue its execution and does not need to be re-compiled, re-linked, or restarted. DynInst manipulates the address-space image of the running program and thus this library needs access only to a running program, not to its source code.

The DynInst API is based on the following abstractions:

- point – a location in a program where new code can be inserted, i.e. function entry, function exit
- snippet – a representation of a piece of executable code to be inserted into a program at a point; a snippet must be build as an AST (Abstract Syntax Tree).

Taking into account the possibilities offered by the DynInst library, it is possible to insert code in the running application for two main objectives:

- Insert code for monitoring purposes to collect information about the behavior of the application.
- Insert code for performance tuning. The main goal of the dynamic tuning is to improve the performance on the fly. Therefore, it is necessary to insert new code in the application.

Thus, the *monitor* and the *tuner* have been designed using the DynInst API.

2.3 Pattern Based Application Design for Performance Tuning

Dynamic performance tuning of parallel applications is a task that must be carried out during the application execution and therefore, there are some points to be considered:

1. It is necessary to introduce the smallest possible intrusion. Besides the classical monitoring intrusion in dynamic performance tuning there is some extra intrusion due to the monitors' communication, the performance analysis and the program modification.
2. The analysis must be quite simple because the decisions must be taken in a short time to be effective in the execution of the program.
3. The modifications must not involve a high degree of complexity, because it is not realistic to assume that any modification can be done on the fly.

For all these reasons, the analysis and modifications cannot be very complex. However, if the programmer can use any structure, the generated bottlenecks can be extremely complicated and the analysis and the modifications are extremely difficult.

A good compromise between performance improvement and application development is to offer the programmer a pattern based application design and development environment. Using this environment the dynamic performance tuning tool is simplified, because the set of performance bottlenecks to be analyzed and tuned are only those related to the programming patterns offered to the user.

On the other hand, this approach also facilitates application design and development. The user is constrained to use a set of programming patterns, but using them he/she skips the details related to the low level parallel programming. Moreover, the dynamic performance tuning environment (including the application design tool and the dynamic performance tuning tool) allows the programmer to concentrate on the application design and not to worry about the program performance.

3 Application Design Tool

It is well known that designing, developing and tuning parallel/distributed applications is a hard task. There is a lack of useful environments that facilitates these tasks. Our "pattern based" application design tool is useful to achieve two main goals:

- On the one hand, it facilitates modification of the application on the fly to improve the performance. The defined patterns are well-known structures that may present certain well-known performance bottlenecks. Therefore, the points that must be monitored to detect the possible bottlenecks as well as the actions that must be carried out to break them are well defined. Actually, each abstract pattern is characterized by a set of parameters that determines the dynamic behavior of the pattern. Thus, changes in the application behavior, to improve performance, could be carried out by modifying the values of these parameters.
- On the other hand, it simplifies the application design to the programmer offering a set of well-known useful programming structures. When one of the abstract patterns has been selected by the programmer, the low-level details related to process communication are automatically created in such a way that the

programmer must only fill in some methods corresponding to the particular details of the application being developed. This approach has been proposed many times in the literature as in [6, 7]. The main drawback of this approach is the lost of efficiency when compared with expert programming using low level primitives. However, our approach includes hidden performance improvement. Using our environment the programmer does not have to care about performance issues since the application will be tuned on the fly.

We have adopted a general methodology to characterize patterns. This methodology allows using a unified approach to the definition, analysis and implementation of each pattern, but also defines a way to include new patterns in the future. The methodology includes:

- General description of the pattern.
- Define the elements to specify the user application in terms of the selected pattern (interface). It includes initialization and ending, functional description, and communication management.
- Characterize the associated pattern bottlenecks.
- Determine the magnitudes that have to be calculated to detect these bottlenecks: which must be monitored.
- Determine the parameters that could be changed to overcome these bottlenecks and the actions that could be taken on them.

Using this application design tool the programmer is constrained to choose and combine the defined patterns. To ensure that the design tool is really useful it is necessary to include the most used programming patterns. Therefore, it is necessary to define a limited set of patterns that can be easily analyzed and tuned on the fly, but that also offer the possibility to design a wide range of parallel/distributed applications. The patterns included so far are the following ones:

- **Master/Worker**: *Description:* this pattern contains a master process that generates requests to other processes called workers, these requests are represented by data units called tasks. These workers make some computation on these tasks and then send the results back to the master. *Interface:* how master generates tasks (Task Generation), the actual computation that each worker must do (Task Processing) and the processing that the master must do on the received results (Results Processing). *Bottlenecks:* execution time differences among workers, too few workers, or too many workers. *Detection magnitudes:* communications time, workers computation time. *Adjustable parameters:* task distribution, and number of workers.
- **Pipeline**: *Description:* this pattern represents those algorithms that can be divided in an ordered chain of processes, where the output of a process is forwarded to the input of the next process in the chain. *Interface:* work that must be carried out at each stage of the pipe, input and the output data and connection among stages. *Bottlenecks:* significant executions time differences among stages, bad communication/computation ratio. *Detection magnitudes:* computing time and data load of each stage, stage waiting time. *Adjustable parameters:* number of consecutive stages per node, number of instances of a stage.

- **SPMD (Single Program Multiple Data)**: *Description:* represents those algorithms where the same processing is applied on different data portions. *Interface:* specify the task that must be carried out for all the processes, the interconnection pattern (all-to-all, 2D mesh, 3Dcube, and so on) and the data that must be sent/received for each process. *Bottlenecks:* load imbalance, execution time differences among processes. *Detection magnitudes:* computing time and data load of each process, waiting time for other processes. *Adjustable parameters:* number of inter-communicating processes per node, number of processes, and, in some cases, data distribution.
- **Divide and Conquer:** *Description:* each node receives some data and decides to process it or to create some new processes with the same code and distribute the received data among them. The results generated at each level are gathered to the upper level. There each process receives partial results, makes some computation on them and passes the result to the upper level. *Interface:* processing of each node, the amount of data to be distributed and the initial configuration of nodes. *Bottlenecks:* important differences among branch completion time due to branch depth or process execution time. *Detection magnitudes:* completion time of each branch, computation time of each process, branch depth. *Adjustable parameters:* number of branches generated in each division, data distribution among branches, and branch depth.

Object oriented programming techniques are the natural way for implementing patterns, not only due to its power to encapsulate behavior, but also to offer a well defined interface to the user. For these reasons, we have designed a class hierarchy, which encapsulates the pattern behavior, and also a class to encapsulate the communication library. We use C++ language to implement our environment and we support PVM-based applications.

In next section we show our dynamic performance tuning environment, presenting the main aspects related to design, implementation, monitoring, performance analysis and tuning of a real application based on the Master/Worker pattern.

4 Case Study: Forest Fire Propagation

The forest fire propagation application [8] is an implementation of the "fireline propagation" simulation based on the Andre-Viegas model [9]. The model describes the fireline as a set of sections that can be desegregated to calculate the individual progress of each section for a time step. When the progress of all the sections have been calculated, it is necessary to aggregate the new positions to rebuild the fireline. The general algorithm of this application using the master/worker paradigm is:

Master:
1. Get the initial fireline
2. Generate a partition of the fireline and distribute it to the workers.
3. Wait for the workers answer.
4. **If** the simulation time has been finished **then** terminate
   else Compose the new fire line, adding points if needed and go to step 2.

Worker:
1. Get the fireline section sent by the master
2. Calculate the local propagation of each point in the section (to calculate the new position of a point the model needs to know its left and right neighbours).
3. Return the new section to the master.

Next we present the specification of the associated pattern, and then we describe the on the fly performance analysis and the results of the dynamic performance tuning of the application.

4.1 Pattern Specification

Once a pattern has been chosen for the application, the user must implement the interface elements of the pattern and define the data structures for tasks and results. Specification of the master-worker pattern associated with this application includes:

For the master.
    Initialization: Load initial data (initial fireline).
    Task Generation: Convert fireline into a set of tasks (groups of three contiguous
                    points).
                    Send tasks.
    Results Processing: Get results.
                    Merge results to calculate the new fireline (adding new points
                    if needed).
                    If the simulation is completed indicate this fact.
    Terminate: Show or save the final results (final fireline)

For the worker.
    Task Processing: For each received task do
- Calculate new position for the central point (using the simulation model and information about neighbors)
- Generate result - the new point position

Data structures definition:
- Task structure: given that the simulation model is applied on groups of three contiguous points, a task must include three points.
- Result structure: for each group of three contiguous points the new position of the central point is calculated, then a result consists of a single point.

4.2 Monitoring and Performance Analysis

Once the application has been designed it is necessary to analyze the performance on the fly. The *monitor* inserts instrumentation to measure the time taken by each worker and the communication delays among the master and the workers (*detection magnitudes*). The instrumentation is inserted in those code segments where master sends and receives data, it is just after Task Generation and before Results Processing. In the worker, instrumentation is inserted before and after Task Processing.

In this application all the workers spend approximately the same amount of time (the application is executed on a homogeneous system). Therefore, in the first steps of the propagation simulation, the adequate number of workers is calculated according to the performance parameters of the pattern. However, when the fire propagates, new sections must be interpolated to accomplish the continuity constraint required by the propagation model. This means that as the fireline grows, each worker receives more data to proceed. After a certain number of iterations, the *analyzer* detects that the master is mostly waiting for results from the workers (*too few workers bottleneck*), because they must calculate a bigger amount of tasks increasing its computation time (*workers computation time magnitude*). When the *analyzer* detects this fact, it calculates the ideal number of workers for the new situation. In the case when this number is bigger from the current one, the *analyzer* decides to spawn a new worker (or several) (*increasing workers number parameter*).

4.3 Dynamic Performance Tuning

The *tuner* receives the decision from the *analyzer* to improve the performance of the application by spawning a new worker (or several) in a new machine. The *tuner* modifies the *adjustable parameter* "number of workers" of the master to let it know that there is a new worker (or several) and in the beginning of the next iteration the data must be distributed among all the workers, the old ones and the new ones. Using the dynamic performance tuning environment, the number of workers grows according to the requirements of the application.

In Table 1 the obtained results on an example fireline that starts with 50 points and reaches 850 points after 200 iterations are presented. For this example, the starting number of workers is 5 and it increases till 20. The table summarises the evolution of the number of workers and the execution times (in ms) for this particular example. In this table *Iter.* is the iteration step in the forest fire simulation, *No. points* is the number of points in the fire line for that particular iteration, *No. workers* is the number of workers required by the performance model. $T_{i\,min}$, $T_{i\,max}$ and $T_{i\,ideal}$ are the execution times for that particular iteration when executed with 5, 20 or ideal number of workers (determined by the *analyzer*), and $T_{t\,min}$, $T_{t\,max}$ and $T_{t\,ideal}$ are the total execution times when executed with 5, 20 or dynamic number of workers (ideal number for each iteration).

Table 1. Evolution of the number of workers and the execution times for forest fire example

Iter.	No. points	No. workers	$T_{i\,min}$	$T_{i\,max}$	$T_{i\,ideal}$	$T_{t\,min}$	$T_{t\,max}$	$T_{t\,ideal}$
1	50	5	11660	22902	11660	11660	22902	11660
50	250	11	34300	30512	26635	1171960	1362057	1017880
100	450	15	56940	38122	36880	3464260	3081712	2621468
200	850	20	102220	53342	53342	11444860	7662522	7171129

It can be observed that the dynamic creation of new workers provides the best execution time. It must be considered that, with dynamic tuning, resources are supplied only when needed. Using the right number of workers at each stage is even better than spawning the maximum number from the beginning. In the initial iterations a low number of workers provide better results than a bigger number because of the computation/communication relationship (compare T_i's for a low number of iterations). In the last iterations a higher number of workers provides better results. The overall execution times show that the dynamic creation of workers provides the shorter execution time.

5 Conclusions

A new approach to parallel/distributed performance analysis and tuning has been presented. The developed environment includes a pattern based application design tool and a dynamic performance tuning tool. The sets of patterns included in the pattern based application design tool have been selected to cover a wide range of applications. They offer a well defined behavior and the bottlenecks that can occur are also very well determined. In this sense the analysis of the application and the performance tuning on the fly can be carried out successfully. Using this environment the programmer can design its application in a quite simple way, and then he/she does not need to worry about any performance analysis or tuning, because the dynamic performance tuning takes care of these tasks automatically. The methodology has been tested on a real application and the preliminary results are very successful.

References

1. D. A. Reed, P. C. Roth, R. A. Aydt, K. A. Shields, L. F. Tavera, R. J. Noe, B. W. Schwartz: *"Scalable Performance Analysis: The Pablo Performance Analysis Environment"*. Proceeding of Scalable Parallel Libraries Conference, pp. 104-113, IEEE Computer Society, 1993.
2. W. Nagel, A. Arnold, M. Weber, H. Hoppe: *"VAMPIR: Visualization and Analysis of MPI Resources"*, Supercomputer, vol. 1 pp. 69-80, 1996.
3. A. Espinosa, T. Margalef, E. Luque: *"Integrating Automatic Techniques in a Performance Analysis Session"*. Lecture Notes in Computer Science, vol. 1900 (EuroPar 2000), pp. 173-177, Springer-Verlag, 2000.
4. Y. C. Yan, S. R. Sarukhai: *"Analyzing parallel program performance using normalized performance indices and trace transformation techniques"*, Parallel Computing, vol. 22, pp. 1215-1237, 1996.
5. J. K. Hollingsworth, B. Buck: *"Paradyn Parallel Performance Tools, DynInstAPI Programmer's Guide"*, Release 2.0, University of Maryland, Computer Science Department, April 2000.
6. J. Schaffer, D. Szafron, G. Lobe, and I. Parsons: *"The Interprise model for developing distributed applications"*, IEEE Parallel and Distributed Technology, 1(3):85-96, 1993.
7. J. C. Browne, S. Hyder, J. Dongarra, K. Moore, and P. Newton. *"Visual Programming and Debugging for parallel computing"*, IEEE Parallel and Distributed Technology, 3(1):75-83, 1995.
8. J. Jorba, T. Margalef, E. Luque, J. Andre, D. X. Viegas: *"Application of Parallel Computing to the Simulation of Forest Fire Propagation"*, Proc. 3rd International Conference in Forest Fire Propagation, Vol. 1, pp. 891-900, Luso, Portugal, Nov. 1998.
9. J. C. S. Andre and D. X. Viegas: "A Strategy to Model the Average Fireline Movement of a light-to-medium Intensity Surface Forest Fire", Proc. of the 2nd International Conference on Forest Fire Research, pp. 221-242, Coimbra, Portugal, 1994.

Self-Organizing Hierarchical Cluster Timestamps

Paul A.S. Ward and David J. Taylor*

Shoshin Distributed Systems Group, Department of Computer Science, University of Waterloo
Waterloo, Ontario N2L 3G1, Canada
{pasward,dtaylor}@shoshin.uwaterloo.ca

Abstract. Distributed-system observation tools require an efficient data structure to store and query the partial-order of execution. Such data structures typically use vector timestamps to efficiently answer precedence queries. Many current vector-timestamp algorithms either have a poor time/space complexity tradeoff or are static. This limits the scalability of such observation tools. One algorithm, centralized hierarchical cluster timestamps, has potentially a good time/space tradeoff provided that the clusters accurately capture communication locality. However, that algorithm, as described, uses pre-determined, contiguous clusters. In this paper we extend that algorithm to enable a dynamic selection of clusters. We present experimental results that demonstrate that our extension is more stable with cluster size and provides timestamps whose average size is consistently superior to the pre-determined cluster approach.

1 Motivation

Tools for distributed-system observation and control, such as ATEMPT [9,10], Object-Level Trace [6], and POET [11], can be broadly described as having the architecture shown in Fig.1. The distributed system is instrumented with monitoring code that captures process identifier, event number and type, and partner-event information. This information is forwarded from each process to a central monitoring entity which, using this information, incrementally builds and maintains a data structure of the partial order of events that form the computation [12]. That data structure may be queried by a variety of systems, the most common being visualization engines and control entities, which in turn may be used to control the distributed computation. It is the efficient representation of this partial-order data structure that is the focus of this paper.

Systems we are aware of maintain the transitive reduction of the partial order, typically accessed with a B-tree-like index. This enables the efficient querying of events given a process identifier and event number. It does not, however, enable efficient event-precedence querying, which is one of the most common query types on such structures. To enable efficient precedence testing, the Fidge/Mattern vector timestamp [1,14] is computed for each event and stored with that event

---

* The authors would like to thank IBM for supporting this work.

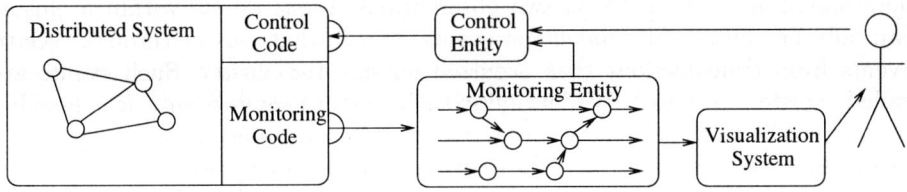

Fig. 1. Distributed-System Observation and Control

in the data structure (Note that for distributed-system observation, these timestamps are computed centrally in the monitoring entity, rather than within the distributed computation.). The choice of the Fidge/ Mattern timestamp is dictated by its ability to answer precedence queries in constant time and the fact that it is dynamic (that is, computable without requiring complete knowledge of the event set). Unfortunately, the Fidge/Mattern timestamp requires a vector of size equal to the number of processes in the computation. Such a requirement does not allow the data structure to scale with the number of processes.

Recently we proposed centralized hierarchical cluster timestamps [17]. These timestamps are also dynamic and can efficiently answer precedence queries, but require up to order-of-magnitude less space than do Fidge/Mattern timestamps. The drawback with such cluster timestamps is that the space consumption is heavily dependent on whether or not the clusters used accurately capture locality of communication. If they do not, then the space-consumption saving is substantially impaired. The algorithm described in that paper uses pre-determined, contiguous clusters. That is, the clusters represent a continuous range of the Fidge/Mattern timestamp. The results show a significant variation in average cluster-timestamp size with small variations in cluster choice. In this paper, we address this problem by extending that algorithm to enable a dynamic selection of clusters. We call this new algorithm self-organizing cluster timestamps. The actual method of selecting clusters is orthogonal to our timestamp algorithm extension, though it must be made dynamically, which substantially limits the choice of clustering method. For our experimental analysis we use a relatively simple dynamic clustering based on first communication.

In the remainder of this paper we first briefly review related work. In Sect.3 we will describe our extension to the hierarchical cluster algorithm to provide self-organizing clusters. We do this in two steps, first dealing with a flat collection of non-overlapping clusters, and then extending it to an arbitrary hierarchy of clusters. We then present experimental results that demonstrate the value of our algorithm.

2 Related Work

The centralized hierarchical cluster timestamp [17] is an attempt to reduce the space requirement of vector timestamps while still providing efficient precedence determination. It is based on two observations. First, events within a cluster can only be causally dependent on events outside that cluster through receive events from transmissions that occurred outside the cluster. Such events are called "cluster receives." By identifying such cluster-receive events, it is possible to shorten the timestamp of all other events within the cluster to the number of processes in the cluster. Second, in many parallel and distributed computations, most communication of most processes is with a small number of other processes. If the clusters capture this communication locality, then there should be few cluster-receive events, and so the average space-consumption per timestamp will be significantly less than with the Fidge/Mattern timestamp. Unfortunately, the algorithm as described in [17] does nothing to select good clusters. Rather it uses pre-determined, contiguous clusters. The contribution of this paper is to extend that algorithm to enable the dynamic selection of clusters, and to show experimentally that this improves the stability of the timestamp algorithm, even when using a rather poor dynamic clustering algorithm.

There are various other approaches that have been taken to the problem of reducing the size of vector timestamps. Fowler and Zwaenepoel [3] create direct-dependency vectors. While these vectors can be substantially smaller than Fidge/Mattern timestamps, precedence testing requires a search through the vector space, which is in the worst case linear in the number of messages. Jard and Jourdan [7] generalize the Fowler and Zwaenepoel method, but have the same worst-case time bound. Singhal and Kshemkalyani [15] take the approach of transmitting just the information that has changed in the vector between successive communications. While not directly applicable in our centralized context, it is possible to use a differential technique between events within the partial-order data structure. However, when we evaluated such an approach we were unable to realize more than a factor of three in space saving. Ward [16] has an approach based on Ore timestamps [13], though it is only applicable to low-dimension computations. There is also some amount of work on dynamic transitive closure (e.g. [8]), though the problem being addressed is more general than is our problem, and the results are not as good for our application.

3 Self-Organizing Cluster Timestamps

We now describe our algorithm in two steps. We start by extending the two-level cluster timestamp to incorporate self-organizing clusters. We then merge this with the arbitrary-depth hierarchical cluster algorithm to produce self-organizing hierarchical cluster timestamps.

3.1 Self-Organizing Two-Level Clusters

Our extension to the two-level cluster timestamp to incorporate self-organizing clusters required several changes. The core change is that clusters are no longer pre-determined, contiguous entities. Rather, each process is defined as initially belonging to a cluster of size one. When timestamping an event that would be

```
1: timestamp(e) {
2:     e.FM = Fidge/Mattern(e);
3:     if (e.type == RECEIVE && e.cluster().inverseMap[e.partner().process] == -1
4:           && !mergable(e, e.partner())) {
5:        e.clusterTimestamp = e.FM;
6:        GCR[e.process] = e.clusterReceive = e.eventNumber;
7:     } else {
8:        if (e.type == RECEIVE && e.cluster().inverseMap[e.partner().process] == -1)
9:           mergeClusters(e, e.partner());
10:       for (j = 0 ; j < e.cluster().size ; ++j)
11:          e.clusterTimestamp[j] = e.FM[e.cluster().map[j]];
12:       e.clusterReceive = GCR[e.process];
13:    }
14:    Clean up Fidge/Mattern timestamps;
15: }
```

Fig. 2. Two-Level Self-Organizing Cluster Timestamps

a cluster receive (that is, the event is a receive event with a partner transmit event that occurred in a different cluster), the algorithm first determines if the two clusters are mergable. If they are, then they are merged, and the event is given the shorter cluster timestamp. Only if they are not mergable is the event left with its Fidge/Mattern timestamp. Insofar as the dynamic clustering algorithm captures communication locality patterns, future communication is also in-cluster, and will likewise receive the shorter cluster timestamp.

The determination of the mergability of clusters is an orthogonal function in our timestamping algorithm, and not the core subject of this paper. However, there is an implicit constraint on acceptable clustering methods. Specifically, the method must be relatively dynamic. It cannot look at more than a few events within a couple of clusters before deciding that the clusters are mergable. The reason is that after an event is timestamped, its timestamp will never change. Therefore, if clusters are to merge, the sooner the merger occurs, the less false cluster-receive events there will be (that is, events that are timestamped as cluster receives, since the merger had not occurred at the time the event was timestamped.). This substantially constrains the possible clustering methods, since most clustering algorithms must look at the entire data set, or at least a randomly selected sample of it, and require multiple iterations rather than clustering in one pass.

For our experimental analysis we used a simple greedy heuristic of merging two clusters whenever processes in the clusters communicate, subject to an upper bound on cluster size. This is probably a worst-case dynamic clustering algorithm, and so insofar as it provides good results, better clustering methods will only improve the results.

The timestamp-creation algorithm is shown in Fig.2. Before we describe the algorithm, a few notation points will help the reader understand the code. Each event is an object in the event class which contains, among other things, the event number (e.eventNumber), process identifier (e.process), a reference to the event's greatest preceding cluster receive within the process (e.clusterReceive), a pointer to the FidgeMattern timestamp (e.FM), if it exists, and a pointer to the cluster timestamp (e.clusterTimestamp). The event class also contains two important methods: cluster() and partner(). The cluster() method returns a reference to the cluster that the process belonged to at the time the event was timestamped. We note at this point that we have designed our algorithm such that the cluster information for any cluster will be maintained as it was at the time an event was timestamped even after cluster mergers. We will explain this point in more detail when we describe the cluster merging algorithm of Fig.3. The partner() method returns a reference to the event's partner event, if any.

Cluster information is maintained in an array of clusters, one for each process in the initial instance. The information that a cluster maintains is its current size, a mapping from cluster timestamp vector locations to process identifiers (this is, a simple array indicating which process each vector element corresponds to), and an inverse mapping from process identifiers to cluster timestamp vector locations (this is, a hash array, since most processes will not have entries in a cluster timestamp). Information pertaining to the merging of clusters is maintained by an array of lists of merge points, which indicate at what event a given cluster merged with another cluster, and what cluster it merged with. As with the original cluster timestamp algorithm, this algorithm maintains a vector of all greatest cluster-receive events in all processes, referred to as GCR, initialized to 0. Process identifiers range from 0 to $N-1$, as do cluster identifiers. Events are numbered starting at 1.

The algorithm first computes the Fidge/Mattern timestamp. For events that are non-mergable cluster receives, it simply uses the Fidge/Mattern timestamp, and adjusts the vector of greatest cluster receives to identify this new event. The determination of mergability, as we have noted, is an orthogonal issue.

For events that are mergable cluster receives, we merge the clusters. This is done as shown in Fig.3. Note that the process for merging consists of appending to the mapping and inverse mapping vectors of the merged-into cluster those values from the merged-from cluster (lines 3 and 4). This ensures that all events in the merged-into cluster that were timestamped prior to the merger will still see the same mapping and inverse mapping data as was present at the time the events were timestamps. In addition, the processes in the merged-from cluster must for future events be identified as belonging to the merged-into cluster (lines 5 to 8).

After merging clusters, if required, the timestamp algorithm sets the cluster timestamp to the projection of the Fidge/Mattern timestamp over the cluster processes. This is sufficient to determine precedence within the cluster. To enable precedence determination beyond the cluster, it also records the greatest preceding cluster receive in the event's process. Finally, the algorithm deletes Fidge/Mattern timestamps that are no longer needed. The computation cost of

```
1: mergeClusters(e,f) {
2:   for (i = 0 ; i < f.cluster().size ; ++i) {
3:     e.cluster().map[e.cluster().size + i] = f.cluster().map[i];
4:     e.cluster().inverseMap[f.cluster().map[i]] = e.cluster()size + i;
5:     clusterMerges[f.cluster().map[i]][CMP[f.cluster().map[i]]].event =
6:         maxEvent[f.cluster().map[i]] + 1;
7:     clusterMerges[f.cluster().map[i]][CMP[f.cluster().map[i]]].cluster = e.process;
8:     ++CMP[f.cluster().map[i]];
9:   }
10:  e.cluster().size += f.cluster().size;
11: }
```

Fig. 3. Two-Level Cluster Merging

```
1: precedes(e,f) {
2:   if (f.cluster().inverseMap[e.process] != -1)
3:     return (e.clusterTimestamp[e.cluster().inverseMap[e.process]] <
4:             f.clusterTimestamp[f.cluster().inverseMap[e.process]]);
5:   else {
6:     for (j = 0 ; j < f.cluster().size ; ++j) {
7:       g = f.clusterTimestamp[j] - (f.process == f.cluster().map[j] ? 0 : 1);
8:       r = event(f.cluster().map[j],g).clusterReceive;
9:       if (e.clusterTimestamp[e.cluster().inverseMap[e.process]] <
10:          event(f.cluster().map[j],r).FM[e.process]);
11:        return true;
12:    }
13:  }
14:  return false;
15: }
```

Fig. 4. Two-Level Self-Organizing Timestamp Precedence Test

this algorithm is $O(N)$, where N is the number of processes. This cost arises because of the need to compute the Fidge/Mattern timestamp in line 2.

The precedence-test algorithm for the two-level self-organizing cluster timestamp is shown in Fig.4. The algorithm first determines if event f's cluster contains the process that contains event e (line 2). This is a simple matter of checking f's cluster's inverse mapping for e's process identifier. A -1 is returned from the hash if the value is not found. If f's cluster contains e, the algorithm applies the Fidge/Mattern test, using the inverse mapping function to select the correct elements of the vectors (lines 3 and 4). If the events are in different clusters, then the algorithm needs to determine if there is a cluster receive causally prior to f that is a successor of e. The test computes this by determining f's set of greatest preceding cluster receives (lines 7 and 8) and checking each in turn to see if e is prior to it (lines 9 and 10). The computation cost of this test is constant for events within the same cluster and $O(f.cluster().size)$ between clusters.

```
1: timestamp(e) {
2:     e.FM = Fidge/Mattern(e);
3:     k = 1;
4:     while (e.type == RECEIVE && e.cluster(k).inverseMap[e.partner().process] == -1
5:            && !mergable(k, e, e.partner())) {
6:         e.clusterReceive[k] = GCR[k][e.process] = e.eventNumber;
7:         ++k;
8:     }
9:     if (e.type == RECEIVE && e.cluster(k).inverseMap[e.partner().process] == -1)
10:        mergeClusters(k, e, f);
11:    e.clusterReceive[k] = GCR[k][e.process];
11:    for (j = 0 ; j < e.cluster(k).size ; ++j)
12:        e.clusterTimestamp[j] = e.FM[e.cluster(k).map[j]];
13:    Clean up Fidge/Mattern timestamps;
14: }
```

Fig. 5. Hierarchical Dynamic Cluster Timestamping

3.2 Hierarchical Self-Organizing Clusters

We now merge the two-level self-organizing algorithm with the hierarchical cluster algorithm of [17]. The resulting algorithm is presented in Fig.5. Clusters are now organized in a hierarchy and assigned a level, starting at 0, which is the innermost cluster. At the highest level is a cluster that comprises the entire computation. The event class now has a cluster(k) method which returns a reference to the level-k cluster that the process belonged to at the time the event was timestamped. The cluster class itself remains unaltered, though the array of clusters now becomes an array of levels of clusters. The cluster-merging data structures likewise have an additional parameter for cluster level, but are otherwise unaltered.

As with the two-level algorithm, the starting point is computing the Fidge/Mattern timestamp of the event (line 2). The **while** loop of lines 4 to 8 then identifies either the cluster in which both events reside, or two clusters, at level-k in the hierarchy, that should be merged. In the event of the latter, we perform essentially the same cluster merge operation as for the two-level algorithm, but adjust the cluster method calls to include the value k, so as to merge the correct clusters. Note also that the algorithm can no longer maintain just one GCRvector, but must maintain such a vector for every cluster level, per the algorithm of [17]. Other than these points, the algorithm is identical to the two-level algorithm of Fig.2. The computation cost of this timestamp-creation algorithm is $O(N)$ as it requires the calculation of the Fidge/Mattern timestamp for each event.

The precedence-test algorithm, shown in Fig.6 is essentially identical to that of hierarchical cluster timestamps. The primary differences are the same as those that occurred in the two-level algorithm, except the cluster method calls now require a cluster level. The computation cost of this test is iden-

```
1: precedes(e,f) {
2:    if (f.cluster(1).inverseMap[e.process] == -1)
3:       return (e.clusterTimestamp[e.cluster(1).inverseMap[e.process]] <
4:              f.clusterTimestamp[f.cluster(1).inverseMap[e.process]]);
5:    k = 1;
6:    currentTimestamp = f.clusterTimestamp;
7:    while (f.cluster(k).inverseMap[e.process] == -1 {
8:       newTimestamp = 0;
9:       for (j = 0 ; j < f.cluster(k).size ; ++j) {
10:         g = currentTimestamp[j] - (f.process == f.cluster(k).map[j] ? 0 : 1);
11:         r = event(f.cluster(k).map[j],g).clusterReceive[k];
11:         newTimestamp = max(event(f.cluster(k).map[j],r).,newTimestamp);
12:      }
13:      ++k;
14:      currentTimestamp = newTimestamp;
15:   }
16:   for (j = 0 ; j < f.cluster(k).size ; ++j) {
17:      g = currentTimestamp[j] - (f.process == f.cluster(k).map[j] ? 0 : 1);
18:      r = event(f.cluster(k).map[j],g).clusterReceive[k];
19:      if (e.clusterTimestamp[e.cluster(1).inverseMap[e.process]] <
20:         event(f.cluster(k).map[j],r).clusterTimestamp[e.cluster(k+1)
                                                     .inverseMap[e.process]]);
21:         return true;
22:   }
23:   return false;
24: }
```

Fig. 6. Hierarchical Cluster Timestamp Precedence Test

tical to that of the original hierarchical cluster timestamp algorithm, being $O(\text{f.cluster(k-2).size f.cluster(k-1).size})$ in general, where the events are in the same level-k cluster. It is $O(\text{f.cluster(1).size})$ if the events are in the same level-1 cluster, and constant if they are in the same level-0 cluster.

4 Experimental Results

We have evaluated our algorithms over several dozen distributed computations covering a variety of different environments, including Java [5], PVM [4] and DCE [2], with up to 300 processes. The PVM programs tended to be SPMD style parallel computations. As such, they frequently exhibited close neighbour communication and scatter-gather patterns. The Java programs were web-like applications, including various web-server executions. The DCE programs were sample business application code.

For our experiments we compared the space requirements for three algorithms: Fidge/Mattern timestamps, pre-determined contiguous cluster timestamps, and self-organizing cluster timestamps. The clustering method used

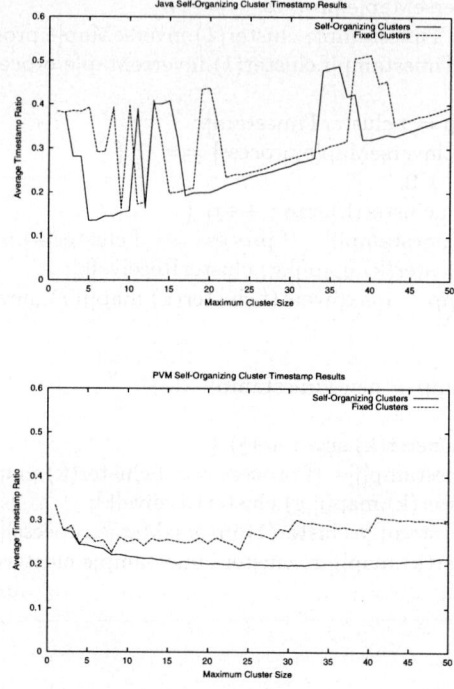

Fig. 7. Ratio of Cluster to Fidge/Mattern Timestamp Sizes

for the self-organizing clusters was to merge clusters on first communication, up to a maximum cluster size. The form of the experiments was to vary the cluster size (maximum cluster size in the case of the self-organizing clusters) from 1 to 50 and observe the ratio of the average cluster timestamp size to the Fidge/Mattern timestamp size. We presumed that the observation tool knew the number of processes in the computation, and encoded the Fidge/Mattern timestamp as a vector of that size.

Sample results for Java and PVM respectively are shown in Fig.7. We can see from these results that the primary objective of this work has been largely achieved. The self-organizing cluster timestamps typically require less space than do the pre-determined cluster timestamps. Of far greater significance, however, is the fact that the self-organizing clusters are far more stable in their space-consumption requirement than are the pre-determined clusters. Note that the Java example demonstrates a size ratio of between 12 and 15 percent of Fidge/Mattern over a range of maximum cluster size from 5 to 10. By contrast, the pre-determined cluster algorithm experienced a size ratio of between 15 and 40 percent of Fidge/Mattern over the same range of cluster size. While there are still spikes in the Java results, they are less frequent, and more easily avoided by our observation tool. Likewise, in the PVM case, the size requirement is both lower, and the range of cluster size in which average cluster timestamp size is within a small factor of that minimum is much larger.

This effect of more consistent and slightly better space-consumption was observed over almost all experiments that we ran. In no instance did our self-organizing cluster timestamps achieve worse results than pre-determined clusters. In the cases where the results were no better, it was readily observed that the pre-determined clusters happened to be a good selection. This typically happened in PVM programs where the communication was extremely regular and coincided with the pre-determined clusters. It should be noted that had the communication been regular but counter to the pre-determined clusters, then the pre-determined cluster approach would have produced very poor results. The self-organizing clusters do not suffer from this problem. Indeed, this is precisely what they overcome.

The full raw result information for our experiments are available on our web site at http://www.shoshin.uwaterloo.ca/~pasward/ClusterTimestamp.

5 Conclusions and Future Work

We have presented an algorithm for self-organizing hierarchical cluster timestamps. These timestamps capture the communication locality that is required for cluster timestamps to be effective. We have presented experimental results that demonstrate that our algorithm is more stable with cluster size and provides timestamps whose average size is consistently superior to a pre-determined cluster approach, even with a poor clustering algorithm.

There are several areas of future work that we are actively exploring. First, we are looking at alternate, more sophisticated, dynamic clustering algorithms. Specifically, we are developing a clustering algorithm that observes several communication events before deciding on the suitability of a cluster merger. The tradeoff is an increase in the number of false cluster-receive events. Second, and in a similar vein, we are extending this work to enable dynamically reconfigurable clusters. This is needed when communication patterns are not stable in long running computations or to correct mistakes made by the dynamic clustering algorithm. Third, we are looking at a technique to allow for overlapping clusters at the same level in the hierarchy. This may be a significant benefit when neighbouring processes communicate. Specifically, while it increases the cluster vector size slightly, it can reduce the precedence-test time by enabling in-cluster testing.

Fourth, we plan to more thoroughly explore the tradeoffs in cluster size and arrangement for the hierarchical algorithm with three or more cluster levels. This is a complex tradeoff between average timestamp size, timestamp-creation time, precedence-test time, and greatest-predecessor-set computation time.

Finally, we are investigating the integration of this timestamp technique with the POET system. The primary issue is that the POET system is based on fixed-size FidgeMattern timestamps, with their distributed-precedence-testing capability. The implications of variable-size timestamps requiring centralized-timestamp testing are unclear.

References

1. Colin Fidge. Logical time in distributed computing systems. *IEEE Computer*, 24(8):28–33, 1991.
2. Open Software Foundation. *Introduction to OSF/DCE*. Prentice-Hall, Englewood Cliffs, New Jersey, 1993.
3. Jerry Fowler and Willy Zwaenepoel. Causal distributed breakpoints. In *Proceedings of the 10th IEEE International Conference on Distributed Computing Systems*, pages 134–141. IEEE Computer Society Press, 1990.
4. Al Geist, Adam Begulin, Jack Dongarra, Weicheng Jiang, Robert Manchek, and Vaidy Sunderam. *PVM: Parallel Virtual Machine*. MIT Press, Cambridge, Massachusetts, 1994.
5. James Gosling, Bill Joy, and Guy Steele. *The Java Language Specification*. Addison-Wesley, 1996. Available at http://java.sun.com/docs/books/jls/.
6. IBM Corporation. IBM distributed debugger for workstations. Online documentation available at: http://www-4.ibm.com/software/webservers/appserv/doc/v35/ae/infocenter/olt/index.html.
7. Claude Jard and Guy-Vincent Jourdan. Dependency tracking and filtering in distributed computations. Technical Report 851, IRISA, Campus de Beaulieu – 35042 Rennes Cedex – France, August 1994.
8. Valerie King and Garry Sagert. A fully dynamic algorithm for maintaining the transitive closure. In *Proceedings of the Thirty-First Annual ACM Symposium on Theory of Computing*, pages 492–498. ACM, 1999.
9. Deiter Kranzlmüller, Siegfried Grabner, R. Schall, and Jens Volkert. ATEMPT — A Tool for Event ManiPulaTion. Technical report, Institute for Computer Science, Johannes Kepler University Linz, May 1995.
10. Dieter Kranzlmüller. *Event Graph Analysis for Debugging Massively Parallel Programs*. PhD thesis, GUP Linz, Linz, Austria, 2000.
11. Thomas Kunz, James P. Black, David J. Taylor, and Twan Basten. POET: Target-system independent visualisations of complex distributed-application executions. *The Computer Journal*, 40(8):499–512, 1997.
12. Leslie Lamport. Time, clocks and the ordering of events in distributed systems. *Communications of the ACM*, 21(7):558–565, 1978.
13. Oystein Ore. *Theory of Graphs*, volume 38. Amer. Math. Soc. Colloq. Publ., Providence, R.I., 1962.
14. Reinhard Schwarz and Friedemann Mattern. Detecting causal relationships in distributed computations: In search of the holy grail. *Distributed Computing*, 7(3):149–174, 1994.
15. M. Singhal and A. Kshemkalyani. An efficient implementation of vector clocks. *Information Processing Letters*, 43:47–52, August 1992.
16. Paul A.S. Ward. A framework algorithm for dynamic, centralized dimension-bounded timestamps. In *Proceedings of the 2000 CAS Conference*, November 2000.
17. Paul A.S. Ward and David J. Taylor. A hierarchical cluster algorithm for dynamic, centralized timestamps. In *Proceedings of the 21st IEEE International Conference on Distributed Computing Systems*. IEEE Computer Society Press, 2001.

A Tool for Binding Threads to Processors

Magnus Broberg, Lars Lundberg, and Håkan Grahn

Department of Software Engineering and Computer Science
Blekinge Institute of Technology, P.O. Box 520, S-372 25 Ronneby, Sweden
{Magnus.Broberg, Lars.Lundberg, Hakan.Grahn}@bth.se

Abstract. Many multiprocessor systems are based on distributed shared memory. It is often important to statically bind threads to processors in order to avoid remote memory access, due to performance. Finding a good allocation takes long time and it is hard to know when to stop searching for a better one. It is sometimes impossible to run the application on the target machine. The developer needs a tool that finds the good allocations without the target multiprocessor. We present a tool that uses a greedy algorithm and produces allocations that are more than 40% faster (in average) than when using a binpacking algorithm. The number of allocations to be evaluated can be reduced by 38% with a 2% performance loss. Finally, an algorithm is proposed that is promising in avoiding local maxima.

1 Introduction

Parallel processing is a way of increasing application performance. Applications made for parallel processing are also likely to have high performance requirements. Many multiprocessor systems are based on a distributed shared memory system, e.g., SGI Origin 2000, Sun's WildFire [4]. To minimize remote memory accesses, one can bind threads statically to processors. This can also improve the cache hit ratio [8] in SMPs. Moreover, some multiprocessor systems do not permit run-time reallocation of threads. Finding an optimal static allocation of threads to processors is NP-complete [7].

Parallel programs are no longer tailored for a specific number of processors, this in order to reduce the maintenance etc. This means that different customers, with different multiprocessors, will share the same application code. The developer have to make the application run efficiently on different numbers of processors, even to scale-up beyond the number of processors available in a multiprocessor today in order to meet future needs. There is thus no single target environment and the development environment is often the (single processor) workstation on the developer's desk.

Heuristics are usually able to find better bindings if one lets them run for a long period of time. There is a trade-off between the time spent searching for good allocations and the performance of the program on a multiprocessor. Another property of the heuristics is that the improvement per time unit usually decreases as the search progresses. It is thus not trivial to decide when to stop searching for a better best allocation.

In operating systems like Sun Solaris there is little support to make an adequate allocation. A tool called `tha` [10] only gives the total execution time for each thread enough for an algorithm like binpacking [7] which does not take thread synchronization into consideration. The result is quite useless, since the synchronizations do impact.

In this paper we present a tool for automatically determining an allocation of threads to processors. The tool runs on the developer's single-processor workstation, and does not require any multiprocessor in order to produce an allocation. The tool considers thread synchronizations, thus producing reliable and relevant allocations.

In Sect. 2 an overview of the tool is found. Empirical studies are found in Sect. 3. In Sect. 4 related and future work is found. The conclusions are found in Sect. 5.

2 Overview of the Tool

The tool used for evaluation of different allocations is called VPPB (Visualization of Parallel Program Behaviour) [1] and [2] and consists of the Recorder and the Simulator. The *deterministic* application is executed on a single-processor workstation, the Recorder is automatically placed *between* the program and the thread library. Every time the program uses the routines in the thread library, the call passes through the Recorder which records information about the call. The input for the simulator is the recorded information and an allocation of threads generated by the Allocation Algorithm. The output from the Simulator is the execution time for the application on a multiprocessor with the given size and allocation. The predicted execution time is fed into the Allocation Algorithm and a new allocation is generated. Simulations are repeated until the Allocation Algorithm decides to stop. The evaluation of a single allocation by the Simulator is called a *test*. The VPPB system works for C/C++ programs with POSIX [3] or Solaris 2.X [11] threads. In [1] and [2] the Simulator was validated with dynamically scheduled threads. We validated the tool on a Sun Enterprise 4000 with eight processors with statically bound threads and used nine applications with 28 threads, generated as in Sect. 3. The maximum error is 8.3%, which is similar to the previous errors found in [1] and [2].

3 Empirical Studies with the Greedy Algorithm

3.1 The Greedy Algorithm

The Greedy Algorithm is based on a binpacking algorithm and makes changes (swap and move) to the initial allocation and test it. If the new allocation is better it is used as the base for next change and so it continues, see Fig. 1. The algorithm keeps track of all previous allocations in order to not test the same allocation several times.

3.2 The Test Applications Used in This Study

In this study we used 4,000 automatically generated applications divided into eight groups of 500 applications with 8, 12, 16, 20, 24, 28, 32, and 36 threads, respectively. Each application contains critical sections protected by semaphores. The number of critical sections is between two and three times the number of threads. Each thread executes first for 2^x time units, x is 0 to 15 throughout this section. Then, with a probability of 50%, the thread enters (if possible) a critical section or exits (if possible) a critical section. Deadlocks are avoided by a standard locking hierarchy. The threads are divided into groups. Threads within one group only synchronizes with each other. The number of groups is between one up to half of the number of threads. With a probability of 93.75% the thread continues to execute for 2^x time units then enter or exit a critical section and so on. With a probability of 6.25% the thread will start terminating by releasing it's critical sections. Exiting each critical section is proceeded with an execution for 2^x time units. Finally, the thread executes for 2^x time units.

```
Allocation bestAlloc = allocateAccordingToBinpack();
Time bestExecutionTime = simulate(bestAlloc);
addToAllocationHistory(bestAlloc);
algorithm(bestAlloc);

procedure algorithm(Allocation alloc) {
  Time executionTime;
  if(random() > 0.5 and allThreadsAreNotOnTheSameProcessor())
    swapARandomThreadWithARandomThreadOnAnotherProcessor(alloc);
  else
    moveARandomThreadToAnotherRandomProcessor(alloc);
  if(allocationIsAlreadyInAllocationHistory(alloc))
    { alogrithm(bestAlloc); return; }
  addToAllocationHistory(alloc);
  executionTime = simulate(alloc);
  if(executionTime == bestExecutionTime)
    { alogrithm(alloc); return; }
  if(executionTime < bestExecutionTime)
    { bestAlloc = alloc; bestExecutionTime = executionTime; }
  alogrithm(bestAlloc);
}
```

Fig. 1. The greedy algorithm in pseudo code

3.3 Characterizing the Greedy Algorithm

The Greedy Algorithm presented in Sect. 3.1 will actually never stop, thus in order to investigate its performance we had to manually set a limit. We chose to continue the algorithm until 500 tests had been performed. We also stored the so far best allocation when having done 20, 60, ... , 460, 500 tests, shown in Fig. 2. When the number of tests is high yet another 40 tests will not decrease the application's execution time much.

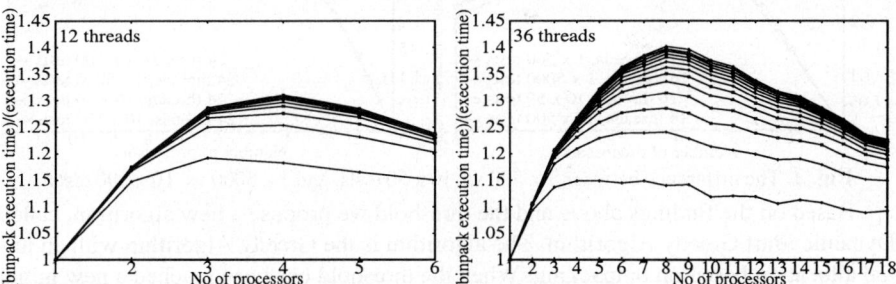

Fig. 2. The average gain by using the Greedy Algorithm as compared to binpacking

3.4 A Threshold for the Greedy Algorithm

The graphs in Fig. 2 clearly shows that it should be possible to define a threshold that stops the Greedy Algorithm to do more tests when the gain will not be significant. The stop criterion for the Greedy Algorithm is defined as to stop when a number of consecutive tests have not gained anything in execution time. We have empirically found that 100 consecutive tests is a good stop criterion if we accept a 2% loss in performance compared to performing 500 tests. By reducing the gain by 2% we reduce the number of tests by 38%. This is of important practical value since the number of tests performed is proportional to the time it takes to calculate the allocation. Performing 500 tests took at most two minutes for any application in the population used in this study.

3.5 Local Maxima and Proposing a New Algorithm

There is always the danger of getting stuck in a local maximum and the Greedy Algorithm is not an exception. In order to investigate if the algorithm runs into a local maximum we used the previous application population with 16 and 24 threads. By giving the Greedy Algorithm a random initial allocation, instead of an allocation based on binpacking, we reduced the risk of getting stuck in the same local maximum.

The result of using 10 x 500 vs. 1 x 5000 tests and 10 x 50 vs. 1 x 500 tests is shown in Fig. 3. As can be seen, sometimes it is better to run ten times from different starting allocations than running the Greedy Algorithm ten times longer from a single starting allocations and sometimes it is not. The reason is found in Fig. 2. As the number of tests increases the gain will be less and less for each test. Thus, when the number of tests reaches a certain level the Greedy Algorithm is close to a local maximum and ten times more tests will gain very little. By using ten new initial allocations that particular local maximum can be avoided, and if the new initial allocations are fortunate a better result is found when reaching the same number of tests. This is what happened in the case with 10 x 500 and 1 x 5000. On the other hand if the number of tests is low the Greedy Algorithm still can gain much with running the same initial allocation for ten times longer. This opposed to running ten Greedy Algorithm with random initial allocation to the previously low tests. This is the case for 10 x 50 and 1 x 500.

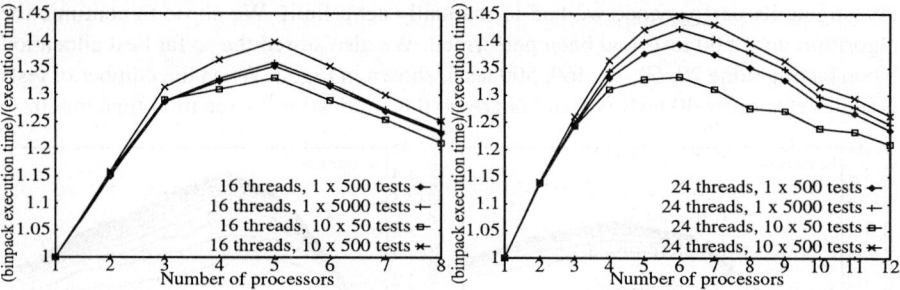

Fig. 3. The difference between 1 x 500 vs. 10 x 50 tests, and 1 x 5000 vs. 10 x 500 tests

Based on the findings above and the threshold we propose a new algorithm, called Dynamic Start Greedy Algorithm. The algorithm is the Greedy Algorithm with an initial allocation based on binpacking. When the threshold has been reached a new initial allocation is created and the algorithm continues until the threshold is reached again. The new algorithm uses the threshold in order to determine whether it is useful to continue running or not. At the same time the algorithm is able to stop running and choose a new initial allocation before it runs too long time with an initial allocation The history of already tested allocations should be kept from one initial allocation to the next.

The Dynamic Start Greedy Algorithm continues with an initial allocation until it reaches a local maximum, then it jumps to a new initial allocation to investigate if it is better. This is the inverse of simulated annealing [6] that jumps frequently in the beginning and more seldom after a while.

4 Related and Future Work

The GAST tool [5] is somewhat similar to the tool described here. GAST originates from the real-time area. With GAST it is possible to automate scheduling, by defining different scheduling algorithms. The GAST tool needs a specification of all tasks, their worst case execution time, period, deadline and dependencies. This specification must be done by hand, which could be a very tedious task to do. Also, high performance computing does not necessarily have either periods or deadlines and a task in GAST may only be a fraction of a thread, since a task can not synchronize with another task inside the task. Each thread must then (by hand) be split into several tasks.

The Greedy Algorithm could be compared, using the tool described in this paper, by replacing the algorithm with simulated annealing [6], etc. This, however, is considered to be future work.

5 Conclusion

We have presented and validated a tool that makes it possible to execute an application on a single processor workstation and let the tool find an allocation for the application on a multiprocessor with any number of processors. The tool uses a Greedy Algorithm that may improve the performance of an application with more than 40% (in average) compared to the binpacking algorithm. We have also shown that it is possible do define a stop criterion that stops the algorithm when there have been no gain for a certain time. By trading off a speed-up loss of 2% we reduced the number of tests performed with 38%. Finally, a new algorithm is proposed that seems promising in giving even better allocations and reducing the risk of getting stuck in a local maxima.

References

1. Broberg, M., Lundberg, L., Grahn, H.: Visualization and Performance Prediction of Multi-threaded Solaris Programs by Tracing Kernel Threads. Proc. IPPS (1999) 407-413
2. Broberg, M., Lundberg, L., Grahn, H.: VPPB - A Visualization and Performance Prediction Tool for Multithreaded Solaris Programs. Proc. IPPS (1998) 770-776
3. Butenhof, D.: Programming with POSIX Threads. Addison-Wesley (1997)
4. Hagersten, E., Koster, M.: WildFire: A Scalable Path for SMPs. Proc. 5th Int Symp. on High Performance Computer Architecture (1999) 172-181
5. Jonsson, J.: GAST: A Flexible and Extensible Tool for Evaluating Multiprocessor Assignment and Scheduling Techniques. Proc. ICPP, (1998) 441-450
6. Kirkpatrick, S.: Optimization by Simulated Annealing: Quantitative Studies. J. Statistical Physics **34** (1984) 975-986
7. Krishna, C., Shin, K.: Real-Time Systems. The McGraw-Hill Companies, Inc. (1997)
8. Lundberg, L.: Evaluating the Performance Implications of Binding Threads to Processors. Proc. 4th Int Conf. on High Performance Computing (1997) 393-400
9. Powell, M., Kleiman, S., Barton, S., Shah, D., Stein, D., Weeks, M.: SunOS 5.0 Multithreaded Architecture. Sun Soft, Sun Microsystems, Inc. (1991)
10. Sun Man Pages: tha, Sun Microsystems Inc. (1996)
11. Sun Soft: Solaris Multithreaded Programming Guide. Prentice Hall (1995)

VizzScheduler - A Framework for the Visualization of Scheduling Algorithms

Welf Löwe and Alex Liebrich

Institut für Programmstrukturen und Datenorganisation, Universität Karlsruhe
Postfach 6980, 76128 Karlsruhe, Germany
{loewe,liebrich}@ipd.info.uni-karlsruhe.de

Abstract. Efficient scheduling of task graphs for parallel machines is a major issue in parallel computing. Such algorithms are often hard to understand and hard to evaluate. We present a framework for the visualization of scheduling algorithms. Using the *LogP* cost model for parallel machines, we simulate the effects of scheduling algorithms for specific target machines and task graphs before performing time and resource consumptive measurements in practice.

1 Introduction

Parallel programs can be modeled by task graphs defining a set of parallel tasks and control and data dependencies between them. A schedule of a task graph is a mapping of its tasks to processors. Finding an optimal mapping is an *NP* hard problem for many task graph classes and many models of parallel machines.

A great variety of scheduling algorithms for different task graph classes and cost models has been published. However, it is hard to evaluate their performance in practice. It depends on the ratio for computation and communication costs on a specific architecture (granularity of the problem), the structure of the task graph, the ratio of tasks that may potentially run in parallel and the actual number of processor in a specific parallel machine etc. Evaluations varying these factor are extremely time and resource consumptive. On the other hand, it is quite disappointing to take the effort of evaluation for some theoretical promising algorithm and to find it poor in its actual performance. We therefore designed a framework allowing a rapid evaluation of scheduling algorithms. We restrict the experimental evaluations to only those scheduling algorithms that passed successfully our simulations.

Another problem with scheduling algorithms addresses their understanding. We found scheduling algorithms published imprecise, misunderstanding of even wrong. As the feed back showed, our own publications were no exceptions. It often requires some attempts to finally find the intended implementation. Therefore, the framework allows a step-by-step execution visualizing together the task being scheduled, the schedule (as computed so far) and the current line of program code in the scheduling algorithm. This execution mode is a good tool for testing and debugging the algorithms before applying or publishing them. As a by-product, it turned out that communicating new scheduling algorithms in presentations became much easier when using our VizzScheduler.

2 Basics

To abstract from the diversity of parallel machines, we need an abstract *machine model*. To evaluate schedules, a cost model is required reflecting the latency for point-to-point communication in the network, the overhead of communication on processors themselves, and the network bandwidth. The *LogP* machine [1] models these communication costs with parameters *Latency*, *overhead*, and *gap* (which is actually the inverse of the bandwidth per processor). An additional parameter describes the number of *Processors*. These parameters have been determined for a number of parallel machines including the CM-5 [1], the IBM SP1 machine [3], a network of workstations and a powerXplorer [2]. Moreover, we need the input size of the problem and the runtime of the single tasks to predict the runtime of the scheduled program. The latter is usually obtained from measurements of the sequential program or a simple scheduled parallel program. It is clear that this leads to errors due to different caching effect and tasks with input dependent load cannot be captured at all. However, this approach leads to precise predictions of parallel programs for a large class of problems. In practice, the runtime measurements of parallel program confirmed their *LogP* based predictions. There are quite a few *LogP* scheduling algorithms published, e.g. in [1,2,5,6]. In order to evaluate them, we only need the *LogP* runtime prediction for a given problem of a given size. To debug or explain the algorithms, we additionally need an architecture allowing to load a scheduling algorithm, execute it step-by-step and draw temporary results. The *Java Debug Architecture* [4] provides access the relevant internal data structures for Java programs. It allows to launch a runtime environment for a program, to start a debugee (scheduling algorithm) and to control its execution by another program. In each execution step, the control program can access the state of the debugee.

The two main data structures that should be visualized are the task graph and its schedule generated by the scheduling algorithm. The former is a directed, acyclic graph; its node represent computational tasks its edges essential dependencies between them. The latter is usually visualized by Gantt charts, a graph showing the computations of the single processors over time. Gantt charts are quite easy to handle since the fix coordinates system of processors and time reduce the drawing problem to a simple scaling. Actually, we could try to find a permutation of the processors minimizing the edge crossings. In practice we do not. As the layout is computed online while the scheduling algorithm runs, this approach would lead to animations that potentially change the order of processors whenever an edge is inserted. Tasks graphs, or directed acyclic graphs (*DAG*s) in general, do not have such a canonical drawing. An optimal drawing also minimizes edge crossings, its efficient computation is not possible, unless *P=NP*. Our framework does not try to innovate *graph drawing*. Good approximation algorithms are known, e.g. heuristic spring embedding approaches, Sugiyama's algorithm [7] (preserving the layered structure of *DAG*s, i.e. nodes with the same depth are drawn on the same y-coordinate) or so called upward drawings. These approaches are sufficient for our purpose and used in the framework.

3 The Architecture

We developed a more general framework, the VizzEditor, supporting the rapid design of visualizations of general algorithms. The VizzScheduler is an instance of the VizzEditor. The VizzEditor accesses the Java Debug Interface and provides certain imaging tools. It enables the integration of user defined graphical tools viewing aspects of the programs that are chosen by the user. In addition to some static information the VizzEditor can draw dynamic program information. Therefore, the information is read at certain user-defined breakpoints and mapped to drawing operations of the graphical views. A general controller coordinates the synchronous update of the program to visualize and the graphical views. Each breakpoint hit generates an event object sent to the controller. This object holds information about the breakpoint (necessary for some filtering) and entries to access the program state (necessary to obtain the runtime data). It passes this object to the mapping program which in turn performs filtering and calls the drawing operations. In many cases the predefined graphical tools are sufficient. To visualize an algorithm, the user implements a mapping program, a Java class, and determines the breakpoint in the algorithm implementation.

We can even reduce these user tasks to a minimum if we know the class of animated algorithms in advance. Then we write an abstract class that captures the class specific data and operations. The new algorithm extends this abstract class and, thus, runs in the predefined environment. If the breakpoints are placed in the predefined code, we can predefine a general mapping program for all algorithms of this class. We applied this approach to the class of scheduling algorithms leading to the VizzScheduler. It restricts the algorithms to visualize to *simulations of parallel programs* and *scheduling algorithms* for task graphs. Simulations are visualized by task graph constructions. A step-by-step execution of a parallel program (simulation) shows the task graph construction; it visualizes program points corresponding to computations and communications. The scheduling algorithms take arbitrary task graphs (as generated by a parallel program simulation) and generate a mapping to an instance of the *LogP* machine. Scheduling algorithms are visualized by Gantt charts. A step-by-step execution shows the decision of the algorithm to place a task on a certain processor starting at a certain time. Four major classes represent our application context:

1. The class modeling *task graphs* as generated by simulations of parallel programs.
2. The abstract class modeling *simulations of parallel programs*. It captures the input and input size of the algorithm. Each simulation constructs an instance of the task graph class. This instance is passed to the subclasses of *scheduling algorithms*.
3. The abstract class modeling *scheduling algorithms*. It accesses the *LogP* parameters (captured in an auxiliary class) and the task graph to be scheduled. Each scheduling algorithm must construct an instance of *schedules*.
4. The class modeling the *schedules* themselves contains the constructors for well-defined *LogP* schedules and captures the schedule information.

The breakpoints are set on the constructor methods of the task graph and schedule classes. This is sufficient to animate the task graph and schedule construction algorithms, respectively. Therefore, we predefined also the two programs (classes) mapping the breakpoint events to drawings.

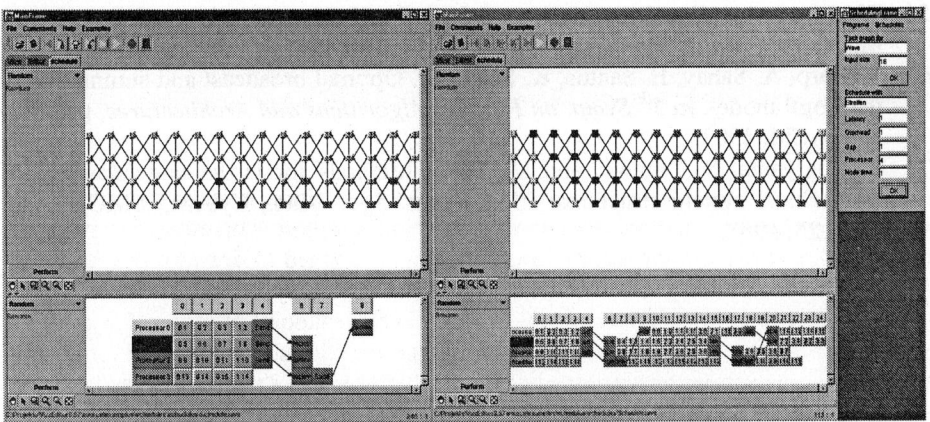

Fig. 1. Left frame: scheduling in action. Right frame: the final schedule

The user of the VizzScheduler looks for a simulation of a parallel program in the library or implements a new simulation class (inheriting form the corresponding abstract class that is predefined in the framework). Such a simulation calls the constructor methods in the class modeling the task graph. Running a simulation automatically triggers the drawing of the corresponding task graph. Then the user looks for a scheduling algorithm in the library or implements a new scheduling algorithm class (inheriting form the corresponding abstract one). The schedule construction uses the construction methods provided by the schedule class. Each run automatically triggers the drawing of the corresponding Gantt chart. In the VizzScheduler GUI, the user may vary the LogP parameters, the input size and the computation times of the task graph nodes. Fig. 1 displays a scheduling for an algorithm implementing a one-dimensional wave simulation. Get your free copy from
http://i44pc29.info.uni-karlsruhe.de/VizzWeb

References

1. D. Culler, R. Karp, D. Patterson, A. Sahay, K. Schauser, E. Santos, R. Subramonian, T. von Eicken. LogP: Towards a realistic model of parallel computation. In 4th *ACM SIGPLAN Symp. on Principles and Practice of Parallel Programming (PPOPP 93)*, pp 235-261, 1993.
2. J. Eisenbiegler, W. Löwe, W. Zimmermann. Optimizing parallel programs on machines with expensive communication. In *Europar' 96*, LNCS 1124, pp. 602-610. Springer, 1996.
3. B. Di Martino and G. Ianello. Parallelization of non-simultaneous iterative methods for systems of linear equations. In *Parallel Processing: CONPAR 94 - VAPP VI*, LNCS 854, pp. 253-264. Springer, 1994.
4. Java Debug Architecture:
http://java.sun.com/j2se/1.3/docs/guide/jpda/index.html.

5. W. Löwe and W. Zimmermann. Scheduling balanced task graphs to LogP-Machines. *Parallel Computing* 26, pp. 1083-1108, 2000.
6. R. Karp, A. Sahay, E. Santos, K. Schauser. Optimal broadcast and summation in the LogP model. In *5th Symp. on Parallel Algorithms and Architectures*, pp. 142-153. ACM, 1993.
7. K. Sugiyama, S. Tagawa, and M. Toda: Methods for visual understanding of hierarchical system structures. IEEE Trans. Syst. Man., Cybern,, SMC-11, pp. 109-125, 1981.

A Distributed Object Infrastructure for Interaction and Steering[*]

Rajeev Muralidhar and Manish Parashar

The Applied Software Systems Laboratory, Department of Electrical and Computer
Engineering, Rutgers, The State University of New Jersey
94 Brett Road, Piscataway, NJ 08854
{rajeevdm,parashar}@caip.rutgers.edu

Abstract. This paper presents the design, implementation and experimental evaluation of DIOS, an infrastructure for enabling the runtime monitoring and computational steering of parallel and distributed applications. DIOS enables existing application objects (data structures) to be enhanced with sensors and actuators so that they can be interrogated and controlled at runtime. Application objects can be distributed (spanning many processors) and dynamic (be created, deleted, changed or migrated). Furthermore, DIOS provides a control network that manages the distributed sensors and actuators and enables external discovery, interrogation, monitoring and manipulation of these objects at runtime. DIOS is currently being used to enable interactive monitoring and steering of a wide range of scientific applications, including oil reservoir, compressible turbulence and numerical relativity simulations.

1 Introduction

Simulations are playing an increasingly critical role in all areas of science and engineering. As the complexity and computational costs of these simulations grows, it has become important for the scientists and engineers to be able to monitor the progress of these simulations, and to control and steer them at runtime. Enabling seamless monitoring and interactive steering of parallel and distributed applications however, presents many challenges. A significant challenge is the definition and deployment of *sensors* and *actuators* to monitor and control application objects (algorithms and data structures). Defining these interaction interfaces and mechanisms in a generic manner, and co-locating them with the application's computational objects can be non-trivial. This is because the structure of application computational objects varies significantly, and the objects can span multiple processors and address spaces. The problem is further compounded in the case of adaptive applications (e.g. simulations on adaptive meshes) where the computational objects can be created, deleted, modified, migrated and redistributed on the fly. Another issue is the construction of a *control*

---

[*] Research supported by the National Science Foundation via grants number ACI 9984357 (CAREERS) awarded to Manish Parashar.

network that interconnects these sensors and actuators so that commands and requests can be routed to the appropriate set(s) of computational objects (depending on current distribution of the object), and the returned information can be collated and coherently presented. Finally, the interaction and steering interfaces presented by the application need to be exported so that they can be accessed remotely, to enable application monitoring and control.

This paper presents the design and evaluations of DIOS (Distributed Interactive Object Substrate), an interactive object infrastructure that supports application interaction and steering. DIOS addresses three key challenges - (1) Definition and deployment of interaction objects that encapsulate sensors and actuators for interrogation and control. Interaction objects can be distributed and dynamic, and can be derived from existing computational data-structures. Traditional (C, Fortran, etc.) data-structures can also be transformed into interaction objects using C++ wrappers. (2) Definition of a scalable control network interconnecting the interaction objects that enables discovery, interaction and control of distributed computational objects, and manages dynamic object creation, deletion, migration, and redistribution. The control network is hierarchical and is designed to support applications executing on large parallel/distributed systems. An experimental evaluation of the control network is presented. (3) Definition of an Interaction Gateway that uses JNI (Java Native Interface) to provide a Java enabled proxy to the application for interaction and steering. The interaction gateway enables remote clients to connect to, and access an application's computational objects (and thus its interaction interfaces) using standard distributed object protocols such as CORBA and Java RMI.

DIOS has been implemented as a C++ library and is currently being used to enable interactive monitoring, steering and control of a wide range of scientific applications, including oil reservoir, compressible turbulence and numerical relativity simulations. DIOS is a part of DISCOVER [3][1], an ongoing project aimed at developing an interactive computational collaboratory that enables geographically distributed clients to collaboratively connect to, monitor and steer applications using web-based portals.

The rest of the paper is organized as follows. Section 2 presents related work. Section 3 presents the design and operation of DIOS. Section 4 presents an experimental evaluation of DIOS. Section 5 presents concluding remarks.

2 Related Work

This section briefly describes related work in computational interaction and steering. A detailed classification of existing interactive and collaborative PSEs (Problem Solving Environments) is presented in [5]. Other surveys have been presented by Vetter et. al in [2] and van Liere et. al in [4]. Run-time interactive steering and control systems can be divided into two classes based on the type and level of the interaction support provided. (1) *Event based steering systems:*

---

[1] Information about the DISCOVER project can be found at *http://www.caip.rutgers.edu/TASSL/Projects/DISCOVER/*.

In these systems, monitoring and steering actions are based on low-level system "events" that occur during program execution. Application code is instrumented and interaction takes place when pre-defined events occur. The Progress [6] and Magellan [7] systems use this approach. (2) *High-level abstractions for steering and control:* The Mirror Object Steering System (MOSS) ([1]) provides a high-level model for steering applications. Mirror objects are analogues of application objects (data structures) and export application methods for interaction. We believe that high-level abstractions for interaction and steering provide the most general approach for enabling interactive applications. DIOS extends this approach.

3 DIOS: Distributed Interactive Object Substrate

DIOS is composed of 2 key components: 1) interaction objects that extend computational objects with sensors and actuators, and 2) a hierarchical control network composed of *Discover Agents, Base Stations,* and an *Interaction Gateway,* that interconnects the interaction objects and provides access to them.

3.1 Sensors, Actuators and Interaction Objects

Computational objects are the objects (data-structures, algorithms) used by the application for its computations. In order to enable application interaction and steering, these objects must export interaction interfaces that enable their state to be externally monitored and changed. Sensors provide an interface for viewing the current state of the object, while actuators provide an interface to process commands to modify the state. Note that the sensors and actuators need to be co-located in memory with the computational objects and have access their internal state. If the computational objects are distributed across multiple processors and can be dynamically created, deleted, migrated and redistributed on-the-fly, multiple sensors and actuators now have to coordinate and collectively process interaction requests.

DIOS provides an API to enable applications to define sensors and actuators. This is achieved by simply deriving the computational objects from a virtual interaction base class provided by DIOS. The derived objects can then selectively overload the base class methods to define their interaction interface as a set of views (sensors) that they can provide and a set of commands (actuators) that they can accept. For example, a Grid object might export views for its structure and distribution. Commands for the Grid object may include refine, coarsen, and redistribute. This process requires minimal modification to original computational objects. Interaction interfaces are exported to the interaction server using a simple Interaction IDL (Interface Definition Language). The Interaction IDL contains metadata for interface discovery and access and is compatible with standard distributed object interfaces like CORBA and RMI. In the case of applications written in non-object-oriented languages such as Fortran, application data structures are first converted into computation objects using a C++ wrapper object. These objects are then transformed into interaction objects.

Interaction objects can be *local*, *global* or *distributed* depending on the address space(s) they span during the course of the computation. Local objects belong to a single address space and there could be multiple instances of a local object on different processors. They can also migrate to another processor at run time. Global objects are similar, but have exactly one instance (that could be replicated on all processors). A distributed interaction object spans multiple processors' address spaces. An example is a distributed array partitioned across available computational nodes. These objects contain an additional distribution attribute that maintains its current distribution type (blocked, staggered, inverse space filling curve-based, or custom) and layout. This attribute can change during the lifetime of the object, e.g. when the object is redistributed. Each distribution type is associated with *gather* and *scatter* operations. Gather aggregates information from the distributed components of the object, while scatter performs the reverse operation. For example, in the case of a distributed array object, the gather operation would collate views generated from sub-blocks of the array while the scatter operator would scatter a query to the relevant sub-blocks. An application can select from a library of gather/scatter methods for popular distribution types provided by DIOS, or can register gather/scatter methods for customized distribution types.

3.2 DIOS Control Network and Interaction Agents

The control network has a hierarchical structure composed of three kinds of interaction agents, Discover Agents, Base Stations, and Interaction Gateway, as shown in Figure 1. Computational nodes are partitioned into interaction cells, each cell consisting of a set of Discover Agents and a Base Station. The number of nodes per interaction cell is programmable. The control network is automatically configured at run-time using the underlying messaging environment (e.g. MPI) and the available number of processors.

Each compute node in the control network houses a Discover Agent that maintains a local interaction object registry containing references to all interaction objects currently active and registered by that node. At the next level of hierarchy, Base Stations maintain registries containing the Interaction IDL for all the interaction objects in an interaction cell. The Interaction Gateway represents an interaction proxy for the entire application and manages a registry of the interaction interfaces for all the interaction objects in the application, and is responsible for interfacing with external interaction servers or brokers. During initialization, the application uses the DIOS API to create and register its interaction objects with local Discover Agents. The Discover Agents export the interaction IDL's for all these objects to their respective Base Stations. Base Stations populate their registries and then forward the interaction IDL's to the Interaction Gateway. The Interaction Gateway, after updating its registry communicates with the DISCOVER server, registering the application and exporting all registered objects. The application now begins its computations. The interaction between the Interaction Gateway and the DISCOVER server is managed by initializing a Java Virtual Machine and using the Java Native Interface to create Java mirrors of all registered interaction objects. These mirrors are registered with a RMI (Remote Method Invocation) registry service executing at the Interaction Gateway. This enables the Server to gain access to and control the interaction objects using the Java RMI API.

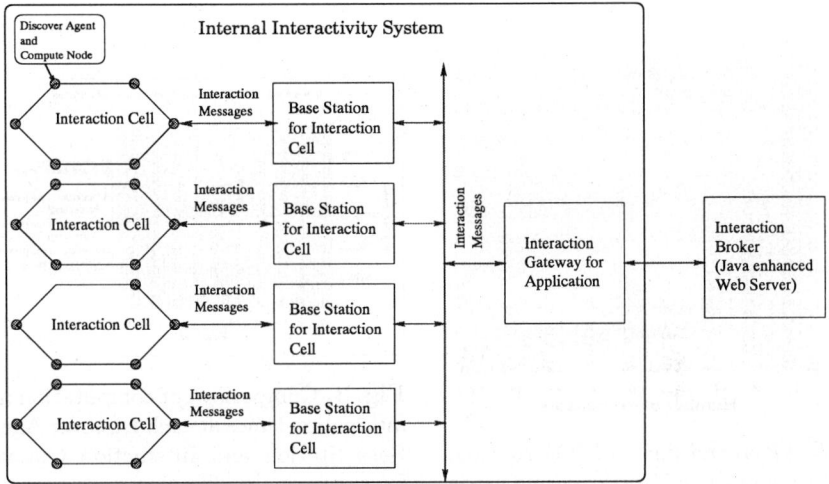

Fig. 1. The DIOS Control Network

During interaction phases, the Interaction Gateway delegates incoming interaction requests to the appropriate Base Stations and Discover Agents, and combines and collates responses (for distributed objects). Object migrations and re-distributions are handled by the respective Discover Agents (and Base Stations if the migration/re-distribution is across interaction cells) by updating corresponding registries. A more detailed description of the DIOS framework including examples for converting existing applications into interactive ones, registering them with the DISCOVER interaction server, and the operation of the control network can be found in [5].

4 Experimental Evaluation

DIOS has been implemented as a C++ library and has been ported to a number of operating systems including Linux, Windows NT, Solaris, IRIX, and AIX. This section summarizes an experimental evaluation of the DIOS library using the IPARS reservoir simulator framework on the Sun Starfire E10000 cluster. The E10000 configuration used consists of 64, 400 MHz SPARC processors, a 12.8 GBytes/sec interconnect. IPARS is a Fortran-based framework for developing parallel/distributed reservoir simulators. Using DIOS/DISCOVER, engineers can interactively feed in parameters such as water/gas injection rates and well bottom hole pressure, and observe the water/oil ratio or the oil production rate. The transformation of IPARS using DIOS consisted of creating C++ wrappers around the IPARS well data structures and defining the appropriate interaction interfaces in terms of views and commands. The DIOS evaluation consists of 5 experiments:

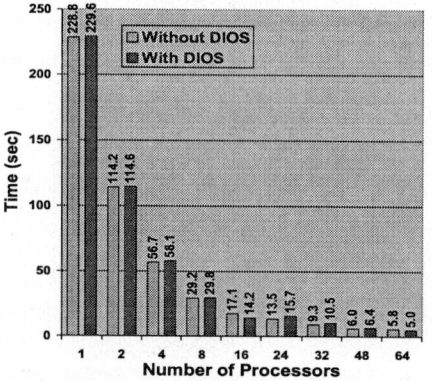

Fig. 2. Overhead due to DIOS runtime monitoring in the minimal steering mode

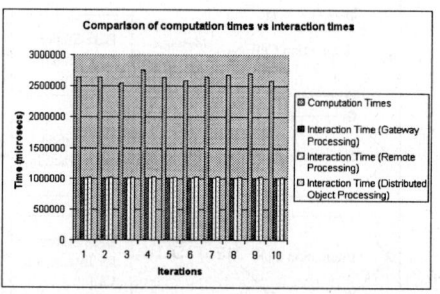

Fig. 3. Comparison of computation and interaction times at each Discover Agent, Base Station and Interaction Gateway for successive application iterations

Interaction Object Registration: Object registration (generating the Interaction IDL at the Discover Agents and exporting it to Base Station/Gateway) took 500 μsec per object at each Discover Agent, 10 ms per Discover Agent in the interaction cell at the Base Station, and 10 ms per Base Station in the control network at the Gateway. Note that this is a one-time cost.

Overhead of Minimal Steering: This experiment measured the runtime overheads introduced due to DIOS monitoring during application execution. In this experiment, the application automatically updated the DISCOVER server and connected clients with the current state of its interactive objects. Explicit command/view requests were disabled during the experiment. The application contained 5 interaction objects, 2 local objects and 3 global objects. The application's run times with and without DIOS are plotted in Figure 2. It can be seen that the overheads due to the DIOS runtime are very small and typically within the error of measurement. In some cases, due to system load dynamics, the performance with DIOS was slightly better. Our observations have shown that for most applications, the DIOS overheads are less that 0.2% of the application computation time.

View/Command Processing Time: The query processing time depends on - (a) the nature of interaction/steering requested, (b) the processing required at the application to satisfy the request and generate a response, and (c) type and size of the response. In this experiment we measured time required for generating and exporting different views and commands. A sampling of the measured times for different scenarios is presented in Table 1.

Table 1. View and command processing times

View Type	Data Size (Bytes)	Time Taken	Command	Time Taken
Text	65	1.4 ms	Stop, Pause or Resume	250 μsec
Text	120	0.7 ms	Refine GridHierarchy	32 ms
Text	760	0.7 ms	Checkpoint	1.2 sec
XSlice Generation	1024	1.7 ms	Rollback	43 ms

DIOS Control Network Overheads: This experiment consisted of measuring the overheads due to communication between the Discover Agents, Base Stations and the Interaction Gateway while processing interaction requests for local, global and distributed objects. As expected, the measurements indicated that the interaction request processing time is minimum when the interaction objects are co-located with the Gateway, and is the maximum for distributed objects. This is due to the additional communication between the different Discover Agents and the Gateway, and the `gather` operation performed at the Gateway to collate the responses. Note that for the IPARS application, the average interaction time was within 0.1 to 0.3% of the average time spent in computation during each iteration. Figure 3 compares computation time with interaction times at the Discover Agent, Base Station and Interaction Gateway for successive application iterations. Note that the interaction times include the request processing times in addition to control network overheads. Finally, Figure 4 shows the breakdown of the interaction time in the case of an object distributed across 3 nodes. The interaction times are measured at the Interaction Gateway in this case.

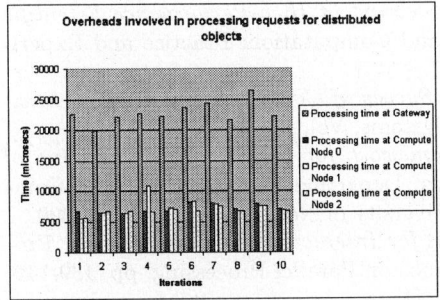

Fig. 4. Breakdown of request-processing overheads for an object distributed across 3 compute nodes. The interaction times is measured at the Interaction Gateway

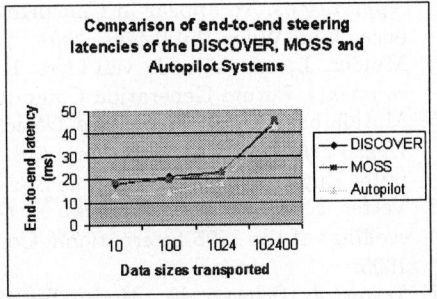

Fig. 5. Comparison of end-to-end steering latencies for DISCOVER, MOSS and Autopilot systems

End-to-end steering latency: This measured the time to complete a round-trip steering operation starting with a request from a remote client and ending with the response delivered to that client. These measurements of course depend on the state of the client, the server and the network interconnecting them. The DISCOVER system exhibits end-to-end latencies (shown in Figure 5) comparable to steering systems like the MOSS and Autopilot systems, as reported in [1].

5 Concluding Remarks

This paper presented the design, implementation and experimental evaluation of DIOS, an interactive object infrastructure for enabling the runtime monitoring and computational steering of parallel and distributed applications. The DIOS interactive object framework enables high-level definition and deployment of sensors and actuators into existing application objects. Furthermore, the DIOS control network and runtime system supports distributed and dynamic objects and can manage dynamic object creation, deletion, migration and redistribution. The Interaction Gateway provides an interaction proxy to the application and enables remote access using distributed object protocols and web browsers. An experimental evaluation of the DIOS framework was presented. DIOS is currently operational and is being used to provide interaction and steering capabilities to a number of application specific PSEs.

References

1. Eisenhauer, G.: *An Object Infrastructure for High-Performance Interactive Applications.* PhD thesis, Department of Computer Science, Georgia Institute of Technology, May 1998.
2. Gu, W., Vetter, J., Schwan, K.: *Computational steering annotated bibliography.* Sigplan notices, 32 (6): 40-4 (June 1997).
3. Mann, V., Matossian, V., Muralidhar, R., Parashar, M.: *DISCOVER: An Environment for Web-based Interaction and Steering of High-Performance Scientific Applications.* To appear in Concurrency and Computation: Practice and Experience, John Wiley Publishers, 2001.
4. Mulder, J., van Wijk, J., van Liere, R.: *A Survey of Computational Steering Environments.* Future Generation Computer Systems, Vol. 15, nr. 2, 1999.
5. Muralidhar, R.: *A Distributed Object Framework for the Interactive Steering of High-Performance Applications.* MS thesis, Department of Electrical and Computer Engineering, Rutgers, The State University of New Jersey, October 2000.
6. Vetter, J., Schwan, K.: *Progress: A Toolkit for Interactive Program Steering.* Proceedings of the 1995 International Conference on Parallel Processing, pp. 139-149. 1995.
7. Vetter, J., Schwan, K.: *Models for Computational Steering.* Third International Conference on Configurable Distributed Systems, IEEE, May 1996.
8. Wheeler, J., et al: *IPARS: Integrated Parallel Reservoir Simulator.* Center for Subsurface Modeling, University of Texas at Austin.
http://www.ticam.utexas.edu/CSM.

Checkpointing Facility on a Metasystem*

Yudith Cardinale and Emilio Hernández

Universidad Simón Bolívar,
Departamento de Computación y Tecnología de la Información,
Apartado 89000, Caracas 1080-A, Venezuela
{yudith,emilio}@ldc.usb.ve
http://suma.ldc.usb.ve

Abstract. A metasystem allows seamless access to a collection of distributed computational resources. Checkpointing is an important service in high throughput computing, especially for process migration and recovery after system crash. This article describes the experiences on incorporating checkpointing and recovery facilities in a Java-based metasystem. Our case study is SUMA, a metasystem for execution of Java bytecode, both sequential and parallel. This paper also shows preliminary results on checkpointing and recovery overhead for single-node applications.

1 Introduction

The access to distributed high performance computing facilities for execution of Java programs has generated considerable interest [3,1,12,7]. A metacomputing system, or metasystem, allows uniform access to heterogeneous resources, including high performance computers. This is achieved by presenting a collection of different computer systems as a single computer.

This work addresses some aspects related to the implementation of a checkpointing facility in a metasystem, with application to SUMA, a metasystem for execution of Java bytecode, both sequential and parallel. We compared several approaches for adding object persistence to the Java execution environment and selected the approach proposed in [2], which uses an extended Java Virtual Machine (JVM). We modified the architecture of SUMA for supporting remote checkpointing and recovery facility based on this extended JVM. This approach is semi-transparent at the user level, because the requirements for using this facility can be easily hidden. We obtained preliminary results on the overhead produced by the selected approach for single-node applications.

The rest of this document is organized as follows. Section 2 describes different approaches to implement persistent Java environments, as a base for Java checkpointing. Section 3 explains the implementation of the aforementioned services in SUMA. Section 4 presents the preliminary results of our research and section 5 presents the conclusions.

---

* This work was partially supported by grants from Conicit (project S1-2000000623) and from Universidad Simón Bolívar (direct support for research group GID-25)

2 Checkpointing Java on a Metasystem

Checkpointing involves capturing the state of a computation in terms of the data necessary to restart it from that state. An advantage of using Java, as far as checkpointing is concerned, is that checkpoints can be taken in a machine independent format. It is necessary to achieve Java object persistence for implementing architecture-independent Java checkpointing.

Several strategies have been proposed for adding persistence to the Java execution environment [4]. Some approaches are based on using language-level mechanisms through libraries [5,10]. Other approaches extend the JVM in order to make the computation state accessible from Java threads, which take the checkpoints [9,2]. Other approaches consist in running the whole JVM over an operating system that supports persistence or inserting a checkpointing layer between the JVM and a traditional operating system, as in [6].

All of the formerly described checkpointing approaches have their advantages and disadvantages. However, the implementation of a checkpointing facility in a metasystem requires some particular considerations. The selection of an appropriate checkpointing approach for a metasystem should take into account:

– Portability, due to the heterogeneity of the systems that comprise a metasystem. This consideration discards the approaches that save the machine state at the operating system level or the JVM level. From a portability viewpoint, the best options are those that keep the state of the computation in terms of Java objects, which can be restarted in another JVM.
– Transparency, which may also be a desirable feature for stand-alone JVM's. However, the need for efficient use of resources in a metasystem may be a reason for activating the checkpointing and recovery/migration services even if the user does not explicitly invoke them.
– Low intrusiveness of the checkpointing process, in terms of performance, especially if the metasystem design aims at high performance computing. Taking a checkpoint is itself a process that may consume a significant amount of time and should be optimized as much as possible. The checkpointing approaches based on adding instructions to the source code or bytecode have the risk of producing further performance reductions.

These aspects of metasystem design lead us to consider checkpointing approaches based on extending the JVM. We evaluated several projects that extend the JVM for implementing object persistence [11,8,9,2]. We are using the approach proposed in [2] because it provides a fine-grained Java thread state capture/restoration facility. This solution requires the checkpointable threads to be defined as extensions of the class "CapturableThread", contradicting the transparency requirement. However, it is potentially transparent because automatic preprocessing of the source code before compilation can easily be implemented.

3   Checkpointing and Recovering Services in SUMA

SUMA is intended to provide services for checkpointing and profiling, as an added value to on-line and off-line remote execution of Java applications. These services are mainly implemented within the Execution Agents, which are the SUMA components that actually execute the applications. On the client side, if a user wants to use the checkpointing service, under the current version she should program her applications based on threads that both extend the class CapturableThreads and implement the Serializable interface. More specifically, the programmer has only to include the statement "import java.lang.threadpack.*" and extend all threads from CapturableThreads.

Figure 1 shows the steps during the development and execution of an user application with checkpointing support on SUMA. On the client side there is no need to install the extended JVM. A stub package is provided for the programmer to compile the modified program. The code instrumentation on the client side can be done automatically, by using a preprocessor of source or byte code (step 1).

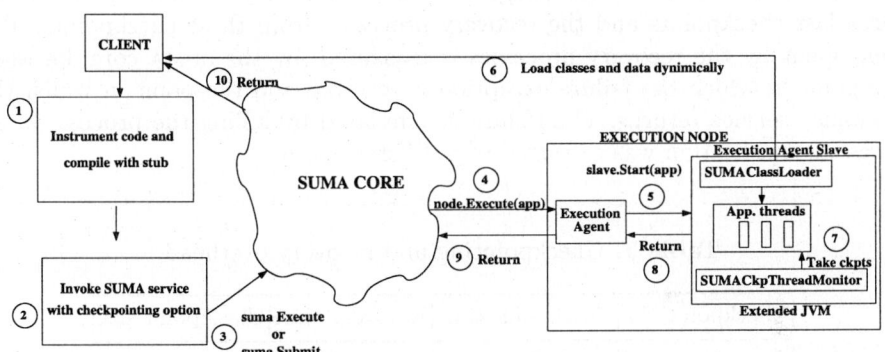

Fig. 1. Application execution on SUMA

The user requests the checkpointing service explicitly when submitting the application for execution in SUMA (step 2). This can be executed from a *suma-Client*, which can invoke either *sumaExecute* or *sumaSubmit* services. These services provide the checkpointing option.

After the SUMA client invokes the remote execution with the checkpointing option, SUMA builds an object that contains all information needed for application execution (step 3), finds a node with checkpointing support and sends the object to the Execution Agent at the selected node (step 4). Once this Execution Agent has received the object representing the application, it starts an Execution Agent Slave in a extended JVM (step 5). Two threads are started initially within this extended JVM: the SUMAClassLoader, whose function is to load classes and data from the client during the execution (it communicates with the client through CORBA callbacks), and the SUMACkpThreadMonitor, which will take the checkpoints. Then the main thread of the application is loaded directly from the client and started. The checkpoints will be taken from this moment on (step 7).

If the execution finishes successfully, the Execution Agent Slave informs the Execution Agent of this and finishes (step 8). The Execution Agent passes this information back to the SUMA core (step 9), which returns the results to the client (step 10). If the execution is interrupted, an exception is caught in the SUMA core, which launches the recovery process. The application will be restarted from the last checkpoint, typically in a different execution node.

4 Experimental Results

We conducted experiments to evaluate the checkpointing intrusiveness and the overhead of the recovery process. The platforms used in the experiments are several 143 MHz SUN Ultra 1 workstations connected through Ethernet. We executed a Java program ("Primes") to calculate the first "n" prime numbers. The prime numbers are saved in a vector, which means that the checkpoint size increases as the program progresses. Table 1 shows the time spent by the three last checkpoints and the recovery processes from these checkpoints. The time spent by the recovery processes is measured, by the SUMA core, between the point in which the failure exception is received and the point in which the "resume" service returns. The failure is simulated by killing the process. In all cases the application was restarted in a different node.

Table 1. Checkpointing and recovery overhead

Checkpoint No.	Checkpoint time	Recovery time	Checkpoint size
2	55.1 sec.	45 sec.	95KB
3	2 min. 5 sec.	1 min. 1 sec.	162KB
4	3 min. 8 sec.	1 min. 56 sec.	393KB

In this example every checkpoint is taken approximately two minutes after the previous one was saved. The overhead is currently very high, for instance, the case in which 4 checkpoints are taken incurs an overhead of about 40%. However, several improvements to this implementation can be done, such as the use of native threads instead of green threads. On the other hand, the number of checkpoints should be related to the probability of hardware failure.

5 Conclusions and Future Work

This work addressed some aspects related to the implementation of a checkpointing facility in a metasystem, with application to the SUMA metasystem.

This approach is almost transparent at the user level, because the requirements for using this facility can be easily hidden. This requirements are (1) modify the thread declarations, which can be done by a pre-processor just before compilation and (2) link locally with a stub that provides extensions for persistent threads. Future work will include the development of the aforementioned pre-processor.

The experiences shown in this article are limited to checkpointing of single-node applications on SUMA. Ongoing research is focusing on reducing performance overhead as well as incorporating a multiple-node (parallel) checkpointing algorithm, implemented with mpiJava. We are currently working on an Execution Agent for parallel checkpointing.

References

1. A. Baratloo, M. Karaul, Z. M. Kedem, and P. Wyckoff. Charlotte: Metacomputing on the web. *Future Generation Computer Systems*, 15(5–6):559–570, October 1999.
2. S. Bouchenak. Making Java applications mobile or persistent. In *Proceedings of 6th USENIX Conference on Object-Oriented Technologies and Systems (COOTS'01)*, January 2001.
3. T. Brench, H. Sandhu, M. Shan, and J. Talbot. ParaWeb: Towards world-wide supercomputing. In *Proceedings of the 7th ACM SIGOPS European Worshop*, 1996.
4. J. Eliot, B. Moss, and T. Hosking. Approaches to adding persistence to Java. In *Proceedings of the First International Workshop on Persistence and Java*, September 1996.
5. S. Funfrocken. Transparent migration of Java-based mobile agents (capturing and reestablishing the state of Java programs). *Proceedings of Second International Workshop Mobile Agents 98 (MA'98)*, September 1998.
6. Jon Howell. Straightforward Java persistence through checkpointing. *In Advances in Persistent Object Systems*, pages 322–334, 1999.
7. Michael O. Neary, Bernd O. Christiansen, Peter Capello, and Klaus E. Schauser. Javelin: Parallel computing on the internet. *Future Generation Computer Systems*, 15(5–6):659–674, Octuber 1999.
8. J. Plank and M. Puening. Checkpointing Java. http://www.cs.utk.edu/~plank/javackp.html.
9. T. Printezis, M. Atkinson, L. Daynes, S. Spence, and P. Bailey. The design of a new persistent object store for pjama. In *Proceedings of the Second International Workshop on Persistence and Java*, August, 1997.
10. T. Sakamoto, T. Sekiguchi, and A. Yonezawa. Bytecode transformation for portable thread migration in Java. *Proceedings of Second International Workshop Mobile Agents 2000 (MA'2000)*, 1(3):123–137, September 2000.
11. T. Suezawa. Persistent execution state of a Java Virtual Machine. *Proceedings of the ACM 2000 Java Grande Conference*, June 2000.
12. H. Takagi, S. Matsouka, H. Nakada, S. Sekiguchi, M. Satoh, and U. Nagashima. Ninflet: a migratable parallel object framework using Java. In *in Proc. of the ACM 1998 Worshop on Java for High-Performance Network Computing*, 1998.

Optimising the MPI Library for the T3E

Stephen Booth

EPCC, University of Edinburgh
Mayfield Road, Edinburgh EH9 3JZ
s.booth@epcc.ed.ac.uk

Abstract. This paper describes an optimised MPI library for the T3E.[1]
Previous versions of MPI for the T3E were built on top of the SHMEM
interface. This paper describes an optimised version that also uses additional capabilities of the low-level communication hardware.

The MPI library[1] is a fundamental part of many parallel applications. Almost any improvement to the performance of the MPI library will benefit a large number of application codes. This paper describes optimisation work for the T3E MPI library. We were able to utilise some special features in the T3E communication hardware to reduce message latency and improve the performance of global barriers.

1 Implementation of the MPI Library

The original implementation of MPI for the T3D was developed at EPCC[4]. This formed the basis for the MPI library shipped as part of the Cray Message passing Toolkit (MPT) for the T3E. The T3D communication hardware provided remote memory access between processors and some additional features such as atomic swap and barrier. The T3D MPI library was built on top of the Cray SHMEM library that provided direct access to all of these capabilities.

The fundamental building blocks of the library are "protocol messages". The sending and receiving processors need to exchange protocol messages to allow matching pairs of send and receive calls to be coupled together. Once the calls are coupled data is copied between processors using SHMEM put or get calls. Each processor needs to maintain a queue of incoming messages and be able to insert messages into remote queues. In the T3D library the queue was implemented using the SHMEM library. Protocol messages were 4-word data packets (corresponding to the packet size on the T3D network) and the queue was a symmetrically allocated (same address on all processors) buffer and lock variable. The lock was always manipulated using the SHMEM atomic swap, so in addition to a shmem_put to transfer the data at least 2 atomic swaps were needed to send a protocol message, one to lock and one to unlock the queue.

Several different protocols were used to implement the point to point communications depending on the size of the message.

---

[1] An earlier version of this paper was presented at the 6th European SGI/Cray MPP workshop Manchester, UK 7-8 September 2000.

- T Very small messages (< 3 words) were packed into the protocol message.
- Tn Medium sized messages were packed into several contiguous queue slots.
- RTA In the Request Transfer Acknowledge protocol the sending processor sends a request to the receiver. When the receiver matches this send to a receive it uses `shmem_get` to fetch the data and sends an acknowledge back to the sender. RTA had a higher latency than Tn but better bandwidth due to fewer memory copies so it was used for larger messages.
- RAT The Request Acknowledge Transfer protocol introduced an additional protocol message but allowed data to be sent using `shmem_put` which had better performance than `shmem_get` on the T3D. However unless the send was synchronous (e.g. `MPI_Ssend`) extra memory copies were needed so this mode was only used in special cases.

2 T3E Optimisations

The T3D MPI library was ported to the T3E almost without change. The hardware differences of the two machines were hidden behind the SHMEM interface. The MPI communication bandwidth is determined by the SHMEM put/get bandwidth so there was little scope for improving this. However the message latency was improved by making protocol messaging more efficient. The T3E communication hardware is quite different to that of the T3D, in addition to capabilities needed to implement SHMEM there is direct hardware support for message queues. These queues are *very* similar to the protocol queue used by MPI. The only major difference is that the packet size is 8 words (64 bytes) instead of 4. Messages are atomically inserted into the remote queue so no locks are required. No routines were provided by Cray to access these functions so it was necessary to write two additional custom routines to send and receive using the hardware message queues[2]. These were then integrated into the MPI library by modifying two macros in the code:

1. PUTP This sent a protocol message to a remote processor.
2. BC_ABSORB This processed any incoming protocol messages in the queue.

The RAT protocol was introduced to take advantage of the better `shmem_put` performance on the T3D. This was only used for large messages where the impact of the additional protocol messages is small so it was retained where convenient to do so. The Tn protocol cannot be implemented with the hardware messaging and was removed completely.

The following results were generated using the MPICH mpptest program[2]. All runs were performed on 8 processors of the 344 PE T3E-900 at EPCC using MPI standard sends. Message buffering was suppressed by setting the environment variable `MPP_BUFFER_MAX=0`.

For large messages (16 Kb and above) performance can be fit to a straight line and the asymptotic latency from these fits has been reduced from 51 to 12 microseconds.

---

[2] Thanks to David Tanqueray of Cray-UK for assistance with this.

The behaviour for short messages is shown in Figure 1; again message latency has been significantly reduced. This is especially true for very short messages using the T protocol where the latency is almost the same as for a SHMEM operation. As the protocol messages are larger up to 7 words of data can now be sent using the T protocol. This graph also shows an improved message bandwidth because for the larger message sizes on this graph the new version is using the RTA protocol instead of Tn which required an additional memory copy.

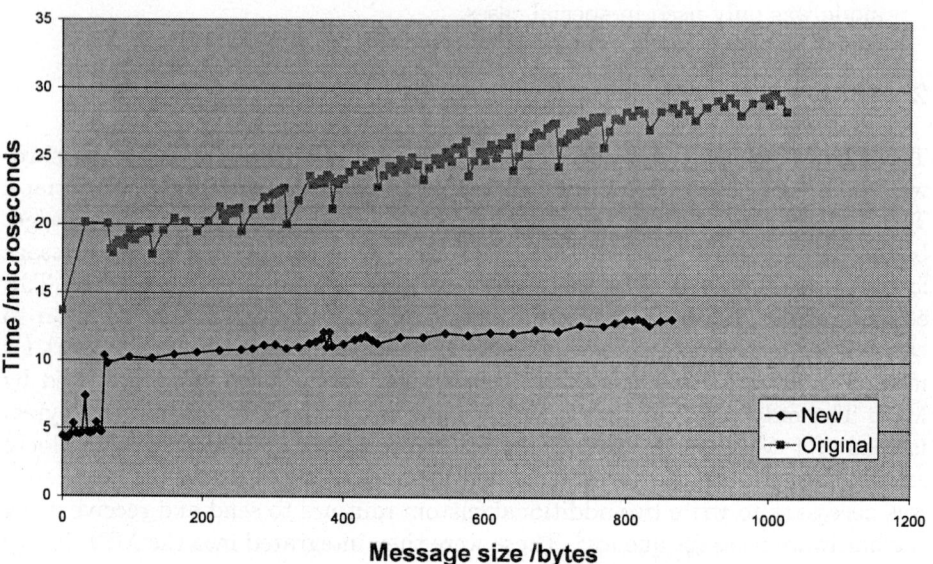

Fig. 1. Short message performance

This figure shows the performance of short messages for the two versions of the library.

The MPI standard mandates that point to point messages must continue to progress while a processor is blocked in a MPI_Barrier call. On the T3D this prevented the use of the hardware barrier. On the T3E the Barrier hardware can be polled. This allows global MPI barriers to utilise the barrier hardware for barriers across MPI_COMM_WORLD or other global communicators. This increased performance of global barriers is shown in Figure 2. This benefit increases as a larger number of processors are used.

All of the above optimisations are incorporated in the Cray MPT release 1.3.0.5 or above.

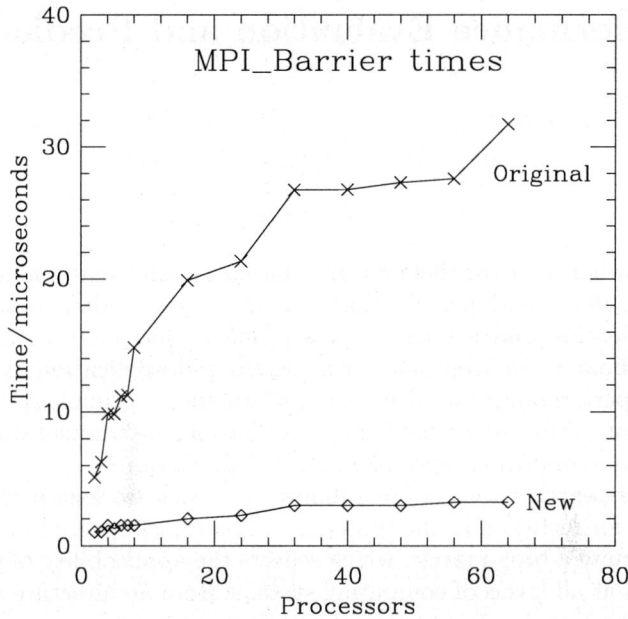

Fig. 2. Global barrier performance

This figure shows the time taken to complete a global barrier as a function of the number of processors being synchronised.

3 Conclusion

By dropping below the SHMEM interface, significant performance improvements have been made to the MPI library. This should improve the performance of any application code that makes extensive use of global MPI barriers or is sensitive to MPI message latency.

References

1. Message Passing Interface Forum: MPI: A Message-Passing Interface Standard June 1995 http://www.mpi-forum.org/
2. W. Gropp, E. Lusk, N. Doss, A. Skjellum: A high-performance, portable implementation of the MPI message passing interface standard, Parallel Computing 22 789-828 September 1996.
3. R. Barriuso, A. Knies: SHMEM User's Guide for C., Cray Research Inc., August 1994.
4. K. Cameron, L. Clarke, A. Smith: "CRI/EPCC MPI for CRAY T3D", 1st European Cray T3D Workshop, EPFL, 6 September 1995.

Topic 02
Performance Evaluation and Prediction

Allen D. Malony, Graham D. Riley, Bernd Mohr,
Mark Bull, and Tomàs Margalef

Topic Chairpersons

The performance of parallel and distributed systems and applications — its evaluation, analysis, and optimization — is at once a fundamental topic for research investigation and a technological problem that requires innovations in tools and techniques to keep pace with system and application evolution. This dual view of performance "science" and performance "technology" jointly spans broad fields of performance modelling, evaluation, instrumentation, measurement, analysis, monitoring, optimization, and prediction.

Fourteen research papers were submitted to this workshop of which eight were selected for inclusion in the conference. The topics covered by the accepted papers have quite a broad range, which reflects the applicability of performance-related topics at all levels of computing systems from architecture and networking through to high level application development in the many programming paradigms which are in current use. A continuing challenge to the area is to seek abstractions and generic techniques which apply across these boundaries. Two themes particularly dominate the accepted papers and these form the basis of the two sessions of the Topic: first, the prediction of performance and performance modelling, and second, techniques to analyse actual performance and practical reports of analyses in specific cases.

Performance Prediction and Modelling

In the area of modelling, *Ponomarev et al.* use a theoretical approach to demonstrate how network queueing behaviour may be improved by using polling rather than more conventional interrupt driven servicing mechanisms. In the search for generic performance prediction methods, one approach is to seek methods which support particular programming paradigms, and this approach is seen in the paper, *Performance Prediction of Oblivious BSP Programs* by González et al. An alternative approach is to focus on classes of algorithms which occur in real applications. This approach is taken in the papers by *Gautama et al.* and *Moreno et al.*, each targeting a different algorithm type. In *Performance Prediction of Data-Dependent Task Parallel Programs*, recent new analysis techniques are used to overcome challenges to prediction for general task parallel programs with dependent behavior. In *The Tuning Problem on Pipelines*, focus is given on *pipeline algorithms* and it is shown that good prediction accuracy can be achieved with careful consideration of all algorithm features.

Performance Analysis and Support Tools

Performance tools for effective empirical performance analysis must address both technological and methodological concerns. The papers in the second session consider three different but related aspects of the problem. First, requirements for effective implementation and use of performance measurement tools is explored in *The Hardware Performance Monitor Toolkit* by *Luiz A. DeRose*. As the title implies, this paper focuses on the use of hardware monitoring facilities and what can be learned from hardware performance data. A second aspect is that of conducting and reporting the results of performance analysis on real systems. The papers by *Baker et al.* on *VIA Communication Performance on a Gigabit Ethernet Cluster* and *Strey and Bange* on *Performance Analysis of Intel's MMX and SSE: A Case Study* are two examples of quality performance analysis in practice. Third, questions of performance analysis methodology are addressed in the paper, *Group Based Performance Analysis for Multithreaded SMP Cluster Applications* by *Brunst et al.* This paper proposes innovative hierarchical viewing methods to support the exploration of larger-scale performance data.

Optimal Polling for Latency–Throughput Tradeoffs in Queue–Based Network Interfaces for Clusters[1]

Dmitry Ponomarev[2], Kanad Ghose[2], and Eugeny Saksonov[3]

[2] Dept. of Computer Science, State University of New York, Binghamton, NY 13902–6000
{dima, ghose}@cs.binghamton.edu
[3] Moscow Institute of Electronics and Mathematics, Moscow, Russia
saks@miem.edu.ru

Abstract. We consider a networking subsystem for message–passing clusters that uses two unidirectional queues for data transfers between the network interface card (NIC) and the lower protocol layers, with polling as the primary mechanism for reading data off these queues. We suggest that for accurate mathematical analysis of such an organization, the values of the system's states probabilities have to be taken into consideration, in addition to the well–known mean–value estimates. A single server single queue polling system with server's "vacations" is then articulated via an M/G/1 queueing model. We present a method for obtaining the values of system's states probabilities in such a scheme that can be used to identify "sweet spots" of the polling period that result in a reasonable compromise between the message passing latency and the overall system's throughput.

1 Introduction

We consider the problem of tuning the performance of message passing in clusters where low latency as well as high system throughput are desirable performance goals. These requirements dictate the use of non–traditional network subsystems for the clusters [4]. Throughput, in this context, refers to the throughput of the system as a whole, including the networking subsystem (which comprises of the protocol layers, OS services, drivers and the network interface card). Traditional network interfaces are interrupt–driven. When the network interface card (NIC) lacks bus mastering capabilities, the arrival of a packet causes the NIC to generate an interrupt. The handler for this interrupt initiates the DMA operation that moves the data from the NIC to the RAM. When the NIC is a bus master, the arrival of a packet does not generate an interrupt as the NIC can initiate the DMA transfer on its own. Interrupts are also generated after the completion of DMA transfers between the host memory and the NIC, specifically when a packet is DMA–ed from RAM–resident outgoing buffers to the NIC in the course of sending a packet and after the completion of a DMA transfer from the NIC to the RAM–resident incoming buffers in the course of receiving a message. These interrupts are needed to trigger protocol layer actions, such as message demultiplexing or actions that initiate further transmissions.

The impact of such interrupt driven interfaces on the overall system performance – that of the network subsystem, as well as that of the host – are two–fold. First, The NIC cannot sustain large data movements on its own, and arrival of data at a high rate can cause overflows from the buffers within the NIC. This is particularly true as the raw hardware data rate of the network increases and approaches that of the bus on which the

---

[1] supported in part by the NSF thru award Nos. EIA 991109, CDA 9700828 & an equipment donation from CISCO Systems

NIC resides (typically, the I/O bus). Such overflows from the NIC buffers result in retransmission of the dropped packets (when reliable delivery is needed), resulting in an overall performance degradation. Message transmission latency, as well as the overall message transfer rates are both affected adversely. Second, frequent interrupts generated by the NIC cause a commensurate increase in the rate of context switching (which can be relatively expensive in terms of cycles), impacting the throughput of the interrupted application adversely.

As NICs continue to evolve and begin to incorporate additional logic for DMA streaming and message demultiplexing (i.e., identifying the end–point of a packet), it is imperative to move away from an interrupt–driven interface to the NIC and seek solutions that exploit the full performance potentials of these NICs [4].

Polled unidirectional queues for incoming and outgoing messages maintained in the RAM provide the basis for implementing efficient interfaces in–between the NIC and the software of the networking subsystem. Typically, in these systems, both the NIC and the networking subsystem software operate autonomously until queue limits, as known to the software or the NIC, are reached. At that point, usually, interrupts are generated to update queue limits and take any other actions that are needed. The incoming and outgoing queues can be global (i.e., common to all connections/channels) or independent queues could be used for each open channel/connection. The latter is preferred when differentiated services (to implement connections with different quality of service, for example) are implemented, with additional logic in the NIC to perform message demultiplexing. For example, Myrinet [5], and the semi–custom field–programmable gate array based NIC described in [2]) use unidirectional queues in this manner to implement low latency communication facilities. In these systems, two unidirectional queues are used, one is written to by the lower protocol layers and read by the NIC while the other is written to by the NIC and read by the software.

Instead of interrupts, both the software and the NIC use polling to read their corresponding queues. The Virtual Interface Architecture specification [Via] [Den+ 98] represents a general form of these interfaces. The motivation behind such a design is a reduction of the frequency of interrupts. A polling agent, such as a daemon or process/thread activated by applications can poll the outgoing and incoming queues. Several incoming messages may accumulate in the queue before it is polled by the application, resulting in a single context–switch to process all these messages as opposed to a per–message context switch, as in traditional designs. Similarly, the NIC can poll the outgoing queue(s) to determine if any message has to be sent out.

When polling is performed by software, the period at which each queue is polled is critical – if polling is performed too often, the overhead for the polling process itself can be detrimental to performance, and in addition, the queue may not have useful data to process. On the other hand if polling is performed infrequently, packets may end up spending a longer time on the queues, increasing the overall latency. The goal of this paper is to analytically model queue–based networking subsystems as described above and identify optimal polling intervals. We concentrate on systems that use global queues; the analysis can be generalized to systems that use multiple sets of queues.

The rest of the paper is organized as follows. Section 2 gives an overview of a queue–based polling–driven networking subsystem, outlining its advantages and hardware modifications that have to be incorporated into a fairly simple NIC to support the design. In section 3, we describe how a single M/G/1 queue with server's "vacations" maps to the situation encountered in a queue–based networking followed by a formal description of the queueing system and the presentation of a method for computing the system's states probabilities. It is also shown in this section how the errors in computations can be estimated over a compact domain in a recursive manner. Section 4 discusses new performance metrics and possible optimizations followed by our conclusions in section 5.

2 Queue–Based Polling–Driven Networking Subsystem

In a queue–based polling–driven networking subsystem, two unidirectional queues are used for interfacing between the device driver software and the NIC. These queues are located in the main memory and serve as the intermediate buffers between the software and the hardware. One of the queues is typically used for passing the commands from the software to the NIC. For example, when an application calls a *send ( )* routine, the message is authenticated, processed by the protocol layers and then passed to the NIC driver, which initiates the DMA indirectly by putting a *do–send* command into the queue, perhaps passing the message descriptor as a parameter. Other commands may also be placed on this queue, for example *do_fast_hardware_retransmit ()* etc. depending on the implementation. The NIC polls this queue periodically and executes commands placed by the software as it finds appropriate.

The second queue is used for the receive path. When the NIC receives a message from the network (we assume that the NIC is a bus master), it DMAs the message into the RAM and acknowledges the completion of this event by placing an appropriate information into the queue. Also, the NIC may signal the occurrence of other events through this queue, including transmission error and acknowledgement that the message has been successfully sent out to allow the driver to free up some buffer space for the upcoming messages. A separate kernel process, or even a thread, polls this queue with some frequency and calls appropriate driver or protocol stack functions to further manipulate the incoming message. No interrupts are normally generated during the course of message reception. The only time when the NIC generates an interrupt is when the queue becomes full. Even when the transmission error is encountered, it is sufficient to associate this event with the higher priority and sort all accumulated requests in the queue according to their priorities. Should such operation seem to be an expensive endeavor, a traditional interrupt can simply be generated on this rare occasion.

Such an organization de–couples the NIC from the driver software, allowing each to execute at their own speeds. The frequency of interrupts comes down, since the interrupts are only generated when the queue becomes full. Moreover, if polling is designed carefully, the number of expensive context switches should also decrease because at a polling instant, the software may very well find several requests already posted by the NIC, thus amortizing the cost of the context switch. However, if polling frequency is chosen badly, polling–driven networking may even increase the number of context switches – this is, of course, the result of polling the empty queue.

Design of such a subsystem requires quite modest modifications to the NIC hardware: a pair of registers has to be added to the NIC for addressing the queues, interrupts have to be turned off, and logic has to be added for generating an interrupt when the queue is full and performing polling on one of the queues. A few changes have to be also made to the driver code, those mainly include adding the functions for accessing the queues.

However, applications and higher–level networking software remain oblivious to these modifications.

Clearly, the performance of a system employing such queues is highly dependent on a carefully chosen frequency of polling a queue. Traditional analysis based on mean–value estimates, such as the average waiting time in the queue, may suggest the necessity of a high polling frequency, because this results in low message–passing latency. Indeed, a message descriptor placed in the queue by the NIC, corresponding perhaps to a completion of a DMA operation upon reception of a message, could receive the almost immediate attention of the polling server in this scenario. However, every attempt to poll the queue results in a performance hit for other processes currently in the system. In the least, when the polling server is scheduled, the context switch has to be performed. Unless the server can execute in the same virtual address space as the interrupted user process (as the case is in UNIX–based systems), this context switch involves saving the page mapping information of the user process and flushing the TLBs, that are quite expensive operations by all standards. In addition, if a polling process is scheduled frequently, all processes in the ready queue will experience longer delays before receiving their time slices. In this context, the polling frequency should be kept to a reasonable minimum. It is especially important to minimize the probability of a situation when the server polls the empty queue. In some ways, this is analogous to a process doing a busy–wait on a software lock issued by another process in a critical section. If the duration of a busy–wait is a short one, the exploring process spins on the lock even more rapidly making it an expensive waiting. If, on the other hand, the busy–wait is one of a longer duration, the process might find its critical section available at its next try. Polling the queue containing only one request may not be very efficient either, in the best case such a situation will not be different from a traditional interrupt–based networking subsystem where an interrupt is generated by the NIC upon the reception of every message.

Thus, to carefully analyze the effects of polling on the performance of the entire system, one should attend to such nuances as the values of system's states probabilities (system's state is defined as the number of requests in the queue), that were largely ignored in favor of more easily obtainable mean value estimates. In what follows, we show how these values can be computed for a single queue system.

3 Analytical Model

Some performance aspects of a queue–based networking subsystem can be analytically modelled using an M/G/1 queue. Hereafter, we shall refer to the process performing polling operation on the queue as the server. If the server finds any requests in the queue at the polling instant, it serves all those requests in accordance with gated service discipline, that is, only those requests that were on the queue at the moment of server's arrival there are served. Requests entering the queue while it is being served must wait until the next cycle and will receive service in the next service period. The state of such system at any moment of time is defined as the number of requests in the queue.

A single server single queue M/G/1 model with server's "vacations" is a degeneration of a multiqueue polling system where several queues are served in a cyclic order. Requests arrive at the queue according to Poisson process, that is, the interarrival time is governed by the probability distribution $1-e^{-\lambda t}$ with average interarrival time $1/\lambda$. Probability distribution of the time required to serve a request is denoted as $B(t)$ with finite first and second moments ($0 < \beta_1 < \infty$ and $0 < \beta_2 < \infty$). After servicing all requests in the queue, the server goes for a vacation. Vacation time is generally distributed in accordance with some probability law and its probability distribution function is denoted as $G(t)$ with finite first and second moments ($0 < \nu_1 < \infty$ and $0 < \nu_2 < \infty$). After vacation period completes, the server switches to the queue again and continues to serve the requests sitting there. We consider the system at the time epochs of the initiation of service at the queue, that is, the moments when vacation periods complete. Assuming that the system operates in the equilibrium mode (the existence of such mode is conditioned by the inequality $\lambda \beta_1 < 1$), we attempt to obtain the values of system's states probabilities at the moments of service initiation. We also derive the upper bounds for errors in the computations.

At the moments of service initiation, the system can be considered as an embedded Markov chain with a finite number of states. The stationary probabilities are connected by the following system of linear equations [6]:

$$n_i = \sum_{k=0}^{\infty} n_k \int_0^{\infty} \frac{(\lambda t)^i}{i!} e^{-\lambda t} d(\varkappa_k(t) \oplus G(t)),$$

where n_i is the stationary probability of state i, $\varkappa_k(t)$ is the service time distribution of k customers and $\oplus$ is the convolution symbol for the two distributions.

Using the generating function $\pi(x) = \sum_{i=0}^{\infty} x^i n_i$, one obtains:

$$\pi(x) = \nu(\lambda(1-x))\pi(\beta(\lambda(1-x))), \qquad (1)$$

where $\nu(.)$ and $\beta(.)$ are the Laplace–Stieltjese transforms of functions $G(t)$ and $B(t)$ respectively. This result is well–known and it had been shown in [6] how the approximate values of system states probabilities can be computed from (1). In what follows, we outline how one could compute these probabilities, in particular, n_0 and n_1 respectively, with a bounded estimation of the error.

Consider the sequence $\{x_k\}$ $k=0,1,2,...;$ $0 \le x \le 1$, the elements of which are connected by the following recursive expression:

$$x_{k+1} = \beta(\lambda(1-x_k)). \qquad (2)$$

Sequence $\{x_k\}$ converges to 1 for any $0 \le x_0 \le 1$ if $k \to \infty$ due to the properties of function $\beta(s)$. Indeed, $\beta(s) \le 1$ when $s \ge 0$ and by differentiating the equality $\beta(\lambda(1-x)) = \int_0^{\infty} e^{-\lambda(1-x)t} d\varkappa(t)$ it can be shown that $\beta'(\lambda(1-x)) \le \beta_1 \lambda < 1$.

3.1 Computing Probability of State 0

For computing n_0 we introduce the following sequence:

$$\pi(x_k) = \nu(\lambda(1-x_k))\pi(x_{k+1}). \qquad (3)$$

The limit of the sequence $\{\pi(x_k)\}$ when $k \to \infty$ exists because of two reasons:
a) there exists the limit of the sequence $\{x_k\}$ and,
b) function $\pi(x)$ is continuous on the closed interval $[0,1]$.
Since $\pi(1) = 1$, the limiting value of this sequence is 1.
From (3) one obtains:

$$\pi(x_0) = \prod_{i=0}^{k} v(\lambda(1-x_i))\pi(x_{k+1}). \qquad (4)$$

In the limit $k \to \infty$ and under the condition $\lambda B_1 < 1$, noting that $\pi(1) = 1$, this results in:

$$\pi(x_0) = \prod_{i=0}^{\infty} v(\lambda(1-x_i)). \qquad (5)$$

Using equality (5), the value of $\pi(x_0)$ can be approximately computed at any point $0 \leq x_0 \leq 1$. To do so, we introduce another sequence, the elements of which $\{\pi_{0k}(x_0)\}$ are defined as products of the first k terms from the equation (5).

$$\pi_{0k}(x_0) = \prod_{i=0}^{k} v(\lambda(1-x_i)). \qquad (6)$$

If $x_0 = 0$ then $\pi(x_0) = n_0$ (exact value of the probability that the queue is empty at the moment of service initiation) and $\pi_{0k}(x_0)$ gives an approximation of n_0. Clearly, when $k \to \infty$ the sequence $\{\pi_{0k}(x_0)\}$ converges to $\pi(x_0)$ and the accuracy of formula (6) improves.

3.2 Error Estimation

The major advantage of the technique shown in the previous section is the possibility to estimate the accuracy of computing $\pi(x_0)$ as a function of k using formula (6) by deriving the expression for the upper bound in computational error.
Indeed, from (2) we obtain that $x_{k+1} \leq x_k + (x_k - x_{k-1})^{**}$ and, hence, $(x_{k+1} - x_k) \leq (x_k - x_{k-1})^{**} \leq (x_1 - x_0)^{**k}$, where $** = \max\{\beta'(\lambda(1-x))\} = \lambda B_1 = o$. $0 \leq x \leq 1$.
Analogously, for $\pi(x_k)$ and $\pi(x_{k+1})$: $\pi(x_{k+1}) \leq \pi(x_k) + (x_{k+1} - x_k)^{**}_1$, or

$\pi(x_{k+1}) \leq \pi(x_k) + (x_1 - x_0)^{**k**}_1$ where $**_1 = \max\{\pi'(x)\} = \pi'(1) = \dfrac{v_1 \lambda}{1-o}$.
$0 \leq x \leq 1$.
Using the last expression, it can be shown that for any N and k such that $N > k$

$$\pi(x_N) - \pi(x_k) \leq \sum_{i=k}^{N} (x_1 - x_0)^{**i**}_1.$$

In the limit $N \to \infty$ we have $\pi(x_\infty) = 1$. Thus,

$$1-\pi(x_k) \leq \sum_{l=k}^{\infty} (x_1-x_0)^{**l**}1 = (x_1-x_0)^{**k}1\frac{1}{1-**} = \frac{(x_1-x_0)^k \lambda v_1}{(1-o)^2}.$$

Consider now the difference $\pi_{0k}(x_0)-\pi(x_0)$. From the equalities obtained earlier, it follows that:

$$0 \leq (\pi_{0k}(x_0)-\pi(x_0)) \leq \prod_{l=0}^{k} v(\lambda(1-x_l))\frac{(x_1-x_0)\lambda o^k v_1}{(1-o)^2} \tag{7}$$

If $o < 1$ and $k \to \infty$, the difference in (7) tends to the limiting value 0. Expression (7) provides an upper bound for the error in computations of n_0 using formula (6).

3.3 Computing Probability of State 1

Differentiating equality (1) with respect to x and using the sequence $\{x_k\}$, it is possible to construct another sequence $\{\pi'(x_k)\}$ in the following way:

$$\pi'(x_k) = -\lambda v'(\lambda(1-x_k))\pi(x_{k+1})-\lambda\beta'(\lambda(1-x_k))\,v(\lambda(1-x_k))\pi'(x_{k+1}). \tag{8}$$

where $v'(\lambda(1-x_k)) = \frac{d}{ds}v(s)|_{s=\lambda(1-x_k)}$, k=0,1,2....

From equations (3) and (8) we construe for any integer k:

$$\pi'(x_0) = \pi(x_0)\sum_{l=0}^{\infty}(-1)^{l+1}\frac{\lambda v'(\lambda(1-x_l))}{v(\lambda(1-x_l))}\prod_{j=0}^{l-1}\lambda\beta'(\lambda(1-x_j)) \tag{9}$$

The convergence of the series is guaranteed here because both $v'(x)$ and $v(x)$ are continuous functions in the closed interval [0,1]. As before, the approximate value of n_1 can be computed using formula (9) by taking into account the first k terms of the summation. Accuracy of such an approximation can be estimated by a method similar to that presented in section 3.2.

4. Performance analysis and optimizations

In this section, we show how the results obtained in the previous section can be applied to performance analysis. We assume that the offered network load is 150Mbytes/sec and we consider two average packet sizes: one is 1500 bytes and the other is 600 bytes. This translates into the arrival rates of 0.1 packets/microsecond and 0.25 packets/microsecond. Accepting a microsecond as a unit of time, we assume that the packets arrive at the host according to the Poisson distribution with $\lambda = 0.1$ and $\lambda = 0.25$ respectively. We further assume that the average service time of a packet by the polling server is 2 microseconds ($a = 0.5$) and the service discipline is gated and context switch latency in such a system is 1 microsecond. Figure 1 shows the values of average waiting time of a packet in the queue (as defined in [7]), probability n_0 (computed using formula (6)), and probability n_1 (formula (9)) as functions of the average vacation period. We assumed that the context switch is a part of a vacation, therefore the minimum value of a vacation period is 1 microsecond.

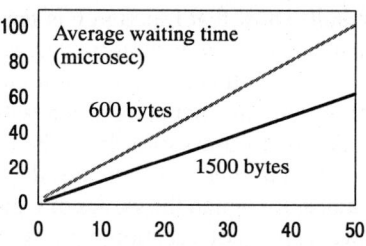 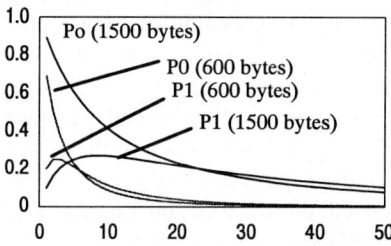

Fig. 1. The graph on the left shows the average waiting time of a packet as a function of the average vacation interval (in microsecs.) for different packet sizes. The graph on the right shows the value of P0 and P1 as functions of the average vacation interval

As can be seen from the Figure 1, short "vacation" periods indeed reduce the average waiting time in the queue, but this comes at the expense of having a higher probability of polling the empty queue (n_0), thus wasting a considerable number of cycles for such useless switchings. The value of probability n_1 also carries some importance because it measures the frequency of finding exactly one request in the queue at the polling instant. Though not resulting in a total waste of CPU time, such service does not offer any improvement compared to a traditional interrupt–based mechanism, since one context switch is required per packet. In a properly designed networking subsystem, each of these parameters has to be given a balanced attention. One simple way to achieve this is to define a cost function (F) depending on the values of n_0 and the average waiting time of a request in the system (w) along with a pair of appropriate coefficients that can be tuned up based on the needs of specific applications and timings obtained by instrumenting the OS kernel. A simple cost function, for instance, can be represented as follows:

$$F(v_1) = c_1 n_0 + c_2 w \tag{10}$$

Here, the coefficient c_1 is the cost of switching to the empty queue and the coefficient c_2 is the cost of a unit of time that an incoming message spends in the queue. If the latency of message passing is more important design goal, then higher waiting cost should be assumed and thus the value of c_2 must be set higher than the value of c_1. However, the opposite is true if the more important characteristic is the overall system's throughput – that is, the amount of work done in a unit of time, and higher latency can be tolerated. Of course, these values can be readjusted dynamically according to the changing workload. As shown in Figure 1, both n_0 and w depend on the average vacation interval which is the single argument of the function F as expressed by formula (10). Any good design should aim at minimizing the value of F by selecting the optimal vacation period.

Figure 2 shows the function F for the two networking subsystem configurations considered in this section. The first graph is for the average packet size of 1500 bytes, the second is for that of 600 bytes. The value of n_0 was multiplied by 100 to keep it in the interval [0..100] and this new value was then used in the formula for F. We computed the value of F for three different sets of cost coefficients. First, c_1 was assumed to be equal to c_2 (for simplicity, we considered the case of both coefficients being set to 1). Second, c_1 was assumed to be greater than c_2 (we set the first coefficient to 1 and the second coefficient to 2). Third, c_2 was assumed to be greater than c_1, so the value of 2 was assigned to c_2 while keeping c_1 at 1. The results show that function F is sensitive to the values of these coefficients, and the system can be effectively controlled by careful selection of the values of c_1 and c_2. In all three cases, the function F has a minimum, and the average vacation period that provides this minimum increases along with the increasing cost of switchings to the empty queue. Another observation from the results shown in the Figure 2 is that the minimums formed by the function F are not the sharp ones. Indeed, there is a sizable range of argument values, for which the values of F deviate only slightly from the minimum value. Thus, a "sweet spot" of vacation periods can be identified, where the value of F is either a minimum or its deviation from the minimum does not exceed a predefined threshold.

Other variations of cost functions obviously exist, where the value of n_1 can be included in some form. To be practical, however, any expression for the cost function has to be fairly simple, so that the optimal vacation period could be computed quickly. This is especially important when the behavior of the applications changes frequently and the vacation period has to be adjusted accordingly to respond to the changing environment.

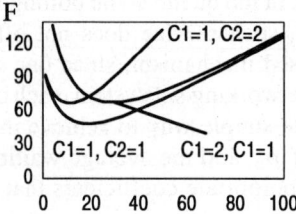
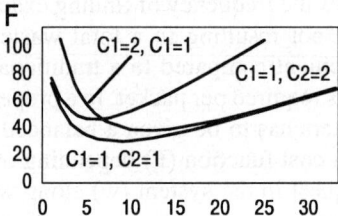

Fig. 2. Cost function F for various average vacation intervals. Graph on the left shows the results for the average packet length of 1500 bytes, and graph on the right – for 600 bytes.

Alternative ways to employ the value of n_0 in system's performance analysis also exist. With the capability of computing the system's states probabilities with high degree of accuracy, the traditional mean–value estimates no longer represent an exclusive gauge of system's performance. In fact, the new metrics, in the very least taking into account the value of n_0, should be considered. One such simple indicator (S) is the average number of switches (vacations) for the service of one request.

Specifically, S=Q/N, where Q is the average number of consecutive switches between two service periods, and N is the average queue length at the polling instant. Q can be easily computed from n_0 in the following way:

$$Q = 1 + (1-n_0) \sum_{k=0}^{\infty} k(n_0)^k = \frac{1}{(1-n_0)}.$$ The minimum value of Q is 1, because at least one switch between two consecutive service periods always occurs. The value of (Q–1) is the indicator of the fraction of switches that find the target queue empty. Parameter S can be controlled by varying the average vacation interval. As the vacation period increases, $Q \to 1$, $N \to \infty$ and thus, $S \to \infty$ which is advantageous from the perspective

of overall system's throughput. Apparently, by varying the average vacation period, one can tune the system in such a way that the value of S is minimized under the constraint that the average queue length does not fall below certain threshold, which can be defined as the level of system's tolerance to the increase in message passing latency.

5. Conclusions

This paper argues that intelligent selection of polling frequency is a key to performance of a system, where the number of interrupts within the networking subsystem is reduced through the use of two polled, unidirectional queues to provide an interface between the NIC and the networking software on the host. Such polling should not only aim at servicing the requests in the queue fast, thus effectively reducing the latency of a message passing, but also attend to the needs of other processes running in the system. In this realm, polling of an empty queue should be avoided and polling of the queue that contains only one request should be minimized, thus amortizing the cost of expensive context–switch operation. The numerical method for computing the probabilities of system's states in the single queue polling system is then presented. In contrast to previously suggested techniques, our mechanism allows to estimate the errors in computations of the state probabilities and accurately derive the probability of polling the empty queue or polling the queue that contains only one request. These values, in conjunction with the mean–value estimates like the average number of customers in the queue and the average queue length, are instrumental in the design of efficient polling in a queue–based networking subsystem. This is illustrated by constructing the cost function, which depends on the probability of switching to the empty queue and the average waiting time in the queue. This cost function can be minimized by selecting the appropriate value of average vacation period.

References :
1. Danning, D. et.al.: The Virtual Interface Architecture. IEEE Micro vol. 18 N2 (1998)
2. Ghose, K., Melnick, S., Gaska, T., Goldberg, S., Jayendran, A. and Stien, B.: The Implementation of Low Latency Communication Primitives in the SNOW Prototype. Proceedings of the 26–th Int'l. Conference on Parallel Processing (ICPP) (1997) 462–469
3. Leibowitz, M.: An Approximate Method for Treating a Class of Multiqueue Problems. IBM J. Research Dev. Vol.5 N3 (1961) 204–209
4. Mukherjee, S. and Hill, M.: The Impact of Data Transfer and Buffering Alternatives on Network Interface Design. Proceedings of the Fourth Int'l Symposium on High–Performance Computer Architecture (HPCA) (1998)
5. Myrinet on–line documentation/specs at:http://www.myri.com
6. Saati, T.: Elements of Queueing Theory with Applications. McGraw–Hill (1961)
7. Takagi, H.: Queueing Analysis of Polling Models. ACM Computer Surveys, Vol.20, N1 (1988)
8. Virtual Interface Architecture on–line documentation/specs at: http://www.viarch.org

Performance Prediction of Oblivious BSP Programs

Jesús A. González[1], Coromoto León[1], Fabiana Piccoli[2], Marcela Printista[2],
José L. Roda[1], Casiano Rodríguez[1] and Francisco de Sande[1]

[1] Dpto. Estadística, Investigación Operativa y Computación,
Universidad de La Laguna, Tenerife, Spain
casiano@ull.es
[2] Universidad Nacional de San Luis
Ejército de los Andes 950, San Luis, Argentina
mprinti@unsl.edu.ar

Abstract. The BSP model can be extended with a zero cost synchronization mechanism, which can be used when the number of messages due to receives is known. This mechanism, usually known as "oblivious synchronization" implies that different processors can be in different supersteps at the same time. An unwanted consequence of this software improvement is a loss of accuracy in prediction. This paper proposes an extension of the BSP complexity model to deal with oblivious barriers and shows its accuracy.

1 Introduction

The asynchronous nature of some parallel paradigms like farms and pipelines hampers the efficient implementation in the scope of a flat-data-parallel global-barrier Bulk Synchronous Programming (BSP [7]) software like the BSPLib [6]. To overcome these limitations, the Paderborn University BSP library (PUB [5]) offers the use of collective operations, processor-partition operations and oblivious synchronization. In addition to the BSP most common features, PUB provides the capacity to partition the current BSP machine into several subsets, each of which acts as an autonomous BSP computer with their own processor numbering and synchronization points. One of the most novel features of PUB is the oblivious synchronization. It is implemented through the *bsp_oblsync(bsp,n)* function, which does not return until n messages have been received. Although its use mitigates the synchronization overhead, it implies that different processors can be in different supersteps at the same time. The BSP semantic is preserved in PUB by numbering the supersteps and by ensuring that the receiver thread buffers messages that arrive out of order until the correct superstep is reached. Some authors claim that an unwanted consequence of these software improvements imply a possible loss of accuracy [3, page 18].

Some runtime systems oriented to the flat BSP model try to bring actual machines closer to the BSP ideal machine by packing individual messages generated during a superstep and optimizing communication time by rearranging the order in which messages are sent at the end of the superstep [6]. This policy reduces the influence of the communication pattern, since it gives place to an *AllToAll* communication pattern at the end of each superstep. The actual overlapping of supersteps produced by PUB machine partitioning and oblivious synchronization makes unfeasible the former implementation approach and may lead to congestion (hot spots) and therefore to a wider variability in the observed bandwidth.

In the next section we propose an extension of the BSP model for PUB parallel programs: the **Oblivious BSP** model. The accuracy of predictions is studied in three representative examples presented in the following two sections. The first case is the Parallel Binary Search example used by the authors of PUB in the introduction of their library. The second example is a pipeline algorithm involving a large number of small messages and oblivious synchronization. While the predicted time by the Oblivious BSP model for computation intensive algorithm fits the actual measured time with a negligible error, less than 3%, the results obtained for the two other intensive communication examples is much larger, reaching 30%.

2 The Oblivious BSP Model

As in ordinary BSP, the execution of a PUB program on a BSP machine $X=\{0,...,P-1\}$ consists of supersteps. However, as a consequence of the oblivious synchronization, processors may be in different supersteps at a given time. Still it is true that:

- Supersteps can be numbered starting at 1.
- The total number of supersteps R, performed by all the P processors is the same.
- Although messages sent by a processor in superstep s may arrive to another processor executing an earlier superstep $r<s$, communications are made effective only when the receiver processor reaches the end of superstep s.

Lets assume in first instance that no processor partitioning is performed in the analyzed task T. If the superstep s ends in an oblivious synchronization, we define the set $\Omega_{s,i}$ for a given processor i and superstep s as the set

$$\Omega_{s,i} = \{j \in X\ /\ \text{Processor } j \text{ sends a message to processor } i \text{ in superstep } s\} \cup \{i\} \quad (1)$$

while $\Omega_{s,i} = X$ when the superstep ends in a global barrier synchronization. In fact, this last expression can be considered a particular case of formula (1) if it is accepted that barrier synchronization carries an *AllToAll* communication pattern. Processors in the set $\Omega_{s,i}$ are called "**the incoming partners of processor i in step s**". Usually it is accepted that all the processors start the computation at the same time. As it will be explained later, the presence of partition functions forces us to consider the most general case in which each processor i joins the computation at a different initial time ξ_i. Denoting by $\xi = (\xi_0, ..., \xi_{P-1})$ the vector for all processors, the **Oblivious BSP** time $\Phi_{s,i}(T, X, \xi)$ taken by processor $i \in X$ executing task T to finish its superstep s is recursively defined by the formulas:

$$\Phi_{1,i}(T, X, \xi) = \max\ \{w_{1,j} + \xi_j\ /\ j \in \Omega_{1,i}\} + (g*h_{1,i} + L_b),\ i = 0,..., P-1, \quad (2)$$

$$\Phi_{s,i}(T, X, \xi) = max \ \{\Phi_{s-1,j}(T, X, \xi) + w_{s,j} \ / j \in \Omega_{s,i}\} + (g^*h_{s,i} + L_b), \ s = 2,..,R,$$
$$i = 0,..., P-1$$

where $w_{s,j}$ denotes the time spent in computing by processor j in step s, R is the total number of supersteps and $h_{s,i}$ is defined as the number of bytes communicated by processor i in step s, that is:

$$h_{s,i} = max \ \{in_{s,j} @ \ out_{s,j} / j \in \Omega_{s,i}\}, \ s = 1,...,R, \ i = 0,...,P-1 \qquad (3)$$

and $in_{s,j}$ and $out_{s,j}$ respectively denote the number of incoming/outgoing bytes to/from processor j in the superstep s. The @ operation is defined as *max* or *sum* depending on the input/output capabilities of the network interface. Rather than exhibiting a linear behavior, the actual communication time $T(h)$ takes the form of a piecewise linear function [1, 2]. We define the *OBSP Packet Size* as the message size h_{PS} in which the curve $T(h)$ has its first inflection point. This size depends on the target architecture. Only for packet sizes larger than the OBSP packet size, such a curve can be approached by a linear function with gap g. The value L_b is the oblivious latency, which is different from the barrier synchronization latency value L used in global synchronization supersteps. L_b is adjusted to optimize the linear fit approach to $T(h)$ for h-relation values larger than the OBSP packet size. Special gap g_0 and latency L_{b0} values have to be used for messages sizes smaller than the OBSP packet size. Thus, the communication capabilities of an OBSP machine are characterized by the five parameters (g, L, L_b, g_0, L_{b0}), which, as in the BSP model, depend on the number of processors.

At any time, processors are organized in a *hierarchy of processor sets*. A processor set in PUB is represented by a structure called a *BSP object*. Let $Q \subseteq X$ be a set of processors (i.e. a BSP object) executing task T. When processors in Q execute function *bsp_partition(t_bsp *Q, t_bsp *S, int r, int *Y)*, the set Q is divided in r disjoint subsets S_i such that,

$$Q = \cup_{0 \leq i \leq r-1} S_i, \qquad (4)$$
$$S_0 = \{0,..., Y[0]-1\},$$
$$S_i = \{Y[i-1],..., Y[i]-1\}, \ 1 \leq i \leq r-1$$

After the partition step, each subgroup S_i acts as an autonomous BSP computer with its own processor numbering, messages queue and synchronization mechanism. The time that processor $j \in S_i$ takes to finish its work in task T_i executed by the BSP object S_i is given by

$$\Phi_{Ri, j}(T_i, S_i, \Phi_{s-1,j} + w^*_{s,j}) \ \text{such that} \ j \in S_i, \ i = 0,...,r-1, \qquad (5)$$

where R_i is the number of supersteps performed in task T_i and $w^*_{s,j}$ is the computing time executed by processor j before its call to the *bsp_partition* function in the s-th superstep of original set Q. Observe that subgroups are created in a stack-like order, so function *bsp_partition* and *bsp_done* incur no communication. This implies that different processors in a given subset can arrive at the partition process (and leave it) at different time. From the point of view of the parent machine, the code executed between the call to *bsp_partition* and *bsp_done* behaves as computation (i.e. like a call to a subroutine).

Another essential difference of the Oblivious Model proposed here with respect to the BSP model, is the way the computing time W is carried out. Our proposal is to associate a computational constant with each basic block (maximal segment of code without jumps).

Table 1. OBSP values of L_{b0}, g and L_b for the CRAY T3E

L_{b0}	g	L_b
2E-04 sec	0.558E-09 sec/byte	3.62E-04 sec

3 Predicting Groups: The Parallel Binary Search (PBS)

The *PBS* problem [5] consists in locating $SIZE = m*P$ queries (where P is the number of processors) in a butterfly data structure of $N = n*P$ keys. The root of the tree is replicated P times, and each other level is replicated half as many times as the level above. Fig. 1 shows the PUB implementation of the parallel binary search. The code in lines 7-12 routes each query to its correct sub-tree. Variable *temp* stores the queries that have to be routed to the other half of the butterfly. The counter *new_m* carries the number of queries that will remain in the local processor. In line 14 the unbuffered function *bsp_sendmsg()* is used to send a message (pointed by *temp*), which was created by *bsp_createmsg()* (line 3). In lines 23-29, the search is either finished locally, or the function *bin_search()* is called recursively on different subsets of processors. The call to *bsp_partition()* in line 26 divides the processors in two groups of equal size. Since the number of messages to receive is known in advance, the code makes use of the oblivious synchronization function *bsp_oblsync(bsp, n)*, which does not return until n messages have been received (line 16).

Let be $m = SIZE/P$ the number of queries that each processor has to locate. The algorithm will create a new BSP-machine in each new level of the tree. Hence, the computation in each recursion level takes two supersteps; the first one involves the routing process and the second the recursive partition process.

After the first superstep a new BSP-machine is created. For these new BSP-machine, the computing time executed by a processor j before its call to the *bsp_partition* function is:

$$w^*_{s,j} = (C_0 * m/2 + C_1) + B$$

The $m/2$ factor is due to the assumption that queries are uniformly distributed.

```
1.   void bin_search(pbsp bsp, int d, int m) {
2.
3.     msg = bsp_createmsg(bsp,m*OVERSAMPLE * sizeof(int))
4.     temp = bspmsg_data(msg);
5.     pid=bsp_pid(bsp); nprocs=bsp_nprocs(bsp);
6.
7.     for (i=new_m=other=0; i < m; i++)
8.        if (query[i]<=bkey[d] && pid>=nprocs/2 ||
9.            query[i]> bkey[d] && pid<nprocs/2)
10.           temp[other++] = query[i];
11.       else
12.          query[new_m++] = query[i];
13.
14.    bsp_sendmsg(bsp,(pid+ nprocs/2) %
15.                nprocs,msg,other*sizeof(int));
16.    bsp_oblsync(bsp,1);
17.    msg = bsp_getmsg(bsp, 0);
18.
19.    memcpy(&query[new_m], bspmsg_data(msg),
20.           bspmsg_size(msg));
21.    new_m += bspmsg_size(msg)/sizeof(int);
22.
23.    if (d==0) local_search(new_m);
24.    else {
25.       part[0]= nprocs/2; part[1]= nprocs;
26.       bsp_partition(bsp, &subbsp, 2, part);
27.       bin_search(subbsp, d-1, new_m);
28.       bsp_done(&subbsp);
29.     }
30. }
```

Lines 3–12: A_0*m+A_1
Lines 14–17: $g*m*sizeof(int)/2+L_b$
Lines 19–21: $C_0*m/2+C_1$
Line 23: Seq
Line 24: T
Lines 25–26: B
Line 28: D

Fig. 1. Parallel Binary Search with partition operations

Therefore, the initial distributions of times ($\xi_{i,d}$) when processor i starts the *bin_search* function at depth level d is given by:

$$\xi_{i,d} = \begin{cases} 0 & \text{for } d=0 \\ \phi_{1,i}(PBS, S_{d-1}, \xi_{i,d-1}) + (C_0 * m/2 + C_1) + B & \text{for } d=1,...,\log_2(P)-1 \end{cases}$$

Where $\phi_{1,i}(PBS, S_{d-1}, \xi_{i,d-1})$ is the time when processor i finishes the first superstep (that is, reaches line 16 in Fig. 1). Constants C_0 and C_1 are associated with lines 19 to 21 and constant B corresponds to the partition process (lines 25-26).

Let us compute $\phi_{1,i}(PBS, S_{d-1}, \xi_{i,d-1})$. As the queries are equally distributed, the value m can be considered constant. The time spent by processor i in lines 3-12 is $w_{1,i} = (A_0 * m + A_1)$. The *h*-relations in all supersteps are the same:

$$h_{1,i} = (m* sizeof(int))/2$$

The incoming partners of processor i in superstep *1* are:

$$\Omega_{1,i} = \{ i, i \text{ xor } 2^{\log(|Sd|)-1} \} \quad \text{for all } (PBS, S_d, \xi_{i,Sd}) \text{ and } d =0, 1,...,\log(P)-1$$

The Oblivious Time taken by processors in the first superstep is calculated by formula:

$$\phi_{1,i}(PBS, S_d, \xi_{i,d}) = ((A_0 * m + A_1) + \xi_{i,d}) + g\, m/2 * sizeof(int) + L_b \text{ for } d = 0,...,\log(P)-1$$

The time when processor i finishes step 2 at depth d is given by:

$$\phi_{2,i}(PBS, S_d, \xi_d) = \begin{cases} \phi_{2,i}(PBS, S_{d+1}, \xi_{i,d+1})+D & \text{for } d = 0...log(P)-2 \\ \phi_{1,i}(PBS, S_d, \xi_{i,d})+(C_0*m/2+C_1)+ SeqT+g* h_{2,i}+L_b & \text{for } d =log(P)-1 \end{cases}$$

The time $\phi_{2,i}(PBS, S_{d+1}, \xi_{i, d+1})$ stands for the instant when the recursive call at line 27 (recursion level $d+1$) finishes. The constant D corresponds to the *bsp_done()* call at line 28. The $(PBS, S_{log(P)-1}, \xi_{i,log(P)-1})$-machines are the last BSP-machines created, and their second superstep includes the calling to the sequential binary search ($SeqT$). Since our study concentrates in the prediction accuracy of the communication stages, in the experiments, we have substituted the sequential binary search by an empty body.

The oblivious BSP time $\phi_{2,0}(PBS, S_0, \xi_{i,0})$ of the *PBS* algorithms in a BSP-machine with P processors at the outmost level can be obtained by successive substitutions:

$$\Phi_{2i}(PBS,P,0)= log(P)*[A_0*m+A_1+ g*m/2*sizeof(int)+L_b+(C_0*m/2+C_1)] \\ +(log(P)-1)* [B+D]+SeqT$$

Table 2 presents the prediction accuracy of the OBSP model. The percentage of error entries in the last row have been computed as

$$\%Error=(Real-Predicted\ OBSP)*100/Real$$

Table 2. 2 097 152 Items. Real and OBSP predicted times for the PBS algorithm in the CRAY T3E. Time is in seconds.

Processors	2	4	8	16
Real	0.1776	0.1600	0.1202	0.0838
Predicted OBSP	0.1145	0.1152	0.0883	0.061
% Error	35%	28%	26%	27%

We also considered a computationally intensive experiment: the Fast Fourier Transform. The errors observed for this application are under 1%.

4 Pipelines in PUB

This section illustrates the OBSP model through a fine-grain intensive-communication application. A virtual pipeline is cyclically mapped onto a set of processors. The Resource Allocation Problem (RAP) asks to map limited resources to a set of tasks by way of maximizing their effectiveness [4]. Assume that we have M units of an indivisible resource and N tasks. For each task j, function $f_j(x)$ gives the income obtained when a quantity x of resource is allocated to the task j. The problem can be formally expressed as:

$$Max\ \sum_{j=1,...,N} f_j(x_j), \quad s.t.\ \sum_{j=1,...,N} x_j=M,\ x_j \in N$$

where N denotes the set of non negative integer numbers. Let us denote by $Q[k][m]$ the optimal income for the resource allocation sub-problem constituted by the first k tasks and m units of resource. Applying the Dynamic Programming Principle to this problem leads to the following state equation:

$$Q[1][m] = f_1(m),\ 0 \leq m \leq M,$$
$$Q[k][m] = \max\{Q[k-1][m-x] + f_k(x) / 0 \leq x \leq m\},\ 1 < k \leq N$$

This formula leads to a very simple sequential algorithm solving the problem in time $O(N \cdot M^2)$. Observe that dependencies with respect to the activities of the values $Q[k][m]$ occur only among adjacent values of k. Based in this idea, we have designed a pipeline algorithm with N virtual stages which are cyclically mapped over the P physical processors (Fig. 2). Due to this virtualization process, computation is performed in *Num_bands* bands (line 1). During the execution of the band b, the physical processor *Name* simulates the virtual processor *NAME* (line 7). This simulation consists of computing the optimal values $Q[NAME][m]$ for all the resource values m between 0 and M. This is done by the call to function *rap_spaa()* (line 11), whose code is presented in Fig. 3. Physical processor 0 deals with the management of a buffer needed to store the incoming messages from processor $P-1$. Fig. 4 corresponds to the function *rap_spaa0()* that is called by processor 0 at line 9, and previously has initialized this *buffer* to 0's in the *calloc()* (line 3).

```
1.   Num_Bands = (N%P) ? N/P+1 : N/P;
2.   if(Name == 0) {
3.       buffer = (int*)calloc(M+1, sizeof(int));
4.       front = 0; end = M;
5.   }
6.   for(b = 0; b<Num_Bands; b++) {
7.       NAME=b*P+Name;
8.       if(Name==0)
9.           Sol=rap_spaa0(&bsp, M, NAME, P, NAME==N-1, b==Num_Bands-1);
10.      else if(NAME<N)
11.          Sol=rap_spaa(&bsp, M, NAME, P, NAME==N-1);
12.      else
13.          dummy_stage(&bsp, M, P);
14.  }
```

Fig. 2. Mapping cyclically a virtual pipeline with N stages

To make a detailed OBSP analysis of this pipeline algorithm, we only study the steps in the first band corresponding to Figs. 3 and 4. The behavior is similar in the rest of the bands, except in the last one where some processors only have to synchronize performing dummy steps (line 13).

In the first superstep, each processor initializes its vector Q (line 3). Condition in line 6 imposes that the processor *Name* has to wait *Name* supersteps before receiving its first message.

Only processor 0 complies with this condition in the first step, so it takes one value from the buffer (line 11), updates its vector Q (line 12) and sends a message (one integer) to processor 1 (line 13). In this superstep, it holds that:

$$\Omega_{1,1} = \{0,1\};\ \Omega_{1,i} = \{i\},\ i \neq 1,$$
$$h_{1,0} = h_{1,1} = sizeof(int);\ h_{1,i} = 0,\ 1 < i < P$$

```
1.   int rap_spaa(t_bsp *bsp, int M, int NAME, int P, int bLast) {
2.     int *Q, q, m, d, Step, Status;
3.     Q=(int*)calloc(M+1, sizeof(int));
4.     if(Q==NULL) bsp_abort(bsp, "Memory Error\n");
5.     for(Step=0, m=0; Step<=M+P; Step++) {
6.       if((bsp_pid(bsp)<=Step) && (m<=M)) {
7.         q = *((int*)bspmsg_data(bsp_getmsg(bsp, 0)));
8.         for(d=m; d<=M; d++) Q[d]=max(Q[d], q+f(NAME, d-m));
9.         if(!bLast) bsp_send(bsp, NEXT, &Q[m], sizeof(int));
10.        m++;
11.      }
12.      Status = (Step >= bsp_pid(bsp)-1) && (Step < bsp_pid(bsp)+M);
13.      bsp_oblsync(bsp, Status);
14.    }
15.    q=Q[M];
16.    free(Q);
17.    return q;
18. }
```

Fig. 3. Pipeline algorithm for the RAP. Code for virtual processor *NAME*

Under the assumption that the OBSP packet size is much larger than an integer size, the appropriate values of g and L to use in formula (2) are g_0 and L_{b0}:

$$\Phi_{1,0} = A_0*(M+1) + A_1 + B_0*(M+1) + B_1 + g_0* h_{1,0} + L_{b0},$$
$$\Phi_{1,1} = max\{w_{1,0}, w_{1,1}\} + g_0* h_{1,1} + L_{b0}$$
$$= A_0*(M+1) + A_1 + B_0*(M+1) + B_1 + g_0* h_{1,1} + L_{b0},$$
$$\Phi_{1,i} = A_0*(M+1) + A_1, \ 1 < i < P$$

where A_0 and A_1 are the constants associated with the execution OF *calloc()*, and the constants B_0 and B_1 correspond to update the values $Q[NAME-1][m]$. Since all processor start computation at the same initial time, $\xi_i = 0$ for all processors.

In each subsequent superstep, one processor complies with condition in line 6 and receives its first message. This processor dominates the computing cost because it has to perform the largest updating process. During the next $P-1$ supersteps it holds that:

$$\Omega_{s,i} = \{i-1, i\}, \ h_{s,i} = sizeof(int), \ 0 < i \leq s < P,$$
$$\Omega_{s,i} = \{i\}, \ h_{1,i} = 0, \ s < i < P$$

and the OBSP time is given by:

$$\Phi_{s,i} = max\{\Phi_{s-1,i-1} + B_0*(M+1-s+i) + B_1, \ \Phi_{s-1,i} + B_0*(M+2-s+i) + B_1\} + g_0*h_{s,i} + L_{b0},$$
$$0 < i \leq s < P,$$
$$\Phi_{s,i} = A_0*(M+1) + A_1, \ s < i < P$$

After the P-th superstep, each processor receives one message per superstep. As processor $P-1$ is the last to finish its computation and taking into account that it has the largest computing time, the cost for the subsequent supersteps is:

$$\Omega_{s,i} = \{i-1, i\}, \ h_{s,i} = sizeof(int), \ 0 \leq i < P \leq s,$$
$$\Phi_{s,i} = max\{\Phi_{s-1,i-1} + B_0*(M+1-s+i) + B_1, \ \Phi_{s-1,i} + B_0*(M+2-s+i) + B_1\} + g_0*h_{s,i} + L_{b0},$$
$$0 \leq i < P \leq s$$

```
1.   int rap_spaa0(t_bsp *bsp,int M,int Name,int P,int bLast,int
     pLast) {
2.      int *Q, q, m, d, Step, Status;
3.      Q=(int*)calloc(M+1, sizeof(int));
4.      if(Q==NULL) bsp_abort(bsp, "Memory Error\n");
5.      for(Step=0, m=0; Step<=M+P; Step++) {
6.         if((!pLast) && (Step >= P)){
7.            q = *((int*)bspmsg_data(bsp_getmsg(bsp, 0)));
8.            end=(++end)%(M+1);   buffer[end]=q;
9.         }
10.        if(m<=M) {
11.           q=buffer[front]; front=(++front)%(M+1);
12.           for(d=m; d<=M; d++) Q[d]=max(Q[d], q+f(Name, d-m));
13.           if (!bLast) bsp_send(bsp, NEXT, &Q[m], sizeof(int));
14.           m++;
15.        }
16.        Status = !pLast && (Step >= P-1) && (Step < P+M);
17.        bsp_oblsync(bsp, Status);
18.     }
19.     q=Q[M];
20.     free(Q);
21.     return q;
22.  }
```

Fig. 4. Pipeline Algorithm for the RAP. Code for processor 0

where all the arithmetic operations are modulo P. The number of supersteps in a band is $(M+P+1)$, so the algorithm performs $R = (M+P+1) * \lceil N/P \rceil$ supersteps. By successive substitutions we arrive to:

$$\Phi_{R, P-1} = \lceil N/P \rceil * \{(A_0*(M+1)+A_1 + P*\{B_0*(M+1)+B_1 + L_{b0} + g_0*h\} + M*\{(B_1+L_{b0} + g_0*h) + B_0*(M+1)/2\} + C + L_{b0} + g_0*h\}$$

where constant C is related with the computation in lines 15-17 in Fig. 3 (respectively lines 19-21 in Fig. 4), and $h = sizeof(int)$.

Table 3 presents the values for the computational constants measured on the CRAY T3E. Actual and predicted time are shown in Table 4.

Table 3. Computational and communication constants (CRAY T3E). Time is in seconds

A_0	A_1	B_0	B_1	C
2.39E-08	4.21E-05	1.19E-07	1.92E-05	3.50E-05

Table 4. Real and OBSP predicted times for the RAP algorithm. Time is in seconds

Processors	2	4	8	16
Real	181.81	91.13	45.72	23.30
Predicted OBSP	142.82	71.58	35.96	18.30
% Error	27.30%	27.31%	27.13%	27.33%

5 Conclusions

This paper presents an extension of the BSP model to deal with oblivious synchronization and machine partitions. It also introduces a different approach to the prediction of the computing time. The model parameters for PUB have been evaluated on a CRAY T3E. While the predicted time by the Oblivious BSP model for computation intensive algorithm fits the actual measured time with a negligible error, less than 3%, the results obtained for the two intensive communication examples are below 30%. These figures are comparable to what is obtained for classical BSP algorithms (ranging from 18% to 65%) [8].

Acknowledgements

This research has been partially supported by Comisión Interministerial de Ciencia y Tecnología under project TIC1999-0754-C03.

References

1. Abandah, G. A., Davidson, E. S. Modelling the Communication Performance of the IBMP-SP2. 10th IPPS. 1996.
2. Arruabarrena, J. M., Arruabarrena A., Beivide R., Gregorio J. A. Assessing the Performance of the New IBM-SP2 Communication Subsystem. IEEE Parallel and Distributed Technology. pp.12-22. 1996.
3. Goudreau, M. Hill, J., Lang, K. McColl, B., Rao, S., Stephanescu, D., Suel, T., Tsantilas, T. A Proposal for the BSP Worldwide Standard Library.
http://www.bsp-worldwide.org/standard/stand2.htm. 1996.
4. Morales, D. G. Almeida F., García F., Roda J. L., Rodríguez C. Design of Parallel Algorithms for the Single Resource Allocation Problem. European Journal of Operational Research. 126 pp.166-174. 2000.
5. Olaf Bonorden, Ben Juurlink, Ingo von Otte, Ingo Rieping- The Paderborn University BSP (PUB) Library- Desing, Implementation and Performance- 13th International Parallel Processing Symposium & 10th Symposium on parallel and Distributed Processing (IPPs/SPDP). 1999.
6. Hill J. McColl W. Stefanescu D. Goudreau M.. Lang K. Rao S. Suel T. Tsantilas T. Bisseling R. BSPLib: The BSP Programming Library. Parallel Computing. 24(14) pp. 1947-1980. 1988.
7. Valiant L. G. A Bridging Model for Parallel Computation. Communications of the ACM. 33(8). pp. 103-111. 1990.
8. Zavanella, A. Milazzo, A. Predictability of Bulk Synchronous Programs Using MPI. 8th Euromicro PDP pp. 118-123. 2000.

Performance Prediction of Data-Dependent Task Parallel Programs

Hasyim Gautama and Arjan J. C. van Gemund

Faculty of Information Technology and Systems, Delft University of Technology
P.O. Box 5031, NL-2600 GA Delft, The Netherlands
{H.Gautama, A.J.C.vanGemund}@ITS.TUDelft.NL

Abstract. Current analytic solutions to the execution time prediction Y of binary parallel compositions of tasks with arbitrary execution time distributions X_1 and X_2 are either computationally complex or very inaccurate. In this paper we introduce an analytical approach based on the use of lambda distributions to approximate execution time distributions. This allows us to predict the first 4 statistical moments of Y in terms of the first 4 moments of X_i at negligible solution complexity. The prediction method applies to a wide range of workload distributions as found in practice, while its accuracy is better or equal compared to comparable low-cost approaches.

1 Introduction

A well-known problem in the performance analysis of parallel and distributed systems is to predict the execution time of a parallel composition of tasks having stochastic execution time. Parallel task compositions can be distinguished into n-ary compositions and binary compositions. The n-ary compositions typically result from data parallelism (e.g., parallel loops) where each task essentially involves the same computation on different data. Binary compositions, in contrast, typically result from task parallelism where the computation involved in the composition may be totally *different*. Consequently, performance prediction of task parallel programs frequently requires the evaluation of binary (heterogeneous) parallel compositions, a problem that, unlike n-ary compositions, has not received much attention.

Consider a binary parallel composition of two tasks having execution time X_1 and X_2, respectively. The resulting execution time Y of the parallel composition is given by

$$Y = \max(X_1, X_2) \qquad (1)$$

Many authors have used Eq. (1) as part of a compile-time static prediction technique [1,3,11,14]. In these approaches X_i (and Y) are implicitly assumed to be deterministic. While Eq. (1) indeed yields a correct prediction when X_i are deterministic, interpreting Eq. (1) in terms of mean values when X_i are *stochastic* (i.e., $\mathsf{E}[Y] = \max(\mathsf{E}[X_1], \mathsf{E}[X_2])$) introduces a severe error which increases monotonically with the variance of X_i [7]. For example, consider the binary composition of two tasks whose execution time are independent, normally distributed with $E[X_1] = E[X_2] = 1$, $Var[X_1] = 1$ and $Var[X_2] = \sigma^2$. Our measurements show that the relative error of the predicted $E[Y]$ is almost 40% and 70% for $\sigma = 1$ and 5, respectively. Yet, in many practical circumstances X_i are typically modeled as stochastic parameters, reflecting the execution time distribution of possibly time-critical tasks over a large spectrum of possible input data sets, and/or the inherent stochastic behavior of the underlying virtual machines. While such a stochastic approach is more effective and realistic than using deterministic parameters [15], solving Eq. (1) now becomes a non-trivial problem well-known in the field of order statistics.

There are a number of approaches to express an execution time distribution, the choice of which largely determines the trade-off between accuracy and cost involved in solving Y. An exact, closed-form, solution for the distribution of Y can be obtained using the cumulative density function (cdf). Let $F_{X_i}(x)$ denote the cdf of X_i. For independent X_i from order statistics [17] it follows that $F_Y(x)$ is given by

$$F_Y(x) = F_{X_1}(x) F_{X_2}(x) \qquad (2)$$

While Eq. (2) is exact, only parametric solutions are of practical use.

Recently a method has been proposed [4] where a distribution is represented in terms of a limited number of statistical moments. The kth moment of X, denoted $E[X^k]$, is defined by

$$E[X^k] = \int_{-\infty}^{\infty} x^k dF_X(x) \qquad (3)$$

This method has been successfully applied to the analysis of sequential and conditional task compositions [5], such that the first four moments of the execution time ($E[Y^k]$) of an arbitrary composition of loops and branches can be recursively expressed in terms of the first four moments of each loop bound, branch probability, and basic block execution time ($E[X^k]$) at $O(1)$ cost. Although the approach is straightforward in the sequential domain, for parallel composition there is in general no analytic, closed-form solution for $E[Y^k]$ in terms of $E[X^k]$ due to a fundamental integration problem [4].

In this paper we present a method based on the use of lambda distributions as intermediate approximation of an execution time distribution in terms of the first four moments. Our contribution has the specific advantage that the approximation of $E[Y^k]$, now readily expressed in terms of the input moments $E[X_i^k]$, has $O(1)$ solution complexity while the approximation error is acceptable. Recently the use of lambda distributions has already been successfully introduced to solve a related integration problem for n-ary parallel compositions of tasks with independent, identically distributed (iid) execution times [4]. Experiments show that the estimation error of the mean value of the parallel execution time is less than 4% for parallel sections comprising up to 10,000 tasks whose execution times are normally distributed. Measurements on real programs (NAS-EP benchmark, PSRS sorting program, and WATOR simulator) confirm these results provided the task execution distributions are independent and unimodal [4].

However, the requirements of X_i being identical restricts these results to binary parallel compositions with *identical* work loads while *non*-identical work loads frequently occur in practice.

The results for binary compositions of *non*-identical tasks as presented in this paper therefore extends the general applicability of the moments approach from the data parallel computing domain to the task parallel computing domain, where task heterogeneity is common. Combining with the results for sequential programs the moment method constitutes an integrated approach to the analysis of any parallel program that can be modeled by Series-Parallel stochastic graphs (SP-graphs). To the best of our knowledge such an approach towards solving $\mathsf{E}[Y^k]$ for binary parallel task compositions in terms of $\mathsf{E}[X^k]$ has not been described elsewhere.

The remainder of the paper is organized as follows. In Section 2 we review current approaches towards performance estimation of binary parallel task composition. In Section 3 we present our approximation method using lambda distributions. In Section 4 we test the our method using well-known standard distributions as well as distributions measured from real applications.

2 Related Work

There have been a number of analytic approaches to predicting the execution time of a binary parallel composition of tasks having stochastic execution time. One approach is to restrict the type of distributions allowed for X to those, for which exact analytical solutions can be derived, such as the class of discrete distributions using the traditional z-transform [9], exponential and uniform distributions [10], and the class of exponomial distributions [13]. While the solution is exact, such execution time distributions are seldom found in practical programs.

Another approach is by approximating X in terms of increasing failure rate random variables [8] or in terms Gram-Charlier series of type A from which the integration problem can be solved [4]. Again, let $\mathsf{E}[X^k]$ be the moments that characterize the distribution of X. Then the approximating probability density function (pdf) of X, denoted by $f(x)$, can be expressed by the Gram-Charlier series [4]. While asymptotically exact, it can be shown, unfortunately, that the number of Gram-Charlier terms needed for a sufficiently accurate approximation is prohibitive [4].

While the above approaches allow X_i to have different distributions, other methods approach the binary composition problem from the n-ary perspective [4,6,7], i.e., by solving $Y = \max(X_1, \ldots, X_N)$ for $N = 2$. However, all these approaches assume X_i to be iid which significantly narrows the application space.

As a result of the difficulties in finding a low-cost, accurate, analytical solution to solving the binary parallel composition problem, also a number of heuristic approaches have been proposed. A good example of such an approach is found in [15]. Y is calculated by simply choosing X_i with the largest mean or by selecting the stochastic value with the largest magnitude value in its entire range.

For example (adapted from [15]), to compute the maximum of $X_1 = 4 \pm 0.5$ and $X_2 = 3 \pm 2$, X_1 has the largest mean, and X_2 has the largest value within its range. On average however, the values of X_1 are likely to be higher than the values of X_2. We formulate the heuristic as described in [15] as follows

$$Y = \begin{cases} X_1, & \mathsf{E}[X_1] > \mathsf{E}[X_2] \\ X_1, & \mathsf{E}[X_1] = \mathsf{E}[X_2] \text{ and } \mathsf{E}[X_1^2] > \mathsf{E}[X_2^2] \\ X_2, & \text{otherwise.} \end{cases} \quad (4)$$

Being a simple heuristic, despite its attractive low-cost property, Eq. (4) only takes into account the first two moments $\mathsf{E}[X_i^k]$, and, amongst other things, does not compute the offset in $\mathsf{E}[Y]$ as established by the order statistics. Nevertheless, next to our positive prior experience with lambda distributions, this heuristic has partly been the inspiration for our low-cost, analytic solution to the binary parallel composition problem.

3 Methodology

In this section we present our approximation approach using lambda distributions. Due to space limitations the background of lambda distributions is omitted, while the interested reader is referred to [12]. First, we describe the principle behind our approach, after which we present our main result for binary parallel composition.

3.1 Principle

To illustrate the principle of our approach consider the following example. Let X_1 and X_2 be uniform distributions with sample spaces $[0, 1/m]$, where $m > 0$ is a shape parameter, and $[1, 3/2]$, respectively. Figure 1 shows F_{X_1} for $m = 1$ and F_{X_2} which represents a trivial case to obtain Y. From Eq. (2) we immediately obtain $F_Y = F_{X_2}$ since $F_{X_1} = 1$ for $F_{X_2} > 0$. In contrast, Figure 2 shows the resulting F_Y (dashed line) using Eq. (2) for $m = 1/2$. Due to the integration problem this exact solution F_Y cannot be evaluated explicitly in terms of $\mathsf{E}[X_i^k]$. Applying heuristic Eq. (4) would simply yield $Y = X_2$ independent of $\text{Var}[X_1]$. Consequently this heuristic causes a large estimation error shown by area between F_{X_2} and F_Y which increases monotonically as function of $\text{Var}[X_1]$.

A better approximation can be obtained by taking the *minimum* of F_{X_1} and F_{X_2} as shown by the bold solid line in Figure 2. In contrast to heuristic Eq. (4) this approach implicitly takes $\text{Var}[X_1]$ into account such that the estimation error is less sensitive to $\text{Var}[X_1]$.

Since the execution time distribution in our method is expressed in terms of statistical moments, we have to evaluate the moments of Y which can be time consuming because the cdf of Y may range from $-\infty$ to ∞. Due to the specific (inverse) formulation of the lambda distribution, however, the moments can be easily obtained while the cdf range is significantly reduced from 0 to 1 (as shown

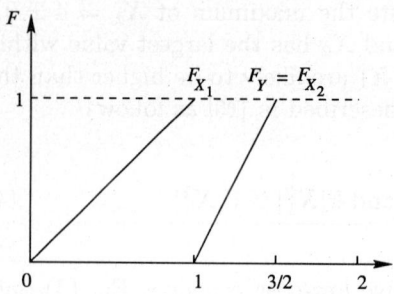
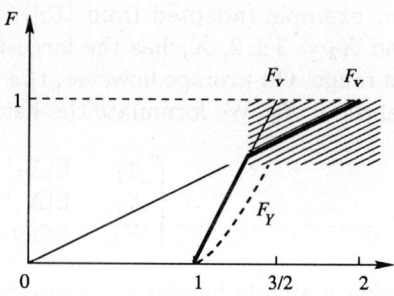

Fig. 1. $Y = \max(X_1, X_2)$ for $m = 1$

Fig. 2. $Y = \max(X_1, X_2)$ for $m = 1/2$

in Section 3.2). A second reason for using the lambda distribution is that its parameters (λ values) can be obtained from $\mathsf{E}[X^k]$ in a straightforward manner. Thus $\mathsf{E}[Y^k]$ can be easily evaluated directly from $\mathsf{E}[X^k]$ using the λ values as intermediate parametric representation.

3.2 Binary Parallel Composition

We now present our new result for general binary parallel compositions in Theorem 1 based on the use of the lambda distribution.

Theorem 1. *Let random variable Y be defined as*

$$Y = \max(X_1, X_2)$$

where X_i are independent random variables for which $\mathsf{E}[X^k]$, $k = 1, 2, 3, 4$ exists. Let X_i be expressed in terms of the lambda distribution as

$$X_1 = R_{X_1}(F) = \alpha_1 + \frac{(F^{\alpha_3} - (1-F)^{\alpha_4})}{\alpha_2}$$

$$X_2 = R_{X_2}(F) = \beta_1 + \frac{(F^{\beta_3} - (1-F)^{\beta_4})}{\beta_2}$$

where α_i and β_i are constants evaluated from a simple function of X_1 and X_2, respectively. Then the moments of Y are approximated by

$$\mathsf{E}[Y^k] = \int_0^1 (\max(R_{X_1}(F), R_{X_2}(F)) + \Delta x)^k \, \mathrm{d}x \tag{5}$$

where Δx is the approximation error. □

Due to space limitations the proof of Theorem 1 is given in [4]. It can be proven that Δx reaches a maximum when $\mathsf{E}[X_1] = \mathsf{E}[X_2]$ and approaches zero when $|\mathsf{E}[X_1] - \mathsf{E}[X_2]|$ is large. As mentioned earlier, due to specific formulation of λ distribution the distribution of Y may range from 0 to 1 rather than from $-\infty$ to ∞ which significantly reduces the solution cost. Note that Eq. (5) conserves the commutative property of the binary parallel composition.

4 Synthetic Distributions

This section describes the quality of our prediction approach when applied to some of the frequently-used standard distributions. The estimation quality is defined by the relative error ε_k evaluated from the predicted moments $\mathsf{E}[Y_p^k]$ in Eq. (5) and the measured moments $\mathsf{E}[Y_m^k]$, according to

$$\varepsilon_k = \frac{|\mathsf{E}[Y_p^k] - \mathsf{E}[Y_m^k]|}{\mathsf{E}[Y_p^k]} \qquad (6)$$

In our applications we use ε_k to determine the estimation error of our method (Eq. (5)) as well as the heuristic (Eq. (4)).

The first synthetic distribution is the continuous uniform distribution. Let X_1 and X_2 be continuous uniform distributions with sample spaces $[0, 1/m]$ and $[1, 3/2]$, respectively, where m in X_1 is introduced to evaluate the relative error between X_1 and X_2 for various scenarios. For $0.1 \leq m < 2/3$ our method is much better than the heuristic as shown in Figure 3 while for $2/3 \leq m < 1$ both methods yield the same error. For $m \geq 1$ both methods have no error since the cdf's are disjunct (i.e., $Y = X_2$). The maximum error of our method is 15% while ε_1 is even less than 5%.

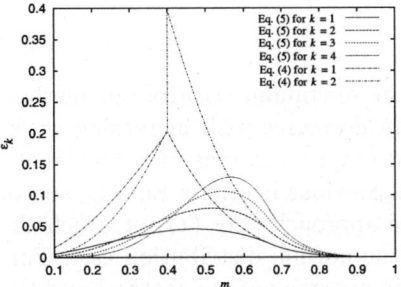
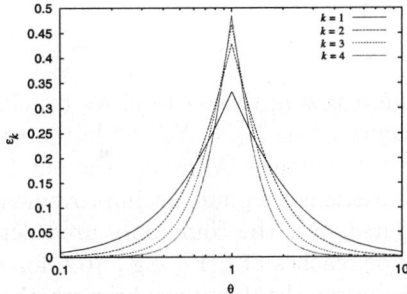

Fig. 3. ε_k for uniform distribution

Fig. 4. ε_k for exponential distribution

A similar scenario is also used for the exponential distribution where $\mathsf{E}[X_1] = 1$, and $\mathsf{E}[X_2] = 1/\theta$ with θ varying from 0.1 to 10. The relative error is shown in Figure 4. Again as a consequence of the prediction principle described in Section 3.1, the error is the largest when $\mathsf{E}[X_1] = \mathsf{E}[X_2]$. Note that in this case the heuristic Eq. (4) has the same performance since $F_{X_2} < F_{X_1}$ in the entire range causes both methods to return the X with the greatest mean value. Note also that in Figure 4 ε_k is symmetric around $\theta = 1$ when θ is plotted in logarithmic scale. The maximum error for $\mathsf{E}[Y]$ is 33%, which sharply decreases for diverging workloads.

The third synthetic distribution is the normal distribution where $E[X_1] = 1$ and $\text{Var}[X_1] = 1$, while $E[X_2] = \mu$ and $\text{Var}[X_2] = \sigma^2$. We vary μ and σ as shown in Figures 5 and 6, respectively. Again, the estimation error decreases as the workloads diverge, while for larger variance our method outperforms the heuristic. In Figure 5 both methods have the same error since the predicted Y is X_2. Note that in Figure 6 the decreasing ε_k for $k = 2$ and $\sigma = 2$ is due to $E[Y^2] > E[X_2^2]$ for $1 < \sigma < 2$ while $E[Y^2] < E[X_2^2]$ for $\sigma > 2$. The maximum error of $E[Y]$ is 35%, while the error decreases with $\text{Var}[X_2]$ whereas the error of heuristic Eq. (4) steadily increases.

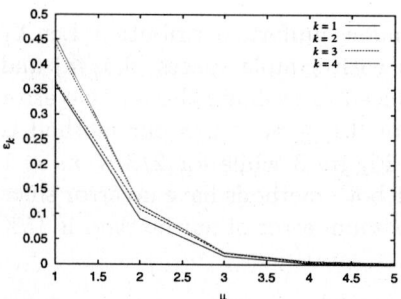

Fig. 5. ε_k for normal distribution $\sigma = 1$

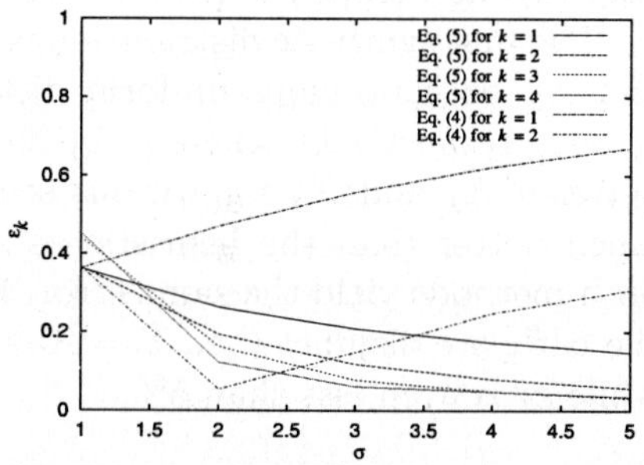

Fig. 6. ε_k for normal distribution $\mu = 1$

Summarizing this section, we conclude that the maximum error of our method occurs when $X_1 = X_2$, while the error quickly *decreases* with increasing workload unbalance. Although the maximum error ranges into tens of percents, the heuristic is a significant improvement over the previous heuristic Eq. (4), and of course, over the commonly used deterministic approach (Eq. (1)) of which the error reaches of $E[Y]$, e.g., 70% for $\sigma = 5$ in the normal distribution case. Furthermore, the difference between the prediction accuracy of our method and the previous heuristic and deterministic approaches increases in favor of our method for increasing task execution time variance.

A significant point of our results is that our method *gains* accuracy for *different* workloads, a situation typical for task parallelism, which indeed is the focus of our method. In this sense our method is complementary to our n-ary (data parallel) prediction method which adequately covers the situation where $E[X_1]$ is *close* to $E[X_2]$ [4].

5 Empirical Distributions

5.1 Pipeline

In this section we determine the quality of our approximation when applied to a pipelined application of two tasks whose execution times are denoted by X_1

and X_2, respectively. The pipeline comprises a Gaussian random generator task that supplies one-dimensional, real-valued vectors of length N to a PSRS sorting task. In steady state the total execution time per vector of the pipelined application is given by $Y = \max(X_1, X_2)$, assuming both tasks use different resources.

The generator task is implemented using the data parallel NAS-EP benchmark [2]. The PSRS sorting task is a data parallel application that sorts the input array by first dividing the array in P equal subarrays where P also denotes the number of processors. Each partition is sorted in parallel, after which a number of global pivots are determined. Based in these pivots, the subarrays are cyclically merged. As a result, a sorted array is obtained. A description of the algorithm can be found in [16].

To have an interesting scenario for our experiment (i.e., the worst case for Eqs. (5) and (4)), we adjust the parameters such that both tasks have approximately equal workload (which also balances the pipeline). We choose $P = 1$ processor for NAS-EP and $P = 24$ for PSRS. The pipeline processes 6,000 arrays per experiment. A number of experiments, based on 6,000 simulation runs, are performed where N varies from $N = 4 \; 10^4$ to $N = 10^5$. For $N = 10^5$ the pdf's of X_1 and X_2 are given in Figure 7. In this figure X_1 is approximately normal while X_2 has a long right tail. Furthermore, the variance of X_2 (the sorting task) is much larger than that of X_1.

Figure 8 shows ε_k of our method and the heuristic. For both methods ε_k is decreasing for increasing N due to the disjunction of X_1 and X_2. Although $\mathsf{E}[X_1] = \mathsf{E}[X_2]$ ε_k is excellent since the coefficient of variation is small (in practice, task variance is indeed much smaller than we have assumed in our theoretic evaluation in Section 4).

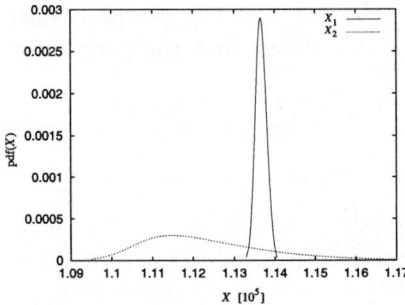

Fig. 7. pdf(X_1) and pdf(X_2) for $N = 10^5$

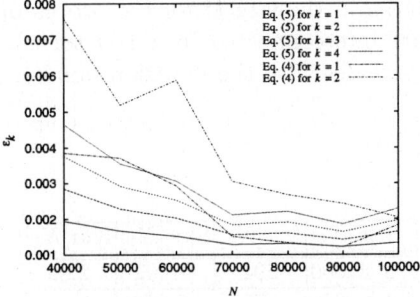

Fig. 8. ε_k for pipeline

5.2 WATOR

In this section we predict the performance of WATOR, an application where the task workload balance changes significantly over the time. WATOR is a Monte Carlo simulation in which idealized fish and sharks live, move randomly, breed, and eat one another in a two-dimensional ocean with toroidal topology. The characteristic of such an algorithm is that the workload can be severally unbalanced because of the computational scenario. Hence the workload in each processor is changing with increasing iteration number i (i.e., simulated time). The load unbalance comes about naturally because of the dynamics of the problem: the fish and sharks tend to aggregate in schools as the they breed, move and eat each other. More information on the algorithm can be found in [4].

In our experiment we perform a simple rectangular subdomain decomposition of the ocean for $P = 2$ processors such that each processor is assigned to process 2,500 grid points. As workload X we choose the number of fish within each processor, which on initialization is generated randomly over each location in the ocean. The workload X_1 for i ranging from 0 to 256 is given in Figure 9 in terms of central moments based on 6,000 simulation runs. The pdf of X_1, where X_1 is normalized, is given in Figure 10. As shown by the table and the figure, the workload changes over time, exhibiting a bimodal distribution for $i = 256$. The estimation error is given in Figure 12 for iteration number $i = 2, \ldots, 128$. Although initially below 5%, the error quickly increases with the iteration number i as a result of the large correlation between X_1 and X_2, which implies that X_1 and X_2 are no longer independent (populations in different processors influence one-another). This dependence also causes the error to be the same for both methods.

In Figure 11 the correlation is shown between P_1 and P_j for $P = 16$ processors. Despite the small coefficient of correlation the actual covariance is large due to large variance values. As to be expected Figure 11 shows that the correlation is the largest for the processors nearest to P_1 (P_2 and P_{16}, the processors are interconnected in a 1-D torus). Figure 11 also shows that the correlation increases with the iteration number i.

i	$E[X_1]$	$Var[X_1]$	$Skw[X_1]$	$Kur[X_1]$
0	1,000	594	−0.02	2.99
4	491	175	0.07	3.01
16	895	7,421	0.36	2.80
64	1,762	208,695	−0.40	2.50
128	1,278	230,641	1.02	3.32
256	1,487	495,116	0.22	1.86

Fig. 9. The first four central moments of X_1 for WATOR ($P = 2$)

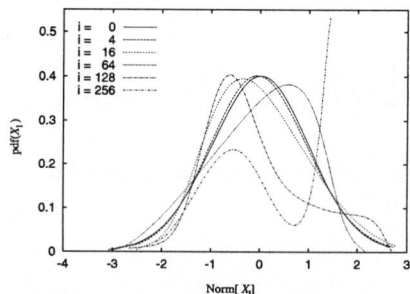

Fig. 10. Normalized pdf(X_1) for WATOR

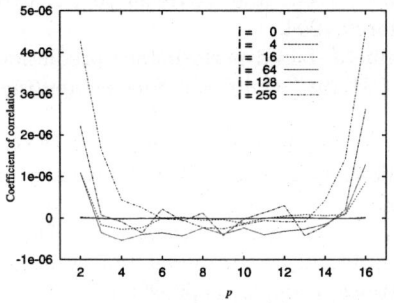
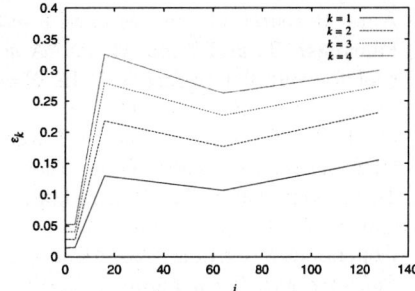

Fig. 11. Measured correlation for WATOR

Fig. 12. ε_k for WATOR

In summary, our measurements of the two above applications show that the error of $E[Y]$ is in the percent range, rather than in the ten percent range, as in practice task execution time variance is less than our theoretic experiments might suggest. Provided the task execution times are independent these results suggest that this is even a worst case as in the corresponding experiments the tasks had equal workloads.

6 Conclusion

In this paper we have presented an analytical model of the execution time distribution Y of binary parallel composition of tasks X_1 and X_2 with stochastic workloads. Our approach is based on approximating the distributions X and Y in terms of the first four moments, in conjunction with the use of the lambda distribution as an intermediate vehicle, to derive a closed-form, $O(1)$ complexity expression for $E[Y^k]$ in terms of $E[X^k]$.

We have investigated to what extent the moments approximation and the lambda distribution approximation have affected the accuracy of our model. Measurements using three well-known synthetic workload distributions show that the worst case error of $E[Y]$ is 35%, occurring for equal workloads, while sharply decreasing for diverging workloads. Empirical data obtained from two real programs suggest that the worst case error may actually be much less (our measurements indicate 5%), provided the task workloads are independent.

As an adequate solution already exists for parallel compositions where tasks have equal workloads, our method focuses on filling the gap where workloads are different. The results show that in this sense our approach provides a low-cost solution that outperforms comparable methods known to date.

References

1. Allen, F., Burke, M., Cytron, R., Ferrante, J., Hsieh, W., and Sarkar, V.: "A Framework for Determining Useful Parallelism." In *Proc. 1988 Int. Conf. Parallel Proc.*, IEEE, Aug. 1988, pp. 207–215.

2. Bailey, D. et al.: The NAS Parallel Benchmarks, Tech. Rep. RNR-94-007, NASA Ames Research Center, Moffett Field, CA, March 1994.
3. Fahringer, T. and Zima, H. P.: "A static parameter-based performance prediction tool for parallel programs." In *Proc. 7th ACM Int'l Conf. on Supercomputing*, Tokyo, July 1993, pp. 207–219.
4. Gautama, H.: On the Use of Lambda Distributions in the Prediction of Parallel Program Execution Time, Tech. Rep. 1-68340-44(2000)02, Delft University of Technology, Delft, The Netherlands, Feb. 2000.
5. Gautama, H. and van Gemund, A. J. C.: "Static Performance Prediction of Data-Dependent Programs." In *ACM Proc. on The Second International Workshop on Software and Performance (WOSP 2000)*, Ottawa, Canada, Sept. 2000.
6. Gelenbe, E., Montagne, E., Suros, R.: "A Performance Model of Block Structured Parallel Programs." In Cosnard, M. et al. (eds.): *Parallel Algorithms and Architectures*, Elsevier Science Publishers B. V. North-Holland, 1986, pp. 127–138.
7. Gumbel, E. J.: "Statistical theory of extreme values (main results)." In *Contributions to Order Statistics* (Sarhan, A. E. and Greenberg, B. G. eds.), John Wiley & Sons, 1962, pp. 56–93.
8. Kruskal, C. P. and Weiss, A.: "Allocating Independent Subtasks on Parallel Processors." In *IEEE Transactions on Software Engineering* Vol. 11, Oct. 1985, pp. 1001–1016.
9. Lester, B. P.: "A system for Computing The Speedup of Parallel Programs." In *Proc. 1986 Int. Conf. Parallel Proc.*, IEEE, Aug. 1986, pp. 145–152.
10. Madala, S. and Sinclair, J.: "Performance of Synchronous Parallel Algorithms with Regular Structures." In *IEEE Trans. on Parallel and Distributed Systems*, Vol. 2, No. 1, Jan, 1991, pp. 105–116.
11. Mendes, C. L. and Reed, D. A.: "Integrated compilation and scalability analysis for parallel systems." In *Proc. Int'l Conf. on Parallel Architectures and Compilation Techniques (PACT '98)*, Paris, Oct. 1998, pp. 385–392.
12. Ramberg, J. S. et al.: "A Probability Distribution and Its Uses in Fitting Data." In *Technometrics*, Vol. 21, No. 2, May, 1979, pp. 201–214.
13. Sahner, R. A. and Trivedi, K. S.: "Performance and Reliability Analysis Using Directed Acyclic Graphs." In *IEEE Transactions on Software Engineering*, Vol. SE-13, No. 10, Oct. 1987, pp. 1105–1114.
14. Sarkar, V.: "Determining Average Program Execution Times and their Variance." In *Proc. 1989 ACM SIGPLAN Conf. Prog. Language Design and Implementation*, pp. 298–312.
15. Schopf, J. M. and Berman, F.: "Performance Prediction in Production Environments." In *Proc. of 1998 IPPS/SPDP, 12th Int. Parallel Processing Symp. on Parallel and Distributed Processing*, Orlando, Florida, 1998, pp. 647–653.
16. Shi, H. and Schaeffer, J.: "Parallel Sorting by Regular Sampling." In *Journal of Parallel and Distributed Computing*, Vol. 14, No. 4, 1992, pp. 361-372.
17. Trivedi, K. S.: *Probability and Statistics with Reliability, Queueing, and Computer Science Applications*, Prentice-Hall, INC. , Englewood Cliffs, NJ. 1982.

The Tuning Problem on Pipelines[1]

Luz Marina Moreno, Francisco Almeida, Daniel González, Casiano Rodríguez

Dpto. Estadística, I. O. y Computacion, Universidad de La Laguna,
La Laguna, Spain
{falmeida,dgonmor,casiano}@ull.es

Abstract.. Performance analysis and prediction is an important factor determining the efficiency of parallel programs. Considerable efforts have been made both in pure theoretical analysis and in practical automatic profiling. Unfortunately, contributions in one area seem to ignore the results of the other. We introduce a general performance prediction methodology based on the integration of analytical models and profiling tools. According to this approach we have developed a tool that automatically solves the prediction of the parameters for optimal executions of parallel pipeline algorithms. The accuracy of the proposal has been tested on a CRAY T3E for pipeline algorithms solving combinatorial optimization problems. The results obtained suggest that the technique could be successfully ported to other paradigms.

1 Introduction

One disappointing contrast in parallel systems is between the peak performance of the parallel systems and the actual performance of parallel applications. Performance prediction is important in achieving efficient execution of parallel programs, since it allows to avoid the coding and debugging cost of inefficient strategies. Most of the approaches to performance analysis fall into two categories: Analytical Modeling and Performance Profiling.

Analytical methods use models of the architecture and the algorithm to predict the program runtime and the analysis can be independent from the target architecture. Parallel performance analysis typically studies the sensitivity of application performance as a function of the system size and problem size. Profiling may be conducted on an existing parallel system to recognize current performance bottlenecks, correct them, and identify and prevent potential future performance problems.

Currently, the majority of performance metrics and tools devised for performance evaluation and tuning rarely provide predictions of performance for executions that have not been measured. Many projects have been developed to create trace files of

---

[1] The work described in this paper has been partially supported by the Spanish Ministry of Science and Technology (CICYT) TIC1999-0754-C03.

events with associated time stamps and then examine them in post-mortem fashion by interpreting them graphically. The ability to generate trace files automatically is an important component of many tools like PICL [2], Dimemas [3], Kpi [1].

Although much work has been developed in Analytical Modeling and in Parallel Profiling. We claim that to obtain automatic and effective practical tools with predictive ability, both fields should be integrated. When executing an algorithm, the user should know the analytical model and provide the complexity analytical formula of the algorithm implemented. According to this formula, the profiler could compute the parameters needed by this formula for the performance prediction and use them on the optimal execution of the algorithm.

In section 2 we formalize the General Tuning Problem and propose a generic methodology to approach it. In section 3 we apply this technique to the Pipeline Paradigm. We have extended the La Laguna Pipeline tool, *llp* [4], with automatic profiling facilities. The new system measures the relevant code sections, finds the constants involved, minimizes the complexity function and finds the optimal parameters for the execution on the current input and architecture. The feasibility of the technique and its accuracy has been contrasted over pipeline algorithms for combinatorial optimization problems.

2   The Problem and the Methodology

As is common in Computability Theory, any algorithm A determines a function F_A from an input domain D to an output domain. Usually the input domain D is a cartesian product $D = D_1 x...xD_n$, where D_i is the domain for the *i-th* parameter

$$F_A : D = D_1 x...xD_n \subset \Sigma^* \to \Sigma^*$$

such that $F_A(z)$ is the output value for the entry z belonging to D. This algorithm A, when executed with entry z on a machine M, spends a given *execution time*, denoted $Time_M(A(z))$. In most cases this $Time_M(A(z))$ function can be approximated by an analytical Complexity Time formula $CTime_M(A(z))$. We assume that $CTime_M(A(z))$ represents with enough accuracy the actual function time $Time_M(A(z))$.

We will classify the parameters $D_1 x...xD_n$ of F_A into two categories T (T comes for tuning parameters) and I (for true Input parameters).

We define that $x \in D_i$ is a *"tuning parameter"*, $x \in T$ if and only if, occurs that x has only impact in the performance of the algorithm but not in its output. We can always reorder the tuning parameters of A, to be the first ones in the algorithm:

$$T = D_1 x...xD_k \text{ and } I = D_{k+1} x...xD_n$$

With this convention is true that $F_A(x, z) = F_A(y, z)$ for any x and $y \in T$, but, in general, $Time_M(A(x, z)) \neq Time_M(A(y, z))$.

The "Tuning Problem" is to find $x_0 \in T$ such that,

$$CTime_M(A(x_0, z)) = min \{ CTime_M(A(x, z)) / x \in T\} \text{ (1)}.$$

The general approach that we propose to solve the tuning problem is:

1. Profiling the execution to compute the parameters needed for the Complexity Time function $CTime_M(A(x, z))$.
2. Compute $x_0 \in \mathcal{T}$ such that minimizes the Complexity Time function $CTime_M(A(x, z))$.
3. At this point, the predictive ability of the Complexity Time function can be used to predict the execution time $Time_M(A(z))$ of an optimal execution or to execute the algorithm according to the tuning parameter $\mathcal{T}$.

3 The Pipeline Tuning Problem

We will restrict our study to the case where the code executed by every processor of the pipeline is the M iteration loop of figure 1. In the loop that we consider, *body0* and *body1* take constant time, while *body2* depends on the iteration of the loop. This loop represents a wide range of situations, as is the case of many parallel Dynamic Programming algorithms [4].

```
void f() {
  Compute(body0);
  i = 0;
  While(i < M) {
    Receive();
    Compute(body1);
    Send();
    Compute(body2, i);
    i++
  }
}
```

Fig. 1. Standard loop on a pipeline algorithm.

The virtual processes running this code must be assigned among the p available processors following a mixed block-cyclic mapping on a one way ring topology. The grain G of processes assigned to each processor is the second tuning parameter to ponder. Buffering data reduces the overhead in communications but can introduce delays between processors increasing the startup of the pipeline. The size B of the buffer is our third tuning parameter.

The Analytical Model and the Pipeline Tuning Solver

The optimal tuning parameters $(p_o, G_o, B_o) \in \mathcal{T} = \{ (p, G, B) / p \in \mathbb{N}, 1 \leq G \leq N/p, 1 \leq B \leq M \}$ must be calculated assumed that the constants characterizing the architecture and the constants associated to the algorithm have been provided. As the Analytical Model we will follow the general model presented in [4].

In this model, the time to transfer B words between two processors is given by $\beta + \tau B$, where β is the message startup time and τ represents the per-word transfer time. An external reception is represented by (β^E) and an internal reception by (β^I), including the time spent in context switching. The variables t_o, t_1, t_{2i} respectively denote the times to compute *body0*, *body1* and *body2* at iteration i.

The startup time between two processors T_s includes the time needed to produce and communicate a packet of size B

$$T_s = t_0*(G-1) + t_1 * G * B + G*\Sigma_{i=1,(B-1)} t_{2i} + 2*\beta' * (G-1)*B + \beta^E * B + \beta + \tau *B$$

T_c denotes the whole evaluation of G processes, including the time to send M/B packets of size B:

$$T_c = t_0*(G-1) + t_1*G*M + G*\Sigma_{i=1,M} t_{2i} + 2*\beta' *(G-1)*M + \beta^E*M + (\beta + \tau*B)* M/B$$

For a problem with N stages on the pipeline (N virtual processors) and a loop of size M (M iterations on the loop), the execution time is determined by:

$$T(p, G, B) = \max \{ T_s * (p - 1) + T_c * N/(G*p),\ T_s * (N/G - 1) + T_c \}$$

with $1 \leq G \leq N/p$ and $1 \leq B \leq M$. $T_s * (p-1)$ holds the time to startup processor p and $T_c * N/(G*p)$ is the time invested in computations after the startup. The tuning parameter is $\mathcal{T} = (p, G, B)$ and the input parameter is $I = (N, M, t_0, t_1, t_2)$.

The La Laguna Pipeline tool, *llp*, enrolls a virtual pipeline into a simulation loop according to the mapping policy specified by the user. This policy is determined by the grain parameter, G. *llp* also provides a directive to pack the data produced on the external communications. The directive establishes the number of elements B to be buffered. We have instrumented *llp* to solve automatically the Pipeline Tuning Problem. The profiling step runs sequentially just one stage of the pipeline so that the whole set of input parameters is known in advance. The minimization function for the analytical model supplying the parameters for an optimal execution is then applied.

To solve the tuning problem the input parameters $I = (N, M, t_0, t_1, t_2)$ must be known before the minimization function be called. Given that N and M are provided by the user, (t_0, t_1, t_2) must be computed for each instance. Since the computations on the pipeline code (fig 1) are embedded into two *llp-communications* calls, during the profiling phase, these *llp* routines are empty and just introduce timers.

Computational Results

To contrast the accuracy of the model we have applied it to estimate (p_0, G_0, B_0) for the pipeline approach on the dynamic programming formulation of the knapsack problem (KP) and the resource allocation problem (RAP). The machine used is a CRAY T3E providing 16 processors. For the problems considered, we have developed a broad computational experience using *llp*. The computational experience has been focused to finding experimentally the values (p_0, G_0, B_0) on each problem. The tables denote the optimal experimental parameters as *G-Real*, *B-Real*. These were found by an exhaustive exploration of the *GxB* search space. *Best Real Time* denotes the corresponding optimal running time. The running time of the parallel algorithm for parameters (G_0, B_0) automatically calculated solving equation (1) is presented in column *Real Time*. The tables also show the error made ((*Best Real Time* - *Real Time*) / *Best Real Time*) by considering the parameters automatically provided by the tool. The very low error made with the prediction makes the technique suitable to be considered for other parallel paradigms.

Table 1. (G_o, B_o) prediction.

P	G_o	B_o	Real Time	G-Real	B-Real	Best Real Time	Error
Knapsack Problem (KP12800)							
2	10	3072	138.61	20	5120	138.24	0.0026
4	10	1536	70.69	20	1792	69.47	0.017
8	10	768	35.69	20	768	35.08	0.017
16	10	256	18.14	10	768	17.69	0.025
Resource Allocation Problem (RAP1000)							
2	2	10	74.62	5	480	70.87	0.053
4	2	10	37.74	5	160	36.01	0.048
8	2	10	19.26	5	40	18.45	0.044
16	2	10	10.06	5	40	9.76	0.031

4 Conclusions

We have presented a formal definition of the General Tuning Problem and proposed a generic methodology to approach it. A special case for Pipelines has been approached. We have extended the La Laguna Pipeline tool with automatic profiling facilities to solve the Tuning Problem for Pipelines. The feasibility of the technique and its accuracy has been contrasted on combinatorial optimization Problems on a CRAY T3E.

References

1. Espinosa A., Margalef T., Luque E.. Automatic Performance Evaluation of Parallel Programs. Proc. Of the 6th EUROMICRO Workshop on Parallel and Distributed Processing. IEEE CS. 1998. 43-49.
2. Geist A., Heath M., Peyton B., Worley P.. PICL: Aportable Instrumented Communications Lybrary, C Reference Manual. Technical Report TM-11130. Oak Ridge National Laboratory. 1990.
3. Labarta J., Girona S., Pillet V., Cortes T., Gregoris L.. Dip: A Parallel Program Development Environment. Europar 96. Lyon. August 1996.
4. Morales D., Almeida F., Moreno L. M., Rodríguez C.. Optimal Mapping of Pipeline Algorithms. EuroPar 2000. Munich. Sept. 2000. 320-324

The Hardware Performance Monitor Toolkit

Luiz A. DeRose

Advanced Computing Technology Center, IBM T. J. Watson Research Center
Yorktown Heights, NY, USA
laderose@us.ibm.com

Abstract. In this paper we present the Hardware Performance Monitor (HPM) Toolkit, a language independent performance analysis and visualization system developed for performance measurements of applications running on the IBM Power 3 with AIX and on Intel clusters with Linux. The HPM Toolkit supports analysis of applications written in Fortran, C, and C++. It was designed to collect hardware events with low overhead and minimum measurement error, and to display a rich set of metrics, including hints to help users in optimizing applications, without requiring modifications in the software infrastructure.

1 Introduction

Application developers have been facing new and more complex performance tuning and optimization problems as parallel architectures become more complex, with clustered SMPs, deep-memory hierarchies managed by distributed cache coherence protocols, and more intricate distributed interconnects. The sensitivity of parallel system performance to slight changes in application code, together with the large number of potential application performance problems (e.g., load balance, false sharing, and data locality) and continually evolving system software, make application tuning complex and often counter-intuitive. Thus, it is not surprising that users of parallel systems often complain that it is difficult to achieve a high fraction of the theoretical peak performance.

Correlating parallel source code with dynamic performance data from both software and hardware measurements, while still providing a portable, intuitive, and easy to use interface, is a challenging task [6]. In order to understand the execution behavior of application code in such complex environments, users need performance tools that are able to access hardware performance counters and map the resulting data to source code constructs. Moreover, these tools should be able to help the user to identify the causes of the performance problems, and not only display raw values for the hardware metrics. Without such tools, the optimal use of high-performance parallel systems will remain limited to a small group of application developers willing to master the intricate details of processor architecture, system software, and compilation systems.

To provide a system for performance measurements and visualization of applications, we developed the *Hardware Performance Monitor (HPM) Toolkit*, which is currently composed of three modules: an utility to start an application, providing performance data at the end of execution, an instrumentation library with multi-language support, and a graphical user interface for performance visualization. The HPM Toolkit supports performance data capture, analysis, and presentation for applications written in Fortran, C, and C++, executing on sequential or parallel systems, running shared memory applications, message passing, or both paradigms.

During the execution of the instrumented code, the HPM library captures hardware performance data from each instrumented section of the program on each thread of execution. At the end of the execution it combines the collected information to compute derived metrics, such as cache hit ratio and MFLOPS rates, generating one *performance file* for each task. To allow multi language cross-architecture support, as well as, flexibility in metrics selection, the performance file is represented with a self-defined format in XML.

The main contributions of the HPM Toolkit described in this paper are: First, the exploitation of the hardware performance counters to compute and present a rich set of derived metrics. These derived metrics allow users to correlate the behavior of the application to one or more of the components of the hardware. Second, an analysis of the measurement error and a technique to reduce this error. Third, an approach to analyze the derived metrics and provide hints to help users to identify the causes of performance problems, and finally, a flexible interface, defined in XML, that is able to separate performance data presentation from language and architecture peculiarities, allowing multi-language support and architecture independence.

The remainder of this paper is organized as follows: §2 describes the components of the HPM Toolkit used to collect application performance data. §3 discuss the hardware performance counters support. §4 describes the HPM Toolkit performance visualization interface and the XML interface used to allow flexibility in metric selection. Finally, §5 presents our conclusions.

2 The HPM Data Collection System

Unfortunately, most users do not have the time or desire to learn how to use complex tools. Hence, one of the main design goals of the HPM Toolkit was to create an easy to use environment for performance analysis. The first component of the HPM Toolkit is the *hpmcount* utility. It allows users to start serial or parallel applications, and at the end of execution, it provides a summary output with wall clock time (WCT), hardware performance counters information, derived hardware metrics, and resource utilization statistics.

The hpmcount utility provides a general view of the performance of an application. However, in general, this is not enough for a more complete understanding of the application behavior. Thus, the HPM Toolkit also provides an instrumentation library, so users can place instrumentation calls in selected program regions to measured the performance of the program at a finer granularity.

The HPM library supports multiple instrumentation sections, nested instrumentation, and multiple calls to the same instrumented section. During program execution, the HPM library accumulates counts and durations for all instrumented sections of the program. When nested instrumentation is used, exclusive duration is generated for the outer sections. Average and standard deviation are provided when an instrumented section is activated multiple times. As we shall see in Section 4, performance metrics are shown for each instrumented section, allowing users to instrument an application, examine the correlation of performance metrics and source code, and use the graphical interface to re-instrument the application with the knowledge obtained.

Currently, the HPM instrumentation is inserted statically by the user. A new HPM Toolkit component under development is an utility for dynamic instrumentation of programs. This utility uses the Dynamic Probe Class Library [2] (DPCL), a layer built on top of the Dyninst API [1], to support dynamic instrumentation on multiple nodes.

One important aspect of the HPM Toolkit is the support for multi-threaded applications. Due to the current trend in computer architecture, parallel systems are being built as clusters of shared memory processor. Thus, support for the shared-memory programming paradigm (e.g., pThreads or OpenMP) is a necessary requirement for any new performance tool. In order to provide multi-thread support, the HPM library has two pairs of functions to indicate the start and end of each code region to be instrumented. One pair of functions is used for instrumentation within a parallel region on a multi-threaded application, while the other pair is used outside of parallel regions. The main difference between these functions is that the former only counts the activity of the calling thread, while the latter counts the activity of a process and all of its children.

3 Hardware Performance Counters

Although software instrumentation can capture the interaction of compiler-synthesized code with runtime libraries and system software, understanding the effects of deep-memory hierarchies, cache coherence protocols, and branch prediction requires concurrent capture of both software and hardware performance metrics. Fortunately, new microprocessors provide a set of registers for access to hardware performance data.

Hardware performance counters are special purpose registers that keep track of programmable hardware events. Since they are provided at hardware level, their main strengths are low intrusion cost, accuracy, and low overhead. On the other hand, they are still a limited resource, with current processors having between 2 and 8 counters. Moreover, hardware counters tend to be specific to each processor, are generally 32 bit, and are normally programmed at kernel level, which make them prone to frequent overflows and difficult to program.

To address these problems, vendors normally provide a software API for access to the hardware counters. On IBM systems, we use the system and kernel thread performance monitor API (PMAPI), which takes care of most of the lower level issues related to accessing hardware counters, such as handling of overflows, context switches, and thread level support. However, since a particular vendor

API does not provide portability across processors from different vendors, the HPM Toolkit was also implemented on top of PAPI [3], a system-independent interface for hardware performance counters. Using the PAPI interface, the HPM Toolkit was ported to Intel platforms under Linux, and can be easily extended to any other system supported by PAPI. This paper, however, concentrates on issues related to IBM Power 3 systems. In the reminder of this section we discuss the derived metrics supported by the HPM Toolkit, and present an analysis of overhead and measurement error.

3.1 Derived Hardware Metrics

Another weakness of hardware performance counters is that they provide only raw counts, which does not necessarily help users to identify which events are responsible for bottlenecks in the program performance. For example, the information that an executed program had x million cache misses tend to be useless for a user, unless he or she can correlate this number with other data, such as number of loads and stores. To address this problem, the HPM Toolkit calculates a rich set of derived metrics that combine hardware events and time information to provide more meaningful information, such as cache miss rates, branches miss-predicted percentage, MIPS, and MFLOPS rates. Fortunately, the IBM Power 3 processor has 8 counters, which provides enough information for the generation of several derived metrics on each program execution. On systems that have less hardware counters available, multiplexing [5] could be used under PAPI, increasing coverage, but reducing accuracy.

The HPM library allows users to specify via an input file the desired set of hardware events to be used. To facilitate use, the HPM Toolkit also provides sets of pre-defined events that can be selected via environment variables. Independently of the mechanism used to select the hardware events, the library identifies the events being used and generates all possible derived metrics for the events selected. A list of the current set of derived metrics supported for the IBM Power 3 is presented in Table 1. Each of these metrics allows users to correlate the behavior of the application to one or more of the components of the hardware.

3.2 Instrumentation Overhead and Measurement Errors

As mentioned above, some of the strengths of hardware performance counters are low overhead and accuracy. Thus, it is important that performance tools based on hardware performance counters preserve these features. Two issues are considered here: *instrumentation overhead* and *measurement error*. Any software instrumentation is expected to incur in some overhead [4]. Thus, since it is not possible to eliminate the overhead, our goal was to minimize it. On the HPM library, the observed overhead for each instrumented code section, generated by the start and stop of data collection calls, is in the order of 2500 cycles (about 6.7 μsec on a 375 MHz processor). During this time, the library executes about 3000 instructions. The bulk of these operations are fixed point (about 2100),

Table 1. Supported derived metrics on the IBM Power 3

Derived Metric	Method
Total time in user mode	Cycles/CPU frequence
Utilization rate	Total time in user mode/WCT
IPC	Instructions completed/Cycles
MIPS	Instructions completed/(1000000 × WCT)
Instructions per IC Miss	Instructions completed/Instructions cache misses
Total LS operations	Loads + Stores
% of cycles LSU is idle	100 × LSU idle/Cycles
Instructions per LS	Instructions completed/Total LS
Loads per load miss	Loads/L1 Load misses
Stores per store miss	Stores/L1 Store misses
Loads per L2 load miss	Loads/L2 Load misses
Stores per L2 store miss	Stores/L2 Store misses
Loads per TLB miss	Loads/TLB misses
Load stores per D1 miss	Total LS/(L1 Load misses + Store misses)
L1 cache hit rate	100 × (1 − ((L1 Load misses + Store misses)/Total LS)
L2 cache hit rate	100 × (1 − ((L2 Load misses + Store misses)/Total LS)
Snoop hit ratio	100 × Snoop hits/Snoop requests
HW FP instructions per cycle	$(FPU_0 + FPU_1)$/Cycles
Float point operations	$FPU_0 + FPU_1 + FMAs$
Float point operations rate	$(FPU_0 + FPU_1 + FMAs)/(1000000 \times WCT)$
Computation intensity	$(FPU_0 + FPU_1 + FMAs)$/Total LS
FMA %	$100 \times (FMAs\ executed \times 2)/(FPU_0 + FPU_1 + FMAs)$
Fixed point instructions	$FXU_0 + FXU_1 + FXU_2$
Branches Misspredicted %	100 × Branches Misspredicted/Branches

loads (445), and stores (325). Most of the overhead is due to time measurement, since for portability we use the function gettimeofday, that unfortunately tends to be an expensive operation in most systems. Since we are accessing the hardware counters, we could have avoided this overhead by deriving time using cycles and the frequency rate of the processor. However, this approach would reduce the number of available counters for user selection, which could be a problem, specially when only a few hardware counters are available. Moreover, since the PMAPI takes care of context switches and thread accumulation, this approach would measure the total time in user mode, not wall clock time, which is a more interesting metric for program optimization. Therefore, we decided not to use this approach.

Several issues were considered in order to reduce measurement error. First, most of the library operations are executed before starting the counters, when returning the control to the program, or after stopping the counters, when the program calls a "stop" function. However, even at the library level, there are a few operations that must be executed within the counting process, as for ex-

Table 2. Counter measurements for timing and counting functions within HPM

Function	Cycles	Instr.	Stores	Loads	FX Ops
Count	285	234	40	69	93
Time	2000	2200	48	53	2048

Table 3. Average metric values and standard deviation for the start and stop functions

	Cycles	IC Miss	LD Miss	TLB Miss
Average	285	0.350	0.004	0.023
Standard deviation	15.27	1.216	0.077	0.150

ample, releasing a lock. Second, since timing collection and capture of hardware counters information are two distinctive operations, we had to decide between timing the counters or counting the timer. We used the hardware counters to measure the overhead of both operations (i.e., start and stop the counters, and calling the timing function twice, which would correspond to the timing calls at the beginning and end of one instrumented section). As shown in Table 2, timing is about one order of magnitude more expensive than counting. Thus, the counters calls are wrapped by the timer calls, generating a small error in the time measurement (in the order of 0.8 μsec on a 375 MHz processor), but minimal error in the counting process.

However, in order to access and read the counters, the library still has to call lower level routines from the PMAPI. Although one of the last instructions executed by the library before returning the control to the program is a PMAPI call to start the counters, and the first instruction executed by a "stop" function is a call to stop the counters, there are always some instructions executed by the kernel that are accounted as part of the program. Also, cache or TLB misses occurred while executing library calls can generate measurement errors. So, in order to compensate for these measurement errors, we use the hardware counters to measure the cost of one call to the start and stop functions. This measurement is performed twice, during initialization and finalization of the library, and we consider the minimum of these calls as measurement error, and subtract these values from the values obtained on each instrumented code section.

In order to estimate the final measurement error, we called the start and stop functions 1000 times, counting all pre-defined set of events provided in the library. We observed that the number of completed instructions, loads, and stores were constant (the values shown on Table 2), while there was a small variation on cycles and number of misses (TLB, instruction, and loads[1]), as shown in Table 3. The standard deviations presented in Table 3 correspond to the measurement error for each of the main hardware events measured by the library.

---

[1] The number of store misses was always zero.

4 Performance Visualization

One of the design goals of the HPM Toolkit was to create an easy to use cross-architecture, language independent performance analysis interface. Hence, the implementation of the performance visualization component (*hpmviz*) relies on a single interface for performance visualization that provides a source code editor. This editor allows users to refine the performance analysis by re-instrumenting the application, while visualizing performance data from earlier executions. Additionally, one can access and load performance data from multiple executions, including different numbers of processors and different hardware count events. This functionality allows users to compare executions, in order to better understanding hardware and software interactions. In this section we present the main functionality of hpmviz, and a description of the XML interface used as input.

4.1 Hpmviz

Hpmviz takes as input the performance files generated by the HPM library. Users can visualize a single performance file from a parallel execution or multiple files from the same execution. In the latter case, hpmviz takes care of merging the files. As Shown in Figure 1, which displays an instrumented version of a mixed mode implementation of the swim code from the SPEC CPU benchmark, the main window of hpmviz is divided in two panes. The left pane displays for each instrumented section an identification, inclusive duration, exclusive duration, and count[2]. The instrumented sections are sorted by exclusive duration, so users can quickly identify the major time consuming portions of the application.

Left clicking on an instrumentation point in the left pane refocus the corresponding section in the source code pane. Right clicking on any instrumentation section in the left pane, brings a "metrics" window, shown in Figure 2, which displays all metrics for the corresponding instrumented section.

4.2 Identifying Possible Performance Problems

In order to help users identify performance problems based on the values of the derived metrics, the HPM Toolkit uses heuristics based on the characteristics of the architecture, to define a range of values considered satisfactory for some of the metrics (the metrics in bold in Table 1). When a metric value is below the threshold predefined as minimum recommended value for the metric, it appears in the metrics window highlighted with red. Similarly, when the metric value is above the predefined threshold value, it appears highlighted with green.

These threshold values were defined and fine-tuned based on the understanding of the architecture and feedback from application experts. A green value indicates that the hardware components addressed by the metric are being well utilized, while a red value indicates that the corresponding section of the code may

---

[2] These values correspond to the maximum value of the metric, across the parallel execution of the program.

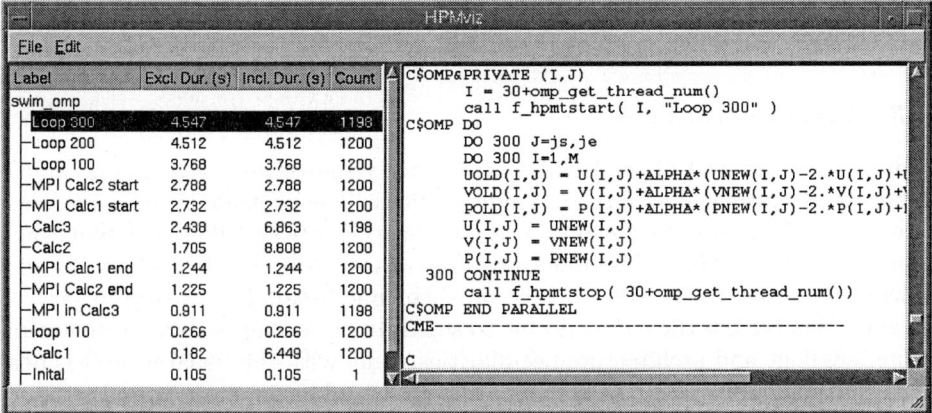

Fig. 1. Hpmviz main window

Task	Thread	Count	ExcSec	IncSec	Ld/TLB miss	Total LS	Instr/LS	MIPS	Instr/Cycles	HW FP/Cycle	FPI+FMA	MFLIp/s	FMA %
0	30	1198	4.547	4.547	426.97	183.151	1.731	69.714	0.422	0.125	156.734	34.471	79.844
0	31	1198	4.516	4.516	440.064	171.494	1.694	64.319	0.35	0.113	156.73	34.708	79.844
0	32	1198	4.522	4.522	461.441	161.485	1.657	59.194	0.292	0.103	156.732	34.662	79.844
0	33	1198	4.498	4.498	424.573	158.184	1.755	61.73	0.385	0.108	129.073	28.693	79.844
1	30	1198	4.335	4.335	439.779	176.707	1.711	69.749	0.4	0.125	156.738	36.157	79.843
1	31	1198	4.3	4.3	477.445	166.656	1.677	64.982	0.339	0.114	156.728	36.446	79.844
1	32	1198	4.304	4.304	467.948	166.475	1.676	64.832	0.337	0.114	156.728	36.415	79.844
1	33	1198	4.304	4.304	450.622	153.271	1.739	61.93	0.373	0.109	129.084	29.994	79.844
2	30	1198	4.344	4.344	438.126	191.055	1.753	77.103	0.515	0.145	156.726	36.078	79.844
2	31	1198	4.333	4.333	455.151	166.576	1.676	64.452	0.337	0.114	156.729	36.173	79.844
2	32	1198	4.334	4.334	468.255	166.796	1.677	64.554	0.339	0.114	156.736	36.167	79.844
2	33	1198	4.316	4.316	464.372	151.838	1.734	60.991	0.373	0.11	129.081	29.905	79.844
3	30	1198	4.494	4.494	437.881	182.978	1.73	70.453	0.43	0.128	156.732	34.879	79.844
3	31	1198	4.471	4.471	470.266	168.574	1.684	63.473	0.338	0.112	156.736	35.053	79.844

Fig. 2. Metrics window

need optimization with regards to the utilization of the hardware components covered by the metric. Consider for example the derived metric computation intensity, which is the ratio of number of floating-point operations by the number of array loads and stores. The Power 3 architecture has two floating-point units (FPU) and two load-store units (LSU). Each FPU can execute a multiply, an add, or a fused-multiply-add (FMA) per cycle. Therefore, computation intensity of 2 would represent the best utilization of these hardware components (FPU and LSU) when performing floating-point operations. Similarly, to achieve the best possible utilization of the FPU, the program should have FMA percentage close to 100%. However, since the threshold values depend on the context of the program, the red and green colors are only considered as hints to the user, and not as hard indication of a performance problem. For instance, if the measured section of the program, in the example above, was performing mostly communications or fixed-point operations, The tool would probably indicate a poor FPU utilization, which is true, but would not be necessarily the reason for a performance problem.

4.3 Performance Files

An important aspect of the HPM performance visualization system is its multi-language support and architecture independence. The problem in providing such functionality is that the performance visualization system should be built such that it can work with minimum knowledge of the data that is going to be displayed. In order to be able to provide such functionality, it was necessary to define a flexible interface that is able to separate performance data presentation from language and architecture peculiarities. Only with this separation it is possible to display any kind of metrics, as well as, add new metrics and support new languages and architectures, without requiring extensive modifications to the graphical user interface. The HPM Toolkit performance file was designed to provide the generality and extensibility necessary to represent a diverse set of performance metrics. XML was chosen as the language for the data format because it provides this flexibility. In addition, by using XML, we could use its parsing framework, which allowed a quicker development, since very little new code had to be built over the framework.

The performance file consists of one set of data for each instrumented record in the code. Due to the support of threaded and MPI programs, an instrumented section of the program may generate several instrumentation records. To be able to present the performance data grouped by instrumented sections of the program, and not by records, we defined a unique identification for each instrumented section based on the file name and the line numbers. This information is transparently inserted into the library calls during a pre-processor phase at compile time. Each of these performance records contains specifications that include both mandatory and optional data fields, as shown in Figure 3, which displays the XML definition for one instrumentation record.

The combination of metadata and data defined for the performance file is the key to the HPM Toolkit extensibility. It allows hpmviz to render the necessary information for presentation, such as the metrics being displayed, as well as, presentation characteristics, like the range of pre-defined thresholds and display defaults (e.g., if the metric should be displayed or not).

5 Conclusions

In this paper, we described the HPM Toolkit, a language independent performance analysis and visualization system developed for performance measurements of sequential and parallel applications running on the IBM Power 3 and on Intel clusters with Linux.

The HPM Toolkit supports instrumentation and analysis of MPI and multi-threaded applications written in Fortran, C, and C++. One of its main strengths

```
<InstrumentationPt lid="swim.f775" disp="true" tid="37" task="0"
     label="Loop 300" file="swim.f" linestart="775" lineend="786" >
  <data name="Count" value="1198" />
  <data name="ExcSec" value=" 2.918" />
  <data name="IncSec" value=" 2.918" />
  <data name="PM_CYC" value=" 169719339" disp="false" />
  <data name="PM_INST_CMPL" value=" 135603862" disp="false" />
  <data name="PM_ST_CMPL" value=" 8255773" disp="false" />
  <data name="PM_LD_CMPL" value=" 56883532" disp="false" />
  <data name="PM_FPU0_CMPL" value=" 6463248" disp="false" />
  <data name="PM_FPU1_CMPL" value=" 5122784" disp="false" />
  <data name="PM_EXEC_FMA" value=" 7697521" disp="false" />
  <data name="User time" value=" 0.764" />
  <data name="Use rate" value=" 0.262" />
  <data name="Total LS" value=" 65.139" />
  <data name="Instr/LS" value=" 2.082" sbad="-1.0" sgood="2.5" dbad="-1.0" dgood="2.5" />
  <data name="MIPS" value=" 46.476" />
  <data name="IpC" value=" 0.799" sbad="-1.0" sgood="2.0" dbad="-1.0" dgood="2.0" />
  <data name="HW FP/Cyc" value=" 0.068" />
  <data name="FPI+FMA" value=" 19.284" />
  <data name="Mflip/s" value=" 6.609" />
  <data name="FMA %" value=" 79.835" sbad="-40.0" sgood="70.0" dbad="-40.0" dgood="70.0" />
  <data name="Comp Int." value=" 0.296" sbad="-0.7" sgood="1.4" dbad="-0.7" dgood="1.4" />
</InstrumentationPt>
```

Fig. 3. XML definition for one instrumentation record

is the collection of hardware events with low overhead and minimum measurement error, for the presentation of a rich set of derived metrics, including hints to help users in optimizing applications.

In order to provide multi-language support and architecture independence, we defined a flexible and extensible format for the performance file, which allows measurement of different metrics, without requiring major modifications in the software infrastructure.

References

1. BUCK, B. R., AND HOLLINGSWORTH, J. K. An API for Runtime Code Patching. *Journal of High Performance Computing Applications 14*, 4 (Winter 2000).
2. DEROSE, L., HOOVER JR., T., AND HOLLINGSWORTH, J. K. The Dynamic Probe Class Library - An Infrastructure for Developing Instrumentation for Performance Tools. In *Proceedings of 2001 International Parallel and Distributed Processing Symposium* (April 2001).
3. BROWNE, S., DONGARRA, J., GARNER, N., HO, G., MUCCI, P. A Portable Programming Interface for Performance Evaluation on Modern Processors. *The International Journal of High Performance Computing Applications*, 14:3, Fall 2000.
4. MALONY, A. D., REED, D. A., AND WIJSHOFF, H. A. G. Performance Measurement Intrusion and Perturbation Analysis. *IEEE Transactions on Parallel and Distributed Systems 3*, 4 (July 1992), pp. 433–450.
5. MAY, J. M. MPX: Software for multiplexing hardware performance counters in multithreaded programs. In *Proceedings of 2001 International Parallel and Distributed Processing Symposium* (April 2001).
6. PANCAKE, C. M., SIMMONS, M. L., AND YAN, J. C. Performance Evaluation Tools for Parallel and Distributed Systems. *IEEE Computer 28*, 11 (November 1995).

VIA Communication Performance on a Gigabit Ethernet Cluster*

Mark Baker[1], Paul A. Farrell[2], Hong Ong[3], and Stephen L .Scott[4]

[1] School of Computer Science, University of Portsmouth
Portsmouth, UK, PO1 2EG
Mark.Baker@computer.org
[2] Dept. of Mathematics and Computer Science, Kent State University
Kent, OH 44242, USA
farrell@mcs.kent.edu
[3] Dept. of Mathematics and Computer Science, Kent State University
Kent, OH 44242, USA
hong@mcs.kent.edu
[4] Oak Ridge National Laboratory, Oak Ridge, TN 37831-6367, USA
scottsl@ornl.gov

Abstract. As the technology for high-speed networks has evolved over the last decade, the interconnection of commodity computers (e.g., PCs and workstations) at gigabit rates has become a reality. However, the improved performance of high-speed networks has not been matched so far by a proportional improvement in the ability of the TCP/IP protocol stack. As a result the Virtual Interface Architecture (VIA) was developed to remedy this situation by providing a lightweight communication protocol that bypasses operating system interaction, providing low latency and high bandwidth communications for cluster computing. In this paper, we evaluate and compare the performance characteristics of both hardware (Giganet) and software (M-VIA) implementations of VIA. In particular, we focus on the performance of the VIA send/receive synchronization mechanism on both uniprocessor and dual processor systems. The tests were conducted on a Linux cluster of PCs connected by a Gigabit Ethernet network. The performance statistics were collected using a local version of NetPIPE adapted for VIA.

1 Introduction

The advent of high performance microprocessors coupled with high-speed interconnects has made clusters an attractive platform for parallel and distributed computing. There are many research institutes and academic departments involved in building low cost Beowulf-class clusters to fulfill their computing needs at a fraction of the price of a traditional mainframe or supercomputer.

---

* This work was supported in part by NSF CDA 9617541, NSF ASC 9720221, NSF ITR 0081324, by the OBR Investment Fund Ohio Communication and Computing ATM Research Network (OCARnet), and through the Ohio Board of Regents Computer Science Enhancement Initiative

Interconnecting the nodes in a cluster requires network hardware and software that is scalable, reliable, and provides high bandwidth and low latency communications. Gigabit Ethernet [1], among the other high-speed networks, can in principle provide the required performance needed for cluster computing. However, the improved performance of Gigabit Ethernet is not realized at the application layer of the network. This is due primarily to the overheads incurred in communicating between processor, memory, and I/O subsystems that are directly connected to a network. In particular, this communication overhead is caused by the time accumulated when messages move through different layers of the TCP/IP stack in the operating system. The source of these overheads is multiple memory copies and use of the operating system for receiving and transmission of packets [2]. In the past, the end-to-end Internet protocol overhead did not significantly contribute to the poor network performance, since the latency was primarily dominated by the speed of the underlying network links. However, Gigabit Ethernet technologies coupled with high-speed processors now mean that the overhead of the Internet protocol stack is the dominant bottleneck in the performance of this technology.

Many research projects have been proposed to address network performance issues. Examples of these projects include U-Net [3], Fast Messages [4], and Active Messages [5]. More recently, the Virtual Interface Architecture (VIA) [6] has been developed to standardize efforts in this area. VIA defines mechanisms that will bypass the intervention of the operating system layers and avoid excess data copying during sending and receiving of packets. This effectively reduces latency and lowers the impact on bandwidth. Since the introduction of VIA, several software and hardware implementations of VIA have become available. Examples include Giganet [7], ServerNet-II [8], Myrinet [9], and M-VIA [10].

This paper evaluates and compares the performance of both hardware and software implementations of VIA technology on a Linux-based cluster connected by a Gigabit Ethernet Network. The layout of this paper is as follows: Section 2 gives an overview of the VIA technology. Section 3 gives an overview of NetPIPE and the implementation of NetPIPE-VIA. Section 4 presents the test environments used. Section 5 discusses the results from our performance tests. Finally, the conclusions and future work are presented in Section 6.

2 VI Architecture Overview

The VI Architecture is an industry trade effort to provide low latency and high bandwidth message-passing support over a System Area Network (SAN). Figure 1 illustrates the VIA design. The VIA design consists of two major components: the *VI Provider* and the *VI Consumer*.

The *VI Provider* is a combination of a media dependent *VI Network Interface Card* (NIC) and the *VI Kernel Agent*. The VI Kernel Agent is a software component that includes the device driver for the VI NIC and a set of kernel routines needed to perform privileged operations such as connection management and memory registration on behalf of applications.

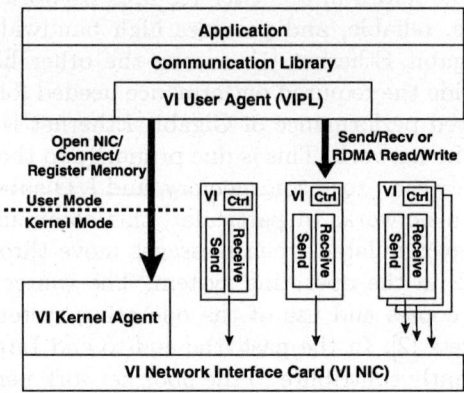

Fig. 1. VI Architecture

The *VI Consumer* is an application process that communicates using the *VI Provider Library* (VIPL) primitives. The software component that implement the VIPL is known as the *VI User Agent*. It provides a protected and directly accessible interface, know as *Virtual Interface* (VI), to the network interface. Each VI represents a communication endpoint and pairs of such VIs can be connected to form a communication channel for bi-directional point-to-point data transfer. A VI Consumer can have multiple VIs.

Each VI is associated with a send queue and a receive queue (also known as work queue). For data transmission, the sender and the receiver post packet descriptors to its work queue. A mechanism known as a *doorbell* is used to notify the VI Kernel Agent that a descriptor has been added to a work queue. A doorbell is a control register associated with each work queue which is mapped into the virtual address space of the application process that owns the VI.

A VI Consumer must register the memory region of its packet descriptors and data buffers with the VI Kernel Agent before being used for communication. Memory registration takes the expensive operations of mapping memory and doing virtual to physical translation out of the critical performance path. As a consequence, this eliminates the need for copying data from the user buffer space to the kernel buffer space, which is typically used in traditional communication models.

The VI Architecture supports send/receive and remote direct memory access (RDMA) read/write types of data movements. The current revision of the VI architecture specification defines the semantics of a RDMA Read operation but does not require that the network interface support it.

3 NetPIPE Benchmark and Implementation of NetPIPE-VIA

NetPIPE [11] is a network protocol independent performance evaluation tool developed by Ames Laboratory. The design of NetPIPE consists of a protocol independent driver, and a set of well defined communication APIs.

The device independent driver implements a ping-pong like program which increases the transfer block size from a single byte to large blocks until transmission time exceeds 1 second. Specifically, for each block size c, three measurements are taken for block sizes $c - p$ bytes, c bytes and $c + p$ bytes, where p is a perturbation parameter with a default value of 3. This allows examination of block sizes that are possibly slightly smaller or larger than an internal network buffer.

The communication APIs implement the protocol specific module. Currently, NetPIPE supports TCP, PVM, and MPI communication protocols. For our performance evaluation, we implemented a VIA communication protocol module for NetPIPE.

The set of NetPIPE communication APIs needed for the protocol specific module includes those for establishing a connection, closing a connection, sending and receiving data, and performing synchronization. We implemented all the communication APIs using the VIPL library.

To keep the implementation simple, NetPIPE-VIA creates a pair of VI endpoints per connection. A fixed number of send and receive packet descriptors are pre-allocated and each descriptor has a fixed size of registered (pinned) memory, which is equal to the maximum data buffer size supported by the VI Provider. The descriptors are chained together to form a ring. To send a message, NetPIPE-VIA gets a descriptor from the send ring and posts the descriptor to the send queue. After the completion of a send operation, the descriptor is inserted back into the ring. VIA requires packet descriptors to be posted on the receive queue before any message arrives. Otherwise, the message will be lost. Therefore, NetPIPE-VIA pre-posts all the receive descriptors before the reception of messages occurs. Whenever a packet arrives, it gets a descriptor out of the receive queue, processes the packet, and posts the descriptor back to the receive queue again.

For each measurement, the protocol independent driver determines the size of the data block either linearly or exponentially depending on a user specified command line option. Hence, the memory buffer for a data block of size c is dynamically allocated at run time. In order to achieve zero-copying and avoid the extra overhead of pining and unpining the memory buffer for each data block, NetPIPE-VIA pre-allocates and pre-registers a pool of memory buffers. All memory requirements of the independent protocol driver are satisfied from this memory pool. This also keeps the memory management in NetPIPE-VIA simple.

When transmitting a large data block, the message will be fragmented in order to fit into a descriptor's data segment. This implies that multiple descriptors are needed to either transmit or receive large messages. Consequently, flow control is required to prevent the sender from overflowing the receiver's pre-posted receive descriptors. NetPIPE-VIA implements a simple flow control scheme. On the sender side, it continues to transmit until either the entire data block c is sent or the number of sends reaches the maximum number of pre-posted descriptors of the receiver. For the latter case, the sender waits for a "continue" message from the receiver before sending more packets. On the receiver side, it continues to receive packets until either the entire data block c is received or it reaches the maximum number of pre-posted descriptors. If the receiver runs out of pre-posted descriptors, it stops receiving and waits for all receive requests to complete. Then, it sends a "continue" message to inform the sender to continue to send more packets.

4 Testing Environment

The testing environment for collecting VIA performance data was a cluster of 32 dual processor Pentium III 450MHz PCs using the Intel 440BX chipset. The PCs were equipped with 256MB of 100MHz (PC100) SD-RAM. The PCs were connected together through a Foundry FastIron 10/100/1000Mbps switch using SysKonnect *SK-9821* NICs. Four of these PCs were also connected together through a Giganet cLAN5000 switch using cLAN1000 NICs. In addition, two PCs were connected back to back using Packet Engine *GNIC-II* NICs. All the NICs were installed in 33MHz/32bit PCI slots. The PCs were running the Red Hat 6.2 distribution with the 2.2.16 Linux kernel. For testing the software implementations of VIA, M-VIA v1.0 was installed. All performance results were collected using the NetPIPE-VIA benchmark tool.

5 Performance Results

In VIA terminology, the term synchronization is used to refer to the process by which a VI Consumer detects, or is notified of, the completion of a communication request. For each of the Gigabit Ethernet NIC mentioned earlier, we evaluated the performance characteristics of the polling and blocking synchronization schemes for a uniprocessor system and a dual processor system. In particular, we present and compare the point-to-point latency and throughput performance of both hardware and software implementation of VIA. For completeness, we have also included the TCP performance[1]. Latency is measured by taking half the average round-trip time for a 1 byte transfer. The throughput rate is calculated from half the round-trip time for a data block of size c bytes.

5.1 VIA Latency Discussion

Table 1 summarizes the latency performance for the various NICs on uniprocessor and dual processor systems. One obvious observation is that the TCP latency, on both the uniprocessor and dual processor systems, is at least 50% higher

---

[1] The LAN emulation driver *lanevi* was used to collect TCP performance for the cLAN 1000 NIC

Table 1. Latency Performance in μ secs

	Uni-Processor			Dual Processor		
	Socket	VI		Socket	VI	
	Read/Write	Send/Recv		Read/Write	Send/Recv	
NIC	TCP	Poll	Block	TCP	Poll	Block
CLAN	58	9	9	116	10	45
GNIC-II	57	19	19	94	42	42
SK-9821	63	29	29	101	51	53

than the VIA latency regardless of which synchronization schemes are used. This highlights that VIA can, in practice, deliver the low latency needed for communication intensive applications. In general, the latency of hardware implemented VIA (cLAN) is at least 40% lower than software implemented VIA (GNIC-II and SK-9821). With hardware support, the VI Kernel agent is able to offload much of the processing to the network card resulting in lower processing overhead.

For the uniprocessor system, the latency for both synchronization schemes is almost identical for all NICs. For a dual processor system, the latency using the polling scheme is slightly less than the blocking scheme. However, it is more obvious for the cLAN NIC. The primary cause for such a difference is due to the implementation of the doorbell mechanism in the VI Kernel agent. cLAN's doorbell mechanism is supported directly in hardware as a true memory mapped doorbell. cLAN's VIPL uses the `ioctl` system call to provide the time-sensitive services. On the other hand, M-VIA's VIPL uses `fast_traps` system calls to emulate the doorbell mechanism. In Linux kernel 2.2.16, there is a big variance when timing both the `ioctl` and `fast_trap` calls. However, when we take the average of the overhead for each system call, it yields lower overhead per wait operation on a dual-processor system then on a uniprocessor system. However, this effect is less on a uniprocessor system resulting in little or no difference in latency.

For M-VIA, the latency for both VIA synchronization schemes on the dual processor system is higher when compared to the uniprocessor system. This is because M-VIA uses the Linux `spinlock` primitives to protect the data structure of each VI. For an SMP, the overhead of using `spinlock` primitives to perform mutual exclusion across CPUs is higher than in the uniprocessor case. This overhead comes from disabling interrupts when making `spinlock` calls to lock the VI data structure. Although it is expensive, the `spinlock` mechanism is safe as compared to other implementations. On the other hand, the latency for cLAN on the dual processor system is only about 1μ second higher than the uniprocessor system. This is because cLAN uses the Linux `pthread` primitives to provide protected access to the VI data structure. It is relatively cheap in terms of CPU cost and does not require the calling thread to disable interrupts.

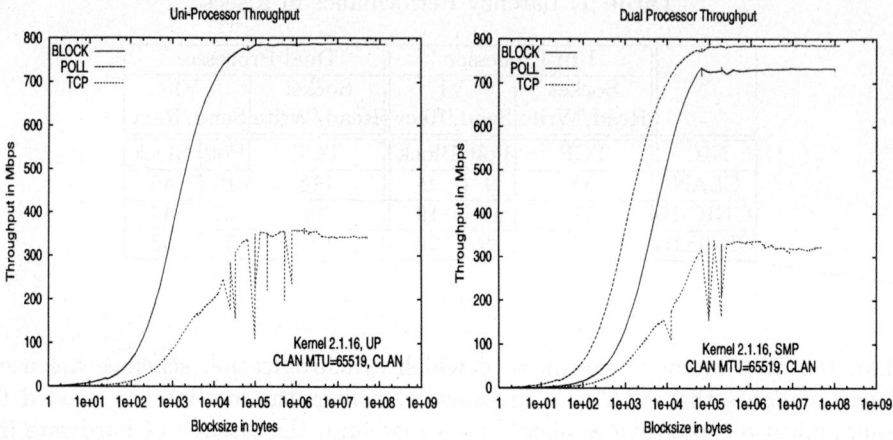

Fig. 2. cLAN: Send/Recv Mode

5.2 VIA Throughput Discussion

Figure 2 shows the communication performance using cLAN. For a uniprocessor system, cLAN achieves maximum throughput of approximately 362Mbps for TCP and 788Mbps for both polling and blocking synchronization schemes. For a dual processor system, cLAN achieves maximum throughput of approximately 339Mbps, 738Mbps, and 768Mbps for TCP, the blocking scheme, and the polling scheme, respectively. The advantage of using the polling scheme is more obvious for the dual processor system. Recall that cLAN uses a software layer to emulate TCP transmission. The actual transmission still uses the cLAN VI Kernel agent and the VIA-aware hardware. One would expect TCP to perform well in such a configuration. However, we observe that there were many severe dropouts in the cLAN TCP graph especially for larger data blocks. This could be interpreted as the overhead involved in maintaining the VI's work queues, the cost of the memory copy from the user's data buffer to the packet descriptor's data buffer, and the overhead of the cLAN's TCP emulated device driver (lanevi) in fragmenting the data block to 1500 bytes (the default maximum transmission unit (MTU) specified in the Ethernet standard 802.3).

Figure 3 shows the communication performance using the GNIC-II. For a uniprocessor system, the GNIC-II achieves maximum throughput of approximately 258Mbps for TCP and 510Mbps for both polling and blocking synchronization schemes. For a dual processor system, the GNIC-II achieves maximum throughput of approximately 261Mbps for TCP and 273Mbps for the polling scheme and blocking scheme, respectively. In the dual processor system, the VIA performance drops drastically whereas the performance of TCP increases slightly.

Figure 4 shows the communication performance using the SK-9821 NICs. For the uniprocessor system, SK-9821 achieves maximum throughput of approximately 296Mbps for TCP and 520Mbps for both polling and blocking syn-

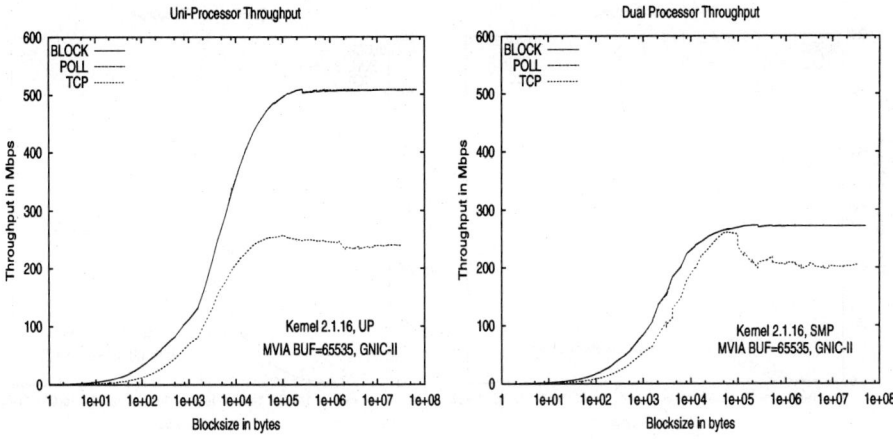

Fig. 3. GNIC-II: Send/Recv Mode

chronization schemes. For dual processor system, SK-9821 achieves maximum throughput of approximately 260Mbps for TCP and 269Mbps for polling scheme and blocking schemes, respectively.

The poor VIA throughput performance on the dual processor system is related to the implementation of the doorbell mechanism in M-VIA as explained above. In general, the throughput performance using the polling mechanism is slightly better (about $1 - 3\%$) than the blocking mechanism for all NICs under both systems. However, this effect can only be observed when the data block size is large, e.g $> 4Mbytes$.

5.3 Effect of Hardware MTU on Throughput Performance

In M-VIA, the GNIC-II and SysKonnect NICs hardware MTU is 1500 bytes. This is because the Gigabit Ethernet standard still limits the MTU to 1500 bytes. In [12], it has been observed that a larger MTU improves TCP throughput.

To confirm that hardware MTU will also improve VIA performance, we tested the SK-9821 NIC using an MTU of 9000 bytes. Since the Foundry switch does not support MTU greater than 1500 bytes, we connected two PCs back to back using the SK-9821 NICs. Figure 5 shows the VIA communication performance as well as the TCP performance. For the uniprocessor system, the SK-9821 achieved maximum TCP throughput of approximately 574Mbps with latency of 54μ secs. The M-VIA performance attains maximum throughput of roughly 632Mbps using the blocking scheme and 648Mbps using the polling synchronization scheme. The latency for both schemes is approximately 24μ secs. This represents an increase of a factor of 2 for TCP throughput and approximately a 20% increase for the VIA throughput when compared to using MTU of 1500 bytes. Moreover, the latency has also decreased.

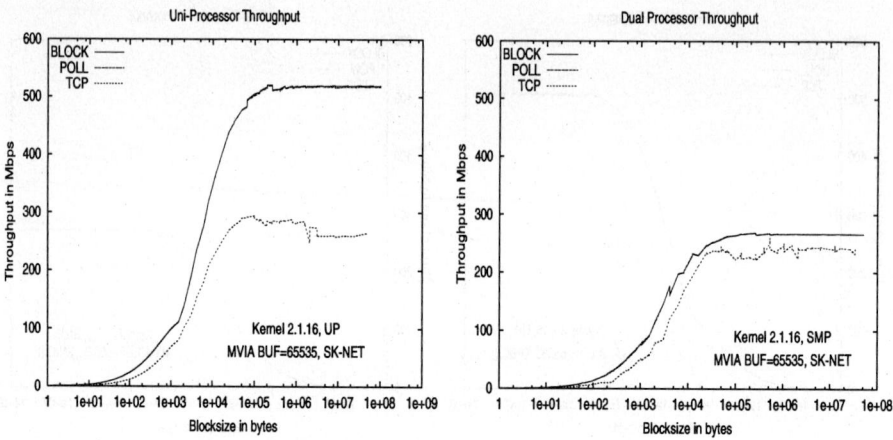

Fig. 4. SK-9821: Send/Recv Mode

For the dual processor system, the SK-9821 achieves a maximum TCP throughput of approximately 504Mbps with latency of 93μ secs. The M-VIA maximum throughput is approximately 535Mbps for both the polling and blocking schemes. The latency of the polling scheme has increased by 3μ secs. However, the latency of the blocking scheme remains unchanged. As compared to MTU of 1500 on the dual processor system, the M-VIA throughput has improved by approximately 200Mbps.

6 Conclusion

This paper has presented the performance of both hardware and software implementation of VIA on uniprocessor and dual processor systems. From the performance figures, we have verified that the VI architecture can give higher throughput and lower communication latency to applications. We have also confirmed that eliminating the TCP protocol stack provides higher throughput performance. VIA technology can take advantage of the VIA-aware hardware. For instance, cLAN achieves higher throughput and lower latency when compared to a software-only implementation such as M-VIA. The effectiveness of polling and blocking synchronization schemes depends on the implementation of the doorbell mechanism. Further investigation of other VIA features such as multiple VIs and RDMA is warranted. Moreover, we suspect that using multiple VIs on a SMP system may yield higher throughput.

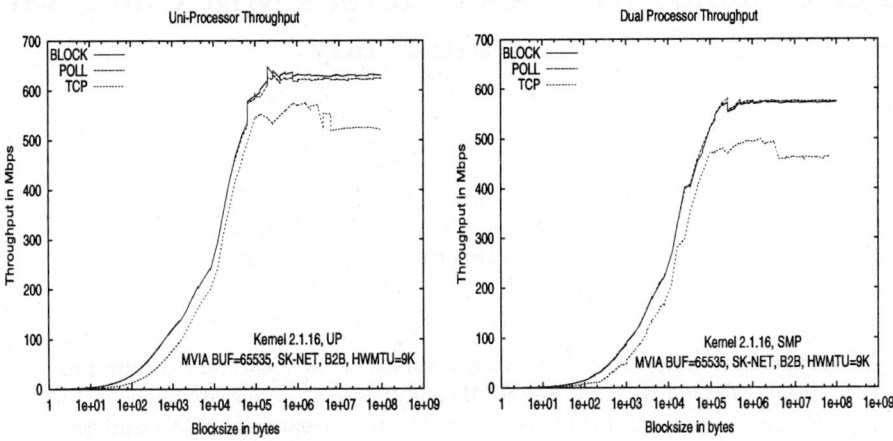

Fig. 5. SK-9821: Send/Recv Mode with MTU=9000

References

1. Gigabit Ethernet Alliance: Gigabit Ethernet Overview, www.gigabit-ethernet.org (1997)
2. R. P. Martin, A. M. Vahdat, D. E. Culler, T. E. Anderson: Effects of Communication Latency, Overhead, and Bandwidth in a Cluster Architecture. Proc. 24th Annual Int'l Symp. on Computer Architecture (ISCA). (1997)
3. T. Von Eicken, A. Basu, V. Buch, W. Vogels: U-NET: A User Level Network Interface for Parallel and Distributed Computing. Proc. of the 15th SOSP. (1995)
4. S. Pakin, M. Lauria, A. Chien: High Performance Messaging on Workstation: Illinois Fast Message (FM) for Myrinet. Proc. of Supercomputing'95. (1995)
5. Richard P. Martin, Amin M. Vahdat, David E. Culler, Thomas E. Anderson: Effects of Communication Latency, Overhead, and Bandwidth in a Cluster Architecture. ISCA 24. (1997)
6. Compaq Computer Corp., Intel Corp., Microsoft Corp: Virtual Interface Architecture Specification version 1.0, developer.intel.com/design/servers/vi/ (1997)
7. Giganet Inc.: cLAN Performance, www.giganet.com/products/performance.html
8. E. Speight, H. Abdel-Shafi, J. K. Bennett: Realizing the Performance Potential of the Virtual Interface Architecture. Proc. of Supercomputing'99. (1999)
9. N. J. Boden, D. Cohen, R. E. Felderman, A. E. Kulawik, C. L. Seitz, J. N. Seizovic, W. Su: Myrinet - A Gigabit per second Local Area Network. IEEE Micro. (1995)
10. National Energy Research Scientific Computing Center: M-VIA: A High Performance Modula VIA for Linux, www.nersc.gov/research/FTG/via/
11. Q. O. Snell, A. R. Mikler, J. L. Gustafson: NetPIPE: Network Protocol Independent Performance Evaluator. Ames Lab., Scalable Comp. Lab., Iowa State. (1997)
12. Paul A. Farrell, Hong Ong: Communication Performance over a Gigabit Ethernet Network. IEEE 19th Proc. of IPCCC. (2000)

Performance Analysis of Intel's MMX and SSE: A Case Study

Alfred Strey and Martin Bange

Department of Neural Information Processing
University of Ulm, D-89069 Ulm, Germany
strey@neuro.informatik.uni-ulm.de

Abstract. The MMX and SSE extensions of current Intel Pentium processors offer a 4-way or 8-way SIMD parallelism to accelerate many vector or matrix applications. In this paper the performance of MMX and SSE for the implementation of neural networks is evaluated. It is shown that a speedup in the range from 1.3 to 9.8 for single neural operations and a total speedup of up to 4.1 for the simulation of a complete neural network can be achieved. A detailed performance counter analysis is provided.

1 Motivation

In 1997, Intel introduced the first multimedia extension called MMX to its x86 architecture [4]. It is mainly designed for accelerating many video, image or speech processing algorithms that apply simple operations to large arrays composed of 8-bit or 16-bit elements. Eight 8-bit or four 16-bit integer data elements can be packed into 64-bit registers and several calculations can be performed simultaneously according to the SIMD execution model. Pentium III processors, available since 1999, offer additionally the SSE (*Streaming SIMD Extension*) unit that supports data-parallel operations on four single-precision 32-bit floating point numbers packed in new 128-bit registers. It is designed to improve the speed of advanced 3D geometry calculations that require a higher precision.

Although the instruction sets of both units were inspired by popular multimedia algorithms, also many other applications can take profit of the internal SIMD parallelism. Bhargava and al. have evaluated the performance of MMX for several digital signal processing algorithms and have measured a speedup in the range from 0.49 to 5.5 for various applications [2]. Gaborit et al. have shown, that MMX can accelerate the calculation of the Mahalanobis distance required for several neural network models [3]. They achieve a speedup of more than 3, but they do not consider the compute-intensive neural network training phase.

In this paper the suitability of both MMX and SSE for neural network applications is studied. The performance is evaluated for seven important neural operations presented in the next section. Section 3 describes our methodology and Section 4 discusses the main results of our experimental performance study. In Section 5 the results are explained by a performance counter analysis. Section 6 concludes this paper.

2 Neural Network Operations

Fig. 1 shows a Radial Basis Function (RBF) network that represents a typical artificial neural network model suitable for classification and approximation tasks. It is trained by a gradient descent algorithm which adapts the positions of the centers c_{ij}, the heights w_{jk} and the widths of all Gaussian bells in the hidden layer. Eq. 1 to 7 shown in the right half of Fig. 1 are the basic neural operations that will be analyzed throughout this paper. They are not only essential for the RBF network but also for many other important neural network algorithms. The calculation of the exponential function in line 2 of the algorithm cannot be accelerated by the multimedia units. In all equations $s_j = 1/2\sigma_j$ is used instead of σ_j to eliminate divisions that cannot be realized on MMX.

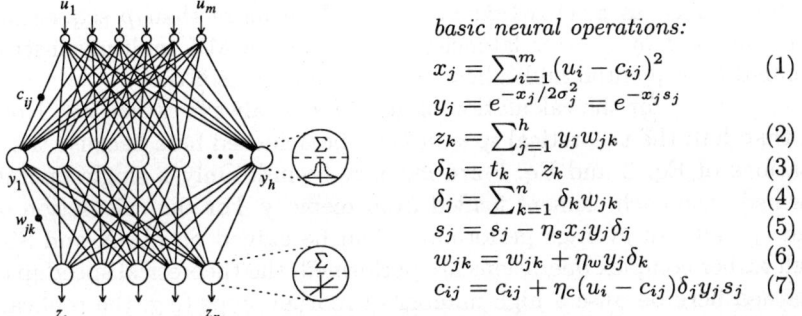

basic neural operations:

$$x_j = \sum_{i=1}^{m}(u_i - c_{ij})^2 \quad (1)$$
$$y_j = e^{-x_j/2\sigma_j^2} = e^{-x_j s_j} \quad (2)$$
$$z_k = \sum_{j=1}^{h} y_j w_{jk} \quad (3)$$
$$\delta_k = t_k - z_k \quad (3)$$
$$\delta_j = \sum_{k=1}^{n} \delta_k w_{jk} \quad (4)$$
$$s_j = s_j - \eta_s x_j y_j \delta_j \quad (5)$$
$$w_{jk} = w_{jk} + \eta_w y_j \delta_k \quad (6)$$
$$c_{ij} = c_{ij} + \eta_c (u_i - c_{ij}) \delta_j y_j s_j \quad (7)$$

Fig. 1. Architecture and training algorithm of a m-h-n RBF network

3 Methodology

All neural operations according to Eq. 1 to 7 were encoded in assembly language (according to the x86 instruction set enhancements for MMX and SSE), translated by the Gnu assembler and evaluated on a PC with a 500 MHz Pentium III processor running the Linux operating system. Either 32-bit float or 16-bit fixed point (mapped to 16-bit integer) parallel data types were used. Special care was taken for the correct alignment of all data elements because the penalty for misaligned data is high on both multimedia units. For reference, all neural operations were also implemented in C using the `float` data type and compiled by the Gnu C compiler. Compiler optimizations were switched on. The execution times of all seven neural operations related to three different neural network sizes (16-104-16, 64-416-64 and 128-832-128 neurons in the input, hidden and output layer) were measured for the MMX code, for the SSE code and for the sequential floating point code. Furthermore, the time for a complete adaptation of all neural network variables according to a single input vector **u** was determined. A first series of experiments revealed a rather low speedup on MMX for all those neural operations consisting of several succeeding multiplications. Therefore optimized versions of Eq. 5 and 6 have been implemented that offer faster multiplications but cause additional loss of precision.

4 Results

Table 1 contains the measured speedup for all seven neural operations compared to the reference float implementation. The theoretical speedup for all implementations is equivalent to the parallelism degree p which is 4 for both MMX and SSE because four 16-bit fixed or four 32-bit floating point calculations can be performed simultaneously. It can be seen that for certain operations a very high speedup can be obtained that exceeds the theoretical speedup p by far. On MMX especially the computation of x_j and z_k is 5 to 10 times faster than the reference float implementation. This anomaly can be explained by special MMX instructions such as `multiply&add` that replace more than p sequential float instructions and by shorter latencies provided by MMX multiply instructions (compared to sequential multiplications on the processor core).

The speedup for the calculation of δ_k and s_j is always rather low. Not much more than half the theoretical speedup can be achieved here because the implementations of Eq. 3 and Eq. 5 are memory-bound: Only a single operation is performed with each element loaded from memory. For the calculation of w_{jk}, δ_j and c_{ij} only an average performance can be gained on MMX and SSE. Although rather complex operations are performed, the theoretical speedup cannot be reached here because a high number of reorder steps (e.g. the replication of scalar operands) must be executed. On MMX also a high number of instructions is required for the precise computation of each 16 by 16 bit product. The 4th column of Table 1 shows that the optimized implementations of Eq. 5 and 6 based on simpler multiply instructions provide a significantly improved speedup.

In Fig. 2 the total neural network simulation time for all three network sizes on MMX (only optimized version), on SSE and on the floating point unit of the Pentium III processor core are compared. For small networks a high speedup in the range from 3.7 (on SSE) up to 4.1 (on MMX) compared to the reference float implementation can be achieved. When the network size is varied, two interesting effects can be observed in Table 1 and Fig. 2. On the one hand the speedup of

Table 1. Measured speedup for seven neural operations on MMX and SSE (with three network sizes 16-104-16 / 64-416-64 / 128-832-128)

Eq.	calc. of	MMX	MMX (optimized)	SSE
1	x_j	6.7/6.3/6.9	not applicable	3.7/3.5/3.2
2	z_k	6.6/7.4/9.8	not applicable	4.7/4.2/3.5
3	δ_k	1.7/2.0/2.3	not applicable	1.3/1.6/1.8
4	δ_j	2.6/2.7/4.5	not applicable	3.7/3.6/3.4
5	s_j	1.3/1.3/1.3	2.1/2.3/2.4	2.1/2.3/2.3
6	w_{jk}	1.7/1.9/2.6	5.7/3.7/5.4	3.7/2.0/2.0
7	c_{ij}	2.9/2.5/3.2	not applicable	3.3/1.5/1.1

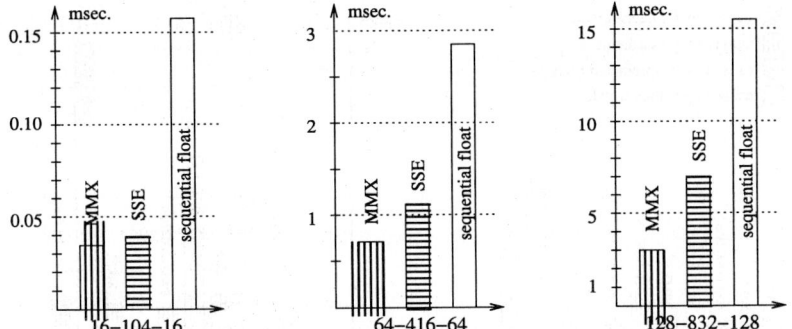

Fig. 2. Time for a RBF network training step after the presentation of a new pattern

several fixed point implementations on MMX (e.g. the calculation of x_j, z_k and δ_j) is increased if the network is enlarged. On the other hand the floating point implementations on SSE show the reverse effect: The speedup is reduced if the network size is increased.

5 Performance Counter Analysis

To explain some of the surprising effects described above all implementations on both MMX and SSE were analyzed by accessing the performance counters of the Pentium III processor with the PCL performance counter library [1]. As performance metrics the number I of instructions executed for each neural operation, the number of clock cycles per instruction (CPI), the number of L1 and L2 cache misses, the resource stalls and the number of mispredicted branches were recorded. For both MMX and SSE, the ratios of the number of instructions required by the reference implementation to the number of instructions required by MMX and SSE were computed (see Table 2). It can be seen that for all implementations on MMX the ratio I_f/I_{MMX} and the corresponding speedup listed in Table 1 are strongly correlated. Thus, the higher speedup for some operations (e.g. x_j and z_k) results essentially from a lower dynamic instruction count on MMX. For the memory-bound neural operations (e.g. s_j and δ_k) the ratio I_f/I_{MMX} is not higher than 2 because on MMX half the number of memory accesses compared to the float implementation are required.

The increasing speedup of several MMX implementations for larger networks can be explained partly by an increasing I_f/I_{MMX} ratio (caused by a diminishing initialization overhead on MMX) and partly by an increasing CPI value of the reference implementation. The latter effect is particularly evident for the δ_j calculation and is mainly due to L1 cache misses (compare Fig. 3a).

The diminishing speedup of SSE implementations for larger networks cannot be explained by the I_f/I_{SSE} ratio. Instead it corresponds to increasing CPI_{SSE} values (see Table 2). For some operations (e.g. Eq. 4, see Fig. 3a) this effect is due to L1 and L2 cache misses. For other operations containing several succeeding

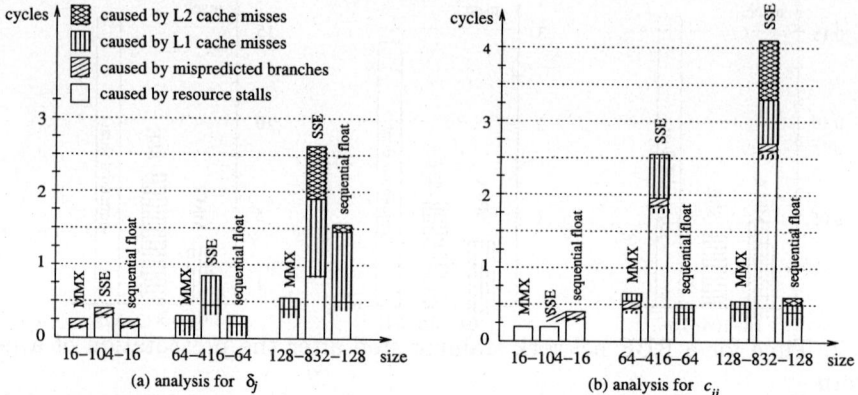

Fig. 3. Number of lost cycles per instruction due to L1 or L2 cache misses, resource stalls and branch mispredictions

multiplications (e.g. Eq. 7, see Fig. 3b) the high CPI_{SSE} count results from a high number of resource stalls. Here internal data dependencies prevent the pipelined SSE unit from executing several instructions simultaneously.

6 Summary and Conclusions

This case study shows that both MMX and SSE are fairly well suited for neural network simulations. Especially for small networks a speedup approximately equal to the internal parallelism degree of 4 can be achieved. On MMX all operations required for a neural classification with an already trained large network can even be accelerated by a factor of up to 9.8. Thus, MMX is the preferable multimedia unit for neural network simulation if only speed is considered and the loss of precision is acceptable. The SSE implementation revealed to be always slower than the MMX implementation. For larger networks, L1 or L2 cache misses and resource stalls cause a drastic decrease of the achievable speedup.

Table 2. Selected results from the performance counter analysis (for 3 network sizes)

calc. of	I_f/I_{MMX}	I_f/I_{SSE}	CPI_{MMX}	CPI_{SSE}	CPI_f
x_j	4.3/5.5/5.7	4.3/5.5/5.7	0.6/0.9/0.9	1.0/1.6/2.0	0.9/1.0/1.1
z_k	5.6/6.1/6.2	5.6/6.1/6.2	0.7/0.8/0.8	1.0/1.4/2.0	0.9/1.0/1.1
δ_k	1.3/1.8/2.0	1.3/1.8/2.0	1.5/1.2/1.0	1.4/1.3/1.2	1.2/0.9/0.8
δ_j	2.7/2.7/2.7	4.6/4.7/4.8	0.8/0.8/0.9	1.0/1.1/2.1	0.8/0.8/1.5
s_j	1.5/1.6/1.6	2.1/2.6/2.7	0.9/0.7/0.7	1.4/1.2/1.8	1.0/1.0/1.1
w_{jk}	4.2/4.3/4.3	4.1/4.3/4.5	0.6/0.9/0.9	0.9/1.7/2.2	0.7/0.8/1.5
c_{ij}	2.3/2.5/2.5	4.0/4.7/4.8	0.7/0.9/0.9	1.1/2.8/4.9	0.8/0.9/1.1
RBF net	3.4/3.7/3.8	4.3/5.0/5.1	0.7/0.9/0.9	1.0/1.7/2.7	0.8/0.9/1.3

References

1. R. Berrendorf and B. Mohr. PCL –The Performance Counter Library. Research Centre Juelich (Germany), available from http://www.fz-juelich.de/zam/PCL.
2. R. Bhargava, L. K. John, B. L. Evans, and R. Radhakrishnan. Evaluating MMX technology using DSP and multimedia applications. In *Proc. of the 31st ACM/IEEE Int. Symp. on Microarchitecture (MICRO-98)*, pages 37–48, IEEE, 1998.
3. L. Gaborit, B. Granado, and P. Garda. Evaluating micro-processors' multimedia extensions for the real time simulation of RBF networks. In *Proc. of MicroNeuro 99*, pages 217–221. IEEE, 1999.
4. A. Peleg, S. Wilkie, and U. Weiser. Intel MMX for multimedia PCs. *Communications of the ACM*, 40(1):24–38, 1997.

Group-Based Performance Analysis for Multithreaded SMP Cluster Applications

Holger Brunst[1], Wolfgang E. Nagel[1], and Hans-Christian Hoppe[2]

[1] ZHR, Dresden University of Technology, Germany
{brunst,nagel}@zhr.tu-dresden.de
[2] Pallas GmbH, Germany
hch@pallas.com

Abstract. Performance optimization remains one of the key issues in parallel computing. With the emergence of large clustered SMP systems, the task of analyzing and tuning scientific applications actually becomes harder. Tools need to be extended to cover both distributed and shared–memory styles of performance analysis and to handle the massive amount of information generated by applications on today's powerful systems. This paper proposes a flexible way to define hierarchies of event streams and to enable the end–user to traverse these hierarchies, looking at sampled or aggregated information on the higher levels. The concept will be implemented and evaluated in practice within the scope of the US DOE ASCI project.

Keywords: performance visualization, application tuning, massively parallel programming, scalability, message passing, multi-threading.

1 Introduction

The emergence of clustered SMP platforms with a moderate number of CPUs per node, coupled by a shared memory and a potentially large number of these nodes coupled with an off–the–shelf interconnection network, but not sharing the same memory, changes the scene for the authors of parallel scientific applications. In the following paper, we will discuss the challenges associated with clusters of SMPs and present the generic concept of flexible grouping of event streams and its application to the performance analysis of parallel applications on hierarchical systems.

2 New Challenges for Performance Analysis

Up to now, the predominant parallel architecture classes have been the classic shared–memory systems with limited scalability and the scalable distributed–memory MPP systems. For each class, performance analysis methodologies and tools (AIMS[7], PABLO [1], PARADYN[4], Paragraph[2], Paraver[3], Vampir [5], et. al. [6]) had been developed and the significant scientific and engineering codes had been ported and optimized. For clustered SMP platforms, the picture changes. To achieve a good price / performance ratio, these systems do not provide an efficient virtual–shared–memory system, but expose their structure to the applications. An application programmer aiming at scalability beyond one SMP node has to make a choice between the message–passing programming model, or a combination of message–passing between SMP nodes, most probably MPI and a shared–memory model within one node, most probably OpenMP. In both cases, performance analysis faces new challenges which result in the urge to extend the current MPP performance–analysis tools by

- support for multi–threading,
- analysis of memory and CPU statistics,
- display of scheduler events and interactions.

The challenge here is mostly an appropriate organization of performance data, both internally to the tools and more importantly to the end–user: the potentially enormous amount of performance information (in particular if event tracing is used) has to be processed and displayed in a way that an ordinary user can understand. The following section will present a generic model for flexibly organizing the hierarchy levels of clustered SMP systems into a top–down scheme. This will enable the end–user to proceed from a bird's eye view of an application run to a detailed view of those 'suspicious' parts of the application execution that may indicate an actual performance problem.

3 A Generic Model for Event Trace Data Grouping

Event-based performance analysis is capable of giving a detailed insight into the application's behavior to the end user. However, this advantage compared to standard profiling techniques introduces certain difficulties regarding the huge amount of data that is typically generated. The two major problems are:

1. Large trace data buffers with fast access methods;
2. Appropriate presentation of the data to the end-user.

While work has been carried out on the trace data buffer mechanisms, trace data presentation still poses a lot of unanswered questions. In this paper we concentrate on structuring the data in a way that provides a good overview of the application's performance, but also allows quick access to multiple levels of detail.

3.1 Event Traces to be Stored in the Model

The event trace data that needs to be grouped and stored in our model can be subdivided into four major categories:

1. Program State Changes
2. Point to Point Communication

3. Collective Operations
4. Hardware Performance Monitors.

Each of these categories has specific properties that need to be related to each other in order to create a complete view of an application's runtime behavior.

3.2 Requirements of the Model

Single event traces without a context are of limited use for performance analysis. Grouping and linking of event traces is essential for successful performance analysis. In the design procedure of our grouping model, we identified the following requirements:

- Use simple event records to allow a fast linear tracing mechanism, in order to minimize the influence of the tracer on the application and to keep execution time costs small.
- Keep event traces independent of each other on the tracing level to allow filtering and reduction in a post–processing phase.
- Enable event trace re–grouping depending on custom search criterion.
- Keep the grouping as flexible as possible regarding existing computer architectures to be modeled.
- The level of abstraction and detail must not be limited by any static constraints of the model.
- Keep things simple and readable for human beings! In other words, we support both ASCII and binary trace file output.

3.3 The Grouping Model

As already stated above, the grouping model is built around the various types of event traces we want to relate to each other. To increase the readability, while reducing the amount of space needed, our model description is rather informal and only paraphrases the full specification upon which this is based. A trace file can consist of N state chains which are each to be defined as follows:

DEFSTATECHAIN <ChainID> <ChainName>

The states that can be put in such a chain need to be declared with:

DEFSTATE <StateID> <StateName>

Finally, the state changes themselfves need to be expressed as follows:

<TimeStamp> ENTERSTATE <StateId> INCHAIN <ChainID>
<TimeStamp> EXITSTATE <StateId> INCHAIN <ChainID>

Similar records have to be written for the performance monitor, collective operation and point to point communication chains. For the grouping, declaration records of the following shape need to be written in the declaration header of a trace file:

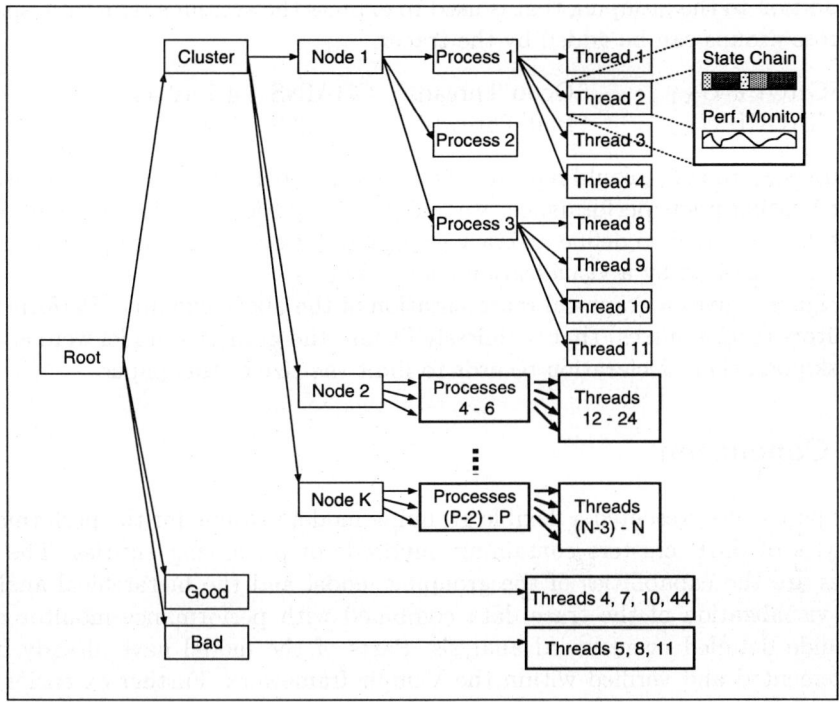

Fig. 1. Hierarchical Grouping of a Multithreaded SMP Cluster Application

DEFGROUP <GroupID> <GroupName> CHAINS <Multiple ChainIDs>
for a group of chains, or
DEFGROUP <GroupID> <GroupName> GROUPS <Multiple GroupIDs>
for a group consisting of other groups.

3.4 An Example

The following example shows the group declaration records that are needed to specify an SMP Cluster consisting of K nodes, P processes and N threads. Each process hosts four threads and every node includes three processes.

DEFSTATECHAIN 1	"Thread 1"		
DEFSTATECHAIN N	"Thread N"		
DEFGROUP G_1	"Process 1"	CHAINS	1 2 3 4
DEFGROUP G_P	"Process P"	CHAINS	N-3 N-2 N-1 N
DEFGROUP G_{P+1}	"Node 1"	GROUPS	$G_1\ G_2\ G_3$
DEFGROUP G_{P+K}	"Node K"	GROUPS	$G_{P-2}\ G_{P-1}\ G_P$
DEFGROUP G_{P+K+1}	"Cluster"	GROUPS	$G_P\ \ldots\ G_{P+K}$
DEFGROUP G_{P+K+2}	"All Threads"	CHAINS	1 2 3 4 ... N

In addition to the grouping that is used to express the system's structure, special purpose groups can be added by the tracer.

DEFGROUP G_{X1} "Good Threads"   CHAINS   4 7 10 44
DEFGROUP G_{X2} "Bad Threads"   CHAINS   5 8 11

Group G_{X1} and G_{X2} could represent good and bad performing threads regarding their floating point performance. Virtually any criterion that is available to the tracer can be used to define arbitary groups and group relationships, which can then be exploited by a visualization component.

Figure 1 gives a graphical representation of the above example. Performance monitors (cache misses) that seamlessly fit into the grouping model were added. We skipped their declaration records to limit the size of this paper.

4 Conclusion

This paper has presented a flexible grouping model suitable for the performance analysis of SMP clusters containing hundreds of processing entities. The key issues are the capabilities of the grouping model and the hierarchical analysis and visualization of the trace data combined with performance monitor data to guide detailed event-based analysis. Parts of the model have already been implemented and verified within the Vampir framework. Further extensions to Vampir, that are currently being worked on, will serve as proof of the concept, demonstrating the benefits of event-based performance analysis to real-world users with applications on the upcoming SMP cluster systems.

References

1. L. DeRose and D. A. Reed. SvPablo: A Multi-Language Architecture-Independent Performance Analysis System. In *Proceedings of the International Conference on Parallel Processing (ICPP'99)*, Fukushima, Japan, September 1999.
2. M. T. Heath, A. D. Malony, and D. T. Rover. Visualization for parallel performance evaluation and optimization. In I. J. Stasko, J. Domingue, M. H. Brown, and B. A. Price, editors, *Software Visualization*, pages 347–365. MIT Press, Cambridge, 1998.
3. J. Labarta, S. Girona, V. Pillet, T. Cortés, and L. Gregoris. DiP: A Parallel Program Development Environment. In *2nd International EuroPar Conference (EuroPar 96)*, Lyon, France, August 1996.
   http://www.cepba.upc.es/paraver.
4. B. P. Miller, M. D. Callaghan, J. M. Cargille, J. K. Hollingsworth, R. B. Irvin, K. L. Karavanic, K. Kunchithapadam, and T. Newhall. The Paradyn Parallel Performance Measurement Tools. *IEEE Computer*, 28(11):37–46, November 1995.
   http://www.cs.wisc.edu/~paradyn.
5. W. E. Nagel, A. Arnold, M. Weber, H.-C. Hoppe, and K. Solchenbach. VAMPIR: Visualization and Analysis of MPI Resources. *Supercomputer 63*, XII(1):69–80, January 1996.
   http://www.pallas.de/pages/vampir.htm.

6. Pointers to tools, modules, APIs and documents related to parallel performance analysis.
   http://www.fz-juelich.de/apart/wp3/modmain.html.
7. J. C. Yan. Performance Tuning with AIMS – An Automated Instrumentation and Monitoring System for Multicomputers. In *Proceedings of the 27th Hawaii International Conference on System Sciences*, volume II, pages 625–633, Wailea, Hawaii, January 1994.
   http://www.nas.nasa.gov/Groups/Tools/Projects/AIMS.

Topic 03
Scheduling and Load Balancing

Ishfaq Ahmad, Henri Casanova, Rupert Ford, and Yves Robert

Topic Chairpersons

Welcome to the Euro-Par 2001 Topic 03 on Scheduling and Load Balancing. Scheduling and load balancing are key areas in the quest for performance in parallel and distributed applications. Relevant techniques can be provided either at the application level, or at the system level, and both scenarios are of interest for this topic.

Twenty papers were submitted to Topic 03, one of which was re-directed to Topic 04. Out of the nineteen remaining papers, three were selected as regular papers, and four as research notes. All papers were reviewed by at least three referees, and the vast majority received four reviews.

The presentation of the seven papers is organized in two sessions. The first session contains three papers. In the first paper, *On Minimising the Processor Requirements of LogP Schedules*, the authors propose different clustering heuristics for task scheduling in the LogP model. These heuristics reduce the number of required processors without degrading the makespan. The second paper, *Exploiting Unused Time Slots in List Scheduling Considering Communication Contention*, presents (two versions of) a contention aware scheduling strategy which is compared to two related methods. It out-performs these other methods, with similar or better complexity, apart from one case where high communication costs mean that a more sequential solution is most apt. The third paper, *An Evaluation of Partitioners for Parallel SAMR Applications*, presents a review of mesh-partitioning tools/techniques for structured meshes, and provides experimental results for the various tools on one selected application, with various numbers of processors, problem size and partition granularity.

The second session contains four papers. The first paper, *Load Balancing on Networks with Dynamically Changing Topology*, presents a load balancing algorithm targeted at synchronous networks with dynamic topologies (e.g. due to link failures), and establishes a convergence result for nearest-neighbor load-balancing techniques. The second paper, *A Fuzzy Load Balancing Service for Network Computing Based on Jini*, addresses the problem of load balancing for servers executing independent tasks generated by clients in a distributed object computing environment implemented with Jini; the results show that the fuzzy algorithm achieves significantly better load balancing than random and round-robin algorithms. The third paper, *Approximation Algorithms for Scheduling Independent Malleable Tasks*, builds on the well-known continuous resource allocation case for scheduling independent non-preemptive tasks. Finally, the fourth paper, *The Way to Produce the Quasi-workload in a Cluster*, addresses the problem of generating synthetic workloads that can serve as input for the simulation of scheduling algorithms in cluster-based architectures.

We wish you an interesting workshop via the presentations, papers, and interactions with fellow researchers. We also hope you have an enjoyable visit to Manchester.

On Minimising the Processor Requirements of LogP Schedules

Cristina Boeres*, Gerson N. da Cunha, and Vinod E. F. Rebello**

Instituto de Computação, Universidade Federal Fluminense (UFF)
Niterói, RJ, Brazil
{boeres,gerson,vinod}@ic.uff.br

Abstract. This paper briefly describes the mechanisms used to reduce the number of processors required by a class of task replication-based scheduling heuristics for the *LogP* model. These heuristics, which are based on the task clustering algorithm design methodology [3], are known to generate schedules with good makespans [3,5]. Results in this paper show that a significant reduction, on average, in the number of processors required can be obtained without degrading the makespan. These mechanisms can also be used to tradeoff *quality* in terms of an increase in the makespan for *quantity* in terms of a further reduction in the number of processors required.

1 Introduction

The principal objective of task scheduling is to find a schedule with the minimal makespan, for a given program representation and communication model on bounded or unbounded number of processors. A secondary objective, though just as important, is minimising the cost of implementing this makespan.

The standard communication model used in the task scheduling problem is the *delay model*, where the *latency* or *delay* for a message transmission is the only communication parameter considered relevant [12]. However, with the advances in technology, the evolution of parallel architectures, and the use of software-based communication libraries to support portability, other communication characteristics have been shown to influence performance significantly [10].

A well-known and now established abstract model of parallel computation, the *LogP* model, has attemped to address this fact [7]. The principal feature encompassed in this model is that inter-processor communication also requires processing time by the communicating processors. This model identified four architectural parameters: L is the *latency* incurred when transmitting a message; o, the processing *overhead* incurred when sending or receiving (during which time the processor cannot execute tasks nor send or receive other messages); g, the

---

* This work is funded by grants from the the Fundação de Amparo à Pesquisa do Estado do Rio de Janeiro (FAPERJ). The authors are partially supported by grants from Conselho Nacional de Desenvolvimento Científico e Tecnológico (CNPq).
** On leave from the Universidade Católica de Petrópolis, Petrópolis, RJ, Brazil.

minimum *gap* between two consecutive message sends or receives by a processor; and P, the number of processors available. These parameters also capture the fact that networks have a limited capacity for message transmissions. While recent, more accurate models have also been proposed [1,13], these appear to be refinements of the *LogP* model rather than radically new models. These *LogP*-type models succeed in modeling a number of parallel machines [1,7,9,10,13].

Since characteristics such as the processing cost to send and receive messages cannot be modeled as part of the message delay [7], poor program performances may result from a schedule based on an inaccurate representation of the target machine [4]. In comparison to the number of scheduling heuristics devised for the delay model, few scheduling strategies based on communication models that specify *LogP*-type characteristics have been proposed [2,4,6,8,9]. Furthermore, these algorithms tend to be limited to specific classes or types of graphs (with the exception of [8]) and restricted *LogP* models (with the exception of [9]). One of the difficulties when handling the *LogP* parameters is that the overheads are communication costs paid for by computation time.

Clustering or grouping tasks together on a processor reduces communication costs. If the successors of a task have been assigned to different processors, it may be advantageous to *replicate* this task on each of the processors containing a successor. Under the *LogP* model, task replication may still be worthwhile even if the copy is not scheduled on the same processor as its successor. Replicating a task which needs to send more than one message avoids the delays (o or g) that would be incurred by the subsequent messages sent by this task.

In [5], a number of task replication-based clustering algorithms were proposed based on the task clustering algorithm design methodology proposed in [2,3]. These algorithms schedule arbitrary task graphs on an unbounded number of processors under an unrestricted *LogP* model and generate schedules whose makespan compare favourably with those produced by existing scheduling algorithms [2,3,5]. The methodology, like most cluster algorithms [11,14], consists of two stages. The *first stage* tries to create a cluster for each task (the task becomes the *owner* of the cluster), made up of copies of ancestor tasks which allow the owner to be scheduled as early as possible. The *second stage* determines the number of copies of each cluster necessary to implement a schedule with the makespan found earlier.

In order to guide the construction process of each cluster, the methodology enforces four cluster design restrictions during the first stage [3]. *Restriction 1* (R1) prevents the owner from being delayed by overheads due to message sends to other clusters. *Restriction 2* (R2) removes the problem of ordering the send overheads by restricting each cluster to sending only one message. *Restriction 3* (R3) forces the receive overheads within the cluster to be scheduled as late as possible, while *Restriction 4* (R4) assumes that these overheads are ordered by the arrival time of their respective messages. While the first two restrictions aid in the process of minimizing the schedule time of each owner, the number of clusters (and thus processors) required to implement this *virtual schedule* (i.e. the schedule obtained by abiding to the restrictions) tends to be extremely high. This problem could be alleviated if the second stage were to carefully relax R1 and/or R2 and remove the copies of clusters which become redundant.

Most scheduling heuristics try to find the smallest makespan by calculating the earliest time that tasks (in the case of clustering algorithms, the owner tasks) can be scheduled. In $LogP$ clustering algorithms, the delaying of both tasks and the transmission of messages can be used to produce time intervals or windows of available processing time in which additional tasks could be included into a cluster, or where more than one send overhead could be scheduled, without compromising the makespan of the virtual schedule.

This work aims to re-design the second stage of the task clustering algorithm design methodology by proposing a series of mechanisms to decrease the number of clusters required by the final schedule without, in the first instance, increasing the makespan. These same mechanisms can be used to trade-off (i.e. decrease further the number of) processors for an increase in the makespan. In this paper, Restriction 2 (R2) is relaxed to permit an owner to send various messages if this eliminates at least some of the copies of the owner's cluster.

The following section presents some terminology used by design methodology. Section 3 defines the concept of processing windows and describes three mechanisms used to increase their size. How these windows are used to reduce the number of clusters required is also discussed. Section 4 summarises the results obtained while Sect. 5 presents some conclusions.

2   Terminology

In task scheduling, a parallel application is often represented by a *directed acyclic graph* or *DAG* $G = (V, E, \varepsilon, \omega)$, where: the set of vertices, V, represents the *tasks*; E, their precedence relationships; $\varepsilon(v_i)$ is the execution cost of task $v_i \in V$; and $\omega(v_i, v_j)$, the amount of data transmitted from task v_i to v_j.

The design methodology associates independent overhead parameters with the *sending* and *receiving* of a message, denoted by o_s and o_r, respectively and separate parameters for the gap between successive message sends (g_s) and receives (g_r) as proposed in [13]. Also, the latency parameter L is treated as the transmission time per unit data.

The emphasis of previous scheduling algorithms based on this two-stage design methodology has been on the design and implementation of the first stage [5]. This stage attempts to create a cluster $C(v)$ for each $v \in V$ (subject to the cluster design restrictions [3]) so that the *schedule time* of v, denoted by $s(v)$, is the earliest possible. Due to task replication, only a subset (the set of *useful clusters*, uc) of the $|V|$ clusters created will be utilized to form the set of *necessary clusters*, i.e. the number of copies of each cluster $\in uc$ (due to R1 and R2) necessary to implement the virtual schedule of G with makespan $\mathcal{M} = \max_{v \in V}\{s(v) + \varepsilon(v)\}$. The second stage starts with the *sink clusters* (clusters whose owners have no successors $\in V$) and visits useful immediate ancestor clusters in reverse topological order. Cluster $C(w)$ is an immediate ancestor of $C(v)$ if owner w is an immediate ancestor of a task in $C(v)$ and $w \notin C(v)$.

3 Relaxing Restriction 2

Even though, the first stage creates $|V|$ clusters, one for each task in G, only $|uc|$ of these clusters will be used. However, due to the replication of clusters, $|nc|$ *necessary clusters* (where $|nc| \geq |uc|$) are required to implement the virtual schedule with makespan $\mathcal{M}$. The mechanisms proposed in this paper study the effects of relaxing restriction R2 in order to reduce $|nc|$ and thus implement the final schedule with a *reduced set of clusters, rsc*.

These mechanisms basically attempt to define a large enough *processing window*, for the clusters $\in nc$, within which the send overheads of more than one message can be scheduled (subject to R1 but not R2) without increasing the makespan. This work extends the idea described in Example 1 and Fig. 1 (a).

Example 1: Assume cluster $C(w)$ has been constructed by the first stage according to the cluster design restrictions and that message (w, u_i) sent by the owner w in cluster $C'(w)$, a copy of cluster $C(w)$, to task u_i in $C(v)$ arrives t time units *earlier* than the *schedule time* of the associated receiving overhead. It would be possible therefore to delay the sending of that message from $C'(w)$ by t time units, creating a *processing window* of size t between the end of the execution of $w \in C'(w)$ and the sending overhead. If t is large enough (i.e. $t \geq \max\{o_s, g_s\}$) this message could also be sent by $C(w)$ since the o_s for (w, u_i) can be scheduled after the o_s of $C(w)$'s message without delaying $C(v)$, thus removing the need for cluster $C'(w)$. The removal of a cluster also eliminates the need for all of its ancestor clusters. These gains are made possible, in part, by R3 which schedules the receive overheads as late as possible within each cluster.

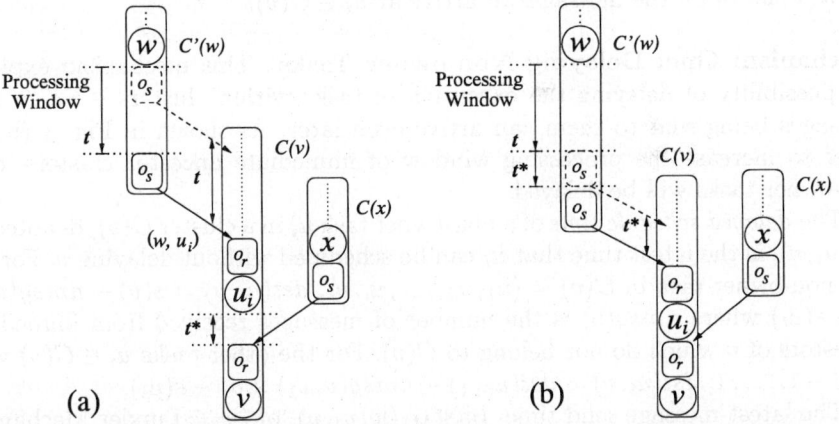

Fig. 1. Both, (a) Example 1: the delaying of message (w, u_i) and (b) Mechanism One: the delaying of task u_i, can be used to increase the processing window of (w, u_i)

Based on this idea, the number of clusters can be reduced by rescheduling communications. However, further gains could be attained by delaying clusters since not all of the owners v need to be scheduled at their $s(v)$ to achieve the makespan $\mathcal{M}$. This section discusses 3 mechanisms used to increase the processing window of $C(w)$, through a combination of delaying tasks and rescheduling communications. Mechanism One delays the non-owner tasks within the cluster $C(v) \in uc$. Mechanism Two reorders message receives within the successors $C'(v) \in rsc$ of $C(w)$. Once the sizes of the processing windows for $C(w)$ have been identified, the messages sent by w are rescheduled and a sufficient number of copies $C'(w)$ of $C(w)$ is defined. Mechanism Three tries to delay the $C'(w)$s in rcs. This process is then repeated for the next reverse-topological cluster $\in uc$.

Defining a Processing Window: A message (w, u_i) may not necessarily be processed immediately on arrival at its destination cluster $C(v)$ due to the execution of other tasks or receive overheads in that cluster. The mechanisms aim to determine, for each cluster $\in nc$, the earliest and latest time that its message can be sent, thus defining a processing window for that message. The earliest message send time of (w, u_i), from the first stage, is $emst(w, u_i, v) = s(w) + \varepsilon(w)$. The latest message send time $lmst(w, u_i, v)$ depends on the latest time that the receive overhead of (w, u_i) can be processed in $C(v)$. The period of time $[emst(w, u_i, v), lmst(w, u_i, v)]$ is the interval during which message (w, u_i) can be sent to $C(v)$ without delaying task v and whose duration defines the processing window $pw(w, u_i, v)$.

The schedule time of non-owner task $u_i \in C(v)$, denoted by $st(u_i, v)$, is the earliest time that task u_i can be scheduled in cluster $C(v)$. Considering Example 1, where only the sending of messages are delayed and not the tasks, $lmst(w, u_i, v) = st(u_i, v) - (o_s + L \times \omega(w, u_i) + n \times o_r)$ when message (w, u_i) is the nth last of all the messages to arrive at $u_i \in C(v)$.

Mechanism One: Delaying Non-owner Tasks. This mechanism explores the possibility of delaying the execution of tasks within clusters $\in uc$ so that messages being sent to them can arrive even later. As shown in Fig. 1 (b), in order to increase the processing window of immediate ancestor clusters, only non-owner tasks will be delayed.

The *delayed schedule time* of a non-owner task u_i in a cluster $C(v)$, denoted by $dst(u_i, v)$, is the latest time that u_i can be scheduled without delaying v. For the last non-owner task in $C(v) = \langle u_1, u_2, \ldots, u_l, v \rangle$, $dst(u_l, v) = s(v) - nmsg(v) \times o_r - \varepsilon(u_l)$ where $nmsg(v)$ is the number of messages received from immediate ancestors of v which do not belong to $C(v)$. For the other tasks $u_i \in C(v)$ with $i = l-1, \ldots, 1$, $dst(u_i, v) = dst(u_{i+1}) - nmsg(u_{i+1}) \times o_r - \varepsilon(u_i)$.

The latest message send time, $lmst_{M1}(w, u_i, v)$, of (w, u_i) under Mechanism One is now defined as a function of $dst(u_i, v)$. This provides the scope to increase both the processing window associated with $C(w)$ due to the message (w, u_i) even further, and the possibility for this copy of $C(w)$ to send other messages.

Let $\mathcal{S} = \{(w_1, u_i), \ldots, (w_j, u_i), \ldots (w_k, u_i)\}$ be the subset of messages sent to task $u_i \in C(v)$ which arrive before u_i's overheads are processed (i.e. $dst(u_i, v) - nmsg(u_i) \times o_r$). The latest message send time of messages (w_j, u_i) in $\mathcal{S}$ is $lmst_{M1}(w_j, u_i, v) = dst(u_i, v) - (o_s + L \times \omega(w_j, u_i) + nmsg(u_i) \times o_r)$. But not all the messages sent to u_i necessarily arrive before this time. Let $\mathcal{L} =$

$\langle(w_1, u_i), \ldots, (w_q, u_i), \ldots, (w_k, u_i)\rangle$ be the list of those messages in non-increasing order of their arrival time. The latest send time for each message in $\mathcal{L}$ is given by $lmst_{M1}(w_q, u_i, v) = dst(u_i, v) - (o_s + L \times \omega(w_q, u_i) + l \times o_r)$, $q = 1, \ldots k$.

Mechanism Two: Ordering the Receive Overheads. In Mechanism One, messages in $\mathcal{S}$ are delayed sufficiently only to allow them to arrive at the same time, i.e., the time at which the first of the respective receive overheads for u_i is processed. The processing windows of respective senders can be increased if these messages were to arrive at $C'(v)$ just in time for the execution of their receive overheads. This mechanism refines the results of Mechanism One, by re-ordering the messages $(w, u_i) \in \mathcal{S}$ (and thus removing restriction R4) according to the number of messages that task w needs to send to its immediate successors $\in rsc$. Delaying the receiving of w's message as much as possible, again increases $pw(w, u_i, v')$.

Defining the Reduced Set of Clusters: Once the mechanisms have been applied to increase the processing window of $C(w) \in uc$, the number of copies of cluster $C(w)$ required to send all of the messages of w to its successors $\in rsc$ has to be found. The list of messages sent by owner w to immediate successor clusters $\in rsc$, denoted by list of tuples $mlist(w) = \langle[u_i, v] \mid u_i \in C'(v) \wedge C'(v) \in rsc \wedge (w, u_i) \in E \wedge w \notin C'(v)\rangle$, can easily be calculated. For each message in the list $mlist(w)$, the *sending order* $so(w, u_i, v) = \lfloor pw(w, u_i, v)/o_s \rfloor + 1$, determines the latest position of (w, u_i) in the sequence of messages sent by a copy of cluster $C(w)$. In order to establish the number of messages that a copy of $C(w)$ can send, the tuples in $mlist(w)$ are organised in non-decreasing order of their respective $so(w, u_i, v)$.

The number of copies of $C(w)$ necessary and the messages that each copy must send are specified as follows. For each tuple $[u_i, v] \in mlist(w)$ with sending order $so(w, u_i, v) = p$, a search is made for a copy of $C(w)$ which has been assigned $p-1$ messages. If no such copy is found, a search for a copy assigned to $p-2$ messages is tried, and so on until, if necessary, a new copy of $C(w)$ is allocated. The objective is to assign the maximum number of messages to a copy of $C(w)$ without increasing the makespan. When all of the tuples in $mlist(w)$ have been visited, those copies of $C(w)$ with assigned messages (denoted as $C'(w)$) are included in rsc.

Mechanism Three: Delaying the Schedule Time of the Owners. It is possible that the send overheads of $C'(w)$ are still executed earlier than necessary. Delaying the messages will allow owner w and the non-owner tasks $\in C'(w)$ to be delayed too, thus increasing the processing windows of messages sent to $C'(w)$. Also, all sink clusters can be delayed so that they complete their execution by makespan $\mathcal{M}$.

Reducing the Schedule's Processor Count: After the cluster copy elimination process, an attempt is made to minimise the number of processors required by mapping the clusters $\in rsc$ appropriately. This phase is common in most clustering algorithms [5,14] and typically the mapping process is simple: multiple clusters can be mapped to the same processor if their execution intervals do not overlap, i.e. as long as the execution of a cluster and its send overheads do not delay the execution of another cluster.

It may be possible to reduce further the number of processors required by allowing the makespan to be increased. The mechanisms (and mapping) can be used to increase the makespan incrementally until a satisfactory number of processors is obtained, or to find the number of processors necessary for a given makespan greater than $\mathcal{M}$.

4 Results

This section summarises the results obtained from 5 experiments using the $LogP$ scheduling algorithm, named Configuration 2 (C2) in [5], and a version of C2 (RPM) in which the second stage has been modified to incorporate the mechanisms described earlier. Experiment 1 compares the reduction in the number of both clusters and processors using the same benchmark suite of DAGs [4] (which includes various sizes of in-trees, diamond DAGs and a set of randomly generated DAGs as well as irregular DAGs) and variety of $LogP$ communication parameter values used in [3]. Experiment 2 attempts to analyse the relative merits of each of the proposed mechanisms. Both this experiment and Experiment 3 focus on diamond DAGs since the schedules produced tend to require an exorbitant number of processors. Experiment 3 investigates how the reduction in the number of required clusters is affected by the granularity of the graphs and by the $LogP$ parameters. Experiments 4 and 5 compare the modified scheduling algorithm with another $LogP$ scheduling algorithm, MSA [4], proposed for the bounded processor scheduling problem. Earlier published work showed that, on the whole, while the schedules produced by MSA had poorer makespans, the number of processors required were significantly smaller compared to the schedules of C2 [2]. Experiment 4 identifies the differences in processor requirements for MSA and the modified algorithm. Experiment 5 compares the processor requirements of schedules produced by these two algorithms when the makespans are fixed by MSA, i.e. RPM increases the makespan in an attempt to reduce further the number of processors required.

Experiment 1: Compares the results of 77 schedules for a variety of graphs and $LogP$ conditions. The average reduction in the number of clusters and processors achieved without increasing the makespan was 60.2% and 63% respectively. The average degree of cluster replication ($adcr = |rsc|/|uc|$), which is related to the efficiency of the schedule, improved from 7 to 3.1. In 58 of the 77 cases (75.3%), the number of clusters required ($|rsc|$) was less than that of C2 ($|nc|$) and equal in the remaining 19. In 12 of these 19 cases, the schedules produced contained no replicated clusters ($|rsc| = |uc|$) so no gains were possible. However, a reduction in the number of processors (np) was obtained in 65 (84.4%) cases. This shows that in 7 (9.1%) cases where the mechanisms appeared unsuccessful, the rescheduling of the clusters improved the processor mapping.

Experiment 2: In order to compare the merits of the different mechanisms, four second stage algorithms were implemented: Alg1 delays the messages so that they arrive in time for the processing of their receive overhead (see Example 1 in Section 3); Alg2 is Alg1 together with Mechanism One; Alg3 is Alg2 with Mechanism Two; and Alg4 implements all three mechanisms.

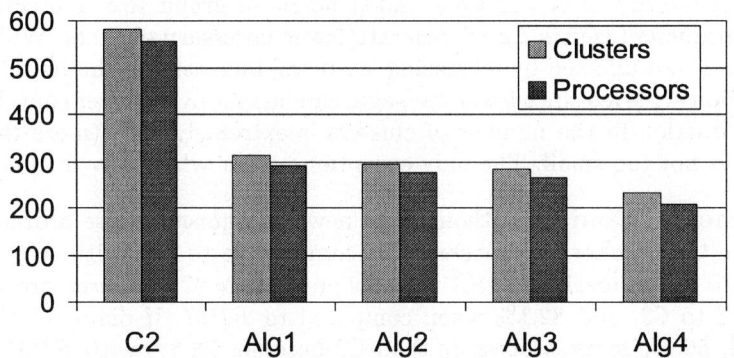

Fig. 2. The average number of clusters and processors required

Alg1: This technique is particularly useful when the communication costs are low, since the schedules contain many copies of small clusters and thus intensive communication, particularly for diamond and random graphs. As the communication costs increase (especially o_s) there is a degradation in the reductions acheived. The average reduction compared to C2 for the same 77 cases was 46.6% for rsc and 47.5% for np. The $adcr$ decreased to 4.1. In addition to the 19 cases cited for C2 in Experiment 1, Alg1 found the smallest rsc (i.e., the other mechanisms were unable to decrease this number) in a further 9 (11.7%). In 6 of these 9 cases, Alg1 eliminated all of the replicated clusters ($|rsc| = |uc|$). The smallest np was attained in 4 cases. In 52 (67.5%) of the cases, $|rc|$ and np were less than C2. These results show that the simple fact of having messages arrive just in time can provide a significant improvement in schedule efficiency.

Alg2: The results, in general, appear to show that there is little to be gained from delaying non-owner tasks within clusters. In comparison to C2, the reduction in rsc was 49.3% and 50.4% for np, up 3% from Alg1 and can be attributed mainly to the diamond DAGs. These results reflect the characteristics of the cluster design process, indicating that clusters contain few idle periods.

Alg3: The reduction in rsc and np now improved to 51.2% and 52.2%, respectively. Here, the gains were achieved principally by the random graphs. In 56 (70.1%) and 61 (79.2%) of the cases, $|rsc|$ and np were less than C2, respectively. To exploit the advantages of re-ordering message receptions, it is necessary to have clusters in which a task has various immediate ancestor clusters.

Alg4: In addition to the results presented earlier in Experiment 1, one further point re-emphasises the importance of Mechanism 3 to the mapping process. All of the mechanisms are necessary to attain the smallest rsc in only 19 (24.7%) cases, while they are necessary in 58 (75.3%) in order to find the smallest np.

Experiment 3: Diamond DAGs were used because of their regularity and high degree of cluster replication in the schedules produced by algorithms based on the design methodology. The results show, firstly, as the tasks in the graph increases so does the % reduction in the number of clusters achieved by RPM, independent of the communication parameters. As the number of tasks in G increases, so does $|nc|$ but at much faster rate due to replication. The % reduction also increases as the granularity of G increases, independent of graph size. Increases in the $LogP$ parameters causes C2 to generate fewer necessary clusters. While the % reduction is not affected by increasing latencies, increasing o_s limits the amount of reduction achieved since fewer messages can be sent by a cluster copy. However, the % reduction in the number of clusters is extremely high (more than 80%) when o_r is not too small. The only exceptions occur when $adcr$ is almost one.

Experiments 4 and 5: Although the new mechanisms cause a dramatic decrease in the number of processors in comparison to C2, with MSA [4] the results are not as marked. MSA requires on average 92.8% *fewer* processors [3] compared to C2, and 82.1% when compared to RPM. If diamond DAGs are excluded, 56.6% fewer processors than C2 becomes 24.8% with RPM. Bear in mind that this represents the fact that C2 employs, on average, almost 13.9 times as many processors as MSA. RPM uses 5.6 times as many, with the benefit of a better makespan in 95.3% of the 107 cases tested.

When RPM degrades the makespan to that found by MSA, np decreases further. MSA now only requires 33.8% (and 24.3%, when excluding diamond DAGs) fewer processors than RPM. This is equivalent to RPM using, on average, 1.5 times as many processors. MSA performs better since it does not replicate clusters but instead bundles messages sent to common processor destinations in order to minimise the number of send and receive overheads incurred.

5 Conclusions

This paper presented a series of mechanisms to be used in the second stage of a existing clustering algorithm design methodology [3] for task replication based $LogP$ scheduling heuristics. The first stage of heuristics based on this design methodology is responsible for the creation of clusters from which a (virtual) schedule can be constructed. While the makespans of these schedules are good, their implementation cost in terms of processor numbers can be extremely high [2,3,5]. The mechanisms proposed in this paper, reduce the number of processors required by schedules (generated by one of the best heuristics based on the methodology [5]), on average, by 63%. Using these same mechanisms, it is possible to further reduce the processor requirements at the expense of an increase in the makespan for the given schedule. This can be viewed as an alternative approach to the problem of scheduling on a fixed number of processors, but with the advantage of knowing the performance benefits of increasing the number of available processors.

Note that the schedules produced by $LogP$ heuristics which employ these mechanisms satisfy the $LogP$ network capacity constraint of there being at most

$\lceil L/g \rceil$ messages in transit to any processor or from any processor at any time[7]. The gains obtained by these mechanism are achieved by relaxing two of the four cluster design restrictions (R2 and R4) used by the first stage.

References

1. A. Alexandrov, M. Ionescu, K. E. Schauser, and C. Scheiman. LogGP: Incorporating long messages into the LogP model - one step closer towards a realistic model for parallel computation. *7th Annual Symposium on Parallel Algorithms and Architectures (SPAA'95)*, 1995.
2. C. Boeres, A. Nascimento, and V. E. F. Rebello. Scheduling arbitrary task graphs on LogP machines. In P. Amestoy et al., editors, *The Proceedings of the 5th International Euro-Par Conference on Parallel Processing (Euro-Par'99)*, LNCS 1685, pages 340–349, Toulouse, France, August 1999. Springer.
3. C. Boeres, A. P. Nascimento, and V. E. F. Rebello. Cluster-based task scheduling for LogP model. *International Journal of Foundations of Computer Science*, 10(4):405–424, 1999.
4. C. Boeres and V. E. F. Rebello. A versatile cost modelling approach for multicomputer task scheduling. *Parallel Computing*, 25(1):63–86, 1999.
5. C. Boeres and V. E. F. Rebello. On the design of clustering-based scheduling algorithms for realistic machine models. In *The Proceedings of the 15th International Parallel and Distributed Processing Symposium (IPDPS'01)*, San Francisco, USA, April 2001. IEEE Computer Society Press.
6. C. Boeres, V. E. F. Rebello, and D. Skillicorn. Static scheduling using task replication for LogP and BSP models. In D. Pritchard and J. Reeve, editors, *The Proc. of the 4th International Euro-Par Conference on Parallel Processing (Euro-Par'98)*, LNCS 1470, pages 337–346, Southampton, UK, September 1998. Springer.
7. D. Culler et al.. LogP: Towards a realistic model of parallel computation. In *Proceedings of the 4th ACM SIGPLAN Symposium on Principles and Practice of Parallel Programming*, San Diego, CA, USA, May 1993.
8. T. Kalinowski, I. Kort, and D. Trystram. List scheduling of general task graphs under LogP. *Parallel Computing*, 26(9):1109–1128, 2000.
9. W. Lowe and W. Zimmermann. Scheduling balanced task-graphs to LogP-machines. *Parallel Computing*, 26(9):1083–1108, 2000.
10. R. P. Martin, A. M. Vahdat, D. E. Culler, and T. E. Anderson. Effects of communication latency, overhead, and bandwidth in a cluster architecture. In *Proc. of the 24th International Symposium on Computer Architecture*, pages 85–97, June 1997.
11. M. A. Palis, J.-C Liou, and D. S. L. Wei. Task clustering and scheduling for distributed memory parallel architectures. *IEEE Transactions on Parallel and Distributed Systems*, 7(1):46–55, January 1996.
12. C. H. Papadimitriou and M. Yannakakis. Towards an architecture-independent analysis of parallel algorithms. *SIAM J. Comput.*, 19:322–328, 1990.
13. A. Tam and C. Wang. Realistic communication model for parallel computing on cluster. In *Proc. of the 1st IEEE International Workshop on Cluster Computing*, pages 92–101, Melbourne, Australia, December 1999. IEEE Computer Soc. Press.
14. T. Yang and A. Gerasoulis. DSC: Scheduling parallel tasks on an unbounded number of processors. *IEEE Transactions on Parallel and Distributed Systems*, 5(9):951–967, 1994.

Exploiting Unused Time Slots in List Scheduling Considering Communication Contention

Oliver Sinnen and Leonel Sousa

Universidade Técnica de Lisboa, IST / INESC-ID
Rua Alves Redol 9, 1000 Lisboa, Portugal
{oliver.sinnen,las}@inesc.pt

Abstract. Static scheduling is the temporal and spatial mapping of a program to the resources of a parallel system. Scheduling algorithms use the Directed Acyclic Graph (DAG) to represent the sub-tasks and the precedence-constraints of the program to be parallelised. This article proposes an extention to the classical list scheduling heuristic that allows to schedule DAGs to arbitrary processor architectures considering link contention. In this extension, communication links are treated as shared resources likewise the processors and we improve the extended algorithm by exploiting unused time slots on the resources. The algorithm is experimentally compared to the existing heuristics BSA and DLS.

1 Introduction

The scheduling of a DAG (or task graph) is in its general form an NP-hard problem [1], i.e. an optimal solution cannot be calculated in polynomial time (unless $NP = P$). Many scheduling heuristics for near optimal solutions have been proposed in the past, e.g. surveys [2,3], following different approaches. Early scheduling algorithms did not take communication into account, but due to the increasing importance of communication for parallel performance, the consideration of the communication was included in the scheduling algorithms recently proposed. Most of these algorithms assume the target system as a homogenous system with fully connected processors and contention free communication resources. Very few algorithms model the target system as an arbitrary processor network and incorporate contention in the scheduling heuristic [4,5]. In [6], however, Macey and Zomaya showed that the consideration of link contention is significant to produce an accurate and efficient schedule.

This article presents an extension to the classical list scheduling heuristic [1] for scheduling on arbitrary processor networks with the consideration of link contention. The enhancement of the heuristic is achieved by treating communication links as shared resources likewise the processors. The new algorithm is further improved by exploiting unused time slots.

2 Models and Definitions

The DAG, as a graph theoretic representation of a program, is a directed and acyclic graph, where the nodes represent computation and the edges communication. A weight $w(n_i)$ assigned to a node n_i represents its computation cost and a weight c_{ij} assigned to an edge e_{ij} represents its communication cost.

The topology of an arbitrary target system is represented as an undirected graph, where a vertex P_i represents a processor and an undirected edge L_{ij} represents a communication link between the incident processors P_i and P_j. Most scheduling algorithms, like the ones discussed here, assume a dedicated communication system.

We denote the start time of node n_i scheduled to processor P_k as $ST(n_i, P_k)$ and its finish time as $FT(n_i, P_k)$. The finish time of processor P_k is defined as $FT(P_k) = \max_i\{FT(n_i, P_k)\}$. After all nodes and edges of the DAG have been scheduled to the target system the schedule length is defined as $\max_k\{FT(P_k)\}$.

3 Extended List Scheduling

The first phase of list scheduling is the attribution of priorities to the nodes of the DAG and their ordering according to these priorities. Our Extended List Scheduling (ELS) heuristic uses the node's *bottom-level* $bl(n_i)$ as the measure for its priority . The bottom-level of a node is the longest path beginning with the node, where the length of a path is defined as the sum of the weights of its nodes and edges. The bottom-level has several properties beneficial for communication and contention aware list scheduling [7], and ordering the nodes by its bottom-levels in descending order automatically establishes an order according to the precedence-constraints of the graph [7]. Furthermore, in [8], eight priority schemes for contention aware list scheduling were experimentally compared and the bottom-level scheme performed best.

The main part of ELS iterates over the ordered node list and determines for every node the processor that allows its earliest *finish* time. Using the finish time instead of the starting time, takes the processor speed into account and allows the algorithm to be easily applied to heterogeneous target systems [8]. The node is scheduled on the chosen processor and the incoming edges of the node are scheduled on the corresponding communication links. By scheduling not only the nodes to the processors, but also scheduling the edges to the links, the algorithm achieves awareness of contention. Communication conflicts are detected as occupied links and the conflicting edge is delayed until the link is free. The route for the communication is determined by the static routing algorithm of the target architecture. Analogous to the processor, the start time and finish time of an edge on a link are denoted $ST(e_{ij}, L_{lk})$ and $FT(e_{ij}, L_{lk})$, respectively. Now, the data ready time $DRT(n_i, P_k)$ of a node n_i on processor P_k is defined as the time when the last communication from its parent nodes arrives, $DRT(n_i, P_k) = \max_j\{FT(e_{ji}, L_{lk})\}$. For a valid schedule, $ST(n_i, P_k) \geq DRT(n_i, P_k)$ must be true for all nodes.

The basic ELS algorithm determines the start and the finish time of a node on a processor at the end of the nodes already scheduled to that processor. The earliest start time of a node at the end is equal or greater to the finish time of processor P. The node's finish time is then its start time plus its computation time.

$$ST(n_i, P) = \max\{FT(P), DRT(n_i, P)\}$$
$$FT(n_i, P) = ST(n_i, P) + w(n_i)$$

For the improvement of the basic ELS algorithm (called ELS-slot), we utilise unused time slots between nodes. To schedule a node n_i between two already scheduled nodes, a time slot large enough to accommodate n_i must be found. Assume the l nodes $n_{p_1}, n_{p_2}, \ldots n_{p_l}$ are scheduled in this order on the processor P. Let k_0 be the smallest k ($1 \leq k \leq l-1$) that fulfils $w(n_i) \leq ST(n_{p_{k+1}}, P) - \max\{FT(n_{p_k}, P), DRT(n_i, P)\}$. The start and finish time of n_i are then

$$ST(n_i, P) = \max\{FT(n_{p_{k_0}}, P), DRT(n_i, P)\}$$
$$FT(n_i, P) = ST(n_i, P) + w(n_i).$$

If there is no such k_0, then the start and finish time are determined as in ELS, i.e. the node is scheduled at the end. k_0 corresponds to the node's earliest start and finish time.

The start and the finish time of an edge on a link are determined correspondingly. ELS's complexity is $O(V lg(V) + P(V + E \cdot O(Routing))$ and ELS-slot has a complexity of $O(V^2 + P \cdot E \cdot O(Routing) + P^2 E^2)$, where $O(Routing)$ is the routing complexity of the target machine.

4 Experiments and Conclusions

ELS and ELS-slot were implemented and used to schedule random graphs to different architectures. The obtained schedule lengths are compared to the ones of BSA [4] and DLS [5] (streamlined version for homogeneous processors), which are also contention aware scheduling algorithms for arbitrary processor networks. DLS's complexity is similar to ELS's and BSA's complexity is similar to that of ELS-slot. The random graphs generated had the following characteristics: graph size 50-500 nodes; average number of edges per node 1.5, 2 or 5; node weight was uniformly distributed in [0.1, 1.9], i.e. average 1; edge weight was determined in a way that the global Communication-to-Computation Ratio (CCR) was 0.1, 1 or 10. The target machine architectures are (cyclic) meshes, rings and fully connected machines with 4, 8 and 16 processors. The results shown in Fig. 1 - every point corresponds to the average of 10 graphs - are for 16 processors and graphs with 2 average edges per node. The other results are similar in nature.

For low (CCR 0.1, Fig. 1a) and medium communication (CCR 1, Fig. 1b), BSA performs worse than the other algorithms (> 300% for CCR 0.1 and > 60% for CCR 1). The difference between ELS and DLS is negligible and ELS-slot performs best for CCR 1, with an improvement of about 30 % over ELS.

For high communication (CCR 10, Fig. 1c-1e), the relevance of the target system's topology increases and BSA yields the best results for the ring topology, where links are sparse (Fig. 1e), even though with a minimal speedup (< 25%).

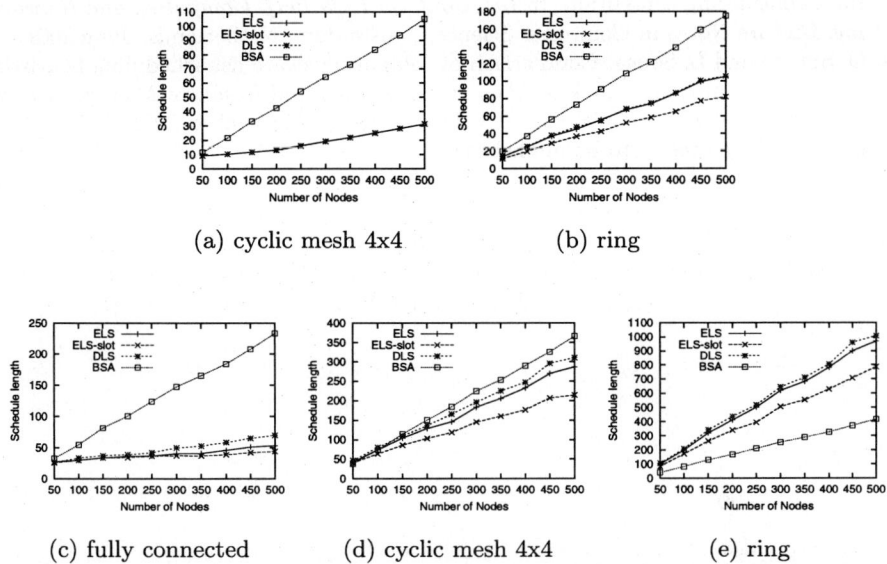

Fig. 1. Schedule results with CCR 0.1 (a), CCR 1 (b), CCR 10 (c-e)

While the other algorithms yield here schedule lengths higher than the sequential execution time, they perform better than BSA on the other architectures (Fig. 1c, 1d). ELS performs always better than DLS (about 5%-20%), due to a better priority choice and ELS-slot can improve ELS by about 20%-30%.

References

1. M. Cosnard and D. Trystram. *Parallel Algorithms and Architectures.* Int. Thomson Computer Press, London, UK, 1995.
2. A. Gerasoulis and T. Yang. A comparison of clustering heuristics for scheduling DAGs on muliprocessors. *Journal of Parallel and Distributed Computing,* 16(4):276–291, December 1992.
3. Y. Kwok and I. Ahmad. Benchmarking the task graph scheduling algorithms. In *Proc. of Int. Par. Processing Symposium/Symposium on Par. and Distributed Processing (IPPS/SPDP-98),* pages 531–537, Orlando, Florida, USA, April 1998.
4. Y. Kwok and I. Ahmad. Bubble Scheduling: A quasi dynamic algorithm for static allocation of tasks to parallel architectures. In *Proc. of Symposium on Parallel and Distributed Processing(SPDP),* pages 36–43, Dallas, Texas, USA, October 1995.
5. G. C. Sih and E. A. Lee. A compile-time scheduling heuristic for interconnection-constrained heterogeneous processor architectures. *IEEE Transactions on Parallel and Distributed Systems,* 4(2):175–186, February 1993.
6. B. S. Macey and A. Y. Zomaya. A performance evaluation of CP list scheduling heuristics for communication intensive task graphs. In *Parallel Processing Symposium, 1998. Proc. of IPPS/SPDP 1998,* pages 538 –541, 1998.

7. O. Sinnen and L. Sousa. Scheduling task graphs on arbitrary processor architectures considering contention. In *Int. Conf. on High Perf. Computing and Networking*, Lecture Notes in Computer Science, Amsterdam, Netherlands, June 2001.
8. O. Sinnen and L. Sousa. Comparison of contention aware list scheduling heuristics for cluster computing. In *Workshop on Scheduling and Resource Management for Cluster Computing (ICPP 2001)*, Valencia, Spain, September 2001. IEEE Computer Society Press. (to be published).

An Evaluation of Partitioners for Parallel SAMR Applications*

Sumir Chandra and Manish Parashar

TASSL/ECE Department, Rutgers, The State University of New Jersey
94 Brett Road, Piscataway, NJ 08854 USA
{sumir,parashar}@caip.rutgers.edu

Abstract. This paper presents an experimental evaluation of a suite of dynamic partitioning/load-balancing techniques for adaptive grid hierarchies that underlie parallel structured adaptive mesh refinement applications. Partitioners evaluated include those included in popular software libraries such as GrACE, Vampire, and ParMetis. The overall goal of the research presented in the paper is an application-centric characterization of the partitioners as a function of the number of processors, problem size, and partitioning granularity.

1 Introduction

Dynamic adaptive mesh refinement (AMR) methods for the solution of partial differential equations, that employ locally optimal approximations, can yield highly advantageous ratios for cost/accuracy when compared to methods based upon static uniform approximations. These techniques seek to improve the accuracy of the solution by dynamically refining the computational grid in regions of high local solution error. Distributed implementations of these methods lead to interesting challenges in dynamic resource allocation, data-distribution and load balancing, communications and coordination, and resource management. Critical among these is the partitioning of the adaptive grid hierarchy to balance load, optimize communications and synchronizations, minimize data migration costs, and maximize grid quality (aspect ratio) and available parallelism.

This paper presents an experimental evaluation of a suite of dynamic domain-based partitioning and load-balancing techniques for distributed adaptive grid hierarchies that underlie parallel structured adaptive mesh refinement (SAMR) methods for the solution to partial differential equations. The partitioners evaluated include existing (ISP and G-MISP) as well as new (G-MISP+SP, pBD-ISP, and SP-ISP) techniques, and constitute a selection from popular software libraries, viz. GrACE [2], Vampire [3], and ParMetis [1]. A 3-D compressible turbulence application kernel solving the Richtmyer-Meshkov instability is used as the driving application in the evaluation. The primary motivation for the

---

* Research supported by NSF via grants WU-HT-99-19 P029786F (KDI) and ACI 9984357 (CAREERS) awarded to Manish Parashar. The authors thank Johan Steensland and Ravi Samtaney for providing access to Vampire and RM3D.

Table 1. Summary of evaluated partitioning techniques

Scheme	Suite	Description
SFC (ISP)	GrACE	Decomposition of the recursive linear representation of multi-dimensional hierarchy, generated using space-filling mappings
G-MISP	Vampire	Successive refinement of one-vertex graph (of workloads) by splitting vertices with total weight greater than a threshold
G-MISP+SP	Vampire	Similar to G-MISP scheme but uses sequence partitioning to assign internal blocks to processors
pBD-ISP	Vampire	Binary dissection of domain into p partitions with orientation of the cuts determined by the Hilbert space-filling curve
SP-ISP	Vampire	Dual-level parameterized binary dissection, with SFC-ordered one dimensional list partitioned using sequence partitioning
WD	ParMetis	Global workload algorithm for unstructured grids employing multi-level k-way graph partitioning

research presented in this paper is the observation that *even for a single application, the most suitable partitioning technique depends on input parameters and its run-time state* [4]. The goal of this work is an application-centric characterization of the partitioners as a function of the number of processors, problem size, and partitioning granularity. Such a characterization will enable the run-time selection of partitioners based on the input parameters and application state.

2 Experimental Evaluation of Partitioning Techniques

This paper evaluates a suite of six domain-based partitioning techniques [4], namely, space-filling curve based partitioning (SFC), geometric multi-level inverse space-filling curve partitioning (G-MISP), geometric multi-level inverse space-filling curve partitioning with sequence partitioning (G-MISP+SP), p-way binary dissection inverse space-filling curve partitioning (pBD-ISP), "pure" sequence partitioning with inverse space-filling curves (SP-ISP), and wavefront diffusion (WD) based on global work load. Table 1 summarizes these techniques.

The partitioners described above were evaluated using a 3-D "real-world" compressible turbulence application solving the Richtmyer-Meshkov (RM) instability. The RM3D application is part of the virtual test facility developed at the ASCI/ASAP center at the California Institute of Technology[1]. The Richtmyer-Meshkov instability is a fingering instability which occurs at a material interface accelerated by a shock wave. The experiments were performed on the NPACI IBM SP2, *Blue Horizon*, at the San Diego Supercomputing Center. Blue Horizon is a teraflop-scale Power3 based clustered SMP system from IBM with 1152 processors and 512 GB of main memory and AIX operating system.

The experiments used a base (coarse) grid of 128x32x32 with 3 levels of factor 2 space-time refinements with dynamic regridding and redistribution at regular

---
[1] http://www.cacr.caltech.edu/ASAP.

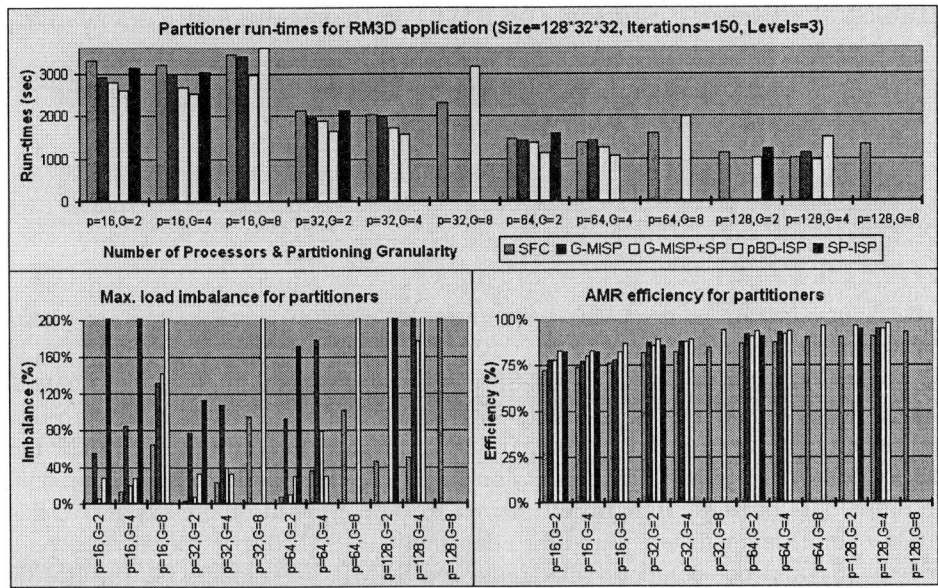

Fig. 1. Performance of partitioning techniques for RM3D application

intervals. The application ran for 150 coarse level time-steps in each case. The experiments consisted of varying the partitioner used, the number of processors (16 - 128), and the partitioning granularity (2x2x2 - 8x8x8). The metrics used for evaluation include the total run-time, maximum load imbalance, and the corresponding AMR efficiency. AMR efficiency is the measure of effectiveness of AMR and affects partitioning and load balancing requirements. High AMR efficiency leads to finer granularity refinements. The experimental results for the three metrics are summarized in Fig. 1 and tabulated for 16 processors with granularity 2 in Table 2. Note that the absence of a bar for a partitioner in the graph indicates that the partitioner was not suitable for that combination.

The RM3D application required rapid refinement and efficient redistribution due to the shock wave introduced. The pBD-ISP, G-MISP+SP, and SFC partitioning schemes are best suited to the RM3D application as they are high-speed partitioners that attempt to distribute the workload as evenly as possible while maintaining good communication patterns. The pBD-ISP scheme is the fastest partitioner but generates average load balance which worsens with higher granularity. G-MISP+SP and SFC techniques yield excellent load balance but are relatively slower. The G-MISP scheme favors speed over load balance and has an average overall performance. The SP-ISP technique fares poorly due to partitioning overheads and high computational costs, resulting in higher partitioning time and poor load balance. All evaluated partitioning techniques scale reasonably well. The optimal partitioning granularity for an application may require a trade-off between the execution speed and the load imbalance. In the case of

Table 2. Partitioner performance for RM3D on 16 processors with granularity 2

Partitioner	Run-time(s)	Max. Load Imbalance(%)	AMR Efficiency(%)
SFC	3315.22	1.629	72.388
G-MISP	2931.08	55.431	77.745
G-MISP+SP	2805.54	5.834	77.851
pBD-ISP	2601.05	28.498	83.169
SP-ISP	3136.32	204.548	82.207

RM3D application, a granularity of 4 gives the lowest execution time and yields acceptable load imbalance.

SP-ISP, G-MISP and G-MISP+SP partitioning schemes fail for experiments on large number of processors using a higher granularity. SP-ISP scheme fails due to the large number of blocks created. G-MISP and its variant G-MISP+SP fail due to the effects of high granularity on the underlying partitioning mechanism. Finally, our ParMetis integration proved to be computationally expensive due to the additional effort required for adapting it to SAMR grid hierarchies. As a result, it could not compete with dedicated SAMR partitioners for the RM3D application and is not part of the results.

3 Conclusions

This paper presented an application-centric experimental evaluation of a suite of dynamic domain-based partitioning and load-balancing techniques for the SAMR RM3D compressible turbulence application. Each of the partitioners evaluated represented a unique compromise between partitioning speed and partitioning/load-balancing quality. The experiments focussed on the effect of the choice of partitioner and partitioning granularity on execution time. Metric included the overall run-time, load-balance achieved, and AMR efficiency. It was observed that partitioners with high partitioning speed and average-to-good load balance performed better for the RM3D application. The pBD-ISP and G-MISP+SP schemes generated acceptable load balance with high partitioning speed and high AMR efficiency.

References

1. Karypis, G., Schloegel, K., Kumar, V.: *ParMetis - Parallel Graph Partitioning and Sparse Matrix Ordering Library, ver. 2.0.* University of Minnesota, 1998.
2. Parashar, M., et al: *A Common Data Management Infrastructure for Adaptive Algorithms for PDE Solutions.* Technical Paper at Supercomputing, 1997.
3. Steensland, J.: *http://www.caip.rutgers.edu/~johans/vampire.* Vampire, 2000.
4. Steensland, J., Chandra, S., Thuné, M., Parashar, M.: *Characterization of Domain-Based Partitioners for Parallel SAMR Applications.* IASTED International Conference on Parallel and Distributed Computing and Systems, 2000.

Load Balancing on Networks with Dynamically Changing Topology

Jacques M. Bahi[1] and Jaafar Gaber[2]

[1] LIFC, Université de Franche-Comté, France
[2] Université de Technologie de Belfort-Montbéliard, France

Abstract. In this paper, we present a time dependent diffusion model for load balancing on synchronous networks with dynamically changing topology. This situation can arise for example from link failures. Our model is general and include Cybenko's diffusion models for fixed topology networks. We will show that under some assumptions, the time dependent load balancing algorithm converges and balances the total work load among the processors in the distributed network.

1 Introduction

One of the most fundamental problems in distributed processing is to balance the work that must be performed among all the processors in a distributed network or a parallel machine. The distributed load balancing problem is the following. The processor network is modeled by an undirected connected graph $G = (V, E)$ in which each node contains a number w_i of current work load. The load balancing problem was studied by several authors from different perspectives [2,9,4,3,7]. The goal of a load balancing algorithm is to determine how to move amounts of work load across edges so that finally, the weight on each node is equal. The schedules of the load balancing problem are iterative in nature and their behavior can be characterized by iterative methods derived from linear system theory. Local iterative load balancing algorithms were first proposed by Cybenko in [2]. These algorithms iteratively balance the load of a node with its neighbors until the whole network is globally balanced. The are mainly two iterative load balancing algorithms : diffusion algorithms [2,3] and their variant the dimension exchange algorithms [2,9]. Diffusion algorithms assume that a processor exchanges load between neighbor processors simultaneously, whereas dimension exchange algorithms assume that a processor exchanges load with a neighbor processor in each dimension at each time step.

These algorithms, however, have been derived for use on synchronous networks with fixed topology. In a synchronous network, the nodes share a global clock. In each time step, each edge can transmit a message in each direction. In a network with dynamically changing topology (i.e., a dynamic synchronous network), the set of edges in the network may vary at each time step. In any time step, a *live* edge is one that can transmit one message in each direction [5,8]. We assume that at each time step, each node in a synchronous dynamic network knows which of its edges are live. A dynamic network can be viewed here as a network in which some edges fail during the execution of an algorithm. The fault tolerance properties of many specific network have been analyzed [1,8]. Typically the goal is to show that a network with faults can emulate a fault-free network with little slowdown [5]. The locations of the faults are assumed to be known or at least locally detectable. In the following, we do not make any assumption on either the pattern of link failures or the topology of the network.

In this paper, we extend the diffusive local load balancing scheme to be used on synchronous networks with dynamically changing topology. We show that under some suitable assumptions, a load balancing algorithm converges to the uniform distribution. We address in this paper the static load balancing problem. The uniform distribution allocates the same amount of work to every processor while keeping the total amount of work in the network constant.

This paper is organized as follows. In section 2 we review the diffusion load balancing approach developed by G.Cybenko for synchronous networks with a fixed topology. In section 3, we describe a time dependent load balancing approach that can be used in synchronous networks with dynamically changing topology. This approach is a generalization of Cybenko's diffusion algorithms as it will be showed in section 4. We analyze then the proposed approach in section 4 and we give some examples in section 5. We end this paper by some concluding remarks and by a discussion of future work. Notations and mathematical background needed for this paper are given in the appendix.

2 Fixed Topologies Diffusion Load Balancing Schemes

2.1 Standard Diffusion Approach

In the rest of the paper, M^k denotes the kth power of the matrix M, and u^T denotes the transpose vector of $u \in \mathbb{N}$.

Assume that we have a distributed system represented by a graph $G = (V, E)$ with n nodes, V is the set of nodes (i.e., processors) and E is the set of edges (communication links). Let $w_i(t) \geq 0$ be the load handled by processor i at time t, where t is a nonnegative integer time variable. The diffusion load balancing model defined by G. Cybenko is the following

$$w_i(t+1) = w_i(t) + \sum_{j \neq i} \alpha_{ij}(w_j(t) - w_i(t)), \tag{1}$$

where the α_{ij} are *constants* and satisfy the following conditions:

- $\alpha_{ij} \geq 0$ for all i, j,
- if $(i,j) \notin E$, then $\alpha_{ij} = \alpha_{ji} = 0$,
- $1 - \sum_{j=1}^{n} \alpha_{ij} \geq 0$.

we rewrite (1) as a simple vector equation $w(t+1) = Mw(t)$, where $w(t) = (w_1(t), ..., w_n(t))^T$ denotes the work distribution and $M = (m_{ij})$ is a *constant matrix* given by

$$m_{ij} = \begin{cases} \alpha_{ij} \text{ if } i \neq j \\ 1 - \sum_{j=1}^{n} \alpha_{ij} \text{ if } i = j. \end{cases}$$

G. Cybenko showed the following result

Theorem 1 (Cybenko, [2]). *If the network is connected and the associated constant diffusion matrix M is symmetric, doubly stochastic and not bipartite, then the iterative process (1) converges to the uniform distribution that balance the total load among the nodes.*

2.2 Dimension Exchange Approach

Given a d-dimensional network, the dimension exchange load balancing model presented by G. Cybenko [2] and extended in [4,7] is the following

$$w(t+d) = Mw(t), \quad (2)$$

where $M = M_{d-1} \times ... \times M_0$.
If $w(t)$ is the load distribution at time t, then $Mw(t)$ is the new distribution of loads at time $t + d$ resulting from applying successively the balance operations for the consecutive dimensions $0, 1, ..., d-1$ in consecutive steps. In other words, a single iteration of the diffusion approach is serialized in one sweep through all dimensions of the network.
$M_\ell = (m_\ell)_{ij}$ is a *constant matrix* across the ℓth dimension, $0 \leq \ell < d$, given by

$$(m_\ell)_{ij} = \begin{cases} \alpha_{ij} \text{ if } j \text{ is the neighbor of } i \text{ across the } d\text{th dimension} \\ 1 - \sum_{j=1}^{n} \alpha_{ij} \text{ if } i = j \\ 0 \text{ otherwise.} \end{cases}$$

G. Cybenko has presented this model for a d-dimensional hypercube in [2]. Note that the comparison between diffusion algorithm and the dimension exchange algorithm is similar to the differences between Jacobi and Gauss-Seidel methods for iterative matrix methods.

It is worth noting that the matrices used by both the two schemes are constant matrices. In the standard diffusion scheme, all the entries of the matrix M are constants and remain unchanged during the load balancing process. In the dimension exchange scheme, the matrix M consists of d matrices, when we have a d-dimensional network, all their entries are constants. During the iterative load balancing process, we cycle through the dimension sequence of the network in consecutive steps [2]. In the rest of the paper, we refer to the two Cybenko's load balancing schemes as diffusion load balancing scheme

Our approach in this paper is quite different from the Cybenko's approach. We assume that the network can have a dynamically changing topology (a dynamic network): communication links may go up and down dynamically. Cybenko's diffusion scheme fails in a dynamic network because it assumes that the topology is fixed: in each step of the iterative process, load can be moved across fixed set of communication links. This is why it proceeds with constant matrices.

In what follows, we will describe a time dependent diffusion approach that can be used on a synchronous network with dynamically changing topology.

3 Diffusion Load Balancing on Dynamically Changing Topology

3.1 Description

In this paper, we propose the following load balancing model defined by

$$w_i(t+1) = w_i(t) + \sum_{j \neq i}(\alpha_t)_{ij}(w_j(t) - w_i(t)), \qquad (3)$$

where the $(\alpha_t)_{ij}$ are *time dependent coefficients*.
we rewrite (3) as a simple vector equation

$$w(t+1) = M_t w(t), \qquad (4)$$

where $w(t)$ denotes the work distribution and $M_t = (m_t)_{ij}$ is given by

$$(m_t)_{ij} = \begin{cases} (\alpha_t)_{ij} & \text{if } i \neq j \\ 1 - \sum_{j=1}^{n}(\alpha_t)_{ij} & \text{if } i = j. \end{cases}$$

The load assignment given by (3) is similar to Cybenko diffusion scheme [2] given by (1) except that the term $(\alpha_t)_{ij}$, as suggested by its notation, is not a constant but it depends on the time t.
The main result of this paper is the following.

Result *If there exist integers $\ell(k)$, where k is a nonnegative integer time variable such that*
i) at times, $\ell(k)$ successive diffusion matrices appearing in (4) are all equal to a fixed matrix T,
ii) for a sufficiently large time k, $T^{\ell(k)}$ is a constant positive matrix,
then the time depend load balancing scheme (3) converges to a vector distribution of loads among the nodes of the form $w^* = (\bar{w}, ..., \bar{w})^T$.
In addition, if the diffusion matrices are doubly stochastics then $\bar{w} = \frac{\sum_{i=1}^{n} w(0)}{n}$ where $w(0)$ is the initial load distribution.

3.2 Convergence Analysis

The mathematical formulation of the above result is the following

Theorem 2. *Suppose that there exists a matrix T, a sequence $\{p_k\}_{k \in \mathbb{N}}$ and integers $\ell(k)$ such that*

i) $M_{p_k} = M_{p_k+1} = \ldots = M_{p_k+\ell(k)} = T$,
ii) $\lim_{k \to \infty} T^{\ell(k)} = Q$,

where Q is a positive matrix
then the time dependent load balancing scheme (3) converges to a vector $w^* = k(1,1,\ldots,1)^T$.
in addition, if the matrices M_t are doubly stochastic then w^* is the uniform distribution of loads among the nodes, i.e.

$$\bar{w} = \frac{\sum_{i=1}^{n} w_i^0}{n}$$

where $w^0 = (w_1^0, \ldots, w_n^0)^T$ is the initial load distribution vector.

Proof. For $w = (w_1, \ldots, w_n)^T$, let $|w|_\infty$ denotes the maximum norm of w, $|w|_\infty = \max_{1 \le i \le n} |w_i|$.

Since M_{p_k} is a stochastic matrix, $|M_{p_k}| = 1$. We prove that the sequence $\{w(p_k)\}_{k \in \mathbb{N}}$ is bounded and thus it contains a convergent subsequence (Borel-Lebesgue theorem). Let $\{w(p_{k_m})\}_{m \in \mathbb{N}}$ denotes this subsequence,

$$\lim_{m \to \infty} w(p_{k_m}) = w^*. \tag{5}$$

We have $|w(t+1)|_\infty = |M_t w(t)|_\infty \le |M_t|_\infty |w(t)|_\infty \le |w(t)|_\infty \ldots \le |w(0)|_\infty$, so the sequence $\{|w(t)|_\infty\}_{t \in \mathbb{N}}$ is a decreasing bounded sequence thus it is convergent and $\lim_{t \to \infty} |w(t)|_\infty = \lim_{m \to \infty} |w(p_{k_m})|_\infty = |w^*|_\infty$.
Let's denote by $M_{p_k, \ell(k)} = M_{p_k+\ell(k)} \ldots M_{p_k+1} M_{p_k}$. We have

$$M_{p_{k_m}, \ell(k_m)} w(p_{k_m}) = M_{p_{k_m}+\ell(k_m)} \ldots M_{p_{k_m}+1} M_{p_{k_m}} w(p_{k_m})$$
$$= M_{p_{k_m}+\ell(k_m)} \ldots M_{p_{k_m}+1} w(p_{k_m}+1)$$
$$\vdots$$
$$= w(p_{k_m} + \ell(k_m) + 1).$$

Note that by hypothesis *i)* of theorem 2, $M_{p_{k_m}, \ell(k_m)} = T^{\ell(k_m)+1}$. We can check that

$$\lim_{m \to \infty} |Qw^* - w(p_{k_m} + \ell(k_m) + 1)|_\infty \le \lim_{m \to \infty} |(Q - T^{\ell(k_m)+1})w^*|_\infty + |(w^* - w(p_{k_m}))|_\infty.$$

By hypothesis *ii)* of theorem 2 and (5) we obtain

$$\lim_{m \to \infty} |Qw^* - w(p_{k_m} + \ell(k_m) + 1)|_\infty = 0.$$

Thus
$$|Qw^*|_\infty = \lim_{m \to \infty} |w(p_{k_m} + \ell(k_m) + 1)|_\infty = |w^*|_\infty. \tag{6}$$

We prove now that the sequence $\{w(t)\}_{t \in \mathbb{N}}$ converges to w^*. We have

$$M_t w^* = w^*,$$

and
$$\lim_{t\to\infty} |w(t+1) - w^*|_\infty = \lim_{m\to\infty} |w(p_{k_m}) - w^*|_\infty = 0.$$
Since for all $t \in \mathbb{N}$, M_t is doubly stochastic then

$$\sum_{i=1}^n w_i(1) = \sum_{i=1}^n \sum_{j=1}^n (m_0)_{ij} w_j(0) = \sum_{j=1}^n w_j(0) \underbrace{\sum_{i=1}^n (m_0)_{ij}}_{1} = \sum_{j=1}^n w_j(0),$$

by induction we obtain that for all $t \in \mathbb{N}$, $\sum_{i=1}^n w_i(t) = \sum_{j=1}^n w_j(0)$, and $\sum_{i=1}^n w_i^* = \sum_{i=1}^n w_i(0)$.
Since $w_i^* = k$, we have $\sum_{i=1}^n w_i(0) = \sum_{i=1}^n w_i^*(t) = nk$ which yields

$$\bar{w} = \frac{\sum_{i=1}^n w_i(0)}{n},$$

as desired.

3.3 Specific Schemes Derived from Theorem 2

First if we suppose that we have a fixed topology network, then we obtain the classical Cybenko algorithm stated in theorem 1.

Corollary 1. *Theorem 1 is a particular result of theorem 2.*

Proof. In theorem 1 it is assumed that the network is connected which means that M is an irreducible matrix. It is also assumed that M is symmetric so it is doubly stochastic. The not bipartite assumption implies that -1 is not an eigenvalue of M, hence $\lim_{k\to\infty} M^k$ exists.
A classical result in [6], (page 28, theorem 1.7) states that
-1 is not an eigenvalue of M and M is irreducible $\iff \exists L \in \mathbb{N}$, M^L is a positive matrix (M is a primitive matrix).
So $\lim_{k\to\infty} M^k = Q$ which is positive and doubly stochastic.
If we choose in theorem 2, $\{p_k\}_{k\in\mathbb{N}} = \{k\}_{k\in\mathbb{N}}$ and $\ell(k) = k$ for all $k \in \mathbb{N}$, and $T = M$ a doubly stochastic matrix then for all $t \in \mathbb{N}$, $M_t = T = M$ is obtained by assumption i) and $\lim_{k\to\infty} M^k = Q$ is obtained by assumption ii); theorem 1 becomes a particular case of theorem 2.

Corollary 2. *If for all $t \in \mathbb{N}$, M_t is a doubly stochastic matrix and if there exist a matrix T such that*

$$\lim_{k\to\infty} T^k = Q$$

where Q is a positive doubly stochastic matrix and if there exist an increasing subsequence $\{\ell(k)\}_{k\in\mathbb{N}}$ such that

$$M_{p_k} = M_{p_k+1} = ... = M_{p_k+\ell(k)} = T$$

then the time dependent load balancing scheme (3) converges to a vector $w^* = \frac{\sum_{i=1}^n w_i^0}{n}(1,1,...,1)^T$.

Proof. Since $\ell(k)$ is an increasing sequence, we have $\lim_{k\to+\infty} \ell(k) = +\infty$, so $\lim_{k\to+\infty} T^{\ell(k)} = \lim_{k\to\infty} T^k = Q$ which is a positive doubly stochastic matrix. This corollary corresponds to the situation below

$$\underrightarrow{M_0 * ... * T * * ... * * TTT * * ... * * TTTTT * * ... * * TTTTTTT * ....}_{\text{time axis}}$$

Example

Consider the behavior of the load balancing algorithm on a d-dimensional hypercube with $d = 2$, when matrix T is

$$T = \begin{bmatrix} 0 & 1/3 & 0 & 2/3 \\ 1/3 & 0 & 2/3 & 0 \\ 2/3 & 0 & 1/3 & 0 \\ 0 & 2/3 & 0 & 1/3 \end{bmatrix}$$

if a live edge that connect two nodes i and j fails during the course of the computation then its correspondent entry $(m_t)_{ij}$ in M_t becomes equal to 0. If there are no faults then the we obtain the matrix T. We remark that for large enough k ($k \geq 18$), $T^k = Q$, where Q is a positive matrix all its entries are equal to $1/4$. By Corollary 2, we know that if $\lim_{k\to\infty} T^k = Q$ and if we encounter the matrix T successively in an increasing consecutive steps then the time dependent load balancing balances the total work distribution among the processors regardless of possibly faults occurring in the network.

Another particular case corresponds to the following situation

Corollary 3. *If there exists a subsequence $\{p_k\}_{k\in\mathbb{N}}$ such that*

$$M_{p_k} = Q$$

where Q is the matrix wherein all its entries are equal to $1/n$, then the time dependent load balancing scheme (3) converges to $w^* = \frac{\sum_{i=1}^n w_i^0}{n}(1, 1, ..., 1)^T$.

Proof. This is a particular situation of theorem 2 where we choose $\ell(k) = 1$.

$$\underrightarrow{M_0 * ... * Q * * ...}_{\text{time axis}}$$

Remark 1. As soon as we meet a positive doubly stochastic matrix the distribution load of work is uniform.

Corollary 4. *If there exists an integer L and a matrix T such that $T^L = Q$, where Q is a doubly stochastic matrix and if there exists a subsequence $\{p_k\}_{k\in\mathbb{N}}$ such that*

$$M_{p_k} = M_{p_k+1} = ... = M_{p_k+L} = T$$

then the time depend load balancing scheme (3) converges to the vector $w^* = \frac{\sum_{i=1}^n w_i^0}{n}(1, 1, ..., 1)^T$.

Proof. This is a particular situation of theorem 2 where we choose $\ell(k) = L$.

The above corollary corresponds to the following situation

$$\underrightarrow{M_0 * ... * \overbrace{TT..TT}^{L \text{ times}} * * ...}_{\text{time axis}}$$

4 Conclusion

A new model of time dependent local load balancing is proposed in this paper. This model can be used on synchronous networks with fixed topology and synchronous networks with dynamically changing topology. This is useful when the topology might change owing to failures in communication links. This is well-suited for large problems that need to share computations among distant processors of a NOW or COW(Network or Cluster of Workstations) as well as large networks. It is worth pointing out that our approach makes no assumptions on either the topology of the network or the pattern of possibly link failures. It is shown that under some assumptions, a time dependent load balancing algorithm converges and balances the total work load among the processors in the distributed network. Our next further investigation concerns the study of local load balancing algorithms on asynchronous networks.

References

1. W. Aiello, T. Leighton: Coding theory, hypercube embeddings, and fault tolerance. 3rd Annual ACM Symposium on Parallel Algorithms and Architectures (1991) July.
2. G. Cybenko: Dynamic load balancing for distributed memory architecture. Journal of Parallel and Distributed Computing, **7**, (1989), 279-301.
3. J. E. Boillat: Load balancing and poisson equation in a graph. Concurrency-Practice and Experiencen, **2**, (1990), 289-313.
4. S. H. Hosseini, B. Litow, M. Malkawi, J. McPherson, K. Vairavan: Analysis of a graph coloring based distributed load balancing algorithm. Journal of Parallel and Distributed Computing, **10**, (1990), 160-166.
5. W. Aiello , B. Awerbush, B. Maggs, S. Rao: Approximate load balancing on dynamic and asynchronous networks. Proc. of the 25th Annual ACM Symposium on on the Theory of Computing STOC (1993) May, 632-641.
6. A. Berman, R. J. Plemmons: Nonnegative matrices in the Mathematical sciences. Academic Press, New York (1979) reprinted by SIAM, Philadelphia, 1994.
7. B. Litow, S. H. Hosseini, K. Vairavan and G. S. Wolffe: Performance characteristics of a load balancing algorithm. Journal of Parallel and Distributed Computing, **31**, (1995), 159-165.
8. F. T. Leighton, B. M. Maggs, R. K. Sitaraman: On the fault tolerance of some popular bounded-degree networks. SIAM Journal on computing (1998) October, 1303-1333.
9. R. Diekmanand, A. Frommer, B. Monien: Efficient schemes for nearest neighbor load balancing. Parallel Computing, **25**, (1999), 289-313.
10. M.-J. Bahi: Parallel chaotic algorithms for singular linear systems. Parallel algorithms and Applications, **14**, (1999), 19-35.
11. M.-J. Bahi: Asynchronous iterative algorithms fo nonexpansive linear systems. Journal of Parallel and Distributed Computing, **60**, (2000), 92-112.

A Fuzzy Load Balancing Service for Network Computing Based on Jini[†]

Lap-Sun Cheung and Yu-Kwong Kwok

Department of Electrical and Electronic Engineering
The University of Hong Kong, Pokfulam Road, Hong Kong
Email: {lscheung, ykwok}@eee.hku.hk

Abstract. Distributed object computing systems are widely envisioned to be the desired distributed software development paradigm due to the higher modularity and the capability of handling machine and operating system heterogeneity. As the system scales up (e.g., with larger number of server and client objects, and more machines), a judicious load balancing system is required to efficiently distributed the workload (e.g., the queries, messages/objects passing) among the different servers in the system. However, in existing distributed object middleware systems, such a load balancing facility is lacking. In this paper, we describe the design and implementation of a dynamic fuzzy-decision based load balancing system incorporated in a distributed object computing environment. The proposed approach works by using a fuzzy logic controller which informs a client object to use the most appropriate service such that load balancing among servers is achieved. We have chosen Jini to build our experimental middleware platform, on which our proposed approach as well as other approaches are implemented and compared. Extensive experiments are conducted to investigate the effectiveness of our fuzzy-decision based approach, which is found to be consistently better than other approaches.
Keywords: distributed object computing, load balancing, fuzzy decision, Java, Jini, remote method invocation, middleware.

1 Introduction

With the great advancement of hardware technologies, powerful distributed computing systems are becoming ubiquitous. Indeed, with commodity hardware components, a high performance network of PCs can be set up to execute applications developed using new software structuring paradigms, such as object based systems and object brokerage protocols, which have also advanced tremendously parallel to the development of hardware technologies. Such new distributed software development paradigms, while have the advantages of modularity and capable of handling platform heterogeneity, were conceived as impractical in mere five to ten years ago because many complex operations such as object serialization and data marshalling, were too time consuming to be efficiently run on the hardware platforms. Currently, many commercial software projects are using distributed object based approaches such as CORBA (common object request broker architecture), DCOM, and Java RMI (remote method invocation). Using a distributed object based approach, an application is constructed as a group of interacting objects. These objects are distributed over multiple machines which interact with each other through well predefined protocols (e.g., RMI in Java). Usually, the interactions are queries or remote services invocation.

It is common that in such a distributed object computing system, there are multiple objects (possibly on heterogeneous platforms) that provide the same service. This is done to achieve a higher availability and scalability. Even the lookup service object may have several instances in the network. Under light load conditions (i.e., few number of remote service invocations or

---

[†] This research was jointly supported by the Hong Kong Research Grants Council under contract numbers HKU 7124/99E and HKU 7024/00E), and by a HKU URC research grant under contract number 10203413.

object passing), the system can perform reasonably well. However, as the system scale up to a moderate size (e.g., 10 machines), the number of requests generated in the system can be of a very large volume and be very bursty. As a result, some machines might be overloaded while other machines are idle or lightly loaded. In order to improve the performance, specifically the client request response time of a distributed application, load balancing techniques can be introduced to distribute workload in a judicious manner among various machines [14].

We focus on the middleware based approach to perform load balancing in a distributed object network. The major requirements of a middleware based load balancing service in a object computing system are:

- *Client transparency*: Client programs need not be modified in order to use load balancing service. Client should not be aware of the changes due to incorporating of a new load balancing algorithm in the load balancing service.
- *Avoid changing middleware layer*: Middleware layer should not be modified. Once the middleware layer has been modified, it will become proprietary and incompatible with other existing applications developed using the original middleware.
- *Server transparency*: Like client transparency, server applications need not be changed so as to take the advantage of load balancing service.
- *Scalability and fault-tolerance*: To avoid a single point of failure, several load balancers can coexist in a federation. Load balancers can be configured to work cooperatively to form a single logical load balancing service.
- *Integrating new load balancing algorithms*: The load balancing service should be designed in such a way that different load balancing algorithms can be easily integrated without extensive modification of the source code of the load balancing service, i.e., modular design pattern should be employed to develop the load balancing service.
- *Minimal overhead*: Network overhead caused by load balancing service should be minimized. A load balancing service should be designed such that unnecessary message/ object exchanges between the load balancing service with other network components should be avoided; otherwise, the overall system performance cannot be guaranteed.

Existing load balancing algorithms used in distributed object computing systems are usually based on simple techniques such as round-robin or random, which may not give optimized performance. Thus, in our study we propose, implement, and evaluate a new approach for load balancing in a distributed object system. We incorporate our load balancing scheme in a dynamic network service system called Jini [7]. Our proposed load balancing algorithm employs fuzzy-decision control [8]. An effective load balancing scheme requires the knowledge of the global system state (e.g., the workload distribution). However, in a distributed computing system, the global state is swiftly and dynamically changing and it is very difficult to accurately model the system analytically [4], [6]. Thus, in order to tackle the load balancing problem in such an environment where state uncertainty is unavoidable, we employ a fuzzy-decision approach to model those state variables that cause uncertainty in global states. Our approach is novel in that it is seamlessly incorporated into the Jini middleware. Our fuzzy-decision control is also effective and robust, as evident in the experimental results in a real Jini network, due to the concise fuzzy rules set. There have been some recent attempts in using fuzzy-based approaches for load balancing [2], [3], [5], [13], but those approaches are either too restrictive or not suitable for a middleware based environment considered in our study.

This paper is organized as follows. In the next section, we describe our proposed fuzzy-decision based approach. Section 3 contains the experimental results we obtained in our Jini-based testbed built on a Pentium PCs network. The last section concludes this paper.

2 The Proposed Fuzzy-Decision Based Load Balancing Scheme

In this section, the design of the our proposed fuzzy-decision based load balancing service is described. We first describe the fuzzy logic controller, which is the core part of the fuzzy load balancing service. The dynamic interactions between the fuzzy load balancing service and other components are discussed in detailed in subsequent subsections.

To handle a complex system such as a high speed computer network where a lot of uncertain parameters exist, a model with complex and nonlinear relationships between a lot of variables have to be devised, making a conventional control theory based approach intractable. To overcome this problem, fuzzy logic control theory [8] can be applied instead of the conventional one. Fuzzy logic control attempts to capture intuition in the form of IF-THEN rules, and conclusions are drawn from these rules [8]. Based on both intuitive and expert knowledge, system parameters can be modeled as linguistic variables and their corresponding membership functions can be designed. Thus, nonlinear system with great complexity and uncertainty can be effectively controlled based on fuzzy rules without dealing with complex, uncertain, and error-prone mathematical models [8]. The architecture of the fuzzy logic controller shown in Figure 1 includes five components: Fuzzifier, Rule Base, Membership functions, Fuzzy Inference Engine, and Defuzzifier. The fuzzifier is the input interface which maps a numeric input to a fuzzy set so that it can be matched with the premises of the fuzzy rules defined in the application-specific rule base. The rule base contains a set of fuzzy if-then rules which define the actions of the controller in terms of linguistic variables and membership functions of linguistic terms. The fuzzy inference engine applies the inference mechanism to the set of rules in the fuzzy rule base to produce a fuzzy set output. This involves matching the input fuzzy set with the premises of the rules, activation of the rules to deduce the conclusion of each rule that is fired, and combination of all activated conclusions using fuzzy set union to generate fuzzy set output. The defuzzifier is an output mapping which converts fuzzy set output to a crisp output. Base on the crisp output, the fuzzy logic controller can drive the system under control.

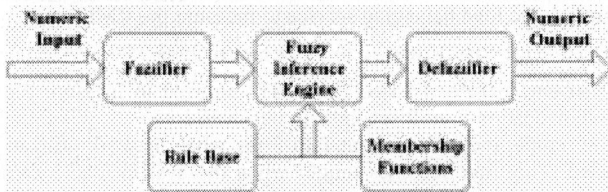

Figure 1: The architecture of the fuzzy logic controller.

The fuzzy rule base contains a set of linguistic rules. These linguistic rules are expressed using linguistic values and linguistic variables. Different linguistic values can be assigned to a linguistic variable. For instance, very_long or moderately_short can be used in the variable remote_method_Invocation_time. These linguistic values are modeled as fuzzy sets. Based on the linguistic values, their corresponding membership functions can be expressed based on application requirements.

In the Jini computing model, client objects basically have no idea on which service they should send requests to in order to achieve the best QoS (quality of service) or more specifically, the shortest response time. Generally, a request router or load balancer can be implemented to route client requests to the most appropriate service. The request router can make such decisions based on the current state of server objects. However, such state information may not be updated and reliable as client requests reach servers [11]. That is the state information cannot reflect the state of servers accurately due to network delay. The request router needs to use approximate reasoning to handle the fuzzy information so as to make the system efficient. In order to make a correct routing decision, linguistic variables, server load, remote method invocation time, and service rank, are used in the fuzzy logic algorithm and are defined as follows.

We define server load, denoted as SL, with the fuzzy set definition: {low (L), medium (M), high (H)}. Accurate estimate of load is notoriously difficult to obtain [9], [10]. We employ an indirect approach in determining SL. Instead of directly measuring each process execution time, we measure the execution time of a benchmark program which consists of several benchmark kernel loops. The benchmark program runs perpetually without stopping in the system as a background process. By observing the running times of the benchmark program, we can infer the instantaneous load level in the system. Figure 2 shows the membership graph for SL.

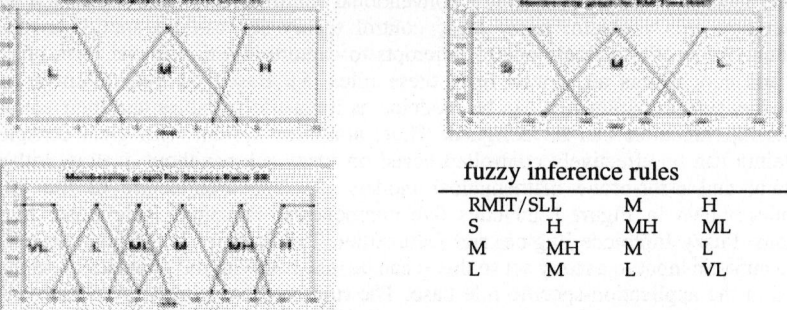

fuzzy inference rules

RMIT/SLL	M	H
S	H	MH	ML
M	MH	M	L
L	M	L	VL

Figure 2: The membership graphs for server load (SL), RMI time (RMIT), service rank (SR), and the fuzzy inference rules.

In order to measure the responsiveness of servers to client requests as well as the overhead introduced into the network by distributed processing (i.e., message/object exchanges), network utilization needs to be determined. This is done by measuring the time for Remote Method Invocation. We define a benchmark remote method which simply returns a primitive data type from server to our fuzzy logic load balancing service to measure the RMI time:

`int n; public int getNumber() {return n;}`

The method `System.currentTimeMillis()` is used to measure the time elapsed during remote method invocation in milliseconds. In our measurements, it is found that the time needed to execute the remote method is about 2 to 3 ms when network utilization is low and server is lightly loaded. The time becomes longer when the system load increases. Thus the benchmark remote method can approximately reflect the network load and the responsiveness of servers. The fuzzy set of remote method invocation time (RMIT) is defined as: {`short(S)`, `medium (M)`, `long (L)`}. Figure 2 shows the membership graph for remote method invocation time RMIT.

We use service rank (SR) to classify services into six different categories. The fuzzy set of SR is: {`very low (VL)`, `low (L)`, `medium low (ML)`, `medium (M)`, `medium high (MH)`, `high (H)`}. The membership graph of service rank is shown in Figure 2. The higher the rank that a service gets, the more appropriate that it can accept client requests. After defining the above fuzzy variables, a set of inference rules is defined as shown in Figure 2. By applying the fuzzy inference rules, a decision can be generated based on both antecedents. That is, if RMIT is short and SL is low, then SR is high. Having these fuzzy inference rules and membership graphs, the fuzzification and defuzzification processes can be carried out as follows. First, the input values of RMIT and SL are mapped to their respective membership degree values on their membership graphs. These degree values are compared and the minimum of the two is then projected onto the membership function of their consequence graph. The output graph, usually in the shape of a trapezium [8], then represents the output of one inference rule. After the output graph is generated, defuzzification of the fuzzy output into a crisp or numeric value can be carried out. We used the centroid method [8] to defuzzify the output. It has been noted that the thundering herd effect [12] may occur if the load balancer immediately forwards all requests to a server that is assigned to the highest service rank. It will lead to a sudden degradation in the overall system performance. In order to minimize such effect, the fuzzy logic load balancing service schedules client requests to servers based on a prioritized round-robin algorithm [1]. In our implementation using the Jini platform, the system consists of a lookup service, a fuzzy logic load balancing service, several server objects (providing services) and client objects. In the following, we discuss the structure and the function of each component.

Each standard Jini service consists of basic functions such as finding lookup service and registering to it. These actions can be accomplished by installing a `JoinManager`, which is a standard Jini feature, into the service. Figure 3 shows the services residing in the server host. In our implementation, there is a general service in which clients are interested. The service consists of a `JoinManager`, `Remote Service Object` and `Remote Service Admin Object`. `Remote Service Object` is a remote object which implements the remote interface that is known to client. Client can invoke methods on service object based on the remote interface. `Remote Service Admin Object` provides an interface so that the service attributes can be modified by other administrative components in the network. We also incorporate a load monitor service in the server host. Like other Jini services, load monitor service registers itself with the lookup service with the help of `JoinManager`. The remote load monitor service object is being used when the fuzzy logic load balancing service registers as a listener for the remote event generated by load monitor service. The event consists of information such as server location and server load.

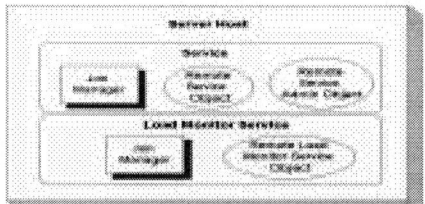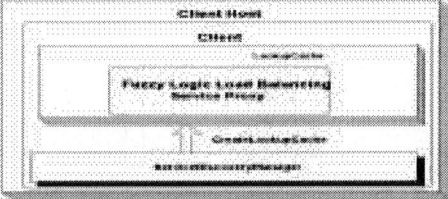

Figure 3: Structure of the server and client hosts.

Basically, a client locates lookup service and gets the services proxies available in the lookup service. Then the client, based on the service interface, generates a request to fuzzy logic load balancing service and gets the result after the service has finished the execution. The structure of the client is shown in Figure 3. The client consists of a `LookupCache` which is created by `ServiceDiscoveryManager`. Inside the cache, it stores the fuzzy logic load balancing service proxy to which client can send request. `ServiceDiscoveryManager` is a standard Jini feature of which the main use is to help clients to locate services and cache service proxies. Fuzzy logic load balancing service is the core part of the system. Its main function is to analyze information passed from the load monitor, and then make a decision to forward client request to appropriate server. The structure of the fuzzy logic load balancing service is shown in Figure 4. The fuzzy logic load balancing service performs actions such as registering itself to the lookup service and obtaining service proxies available in the lookup service. Thus, it acts as both a server and client as it consists of both the `JoinManager` and `ServiceDiscoveryManager`. Our proposed fuzzy logic load balancing algorithm is implemented in the fuzzy logic controller.

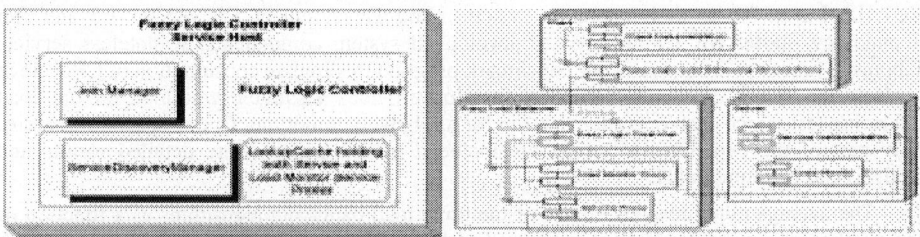

Figure 4: Structure of the fuzzy logic based load balancing service host and the overall load balancing system.

With the above components, the load balancing mechanism can be summarized as follows (illustrated in Figure 5).
1. A client obtains a fuzzy logic load balancing service proxy and sends request to the service.
2. Load monitor asynchronously sends information to fuzzy logic controller for analysis.
3. Fuzzy logic load balancing service periodically measures the remote method invocation time from the load balancer to the server.
4. When a new piece of information such as remote method invocation time or server load arrive at the fuzzy logic controller, the fuzzy inference engine will start to analyze and assign ranks to different servers.
5. After determining which server is the appropriate candidate, the fuzzy logic controller forwards the client request to that server.

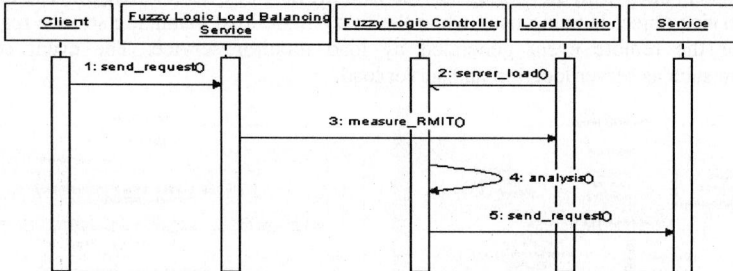

Figure 5: The fuzzy-decision based load balancing mechanism.

3 Performance Results

To evaluate our approach, we have implemented a distributed object platform using Jini and experiments were performed to analyze the client response time and throughput of different load balancing schemes. In order to simulate real client access patterns, a request sequence was generated by using a random number generator to place requests in a given time interval. The request sequences consist of request bursts and intervals of silence. For comparison, we also implemented a system with load balancing algorithm using random and round-robin load distribution by incorporating these algorithms into our fuzzy logic load balancing service. We have set up the testing environment as follows. Six machines are assigned as Jini services and two others are assigned as Jini clients. All the machines are connected by an Ethernet hub with bandwidth of 10Mbps. The configuration of six server machines are: (1) two 500MHz CPU Intel Pentium III workstations, (2) two 667MHz CPU Intel Pentium III workstations, and (3) two 450MHz CPU Intel Pentium III workstations. All machines are equipped with 128MB memory. We have another two machines, which are 600MHz CPU Intel Pentium III workstations with 128MB memory, holding lookup services and fuzzy logic load balancing service. The client machines we used are all 200MHz CPU Pentium with 64MB memory. All machines are running Red Hat Linux 7.0 as their operating systems. Java Development Kit version 1.3 and Jini Technology Starter Kit 1.1 are used to develop all system components. A stateless service, Fibonacci function, is chosen as our benchmark program to simulate consumption of CPU clock cycle in the server machines. Fibonacci function provides a suitable workload for our load balancing tests since each operation can run for a relatively long time. Due to space limitations, only part of the experimental results are included in this paper. More detailed results and analysis can be found in [1].

The average client response times of the three load balancing algorithms as a function of the number of servers are shown in Figure 6, which illustrates that the fuzzy-based approach outperforms the other algorithms consistently for different number of servers. The average client response time of random load balancing algorithm is the highest under all the cases because

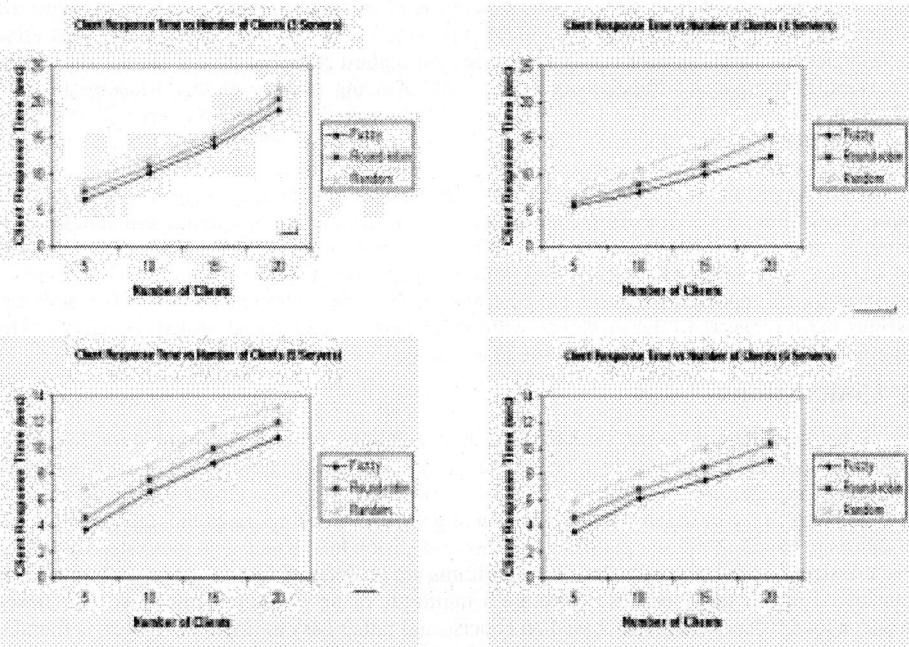

Figure 6: Average response times of the clients.

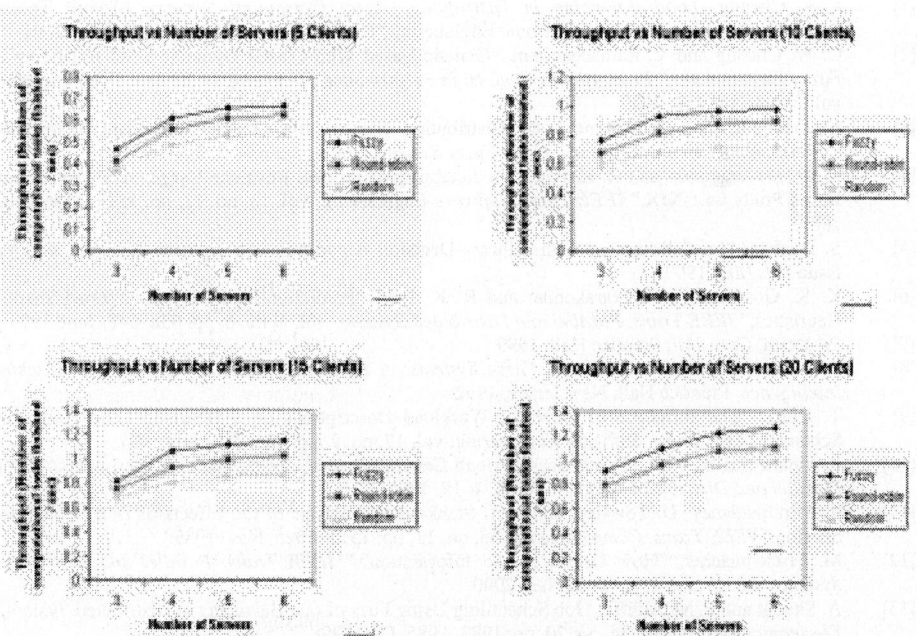

Figure 7: Average throughput of the clients.

uneven distribution of load exists in the random load balancing algorithm. A server with less computing power causes a higher response time when it is suddenly overloaded. This effect deteriorates the overall performance and causes the highest response time. Figure 7 shows how the average throughput differs between each load balancing strategy. In this measurement, 5 to 20 clients were used and each client generated 50 requests. Each client request will generate a computational task using Fibonacci function. The experiment is repeated 100 times for different number of servers. As can be seen from Figure 7, throughput increases as the number of servers increases. Again, the throughput of random load balancing algorithm is the worse among the three algorithms due to the fact than an overloaded computing machines will lengthen the completion time of a task and thus, reducing the overall throughput. For throughput-sensitive application, random load balancing algorithm is not suitable. On the other hand, the throughput of fuzzy-based approach performs the best among the three. The reason is that our approach assigns more requests to the machines with better performance based on fuzzy analysis. This significantly reduces the completion time of a task.

4 Conclusions

Load balancing is an old problem. But new solutions are required in modern distributed object computing platforms, which are increasingly being used in developing many commercial distributed applications. In this paper, we describe the design, implementation, and evaluation of our proposed fuzzy-decision based load balancing algorithm incorporated in a distributed object middleware based on the Jini platform. Our fuzzy-decision load balancer is motivated by the fact that classical and recent load balancing algorithms are inadequate for use in the target platforms considered in our study because there are a multitude of new requirements exist. Our fuzzy-decision load balancing service, based on concise and rather easy to implement rules, is found to be very effective in our extensive experimental studies using a real Jini-based testbed.

References

[1] L.-S. Cheung, *Load Balancing in Distributed Object Computing Systems*, M.Phil. Thesis, Department of Electrical and Electronic Engineering, The University of Hong Kong, May 2001.
[2] C. W. Cheong and V. Ramachandran, "Genetic Based Web Cluster Dynamic Load Balancing in Fuzzy Environment," *Proc. 4th Intl Conf. High Performance Computing in the Asia-Pacific Region*, vol. 2, pp. 714–719, 2000.
[3] E. Damiani, "An Intelligent Load Distribution System for CORBA-Compliant Distributed Environments," *Proc. IEEE Int'l. Conf. Fuzzy Systems*, vol. 1, pp. 331–336, 1999.
[4] M. V. Devarakonda and R. K. Iyer, "Predictability of Process Resource Usage: A Measurement-Based Study on UNIX," *IEEE Trans. Software Engineering*, vol. 15, no. 12, pp. 1579–1586, Dec. 1989.
[5] S. Dierkes, "Load Balancing with a Fuzzy-Decision Algorithm," *Information Sciences*, vol. 97, Issue 1-2, Mar. 1997.
[6] K. K. Goswami, M. Devarakonda, and R. K. Iyer, "Prediction-Based Dynamic Load-Sharing Heuristics," *IEEE Trans. Parallel and Distributed Systems*, vol. 4, no. 6, pp. 638–648, June 1993.
[7] W. Keith, *Core Jini*, Prentice Hall, 1999.
[8] B. Kosko, *Neural Networks and Fuzzy Systems: A Dynamical Systems Approach to Machine Intelligence*, Prentice Hall, New Jersey, 1992.
[9] T. Kunz, "The Influence of Different Workload Descriptions on a Heuristic Load Balancing Scheme," *IEEE Trans. Software Engineering*, vol. 17, no. 7, pp. 725–730, July 1991.
[10] P. Mehra and B. Wah, "Synthetic Workload Generation for Load-Balancing Experiments," *IEEE Parallel and Distributed Technology*, pp. 4–19, 1995.
[11] R. Mirchandaney, D. Towsley, and J. A. Stankovic, "Analysis of the Effects of Delays on Load Sharing," *IEEE Trans. Computers*, vol. 38, no. 11, pp. 1513–1525, Nov. 1989.
[12] M. Mitzenmacher, "How Useful Is Old Information?," *IEEE Trans. Parallel and Distributed Systems*, vol. 11, no. 1, pp. 6–20, Jan. 2000.
[13] A. Shaout and P. McAuliffe, "Job Scheduling Using Fuzzy Load Balancing in Distributed System," *Electronics Letters*, vol. 34, no. 20, pp. 1983–1985, Oct. 1998.
[14] N. G. Shivaratri, P. Krueger, and M. Singhal, "Load Distributing for Locally Distributed Systems," *Computer*, vol. 25, no. 12, pp. 33–44, Dec. 1992.

Approximation Algorithms for Scheduling Independent Malleable Tasks[*]

J. Błażewicz, M. Machowiak[1], G. Mounié, and D. Trystram[2]

[1] Instytut Informatyki Politechnika Poznanska
ul. Piotrowo 3a, 60 - 965 Poznan, Poland
[2] ID-IMAG, 51 rue Jean Kuntzman
38330 Montbonnot Saint Martin, France

Abstract. Malleable tasks consist in considering the tasks of a parallel program as large computational units that may be themselves parallelized. In this paper we investigate the problem of scheduling a set of n independent malleable tasks on a m processors system, starting from the continuous version of the problem.

1 Introduction

The malleable task model is a recent model in parallel processing introduced in order to solve efficiently some practical problems [5,6,7]. These problems have complex behavior at the finest level of execution which brings classical methods of scheduling to their limits, mainly due to the explicit management of the communications. The idea of a malleable task (MT) results in solving the problem at a different level of granularity in order to globally take into account communication costs and parallelization overheads with a simple penalty factor.

Malleable tasks can be distinguished from multiprocessor tasks, considered for example in [1], where the number of processors allotted to each task is known. The latter model has received a considerable attention in the literature. The problem of scheduling independent MT without preemption (it means that each task is computed on a constant number of processors from its start to completion) is NP-hard [2], thus, an approximation algorithm with performance guarantee has been looked for. While the problem has an approximation scheme for any fixed value m, the number of processors, [4], no general practical polynomial approximation better than 2 is known [5].

In this paper starting from the continuous version of the problem (i.e. where the tasks may require a fractional part of the resources), we propose a different approximation algorithm with a performance guarantee equal to 2. Then, some improvements are derived.

---

[*] This work was realized when J. Błażewicz was visiting ENSGI, Grenoble, in Spring 2000 and was partially supported by KBN Grant 8T11A01618

2 Problem Formulation

We consider a set of m identical processors $\mathcal{P} = \{P_1, P_2, \ldots, P_m\}$ used for executing the set $\mathcal{T} = \{T_1, T_2, \ldots, T_n\}$ of n independent, non-preemptable malleable tasks (MT). Each MT needs for its execution at least 1 processor. The number of processors allotted to a task is unknown in advance. The *processing speed* of a task depends on the number of processors allotted to it: namely, function f_i relates processing speed of task T_i to a number of processors allotted. The criterion assumed is schedule length.

Now, the problem may be stated as the one of finding a schedule (a processor allocation to tasks) of minimum length ω, provided that the processing speed functions of the tasks are all *concave*. Let us note, that this is a realistic case, more often appearing in practice. We will denote this minimum value as $\omega_m^\star$.

As far as processors are concerned, functions f_i are discrete. However, in general, it would be also possible that these functions are continuous. In what follows we will use the results of optimal continuous resource allocation to construct good processor schedules. The reader will find the basic results from the optimal continuous resource allocation theory in [10]. To distinguish it from a discrete case, an optimal schedule length of a continuous case will be denoted by $C_{cont}^\star$. Basically, in the continuous case, all tasks are executed from time 0 to $C_{cont}^\star$ on a fraction of the available processors.

3 An Approximation Algorithm and Its Worst Case Behavior

In this section we propose an algorithm to transform a schedule obtained from the continuous version into a feasible schedule for the discrete MT model and prove that it has a performance guarantee of 2.

Every task T_i with an allocation $r_i \geq 1$ in the continuous solution is scheduled on $\tilde{r}_i = \min(r, t_i(r) \leq 2 \times C_{cont}^\star)$ processors in the malleable scheduling. All parallel tasks (allotment strictly larger than 1) start at time 0. Other tasks, for which a continuous allotment $r_i < 1$, receive one processor and are scheduled in free time slots (cf Algorithm 1).

Algorithm 1 Generic transformation algorithm.

Compute $C_{cont}^\star$ and $\forall i, r_i$
for $i = 1$ to n, $\tilde{r}_i = \min(r, t_i(r) \leq 2 \times C_{cont}^\star)$
for $i = 1$ to n
    if $r_i < 1$ then $\tilde{r}_i = 1$
    else if $\tilde{r}_i > 1$ then $Start(i) = 0$
for $i = 1$ to n
    if $\tilde{r}_i = 1$ then
        $Start(i) = MinimumDateAvailableProcessor()$

Note, that the complexity of the above transformation algorithm is $O(n \log(m))$, as it required to maintain a heap of processor load.

Theorem 1 *Algorithm 1 has a performance guarantee of 2.*

Proof The continuous solution consists in executing simultaneously all the tasks on a fractional number of processors. This solution realizes the trade-off between the total work (task duration by allotted processors) and the length of the tasks. Thus C^*_{cont}, is a lower bound on ω^*_m.

For all the tasks which continuous allotment $r_i \geq 1$, by construction of the Algorithm 1, their duration are less than $2\ C^*_{cont}$. Their work decreases. Moreover, the sum of the processors allotted to these tasks after the transformation stays lower than m. Thus, these tasks, whose duration is between C^*_{cont} and $2\ C^*_{cont}$, can be executed on less than m processors starting at time 0, and their work is smaller than mC^*_{cont}.

The tasks which continuous allotment $r_i < 1$ are assigned on one processor. Their execution times decrease but their work increases. This surface is still the minimal one that these tasks can have in any discrete malleable schedule. Thus these tasks have a duration lower than C^*_{cont} and their total surface is less than $m\ \omega^*_m$.

The sum of the surfaces of the tasks is lower than $m\ C^*_{cont} + m\ \omega^*_m$. An analysis similar to Graham's one can be now applied [3]. The last task that is allotted starts at a time when all the processors are busy (otherwise, it could have been started earlier). Thus, the schedule length of the malleable (discrete) schedule, ω_m is lower than $max\{2\ C^*_{cont}, \frac{m\ C^*_{cont} + m\ \omega^*_m}{m} + C^*_{cont}\}$, that is $2\ C^*_{cont} + \omega^*_m$. If $\omega^*_m \geq 2\ C^*_{cont}$, we obtain directly a guarantee of 2.

When $\omega^*_m \leq 2\ C^*_{cont}$, as $2\ C^*_{cont}$ is greater than ω^*_m, by construction, the allotment chosen for all the tasks is lower than the allotment in the optimal malleable schedule. The work of all the tasks is lower than $m\omega^*_m$. Using the same analysis, we obtain $\omega_m \leq \frac{m\ \omega^*_m}{m} + C^*_{cont} \leq 2\ \omega^*_m$

Thus Algorithm 1 has the worst case behavior bounded by 2.

4 An Improved Algorithm with Better Average Behavior

The 2-approximation presented in [5] is based on a clever reduction of MT scheduling to the strip-packing problem, using the earliest result of [9]. It is worth stressing that the algorithm of Ludwig [5], on average behaves similarly to its worst case behavior.

Algorithm 1 has also a worst case bound equal to 2. In average it will behave similarly, most often approaching this bound. For this reason we propose a slightly more sophisticated algorithm. Its main idea for refinement is to pack more cautiously small tasks (requiring one processor only) and to use several steps of rounding off. These changes allow an improved average behavior.

Algorithm 2

procedure Algorithm2()
    Compute C^*_{cont} and $\forall i, r_i$
    for $i = 1$ **to** n
        if $r_i \leq 1$ **then** $\tilde{r}_i := 1$
        else if $(r_i > 2)$ *or* $(r_i < 1.5)$ **then** $\tilde{r}_i = \lfloor r_i \rfloor$
        else $\tilde{r}_i = 2$ {refinement when $1.5 \leq r_i \leq 2$}
    $\tilde{m} = \sum_{i=1}^{n}(\tilde{r}_i)$.
    find k, such that $t_k(r_k) = max_{1 \leq i \leq n}\{t_i(r_i)\}$
    while $\tilde{m} < m$
        $r_k = r_k + 1; \tilde{m} = \tilde{m} + 1$
        find k, such that $t_k(r_k) = max_{1 \leq i \leq n}\{t_i(r_i)\}$
    Schedule1 =
        find k, such that $r_k = max_{1 \leq i \leq n}\{r_i\}$
        $d = MinimumDateAvailableProcessor(r_k)$
        while $d + t_k(r_k) < max(C^*_{cont}, \sum_{i=1}^{n} t_i(1))$
            $Start(k) = d$; $Scheduled(t_k) = $ True
            find k, such that $r_k = max_{1 \leq i \leq n}\{r_i\}$
            $d = MinimumDateAvailableProcessor(r_k)$
        Algorithme2($\mathcal{T} - Scheduled(\mathcal{T})$)
    if $\tilde{m} > m$ **then**
        Schedule2 =
        do
            find k, such that $r_k = max_{1 \leq i \leq n}\{r_i\}$
            $old_k = r_k$
            if $r_k > 1$ **then** $r_k = r_k - 1$
            $d = MinimumDateAvailableProcessor(r_k)$
            while $d + t_k(r_k) < max_{1 \leq i \leq n}\{t_i(r_i)\}$
                $Start(k) = d$; $Scheduled(t_k) = $ True
                find k, such that $r_k = max_{1 \leq i \leq n}\{r_i\}$
                $d = MinimumDateAvailableProcessor(r_k)$
        until $Scheduled(\mathcal{T}) == \mathcal{T}$ or $old_k == 1$
    else
        Schedule2 = $+\infty$
    Choose the better between Schedule1 and Schedule2

To evaluate the mean behavior of Algorithm 2 we use the following measure:

$$S_{Alg2} = \min\{\omega_m/C^*_{cont}, \omega_m/C_{area})\},$$

where: ω_m - a schedule length obtained by Algorithm 2, C^*_{cont} - an optimal schedule length of the continuous solution, $C_{area} = \sum_{i=1}^{n} t_i(1)/m$ - a schedule length for the uniprocessor allocation for all the tasks. Clearly, the maximum of the two values C^*_{cont} and C_{area} is the lower bound on the optimal schedule length ω^*_m for malleable tasks (discrete case), thus, S_{Alg2} indicates properly a behavior of Algorithm 2.

5 Experiments

To test mean behavior of Algorithm 2, experiments have been conducted as follows. Task processing times $t_i(1)$ have been generated from a uniform distribution in interval [1..100]. Processing speed functions is $f_i(r) = r^{1/a}, a \geq 1$. Values of parameter a have been generated from a uniform distribution in interval [1..10]. The results of the experiments are gathered in Tables 1 through 2. Each entry in these tables is a mean value for 10 instances randomly generated.

Processors	a - different for each task			$a = 4$		
	ω_m/C^*_{cont}	ω_m/C_{area}	S_{alg2}	ω_m/C^*_{cont}	ω_m/C_{area}	S_{alg2}
4	7.96	1.00	1.00	8.48	1.01	1.01
8	5.16	1.02	1.02	5.22	1.02	1.02
16	3.35	1.28	1.28	3.12	1.18	1.18
32	3.26	1.54	1.54	3.11	1.29	1.29
64	1.93	1.48	1.48	2.98	1.32	1.32
128	1.60	1.41	1.41	1.87	1.36	1.36
256	1.21	2.12	1.21	1.30	2.03	1.30
512	1.12	3.79	1.12	1.10	3.09	1.10

Table 1 ($n = 100$) illustrates an influence of a number of processors on the average behavior of Algorithm 2. Table 2 ($m = 64$) shows the impact of the number of tasks on the performance of Algorithm 2. Figure 1 illustrates an impact on the behavior of Algorithm 2 by a number of tasks with varying speed functions.

Tasks	a - different for each task			$a = 4$		
	ω_m/C^*_{cont}	ω_m/C^*_{area}	S_{alg2}	ω_m/C^*_{cont}	ω_m/C_{area}	S_{alg2}
20	1.09	4.26	1.09	1.07	3.19	1.07
40	1.11	2.60	1.11	1.33	3.05	1.33
60	1.19	1.62	1.19	1.15	1.83	1.15
80	1.17	1.68	1.17	1.28	1.52	1.28
100	1.51	1.47	1.47	1.30	1.42	1.30
120	1.48	1.41	1.41	1.43	1.18	1.18
140	1.61	1.40	1.40	1.45	1.19	1.19
160	1.78	1.25	1.25	1.57	1.18	1.18
180	2.23	1.26	1.26	1.85	1.09	1.09
200	2.05	1.10	1.10	6.01	1.00	1.00

From the experiments conducted we see that the mean behavior of the algorithm (as obtained in the above computational experiments) does not exceed value 1,54 of the assumed lower bound of the optimal schedule length for the discrete case. The experiments show that when a number of tasks greatly exceeds a number of processors, the optimal continuous solution does not approximate well the discrete malleable one.. On the other hand, for a number of tasks being

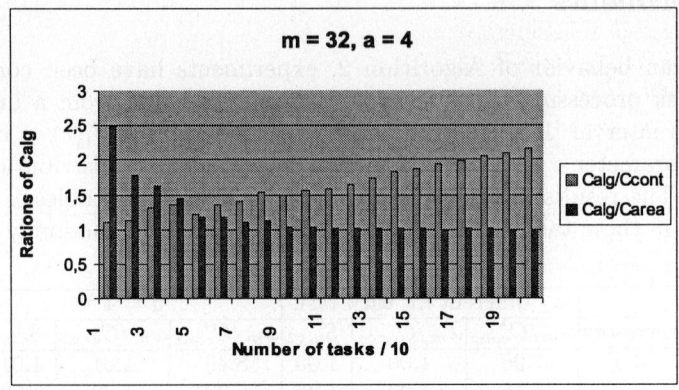

Fig. 1. Impact of a number of tasks on behavior of Algorithm 2

close to a number of processors, the continuous solution may be a good starting point for a construction of an optimal malleable schedule. Since the first is constructed in polynomial time, the second (of a good quality) may be also constructed in a short time.

6 Perspectives

Further investigations could take into account a construction of the proposed algorithm with a better worst case performance guarantee, as well as an analysis of some special (but practically important) cases, involving few parallel tasks in the system only, each requiring many processors at the same time.

References

1. J. Błażewicz, M. Drabowski, J. Węglarz: Scheduling multiprocessor tasks to minimize schedule length, *IEEE Transactions on Computers* **35**, 1986, 389–393.
2. J. Du, J. Y.-T. Leung: Complexity of scheduling parallel tasks systems. *SIAM Journal on Discrete Mathematics* **2**, 1989, 473–487.
3. R. L. Graham: Bounds for certain multiprocessing anomalies, *Bell System Tech. J.*, **45**, 1966, 1563-1581.
4. K. Jansen, L. Porkolab: Linear-Time Approximation Schemes for Scheduling Malleable Parallel Tasks, In *Tenth Annual ACM-SIAM Symposium on Discrete Algorithms (soda99)*, ACM-SIAM, 1999, 490–498.
5. W. T. Ludwig: *Algorithms for scheduling malleable and non-malleable parallel tasks*, PhD thesis, University of Wisconsin - Madison, Department of Computer Sciences, 1995.
6. G. Mounié, C. Rapine, D. Trystram: Efficient approximation algorithms for scheduling malleable tasks, In *Eleventh ACM Symposium on Parallel Algorithms and Architectures (SPAA'99)*, ACM, 1999, 23–32.

7. G. N. S. Prasanna, B. R. Musicus: The optimal control approach to generalized multiprocessor scheduling, *Algorithmica*, 1995.
8. A. Steinberg: A Strip-Packing Algorithm with Absolute Performance Bound 2, *SIAM Journal on Computing* **26 (2)**, 1997, 401–409.
9. J. Turek, J. Wolf, P. Yu: Approximate algorithms for scheduling parallelizable tasks, In *4th Annual ACM Symposium on Parallel Algorithms and Architectures*, 1992, 323–332.
10. J. Węglarz: Modelling and control of dynamic resource allocation project scheduling systems, In S. G. Tzafestas (ed.), *Optimization and Control of Dynamic Operational Research Models*, North-Holland, Amsterdam, 1982.

The Way to Produce the Quasi-workload in a Cluster

Fumie Costen and John Brooke

MRCCS, Manchester Computing, The University of Manchester
Oxford Road, Manchester, M13 9PL, United Kingdom

Abstract. Resource Management Systems (RMS) can be used to improve the utilization of a cluster of workstations or processors. In a system which has a mixture of interactive and batch work and a mixture of serial and parallel jobs there is no single measure which determines the effective utilization of the cluster. We propose a mathematically well-defined procedure for determining an ensemble of states "sufficiently close" to the measured workload of the cluster. We call these states quasi-workloads and suggest how they can provide a basis for simulations which predict the changes in cluster performance for differing RMS policies and schedules.

1 Motivation of this Work

In previous work we have investigated the ability of Resource Management Systems (e.g. LSF, PBS) to improve the performance of Clusters of Workstations (CoW) [1]. Our previous work suffered from the disadvantage that we used a workload based on clones of a small number of template jobs running the same program on different numbers of processors. This does not represent the loading provided by multiple users submitting a range of jobs, using both batch and interactive job submission. We therefore wish to test the method by using data from a real cluster. Hoewver we also wish to get some estimates of variation in the effects of the RMS policy under similar but not identical loads. We therefore describe here a method of creating what we call "quasi-workloads". These are derived from the real workload but in such a way as to be "close", in a manner which we describe precisely in this article, but not identical. Thus if we create M quasi-workloads we run our simulation over the whole set and come up with mean and standard deviation representing the effect of the RMS policy being tested on a cluster with a "typical" loading which includes variation around the real loading.

The novelty of our method is that we can dispense with the need to make assumptions about the underlying statistical distribution of the observed data. Thus we do not need to impose some assumed static distribution, e.g. Gaussian profile, on data whose distribution may change over time. This enables the method to handle cyclic and secular trends in the pattern of cluster usage over an extended time period, and real cluster loads often do exhibit such trends, e.g. weekends, seasonal holidays. This method is based on a statistical method that produces a probability density function, this is also called likelihood in the conventions of the particular statistical literature.

The structure of the paper is as follows: in Section 2 we descibe the mathematical basis of our method, in Section 3 we apply it to real data, in Section 4 we contrast this method with other possible statistical approaches and in Section 5 we suggest how this work could be applied.

2 Extracting Workload Characteristics

We gathered information from two SGI Origin2000 machines with differing types of workloads. Although these machines can be regarded as MPP machines, they can also be considered as a cluster of nodes with a single memory address space and thus can be considered as a tightly coupled cluster with additional hardware and software features to provide virtual shared memory and a very rich network interconnect. The two Origins are called Kilburn and Fermat. Kilburn is a 40 processor Silicon Graphics Origin 2000, with a peak performance of 16 Gflops, 10 Gbytes of main memory and about 250 Gbytes of disk storage. Fermat is a SGI Origin2000 with 16 processors, 8Gb memory and another 2Tb of disk space. There is no CPU restriction on interactive jobs. Both machines run the NQE (Network Queueing Environment) batch queuing system. The batch and interactive jobs run on Kilburn and Fermat were using either 1, 2, 4, or 8 CPUs.

We now show how we produce quasi-workloads from a real observed workload. The workload can apply to a number of measures, e.g number of jobs launched in a given time span, memory usage as a function of time. The shared memory architecture of the Origin2000 permits certain quantities to be described by a single measure, in a distributed memory cluster they would be per processor.

One of the methods for univariate probability density estimation is the histogram, which is the oldest, simplest, and most widely used. However, the histogram's mathematical drawback translates itself into inefficient use of the data if histograms are used as density estimates in procedures like cluster analysis and nonparametric discriminant analysis. The discontinuity of histograms causes extreme difficulty if derivatives of the estimates are required. Another point is that the choice of the origin can have a considerable effect on the histogram profile effect and also we require a choice of the amount of smoothing and treatment of the tails of the sample. The alternative and more fundamental way of constructing an estimate of the density function (likelihood) from the observed data (in our case, the real workload), assumed to be a sample from an unknown probability function, is called em density estimation. M. Rosenblatt [3] and E. Parzen [4] introduced the kernel density estimator and B. Silverman [5] gives a good introduction to kernel estimators and bandwidth selection.

Given the ϱ observed data $\xi_1 \cdots \xi_\varrho$ drawn from the unknown probability density Ψ, the standard kernel estimator is the single bandwidth estimator:

$$\Psi(x) = \frac{1}{\beta\varrho} \sum_{i=1}^{\varrho} \mathcal{K}\left(\frac{x - \xi_i}{\beta}\right) \qquad (1)$$

where $\mathcal{K}$ is a kernel function integrating to one and β is the window width, also called the smoothing parameter or bandwidth. In the method we are free to choose the kernel function, and through this the "experience" of previous analysis of such data can be used to optimise the mapping of discrete data observations to a continuous probability density (likelihood).

Just as the histogram uses a bin width to define the bins of the histogram and to control the amount of smoothing inherent in the procedure, the kernel estimator uses a window width to determine the width of the observation area. The kernel function determines the shape of the local peaks while the window width determines the width of the individual peaks. The kernel estimate is constructed by adding the peaks up. There has been much reseach on selecting the optimal bandwidth β under different assumptions on Ψ or different optimality criteria. D. Marchette [6] et al proposed the filtered kernel density estimation which uses a small number of bandwidths and the gaussian function as the density function and is superior in performance to the standard kernel estimator, provided appropriate filter functions and bandwidths can be chosen.

We apply the above method to produce likelihoods (probability density functions) for the following characteristics of the measured workload for a given time interval: Ψ_m the required memory of a job and Ψ_{njob} the number of jobs started a day. We define ν_m, ν_{njob} as the maximum values of the likelihoods Ψ defined above. We also define η_m and η_{njob} as the maximum values (from the raw data directly) of the required memories and the number of jobs started per day. These two measures are just examples of the range of methods we could apply to any scalar measure of machine or cluster performance. Our likelihood estimation method is the same for any scalar measure with an obvious generalisation to vector measures (e.g. CPU utilization over multiple processors).

Figure 1 shows the likelihood obtained from this data for memory required per job on Kilburn.

3 An Ensemble of Quasi-workloads

Here, we explain the procedure for producing an ensemble of quasi-workloads. We choose, for illustration, a single characteristic, number of jobs per day, the method is the same for all other scalar measures. The function $\Psi_{njob}(n_{job})$ gives a likelihood of a particular number of jobs being started in a day. This looks like a smoothed histogram, but it is determined by a minimization procedure that makes it stable to changes in the origin chosen for the bins. Figure 2 shows the comparison between the likelihood function and histograms of varying bin width and bin origin. The sensitivity of the shape of the histogram curve to variations in the choice of bins can be clearly seen, thus it is not stable for producing quasi-workloads.

We then use a Monte Carlo procedure to determine different values of quasi-values N for the number of jobs started per day in our ensemble. We determine each N subject to a bounding norm as follows,

$$0 \leq \nu_{njob} \times \gamma_b \leq \Psi_{njob}(njob = \eta_{njob} \times \gamma_a) \qquad (2)$$

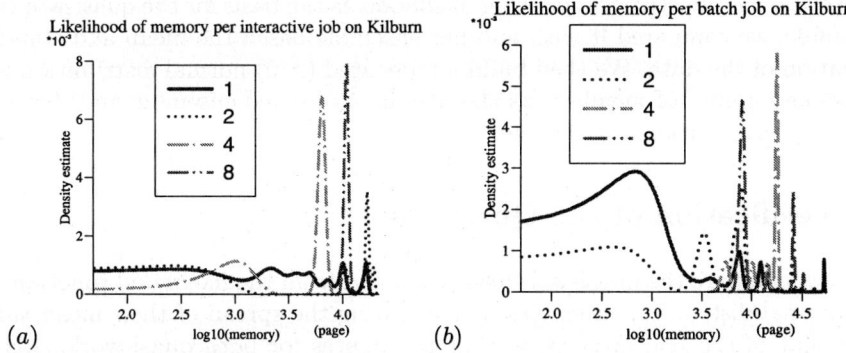

Fig. 1. Normalized likelihood of memory used per: (a) interactive job on Kilburn, (b) batch job on Kilburn. X-axis is the logarithm base 10 of memory size in page where 1 page is 16384 bit. Y-axis is the density estimate of the required memory per job. A solid line, a dotted line, a broken line with one dot, and a broken line with two dots show the likelihood of memory of 1, 2, 4, and 8 CPU jobs, respectively

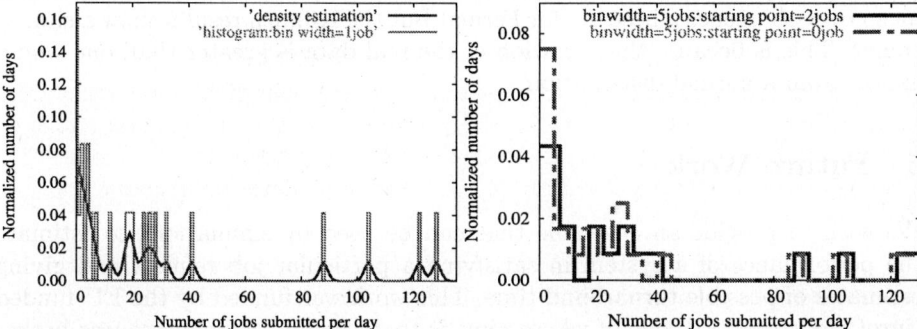

Fig. 2. Left: relative frequency of the number of days for a certain number of 1 CPU batch jobs started a day on Kilburn. The bin width of the histogram is 1 day. The solid line is the result of the density estimation. Right: the same data showing the sensitivity to the histogram bin width and choice of origin, comparing 2 and 5 day bins

$$N = Int(\eta_{njob} \times \gamma_a) \qquad (3)$$

where γ_a, γ_b are random numbers in the range $[0, 1]$ When the bounding condition 2 is not satisfied, we reject N and reiterate with different random numbers until it is satisfied. We iterate this whole procedure as many times as we require quasi-workloads in our ensemble, and for all the characteristic quantities defining our quasi-workload.

To test the effectiveness of using likelihood as the basis for the quasi-workload ensemble, we compared it with another ensemble based the mean and standard deviation of the data. We then build a truncated (> 0) normal distribution with the same number of members as the likelihood-derived ensemble and discretize it with a simple rounding scheme.

4 Verification of the Quasi-data

We now compare the quasi-workloads obtained from the likelihood function and the normal distribtion ensembles by comparing the spread of their mean values with that of the real data. Note that the figures for both quasi-workloads are also derived from averaging over an ensemble of 10 quasi-workloads. Thus they have two levels of averaging, the real data has only the time average.

We obtain error rates for any measure ψ by $|(\psi_r - \psi_q)|/\psi_r$ where the subscripts stand for the real and quasi data respectively. Our chief result is that the average error rates of Gaussian model on Fermat and Kilburn are 85% and 40%, respectively, whilst those of density estimate model on Kilburn and Fermat are 23% and 27%, respectively. This is reinforced by comparing the means from the different categories of jobs shown in Figure 3. The probability density (likelihood) quasi-workloads give values which are consistently closer to the real mean over all queues (these are for Fermat but the Kilburn results show a similar trend). This is because the variation of the real data is greater than one would expect from a normal distribution.

5 Future Work

We wish to provide an ensemble that can be used by simulations to estimate the performance of a system in satisfying a particular job request and giving estimates of possible turnaround time. This work was funded by the EU-funded EuroGrid project [7], one of whose aims is to develop a reliable resource broker for a European wide network of HPC Centres. Although our method of likelihood estimation takes an order of magnitude more CPU time than using an assumption such as normal distribution, it only has to be performed once a day (say) and can be used by multiple simulations to estimate the mean performance of incoming jobs, and equally importantly the likely variance around this mean. Thus a resource broker submitting from a Grid network could obtain information as to the performance and the "risk" associated with placing a particular request on the system at that time. Our method is thus fundamentally to use recent system history as the basis for such estimates but via a more elegant and statistically well-founded method than just using the raw data.

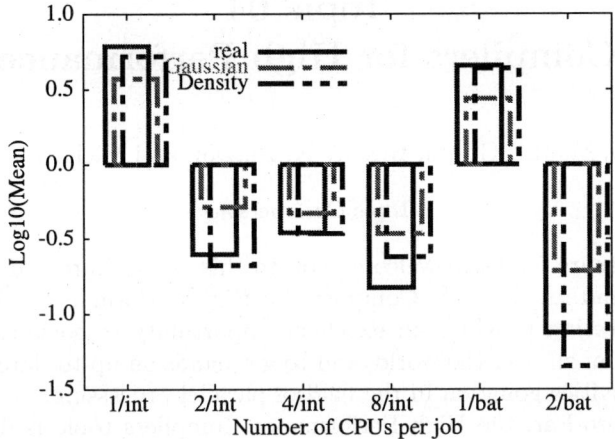

Fig. 3. Mean of the number of started jobs per day on Fermat. X-axis is the number of CPUs per interactive or batch job and Y-axis is the mean of the number of jobs started on Fermat. 4/int and 8/bat in X-axis mean the interactive job which requires 4 cpus and the batch job which requires 8 cpus, respectively. A solid line, a broken line with 1 dot, and a broken line with 2 dots, mean real job, quasi jobs from the Gaussian derivative model, and quasi job from the density estimate model, respectively

References

1. F. Costen, J. M. Brooke, M. Pettipher, "Investigation to Make Best Use of LSF with High Efficiency" IEEE International Workshop on Cluster Computing (IWCC'99), Melbourne, Australia, pp.211-220, Dec. 2-3, 1999
2. S. Zhou, "LSF: Load sharing in large-scale heterogeneous distributed systems ", Proc. Workshop on Cluster Computing, 1992
3. M. Rosenblatt, "Remarks on some Nonparametric Estimates of a Density Function", Ann.Math.Statist.,27,832-835, 1956
4. E. Parzen, "On Estimation of a Probability Density Function and Mode", Ann.Math.Statist.,33,1065-1076, 1962
5. B. W. Silverman, "Density Estimation for statics and data analysis", Chapman & Hall, London, 1986
6. D. J. Marchette et al, "Filtered Kernel Density Estimation", www.nswc.navy.mil/compstat/FKE/fke.html
7. EuroGrid, EU IST 5th Framework, details at http://www.eurogrid.org

The authors would like to thank D. Marchette et al in Naval Surface Warfare Center for their support in the programming of the filtered kernel density estimation. We acknowledge funding from the EU 5th Framework IST under the EuroGrid project. We thank the Europar referees for their very helpful comments and suggestions.

Topic 04
Compilers for High Performance

Jens Knoop, Manish Gupta, Keshav K. Pingali, and Michael F. P. O'Boyle

Topic Chairpersons

It is a pleasure for us to welcome you to this year's Euro-Par conference in Manchester, and its topic on "Compilers for High Performance." As in previous years, this meeting provides an excellent opportunity to socialize with fellow researchers from all over the world, and to get hands on up-to-date research and the many activities going on in the field of parallel processing.

Within Euro-Par, the High Performance Compilers topic is devoted to research in all subjects concerning technology for compilation of programs for high performance systems, including, but not limited to, optimizing the utilization of system resources such as power consumption, code size, and memory requirements. Contributions were sought in all related areas, including the traditional fields of compiler technology such as static program analysis and transformation (including automatic parallelization), mapping programs to processors (including scheduling, and allocation and mapping of tasks), and code generation, but also dynamic and feedback directed optimization, compiling for embedded, hybrid and heterogeneous systems, and the interplay between compiler technology and development and execution environments. The focus on the application of these techniques to the automatic extraction and exploitation of parallelism distinguishes the topic from the other compiler oriented topics in Euro-Par (#03, #07, #13, and #20).

This year fifteen papers, contributed by an international mix of authors from three continents and eight countries, were submitted, one of which was moved from Topic 03 on "Scheduling and Load Balancing" to Topic 04. Each of these papers was reviewed by at least three referees, with an average of 3.66 reports per paper. Using the referees' reports as guidelines, the topic committee selected after intensive e-mail discussions eight of the submitted papers for publication and presentation at the conference. Of these, five papers were elected as regular papers, and three as research notes. These papers were presented in two consecutive sessions on Friday morning.

The topics covered by this year's submissions reflect the wide spectrum of current research in the field of high performance compilers. This heterogeneity is still visible in the papers accepted for presentation at the conference. However, there are some superordinate themes predominating in this year's submissions. Above all, these are novel uses of elsewhere developed and approved means and techniques for new applications and new application scenarios, and the integration of dynamic and static approaches to benefit from the best of both worlds. Additionally, much emphasis is given to the comparing exploration of the efficacy of competing approaches, and the extraction of their specific application profiles. Considering the accepted papers in more detail makes this evident.

The first session of the High Performance Compilers topic is devoted to program analysis and transformation. It begins with a paper by Sebastian Unger and Frank Mueller, in which they reconsider the handling of irreducible code in optimization, a classical problem getting new relevance with the growing dissemination of modern VLIW-like architectures supporting instruction-level parallelism such as Intel's IA-64. The authors present a novel approach for transforming irreducible loops into reducible ones, which is guided by a new heuristic for node splitting based on computing the dominator tree of a program. They explore the efficacy and adequacy of the new approach for subsequent optimizations in comparison to both the traditional node-splitting approach, and an approach using DJ-graphs for representing and optimizing irreducible code. Their findings will be useful for anyone (re-) designing a compiler. The next two papers are concerned with redundancy elimination. The first of these, by Manel Fernández, Roger Espasa, and Saumya Debray, targets the elimination of (partially) redundant loads in executable code by replacing expensive loads from memory by inexpensive register transfers. Conceptually similar to classical *partial redundancy elimination*, the specific constraints of the setting such as the fixed number of hardware registers, require original solutions, for which the authors develop three algorithms of different power and complexity. In the next paper, by Peter Faber, Martin Griebl, and Christian Lengauer, the elimination of loop-carried redundancies among computations involving arrays is targeted, a subject not considered by classical redundancy elimination techniques. Focusing on a typical setting for scientific code, where loop bounds and array subscripts are often expressible as affine functions, they show how to re-orchestrate and utilize techniques for scheduling and automatic parallelization to restructure such loops making them amenable to redundancy elimination involving array expressions. The final paper of this session, by Apan Qasem, David Whalley, Xin Yuan, and Robert van Engelen, describes an alternative approach to that of Fernández and colleagues to reducing the number of load and store instructions in a program. They explore the adequacy of using swap instructions, which are typically used for process synchronization, to coalescing load and store operations. Their results are promising, showing that both the number of executed instructions and of accesses to the memory system are reduced.

The second and final session of the High Performance Compilers topic is devoted to automatic parallelization and compiler support techniques. The first paper, by Daniel Chavarría-Miranda, John Mellor-Crummey, and Trushar Sarang, targets the automatic parallelization of data-parallel programs using multipartitioned data distributions. These are known to offer better parallel efficiency and scalability for multi-directional line-sweep computations than block unipartitionings. In their paper, the authors present a comprehensive study of the compiler techniques implemented in the dHPF compiler supporting the automatic generation of multipartitioned code. The reported performance results are impressive showing that the generated code is most competitive to that of hand-coded parallelizations using multipartitioning. The second paper, by Peter M. W. Knijnenburg, Toru Kisuki, and Kyle Gallivan, deals with iterative compilation, a highly effective, but time-consuming approach searching for the best program optimizations by profiling many variants and selecting the most efficient one. The authors show that iterative compilation can effectively be guided by static models. Considering loop unrolling and tiling for illustration, they demonstrate that the usage of static cache models allows substantial reductions of the computation costs essentially without any performance deductions of the final code. The next paper, by Vincent Loechner, Benoît Meister, and Philippe Clauss, targets the efficient usage of the memory hierarchy. The reduction of cache misses is here an important source for getting performance improvements, addressed for example by methods for enhancing temporal locality. The authors present an architecture-independent generalization of these methods focusing on innermost loops to non-perfect loop nests. Essentially, this works by minimizing the number of iterations between consecutive accesses of the data in memory. In effect, this reduces cache misses as well as TLB (translation lookaside buffer) misses, while still allowing the additional application of specific architecture-dependent transformations such as blocking. The final paper of this session, by Vivek Sarkar and Stephen Fink, targets dependence analysis for arrays in Java programs that is efficiently enough for usage in just-in-time compilers in contemporary Java Virtual Machines. Features such as the dynamic allocation of arrays in Java requiring pointer-induced aliases of array objects make this a difficult task. The authors address this by a new approach based on sparse congruence partitioning representations built on the so-called array SSA form. Preliminary experimental results reported are encouraging, but underline also the importance of, e.g., enhanced interprocedural information for further improving the precision of the analysis results.

In closing, we would like to express our gratitude to the many people, whose contributions made this conference, and the High Performance Compilers track possible. Above all, we thank the authors who submitted a paper, the Euro-Par Organizing Committee, and the numerous referees, whose excellent work was an invaluable help for the topic committee. We hope you will enjoy the presentations, as well as the papers in the proceedings, finding (many of) them useful for your work and research.

Handling Irreducible Loops: Optimized Node Splitting vs. DJ-Graphs

Sebastian Unger[1] and Frank Mueller[2]

[1] DResearch Digital Media Systems
Otto-Schmirgal-Str. 3, 10319 Berlin (Germany)
[2] North Carolina State University, CS Dept.
Box 8206, Raleigh, NC 27695-7534
fax: +1.919.515.7925
mueller@cs.ncsu.edu

Abstract. This paper addresses the question of how to handle irreducible regions during optimization, which has become even more relevant for contemporary processors since recent VLIW-like architectures highly rely on instruction scheduling. The contributions of this paper are twofold. First, a method of optimized node splitting to transform irreducible regions of control flow into reducible regions is derived. This method is superior to approaches previously published since it reduces the number of replicated nodes by comparison. Second, three methods that handle regions of irreducible control flow are evaluated with respect to their impact on compiler optimizations: traditional and optimized node splitting as well as loop analysis through DJ graphs. Measurements show improvements of 1-40% for these methods of handling irreducible loop over the unoptimized case.

1 Introduction

Compilers heavily rely on recognizing loops for optimizations. Most loop optimizations have only been formulated for natural loops with a single entry point (header), the sink of the backedge(s) of such a loop. Multiple entry loops cause *irreducible regions* of control flow, typically *not* recognized as loops by traditional algorithms. These regions may result from goto statements or from optimizations that modify the control flow. As a result, loop transformations and optimizations to exploit instruction-level parallelism cannot be applied to such regions so that opportunities for code improvements may be missed.

Modern architectures, such as very long instruction word (VLIW) architectures (Phillips TriMedia, IA-64), require aggressive instruction scheduling to exploit their performance [6] but this requires knowledge about the structure of a program, which contemporary compilers generally do not support for irreducible regions of code. In addition, aggressive global instruction scheduling, enhanced modulo scheduling [13], trace scheduling and profile-guided code positioning combined with code replication [8,9] or applied during binary translation may result in branch reordering and code replication, which itself may introduce irreducible regions. This paper briefly discusses traditional loop splitting, contributes a new approach of optimized node splitting and reports on a performance study of these approaches with DJ-graphs that recognize irreducible loops.

2 Traditional Node Splitting

Node splitting is based on T1/T2-interval analysis that detects irreducible regions in a flow graph. T1/T2 are iteratively applied on the flow graph reducing it to a simpler one:

T1 Remove any edge that connects a node to itself.
T2 A node with only one predecessor are merged into a single *abstract* node while preserving incoming edges of the predecessor and outgoing edges of the original node.

If these transformations are applied as long as possible the resulting graph is called the *limit graph*. If the final graph is trivial (a singleton node), then the original flow graph was reducible. Otherwise, all of its nodes either have none or *more* than one predecessor. Node splitting defines a transformation T3, which is applied on the limit graph:

T3 Duplicate a node with multiple predecessors (one copy per predecessor). Connect each predecessor to a distinct copy and duplicate outgoing edges of the original node.

After the application of T3, apply T1/T2 again and repeat this process. The resulting limit graph is always trivial. If the above process is reversed, leaving the duplicated nodes in place, the result is a *reducible* flow graph that is equivalent to the original one. This algorithm is inefficient because it does not consider which nodes form the irreducible loops. In this work, algorithms will be presented that exactly analyze the extent, structure and nesting of irreducible loops. Based on such an analysis a much better algorithm than that above will be constructed.

3 Properties of Irreducible Regions of Code

The motivation of this work is to develop an algorithm that converts an arbitrary irreducible control flow graph into an *equivalent reducible* one with the minimal possible growth in code size. This first involves the construction of an algorithm. This work builds on Janssen and Corporaal [7] who found that each irreducible loop has exactly one maximal subset of at least two of its nodes that have the same immediate dominator, which in turn is *not* part of the loop. They also discovered that these sets play an important role when minimizing the number of splits. Their definition of so-called Shared External Dominator sets was:

Definition 1 (Loop-set). *A loop in a flow graph is a path* $(n_1, \ldots, n_k)$ *where* n_1 *is an immediate successor of* n_k. *The nodes* n_i *do not have to be unique. The set of nodes contained in the loop is called a loop-set.*

Definition 2 (SED-set). *A Shared External Dominator set (SED-set) is a subset of a loop-set L whose elements share the same immediate dominator and whose immediate dominator (idom) is not part of L. A SED-set of L is defined as:* $SED\text{-}set(L) = \{n_i \in L \mid \text{idom}(n_i) = e \notin L\}$.

Definition 3 (MSED-set). *A Maximal Shared External Dominator set (MSED-set) K of a loop-set L is defined as:*
SED-set K is maximal $\iff \nexists$ SED-set M, such that $K \subset M$ and $K, M \subseteq L$.

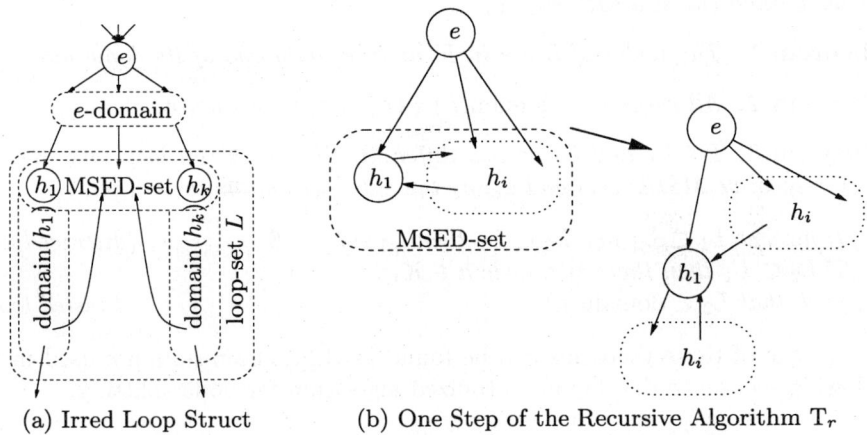

(a) Irred Loop Struct (b) One Step of the Recursive Algorithm T_r

Fig. 1. Analyzing Irreducible Loop Structures and Optimized Node Splitting

The MSED-set is a generalization of the single entry block in natural loops, which consists of just one node. In the following, the nodes of MSED-sets will be simply called the header nodes or headers. Building on that, new generalized definitions can also be found for the bodies (an irreducible loop can have more than one), backedges and the nesting of irreducible loops. Figure 1(a) illustrates this generalized structure. Domains represent the body of a natural loop. Edges from a domain back into the MSED-sets are backedges. The node e is the immediate dominator of the header nodes. The region called e-domain will be defined and used in the next section.

The following, generalized definitions of backedges and domains are based on MSED-sets whose definition in turn depends on the loop-set. This means that the extension of the loop-set cannot be defined using backedges as it is for natural loops. This is only a problem because the definition of MSED-sets does in no way require the loop-set to be maximal. However, several of the following theorems only hold if the loop-sets are SED-maximal.

Definition 4 (SED-maximal loop-sets). *A loop-set L is SED-maximal if there is no other loop-set L' such that $L \subset L'$ and MSED-set$(L) \subseteq$ MSED-set(L').*

Definition 5 (Domains). *Let L be an irreducible SED-maximal loop-set, K be its MSED-set and h_i be the nodes of K. The domain of h_i is then defined as:*
$$\text{domain}(h_i) = \{ n_j \in L \mid h_i \text{ dominates} n_j \}$$

Definition 6 (backedges). *Let L be an irreducible SED-maximal loop-set, K be its MSED-set and h_i be the nodes of K. An edge (m,n) with $m \in L$ and $n \in K$ is then called a back-edge of L.*

Theorem 1. *The nodes of L are in K or in exactly one of its domains.*

Theorem 2. *All edges into* domain$(h) \setminus \{h\}$ *originate from h.*

Theorem 3. *Let L_1 and L_2 be two different, SED-maximal loop-sets, K_1, K_2 their respective MSED-sets and e_1, e_2 the external dominators. Then*

- *If neither $L_1 \subset L_2$ nor $L_2 \subset L_1$ then $L_1 \cap L_2 = \emptyset$.*   (distinct loops)
- *If $L_2 \subset L_1$ then there is a node $h \in K_1$ such that $L_2 \subset$ domain(h).*   (nested loops)

The proofs of these theorems can be found in [12]. The results are used in the following section to develop an optimized algorithm for node splitting.

4 Optimized Node Splitting

The knowledge about the structure of irreducible loops can be used to guide the T3 transformation to some extend. Repeated application of T1/T2 will collapse domains into their headers leaving an MSED-set. Applying T3 to a node in the MSED-set then splits a header and its *entire* domain.

As the domains are collapsed into one abstract node, multiple edges from one domain to a single header node will reduce to just one edge from the abstract node to the header node. This reduces the number of copies of that node and is also true for multiple edges from the outside. Figure 1(a) suggests by the naming that the region called e-domain (defined below) should be handled just as any other domain. That is, transformations T1 and T2 should collapse it into e, thereby reducing multiple edges from that domain to any header node into one edge. Of course, T3 should not be applied to this abstract node.

Definition 7 (e-domain). *Let L be an irreducible SED-maximal loop-set, K be its MSED-set and e the external dominator. That is: If e is the immediate dominator of the nodes in K, then the set e-domain is defined as:*

$$\text{e-domain} = \left\{ n_i \in N \;\middle|\; \begin{array}{l} e \text{ dominates } n_i, \; n_i \notin L \text{ and} \\ \exists \text{ a path } p \text{ from } n_i \text{ into } L \text{ with} \\ e \notin p. \end{array} \right\}$$

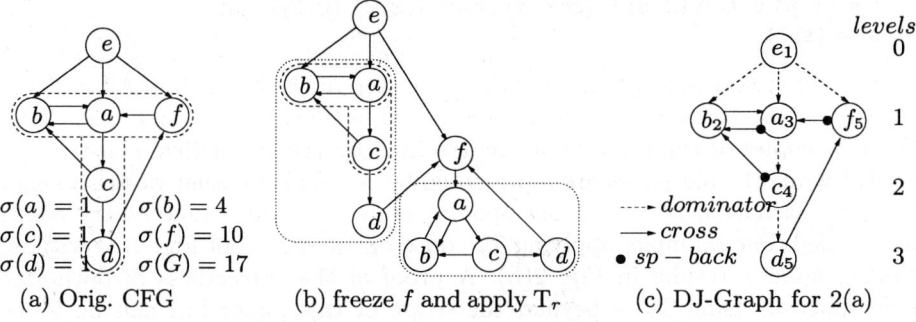

Fig. 2. T3 Cannot Split this Graph with Weights σ in a Minimal Way

Does this algorithm always produce the minimal reducible equivalent flow graph? Unfortunately not, as counter-examples show that selecting the nodes to split just by their weight is not sufficient. Another question is if there is always an order that leads to the minimum. Alas, not even that is true. Figure 2 gives a flow graph where no order will split the nodes to yield a minimal graph.

A new approach has been developed, based on the observation that all of the counter-examples contained one of the header nodes that was not split at all. The new approach chooses a single header node (plus its domain, of course) that *not split at all*. All other nodes of the loop-set are split once. This is illustrated in Figure 1(b). The regions containing the copies of the remaining nodes of L are not yet guaranteed to be reducible but they are guaranteed to be smaller than L by at least one node. Hence, the above step can be applied recursively to these copied regions. This new approach also needs a scheme for selecting the node h_1 with the advantage over the previous approach that for any flow graph there is a selection scheme that leads to a minimal result. All that remains is to actually find this scheme. First, however, the algorithm is defined more precisely. The following notation will be used in the following: If f is a function over the nodes of any control flow graph, then $f(X)$, where X is a subset of these nodes, stands for the set $\{f(x) | x \in X\}$.

Definition 8 (Transformation T_r). *Let $G = (N, E, s)$ be an arbitrary (irreducible) control flow graph, L an SED-maximal, irreducible loop-set of G, K its MSED-set, e the external dominator and h an arbitrary node from K. Then the transformation $G' = (N', E', s') = T_r(G, L, h)$ is defined as follows (with $S = (L \setminus \text{domain}(h))$):*

- $N' = (N \times \{1\}) \cup (S \times \{2\})$
- $E' \subset N' \times N'$ *such that the following restrictions hold:*
  - $(x, y) \in E \wedge (x, y) \notin (\text{domain}(h) \times S) \iff ((x, 1), (y, 1)) \in E'$
  - $(x, y) \in E \wedge (x, y) \in (\text{domain}(h) \times S) \iff ((x, 1), (y, 2)) \in E'$

- $(x,y) \in E \wedge (x,y) \in (S \times (N \setminus S)) \iff ((x,2),(y,1)) \in E'$
- $(x,y) \in E \wedge (x,y) \in (S \times S) \iff ((x,2),(y,2)) \in E'$
- $s' = (s,1)$

The above transformation represents one step of the algorithm. All nodes of the loop-set L, except for those in the selected header node's domain, are split. The new copies of these nodes are represented by the syntactical construction $S \times \{2\}$ while the old nodes are represented by $N \times \{1\}$. In other words, a single T_r transformation results in one split to copy S so that unnecessary copies are avoided. For example, applying T_r once on the graph of Fig. 2(a) without copying node f results in Fig. 2(b). A proof of the correctness of optimized node splitting using T_r is beyond the scope of this paper but can be found elsewhere [12]. The recursive algorithm for T_r is shown in the appendix.

5 Using DJ Graphs to Optimize Irreducible Loops

The representation of DJ Graphs [11] may be used for incremental data-flow analysis but it also provides the means to perform loop optimizations on irreducible loops. By constructing the DJ Graph of a control-flow graph, natural and irreducible loops and their nesting hierarchy can be detected.

An example is depicted in Figure 2(c). The DJ-Graph consists of the edges of the dominator tree (dashed), backedges, and the remaining edges of the control flow called cross edges (solid). Furthermore, sp-back edges are control-flow edges $x \to y$ where $x = y$ or y is an ancestor of x is a spanning tree resulting from a depth-first search. In the example, a search in the order of the indicies of the nodes indicates that the edges marked with bullets are sp-back. Loops in the DJ-Graph can then be found starting from the lowest dominator level (level 3). If a backedge exists at the current level, then nodes corresponding to its natural loop are collapsed into one node. Afterwards, if a cross edge is also sp-back, all strongly connected components at the current level or below represent an irreducible loop and are collapsed to a single node before considering the next higher level. In the example, there are no backedges but several cross edges at level 1 that are also sp-back. The only strongly connected component comprises all nodes at level 1 or below, i.e., exactly one irreducible loop is found. However, Figure 2(b) shows that an inner loop $\{a,b\}$ and an outer loop $\{a,b,c\}$ may be distinguished by optimized node splitting. Nonetheless, DJ-Graphs still allow the distinction of irreducible loop bodies either if they comprise different levels or if they represent distinct strongly connected components. Furthermore, DJ-Graphs also allow the detection of reducible loops within irreducible ones. Had there been an edge $d \to c$ in Figure 2(c), then this edge would have been recognized as a backedge whose source and sink comprise a loop at level 2.

There are other differences between natural loops and DJ-graphs representations of irreducible loops. Instead of one loop header for natural loops, irreducible loops have multiple entry blocks with predecessor blocks outside the loop. Furthermore, there is no block in an irreducible loop that dominates all other blocks within the loop. Notice, however, that we allow a natural loop to share a header with an irreducible loop. We still distinguish both loops in this case. These differences require changes to other loop optimizations.

Code motion moves invariant operations out of the body of a natural loop into the preheader block. For irreducible loops, the set of entry blocks can be augmented by a set of preheader blocks. Then, a copy of a loop-invariant operation is moved into all preheaders at once. Code motion as stated in [1] applies with minor changes, *e.g.*, to find invariant statements in loop l:

1. $dst = src$ is invariant if src is constant or its reaching definitions are outside l, as indicated by registers live on entry for *each* preheader of l.
2. transitively mark statements in step 3 until no more unmarked invariant statements are found.
3. $dst = src$ is invariant if src is constant, if its sole reaching definition inside l is marked invariant or if its reaching definitions are outside l.

For each entry of an irreducible loop, we delete all other entries and collect the sources of all backedges within the resulting region. Notice that such a region may contain more than one natural loop now. We call the collected blocks the sources of *pseudo-backedges* of the irreducible loop. A block of an irreducible loop is executed during each iteration if it dominates all sources of pseudo-backedges within the corresponding reducible regions. This requires dominator information of the reducible pseudo-regions to be associated with an irreducible loop.

Finding induction variables becomes more complicated due to irreducible loops. We limit our approach by requiring that changes to induction variables are performed in blocks which are executed on each loop iteration. This information is already available from code motion for memory reads. In addition, one could allow balancing modifications in corresponding conditional arms. These arms range from a split at an always iterated block to a join at the next block that is always executed during each loop iteration. We did not implement this extension. Once induction variables are identified, strength reduction and induction variable elimination are performed as for natural loops, except that invariant operations of register loads are moved into *all* preheaders of the irreducible loop.

Similar to the handling of induction variables, recurrences can be optimized by moving the prologue into all preheaders, given that the memory access originates in a block that is executed on each loop iteration. Other optimizations also benefit from the additional loop information. For example, global register allocation is performed by prioritized graph coloring in VPO. The priority is based on the loop frequency, which is readily available even for irreducible loops and their nesting within other loops. No modification was required to such optimizations.

6 Measurements

We chose VPO [3] as a platform to conduct a performance evaluation. VPO only recognizes natural loops with a single header, just as all contemporary optimizing compilers we know of. Irreducible regions of code remain unoptimized. First, we added the recognition of DJ Graphs to VPO, extended code motion, strength reduction, induction variable elimination and recurrences. Second, we implemented optimized node splitting through T_r. The heuristic driving node selection was to choose the header of the domain with the most instructions. This node (and its domain) were not split while all other nodes in the loop set were split. Third, traditional node splitting using T1/T2/T3 was integrated. The heuristic considers for each header the number of instructions times predecessors. The header with the smallest heuristic value is then chosen.

Test programs with irreducible loops were used to measure the effect of the three different approaches. Dfa simulates a deterministic finite automata representing an irreducible loop containing two independent natural loops (see Fig. 2a in [11]). Arraymerge, extracted and translated from a Fortan application, merges two sorted arrays. The remaining programs are common UNIX utilities.

The measurements were collected for the Sun SPARC architecture using the environment for architectural study and experimentation (EASE) that is integrated into VPO. The left part of Table 1 depicts the number of dynamically executed instructions of a function that was originally irreducible. Changes in percent are reported relative to not optimizing irreducible loops. The table shows comparable reductions of 1-40% in the number of executed instructions for DJ, T3 and /TR. The improvements for T_r can be attributes in part to VPO, which still applies loop optimizations to reducible loops contained in the same function as irreducible ones. Other compilers may suppress optimizations resulting in even higher gains for DJ or T_r. The quantity of improvements are subject to the execution frequency of irreducible regions within the enclosing function. For example, Arraymerge contains a central loop for sorting that was irreducible. Tail, on the other hand, contains an irreducible loop for block reads, which is executed infrequently relative the the other instructions within the function. The function "skipcomment" in Unifdef1 showed worse results for T_r, which is corre-

Table 1. Instructions and their Changes for Irreducible Regions

Program	DJ Graph	Node Splitting		DJ Graph	Node Splitting	
		T3(trad.)	T_r(opt.)		T3(trad.)	T_r(opt.)
dfa	-13.91%	-13.85%	-13.88%	-4.79%	+30.54%	+21.56%
arraymerge	-36.76%	-39.70%	-39.70%	-0.83%	+32.50%	+19.17%
tail	0.00%	0.00%	0.00%	+1.70%	+6.60%	+3.83%
unifdef1	-0.36%	+9.01%	+10.37%	+7.14%	+26.79%	+28.57%
unifdef2	-4.40%	-7.23%	-1.10%	+1.79%	+21.43%	+25.00%
hyphen	+0.01%	+0.01%	+0.01%	+8.93%	+20.24%	+20.24%
cpp	+0.05%	-1.61%	-1.18%	-0.27%	+1.64%	+2.33%
nroff1	-8.28%	-7.19%	-13.50%	+0.84%	+35.15%	+10.46%
nroff2	-4.37%	-4.42%	-0.19%	+0.47%	+25.58%	+1.86%
nroff3	0.00%	+0.06%	+0.13%	0.00%	+16.67%	+9.80%
sed	-0.59%	-4.02%	-4.49%	+2.06%	-0.40%	-1.27%
	Dynamically Executed Instr.			Static Code Size (Instr.)		

lated to fewer delay slots of branches being filled. Similar effects were observed for cases where little changes were observed.

The right part of Table 1 depicts for a function of a program containing an irreducible loop the size of the function in number of instructions. The code size only changes insignificantly for DJ-Graphs. These small changes are due to other optimizations. The quantity of changes depends on the number of preheaders and the compensation by other optimizations, such as peephole optimization. For T_r, the code size changes between -1% and 28%. This change in size is measured relative to the original function containing an irreducible loop. The change in code size relative to the *entire program* was between 0.5% and 3.5% for larger test programs and 8-17% where the irreducible loop comprised most of the test program (Dfa, Arraymerge and Hyphen). The fact that node splitting stops at function boundaries limits the overall increase in code size for the entire program so that exponential growth was not encountered in the experiments and is unlikely in general. T3 resulted in more code growth (up to 35%). T3 mostly shows a differnt dynamic instruction count than T_r indicating that T_r reduces the amount of code duplication while preserving the performance.

The differences between the two node splitting techniques are further illustrated in Table 2 depicting the number of copied register transfer lists (RTLs) for T3 and T_r (changes relative to T3 parenthesis). Since both node splitting approaches are performed as one of the first optimizations, each RTL of the intermediate code representation resembles a very simplistic instruction. The numbers show that the traditional method results in significantly more replicated code after node splitting than the T_r, which only requires 1-30% of copied RTLs under T_r relative to T3. T3 may yield considerably inferior results that T_r for optimizing compilers with less aggressive optimizations than VPO. These findings indicate that T_r is superior to the traditional approach but actual savings depend on the phase ordering of optimizations and the infrastructure of the optimizing compiler as such.

In addition, we compared the node splitting methods T3 and T_r with the controlled node splitting (CNS) with heuristic by Janssen and Corporaal [7]. The CNS approach is detailed in the related work section. The measurements indicated that CNS differed only insignificantly from our T3 approach, both in the number of executed instructions and the change in code size. Careful analysis revealed that the heuristic used for T3 almost always picked

Table 2. RTLs copied during Node Splitting

Program(Function)	T3	T_r(opt.)
dfa(main)	701	204 (-70.90%)
arraymerge(MergeArrays)	306	50 (-83.66%)
tail(main)	1906	100 (-94.75%)
unifdef1(skipcomment)	218	56 (-74.31%)
unifdef2(skipquote)	191	44 (-76.96%)
hyphen(main)	914	153 (-83.26%)
cpp(cotoken)	2791	71 (-97.46%)
nroff1(text)	975	138 (-85.85%)
nroff2(getword)	787	103 (-86.91%)
nroff3(suffix)	417	28 (-93.29%)
sed(fcomp)	4897	38 (-99.22%)

the same nodes for splitting as CNS. Further restrictions on node selection by CNS only occurred in one case (nroff) but had hardly any effect on the results.

Finally, we also measured the instruction cache performance for a 4kB and 512B direct-mapped cache using VPO and EASE. The hit ratio did not change significantly (less than 1%) for the tested programs, regardless of the cache size. For changing code sizes, the cache work is often a more appropriate measurement [8], where a miss accounts for 10 cycles delay (for going to the next memory level) and a hit for one cycle. The methods of handling irreducible loops all resulted in reduced cache work for most cases, varying between a reduction of 6% and 28%. This reduction seems to indicate that execution in replicated regions tends to be localized, *i.e.*, once such a region is entered, executing progresses within this replica rather than transferring control between different replicas.

7 Related Work

Reducible flow graphs were first mentioned by Allen [2]. The idea of node splitting stems from Cocke and Miller [4]. DJ Graphs are due to Sreedhar *et. al.* [11]. Havlak proposed a method for recognizing reducible and irreducible loops as well as the nesting of either ones [5]. His algorithm used node splitting only for headers of natural loops contained within irreducible loops as a means to have distinct header nodes. This work did not use node splitting to make irreducible loops reducible, whereas our work did. Furthermore, our notion of backedges is independent of any graph traversals while Havlak's backedges for irreducible loops depend on the order of a traversal of the control flow. Ramalingam [10] contributed performance improvements and a common formal framework for three schemes for recognizing loop structures, including those by Sreedhar *et al.* and Havlak. Since our study is concerned with the performance of the *compiled programs* rather than the performance of the *compiler*, we did not implement his improvements. However, we strengthen the results of [10] through our structural definition of loops and our SED-maximal loop sets that capture the loop descriptions of previous work and represent a *minimal loop nesting forest*. In particular, we reduce irreducible loops into reducible ones in a bottom-up fashion (wrt. the level in the dominator tree) by isolating (and freezing) the largest domain and its header while splitting the remaining nodes in the loop set. Recursive splitting ensures that different loops within one irreducible region can be isolated. Hence, we go beyond the approach by Sreedhar *et al.* although our algorithm uses the same data structures. We also showed how several optimization methods for reducible graphs can be transformed into methods for irreducible graphs, which, once again, strengthens Ramalingam's results [10].

The notion of MSED-sets is introduced by Janssen and Corporaal [7], and a node-splitting algorithm, called "Controlled Node Splitting", is presented that tries to minimize the number of splits. However, their algorithm differs from our approach in that they use the traditional approach of splitting *one* node while we exclude one node from splitting and split *all other nodes* in the MSED-set. They report reductions in code sizes to almost 1/10 of the original size. Our measurements indicated that these savings were mostly due to the heuristic for node selection. We can also show that their formulation seldom leads to savings in practise while ours handles nested irregular regions more elegantly [12].

8 Conclusion

We derived a new approach for optimized node splitting that transforms irreducible regions of control flow into reducible ones. This method is superior to approaches previously published since it reduces the number of replicated nodes by comparison. We also discussed the application of DJ Graphs to recognize the structure of irreducible loops and implemented extensions to common code optimizations to handle these new types of loops. Measurements show improvements of 1-40% in the number of executed instructions for the approaches of handling irreducible loops. Optimized node splitting has the advantage that it does not require changes to other code optimizations within the compiler but may increase the code size of large programs by about 2% and the size of small programs by about 12%. On the average, it results in less code growth than traditional node splitting and, hence, is superior to it.

References

1. A. V. Aho, R. Sethi, and J. D. Ullman. *Compilers - Principles, Techniques, and Tools.* Addison-Wesley, 1986.
2. F. Allen. Control flow analysis. *Sigplan Notices*, 5(7):1-19, 1970.
3. M. E. Benitez and J. W. Davidson. A portable global optimizer and linker. In *ACM SIGPLAN Conf. on Programming Language Design and Impl.*, pages 329-338, June 1988.
4. J. Cocke and J. Miller. Some analysis techniques for optimizing computer programs. In *2nd Hawaii Conference on System Sciences*, pages 143-146, 1969.
5. P. Havlak. Nesting if reducible and irreducible loops. *ACM Trans. Programming Languages and Systems*, 19(4):557-567, July 1997.
6. J. Hoogerbrugge and L. Augusteijn. Instruction scheduling for trimedia. *Journal of Instruction-Level Parallelsim*, 1(1-2), 1999. www.jilp.org.
7. J. Janssen and H. Corporaal. Making graphs reducible with controlled node splitting. *ACM Trans. Programming Languages and Systems*, 19(6):1031-1052, November 1997.
8. F. Mueller and D. B. Whalley. Avoiding unconditional jumps by code replication. In *ACM SIGPLAN Conf. on Programming Language Design and Impl.*, pages 322-330, June 1992.
9. F. Mueller and D. B. Whalley. Avoiding conditional branches by code replication. In *ACM SIGPLAN Conf. on Programming Language Design and Impl.*, pages 56-66, June 1995.
10. G. Ramalingam. On loop, dominators, and dominance frontier. In *ACM SIGPLAN Conf. on Programming Language Design and Impl.*, pages 233-241, June 2000.
11. V. Sreedhar, G. Gao, and Y. Lee. Identifying loops using DJ graphs. *ACM Trans. Programming Languages and Systems*, 18(6):649-658, November 1996.

12. S. Unger and F. Mueller. Handling irreducible loops: Optimized node splitting vs. dj-graphs. TR 146, Inst. f. Informatik, Humbolt University Berlin, January 2001. www.informatik.hu-berlin.de/~mueller.
13. Nancy J. Warter, Grant E. Haab, Krishna Subramanian, and John W. Bockhaus. Enhanced modulo scheduling for loops with conditional branches. In *25th Annual International Symposium on Microarchitecture (MICRO-25)*, pages 170–179, 1992.

Algorithm for Optimized Node Splitting

In the following, the recursive algorithm for T_r is given. Transformations are initiated by a call splt_loops(start node, empty set). The first argument to splt_loops is the node dominating all nodes that have yet to be processed. The second argument is a set of nodes that, if non-empty, defines a region that should be handled since all nodes outside of it have already been processed and did not changed. The function returns true if the given node has any edges that indicate an irreducible loop at its level.

```
bool splt_loops(top, set) {
  cross = false;
  foreach (child in domtree.successors(top))
    if (set is empty OR child in set)
      if (splt_loops(child, set))
        cross = true;
  if (cross) handle_ir_children(top, set);
  foreach (predecessor in controlflow.preds(top))
    if (is_sp_back(pred, top) AND !(top dominates pred))
      return true;
  return false;
}
```

At first, splt_loops handles all levels below the given node (but only within the current region). If any of these calls return true, then a child of top contains an irreducible loop on the level just below top. This is handled in a bottom-up fashion so that the domains in that loop are already reducible. After the children of the current top have been handled completely, it is checked if there exits any edge that indicates an irreducible loop on the level of top itself and the result is returned. The function handle_ir_children is called with the external dominator node as an argument. It has to find all SED-maximal loop-sets and then split the irreducible ones one after another.

```
void handle_ir_children(top, set) {
  // find all strongly conntected components (SCCs)
  scclist = find_sccs(child, set, top.level);
  foreach (scc in scclist)
    if (size_list(scc) > 1) // non-trivial component
      handle_scc(top, scc);
}
```

After all SCCs have been found, they are now converted one by one into reducible regions by `handle_scc`.

```
void handle_scc(top, scc) {
  ComputeWeights(top, scc);
  // find header w/ max sum(weights(nodes in domain))
  hdr = ChooseNode(msed);
  // split nodes in scc (except hdr and it domain)
  SplitSCC(hdr, scc);
  RecomputeDJG(top); // renew control-flow and DJ info
  // add copies that are headers to tops
  tops = find_top_nodes(scc);
  foreach (hdr in tops)
    splt_loops(hdr, scc); // recurse: split all headers
}
```

SplitSCC then splits all nodes in the SCC except the chosen node and its domain, rearranges the control flow graph and changes the dominator information such that the copied regions are independent subtrees in the dominator tree.

```
void SplitSCC(header, scc) {
  make a copy of nodes in {scc - domain(header)};
  connect copies (within loop set and immediate
    neighbors outside loop set), renew DJ info;
  scc = scc + copies;
}
```

The heuristic selects the node with the maximum weight out of headers in the MSED-set.

```
node ChooseNode(msed) {
  MaxWeight = 0;
  foreach (node in msed)
    if (node.weight > MaxWeight) {
      MaxWeight = node.weight;
      MaxNode = node;
    }
  return MaxNode;
}
```

Weights of header nodes are computed as the sum of the weights of nodes in the domain of the header. The weight of a single node `sigma` is determined as the number of RTLs of this nodes (instructions in the intermediate representation) excluding branches and jumps.

```
void ComputeWeights(top, scc) {
  foreach (node in scc)
    if (node.level == top.level + 1) {
      GetWeight(node, node, scc);
      add_list(node, msed);
    }
}
```

```
void GetWeight(node, header, scc) {
  node.weight = sigma(node);
  foreach (child in domtree.successors(node))
    if (in_list(child, scc)) {
      GetWeight(child, header, scc);
      node.weight = node.weight + child.weight;
    }
  node.header = header;
}
```

See [12] for more details including an adapted algorithm for finding strongly connected components (SCCs).

Load Redundancy Elimination on Executable Code*

Manel Fernández[1], Roger Espasa[1], and Saumya Debray[2]

[1] Computer Architecture Department, Universitat Politècnica de Catalunya
Barcelona, Spain
{mfernand,roger}@ac.upc.es
[2] Department of Computer Science, University of Arizona
Tucson AZ, USA
debray@cs.arizona.edu

Abstract. Optimizations performed at link time or directly applied to final program executables have received increased attention in recent years. This paper discuss the discovery and elimination of redundant load operations in the context of a link time optimizer, an optimization that we call *Load Redundancy Elimination (LRE)*. Our experiments show that between 50% and 75% of a program's memory references can be considered redundant because they are accessing memory locations that have been referenced less than 200–400 instructions away. We then present three profile-based LRE algorithms targeted at optimizing away these redundancies. Our results show that between 5% and 30% of the redundancy detected can indeed be eliminated, which translates into program speedups in the range of 3% to 8%. We also test our algorithm assuming different cache latencies, and show that, if latencies continue to grow, the load redundancy elimination will become more important.

1 Introduction

Optimizations performed at link time or directly applied to final program executables have received increased attention in recent years [13,3,11]. First, large programs tend to be compiled using separate compilation, that is, one or a few files at a time. Therefore, the compiler does not have the opportunity to optimize the full program as a whole, even performing sophisticated inter-procedural analysis. A second reason is the emergence of profile-directed compilation techniques [12,7]. However, the same problem of separate compilation plagues the use of profile feedback: large projects will be forced to re-build every file to take advantage of the profiling information. Link time optimizations are able to re-optimize the final binary using profile data without recompiling source code.

This paper presents an optimization to be applied in the context of link time optimizers. We discuss the discovery and elimination of load operations

---

* This work is being supported by the Spanish Ministry of Education under grants CYCIT TIC98-0511 and PN98 46057403-1. The research described in this paper has been developed using the resources of the CEPBA.

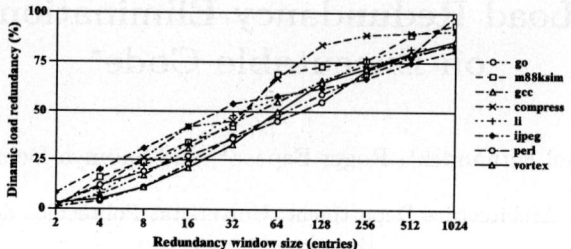

Fig. 1. Dynamic amount of load redundancy for the whole SPECint95 (Compaq/Alpha executables compiled with full optimizations). X-axis is logarithmic

that are redundant and can be safely removed in order to speed up a program, an optimization that we call *Load Redundancy Elimination (LRE)*. Unnecessary memory references appear in a binary due to a variety of reasons: a variable may not have been kept in a register by the compiler because it was a global, or maybe the compiler was unable to resolve aliasing adequately. We then present three profile-based LRE algorithms targeted at optimizing away these redundancies: a basic LRE algorithm for extended basic blocks, and two general algorithms that work over regions of arbitrary control flow complexity: one for removing fully redundant loads and the other for removing partially redundant loads.

2 Dynamic Amount of Load Redundancy

We start motivating our work by measuring a potential upper bound on how many loads could be removed from a program. Our goal is to measure how often a load is re-loading data that has already been loaded in the near past. Thus, we instrument the SPECint95 programs to catch all their memory references. Dynamic load redundancy is measured by recording the most recent n memory references into a *redundancy window*. This is a simple FIFO queue, where new references coming into it displace the oldest reference stored in the window. A dynamic instance of a load is then redundant if its effective address matches the address of any prior load or store that is still in the redundancy window.

The results of our measures are shown in Figure 1, for various redundancy window sizes. Clearly, a lot of redundancy exists even in these highly optimized binaries. As an example, for m88ksim, almost 75% of all load references were to memory locations that had been referenced by at least one of the most recent 256 memory instructions. In general, almost 50% of all loads are re-loading a data item that was read/written less than 100 memory instructions ago. Today's optimizing compilers are clearly able to deal with regions larger than this size, and should be expected to optimize all this redundancy away.

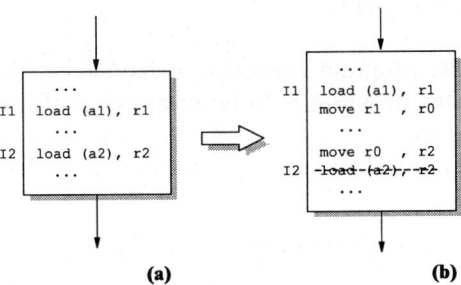

Fig. 2. Elimination of redundant load inside a machine code basic block

3 LRE on Executable Code

The simplest example of Load Redundancy Elimination (LRE) is shown in Figure 2. Suppose that an instruction I_1 loads a value into register r_1 from memory location pointed by a_1. This load is followed after some instructions by another instruction I_2 within the same basic block, which puts its value from location pointed by a_2 into register r_2. If it can be proved that both memory locations are the same, and this location is not modified between these two instructions, then I_2 is *redundant* in front of I_1[1]. Once a redundant load has been identified, we may try to eliminate it by *bypassing* the value from the first load to the redundant one, as shown in Figure 2b. This is accomplished by inserting a couple of move operations that use a new *available* register (r_0 in the example).

Although this is the most simple case of LRE, it already introduces the three fundamental problems that this optimization has to deal with. The first problem is to decide if both loads are really accessing the same memory location, and also that there is no store between them that *may* be in conflict with that location. There is an extensive work on *alias analysis* [1,9], but they are typically formulated in terms of source-level constructs that do not handle features encountered in executable programs [4]. The second problem is to find a register to bypass the source value to the redundant load. *Register liveness analysis* computes which registers are live at every point in the code [6,10]. Finally, the example shows that eliminating a load doesn't come without a cost: we have inserted "move" instructions in the code in the hope that (a) they can be removed by a copy propagator and (b) even if they are not, their cost will be lower than that of the original redundant load. In any case, a careful *cost-benefit* analysis is required.

Alias and register liveness analysis are well-known data-flow problems already described in the literature [9]. From now on, we assume that both of them have been computed before applying the LRE optimization. The more accurate are these analysis, the more opportunities appear for LRE.

---

[1] Note that the redundancy is also present if the instruction I_1 is a store operation.

4 Profile-Guided LRE

Information about the program execution behavior can be very useful in optimizing programs. Our proposal is to be aware of *profile information* to guide LRE. We next outline the algorithms used and present the cost-benefit equations that use the profile information to choose the candidates for removal.

4.1 Eliminating Close Redundancy

The results presented in Section 2 show that between 25% and 40% of all the redundancy detected can be captured using a redundancy window of just 16 entries. This indicates that the first source of redundancy that we should target our optimization at is located within small groups of basic blocks.

A natural extension of the example given in Figure 2 is to perform LRE on Extended Basic Blocks[2]. For every load in the EBB, we search bottom-up for other load or store that may be a source of redundancy, as shown in Figure 3a. But what if the hot path does not flow through BB2? A move instruction has been inserted in the critical path, although the bypassed value will be most often unused. There is no benefit in applying LRE and we might risk lowering performance. The lesson to learn is that it is not always beneficial to remove a redundant load, and it is necessary to apply LRE carefully. We need to be compute as precisely as possible the benefit (B) and cost (C) of applying the optimization for each particular load. The equations we use are as follows:

$$B = lat_{load} \times BB_2^{freq}$$
$$C = lat_{move} \times (BB_1^{freq} + BB_2^{freq})$$
$$LRE \Leftrightarrow C \leq B$$

The benefit includes the latency of the load being eliminated times the frequency of its basic block. The costs include the latencies of the *new* two "move" instructions weighted by the execution frequencies of their corresponding basic blocks. Note that the costs are pessimistic, as they always include *both* "move" instructions even though they might be later removed by a copy propagator.

4.2 Eliminating Distant Redundancy

Going back to Figure 1, there is still a lot of redundancy that can be caught if we can explore larger distances between instructions. To catch this redundancy, we need to apply LRE to regions of code that expand beyond an EBB.

The second algorithm we present is targeted at detecting *fully redundant loads*, that is, loads that are redundant with respect to *all* the control flow paths that reach them. For every load, we scan all potential paths looking for a source instruction that may render it. As shown in Figure 3b, if redundancy is found on all paths and all intervening stores do not alias with the load, the

---
[2] An EBB is a set of basic blocks with a single entry point but multiple exit points.

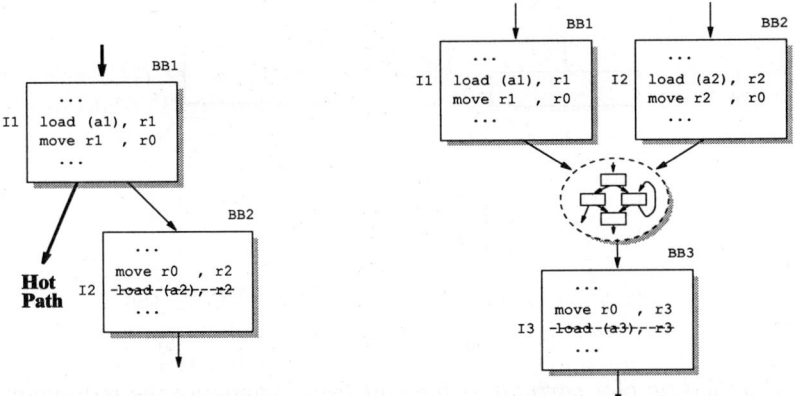

Fig. 3. Elimination of *fully redundant* loads: (a) within extended basic blocks, (b) for multi-path redundant loads. LRE should be applied coupled to a cost-benefit analysis

load becomes a candidate for removal. Then we apply the cost-benefit equations already described, although we have to extend the cost (C) to account for all the move instructions that must be inserted on each of the redundancy paths:

$$C = lat_{move} \times \left(BB_{red}^{freq} + \sum_{i=1}^{n} BB_{src_i}^{freq} \right)$$

If the benefit of removing the candidate out-weight the cost of adding the "move" instructions, the algorithm starts looking for an available register to bypass the value [5]. If no register is found, then the load can not be removed.

In the LRE algorithms discussed so far, the removal of a load is a safe transformation because there is always a static source of redundancy. However, a high percentage of dynamic redundancy comes from *partially redundant loads*, that is, loads that are redundant only on some control flow paths. Imagine that instruction I_2 in Figure 4 is an invariant inside the loop. The previous algorithm will fail to remove the load because it is not fully redundant: I_2 is redundant on the loop back-edge with I_1, but it is not on the entry point of the loop. This situation arises frequently, even without considering loops.

Partial LRE involves insertion of new instructions. As insertions are usually done on a different EBB, the inserted instructions become *speculative*. In general, it is safe to perform speculation for instructions that cannot cause exceptions, but this is not the case for speculative loads. In order to deal with safe insertions only, our implementation of partial LRE is restricted to global and stack references. We have followed the approach described by Horspool and Ho [8], that proposed a general profile driven PRE algorithm based upon edge profiles. The idea is to insert copies on less frequently executed paths in favor of more frequently executed paths. We have adapted their algorithm to (a) only consider redundant load operations, and (b) to deal with our cost-benefit analysis. Being n the

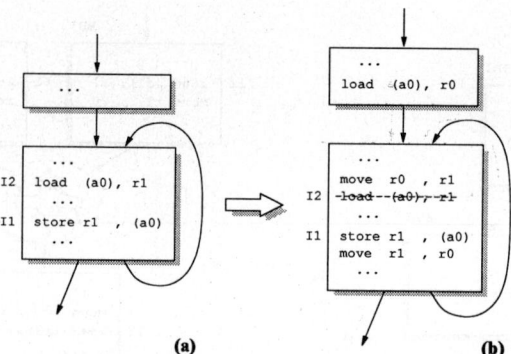

Fig. 4. Elimination of a *partially redundant load*. Removing the redundant load requires to insert instances in less-frequent paths, in order to make the load fully redundant

number of partial redundancies and m the number of load insertions needed, the cost of removing a load is then:

$$C_{bypass} = lat_{move} \times \left(BB_{red}^{freq} + \sum_{i=1}^{n} BB_{src_i}^{freq} \right)$$
$$C_{insert} = lat_{load} \times \sum_{i=1}^{m} EDG_i^{freq}, \quad C = C_{bypass} + C_{insert}$$

Cost involves not only bypassing the value, but inserting the new load operations that make the candidate become fully redundant. We use the same algorithm as before for obtaining available registers, but it has been extended to also look for register availability at the new load insertion points.

5 Performance Evaluation

We have implemented the proposed LRE approaches within the `alto` link-time optimizer [11,5]. The SPEC95 integer benchmarks were compiled with full optimizations using the vendor-supplied C compiler, on an AlphaServer equipped with an Alpha 21264 microprocessor. The programs were instrumented using Pixie and executed on the SPEC training inputs to obtain an execution frequency profile. Finally, these binaries and were processed by Alto with/without using different degrees of profile-guided LRE: LRE on EBB for catching close redundancy, and fully- and partial-LRE for catching distant redundancy.

We start evaluating the effectiveness of the three LRE algorithms under study by comparing the number of dynamic loads executed, for each benchmark. As it can be seen in Figure 5a, all programs show improvements around 5%, with some rather better cases such as `m88ksim` and `compress`. The results also show that working only on EBBs is not enough to catch the close-redundancy we presented in Section 2. Except for `perl` and `vortex`, LRE applied to EBBs yields a small reduction in dynamic loads. By contrast, fully-LRE improves the overall results

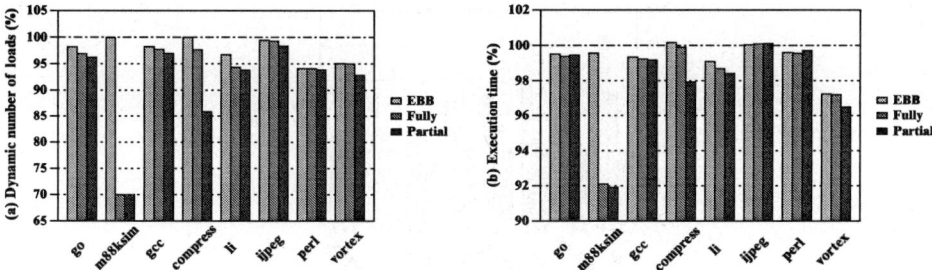

Fig. 5. Effect of different LRE degrees in (a) number of loads at run time, and (b) execution time. The baseline is optimized binaries by Alto without any LRE at all

for five programs and partial-LRE only yields extra improvements for compress. Additional number to better understand this results are presented in [5].

We are also interested in quantifying the percentage of reduction in execution time. We have decided to use the SimpleScalar toolset [2] that models a Compaq Alpha 21264 to get an accurate measure of the differences between the LRE algorithms. Results are presented in Figure 5b. Since loads are only a fraction of all instructions executed in a program, reduction in execution time is smaller than the corresponding reduction in number of dynamic loads. Thus, for example, the 30% reduction in dynamic loads in m88ksim only translates into an 8% reduction in execution time. However, the decrease in execution time shows that we have removed some loads that indeed were on the program's critical path.

Another interesting measure is to see what will happen in the future, as L1-cache latency continues to increase. Current CPUs are typically at a 2-cycle or 3-cycle latency and the trend is towards hyper-pipelining and, therefore, longer latencies. We re-simulated all the benchmarks changing the L1-cache latency to 3, 4 and 5 cycles. We also re-compiled every benchmark, since our cost/benefit analysis is dependent on the latency of the loads. Results can be seen in Figure 6. As expected, the longer the latency the worse the execution time of all programs. However, as latency increases, the importance of performing LRE also grows. For example, after applying partial-LRE in vortex, the execution time at a 5-cycle latency is *better* than the original execution time using a 3-cycle latency.

6 Summary and Future Directions

This paper has presented three algorithms to perform load redundancy elimination on executable files. We have shown that between 50% and 75% of all memory references in the SPECint95 programs can be considered "redundant"', since they access memory locations that had already been referenced by another load or store within a close dynamic distance. The first algorithm, LRE within extended basic blocks, is able to remove less than 5% of all loads, and yields speedups below 4% in execution time. The results indicate that an extended

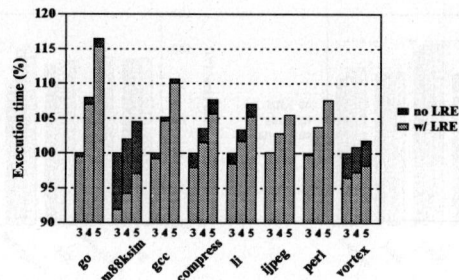

Fig. 6. Effect of load latency in execution time (from 3-cycle to 5-cycle hit latency)

basic block is too small to catch the redundancy measured in our experiments. The second algorithm, LRE for fully redundant loads on arbitrary control flow regions, yields an average increase of a 10% in loads to be removed. Despite this small increase, fully-LRE does detect some of the critical loads and thus increases speedups up to an 8%. The third algorithm, LRE for partially redundant loads, significantly increases the number of static loads removed (a 30% over the EBB algorithm). However, the algorithm only shows its strengths on compress, where an extra 12% of dynamic loads are removed over the fully-LRE algorithm. We believe that we need to explore better alias analysis algorithms to fully obtain the potential of the LRE optimization. We also test our algorithms assuming different cache latencies, and show that, if latencies continue to grow, LRE will become more important.

References

1. A. V. Aho, R. Sethi, and J. D. Ullman. *Compilers principles, techniques, and tools*. Addison-Wesley, Reading, MA, 1986.
2. D. Burger and T. M. Austin. The SimpleScalar tool set, version 2.0. Technical Report CS-TR-97-1342, CS Department, University of Wisconsin-Madison, 1997.
3. R. Cohn, D. Goodwin, P. G. Lowney, and N. Rubin. Spike: An optimizer for Alpha/NT executables. In USENIX, editor, *The USENIX Windows NT Workshop 1997*, pages 17–23, Seattle, Washington, August 11–13 1997.
4. S. Debray, R. Muth, and M. Weippert. Alias analysis of executable code. In *The 25th ACM SIGPLAN-SIGACT Symposium on Principles of Programming Languages*, pages 12–24, Orlando, Florida, January 19–21 1998.
5. M. Fernández, R. Espasa, and S. Debray. Load redundancy elimination on executable code. Technical Report UPC-DAC-2001-3, Computer Architecture Department, Universitat Politècnica de Catalunya-Barcelona, 2001.
6. D. W. Goodwin. Interprocedural dataflow analysis in an executable optimizer. In *Proceedings of the ACM SIGPLAN '97 Conference on Programming Language Design and Implementation*, pages 122–133, Las Vegas, Nevada, June 15–18 1997.
7. R. Gupta, D. A. Berson, and J. Z. Fang. Path profile guided partial redundancy elimination using speculation. In *Proceedings of the 1998 International Conference on Computer Languages*, pages 230–239, Chicago, May 14–16 1998.

8. R. N. Horspool and H. C. Ho. Partial redundancy elimination driven by a cost-benefit analysis. In *8th Israeli Conference on Computer System and Software Engineering*, pages 111–118, Herzliya, Israel, June 1997.
9. S. S. Muchnick. *Building an Optimizing Compiler*. Morgan Kaufman, 1997.
10. R. Muth. *Alto: A Platform for Object Code Modification*. PhD thesis, Department of Computer Science, University of Arizona, 1999.
11. R. Muth, S. Debray, S. Watterson, and K. de Bosschere. alto: A link-time optimizer for the DEC Alpha. Technical Report TR98-14, Department of Computer Science, University of Arizona, 1998.
12. K. Pettis and R. C. Hansen. Profile guided code positioning. In *Proceedings of the ACM SIGPLAN '90 Conference on Programming Language Design and Implementation*, pages 16–27, June 1990.
13. A. Srivastava and D. W. Wall. A practical system for intermodule code optimization at link-time. *Journal of Programming Languages*, 1(1):1–18, Dec. 1992.

Loop-Carried Code Placement

Peter Faber, Martin Griebl, and Christian Lengauer

Fakultät für Mathematik und Informatik. Universität Passau
D–94030 Passau, Germany
{faber,griebl,lengauer}@fmi.uni-passau.de

Abstract. Traditional code optimization techniques treat loops as non-predictable structures and do not consider expressions containing array accesses for optimization. We show that the polyhedron model can be used to implement code placement techniques that exploit equalities of expressions that hold between loop iterations. We also present preliminary results for a simple example.

1 Introduction

Traditional code optimization techniques treat loops as non-predictable structures. In order to exploit the equality of expressions across loop iterations in code placement or code motion, loops may be partially unrolled [9,5]. However, a loop may have to be unrolled infinitely often to remove *all* redundancies, which would lead to data structures that are unbounded in size. The polyhedron model [3,7] offers a way to analyze memory accesses in loops by considering symbolically expressible sets of loop iterations. These descriptions are usually restricted to affine expressions in the index variables of surrounding loops and constants. Thus, in general, it is only possible to analyze code fragments. The representation of loop iterations in the polyhedron model provides a means for transformations based on the analysis of array accesses in loop nests: Wonnacott extended constant propagation and dead code elimination to arrays [10].

In this work, we use the polyhedron model to extend a further class of optimization techniques to arrays – namely code placement optimizations. Our aim is to improve code written by a programmer without attention to possible recomputations of the same value in different loop iterations. Although the method is in principle also applicable to WHILE-loops, we only consider DO-loops here.

2 Loop-Carried Code Placement

The central question of code placement is where to put the computation of an expression in order to ensure this computation to be performed only once and only if needed. Relevant data flow information is gathered in most approaches by syntactic analysis. There are also approaches for the analysis of scalars that introduce semantic properties, such as the one employed by Steffen, Knoop and Rüthing [5], which exploits equalities resulting from assigning terms to variables.

We restrict ourselves to a syntactic – but loop-carried – equivalence of expressions: we use affine expressions in loop indices to infer equality. This enables us to prove the equality of terms that are not syntactically identical, e.g., C(i,i) and C(i,j) in Ex. 1, which represent the same value for i = j.

We minimize the amount of computations performed during the execution of a loop nest by replacing computations of already computed values with array lookups. As a cost model, we employ the number of function calls and arithmetic operations executed, while we view reads and writes as zero-cost operations.

Example 1.

```
DO j=1,n
  DO i=1,n+1
  ! Statement S1
  ! Occurrences:
  !  [7]     [6]  [1]  [3]  [2]  [5]  [4]
     D(i,j)  =  A(i)  **  B(j)  +  C(i,i)
  ! Statement S2
  ! Occurrences:
  !  [14]  [13]  [8]  [10]  [9]  [12]  [11]
     E(i,j)  =  A(i)  **  B(j)  +  C(i,j)
  END DO
END DO
```

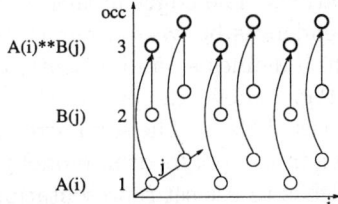

Fig. 1. OIG for A(i) ** B(j) of Ex. 1 (n = 2)

In the program text above, the term A(i)**B(j) occurs twice and represents the same value in both locations, so it suffices to compute this term once. However, if i = j, the complete terms on the right hand side (RHS) of the assignments are identical; in this case, it suffices to compute the RHS once. We remove the redundant computations that occur in the second statement (the computation of A(i)**B(j) for all i, j, and the computation of A(i)**B(j)+C(i,j), i = j), replacing them by memory lookups.

2.1 Basic Structures

We use generalizations of the usual structures in the polyhedron model that are described in detail, e.g., by Cohen [1] and by Lengauer [7].

A subroutine is a term combined of statements, which are terms composed of an operator and, possibly, a list of arguments. Each term is identified with a unique number, its *occurrence*. In contrast to the conventional polyhedron model, which is based on read and write *accesses*, we base our method on occurrences, enabling references to any point in the program text. In Ex. 1, the occurrences are placed in brackets on the comment lines above the corresponding code. Note that the order of occurrences corresponds to the order of target code a compiler would generate. Analogously to the conventional polyhedron model, we consider different *occurrence instances*. These are – in a nest of n loops – represented by a vector $\alpha \in \mathbb{Z}^{n+1}$ with the first n components given by the *index vector* defining the loop iteration and the last component given by the occurrence. The set of occurrence instances is denoted OI. Fig. 1 shows the instances of occurrences

1–3 from Ex. 1, for n = 2. The index space spans the i×j-plane of the diagram, while occurrences are assigned to the vertical occ-axis.

The usual dependence analysis in the polyhedron model – such as Feautrier's [2] – captures dependences between occurrences that represent accesses. However, in order to model execution on the level of occurrences, we have to include dependences arising from the combination of occurrences. For flow dependences, the application of a function or operator depends on its input arguments, and the output arguments depend on the function application. Anti and output dependences do not occur between compound occurrences. We combine all these dependences in a relation E.

With E as edge relation, we create a graph (OI, E) that mimics the structure of the terms of the loop body and enables us to argue about different loop iterations. The edges in this *occurrence instance graph* (OIG) are the "normal" dependences between occurrence instances: any order on OI that is compatible with E defines a valid execution of the program.

Fig. 2 shows the part of the OIG that contains the compound occurrence instances of Ex. 1. The solid arrows represent the dependences in E. The approach taken in the polyhedron model to represent such structures that are unbounded in size is to use set representations to combine different instances to a single set. E.g., the Omega tool [4] provides this functionality.

2.2 Code Placement by Affine Scheduling

In order to determine whether a value is computed twice, we have to introduce a notion of equality. Our equality relation $\equiv$ is based on the input dependence relation δ^i. We are only interested in dependences between reads that are executed without any conflicting write in between. Fig. 2 shows the OIG of the compound terms of Ex. 1 with dashed arrows indicating equivalences as defined above (the arrows indicate the ordered, non-reflexive part of $\equiv$).

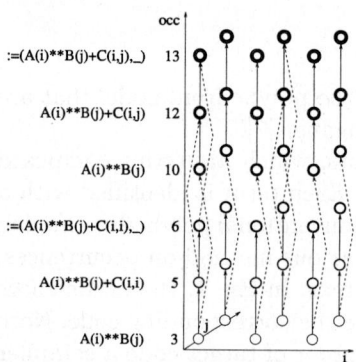

Fig. 2. OIG for the compound terms of Ex. 1 (n = 2)

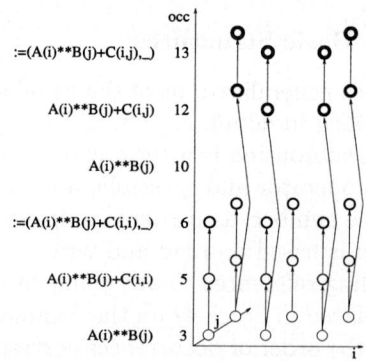

Fig. 3. COIG representation for the compound terms of Ex. 1 (n = 2)

The relation $\equiv$ divides the OI into equivalence classes $OI/\equiv$. The occurrence instances in a single equivalence class are guaranteed to represent the same value. So, in order to compute a value only once, we have to generate a single computation for each element in $OI/\equiv$. Still, these computations must be executed in an order compatible with E. We assert this by computing a schedule for the equivalence classes. I.e., we construct the condensation of the OIG and compute a schedule for the vertices of this *condensed occurrence instance graph* (COIG).

A representation of the COIG that can be directly passed to a scheduler can be obtained by choosing a single representative of an equivalence class – we choose the lexicographic minimum – and adjusting dependence information appropriately. Fig. 3 shows this representation for Ex. 1 (n = 2).

We may now compute a schedule for the vertices $OI/\equiv$ using, e.g., Feautrier's scheduler [3] – just as one would compute a schedule for the *statement instances* in conventional loop parallelization – and obtain a transformation that is applied to the index space of $OI/\equiv$. The resulting index space description defines a legal execution order and places lookups as early as possible. From this description, we can generate code using scanning techniques as the one employed by Omega [4] or the one of Quilleré and Rajopadhye [8]; this code is then rewritten to use newly introduced arrays for storing the value of scheduled occurrence instances.

3 Results and Final Remarks

We applied our method to Ex. 1. We transformed the loop nest according to Feautrier's scheduler, scanned the resulting polyhedron with the Omega code generator, and introduced auxiliary variables. This resulted in the following code:

```
DO t2=1,n
    DO t3=1,t2-1
        TMP1(t3,t2)=A(t3)**B(t2)
    END DO
    TMP2(t2)=A(t2)**B(t2)+C(t2,t2)
    D(t2,t2)=TMP2(t2)
    E(t2,t2)=TMP2(t2)
    DO t3=t2+1,n+1
        TMP1(t3,t2)=A(t3)**B(t2)
    END DO
END DO
DO t2=1,n
    DO t3=1,t2-1
        D(t3,t2)=TMP1(t3,t2)+C(t3,t3)
        E(t3,t2)=TMP1(t3,t2)+C(t3,t2)
    END DO
    DO t3=t2+1,n+1
        D(t3,t2)=TMP1(t3,t2)+C(t3,t3)
        E(t3,t2)=TMP1(t3,t2)+C(t3,t2)
    END DO
END DO
```

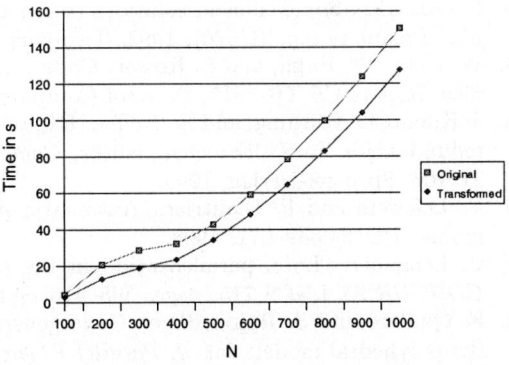

Fig. 4. Timings on a 1 GHz Pentium III

Fig. 4 shows the timing results on a 1 GHz Pentium III Xeon running Linux. The times are accumulated over 500 runs of the code fragment. The transformed code performs 12% to 37% better than the original one.

Our method is aimed at speeding up source code written by a human, where most time is spent in the computation on array elements (in scientific codes, these are usually expensive floating-point operations).

We are currently in the process of incorporating our method into our code restructurer *LooPo*. We plan to perform more substantial performance measurements when the implementation is available.

An optimization that has to be performed when applying this method to real codes is minimizing array sizes following, e.g., Feautrier and Lefebvre [6].

We have only used syntactic equivalence, augmented by equivalence on expressions that could be identified as affine for a certain vector space. Especially for the improvement of code written by a human, further exploitation of associativity and commutativity is important. Also, the possible impact of different schedulers on the transformed program remains to be investigated.

We chose computations as the cost-determining factor. A more realistic cost model should consider different costs for memory accesses, e.g., cache vs. main memory. This is a crucial point that remains for future work. Additionally, the overhead introduced by the new arrays and possibly complicated index functions still has to be reduced; ideally, the cost model should be made sensitive to computations in index functions and the time spent in memory lookups.

Acknowledgements This work is supported by the DAAD through project PROCOPE and by the DFG through project *LooPo/HPF*.

References

1. A. Cohen. *Program Analysis and Transformation: From the Polytope Model to Formal Languages.* PhD thesis, PRiSM, Université de Versailles, 1999.
2. P. Feautrier. Dataflow analysis of array and scalar references. *Int. J. Parallel Programming*, 20(1):23–53, Feb. 1991.
3. P. Feautrier. Some efficient solutions to the affine scheduling problem. *Int. J. Parallel Programming*, 21(5/6), 1992. Two-part paper.
4. W. Kelly, W. Pugh, and E. Rosser. Code generation for multiple mappings. Technical Report CS-TR-3317, Dept. of Computer Science, Univ. of Maryland, 1994.
5. J. Knoop, O. Rüthing, and B. Steffen. Expansion-based removal of semantic partial redundancies. In S. Jähnichen, editor, *Compiler Construction*, LNCS 1575, pages 91–106. Springer-Verlag, 1999.
6. V. Lefebvre and P. Feautrier. Automatic storage management for parallel programs. *PC*, 24:649–671, 1998.
7. C. Lengauer. Loop parallelization in the polytope model. In E. Best, editor, *CONCUR'93*, LNCS 715, pages 398–416. Springer-Verlag, 1993.
8. F. Quilleré and S. Rajopadhye. Code generation for automatic paralelization in the polyhedral model. *Int. J. Parallel Programming*, 28(5):469–498, 2000.
9. B. Steffen. Property-oriented expansion. In R. Cousot and D. A. Schmidt, editors, *Static Analysis, 3rd International Symposium (SAS '96)*, LNCS 1145, pages 22–40. Springer-Verlag, 1996.
10. D. Wonnacott. Extending scalar optimizations for arrays. In M. Gupta and S. M. J. Moreira, editors, *13th Workshop on Languages and Compilers for Parallel Computing (LCPC 2000)*, LNCS. Springer-Verlag, 2000. To appear.

Using a Swap Instruction to Coalesce Loads and Stores

Apan Qasem, David Whalley, Xin Yuan, and Robert van Engelen

Department of Computer Science, Florida State University
Tallahassee, FL 32306-4530, U.S.A.
phone: (850) 644-3506
{qasem,whalley,xyuan,engelen}@cs.fsu.edu

Abstract. A *swap* instruction, which exchanges a value in memory with a value of a register, is available on many architectures. The primary application of a swap instruction has been for process synchronization. As an experiment we wished to see how often a swap instruction can be used to coalesce loads and stores to improve the performance of a variety of applications. The results show that both the number of accesses to the memory system (data cache) and the number of executed instructions are reduced.

1 Introduction

An instruction that exchanges a value in memory with a value in a register has been used on a variety of machines. The primary purpose for these *swap* instructions is to provide an atomic operation for reading from and writing to memory, which has been used to construct mutual-exclusion mechanisms in software for process synchronization. In fact, there are other forms of hardware instructions that have been used to support mutual exclusion, which include the classic *test-and-set* instruction. We thought it would be interesting to see if a swap instruction could be exploited in a more conventional manner. In this paper we show that a swap instruction can also be used by a low-level code-improving transformation to coalesce loads and stores into a single instruction, which results in a reduction of memory references and executed instructions.

A swap instruction described in this paper exchanges a value in memory with a value in a register. This is illustrated in Fig. 1, which depicts a load instruction, a store instruction, and a swap instruction using an RTL (register transfer list) notation. Each assignment in an RTL represents an effect on the machine. The list of effects within a single RTL are accomplished in parallel. Thus, the swap instruction is essentially a load and store accomplished in parallel.

2 Opportunities for Exploiting a Swap

A swap instruction can potentially be exploited when a load is followed by a store to the same memory address and the value stored is not computed using the value

```
r[2] = M[x];           M[x] = r[2];           r[2] = M[x]; M[x] = r[2];
```
(a) Load Instruction   (b) Store Instruction   (c) Swap Instruction

Fig. 1. Contrasting the Effects of Load, Store, and Swap Instructions

```
                                    for (j = n-1; j > 1; j -= 2) {
    for (j = n-1; j > 1; j--)           d[j]   = d[j-1]-dd[j];
        d[j] = d[j-1]-dd[j];            d[j-1] = d[j-2]-dd[j-1];
                                    }
         (a) Original Loop                  (b) Loop after Unrolling
```

Fig. 2. Unrolling a Loop to Provide an Opportunity to Exploit a Swap Instruction

that was loaded. We investigated how often this situation occurs and we have found many direct opportunities in a number of applications. The most common situation is when the values of two variables are exchanged. However, there are also opportunities for exploiting a swap instruction after other code-improving transformations have been performed. It would appear in the code segment of Fig. 2(a) that there is no opportunity for exploiting a swap instruction. However, consider Fig. 2(b) which shows the loop unrolled by a factor of two. Now the value loaded from d[j-1] in the first assignment statement in the loop is updated in the second assignment statement and the value computed in the first assignment is not used to compute the value stored in the second assignment.

Sometimes apparent opportunities at the source code level for exploiting a swap instruction are not available after other code-improving transformations have been applied. Many code-improving transformations either eliminate (e.g. register allocation) or move (e.g. loop-invariant code motion) memory references. Coalescing loads and stores into swap instructions should only be performed after all other code-improving transformations that can affect the memory references have been applied. Fig. 3(a) shows an exchange of values after the two values are compared in an if statement. Fig. 3(b) shows a possible translation of this code segment to machine instructions. Due to common subexpression elimination, the loads of x and y in the block following the branch have been deleted in Fig. 3(c). Thus, the swap instruction cannot be exploited within that block.

3 A Code-Improving Transformation to Exploit the Swap Instruction

Fig. 4(a), shows an exchange of the values of two variables, x and y, at the source code level. Fig. 4(b) shows similar code at the SPARC machine code level, which is represented in RTLs. The variable t has been allocated to register r[1]. Register r[2] is used to hold the temporary value loaded from y and stored in x. At this point a swap could be used to coalesce the load and store of x or the load and store of y. Fig. 4(c) shows the RTLs after coalescing the load and

if (x > y) {
  t = x;
  x = y;
  y = t;
}
(a) Exchange of Values in x and y at the Source Code Level
	r[1] = M[x];
	r[2] = M[y];
	IC = r[1] ? r[2];
	PC = IC <= 0, L5;
	r[1] = M[x];
	r[2] = M[y];
	M[x] = r[2];
	M[y] = r[1];
	(b) Loads are Initially Performed in the Exchange of Values of x and y
		r[1] = M[x];
		r[2] = M[y];
		IC = r[1] ? r[2];
		PC = IC <= 0, L5;
		M[x] = r[2];
		M[y] = r[1];
		(c) Loads Are Deleted in the Exchange of Values Due to Common Subexpression Elimination

Fig. 3. Example Depicting Load Instructions Being Deleted

t = x;
x = y;
y = t;
(a) Exchange of Values in x and y at the Source Code Level
	r[1] = M[x];
	r[2] = M[y];
	M[x] = r[2];
	M[y] = r[1];
	(b) Exchange of Values in x and y at the Machine Code Level
		r[2] = M[y];
		M[x] = r[2]; r[2] = M[x];
		M[y] = r[2];
		(c) After Coalescing the Load and Store of x

Fig. 4. Example of Exchanging the Values of Two Variables

store of x. One should note that r[1] is no longer used since its live range has been renamed to r[2]. Due to the renaming of the register, the register pressure at this point in the program flow graph has been reduced by one. Reducing the register pressure can sometimes enable other code-improving transformations that require an available register to be applied. Note that the decision to coalesce the load and store of x prevents the coalescing of the load and store of y.

The transformation to coalesce a load and a store into a swap instruction was accomplished using an algorithm described in detail elsewhere [4]. The algorithm finds a load followed by a store to the same address and coalesces the two memory references together into a single swap instruction if a number conditions are met. Due to space constraints, we only present a few of the conditions.

The instruction containing the first use of the register assigned by the load has to occur after the last reference to the register to be stored. For example, consider the example in Fig. 5(a). A use of r[a] appears before the last reference to r[b] before the store instruction, which prevents the load and store from being coalesced. Fig. 5(b) shows that our compiler is able to reschedule the instructions between the load and the store to meet this condition. Now the load can be moved immediately before the store, as shown in Fig. 5(c). Once the load and store are contiguous, the two instructions can be coalesced. Fig. 5(d) shows the code sequence after the load and store have been deleted, the swap instruction has been inserted, and r[a] has been renamed to r[b].

r[a] = M[v]; ... ... = ... r[a] ...; ... = ... r[b] ...; ... M[v] = r[b];	r[a] = M[v]; ... ... = ... r[b] ...; ... = ... r[a] ...; ... M[v] = r[b];	... ... = ... r[b] ...; r[a] = M[v]; M[v] = r[b]; ... = ... r[a] ...; ...	... ... = ... r[b] ...; r[b] = M[v]; M[v] = r[b]; ... = ... r[b] ...; ...
(a) Use of r[a] Appears before a Reference to r[b]	(b) First Use of r[a] Appears after the Last Reference to r[b]	(c) Load and Store Can Now Be Made Contiguous	(d) After Coalescing the Load and Store and Renaming r[a] to r[b]

Fig. 5. Scheduling Instructions to Exploit a Swap

Table 1. Test Programs

Program	Description
bandec	constructs an LU decomposition of a sparse representation of a band diagonal matrix
bubblesort	sorts an integer array in ascending order using a bubble sort
chebpc	polynomial approximation from Chebyshev coefficients
elmhes	reduces an $N \times N$ matrix to Hessenberg form
fft	fast fourier transform
gaussj	solves linear equations using Gauss-Jordan elimination
indexx	cal. indices for the array such that the indices are in ascending order
ludcmp	performs LU decomposition of an $N \times N$ matrix
mmid	modified midpoint method
predic	performs linear prediction of a set of data points
rtflsp	finds the root of a function using the false position method
select	returns the k smallest value in an array
thresh	adjusts an image according to a threshold value
transpose	transposes a matrix
traverse	binary tree traversal without a stack
tsp	traveling salesman problem

4 Results

Table 1 describes the numerous benchmarks and applications that we used to evaluate the impact of applying the code-improving transformation to coalesce loads and stores into a swap instruction. The code-improving transformation was implemented in the *vpo* compiler [1]. *Vpo* is a compiler backend that is part of the *zephyr* system, which is supported by the National Compiler Infrastructure project. The programs depicted in boldface were directly obtained from the Numerical Recipes in C text [3]. The code in many of these benchmarks are used as utilities in a variety of programs. Thus, coalescing loads and stores into swaps can be performed on a diverse set of applications.

Table 2 depicts the results that were obtained on the test programs for coalescing loads and stores into swap instructions. We unrolled several loops in these programs by an unroll factor of two to provide opportunities for coalescing a load and a store across the original iterations of the loop. In these cases, the *Not Coalesced* column includes the unrolling of these loops to provide a fair comparison. The results show decreases in the number of instructions executed and memory references performed for a wide variety of applications. The amount of the decrease varied depending on the execution frequency of the load and store

Table 2. Results

Program	Instructions Executed			Memory References Performed		
	Not Coalesced	Coalesced	Decrease	Not Coalesced	Coalesced	Decrease
bandec	69,189	68,459	1.06%	18,054	17,324	4.04%
bubblesort	2,439,005	2,376,705	2.55%	498,734	436,434	12.49%
chebpc	7,531,984	7,029,990	6.66%	3,008,052	2,507,056	16.66%
elmhes	18,527	18,044	2.61%	3,010	2,891	3.95%
fft	4,176,112	4,148,112	0.67%	672,132	660,932	1.67%
gaussj	27,143	26,756	1.43%	7,884	7,587	3.77%
indexx	70,322	68,676	2.34%	17,132	15,981	6.72%
ludcmp	10,521,952	10,439,152	0.79%	854,915	845,715	1.08%
mmid	267,563	258,554	3.37%	88,622	79,613	10.17%
predic	40,827	38,927	4.65%	13,894	11,994	13.67%
rtflsp	81,117	80,116	1.23%	66,184	65,183	1.51%
select	19,939	19,434	2.53%	3,618	3,121	13.74%
thresh	7,958,909	7,661,796	3.73%	1,523,554	1,226,594	19.49%
transpose	42,883	37,933	11.54%	19,832	14,882	24.96%
traverse	94,159	91,090	3.26%	98,311	96,265	2.08%
tsp	64,294,814	63,950,122	0.54%	52,144,375	51,969,529	0.34%
average	6,103,402	6,019,616	3.06%	3,689,893	3,622,568	8.52%

instructions that were coalesced. As expected the use of a swap instruction did not decrease the number of data cache misses.

5 Conclusions

In this paper we have experimented with exploiting a swap instruction, which exchanges the values between a register and a location in memory. While a swap instruction has traditionally only been used for process synchronization, we wished to determine if a swap instruction could be used to coalesce loads and stores. Different types of opportunities for exploiting the swap instruction were shown to be available. A number of issues related to implementing the coalescing transformations were described. The results show that this code-improving transformation could be applied on a variety of applications and benchmarks and reductions in the number of instructions executed and memory references performed were observed.

Acknowledgements

This research was supported in part by the National Science Foundation grants EIA-9806525, CCR-9904943, CCR-0073482, and EIA-0072043.

References

1. M. E. Benitez and J. W. Davidson, "A Portable Global Optimizer and Linker," *Proceedings of the SIGPLAN'88 Symposium on Programming Language Design and Implementation*, Atlanta, GA, pp. 329–338, June 1988.

2. J. W. Davidson and S. Jinturkar, "Memory Access Coalescing: A Technique for Eliminating Redundant Memory Accesses," *Proceedings of the SIGPLAN'94 Symposium on Programming Language Design and Implementation,* pp. 186–195, June 1994.
3. W. H. Press, S. A. Teukolsky, W. T. Vetterling, and B. P. Flannery, *Numerical Recipes in C: The Art of Scientific Computing, Second Edition,* Cambridge University Press, New York, NY, 1996.
4. A. Qasem, D. Whalley, X. Yuan, R. van Engelen, "Using a Swap Instruction to Coalesce Loads and Stores," *Technical Report TR-010501,* Computer Science Dept., Florida State University.

Data-Parallel Compiler Support for Multipartitioning*

Daniel Chavarría-Miranda, John Mellor-Crummey, and Trushar Sarang

Dept. of Computer Science MS132, Rice University
Houston, TX 77005
{danich,johnmc}@cs.rice.edu

Abstract. Multipartitioning is a skewed-cyclic block distribution that yields better parallel efficiency and scalability for line-sweep computations than traditional block partitionings. This paper describes extensions to the Rice dHPF compiler for High Performance Fortran that enable it to support multipartitioned data distributions and optimizations that enable dHPF to generate efficient multipartitioned code. We describe experiments applying these techniques to parallelize serial versions of the NAS SP and BT application benchmarks and show that the performance of the code generated by dHPF is approaching that of hand-coded parallelizations based on multipartitioning.

1 Introduction

High Performance Fortran (HPF) and OpenMP provide a narrow set of choices for data and computation partitioning. While their standard partitionings can yield good performance for loosely synchronous computations, they are problematic for more tightly-coupled computations such as line sweeps. Line sweep computations are the basis for Alternating Direction Implicit (ADI) integration—a widely-used numerical technique for solving partial differential equations such as the Navier-Stokes equation [5,10], as well as a variety of other computational methods [10]. Recurrences along each dimension of the data domain make this class of computations difficult to parallelize effectively.

To support effective parallelization of line-sweep computations, a sophisticated strategy for partitioning data and computation known as *multipartitioning* was developed [5,10]. Multipartitioning distributes arrays of two or more

---

* This work has been supported in part by NASA Grant NAG 2-1181, DARPA agreement number F30602-96-1-0159, and the Los Alamos National Laboratory Computer Science Institute (LACSI) through LANL contract number 03891-99-23, as part of the prime contract (W-7405-ENG-36) between the Department of Energy and the Regents of the University of California. The U.S. Government is authorized to reproduce and distribute reprints for Governmental purposes notwithstanding any copyright annotation thereon. The views and conclusions contained herein are those of the authors and should not be interpreted as representing the official policies or endorsements, either expressed or implied of sponsoring agencies.

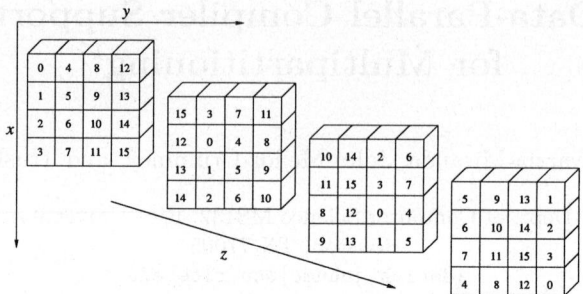

Fig. 1. 3D Multipartitioning on 16 processors

dimensions among a set of processors so that for computations performing a line sweep along any one of the array's data dimensions, (1) all processors are active in each step of the computation, (2) load-balance is nearly perfect, and (3) only a modest amount of coarse-grain communication is needed. These properties are achieved by carefully assigning each processor a balanced number of tiles between each pair of adjacent hyperplanes that are defined by the cuts along any partitioned data dimension. Figure 1 shows a 3D multipartitioning for 16 processors; the number in each tile indicates the processor that owns the block. For 3D problems, "diagonal" multi-partitionings [10] can be applied when $\sqrt{p}$ is integral, where p is the number of processors. This strategy involves partitioning the data domain into $p^{\frac{3}{2}}$ tiles. Each processor handles $\sqrt{p}$ tiles arranged along diagonals through the data domain. Recently, we developed an algorithm for applying multipartitionings efficiently on an arbitrary number of processors, which significantly broadens their applicability [7].

A study by van der Wijngaart [11] of implementation strategies for hand-coding parallelizations of Alternating Direction Implicit Integration (ADI) found that 3D multipartitioning was superior to both static block partitionings with wavefront parallelism, and dynamic block partitionings in which each phase of computation is perfectly parallel but data is transposed between phases.

Our earlier research on data-parallel compilation technology to support effective, semi-automatic compiler-based parallelizations of ADI line-sweep computations focused on exploiting wavefront parallelism with static block partitionings by using a coarse-grain pipelining strategy [1]. Although the performance we achieved with this approach was superior to that achieved for a version of the codes using dynamic block partitionings compiled with the Portland Group's *pghpf* compiler [4], both of the compiler-based parallelization strategies fell significantly short of the performance achieved by hand-coded parallelizations of the applications based on multipartitioning [1].

To closer approach the performance of hand-coded line-sweep computations with compiler-based parallelizations, we have been developing data-parallel compiler support for multipartitioning. A previous paper [6] describes basic compiler and runtime techniques necessary to support multipartitioned data distributions and a prototype implementation in the Rice dHPF compiler. Measurement of code generated with this early prototype identified several opportunities for improving performance. This paper describes the design and implementation of key techniques that address problems identified by reducing communication frequency, reducing message volume, and simplifying generated code.

Section 2 briefly introduces the Rice dHPF compiler and sketches its implementation of multipartitioning. Section 3 describes new optimizations that address performance issues with multipartitioning. Section 4 describes general optimizations that were crucial to generating efficient code for the complex iteration spaces that arose with multipartitioned code. Section 5 compares the performance of our compiler-based multipartitionings of the NAS SP and BT application benchmarks [3] (two codes that use ADI integration to solve the Navier-Stokes equation in three dimensions) and with the performance of hand-coded multipartitionings. Section 6 presents our conclusions.

2 The dHPF Compiler

The dHPF compiler [1,2] translates HPF programs into single-program-multiple-data node programs in Fortran 77 that use MPI message-passing primitives for communication. dHPF is based on an abstract equational framework that expresses data parallel program analyses and optimizations in terms of operations on sets of integer tuples. These tuples represent data elements, processors and iterations [2]. The Omega Library [9,8] serves as the implementation technology for the framework. Our equational framework has enabled us to implement simple, concise, and general formulations of analyses and optimizations. Because of the generality of these formulations, it has been possible to implement a comprehensive collection of advanced optimizations to support semi-automatic parallelization of scientific programs that are broadly applicable.

To support multipartitioned arrays, we extended dHPF to treat each data tile for a multipartitioned array as a block in a block partitioned array that is assigned to its own virtual processor and augmented code generation to map an appropriate collection of virtual processors to each physical processor [6]. Each data tile is extended using shadow regions to hold non-local data received from adjacent tiles. On each processor, all local tiles for a multipartitioned array are dynamically allocated as contiguous data. Storage is indexed in column-major order, where the leftmost dimensions are the original array dimensions and a new rightmost dimension corresponds to the *tile index*. All communication and computation for a tile is defined in terms of the data mapped to that tile.

Code generation for multipartitioned loop nests is a two step process. First we generate code for executing a loop nest for a single tile. Then, we wrap this code in a loop that iterates over all the tiles assigned to a physical processor. Communication generation for tiles is handles similarly. Communication pinned inside a computational loop by data dependences is handled for a tile as if its virtual processor is a physical processor. Communication operations that are vectorized outside of all computational loops over data dimensions are each enclosed in their own tile enumeration loop.

3 Multipartitioning Optimizations

From a processor's perspective, a multipartitioned computation is organized as computation on each of a series of tiles. To avoid unnecessary serialization between physical processors, each processor's tile computations must be scheduled in the proper order. To achieve good scalability, communication between processors must be as infrequent as possible. We describe optimizations that address these two issues for compiler-generated multipartitioned computations.

Tile Scheduling & Tile Loop Placement. A loop nest operating on multipartitioned data involves having each processor perform the portion of the loop's computation associated with each of its tiles. When communication is required to satisfy loop-carried data dependences between tiles, the tile enumeration order must be chosen carefully to avoid unnecessary serialization. This problem is unique to multipartitioning. Because of the way tiles are assigned to processors in multipartitioned distributions, choosing to iterate through a processor's tiles along any one multipartitioned data dimension determines the processor's iteration order along other multipartitioned dimensions as well. (This can be appreciated by considering a directional sweep over any processor's tiles in Fig. 1.)

If there are no loop-carried, processor-crossing true dependences that require communication, then any tile enumeration order is equally good. Otherwise, the data dimension along which the communication is flowing is selected as the tile dimension driving the enumeration order, and the tile iteration direction is selected to flow in the same direction as the communication. With dHPF's general computation partitioning model, we can always choose computation partitionings for statements in a loop nest so that all communication caused by loop-carried dependences in one data dimension flows in the same direction.

As long as processor-crossing dependences flow along only one dimension of multipartitioned array, any tile enumeration order that does not sweep in the opposite direction of the communication will be correct. However, full parallelism will be realized for a loop nest only if the tile dimension is the same as the dimension along which communication occurs, and the tile enumeration order is the same as the direction of the communication. If a multipartitioned computation involves communication along more than one dimension, the computation will be partially serialized regardless of tile enumeration order.

Communication Placement. In a loop nest, a processor-crossing true data dependence on a reference can be preserved by placing communication at the proper loop level. Loop-carried dependences can be preserved by placing communication within the loop carrying the dependence. Loop-independent dependences can be preserved by placing it within the loop that is the least common ancestor of the dependence source and sink.

Loop nests iterating over the data dimensions of a multipartitioned array possess the unique property that if there is only communication along a single direction of a single data dimension, it can be hoisted out of all enclosing loops over data dimensions without reducing parallelism. dHPF exploits this property to vectorize communication for processor crossing true dependences (both loop-carried and loop-independent) out of multipartitioned loops. This optimization enables loops to iterate over multipartitioned data in stride-1 order, regardless of where processor-crossing dependences exist. Without this optimization, communication would be pinned at some level in the loop nest, resulting in more messages of smaller size, which is more costly.

Communication placement in dHPF occurs in two steps. First, the compiler computes an initial placement in which data dependences are used to determine for each reference the loop level at which communication might be needed. This placement is safe for any data layout and any possible computation partitioning for each of the program's statements. Second, we apply a placement refinement algorithm that uses information about the data layout and computation partitionings selected to attempt to improve the initial placement. Placement refinement can hoist communication out of a loop, if it flows along the tile iteration dimension and direction and all statements in the loop nest are multipartitioned.

Aggregating Communication Across Tiles. A key property of multipartitionings is that a single physical processor owns all of the tiles that are neighbors of a particular processor's tiles along any given direction. For example, in Fig. 1 the right neighbor (if any) of each of processor 1's tiles along the y dimension belongs to processor 5. Thus, if a processor's tiles need to shift data to neighbors along a particular dimension, the processor needs to send values to only one other processor. For communication that has been vectorized completely out of loops over multipartitioned data dimensions, this property must be exploited to achieve scalable performance. Otherwise, in a 3D multipartitioning, a vectorized communication would require a processor to send $\sqrt{p}$ messages—one per tile.

To avoid this scaling problem, when the dHPF compiler generates code for each fully vectorized communication event, it sends data from all tiles of an array on the owning processor in a single message to the corresponding recipient. This optimization is a major factor in reducing communication frequency, although it doesn't reduce its volume.

4 General Optimizations

Our quest to achieve hand-coded performance with multipartitioned code generated by dHPF led us to devise several new types of optimizations that are universally applicable. Most of these optimizations are refinements of dHPF's analysis and code generation strategies for constructing and manipulating sets of integer tuples using the Omega Library [8]. The set-based optimizations we describe here improve the ability of dHPF to analyze and optimize set representations that arise with complex programs.

Formulating Compact Sets. The Omega Library has enabled us to develop very general formulations of sophisticated optimizations in the dHPF compiler. However, sophisticated optimizations such as partially replicating computation to reduce communication can give rise to unnecessarily complex sets. Complex sets can cause Omega Library set manipulation operations to exhaust resources or generate inefficient code. Analysis of sets that arose during compilation showed that disjunctions of sets in which some tuple dimensions were drawn from a range of adjacent constants were not being collapsed together. We discovered that sets with compact ranges of constant terms could be collapsed by recomputing a set S as $\text{ConvexHull}(S) - (\text{ConvexHull}(S) - S)$. This process forces the set to be recomputed as a difference from a single conjunct, which has the effect of reducing the set to its most compact form. This optimization enabled us to partially-replicate computation for some unrolled code and save a factor of 5 in communication volume as described in the experiments.

Communication Factoring. As a consequence of partially-replicated computation partitionings, a single reference can cause communication in multiple directions. With multipartitioned or block distributions, partial replication of computation around block boundaries will cause right-hand-side array references to require communication in both directions along each partitioned array dimension. While the integer tuple representation of communication sets used in dHPF can represent nearest-neighbor communication to each of a block's neighbors, the code generated for such communication is inefficient because for each neighbor, it must check which face of the non-convex communication set is needed. By factoring the communication event into simpler communication events—in this case, a separate one for each data dimension and each communication direction—the resulting communication is more efficient and the generated code is much shorter. After factoring the communication, each communication typically is represented by a simple convex set.

Communication Set Construction. The form of set representations based on the Omega Library is largely determined by how the sets are constructed. Carefully constructing sets yields equivalent but simpler forms, speeds up analysis and code generation, and produces cleaner and simpler output. To simplify the representation of communication sets, we group data references contributing to a communication set into equivalence classes. Equivalence classes are formed by inspecting the value number of each subscript expression in the communication-causing dimension and grouping conformant references together. References with different value numbers in partitioned dimensions should be grouped into different equivalence classes. Each equivalence class has a simple convex representation. The final communication set is constructed by unioning together sets constructed for each equivalence class.

Communication Coalescing. Communication is initially scheduled independently for each data reference. Then, multi-directional communication for any single reference (caused by partially-replicated computation partitionings) is factored into separate operations. At this point, there may exist many communication events that send and receive overlapping sets of data. To avoid redundant communication, we merge conformant communication events moving overlapping sets of data. Since communication events draw their representation from data references and computation partitionings, comformance between two communication events is not easily determined. For example, the data reference a(i,j,k) with a computation partitioning of ON_HOME a(i+1,j,k) causes communication for the last row of data in each tile. The data reference a(i-1,j,k) with a partitioning of ON_HOME a(i,j,k) requires exactly the same data to be communicated. To detect such redundancy, we convert them into a normal form by removing offsets in ON_HOME references and adjusting data references accordingly.

General Communication Aggregation. Rather than sending separate messages for each distributed array to be communicated, we extended the dHPF compiler to combine messages at the same point in the code that are addressed to the same recipient from a particular sender into a single message. Two single logical shift communication events for different distributed arrays may be safely aggregated if both arrays are mapped to the same HPF template, and communication flows in one direction along the same dimension of the template.

Code Generation. Generating SPMD code templates (that contain appropriately bounds-reduced loops and conditionals which partition the computation among the available processors) for vectors of disjunctive iteration spaces is a complex problem we encounter when generating code for iteration spaces that have been partially-replicated along data partitioning boundaries.

While Omega contains a sophisticated procedure for generating code templates for complex iteration spaces [9], we found that applying Omega's code generation algorithm to vectors of disjunctive iteration spaces often produced inefficient code templates in which a set of guards terms is repeatedly tested and placeholders for code fragments may repeat many times. In the dHPF compiler, we take several steps to generate high-quality code for such complex iteration spaces. First, we exploit context information present at the enclosing scope to avoid testing conditions already known to be true. Second, when generating code for a vector of iteration sets, we avoid repeatedly testing the same conditions by (a) projecting out satisfiability constraints that are common to all of the iteration sets and test them only once, and (b) refining Omega's code generation algorithm for vectors of iteration spaces to merge adjacent statements subject to the same guards. Third, to avoid unnecessarily complex guards and code replication, we merge together adjacent instances of the same statement and simplify guards from disjoint disjunctive form to simple disjunctions. Finally, to avoid enforcing the same constraints twice, we project away satisfiability constraints from guards around a loop nest that are enforced by the loop bounds.

Generating Optimizable Code. The dHPF compiler translates an HPF program into SPMD Fortran 77 code with MPI communication. The generated code will run fast only if the target system's Fortran compiler can generate good machine code for it. Our experimentation with multipartitioned code generated by dHPF has been performed on an SGI Origin 2000 with MIPS R10000 processors using SGI's MIPSpro Fortran compiler. Achieving good cache utilization on this architecture is essential for good performance. The two key issues that had to be addressed were *avoiding conflict misses*, and *exploiting software prefetching*. We avoid conflict misses that arise with dynamically-allocated tiles in multipartitioned arrays by padding each tile dimension to an odd length. Since we depend on the target system's Fortran compiler to insert software prefetches to hide the latency of memory accesses, the multipartitioned Fortran code that dHPF generates must be readily analyzable. We had to adjust our generated code so the backend compiler did not erroneously infer aliasing between separate arrays, and we had to avoid product terms in subscripts (including those that might arise by forward substitution). One significant change this required was using Cray pointer notation for accessing multi-dimensional dynamically-allocated arrays rather than using linearized subscripts.

5 Experimental Results

We applied the dHPF compiler to generate optimized multipartitioned parallelizations of serial versions (NPB2.3-serial release) of the NAS BT and SP application benchmark codes [3] developed by NASA Ames. BT and SP solve systems of equations resulting from an approximately factored implicit finite-difference discretization of three-dimensional Navier-Stokes equations. While BT solves block-tridiagonal systems of 5x5 blocks, SP solves scalar penta-diagonal systems. Both codes are iterative computations. In each time step, the codes calculate boundary conditions and then compute the right hand sides of the equations. Next, they solve banded systems in computationally-intensive bi-directional sweeps along each of the 3 spatial dimensions. Finally, they update flow variables. Parallel versions of these computations require communication to compute the right hand sides and during the forward and backward line sweeps.

We lightly modified the serial versions of SP and BT for use with dHPF. We added HPF data distribution directives, HPF INDEPENDENT and NEW directives (for array privatization), and a few one trip loops (around a series of loops to facilitate fusing communication). Multipartitioning is specified using a new MULTI distribution keyword for template dimensions. Our experiments were performed on an SGI Origin 2000 node of ASCI Nirvana (128 250MHz R10000, 32KB (I)/32KB (D) L1, 4MB L2 (unified)).

5.1 NAS BT

Effectively parallelizing the NPB2.3-serial version of BT with dHPF required a broad spectrum of analysis and code generation techniques. Multipartitioning and new optimizations in dHPF greatly improved both the performance and scalability of the generated code compared to our earlier parallelizations [1] based on block partitionings. Both the sequential and parallel performance of dHPF's compiler-multipartitioned code is much closer to the hand-coded version. Figure 2 shows a 16-processor parallel execution trace for one steady-state iteration

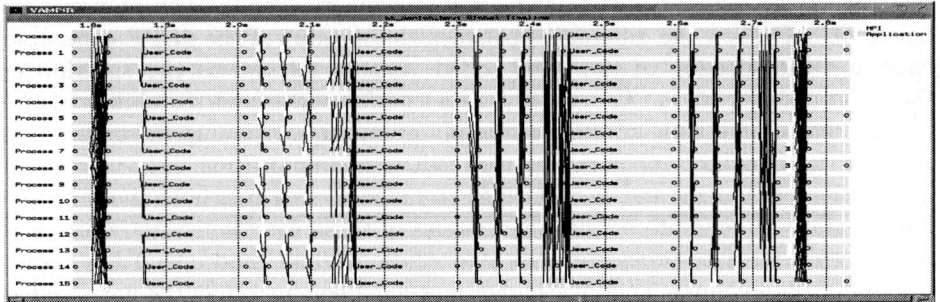

Fig. 2. dHPF-generated NAS BT using 3D multipartitioning

# CPUs	hand-coded	dHPF	% diff.
1	1.06	1.09	-2.64
4	3.28	3.34	-1.77
9	7.73	7.26	6.14
16	14.21	13.49	5.10
25	21.08	20.66	1.98
36	29.78	28.77	3.40
49	39.73	33.73	15.10
64	48.13	51.15	-6.28

Class A: $64 \times 64 \times 64$

# CPUs	hand-coded	dHPF	% diff.
1	0.98	0.92	5.85
4	3.37	2.91	13.48
9	4.91	5.63	-14.70
16	12.30	12.83	-4.34
25	19.09	19.91	-4.30
36	30.95	28.80	6.93
49	52.82	37.04	29.88
64	66.04	47.03	28.78
81	82.28	53.57	34.89

Class B: $102 \times 102 \times 102$

Fig. 3. Comparison of hand-coded and dHPF speedups for NAS BT

of our compiler-generated multipartitioned code for the class A (64^3) problem size. This parallelization is quite similar to the hand-coded multipartitioning.

Using non-owner computes computation partitionings to partially replicate computation along multipartitioned tile boundaries led to dramatic reductions of communication volume. In BT's compute_rhs subroutine, partially replicating the computation of the privatizable temporary arrays rho_q, qs, us, vs, ws, and square along the boundaries of a multipartitioned tile avoided communication of these six variables. No additional communication was needed to partially-replicate this computation because the boundary planes of the multipartitioned u array needed by the replicated computation were already being communicated. This optimization cut the communication volume of compute_rhs by nearly half. In BT's lhsx, lhsy, and lhsz subroutines, partially replicating computation along the partitioning boundaries of two arrays, fjac and njac, whose global dimensions are (5,5,IMAX,JMAX,KMAX), saved a factor of five in communication. Rather than communicating planes of computed values for these arrays across partitions in the i, j, and k dimensions, we communicated sections of rhs(5,IMAX,JMAX,KMAX), which is a factor of five smaller.

Figure 3 compares speedups of NASA Ames' hand-coded parallelization using multipartitioning with those of our dHPF-generated code. All speedups are relative to the performance of the original sequential code. The columns labeled "% diff" show the differences between the speedup of the dHPF-generated code and the speedup of the hand-coded version, relative to the speedup of the hand-coded version. The good parallel performance and scalability of the compiler-generated code comes from applying multipartitioning in conjunction with partially-replicated computation to reduce communication, aggressive communication placement, and aggregating communication across both tiles and different arrays. A measure of the effectiveness of these communication optimizations is that for a 16-processor class A execution, dHPF had only 1.5% higher communication volume, and 20% higher message frequency than the hand-coded implementation.

While the performance of dHPF-generated code closely tracks that of the hand-coded version for the 64^3 problem size, for the 102^3 size the parallel efficiency of dHPF's generated code begins to lag at 49 processors. As the number of processors increases, the surface-to-volume ratio of multipartitioned tiles grows proportional to $\sqrt{p}$ and dHPF's packing and unpacking of data in array overlap regions causes an increase in secondary data cache misses. This degrades the performance of communication-sensitive line sweeps the most. The hand-coded implementation uses data in communication buffers without unpacking.

5.2 NAS SP

Effectively parallelizing SP also required a broad spectrum of optimizations as with BT. Despite the fact that the dynamic communication patterns of dHPF's multipartitioned parallelization resemble those of the hand-coded parallelization, there is still a performance gap between the two implementations. Figure 4 compares speedups of NASA Ames' hand-coded parallelization using multipartitioning with those of our dHPF-generated code. All speedups are relative to the performance of the sequential code for the respective NPB2.3-serial distribution. Most of the difference comes from extra communication volume present in the compiler-generated code for SP's lhs<xyz> routines.

Currently, the dHPF compiler uses a procedure-local communication placement analysis. This approach schedules communication in each procedure even though the values might already be available locally. Interprocedural communication analysis and placement analysis would be needed to eliminate this additional communication. We measured a significant increase in secondary cache misses in the sweep routines caused by how dHPF manages communication buffers and unpacks non-local data into overlap regions. For z_solve, the overhead was 100%. This cost could be reduced by accessing remote data directly from the packed buffers, but would prove challenging to implement due to the non-contiguous nature of the data.

For SP, non-local values gathered by the compute_rhs routine cover the non-local values needed by the lhsx, lhsy and lhsz routines. In a 16-processor execution for a class A problem size, this unnecessary communication in lhsx, lhsy and lhsz causes the communication volume of our dHPF-generated code

# CPUs	hand-coded	dHPF	% diff.
1	1.01	0.96	5.50
4	4.21	3.29	21.83
9	11.60	7.75	33.24
16	16.21	14.43	10.98
25	21.00	22.68	-7.98
36	30.69	28.44	7.31
49	42.43	30.89	27.19
64	67.57	35.15	32.42

Class A: $64 \times 64 \times 64$

# CPUs	hand-coded	dHPF	% diff.
1	0.80	0.78	2.67
4	2.86	2.52	12.13
9	7.74	6.17	20.26
16	13.01	11.36	12.63
25	22.15	17.77	19.75
36	36.52	25.72	29.57
49	51.78	33.22	35.85
64	58.35	41.52	28.84
81	74.95	45.52	39.26

Class B: $102 \times 102 \times 102$

Fig. 4. Comparison of hand-coded and dHPF speedups for NAS SP

to be 14.5% higher than for the hand-coded parallelization. Although the additional volume is modest, since this extra communication is forward and backward along each of the spatial dimensions, the communication frequency of the dHPF-generated code to be 74% higher than the hand-coded parallelization.

Like with BT, partially-replicating computation at the boundaries of multipartitioned tiles offered significant benefits for SP. In SP's lhsx, lhsy, and lhsz routines, replicating computation of boundary values of cv, a partitioned 1-dimensional vector aligned with a multipartitioned template, eliminated the need to communicate these boundary values at loop depth two between their definition and use. Although partially replicating computation of cv required communicating two additional planes of the three-dimensional multipartitioned array us in each of these routines, this communication was fully vectorizable, whereas the communication of cv we avoided was not. In SP's x_solve, y_solve, and z_solve routines, dHPF's ability to vectorize loop-carried communication out of the entire loop nest over a multipartitioned tile was the key to achieving one message per tile.

6 Conclusions

Van der Wijngaart showed that multipartitioning yields superior parallel performance for tightly-coupled line sweep computations than other partitioning choices [11]. In the dHPF compiler, we successfully implemented support for multipartitioning. We were able to apply aggressive optimizations in dHPF in the complicated circumstances arising in multipartitioned code principally because our compiler optimizations are formulated in a very general way—as manipulation of sets of integer tuples [2]. Only the combination of multipartitioning and aggressive optimizations enabled us to approach hand-coded performance on the NAS SP and BT benchmarks. Achieving high performance with compiler-generated parallelizations requires paying attention to *all* the details. Multipartitioning by itself leads to balanced computation, but matching the hand-coded communication frequency and volume, and also the scalar performance is necessary to achieve competitive performance.

Remaining differences in performance between the dHPF-generated code and the hand-coded parallelizations result from three factors. First, dHPF-generated code incurs higher data-movement overheads in its communication support code than the hand-coded implementations, which carefully reuse buffers and use communicated data directly out of buffers rather than unpacking. Second, dHPF-generated code contains extra communication that comes from a lack of interprocedural analysis and placement. Third, the hand-coded implementation hides communication latency by scheduling local computation while data is in flight. Since in the serial version of the code analyzed by dHPF, the overlapped local computation is in another routine, achieving this optimization would require more global analysis and transformation.

Our experiments with two line-sweep codes show that our compiler technology is able to simultaneously optimize all aspects of program performance. We have demonstrated that it is possible to use data-parallel compiler technology to effectively parallelize tightly-coupled line-sweep applications and yield performance that is approaching that of sophisticated hand-coded parallel versions.

Acknowledgments

We thank Vikram Adve for his involvement in the early design and implementation discussions of this work.

References

1. V. Adve, G. Jin, J. Mellor-Crummey, and Q. Yi. High Performance Fortran Compilation Techniques for Parallelizing Scientific Codes. In *Proceedings of SC98: High Performance Computing and Networking*, Orlando, FL, Nov 1998.
2. V. Adve and J. Mellor-Crummey. Using Integer Sets for Data-Parallel Program Analysis and Optimization. In *Proceedings of the SIGPLAN '98 Conference on Programming Language Design and Implementation*, Montreal, Canada, June 1998.
3. D. Bailey, T. Harris, W. Saphir, R. van der Wijngaart, A. Woo, and M. Yarrow. The NAS parallel benchmarks 2.0. Technical Report NAS-95-020, NASA Ames Research Center, Dec. 1995.
4. Z. Bozkus, L. Meadows, S. Nakamoto, V. Schuster, and M. Young. Compiling High Performance Fortran. In *Proceedings of the Seventh SIAM Conference on Parallel Processing for Scientific Computing*, pages 704–709, San Francisco, CA, Feb. 1995.
5. J. Bruno and P. Cappello. Implementing the beam and warming method on the hypercube. In *Proceedings of 3rd Conference on Hypercube Concurrent Computers and Applications*, pages 1073–1087, Pasadena, CA, Jan. 1988.
6. D. Chavarría-Miranda and J. Mellor-Crummey. Towards compiler support for scalable parallelism. In *Proceedings of the Fifth Workshop on Languages, Compilers, and Runtime Systems for Scalable Computers*, Lecture Notes in Computer Science 1915, pages 272–284, Rochester, NY, May 2000. Springer-Verlag.

7. A. Darte, J. Mellor-Crummey, R. Fowler, and D. Chavarría-Miranda. On efficient parallelization of line-sweep computations. In *9th Workshop on Compilers for Parallel Computers*, Edinburgh, Scotland, June 2001.
8. W. Kelly, V. Maslov, W. Pugh, E. Rosser, T. Shpeisman, and D. Wonnacott. The Omega Library Interface Guide. Technical report, Dept. of Computer Science, Univ. of Maryland, College Park, Apr. 1996.
9. W. Kelly, W. Pugh, and E. Rosser. Code generation for multiple mappings. In *Frontiers '95: The 5th Symposium on the Frontiers of Massively Parallel Computation*, McLean, VA, Feb. 1995.
10. N. Naik, V. Naik, and M. Nicoules. Parallelization of a class of implicit finite-difference schemes in computational fluid dynamics. *International Journal of High Speed Computing*, 5(1):1–50, 1993.
11. R. F. Van der Wijngaart. Efficient implementation of a 3-dimensional ADI method on the iPSC/860. In *Proceedings of Supercomputing 1993*, pages 102–111. IEEE Computer Society Press, 1993.

Cache Models for Iterative Compilation

Peter M. W. Knijnenburg[1], Toru Kisuki[1], and Kyle Gallivan[2]

[1] LIACS, Leiden University, the Netherlands
{peterk,kisuki}@liacs.nl
[2] Department of Computer Science, Florida State University, USA
gallivan@cs.fsu.edu

Abstract. In iterative compilation we search for the best program transformations by profiling many variants and selecting the one with the shortest execution time. Since this approach is extremely time consuming, we discuss in this paper how to incorporate static models. We show that a highly accurate model as a filter to profiling can reduce the number of executions by 50%. We also show that using a simple model to rank transformations and profiling only those with highest ranking can reduce the number of executions even further, in case we have a limited number of profiles at our disposal. We conclude that a production compiler might perform best using the last approach.

1 Introduction

An important task of a compiler is to transform a source program into an efficient variant for a specific target platform. Traditionally, compilers use static, simplified machine models and hardwired strategies to determine the order in which to apply certain transformations and their parameter values, such as tile sizes or unroll factors. However, actual machines and their back end compilers have so complex an organization that this approach will likely not deliver optimal code. In order to solve this problem, we have proposed *iterative compilation* where many variants of the source program are generated and the best one is selected by actually profiling these variants on the target hardware [7]. This framework is essentially target neutral since it consists of a driver module that navigates through the optimization space and a source to source restructurer that allows the specification of the transformations it employs. The native compiler is used as back end compiler and it is treated together with the platform as a black box. We have shown [7] that this approach outperform existing static approaches significantly, albeit at the price of being extremely time consuming. In this paper, we propose to use static models that cover part of the behavior of the target platform, to estimate the effect of transformations and to exclude transformations that are likely to produce poor results. We distinguish two approaches.

Execution driven The driver searches through the optimization space and the model is used to filter out bad candidate transformations during the search. Only if the model predicts that a transformation may be better than the best one found so far, profiling of the transformed program will take place.

R. Sakellariou et al. (Eds.): Euro-Par 2001, LNCS 2150, pp. 254–261, 2001.
© Springer-Verlag Berlin Heidelberg 2001

Model driven The models are used to rank a collection of transformations before any profiling takes place. Only the transformations with highest ranking are profiled. The transformation that gives rise to the shortest execution time is chosen.

We restrict attention to two well-known program transformations: loop tiling [5,8] and unroll-and-jam [4]. Both transformations are targeted towards cache exploitation. Unroll-and-jam, moreover, duplicates the loop body to expose more instructions to the hardware that can be executed in parallel. These two transformations, therefore, are highly interdependent and their compound result gives rise to a highly irregular optimization space [3]. Since the dominant effect of the transformations is their effect on cache behavior, static cache models are the prime models of interest.

Recently, there have been approaches where the compiler searches the transformation space using static models [4,13]. These approaches, however, do not use profile information. Also, there have been several approaches to *feedback directed optimization*, in which run time information is exploited to alter a program [10]. We can distinguish between on-line and off-line approaches. On-line approaches optimize at runtime or during the lifetime of a program [1,6,11]. Off-line approaches include architectural tuning systems for BLAS [2,12] or DSP kernels [9]. For embedded systems an off-line approach is best suited since high compilation times can be amortized across the number of systems shipped.

This paper is organized as follows. In Section 2 we discuss the cache models used, the iterative search algorithms and the benchmarks and platforms. In Section 3 we discuss the performance of iterative compilation with cache models and give a detailed analysis of the levels of optimization that can be reached with a limited number of program executions. In section 4 we discuss the results obtained in this paper and we draw some concluding remarks in section 5.

2 Experiment

Cache Models First, as an upperbound for the present approach, we use a full level 1 cache simulator to compute hit rates. This model is too expensive to be used in practice but we include it since it is more accurate than any other static model. We interpret results obtained for the simulator as upperbound results with which we can compare other models. Second, as a realistic case, we use a simple model proposed by Coleman and McKinley [5] that uses an approximation of the working set WS and selects the tile size giving rise to the largest working set that still fits in the cache. In order for models to be effective, we assume that they are far less costly to evaluate than profiling the program.

Execution driven search We consider the following two strategies.

- **EXEC-CS** A new point next is selected and evaluated if the cache hit rate $H(\text{next})$ is within a factor α of the current best cache hit rate $H(\text{current})$. By experimentation, we found that a slack factor $\alpha = 99.9\%$ is optimal. The search algorithm will stop after N combinations are executed.

  ```
  current = initial transformation
  REPEAT
      next = next transformation
      IF H(next) ≥ α × H(current)
      THEN execute(next)
           IF exec_time(next) < exec_time(current)
           THEN current = next
  ```

- **EXEC-CM** is based on the Coleman/McKinley model [5]. CS denotes the cache size and WS is the working set of one tile. This strategy selects on an lower and upper bound for the working set, so that only programs with a large working set are profiled. By experimentation, we found that optimal values are $\beta = 40\%$ and $\gamma = 50\%$.

  ```
  current = initial transformation
  REPEAT
      next = next transformation
      IF WS(next) ≥ β × CS &&
         WS(next) ≤ γ × CS
      THEN execute(next)
           IF exec_time(next) < exec_time(current)
           THEN current = next
  ```

Model driven search We consider the following three strategies.

- **MOD-CS1** First, we calculate the cache hit rate of a large collection of tile sizes and unrolling factors using the cache simulator. The N combinations with the highest hit rates are executed.

  ```
  calculate cache hit rates
  rank transformations on hit rate
  current = best transformation
  REPEAT
      next = next best transformation
      execute(next)
      IF exec_time(next) < exec_time(current)
      THEN current = next
  ```

- **MOD-CS2** We consider each unroll factor from 1 to 20 and compute the cache hit rate for a large set of tile sizes and that unroll factor. Then, for each unroll factor, the $N/20$ combinations with highest hit rate are selected and executed.

```
calculate cache hit rates
FOREACH Unroll Factor
    rank transformations using hit rate
current = initial transformation
FOREACH Unroll Factor
    next = next best for this unroll factor
    execute(next)
    IF exec_time(next) < exec_time(current)
    THEN current = next
```

- **MOD-CM** In this strategy, we select for each unroll factor the largest tile size such that the working set WS is within $\gamma\%$ of the cache size CS. $N/20$ combinations with largest tile size are selected for each unroll factor.

```
current = initial transformation
FOREACH Unroll Factor
    next = next largest tile size
          s.t. WS(next) ≤ γ × CS
    execute(next)
    IF exec_time(next) < exec_time(current)
    THEN current = next
```

Benchmarks and Platforms The benchmarks considered are the most important and compute intensive kernels from multimedia applications. We use all 6 possible loop permutations of matrix-matrix multiplication on 3 data input sizes of 256, 300 and 301. We use the 2 loop orders in matrix-vector multiplication on data input sizes 2048, 2300 and 2301. We use 6 loop orders in Forward Discrete Cosine Transform (FDCT), one of the most important routines from the low level bit stream video encoder H263. We also use the 6 variations of the second main computation loop from FDCT that consists of a multiplication of a transposed matrix. We use data input sizes of 256, 300 and 301. Finally, we use a Finite Impulse Response filter (FIR), one of the most important DSP operations, with data sizes of 8192, 8300 and 8301. We executed on the following platforms: Pentium II, Pentium III, HP-PA 712, UltraSparc I. We used the native Fortran compiler or g77, with full optimization on. Loop tiling uses tile sizes of 1 to 100, and loop unrolling uses unroll factors of 1 to 20. We allow a maximum of 400 program executions.

3 Results

In this section we discuss the results we obtained for iterative compilation incorporating cache models. For practical purposes, it is important to restrict the number of program executions to be small. To analyze the efficiency of iterative compilation for this case, we use a *trade-off graph* [7]. This graph contains a number of *equi-optimization curves* indicating the percentage of benchmarks that reach a certain percentage of the maximal speedup as a function of the number of program executions. The trade-off graph for the algorithm that only uses profiles and no models and that is studied in [7], is depicted in Figure 1(a). We call this algorithm the Execution-Only Algorithm (EO) and it is used as the base case with which to compare the other algorithms. From this graph we can deduce, for example, that after 100 executions, 48% of the benchmarks were fully optimized and thus reached 100% of the maximal speedup. Likewise, after 50 executions, 77% of the benchmarks reached at least 90% of the maximal speedup. After 20 executions, almost every benchmark reached at least 60% of this speedup.

Execution driven search Inspecting Figures 1(a) and 1(b), we see that EXEC-CS only needs about half as many executions as the Execution-Only Algorithm and still obtains the same trade-off. For example, we can see that the levels of optimization obtained after 25 program executions is about the same as the levels of optimization obtained by EO after 50 executions, and likewise after 50 executions it is the same as EO obtains after 100 executions. Comparing the trade-off graph for EXEC-CM in Figure 1(c) to the trade-off graph for EXEC-CS in Figure 1(b), we see that for 10 to 30 program executions both strategies perform equally well and improve the Execution-Only Algorithm substantially. For more than 30 executions, EXEC-CS is superior to EXEC-CM.

Model driven search From Figure 1(d) it follows that for up to 10 executions, the strategy MOD-CS1 is as effective as EXEC-CS. For more executions, EXEC-CS is superior. This shows that a cache model that assumes that all memory references go through the cache is not an adequate model for real platforms. Moreover, the left-most point in the trade-off graph for EXEC-CS1 corresponds to a strategy where we only use static model information, as is customarily done in traditional compilers. It follows that such a strategy is not able to reach levels of optimization that iterative compilation can.

In the strategies MOD-CS2 and MOD-CM we execute programs in batches of 20 (one for each unroll factor). From Figure 1(e) it follows that MOD-CS2 performs equally well for 20 executions as EXEC-CS. It is inferior to EXEC-CS for more executions. At the same time, it is superior to MOD-CS1 for every number of execution that we would allow.

Finally, Figure 1(f) shows that MOD-CM is superior to EXEC-CS for 20 executions and reaches about the same levels of optimization for 40 executions. Comparing the trade-off graphs from Figures 1(b) and 1(f), we see that after 20 executions using the MOD-CM strategy, we reach the same level of optimization as EXEC-CS does after 30 to 40 executions. Comparing Figure 1(f) to Figure 1(a), we see that these levels of optimization are reached in the Execution-Only approach after about 70 executions. MOD-CM is also superior to EXEC-CS1 and EXEC-CS2 for up to 80 executions. Only if we would allow 100 executions, these latter strategies prove to be better than MOD-CM. This shows that, although it is only a crude approximation of the exact hit rate, the working set size constraint is highly effective.

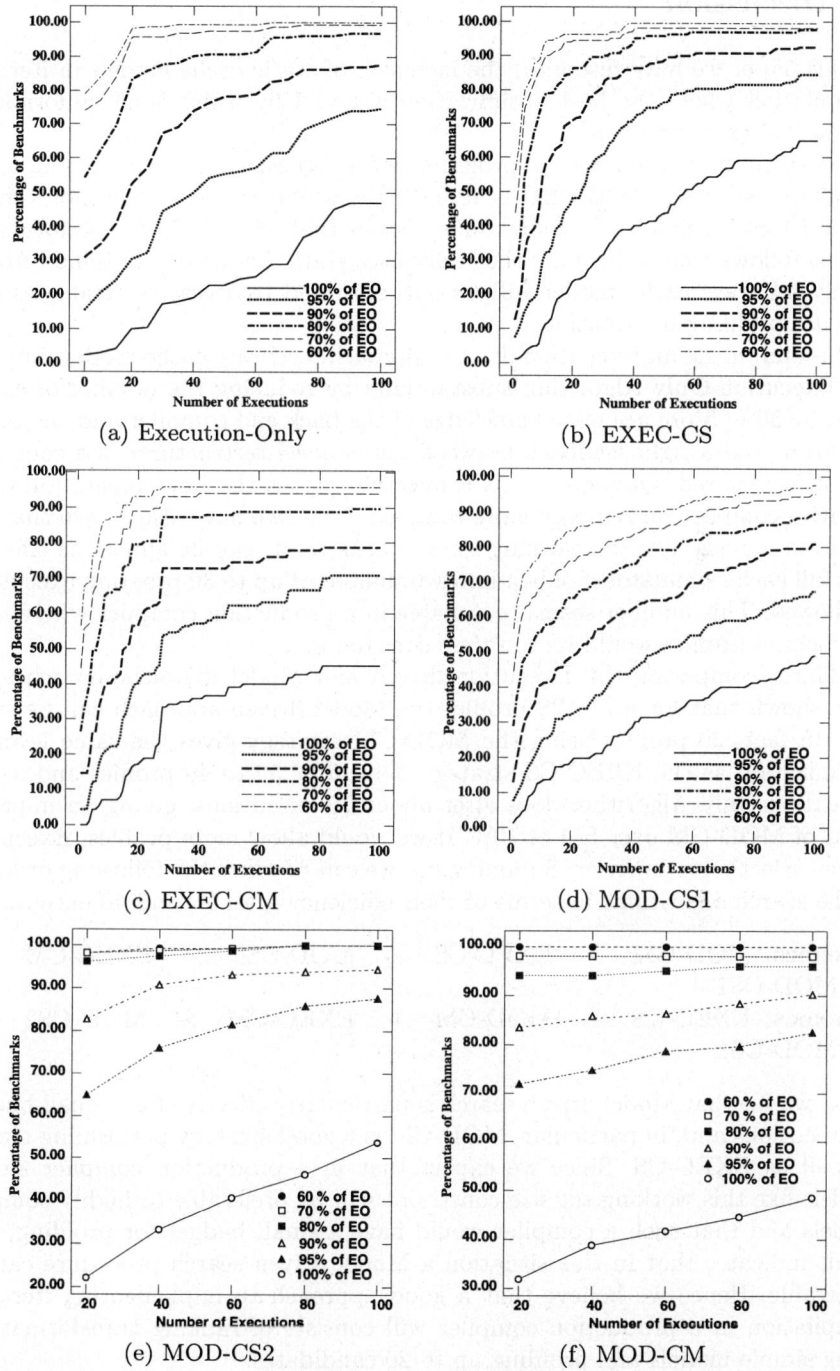

Fig. 1. Trade-off graphs

4 Discussion

In this paper we have discussed the inclusion of static cache models in iterative compilation where the best optimization is found by using model information and actual execution times.

First, profiling a number of programs with highest hit rates according to the simulator (strategy MOD-CS1) is actually the worst strategy. This shows that a static L1 cache simulator ignores many issues that are crucial for performance. It also follows that a strategy that only uses static knowledge obtained from a highly accurate cache model will be outperformed by iterative strategies that also use profiling information.

Second, using an Execution driven approach, accurate cache models improve the Execution-Only Algorithm substantially by reducing the number of executions by 50%. More accurate knowledge of the back end compiler and the target platform, and a tight feedback between source level restructurer and code generator is required. Obviously, this connection makes the implementation of an iterative compilation strategy more complex. Next, we have also shown that less accurate models, like the working set size constraint, can be almost as effective as a full cache simulator if only a limited number of up to 30 program executions is allowed. This number seems reasonable in a production compiler where large numbers of profiles would be too time consuming.

Third, comparing the Execution driven and Model driven approaches, we have shown that for up to 20 profiles the Model driven approach can be superior. In fact, 20 profiles using the MOD-CM strategy gives the same levels of optimization as the EXEC-CS strategy does after 30 to 40 profiles and as the Execution-Only Algorithm does after about 70 executions, giving an improvement of MOD-CM over EO of 70%. If we would allow more profiles, Execution driven selection is superior. Summing up, we can produce the following ordering of the search algorithms in terms of their efficiency after 20 and 40 executions.

20 execs. MOD-CM $\succ$ EXEC-CS $\sim$ MOD-CS2 $\succ$ EXEC-CM $\succ$ MOD-CS1

40 execs. EXEC-CS $\succ$ MOD-CM $\succ$ EXEC-CM $\succ$ MOD-CS2 $\succ$ MOD-CS1

Next, we see that Model driven search is particularly effective for a small budget of executions and, in particular, MOD-CM is a good strategy performing almost as well as EXEC-CS. Since we expect that in a production compiler simple models like this working set size constraint will be preferable to highly complex models and that such a compiler would have a small budget for profiling, this result indicates that in this situation a Model driven search procedure can be preferable. Hence we believe that a good approach to implementing iterative compilation in a production compiler will consists of ranking transformations using simple models and profiling up to 20 candidates.

5 Conclusion

In this paper we have discussed the inclusion of cache models in iterative compilation where we search for the best optimization. We have considered Execution driven and Model driven search strategies, based on two types of model. First, we have shown that a highly accurate model alone and using no profiling is not capable of producing levels of optimization as high as iterative compilation can. Second, we have shown that Execution driven search using accurate models is capable of reducing the number of required program executions by 50% and still obtain the same levels of optimization as Execution-Only iterative compilation does for any given budget of profiling. Third, we have shown that Model driven search using a simple model can improve Execution-Only iterative compilation by 70% in case there is a small budget of profiles. We conclude that, for a production compiler that would likely prefer simple models and few profiles, Model driven iterative compilation can be highly effective.

References

1. J. Auslander, M. Philipose, C. Chambers, S. J. Eggers, and B. N. Bershad. Fast, effective dynamic compilation. In *Proc. PLDI*, pages 149–159, 1996.
2. J. Bilmes, K. Asanović, C. W. Chin, and J. Demmel. Optimizing matrix multiply using PHiPAC: A portable, high-performance, ANSI C coding methodology. In *Proc. ICS*, pages 340–347, 1997.
3. F. Bodin, T. Kisuki, P. M. W. Knijnenburg, M. F. P. O'Boyle, and E. Rohou. Iterative compilation in a non-linear optimisation space. In *Proc. Workshop on Profile and Feedback Directed Compilation*, 1998.
4. S. Carr. Combining optimization for cache and instruction level parallelism. In *Proc. PACT*, pages 238–247, 1996.
5. S. Coleman and K. S. McKinley. Tile size selection using cache organization and data layout. In *Proc. PLDI*, pages 279–290, 1995.
6. P. Diniz and M. Rinard. Dynamic feedback: An effective technique for adaptive computing. In *Proc. PLDI*, pages 71–84, 1997.
7. T. Kisuki, P. M. W. Knijnenburg, and M. F. P. O'Boyle. Combined selection of tile sizes and unroll factors using iterative compilation. In *Proc. PACT*, pages 237–246, 2000.
8. M. S. Lam, E. E. Rothberg, and M. E. Wolf. The cache performance and optimizations of blocked algorithms. In *Proc. ASPLOS*, pages 63–74, 1991.
9. B. Singer and M. Veloso. Learning to predict performance from formula modeling and training data. In *Proc. Conf. on Machine Learning*, 2000.
10. M. D. Smith. Overcoming the challenges to feedback-directed optimization. In *Proc. Dynamo*, 2000.
11. M. J. Voss and R. Eigenmann. ADAPT: Automated de-coupled adaptive program transformation. In *Proc. ICPP*, 2000.
12. R. C. Whaley and J. J. Dongarra. Automatically tuned linear algebra software. In *Proc. Alliance*, 1998.
13. M. E. Wolf, D. E. Maydan, and D.-K. Chen. Combining loop transformations considering caches and scheduling. *Int'l. J. of Parallel Programming*, 26(4):479–503, 1998.

Data Sequence Locality:
A Generalization of Temporal Locality

Vincent Loechner, Benoît Meister, and Philippe Clauss

ICPS/LSIIT, Université Louis Pasteur
Strasbourg, France.
http://icps.u-strasbg.fr

Abstract. A significant source for enhancing application performance and for reducing power consumption in embedded processor applications is to improve the usage of the memory hierarchy. Such objective classically translates into optimizing spatial and temporal data locality especially for nested loops. In this paper, we focus on temporal data locality. Unlike many existing methods, our approach pays special attention to TLB (Translation Lookaside Buffer) effectiveness since a TLB miss can take up to three times more cycles than a cache miss. We propose a generalization of the traditional approach for temporal locality improvement, called data sequence localization, which reduces the number of iterations that separates accesses to a given array element.

Keywords: Memory hierarchy, cache and TLB performance, temporal locality, loop nests, parameterized polyhedra, Ehrhart polynomials.

1 Introduction

Efficient use of memory resources is a significant source for enhancing application performance and for reducing power consumption for embedded processor applications [16]. Nowadays computers include several levels of memory hierarchy in which the lower levels are large but slow (disks, memory, etc.) while the higher levels are fast but small (caches, registers, etc.). Hence, programs should be designed for the highest percentage of accesses to be made to the higher levels of memory. To accomplish this, two basic principles have to be considered, both of which are related to the way physical cache and memory are implemented: spatial locality and temporal locality. Temporal locality is achieved if an accessed memory location is accessed again before it has been replaced. Spatial locality is achieved if several closely located memory locations are accessed before the cache line or page is replaced, since a cache miss or page fault for a single data element will bring an entire cache line into cache or page into main memory. Taking advantage of spatial and temporal locality translates into minimizing cache misses, TLB (translation lookaside buffer) misses and page faults and thus increases performance.

The TLB holds only a limited number of pointers to recently referenced pages. On most computers, this number ranges from 8 to 256. Few microprocessors have a TLB reach larger than the secondary cache when using conventional page sizes. If the TLB reach is smaller than the cache, the processor will get TLB misses while accessing data from the cache. Many microprocessors like the MIPS R12000/R10000, Ultrasparc II and PA8000 use selectable page sizes per TLB entry in order to increase the TLB reach. For example, the MIPS R12000 processor TLB supports 4K to 16M page sizes per TLB entry, which means the TLB reach ranges from 512K to 2G. Unfortunately, while many processors support multiple page sizes, few operating systems make full use of this feature [18].

Recent work has provided advances in loop and data transformation theory. By using affine representation of loops, several loop transformations have been unified into a single framework using a matrix representation of these transformations [22]. These techniques consist either in unimodular [1] or nonunimodular [11] iteration space transformations as well as tiling [10,20,21]. More recently, Kandemir et al. [9] and O'Boyle and Knijnenburg [14] have proposed a unifying framework for loop and more general data transformations. In [14], the authors propose an extension to nonsingular data transformations.

Unfortunately, these approaches do not pay special attention to TLBs. Hence, a program that exhibits good cache locality can yield a very poor performance. This is mainly due to the fact that only the innermost loop level is considered in most of these methods. In the resulting programs, accesses with large strides can occur each time indices of the outer loops are incremented. This can yield many expensive TLB misses.

Spatial locality is classically improved by computing new memory data layouts yielding stride-one accesses in the innermost loop, and temporal locality is improved by transforming loops such that constant data are accessed in the innermost loop for some array references (blocking will also be discussed hereunder). We have proposed a different approach for spatial locality in [6], by determining new data layouts from the computation of Ehrhart polynomials [5].

In this paper, we only focus on temporal locality optimization by defining a more general and efficient approach: temporal locality can be improved by reducing the number of iterations that separates two successive accesses to a given reused data. Similar approaches of some other work are discussed in Sect. 4.

Let us consider the first example presented in Tab. 1. Observe in this example that reference $A(j,i)$ exhibits good temporal locality since any iteration between $(i,j,1)$ and (i,j,N) will access the same data. Although temporal reuse occurs for reference $B(k,j)$, there is no possible loop transformation that could result in a good temporal locality in the innermost loop for both references. Hence, any classical optimization method would consider such a loop nest as acceptable. Observe that all elements of array B are reused each time index i is incremented. If all these elements cannot be loaded simultaneously in the cache due to a too large value of N, any reused element is no longer present in the cache when it has to be accessed again. Moreover, accessing all elements of array B will generate TLB misses if B is stored in several memory pages. These unavoidable TLB misses are repeated each time i is incremented.

We made some performance mesures on a MIPS R12000 processor, with 2-way set-associative 32KB data L1 cache, 8MB L2 cache, and 64-entry TLB. We

Table 1. Two versions of a loop nest

first version	second version

do i = 1,N
  do j = 1,N
    do k = 1,N
      A(j,i) = A(j,i) + B(k,j)
	do j = 1,N
	  do i = 1,N
	    do k = 1,N
	      A(j,i) = A(j,i) + B(k,j)

# L1 cache misses: 15,638,299,806 # L2 cache misses: 3,906,794,992 # TLB misses: 16,120,451 computation time: 2712.14s	# L1 cache misses: 91,642,448 # L2 cache misses: 1,899,471 # TLB misses: 16,290,785 computation time: 425.21s

ran this loop nest for $N = 5000$ and measured data cache and TLB misses with the performance tool *perfex* using hardware counters. Computation time was measured using the system clock. We obtain the results presented in Tab. 1.

Let us now consider another semantically equivalent version of this loop nest, presented on righthand side of Tab. 1. Loops i and j have been interchanged in order to improve temporal locality for the smallest possible sequence of elements of B: $B(1,j), B(2,j), ..., B(N,j)$. The measures show important savings in the number of cache misses, due to the elimination of strides of size N^2.

This transformation seems quite similar to blocking: if the N elements of B can be loaded simultaneoulsly in the cache, then the same result could have been obtained by defining blocks of size $N \times 1 \times N$: If the N elements cannot be loaded entirely in the cache, blocking should result in better performance by adjusting the block size to a proper value. However, this is a difficult task greatly dependent on the cache parameters (size, associativity, hierarchy, etc.). Moreover, performance of blocking can often be reduced by cache conflicts effects, and blocking may break temporal locality. By allowing autoblocking and interchange of loops (-LNO:blocking=on:interchange=on) while compiling the previous initial example for $N = 5000$ with the SGI F90 compiler, loop k is divided into blocs of 1820 iterations. In the initial program and in our optimized version, each array element $A(j, i)$ is consecutively reused N times and is not further reused. Hence it is register-stored during the computation of these N iterations. In the blocked version, each $A(j, i)$ is consecutively reused 1820 times. Then all other array elements are reused in the same way before the same element $A(j, i)$ is reused again 1820 times and so on. Therefore, register locality is broken $N/1820$ times in this blocked version. For this example, lower performance is observed for the blocked version in particular in the number of TLB misses (48,567,268 versus 16,290,785 in our version).

Our proposed approach is independent of the target architecture and will improve performance in any situation. In any case it does not prevent additional blocking transformations. Although applying a blocking transformation on our optimized version for this example does not improve performance at all.

The example shows a simple loop interchange transformation, but our approach is not reduced to deduce opportune loop interchanges. All references in an imperfectly nested loop are examined, and eventually new iteration directions are computed with respect to data dependences. We propose a step by step algorithm consisting in optimizing a maximum number of references at the most inner possible loop level. Our techniques use the polytope model [8] with an intensive use of its parametric extensions [13,5] and of their implementations in the polyhedral library *PolyLib* [19].

Temporal locality can be fully optimized, *i.e.* in the innermost loop, only for a subset of occuring references. *Data sequence localization* consists in considering the remaining references at next loop levels, in order to minimize the number of occuring iterations between two successive reuses of the same data. It results in optimizing temporal locality for the sequence of data that is referenced between two such reuses. The smaller the reused data sequences are, the more successful is the opportunity that these sequences can be entirely loaded in the highest levels of the memory. Notice that the most favorable case corresponds to the smallest data sequence containing one single data. Hence we can observe that classical temporal optimization in the innermost loop is a particular case of data sequence localization.

Our temporal locality optimization method is presented in Sect. 2. Some prerequisites on unimodular transformations and data dependences are given first. Then the method is detailed step-by-step by presenting our temporal optimization algorithm for one reference, then for any number of references. Section 3 describes the positive effects of our method on parallel programs. After some comparisons with closer related work have been detailed in Sect. 4, conclusions and future objectives are given in Sect. 5.

2 Loop Transformations for Temporal Locality

Loop nests and array references. We assume that loops are normalized such that their step is one. The iteration space of a loop nest of depth d is a d-dimensional convex polyhedron D_P. It is bounded by parameterized linear inequalities imposed by the affine loop bounds and hence is a parameterized convex polyhedron, where P is a p-vector of integer parameters: $P = (N_1, ..., N_p)$.

The references are affine combinations of the indices and the parameters. A reference to a d'-dimensional array element inside a d-dimensional loop nest is represented by a *homogeneous* integer reference matrix R, of size $(d' + p + 1) \times (d + p + 1)$. This matrix defines a reference in a space including the index variables, as well as the parameters and the constant. A reference is an affine mapping $f(I, P) = R\,(I, P, 1)^\top$, where $^\top$ denotes the transpose vector.

We consider one loop nest containing some references to optimize. Each reference i in the loop nest is associated to an accessed set of data $Data_i$, and all references are ordered by decreasing sizes of their data sets. The largest data sets are more likely to induce large strides resulting in many cache and TLB misses. Hence, our heuristics selects the different reuse directions associated with loops ordered from the innermost to the outermost loop, following the descending size of the associated sets of accessed data $\#Data_i$. For any given reference i and its associated iteration space D_i, the size of its data set $\#Data_i$ is given by the Ehrhart polynomial of the affine transformation R_i of D_i, where R_i is the reference matrix [4].

Temporal locality is achieved by applying a transformation to the original loop. In this paper, we consider unimodular transformations, being equivalent to any combination of loop interchange, reversal and skewing [22].

Unimodular transformations. Let T be a unimodular $(d+p+1) \times (d+p+1)$ matrix. This matrix defines a *homogeneous* affine transformation t of the iteration domain as:
$$t : D_P \subset \mathbb{Z}^d \to D'_P = t(D_P) \subset \mathbb{Z}^d$$
$$I \mapsto I' = t(I) \text{ such that } (I', P, 1)^\top = T\,(I, P, 1)^\top.$$

The transformed domain D'_P corresponds to a new scanning loop nest, obtained by applying the Fourier-Motzkin algorithm [2] to a perfect loop nest. This algorithm computes the lower and upper bounds of each iteration variable I'_k as a function of the parameters and the variables $I'_1 ... I'_{k-1}$ only. The body of the loop also has to be transformed in order to use vector I': all references to vector I are replaced by $t^{-1}(I')$.

If the loop nest is not perfect then some more work has to be done. First, we have to compute the set of iteration domains corresponding to the original loop nest. All these iteration domains have to be defined in the same geometrical space (same dimension and same variables). This can be done by using a variant of code sinking [12,22]. Then, the transformation is applied to all these iteration domains. To get the resulting loop nest we apply Quilleré's algorithm [15], which constructs an optimized loop nest scanning several iteration domains.

Data dependences and validity of loop transformations. In order to be valid, the transformation has to respect the dependences of the loop. From this point, by 'dependence' we will mean flow, anti-, and output dependences only. Input dependence does not play a role, since distinct reads of the same memory location can be done in no particular order [2]. We denote by $\preceq$ the lexicographical *lower or equal* operator.

Let $\mathcal{D}$ be the set of *distance vectors* related to data dependences occurring in the original loop nest: $\delta \in \mathcal{D}$ iff there exist two iterations $I \preceq J$, such that $J = I + \delta$, and there is a data dependence from iteration I to iteration J. Notice that all distance vectors are lexicographically non-negative.

The condition for equivalence between the transformed loop nest and the original loop nest is that [2]: $t(\delta) \succ 0$ for each positive δ in $\mathcal{D}$.

Optimizing one reference. Let us consider an iteration domain D_P of dimension d, referencing one array through a homogeneous reference matrix R of size $(d' + p + 1) \times (d + p + 1)$, where d' is the dimension of the array. There is temporal reuse if the data accessed by the loop has smaller geometric dimension than the iteration domain. As a consequence, in order for the reference to be temporally optimized, the rank of matrix R has to be lower than $(d + p + 1)$.

The image defined by matrix R to the iteration space results in a polytope containing all the accessed data, and is called the data space. Each integer point d_0 of the data space, or each data, corresponds to a polytope to be scanned by the optimized inner loops. It is a polytope depending on parameter d_0. It is computed by applying function preimage R^{-1} to d_0, intersected with the iteration domain D_P. Let $\mathcal{H} = Affine.Hull(R^{-1}d_0 \cap D_P)$. Let matrix B_T be the set of column-vectors generating $\mathcal{H}$. This matrix contains the scanning directions of the optimized inner loops.

Let $B = \left(\begin{array}{c|c} (B_D|B_T) & 0 \\ \hline 0 & Id \end{array} \right)$ in the homogeneous space. Matrix B_D is a basis of the space scanning each accessed data. It must be chosen in order for B to be unimodular and full rank (using the Hermite normal form theorem for example), and also to satisfy the dependences. As a result, B is a basis for the optimized scanning loops, the outermost loop corresponding to the leftmost column vector of B. Transformation matrix T is equal to B^{-1}.

Example 1. Consider the loop nest presented on the left of Tab. 2. There is an output dependence for array A, of distance vector $\delta = (0, 1, -1)^\top$. The reference matrix to variable A, is $R = \begin{pmatrix} 1 & 0 & 0 & 1 & 0 \\ 0 & 1 & 1 & 0 & -1 \\ 0 & 0 & 0 & 1 & 0 \\ 0 & 0 & 0 & 0 & 1 \end{pmatrix}$.

Table 2. Optimizing a loop nest containing one reference

original loop nest	optimized loop nest
do i = 1, N	do u = 1, N
do j = 1, N	do v = 2, N+u
do k = 1, i	do w = max(1,v-N), min(u,v-1)
A[i+N, j+k-1] = f(i,j,k)	A[u+N, v-1] = f(u,v-w,w)

Each point $d_0 = (x_0, y_0)^\top$ of the data space corresponds to the scanning of the following polytope: $R^{-1}d_0 \cap D_N = \{(x_0, y_0 - k, k)^\top \in D_N\}$, where D_N is the iteration domain. The vector supporting the affine hull of this polytope is $B_T = \begin{pmatrix} 0 \\ -1 \\ 1 \end{pmatrix}$. The dependence is satisfied with $B_D = \begin{pmatrix} 1 & 0 \\ 0 & 1 \\ 0 & 0 \end{pmatrix}$.

The transformed loop nest is obtained by applying $T = B^{-1}$ to the iteration domain, and by transforming the references to I by $t^{-1}(I')$. The result is given Tab. 2, with $I' = (u, v, w)^\top$. Reference to variable A has been temporally optimized in the innermost loop: index w does not appear in the reference.

Multiple references optimization. The main objective of our approach is to reduce stride sizes generated from any reference. The largest stride that can be generated by a reference is the size of its associated data set. Hence, our heuristic states that references associated with the largest data sets should be optimized first. This introduces the concept of *data sequence localization*. Consider a loop nest containing n references to the same or to different arrays. The data set sizes are determined by computing the Ehrhart polynomials of the affine transformation of D_P by the reference matrices [4]. Then we compute the subspaces $\mathcal{H}_i$ where temporal reuse occurs for each reference i, as described below: $\mathcal{H}_i = Affine.Hull(R_i^{-1}d_0 \cap D_P)$.

The algorithm consists in building a basis for the scanning loops represented as matrix B, from right to left. The rightmost scanning vector is chosen so that it optimizes as many references as possible. The algorithm then successively selects the scanning vectors in order to optimize as many non yet optimized references as possible. In case of equality, the references having the largest data set sizes are chosen:

1. Order the n references by decreasing data set sizes.
2. Compute the spaces $\mathcal{H}_i$ for each reference, $1 \leq i \leq n$.
3. for $col = d$ downto 1 do
   (a) Find the direction $\mathcal{T}$ that optimizes as many references as possible, in the set of references that have been optimized the least. This is done by computing successive intersections of the sets $\mathcal{H}_i$. If there are no more references to optimize choose a direction such that B is unimodular.
   (b) Put the vector $\mathcal{T}$ in the column col of matrix B. Check the dependences and the unimodularity of B; if they are not satisfied, go back to step 3a and choose another direction.

The unimodularity of B is checked using the Hermite normal form theorem ([17], corollary 4.1c): at each step of the algorithm, the column vectors of B should generate a dense lattice subspace. This condition is verified if and only if the *gcd* of the subdeterminants of order $d - col$ of these column vectors is 1.

Example 2. Consider the 4-dimensional loop nest presented in Tab. 3. We choose first to optimize temporal reuse for reference $A[k, j, i]$, since it has the largest data set (N^3). The two references to B have the same data set size (N^2). Let us call R_1 the reference to $A[k, j, i]$, R_2 and R_3 the references to $B[l, j]$ and $B[i, l]$ respectively. There is one dependence on variable A, of distance vector $(0, 0, 0, 1)^\top$.

Table 3. A loop nest containing 3 references

```
do i = 1, N
  do j = 1, N
    do k = 1, N
      do l = 1, N
        A[k,j,i] = A[k,j,i] + B[l+k,j] + B[i,l+k]
```

The first step of the algorithm consists in computing the linear spaces of temporal reuse $\mathcal{H}_i$, for $i = 1, 2, 3$. $\mathcal{H}_1$ is supported by vector $(0, 0, 0, 1)^\top$,

Table 4. Optimized loop nest

```
do u = 1, N
  do v = 1, N
    do w = 2, 2*N
      do x = max(w-N,1),min(w-1,N)
        A[x,u,v] = A[x,u,v] + B[w,u] + B[v,w]
```

Table 5. Performance results

$N = 700$	Original loop	Loop blocking	Optimized loop
# L1 data cache misses	52,283,667,715	747,493,318	777,072,089
# L2 data cache misses	23,082,872	53,590,447	19,351,070
# TLB misses	1,345,342,838,661	127,516,826	124,344,788
computation time	10,873s	1,757s	1,688s

$\mathcal{H}_2$ is supported by $(1, 0, 0, 0)^T$ and $(0, 0, 1, -1)^T$, and $\mathcal{H}_3$ is supported by $(0, 1, 0, 0)^T$ and $(0, 0, 1, -1)^T$. The algorithm then selects four new scanning vectors in this order:

- vector $(0, 0, 1, -1)^T$ is chosen first, since it optimizes both references R_2 and R_3 (but not R_1).
- vector $(0, 0, 0, 1)^T$ then optimizes reference R_1, which has not been optimized yet. Notice that reference R_1 cannot be better optimized in a further step, since $dim(\mathcal{H}_1) = 1$.
- vector $(1, 0, 0, 0)^T$ optimizes reference R_2.
- vector $(0, 1, 0, 0)^T$ optimizes reference R_3.

Finally, we get $B = \begin{pmatrix} 0 & 1 & 0 & 0 & 0 & 0 \\ 1 & 0 & 0 & 0 & 0 & 0 \\ 0 & 0 & 0 & 1 & 0 & 0 \\ 0 & 0 & 1 & -1 & 0 & 0 \\ 0 & 0 & 0 & 0 & 1 & 0 \\ 0 & 0 & 0 & 0 & 0 & 1 \end{pmatrix}$ and $T = B^{-1} = \begin{pmatrix} 0 & 1 & 0 & 0 & 0 & 0 \\ 1 & 0 & 0 & 0 & 0 & 0 \\ 0 & 0 & 1 & 1 & 0 & 0 \\ 0 & 0 & 1 & 0 & 0 & 0 \\ 0 & 0 & 0 & 0 & 1 & 0 \\ 0 & 0 & 0 & 0 & 0 & 1 \end{pmatrix}$.

The dependence is satisfied and the resulting loop nest is presented in Tab. 4. Table 5 shows our experimental results for $N = 700$, on three version of the loop: the original loop nest without blocking nor interchange optimization, the SGI F90 compiler version allowing autoblocking and interchange of loops, and our version. These mesures show an important performance improvement from the original loop to the two optimized versions, and some more gain in the number of L2 data cache misses and TLB misses from the blocking version to our optimized version. These L2 and TLB misses have been transformed into L1 misses in our version, since the reused data sequences fit the lower memory hierarchy level. Getting even better results could be possible by now through our spatial locality optimization [6].

3 Consequences on Parallel Optimizations

Although our method is devoted to improving savings in cache and TLB miss rates, it also has an important impact on processor locality on massively parallel architectures: when a processor brings a data page into its local memory, it will reuse it as much as possible due to our temporal optimization. This yields significant reductions in page faults and hence in network traffic.

We can also say, as mentioned by Kandemir et al. in [9], that optimized programs do not need explicit data placement techniques on shared memory NUMA architectures: when a processor uses a data page frequently, the page is either replicated onto that processor's memory or migrated into it. In either cases, all the remaining accesses will be local.

Temporal optimizations presented in Sect. 2 often generate outer loops that carry no reuse and no data dependences. Hence, these outer loops are perfect candidates for parallelization since distinct iterations do not share any data.

All these facts allow the generation of data-parallel codes with significant savings in interprocessor communication.

4 Related Work

In [7], Ding and Kennedy define the concept of *reuse distance* as being the number of distinctive data items appearing between two closest references to a same data. Although their objective of minimizing such distances seems quite similar to ours, they rather consider fusion of data-sharing loops. Reuse distance minimization inside a loop nest with multiple references is not considered at all.

Ciernak and Li in [3] introduce the concept of *reference distance* as being the number of different cache lines accessed between two references to the same cache line. However this item does not guide their optimization process, but is used as a metric of quality. They also define *stride vectors* as being vectors composed of the strides associated to each loop level. Their objective is to obtain such a vector with elements in decreasing order, whereas our objective is to minimize all elements of this vector, while breaking the largest strides into smaller ones. For example, in our method, stride vector (N, N) will be prefered to vector $(N^2, 1)$.

5 Conclusion

We have shown that significant performance improvements can be obtained in programs through data sequence localization. Our method, compared to blocking, is independent from the target architecture and hence does not need fine tuning relatively to the memory hierarchy specifications. We also have proposed an original approach for spatial locality optimization [6] which can be naturally unified with the temporal optimization method of this paper in order to get even better program performance.

All the geometric and arithmetic tools we used are implemented in the polyhedral library *PolyLib* (http://icps.u-strasbg.fr/Polylib). We are currently implementing the method presented in this paper in an environment for source to source transformations of Fortran programs. Once implemented, we are going to validate our method on some larger benchmarks.

We are now studying other important issues such as memory compression, since further performance improvements can be expected, and memory size minimization which is essential in embedded systems. We also investigate another approach, by considering architectural parameters characterizing the target architecture: cache size, cache associativity, cache line size, TLB reach, etc. In addition to data locality optimization, other important issues related to efficient memory use can be considered, such as array padding and cache set conflicts.

References

1. U. Banerjee. Unimodular transformations of double loops. In *Advances in Languages and Compilers for Parallel Processing*. MIT Press, Cambridge, MA, 1991.
2. U. Banerjee. *Loop Transformations for Restructuring Compilers - The Foundations*. Kluwer Academic Publishers, 1993. ISBN 0-7923-9318-X.
3. M. Cierniak and W. Li. Unifying data and control transformations for distributed shared-memory machines. In *Proc. Prog. Lang. Design and Implementation*, 1995.
4. Ph. Clauss. Handling memory cache policy with integer points countings. In *Euro-Par'97*, pages 285–293, Passau, August 1997. Springer-Verlag, LNCS 1300.
5. Ph. Clauss and V. Loechner. Parametric analysis of polyhedral iteration spaces. *Journal of VLSI Signal Processing*, 19(2):179–194, 1998. Kluwer Academic Pub.
6. Ph. Clauss and B. Meister. Automatic memory layout transformations to optimize spatial locality in parameterized loop nests. *ACM SIGARCH Computer Architecture News*, 28(1):11–19, March 2000.
7. C. Ding and K. Kennedy. Improving effective bandwidth through compiler enhancement of global cache reuse. In *Proc. of the 2001 International Parallel and Distributed Processing Symposium, San Francisco*, April 2001.
8. P. Feautrier. *The Data Parallel Programming Model*, volume 1132 of *LNCS*, chapter Automatic Parallelization in the Polytope Model, pages 79–100. Springer-Verlag, 1996. G.-R. Perrin and A. Darte, Eds. ISBN 3-540-61736-1.
9. M. Kandemir, A. Choudhary, J. Ramanujam, and P. Banerjee. A matrix-based approach to global locality optimization. *Journal of Parallel and Distributed Computing*, 58:190–235, 1999.
10. M. Lam, E. Rothberg, and M. Wolf. The cache performance of blocked algorithms. In *Int. Conf. ASPLOS*, April 1991.
11. W. Li. *Compiling for NUMA parallel machines*. PhD thesis, Dept. Computer Science, Cornell University, Ithaca, NY, 1993.
12. V. Loechner, B. Meister, and Ph. Clauss. Precise data locality optimization of nested loops. Technical report, ICPS, http://icps.u-strasbg.fr, 2001.
13. V. Loechner and D. K. Wilde. Parameterized polyhedra and their vertices. *International Journal of Parallel Programming*, 25(6):525–549, December 1997.
14. M. O'Boyle and P. Knijnenburg. Nonsingular data transformations: Definition, validity, and applications. *Int. J. of Parallel Programming*, 27(3):131–159, 1999.
15. F. Quilleré, S. Rajopadhye, and D. Wilde. Generation of efficient nested loops from polyhedra. *Int. J. of Parallel Programming*, 28(5):469–498, October 2000.
16. J. M. Rabaey and M. Pedram. *Low Power Design Methodologies*. Kluwer Academic Publishers, 1995.

17. A. Schrijver. *Theroy of Linear and Integer Programming.* John Wiley and Sons, New York, 1986. ISBN 0-471-90854-1.
18. M. R. Swanson, L. Stoller, and J. Carter. Increasing TLB reach using superpages backed by shadow memory. In *Proceedings of the 25th Annual International Symposium on Computer Architecture*, pages 204–213, June 1998.
19. D. K. Wilde. A library for doing polyhedral operations. Master's thesis, Oregon State University, Corvallis, Oregon, 1993.
20. M. Wolfe. More iteration space tiling. In *Proc. Supercomputing'89*, pages 655–664, November 1989.
21. M. Wolfe. The tiny loop restructuring research tool. In *International Conference on Parallel Processing*, pages II. 46–53, 1991.
22. M. Wolfe. *High Performance Compilers for Parallel Computing.* Addison Wesley, 1996. ISBN 0-8053-2730-4.

Efficient Dependence Analysis for Java Arrays

Vivek Sarkar and Stephen Fink

IBM Thomas J. Watson Research Center
P. O. Box 704, Yorktown Heights, NY 10598, USA

Abstract. This paper studies dependence analysis for Java arrays, emphasizing *efficient solutions* that avoid a large compile-time overhead. We present a new approach for dependence analysis based on sparse congruence partitioning representations in SSA form. Since arrays in Java are dynamically allocated, our approach takes pointer-induced aliasing of array objects into account in conjunction with analysis of index values. We present experimental results to evaluate the effectiveness of our approach, and outline directions for further improvements.

1 Introduction

Parallelizing and optimizing compilers perform array dependence analysis to aid parallelizing transformations and enhance back-end optimizations. The core problem addressed by dependence analysis ask whether and under what conditions two array references may interfere. The bulk of past work on array dependence analysis has focused on imperative programming languages such as Fortran and C, and has resulted in a wide range of data dependence tests based on *symbolic analysis of index values* (*e.g.*, see [14,2,8,10,9,11,3]). Java, with dynamically allocated arrays, also requires *pointer-induced alias analysis* (*e.g.*, see [5,13,12]) of array objects as part of array dependence analysis.

We examine an approach to dependence analysis for Java arrays, based on sparse congruence partitioning in SSA form and accounting for pointer-induced aliasing of array objects. The main features of our approach are:

1. *Congruence Partitioning* [1] based on SSA form provides an efficient approximate analysis of when two index values are "definitely same" (DS).
2. A new *Uniformly-Generated Partitioning* provides provides an efficient approximate analysis of when two index values are "uniformly generated" [7] *i.e.*, when the two index values differ by a compile-time constant.
3. The *Inequality Graph* representation from [3] provides an efficient approximate analysis of when two index values are related by a $<$ or $>$ inequality.

These representations all rely on an extended SSA form. Since the compiler uses only efficient *sparse* dataflow techniques, these techniques are ameneble for runtime or dynamic (JIT) compilation. Experimental results show that congruence partitioning techniques catch a substantial number of cases, but also indicate significant opportunities for improvement with better algorithms and inter-procedural analysis.

2 Background

The dependence analysis approach presented in this paper builds on the SSA congruence partitioning algorithm introduced in [1], and the Inequality Graph from [3].

We first partition SSA reference variables into equivalence classes. The result is represented as REF$_\simeq$, where REF$_\simeq(a)$ is the equivalence class for variable a. Given two SSA variables containing object references, a and b, if REF$_\simeq(a)$ = REF$_\simeq(b)$ then the (unique) definitions of a and b are guaranteed to be "definitely same" i.e., REF$_\simeq.DS(a,b)$ = true.

Further, as described in [6], if REF$_\simeq(a) \neq$ REF$_\simeq(b)$, and both a and b belong to equivalence classes that included the result of a **new** operation, then a and b are guaranteed to be "definitely different" i.e., REF$_\simeq.DD(a,b)$ = true. This also holds if a's equivalence class includes the result of a **new** operation, and b's equivalence class includes a parameter.

The *Inequality Graph* (*IG*) representation is used to provide an efficient approximate solution to the problem of determining when two index values are related by a $<$ or $>$ inequality. As described in [3], a demand-driven traversal of the inequality graph can establish that two index values belong to an inequality relation. We omit further details due to space constraints; see [3] for more details.

3 Uniformly-Generated Partitioning of Integer Variables

Past work has shown that the most common case in data dependence analysis compares index expressions that differ by a compile-time constant [8,10]. Such index expressions are said to be "uniformly-generated" [7]. In this section, we describe the *uniformly-generated partitioning* representation, which is as an extension to congruence partitioning and applies to all integer-like variables.

The partitioning is represented by three structures – INDEX$_\simeq$, INDEX_OFFSET, and INDEX_REP, where INDEX$_\simeq(a)$ is the "uniformly-generated" equivalence class for variable a. Given two SSA variables, a and b, if INDEX$_\simeq(a)$ = INDEX$_\simeq(b)$ then the (unique) definitions of a and b are guaranteed to compute values that differ by a compile-time constant. The values of a and b are related by the identity, $a = b + $ INDEX_OFFSET$(a) -$ INDEX_OFFSET(b), where INDEX_OFFSET(a) contains a constant offset that relates the value of a to the value of a hypothetical *representative variable*, INDEX_REP(a) for the equivalence class containing variable a by the identity, $a = $ INDEX_REP$(a) + $ INDEX_OFFSET(a).

If INDEX$_\simeq(a)$ = INDEX$_\simeq(b)$ and INDEX_OFFSET(a) = INDEX_OFFSET(b), then the definitions of a and b are guaranteed to be "definitely same", indicated by INDEX$_\simeq.DS(a,b)$ = true. If INDEX$_\simeq(a)$ = INDEX$_\simeq(b)$ and INDEX_OFFSET$(a) \neq$ INDEX_OFFSET(b), then the definitions of a and b are guaranteed to be "definitely different" i.e., INDEX$_\simeq.DD(a,b)$ = true.

The three structures are initialized as follows. First, congruence partitioning is performed on integer variables, and INDEX$_\simeq$ is initialized to the resulting partition. A representative variable is arbitrarily selected from each equivalence class in the partitioning. For each integer variable, a, INDEX_OFFSET(a) is set $= 0$, and INDEX_REP(a) is set to the representative variable for a's equivalence class.

Next, we merge congruence classes as follows. For each instruction of the form, $a := b + constant$, the equivalence classes containing a and b are merged. REF$_\simeq$ is updated to reflect the result of the merge. INDEX_REP(a), the representative variable for a's class is arbitrarily chosen as the representative variable for the merged class. Further, the offset values for b and all variables that were in the same class as b are updated such that INDEX_OFFSET(b) := INDEX_OFFSET(a) − $constant$.

4 Algorithm

This section lays out the entire approach for intraprocedural dependence analysis considered in this paper. First we construct the sparse data structures as described; namely, SSA form, the congruence partitioning, and the uniformly-generating congruence partitions, and the inequality graph.

Next, we query these data structures to compare. a pair of one-dimensional array accesses, $a[i]$ and $b[j]$, in the extended SSA form. We perform the following steps in an attempt to determine whether these array accesses are "definitely-different" or "definiately-same". If none of the previous steps has a a conclusive answer, Step 6 returns *unknown* as a conservative default solution.

1. *Type propagation and disambiguation*
   if a and b cannot have overlapping types **then return** *definitely-different*;
2. *Definitely-different test for object references using* REF$_\simeq$
   if REF$_\simeq$.$DD(a, b)$ = *true* **then return** *definitely-different*;
3. *Definitely-different test for index values using* INDEX$_\simeq$
   if INDEX$_\simeq$.$DD(a, b)$ = *true* **then return** *definitely-different*;
4. *Definitely-same test using* REF$_\simeq$ *and* INDEX$_\simeq$
   if REF$_\simeq$.$DS(a, b)$ = *true* **and** INDEX$_\simeq$.$DS(a, b)$ = *true* **then**
   return *definitely-same*;
5. *Traversals of the Inequality Graph, IG*
   Traverse IG starting at i and attempt to prove $i < j$ or $j > i$.
6. *Otherwise*
   return *unknown*;

5 Experimental Results

We present results using the implementation of extended SSA form in the Jalapeño dynamic optimizing compiler [4,6]. We performed the dependence analysis test for each pair of distinct array references in each innermost loop of each method executed.

Table 1 presents "static" counts of array reference pairs examined. The aload and astore columns represent the total number of aload and astore instructions encountered in innermost loops. The # pairs column contains the number of pairs of distinct aload/astore instructions found in innermost loops. The remaining columns break down the number of pairs into six categories:

Table 1. Summary of dependence test results on pairs of array references in innermost loops. The table reports on the 7 SPECjvm98 codes, and on two parallel computational fluid dynamics codes described in [?]

Benchmark	aload	astore	# pairs	type.DD	ref.DD	index.DD	graph.DD	DS	unresolved
compress	20	15	13	0	0	0	0	1 (7.7%)	12 (92.3%)
jess	255	42	793	335 (42%)	0	3 (0.4%)	1 (0.1%)	32 (4.0%)	422 (53%)
db	44	13	37	0	0	0	0	7 (19%)	30 (81%)
javac	192	71	181	30 (17%)	1 (1.2%)	12 (6.6%)	0	22 (12%)	116 (64%)
mpegaudio	172	43	658	295 (45%)	0	103 (16%)	2 (0.3%)	26 (4.0%)	232 (35%)
mtrt	78	13	134	28 (21%)	3 (2.2%)	5 (3.7%)	0	6 (4.5%)	92 (69%)
jack	60	11	60	0	0	0	0	2 (3.3%)	58 (97%)
laura	122	54	343	127 (37%)	22 (6.4%)	105 (31%)	0	6 (1.7%)	83 (24%)
2dtag	24	22	247	123 (50%)	0	11 (4.5%)	0	4 (1.6%)	109 (44%)
section2	123	53	403	79	0	92	0	45	187

type.DD The number of pairs which type propagation determines to be *definitely-different* (Step 1).

ref.DD The number of pairs which simple alias analysis determines to be *definitely-different* (Step 2).

index.DD The number of pairs which uniformly-generated congruence partitions determine to be *definitely-different* (Step 3).

graph.DD The number of pairs which the inequality graph traversal determines to be *definitely-different* (Step 5).

DS The number of pairs which congruence partitioning determines both the index and array reference to be *definitely-same* (Step 4).

unknown All remaining pairs (Step 6).

The results show that Java's strong type system helps disambiguate many array references. The two variants of congruence partitioning are the next most effective. The simple alias analysis and inequality graph traversals are mostly ineffective. The totality of techniques appears to be most effective on the two numerical CFD codes (laura and 2dtag). The number of unresolved pairs ranges from 24% to 97%. However, as some pairs are neither DD nor DS, even exact analysis would have non-zero unresolved pairs. A limit on analysis precision remains open for future work.

These results suggest that there may be room for increased precision with more powerful techniques. It is not surprising that intra-procedural alias analysis provided little help for DD. We experimented with assuming that distinct parameters are not aliased, which determined 3 additional pairs to be DD. We are also investigating more powerful variants of the inequality graph and other sparse demand-driven dataflow techniques.

6 Conclusions and Future Work

This paper presented a new approach for dependence analysis based on sparse congruence partitioning representations built on SSA form. Our experimental results demonstrate some effectiveness for dependence tests on array references based on standard and uniformly generated congruence partitioning. However, there may be significant opportunities for improvement with interprocedural analysis and/or improved dataflow propagation of inequalities.

References

1. B. Alpern, M. N. Wegman, and F. K. Zadeck. Detecting equality of variables in programs. In ACM, editor, *POPL '88. Proceedings of the conference on Principles of programming languages, January 13–15, 1988, San Diego, CA*, pages 1–11, New York, NY, USA, 1988. ACM Press.
2. U. Banerjee. *Loop transformations for restructuring compilers: the foundations.* Kluwer Academic Publishers, Boston, MA, 1993.
3. R. Bodik, R. Gupta, and V. Sarkar. ABCD: Eliminating Array Bounds Checks on Demand. In *SIGPLAN 2000 Conference on Programming Language Design and Implementation*, June 2000.
4. M. Burke, J.-D. Choi, S. Fink, D. Grove, M. Hind, V. Sarkar, M. Serrano, V. Sreedhar, H. Srinivasan, and J. Whaley. The Jalapeño Dynamic Optimizing Compiler for Java. In *ACM Java Grande Conference*, June 1999.
5. M. Emami, R. Ghiya, and L. J. Hendren. Context-sensitive interprocedural points-to analysis in the presence of function pointers. In *SIGPLAN '94 Conference on Programming Language Design and Implementation*, pages 242–256, June 1994. SIGPLAN Notices, 29(6).
6. S. Fink, K. Knobe, and V. Sarkar. Unified analysis of array and object references in strongly typed languages. In *Seventh International Static Analysis Symposium (2000)*, June 2000.
7. K. Gallivan, W. Jalby, and D. Gannon. On the Problem of Optimizing Data Transfers for Complex Memory Systems. *Proceedings of the ACM 1988 International Conference on Supercomputing*, pages 238–253, July 1988.
8. G. Goff, K. Kennedy, and C.-W. Tseng. Practical dependence testing. In *SIGPLAN '91 Conference on Programming Language Design and Implementation*, pages 15–29, 1991. SIGPLAN Notices, 266.
9. M. R. Haghighat and C. D. Polychronopoulos. Symbolic analysis for parallelizing compilers. *ACM Transactions on Programming Languages and Systems*, 18(4):477–518, July 1996.
10. D. E. Maydan, J. L. Hennessy, and M. S. Lam. Efficient and exact data dependence analysis. In *SIGPLAN '91 Conference on Programming Language Design and Implementation*, pages 1–14, 1991. SIGPLAN Notices, 266.
11. W. Pugh and D. Wonnacott. Eliminating false data dependences using the omega test. *Proceedings of the ACM SIGPLAN '92 Conference on Programming Language Design and Implementation, San Francisco, California*, pages 140–151, June 1992.
12. B. Steensgaard. Points-to analysis in almost linear time. In *23rd Annual ACM SIGACT-SIGPLAN Symposium on the Principles of Programming Languages*, pages 32–41, Jan. 1996.
13. R. P. Wilson and M. S. Lam. Efficient context-sensitive pointer analysis for C programs. In *SIGPLAN '95 Conference on Programming Language Design and Implementation*, pages 1–12, June 1995. SIGPLAN Notices, 30(6).
14. M. J. Wolfe. *Optimizing Supercompilers for Supercomputers.* Pitman, London and The MIT Press, Cambridge, Massachusetts, 1989. In the series, Research Monographs in Parallel and Distributed Computing.

Topic 05
Parallel and Distributed Databases, Data Mining and Knowledge Discovery

Harald Kosch, Pedro R. Falcone Sampaio, Abdelkader Hameurlain, and Lionel Brunie

Topic Chairpersons

We would like to welcome you to the Euro-Par 2001 topic on Parallel and Distributed Databases and Data Mining. It is the first time that the parallel and distributed processing in databases topic at the Euro-Par Conference Series has expanded to incorporate contributions coming from the Data Mining area. From the scope and nature of the submissions received, we were quick to recognize the fruitfulness of this symbiosis, stemming from the fact that many technical challenges and solutions can be shared (for instance, the problem of parallel access to multidimensional data structures). As a result of the topic expansion, we are proud to present two sessions with 6 paper presentations for which we expect some controversy, as well as instructive insights originating from the research discussions. We also hope that you enjoy your visit to Manchester.

Today, the World Wide Web is regarded as a distributed global information resource, which is not only important to individual users, but also to business organizations. New intensive data consuming applications (e.g. Multimedia Content Management, Data Mining, Decision Support, E-Commerce) emerged in this environment. They often suffer from performance problems and single database source limitations. Introducing data distribution and parallel processing helps to overcome resource bottlenecks and to achieve guaranteed throughput, quality of service, and system scalability. Recent developments in parallel and distributed architectures supported by high performance networks and intelligent middleware offer parallel and distributed databases a great opportunity to make a step from being highly specialized systems to supporting cost-effective every day applications.

This year 10 papers were submitted, a considerable increase with regard to the previous edition of the topic at Euro-Par. The quality and range of the 10 submitted papers was remarkable, and we needed intensive peer discussions to select the best ones. The growing number of submissions shows the popularity of research on parallel and distributed databases, as well as the strong link with its 'sister' field of data mining. All papers were reviewed by four reviewers, where, besides the PC members, 19 external reviewers supported the process. The feedback to the authors were thorough and detailed, and many reviewers took additional efforts to point out further possible research directions. Using these referee's reports as guidelines, the program committee chose six papers for publication and presentation at the conference. Four were selected as regular papers, and two as research notes. These were scheduled to be presented in two sessions, on Wednesday 29th of August during the afternoon. One session is dedicated to aspects focusing on performance and implementation in parallel and distributed databases and the other session on parallel data-mining oriented aspects.

The first full session focuses on performance and implementation techniques in parallel and distributed databases. The three papers chosen for this session bring new results in classical areas of parallel and distributed database research.

Highlighting the consolidation of the ODMG as a step forward in providing standards for object database systems, and the increasing importance of efficient parallel implementations of query processing operators in ODMG compliant object databases, the first paper by Sandra de F. Mendes Sampaio, Jim Smith, Norman W. Paton and Paul Watson presents experimental results of several join algorithms implemented in the Polar ODMG compliant parallel object database system. The second paper, by Holger Märtens, brings new insights on the relation between different skew types and load balancing methods in parallel database systems, suggesting some anti-skew measures to alleviate skew effects. The third paper, by Azzedine Boukerche and Terry Tuck, addresses the problem of improving concurrency control in distributed databases, by using implementation techniques based on predeclaring tables that will be updated when a transaction begins.

The second full session focuses on parallel processing in data mining. Reflecting the increasing importance of data mining techniques in industrial applications, all three papers contribute to a more efficient processing of these complex and resource-hungry techniques.

In the first paper, Valerie Guralnik, Nivea Garg and George Karypis present two parallel formulations (using once a data and once a task parallelisation) of a serial sequential pattern discovery algorithm based on tree projection that are well suited for distributed memory parallel computers. The discovery of sequential patterns is becoming increasingly useful and essential in many commercial applications and an acceptable mining performance is critical to these applications. In the second paper Attila Gürsoy and İlker Cengiz have developed and evaluated two parallelisation schemes for a tree-based k-means method on shared memory architectures. They use a data-parallelization paradigm and study data pattern composition necessary for efficient processing. This paper is highly related to the first one and we expect some interesting comparative discussions in this session. In the third paper, Domenica Arlia and Massimo Coppola have developed and implemented a parallelisation of DBSCAN, a broadly used Data Mining algorithm for density-based spatial clustering. Interesting, here, is the applicability of the developed methods to multimedia, or spatial parallel databases and makes therefore a link to the first session.

In closing, we would like to thank the authors who submitted a contribution, as well as the Euro-Par Organizing Committee, and the referees with their highly useful comments, and whose efforts have made this conference, and Topic 05 possible.

An Experimental Performance Evaluation of Join Algorithms for Parallel Object Databases

Sandra de F. Mendes Sampaio[1], Jim Smith[2], Norman W. Paton[1], and Paul Watson[2]

[1] Department of Computer Science, University of Manchester
Manchester, M13 9PL, UK
{sampaios,norm}@cs.man.ac.uk
[2] Department of Computing Science, University of Newcastle upon Tyne
Newcastle, NE1 7RU, UK
{Paul.Watson,Jim.Smith}@newcastle.ac.uk

Abstract. Parallel relational databases have been successful in providing scalable performance for data intensive applications, and much work has been carried out on query processing techniques in such systems. However, although many applications associated with object databases also have stringent performance requirements, there has been much less work investigating parallel object database systems. An important feature for the performance of object databases is the speed at which relationships can be explored. In queries, this depends upon the effectiveness of different join algorithms into which queries that follow relationships can be compiled. This paper presents the results of empirical evaluations of four parallel join algorithms, two value based and two pointer based. The experiments have been run on Polar, a parallel ODMG object database system.

1 Introduction

Applications associated with object databases are demanding in terms of their complexity and performance requirements. However, there has not been much work on parallel object databases, and few complete systems have been constructed. There has been still less work on systematic assessment of the performance of query processing in parallel object databases. This paper presents a performance evaluation of different algorithms for exploring relationships in the parallel object database system Polar [9].

The focus in this paper is on the performance of OQL queries over ODMG databases, which are compiled in Polar into a parallel algebra for evaluation. The execution of the algebra, on a network of PCs, supports both inter and intra operator parallelism. The evaluation focuses on the performance of three parallel join algorithms, one of which is value based (hash join) and two of which are pointer based (materialize and hash loops). Figures are presented for queries running over the medium OO7 database [2].

The experiments and the resulting performance figures can be seen to serve two purposes: (i) they provide insights on algorithm selection for implementers of parallel object databases; (ii) they provide empirical results against which cost models for parallel query processing can be validated (e.g., [8]).

There is a considerable body of work on pointer based join algorithms. For example, six uni-processor join algorithms are compared in [8], including algorithms based on nested loop, sort merge and hybrid hash. A more recent study [1] both proposes a new pointer based join algorithm and provides a comprehensive comparison with several other approaches. Although [1] contains a few empirical results, the evaluations are based principally on analytical models, and parallelism is not considered.

There have been a few investigations into query evaluation in parallel object database systems. Four hash-based parallel pointer based join algorithms, including hash-loops, are compared in [3]. The comparison, which uses an analytical model, focuses on issues such as the need for extents for both classes participating in a join. Another model-based evaluation is provided by [10], in which their multiwavefront algorithm is compared with a more conventional pointer-based algorithm. There are few empirical evaluations of parallel pointer-based joins, although [4] describes how ParSets can be used to support parallel traversals over object databases for application development rather than query processing.

We see this paper as adding to the results mentioned above by providing comprehensive experimental evaluations over a parallel object database system. The paper is organized as follows: The architecture of the Polar parallel object database is outlined in Section 2. The parallel join algorithms evaluated are described in Section 3. Section 4 describes the experiments in detail, reviewing the OO7 database, and presenting the queries used in the experiments. Section 5 presents results of the experiments and their interpretation. Finally, Section 6 concludes.

2 The Polar System

Polar is a shared-nothing ODMG compliant object database server. For the experiments reported in this paper, it was running on 8 PCs, interconnected by Fast Ethernet. One of these processors serves as a coordinator, running the compiler/optimizer, while the remaining seven serve as object stores, running an object manager and execution engine.

In Polar, OQL queries are compiled into parallel query execution plans (PQEPs) expressed in an object algebra based on that of [5]. All the algebraic operators are implemented as iterators [7]. As such, the operators support three main functions, *open*, *next* and *close*, which define the main interface through which they interact with one another. The implementation of the algebra is essentially sequential, and most of the functionality that relates to parallelism, such as flow control, inter-process communication and data distribution, is encapsulated in the exchange operator, following the operator model of parallelization [6].

Figure 1 illustrates two possible PQEPs for query Q1 in figure 2. The query is over the OO7 benchmark schema. The plan on the left in figure 1 executes the example query using the value-based hash-join, while the plan on the right executes the same query using the pointer-based hash-loops.

In both plans, *CompositePart* objects are obtained from store through a seq_scan operator. The apply operators perform projections on the input tuples, discarding attributes that are not relevant to the subsequent steps of the execution. The exchange operators are responsible for sending tuples from a producer processor to its consumer(s) and for receiving the tuples on the consumer processors using the network. Thus exchange defines a partitioning of PQEPs into sub-plans, as indicated in the figure. The exchange in the boundary between sub-plans 1 and 2 redistributes the input tuples for the join operator according to the join attribute. The policy used for tuple distribution is chosen at query compile time, e.g. *select_by_oid* or *round_robin*. The exchange in the boundary between sub-plans 2 and 3 is responsible for directing the intermediate results to a single processor (the coordinator) for building the final result and sending it to the user.

Object identifiers in Polar contain a volume identifier, and a logical identifier within the volume. Tables are maintained that allow the node of a volume to be identified from the volume id, and to allow the page of an object to be identified from its logical identifier.

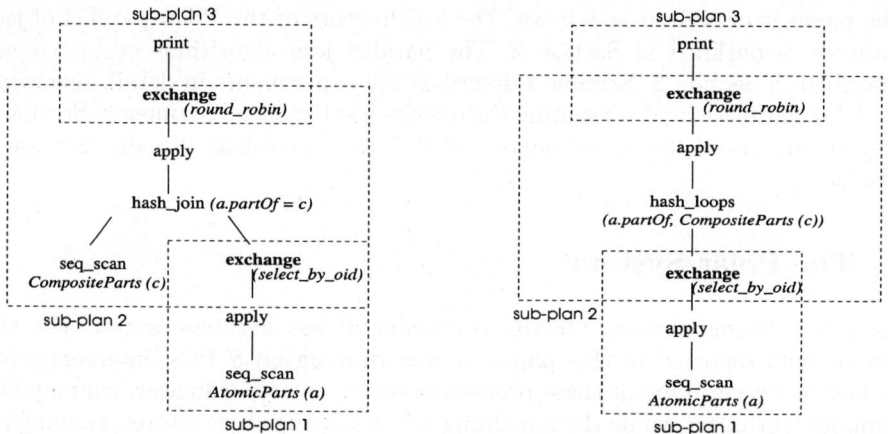

Fig. 1. On the left hand side: Possible PQEP, based on hash-join, for example query Q1. On the right hand side: Possible PQEP, for hash-loops, for example query Q2

3 Algorithms

This section describes the design of the three join algorithms evaluated in Polar.

Hash-join: The Polar version of hash-join is a one-pass implementation of the relational hash-join implemented as an iterator. This algorithm hashes the tuples of the smallest input on their join attribute(s), and places each tuple into a main memory hash table. Subsequently, it uses the tuples of the largest input to probe the hash table using the same hash function, and tests whether the tuple and the tuples that have the same result for the hash function satisfy the join condition.

Materialize: The materialize operator is the simplest pointer-based join, which performs naive pointer chasing. It iterates over its input tuples, and for each tuple reads an object, the OID of which is an attribute of the tuple. Dereferencing the OID has the effect of following the relationship represented by the OID-valued attribute. Unlike the hash-join described previously, materialize does not retain (potentially large) intermediate data structures in memory, since the only input to materialize does not need to be held onto by the operator after the related object has been retrieved from the store.

Hash-loops: The hash-loops operator is an adaptation for the iterator model of the pointer-based hash-loops join proposed in [3]. The main idea behind hash-loops is to minimize the number of repeated accesses to disk pages without retaining large amounts of data in memory. The first of these conflicting goals is addressed by collecting together repeated references to the same disk pages, so that all such references can be satisfied by a single access. The second goal is addressed by allowing the algorithm to consume its input in chunks, rather than all at once. Thus, hash-loops may fill and empty a main memory hash table multiple times to avoid keeping all of the input tuples in memory at the same time. Once the hash-table is filled with *window_size* tuples, each bucket in the hash table is scanned in turn, and its contents matched with objects retrieved from the store. Since the tuples in the hash table are hashed on the page number of the objects specified in the inter-object relationship, each disk page is retrieved from the store only once within each window. Once all the tuples that reference objects on a particular page have been processed, the corresponding bucket is removed from the hash table, and the next page, which corresponds to the next bucket to be probed, is retrieved from the store. Thus, hash-loops seeks to improve on materialize by coordinating accesses to persistent objects, which are likely to suffer from poor locality of reference in materialize.

4 The Experiments

OO7 Database The OO7 Benchmark [2] provides three different sizes for its database: small, medium and large. The differences in size are reflected in the cardinalities of extents and inter-object relationships. The following table shows the cardinalities of the extents and relationships used in the experiments for the medium OO7 database, which is used here.

Extent	Cardinality	Cardinality of Relationships
AtomicParts	100,000	partOf: 1
CompositeParts	500	parts: 200, documentation 1
Documents	500	
BaseAssemblies	729	componentsPriv: 3

To give an indication of the sizes of the persistent representations of the objects involved in OO7, the following are the sizes of individual objects obtained by measuring the collections stored for the medium database: AtomicPart – 190 bytes; CompositePart – 2,761 bytes; BaseAssembly – 190 bytes; Document – 24,776 bytes.

Experiment Queries The benchmark queries, Q1 to Q4, are given in Figure 2. Q1 and Q2 explore single-valued relationships, whereas Q3 and Q4 explore multiple-valued relationships. The predicate in the `where` clauses in Q1 and Q3 are used to vary the selectivity of the queries over the objects of the input extents, which may affect the join operators in different ways. The selectivities are varied to retain 100%, 10%, 1%, and 0.1% of the input extents.

```
Q1:
select struct(A:a.id,
       B:a.partOf.id)
from a in AtomicParts
where a.id <= v1
  and a.partOf.id <= v2;

Q3:
select struct(A:c.id,B:a.id)
from c in CompositeParts,
     a in c.parts
where c.id <= v1
  and a.id <= v2;
```

```
Q2:
select struct(A:a.id,B:a.docId,
       C:a.partOf.documentation.id)
from a in AtomicParts
where a.docId !=
      a.partOf.documentation.id;

Q4:
select struct(A:b.id,B:c.id)
from b in BaseAssemblies,
     a in b.componentsPriv,
     c in a.parts
where b.buildDate<c.buildDate;
```

Fig. 2. OQL expressions for the experiment queries

4.1 Experiment Context

The environment used in the experiments is a cluster of 233MHz Pentium II PCs running RedHat Linux version 6.2, each with 64MB main memory and a number of local disks, connected via a 100Mbps Fast ethernet hub. For each experiment, data is partitioned in "round robin" style over some number of MAXTOR MXT-540SL disks, of which there is one at each node. All timings are based on cold runs of the queries, with the server shut down and the operating system cache flushed between runs. In each case, the experiments were run three times, and the fastest time obtained is reported.

Several of the algorithms have tuning parameters that can have a significant impact on the way they perform (e.g., the hash table sizes for hash-join and hash-loops). In all cases, we have tried to select values for these parameters that will allow the algorithms to perform at their best. In hash-join, the hash table size is set differently for each join, to the value of the first prime number after the number of buckets to be stored in the hash table by the join. This

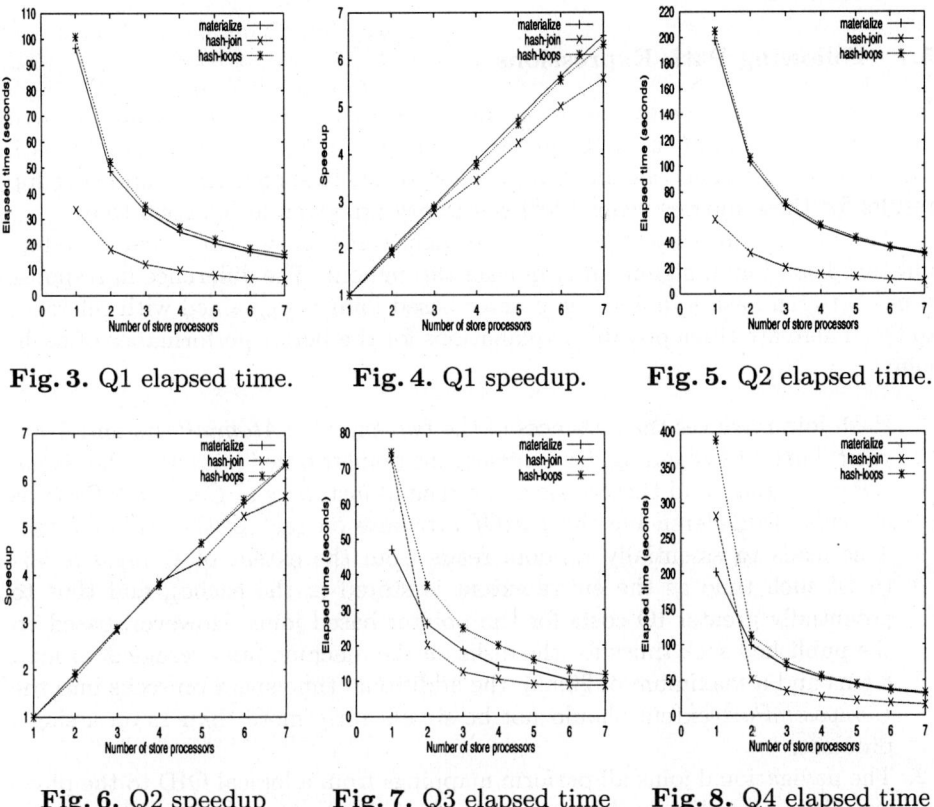

Fig. 3. Q1 elapsed time. **Fig. 4.** Q1 speedup. **Fig. 5.** Q2 elapsed time.

Fig. 6. Q2 speedup **Fig. 7.** Q3 elapsed time **Fig. 8.** Q4 elapsed time

means that there should be few clashes during hash table construction, but that the hash table does not occupy excessive amounts of memory. In hash-loops, the hash table size is also set differently for each join, to the value of the first prime number after the number of pages occupied by the extent that is being navigated to. This means that there should be few clashes during hash table construction, but that the hash table does not occupy an excessive amount of memory. The other parameter for hash-loops is the window size, which is set to the size of the input collection, except where otherwise stated. This decision minimizes the number of page accesses carried out by hash-loops, at the expense of some additional hash table size. None of the experiments use indexes, although the use of explicit relationships with stored OIDs can be seen as analogous to indexes on join attributes in relational databases.

5 Results

5.1 Following Path Expressions

Path expressions, whereby one or several single-valued relationships are followed in turn, are common in OQL queries. Test queries Q1 and Q2 contain path expressions, of lengths one and two, respectively[1]. Response times and speedup results for these queries using 100% selectivity are given in figures 3 to 6.

The graphs illustrate that all three algorithms show near linear speedup, but that hash-join is significantly quicker throughout. The difference in response times between hash-join and the pointer based joins is explained with reference to Q1. There are three possible explanations for the better performance of hash-join:

1. Hash join retrieves the instances of the two extents (*AtomicParts* and *CompositeParts*) by scanning. By contrast, the pointer based joins scan the *AtomicParts* extent, and then retrieve the related instances of *CompositeParts* as a result of dereferencing the *partOf* attribute on each of the *AtomicParts*. This leads to essentially random reads from the extent of *CompositePart* (until such time as the entire extent is stored in the cache), and thus to potentially greater IO costs for the pointer based joins. However, based on the published seek times for the disks on the machine (an average of around 8.5ms and a maximum of 20ms), the additional time spent on seeks into the *CompositePart* extent should not be significantly more than 1s on a single processor.
2. The navigational joins all perform mappings from a logical OID to the physical disk page where an object is stored. If this logical to physical mapping is slow, that would further increase the cost of obtaining access to a specific object within an extent, a feature that is not required by the value-based joins.
3. When an object has been read in from disk, it undergoes a mapping from its disk based format into the nested tuple structure used for intermediate data by the evaluator. Because each *CompositePart* is associated with many *AtomicParts*, the pointer based joins perform the *CompositePart* $\rightarrow$ *tuple* mapping once for every *AtomicPart* (i.e., 100,000 times), whereas this mapping is carried out only once for each *CompositePart* when the extent is scanned for the hash-join (i.e., 500 times).

An additional experiment was carried out to identify the cost of the *CompositePart* $\rightarrow$ *tuple* mapping, which shows that around 50% of the time taken to evaluate Q1 for materialize (and thus also hash-loops) on one processor is spent on the mapping. A further test showed that the essentially random fetching of the pages from the *CompositeParts* extent occupied around 20% of the time taken to evaluate Q1 for materialize.

---

[1] We define the length of a path expression to be the number of joins required to evaluate it.

We note the very similar performance of materialize and hash-loops. Hash-loops seeks to improve on materialize by reducing the number of page reads, through coordinating accesses to related pages. However, this shows no benefit in the example queries, because the complete *CompositeParts* and *Documents* extents can be cached, and thus the potential costs associated with uncoordinated accessing of the disk by materialize have been mitigated.

5.2 Following Multiple-Valued Relationships

Multiple valued relationships are expressed in OQL by iterating over collections that represent relationships in the from clause. Polar uses the same join algorithms for evaluating such relationships as for following path expressions. Test queries Q3 and Q4 follow one and two multiple valued relationships respectively. Response times for these queries using 100% selectivity are given in figures 7 and 8.

A striking feature of the figures for both Q3 and Q4 is the superlinear speedup for both hash-join and hash-loops, especially in moving from 1 to 2 processors. Both hash-join and hash-loops have significant space overheads associated with their hash tables, which causes swapping during evaluation of these algorithms in the configurations with smaller numbers of nodes. Monitoring swapping on the different nodes shows that by the time the hash tables are split over 3 nodes they fit in memory, and thus the effect of swapping on performance is removed for the larger configurations.

Another noteworthy feature is the fact that the relative performance of materialize and hash loops compared with hash join is better in Q3 and Q4 than in Q1 and Q2. This can be explained with reference to Q3. In Q3, the total number of *CompositePart* $\rightarrow$ *tuple* and *AtomicPart* $\rightarrow$ *tuple* mappings is the same for all the join algorithms (in contrast with the situation in Q1 and Q2). Thus the overhead that resulted from repeatedly mapping the same object does not affect materialize or hash loops in Q3.

As mentioned in Section 3, it is possible to reduce the space overhead associated with the hash table in hash loops by constructing several smaller hash tables over parts of the input extent, rather than one hash table over the whole extent. To test the effect of this on the performance of hash loops, figures 9 and 10 show results for different values of the window size parameter of hash-loops, for Q2 and Q4. Note from figure 9 that for Q2 the variation in the window size did not affect the performance. However, for Q4 (figure 10) there is a reduction in the elapsed times for smaller numbers of processors, as a consequence of the reduction of the swapping activity in those configurations.

5.3 Varying Selectivity

The selectivity experiments involve applying predicates to the inputs of Q1 and Q3, each of which carries out a single join. Response times for these queries over the medium OO7 database running on 6 nodes, varying the values for $v1$ and $v2$ in the queries, are given in figures 11 and 12, and figures 13 and 14,

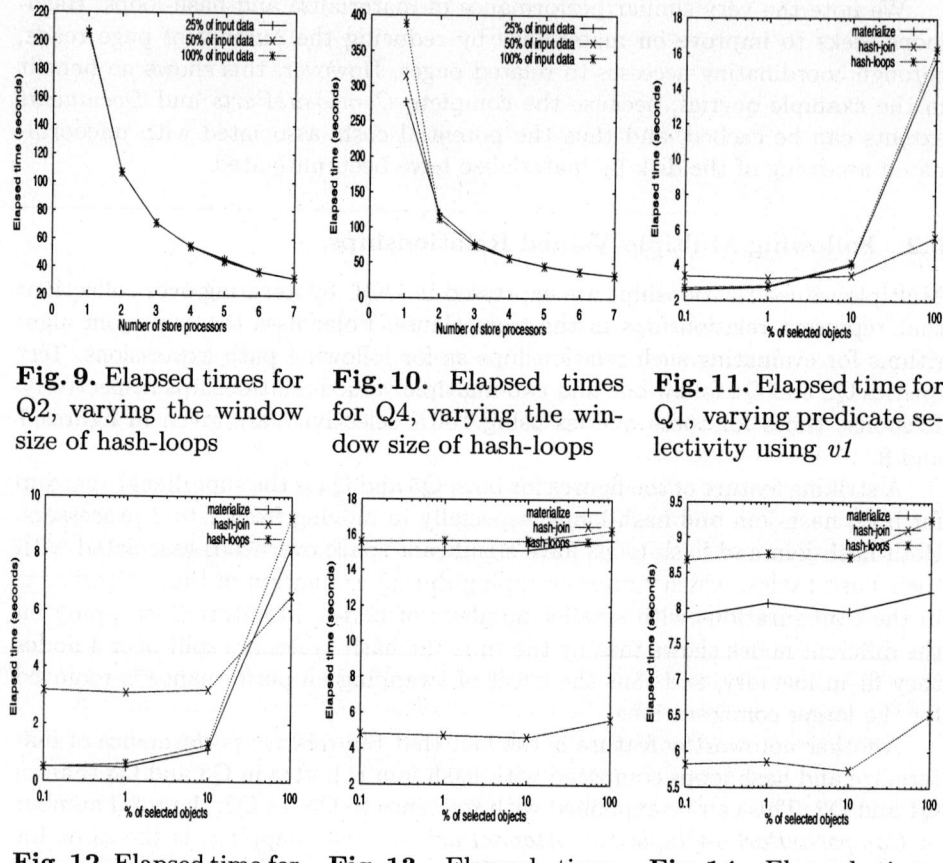

Fig. 9. Elapsed times for Q2, varying the window size of hash-loops

Fig. 10. Elapsed times for Q4, varying the window size of hash-loops

Fig. 11. Elapsed time for Q1, varying predicate selectivity using $v1$

Fig. 12. Elapsed time for Q3, varying predicate selectivity using $v1$

Fig. 13. Elapsed times for Q1, varying predicate selectivity using $v2$

Fig. 14. Elapsed times for Q3, varying predicate selectivity using $v2$

respectively. Note that what is being varied here is the selectivities of the scans of the collections being joined, not the *join selectivity* itself, which is ratio of the number of tuples returned by a join to the size of the cartesian product.

The experiments measure the effect of varying the selectivity of the scans on the inputs to the join thus:

1. *Varying the selectivity of the outer collection (v1):* The outer collection is used to probe the hash table in the hash-join, and is navigated from in the pointer-based joins. The effects of reducing selectivities are as follows:
   hash-join: The number of times the hash table is probed and the amount of network traffic is reduced, although the number of objects read from disk and the size of the hash table remain constant. In Q1, the times reduce to some extent with drops in selectivity, but not all that much, so we can conclude that neither network delays nor hash table probing make substantial

contributions to the time taken to evaluate the hash-join version of Q1. As the reduction in network traffic and in hash table probes is similar for Q1 and Q3, it seems unlikely that these factors can explain the somewhat more substantial change in the performance of Q3. The only significant feature of Q3 that does not have a counterpart in Q1 is the unnesting of the *parts* attribute of *CompositeParts*. The unnest operator creates a large number of new intermediate tuples in Q3 (100,000 in the case of 100% selectivity), so we postulate that much of the benefit observed from reduced selectivity in Q3 results from the smaller number of collections to be unnested.

pointer-based joins: The number of objects from which navigation takes place reduces in line with the selectivity, so reducing the selectivity of the outer collection significantly reduces the amount of work being done. As a result, changing the selectivity of the scan on the outer collection has a substantial impact on the response times for the pointer-based joins in the experiments. As many real queries will have low selectivities, there should be many cases in which pointer based joins will give better performance than value based joins in which full extents are scanned.

2. *Varying the selectivity of the inner collection (v2):* The inner collection is used to populate the hash table in hash-join and to filter the results obtained after navigation in the pointer-based joins. The effects of reducing selectivities are as follows:

hash-join: The number of entries inserted into the hash table reduces, as does the size of the hash table, although the number of objects read from disk and the number of times the hash table is probed remains the same. In Q1 there are at most 500 entries in the hash table (one for each *CompositePart*), which is reduced to 1 for the lowest selectivity. However, in Q3 the corresponding figures are 100,000 (one for each *AtomicPart*) and 100, so the reductions in hash table inserts and in hash table size are much more substantial for Q3 than for Q1. This could explain the pattern observed in figures 13 and 14, although the overall change in response time in each case is modest.

pointer-based joins: The amount of work done by the navigational joins is unaffected by the addition of the filter on the result of the join. As a result, changing the selectivity of the scan on the inner collection has a modest impact on the response times for the pointer-based joins in the experiments.

6 Conclusions

The paper has presented results on the evaluation of queries over a parallel object database server. To the best of our knowledge, the results reported are the most comprehensive to date on the experimental evaluation of navigational joins, and on the performance of parallel object databases in a shared-nothing environment.

To draw very general conclusions from specific experiments would be injudicious, but the results reported certainly demonstrate that the join algorithm of choice depends on many factors, including the sizes of the collections participating in the join, the cardinalities of the relationships explored, the selectivities and locations of predicates on inputs to nodes, and the amount of memory available.

What use are these experiments to others? We hope that the results could be particularly useful to three groups of people: developers of object database systems, who must select appropriate algorithms for inclusion in their systems; researchers working on analytical models of database performance, who stand to benefit from the availability of experimental results against which models can be validated; and the developers of query optimizers, who have to design cost models or heuristics that select physical operators based on evidence of how such operators perform in practice.

References

1. R. Braumandl, J. Claussen, A. Kemper, and D. Kossmann. Functional-join processing. *VLDB Journal*, 8(3+4):156–177, 2000.
2. M. Carey, D. J. DeWitt, and J. F. Naughton. The OO7 benchmark. In *ACM SIGMOD*, pages 12–21, 1993.
3. D. J. DeWitt, D. F. Lieuwen, and M. Mehta. Pointer-based join techniques for object-oriented databases. In *Proc. of the 2nd Int. Conference on Parallel and Distributed Information Systems (PDIS)*, pages 172–181. IEEE-CS, 1993.
4. D. J. DeWitt, J. F. Naughton, J. C. Shafer, and S. Venkataraman. Parallelising OODBMS traversals: A performance evaluation. *VLDB Journal*, 5(1):3–18, January 1996.
5. L. Fegaras and D. Maier. Optimizing object queries using an effective calculus. *ACM Transactions on Database Systems*, December 2000.
6. G. Graefe. Encapsulation of parallelism in the Volcano query processing system. In *ACM SIGMOD*, pages 102–111, 1990.
7. G. Graefe. Iterators, schedulers, and distributed-memory parallelism. *Software-Practice and Experience*, 26(4):427–452, April 1996.
8. E. Shekita and M. J. Carey. A performance evaluation of pointer-based joins. In *ACM SIGMOD*, pages 300–311, Atlantic City, NJ, May 1990.
9. J. Smith, S. F. M. Sampaio, P. Watson, and N. W. Paton. Polar: An architecture for a parallel ODMG compliant object database. In *Conference on Information and Knowledge Management (CIKM)*, pages 352–359. ACM press, 2000.
10. S. Y. W. Su, S. Ranka, and X. He. Performance analysis of parallel query processing algorithms for object-oriented databases. *IEEE TDKE*, 12(6):979–997, 2000.

A Classification of Skew Effects in Parallel Database Systems

Holger Märtens

Universität Leipzig, Institut für Informatik
Postfach 920, D–04009 Leipzig, Germany
`maertens@informatik.uni-leipzig.de`

Abstract. Skew effects are a serious problem in parallel database systems, but the relationship between different skew types and load balancing methods is still not fully understood. We develop and compare two classifications of skew effects and load balancing strategies, respectively, to match their relevant properties.

Our conclusions highlight the importance of highly dynamic scheduling to optimize both the complexity and the success of load balancing. We also suggest the tuning of database schemata as a new anti-skew measure.

1 Introduction

A major performance barrier in parallel database systems (PDBS) are **skew effects**, characterized by an uneven distribution of data and/or workload across the system's resources. Despite numerous proposed **load balancing** strategies, this problem is far from solved, partly because there is no well-structured model of the different types of skew, their causes, consequences, and interdependencies, and the methods to combat them.

To help identify appropriate load balancing methods for different forms of skew, we present two classifications of skew effects and load balancing approaches, respectively, then match the two to find sensible pairs. This allows us to state why some previous approaches are insufficient and to propose some required capabilities of future algorithms.

Our study is on a purely qualitative level and makes no architectural assumptions. Instead, we focus on the fundamental relationships of different types of skew, with each other and with the various load balancing techniques, to reach general conclusions independent of numerical parameters. We find that highly dynamic scheduling methods based on observed execution times are superior in both complexity and attainable load balance. We also suggest the tuning of database schemata as a new anti-skew measure.

We first discuss some related research in Sect. 2. Sects. 3 and 4 present our classifications of load balancing methods and skew effects, respectively. These are matched in Sect. 5, and Sect. 6 offers our conclusions and outlook on the future. The reader interested in more detail is referred to an extended version of this article [9].

2 Related Work

Skew effects have been widely studied in the literature, and a large number of skew-aware load balancing algorithms have been developed, some of which are quite successful. However, a systematic analysis and classification of skew does not yet exist.

A taxonomy of data skew in parallel joins [14] includes the aspects of intrinsic and partition skew. It also defines redistribution and join product skew similar to 'plane skew' and 'solid skew' from [15]. [16] uses the notions of single, double, and 'messy' skew that intermingle attribute value skew and correlation (cf. Sect. 4). Attribute value distributions have been modeled in many complex ways [1, 3, 10]. They are used with histograms [10] or sampling methods [12] to predict result sizes and processing costs. Some researchers have studied the correlation between value distributions of different attributes [11].

Load balancing has been classified as 'static' and 'dynamic' with varying definitions [2, 16]. We have further differentiated dynamic methods [7], while [5] distinguished skew avoidance from skew resolution. 'Adaptive' query processing was surveyed for wide-area networks [4]. Load balancing was also classified outside the DBS field [13].

These approaches are commonly limited to subsets of the different skew types and do not capture the complex interactions between them.

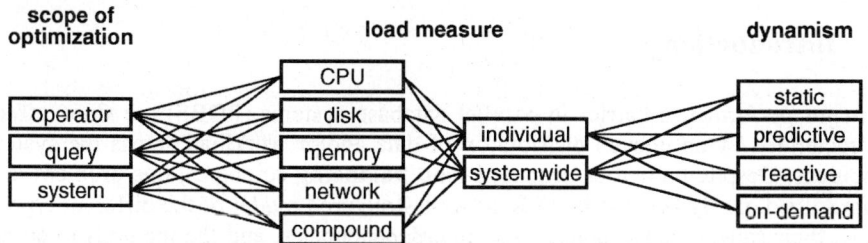

Fig. 1. Overview of load balancing classification

3 Classification of Load Balancing Paradigms

We understand load balancing to comprise these four (not necessarily distinct) steps:

Load Partitioning

The workload is partitioned into **load units** that have two properties: the **partitioning dimension** reflecting the intended type(s) of parallelism (inter- and intra-transaction, -query, and -operator parallelism), and the **load granule**, i.e., the size of single load units. Thus, load units can range from a single sub-operator to a pipeline of several operators to a batch of multiple transactions. Load partitioning may be predetermined by the **data allocation,** prior processing steps or logical dependencies in the data.

Choice of Degree of Parallelism

The **degree of parallelism (DP)** is primarily determined by the total amount of load and its overall resource demands. Other aspects include the current system load and the relative performance of resources, e.g., disks vs. CPUs.

Selection of Processing Nodes

The set of **eligible processors** that can truly process a load unit similarly depends on the load situation, but also on the system architecture (especially for shared-nothing). Ineligible nodes may imply a reduction of the DP.

Load Assignment (Scheduling)

Finally (and perhaps most importantly), load units are assigned to processing nodes, determining the final load distribution and balancing. As above, it may be predetermined by data allocation, system architecture, previous processing, or data dependencies. Scheduling primarily equalizes CPU and main memory load but also affects disk and network utilization, e.g., by selecting the order of data access [8].

3.1 Classification

Our classification, summarized in Fig. 1, is tailored to the purpose of matching algorithms with the types of skew they are capable of resolving. It has three main criteria:

The **scope** of optimization is the portion of load that the algorithm can simultaneously oversee, ranging from one operator to one query to (rarely) the entire system. It reflects the types of parallelism and the load partitioning dimensions given above.

The **measure** of system load can refer either to a single type of resource (CPU, memory, disks, network) or to a compound load measure. Furthermore, the load situation can be regarded either for individual resources or for the overall system.

The **dynamism** of an algorithm denotes the time when load balancing decisions are taken. **Static** methods use, e.g., constant load granules and DPs with random or round-robin load assignment. **Predictive** techniques assign all load in advance for their scope and then strictly execute the resulting schedule [2]. **Reactive** methods use a predictive schedule that is later adapted as needed [5, 6, 15]. **On-demand** algorithms avoid advance planning and assign one load unit at a time as execution proceeds [7, 16]. The latter two are called **runtime** techniques; runtime and predictive methods are labeled **dynamic**.

These criteria are not totally independent of each other. (For instance, a 'high' ranking in all categories would pose a prohibitively complex optimization problem.) Tuning the schema definition and data allocation may be understood as static actions.

4 Classification of Skew Effects

Our classification is depicted in Fig. 2. Intrinsic, query, and partition skew are summarized as **data skew (DS)** [14], as they all relate to the distribution of (values within) data. Capacity and execution skew refer to the processing performance of the system.

4.1 Intrinsic Skew (IS)

Intrinsic skew broadly denotes an uneven distribution of attribute values within the data:

Attribute value skew (AVS) refers to a single attribute of a single relation.

Correlation skew (CoS) depends on the logical correlation of value distributions from more than one attribute. CoS may span several attributes and can be either **intra-relational** or **inter-relational** (concerning attributes of one or several relations).

Intrinsic skew can occur in both base relations and intermediate results. It does not depend on the storage or processing methods applied and is caused only by the properties of the world modeled and by the schema definition that maps them into the database.

4.2 Query Skew (QS)

This term denotes the bias in query predicates, which normally tend to select certain relations, attributes, or values more frequently than others. Like intrinsic skew, query skew derives from the logical view of the data independent of the storage or processing approach, and may also partially depend on the definition of the database schema.

4.3 Partition Skew (PS)

This is the type of skew most widely studied in the literature. It is characterized by an uneven distribution of data across physical resources (processors, disks, main memory) and/or load units. We generalize the categorization by Walton et al. [14] as follows:

Tuple placement skew (TPS) concerns the initial distribution of raw input data (i.e., the base relations) across the disks and processing nodes in the system.

Selectivity skew (SS) is defined by varying selectivity rates for sub-scans on different partitions of data.

Redistribution skew (RS) occurs due to different amounts of data being transferred between different processors.

Result size skew (RSS) denotes disparate result sizes for concurrent load units.

Within queries, TPS and SS refer to load units that scan base relations, whereas RS and RSS can occur only in operations that use intermediate results. This distinction is important because the allocation of base data cannot be changed at query runtime. The different types of PS are related with each other and with intrinsic skew in various ways:

- Tuple placement skew can occur if data allocation is based on attribute values and if the partitioning attribute is burdened with AVS.
- For scans, selectivity skew is likely if a selection involves a partitioning attribute.

- For data redistribution, the distribution key may again refer to the selection attribute from the previous step, or to one having AVS on it, leading to redistribution skew.
- RS alone may lead to result size skew simply because a load unit's output depends on the size of its input. But even with balanced input sizes, result sizes may vary strongly if the redistribution key is referenced by the operation.

If several of these effects occur, they may either amplify or assuage each other. In the last three steps, query skew is also involved through selection and join predicates. All points are also valid for correlated attributes instead of selection or redistribution keys.

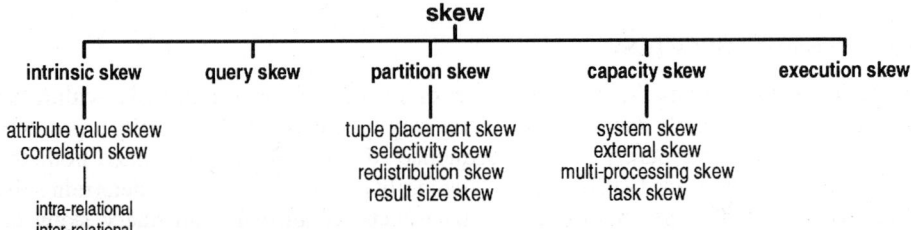

Fig. 2. Overview of skew classification

4.4 Capacity Skew (CS)

Capacity skew refers to the amount of work a processor is capable of performing and thus comprises those effects whose cause lies outside the data distribution:

System skew (SyS) consists in heterogeneities of the hardware and the operating system, such as different processors, memory sizes, or OS versions.

External skew (ExtS) denotes skew effects due to workloads outside the database system, especially application programs on non-dedicated servers.

Multi-processing skew (MPS) comprises the effects caused within the DBS, but outside the current scope of load balancing. Like ExtS, it can denote a skew in the availability of resources to the load units under consideration.

Task skew (TS) is present when two load units work on equal amounts of data but have different tasks to perform (e.g., a scan and a sort operation, or a simple and a complex query), causing disparate resource consumption.

Both multi-processing and task skew may stem from query skew, as the type and order of queries submitted to the system determine the basic sequence of tasks required.

A query optimizer can develop execution plans that may or may not cause capacity skew. For instance, partial parallelism – though often beneficial to reduce the total workload for small queries – is far more likely than full parallelism to lead to multi-processing skew. MPS will turn into PS for load balancing methods with system scope.

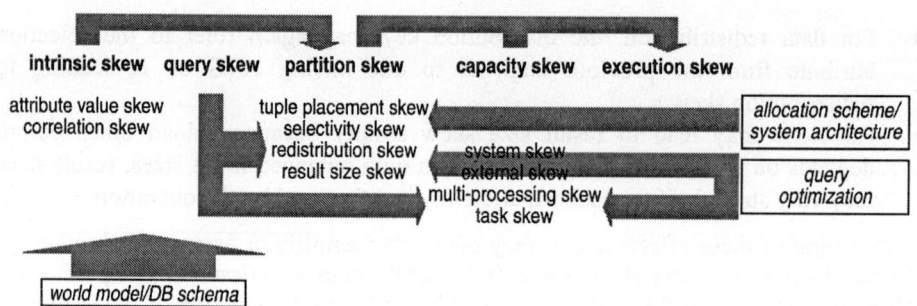

Fig. 3. Overview of skew causes

4.5 Execution Skew (ES)

Execution skew denotes the disparate execution times of concurrent tasks within the database system. Strictly speaking, ES is the only type of skew that is truly a problem for a PDBS. It exists purely as a consequence of other skew types since both the amount of data processed (PS) and the availability of resources (CS) determine the execution speed of a given load unit. The effects of intrinsic and query skew on execution times are indirect.

4.6 Analysis of Causal Relationships

The network of dependencies is illustrated in Fig. 3, which is based on Fig. 2 but enhanced with the causal relationships between the various skew types. The graph allows us to identify three categories of skew types that seem to be the cause of all others:

- intrinsic skew of all shades, due to the properties of the world modeled in the DBS;
- query skew, based on the users' demands;
- system and external skew, which are caused outside the DBMS.

The figure also contains the database and allocation schemata as well as the query optimizer, portrayed as system-inherent components that influence the likelihood of skew at the time of processing. It is these elements in which load balancing can be enacted to combat skew. The system architecture is also shown but must be assumed as fixed.

5 Matching the Classifications

We now compare the two classifications of skew effects and load balancing techniques, proceeding along the categories of skew as given above, in order to analyze which methods are generally capable of alleviating which types of skew. This naturally leads to a list of characteristics that we deem sensible for future load balancing algorithms.

5.1 Intrinsic and Query Skew

As intrinsic and query skew are both caused by the world model itself, they can be treated only by manipulating the database schema. This type of manipulation would be classified as static, with a systemwide scope of optimization. Since it would not be concerned with system load at runtime, the category of measure is irrelevant here.

The chances of tuning the database schema to avoid IS and QS are limited by the inherent biases of the world itself and by the requirements of a 'natural' view allowing convenient querying. Still, routine modeling steps such as **(de)normalization** and **materialized view selection** might be extended to account for skew effects. We are not aware of any existing solution of this kind.

5.2 Partition Skew

The variety of subclasses of PS can be tackled in different ways.

Tuple placement skew is treated statically during data allocation, using either system or query scope to optimize throughput or response times, respectively. Like in Sect. 5.1, the load measure is irrelevant. Simple approaches try to decluster the raw data in equally sized disk partitions, others aim to balance the I/O expected at runtime. The latter require some knowledge of query skew (e.g., through traces of past activity) and a load measure reflecting individual disks.

Selectivity skew is also remedied by data allocation, with the same classification of algorithms, usually by random or hash-based declustering. Range declustering, on the other hand, *intentionally causes* SS in order to restrict range queries to a subset of disks, avoiding full parallelism that can be inefficient.

Redistribution skew and **result size skew** are often inevitable due to intrinsic skew and thus call for dynamic techniques that may be predictive, reactive, or on-demand. System scope has been implemented only for limited workloads, and most solutions work rather well with query or even operator scope. The load measure should comprise all potential bottlenecks, but actual implementations are often limited to CPU load or use the amount of data as representative for overall resource consumption. In all cases, estimates of future load are notoriously error-prone despite the efforts described in Sect. 2, threatening the success of load balancing [6, 16].

5.3 Capacity Skew

By definition, system, external, and multi-processing skew cannot be *avoided* by any load balancing algorithm. Still, they should be *accounted for* by monitoring resource capacity and routing workloads accordingly. This is easier for SyS than for fluctuating ExtS and MPS. In contrast, task skew can be treated by the optimizer through performance cost models, although inaccuracies will multiply with the errors in size estimates noted in Sect. 5.2. On the whole, capacity skew is far more difficult to handle than partition skew and has mostly been passed over in the literature, with most studies addressing single-user mode only and neglecting the problems of multi-user processing.

In any case, a wide scope of optimization and a comprehensive load measure will benefit the treatment of capacity skew. Most importantly, however, load balancing must be highly dynamic to respond to unforeseen changes in processor capacity.

5.4 Execution Skew

Being 'only' the consequence of PS and CS, execution skew might not be considered a problem in its own right, but treating it directly instead of its underlying causes can have several advantages. Specifically, a runtime algorithm (re)assigning single load units based on the progress of execution (cf. Sect. 3.1) could largely do without predictions of data and capacity skew because load balancing would depend on actual resource consumption instead. This would reduce the complexity of load balancing itself by eliminating the work of obtaining cost estimates. More importantly, the workload can be balanced better because in contrast to vague cost estimates, observed execution times are accurate by definition. The benefit increases with more complex and irregular load.

A load balancing technique addressing execution skew is always of the runtime variety. Observed execution times constitute a compound measure including CPU load as well as, for instance, delays caused by disk contention and memory shortage. A large optimization scope may be beneficial by reducing interference between load units.

Table 1. Overview of load balancing requirements for different skew types

skew type		time of correction	scope of optimization	load measure	dynamism
Intrinsic	attribute value	schema design	system		static
	Correlation				
Query		schema design	system		static
Partition	tuple placement	data allocation	system	individual disks	static
	Selectivity				
	Redistribution	load balancing (steps 1 4)	operator/query/ system	CPU, memory	dynamic
	Result size				
Capacity	System				
	External				
	Multi-processing				
	Task	load balancing (2 4)	query	CPU	dynamic
Execution		load balancing (2 4)	operator/query/ system	compound	runtime

5.5 Analysis

Our summary of requirements in Table 1 shows a clear analogy between the causal order of skew types and the temporal order of the load balancing steps where they can be amended. The latter in turn mirrors the dynamism needed for the associated anti-skew techniques, revealing that only highly dynamic methods can successfully treat skew in complex environments. This seemingly simple perception challenges the majority of existing load balancing methods. We think most studies have achieved too optimistic results by neglecting aspects such as correlation and capacity skew or multi-user mode.

Surprisingly, dynamic load balancing need not be excessively complex. While static methods require system scope to account for all possible future load, dynamic algorithms can work well on the query or even operator level. Runtime techniques also work with a single, compound, easily gathered load measure (i.e., actual execution times) while others are enhanced with ever more complex measures and estimates.

Since on-demand schemes cannot analyze the exact cause of processing delays, they should be complemented to observe, for instance, certain memory and I/O limits, possibly based on rough load estimates far less complex than in predictive algorithms. Delays can then be assumed as CPU-based and scheduling can proceed accordingly.

Recommendation

For the development of future load balancing algorithms, we suggest the following twofold strategy that combines static and dynamic aspects:

1. Use static methods to prepare the data in such as way as to limit data skew occurring at the time of query processing. This exploits known techniques of data allocation but should also include some skew-aware schema tuning as outlined in Sect. 5.1.
2. In query processing, employ an on-demand load balancing scheme. Use its reduced complexity either to keep the algorithms lean or to allow for a greater optimization scope. Supplement this with aspects like memory restrictions and disk contention.

6 Conclusions and Future Work

In this paper, we developed classifications for both skew effects and load balancing techniques, then compared the two to achieve a conceptual framework for the assessment of existing processing approaches and for the development of new algorithms.

We found that highly dynamic techniques have great advantages with respect to their own complexity as well as to the expected success of load balancing because they rely on observed execution times rather than inaccurate cost estimates. We particularly favor on-demand scheduling methods treating execution skew and strongly recommend to pursue this approach further. In addition, we noted an unexplored potential for skew treatment in the design of database schemata and materialized views. We consider this an interesting line of research for efficient parallel query processing.

Our own future work will primarily concern the development of new, on-demand load balancing methods. In addition, we will continue our quest for suitable data allocation schemes and proceed with our investigations into the nature of skew effects.

References

1. C. M. Chen, N. Roussopoulos: *Adaptive Selectivity Estimation Using Query Feedback.* Proc. ACM SIGMOD Conf., Minneapolis, 1994.
2. H. M. Dewan, M. Hernández, K. W. Mok, S. J. Stolfo: *Predictive Dynamic Load Balancing of Parallel Hash-Joins Over Heterogeneous Processors in the Presence of Data Skew.* Proc. 3rd PDIS Conf., Austin, 1994.
3. C. Faloutsos, Y. Matias, A. Silberschatz: *Modeling skewed distributions using multifractals and the '80-20 law'.* Proc. 22nd VLDB Conf., Bombay, 1996.
4. J. M. Hellerstein, M. J. Franklin, S. Chandrasekaran, A. Deshpande, K. Hildrum, S. Madden, V. Raman, M. A. Shah: *Adaptive Query Processing: Technology in Evolution.* Data Eng. Bulletin 23 (2), 2000.
5. K. A. Hua, C. Lee: *Handling Data Skew in Multiprocessor Database Computers Using Partition Tuning.* Proc. 17th VLDB Conf., Barcelona, 1991.
6. N. Kabra, D. J. DeWitt: *Efficient Mid-Query Re-Optimization of Sub-Optimal Query Execution Plans.* Proc. ACM SIGMOD Conf., Seattle, 1998.
7. H. Märtens: *Skew-Insensitive Join Processing in Shared-Disk Database Systems.* Proc. IDPT Conf., Berlin, 1998.
8. H. Märtens: *On Disk Allocation of Intermediate Query Results in Parallel Database Systems.* Proc. Euro-Par Conf., Toulouse, 1999.
9. H. Märtens: *A Classification of Skew Effects in Parallel Database Systems.* Techn. Report 3/2001, Dept. of Computer Science, Univ. of Leipzig. (Available at: http://dol.uni-leipzig.de/pub/2001-21/en)
10. Y. Matias, J. S. Vitter, M. Wang: *Wavelet-Based Histograms for Selectivity Estimation.* Proc. ACM SIGMOD Conf., Seattle, 1998.
11. V. Poosala, Y. E. Ioannidis: *Selectivity Estimation Without the Attribute Value Independence Assumption.* Proc. 23rd VLDB Conf., Athens, 1997.
12. S. Seshadri, J. F. Naughton: *Sampling Issues in Parallel Database Systems.* Proc. 3rd EDBT Conf., Vienna, 1992.
13. T. Schnekenburger, G. Stellner (eds.): *Dynamic Load Distribution for Parallel Applications.* Teubner, Leipzig, 1997.
14. C. B. Walton, A. G. Dale, R. M. Jenevein: *A Taxonomy and Performance Model of Data Skew Effects in Parallel Joins.* Proc. 17th VLDB Conf., Barcelona, 1991.
15. X. Zhou, M. E. Orlowska: *A Dynamic Approach for Handling Data Skew Problems in Parallel Hash Join Computation.* Proc. IEEE TENCON Conf., Beijing, 1993.
16. X. Zhou, M. E. Orlowska: *Handling Data Skew in Parallel Hash Join Computation Using Two-Phase Scheduling.* Proc. ICA^{3}PP Conf., Brisbane, 1995.

Improving Concurrency Control in Distributed Databases with Predeclared Tables

Azzedine Boukerche and Terry Tuck

PARADISE Research Laboratory
Dept. of Computer Sciences, Univ. of North Texas
boukerche@cs.unt.edu
terry.tuck@sw.boeing.com

Abstract. In this paper we present a concurrency control algorithm and recovery protocol for distributed databases that produces a schedule that is equivalent to that of a temporally ordered serial schedule. The algorithm is intended to be somewhat practical from the standpoints of both burden on the application developer and realism of the network environment. Accordingly, it allows transactions to be received out of order within a window of tolerance. Moreover, it doesn't require declaration of readsets, and writesets are declared simply at the table level and without predicates. This paper discusses the algorithm, present its analytical studies, and report on the simulation experiments we carried out to evaluate the performance of ours scheme. Our results clearly indicate that with predeclared tables, performance is greatly improved as compared with that from the conservative MVTO algorithm.

1 Introduction

There appears to be a gap in previous database transaction concurrency control studies on practical concurrency control methods that preserve temporal dependencies only in the presence of data dependence. To fill this gap, concurrency control methods are needed that efficiently produce chronologically ordered execution schedules for data-dependent transactions (for the sake of preserving temporal dependencies) while simultaneously taking advantage of potential performance gains by supporting out-of-order (i.e., concurrent) execution of data-independent transactions. This paper addresses the above-mentioned gap in light of these assumptions. We present a transaction concurrency control algorithm that is designed to execute transactions in a high-performance manner while producing conflict-serializable schedules that preserve temporal dependencies that coexist with data dependencies. The algorithm is intended to be (a) useful in real-world on-line transaction processing (OLTP) applications that are conforming to the above assumptions, (b) practical for the application developer, and (c) applicable to both distributed and centralized databases.

The remainder of this paper is organized as follows. In section 2, we describe the DDBS model we used as a basis for this paper. In section 3, we present our algorithm followed by its analytical performance in Section 4. In section 5, we present the simulation set of experiments we carried out to evaluate the performance of our scheme. Finally, in Section 6 we conclude this paper.

2 DDBS Model

We view a database as a persistent store for a collection of named data items partitioned into disjoint sets that we refer to as tables. (Note: although the term 'table' implies the relational data model, the algorithm doesn't appear to be restricted to this application.) A distributed database system (DDBS) is viewed as a collection of logically interrelated databases distributed among a group of computer nodes that are interconnected via an assumed reliable network. In our view of the DDBS, we consider each data item to be tied to a particular database; that is, the DDBS is restricted to the non-replicated case. In our DDBS model, a single Transaction Manager (TM) manages each transaction in a dedicated/centralized fashion, and multiple TMs operate independently of each other. The TM executes each logical database operation in client/server style by dispatching the corresponding message to the target database within DDBS. A concurrency control algorithm governs the various synchronization mechanisms employed by the DDBS to control the execution order of database operations. This execution order is called a schedule, and it is, in general, correct if it is equivalent to any other schedule in which the transactions are executed serially (i.e., the schedule is serializable). The design requirements discussed earlier directly influenced key characteristics of our algorithm and its corresponding DDBMS model. The requirement of immediate execution of *write* operations requires, in turn, support for multiple versions of each data item. Reducing semantic incorrectness associated with the return of an incorrect data item version suggests a non-aggressive, if not conservative, synchronization technique. The requirement for an execution schedule that is equivalent to a timestamp-ordered serial schedule necessitates the use of timestamp ordering. Finally, the requirement for improved concurrency combined with a non-aggressive synchronization technique requires predeclaration of the data items to be accessed. Combining this with the requirement for ease of use for the application developer requires that predeclaration be done at other than the data-item level.

3 Proposed Concurrency Algorithm

The correctness constraint for all schedules produced by our concurrency control algorithm is that they are conflict serializable and computationally equivalent to a temporally ordered serial schedule for the same set of transactions. It has been shown that the problem of concurrency control based on conflict serializability is decomposable into sub-problems of synchronizing operations involved in the two types of conflict, *read-write* and *write-write* [1,5,6]. These two sub-problems can be solved independently as long as their solutions are combined in a manner that yields an overall transaction ordering. Decomposing the overall problem into *write-write* and *read-write* synchronization subproblems also simplifies the presentation of our algorithm.

In accordance with the design constraints, *write* operations are executed immediately upon receipt by a local database. This requires support for coexisting versions of each data item; that is, a multiversion DDBS. With a multiversion database *write-write* synchronization is trivial: each version of a data item is uniquely identified with the globally unique timestamp of its creating transaction. This uniqueness effectively eliminates conflict between any two *writes* targeting the same data item, thereby making the order of their execution inconsequential.

Read-write synchronization, on the other hand, is somewhat more complicated in our scheme. Five rules of operation establish a framework within which *read* operations are synchronized with *writes*. In describing these rules, let $W\text{-}ts(x^k)$ represent the creation timestamp of version k of data item x, and $ts(T_i)$ represent the timestamp of transaction i. The rules are as follows:

Write rule: upon receipt of $write_i(x,y)$ from T_i, create a new data-item version x^k with value y and timestamp $W\text{-}ts(x^k)$ set to $ts(T_i)$.

Read rule: upon receipt of $read_i(x)$ from T_i, return the value of data-item version x^j such that $W\text{-}ts(x^j)$ is the largest timestamp such that $W\text{-}ts(x^j) < ts(T_i)$.

The Read rule, when combined with the design constraint of reducing semantic incorrectness associated with the return of a temporally incorrect value for the targeted data item, suggests that each database delays its response to a *read* request until the correct version is both available and committed. This gives rise to the following delay rule.

Delay rule: A $read_i(x)$ from T_i will not be processed while either (a) an older, uncommitted transaction has declared for update the table containing x, or (b) the creating transaction for the accessed data item version (per the Read rule) is still uncommitted.

The Delay rule ensures that each database will respond to a *read* request with the correct and committed data item version as long as the *begin* message from the version's creating transaction is received at the database prior to its receipt of the *read*. However, it is possible for the writer's *begin* message to be delayed by the network to the extent that it is received at the database after the *read*. Then, depending on the commit state of the reader, one of the following two mutually-exclusive rules is appropriate:

Abort rule: A transaction T_t will be aborted if it reads a data item version that is older than a version (of the same data item) created subsequently by a straggling transaction T_{t-c}, where $ts(T_{t-c}) < ts(T_t)$. In other words, if a database responds to some $read_t(x)$ with a data item version with $W\text{-}ts(x) < ts(T_{t-c})$, and then a $write_{t-c}(x)$ is subsequently received at the database, then transaction T_t will be aborted so that it will repeated and returned the correct data-item version.

Reorder rule: The timestamp $ts(T_t)$ of transaction T_t will be reset if it declares for update any table that has been read by a younger committed transaction T_{t+d}. The new timestamp will be set to a value such that the transaction $T_{t'}$ is made to be younger than any committed reader on any of its declared tables.

The Abort and Reorder rules provide the basis for *read-write* synchronization when the *begin* of a writing transaction is late in reaching one of the participating local databases. The Abort rule is similar to that found in other approaches, with the exception that aborted transactions maintain the timestamp with which they started. The Abort rule is applicable in cases where a *begin* is late, but no reader has yet committed having accessed a table included in the *begin*'s table list declaration. The corrective action in such cases is to abort and restart the reader when a straggling writer creates a data item version with a timestamp that is on the interval of the timestamps of the reader and the erroneously returned version (of the same data item). The Reorder rule, however, is unique to our concurrency scheme.

Table 1: Summary of 2-TM Concurency system parameters

Transaction generation rate, λ	At sites i and j, modeled as independent Poisson processes.
Transaction processing time, S	PDF for time between TM's sending of begin/read and write/commit messages.
Inter-transactional table-level conflict, ϕ_{ji}^{k}	Fraction of writes from site j having table-level conflict at site k with reads from site i.
Inter-transactional data-item-level conflict, γ_{ji}^{k}	Fraction of writes from site j having data-item-level conflict at site k with reads from site i.
Transmission delays, t and t'	PDF for delays, including pipelining delays.

Whenever a transaction's *begin* message arrives at a local database at which some younger reader has already committed, there is a chance that allowing the transaction to proceed will lead to a non-serializable schedule. This chance exists only when a younger reader has read from one of the tables included in the table list of the delinquent *begin*. It actually occurs whenever there is data-item-level conflict between the committed reader and some *write* to be issued by the transaction associated with the delinquent *begin*.

Unfortunately, it appears that true data-item-level conflict with committed readers cannot be verified without employing costly read-tracking mechanisms at the data-item level. Consequently, a pessimistic approach is taken, and any table-level conflict between a committed reader and delinquent older writer is handled as a data-item-level conflict.

In the presence of younger committed readers with table-level conflict, the Reorder rule is applied to a delinquent *begin* in order to reposition its associated transaction in the temporal order to the earliest point at which the transaction can be safely executed in a serializable fashion at all participating local databases. In summary, each local database hosting a table with a younger committed reader replies to the *begin* message with a safe timestamp, the associated Transaction Manager adopts the maximum of all such replies, and then communicates the new temporal position to the application/entity initiating the transaction for a go/no-go decision.

In Boukerche et. al. [2], we present the high-level pseudo code listings which illustrate how the Transaction Manager and Database components operate in order to provide concurrency control according to the stated rules.

4 Analytical Performance of Our Concurrency Scheme

Our analysis focuses on the probabilities and delays attributed to transaction conflict. The most general case of conflict occurs when transactions issue both *read* and *write* operations to each local database, so this case is chosen for all transactions. A context is established by making the following assumptions. First, transactions are generated at different TM sites of the DDBS as independent Poisson processes. Second, local processing delays are negligible in comparison to communication delays. Third, transaction generations and communications delays are independent. Finally, in accordance with prior assumption, all clocks within the system are synchronized.

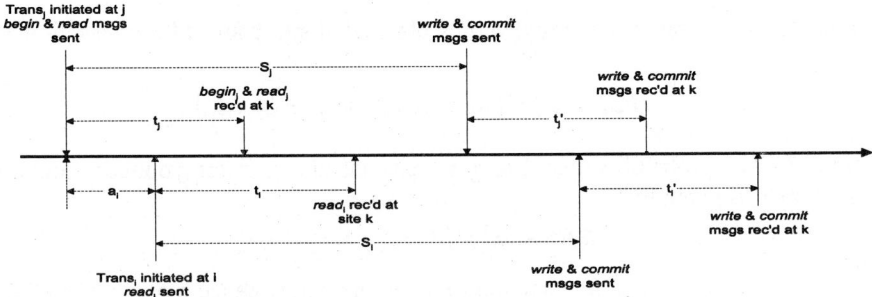

Figure a: Transaction event timeline

The transaction model is modified slightly. Transactions are restricted to be 2-step. In addition, for the purpose of the analysis, the transaction model is such that all *begin* and/or *read* messages are simultaneously dispatched at the exact moment the transaction is started. Similarly, after a period of time for transaction processing, all *write* and *commit* messages are simultaneously dispatched. Finally, a single-phase commit protocol is used. For more details and a complete proof correctness of this scheme, the authors may wish to consult [2].

(i) Conflict Model for a 2-TM MVTC System: Consider two sites hosting TMs, i and j. Suppose that these two sites generate transactions as independent Poisson processes with rates λ_i and λ_j, respectively. Also suppose that a third site, k, exists which hosts a database which will be accessed via a pipelined network by transactions at i and j.

Suppose that transaction T_j is initiated at time $ts(T_j)$ at site j. Further, suppose that this transaction will attempt to write some x_n in table X at site k. At the instant the transaction initiates, $begin_j(X)$ and $read_j(x_n)$ are simultaneously sent to site k in order to register T_j as a writer on table X and to start its *read*. The propagation delay for this message is represented by t_j. Assume that T_j performs local processing that will be concluded with simultaneous transmission of both $write_j(x_n)$ and $commit_j$ messages to site k. The processing time is represented with S_j (See Figure above).

Similarly, suppose that a transaction at site i, T_i, is initiated at time $ts(T_j) + a_i$, which is later than $ts(T_j)$. This transaction will attempt to read some x_m in table X at site k, and at the time of initiation a $read_i(x_m)$ is simultaneously sent site k. The transaction's processing time is represented with S_i.

(ii) Analysis of the 2-TM MVTC System: We now derive the probabilities and expected times associated with the different ways these two transactions can interact. We use ϕ_{ji}^k and γ_{ji}^k to represent the fraction of *writes* from all transactions originating at site j that will conflict at the table level and data-item level, respectively, at site k with *reads* from transactions originating at site i.

Lemma 1: The probability that $read_i$ is blocked at site k for an older transaction T_j is given by

$$BR_{ij}^k = \phi_{ji}^k P\left(t_j < a_i + t_i \wedge S_j + t_j' > a_i + t_i\right)$$

Lemma 2: The probability that $commit_i$ is blocked at site k for older transaction T_j is given by

$$BC_{ij}^k = \phi_{ji}^k P\left(a_i + t_i < t_j < a_i + S_i + t_i'\right).$$

Lemma 3: The probability that $begin_j$ is rejected at site k for younger committed transaction T_i is given by

$$RB_{ji}^k = \phi_{ji}^k P\left(t_j > a_i + S_i + t_i'\right).$$

We now derive expressions that approximate the performance measures in a 2-TM MVTC system.

Theorem 1: *Given exponential approximations for* t_i, t_j, *and* S_j *with respective means of* $1/\mu_i$, $1/\mu_j$, *and* $1/s_j$, *the probability that* $read_i$ *is blocked at site k for an older transaction* T_j *is approximated by*

$$BR_{ij}^k = \phi_{ji}^k \frac{\mu_i \mu_j \lambda_i \left(\lambda_i + \mu_i + \mu_j\right)}{\left(\lambda_i + s_j\right)\left(\mu_i + s_j\right)\left(\lambda_i + \mu_j\right)\left(\mu_i + \mu_j\right)}$$

Theorem 2: *Given exponential approximations for* t_i, t_j, *and* S_j *with respective means of* $1/\mu_i$, $1/\mu_j$, *and* $1/s_j$, *the expected time that* $read_i$ *is delayed by a block at site k for an older transaction* T_j *is approximated by*

$$E\left(dr_{ji}^k\right) = \frac{1}{s_j} \frac{\lambda_i \left(\mu_i + \mu_j\right)}{\lambda_i \left(\mu_i + \mu_j\right) + s_j \left(\mu_i + \lambda_i + s_j\right)} + \frac{1}{\mu_j}$$

Theorem 3: *Given exponential approximations for* t_i, t_j, *and* S_i *with respective means of* $1/\mu_i$, $1/\mu_j$, *and* $1/s_i$, *the probability that* $commit_i$ *is blocked at site k for an older transaction* T_j *is approximated by*

$$BC_{ij}^k = \phi_{ji}^k \frac{\lambda_i \mu_i \mu_j \left(\mu_i + s_i + \mu_j\right)}{\left(\lambda_i + \mu_j\right)\left(s_i + \mu_j\right)\left(\mu_i + \mu_j\right)^2}$$

Corollary 1: *Given exponential approximations for* t_i, t_j, *and* S_i, *with respective means of* $1/\mu_i$, $1/\mu_j$, *and* $1/s_i$, *the probability that transaction* T_i *is restarted because of a missed* $write_j$ *at site k is approximated by*

$$RT_{ij}^k = \gamma_{ji}^k \phi_{ji}^k \frac{\lambda_i \mu_i \mu_j \left(\mu_i + s_i + \mu_j\right)}{\left(\lambda_i + \mu_j\right)\left(s_i + \mu_j\right)\left(\mu_i + \mu_j\right)^2}$$

Theorem 4: *Given exponential approximations for t_i, t_j, S_i, and S_j with respective means of $1/\mu_i$, $1/\mu_j$, $1/s_i$, and $1/s_j$, the expected time that $commit_i$ is delayed by a block at site k for an older transaction T_j is approximated by*

$$E\left(dc_{ji}^k\right) = \frac{1}{s_j} \frac{\left(\lambda_i + \mu_j\right)\left(s_i + \mu_j\right)\left(\mu_i + \mu_j\right)}{\left(\lambda_i + \mu_j\right)\left(s_i + \mu_j\right)\left(\mu_i + \mu_j\right) + \lambda_i\left[\left(s_i + s_j\right)\left(\mu_i + s_j\right) - s_i\mu_i\right]} + \frac{1}{\mu_j}$$

Theorem 5: *Given exponential approximations for t_i, t_j, and S_i, with respective means of $1/\mu_i$, $1/\mu_j$, and $1/s_i$, the probability that $begin_j$ is rejected at site k because of a younger committed transaction T_j is approximated by*

$$RB_{ji}^k = \frac{s_i \lambda_i}{\left(s_i + \mu_j\right)\left(\lambda_i + \mu_j\right)} \left(\frac{\mu_i}{\mu_i + \mu_j}\right)^2$$

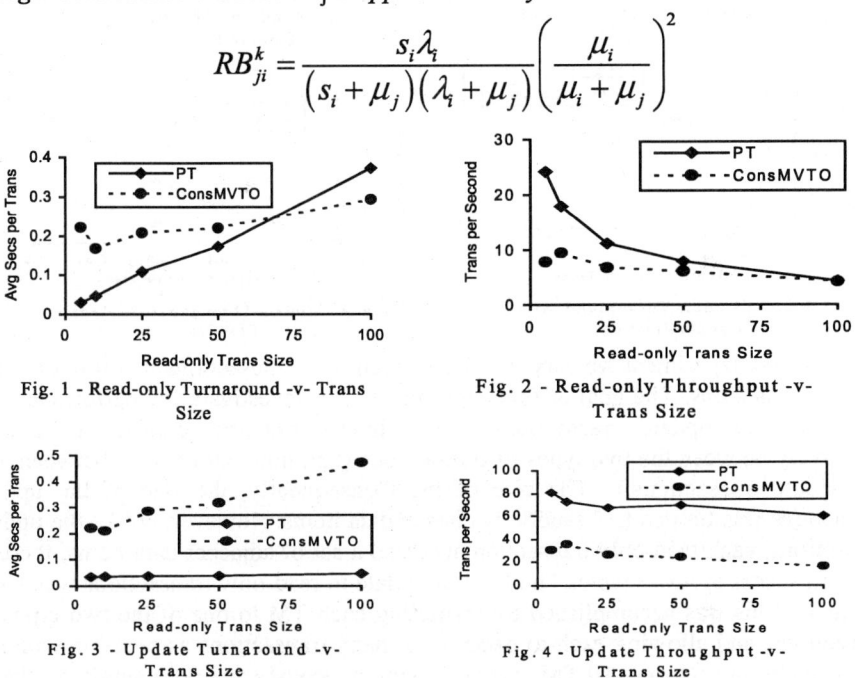

Fig. 1 - Read-only Turnaround -v- Trans Size

Fig. 2 - Read-only Throughput -v- Trans Size

Fig. 3 - Update Turnaround -v- Trans Size

Fig. 4 - Update Throughput -v- Trans Size

5 Simulation Experiments

In order to acquire performance measures, a functional model of a DDBS with our algorithm was implemented in Java. This model includes stand-alone TM and DB components that communicate via Java RMI. To support post-execution analyses, time-stamped operations were recorded within each DB component. Each DB was configured identically with 20 tables of 25 data items ("columns"), for a per-DB total of 500 data items. The experiments were performed on a cluster of Intel Pentium III (350 MHz) PCs running Microsoft Windows NT Workstation 4.0 with Service Pack 5, interconnected with a non-dedicated 10 Mbs LAN, and using the JavaSoft Java™ 2 Runtime Environment, Standard Edition, v 1.2.2_006. Three types of experiments are presented below. These experiments provide insight on the performance of the algorithm when transaction density is high. (At each TM, no delay was induced between the completion of a transaction and the start of the next.) They follow from those in [1,4].

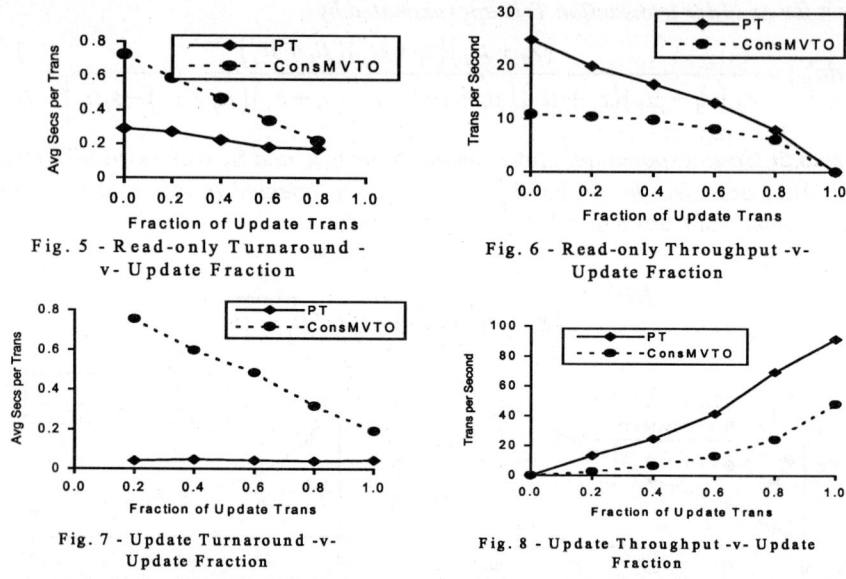

Fig. 5 - Read-only Turnaround -v- Update Fraction

Fig. 6 - Read-only Throughput -v- Update Fraction

Fig. 7 - Update Turnaround -v- Update Fraction

Fig. 8 - Update Throughput -v- Update Fraction

In our first experiment we vary the size of read-only transactions in a mix of small update transactions. The goal of this experiment is to investigate the performance of read-only and update transactions when inter-transaction conflict is almost exclusively between the two types of transactions (i.e., minimal conflict between any two update transactions.) The size of the Consequently, the size of the update transactions was limited to 2 randomly chosen data items. However, unlike the update transactions, each read-only transaction accessed a set of adjacent data items, thereby focusing access to fewer tables. The ratio of update to read-only transactions was fixed at 4 to 1. This was accomplished by restricting each TM to one of the two types of transactions, and allowing each to execute as many transactions as possible within a run. Finally, in each run, 10 TMs executed simultaneously against a single database. Experiment runs were executed with mean sizes of 5, 10, 25, 50, and 100 data items for the read-only transactions. Figs 1-4 show the performance of the read-only and update transactions as measured in turnaround time (i.e., response time) and throughput. The measured values are plotted against the size of the read-only transactions in each run, with "PT" indicating the results with Predeclared Tables, and "ConsMVTO" indicating the performance of the conservative MVTO algorithm. With respect to read-only transactions, the results are expected. For update transactions, the curves for our algorithm, PT, for both throughput and turn-around time would likely be flatter with a more powerful host for the database. The algorithm was designed to eliminate delays on write operations, so the decreased performance with larger read-only transaction sizes appears to result from processor contention at the database host. With the exception of the turnaround time for very large readsets, each of the graphs shows improved performance with the predeclared tables.

In our second set of experiments, we vary the mix of read-only and update transactions to investigate the performance of the two types of transactions. Targeted data items for these types of transactions were selected in the same manner as that in the first experiment. Transaction size for the updates was also the same, and the mean size for the read-only transactions was fixed at 50. Again, 10 TMs were executed simultaneously, with each dedicated to one of the two transaction types. Experiment runs were executed with [0,..,10] of the 10 TMs dedicated to update transactions. Figs 5-8 show the performance of the read-only and update transactions, respectively, as measured in turnaround time and throughput. These metrics are plotted against the fraction of update transactions in each run. In this scenario, the performance of both types of transactions is greatly improved with the predeclared tables.

6 Conclusion

We have described an efficient algorithm for controlling transaction concurrency in a distributed database system that is suitable for environments free of long-lived update transactions. We have presented an analytical study of our scheme as well as a set of simulation experiments to evaluate the performance of our scheme. When compared with the conservative MVTO scheme, the results obtained show a significant improvement, which is a result of our improved concurrency gained by eliminating needless blocks. Our plan for future work is to further investigate the experimental performance of our concurrency scheme. An optimistic version of this algorithm will also be studied [2,3]. It is also aimed at preserving temporal order, but relaxes the constraint on temporal semantic correctness. The relaxation introduces rollback as the recovery mechanism for transactions that have been returned a temporally incorrect data-item value.

Acknowledgments

This work was supported by UNT Research Grant.

References

[Bouk01] A. Boukerche and Terry Tuck, "T3C: A Temporally Correct Concurrency Control Algorithm for Distributed Databases", IEEE/ACM MASCOTS 2000.
[Bouk01] A. Boukerche and Terry Tuck "Concurrency Control Mechanisms in Distributed Database Systems," UNT Tech. Report – In Preparation
[Bouk99] A. Boukerche, S. K. Das, A. Datta, and T. LeMaster, "Implementation of a Virtual Time Synchronizer for Distributed Databases", IEEE/ACM IPDPS'99.
[Care86] M. J. Carey and W. A. Muhanna, "The Performance of Multiversion Concurrency Control Algorithms," ACM Trans. on Comp. Sys., Vo. 4, 1986.
[Özsu99] M. T. Özsu, P. Valduriez, Principles of Distributed Database Systems, Upper Saddle River, NJ: Prentice Hall, 1999.
[Thom96] A. Thomasian, atabase Concurrency Control: Methods, Performance, and Analysis, Boston, MA: Kluwer Academic Publishers, 1996.

Parallel Tree Projection Algorithm for Sequence Mining*

Valerie Guralnik, Nivea Garg, and George Karypis

University of Minnesota, Department of Computer Science and Engineeering/Army
HPC Research Center,
Minneapolis, MN, USA
{guralnik,garg,karypis}@cs.umn.edu

Abstract. Discovery of sequential patterns is becoming increasingly useful and essential in many scientific and commercial domains. Enormous sizes of available datasets and possibly large number of mined patterns demand efficient and scalable algorithms. In this paper we present two parallel formulations of a serial sequential pattern discovery algorithm based on tree projection that are well suited for distributed memory parallel computers. Our experimental evaluation on a 32 processor IBM SP show that these algorithms are capable of achieving good speedups, substantially reducing the amount of the required work to find sequential patterns in large databases.

1 Introduction

Sequence data arises naturally in many applications. For example, marketing and sales data collected over a period of time provide sequences that can be analyzed and used for projections and forecasting. In the past several years there has been an increased interest in using data mining techniques to extract interesting sequential patterns from temporal sequences. The most time consuming operation in the discovery process of such patterns is the computation of the frequency of the occurrences of interesting sub-sequences of set of events (called candidate patterns) in the database of sequences. However, the number of sequential patterns grows exponentially and various formulations have been developed [1,2,3,4] that try to contain the complexity by imposing various temporal constraints, and by consider only those candidates that have a user specified minimum support. Even with these constraints, the task of finding all sequential patterns requires a lot of computational resources (*i.e.*, time and memory), making it an ideal candidate for parallel processing. This was recognized by Zaki [5] which developed a parallel formulation of the SPADE algorithm [6] for shared-memory parallel

---

* This work was supported by NSF CCR-9972519, EIA-9986042, ACI-9982274, by Army Research Office contract DA/DAAG55-98-1-0441, by the DOE ASCI program, and by Army High Performance Computing Research Center contract number DAAH04-95-C-0008. Access to computing facilities was provided by the Minnesota Supercomputing Institute.

computers. However, there has been no work in developing scalable and efficient parallel formulations for this class of algorithms that are suitable for distributed memory parallel computers.

In this paper we present two different parallel algorithms for finding sequential patterns on distributed-memory parallel computers. The first algorithm decomposes the computation by exploiting data parallelism, whereas the other utilizes task parallelism. One of the key contributions of this paper is the development of a static task decomposition scheme that uses a bipartite graph partitioning algorithm to simultaneously balance the computations and at the same time reduce the data sharing overheads, by minimizing the portions of the database that needs to be shared by different processors. We experimentally evaluate the performance of our proposed algorithms on different datasets on a 32-processor IBM SP2 parallel computer. Our experiments show that the proposed algorithms incur small communication overheads, achieve good speedups, and can effectively utilize the different processors.

2 Sequence Mining

The problem of mining for sequential patterns was first introduced by Agrawal et al [1]. The authors showed how their association rule algorithm for unordered data [7] could be adapted to mine for frequent sequential patterns in sequence data. The class of episodes being mined was generalized, and the performance enhancements were presented in [3]. In this section we will summarize the terminology first introduced by Agrawal [1] and being used throughout the paper.

We are given a database $\mathcal{D}$ of sequences called *data-sequences*. Each data-sequence consists of the list of *transactions*, ordered by increasing transaction-time. A transaction has the following fields: sequence-id, transaction-id, transaction-time, and the items present in the transaction. We assume that the set of items $\mathcal{I} = \{i_1, i_2, \ldots, i_m\}$, is the set of literals that can be sorted in lexicographical order. The items in the transaction are sorted in lexicographical order.

An *itemset* i is a non-empty set of items, denoted by $(i_1 i_2 \ldots i_m)$, where i_j is an item. A *sequence* is an ordered list of itemsets, denoted by $< s_1 s_2 \ldots s_n >$, where s_i is an itemset. The *support of a sequence* is defined as the fraction of total data-sequences that contain this sequence. A sequence is said to be *frequent* if its support is above a certain user-specified minimum threshold. Given a database $\mathcal{D}$ of data-sequences, the problem of mining for sequential patterns is to find the *all frequent sequences* among all data-sequences. Each such frequent sequence represents a *sequential pattern*. It is important to note that from now on the term sequential is adjective of pattern, while term serial is adjective of algorithm.

3 Serial Tree Projection Algorithm

The tree projection algorithm represents discovered patterns in the tree structure, called Projection Tree (PT). The tree is grown progressively by the algo-

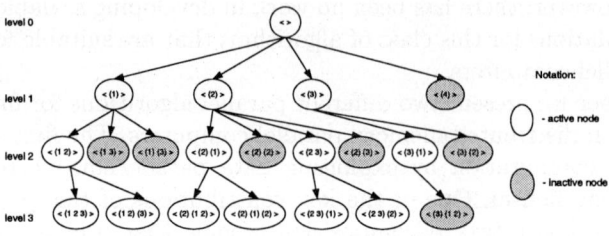

Fig. 1. An example of Projection Tree

rithm such that only the nodes corresponding to frequent patterns are generated. The level-wise version of the algorithm grows the tree in a breadth-first manner. In iteration k, it extends all the nodes at level $k-1$. The candidate extensions of a given node are formed by using only the frequent extensions of its parent. A node can be extended into multiple children nodes via items in two ways as follows. A child of the node can be created by extending the last itemset in a pattern represented by a node with an item that is lexicographically larger than all the items in that itemset (called *itemset extension*) or by extending a pattern with a new 1-item itemset (called *sequence extension*). The new children represent $(k+1)$-item patterns. All the nodes that belong to a sub-tree which potentially can be extended are called *active extensions*. If the node cannot be extended any further it becomes *inactive* and is pruned from the tree.

Figure 1 illustrates an example of Projection Tree. In this example the set of active extensions of node $< (2) >$ is $\{1, 3\}$, where 1 is an active sequence extension and 3 is an active itemset extension. The set of active items is $\{1, 2, 3\}$.

One of the key features of the algorithm is that the supports of the patterns represented by the candidate extensions are gathered by using the set of *projected* data-sequences at the parent. The algorithm maintains a list of *active items* of the node. Active item list of a node consists of items that can be found in itemset represented by its descendants. When a data-sequence is projected on a node, only the items that occur in its active item list are kept. The data-sequence gets recursively projected along the paths determined by active extensions. The idea is, only those items in a data-sequence percolate down the tree that can only potentially be useful in extending the tree by one more level.

The process of counting support of $(k+1)$-item pattern is accomplished as follows. Each node, representing the pattern $P = < s_1 s_2 \ldots s_m >$, at level $k-1$ maintains four count matrices, which are used to count the support of four different types of sequential patterns. Once data-sequences are projected to the node with matrices, the algorithm iterates through them to gather support counts. For more detail refer to [8].

4 Parallel Formulation

The overall structure of the computations performed by the serial tree projection algorithm for discovering sequential patterns (discussed in Section 3)) is encapsulated in the tree that is generated in a breadth-first manner by the algorithm. Given that the computations are structured in this fashion, there are two general ways that can be used to decompose the computations [9]. The first approach exploits the data parallelism that exists in computing the support at each node, whereas the second approach exploits the task parallelism that exists in the tree-based nature of the computation. Our parallel formulations using both of these approaches are described in the rest of this section.

4.1 Data Parallel Formulation

The key idea behind our data parallel formulation (DPF) is to decompose the computations associated with counting the support of the various sequential patterns at each node of the tree. In particular, our parallel formulation works as follows.

If p is the total number of processors, the original database is initially partitioned into p equal size parts, and each one is assigned to a different processor. To compute the support of the candidate sequences at level k, each processor projects its local set of data sequences to the nodes at level $k-2$, and computes their support based on the local data sequences. The global supports are determined by using a reduction operation to add up the individual supports. These global supports are made known to all the processors, and are used to determine which nodes at the kth level meet the minimum support constraints. Note that in this approach, all the processors build the same tree (which is identical to that built by the serial algorithm). This parallel formulation is similar in nature to the count distribution method developed for parallelizing the serial Apriori algorithm for finding associative patterns [1,10]. Even though this approach does lead to load balanced computations it incurs high communication overhead. Furthermore, this algorithm works well only when the tree and count matrices can fit into the main memory of each processor. If the number of candidates is large, then the matrices may not fit into the main memory. In this case, this algorithm has to partition the tree and compute the counts by scanning the database multiple times, once for each partition of the tree.

4.2 Task Parallel Formulation

The key idea behind the task parallel formulation (TPF) is that when the support of the candidate patterns at level k is computed by projecting the databases at the various nodes at the $k-2$ level of the tree, the computations at each of these $k-2$ nodes are independent of each other. Thus, the computations at each node becomes an independent task and the overall computation can be parallelized by distributing these tasks among the available processors.

Our task parallel formulation distributes the tasks among the processors in the following way. First, the tree is expanded using the data-parallel algorithm described in Section 4.1, up to a certain level $k + 1$, with $k > 0$. Then, the different nodes at level k are distributed among the processors. Once this initial distribution is done, each processor proceeds to generate the subtrees (*i.e.*, sub-forest) underneath the nodes that it has been assigned.

In order for each processor to proceed independently of the rest, it must have access to the sequences in the database that may contain the patterns corresponding to the nodes of the tree that it has been assigned. The database sequences (or portions of) that each processor P_i needs to have access to, can be determined as follows. Let S_i be the set of nodes assigned to P_i, A_i be the union of all the active items of the nodes in S_i, and B_i be the union of all the items in each of the frequent patterns that correspond to a node in S_i. Given these definitions, each processor needs to have access to all the sequences that contain items belonging in the set $C_i = A_i \bigcup B_i$. Moreover, since it computes only the frequent patterns that are underneath the nodes in S_i, it needs to only retain the items from the original sequences that are in C_i. We will refer to the set of items C_i as the *sub-forest itemset* of the node set S_i.

In our algorithm, once the distribution of the nodes at level k is determined, the sets $C_0, C_1, \ldots, C_{p-1}$ are determined and broadcasted to all the processors. Each processor then reads the local portion of the database (the one that was used by the data-parallel algorithm), splits it into p parts, one for each processor, and sends it to the appropriate processor. Each processor, upon receiving the sequences corresponding to its portion of the tree, writes them to the disk and proceeds to expand its nodes independently. Note that since the sets C_i for different processors can overlap, processors will end up having overlapping sections of the original database.

The key step in the STPF algorithm is the method used to partition the nodes of the kth level of the tree into p disjoint sets $S_0, S_1, \ldots, S_{p-1}$. In order to ensure load balance, this partitioning must be done in a way so that the work is equally divided among the different processors. A simple way of achieving this is to assign a weight to each node based on the amount of work required to expand that node, and then use a bin-packing algorithm [11] to partition the nodes into p equal-weight buckets. This weight can be either a measure of the actual computational time that is required, or it can be a measure that represents a relative time, in relation to the time required by other nodes. Obtaining relative estimates is much easier than obtaining estimates of the actual execution time. Nevertheless, accurately estimating the relative amount of work associated with each node is critical for the overall success of this load balancing scheme.

A simple estimate of the relative amount of work of a particular node is to use the support of its corresponding sequential pattern. The motivation behind this approach is that if a node has a high support it will most likely generate a deeper subtree, than a node with a lower support. However, this estimate is based on a single measure and can potentially by very inaccurate. A better estimate of the relative amount of work can be obtained by summing up the support of all of its active extensions, that is, the support of all of its children nodes at the $k+1$st level in the tree. This measure by looking ahead at the support of the patterns of length $k+1$, will lead to a more accurate estimate. This is the method that we use to estimate the relative amount of work associated with each node.

Even though this bin-packing-based approach is able to load-balance the computations, it may lead to partitions in which the sub-forest itemsets assigned to each processor have a high degree of overlap. Consequently, the follow-up database partitioning will also lead to highly overlapping local databases. This increases the amount of time required to perform the partitioning, the amount of disk-storage required at each processor, and as we will see in the experiments presented in Section 5.2, it also increases the amount of time required to perform the projection. Ideally, we would like to partition the nodes at the kth level in such a way so that in addition to balancing the load we also minimize the degree of overlap among the different databases assigned to each processor.

Since the degree of overlap in the local databases is directly proportional to the degree of overlap in the sub-forest itemsets, we can minimize the database overlap by minimizing the overlap in the sub-forest itemsets. This later problem can be solved by using a minimum-cut bipartite graph partitioning algorithm, as follows.

Let $G = (V_A, V_B, E)$ be an undirected bipartite graph, where V_A, and V_B are the two sets of vertices and E is the set of edges. The vertices in V_A correspond to the nodes of the tree, the vertices in V_B correspond to the sequence items, and there is an edge $(u, v) \in E$ with $u \in V_A$ and $v \in V_B$, if the item v is an active item of node u. Each vertex $u \in V_A$ has a weight $w(u)$ that is equal to the relative amount of work required to expand its corresponding subtree, and each vertex $v \in V_B$ has a weight of one. Furthermore, each edge (u, v) has a weight of one.

A partitioning of this bipartite graph into p parts that minimizes the edge-cut (*i.e.*, the number of edges that straddle partitions), subject to the constraint that the the sum of the weight of the vertices in V_A assigned to each part is roughly the same, can be used to achieve the desired partitioning of the tasks. Since each partition contains tree-nodes whose total estimated work is roughly the same, the overall computation will be balanced. Furthermore, by minimizing the edge-cut the resulting partition groups nodes together so that their sub-forest itemsets have as little overlap as possible. Note that an edge belonging to the cut-set indicates that the corresponding item is shared between at least two partitions. In general, for each item u, the number of its incident edges that belong to the cut-set plus one, represent the total number of sub-forest itemsets that this node belongs to.

In our algorithm, we compute the bipartite min-cut partitioning algorithm using the multi-constraint graph partitioning algorithm [12] available in the METIS graph partitioning package [13].

Table 1. Parameter values for datasets

Dataset	Avg. no. of transactions per sequence	Avg. no. of items per transaction	Avg. length of maximal potentially frequent sequences	Avg. size of itemsets in maximal potentially frequent sequences	$MinSup(\%)$
DS1	10	2.5	4	1.25	0.1
DS2	10	5	4	1.25	0.25
DS3	10	5	4	2.5	0.33
DS4	20	2.5	4	1.25	0.25

5 Experimental Evaluation

5.1 Experimental Setup

We use the same synthetic datasets as in [3], albeit with more data-sequences. We generated datasets by setting number of maximally potentially frequent sequences $N_S = 5000$, number of maximal potentially frequent itemsets $N_I = 25000$ and number of items. $N = 10000$. The number of data-sequences D was set to 1 million. Table 1 summarizes the dataset parameter settings and shows the minimum support used in experiments reported below.

We ran our experiments on IBM SP cluster. The IBM SP consists of 79 four-processor and 3 two-processor machines with 391 GB of memory. The machines utilize the 222 MHz Power3 processors.

Table 2. Serial execution time for $DS3$

N.of P	DPF	TPF-GP2	TPF-GP3	TPF-BP2	TPF-BP3
2	7914.82s	4370.37s	4263.24s	6128.41s	6885.33s
4	7922.66s	3012.61s	3443.54s	4835.05s	6740.49s
8	8017.73s	2346.55s	2785.41s	3626.02s	6294.13s
16	8135.03s	1992.7s	2595.51s	2903.85s	5508.26s
32	8413.89s	1804.09s	2497.52s	2404.73s	4604.7s

5.2 Results

We evaluated DPF and TPF based on the following criteria: how effective they are in terms of execution time and how effective they are in balancing workload. Additionally, we implemented two approaches for balancing the workload in TPF. One was based on Bipartite Graph Partitioning (TPF-GP) and the other was based in Bin Packing (TPF-BP). Those schemes were also evaluated based on how well they can minimize the overlap between databases assigned to each processor. Both schemes were run starting the task parallelism at level 2 and level 3 and resulting in 4 sets of experiments for each of the datasets (TPF-GP2, TPF-GP3, TPF-BP2, TPF-BP3).

Figure 2 shows the execution time of all five schemes on the four different datasets on 2, 4, 8, 16 and 32 processors. A number of interesting observations can be made looking at these results.

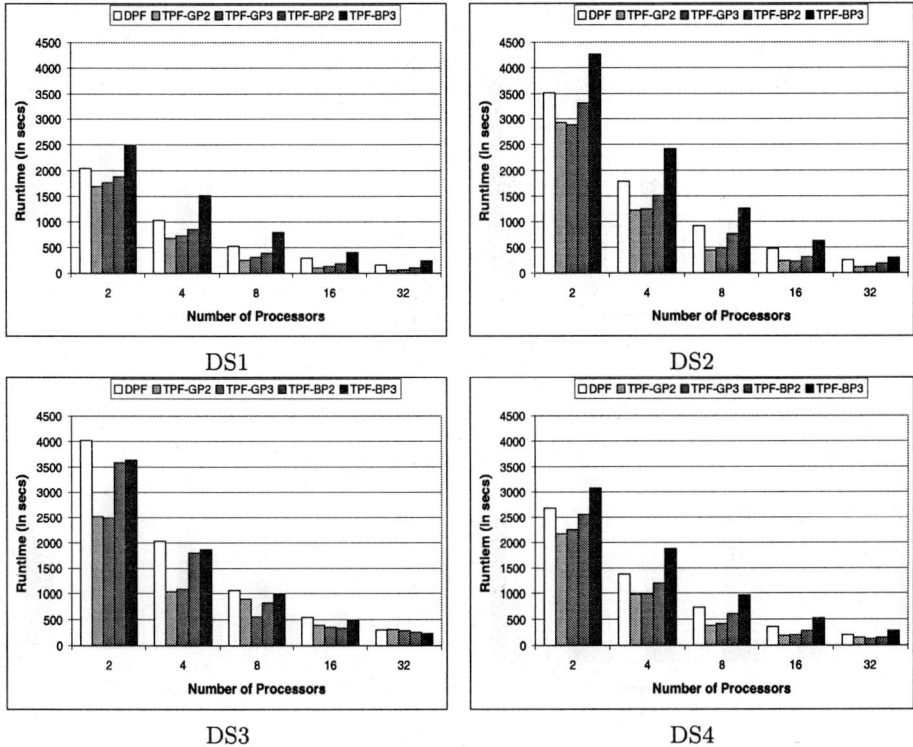

Fig. 2. Execution Time (in secs)

First, the DPF algorithm achieves good speedups for all four data sets. In particular, as we increase the number of processors from 2 to 32 (a factor of 16), the amount of time decreases by a factor of 12.3, 13.9, 13.42 and 13.64 for each one of the four datasets, respectively.

Second, the speedups achieved by the TPF-GP2 algorithm are actually sometimes super-linear. As the number of processors increases from 2 to 32, the runtime for each one of the four datasets decreases by factor of 29.8, 24.5, 8.0 and 14.66, respectively. The super-linear speedup is due to the fact that each processor is assigned a sub-forest of the original tree and the databases are redistributed. As a result, the amount of time spent in projection and disk I/O actually reduces as the number of processors increases. Also the poor result on the third data set is due to the fact that the static tasks assignment leads to unbalanced work distribution.

Third, comparing the bipartite graph partitioning based formulation of TPF to the one based on bin-packing we can see that graph partitioning leads to substantially smaller execution times. This is because of the two reasons. First, as discusses in Section 4.2, the graph partitioning based approach reduces the overlap among the local databases; thus reducing the redistribution cost as well

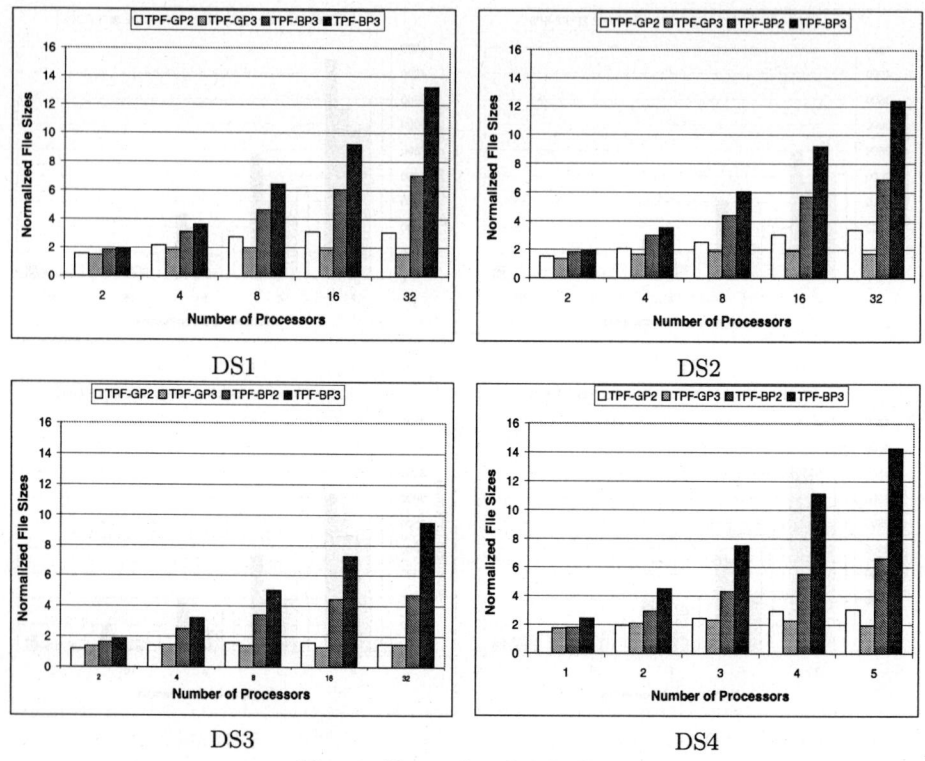

Fig. 3. Normalized File Sizes

as disk I/O. Second, because each processor is assigned fewer distinct items, the projection cost is reduced. To illustrate the reduction in database sizes we plotted the size of local databases (summed over all the processors) for the two sets of schemes. These results are shown in Figure 3. These figures show the database sizes, relative to the size of the databases (after it has been pruned so it only contains the active items) on a single processor. As we can see from those figures, the graph partitioning based schemes lead to local databases whose size up to a factor smaller that the bin-packing scheme.

Also, the reduction in projection time can be seen in Table 2, that shows the total amount of time spent by all the processors in performing the local computation. From this table we can see that the graph partitioning scheme TPF-GP2 spends only 1804 secs versus 2404 secs for TPF-BP2.

Fourth, comparing TPF-GP2 versus TPF-GP3 and TPF-BP2 against TPF-BP3, we can see that the run-times achieved by the schemes that switch to tasks distribution after the second level are in general smaller. The only exception is for the third dataset in which TPF-GP3 does better that TPF-GP2 on 8, 16 and 32 processors. This is due to the fact that TPF-GP3 lead to better load balance and that TPF-GP2 is highly unbalanced.

6 Conclusion and Directions of Future Research

In this paper we presented two algorithms for finding sequential patterns using the tree projection algorithm that are suitable for distributed memory parallel computers. Our experimental results show that both the data parallel and the task parallel formulations are able to achieve good speedups as the number of processors increase. Furthermore, the bipartite graph partitioning based task distribution approach is able to substantially reduce the overlap in the databases required by each processor.

Despite these promising results we believe that the overall performance can be further improved by developing dynamic load balancing schemes.

References

1. R. Aggrawal and R. Srikant. Mining sequential patterns. In *Proc. of the Int'l Conference on Data Engineering (ICDE)*, Taipei, Taiwan, 1996.
2. H. Mannila, H. Toivonen, and A. I. Verkamo. Discovering frequent episodes in sequences. In *Proc. of the First Int'l Conference on Knowledge Discovery and Data Mining*, pages 210–215, Montreal, Quebec, 1995.
3. R. Srikant and R. Agrawal. Mining sequential patterns: Generalizations and performance improvements. In *Proc. of the Fifth Int'l Conference on Extending Database Technology*, Avignon, France, 1996.
4. Mahesh V. Joshi, George Karypis, and Vipin Kumar. Universal formulation of sequential patterns. Technical report, Universit of Minnesota, Department of Computer Science, Minneapolis, 1999.
5. Mohammed J. Zaki. Parallel sequence mining on smp machines. In *Workshop On Large-Scale Parallel KDD Systems (in conjunction 5th ACM SIGKDD International Conference on Knowledge Discovery and Data Mining*, pages 57–65, San Diego, CA, august 1999.
6. M. J. Zaki. Efficient enumeration of frequent sequences. In *7th International Conference on Information and Knowledge Management*, 1998.
7. R. Agrawal and R. Srikant. Fast algorithms for mining association rules. In *Proc. of the 20th VLDB Conference*, pages 487–499, Santiago, Chile, 1994.
8. Valerie Guralnik, Nivea Garg, and George Karypis. Parallel tree projection algorithm for sequence mining. Technical Report 01-017, Department of Computer Science, University of Minnesota, 2001.
9. Vipin Kumar, Ananth Grama, Anshul Gupta, and George Karypis. *Introduction to Parallel Computing: Design and Analysis of Algorithms*. Benjamin/Cummings Publishing Company, Redwood City, CA, 1994.
10. E. H. Han, G. Karypis, and V. Kumar. Scalable parallel data mining for association rules. *IEEE Transactions on Knowledge and Data Eng. (accepted for publication)*, 1999.
11. T. H. Cormen, C. E. Leiserson, and R. L. Rivest. *Introduction to Algorithms*. MIT Press, McGraw-Hill, New York, NY, 1990.
12. G. Karypis and V. Kumar. Multilevel algorithms for multi-constraint graph partitioning. In *Proceedings of Supercomputing*, 1998. Also available on WWW at URL http://www.cs.umn.edu/~karypis.

13. G. Karypis and V. Kumar. metis: Unstructured graph partitioning and sparse matrix ordering system. Technical report, Department of Computer Science, University of Minnesota, 1995. Available on the WWW at URL http://www.cs.umn.edu/~karypis/metis/metis.html.

Parallel Pruning for K-Means Clustering on Shared Memory Architectures

Attila Gürsoy and İlker Cengiz

Computer Engineering Department, Bilkent University
Ankara, Turkey
{agursoy,icengiz}@cs.bilkent.edu.tr

Abstract. We have developed and evaluated two parallelization schemes for a tree-based k-means clustering method on shared memory machines. One scheme is to partition the pattern space across processors. We have determined that spatial decomposition of patterns outperforms random decomposition even though random decomposition has almost no load imbalance problem. The other scheme is the parallel traverse of the search tree. This approach solves the load imbalance problem and performs slightly better than the spatial decomposition, but the efficiency is reduced due to thread synchronizations. In both cases, parallel tree-based k-means clustering is significantly faster than the direct parallel k-means.

1 Introduction

Clustering is an important area which finds application in a variety of fields including data mining, pattern recognition, explorative data analysis, image processing, and more [1] [2]. K-means [3] is a partitional clustering method and it is one of the most commonly used clustering algorithms. In this paper, we focus on parallelization techniques for a faster version of k-means clustering algorithm, a tree-based k-means method [4].

The k-means (direct) algorithm treats input patterns as points in a d dimensional space and employs Euclidean-distance based similarity metric between patterns and cluster centers. The algorithm chooses an initial set of cluster centers and then each pattern is assigned to the cluster represented by the closest cluster center. After all patterns processed and new clusters are formed, cluster centers are updated to represent new clusters. The sequential execution time of k-means can be improved by reducing the number of distance calculations. The algorithm presented in [4] is one of the such approaches. The algorithm organizes patterns in a k-d tree. The root of the tree represents all patterns and children nodes represent patterns in subspaces. In each iteration, the k-d tree is traversed in a depth-first manner starting at the root node. At the root level, all cluster centroids are candidates to be the closest centroid to any pattern in the space represented by the root node. As we traverse the tree, a pruning method is applied to eliminate some of the candidates for the subspace represented by each node visited. That is, the candidate set that comes from the parent node might contain some clusters centroids that cannot be closest to any pattern in the subspace. When the candidate set is reduced to one cluster centroid, all the patterns in the subspace is assigned to that cluster. Otherwise, a leaf node eventually is reached and pairwise distance calculations are performed for all patterns in the leaf node and cluster centroids in the candidate set.

Parallelization of the direct k-means method is relatively easier. However, in the case of tree-based k-means, the traverse of the irregular tree structure complicates parallelization and poses load balancing and synchronization problems. In this paper, we discuss parallelization of the tree-based k-means method and propose two different schemes based on pattern decomposition and parallel search of the k-d tree used in the tree-based algorithm. The main motivation behind this study is to develop and evaluate alternative parallelization schemes. The implementation uses Pthreads which is a standard thread interface available on most multiprocessor systems Although this study is done for shared memory machines, the proposed pattern decomposition scheme can be used for distributed memory machines as well.

2 Parallel Pruning for Tree Based K-Means

The parallelization of the tree-based k-means is more challenging due to the irregular tree decomposition of space (since it depends on pattern distribution), and varying computations during the traversal. The computations done during the traversal can be coarsely divided into two groups: internal-node computations and leaf computations. In the internal nodes, the space covered by a node is compared against the current candidate set of centroids. Since some of the cluster centroids might have been pruned in the upper levels, the number of distance calculations (which is proportional to the size of the candidate set) can vary across internal nodes. At the leaves, similarly, distance calculations among a differing number of remaining patterns and number of candidates results in varying computation loads. With this load imbalancing in mind, a way of distributing computations done at the nodes need to be developed. One approach is to partition patterns among threads such that each thread is responsible for the pruning due to the space covered by its own patterns. A second one would be the parallel traversal of a single tree in a dynamic fashion.

Pattern Decomposition – parallel multiple tree pruning. Pattern decomposition scheme divides patterns into p disjoint partitions where p is the number of processors. Then, each partition is assigned to a different thread. Every thread forms a k-d tree for its own patterns and performs tree based algorithm on its own set of patterns. This way of parallelization is similar to the parallelization of the direct k-means scheme. However, the tree version has two major differences or problems: load imbalance and possibly less pruning compared to the sequential case. For example, consider two threads, one with a set of patterns that are concentrated in a small space, and another one with the same number of patterns but scattered around much larger space. There will be more pruning of candidate cluster centroids at the upper levels of the local tree (that belongs to a thread)) in the case of compact subspace because many cluster centroids possibly will be far from the compact space. In the case of sparse and larger subspace, the pruning might shift towards to the leaves which might result in more distance calculations. In the direct k-means, it does not matter which patterns form a partition. However, in the tree-based case, we have to choose patterns such that the problems mentioned above are addressed. We have tried two different partitioning schemes: (a) **random pattern decomposition** where each thread gets equal number of patterns chosen randomly from the space covered by all patterns, (b) **spatial decomposition** where each thread gets equal of number of patterns that belong to a compact space.

Parallel single tree pruning. The possible load imbalance problem of the static pattern decomposition can be solved by distributing distance calculations (not the patterns) to threads dynamically. In this scheme, we have a single tree representing all the patterns. The tree traverse for pruning is parallelized by maintaining a shared pool of work. A work is a tuple composed of a node (where the traverse to be started) and a set of candidate clusters. An idle thread simply picks a work from the queue and applies the pruning procedure starting from the node possibly going downwards in a depth-first manner. In order to create enough work for other threads, a thread puts more work (some of its sub-trees that need to traversed) into the shared queue if there is no work in the queue for other threads. The advantage of this scheme is dynamic load balancing . An idle thread will always find work to do as long as some parts of the tree still have not been traversed. However, this scheme needs to maintain a shared work queue which requires usage of locks for enqueue and dequeue operations. The frequency of such operations attempted by the threads has significant impact on the performance. Blocking kernel-level threads on a lock results in a switch from user space to kernel space in the operating system and is expensive.

3 Evaluation of the Multiple Tree and Single Tree Pruning

We have conducted some preliminary performance experiments on a Sun system where 8 processors are available. We used two different data sets with 2-dimensional patterns: dataset1 with 100000 patterns and dataset2 with one million patterns. Dataset1 is the same as in used in [4] which contains randomly generated globular 100 clusters. For spatial decomposition, we partitioned the patterns into strips containing equal number of patterns. The execution time and load balancing data are shown in Table 1 for varying number of threads. The spatial decomposition has better execution times than the random pattern decomposition. The reason for this is explained by the amount of pruning done and the computational load imbalance. We collected statistics about the distance calculations done at the leaves of the tree. The more distance calculation means the less pruning done at the interior nodes. For spatial decomposition, the number of distance calculations increases slightly as the number of threads increases. That is, the amount of work done in the parallel version increases with the number of threads, but slightly, which results in reduced efficiency. This effect is more significant in the random decomposition case. The number of distance calculations increases more than 3 times for 8 threads and this causes the parallel execution time of the random decomposition to be significantly worse than the spatial decomposition. On the other hand, random decomposition has better balanced computational load. The spatial decomposition has upto 20% load imbalance whereas random decomposition has no more than 6% load imbalance. As a result, the one dimensional spatial decomposition scheme suffers from load imbalance, random decomposition suffers from increased work due to less pruning, but overall, spatial decomposition is superior to random decomposition.

Table 1. Load balance and execution time results for pattern decomposition

Num. of Threads	Time (seconds)		Num. of distance calc. ($\times 10^6$)		Load imbalance	
	spatial	random	spatial	random	spatial	random
1	18.03	21.34	14.93	14.93	0	0
2	11.92	14.43	14.89	22.64	11	2
3	9.10	14.36	15.73	28.5	12	2
4	7.91	11.52	16.86	34.62	13	6
5	7.15	13.37	17.32	39.02	18	1
6	6.12	16.66	17.40	44.80	20	6
7	6.08	14.90	18.16	50.52	18	2
8	6.40	15.85	19.84	54.25	16	4

Table 2 compares performance of the single tree pruning, spatial-decomposition, and direct k-means (all parallel) for dataset1 and dataset2. First, the execution time of the tree-based parallel k-means is significantly superior than the direct k-means. When we compare single tree pruning and spatial decomposition techniques, we observed that single tree pruning performs better because it does not have a load imbalance problem. However, the efficiency is not as good as the one of the direct k-means. One of the reasons is the locks to access to the shared queue. Although we tried to reduce the use of locks, performance problems after five processors are noticeable. Another reason might be due to cache when the tree is traversed in a dynamic and irregular way. This is particularly noticeable in the execution time of spatial and random decompositions for one thread case (Table 1). Both spatial and random decompositions (one thread) perform exactly the same sequence of computations. However, the random one is 20% slower (which was tested on several different Sun machines). Since the number of threads is one, this difference is not due to parallelism. In the spatial decomposition, the tree is build such that the sequence of memory locations allocated for nodes mimics the order of nodes visited during the depth-first search which (most probably) results in better use of cpu caches. However, in the random case, that order is not valid. A similar case is true for the single tree version (visiting nodes in an arbitrary order). However, both spatial and single-tree cases are significantly superior than the parallel direct k-means.

Table 2. Execution time for single tree, spatial decomp., and direct

Num. of Threads	Dataset 1 (100000 patterns)			Dataset 2 (1000000 patterns)		
	single-tree	spatial	direct	single-tree	spatial	direct
1	17.99	18.03	145.6	167.55	167.03	1987.91
2	11.48	11.92	73.31	98.98	107.85	996.91
3	8.60	9.10	52.54	71.90	80.97	693.69
4	6.51	7.91	39.36	57.29	67.02	524.83
5	5.73	7.15	31.78	48.62	54.41	419.18
6	5.73	6.12	26.58	42.49	50.61	351.92
7	5.60	6.08	22.58	41.31	49.08	302.97
8	5.87	6.40	20.05	39.66	51.81	269.93

4 Conclusion and Future Work

In this work, we developed and evaluated two parallelization schemes for a tree-based k-means clustering on shared memory architectures using Pthreads. One of the schemes is based on pattern decomposition (multiple trees). We determined that spatial decomposition of patterns outperforms random pattern decomposition even though random decomposition has almost no load imbalance problem. The spatial decomposition, on the other hand, can be improved further by forming partitions in a more clever way and can be used also for running the algorithm on distributed memory machines. The other approach is the parallel traverse of the single tree. This approach solves the load imbalance problem, but the overhead of thread synchronizations need to be handled, for example, by employing programming environments with more efficient thread support.

References

1. Jain, A. K., Murty, M. N., Flynn, P. J.: Data Clustering: A Review. ACM Computing Surveys, Vol. 31, No. 3, (1999) 264-323
2. Judd, D., McKinley, P. K., Jain, A. K.: Large-Scale Parallel Data Clustering. In Proc. of the 13th Int. Conf. on Pattern Recognition, (1996)
3. McQueen, J.: Some Methods for Classification and Analysis of Multivariate Observations. Proceedings of the Fifth Berkeley Symposium on Mathematical Statistics and Probability, (1997) 173-188
4. Alsabti, K., Ranka, S., Singh, V.: An Efficient K-Means Clustering Algorithm. IPPS/SPDP 1st Workshop on High Performance Data Mining, (1998)

Experiments in Parallel Clustering with DBSCAN

Domenica Arlia and Massimo Coppola

Università degli Studi di Pisa, Dipartimento di Informatica
Corso Italia 40, 56125 Pisa, Italy
coppola@di.unipi.it

Abstract. We present a new result concerning the parallelisation of DBSCAN, a Data Mining algorithm for density-based spatial clustering. The overall structure of DBSCAN has been mapped to a skeleton-structured program that performs parallel exploration of each cluster. The approach is useful to improve performance on high-dimensional data, and is general w.r.t. the spatial index structure used. We report preliminary results of the application running on a Beowulf with good efficiency.

1 Introduction

The goal of Clustering consists in grouping data items into subsets that are homogeneous according to a given notion of similarity. It is well known [1] that clustering techniques are poorly scalable w.r.t. the amount of data, and to the number of data attributes. There is still an open debate [2] about *effectiveness* of distance measures for clustering data with very high dimensionality. Even if new data structures have recently been developed (like the X-Tree or the M-Tree) the performance of spatial index structures asymptotically degrades to that of a linear scan for high dimensional, ill distributed data.

There are relatively few results about improving practical use of clustering by means of parallel computation, and to the best of our knowledge, little has been done about parallel clustering with spatial access methods. Most of the research about spatial indexes is done in the Database community, and it has to face different and more complex problems like concurrent updates, which are outside the scope of our present work.

On the contrary, we will mainly address the performance of the retrieval operation, assuming that the data are already properly stored. Our contribution is a parallel implementation of the DBSCAN clustering algorithm [3], which is a new achievement. We aim at lowering computation time for those cases where density-based spatial clustering takes too long but it is still appropriate.

The main research line of our group is aimed at high-level structured languages in Parallel Programming Environments (PPE), to enhance code productivity, portability and reuse in parallel software engineering. The coordination language of our programming environment SkIE provides a set of parallel skeletons which express the basic forms of parallelism and encapsulate modules of sequential code. The overall software architecture and the philosophy of the language are more extensively described in other papers, see [4]. Essentially, parallel skeletons are higher-order functionals used to express communication and synchronisation semantics among program modules. Sequential and parallel semantics are thus separated by module interface definitions.

Data Mining (DM) algorithms are an interesting source of problems of dynamic nature involving large data structures. We started a new research, summarized in [5], by looking at the interplay among the design of DM applications and the design and implementation of a PPE.

Here we report the results achieved so far with the DBSCAN algorithm. We started form the sequential source and turned the key functionalities into separate sequential modules. We have devised a parallel cooperation scheme among these modules, explained in §3. We finally mapped this high-level structure to a composition of skeletons in the coordination language of SkIE. We propose a refinement of the simple parallel scheme to control parallel overhead, and report test result for the parallel application.

2 Problem Definition

DBSCAN is a density-based spatial clustering algorithm. The original paper [3] fully explains the algorithm and its theoretical bases, which we briefly summarize in the following. By density-based we mean that clusters are defined as connected regions where data points are dense. If density falls below a given threshold, data are regarded as noise. Given a set of N points in R^d, DBSCAN produces a flat partition of the input into a number of *clusters* and a set of *noise* points. The density threshold is specified by choosing the minimum number *MinPts* of points in a sphere of radius ϵ. As a basic definition, a **core point** is a point whose ϵ-neighborhood satisfies this density condition. Clusters are non-empty, maximal sets of core points and surrounding boundary points. The high level structure of DBSCAN is a linear search for unlabelled core points, each new core point starting the ExpandCluster procedure (Fig. 1a). ExpandCluster is the working core of the algorithm, and its key operation is a spatial query, the operation of retrieving all the points belonging to a given region of the space. It can be shown that clusters are invariant w.r.t. the order of point selection in ExpandCluster, and that the overall complexity is $O(N \cdot r())$, where $r()$ is the complexity of the neighborhood retrieval.

A characteristic of spatial clustering is that spatial index structures are essential to enhance the locality of data accesses. The first implementation of DBSCAN uses a R*-Tree [6] to hold the whole input set. The R*-Tree is a secondary memory tree for d-dimensional data. It can answer to spatial queries with complexity proportional to the tree depth, $O(\log N)$ in time and I/O accesses. With this assumption, the authors of DBSCAN report a time complexity of $O(N \log N)$. As stated in the introduction, if the data distribution is unknown, spatial index structures need $O(N)$ search time for large values of N and d. This is also true for the R*-Tree when too large or dense regions are queried.

ExpandCluster (p, Input_Set, ε, MinPts,
          ClusterID)
  label(p, ClusterID)
  put p in a seed queue
  while queue is not empty
    extract c from the queue
    retrieve the ε-neighborhood of c
    if (there are at least MinPts neighbours)
      foreach neighbour n
        if (n is labelled NOISE)
          label n with ClusterId
        if (n is unlabelled)
          label n with ClusterId
          put n in the queue

Master :
  while (there are pending results)
    get $\{p, s, set_n\}$ from the result queue
    if ($s > MinPts$)
      foreach point $n \in set_n$
        if (n is labelled NOISE)
          label n with ClusterID
        if (n is unlabelled)
          label n with ClusterID
          put n in the candidate queue

Slave :
  forever
    get point c from the candidate queue
    $set_n = $ ε-neighborhood(c)
    put $\{c, \#set_n, set_n\}$ in the result queue

Fig. 1. (a) Pseudo-code of ExpandCluster — (b) Parallel decomposition.

```
farm retrieve in(candidate p) out(neighb n)
    Slave in(p) out(n)
end farm

pipe body in(neighb a) out(neighb b)
    Master in(a) out(candidate p)
    retrieve in(p) out(b)
end pipe

loop dbscan in(neighb i) out(neighb o)
        feedback(i=o)
    body in(i) out(o)
    while test in(o) out(bool cont)
end loop
```

Fig. 2. The skeleton structure of parallel DBSCAN and its template implementation

3 The Parallel DBSCAN

We first addressed the performance of region queries. Region queries account for more than 95% of the computation time even when the R*-Tree fits in memory and contains two-dimensional data. Here we describe a simple replication approach, which has non obvious consequences on the behaviour of the algorithm. Our current target is to trade-off computational resources to increase the bandwidth of the slowest part of DBSCAN. We made no efforts yet in designing parallel access to the R*-Tree. Sequential DBSCAN is general w.r.t. the data structure, and I/O bandwidth is a more immediate limitation than data size.

By relaxing the visit order constraints, we have rewritten ExpandCluster as the composition of two separate processes (Fig. 1b), which actually interact through asynchronous, unordered channels. The parallel visit can be proven correct w.r.t. the sequential one, and can concurrently execute the queries.

The Master module performs cluster assignment, while the Slave module answers neighborhood queries using the R*-Tree. Reading spatial information is decoupled from writing labels, and the Slave has a pure functional behaviour. Having restructured the algorithm to a Master-Slave cooperation, we must ex-

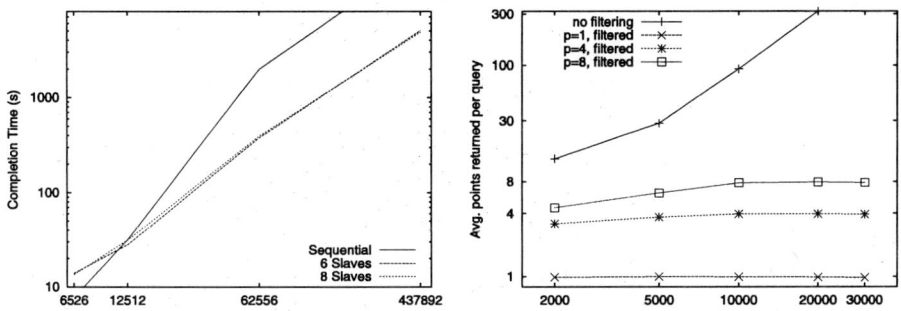

Fig. 3. (a) Completion times ($p = 1, 6, 8$) w.r.t. data size, with $\epsilon = 30000$, log/log scale. (b) Effect of filtering on query answers, $p = 1, 4, 8$, for file ca and varying ϵ.

press its structure using the skeletons of our language. There is pipeline parallelism between Master and Slave, and functional independent replication can be exploited among multiple Slaves. In SkIE, the two skeletons **pipe** and **farm** respectively declare these two basic forms of parallelism. The outer **loop** skeleton in Fig. 2 expresses a data-flow loop, with back flow of information (the query answers) and a sequential module to test program termination.

Unlike the sequential DBSCAN, points already labelled are returned again and again from the slaves. Labels are kept and checked in the Master, which can quickly become a bottleneck, as the upper curve in Fig. 3b shows. This parallel overhead comes from the complete separation of labelling and spatial information. We reduce the overhead by introducing partially consistent information in the Slaves. The Slaves maintain local information used to discard redundant results, by ⓐ returning the set of neighbours for core points only and ⓑ never sending again a previously returned point. The filtering rule ⓐ alone has negligible effect, but is needed for the correctness of rule ⓑ. We see in Fig. 3b that the average number of points returned per query now approaches the degree of parallelism. This is also the upper bound, since no point is sent more than once by the p Slaves.

The program has been tested on a Beowulf class cluster of 10 PCs, with two samples (6K, 12K points), the full ca dataset (62K points) used in [3], and a scaled-up version of the data comprising 437 thousand points. More details can be found in [5]. This data size (the R*-Tree is up to 16 Mbytes) still allows in-core computation. Nevertheless the speedup (up to 6 with 8 slaves) and efficiency are good. From the completion times (Fig. 3a) we can see that a parallelism degree $p = 6, 8$ is the most we can usefully exploit on our architecture with in-core input datasets. We expect that the additional overhead for the out-of-core computation of a larger input set will raise the amount of available parallel work.

4 Conclusions

The program structure we have devised has several advantages. It exploits the modularity of the sequential application, so it helped in reengineering existing code to parallel with minimal effort. It is easily described and implemented using the skeleton coordination patterns. The additional code is simple and general: both sequential DBSCAN and our parallel implementation will still produce identical results when replacing the R*-Tree with another spatial index structure. At present time we duplicate the spatial data structure to gain computation and I/O bandwidth. Saving disk space will be addressed in a later stage.

We deal with the parallel overhead of the simple Master-Slave decomposition through a distributed filtering technique. This solution has been tested for in-core data size with high computational load, showing large saving of computation and communication, and a consistently good speedup w.r.t. the sequential algorithm.

We still have to verify the scalability results for larger input sets, forcing the R*-Tree to be actually stored out-of core. Secondary memory sharing by parallel file system can reduce or avoid the amount of data replication. Comparison of the R*-Tree with newer spatial data structures is also needed, and more complex filtering heuristics can be devised to further reduce the parallel overhead at higher parallelism degree, by exploiting locality and affinity scheduling among the queries. Finally, we are studying the extension of parallel DBSCAN results to OPTICS [7], a DBSCAN-based automatic clustering methodology which relies on a specific visit order in the ExpandCluster procedure.

Acknowledgments

We wish to thank Dr. Jörg Sander and the authors of DBSCAN for making available the source code.

References

1. Daniel A. Keim and Alexander Hinneburg. Clustering techniques for large data sets–from the past to the future. In *Tutorial notes for ACM SIGKDD 1999 international conference on Knowledge discovery and data mining*, pages 141–181, 1999.
2. K. Beyer, J. Goldstein, R. Ramakrishnan, and U. Shaft. When Is "Nearest Neighbor" Meaningful? In C. Beeri and P. Buneman, editors, *Database Theory - ICDT'99 7th International Conference*, volume 1540 of *LNCS*, pages 217–235, January 1999.
3. Martin Ester, Hans-Peter Kriegel, Jörg Sander, and Xiaowei Xu. A Density-Based Algorithm for Discovering Clusters in Large Spatial Databases with Noise. In *Proceedings of KDD '96*, 1996.
4. B. Bacci, M. Danelutto, S. Pelagatti, and M. Vanneschi. SkIE : A heterogeneous environment for HPC applications. *Parallel Computing*, 25(13–14):1827–1852, December 1999.
5. Massimo Coppola and Marco Vanneschi. High-Performance Data Mining with Skeleton-based Structured Parallel Programming. Technical Report TR-06-01, Dipartimento di Informatica, Università di Pisa, May 2001.

6. N. Beckmann, H.-P. Kriegel, R. Schneider, and B. Seeger. The R*-tree: an efficient and robust access method for points and rectangles. In *Proc. of the ACM SIGMOD International Conf. on Management of Data*, pages 322–331, 1990.
7. M. Ankerst, M. M. Breunig, H.-P. Kriegel, and J. Sander. OPTICS: ordering points to identify the clustering structure. In *Proceedings of the 1999 ACM SIGMOD international conference on Management of data*, pages 49–60, 1999.

Topic 06
Complexity Theory and Algorithms

Gianfranco Bilardi, Rainer Feldmann, Kieran Herley, and Bruce Maggs

Topic Chairpersons

The complexity theory and algorithms topic focuses on the theoretical foundations of parallel computing, especially the exploration of fundamental problems and issues from an algorithmic perspective and the formulation, investigation and evaluation of the appropriate computational models that allow such issues to be addressed in a rigorous, quantitative manner. Following a thorough reviewing process in which each paper was assessed by four referees, two papers have been selected for presentation as regular papers. An additional paper that was originally submitted to Topic 09 (and accepted as a research note) was also moved to this session for presentation. The committee would like to extend its sincere thanks to all those who contributed papers and to the many colleagues who helped with the reviewing process.

The paper "Beyond External Computing: Analysis of the Cycle Structure of Permutations" by J. Keller and J. Sibeyn studies the problem of determining the cycle structure of a permutation in parallel given an oracle for the permutation π that for any x returns $\pi(x)$. The theoretical results are nicely complemented by experimental work.

The paper "Heaps Are Better than Buckets: Parallel Shortest Paths on Unbalanced Graphs" by U. Meyer presents a parallel algorithm for solving the single-source shortest path problem on an arbitrary graph in which the weight on every edge is chosen at random between 0 and 1. The algorithm is work-efficient and fast for a natural class of graphs that includes power-law graphs (which have been suggested as a model for the structure of the Internet).

The short paper "Efficient Synchronization of Asynchronous Processes" by S. Lodha, P. Chandra, A. Kshemkalyani and M. Rawat presents a refinement of Bagrodia's algorithm for the efficient implementation of a CSP-like communication/synchronization primitive among asynchronous processes. Experimental results are presented that suggest a significant reduction in message overhead when compared with Bagrodia's original algorithm.

Beyond External Computing: Analysis of the Cycle Structure of Permutations

Jörg Keller[1] and Jop F. Sibeyn[2]

[1] FernUniversität, LG Technische Informatik II, 58084 Hagen, Germany
Joerg.Keller@fernuni-hagen.de
[2] Computing Science Department, Umeå University, Sweden
http://www.cs.umu.se/~jopsi/

Abstract. A parallel algorithm with super-linear speed-up for determining the structure of permutations of n elements for extremely large n is presented and analyzed. The algorithm uses sublinear space. If evaluating a randomly chosen successor oracle π costs c time, then a complete analysis can be performed in expected time $c \cdot (\ln n - \ln(P \cdot N)) \cdot n/P$, where P is the number of available processors, and N gives the size of the secondary memory of each of the processors. A simple refinement reduces this time by a factor $1 - 1/e$. The theoretical analyses are compared with experiments. At the current state of the technology values of n up to about 2^{48} might be handled. We also describe how to perform a screening of π in much less time. If $\pi^{\sqrt{n/(\ln n \cdot P)}}$ can be constructed, then such a screening can be performed in $\mathcal{O}(c \cdot \sqrt{\ln n} \cdot n/P)$ time.

1 Introduction

Consider a permutation given by an oracle, that is, when we specify x, $0 \leq x < n$, we get back $\pi(x)$ from the oracle, but we have no further knowledge about the permutation's structure. How to compute the cycle structure of π for extremely large n? Here "computing the cycle structure of π," means generating a list that gives one element of each cycle of π together with its length. The memory consumption should be much smaller than n. For large values of n, we think of $n \geq 2^{40}$, an efficient parallel algorithm is necessary to obtain acceptable runtime.

We present a parallel algorithm to compute the cycle structure of a permutation π which is chosen from the set of all permutations on n numbers with uniform probability. If c is the time for evaluating π once, and N is the size of the secondary memory of a processor, then the expected runtime on a parallel computer with P processors is just over $c \cdot (1 - 1/e) \cdot (\ln n - \ln(P \cdot N)) \cdot n/P$. In comparison to earlier — sequential — algorithms we reduce the amount of work by about a factor of two. Most important, however, is the almost perfect parallelization. If, as is the case for a cluster of workstations, the PUs all come with their own hard disk of size N, then we even obtain super-linear speed-up. For example, for $n = 2^{48}$, $N = 2^{32}$ and $P = 2^8$, the speed-up lies close to $2 \cdot P$. The algorithms borrow ideas from some recent parallel list ranking algorithms [7,10,8,11]. Any parallel algorithm that works by gradual reduction of the problem size, such as independent-set removal techniques [1], are ruled out because the structure of π is available only implicitly.

The considered problem is relevant in the domains of pseudo-random number generators (PRNGs) and cryptography. In a PRNG, the transitions from one state to the next can be considered as a permutation on the set of states. For a simple PRNG based on linear congruences, its period can be derived analytically. However, analysis of a complex PRNG is often not feasible; the period is estimated from a simplified model. Computing the cycles would reveal the real period and identify the set of unwanted start states if there are additional small cycles besides the main cycle.

In the second place, symmetric encryption with a fixed key can be viewed as a permutation on the set of codewords. A good encryption algorithm should behave like a randomly chosen permutation. One of the criteria that should be satisfied (and that cannot be tested by some simple random probing strategy) is that the cycle structure should not deviate too much from what is expected. The challenge, the size of the permutation, lies in these areas of application: for algorithms like DES and IDEA we have $n = 2^{64}$.

The following notation is used throughout the paper. For the parameters we also indicate some typical values. The algorithms are general.

P=number of proc., 2^8 n=no. of elements in structure, 2^{48}
M=size of main memory per proc., 2^{26} π=successor function
N=size of secondary mem. per proc., 2^{32} c=time for evaluating π once

Here M and N are given in words (of size $\log n$). The processing units, PUs, are indexed from 0 through $P - 1$. The index of element x, $0 \leq x < n$, will also be written as a pair (i, j), with $j = \lfloor x/P \rfloor$ and $i = x \bmod P$. Two such pairs are compared in a reversed lexicographical way. That is, $(i, j) < (i', j')$ when $j < j'$ or when $j = j'$ and $i < i'$. PU k, $0 \leq k < P$, is taking care of the indices (k, j), for all $0 \leq j < n/P$.

2 The Importance of Permuting

Permuting the elements of an array is trivial when it is allowed to use a second array. If space considerations make this undesirable, one should consider *in-situ* algorithms, which require only $o(n)$ additional memory. The known sequential in-situ permutation algorithms [2,4] are *cycle leader* algorithms: first a unique *leader* element is found for every cycle of the permutation. Normally, these leaders are the smallest elements on their cycles. Once the leaders are found, performing the actual permutations takes only $\mathcal{O}(n)$ time. So the time for the whole algorithm is determined by the time for finding the leaders.

Checking whether i is a leader normally proceeds by evaluating $j = \pi^k(i)$, for $k = 1, 2, \ldots$, until $j = i$ or until additional tests indicate that i cannot be a leader. The algorithms differ in their implementations of these tests. The simplest test is $j < i$: if this happens, then i cannot be the smallest element on the cycle, so it cannot be a leader. This test does not help to reduce the worst-case running time below the $\mathcal{O}(n^2)$ achieved by the trivial algorithm, but if each permutation is equally likely then the average runtime is bounded by $\mathcal{O}(n \cdot \log n)$ [4]. The algorithm requires $\mathcal{O}(\log n)$ bits of storage. Storing b additional bits, Melville [6] reduces the worst-case time to $\mathcal{O}(n^2/b)$. For very large n, this worst-case time becomes interesting only for excessive b. In the algorithm by Fich et. al. [2] a hierarchy of local minima is constructed while proceeding along the cycle until it finds that either i is the global minimum on the cycle, or that i is not a leader. This algorithm has $\mathcal{O}(n \cdot \log n)$ worst-case runtime. The algorithm requires storage for $\mathcal{O}(\log n)$ integers, that is for $\mathcal{O}(\log^2 n)$ bits, which is a feasible amount, even for large n.

All these algorithms can be easily parallelized: the n tests whether the elements are leaders are distributed over the available processors. However, because the expected length of the longest cycle in a randomly chosen permutation is linear in n (approximately $0.624 \cdot n$ [9, p. 358]), such straight-forward parallelizations lead to at most $\mathcal{O}(\log n)$ speed-up for any P (taking into account the leading constants of the algorithms, it can be estimated that even for $n = 2^{64}$ the speed-up can never exceed 33). To our knowledge, there is no known way to parallelize the check for a single leader, as methods like pointer doubling cannot be applied. Hence, there is no hope for an efficient parallel algorithm based on the cycle leader algorithms. Hagerup and Keller [3] give a PRAM algorithm for the in-situ permutation problem with worst case runtime $\mathcal{O}(n/P + \log n \cdot \log \log(n/P))$, but, as it needs n additional bits of storage, it is not applicable to our problem.

3 Complete Analysis of Structure

We first consider the parallel algorithm for completely evaluating the cycle structure of π. Clearly any such algorithm requires that π is evaluated at least n times, which may take too long. In that case the structure can only be analyzed partially. If n evaluations are acceptable, however, then our algorithm can be performed, because in practice, applying several refinements, the total number of evaluations is bounded by about $5 \cdot n$, perfectly distributed over the processors.

3.1 Basic Algorithm

The basic algorithm minimizes the communication. It consists of four phases. The first and the third are performed locally without communication, the second is very similar to a parallel-external list-ranking problem, for which efficient algorithms have been designed before, both in theory and in practice [5,8,11]. The fourth is a gather operation.

In Phase 1, every PU k, $0 \leq k < P$, performs the following steps in parallel. Next to some local variables, each PU has arrays nxt and dst for storing a remote successor of a node and the distance thereto. These arrays have length N each (assuming that secondary memory can hold $2 \cdot N$ integers). The elements (k, j) with $0 \leq k < P$ and $j \leq N$ serve as a set of "starting points". PU k, $0 \leq k < P$, follows the cycle going through starting point (k, j), for all $0 \leq j < N$, until it reaches another starting point.

Algorithm PHASE 1

1. Set $cur_k = 0$.
2. Set $(i,j) = (k, cur_k)$ and $cnt_k = 0$.
3. Repeat $(i,j) = \pi(i,j)$ and $cnt_k = cnt_k + 1$, until $j < N$.
4. Set $nxt_k(cur_k) = (i,j)$ and $dst_k(cur_k) = cnt_k$.
5. $cur_k = cur_k + 1$. If $cur_k < N$ then goto Step 2.

The expected number of iterations in Step 3 is clearly $n/(P \cdot N)$ (because in a random experiment with a probability of success equal to p, the expected number of trials until the first success equals $1/p$). So, the total expected time consumption for this phase equals $c \cdot n/P$. For all but specially constructed pathological π the actual value will be only slightly larger. The experimental results in Section 5 confirm this.

As a result of the operations in Phase 1, we have constructed a set of links spanning most of the cycles. The total number of these links is $P \cdot N$. In Phase 2, we compute the lengths of these cycles.

Algorithm PHASE 2

1. Perform the "peeling-off" algorithm from [11] to determine the minimum element on every cycle and the distance thereof. If such a minimum element is found, then the cycle statistics are updated.
2. The additional arrays are no longer needed and can be discarded.

All operations can be performed with $\mathcal{O}(N)$ work, paging and routing per PU. Applying the indicated optimized implementation or one of the others, the constants are small. For example, the total amount of data a PU is sending is about $8 \cdot N$. In comparison to the cost of Phase 1, and the even higher cost of Phase 3, this is negligible, even though integers cannot be pumped into the network at clock rate.

After phase 2 we have found all cycles that contain at least one starting point. Phase 3 serves to find the remaining cycles. It is similar to Phase 1, the main difference being another stopping criterion. Each PU has its own local cycle statistics which are set to zero at the beginning of Phase 3. For every PU k, $0 \leq k < P$, the following steps are performed in parallel. PU k starts from all elements (k, cur_k) which are not starting points, i.e. where $cur_k \geq N$, because they might lie on a cycle without starting point. The cycle is followed until either a starting point is reached, in which case the cycle is already detected, or until (k, cur_k) is reached again, in which case (k, cur_k) is the cycle leader, or until $(i,j) < (k, cur_k)$ is reached in which case (k, cur_k) cannot be the cycle leader.

Algorithm PHASE 3

1. Set $cur_k = N$.
2. Set $(i,j) = (k, cur_k)$ and $cnt_k = 0$.
3. Repeat $(i,j) = \pi(i,j)$ and $cnt_k = cnt_k + 1$, until $(i,j) \leq (k, cur_k)$.
4. If $(i,j) = (k, cur_k)$, then we have found a new cycle. Update the local cycle statistics, using cnt_k.
5. $cur_k = cur_k + 1$. If $cur_k < (n/P)$ then goto Step 2.

At the end we have local cycle statistics, in which the PUs recorded the cycles they have discovered. In Phase 4, the PUs perform a logarithmic-depth reduction with the effect that finally the union of everything that was discovered comes to stand in PU 0, who can output the result. If π is indeed more or less random, then the time for this Phase 4 is very small, because in that case the number of cycles is bounded by $\mathcal{O}(\log n)$.

3.2 Analysis

The following analysis is not new (a slightly simpler result was proven already in [2]). We present it here for comparison purposes.

Lemma 1 *For a random oracle π, the expected number of evaluations of π performed by each of the PUs in Phase 3 is bounded by $(\ln n - \ln(P \cdot N)) \cdot n/P$.*

Proof: Starting with an index (k, l), the probability to hit a node $(i, j) \leq (k, l)$ equals $P \cdot l/n$ (actually, after i hops on a path, this probability equals $P \cdot l/(n-i)$, which is slightly larger). So, for given l, writing $p = P \cdot l/n$ and $q = 1 - p$, the expected number of evaluations is given by

$$t_l = \sum_{i=0}^{\infty}(i+1)\cdot p\cdot q^i = \sum_{j=0}^{\infty}\sum_{i=j}^{\infty} p\cdot q^i = \sum_{j=0}^{\infty} p\cdot q^j/(1-q) = \sum_{j=0}^{\infty} q^j = \frac{1}{1-q} = n/(P\cdot l).$$

Hence, if cur_k is running from N to n/P, then the total expected number of evaluations of π performed by PU_k is given by

$$\sum_{l=N}^{n/P} n/(P \cdot l) \simeq (\ln(n/P) - \ln N) \cdot n/P = (\ln n - \ln(P \cdot N)) \cdot n/P.$$

□

So, in order to minimize the total costs one should indeed test the maximum possible number of indices during Phase 1. For the typical values of P, N and n that were given in Section 1, the time consumption is about $6 \cdot c \cdot n/P$. This is still a very long time, but it will become feasible with foreseeable increases in N, P and processor speed. It also makes sense to look for further reductions of the time consumption.

3.3 A Refinement

With a small modification, we can gain about 40%. The idea is to keep track of the number r of indices that were not yet "found". That is, at any given time r equals n minus the sum of the lengths of all detected cycles. Clearly a new cycle cannot be longer than r. Hence, if we are searching from some index (k, cur_k), and we did not yet hit a node (i, j) with $(i, j) \leq (k, cur_k)$ after r applications of π, we may nevertheless conclude that we are on a cycle that was discovered before and stop. Thus, we should modify Step 3 of Phase 3 as follows:

3. Repeat $(i,j) = \pi(i,j)$ and $cnt_k = cnt_k + 1$, until $(i,j) \leq (k, cur_k)$ or $cnt_k = r$.

In a sequential algorithm it would be trivial to keep r up-to-date. In a parallel algorithm this requires some extra effort. Because we expect to find only few cycles, there is no need to wait: as soon as a cycle is detected by a PU, it can immediately broadcast its length to all other PUs. Such a broadcast can be performed in $\log P$ communication rounds. The involved packets have constant size. Thus, this costs $\mathcal{O}(\log P)$ time, which is negligible in comparison to $c \cdot n/P$. Thus, we may assume, as is done in the following analysis, that r is up-to-date.

Lemma 2 *During pass l of the loop in step 3, the expected value of r is about $n/(P \cdot l)$.*

Proof: From [9] we use the fact that the expected number of cycles of length m equals $1/m$. The possible discovery of such a cycle is an independent event, so the expected number of remaining cycles of length m equals $(1 - m/n)^{P \cdot l}/m$. Thus, substituting $L = P \cdot l$, the expected sum $\bar{r}_l$ of the lengths of these cycles can be estimated as follows:

$$\bar{r}_l = \sum_{m=0}^{n}(1-m/n)^L \simeq \int_0^n (1-m/n)^L \, dm = \frac{-n}{L+1} \cdot (1-m/n)|_0^n = \frac{n}{L+1} \simeq n/L.$$

$\square$

By an analysis similar to the proof of Lemma 1, we obtain

Theorem 1 *For a random oracle π, the expected number of evaluations of π performed by each of the PUs in the modified Phase 3 is bounded by $(1 - 1/e) \cdot (\ln n - \ln(P \cdot N)) \cdot n/P$.*

4 Other Results

Finding the Longest Cycle. For some applications it may be sufficient to know the size L and some elements of the longest cycle. For example, it may be possible to generate several oracles, with the purpose to pick the one that maximizes L. L has expected value $0.624 \cdot n$, but the actual values fluctuate a lot. It is easy to see that the probability that $L > n - m$ is at least m/n. Thus, trying r times will mostly give us an oracle with $L > n - n/r$.

In the previous section we have reduced the running time by a constant factor, but even $c \cdot n/P$ may be beyond feasibility. In a special case a superficial screening can be performed so fast, that it even becomes possible to test many oracles. We assume that after some (maybe quite expensive) preprocessing a new oracle $\rho = \pi^x$ can be constructed, that again can be evaluated in c time[1]. In the following we will use $x = \sqrt{n/(\ln n \cdot P)}$.

---
[1] This assumption is e.g. valid for permutations like $a \cdot x + b \bmod m$, but not for DES.

The algorithm is simple: Each PU randomly chooses $\ln n$ starting points. From each starting point the algorithm applies x times ρ. The indices of all nodes that are visited during these jumps are stored, this information is called a track. It is most convenient if at the end of such a batch of operations all new information is gossiped, so that all PUs have access to it locally. Then for each track, the algorithm x times applies π, while testing whether a track starting from another starting point already covered this sector. Because such a track has left traces every x nodes, this will certainly be detected. If this happens, then this track is not further extended. These operations are repeated until all tracks got stuck. The amount of double work is very small.

Theorem 2 *The described algorithm has running time $\mathcal{O}(c \cdot \sqrt{\ln n \cdot n/P})$. Afterwards, for any given seed it can be tested in $c \cdot \sqrt{n/(\ln n \cdot P)}$ time whether it lies on a sufficiently long cycle or not.*

Proof: Because the number of evaluations of π equals the number of evaluations of ρ, we only need to estimate the latter. Because each PU essentially covers only the gaps between its starting points and those that follow, the work can be estimated on the sum of the sizes of these gaps multiplied by c/x, which gives $\mathcal{O}(c \cdot n/(P \cdot x))$. We must add $\mathcal{O}(c \cdot x)$ for each starting point, thus the total time consumption for each PU is given by

$$\mathcal{O}(c \cdot n/(P \cdot x)) + c \cdot x \cdot \ln n = \mathcal{O}(c \cdot \sqrt{\ln n \cdot n/P}).$$

The length of the cycles can be found by knotting all tracks together. If this should be used as a random generator, then for a seed s it can be tested by performing $\sqrt{n/(\ln n \cdot P)}$ times π whether s lies on a sufficiently long cycle. □

Very Short Cycles. Cycles with length up to l can trivially be detected with $l \cdot n/P$ evaluations of π per PU.

Tree Like Structures. More interesting are oracles that only guarantee outdegree 1, but for which a node may be the successor of several nodes. In that case, the given algorithm may not terminate, because there may be cycles of nodes with high indices to which is attached a tail containing a node with low index. The solution is to throw anchors every now and then, and stopping as soon as an anchor is reached. A possibility is to throw anchors after a number of evaluations that is doubled every time. In this way at most twice as many evaluations are performed as necessary.

Testing on Randomness. For some applications there is no need to find all cycles. In such cases a cheaper screening will suffice. Here, we consider omitting Phase 3. Then, the algorithm runs in just over $c \cdot n/P$ time. In the following we work under the assumption that π is random. If it is not, then it may either still behave as assumed, or it does not, and in that case it will be detected.

Lemma 3 *After Phase 1 and Phase 2, the expected fraction of the cycles of length m that has been found equals $1 - (1 - m/n)^{P \cdot N} \simeq 1 - e^{m \cdot P \cdot N/n}$. For $m \geq n/(P \cdot N) \cdot \ln n$ all cycles have been found, with high probability.*

Proof: For any given cycle of length m, the probability that none of its elements is among the lowest $P \cdot N$, equals $(1 - m/n)^{P \cdot N}$. Substituting $m = n/(P \cdot N) \cdot \ln n$ gives $1/n$. As, for random π there are only $\mathcal{O}(\ln n)$ cycles in total, the probability that any of them is not detected is hardly larger. □

5 Experimental Results

We have implemented a sequential simulation of the basic algorithm together with the simple improvement from Section 3.3 in C. We have run this program on a computer with sufficient internal memory for the size of the experiments that we wanted to perform. So, the random permutations could be generated easily and were stored in arrays. We were not interested in time, but in the number of evaluations made by each PU. Other points of interest are the occurring fluctuations in the numbers of cycles and the load balancing among the PUs.

Table 1. Results of experiments. The columns give $\log_2 n$, $\log_2(P \cdot N)$, the number of tests, the minimum number of cycles that was found, the average number and the maximum number. Ta is the average value of the total number of evaluations divided by P. TM gives the corresponding maximum number. ta is the average of the maximum number of evaluations performed by any of the (virtual) PUs. tM gives the corresponding maximum

log n	log($P \cdot N$)	tests	Cm	Ca	CM	Ta	TM	ta	tM
16	4	10000	2	11.66	26	309647	535040	463808	913248
16	8	10000	2	11.67	26	223927	395357	257792	452864
16	12	100000	1	11.67	28	134846	240286	142400	252576
20	4	2000	5	14.49	27	6451451	10409239	8947232	14887648
20	8	2000	3	14.41	27	5023912	8647220	5561552	9275280
20	12	10000	3	14.41	30	3587918	6467906	3714624	6593576
20	16	10000	4	14.47	30	2157791	3855698	2187328	3884932
24	8	1000	6	17.27	32	103595973	170821183	112231808	183887984
24	12	1000	5	17.39	31	90363923	135110679	82525232	137614384
24	16	1000	6	17.12	30	57065471	98106800	57659024	98444288
24	20	1000	4	17.21	34	34271603	58610751	34389440	58816288
28	12	100	11	19.31	31	1579220642	2371955835	1608459888	2413276912
28	16	100	10	20.35	29	1270724358	1978054028	1278394896	1985230560
28	20	100	9	19.84	30	880985077	1468056382	882947248	1470623392
28	24	500	7	19.50	32	542089349	971220637	542567680	972277488

We have tested for $n = 2^{16}, 2^{20}, 2^{24}, 2^{28}$. For larger n the main problem is that the time consumption does not allow to run sufficiently many tests to draw reliable conclusions. All these n have been investigated for $P \cdot N = n/2^4, n/2^8, n/2^{12}, n/2^{16}$. We have set $P = 16$, this has no implications for the number of evaluations. All results are given in Table 1. We have performed a least square adaptation for determining the values of β and γ in the number T of evaluations per PU:

$$T = (\beta + \gamma \cdot (\ln n - \ln(P \cdot N)) \cdot n/P.$$

The best fit is obtained with $\beta = 0.710$ and $\gamma = 0.486$. These values are smaller than expected, which might be due to the positive effect of stopping when $r = 0$. For all instances with $n \leq 2^{24}$, the deviation is less than 1%. For $n = 2^{28}$, the deviation is slightly larger, due to an insufficient number of experiments.

For each n, the average number of cycles lies close to the value it should have: the harmonic numbers $H_n = \sum_{i=1}^{n} 1/i$. The deviation is at most a few percent and due to an insufficient number of tests.

The maximum number of cycles is bounded by about twice the expected number, though the deviation appears to decrease for larger n. The minimum number of cycles may be very small. For larger n it increases. This is due to two effects: for larger n the probability on very few cycles decreases considerably (the probability that a permutation consists of exactly one cycle equals $1/n$); for large n we could not perform many tests. The experiments do not allow to draw any final conclusion, but it appears that the distribution around the expected value is more or less symmetrical. For example, for $n = 2^{28}$, the expected value is close to 20, and permutations with less than 10 cycles are about equally frequent as permutations with more than 30 cycles (1 or 2 on every 100 permutations).

From the difference between the average and maximum number of evaluations we see that the actual running times may fluctuate a lot (the maximum is up to 70% higher than the average, and exceeds the minimum even by a factor three). There is some correlation with the number of cycles (if there are many cycles, then probably r will be large during the experiment and the last cycle will be found late), but we have seen many exceptions.

Comparing the total number of evaluations divided by P and the maximum number of evaluations performed by any PU, we see that there may be a considerable difference for the smallest n, which are not relevant in real applications. For the larger n, this difference decreases to 1% and less. This is so little, that there is no need for additional load balancing.

In order to estimate c, we have tested the pseudo-random number generator function lrand48. On a workstation with a Pentium II processor running at 333 MHz, FreeBSD operating system and GNU C compiler, we found that about 2^{29} evaluations were performed per minute. Hence, for $n = 2^{48}$, n evaluations would take about 2^{19} minutes or 364 days of processing time. This means, that with sufficiently many processors (which by now are several times faster), a problem of this size may be tackled in a few days.

6 Open Problems and Further Work

Future work will focus on a message-passing implementation for a workstation cluster or multiprocessor to validate our preliminary results. Another permutation to be tested will be the DES encryption algorithm with a fixed key. The number of elements in this permutation is larger than in the lrand48 case by a factor of 2^{16}. Also, evaluation of the DES permutation will take much longer than evaluating the lrand48 permutation. It appears that with the sketched improvements we have fully exploited the available information and memory. Only by storing data more compactly some further gains are possible, but this will not change things dramatically. Hence, there is a need for faster evaluation. A very interesting possibility is to use programmable hardware such as field-programmable gate arrays (FPGAs). In the simplest case, these devices are added to the processors as boards in the cluster scenario. In the case of DES, this could lead to a performance improvement by more than a magnitude. Also, the control flow in our algorithm is quite regular. Thus in a single FPGA, several processing instances to solve the problem could be implemented and multiple FPGAs could be used. It could thus be possible to construct a dedicated FPGA-based machine to solve the cycle-structure problem.

References

1. Cole, R., U. Vishkin, 'Approximate Parallel Scheduling, Part I: the Basic Technique with Applications to Optimal Parallel List Ranking in Logarithmic Time,' *SIAM Journal on Computing*, 17(1), pp. 128–142, 1988.
2. Fich, F. E., J. I. Munro, P. V. Poblete, 'Permuting in Place,' *SIAM Journal on Computing*, 24(2), pp. 266–278, 1995.
3. Hagerup, T., J. Keller, 'Fast Parallel Permutation Algorithms,' *Parallel Processing Letters*, 5(2), pp. 139–148, 1995.
4. Knuth, D. E., 'Mathematical Analysis of Algorithms,' *Proc. of IFIP Congress 1971*, Information Processing 71, pp. 19–27, North-Holland Publ. Co., 1972.
5. Lambert, O., J. F. Sibeyn, 'Parallel and External List Ranking and Connected Components on a Cluster of Workstations,' *Proc. 11th International Conference Parallel and Distributed Computing and Systems*, pp. 454–460, IASTED, 1999.
6. Melville, R. C., 'A Time-Space Tradeoff for In-Place Array Permutation,' *Journal of Algorithms*, 2(2), pp. 139–143, 1981.
7. Reid-Miller, M., 'List Ranking and List Scan on the Cray C-90,' *Journal of Computer and System Sciences*, 53(3), pp. 344–356, 1996.
8. Ranade, A., 'A Simple Optimal List Ranking Algorithm,' *Proc. of 5th High Performance Computing*, Tata McGraw-Hill Publishing Company, 1998.
9. Sedgewick, R., Ph. Flajolet, *An Introduction to the Analysis of Algorithms*. Addison Wesley, Reading, Mass., 1996.
10. Sibeyn, J. F., 'One-by-One Cleaning for Practical Parallel List Ranking,' to appear in *Algorithmica*. Preliminary version in *Proc. 9th Symposium on Parallel Algorithms and Architectures*, pp. 221-230, ACM, 1997.
11. Sibeyn, J. F., 'Ultimate Parallel List Ranking,' *Techn. Rep. MPI-I-99-1005*, Max-Planck-Institut für Informatik, Saarbrücken, Germany, 1999.

Heaps Are Better than Buckets:
Parallel Shortest Paths on Unbalanced Graphs*

Ulrich Meyer

Max-Planck-Institut für Informatik
Stuhlsatzenhausweg 85, 66123 Saarbrücken, Germany
www.uli-meyer.de

Abstract. We propose a new parallel algorithm for the single-source shortest-path problem (SSSP). Its heap data structure is particularly advantageous on graphs with a moderate number of high degree nodes. On arbitrary directed graphs with n nodes, m edges and independent random edge weights uniformly distributed in the range $[0, 1]$ and maximum shortest path weight $\mathcal{L}$ the PRAM version of our algorithm runs in $\mathcal{O}(\log^2 n \cdot \min_i \{2^i \cdot \mathcal{L} \cdot \log n + |V_i|\})$ average-case time using $\mathcal{O}(n \cdot \log n + m)$ operations where $|V_i|$ is the number of graph vertices with degree at least 2^i. For power-law graph models of the Internet or call graphs this results in the first work-efficient $o(n^{1/4})$ average-case time algorithm.

1 Introduction

The *single-source shortest-path problem* (SSSP) is a fundamental and well-studied combinatorial optimization problem with many practical and theoretical applications. However, the fast and efficient SSSP computation still constitutes a major bottleneck in parallel computing.

Let $G = (V, E)$ be a directed graph with $|V| = n$ nodes and $|E| = m$ edges, let s be a distinguished vertex of the graph, and c be a function assigning a non-negative real-valued *weight* to each edge of G. The objective of the SSSP is to compute, for each vertex v reachable from s, the weight of a minimum-weight ("shortest distance") path from s to v, denoted by $dist(s, v)$, abbreviated $dist(v)$; the weight of a path is the sum of the weights of its edges. We are particularly interested in graphs with unbalanced node degrees, i.e., the maximum node degree d is by orders of magnitude bigger than the average node degree in G.

The parallel random access machine (PRAM) [10] is one of the most widely studied abstract models of a parallel computer. A PRAM consists of P independent processors (processing units, PUs) and a shared memory, which these processors can synchronously access in unit time. We assume the *arbitrary* CRCW (concurrent read concurrent write) PRAM, i.e., in case of conflicting write accesses to the same memory cell, an adversary can choose which access is successful.

---

* Partially supported by the IST Programme of the EU under contract number IST-1999-14186 (ALCOM-FT).

A fast and efficient parallel algorithm minimizes both *time* and *work* (product of time and number of processors). Ideally, the work bound matches the complexity of the best (known) sequential algorithm. Dijkstra's sequential approach [8] with Fibonacci heaps [11] solves SSSP on arbitrary directed graphs with non-negative edge weights in $\mathcal{O}(n \log n + m)$ time. It maintains a partition of V into *settled*, *queued*, and *unreached* nodes, and for each node v a *tentative distance* tent(v); In each iteration, the queued node v with smallest tentative distance is removed from the queue, and all edges (v, w) are *relaxed*, i.e., tent(w) is set to $\min\{\text{tent}(w), \text{tent}(v) + c(v, w)\}$. It is well known that tent(v) = dist(v), when v is selected from the queue, hence v is settled and will never re-enter the queue. Therefore, Dijkstra's approach is a so called *label-setting* method.

Label-correcting variants may remove nodes from the queue for which tent(v) $>$ dist(v) and hence have to *re-insert* those nodes until they are finally settled. Linear average-case time for *directed* SSSP can be achieved with a sequential label-correcting approach [17], too. Label-correcting SSSP algorithms are natural candidates for parallelization: using a number of sequential priority queues, several nodes are removed concurrently in one round. A key problem is the efficient selection of a large "provably good" node set for removal.

Previous Work on Parallel SSSP. So far there is no parallel $\mathcal{O}(n \cdot \log n + m)$ work PRAM SSSP algorithm with sublinear running time for arbitrary digraphs with non-negative edge weights. The $\mathcal{O}(n \cdot \log n + m)$ work solution by Driscoll et. al. [9] has running time $\mathcal{O}(n \cdot \log n)$. An $\mathcal{O}(n)$ time algorithm requiring $\mathcal{O}(m \cdot \log n)$ work was presented by Brodal et. al. [5]. Faster algorithms require more work, e.g., the approach by Han et. al. [12] needs $\mathcal{O}(\log^2 n)$ time and $\mathcal{O}(n^3 \cdot (\log \log n / \log n)^{1/3})$ work. The algorithm of Klein and Subramanian [14] takes $\mathcal{O}(\sqrt{n} \cdot \log \mathcal{L} \cdot \log n \cdot \log^* n)$ time and $\mathcal{O}(\sqrt{n} \cdot m \cdot \log \mathcal{L} \cdot \log n)$ work where $\mathcal{L}$ is the maximum shortest path weight. Similar results have been obtained by Cohen [6] and Shi and Spencer [20].

Further work-efficient SSSP algorithms exist for random graphs [4] where each of the n^2 possible edges is present with a certain probability. Under the assumption of independent random edge weights uniformly distributed in the interval $[0, 1]$ the fastest work-efficient label-correcting approach for random graphs [18,19] requires $\mathcal{O}(\log^2 n)$ time and linear work on average; additionally, $\mathcal{O}(d \cdot \mathcal{L} \cdot \log n + \log^2 n)$ time and $\mathcal{O}(n + m + d \cdot \mathcal{L} \cdot \log n)$ work on average is achieved for arbitrary graphs with random edge weights where d denotes the maximum node degree in the graph and $\mathcal{L}$ denotes the maximum weight of a shortest path to a node reachable from s, i.e., $\mathcal{L} = \max_{v \in G, \text{dist}(v) < \infty} \text{dist}(v)$. The algorithms fail for large d. Crauser et. al. [7] gave general criteria that divide Dijkstra's label-setting algorithm into a number of phases, such that the operations within a phase can be done in parallel. The efficiency of the criteria was shown for random graphs where sublinear average-case running time can be obtained.

New Results. We propose a new parallel label-correcting SSSP approach that is particularly suited for graphs with unbalanced node degrees and analyze its average-case performance on arbitrary directed graphs: Let $|V_i|$ denote the number of graph vertices with degree at least 2^i. Assuming independent random edge weights uniformly distributed in $[0, 1]$, our algorithm runs in $\mathcal{O}(\log^2 n \cdot \min_i\{2^i \cdot \mathcal{L} \cdot \log n + |V_i|\})$ time on average using $\mathcal{O}(n \cdot \log n + m)$ operations. This significantly extends the class of inputs for which parallel SSSP can be solved in sublinear average-case time using only $\mathcal{O}(n \cdot \log n + m)$ work. In particular, for some random power-law graph classes which are widely considered to be appropriate models of the Internet or telephone call graphs [1,16] our algorithm is the first to achieve $o(n^{1/4})$ average-case time while still remaining work efficient. Furthermore, we sketch how to extend the average-case analysis of the parallel label-setting approach with heaps [7] from random graphs to arbitrary graphs and compare its performance with our new algorithm.

2 Preliminaries

The parallel SSSP algorithm of [18], called Δ-stepping, and its improved version [19] are label-correcting approaches that work in phases: if M denotes the smallest tentative distance in the queue data structure Q at the beginning of a phase, then they remove all nodes v with tentative distance tent$(v) < M + \Delta$ in parallel. The parameter Δ is called the *step-width*. Those nodes which are removed with non-final distance values are eventually *re-inserted* into Q. In order to bound the number of re-insertions and hence the total work, Δ must not be chosen too big. On the other hand, taking Δ too small can result in many phases, i.e., poor running times:

Lemma 1 ([18]) *Under the assumption of independent random edge weights uniformly drawn from $[0, 1]$, the average-case number of re-insertions for an arbitrary node v_0 in the Δ-stepping algorithm is bounded by $\mathcal{O}(1)$ provided that $\Delta \leq 1/d$ for maximum node degree d.*

Proof: If a node v_0 was removed from Q for the first time in phase i, then a re-insertion of v_0 in phase $i + j$ can be mapped on a simple path $\langle v_j, \ldots, v_0 \rangle$ such that v_k was removed in phase $i + j - k$ and the tentative distance of v_k was improved by relaxing the edge (v_{k+1}, v_k). In any case, the total weight of the path $\langle v_j, \ldots, v_0 \rangle$ must be smaller than the step-width. If d denotes the maximum degree in the graph then there are at most d^l simple paths of l edges into v_0. For l independent random edge weights uniformly distributed in $[0, 1]$, the probability that their sum is at most $\Delta \leq 1$ is bound by $\Delta^l/l!$. Hence, the average-case number of re-insertions for v_0 can be bounded by $\sum_1^\infty (d \cdot \Delta)^l/l! = \mathcal{O}(1)$ for $\Delta \leq 1/d$. □

Parallel node-removal is realized by using a random mapping π of node indices to a number of P sequential priority queues Q_j. Load-balancing for node removals is guaranteed with high probability (whp)[1] by the random distribution

---

[1] *with high probability (whp)* means that the probability for some event is at least $1 - n^{-\beta}$ for any constant $\beta > 0$.

provided that sufficiently many nodes are removed in parallel. Load-balancing for relaxations is done as follows: all relaxations of a phase are first grouped according to their target nodes (semi-sorting with integer keys) and for each node only the relaxation resulting in the smallest tentative distance is forwarded to its priority queue in charge [19].

The sequential priority structure for processor PU_j can be implemented by linear arrays B_j of buckets such a queued node v is kept in $B_{\pi(v)}[i]$ for tentative distances in the range $[i \cdot \Delta, (i+1) \cdot \Delta)$. Let k denote the biggest bucket index such that $B_j[0], \ldots, B_j[k-1]$ are empty for all j. Then a phase removes all nodes from $B_0[k], \ldots, B_{P-1}[k]$. After $\mathcal{O}(\log n)$ phases the smallest tentative distance in the queue has increased by at least Δ whp. This is a simple consequence of the observation that in a graph with maximum degree d and random edge weights there are no simple paths of $\Omega(\log n)$ edges and total weight at most $1/d$ whp [18]. Hence, each bucket is expanded during at most $\mathcal{O}(\log n)$ subsequent phases until it finally remains empty whp. Finding the next bucket index for deletion is done in a sequential fashion, i.e., testing k buckets takes k phases. Thus, for maximum shortest path weight $\mathcal{L}$, at least $\mathcal{L} \cdot d$ phases and at most $\mathcal{O}(\mathcal{L} \cdot d \cdot \log n)$ phases are required whp.

Based on the Δ-stepping algorithm sketched above, a sequential SSSP algorithm with average-case running time $\mathcal{O}(n+m)$ was developed [17]. Starting with buckets of width $\Delta = 1$, it builds a bucket hierarchy in the following way: before the algorithm removes all nodes from the current bucket B_{cur} of width Δ_{cur} it checks the maximum node degree d^* in B_{cur}. If $\Delta_{\mathrm{cur}} > 1/d^*$ then it splits B_{cur} into smaller buckets of size $2^{-\lceil \log_2 d^* \rceil}$ each and continues with the leftmost non-empty bucket among those just generated. Thus, on the one hand, the average-case number of re-insertions and re-relaxations can be bounded by $\mathcal{O}(n+m)$ since nodes with high degree are exclusively expanded from buckets with sufficiently small widths; on the other hand, the number of buckets is bounded by $\mathcal{O}(n+m)$, as well, independent of the maximum shortest path weight $\mathcal{L}$. However, even though the nodes within a bucket can still be expanded in parallel, $\Omega(\mathcal{L} + \max_{v \in V} \mathrm{degree}(v))$ phases are required just to visit all buckets.

3 Degree Heaps

In the following we will use the idea of an adaptive step-width for an alternative data structure that avoids scanning lots of small distance intervals at little extra cost. Our new label-correcting algorithm (called Parallel Degree SSSP) uses a number of sequential priority queues and a simple method to compute an appropriate current step width. Opposite to the algorithm of [17] changing the step-width does not require restructuring of the priority queues themselves.

For a graph with n nodes we define a *sequential Degree Heap* D to be a collection of $h = \lceil \log_2 n \rceil$ *relaxed heaps* $D_1, \ldots, D_h$ such that D_i is in charge of tentative distances for nodes having in-degree in $[2^{i-1}+1, 2^i]$. A relaxed heap allows insertions and decrease_key operations in worst-case constant time, deletions of the minimum in worst-case logarithmic time [9]. There is no heap for nodes with degree zero as they are never reached in the SSSP algorithm anyway. Let M_i be the smallest tentative distance in D_i ($M_i = \infty$ for empty D_i) and let $M = \min_i M_i$. Then we compute

$$\Delta_{\max} := \min_i \{\max\{2^{-i-1}, M_i - M\}\}. \tag{1}$$

Subsequently, for each D_i, the SSSP algorithm removes all nodes $v \in D_i$ satisfying $\text{tent}(v) < M + \Delta_{\max}$.

Property 1 *Up to a multiplicative factor of two, $\Delta_{\max}$ is maximal such that for any queued node v with $\text{tent}(v) < M + \Delta_{\max}$, we have $\text{degree}(v) \leq 1/(2 \cdot \Delta_{\max})$.*

Proof: Consider the index i^* that minimizes (1), i.e., $\Delta_{\max} = \max\{2^{-i^*-1}, M_{i^*} - M\} < \infty$. If $M_{i^*} - M > 2^{-i^*-1}$, then $\Delta_{\max}$ was just chosen small enough in order not to remove any node from D_{i^*} for the current phase. Taking another step-width $\Delta \geq 2 \cdot \Delta_{\max} > 2^{-i^*}$ there is a node $v \in D_{i^*}$ having degree at least $2^{i^*-1} + 1$ and $\text{tent}(v) < M + \Delta$, hence $\text{degree}(v) > 1/(2 \cdot \Delta)$. Similarly, if $M_{i^*} - M \leq 2^{-i^*-1}$, then there is already a node $v \in D_{i^*}$ having degree at least $2^{i^*-1} + 1$ and $\text{tent}(v) < M + 2^{-i^*-1}$. Enlarging $\Delta_{\max}$ by a factor of two leads to the same kind of contradiction. □

Corollary 1 *Nodes of degree d are removed using step-width at most $2^{-\lceil \log_2 d \rceil - 1}$.*

Parallel Degree Heaps are obtained by having a sequential Degree Heap D^j for each processor PU_j. Again, a random mapping π is used to distribute the nodes over the sequential Degree Heaps, i.e., node v with in-degree d, $2^{i-1} + 1 \leq d \leq 2^i$, is kept in the i-th heap of $PU_{\pi(v)}$, $D_i^{\pi(v)}$. The step-width computation is adapted in the obvious way by setting $M_i = \min_j M_i^j$ where M_i^j denotes the smallest tentative distance in the i-th heap of PU_j. The minimum of a relaxed heap can be determined in $\mathcal{O}(\log n)$ time, hence each PU can compute its local minima in $\mathcal{O}(\log^2 n)$ time. After that, the global minima M_i and M can be computed by standard pipelined tree-reductions in $\mathcal{O}(\log n)$ time. Finally, the new largest possible step-width is computed as the minimum of $\lceil \log_2 n \rceil$ expressions.

Lemma 2 *Each step-width computation for Parallel Degree Heaps with $P \leq n$ processors can be performed in $\mathcal{O}(\log^2 n)$ time and $\mathcal{O}(P \cdot \log^2 n)$ work.*

4 Average-Case Analysis of Parallel Degree Heaps SSSP

We exploit the correlation between the maximum degree among the nodes concurrently deleted in a phase and the applied step-width to show:

Lemma 3 *Using Parallel Degree Heaps SSSP for graphs with random edge weights uniformly drawn from $[0, 1]$, each node is re-inserted at most $\mathcal{O}(1)$ times on the average.*

Proof: Consider an arbitrary node v_0 with in-degree d_0. Let M be the minimum of all tentative distances for queued nodes in the Degree Heaps when v_0 is removed for the first time. By then, $\text{tent}(v_0) \leq M + 2^{-\lceil \log_2 d_0 \rceil - 1}$ (Corollary 1). As in the proof of Lemma 1, re-insertions of v_0 can be mapped to appropriate paths $P = \langle v_j, \ldots, v_0 \rangle$ of total weight at most $2^{-\lceil \log_2 d_0 \rceil - 1}$ such that the nodes $v_j, \ldots, v_0$ are subsequently removed from the Degree Heaps and the relaxation of their edges lead to an improvement for $\text{tent}(v_0)$.

Let d_i be the in-degree of node v_i. We can confine our analysis to *degree-weight balanced* paths $\langle v_j, \ldots, v_0 \rangle$ where $c(v_{i+1}, v_i) \leq 2^{-\lceil \log_2 d_i \rceil - 1}$. In order to see this, let k be the smallest index such that $c(v_{k+1}, v_k) > 2^{-\lceil \log_2 d_k \rceil - 1}$ for the path P above. The value of $\text{tent}(v_k)$ is already correct up to at most $2^{-\lceil \log_2 d_k \rceil - 1}$ when v_k is removed for the first time. Either, $\text{dist}(v_{k+1}) < \text{dist}(v_k) - 2^{-\lceil \log_2 d_k \rceil - 1}$, then v_{k+1} must have been settled before v_k was removed, and the edge (v_{k+1}, v_k) will never be re-relaxed again to re-insert v_k (and v_0 in the end). Or $\text{dist}(v_{k+1}) \geq \text{dist}(v_k) - 2^{-\lceil \log_2 d_k \rceil - 1}$, but then after the first removal of v_k no improvement of $\text{tent}(v_k)$ can be obtained via a relaxation of (v_{k+1}, v_k). Hence, re-insertions for v_k that could trigger re-insertions of v_0 require edges into v_k of weight less than $2^{-\lceil \log_2 d_k \rceil - 1}$.

Therefore, in order to bound the number of re-insertions for node v_0 it is sufficient to consider all sub-paths $\langle v_l, \ldots, v_0 \rangle$ into v_0 that are degree-weight balanced and have total weight at most $2^{-\lceil \log_2 d_0 \rceil - 1}$: The expected number of edges with weight at most $\min\{2^{-\lceil \log_2 d_i \rceil - 1}, 2^{-\lceil \log_2 d_0 \rceil - 1}\}$ into node v_i is bounded by $1/2$. Therefore, using elementary results of branching processes [2,13] the expected number of relevant degree-weight balanced paths having l edges can be bounded by $(1/2)^l$. Thus, the expected number of re-insertions for v_0 can be bounded by $\mathcal{O}(\sum_{l \geq 1}(1/2)^l) = \mathcal{O}(1)$. □

Theorem 1 *For graphs with random edge weights uniformly drawn from $[0,1]$, Parallel Degree Heap SSSP needs $r = \mathcal{O}(\min_i \{2^i \cdot \mathcal{L} \cdot \log n + |V_i|\})$ phases on the average where $\mathcal{L}$ denotes the maximum shortest path weight and $|V_i|$ is the number of graph vertices with in-degree at least 2^i. On a CRCW PRAM it can be implemented in $\mathcal{O}(r \cdot \log^2 n)$ time and $\mathcal{O}(n \cdot \log n + m)$ work on the average.*

Proof: We fix some arbitrary integer $x \geq 0$ and consider B-phases having step-width bigger or equal $\Delta_x := 2^{-x-1}$ and S-phases having step-width smaller than Δ_x. By Lemma 3, each node is re-inserted $\mathcal{O}(1)$ times on average, and by Property 1, S-phases do only occur when a node of in-degree at least $2^x + 1$ is deleted. Hence, the expected number of S-phases is bounded by $\mathcal{O}(|V_x|)$. After $\mathcal{O}(\log n)$ B-phases the smallest tentative distance among all queued nodes, M, has increased by Δ_x whp ([18], intermediate S-phases can only increase M). Therefore, the total number of B-phases is bounded by $\mathcal{O}(\frac{\mathcal{L} \cdot \log n}{\Delta_x}) = \mathcal{O}(2^x \cdot \mathcal{L} \cdot \log n)$ whp. Altogether we need $\mathcal{O}(2^x \cdot \mathcal{L} \cdot \log n + |V_x|)$ phases on average. Since we are free to choose x, the average-case bound for all phases can be improved to $\mathcal{O}(\min_i \{2^i \cdot \mathcal{L} \cdot \log n + |V_i|\})$.

For the PRAM algorithm we use the load-balancing approach with semi-sorting from [19] where buckets are replaced by Degree Heaps: if r phases are needed on the average then up to $\Theta(\frac{n}{r \cdot \log n})$ sequential Degree Heaps can be used in a load-balanced way. Hence, determining a new step-width takes $\mathcal{O}(\log^2 n)$ time and $\mathcal{O}(\frac{n \cdot \log n}{r})$ work for each phase by Lemma 2. Since node deletions in a Sequential Degree Heap require $\mathcal{O}(\log n)$ time (as compared to $\mathcal{O}(1)$ time for buckets), the algorithm needs altogether $\mathcal{O}(r \cdot \log^2 n)$ time and $\mathcal{O}(n \cdot \log n + m)$ work on the average. □

5 Parallel Label-Setting on Arbitrary Graphs

In this section we sketch how to improve the analysis of a previous parallel label-setting algorithm [7] that is also based on heaps. It applies an adaptive node-removal criterion, too: let $T = \min\{\text{tent}(u) + c(u,z) : u$ is queued and $(u,z) \in E\}$. The OUT-approach removes all queued nodes v with $\text{tent}(v) \leq T$ in one phase since these nodes cannot lead to further distance reductions.

The analysis for *random* graphs and random edge weights given in [7] is based on two observations: (1) random graphs are expanders, i.e., the priority queue is well-filled during most phases. (2) For q queued nodes, each of which having expected degree d, there is a constant probability that the $\sqrt{q/d}$ queued nodes with smallest tentative distance can be concurrently removed in one phase: Let $v_1, v_2, \ldots, v_q$ be the queued nodes in order of increasing tentative distances, and let T' be the value of T in the previous phase. The distance labels $\text{tent}(v_i)$ are random variables in $[T', T'+1]$. Their values are independent and their distributions are biased towards smaller values since they constitute the minimum of potentially many incoming path weights. The value of $\text{tent}(v_r)$ is therefore less than r/q with constant probability for arbitrary r, $1 \leq r \leq q$. The number of edges out of $v_1, \ldots, v_r$ is $\mathcal{O}(d \cdot r)$ with constant probability. Opposite to the tentative distances of queued nodes, the edge weights are not biased towards smaller values. Therefore, the shortest of these edges has length about $\frac{1}{rd}$. We remove $v_1, \ldots, v_r$ from the queue if $\text{tent}(v_r)$ is smaller than the length of the shortest edge out of $v_1, \ldots, v_r$. This is the case (with constant probability) if $r/q \leq \frac{1}{rd}$ or $r \leq \sqrt{q/d}$.

An improved analysis for arbitrary graphs with random edge weights can be based on "active edges" where all edges of a queued node are active. By the same argument as before, for k active edges, there is a constant probability that $\Omega(\sqrt{k})$ of them are concurrently removed in a single phase. Additionally, we use that $T - T' \geq \sqrt{1/k}$ with constant probability. Note that the smallest tentative distance kept in the queue, M, increases by the same amount as T. Therefore, looking at a number of consecutive phases, either M will significantly increase or many edges will be removed. Altogether, for maximum shortest path weight $\mathcal{L}$ there are at most $\mathcal{O}(\sqrt{\mathcal{L} \cdot m})$ phases that remove at least $\Omega(\sqrt{m/\mathcal{L}})$ edges each. For any of the other phases, there is a constant probability that T is increased by $\Omega(\sqrt{\mathcal{L}/m})$. However, there cannot be more than $\mathcal{O}(\sqrt{\mathcal{L} \cdot m})$ such phases because M will not exceed $\mathcal{L}$. Thus, on the average there are $\mathcal{O}(\sqrt{\mathcal{L} \cdot m})$ phases in total.

Using the OUT-approach together with the load-balancing scheme of [19], SSSP can be solved in $\mathcal{O}(\sqrt{\mathcal{L} \cdot m} \cdot \log^3 n)$ average-case time and $\mathcal{O}(n \cdot \log n + m)$ work. Hence, label-correcting SSSP with Parallel Degree Heaps is faster than the OUT-approach unless the graph contains $\Omega(\sqrt{\mathcal{L} \cdot m})$ nodes of in-degree $\Omega(\sqrt{m/\mathcal{L}})$. In that case, the average-case time of both algorithms is bounded by $\mathcal{O}(\sqrt{\mathcal{L} \cdot m} \cdot \log^3 n)$. In fact, if $\mathcal{L} \cdot m$ is very big, both algorithms require at most n phases since each phase settles at least one node whereas the Δ-stepping may take $\Omega(n^2)$ phases. On the other hand, disregarding logarithmic factors, the OUT-approach (and therefore also the Parallel Degree Heap SSSP) is faster than the Δ-stepping whenever $d^2 \cdot \mathcal{L} > m$.

6 Performance on Power Law Graphs

Many massive graphs such as the WWW graph and telephone call graphs share universal characteristics which can be described by the so-called "power law": the number of nodes, y, of a given in-degree x is proportional to $x^{-\beta}$ for some constant $\beta > 0$. For most massive graphs, $\beta > 2$. Independently, Kumar et. al. [15] and Babarasi et. al. [3] reported $\beta \approx 2.1$ for the in-degrees of the WWW graph, and the same value was estimated for telephone call graphs [1].

Graph models where the targets of edges are drawn *randomly* and the *expected* number of nodes for a certain node degree follow a power-law are widely considered to be appropriate models of real massive graphs like the WWW. For $\beta > 2$, the diameter of such graphs was shown to be $\mathcal{O}(\log n)$ whp [16]. Furthermore, for $\beta \geq 2$, the expected maximum node degree is $\Theta(n^{1/\beta})$ and $m = \mathcal{O}(n)$. Hence, assuming independent random edge weights uniformly distributed in $[0, 1]$, SSSP on WWW-like graphs with Δ-stepping requires about $\mathcal{O}(n^{1/2.1} \cdot \log^2 n) = \mathcal{O}(n^{0.48})$ time and linear work on average. The average-case execution time of the OUT-approach is about the same, $\mathcal{O}(n^{0.5} \cdot \text{polylog}(n))$.

The expected number of nodes having in-degree at least d^* is bounded by $\mathcal{O}(n \cdot \sum_{x \geq d^*} x^{-\beta})$ which for constant $\beta \geq 2$ and arbitrary $d^* \geq \beta$ can be approximated by $\mathcal{O}(n \cdot \int_{d^*}^{\infty} x^{-\beta} dx) = \mathcal{O}(n \cdot d^{*-\beta-1})$. Thus, taking $\beta = 2.1$ and $d^* = n^{10/41}$ one expects $\mathcal{O}(n \cdot n^{-3.1 \cdot 10/41}) = \mathcal{O}(n^{10/41})$ nodes of in-degree at least d^*. Therefore, with Parallel Degree Heaps, the average-case time for SSSP on WWW-like graphs drops to $\mathcal{O}(\log^2 n \cdot (n^{10/41} \cdot \log n \cdot \log n + n^{10/41})) = o(n^{1/4})$ using $\mathcal{O}(n \cdot \log n + m)$ work.

7 Conclusions

We have given a new parallel label-correcting SSSP approach together with a data structure that efficiently supports the required operations. The provable average-case performance depends on the node degree distribution. Improved running times while retaining work-efficiency could be shown for practically important inputs with unbalanced node degrees like the WWW graph. However, for the future it would be desirable to solve the SSSP on Web-like graphs in polylogarithmic time and $\mathcal{O}(n \cdot \log n + m)$ work. Furthermore, any work-efficient algorithm with sublinear running time that is independent of the diameter would be of great interest.

References

1. W. Aiello, F. Chung, and L. Lu. A random graph model for massive graphs. In *Proc. 32nd Annual ACM Symposium on Theory of Computing*, pages 171–180. ACM, 2000.
2. K. B. Athreya and P. Ney. *Branching Processes*. Springer, 1972.
3. A. Barabasi and R. Albert. Emergence of scaling in random networks. *Science*, 286:509–512, 1999.
4. B. Bollobás. *Random Graphs*. Academic Press, 1985.
5. G. S. Brodal, J. L. Träff, and C. D. Zaroliagis. A parallel priority queue with constant time operations. *Journal of Parallel and Distributed Computing*, 49(1):4–21, 1998.
6. E. Cohen. Using selective path-doubling for parallel shortest-path computations. *Journal of Algorithms*, 22(1):30–56, January 1997.
7. A. Crauser, K. Mehlhorn, U. Meyer, and P. Sanders. A parallelization of Dijkstra's shortest path algorithm. In *23rd Symp. on Mathematical Foundations of Computer Science*, volume 1450 of *LNCS*, pages 722–731. Springer, 1998.
8. E. W. Dijkstra. A note on two problems in connexion with graphs. *Num. Math.*, 1:269–271, 1959.
9. J. R. Driscoll, H. N. Gabow, R. Shrairman, and R. E. Tarjan. Relaxed heaps: An alternative to fibonacci heaps with applications to parallel computation. *Communications of the ACM*, 31, 1988.
10. S. Fortune and J. Wyllie. Parallelism in random access memories. In *Proc. 10th Symp. on the Theory of Computing*, pages 114–118. ACM, 1978.
11. M. L. Fredman and R. E. Tarjan. Fibonacci heaps and their uses in improved network optimization algorithms. *Journal of the ACM*, 34:596–615, 1987.
12. Y. Han, V. Pan, and J. Reif. Efficient parallel algorithms for computing all pair shortest paths in directed graphs. *Algorithmica*, 17(4):399–415, 1997.
13. T. Harris. *The Theory of Branching Processes*. Springer, 1963.
14. P. Klein and S. Subramanian. A randomized parallel algorithm for single-source shortest paths. *Journal of Algorithms*, 25(2):205–220, November 1997.
15. R. Kumar, P. Raghavan, S. Rajagopalan, and A. Tomkins. Trawling the web for emerging cyber-communities. In *Proc. 8th International World-Wide Web Conference*, 1999.
16. L. Lu. The diameter of random massive graphs. In *Proc. 12th Annual Symposium on Discrete Algorithms*, pages 912–921. ACM–SIAM, 2001.
17. U. Meyer. Single-source shortest-paths on arbitrary directed graphs in linear average-case time. In *Proc. 12th Annual Symposium on Discrete Algorithms*, pages 797–806. ACM–SIAM, 2001.
18. U. Meyer and P. Sanders. Δ-stepping: A parallel shortest path algorithm. In *6th European Symposium on Algorithms (ESA)*, volume 1461 of *LNCS*, pages 393–404. Springer, 1998.
19. U. Meyer and P. Sanders. Parallel shortest path for arbitrary graphs. In *Proc. Euro-Par 2000 Parallel Processing*, volume 1900 of *LNCS*, pages 461–470. Springer, 2000.
20. H. Shi and T. H. Spencer. Time–work tradeoffs of the single-source shortest paths problem. *Journal of Algorithms*, 30(1):19–32, 1999.

Efficient Synchronization of Asynchronous Processes

Sandeep Lodha[1], Punit Chandra[2], Ajay Kshemkalyani[2], and Mayank Rawat[2]

[1] Riverstone Networks Inc.
Santa Clara, CA 95054, USA.
[2] EECS Department, University of Illinois at Chicago
Chicago, IL 60607-7053, USA.

Abstract. Concurrent programming languages including CSP and Ada use synchronous message-passing to define communication between a pair of asynchronous processes. This paper presents an efficient way to synchronize these processes by improving on Bagrodia's algorithm that provides binary rendezvous. Simulation results are presented to show the better performance of the optimized algorithm for two cases - the case where the interaction set is composed of all possible pairs and the case where the set of next allowable interactions is of cardinality one. For the latter, the optimized algorithm also improves upon the best case delay for synchronization. The client-server computing model, the producer-consumer interaction, and interaction between processes executing parallelized tasks represent some broad classes of computations which can leverage the proposed improvements.

1 Introduction

Concurrent programming languages including CSP [6] and Ada [1] use synchronous message-passing to define communication between a pair of asynchronous processes. Although this synchronous style of programming compromises the possible concurrency in the computation, it offers simplicity in program design and verification. The synchronous programming style is also known as binary rendezvous which is a special case of multiway rendezvous, also known as the barrier or committee coordination problem [5].

The generalized alternate command of CSP allows a process to select any one of several binary rendezvous, identified by the *interaction set*, for the next interaction or rendezvous. Several algorithms implement this rendezvous [3,8,7,9]. Buckley and Silberschatz [4] presented four criteria to determine the "effectiveness" of algorithms that implement this construct. Using these criteria, they pointed out some major drawbacks of previously published algorithms and presented an algorithm that meets the criteria. Bagrodia [2] came up with an algorithm that was simpler and more efficient than [4]. This paper describes an algorithm that improves upon the message overhead of Bagrodia's algorithm, and presents simulation results for the same. Section 2 describes the proposed enhancements. Section 3 gives the results of the simulation. Section 4 concludes.

2 Bagrodia's Algorithm and Proposed Enhancements

2.1 Bagrodia's Algorithm

Bagrodia's algorithm associates a unique token with each synchronization, also known as interaction. The token contains the ProcessIDs of the two processes involved in the interaction. When some process P_i becomes $IDLE$, it determines if an interaction (P_i, P_j) with process P_j can be executed by requesting that interaction. An $IDLE$ process requests interactions from its interaction-set in increasing order of priority. A process may request only those interactions for which it possesses the corresponding token. When P_i requests an interaction (P_i, P_j), it sends the corresponding token to P_j. A process may request at most one interaction at any time.

On receiving a token, a process P_j may either commit to the corresponding interaction, refuse to do so, or delay its response. If P_j is $IDLE$, it commits to the interaction. A process commits to an interaction by sending the token back to the requesting process. On the other hand, if P_j is $ACTIVE$, it refuses the interaction. A process refuses an interaction by capturing the token and sending a $CANCEL$ message to the requesting process. This implies that the process that last refused an interaction has the responsibility to initiate the next request for the interaction. A process that has requested an interaction but has not received a response to its request is a REQ process. A REQ process may receive (zero or more) requests for other interactions, before receiving a response to its own request. A REQ process P_j that receives a token for another interaction E_k delays the request E_k if priority of E_k is more than that of the interaction P_j is currently requesting, otherwise it refuses the interaction and sends a $CANCEL$ message. This prevents deadlocks in the system. If a REQ process P_i delays an interaction, the algorithm guarantees that P_i will either commit to its requested interaction or to the delayed interaction. Thus, it is only necessary for a process to delay at most one interaction. Tokens received by a REQ process that has delayed an interaction can immediately be refused by the process, irrespective of the relative priority of the two interactions.

2.2 Proposed Enhancements

We observe the following two drawbacks of Bagrodia's algorithm that cause some inefficiencies, and propose improvements to overcome them.

- First, when a process that is committed to an interaction or is ACTIVE receives a token from another process, it sends a CANCEL to that process and later bears the responsibility of initiating the interaction with that process. This leads to a total of four messages to set up the interaction. There is a wide range of applications for which the interaction set of at least one of the processes participating in an interaction is one. It is unnecessary to send a CANCEL to such a process and later try to reestablish the interaction. The proposed improvement is that instead of sending the CANCEL, the token requesting the interaction can be queued up and later responded to, thereby cutting down on the message overhead.

Some classes of applications that have an interaction-set size of one are described here. The producer-consumer problem is one example where the producer's interaction-set size is one. The producer needs to interact only with the buffer-process. So once the producer is ready with the data, it cannot proceed unless it delivers the data to the buffer-process. Even if the buffer-process sends a CANCEL message to the producer, the producer cannot proceed. In such cases, we can avoid CANCEL messages by making the producer block on the buffer-process. Client-server applications form another class where this proposed improvement is useful. A client in the client-server model has to interact only with the server; thus all clients have an interaction-set size of one. A client that wants to synchronize (interact) with the server cannot proceed unless synchronized. In such applications, we can avoid CANCEL messages by making clients block on the server. Applications that have a high degree of parallelism form another class where the proposed improvement is particularly useful. All worker processes have to interact only with the master process. Thus all worker processes have an interaction-set size of one. Divide-and-conquer class of problems is an example where the worker processes, when done with the assigned computation, cannot proceed unless synchronized with the central process. In such applications, one can avoid CANCEL messages by making worker processes block on the central process.

– The second drawback of Bagrodia's algorithm is that a process that is ready to synchronize cannot initiate the synchronization if it does not have the token. If both processes involved in an interaction have a token each, then this process can initiate the interaction. Its token could then be kept pending at the other end until that process was ready to perform the interaction, at which time, only a single message transmission overhead would be incurred to complete the interaction setup. This scheme is the proposed enhancement. This scheme also increases concurrency in the system when both processes become ready to interact at the same physical time, and reduces the best case delay for synchronization, as explained below. Thus, each interaction can be assigned two tokens, one for each partner.

The proposed algorithm is an extension to Bagrodia's algorithm and addresses the aforementioned drawbacks. In the proposed algorithm, there are either two tokens or a unique token for each interaction, depending on the interaction-set size. There is a unique token for interactions between P_i and P_j if both P_i and P_j have an interaction-set size of more than one. This avoids the danger of extra CANCEL messages. For a pair of processes P_i and P_j such that one of the processes, say P_i (P_i could be the client/worker/producer process in the application), has an interaction-set size of one (P_i always interacts with P_j), there is either one token or two tokens for this interaction. It is up to the application process to decide. The number of messages is independent of the number of tokens in this case. For interactions between processes P_i and P_j, which have two tokens – one with P_i, the other with P_j – either P_i or P_j can send a REQUEST carrying the correct token to the other. Both processes can send their REQUESTs concurrently. This increases concurrency in the system. If P_i sends a REQUEST to P_j and receives a concurrent REQUEST from P_j, then this REQUEST from P_j acts as a REPLY. On $P'_j s$ side, $P'_i s$ REQUEST serves as a REPLY. This improves the best case delay for synchronization (from round-trip delay to one-way delay).

As mentioned above, in Bagrodia's algorithm, an $ACTIVE$ process P_j always refuses the interaction. In the proposed algorithm, a REQUEST from process P_i, where P_i interacts only with P_j, is not refused. Instead, this request is kept in the $DelaySet_j$ of P_j. P_i should have a way to let P_j know that P_i wants to block on P_j (P_j is the only process that P_i interacts with). So in the proposed algorithm, we have an extra bit in the token, called $BlockFlag$, for this purpose. P_i sets it to $true$ if it wants to block on P_j, else it is $false$. This saves two messages. In the proposed algorithm, a CANCEL message is sent either to prevent a deadlock in the system or when the requesting process does not want to block.

3 Results

To demonstrate the efficiency of the optimized algorithm, we simulated both Bagrodia's algorithm (henceforth called BA) and the optimized BA. We compared the average number of messages of the optimized BA and the BA algorithms. The experiments were conducted using Intel Pentium III 866MHz computers with 128 Mb SDRAM, running RedHat Linux, with the algorithms implemented using C++.

The simulation model explored two cases - the first was a client-server type of communication pattern where clients had interaction set size of one, while the other had interactions between all pairs of processes (completely connected graph). The tokens were distributed randomly for both the cases in BA.

In the experiments, the message transfer time was assumed to be negligible. Thus, we abstracted away network latency. The active time - the time for which the process is in $ACTIVE$ state - was a configurable parameter. For a given number of processes, the simulation was repeated 10 times. The variance in the number of messages was negligible (see full paper for details).

Client-server case: As expected, the optimized BA gives better results. The mean number of messages per interaction for BA is nearly 3.06 while it is 2 for the optimized BA. So in the case of the client-server architecture, optimized BA is 35% more efficient than BA (Figure 1). The performance of the optimized BA is independent of the active time.

Fully connected case: The average number of messages for both BA and optimized BA varies with the active time parameter; the graph (Figure 2) shows the results for 10,000 clock ticks. The optimized algorithm shows only a slight improvement over Bagrodia's algorithm. This is largely because as the interactions complete, the system's communication pattern gradually moves towards a client-server system (where the size of the interaction set of clients is one), for

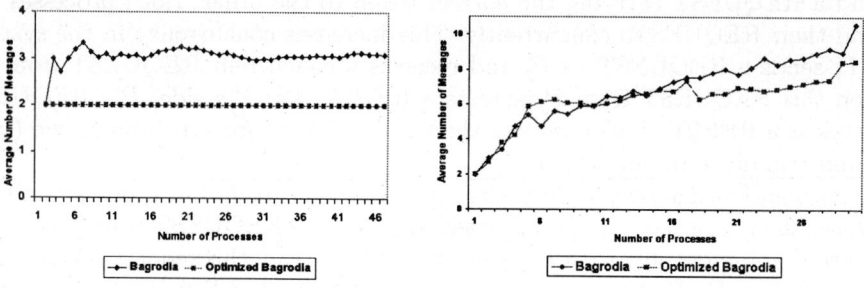

Fig. 1. The client-server case **Fig. 2.** The fully connected case

which the optimized BA algorithm has a lower message overhead. Furthermore, it appears that as the system size increases, the optimized BA seems to behave increasingly better than BA.

4 Concluding Remarks

Concurrent programming languages such as CSP and Ada use synchronous message-passing to define communication between a pair of asynchronous processes. We presented an efficient way to synchronize processes by improving on Bagrodia's algorithm which is one of the best known algorithms to implement synchronous communication between asynchronous processes. Simulation results showed that the optimized BA is always more efficient than BA. An efficiency gain of nearly 35% was achieved for a wide class of applications in which the set of next allowable interactions is of cardinality one.

Acknowledgements

This work was supported by the U.S. National Science Foundation grants CCR-9875617 and EIA-9871345.

References

1. Ada 95 Reference Manual (RM) Version 6.0: Intermetrics, Inc., January 1995. (URL http://lglwww.epfl.ch/Ada/rm95)
2. R. Bagrodia, Synchronization of asynchronous processes in CSP, *ACM TOPLAS*, 11(4):585-597, 1989.
3. A. Bernstein, Output guards and nondeterminism in communicating sequential processes, *ACM TOPLAS*, 2(2):234-238, April 1980.
4. G. Buckley, A, Silberschatz, An effective implementation of the generalized input-output construct of CSP, *ACM TOPLAS*, 5(2):223-235, April 1983.

5. M. Chandy, J. Misra, *Parallel Program Design: A Foundation*, Addison-Wesley, 1978.
6. C. A. R. Hoare, Communication sequential processes, *CACM*, 21(8):666-677, Aug. 1978.
7. F. Schneider, Synchronization in distributed processes, *ACM TOPLAS*, 4(2): 125-148, April 1982.
8. J. Schwarz, Distributed synchronization of communicating sequential processes, *Tech. Report, University of Edinburgh,* July 1978.
9. Van de Snepscheut, Synchronous communication between asynchronous components, *Information Processing Letters*, 13(3): 127-130, Dec. 1981.

Topic 07
Applications on High-Performance Computers

Yoichi Muraoka, Randall Bramley, David F. Snelling, and Harry Wijshoff

Topic Chairpersons

Applications of High-Performance Computers spans a large intellectual area and now includes all the traditional application science and engineering fields. The end goal of all high performance computing research is eventually to support applications, but those applications have traditionally had a strong feedback effect on computer architecture, hardware design, and systems.

This year nine papers were submitted, in areas ranging from weather simulation and prediction to new areas such as bioinformatics. Given the potentially broad spread of topics, what distinguishes the papers accepted for this year's conference is the careful bridging between the application's algorithmic needs and the underlying high performance computing system. Increasingly the efforts of computer architects, compiler writers, software engineers, and software library developers are helping make high performance computing a staple for scientists and engineers. But the papers in this topic session passed the stringent requirement that they not just use high performance techniques, but specifically address how to map the application to the underlying hardware and software systems.

In addition to the traditional areas of high-speed computation and the development of algorithms amenable to it, one theme that has become crucial in recent years is data-intensive computing: how to handle the large volumes of data which scientific and engineering instruments produce, and how to store it. This year's selection of papers also provides valuable insight into the data management issues.

Scanning Biosequence Databases on a Hybrid Parallel Architecture targets an area of increasing importance in high-performance computing, bioinformatics. Scanning sequence databases is possibly the prototypical computational problem in that area, made even more important by the growth of both breadth and depth of genetic database coverage. This paper is an outstanding example of bridging the application area and the underlying hardware and architecture, introducing a unique cluster system that uses a standard PC cluster running Linux, each augmented with a systolic array board. The authors then show how to map the sequence comparison algorithm to the resulting hybrid architecture.

A Parallel Computation of Power System Equations is a good example of the ability to bridge the needs of an application and the underlying hardware and software. Clusters of PCs such as Beowulf systems are increasingly the choice of universities and research laboratories because of their price/performance ratio. Many of these systems use Pentium processors which have SSE instructions — which are essentially vector instructions. This paper shows how to use those effectively in the context of linear system solvers.

Among the most data-intensive computing tasks currently faced by high speed computing is the handling of the flood of data that will result when the Large Hadron Collider at CERN is scheduled to come on-line in 2005. As *Level-3 Trigger for a Heavy Ion Experiment at LHC* describes, a single experiment will produce 15 GBytes/second of data - more than can or should be transferred to permanent storage since only a small number of "events" from the detectors are of interest to physicists. The paper defines the software and hardware architecture being built to recognize interesting patterns in this data flood, and the integration of real-time compression methods on the saved data. Referees agreed that the techniques and ideas used on this problem may well be useful for other applications in other areas with real-time, irreproducible data coming from valuable scientific instruments.

In addition to the real-time acquisition of large volumes of data from instruments, high performance computing simulations produce data which needs to be stored. Even when scientists are only interested in the final results, the increasing use of large scale and distributed platforms makes checkpointing and fault tolerance crucial for reliable computations. *Experiences in Using MPI-IO on Top of GPFS for the IFS Weather Forecast Code* details how to use the MPI-IO standard with IBM's General Parallel File system to store intermediate steps. This is done in the context of the European Centre' for Medium-Range Weather Forecasts' simulation codes which share features common with many emerging parallel applications: hundreds of parallel tasks writing out intermediate time steps every few seconds. This paper provides an understanding of the underlying mechanisms, and timings to help users determine how many nodes should be dedicated to I/O for optimal performance.

In summary, unlike many submitters of papers those in applications areas typically have to satisfy two widely different sets of goals, in furthering both the science in the application area and developing methodologies that constitute high-performance computing research. We thank all of the authors who submitted contributions and succeeded in both goals, and the many referees who helped the committee in spanning the many applications fields represented.

Scanning Biosequence Databases on a Hybrid Parallel Architecture

Bertil Schmidt [1], Heiko Schröder [1] and Manfred Schimmler [2]

[1] School of Computer Engineering, Nanyang Technological University,
Singapore 639798
{asbschmidt,asheiko}@ntu.edu.sg
[2] Institut für Datenverarbeitungsanlagen, TU Braunschweig,
Hans-Sommer-Str. 66, 38106 Braunschweig, Germany
masch@ida.ing.tu-bs.de

Abstract. Molecular biologists frequently scan sequence databases to detect functional similarities between proteins. Even though efficient dynamic programming algorithms exist for the problem, the required scanning time is still very high, and because of the exponential database growth finding fast solutions is of highest importance to research in this area. In this paper we present a new approach to high performance database scanning on a hybrid parallel architecture to gain supercomputer power at low cost. The architecture is built around a PC-cluster linked by a high-speed network and massively parallel processor boards connected to each node. We present the design of a parallel sequence comparison algorithm in order to derive an efficient mapping onto this architecture. This results in a database scanning implementation with significant runtime savings.

1 Introduction

Scanning protein sequence databases is a common and often repeated task in molecular biology. The need for speeding up this treatment comes from the exponential growth of the biosequence banks: every year their size scaled by a factor 1.5 to 2. The scan operation consists in finding similarities between a particular query sequence and all the sequences of a bank. This operation allows biologists to point out sequences sharing common subsequences. From a biological point of view, it leads to identify similar functionality.

Comparison algorithms whose complexities are quadratic with respect to the length of the sequences detect similarities between the query sequence and a subject sequence. One frequently used approach to speed up this time consuming operation is to introduce heuristics in the search algorithms [1]. The main drawback of this solution is that the more time efficient the heuristics, the worse is the quality of the results [11].

Another approach to get high quality results in a short time is to use parallel processing. There are two basic methods of mapping the scanning of protein sequence databases to a parallel processor: one is based on the systolisation of the sequence comparison algorithm, the other is based on the distribution of the computation of pairwise comparisons. Systolic arrays have been proven as a good candidate structure for the first approach [4,12], while supercomputers and networks of workstations are suitable architectures for the second [9]. This paper presents a new approach to high performance sequence database scanning that combines both strategies on a new hybrid parallel architecture, in order to achieve even higher speed.

Hybrid computing is the combination of the SIMD and MIMD paradigm within a parallel architecture, i.e. within the processors of a computer cluster (MIMD) massively parallel processor boards (SIMD) are installed in order to accelerate compute intensive regular tasks. The driving force and motivation behind hybrid computing is the price/performance ratio. Using PC-cluster as in the Beowulf approach is currently the most efficient way to gain supercomputer power. Installing in addition massively parallel processor cards within each PC can further improve the cost/performance ratio significantly. We designed a parallel sequence comparison algorithm in order to fit the characteristics of the hybrid architecture for a protein sequence database scanning application. Its implementation is described on our hybrid system consisting of Systola 1024 cards within the 16 PCs of a PC-cluster connected via a Myrinet switch.

This paper is organised as follows. In Section 2, we introduce the basic sequence comparison algorithm for database scanning and highlight previous work in parallel sequence comparison. Section 3 provides a description of our hybrid architecture. The new parallel algorithm and its mapping onto the hybrid architecture are explained in Section 4. The performance is evaluated and compared to previous implementations in Section 5. Section 6 concludes the paper with an outlook to further research topics.

2 Parallel Sequence Comparison

Surprising relationships have been discovered between protein sequences that have little overall similarity but in which similar subsequences can be found. In that sense, the identification of similar subsequences is probably the most useful and practical method for comparing two sequences. The Smith-Waterman (SW) algorithm [17] finds the most similar subsequences of two sequences (the local alignment) by dynamic programming.

The algorithm compares two sequences by computing a distance that represents the minimal cost of transforming one segment into another. Two elementary operations are used: substitution and insertion/deletion (also called a gap operation). Through series of such elementary operations, any segments can be transformed into any other segment. The smallest number of operations required to change one segment into another can be taken into as the measure of the distance between the segments.

Consider two strings $S1$ and $S2$ of length $l1$ and $l2$. To identify common subsequences, the SW algorithm computes the similarity $H(i,j)$ of two sequences ending at position i and j of the two sequences $S1$ and $S2$. The computation of $H(i,j)$ is given by the following recurrences:

$$H(i,j) = \max\{0, E(i,j), F(i,j), H(i-1,j-1)+Sbt(S1_i,S2_j)\}, \quad 1 \le i \le l1, 1 \le j \le l2$$
$$E(i,j) = \max\{H(i,j-1)-\alpha, E(i,j-1)-\beta\}, \quad 0 \le i \le l1, 1 \le j \le l2$$
$$F(i,j) = \max\{H(i-1,j)-\alpha, E(i-1,j)-\beta\}, \quad 1 \le i \le l1, 1 \le j \le l2$$

where Sbt is a character substitution cost table. Initialisation of these values are given by $H(i,0)=E(i,0)=H(0,j)=F(0,j)=0$ for $0 \le i \le l1$, $0 \le j \le l2$. Multiple gap costs are taken into account as follows: α is the cost of the first gap; β is the cost of the following gaps. Each position of the matrix H is a similarity value. The two segments of $S1$ and $S2$ producing this value can be determined by a backtracking procedure. Fig. 1 illustrates an example

	Ø	A	T	C	T	C	G	T	A	T	G	A	T	G
Ø	0	0	0	0	0	0	0	0	0	0	0	0	0	0
G	0	0	0	0	0	0	2	1	0	0	2	1	0	2
T	0	0	2	1	2	1	1	4	3	2	1	1	3	2
C	0	0	1	4	3	4	3	3	3	2	1	0	2	2
T	0	0	2	3	6	5	4	5	4	5	4	3	2	1
A	0	2	2	2	5	5	4	4	7	6	5	6	5	4
T	0	1	4	3	4	4	4	6	5	9	8	7	8	7
C	0	0	3	6	5	6	5	5	5	8	8	7	7	7
A	0	2	2	5	5	5	5	4	7	7	7	10	9	8
C	0	1	1	4	4	7	6	5	6	6	6	9	9	8

Fig. 1: Example of the SW algorithm to compute the local alignment between two DNA sequences ATCTCGTATGATG and GTCTATCAC. The matrix $H(i,j)$ is shown for the computation with gap costs $\alpha=1$ and $\beta=1$, and a substitution cost of +2 if the characters are identical and −1 otherwise. From the highest score (+10 in the example), a traceback procedure delivers the corresponding alignment (shaded cells), the two subsequences TCGTATGA and TCTATCA

The dynamic programming calculation can be efficiently mapped to a linear array of processing elements. A common mapping is to assign one processing element (PE) to each character of the query string, and then to shift a subject sequence systolically through the linear chain of PEs (see Fig. 2). If $l1$ is the length of the first sequence and $l2$ is the length of the second, the comparison is performed in $l1+l2-1$ steps on $l1$ PEs, instead of $l1 \times l2$ steps required on a sequential processor. In each step the computation for each dynamic programming cell along a single diagonal in Fig. 1 is performed in parallel.

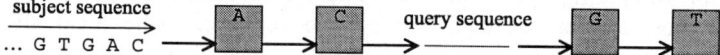

Fig. 2: Sequence comparison on a linear processor array: the query sequence is loaded into the processor array (one character per PE) and a subject sequence flows from left to right through the array. During each step, one elementary matrix computation is performed in each PE

A number of parallel architectures have been developed for sequence analysis. In addition to architectures specifically designed for sequence analysis, existing programmable sequential and parallel architectures have been used for solving sequence problems.

Special-purpose systolic arrays can provide the fastest means of running a particular algorithm with very high PE density. However, they are limited to one single algorithm, and thus cannot supply the flexibility necessary to run a variety of algorithms required analyzing DNA, RNA, and proteins. P-NAC was the first such machine and computed edit distance over a four-character alphabet [10]. More recent examples, better tuned to the needs of computational biology, include BioScan and SAMBA [4,12].

Reconfigurable systems are based on programmable logic such as field-programmable gate arrays (FPGAs), e.g. Splash-2, Biocellerator [5,6], or custom-designed arrays, e.g. MGAP [2]. They are generally slower and have far lower PE densities than special-purpose architectures. They are flexible, but the configuration must be changed for each algorithm, which is generally more complicated than writing new code for a programmable architecture.

Our approach is based on instruction systolic arrays (ISAs). ISAs combine the speed and simplicity of systolic arrays with flexible programmability [7], i.e. they achieve a high performance cost ratio and can at the same time be used for a wide range of applications, e.g. scientific computing, image processing, multimedia video compression, computer tomography, volume visualisation and cryptography [13-16]. The Kestrel design presented in [3] is close to our approach since it is also a programmable fine-grained parallel architecture. Unfortunately, its topology is purely a linear array. This has limited so far its widespread usage to biosequence searches and a computational chemistry application.

3   The Hybrid Architecture

We have built a hybrid MIMD-SIMD architecture from general available components (see Fig. 3). The MIMD part of the system is a cluster of 16 PCs (PentiumII, 450 MHz) running Linux. The machines are connected via a Gigabit-per-second LAN (using Myrinet M2F-PCI32 as network interface cards and Myrinet M2L-SW16 as a switch). For application development we use the MPI library MPICH v. 1.1.2.

For the SIMD part we plugged a Systola 1024 PCI board [8] into each PC. Systola 1024 contains an ISA of size 32×32. The ISA [7] is a mesh-connected processor grid, where the processors are controlled by three streams of control information: instructions, row selectors, and column selectors (see Figure 4). The instructions are input in the upper left corner of the processor array, and from there they move step by step in horizontal and vertical direction through the array. The selectors also move systolically through the array: the row selectors horizontally from left to right, column selectors vertically from top to bottom. Selectors mask the execution of the instructions within the processors, i.e. an instruction is executed if and only if both selector bits, currently in that processor, are equal to one. Otherwise, a no-operation is executed.

Every processor has read and write access to its own memory (32 registers). Besides that, it has a designated *communication register (C-register)* that can also be read by the four neighbour processors. Within each clock phase reading access is always performed before writing access. Thus, two adjacent processors can exchange data within a single clock cycle in which both processors overwrite the contents of their own C-register with the contents of the C-register of its neighbour. This convention avoids read/write conflicts and also creates the possibility to broadcast information across a whole processor row or column with one single instruction. This property can be exploited for an efficient calculation of row broadcasts and row ringshifts, which are the key-operations in the algorithm in Section 4.

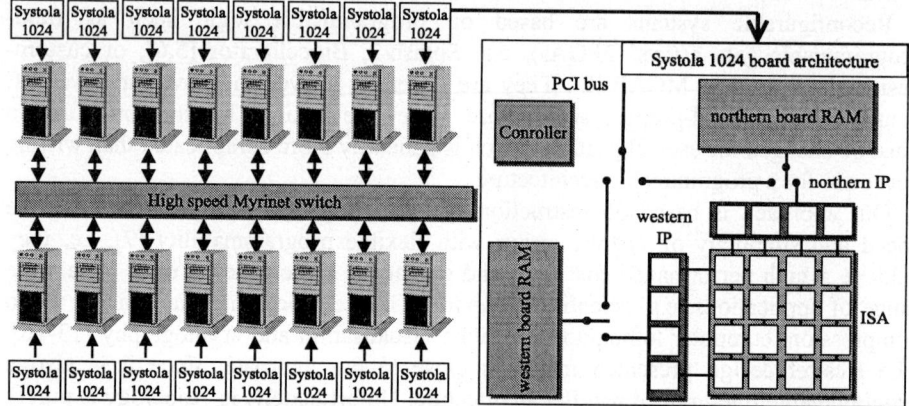

Fig. 3: Architecture of our hybrid system: A cluster of 16 PCs with 16 Systola 1024 PCI boards (left). The data paths in Systola 1024 are depicted on the right

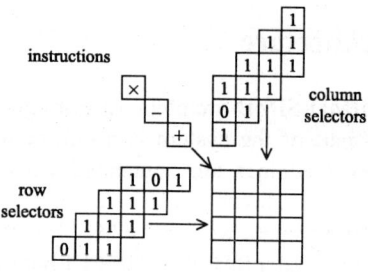

Fig. 4: Control flow in an ISA

For the fast data exchange with the ISA there are rows of intelligent memory units at the northern and western borders of the array called *interface processors* (IPs). Each IP is connected to its adjacent array processor for data transfer in each direction. The IPs have access to an on-board memory, those at the northern interface chips with the northern board RAM, and those of the western chips with the western board RAM. The northern and the western board RAM can communicate bidirectionally with the PC memory over the PCI bus.

At a clock frequency of $f = 50$ MHz and using a word format of $m=16$ bits each (bitserial) processor can execute $f/m = 50/16 \cdot 10^6 = 3.125 \cdot 10^6$ word operations per second. Thus, one board with its 1024 processors performs up to 3.2 GIPS. This adds up to a theoretical peak performance of 51.2 GIPS for 16 boards inside the cluster.

4 Mapping of Sequence Comparison to the Hybrid Architecture

The mapping of the database scanning application on our hybrid computer consists of two forms of parallelism: a fine-grained parallelelisation on Systola 1024 and a coarse-grained on the PC-cluster. While the Systola implementation parallelises the cell computation in the SW algorithm, the cluster implementation splits the database into pieces and distributes them among the PCs using a suitable load balancing strategy. We will now describe both parts in more detail.

Systolic parallelisation of the SW algorithm on a linear array is well-known. In order to extend this algorithm to a mesh-architecture, we take advantage of ISAs capabilities to perform row broadcast and row ringshift efficiently. Since the length of the sequences may vary (several thousands in some cases, however commonly the length is only in hundreds), the computation must also be partitioned on the $N \times N$ ISA. For sake of clarity we firstly assume the processor array size N^2 to be equal to the query sequence length M, i.e. $M=N^2$.

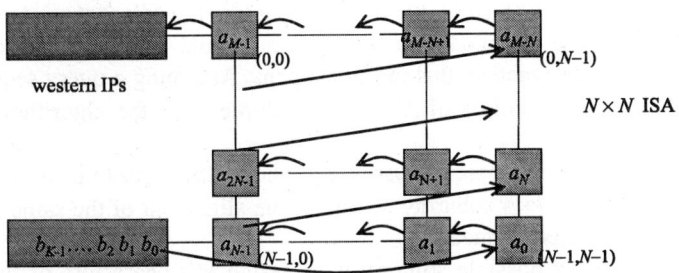

Fig. 5: Data flow for aligning two sequences A and B on an $M=N \times N$ ISA: A is loaded into the ISA one character per PE and B is completely shifted through the array in $M+K-1$ steps. Each character b_j is input from the lower western IP and results are written into the upper western IP

Fig. 5 shows the data flow in the ISA for aligning the sequences $A = a_0a_1...a_{M-1}$ and $B = b_0b_1...b_{K-1}$, where A is the query sequence and B is a subject sequence of the database. As a preprocessing step, symbol a_i, $i = 0,...,M-1$, is loaded into PE (m,n) with $m = N-i$ div $N-1$ and $n = N-i$ mod $N-1$ and B is loaded into the lower western IP. After that the row of the substitution table corresponding to the respective character is loaded into each PE as well as the constants α and β. B is then completely shifted through the array in $M+K-1$ steps as displayed in Fig. 5.

In iteration step k, $1 \leq k \leq M+K-1$, the values $H(i,j)$, $E(i,j)$, and $F(i,j)$ for all i,j with $1 \leq i \leq M$, $1 \leq j \leq K$ and $k=i+j-1$ are computed in parallel in the PEs (m,n) with $m = N-i$ div $N-1$ and $n = N-i$ mod $N-1$. For this calculation PE (m,n) receives the values $H(i-1,j)$, $F(i-1,j)$, and b_j from its eastern neighbour $(m,n+1)$ if $n < N-1$, or from PE $(m+1,0)$ if $n = N-1$ and $m < N-1$, while the values $H(i-1,j-1)$, $H(i,j-1)$, $E(i,j-1)$, a_i, α, β, and $Sbt(a_i,b_j)$ are stored locally. The lower right PE $(N-1,N-1)$ receives b_j in steps j with $0 \leq j \leq K-1$ from the lower western IP and zeros otherwise.

These routing operations can be accomplished in constant time on the ISA. Thus, it takes $M+K-1$ steps to compute the alignment cost of the two sequences with the SW algorithm. However, notice that after the last character of B enters the array, the first character of a new subject sequence can be input for the next iteration step. Thus, all subject sequences of the database can be pipelined with only one step delay between two different sequences. Assuming k sequences of length K and $K=O(M)$, we compute K sequence alignments in time $O(K \cdot M)$ using $O(M)$ processors. As the best sequential algorithm takes $O(K \cdot M^2)$ steps, our parallel implementation achieves maximal efficiency.

Because of the very limited memory of each PE, only the highest score of matrix H is computed on Systola 1024 for each pairwise comparison. Ranking the compared sequences and reconstructing the alignments are carried out by the front end PC. Because this last operation is only performed for very few subject sequences, its computation time is negligible. In our ISA algorithm the maximum computation of the matrix H can be easily incorporated with only a constant time penalty: After each iteration step all PEs compute a new value *max* by taking the maximum of the newly computed *H*-value and the old value of *max* from its neighbouring PE. After the last character of a subject sequence has been processed in PE (0,0), the maximum of matrix H is stored in PE (0,0), which is written into the adjacent western IP.

So far we have assumed a processor array equal in size of the query sequence length ($M=N^2$). In practice, this rarely happens. Assuming a query sequence length of $M = k \cdot N$ with k a multiple of N or N a multiple of k, the algorithm is modified as follows:

1. **$k \leq N$:** In this case we can just replicate the algorithm for a $k \times N$ ISA on an $N \times N$ ISA, i.e. each $k \times N$ subarray computes the alignment of the same query sequence with different subject sequences.

2. **$k > N$:** A possible solution is to assign k/N characters of the sequences to each PE instead of one. However, in this case the memory size has to be sufficient to store k/N rows of the substitution table (20 values per row, since there are 20 different amino acids), i.e. on Systola 1024 it is only possible to assign maximally two characters per PE. Thus, for $k/N > 2$ it is required to split the sequence comparison into $k/(2N)$ passes: The first $2N^2$ characters of the query sequence are loaded into the ISA. The entire database then crosses the array; the *H*-value and *F*-value computed in PE (0,0) in each iteration step are output. In the next pass the following $2N^2$ characters of the query sequence are loaded. The data stored previously is loaded together with the corresponding subject sequences and sent again into the ISA. The process is iterated until the end of the query sequence is reached. Note that, no additional instructions are necessary for the I/O of the intermediate results with the processor array, because it is integrated in the dataflow (see Fig. 5).

For distributing of the computation among the PCs we have chosen a static split load balancing strategy: A similar sized subset of the database is assigned to each PC in a preprocessing step. The subsets remain stationary regardless of the query sequence. Thus, the distribution has only to be performed once for each database and does not influence the overall computing time. The input query sequence is broadcast to each PC and multiple independent subset scans are performed on each Systola 1024 board. Finally, the highest scores are accumulated in one PC. This strategy provides the best performance for our homogenous architecture, where each processing unit has the same processing power. However, a dynamic split load balancing strategy as used in [9] is more suitable for heterogeneous environments.

5 Performance Evaluation

A performance measure commonly used in computational biology is *millions of dynamic cell updates per second* (MCUPS). A CUPS represents the time for a complete computation of one entry of the matrix H, including all comparisons, additions and maxima computations. To measure the MCUPS performance on Systola 1024, we have given the instruction count to update two H-cells per PE in Table 1.

Table 1: Instruction count to update two H-cells in one PE of Systola 1024 with the corresponding operations

Operation in each PE per iteration step	Instruction Count
Get $H(i-1,j)$, $F(i-1,j)$, b_j, max_{i-1} from neighbour	20
Compute $t = \max\{0, H(i-1,j-1) + Sbt(a_i,b_j)\}$	20
Compute $F(i,j) = \max\{H(i-1,j)-\alpha, F(i-1,j)-\beta\}$	8
Compute $E(i,j) = \max\{H(i,j-1)-\alpha, E(i,j-1)-\beta\}$	8
Compute $H(i,j) = \max\{t, F(i,j), E(i,j)\}$	8
Compute $max_i = \max\{H(i,j), max_{i-1}\}$	4
Sum	68

Because new H-values are computed for two characters within 68 instruction in each PE, the whole 32×32 processor array can perform 2048 cell updates in the same time. This leads to a performance of $(2048/68) \times f$ CUPS $= (2048/68) \times (50/16) \times 10^6$ CUPS = 94 MCUPS. Because MCUPS does not consider data transfer time and query length, it is often a weak measure that does not reflect the behaviour of the complete system. Therefore, we will use execution times of database scans for different query lengths in our evaluation.

The involved data transfer in each iteration step is: input of a new character b_j into the lower western IP of each $k \times N$ subarray for query lengths ≤ 2048 (case 1. in Section 4) and input of a new b_j and a previously computed cell of H and F and output of an H-cell and F-cell from the upper western IP for query lengths > 2048 (case 2. in Section 4). Thus, the data transfer time is totally dominated by above computing time of 68 instructions per iteration step.

Table 2: Scan times (in seconds) of TrEMBL 14 for various length of the query sequence on Systola 1024, a PC cluster with 16 Systola 1024, and a Pentium III 600. The speed up compared to the Pentium III is also reported

Query sequence length	256	512	1024	2048	4096
Systola 1024 (*speed up*)	294 (*5*)	577 (*6*)	1137 (*6*)	2241 (*6*)	4611 (*6*)
Cluster of Systolas (*speed up*)	20 (*81*)	38 (*86*)	73 (*91*)	142 (*94*)	290 (*92*)
Pentium III 600 MHz	1615	3286	6611	13343	26690

Table 2 reports times for scanning the TrEMBL protein databank (release 14, which contains 351'834 sequences and 100'069'442 amino acids) for query sequences of various lengths with the SW algorithm. The first two rows of the table give the execution times for Systola 1024 and the cluster with 16 boards compared to a sequential C-program on a Pentium III 600. As the times show, the parallel implementations scale almost linearly with the sequence length. Because of the used static split strategy the cluster times scale also almost linearly with the number of PCs. A single Systola 1024 board is 5-6 times faster than a Pentium III 600. However, a board redesign based on technology used for processors such as the Pentium III (Systola has been built in 1994 [8]) would make this factor significantly higher.

Fig. 6 shows time measurements of sequence comparison with the SW algorithms on different parallel machines. The data for the other machines is taken from [3]. Systola 1024 is around two times faster than the much larger 1K-PE MasPar and the cluster of 16 Systolas is around two times faster than a 16K-PE MasPar. The 1-board Kestrel is 4-5 times faster than a Systola board. Kestrel's design [3] is also a programmable fine-grained parallel architecture implemented as a PC add-on board. It reaches the higher performance, because it has been built with 0.5-μm CMOS technology, in comparison to 1.0-μm for Systola 1024. Extrapolating to this technology both approaches should perform equally. However, the difference between both architectures is that Kestrel is purely a linear array, while Systola is a mesh. This makes the Systola 1024 a more flexible design, suitable for a wider range of applications, see e.g. [13-16].

6 Conclusions and Future Work

In this paper we have demonstrated that hybrid computing is very suitable for scanning biosequence databases. By combining the fine-grained ISA parallelism with a coarse-grained distribution within a PC-cluster, our hybrid architecture achieves supercomputer performance at low cost. We have presented the design of an ISA algorithm that leads to a high-speed implementation on Systola 1024 exploiting the fine-grained parallelism.

The exponentially growth of genomic databases demands even more powerful parallel solutions in the future. Because comparison and alignment algorithms that are favoured by biologists are not fixed, programmable parallel solutions are required to speed up these tasks. As an alternative to special-purpose systems, hard-to-program reconfigurable systems, and expensive supercomputers, we advocate the use of specialised yet programmable hardware whose development is tuned to system speed.

Our future work in hybrid computing will include identifying more applications that profit from this type of processing power, like scientific computing and multimedia video processing. The results of this study will influence our design decision to build a next-generation Systola board consisting of one large 128×128 ISA or of a cluster of 16 32×32 ISAs.

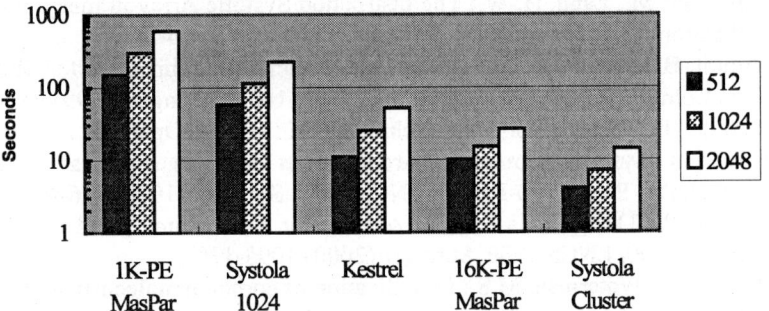

Fig. 6: Time comparison for a 10Mbase search with the SW algorithm on different parallel machines for different query lengths. The values for 1K-PE MasPar, Kestrel, and 16K-PE MasPar are taken from [3], while the values for Systola are based on the TrEMBL 14 scanning times (see Table 2) divided by a normalisation factor of 10

References

1. Altschul, S. F., Gish, W., Miller, W., Myers, E. W., Lipman, D. J.: Basic local alignment search tool, J. Mol. Biol., 215 (1990) 403-410.
2. Borah, M., Bajwa, R. S., Hannenhalli, S., Irwin, M. J.: A SIMD solution to the sequence comparison problem on the MGAP, in Proc. ASAP'94, IEEE CS (1994) 144-160.
3. Dahle, D., et al..: The UCSC Kestrel general purpose parallel processor, Proc. Int. Conf. Parallel and Distributed Processing Techniques and Applications, (1999) 1243-1249.
4. Guerdoux-Jamet, P., Lavenier, D.: SAMBA: hardware accelerator for biological sequence comparison, CABIOS 12 (6) (1997) 609-615.
5. Hoang, D. T.: Searching genetic databases on Splash 2, in Proc. IEEE Workshop on FPGAs for Custom Computing Machines, IEEE CS, (1993) 185-191.
6. Hughey, R.: Parallel Hardware for Sequence Comparison and Alignment, CABIOS 12 (6) (1996) 473-479.
7. Lang, H.-W.: The Instruction Systolic Array, a parallel architecture for VLSI, Integration, the VLSI Journal 4 (1986) 65-74.
8. Lang, H.-W., Maaß, R., Schimmler, M.: The Instruction Systolic Array - Implementation of a Low-Cost Parallel Architecture as Add-On Board for Personal Computers, Proc. HPCN'94, LNCS 797, Springer (1994) 487-488.
9. Lavenier, D., Pacherie, J.-L.: Parallel Processing for Scanning Genomic Data-Bases, Proc. PARCO'97, Elseiver (1998) 81-88.
10. Lopresti, D. P.: P-NAC: A systolic array for comparing nucleic acid sequences, Computer 20 (7) (1987) 98-99.
11. Pearson, W. R.: Comparison of methods for searching protein sequence databases, Protein Science 4 (6) (1995) 1145-1160.
12. Singh, R. K. et al.: BIOSCAN: a network sharable computational resource for searching biosequence databases, CABIOS, 12 (3) (1996) 191-196.

13. Schimmler, M., Lang, H.-W.: The Instruction Systolic Array in Image Processing Applications, Proc. Europto 96, SPIE 2784 (1996) 136-144.
14. Schmidt, B., Schimmler, M.: A Parallel Accelerator Architecture for Multimedia Video Compression, Proc. EuroPar'99, LNCS 1685, Springer (1999) 950-959.
15. Schmidt, B., Schimmler, M., Schröder, H.: Long Operand Arithmetic on Instruction Systolic Computer Architectures and Its Application to RSA cryptography, Proc. Euro-Par'98, LNCS 1470, Springer (1998) 916-922.
16. Schmidt, B.: Design of a Parallel Accelerator for Volume Rendering. In Proc. Euro-Par'2000, LNCS 1900, Springer (2000) 1095-1104.
17. Smith, T. F., Waterman, M.S.: Identification of common molecular subsequences, J. Mol. Biol. 147 (1981) 195-197.

A Parallel Computation of Power System Equations

Y. F. Fung[1], M.F. Ercan[2], T.K. Ho[1], and W. L. Cheung[1]

[1] Dept. of Electrical Eng., The Hong Kong Polytechnic University,
Hong Kong SAR
{eeyffung,eetkho,eewlcheung}@polyu.edu.hk
[2] School of Electrical and Electronic Eng., Singapore Polytechnic, Singapore
mfercan@sp.edu.sg

Abstract. Streaming SIMD Extensions (SSE) is a unique feature embedded in the Pentium III and P4 classes of microprocessors. By fully exploiting SSE, parallel algorithms can be implemented on a standard personal computer and a theoretical speedup of four can be achieved. In this paper, we demonstrate the implementation of a parallel LU matrix decomposition algorithm for solving power systems network equations with SSE and discuss advantages and disadvantages of this approach.

1 Introduction

Personal Computer (PC) or workstation is currently the most popular computing system for solving various engineering problems since it is very cost-effective. With the advanced integrated circuit technology, the computing power that can be delivered by a microprocessor is increasing. The computing performance of a microprocessor is primarily dictated by two factors, namely the operating frequency (or clock rate), and the internal architecture.

The Streaming SIMD Extensions (SSE) is a special feature available in the Intel Pentium III and P4 classes of microprocessors. The SSE enables the execution of SIMD (Single Instruction Multiple Data) operations within the processor and therefore, the overall performance of an algorithm can be improved significantly. The SSE can be considered as an extension of the MMX technology implemented in the Intel Pentium processors [1]. The SSE registers are 128-bit wide and they can store floating-point values, as well as integers whereas MMX registers are limited to characters and integer values. There are eight SSE registers, each of which can be directly addressed using the register names [2]. Utilization of the registers is straightforward with a suitable programming tool. In the case of integers, eight 16-bit integers can be stored and processed in parallel. Similarly, four 32-bit floating-point values can be manipulated. Once two vectors of four floating-point values are loaded into two SSE registers, SIMD operations, such as add, multiply, etc., can be applied to these two vectors in a single operational step. Hence, applications relying heavily on floating-point operations can be substantially accelerated. Moreover, the support of floating-point values in the SSE operations has tremendously widened its applications in other problems including the power systems network problem described in this paper. Programming with the SSE can be achieved by either invoking them using assembly codes included in a standard C/C++ program or by utilizing the special data type hence avoiding assembly coding. The new data type designed for the manipulation of the SSE operation is *F32vec4* [3]. It represents a 128-bit storage, which can be applied to store four 32-bit floating-point data (similarly, type *F32vec8* stores eight 16-bit values). These data types are defined as C++ classes and they can be applied in a C/C++ program directly. Once data stored into the 128-bit data structure, functions that can manipulate the *F32vec4* type data can be called. This will result in parallel processing in two sets of four floating-point values.

The power network problem is computationally intensive and in order to reduce the computation time many researchers have proposed solutions [4] based on parallel hardware systems. However, most of those hardware platforms are expensive and may not be available to most researchers. In following sections we present application of SSE feature to speed up power system network computations and performance obtained accordingly.

2 Power System Network Equations and Parallel Solution with SSE

The power systems network equations usually involve identifying solutions for a set of linear equations in the form of:

$$Ax = b \qquad (1)$$

where A is an incidence symmetric sparse matrix of order n, b is a given independent vector and x is an unknown solution vector. This problem is computationally intensive. In addition, for some applications such as real-time power systems simulation, solution for equation (1) must be determined in a short time-interval, e.g. 10 ms, this also demands a very fast solution time.

A common procedure for solving equation 1 is to factor A into lower and upper triangular matrices L and U such that $LUx = b$ and then this is followed by forward/backward substitution. Details of LU decomposition can be found in [5].

A realistic power system network is comprising of a number of sub networks A_i connected via t_i-lines, to a group of busbars known as cut-nodes [6]. If the network admittance matrix is arranged to follow the sub-network configuration, it can be re-arranged into the Bordered Block Diagonal Form (BBDF). Then, the BBDF matrix can be grouped into sub-matrices where each matrix can be solved by LU decomposition. The sub-matrix is now a dense matrix and therefore, traditional dense matrix algorithm can be applied to determine the L, U triangular matrices. On the other hand, the BBDF, which is a sparse matrix, should be solved by sparse matrix solutions, such as the Choleski method [7].

During LU decomposition the elements in the matrix A are processed along the diagonal and on a row-by-row basis. The following pseudo code illustrates the steps performed to implement LU decomposition using SSE functions.

```
F32vec C, A1, A2;   /* 128-bit values */
Float x;
For (k=0; k<n-2; k++)
For (i=k+1; i<n-1; i++) {x =  a_{i,k}/a_{k,k} ; _mm_load_ps1(C, x);
for (j=k+1; j<n-1; j+=4){
pack four values from a(k,j) to a(k,j+3) into A1;
pack four value from a(i,j) to a(i,j+3) into A2;
A2 = A2 - (A1*C); Unpack the results from A2 and store
in output matrix
}}
```

Data stored in a row of the matrix map naturally into the *F32vec4* data and therefore, four elements in a row can be evaluated in one single step. The term $\frac{a_{i,k}}{a_{k,k}}$ is a constant, which represents the multiplying factor for rows underneath the diagonal element $a_{k,k}$, when elements in row j are being processed. It can be, therefore, stored in a *F32vec4* value with the command _mm_load_ps1, which loads a single 32-bit floating-point value by copying it into all four words. The steps following the LU decomposition are forward and backward substitution. In forward substitution phase, SSE operations can be applied to multiplication of elements of x and $[L]$ matrix. Similarly in backward substitution, the multiplication of x and U can be executed by using SSE functions.

3 Experimental Results

In this section, results obtained for different dimensions of the matrix A are given in Table 1. Two different cases are being compared, namely, (1) conventional approach that is without using SSE, (2) solution obtained by using SSE. The speedup ratios, by taking the processing time of the traditional approach as reference, are also illustrated in Table 1.

Table 1. Performance of different approaches for the solution of $Ax = b$

	Size of Matrix A						
	100	200	400	500	1000	2000
Traditional	9 ms	59 ms	525 ms	758ms	11707ms	94224ms
SSE	5 ms	37 ms	368 ms	507ms	8425ms	65713ms
SSE (speed-up)	1.8	1.59	1.42	1.49	1.39	1.43

When using SSE, for a better performance, data should be in 16-byte aligned form. In order to maintain the 16-byte alignment, the size of the matrix must be a multiple of 4. If this is not the case, then extra rows and columns must be added into the matrix to get around the alignment problem. The best result is obtained for a relatively smaller matrix of 100x100 where the speedup rate is about 1.8. The performance of the SSE algorithms is affected by the overhead due to additional steps required to convert data from standard floating-point values to 128-bit *F32vec4* data and vice-versa. In this computation, three packing/unpacking functions were performed when processing elements in a row. We have empirically found that these functions occupy half of the unit processing time. Despite this overhead, using SSE provided an average speedup ratio of 1.5 for different matrix sizes.

4 Conclusions

In this paper, we have examined the application of SSE to the power systems network equations. According to our results, a speedup ratio around 1.5 can be easily obtained. The results are satisfactory and only minor modifications of the original program are needed in order to utilize the SSE feature. Most importantly, additional hardware is not required for this performance enhancement. SSE is a valuable tool for improving the performance of computation intensive problems, and the power systems network equations problem is one of the ideal applications.

Acknowledgements

This project is sponsored by The Hong Kong Polytechnic University for the first, third and fourth authors, and by Singapore Polytechnic for the second author.

References

1. The Complete Guide to MMX Technology, Intel Corporation, McGraw-Hill (1997).
2. Conte G., Tommesani S., Zanichelli F.: The Long and Winding Road to High-performance Image Processing with MMX/SSE, IEEE Int'l Workshop for Computer Architectures for Machine Perception (2000), 302-310.
3. Intel C/C++ Compiler Class Libraries for SIMD Operations User's Guide (2000)
4. Taoka, H., Iyoda, I., and Noguchi, H.: Real-time Digital Simulator for Power System Analysis on a Hybercube Computer. IEEE Trans. On Power Systems. 7 (1992) 1-10.
5. Wu J. Q., and Bose A.: Parallel Solution of Large Sparse Matrix Equations and Parallel Power Flow, IEEE Trans. On Power Systems, 10 (1995) 1343-1349.
6. Chan K. W. and Snider, L. A.: Development of a Hybrid Real-time Fully Digital Simulator for the Study and Control of Large Power Systems, Proc. of APSCOM 2000, Hong Kong, (2000) 527-531.
7. Jess J. A., and Kees, G. H.: A Data Structure for Parallel LU Decomposition, IEEE Trans. C-31 (1992) 231-239.

Level-3 Trigger for a Heavy Ion Experiment at LHC

U. Frankenfeld[1], H. Helstrup[2], J. Lien[2], V. Lindenstruth[3], D. Röhrich[1],
M. Schulz[3], B. Skaali[4], T. Steinbeck[3], K. Ullaland[1], A. Vestbø[1], and
A. Wiebalck[3]

[1] University of Bergen
Allegaten 55, 5007 Bergen, Norway
[2] Bergen College
P.O. Box 7030, 5020 Bergen, Norway
[3] Kirchhoff Institute for Physics, University of Heidelberg
Schröderstrasse 90, 69120 Heidelberg, Germany
[4] University of Oslo
P.O. Box 1048 Blindern, 0316 Oslo, Norway

Abstract. At the upcoming Large Hadron Collider (LHC) at CERN one expects to measure 20,000 particles in a single Pb–Pb event resulting in a data rate of ∼75 MByte/event. The event rate is limited by the bandwidth of the storage system. Higher rates are possible by selecting interesting events and subevents (Level-3 trigger) or compressing the data efficiently with modeling techniques. Both require a fast parallel pattern recognition. One possible solution to process the detector data at such rates is a farm of clustered SMP nodes, based on off-the-shelf PCs, and connected by a high bandwidth, low latency network.

1 Introduction

The ALICE experiment [1] at the LHC accelerator at CERN will investigate Pb–Pb collisions at a center of mass energy of 5.5 A·TeV starting in the year 2006. A multiplicity of 20,000 particles per interaction in its main tracking detector, the Time Projection Chamber (TPC), is expected. The detector is read-out by 600,000 ADC channels, producing a data size of ∼75 MByte/event [2]. The data from the various subdetectors are transferred into the receiver processors. The data acquisition system collects the subevents and assembles them into a single event for permanent storage. The data rate is limited by the bandwidth of the storage system. Without further data reduction or compression ALICE will be able to take events at rates up to 20 Hz. This data flow is 2–3 times higher than for the other LHC experiments (e.g.: ATLAS: 2 MByte at 270 Hz [3]). Higher rates are possible by selecting interesting events and subevents (Level-3 trigger) or compressing the data efficiently with modeling techniques. Both Level-3 triggering and compression by data modeling require a fast pattern recognition. The necessary computing power can be achieved by using a cluster of PCs. A task example for the Level-3 trigger system is to select events which contains e^+-e^- candidates coming from a quarkonium decay. In the case of low multiplicity events from p–p collisions the online pattern recognition system can be used to remove pile-up events from the data stream.

2 Architecture

Processing detector information at a bandwidth of 10–20 GByte/s or even higher (the peak rate into the front-end electronics is 6 TByte/s) requires a massive parallel computing system. Such a system (Level-3 trigger system) is located in the data flow between the front-electronics of the detector and the event-builder of the data acquisition system.

Clustered SMP nodes, based on off-the-shelf PCs, and connected by a high bandwidth, low latency network provide the necessary computing power for on-line pattern recognition and data compression. The system nodes are interfaced to the front-end electronics of the detector via Read Out Receiver Cards (RORC) to their internal PCI-bus. The hierarchy of the parallel farm is adapted both to the parallelism in the data and to the complexity of the pattern recognition. The TPC detector consists of 36 sectors, each sector being divided into 5 subsectors. The data from each subsector are transferred via an optical fiber from the detector into 180 receiver nodes of the PC farm. The receiver processors are all interconnected by a hierarchical network. Each sector is processed in parallel, results are then merged on a higher level, first locally in 144 sector and 72 sextet nodes and finally in 12 event nodes which have access to the full detector data. The first layer of nodes receives the data from the detector and performs the pre-processing task, i.e. cluster and track seed finding on the subsector level. The pre-processing will be done partly in a FPGA chip on the receiver card. The next two levels of nodes exploit the local neighbourhood: track segment finding on a sector level. Finally all local results are collected from the sectors and combined on a global level: track segment merging and final track fitting. The farm has to be fault tolerant and scalable. Possible network technology candidates are amongst others SCI [4] and GigaBit-Ethernet. The operating system will be LINUX, using a generic message passing API for communication with the exception of data transfers, which use directly remote DMA.

3 Realtime Data Compression

Data rate reduction can be achieved by either reducing the event rate (Level-3 trigger) or the data volume. Based on the detector information – clusters and tracks – interesting events or subevents can be selected for further processing, thus reducing the event rate. Reduction of the event size can be achieved by compression techniques. Data compression techniques can be divided into two major families: lossy and lossless. Lossy data compression concedes a certain loss of accuracy in exchange for greatly increased compression. Lossy compression proves effective when applied to graphical images and digitized voice.

Data compression is a two step process: modeling and coding. Compression consists of taking a stream of symbols and transforming them into codes. The decision to output a certain code for a certain symbol is based on a model. The model is simply a collection of data and rules used to process input symbols and determines which code to output. The Huffman algorithm [5] is an example of a minimum redundancy coding based on probabilities; the vector quantizer [6] is a method based on a codebook.

General lossless or slightly lossy methods like entropy coders and vector quantizers can compress tracking detector data only by factors 2–3. The Huffman compression can be done in the front-electronic before transferring the data to the receiver processors. The best compression method is to find a good model for the raw data and to transform the data into an efficient representation. By online tracking and a compressed data representation an event size reduction by a factor 15 can be achieved [2]. The information is stored as model parameters and (small) deviations from the model. The results are coded using Huffman and vector quantization algorithms. All correlations in the data have to be incorporated into the model. The precise knowledge of the detector performance, i.e. analog noise of the detector and the quantization noise, is necessary to create a minimum information model of the data. Realtime pattern recognition and feature extraction are the input to the model.

4 Pattern Recognition

The data modeling scheme is based on the fact that the information content of the TPC are tracks, which can be represented by models of clusters and track parameters. Figure 1 shows a thin slice of the detector, clusters are aligned along the particle trajectories. The local track model is a helix; the knowledge of the track parameters is necessary for the description of the shape of the clusters in a simple model. The pattern recognition reconstructs clusters and associates them with local track segments. Note that pattern recognition at this stage can be redundant, i.e. clusters can belong to more than one track and track segments can overlap. Once the pattern recognition is completed, the track can be represented by helix parameters.

The online pattern recognition in the STAR experiment is realized as a two step process [7,8]: Cluster finding and track finding. A cluster finder searches for local maxima in the raw ADC-data. If an isolated cluster if found, the centroid position is calculated. The cluster centroids are then combined to form tracks. Without the track information during the cluster finding the unfolding of overlapping clusters is a source of inaccuracy. This approach has been adapted to the ALICE experiment. Due to the higher track density in the ALICE experiment and the resulting overlapping clusters fast cluster finding without track information is very difficult.

The Hough transform is an alternative approach for the pattern recognition which is currently adapted to the high cluster densities which are expected in Heavy Ion collisions. The Hough transform is a standard tool in image analysis that allows recognition of global patterns in a image space by recognition of local patterns (ideally a point) in a transformed parameter space. The adaptive, generalized Hough-transform is applied to raw data, i.e. before cluster finding. Local track segments are found and based on the track information, cluster shapes are modeled.

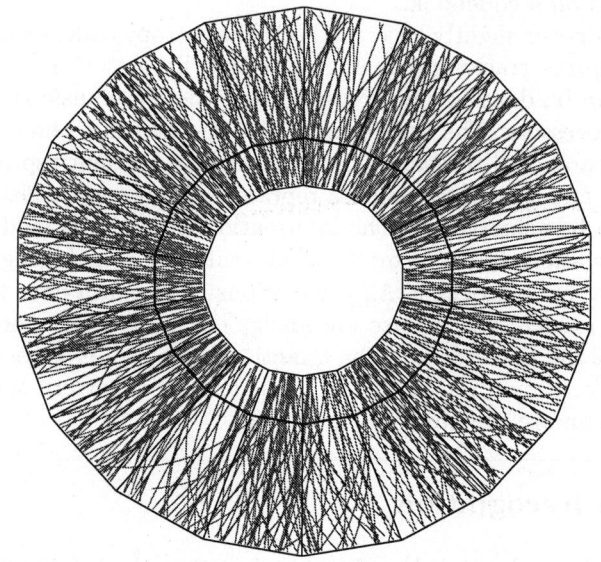

Fig. 1. Simulated collision of two heavy nuclei at LHC. Only a small fraction of the TPC-detector (thin slice) is shown

5 Summary

The Level-3 system for the upcoming Heavy Ion experiments at the LHC accelerator has to process the data at a rate of 10–20 GBytes/s. The architecture and network topology of a PC cluster which fulfills this requirement are currently under study. The information of the Fast Pattern Recognition can be used for data compression, to derive physical quantities (e.g. momentum, impact parameter etc.) for trigger decisions and for online monitoring (Fig. 1).

References

1. ALICE Collaboration, *Technical Proposal*, CERN/LHCC/95-71 (1995).
2. ALICE collaboration, *Technical Design Report of the Time Projection Chamber*, CERN/LHCC 2000-001 (2000).
3. Report of the Steering Group of the LHC Computing Review, CERN/LHCC 2001-004 (2001).

4. SCI (Scalable Coherent Interface) Standard Compliant, ANSI/IEEE 1596-1992.
5. D. A. Huffman, A method for the construction of minimum-redundancy codes, Proceedings of the IRE, Vol. 40, No. 9, (1952) 1098-1101.
6. R. M. Gray, Vector Quantization, IEEE ASSP Magazine April (1984) 4.
7. STAR collaboration, *STAR Conceptual Design Report*, Lawrence Berkleley Laboratory, University of California, PUB-5347 (1992).
8. C. Adler et al., The proposed Level-3 Trigger System for STAR, IEEE Transactions on Nuclear Science, Vol. 47, No.2 (2000).

Experiences in Using MPI-IO on Top of GPFS for the IFS Weather Forecast Code

Nicholas K. Allsopp[1], John F. Hague[2], and Jean-Pierre Prost[3]

[1] IBM Hursley Laboratories, Winchester, UK.
[2] IBM Bedfont Lakes, Feltham, Middlesex, UK.
[3] IBM T.J. Watson Research Center, Yorktown Heights, NY, USA.

Abstract. The Integrated Forecast System (IFS) code is a parallel MPI application running on multiple tasks, a specified number of which, during its execution, writes output to a single global file at the end of several output time intervals. It can therefore write output multiple times during a given run. With the appropriate choice of parallel writing routine the overhead of writing to disk can be effectively hidden from the computation. We shall show how this is possible with careful use of MPI-IO routines on top of the IBM General Parallel File System (GPFS).

1 Introduction

The Integrated Forecast System (IFS) [1,2] code is a parallel MPI [3,4] application running on multiple tasks, a specified number of which, during its execution, writes its outputs to a single global file at the end of several output time intervals. It can therefore write output multiple times during a given run. A serial application can often run out of I/O performance when using a disk system connected to a single processing node. It is already possible to stripe the data across the disks on one node. The next logical step is to stripe the data across multiple nodes thus balancing the I/O activity. The IFS application often needs to write data that is located on a disk which happens to be physically located on a different processor. Usually there is no flexible way to access data on any disk attached to any processor from within the application. The Network File System (NFS) [5] could provide such a solution but its performance is not adequate in many cases. This is particularly true for its write performance.

The IBM General Parallel File System (GPFS) [6] allows the flexibility of access to shared data across multiple nodes. Parallel applications such as IFS need access to disks that are spread across a number of nodes to achieve performance. GFPS allows multiple processors on several nodes to simultaneously access the same file using Posix file system calls. It utilizes the IBM SP [7] switch for fast access and increases the aggregate bandwidth by spreading reads and writes across multiple disks. To maximize the total throughput, it balances the load evenly across all disks. This means that it does not matter to which node the disks are attached. Several studies have been carried out by researchers [8,9,10], aimed at characterizing the behaviour of I/O intensive parallel applications and

Table 1. Possible MPI-IO functions that could be used for writing to a single file

Function	Synchronization	Positioning of File pointer
MPI_FILE_WRITE_ORDERED	Blocking Collective	Shared
MPI_FILE_IWRITE_SHARED	Nonblocking Independent	Shared
MPI_FILE_WRITE_ALL	Blocking Collective	Individual
MPI_FILE_IWRITE	Nonblocking Independent	Individual

at observing the performance gain which can be obtained by restructuring the application code. What we will show in this paper is that with the appropriate choice of parallel writing routine the overhead of writing to disk can be effectively hidden from the computation. This is particularly important when considering an application such as IFS which not only has a lot of calculation but outputs large amounts of data at regular intervals.

2 The IFS Application Code

IFS is the Integrated Forecast System program [1] developed by ECMWF (European Centre for Medium-Range Weather Forecasts) for producing a global 10 day weather forecast. The code is based on a spectral model, with specific development to make it suitable for a distributed memory parallel architecture. The forecast data can be written to a global file system (or database) as frequently as required. Typically, this would be after every 3 hours of prediction, although in this case we chose to output the data for every 15 minutes of prediction to exercise the GPFS system as much as possible.

Within the file writing routine of the IFS code we envisage a scenario where every 30 seconds, each of 1000 MPI tasks outputs 500 messages of 2KB each. This causes 1GB to be written into a single file. The messages have to be fully interleaved in the output file. In the IFS code they are sent by each MPI task either to one master task which writes them out sequentially, or to several (user determined) master tasks which write them out using MPI-IO calls.

3 Choices of MPI-IO Writing Functions

Table 1 shows four functions that could easily be used within the IFS code. For the case where the file pointer is not shared, the user needs to specify the information about the structure of the file to the MPI tasks that are performing the file transfer through the setting of appropriate file views. Of these four MPI-IO functions, MPI_FILE_IWRITE_SHARED appears the most appropriate to be used within the IFS application. This is because it requires the least code modification and the file block sizes might not be the same on each MPI task (therefore using an individual file pointer routine would require a call to MPI_FILE_SET_VIEW function at the beginning of each output phase as well

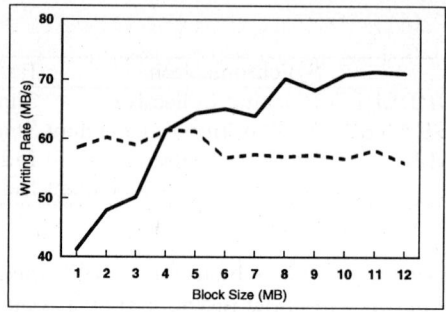

Fig. 1. Speed for writing a single 1GB file to disk from 8 nodes using both a single master task (dotted line) and 8 MPI-IO master tasks (solid line)

as additional communication between MPI tasks). As seen in Figure 1, writing with a single master task gives a maximum bandwidth of around 60MB/s. When using MPI-IO and 8 master tasks the aggregate write bandwidth becomes higher for block sizes over 4 MB to reach 70MB/s for block sizes over 10MB. For larger block sizes, the MPI-IO overhead is compensated by multiple GPFS clients writing in parallel to the file.

Although MPI-IO does not appear to be much faster than a serial write, the important thing here is that, when using MPI-IO, all tasks can participate. It should be noted that although 70MB was perfectly adequate, more comprehensive GPFS configurations are capable of achieving 200 to 300 MB/sec.

4 IFS Test Case

While benchmark programs (like the previous example) can give an indication of the performance of new systems, their extrapolation to real-world application performance is not always straightforward. In this section, we use the IFS code to test the application performance of our GPFS file system. The test case used (T159) is a global forecast spectral model with 60 level, 320 longitudes and 160 latitudes. ECMWF runs much higher resolution models for the actual forecast so we are here concentrating on the I/O aspects of the runtime. This model outputs 44MB of data per calculation step and there were 24 steps per run.

The IFS has the capability to have either a single master task writing all the data to the single file, meaning that all the other tasks must communicate their portion of the output file to the master task, or have a number of parallel writing tasks which use MPI-IO to write to a single file. The number of parallel writing tasks can be the same as or less than the total number of tasks used during the computation. If the number of writing tasks is less than the total number of tasks then there is some inter-task communication involved in order to package the output data ready for file writing.

Table 2. Execution times on the SP test platform of the IFS code using MPI_FILE_IWRITE_SHARED for the parallel write command. The 'dummy' numbers are for IFS codes using dummy parallel write commands. All times are in seconds

# Tasks Total	1 Task writing	2 Tasks writing	2 Tasks 'dummy'	4 Tasks writing	4 Tasks 'dummy'	8 Tasks writing	8 Tasks 'dummy'	16 Tasks writing	16 Tasks 'dummy'
4	1584	1577	1556	1540	1540	-	-	-	-
8	857	816	816	801	800	777	780	-	-
16	564	561	519	527	495	539	499	558	490

The values shown in table 2 were obtained from the IFS test case running on the SP test platform. For comparsion this test was repeated on the most upto date SP2 platform consisting of a single Night Hawk 2 (NH2) node as shown in table 3. Table 2 shows the difference in execution time when using a single master task to write the file compared to using multiple tasks writing to a parallel shared file with MPI-IO. Although it is obvious that the parallel file writing routine outperforms the single master task approach, there is a trade-off between the communication overhead induced by passing the data to a single master task and the MPI-IO overhead of accessing a shared file pointer compensated by the parallel access to the file by several master tasks. This can be seen from the results of using a total number of 16 tasks as the shortest execution time was obtained when using 4 writing tasks. The results of table 2 'dummy' were

Table 3. Execution time on latest SP2 platform using a 16 CPU NH2 node. All times in seconds

# Tasks	1 Task writing	2 Tasks writing	4 Tasks writing	8 Tasks writing	16 Tasks writing
4	908	868	840	-	-
8	469	451	450	448	-
16	275	279	266	266	264

obtained by replacing the MPI-IO file write routines by dummy routines thus removing any file writing whilst retaining all of the file packing algorithms. There is a larger difference shown when using larger numbers of tasks but this is expected because the block size per write is small causing a drop in write performance, as shown in Fig. 1. This shows that actual overhead of the parallel file writing, as performed by MPI-IO on top of GPFS is very small and is not causing a bottleneck for the calculation stage of the IFS test case.

5 Conclusion and Future Work

The results above show that parallel file writing is faster than using a single master writing task. There is a trade-off between the communication overhead induced by passing the data to a single master task and the MPI-IO overhead of accessing a shared file pointer compensated by the parallel access to the file by several master tasks. For this reason, careful consideration is required when choosing the number of master tasks. As can be seen in table 2, it is not straightforward to determine the optimal number of master tasks when using MPI-IO. The main reason for finding the optimal method of file writing is to effectively hide the I/O overhead such that calculation dominates the overall execution time. This is particularly important when considering an application such as IFS which not only has a lot of calculation but outputs large amounts of data at regular intervals. We have shown that this is possible when using an appropriate number of MPI-IO writing tasks compared to using the single master task approach.

In the future, we are planning to run the IFS code on a larger test case and with more tasks, since the typical IFS 10 day forecast model currently runs with a grid size of about 1000 longitudes by 500 latitudes.

Acknowledgment

The authors would like to thank ECMWF for supporting this work.

References

1. Barros, S. R. M., Dent D., Isaksen, I., Robinson, G., Mozdzynski, G., Wollenwever, F., The IFS model: a parallel production weather code. Parallel Computing, **21** No.10 (1995) 1621-1638.
2. The IFS Model Overview and Parallelisation Strategies, Proceedings of the 6th ECMWF workshop, 1994. ISBN 981-01-2211-4.
3. Message Passing Interface Forum, MPI-2: Extensions to the Message-Passing Interface, July 1997. Http://www.mpi-forum.org/docs/docs.html.
4. Gropp, W., Lusk, E., and Thakur, R., Using MPI-2: Advanced Features of the Message-Passing Interface. MIT Press, Cambridge, MA, 1999.
5. The GPFS parallel file system: http://www.almaden.ibm.com/cs/gpfs-spsort.html.
6. The Network File System (NFS): http://www.nfsv4.org/
7. The IBM SP system: http://www.rs6000.ibm.com/hardware/largescale/SP/index.html
8. Kotz, D. and Nieuwejaar, N., Dynamic file-access characteristics of a production parallel scientific workload. In Proceedings of Supercomputing '94, 640-649, (1994). IEEE Computer Society Press.
9. Nieuwejaar, N., Kotz, D., Purakayastha, A., Schlatter Ellis, C., and Best, M., File-access characteristics of parallel scientific workloads. IEEE Transactions on Parallel and Distributed Systems, 7(10) (1996) 1075-1089.
10. Smirni, E., and Reed, D. A., Lessons from characterizing the input/output behavior of parallel scientific applications. Performance Evaluation: An International Journal, 33(1) (1998) 27-44.

Topic 08+13
Instruction-Level Parallelism and Computer Architecture

Eduard Ayguadé, Fredrik Dahlgren, Christine Eisenbeis, Roger Espasa, Guang R. Gao, Henk Muller, Rizos Sakellariou, and André Seznec

Topic Chairpersons

The papers presented in this combined topic consider issues related to the broad theme of computer architecture research. The program reflects the current emphasis of research on the exploitation of instruction-level parallelism and thread-level parallelism, with the papers presented covering several important aspects on both approaches: branch prediction, speculative multitheading, pipelining and superscalar architecture design, SIMD extensions, and dynamic scheduling issues in multithreaded architectures.

The 9 papers selected for presentation were chosen out of a total of 20 submissions (to both the original topics). All submitted papers, except two, received 4 reviews each. We would like to thank sincerely the external referees for their valuable assistance in the reviewing process.

Branch prediction is the common theme of the first four papers presented. A. Ramirez, J. Larriba-Pey, and M. Valero use profiling data to propose a new branch predictor. Y. Chu and M. R. Ito present a branch predictor for indirect branches. Issues related to branch prediction in the context of virtual machine interpreters are discussed by M. A. Ertl and D. Gregg. Branch prediction on speculative multithreading architectures is the subject of the note by C. Iwama, N. D. Barli, S. Sakai, and H. Tanaka.

The second part of the topic starts with a paper by S. Önder and R. Gupta, who propose a mechanism for waking up instructions in superscalar processors. T. Sato and I. Arita investigate the performance of variable latency pipeline on superscalar processors. SIMD extensions to general-purpose microprocessor intruction sets is the subject of the next two papers. J. Sebot and N. Drach-Temam consider the impact of the AltiVec SIMD instruction set on DSP, image and 3D applications. P. Bulić and V. Guštin present a preprocessor and a macro library for exploiting the SIMD extensions. Finally, S. Niar and M. Adda present a dynamic scheduler of parallel threads for the Multithreaded Multiprocessor Architecture.

Branch Prediction Using Profile Data*

Alex Ramirez, Josep L. Larriba-Pey, and Mateo Valero

Universitat Politecnica de Catalunya
Jordi Girona 1–3, D6, 08034 Barcelona, Spain
{aramirez,larri,mateo}@ac.upc.es

Abstract. Branch prediction accuracy is a very important factor for superscalar processor performance. It is the ability to predict the outcome of a branch which allows the processor to effectively use a large instruction window, and extract a larger amount of ILP.

The first approach to branch prediction were static predictors, which always predicted the same direction for a given branch. The use of profile data and compiler transformations proved very effective at improving the accuracy of these predictors.

In this paper we propose a novel dynamic predictor organization which makes extensive use of profile data. The main advantage of our proposed predictor (the *agbias* predictor) is that it does not depend heavily on the quality of the profile data to provide high prediction accuracy.

Our results show that our *agbias* predictor reduces the branch misprediction rate by 14% on a 16KB predictor over the next best compiler-enhanced predictor.

1 Introduction

Branch prediction was first approached using static schemes, which always predict the same direction for a branch, like predicting that all branches would be taken, or that only backwards branches would be taken [23]. Semi-static branch predictors use profile feedback information and encode the most likely branch direction in the instruction opcode, obtaining much higher accuracy than the simple static predictors [9]. Profile data was also used to align branches in the code so that they follow a given static prediction heuristic [3]. Finally, the more accurate dynamic branch predictors, which store the past branch behavior in dynamic information tables, and lookup this data to predict the future branch direction [12,16,18,23,24,25].

We believe this paper contributes in proposing a dynamic prediction scheme which makes extensive use of profile data to provide higher prediction accuracy, even with lower quality or inexact profile data.

The proposed *agbias* predictor is largely based on the static-dynamic predictor combination proposed in [20], and divides branches among four sub-streams: first, among *easy* and *hard* to predict branches; second, among mostly *taken*

---
* This work was supported by the Ministry of Education and Science of Spain under contract TIC-0511/98, by CEPBA, and an Intel fellowship.

and *not taken* branches. This division obtains a significant interference reduction, and allows a separate resource allocation, as not all sub-streams have the same needs.

Our results show that the *agbias* predictor outperforms all other examined predictors (including their compiler enhanced version), reducing branch misprediction rate by 14% on a 16KB predictor.

1.1 Simulation Setup

All the results in the paper were obtained using a simulator derived from the SimpleScalar 3.0 tool set [2]. We run most of the SPECint95 benchmarks (except go, compress, and perl) plus the PostgreSQL 6.3 database system running a subset of the TPC-D queries. All programs were compiled statically and with -O4 optimization level using Compaq's C compiler.

The training and simulation inputs were different to simulate the effect of inaccurate profile data on the prediction accuracy. All simulations were run to completion. All figures in the paper present the arithmetic average of all executed benchmarks, where all codes have the same weight.

We have compared our agbias predictor with the compiler-enhanced versions of most modern de-aliased predictors: a gshare predictor using an optimized code layout [22], agbias using a profiled bias bit [24], bimode using a profiled selector [12,10], gskew [16], and a static-dynamic hybrid using profile data [20].

All predictors simulated use global branch history. The BHR length determines the PHT size: for N bits of history, 2^N PHT entries are allocated. We have used a 4096-entry/4-way set associative BTB to store the bias bit in the agree predictor simulations.

1.2 Paper Structure

The rest of this paper is structured as follows: In Section 2 we present previous related work, and discuss its relevance to this paper. In Section 3 we propose our predictor organization, the *agbias* predictor, and analyze the reasons why it proves more accurate than others, showing that prediction table interference is not the only relevant factor. Finally, in Section 4 we present our conclusions for this work.

2 Related Work

We can classify related work into four groups: basic branch predictors, de-aliased predictors, and compiler support for branch prediction.

Basic branch prediction schemes can be broadly classified into three groups: static, semi-static and dynamic branch predictors.

Static predictors always predict the same outcome for a given branch, and can be based on very simple heuristics, which do not require encoded information for the processor [23]. They can also be based on compiler analysis and more

complex heuristics [1] which are mainly used by the compiler itself to align
branches following a more simple heuristic [3,8]. The compiler can also increase
static prediction accuracy by using code transformations, usually implying code
replication [11,17,21,26].

Semi-static predictors are based on the observation that branches tend to
behave in the same way across different executions of the same code, and use
profile information obtained at run-time [4,9,15]. These predictors predict that
a branch will always follow its most usual direction as observed in the profile
data. Thanks to the use of profile information from an adequate training input
they achieve higher accuracy than simple static predictors based exclusively on
static analysis and heuristics. But the wrong inputs used to obtain the profile
data can lead to decreased accuracy of the predictor.

Dynamic branch predictors store information about the recent behavior of
branches in a given execution of the program, and are predicted to behave in the
same way as they usually did in the same past situation. These predictors differ
mainly in the way they store the past behavior of the branch and the situation in
which it executed, be it relative to the recent outcomes of other branches (global
branch history, path correlation) or the past outcomes of the same branch (self
history) [14,18,23,25].

All dynamic branch prediction schemes use finite tables to store the past
behavior of branches. When two different branches store their information in
the same table entry, aliasing happens. Recent dynamic prediction schemes try
to organize their tables in a clever way to reduce destructive aliasing [7,12,16,24].
We refer to these predictors as de-aliased schemes.

There have been also some dynamic branch prediction studies which have
involved the compiler in the prediction scheme, using profile information to replace some predictor components [10,13,20], or to provide some information that
is better obtained statically [24,19].

An alternative way of reducing prediction table interference is to reduce
the number of branches stored in these tables, filtering out the strongly biased
branches, which would then be predicted with a single bit stored in a separate
table [5,7,19] or statically using profile information [6,13,20]. We show that these
schemes heavily depend on the accuracy of the profile data, and present an
alternative organization which solves this problem, proving equally accurate with
both self-train and cross-train tests.

In [20] the relevance of the static predictors is increased, as they are used to
predict a large fraction of branches, removing them from the dynamic prediction
tables, thus reducing interference, and increasing accuracy. But most of the results shown correspond to the self-trained case, where the profile data is totally
accurate.

3 The Agbias Predictor

Based on the ideas exposed thus far, we propose another combination of static
and dynamic branch predictors which we call *agbias*. The agbias prediction

scheme is shown in Figure 1. Largely based on the prediction scheme proposed in [20], it is composed of two dynamic direction predictors, which use some de-aliasing mechanism (we have chosen the agree mechanism in this paper), and a static meta-predictor which divides branches between the strongly biased sub-stream (the *easy* branches), and the not so biased sub-stream (the *hard* branches). The *easy* branches are those which have the same outcome 95% of the times, that is, they almost never change direction. Both dynamic components share the BHR, which is only updated for the branches belonging to the *hard* sub-stream.

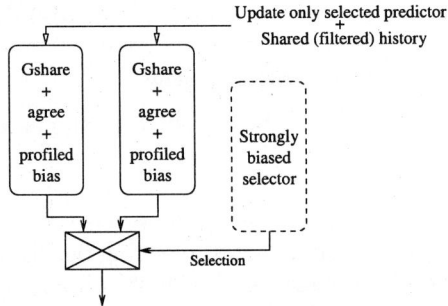

Fig. 1. The agbias predictor scheme

This way, we are dividing branches into four categories: first, using the profiled bias (strongly biased/*easy* or not strongly biased/*hard* branches); second, using their most likely outcome (taken or not taken). The first division is used to distribute branches in two separate dynamic predictors, which allows an independent resource allocation for the *easy* and *hard* sub-streams. The second division is used to minimize negative interference in the prediction tables of both dynamic components, using a de-aliased scheme (we have chosen the agree[p] scheme, hence the name *agbias*). The classification of branches among strongly biased and non-strongly biased using profile data [6] or dynamic tables [5,7,19] has been explored before, but none considered a separate dynamic component for the strongly biased stream.

The static-dynamic combination used in [20] does not allocate any dynamic resources to the *easy* sub-stream, relying entirely on the accuracy of the profile data. Our scheme avoids this too strong dependency by using a small dynamic predictor instead. Even if the profile wrongly classifies a branch as belonging to the easy sub-stream, the dynamic component will be more accurate than a pure semi-static predictor. In this paper we have used a 512 byte agree predictor with compiler enhancements. The agbias predictor used in this paper requires two bits encoded in the instruction: a branch bias bit, and a branch direction bit.

Figure 2 shows the prediction accuracy of the agbias predictor compared to other compiler-enhanced predictors. When not specified, results correspond to the cross-trained test.

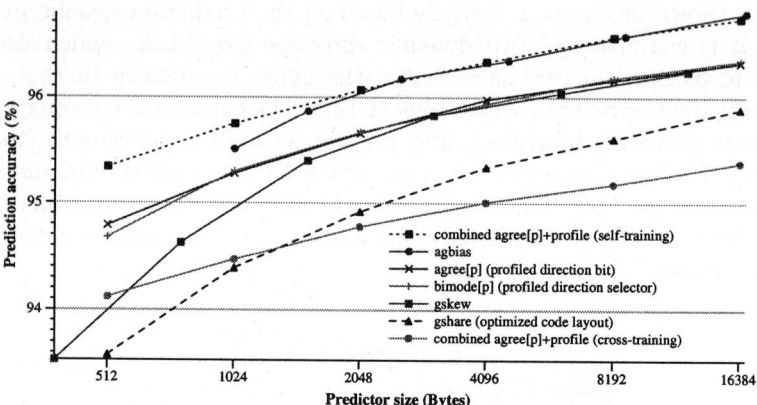

Fig. 2. Prediction accuracy of the agbias predictor compared to other compiler-enhanced predictors

Our results show that the agbias predictor is more accurate than the other predictors examined for all predictor sizes, reaching 96.8% average accuracy for the studied benchmarks, improving on the 96.3% obtained with the compiler-enhanced agree and bimode predictors.

The only comparable predictor is the static-dynamic combination when running the self-trained test, because it obtains the same prediction accuracy but does not require any hardware resources for the *easy* sub-stream prediction. However, note that the accuracy of that static-dynamic combination drops to the level of a gshare predictor with the cross-trained test.

The advantage of the agbias predictor is that it obtains the same performance in the self and cross-trained tests, being less dependent on the profile data accuracy.

3.1 BHR Filtering

Clearly, one major advantage of the agbias predictor is that the *hard* sub-stream predictor has much less interference than other predictors, because it only has to worry about 30% of all branches.

But there is a second difference between the agbias predictor and the other de-aliased schemes: updating the BHR only for branches in the *hard* sub-stream. This selective BHR update achieves an important result: it is increasing the amount of *useful* history information kept in the BHR.

The outcome of the easy branches does not provide the predictor with any extra information, because we *already know* the outcome of the branch. The outcome of the next branches does not depend on it, because it never changes. Not shifting these outcomes into the BHR prevents other -variable- bits from leaving the BHR. This increases the usefulness of the information stored in the first level table, making it easier for the predictor to guess the correct branch outcome.

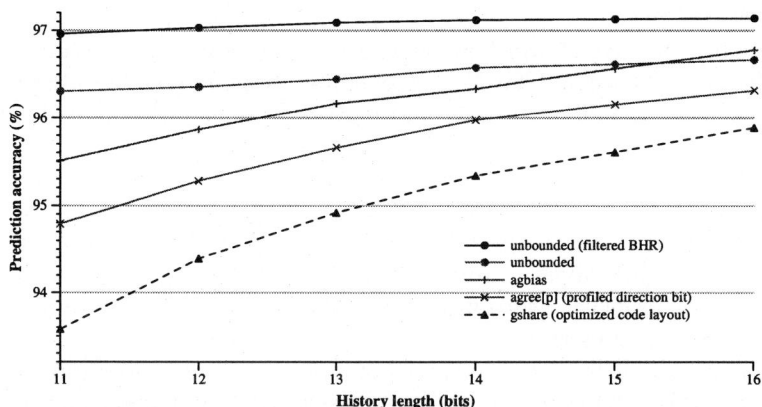

Fig. 3. Effect of BHR filtering on prediction accuracy

Figure 3 shows the prediction accuracy of the agree[p] and the agbias predictors compared to an unbounded predictor using the same history length, and an unbounded predictor with a filtered BHR. The agree and agbias predictors use the history length to determine the PHT size (a 14-bit agree predictor has 2^{14} PHT entries, requiring 4KB of storage, the same 14-bit agbias requires 512 extra bytes for the *easy* sub-stream component). An unbounded predictor has a separate PHT entry for each branch and each possible BHR value, so it is free of interference.

The unbounded predictor increases performance from 96.3% to 96.7% as history length increases, showing that a longer history register represents an advantage to this predictor. The agree and agbias predictors experience larger improvements with increasing history lengths because a longer history also implies a larger PHT, and less interference.

The most remarkable result is that the agbias predictor obtains equivalent performance to an unbounded predictor for 15 bits of history (96.6%), and it actually obtains higher accuracy with 16 bits (96.8% vs 96.7%). But the comparison is not fair, because the agbias predictor also benefits from the BHR filtering: over 70% of all branches do not update the BHR, causing the history length of the agbias predictor to behave like it were 70% larger.

As expected, the unbounded predictor also benefits from a filtered history length, increasing accuracy of a 16-bit history predictor from 96.7% to 97.14%, the same performance as a non-filtered predictor of 22 history bits (not shown). This shows that PHT interference is not the only relevant factor to two-level prediction accuracy: the amount of *useful* information stored in the Level 1 tables is also important.

We have shown how the agbias obtains higher accuracy than any other examined predictor (including their compiler enhanced versions): first, it obtains an important interference reduction in the PHT; second, it increases the usefulness of the BHR information, increasing the potential performance of its two-level adaptive predictor components.

4 Conclusions

In this paper we have shown how we can increase branch prediction accuracy by combining software and hardware techniques, providing yet another example of how the combination of software and hardware techniques can lead to higher performance at a lower implementation cost.

Based on previously proposed predictors and taking full advantage of the compiler, we have presented the *agbias* branch prediction scheme, a static-dynamic hybrid predictor based on the division of the branch stream in four sub streams. A first division among strongly biased (*easy* branches) and not strongly biased branches (*hard* branches), and a second division among mostly *taken* and *not taken* branches.

The agbias predictor uses the *agree* predictions scheme to separate the taken and the not taken sub-streams, and uses two separate dynamic components to separate the easy and the hard sub-streams. Branches are classified using profile information, encoding the class in the instruction opcode.

We outperform all other examined branch prediction schemes for all predictor sizes, obtaining a 96.8% prediction accuracy with a 16KB predictor versus the 96.3% obtained with a compiler enhanced version of agree or bimode, reducing misprediction rate by 14%.

References

1. Thomas Ball and James R. Larus. Branch prediction for free. *Proc. ACM SIGPLAN Conf. on Programming Language Design and Implementation*, pages 300–313, June 1993.
2. D. Burger, T. M. Austin, and S. Bennett. Evaluating future microprocessors: the simplescalar tool set. Technical Report TR-1308, University of Winsconsin, July 1996.
3. Brad Calder and Dirk Grunwald. Reducing branch costs via branch alignment. *Proceedings of the 6th Intl. Conference on Architectural Support for Programming Languages and Operating Systems*, pages 242–251, October 1994.
4. Brad Calder, Dirk Grunwald, and Donald Lindsay. Corpus-based static branch prediction. *Proc. ACM SIGPLAN Conf. on Programming Language Design and Implementation*, pages 79–92, 1995.
5. Po-Yung Chang, Marius Evers, and Yale N. Patt. Improving branch prediction accuracy by reducing pattern history table interference. *Proceedings of the Intl. Conference on Parallel Architectures and Compilation Techniques*, October 1996.
6. Po-Yung Chang, Eric Hao, Tse-Yu Yeh, and Yale N. Patt. Branch classification: a new mechanism for improving branch predictor performance. *Proceedings of the 27th Annual ACM/IEEE Intl. Symposium on Microarchitecture*, pages 22–31, 1994.
7. A. N. Eden and Trevor N. Mudge. The yags branch prediction scheme. *Proceedings of the Intl. Conference on Parallel Architectures and Compilation Techniques*, pages 69–77, 1998.
8. Joseph A. Fisher. Trace scheduling: A technique for global microcode compaction. *IEEE Transactions on Computers*, 30(7):478–490, July 1981.
9. Joseph A. Fisher and Stefan M. Freudenberger. Predicting conditional branch directions from previous runs of a program. *Proceedings of the 5th Intl. Conference on Architectural Support for Programming Languages and Operating Systems*, pages 85–95, 1992.

10. Dirk Grunwald, Donald Lindsay, and Benjamin Zorn. Static methods in hybrid branch prediction. *Proceedings of the Intl. Conference on Parallel Architectures and Compilation Techniques*, pages 222–229, 1998.
11. Andreas Krall. Improving semi-static branch prediction by code replication. *Proc. ACM SIGPLAN Conf. on Programming Language Design and Implementation*, pages 97–106, 1994.
12. Chih-Chieh Lee, I-Cheng K. Chen, and Trevor N. Mudge. The bi-mode branch predictor. *Proceedings of the 30th Annual ACM/IEEE Intl. Symposium on Microarchitecture*, pages 4–13, December 1997.
13. Dondald Lindsay. Static methods in branch prediction. *Ph.D. thesis, Department of Computer Science, University of Colorado*, 1998.
14. Scott McFarling. Combining branch predictors. Technical Report TN-36, Compaq Western Research Lab., June 1993.
15. Scott McFarling and John Hennessy. Reducing the cost of branches. *Proceedings of the 13th Annual Intl. Symposium on Computer Architecture*, pages 396–403, 1986.
16. Pierre Michaud, Andre Seznec, and Richard Uhlig. Trading conflict and capacity aliasing in conditional branch predictors. *Proceedings of the 24th Annual Intl. Symposium on Computer Architecture*, pages 292–303, 1997.
17. Frank Mueller and David A. Whalley. Avoiding conditional branches by code replication. *Proc. ACM SIGPLAN Conf. on Programming Language Design and Implementation*, pages 56–66, 1995.
18. Ravi Nair. Dynamic path-based branch correlation. *Proceedings of the 28th Annual ACM/IEEE Intl. Symposium on Microarchitecture*, pages 15–23, November 1995.
19. Sanjay Jeram Patel, Marius Evers, and Yale N. Patt. Improving trace cache effectiveness with branch promotion and trace packing. *Proceedings of the 25th Annual Intl. Symposium on Computer Architecture*, pages 262–271, June 1998.
20. Harish Patil and Joel Emer. Combining static and dynamic branch prediction to reduce destructive aliasing. *Proceedings of the 6th Intl. Conference on High Performance Computer Architecture*, pages 251–262, January 2000.
21. Jason R. C. Patterson. Accurate static branch prediction by value range propagation. *Proc. ACM SIGPLAN Conf. on Programming Language Design and Implementation*, pages 67–78, 1995.
22. Alex Ramirez, Josep L. Larriba-Pey, and Mateo Valero. The effect of code reordering on branch prediction. *Proceedings of the Intl. Conference on Parallel Architectures and Compilation Techniques*, pages 189–198, October 2000.
23. James E. Smith. A study of branch prediction strategies. *Proceedings of the 8th Annual Intl. Symposium on Computer Architecture*, pages 135–148, 1981.
24. Eric Sprangle, Robert S. Chappell, Mitch Alsup, and Yale N. Patt. The agree predictor: A mechanism for reducing negative branch history interference. *Proceedings of the 24th Annual Intl. Symposium on Computer Architecture*, pages 284–291, 1997.
25. T. Y. Yeh and Y. N. Patt. Two-level adaptive branch prediction. *Proceedings of the 24th Annual ACM/IEEE Intl. Symposium on Microarchitecture*, pages 51–61, 1991.
26. Cliff Young and Michael D.Smith. Improving the accuracy of static branch prediction using branch correlation. *Proceedings of the 6th Intl. Conference on Architectural Support for Programming Languages and Operating Systems*, pages 232–241, October 1994.

An Efficient Indirect Branch Predictor

Yul Chu[1] and M. R. Ito[2]

[1] Electrical and Computer Engineering Department, Mississippi State University,
Box 9571, Mississippi State, MS 39762, USA
chu@ece.msstate.edu
[2] Electrical and Computer Engineering Department,
University of British Columbia, 2356 Main Mall, Vancouver, BC V6T1Z4, Canada
mito@ece.ubc.ca

Abstract. In this paper, we present a new hybrid branch predictor called the GoStay2, which can effectively reduce indirect misprediction rates. The GoStay2 has two different mechanisms compared to other 2-stage hybrid predictors that use a Branch Target Buffer (BTB) as the first stage predictor: Firstly, to reduce conflict misses in the first stage, a new effective 2-way cache scheme is used instead of a 4-way set-associative. Secondly, to reduce mispredictions caused by an inefficient predict and update rule, a new selection mechanism and update rule are proposed. We have developed a simulation program by using Shade and Spixtools, provided by SUN Microsystems, on an Ultra SPARC/10 processor. Our results show that the GoStay2 improves indirect misprediction rates of a 64-entry to 4K-entry BTB (with a 512- or 1K-entry PHT) by 14.9% to 21.53% compared to the leaky filter.

1 Introduction

Speculatively executed instructions used in a branch prediction can degrade system performance since they must be discarded when a branch is mispredicted. Thus, more accurate branch predictors are required for reducing the impact on overall system performance. Single-target direct branches can be predicted with reported hit-ratios of up to 97% [1]. By contrast, indirect branches with multi-targets are harder to predict accurately. The sources of indirect branches are switch statements, virtual function calls, or indirect function calls [2][3].

Conventional branch predictors predict branch direction and generate the target address associated with that direction. In conventional branch schemes, BTB-based prediction schemes are the only predictor for indirect branch prediction in conventional branch schemes since an indirect branch needs a full target address instead of just the direction (taken or not-taken). Chang et al. [4] showed that the small proportion of indirect branches (2 to 3%) for SPECint95 benchmarks can be a critical factor in degrading system performance.

There are two types of indirect branch predictors classified according to the number of component predictors: A single-scheme predictor that has only one predictor and a hybrid predictor that combines two or more single-scheme predictors. The Branch Target Buffer (BTB) represents typical single-scheme predictors. The BTB stores both the branch address and target address. If a current branch is found in the BTB, it is predicted as 'taken' with the target address. If there is a misprediction or a first-miss, the branch and target addresses are updated after the execution. In this paper, we considered hybrid branch predictors consisting of two single-scheme predictors only. Moreover, a BTB is used for the first stage predictor.

Chang et al. [4] proposed a predictor by using the Target Cache to improve the accuracy of indirect branch predictions. The Target Cache is similar to the Pattern History Table (PHT) of a 2-level branch predictor except that the Target Cache records the branch target while the PHT holds branch directions such as taken/not taken. This predictor XORs a pattern- or path-based history bits with the branch address to index the prediction. The Target Cache can reduce the misprediction rates of indirect branches significantly. For example, a 512-entry Target Cache achieved a misprediction rate of 30.4% and 30.9% for gcc and perl, while a 1K–entry 4-way set-associative achieves misprediction rates of 60% and 70.4% [4].

Driesen and Hölzle [3] introduced two variants of the Cascaded Predictor, which has two stages and two different update rules (a leaky or strict filter); a BTB for the first stage and a gshare-like two-level predictor as the second stage. The small-sized BTB works as a filter and the second stage predictor stores indirect branches that need branch history-based prediction. The second stage uses an indexing function similar to the Target Cache such as a path-based branch history XORing with a low-order branch address to index the prediction table.

In this paper, we present a 2-stage hybrid predictor called the GoStay2, which employs a new cache scheme for the first stage, a new selection mechanism, and update rule by using a 2-bit flag for both stages. We show that the GoStay2 outperforms other 2-stage hybrid predictors such as the Cascaded predictor [3] and Target Cache [4] by improving the accuracy of indirect branch predictions.

This paper is organized as follows: section 2 presents the new branch architecture with the two mechanisms for reducing indirect mispredictions; section 3 describes simulation methodology and benchmark programs; section 4 presents our simulation results; and section 5 provides our conclusions.

2   GoStay2 Branch Predictor

Among the several indirect branch predictors in section 1, the leaky filter of the Cascaded predictor offers the most effective misprediction rate for indirect branches [2][3]. However, the leaky filter has some problems that degrade system performance:

- Conflict misses – If a table (BTB) has a small number of entries (say, less than 512 entries), conflict misses might degrade the misprediction rate considerably;
- Inefficient predict rules – If a branch address is found at both stages, the second stage has priority for prediction. If the first stage has a correct target address and the second stage has an incorrect target address, then the assumed priority of the second stage always causes a misprediction; and

- Inefficient update rules – If a predicted target address is wrong, then the resolved target address of the branch address is updated in both stages. This also causes a misprediction if the replaced target address is needed for a following branch.

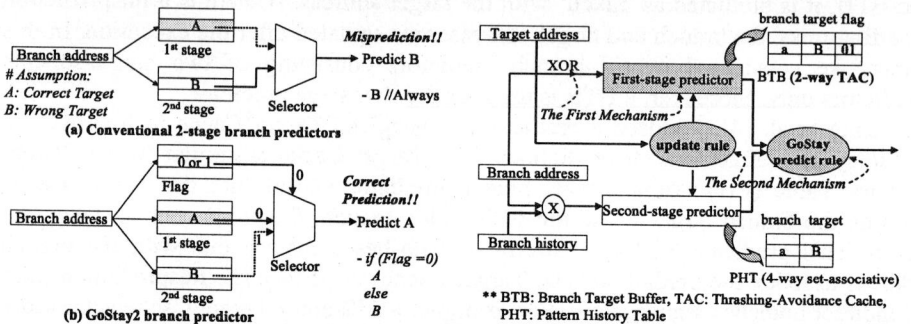

Fig.1. The basic operation of conventional 2-stage and GoStay2 branch predictors

Fig. 2. The overview of a GoStay predictor

Figure 1(a) shows that in a conventional 2-stage branch predictor, if the first stage has a correct target address (A) but the second stage has a wrong one (B), then the prediction (B) leads to misprediction since the second stage always takes priority of prediction.

Figure 1(b) shows the basic operation of the GoStay2 predictor, which can reduce mispredictions effectively. In the GoStay2 predictor, the prediction will be made according to the second flag in the first stage. In Figure 1(b), since the second flag is '0', the prediction (A) is made with the target address in the first stage (A), which leads to correct prediction. The flag is updated to '0' or '1' according to the update rule (refer to section 2.2).

Figure 2 shows the overview of a GoStay2 predictor, which has two different mechanisms compared to other 2-stage hybrid branch predictors. *'GoStay2' implies GoStay predict and update rules, as well as a 2-bit flag in the first stage.* The first bit of the flag is for the replacement policy of the first stage predictor [5], and the second bit is for the GoStay predict and update rule.

2.1 The 2-Way TAC Scheme for the First Stage – The First Mechanism

For the first mechanism, we use a 2-way TAC (Thrashing-Avoidance Cache) developed by Chu and Ito [5] for the first stage to reduce conflict misses. The 2-way TAC scheme employs 2 banks and XOR indexing function [5][6].

Figure 3 shows the main function of the 2-way TAC, which is to place a group of instructions into a bank according to the BSL (Bank Selection Logic) and the BoPLRU (Bank originated Pseudo LRU) replacement policy. Figure 4 shows pseudo code for the basic operation in Figure 3.

The function of the Bank Selection Logic (BSL) is to select a bank initially on a cache miss according to call instructions. The BSL employs a 1-bit counter, which is toggled (0 or 1) whenever a fetched instruction proves to be a call instruction. In Figure 3 and 4, the value of the 1-bit counter represents a selected bank for each instruction. An alternate bank is selected for every procedural call. A group of instructions terminated by a procedure call can be placed into the same bank through the BSL (Bank Selection Logic) and XOR mapping functions (indexing to each bank). The goal of the BSL is to help each bank place instructions in groups according to the occurrence of procedure call instructions.

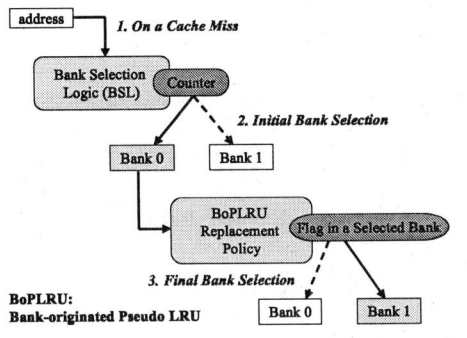

Fig.3. The basic operation of a 2-way TAC scheme

```
// Bank Selection Logic (BSL)
// initial bank selection according to the counter
If the value of the 1-bit counter = 0
      initial bank = bank 0.
else
      initial bank = bank 1.

// Bank originated Pseudo LRU (BoPLRU)
// final bank selection according to the flag
If the flag of the initial bank = 0
      Replace data of the other bank (say, final bank).
      Set the flag of the initial bank to 1.
If the flag of the initial bank = 1
      Replace data of the initial bank (say, final bank).
      Set the flag of the initial bank to 0.
```

Fig.4. Pseudo code for the BSL and BoPLRU policy

In Figure 3 and 4, after the BSL selects a bank on a cache miss, the BoPLRU will determine the final bank for updating a line as a correction mechanism by checking the flag for the selected cache line and set the flag of the initial bank.

The first mechanism helps to improve indirect misprediction rates by reducing conflict misses in a small-sized, say less than 512 entries, first stage predictor table.

2.2 The GoStay Predict and Update Rule – The Second Mechanism

The second mechanism helps to reduce indirect misprediction rates by storing two different target addresses in the two stages and selecting one correct target address from two stages according to a designated flag, which represents a short history of indirect branch predictions.

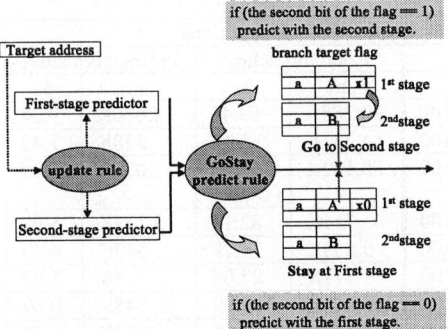

Fig.5. The GoStay predict rule of the second mechanism

Prediction with	Results	Update	Flag (2nd bit)
None	None	Both stages	1
First stage	Correct	None	0
First stage	Incorrect	Both stages	1
Second stage	Correct	None	1
Second stage	Incorrect	Second stage	1

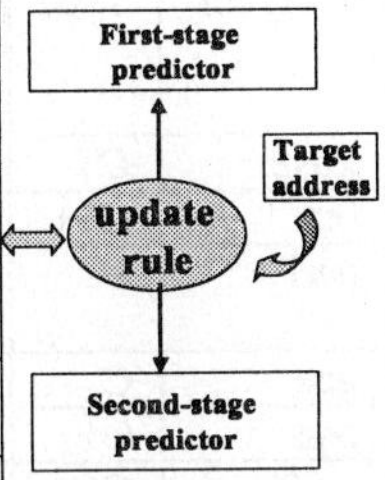

Fig.6. The update rule of the GoStay2 predictor

In Figure 5, if both stages have the same matched branch address, the prediction will be determined according to the GoStay predict rule: if the second bit of the flag in the first stage is '1', the prediction will be done with the target address of the second stage (Go). Otherwise, the prediction will be done with the target address of the first stage (Stay). The goal of the GoStay predict rule is to reduce mispredictions caused by wrong target addresses of the second stage (e.g. as in the leaky filter).

Figure 6 shows the update rule after the branch instruction is resolved. There are three cases for updating both stage predictors:

1) If a prediction with a target address in the first stage is correct, only the second bit of the flag is set to '0'; and
2) If a prediction with a target address in the second stage is correct, there is no update; and
3) Otherwise, the target addresses of both stages are updated and the second bit of the flag is set to '1'.

3 Experimental Environments

An overview of our simulation methodology is described in the following ways: firstly, SPEC95INT and C++ programs were compiled by using a gcc compiler and secondly, the GoS-Sim (branch prediction simulator) ran each executable benchmark with its input data. GoS-Sim was developed by using the Shade and SpixTools. Shade and SpixTools are tracing and profiling tools developed by Sun Microsystems. Shade executes all the program instructions and passes them onto the branch prediction simulator. GoS-Sim not only simulates most indirect branch predictors such as the BTB-based Target Cache and Cascaded Predictor, but it also runs several XOR mapping functions and replacement policies such as the LRU (Least Recently Used) and the Pseudo LRU, etc. The simulator for the proposed predictor was added into the GoS-Sim. Finally, outputs such as misprediction rates, the number of control transfer and procedural call/return instructions, etc. were collected.

Table 1. Benchmark program characteristics

Program	Type	Dynamic instructions	Control Flow Instructions					
			Total		Cond. branches		Indirect branches	
			num.	%	num.	%	num.	%
xlisp	C	189,185K	43,643K	100	30,288K	69.40	4,076K	9.34
ixx	C++	31,830K	7,258K	100	4,731K	65.19	538K	7.42
perl	C	630,281K	130,746K	100	88,162K	67.43	7,656K	5.97
gcc	C	250,495K	53,190K	100	43,711K	82.18	3,177K	5.97
eqn	C++	58,401K	12,080K	100	9,033K	74.78	547K	4.53
m88ksim	C	851K	196K	100	171K	87.02	4K	2.27
go	C	584,163K	82,253K	100	69,163K	84.09	548K	0.67
deltablue	C++	42,149K	9,997K	100	5,122K	51.24	554K	5.54

Table 1 shows the percentages of conditional branches and indirect branches. Five of the SPECint95 programs were used for our simulation –xlisp, perl, gcc, m88ksim, and go. These are the same programs used in [3][7]. The next suite of programs is written in C++ and has been used for investigating the behavior between C and C++ [8][9]. These programs are ixx, eqn, and deltablue. For 'go', since the impact of indirect branch prediction is very low, it will be excluded from all averages in section 4.1. For 'deltablue', it also excludes all averages like 'go' because of the small-sized (less than 500 lines) program.

4 Experimental Results

In this section, we determined the most effective branch predictor among the BTB (Branch Target Buffer, 4-way set-associative), TC (Target Cache), SF (Strict Filter), and LF (Leaky filter). We implemented hybrid predictors (the TC, SF, and LF) with: the first stage as a BTB; the second stage as a 4-way set-associative table with 512-entry; and the 9-bit (512-entry) pattern-based history register. The main differences in update rules for them are: 1) In case of TC, after resolving an indirect branch, the TC (second stage) can only be updated with its target address; 2) For the SF, only branches into the second stage predictor are allowed if the first predictor mispredicts; 3) For the LF, new second stage entries on first-misses are allowed in addition to the update rule of the SF.

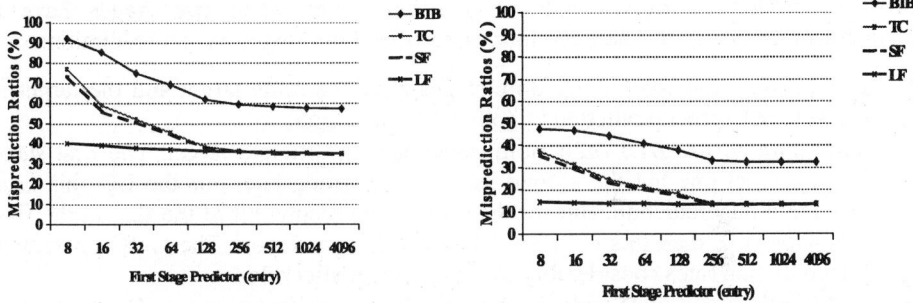

Fig.7. Misprediction rates for C programs   **Fig.8.** Misprediction rates for C++ programs

From the Figure 7 and 8, we determined the LF as the most effective indirect predictor if the first stage has a table with less than 512 entries.

4.1 Misprediction Rates between Leaky Filter (LF) and GoStay2 (GoS)

In this section, we compare the indirect misprediction rates between the LF and GoS predictors. In Figure 9(a), the GoS has lower misprediction rates than the LF for most sizes of the BTB (from 64 entries to 4K entries) and the second-stage predictor (512 entries and 1K entries) for all programs. The number of the LF-512 or LF-1024 means the entry size of the second-stage predictor in LF.

Figure 9 also showed the improvement ratio (IR) between the LF and GoS according to the sizes of the second-stage. We define the IR as: if a misprediction rate of LF-nnn = a and a misprediction rate of GoS-nnn = b, then a/b = 1 + n/100. It shows that 'a' has n% more misprediction rates than 'b'. Where, nnn = 512 or 1024.

So, if n = IR, then IR-nnn = ((a-b)/b)*100 ---------------- (1)

In Figure 9(b), in the case of the IR-512, the IR is increased from 14.9% (64-entry of BTB) to 19.35% (4096-entry of BTB). For the IR-1024, the IR is increased by 17.41% to 21.53%.

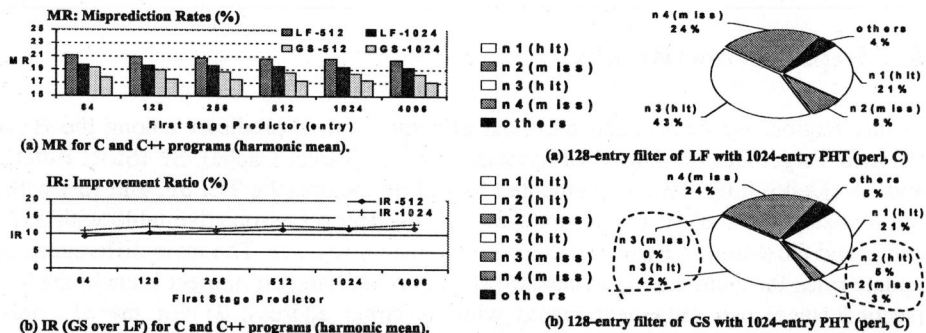

Fig.9. Misprediction rates and Improvements ratios (MR and IR)

Fig.10. Analysis of the prediction rates according to the cases

Most mispredictions of the indirect branches occur when two stages have a simultaneous prediction. There are four cases when both stages have a prediction:

- *addr_both_target_both (n1)*: Both stages have the same target and the target is correct. → Correct prediction in both the LF and GoS;
- *addr_both_target_BTB (n2)*: Both stages have a different target. The first stage has a correct one but the second stage has a wrong one. For the LF, this case leads to a misprediction. But for the GoS, if the second bit of the flag in the first predictor is 0, then this case results in correct prediction. The GoS can reduce misprediction rates considerably by using this predict rule.
- *addr_both_target_PHT (n3)*: Both stages have a different target. The first stage has a wrong one but the second stage has a correct one. In the LF, this case leads to a correct prediction. Meanwhile, for the GoS, if the flag bit is 0, it leads to a misprediction. However, the possibility for this case is very rare, as little as 1%. Otherwise, it is a correct prediction.
- *addr_both_target_none (n4)*: Both stages have a target, but neither target is the correct one. This case always leads to a misprediction in both the LF and GoS.

Figure 10 shows prediction rates according to the cases from the **n1** to **n4** between the LF and GoS with the 128-entry filter (BTB) and the 1024-entry PHT for the 'perl' benchmark program (C program). In Figure 10, 'others' means the prediction rates caused by the cases when one or none of the two stages has a prediction, which can lead to a hit or miss. However, since these rates are small compared to other cases, we ignore them for this section.

The important features provided by Figure 10 are: Figure 10(a) shows that 96% of the total predictions for LF occur within case n1 to n4. Among them, even if there is a correct target in the n2, the predictions caused by the n2 always lead to mispredictions because of the inefficient predict rule. The prediction rate caused by the n2 is 8%, which all lead to misprediction. Figure 10(b) shows that a prediction rate of 95% occurs for GoS in the cases of n1 to n4. However, the differences between the LF and GoS are the hit and miss rates caused by the case of the n2 and n3. In the GoS, more than half of the predictions (5% out of 8%) lead to a hit (n2 hit) instead of a miss (n2 miss). As a result, the misprediction rates can be improved by using the GoStay predict and update rule. Also, even if the predictions of the n3 leads to a hit in LF, part of the predictions for the n3 can lead to mispredictions in GoS. However, since the misprediction rate caused by this case is very small (0% in Figure 6(b)), we can disregard the misprediction rates caused by the n3.

5 Conclusion

For indirect two-stage hybrid branch predictors, the leaky filter was found to be the most effective one. However, the accuracy of this predictor is affected by two factors: The conflict misses for small-sized tables (say, less than 512 entries) considerably degrade the misprediction rate. The other factor is inefficient predict and update rules.

In order to resolve these problems, we have presented new branch architecture, the GoStay2 predictor, which has two mechanisms that are different from the other hybrid branch predictors. The first mechanism is a new cache scheme, TAC, employed as the first stage to reduce conflict misses. The second mechanism is the GoStay predict and update rule to reduce the frequency of wrong predictions caused by inefficient predict and update rules. By using these mechanisms, the GoStay2 reduces indirect misprediction rate of a 64-entry to 4K-entry BTB (with a 512- or 1K-entry PHT) by 14.9% to 21.53% compared to the Cascaded predictor (with leaky filter).

References

1. Tse-Yu Yeh and Yale N. Patt: A comparison of dynamic branch predictors that use two levels of branch history, ISCA, pages 257-266, 1993.
2. John Kalamatianos and David R. Kaeli: Predicting Indirect Branches via Data Compression, IEEE, MICRO 31, 1998.
3. Karel Driesen and Urs Hölzle: The Cascaded Predictor: Economical and Adaptive Branch Target Prediction, IEEE Micro 31, 1998.
4. Po-Yung Chang, Eric Hao, and Yale N. Patt: Target Prediction for Indirect Jumps, Proceedings of the 24th ISCA, Denver, June 1997.
5. Yul Chu and M. R. Ito: The 2-way Thrashing-Avoidance Cache (TAC): An Efficient Instruction Cache Scheme for Object-Oriented Languages, Proceedings of the 17th IEEE ICCD, Austin, Texas, September 2000.
6. F. Bodin, A. Seznec: Skewed-associativity enhances performance predictability, Proc. of the 22nd ISCA, Santa-Margharita, June 1995.
7. R. Radhakrishnan and L. John: Execution Characteristics of Object-oriented Programs on the UltraSPARC-II, Proc. of the 5th Int. Conf. on High Performance Computing, Dec. 1998.

8. B. Calder, D. Grunwald, and B. Zorn: Quantifying Behavioral Differences Between C and C++ Programs, Journal of Programming languages, Vol. 2, No. 4, pp. 313-351, 1994.
9. Urs Hölzle and David Ungar: Do object-oriented languages need special hardware support? Technical Report TRCS 94-21, Department of Computer Science, University of California, Santa Barbara, November 1994.
10. R. F. Cmelik and D. Keppel: Shade: A Fast Instruction-Set Simulator for Execution Profiling, Sun Microsystems Laboratories, Technical Report SMLITR-93-12, 1993.

The Behavior of *Efficient* Virtual Machine Interpreters on Modern Architectures

M. Anton Ertl and David Gregg

[1] Institut für Computersprachen, TU Wien, A-1040 Wien
anton@complang.tuwien.ac.at
[2] Department of Computer Science, Trinity College, Dublin 2, Ireland
David.Gregg@cs.tcd.ie

Abstract. Romer et al (ASPLOS 96) examined several interpreters and concluded that they behave much like general purpose integer programs such as gcc. We show that there is an important class of interpreters which behave very differently. Efficient virtual machine interpreters perform a large number of indirect branches (3.2%–13% of all executed instructions in our benchmarks, taking up to 61%-79% of the cycles on a machine with no branch prediction). We evaluate how various branch prediction schemes and methods to reduce the mispredict penalty affect the performance of several virtual machine interpreters. Our results show that for current branch predictors, threaded code interpreters cause fewer mispredictions, and are almost twice as fast as switch based interpreters on modern superscalar architectures.

1 Introduction

In recent years, interpretive language implementations have become commonplace for many tasks. Despite the importance of interpreters, little effort has been devoted to measuring their behavior on modern pipelined and superscalar architectures. The main work on this topic is by Romer et al. [9] who studied several interpreters (MIPSI, Java, Perl, Tcl). From their measurements, they drew two important conclusions. First, that the interpreters they measured behaved very much like general purpose integer C programs such as gcc, and were unlikely to benefit from any hardware support. Secondly, the interpreters they examined were not particularly efficient. From their experiments, and from examining the code of the interpreters, it was clear that performance was not a central goal of the interpreters' writers. Romer et al concluded that interpreters are likely to benefit far more from an efficient implementation than from hardware support.

In this paper we look at an important class of interpreters which behave very differently. These are efficient virtual machine interpreters. We find that they perform an exceptionally high number of indirect branches. Typical C code performs significantly less than 1% non-return indirect branches; C++ programs (using virtual function calls) perform 0.5%–2% indirect branches [4]; and other interpreters perform less than 1.5% non-return indirect branches. But up to 13% of the instructions executed in the virtual machine interpreters we examine are non-return indirect branches. Consequently, the performance of efficient virtual machine interpreters is highly dependent on the indirect branch prediction accuracy, and the branch misprediction penalty. For one benchmark we see a speedup factor of 2.55 or more (depending on the mispredict penalty) between no predictor and a good predictor.

The main contributions of this paper are (1) to demonstrate that (unlike many interpreters) efficient virtual machine interpreters do not behave like general purpose C programs, (2) to quantify the effects that indirect branches have on such interpreters on modern hardware, and (3) to show that different implementation techniques, especially using a threaded code interpreter, can greatly reduce the effects of indirect branches.

We first introduce VM interpreter implementation techniques (Section 2), then present our benchmarks, and their basic performance characteristics, in particular the high frequency of indirect branches (Section 3), then we introduce ways to make indirect branches fast (Section 4), and evaluate them on our benchmarks using a cycle-accurate simulator (Section 5). Finally we suggest some ways to speed up interpreters on current hardware (Section 6).

2 Efficient Virtual Machine Interpreters

For an efficient interpreter for a general purpose language the design of choice is a virtual machine (VM) interpreter. The program is represented in an intermediate code that is similar in many respects to real machine code: the code consists of VM instructions that are laid down sequentially in memory and are easy to decode and process by software. Efficiently implemented virtual machine interpreters perform well even on programs consisting of many simple operations (5–10 times slower than optimized C, with another factor of 2–3 for run-time type-checking).

The interpretation of a virtual machine instruction consists of accessing arguments of the instruction, performing the function of the instruction, and dispatching (fetching, decoding and starting) the next instruction. The most efficient method for dispatching the next VM instruction is direct threading [1]. Instructions are represented by the addresses of the routine that implements them, and instruction dispatch consists of fetching that address and branching to the routine. Direct threading cannot be implemented in ANSI C and other languages that do not have first-class labels, but GNU C provides the necessary features. Implementors who restrict themselves to ANSI C usually use the giant switch approach (2): VM instructions are represented by arbitrary integer tokens, and the switch uses the token to select the right routine.

When translated to machine language, direct threading typically needs three to four machine instructions to dispatch each VM instruction, whereas the switch method needs nine to ten [6]. The additional instructions of the switch method over direct threading is caused by a range check, by a table lookup, and by the branch to the dispatch routine generated by most compilers.

```
void engine()
{
  static Inst program[] = { &&add /* ... */ };
  Inst *ip; int *sp;

  goto *ip++;

 add:
  sp[1]=sp[0]+sp[1];   sp++;   goto *ip++;
}
```

Fig. 1. Direct threading using GNU C's "labels as values"

```
void engine()
{
  static Inst program[] = { add /* ... */ };
  Inst *ip; int *sp;

  for (;;)
    switch (*ip++) {
    case add:
      sp[1]=sp[0]+sp[1];   sp++;   break;
    /* ... */
    }
}
```

Fig. 2. Instruction dispatch using `switch`

3 Benchmarks

This section describes the interpreters we have benchmarked. It also highlights the differences between the efficient VM intrepreters and the Perl and Xlisp interpreters, which behave more like general purpose C programs. (These benchmarks can be found at
http://www.complang.tuwien.ac.at/anton/interpreter-arch).

Gforth 0.4.9-19990617, a Forth system [5]; it uses a virtual stack machine. We compiled it for indirect threaded code [3] i.e., there is one additional load instruction between the instruction load and the indirect branch (the direct threaded version would not compile for Simplescalar). The workloads we use are *prims2x*, a compiler for a little language, and *bench-gc*, a conservative garbage collector.

Ocaml 2.04, the Objective CAML "bytecode" interpreter, which also implements a virtual stack machine [7]; the VM works on tagged data (with some associated overhead), but does not do run-time type-checking (the tags are probably for the garbage collector). We ran both, a version using direct-threaded code, and a switch-based version. The workloads we use are *ocamllex*, a scanner generator, and *ocamlc*, the Ocaml compiler.

Scheme48 0.53; this interpreter is switch-based, uses a stack-based virtual machine, uses tagged data and performs run-time type checking. We use the Scheme48 compiler as workload (the first 10^8 instructions of building scheme48.image).

Yap 4.3.2, a Prolog system, uses an interpreter based on the WAM, a virtual register machine; it uses tagged data and performs run-time type-checking. We ran a version using direct threaded code and a version using switch dispatch. The workloads we use are *boyer*, part of a theorem prover, and *chat_parser*, a parser for English.

Perl the SPEC95 benchmark. This interpreter uses a linked-list intermediate representation and interprets that. We use the SPEC95 train/jumble benchmark as workload.

Xlisp the SPEC95 benchmark *li*. Xlisp interprets S-expressions (a list/tree-based intermediate representation of Lisp data). We use the SPEC95 ref/boyer program as workload.

We use Gforth, Ocaml, Scheme48, and Yap as examples of efficient VM interpreters. We had hoped to include a Java VM interpreter, but we couldn't find one that was both really efficient and freely available. Apparently everyone is focusing on JIT compilers. We include Perl and Xlisp for comparison with existing work [4], and to demonstrate the difference between many commonly used interpreters and efficient VM interpreters. We selected workloads of non-trivial size and used two workloads for most interpreters in order to exercise significant portions of the interpreters and to avoid overemphasizing some non-representative aspect of the performance. All benchmarks (except Scheme48) were run to completion.

interpreter	workload	inst. exec.	loads	stores	branches	indirect-branches	inst./ind.
gforth	benchgc	64396699	40.7%	10.5%	14.5%	13.0%	8380089	7.6
gforth	prims2x	94962783	39.4%	8.8%	18.4%	10.3%	9841564	9.6
ocaml	ocamlc	66439963	26.4%	10.2%	17.5%	6.3%	4204772	15.8
ocaml (switch)	ocamlc	91550037	21.8%	6.1%	21.5%	4.5%	4204772	21.7
ocaml	ocamllex	69738725	29.5%	10.7%	19.8%	11.3%	7918321	8.8
ocaml (switch)	ocamllex	122558868	22.2%	5.1%	24.3%	6.4%	7918321	15.4
scheme48	build	100000003	27.9%	12.1%	20.0%	3.2%	3275171	30.5
yap	boyer	68153580	32.9%	11.7%	19.7%	5.4%	3681492	18.5
yap (switch)	boyer	97326209	24.8%	8.2%	24.2%	3.7%	3681492	26.4
yap	chat	15510382	33.4%	14.5%	17.1%	5.5%	864703	17.9
yap (switch)	chat	22381662	25.6%	10.0%	22.4%	3.8%	864703	25.8
perl	jumble	2391904893	25.8%	17.8%	19.3%	0.7%	17090181	140.0
xlisp	boyer	173988551	26.1%	16.8%	22.7%	1.1%	1858367	93.6

Fig. 3. Instruction class distribution for our benchmarks

We compiled the interpreters for the SimpleScalar 2.0 microprocessor simulator [2], which simulates a MIPS-like architecture. Some basic data on the behavior of these benchmarks is listed in Fig. 3.

The aspect of these data that is important for this paper is the extremely high proportion of indirect branches in the efficient interpreters: 3.2%–13%. Note also that Gforth requires one load less per indirect branch if it uses direct-threaded instead of indirect-threaded code, resulting in an even higher proportion of indirect branches. In comparison, the benchmarks used in indirect branch prediction research [4] perform at most 2.1% indirect branches.

The reason for all these indirect branches is that every virtual machine instruction performs at least one indirect branch, whether it uses threaded code or switch dispatch. Most virtual machine instructions are quite simple (e.g., add the top two numbers on the stack), and can be implemented in a few native instructions plus dispatch code.

Another issue that can be seen nicely is the effect of threaded code vs. switch dispatch on the instruction count. The threaded and switch based variants of the interpreters were created by using existing compile time options in the interpreters, which use conditional compilation to create the appropriate version. The number of indirect branches is exactly the same in both cases, but the total number of instructions is higher for interpreters using switch dispatch (by a factor of 1.76 for ocamllex). For Ocaml switch dispatch costs 5.9–6.6 instructions more than threaded code, for Yap the difference is 7.9 instructions.

4 Fast Indirect Branches

Unless special measures are taken branches are relatively expensive operations in modern, pipelined processors. The reason is that they typically only take effect after they have reached the execute stage (stage 10 in the P6 micro-architecture, stage 17 in the Pentium 4) of the pipeline, but their result affects the instruction fetch stage (stage 1); i.e., after such a branch the newly fetched instructions have to proceed through the pipeline for many cycles before reaching the execute stage. The resulting delay is known as the misprediction penalty.

One way to avoid the mispredict penalty is to correctly predict the target of the branch and execute instructions there speculatively. Of course, if the prediction is incorrect, the speculatively executed instructions have to be canceled, and the CPU incurs the misprediction penalty.

Profile-Guided Prediction The Alpha architecture supports profile-guided, static indirect branch prediction by having a field in the JMP instruction that specifies 16 bits of the predicted branch target (this should be enough to predict an instruction in the I-cache). However, exploiting this feature requires compiler support for profile feed-back. Unfortunately, the compilers we know don't support this in a way that helps interpreters.

Dynamic Prediction Dynamic branch prediction is a micro-architectural mechanism and works without architectural, compiler or software support. The simplest dynamic indirect branch prediction mechanism is the branch target buffer (BTB), which caches the most recent target address of a branch; it uses the address of the branch instruction as the key for the lookup.

An improvement on the normal BTB is the BTB with 2-bit counters, which replaces a BTB entry only when it mispredicts twice. Actually one bit is sufficient, if the BTB is used only for indirect branch prediction. This halves the mispredictions if a branch usually jumps to just one target, with just a few exceptions.

The best currently-known indirect branch prediction mechanisms are two-level predictors that combine a global history pattern of n indirect branch targets with the branch address and use that for looking up the target address in a table; these predictors were proposed by Driesen and Hölzle [4], and they studied many variations of these predictors. We discuss the effects of various prediction mechanisms on interpreters in Section 5.

5 Evaluation

We added several branch prediction methods to the SimpleScalar-2.0 simulator, and ran the interpreters with the following prediction methods. In all cases, we used an unlimited sized table for the branch predictor, since we are interested in measuring the predicability of the branches with a given model, rather than tuning existing predictors.

No prediction The processor just has to wait until the branch resolves.

Profile-Guided Predicts that an indirect branch always jumps to the address that was most frequent in a training run. We generally use a different interpreted program for the training run (except for Scheme48, but it still gets a very low prediction accuracy).

BTB Predicts that a branch always jumps to the target it jumped to last time.

BTB2 A BTB that only replaces the prediction on the second miss.

2-Level Two-Level predictors that use the branch address and a history register containing the last 1–8 target addresses as a key into a lookup table of predicted targets and two-bit-counters. We use all the bits of the address. The history register is updated speculatively with the predicted target when the instruction fetch from the predicted target occurs.

Figure 4 shows the mispredict rates of our efficient VM interpreters; Fig. 5 shows the resulting execution time in cycles per VM instruction, for SimpleScalar with the shortest mispredict penalty; Fig. 6 shows the execution time when the misprediction penalty is set to 13 cycles (i.e., a Pentium-III-like pipeline length). Note that no results appear for Xlisp or Perl in these two figures, because they are not VM interpreters. Finally, Fig. 7 shows the number of machine cycles per non-return indirect branch executed.

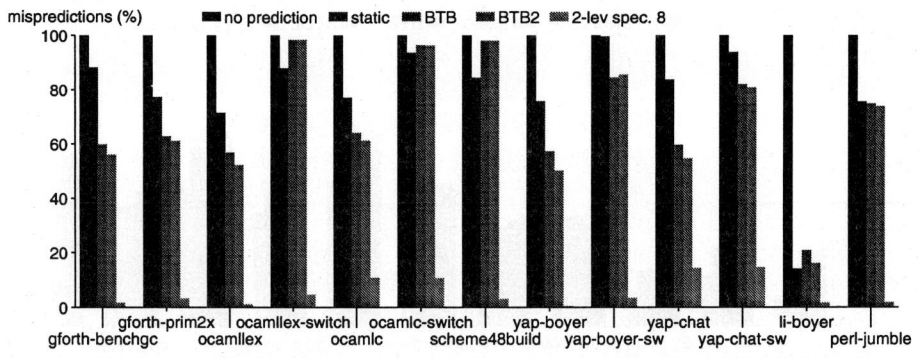

Fig. 4. Mispredict rate of various predictors on interpreters

Even with the smallest mispredict penalty the difference between using the best and the worst predictor can result in a speed difference of 1.36 (yap-boyer) up to 2.55 (gforth-benchgc); with the 13 cycle misprediction penalty the speed differences rise to 1.74–4.77 (yap-chat-sw–gforth-benchgc). So, indirect branch prediction accuracy plays a major role in VM interpreter performance (even more than the instruction counts indicate).

For threaded code, we see 71%–88% mispredictions for profile-guided static prediction, 57%–63% mispredictions for BTB, and 50%–61% for BTB2. With a low mispredict rate, gforth-benchgc takes 3.5 cycles per VM instruction and ocamllex takes 4 cyles, showing that threaded-code interpreters can be very fast, if we can eliminate most mispredictions.

For switch dispatch, we see 84%–100% mispredictions for profile-guided static prediction. The reason for the difference to the threaded-code case is that the switch-based interpreter uses a shared dispatch routine common to all instructions; profile-guided static prediction can therefore predict only the most common VM instruction for the whole training program; with a dispatch routine per VM instruction, profile-guided prediction can predict different next VM instructions, one for each current VM instruction. We expect mispredict rates similar to the threaded-code case, if the C compiler replicates the switch code for every VM instruction. The 100% misprediction result (yap-boyer-sw) is apparently due to differences in VM instruction usage between the training and the reference program.

For BTB and BTB2 we see 98% mispredictions for ocaml and scheme48, and 81%–86% for Yap. Again, the reason for the differences from the threaded-code results is the shared dispatch code: With separate jumps the BTB works quite well if each VM instruction occurs at most once in a loop of the interpreted program; then the BTB will predict all the indirect jumps correctly on the second trip through the loop (and BTB2 on the third trip). With a shared dispatch routine, a BTB will just predict that the present instruction will occur again

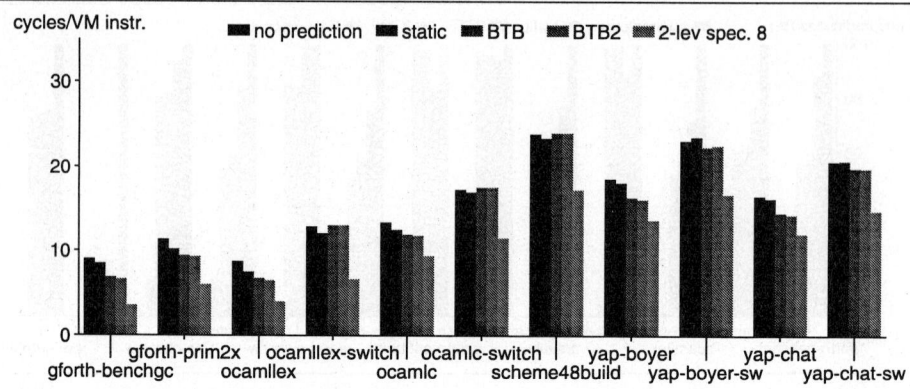

Fig. 5. Execution time of various interpreters with various branch prediction scheme with a mispredict penalty of 4 cycles ("1 cycle" in SimpleScalar terminology)

(which seems to happen about 15% of the time in Yap's register-based VM, but hardly ever in the stack-based VMs of Ocaml and Scheme48).

For the two-level predictors the difference between switch dispatch and threaded code is smaller, probably because the two-level predictors can fall back on the history and are not limited to looking at the address of the current branch.

The overall effect of these differences is that on SimpleScalar with 4 cycles mispredict penalty, switch dispatch takes 4.1–4.5 cycles more without prediction than threaded code, 5.5–6.6 cycles more for BTB2, and 2.6–3.1 cycles more for 2-level spec.(8). Given the short execution time of the threaded-code VM instructions, using switch dispatch is slower by up to a factor of 2.02 (ocamllex with BTB2 and 4 cycles mispredict penalty). Thus threaded code not only needs fewer machine instructions to execute, it also causes substantially fewer mispredictions.

Non-VM Interpreters The behaviour of Xlisp and Perl is very different. Xlisp has a low misprediction rate for all predictors. We examined the code and found that most indirect branches come not from choosing the next operation to execute, but from switches over the type tags on objects. Most objects are the same type, so the switches are very predictable. The misprediction rates for Perl are more in line with other interpreters, but figure Fig. 7 shows that improving prediction accuracy has little effect on Perl. Non-return indirect branches are simply too rare (only 0.7%) to have much effect.

6 Improving Interpreters

To increase the effectiveness of BTBs, each indirect branch should, ideally, have exactly one target, at least within the working set (e.g., an inner loop). The

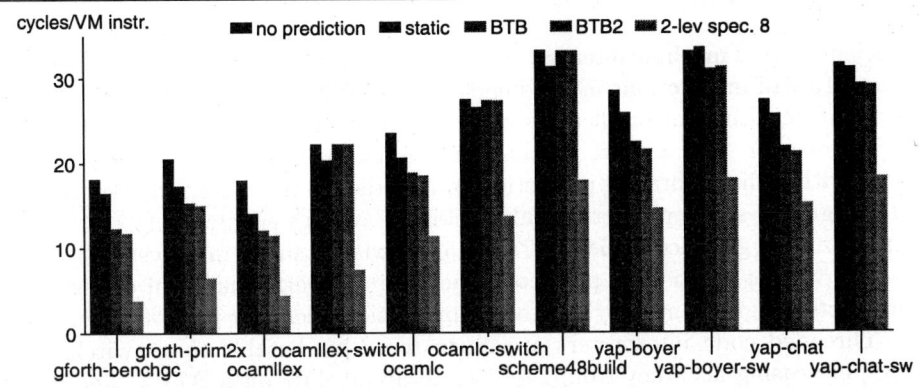

Fig. 6. Execution time of various interpreters with various branch prediction scheme with a mispredict penalty of 13 cycles ("10 cycles" in SimpleScalar terminology)

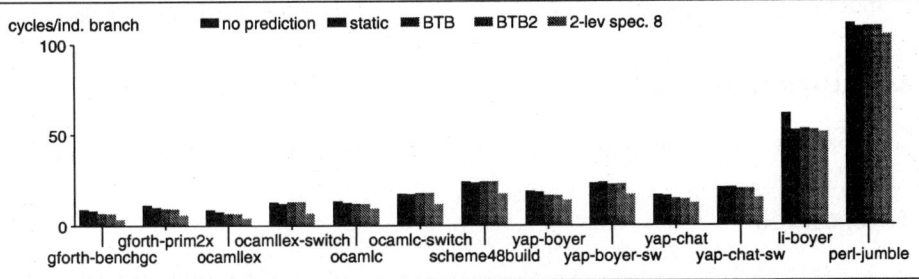

Fig. 7. Execution cycles per non-return indirect branch, with a misprediction penalty of 4 cycles ("1 cycle" in SimpleScalar terminology)

problem with the switch-based interpreters is that there is only a single branch, and usually there are more than one different VM instructions (and thus branch targets) in the working set. Threaded code interpreters improve the accuracy by having one branch per VM instruction; if a VM instruction occurs only once in the working set, its branch will correctly predict its target (the code for the next instruction) all the time.

Another approach is to increase the number of instructions in the VM instruction set. Several optimisations already do this. For example, splitting frequent VM instructions into several variants, preferably specialising them for frequent immediate arguments. Combining common sequences of VM instructions into single "super" instructions [8] will also add context information, and has the added advantage of removing dispatch overhead (and branches) within the sequence. Such specialised instructions should have a smaller number of frequent successors in most programs, and so their indirect branch will be more accurate.

7 Conclusion

Efficient virtual machine interpreters execute a large number of indirect branches (up to 13% of instructions in our benchmarks). Without indirect branch prediction, the resulting mispredictions can take most of the time (up to 62%) even on a processor with a short pipeline (and almost 80% with a longer pipeline). Even with indirect branch prediction, mispredicion rates are remarkably high. Profile guided static prediction only yields an average accuracy of 11%. Branch target buffers give accuracies of 2% to 50%, with a slight improvement for the two-bit variant. Two level predictors increase the performance of efficient VM interpreters significantly, by increasing prediction accuracy to 82%–98%.

Threaded code interpreters are much more predictable than switch based ones, increasing accuracy from 2%–20% to about 45% on a BTB2. The reason is that a switched based interpreter has only a single indirect branch jumping to many targets, whereas a threaded code interpreter has many branches, each of them jumping to a much smaller number of frequent targets. Given that threaded code interpreters also require less overhead for instruction dispatch, they are clearly the better choice for efficiently implementing VM interpreters on modern processors (up to a factor of two speedup for our benchmarks).

Acknowledgements

Vitor Santos Costa was a great help in getting Yap to run on SimpleScalar.

References

1. James R. Bell. Threaded code. *Communications of the ACM*, 16(6):370–372, 1973.
2. Douglas C. Burger and Todd M. Austin. The SimpleScalar tool set, version 2.0. Technical Report CS-TR-1997-1342, University of Wisconsin, Madison, June 1997.
3. Robert B. K. Dewar. Indirect threaded code. *Communications of the ACM*, 18(6):330–331, June 1975.
4. K. Driesen and U. Hölzle. Accurate indirect branch prediction. In *Proceedings of the 25th Annual International Symposium on Computer Architecture (ISCA-98)*, volume 26,3 of *ACM Computer Architecture News*, pages 167–178, New York, June 27–July 1 1998. ACM Press.
5. M. Anton Ertl. A portable Forth engine. In *EuroFORTH '93 conference proceedings*, Mariánské Láznè (Marienbad), 1993.
6. M. Anton Ertl. Stack caching for interpreters. In *SIGPLAN '95 Conference on Programming Language Design and Implementation*, pages 315–327, 1995.
7. Xavier Leroy. The ZINC experiment: an economical implementation of the ML language. Technical report 117, INRIA, 1990.
8. Todd A. Proebsting. Optimizing an ANSI C interpreter with superoperators. In *Principles of Programming Languages (POPL '95)*, pages 322–332, 1995.
9. Theodore H. Romer, Dennis Lee, Geoffrey M. Voelker, Alec Wolman, Wayne A. Wong, Jean-Loup Baer, Brian N. Bershad, and Henry M. Levy. The structure and performance of interpreters. In *Architectural Support for Programming Languages and Operating Systems (ASPLOS-VII)*, pages 150–159, 1996.

Improving Conditional Branch Prediction on Speculative Multithreading Architectures

Chitaka Iwama, Niko Demus Barli, Shuichi Sakai, and Hidehiko Tanaka

Graduate School of Information Science and Technology, The University of Tokyo,
7-3-1 Hongo Bunkyo-ku, Tokyo 113-8654, Japan
chitaka@mtl.t.u-tokyo.ac.jp

Abstract. Dynamic conditional branch prediction is an indispensable technique for increasing performance in modern processors. However, currently proposed schemes suffer from loss of accuracy when applied to speculative multithreading CMP architectures. In this paper, we quantitatively investigate this problem and present a hardware scheme to improve the prediction accuracy. Evaluation results show that an improvement of 1.4% in average can be achieved in SPECint95.

1 Introduction

Speculative Multithreading has been proposed in some Chip Multiprocessors (CMPs) [6,7,8,9] to accelerate performance when executing single thread programs. A speculative multithreading CMP partitions a program into threads and speculatively execute them in parallel across its multiple processing units (PUs). In such execution, however, a number of problems emerged. One of them is the loss of accuracy of conditional branch prediction. Currently proposed conditional branch predictors rely heavily on branch correlations to achieve high accuracy. However, in speculative multithreaded execution, information on these correlations may not be available.

In this paper, we quantitatively investigate this problem and propose a hardware scheme to improve the prediction accuracy. The main idea of this scheme is to exploit the locality of branch correlations within a static thread, and to use a centralized history table to manage branch information from the distributed PUs.

2 Conditional Branch Prediction on Speculative Multithreaded Execution

In this section, we investigate the accuracy of currently available conditional branch predictors when applied to speculative multithreaded execution. We choose five representative predictors for the investigation: bimodal predictor, global predictor, gshare predictor, per-address predictor, and a hybrid predictor of global and per-address predictor.

Bimodal predictor[1] is the simplest among the five predictors. It consists of a table of saturating counters indexed by the program counter. Global predictor, gshare predictor, and per-address predictor are variants of Two-level Predictors[2], which use two levels of branch history. The hybrid predictor[3,4] is a combination of global and per-address predictor, currently adopted in Alpha 21264 processor[5]

For the investigation, we simulated a 4-PU CMP, with a 4-kbyte conditional branch predictor in each PU. The PU is implemented as a 6-stage out-of-order superscalar processor with 64-entry instruction window, four functional units, two load-store units, and a 2k-entry speculative store buffer. We assumed perfect caches and all accesses to memory are completed in two cycles.

We defined a *thread* as a connected subgraph of a control flow graph with exactly one entry point. Inter-thread control and data dependencies are allowed. A program is statically partitioned into threads by a compiler. Innermost loop iterations are first marked as threads. For the rest parts of the control flow graph, the biggest possible subgraphs that meet the thread model's requirements are selected as threads. During the execution, threads are dynamically predicted and scheduled into the PUs. Inter-thread register dependencies are synchronized whereas inter-thread memory dependencies are handled speculatively. If a memory dependence violation is detected, the violating thread and all its successors will be squashed and restarted.

For clarity, we make distinction between static and dynamic threads. *Static thread* is used to refer to a portion of control flow graph identified as thread at compile time, whereas *dynamic thread* is used to refer to a stream of instructions of a static thread actually executed. Unless stated to be *static*, the word *thread* will be used to indicate a *dynamic thread*.

We compared the prediction accuracy in speculative multithreaded execution, with the accuracy in single threaded execution in a single PU. Eight programs from SPECint95 were used for the evaluations. The parameters were adjusted so that there are 10 to 25 millions of conditional branch instructions executed for each simulation run. In the following results, predictions made within misspeculated threads are not accounted.

Figure 1 shows the average prediction accuracy. Except for the bimodal predictor, the results showed a significant loss of prediction accuracy in speculative multithreaded execution. The accuracy degradation of the bimodal predictor is largely due to the increased time to train counter. But other predictors suffered mainly from the unavailability of correct branch information. There are basically two reasons why this information is not readily available.

1. A PU does not have access to the results of branches executed in other PUs. Not only the distributed nature of CMP architecture prevents such accesses, but also the speculative multithreaded execution does not guarantee that the results of branches from predecessor threads are available when a thread is started.
2. Since consecutive threads are scheduled to different PUs, a PU has to execute non-successive threads in sequence. The results of branches from these non-

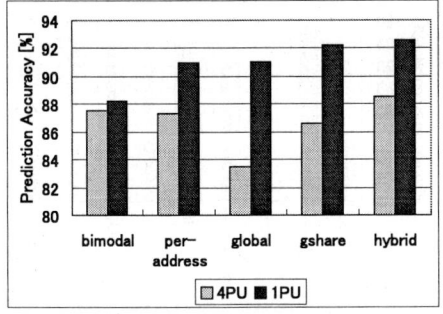 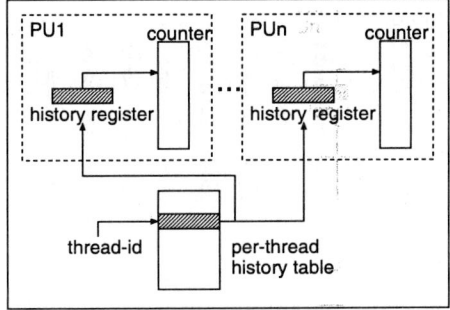

Fig. 1. Speculative multithreading effect on branch prediction accuracy

Fig. 2. Per-thread branch predictor

successive threads, however, are recorded successively, resulting in a broken history information.

3 Improving Prediction Using Per-thread Branch Predictor

To improve the branch prediction on speculative multithreading architectures, information on branch correlations should be used in more effective way. We propose a prediction scheme we call *per-thread branch prediction*. The main idea behind this scheme is to exploit the locality of branch correlations within a static thread.

Figure 2 illustrates the structure of per-thread branch predictor. Each PU has a prediction unit identical to a global predictor. In addition, there is a globally visible *per-thread history table* indexed by static thread identifiers. Each entry of this table records history of branches that belong to the same static thread.

When a PU starts executing a thread, it retrieves the thread's history from the table and initializes its history register with that value. During execution, branches are predicted in the same way as the global prediction scheme. After the execution of the thread is finished, the current value of the history register is written back to the per-thread history table. In case a thread needs to be restarted due to a misspeculation, the corresponding PU reinitializes its history register with the latest history from the per-thread history table. In this way, contamination of history register by misspeculated threads can be reduced.

Per-thread history table tries to maintain correct correlation information of branches that belong to the same static thread. However, when a PU retrieves a history of a thread from the table while a preceding copy of the same thread is still in execution anywhere else, the table cannot provide the PU with the most up-to-date history. Rather, it can only provide history from the last committed thread.

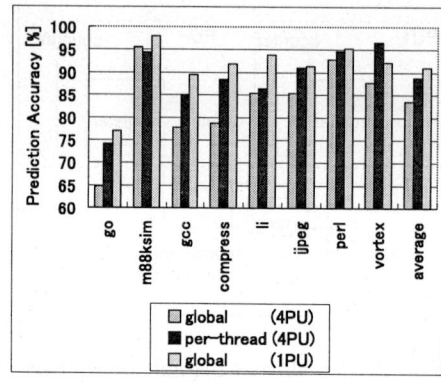 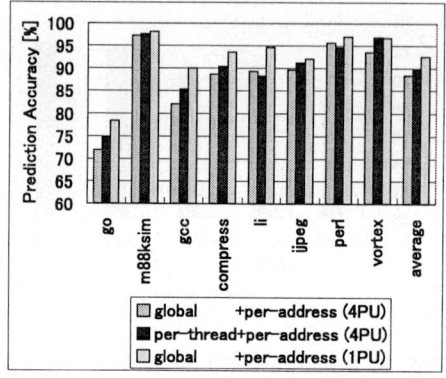

Fig. 3. Prediction accuracy of per-thread predictor and global predictor

Fig. 4. Prediction accuracy of (per-thread + per-address) hybrid predictor and (global + per-address) hybrid predictor

Another possible drawback of the per-thread prediction scheme is that it requires accesses to a centralized table before and after executing a thread. However, since these accesses can be carried out in parallel with other thread initialization/retirement processing, it is unlikely to cause a bottleneck problem to the architecture's critical path.

4 Evaluations

We first compared the performance of the per-thread predictor with that of a global predictor. Evaluation environment is identical to the one previously described in section 2. We assumed that the per-thread predictor consists of four 4-kbyte global predictors, one in each PU, and an additional 3.5-kbyte per-thread history table (2k-entry × 14 bits). Per-thread history table is a direct-mapped table indexed by the lower address bits of the first instruction in the thread. Table access delay is assumed to be two cycles.

Figure 3 shows the prediction accuracy of the global predictor and the per-thread predictor in speculative multithreaded execution. Prediction accuracy of the global predictor in single threaded execution is also shown as reference. It can be observed that the per-thread predictor improved the prediction accuracy of the global predictor on almost all applications, 5.3% in average.

We then combined the per-thread predictor with a per-address predictor to form a new hybrid predictor, and compared its accuracy with the hybrid predictor of global and per-address predictor. The new hybrid predictor is assumed to have four 4-kbyte local predictor structures, one in each PU, and a 3-kbyte per-thread history table (2k-entry × 12 bits). Figure 4 shows the simulation results. Except for *li* and *perl*, prediction accuracy was improved for all applications, by 1.4% in average.

One reason why some applications did not benefit from the per-thread prediction scheme is that, due to the parallel execution of threads, the per-thread history table was not always able to provide a correct per-thread history. Another possible reason is that the scheme only exploits branch correlation within a static thread. Thus, it was not effective for programs that make extensive use of global variables. Branches in these programs have a tendency to be predictable only when global correlation information is used.

5 Concluding Remarks

This paper investigated accuracy loss problem of conditional branch prediction on speculative multithreading CMP architectures and proposed per-thread prediction scheme to overcome the problem. Per-thread prediction uses a centralized history table to manage history of branches that belong to the same static thread. By exploiting the locality of branch correlations within a static thread, our scheme helped to improve the prediction accuracy by 1.4% in average.

The influence of intra-thread branch prediction to the overall performance largely depends on the architecture design. For example, in architectures that have PUs with deep pipeline and operate on threads whose size are relatively large, intra-thread branch prediction should be an important factor for their performance. We plan to make further investigation and perform more detail evaluations on this issue.

References

1. J. Smith: A Study of Branch Prediction Strategies. *Proc. 8th Annual Int'l Symp. Computer Architecture,* 135–148, 1981.
2. T. Yeh, Y. Patt: A Comparison of Dynamic Branch Predictors that use Two Levels of Branch History. *Proc. 20th Annual Int'l Symp. Computer Architecture,* 257–266, 1993.
3. S. McFarling: Combining Branch Predictors. *Technical Report TN-36, Digital Western Research Laboratory,* 1993.
4. P. Chang, E. Hao, T. Yeh, Y. Patt: Branch Classification: A New Mechanism for Improving Branch Predictor Performance. *Proc. 27th Annual Int'l Symp. Microarchitecture,* 22–31, 1994.
5. R. Kessler: The Alpha 21264 Microprocessor. *IEEE Micro, March-April,* 24–36, 1999.
6. K. Olukotun, B. Nayfeh, L. Hammond, K. Wilson, K. Chang: The Case for a Single Chip Multiprocessor. *Proc. 7th Int'l Symp. Architectural Support for Programming Languages and Operating Systems,* 2–11, 1996.
7. L. Hammond, M. Willey, K. Olukotun: Data Speculation Support for a Chip Multiprocessor. *Proc. 8th Int'l Conf. Architectural Support for Programming Languages and Operating Systems,* 48–69, 1998.
8. G. S. Sohi, S. Breach, T. N. Vijaykumar: Multiscalar Processors. *Proc. 22nd Annual Int'l Symp. Computer Architecture,* 414–425, 1995.
9. V. Krishnan, J. Torellas: A Chip-Multiprocessor Architecture with Speculative Multithreading. *IEEE Transactions on Computers, Vol. 48, No. 9.* 866–880, 1999.

Instruction Wake-Up in Wide Issue Superscalars

Soner Önder[1] and Rajiv Gupta[2]

[1] Michigan Technological University
Houghton, MI 49931
[2] The University of Arizona Tucson, AZ 85721

Abstract. While the central window implementation in a superscalar processor is an effective approach to waking up ready instructions, this implementation does not scale to large instruction window sizes. We propose a new wake-up algorithm that dynamically associates explicit wake-up lists with executing instructions according to the dependences between instructions. Instead of repeatedly examining a waiting instruction for wake-up till it can be issued, this algorithm identifies and considers for wake-up a fresh subset of waiting instructions from the instruction window in each cycle. The direct wake-up microarchitecture (DWMA) that we present is able to achieve approximately 80%, 75% and 63% of the performance of a central window processor at high issue widths of 8, 16 and 32 respectively.

1 Introduction

Out-of-order execution allows superscalar processors to take advantage of instruction level parallelism extracted from an instruction stream. However, the potential for speedups supported by the observed levels of instruction level parallelism remain far from being fully realized. To extract high levels of parallelism one problem that must be addressed is that of designing a scalable instruction issue mechanism. A linear increase in extracted parallelism requires a quadratic increase in instruction window size [2].

The implementation of a large instruction window is made difficult by the need for fanning out the wake-up signal to waiting instructions and selecting for issuing the instructions which are ready. When we assume that instructions are woken up by means of broadcasting, as in a central window implementation, we are faced with significant delays which originate from wire delays, tag matching time as well as the associative logic necessary to implement the wake-up functionality. These delays increase significantly for high issue widths because the delay of the wake-up logic of an instruction window is a function of the window size and the issue width. These delays increase quadratically for most building blocks of the instruction window [4].

In this paper we propose a novel wake-up algorithm that dynamically associates wake-up lists with executing instructions. The wake-up list of an instruction identifies a small number of instructions that require for their execution an operand used and/or the result computed by the instruction. We present the design of a microarchitecture, the direct wake-up microarchitecture (DWMA) that implements a wake-up algorithm based upon dynamic construction of wake-up lists. In this algorithm, at each cycle, primarily the instructions belonging to the wake-up lists of instructions that have just completed execution are considered for wake-up as only these instructions could now have become ready.

Our approach is related to the one taken in the design of the dependence based microarchitecture (DBMA) [4] which proposes a solution to the wake-up problem in the context of a conventional superscalar architecture that is of reasonable complexity in comparison to a central window processor. We have implemented a simulator for our architecture and our results show that the DWMA out performs the DBMA architecture due to its flexibility. DWMA captures 80 %, 75 % and 63 % of the performance achievable by a central window processor with the out of order store set memory disambiguator at issue widths of 8, 16 and 32.

2 Direct Wake-Up

The wake-up algorithm proposed by Palacharla et al. in [4] is based upon the observation that if a set of instructions form a dependence chain, then the wake-up mechanism only needs to examine the first instruction in the chain since the other instructions can never be successfully woken before the first instruction. It feeds dependence chains into FIFOs and only the instructions at the heads of the FIFOs are examined for wake-up thereby reducing the complexity of wake-up. However, the window of instructions over which parallelism can be detected by the DBMA mechanism can be sometimes limited because the instruction steering algorithm requires additional empty FIFOs to proceed, and when none are available, it must stall till some FIFOs become empty. While the use of dependence information in guiding the wake-up is an effective approach, the use of FIFOs limits the performance of DBMA.

Our approach provides a large instruction window from which instruction level parallelism is extracted by examining a subset of instructions for wake-up at each cycle. However, unlike the DBMA, instead of continuously examining a waiting instruction at the head of a FIFO till it can be issued, we determine a fresh set of instructions that will be examined by the wake-up mechanism in each cycle. The dependence information is used to identify this set of instructions. If in the current cycle an instruction is expected to complete its execution, then another instruction waiting for the result of the completed instruction may become ready in the next cycle. Thus, such an instruction will be among the set of instructions examined for wake-up and if ready, it will be issued in the next cycle.

To guide the above wake-up heuristic we must dynamically construct a wake-up graph. To obtain an effective hardware design for storing the graph the number of edges emanating from a node cannot be unbounded. In the hardware implementation the wake-up graph is represented by associating with each instruction an explicit wake-up list, W-LIST, which identifies the instructions that will be woken up by that instruction (i.e., the wake-up list is the representation of edges in the graph). Ideally the W-LIST of an instruction should contain all def-use edges emanating from it. But since the number of entries in the W-LIST must be a fixed small number in a practical implementation we place a bound on this number. Therefore we allow an instruction that computes a result to directly wake-up only the first two instructions in the instruction stream that use the result while the others are woken up indirectly by these two instructions. The latter is achieved by introducing use-use edges from the first two instructions and the next four instructions and so on. Thus, there are at most six edges in the W-LIST of an instruction, namely, (d0,d1), (l0,l1) and (r0,r1) corresponding to the result, the left operand and the right operand.

A crucial aspect of our algorithm is that the instructions that are linked through a chain of use-use edges may execute in an order different from the order they appear in the chain. Consider a chain of use-use edges that has been created due to an operand value v. When the value v is computed by its producer, the first instruction in the chain is considered for wake-up. Let us assume that the instruction cannot issue because its other operand is unavailable. In this situation, since the value v is available, we will consider the next instruction in the chain for wake-up even though the previous instruction is still waiting. It is possible that this instruction is found to be ready and thus may execute prior to the preceding instruction in the chain. Thus, the introduction of use-use edges does not restrict out-of-order execution.

While the initial form of the wake-up graph is determined by the original instruction ordering, the graph undergoes transformations determined by execution timing. Let us consider the modifications to the graph that may take place. When an instruction is first added to the wake-up graph, it is linked to the producer of its first unavailable operand, that is, it is added to the W-LIST of the producer of this operand. Now let us assume that this operand becomes available. This will cause the instruction waiting for the value to be considered for wake-up. At this point it may be determined that the second operand of the instruction is also unavailable. In this case the instruction would be added to the W-LIST of the producer of this missing operand. In other words, while one def-use edge has been removed, another one has been added to the wake-up graph. Note that in the worst case an instruction may be woken up at most two times before it can execute.

Consider the example code sequence shown in Figure 1(a). The dependence graph for the code sequence is illustrated in Figure 1(b) and execution of this code sequence on a central window processor ((CW)) with 2 functional units is shown in Figure 1(e). We observe that using our approach the wake-up links for all the instructions except OR and SUB can be established using def-use edges, that is using d0 and d1. This is because the ADD instruction has four children and therefore two result links are not sufficient. We therefore associate XOR and SLL, the first two instructions, directly with the result of ADD through def-use edges, whereas we satisfy the remaining two children OR and SUB using use-use edges emanating from XOR. The resulting wake-up graph is shown in Figure 1(c).

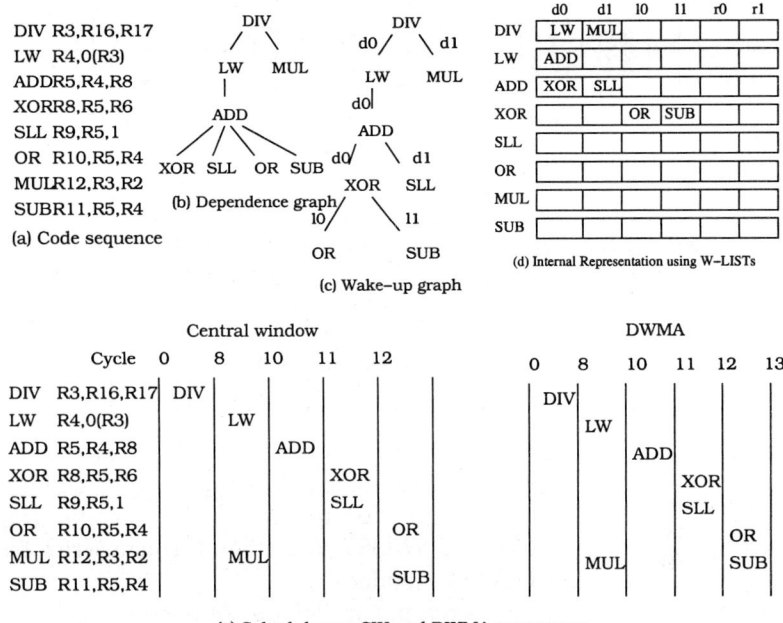

Fig. 1. Example DWMA Schedule

The execution schedule is realized as follows. When the DIV instruction completes its execution, it wakes-up the instructions LW and MUL through its def-use edges d0 and d1. When LW completes its execution, it wakes up the ADD instruction through its d0 edge. Once ADD is completed it activates the XOR and SLL instructions also through d0 and d1 edges. When XOR is activated, it can now activate OR and SUB through its l0 and l1 links. The resulting schedule is given in Figure 1(c). As we can see, in this case, the schedule generated using our wake-up algorithm is the same as that generated by the central window algorithm. In case of the DBMA architecture, the execution of the MUL instruction can be delayed till the dependence chain from DIV to XOR completes execution and releases a FIFO.

3 The Direct Wake-Up Microarchitecture

As shown in Figure 2, DWMA is a highly parallel decoupled superscalar with an eight stage pipeline. The construction of the wake-up graph is begun in the **Decode and Graph GEN-1** stage and completed in the **Rename and Graph GEN-2** stage. The graph is stored in the form of W-LISTs associated with instructions in their respective reorder buffer entries. Therefore the size of the instruction window from which instruction level parallelism is extracted is limited by the

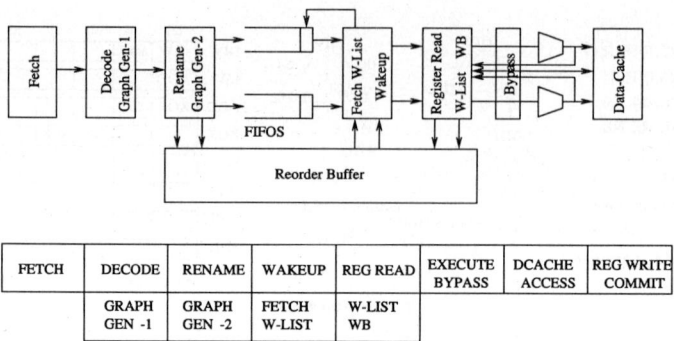

Fig. 2. The Direct Wake-up Microarchitecture

reorder buffer size. The subset of instructions that are to be considered by the wake-up mechanism are fetched and examined from the reorder buffer by the **Fetch W-LIST and Wake-up** stage while the updates to the wake-up graph are performed by the **Register Read and W-LIST WB** stage through write backs to the appropriate entries in the reorder buffer.

The instructions that are executed in parallel are obtained from the heads of the FIFOs and there is a one-to-one correspondence between the FIFOs and the functional units. FIFOs contain instruction descriptors which, in addition to providing the usual opcode and physical register numbers needed for an instruction's execution, also contain information required to carry out the wake-up activities associated with the instruction. Each instruction is entered into the queue when it is first fetched and every time it is woken up. The FIFOs essentially contain those instructions that are likely to be ready for execution.

Reorder Buffer. Each instruction is capable of waking up instructions through its def-use edges as well as use-use edges. In essence, an instruction can wake up to 6 instructions. Therefore large number of ports are required to implement the desired wake-up functionality. DWMA addresses this problem by following a unique reorder buffer design. The reorder buffer is issue-width interleaved and its address space is divided equally among the individual FIFOs. Thus, the reorder buffer index allocated to the instruction number modulo the number of functional units yields the functional unit that will execute this instruction and hence the reorder buffer bank where the wake-up list for the instruction will be stored. Since each functional unit processes a single instruction, only the wake-up list of the currently processed instruction needs to be fetched from the corresponding reorder buffer entry and each functional unit accesses its own reorder buffer bank to fetch the wake-up list of the instruction it is processing.

To provide sufficient number of ports without jeopardizing the processor clock, each reorder buffer bank is composed of 7 columns. The first column stores control information about the instruction as usual in any reorder buffer based superscalar implementation. The remaining 6 columns each store the descriptors that the current instruction should wake-up. As a result, each reorder buffer column element has only a single read and a single write port. As the issue width is increased, only the number of functional units and the number of reorder buffer banks increases.

It should also be noted that the reorder buffer is a collection of simple arrays of data locations since instructions fetch their data values from the provided register file. This design provides a very large instruction window without endangering the clock speed because of the distributed nature of the buffer implementation.

Key Pipeline Stages. Let us consider the operation of the key pipeline stages that construct and process the wake-up graph in greater detail. In the Decode and Graph GEN-1 stage the instruction is decoded and in parallel the producers' W-LISTs, to which the current instruction must be added, are identified from the source register identifiers. A reorder buffer entry is allocated to the instruction by incrementing the tail pointer of the reorder buffer. In Rename and Graph GEN-2 stage the source register identifiers of the instruction are renamed to physical registers and a result register is allocated if necessary. In parallel, the current instruction and its W-LIST are written to the instruction's assigned reorder buffer entry. The instruction is assigned to a functional unit (or FIFO). The assignment is carried out in a round robin fashion. An instruction descriptor is formed and sent to the appropriate FIFO.

In Fetch W-LIST and Wake-up stage the reservation table is accessed to determine whether the operands of the instruction descriptors at the heads of the FIFOs are ready. In parallel, the reorder buffer is accessed to fetch the W-LISTs of these instructions. The instructions corresponding to (l0,l1) are woken up if the left operand is available, the instructions corresponding to (r0,r1) are woken up if the right operand is available, and the instructions corresponding to (d0,d1) are woken up if the instruction takes a single cycle to execute. The ready woken up descriptors are pushed back to the heads of the appropriate FIFOs. The current instruction descriptors, that were initially obtained from the heads of the FIFOs, have now been processed. The ones that are found to be ready and have their functional unit free are sent to the next stage. On the other hand if the functional unit is busy, the ready descriptors are pushed back to the head of their respective FIFOs. If the instruction is not ready, then it is simply forwarded to the next stage. Finally, in Register Read and W-LIST WB stage if the current descriptor is ready, the operand values are read from the register file. If it is not ready the descriptor is written back to the W-LIST of the producer of the missing operand in the reorder buffer.

As we can see from the above description, processing of W-LISTs is done in parallel with the conventional functions of the pipeline stages Decode, Rename, Wake-up and Register Read. Therefore the additional tasks necessary to implement the direct wake-up are juxtapositioned with the conventional pipeline functions in Figure 2.

Graph generation algorithm. For the purpose of graph generation, we provide an array of queues, with each logical register being associated with a single queue. Each entry in a queue is a descriptor identifying a producer for the register's data value. A descriptor contains three fields, namely the reorder buffer index of the producer, the wake-up group of the producer (left operand, right operand, or result) and a one bit counter. When an instruction is being decoded, its source register identifiers are used to access the producer queue array and the descriptor at the head of the queue is copied to the instruction's corresponding operand. The descriptor's counter is incremented, and if it now overflows, the descriptor is removed from the head of the queue. Otherwise, the updated descriptor is left at the head of the queue. This process ensures that there are at most two edges emanating from the instruction corresponding to each of its operands and its result. Two new descriptors are formed, one for each operand which can now serve as new producers of these values and they are inserted at the tail of the corresponding queues. If there is no space left in the queue the new descriptors are simply discarded.

Instruction scheduling. DWMA implements the instruction scheduling uniformly by propagating instruction specific information in the form of instruction descriptors which are hardware pointers uniquely identifying the instruction. The format of the instruction descriptor is shown in Figure 3. The My-ROB-i field is the index of the reorder buffer entry allocated to this instruction. The Op-bits field indicate operand availability; there is one bit per operand. Left and Right register numbers are physical (renamed) registers for this instruction. Finally the PTR-missing field is a pointer to the W-LIST of a producer instruction. When both of the operands are missing, only one of them has to be recorded as part of the instruction descriptor since the descriptor itself is stored into the W-LIST of the other operand.

The actual processing of the instruction descriptors stored into the FIFOs is handled at a rate of one descriptor per FIFO through the Fetch W-List and Wake-up stage. Each descriptor field is used to handle the wake-up process. The processing of each of the descriptors proceeds as follows. The status of the current instruction is determined by accessing the reservation table. For this purpose, the physical register identifiers are sent to the reservation table to fetch the operand availability. Simultaneously with the reservation table access, the stage sends the My-ROB-i field of the instruction descriptor to the reorder buffer to fetch the W-LIST associated with this instruction. Since the descriptor is at the head of the queue, it should now wake-up any instructions which are in its wake-up list.

Once the W-LIST and the operand availability information is obtained, the set of instructions which are ready are identified using the operand availability

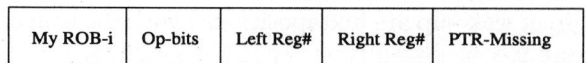

Fig. 3. Instruction descriptor

information for the currently processed instruction descriptor. The instruction itself is ready, if both operands are available. The dependent instructions are ready if they are only missing the data of the source operands of the currently processed instruction, or if the current instruction is a single cycle integer instruction whose result would make them ready. As a result, the following operations are performed in parallel to identify the instructions which would become ready as a result of the wake-up operation carried out by the current instruction:

- if the left operand of the currently processed instruction is available, instructions which are in the left operand group l0,l1 have also one of their operands ready (i.e., through a use-use edge). To update the operand availability information for these instructions, one zero bit from the Op-bits fields of their descriptors is turned on.
- if the right operand of the currently processed instruction is available, instructions which are in the right operand group r0,r1 have also one of their operands ready. The above procedure is applied this time to those instruction descriptors found in the right operand group.
- if the currently processed instruction is a single cycle instruction, instructions which are in the result group d0,d1 will have the required data in the next cycle through a def-use edge. Therefore, for those descriptors found in the result group d0,d1, one zero bit from the Op-bits field of each descriptor is turned on.

The crucial aspect of the above operation is no additional reservation table accesses are necessary to identify those instructions which would be woken-up. Following the operation, we now have a number of descriptors, namely, the original descriptor and its dependent descriptors. We first process the dependent descriptors. If these descriptors are ready they are pushed back to the head of the FIFO. In the next cycle, they can now wake-up their dependents and issue. If they are not ready, they are written back to the reorder buffer by the next stage. If the original descriptor is ready, and the corresponding functional unit is free, the instruction is issued for execution through the Read registers and W-LIST WB stage. If the corresponding functional unit is busy, the descriptor is pushed back to the head of the FIFO.

Longer latency operations need a similar treatment with a different timing. One cycle before the completion of the result, they access their reorder buffer entry to fetch the descriptors in their result wake-up group (d0, d1). These descriptors are inserted to the head of the queue they belong. In the next cycle, these instructions can resume operation if they now have all of their missing operands.

4 Experimental Evaluation

We simulated the DWMA, DBMA and central window algorithms using the FAST system [1]. The experimental set up is shown in Figure 4. We have used a gshare based instruction fetcher for 8 issue processors and an ideal fetcher for 16 and

Issue width	8, 16, 32 instructions
Fetch width	Equal to the issue width
Retire width	Twice the issue width
Instruction Window	Issue width ** 2
Number of FIFOs	Equal to the issue width
Functional Units	Issue width Symmetric Functional units.
Instruction fetch	Aggressive multi-block gshare
Dcache	Perfect
Memory ports	Issue width / 2

(a) Machine parameters

Functional Unit	Latency (cycles)
Load	2
Integer division	8
Integer multiply	4
Other integer	1
Float multiply	4
Float addition	3
Float division	8
Other float	2

(b) Functional Unit latencies

Fig. 4. Machine Configurations

32 issue processors. We employ a modified version of the store set disambiguator described in [3]. Misspeculation recovery is based upon the future file.

The resulting IPCs for all the benchmarks in SPEC95 are shown in Figure 5. An 8/16/32-issue DWMA attains 84/76/71% and 76/74/55% of the 8/16/32-issue central window processor performance for integer and floating point benchmarks respectively. In contrast, the 8/16/32-issue DBMA architecture only achieves 70/47/50% and 54/46/42% of the 8/16/32-issue central window processor performance for integer and floating point benchmarks respectively. The DWMA is significantly more effective than DBMA.

Acknowledgements

Supported by DARPA PAC/C Award. F29601-00-1-0183 and NSF grants CCR-0105355, CCR-0096122, and EIA-9806525 to the University of Arizona.

References

1. S. Önder and R. Gupta. Scalable Superscalar Processing. Ph.D. Thesis, Univ. of Pttsburgh, July 1999.
2. S. Önder and R. Gupta. Superscalar execution with dynamic data forwarding. In *International Conference on Parallel Architectures and Compilation Techniques*, pages 130–135, October 1998.
3. S. Önder and R. Gupta. Dynamic memory disambiguation in the presence of out-of-order store issuing. To appear in the 32nd Annual IEEE-ACM International Symposium on Microarchitecture, November 1999.
4. S. Palacharla, N. P. Jouppi, and J. E. Smith. Complexity-effective superscalar processors. In *Proceedings of the 24th International Conference on Computer Architecture*, pages 206–218, June 1997.
5. S. Vajapeyam and T. Mitra. Improving superscalar instruction dispatch and issue by exploiting dynamic code sequences. In *Proceedings of the 24th International Conference on Computer Architecture*, pages 1–12, June 1997.

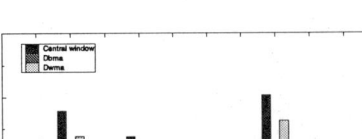
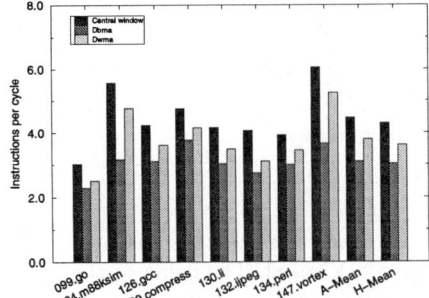
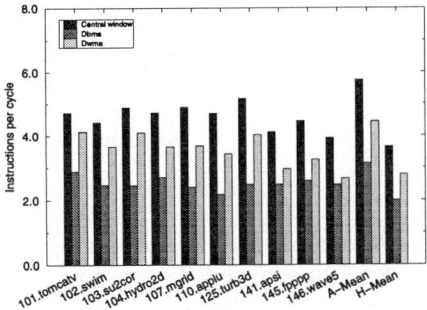
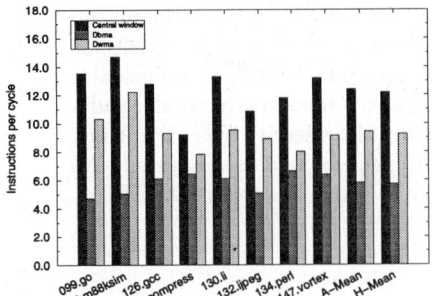
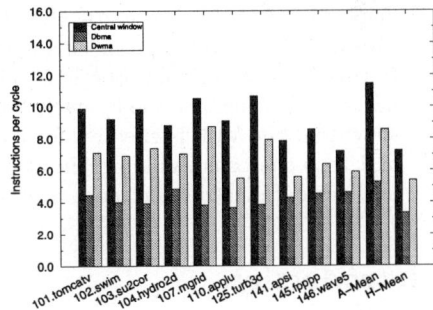
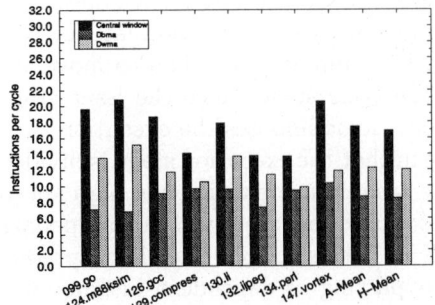
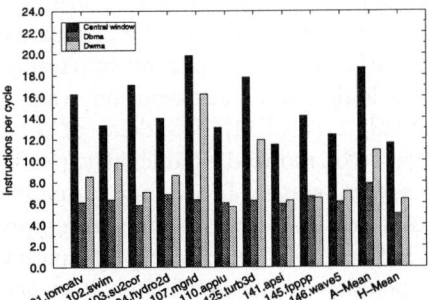

Fig. 5. IPC values for DWMA

Execution Latency Reduction via Variable Latency Pipeline and Instruction Reuse

Toshinori Sato[1] and Itsujiro Arita[2]

[1] Department of Artificial Intelligence
tsato@ai.kyutech.ac.jp
[2] Center for Microelectronic Systems
Kyushu Institute of Technology

Abstract. Operand bypass logic might be one of the critical structures for future microprocessors to achieve high clock speed. The delay of the logic imposes the execution time budget to be reduced significantly, resulting in that the execution stage is divided into several stages. Variable latency pipeline (VLP) structure has the advantages of pipelining and pseudo-asynchronous design techniques. According to source operands delivered to arithmetic units, the VLP changes execution latency and thus it achieves both high speed and low latency for most of the operands. In this paper we evaluate the VLP on dynamically scheduled superscalar processors using a cycle-by-cycle simulator. Our experimental results show that the VLP is effective for reducing the effective execution time, and thus the constraints on the operand bypass logic is mitigated. We also evaluate instruction reuse technique in order to support the VLP.

1 Introduction

Future microprocessors might rely on higher clock speeds, wider instruction issue width, deeper pipeline stages, and larger instruction windows in order to improve performance. As the width and size increases, the scaling of the clock speed becomes difficult to attain. The execution stage consists of execution latency and result drive time for operand bypassing[4]. It is almost impossible to move the bypass logic from the execution stage to the issue stage, since the issue stage is already critical[11]. The delay of the bypass logic imposes the execution time budget to be reduced significantly, resulting in that the execution stage is divided into several stages. Pipelining is one of the techniques realizing the high speed circuits and can improve the throughput of a function. However, deep pipelines can not improve processor performance if it means longer branch misprediction penalty or disallowing back-to-back bypassing of dependent instructions. Therefore, careful considerations are required for applying the pipelining to the bypass logic. On the other hand, asynchronous and pseudo-asynchronous circuits are the other techniques realizing high speed circuits. However, they have the following problems. The asynchronous and pseudo-asynchronous circuits need a completion detector of each operation. The detector becomes the critical path of the circuits and increases processor cycle time. Furthermore, the throughput can be diminished for specific operands. From these considerations, techniques to reduce execution latencies including the operand bypassing are required.

Variable latency pipeline (VLP) structure[6,7] is a microarchitectural technique which has the advantages of the pipelining and the pseudo-asynchronous design techniques. This design technique exploits the fact that the longest path for an individual operation of a logic circuit is generally much shorter than a critical path of the circuit. Furthermore, it utilizes the fact that source operands which decide the critical path are limited to a few variations. Considering the characteristics of logic circuits and their critical paths, the circuits could be designed as the longest path decided by most of the operands for a function[1] is shorter than an expected processor cycle time. For operations which can not be executed in one cycle, pipelined circuits are provided but their execution latencies are increased. This combination of two kinds of the circuits enables that high speed and short latency execution for most of the operations. In this paper, in order to mitigate the constraints on the bypass logic, we evaluate the VLP on platforms of dynamically scheduled superscalar processors using a cycle-by-cycle simulator. In addition, in order to enhance the VLP, we propose to utilize instruction reuse technique[8,10] for the operations which can not be covered by the VLP. The combination of the VLP and the instruction reuse is also evaluated using the simulator.

2 Related Work

This section surveys techniques for reducing the execution latencies.

Oberman et al.[7] develop a variable latency pipelined floating-point adder. In order to achieve maximum system performance, the latency of the floating-point adder becomes variable according to its source operands. This reduces the effective latency while the throughput of the adder is maintained. The effective latency is evaluated using SPECfp92 benchmark suite, but its impact on processor performance is not evaluated.

Kondo et al.[6] propose the VLP structure for integer ALUs. Using properly two kinds of circuits according to the longest path of the circuits for each operation, the effective execution latency can be almost one cycle while processor cycle time achieves 1 GHz. Using SPECint92 benchmark suite, the usefulness of the VLP is confirmed on a platform of an in-order execution scalar processor, but it is not clear for dynamically scheduled superscalar processors.

Richardson proposes result cache[8] which eliminates redundant calculations appeared repeatedly in floating-point units (FPUs). The result cache registers a pair of a floating-point operation and its result. When the same operation emerges, its execution results can be obtained without any calculation in the FPU. Since the latency of the FPU is generally very long, the quick calculation using the table lookup will improve processor performance.

---

[1] In this paper, *operation* and *function* are used properly as follows. A function is one of the executions such as addition, subtract, and so on. An operation is an individual function executed with its own operands.

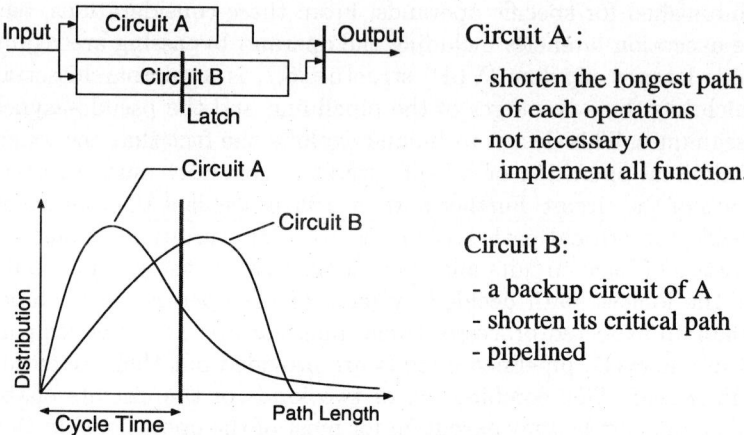

Fig. 1. Variable latency pipeline structure

Reuse buffer proposed by Sodani et al.[10] caches all types of operation results, while the result cache holds only results of floating-point operations. It is indexed by an instruction address while the result cache is indexed by operand values, and thus it can supply execution results at earlier pipeline stages than the result cache. Therefore, the reuse buffer is useful even for operations whose latencies are one. In other words, the effective latency can be less than one.

3 Variable Latency Pipeline Structure

Fig.1 shows the concept of the VLP[6]. A function can be implemented by several kinds of circuits whose design policy are different with each other. In Fig.1, two circuits are used for implementing the function. Circuit A is designed so that most of the longest path of each operation is shorter than a processor cycle time. Circuit B is designed so that the critical path of the circuit is shorter than the cycle time, and is pipelined. Combining these two kinds of circuits reduces the effective latency to execute the function and also maintains the throughput of the function even for the operations which are executed in two cycles. The execution stage consists of execution latency and result drive time for the operand bypassing[4]. Since the effective execution latency can be reduced by the VLP, the constraints on the operand bypass logic is mitigated considerably.

In order to select one from two results, a completion detector for circuit A is required. The detector can be pipelined since the pipelined circuit B works as the backup of the circuit A. Thus, the detector does not increase the critical path. From the above explanation, it can be seen that a high speed and short latency function is implemented. It is true that the total transistor count increases in order to implement two circuits. However, it is possible to reduce the count if the circuits A and B share circuitry.

Fig.2 shows an example of the VLP which is applied to an ALU[6]. There are two kinds of circuits. One is a two stage pipelined circuit consisting of ALU parts I and II, which is used for high speed and high throughput. This circuit is for the circuit B in Fig.1. The other consists of ALU parts I and III and is for the circuit A in Fig.1. That is, its execution latency is one. As can be seen, ALU part I is shared by two circuits. The circuit A in Fig.2 is designed so that any carry propagation over 16 bits is not considered[6]. If the carry propagation for an operation is less than 16 bits, the circuit A consisting of ALU parts I and III supplies its correct result, and most of the operations are included in this case. When the propagation is larger than 16 bits, the circuit A might generate a wrong result and the circuit B works as its backup. Across SPECint95 benchmark programs, over 50% of integer operands are 16 bits or less[2], and thus the percentage of the carry propagation larger than 16 bits is further small. The correct result is obtained in two cycles. Therefore, there is a completion detector of the circuit A which selects one from two results. As described above, the detector does not have any impact on the critical path.

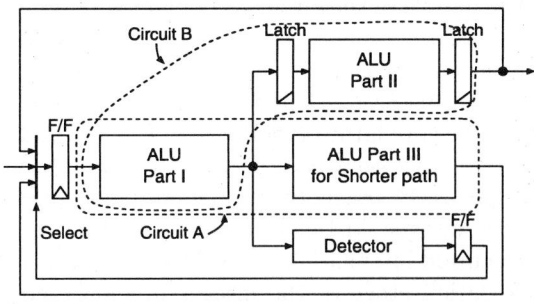

Fig. 2. ALU utilizing VLP

Instruction scheduling is handled as follows. Most schedulers rely on the fact that they know that a simple ALU operations will always take 1 cycle and they are performing wakeup and selection with this knowledge in advance. The VLP breaks this assumption since now some ALU operations take 1 cycle and some take 2 cycles. In the VLP, the execution latency of the ALU operations is assumed to be 1 cycle. Therefore, when an instruction is executed, dependent instructions would be scheduled or may already be scheduled. In the case that the instruction in the ALU takes 2 cycles, the dependent instructions have to be rejected or squashed from the functional unit and re-scheduled. This process is easily implemented. Since the execution latency is at most 2 cycles, the height of dependent instructions is one. There are no instructions which are indirectly dependent upon any two cycle latency operations and are already scheduled. That is, only instructions which are directly dependent upon and located immediately after some two cycle latency operations may violate data dependences. These instructions can be easily detected and invalidated. Re-scheduling the instructions is also easy. Since functional units are already assigned to the instructions, each of them only has to be executed again using correct operands on the same functional unit where it is already assigned. This scheduling scheme resembles that implemented in Compaq 21264 processor[5] and thus could be practical.

4 Evaluation Methodology

We focus on instructions per cycle (IPC) as a metric for evaluating performance. The details of the circuit is explained in [6]. An execution-driven simulator which models wrong path execution caused by branch misprediction is used for this study. We implemented the simulator using SimpleScalar tool set (version 2.0)[3]. The SimpleScalar/PISA instruction set architecture (ISA) is based on MIPS ISA.

The simulator models realistic 4-way and 8-way out-of-order execution superscalar processors based on register update units which have 64 and 128 entries respectively. Each functional unit can execute all functions. We evaluate the VLP integer ALUs[6] explained in Section 3 by comparing with ALUs whose execution latencies are 1 cycle and 2 cycles respectively. That is, we focus on the execution stage of the integer pipelines, considering the operand bypass logic. The latency of the ALU utilizing the VLP is 2 cycles when a carry propagation over 16 bits occurs. Otherwise it is 1 cycle. Candidate functions for the VLP include not only arithmetic and logical instructions but also load, store, and branch instructions. Multipliers and dividers do not utilize the VLP technique. The latency for multiplication is 4 cycles and that for division is 12 cycles. A 4-port, non-blocking, 128KB, 32B block, 2-way set-associative L1 data cache is used for data supply. It has a load latency of 1 cycle after the data address is calculated and a miss latency of 6 cycles. It has a backup of a 8MB, 64B block, direct-mapped L2 cache which has a miss latency of 18 cycles for the first word plus 2 cycles for each additional word. No memory operation can execute beyond a store whose data address is unknown. A 128KB, 32B block, 2-way set-associative L1 instruction cache is used for instruction supply and also has the backup of the L2 cache which is shared with the L1 data cache. For control prediction, a 1K-entry 4-way set associative branch target buffer, a 4K-entry gshare-type branch predictor, and an 8-entry return address stack are used. The branch predictor is updated at the instruction commit stage.

The SPECint95 benchmark suite is used for this study. We use only integer programs because the VLP is applied to only integer ALUs. The test input files which are provided by SPEC are used. We used the object files provided by University of Wisconsin Madison[3], except for 132.ijpeg which is compiled by GNU GCC (version 2.6.3) with the optimization option, -O3. Each program is executed to completion or for the first 100 million instructions. We count only committed instructions.

5 Simulation Results

This section presents simulation results. First in this section, the impact of additional execution latency due to the bypass logic on processor performance is shown. And then, the usefulness of the VLP is evaluated.

5.1 Impact of Long Latency

Fig.3 shows the impact of the additional execution latency due to the bypass logic on processor performance. The processor performance is normalized by that of the processor whose ALU latency is always one. Thus, the lower the bar is, the severer the performance degradation is. For each group of two bars, the left bar indicates the performance of the 4-way processor and the right one indicates that of the 8-way processor. Note that the bars for 4-way and 8-way processors can not be compared with each other. They only indicate the difference from the baseline processor models. The followings are observed. First, the processor performance is significantly degraded. This is different from the belief that dynamically scheduled processors have an ability of long latency tolerance.

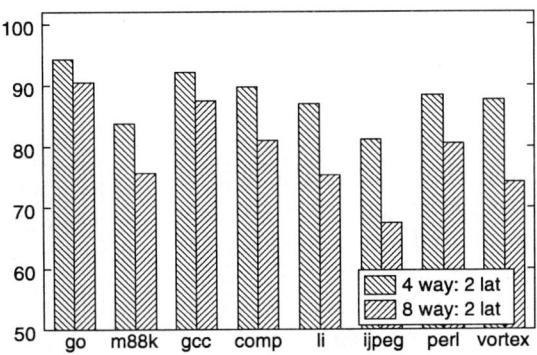

Fig. 3. (%)Impact of long latency

Second, the impact of the long latency is generally much severer for 8-way processor than for 4-way one. The degradation is as much as 30%. This is because 8-way processor can execute more instructions in parallel than 4-way one and because the demand for scheduling becomes higher. In addition, as instruction issue width is larger, the branch resolution time which is longer than that of the baseline model has serious impact on processor performance.

5.2 Effectiveness of VLP

Table 1 shows the percentage of operations whose execution latencies are reduced by the VLP. That is, it presents the VLP hit ratio. Note that it is correct that 4-way and 8-way processors mark different VLP hit ratios. It is because instructions flushed due to branch misprediction are considered for calculating the hit ratios. For most of the programs, approximately 90% of the two cycle latency operations are executed in one cycle by utilizing the VLP. Therefore, only less than 10% of operations must be executed in two cycles. The effective latency is reduced and the performance degradation will

Table 1. (%)VLP hit ratio

program	hit ratio	
	4-way	8-way
099.go	82.00	81.84
124.m88ksim	88.10	88.04
126.gcc	88.86	89.04
129.compress	29.14	33.87
130.li	81.23	81.99
132.ijpeg	93.08	93.02
134.perl	92.28	92.86
147.vortex	87.02	86.93

be compensated. For 129.compress, the VLP hit ratio is considerably lower than others, and hence the effectiveness of the VLP might be smaller than the other programs. The reason why the VLP hit rate is small in the case of 129.compress is as follows. The execution of 129.compress is dominated by a function cl_hash(), which occupies 61.3% of whole execution. In cl_hash(), an integer array which has 69001 values is cleared. This process includes many store operations which occur carry propagations over 16 bits on calculating data addresses. In addition, there are many subtracts with carry propagation over 16 bits on decrementing index variable.

Fig.4 depicts the impact of the VLP on processor performance. For each group of four bars, the first two bars indicate the results for 4-way processor and the remaining two bars indicate those for 8-way processor. The left bar is for the processor consisting of two latency pipelined ALUs. The right bar is for that consisting of the variable latency pipelined ALUs. We can find the followings. First, utilizing the VLP, processor performance for most of the programs is comparable to that of the baseline processors. Second, for 129.compress there is still a significant difference between performance of the processor consisting of one cycle latency ALUs and that of the processor consisting of the VLP ALUs. This is because the VLP hit ratio for the program is very small.

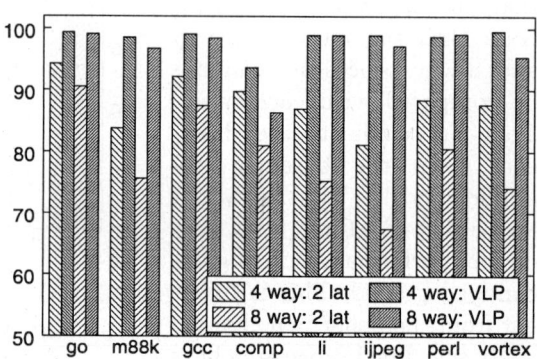

Fig. 4. (%)Effect of VLP

6 Enhancing VLP Using Result Cache

As we have seen in the previous section, the VLP does not always bridge the performance gap between one- and two-cycle latency pipelined ALUs. In this section, we try to enhance the VLP by combining it with the result cache.

6.1 Combining VLP and Result Cache

In order to enhance the VLP, we propose to utilize instruction reuse technique for the operations which are executed in two cycles. Since candidates of the instruction reuse are limited, the utilization of result cache might be improved. Fig.5 explains the case where the result cache is attached to the VLP ALU. When an operation and its operand values are provided to the ALU, they also index the result cache in parallel. Most of the time, the circuit A supplies correct results just like the VLP. When the circuit A can not supply a correct result for an operation, it is supported by the result cache.

Its correct result is obtained from the result cache if the access is hit. In such a case, the execution latency is reduced to be one even though the circuit A is not applicable. When a result cache miss occurs, the execution result from the circuit B is used. As described above, the effective latency is further reduced than the case where only VLP is utilized.

Only operations which can not be covered by the VLP are held in the result cache. This registration policy limiting candidates of the result cache could improve its utilization. Thus, the result cache hit rate might increase and then improve processor performance more efficiently. Note that it is impossible to keep all cases which cause two cycle latency in a lookup table because there are a lot of combinations which occur the carry propagation over 16 bits. However, the execution results have locality and thus the result cache considered in this paper could keep useful combinations efficiently.

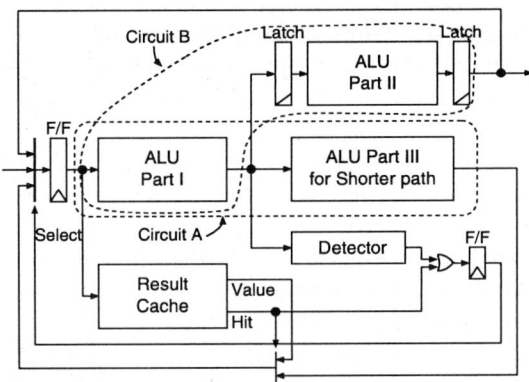

Fig. 5. Enhancing VLP using result cache

6.2 Evaluation Results

We implemented the result cache in the simulator explained in Section 4. It is assumed that the result cache is fully associative and has 64 entries. It is also assumed that the result cache is shared by all functions, and thus it is indexed by opcodes as well as operand values.

Table 2 shows the result cache hit rate. Different from our expectation that the result cache hit rate was high, it is considerably low. This is a discouraging result, especially for 129.compress where the VLP hit ratio is small, and thus it is expected that the contribution of the result cache on processor performance is modest.

Table 2. (%)R-cache hit rate

program	hit rate	
	4-way	8-way
099.go	70.53	69.41
124.m88ksim	89.21	81.73
126.gcc	52.04	51.40
129.compress	15.73	16.04
130.li	78.25	76.43
132.ijpeg	17.78	20.29
134.perl	54.76	46.12
147.vortex	24.15	24.19

Fig.6 depicts the impact on processor performance. For each group of four bars, the first two bars indicate the results for 4-way processor and the remaining two bars indicate those for 8-way one. The left bar is for the processor consisting of the VLP ALUs. The right bar is for that consisting of the VLP ALUs and the result cache. The primal observation is that the performance gap between the baseline model and the VLP model with the result cache is still large for 129.compress. For 8-way processor, it is approximately 10%, even though the result cache efficiently gains the performance by 4% over the VLP model. Since the result cache hit rate for 129.compress is smallest, this simulation result matches with our expectation. The second observation is that the result cache enhances the VLP for most of the cases. The 4-way and 8-way processors are gained by 1.25% and 1.12% on average respectively. Only one exception is 134.perl on 8-way processor. This is due to the following reason. Fig.7 shows the increase of total instruction count which includes instructions flushed by branch misprediction when the result cache is attached. We define the increase by the total number of instructions for the VLP with the result cache model over that for the VLP model. For each group of two bars, the left bar indicates the increase of the 4-way processor and the right bar indicates that of the 8-way one. When the effective execution latency is reduced, instructions executed while branch misprediction is unresolved are increased. On the other hand, the branch resolution time is also reduced. Thus, most of the times, the total instruction count may be reduced. From Fig.7, in the cases of only 132.ijpeg on 4-way processor, 129.compress, 130.li, and 134.perl on 8-way processor, the total instruction increases. For 132.ijpeg, the increase is little, and thus it does not affect processor performance. For 130.li, the result cache hit rate is large, and then its contribution to processor performance is bigger than the negative impact on the increase of the total instruction.

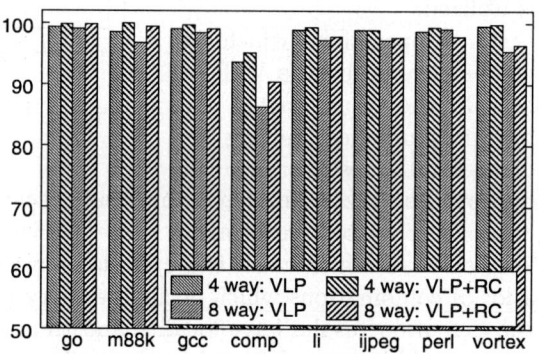

Fig. 6. (%)Effect of result cache

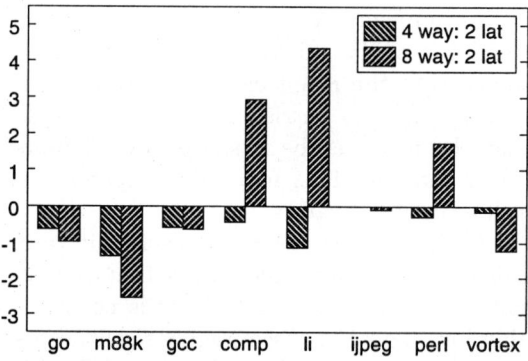

Fig. 7. (%)Increase of total instruction count

For 129.compress and 134.perl, the increase severely affects on performance. And then, processor performance of 134.perl is degraded. Anyway, the result cache has modest contribution for supporting the VLP technique.

7 Concluding Remarks

There is a trend that operand bypass logic is one of the critical structures for future microprocessors to achieve high clock speed. The delay of the bypass logic might impose the execution time budget to be reduced significantly, resulting in that the execution stage is divided into several stages. In this paper, we have evaluated the VLP integer ALUs for attack the problem. We have also proposed to combine the result cache with the VLP structure and evaluated the combination. The findings of this paper are as follows.

- Increase of the execution latency due to the delay of the operand bypass logic is serious, even though it is believed that the dynamically scheduled processors have the ability of latency tolerance.
- The VLP is useful for alleviating the constraints on the bypass logic by reducing the effective execution latencies.
- The combination of the VLP and the result cache has modest contribution to processor performance over the VLP technique.

One of the future studies dealing with the VLP is developing alternative VLP circuits which can cover more operations than the circuit evaluated in this paper. We are also interested in use of the VLP for fault-tolerance. The trends of increasing clock speed and of shrinking transistor size make the transient faults serious, and several fault-tolerant architectures are proposed[1,9]. The two cycle latency ALU in the VLP is effectively a checker ALU for the DIVA[1], and it does not even have to be located on expensive chip real estate. We would like to investigate the VLP both for performance and fault-tolerance.

Acknowledgment

The authors are grateful to Dr. Yoshihisa Kondo at Toshiba Microelectronics Engineering Laboratory for his comments on earlier drafts. Parts of this work were performed while Toshinori Sato was with the laboratory. This work is supported in part by the grant #13558030 from Japan Society for the Promotion of Science.

References

1. Austin T. M.: DIVA: a reliable substrate for deep submicron microarchitecture design. 32nd International Symposium on Microarchitecture (1999)
2. Brooks D., Martonosi M.: Dynamically exploiting narrow width operands to improve processor power and performance. 5th International Symposium on High Performance Computer Architecture (1999)
3. Burger D., Austin T. M.: The SimpleScalar tool set, version 2.0. ACM SIGARCH Computer Architecture News, 25(3) (1997)
4. Hara T., Ando H., Nakanishi C., Nakata M.: Performance comparison of ILP machines with cycle time evaluation. 23rd International Symposium on Computer Architecture (1996)

5. Kessler R. E., McLellan E. J., Webb D. A.: The Alpha 21264 microprocessor architecture. International Conference on Computer Design (1998)
6. Kondo Y., Ikumi N., Ueno K., Mori J., Hirano M.: An early-completion-detecting ALU for a 1GHz 64b datapath. International Solid State Circuit Conference (1997)
7. Oberman S. F., Flynn M. J.: A variable latency pipelined floating-point adder. International Euro-Par Conference (1996)
8. Richardson S. E.: Exploiting trivial and redundant computation. 11th International Symposium on Computer Arithmetic (1993)
9. Rotenberg E.: AR-SMT: a microarchitectural approach to fault tolerance in microprocessors. 29th Fault-Tolerant Computing Symposium (1999)
10. Sodani A., Sohi G. S.: Dynamic instruction reuse. 24th International Symposium on Computer Architecture (1997)
11. Yeager K. C.: The MIPS R10000 superscalar microprocessor. IEEE Micro, April (1996)

Memory Bandwidth: The True Bottleneck of SIMD Multimedia Performance on a Superscalar Processor

Julien Sebot and Nathalie Drach-Temam

LRI - Université Paris Sud - France

Abstract. This paper presents the performance of DSP, image and 3D applications on recent general-purpose microprocessors using streaming SIMD ISA extensions (integer and floating point). The 9 benchmarks benchmark we use for this evaluation have been optimized for DLP and caches use with SIMD extensions and data prefetch. The result of these cumulated optimizations is a speedup that ranges from 1.9 to 7.1.
All the benchmarks were originaly computation bound and 7 becomes memory bandwidth bound with the addition of SIMD and data prefetch. Quadrupling the memory bandwidth has no effect on original kernels but improves the performance of SIMD kernels by 15-55%.

1 Introduction

The SIMD (Single Instruction Multiple Data) extensions to general purpose microprocessor instruction sets have been introduced in 1995 to enhance the performance of multimedia and DSP applications. The goal for these extensions to general purpose microprocessors instruction sets is to accelerate DSP and multimedia application at a small cost. Traditionally in these processors, better ILP exploitation goes through increasing dispatch logic (reorder buffer size, reservation station size) and the number of functional units available. With SIMD instruction sets only the number of functional units is increased (the width of a functional unit). With constantly increasing available transistors in microprocessors there was room for the additional functional units needed by SIMD instruction sets. With SIMD extensions it's up to the programmer or the compiler to extract the ILP that is traditionally extracted by the out of order core of the microprocessor. Multimedia and DSP applications generally work on data vectors, so SIMD programmation is well adapted to these classes of applications.

At the beginning, these extensions were able to process 64 bit integer vectors: Sun with VIS in 1995, HP with MAX in 1995, MIPS with MDMX, Intel with MMX in 1997. The introduction of SIMD extensions able to process single precision floating-point vectors is more recent: AMD with 3DNow! [2] and Intel with SSE in 1998. The multimedia applications use more and more floating-point computations. Currently the main target for these FP SIMD extensions is 3D polygonal rendering that is extensively used in CAD applications and games. The need for single precision floating-point computing power is very important in this class of applications. In 1999 Motorola introduced AltiVec, which is the first SIMD instruction set that can handle both integer and floating-point vectors. Recently, Intel introduced SSE2 with Pentium 4, SSE2 enables double precision floating-point SIMD computation.

In this paper we study the performance of both integer and floating-point applications through DSP, image and 3D kernels on a general purpose microprocessor with SIMD extensions. DSP, image and 3D are the three main classes of multimedia applications and multimedia is the main workload on home computers. We show that SIMD optimizations and data prefetching raise the performance by 1.9 to 7.1 and that memory bandwidth becomes the bottleneck.

2 Related Work and Motivation

This section discusses related work in SIMD instruction sets evaluation.

In [7], Ranganathan and Al. study the performance of several integer image processing kernel including microbenchmarks, jpeg and mpeg compression. They show improvements from 1.1x to 4.2x with VIS, and that data prefetching is very efficient on media kernels. In [1] Bhagarva and Al. show improvements from 1.0x to 6.1x on DSP kernels and jpeg, but don't evaluate the impact of memory hierarchy on the final performance. Yang and Al. study in [3] the impact of paired SIMD floating-point instructions and 4-way SIMD floating-point instructions on 3D geometry transformations. Their study is limited to the impact on ILP and does not look at the memory hierarchy problems. In [6] Nguyen and Al. study the ILP of a small number of micro kernels with AltiVec and show improvements without memory hierarchy between 1.6x and 11.66x.

We have shown preliminary results in [4] about AltiVec performance on floating-point multimedia kernels. In this paper we show the performance improvement of 9 Integer and Floating-Point micro kernels using AltiVec. We focus on the impact of memory hierarchy (latency and bandwidth) on the performance of multimedia kernels using a SIMD instruction set. We show that with AltiVec streaming prefetch enabled, the kernel performance becomes bounded by the memory bandwidth.

3 Methodology

AltiVec is a Single Instruction Multiple Data (SIMD) machine comprised of $32 \times 128 - bit$ "vector" registers, 2 fully pipelined processing units (a vector permute and an ALU) and 170 new instructions. These instructions comprise vector multiply accumulation, all kinds of permutations between two vectors, float to int conversions, pixel packing, logical operations, comparisons, selections and extensions from a scalar to a vector.

AltiVec vector registers can hold either 16 8-bit integers, 8 16-bit integers, 4 32-bit integers than 4 IEEE-754 single precision floats. AltiVec provides streaming prefetch instructions. The programmer can use these instructions to specify the amount of data to be prefetched into the first level cache, with an optional stride. The Motorola PowerPC 7400 is the first microprocessor to implement AltiVec instruction set. There is more informations about the PowerPC 7400 in [5].

We have used Apple MrC compiler through a Metrowerks Codewarrior pro 4 plug-in. MrC allows easy Altivec programming through some extensions which enable the use of Altivec functions in a C program. The C programming model for Altivec used in MrC is designed to look like function calls, but each of this function call represents and generates one Altivec instruction. Variables are defined using C types that match Altivec data types and variables declared using these types are all 16-byte aligned.

We have evaluated the performance of our multimedia kernel by execution on a real PowerPC G4. We have used trace driven simulation to estimate the impact of memory bandwidth impact on these kernel's performance. We couldn't modify the memory bandwidth of our PowerPC G4 (by changing the bus/processor ratio and the memory latency) so we used Motorola G4 simulator v1.1.2 and pitsTT6 v1.4 execution trace generator. PitsTT6 works as a shared library. A call to *startTrace()* launch the trace generation during the execution and a call to *stopTrace()* stops it. It generates a TT6 execution trace which we used as input for the G4 simulator.

4   SIMD Optimizations for DSP Image and 3D Kernels

We have used 9 micro-kernels taken from multimedia and DSP applications. There are 4 single precision floating-point kernels and 5 integer kernels. SOAD: Sum Of Absolute Difference kernel is found in several reference video coder implementations such as MPEG2. It is one of the most computationally intensive aspects of video encoding. RGB2YCbCr converts from Gamma Corrected RGB to the YCbCr Color Space. It is used in video compression algorithms. iDCT: The Inverse Discrete Cosine Transform is used in MPEG2 decompression. The Image filters corresponds to gamma correction filters on static images. The sparse one works only on one component of the image. FIR and IIR filtering are two of the fundamental operations in digital signal processing. DAXPY is used in number of numerical algorithms, it is the heart of matrix-matrix products. The Max micro-kernel is used to find the maximum floating-point element of a vector and the elements corresponding index. It is a very important step in the Viterbi algorithm (speech recognition). The 3D kernel performs the essential steps of the geometry part of the 3D polygonal graphic pipeline. 3D polygonal rendering is used by most of the CAO/CAD applications, virtual reality and many games.

AltiVec provides SIMD instructions able to work on 4 to 16 element wide vectors depending on the data types. The programmer can permute each byte element of a vector as he wants. A simple way to characterize the "theoritical" speedup of a SIMD program is to use as speedup the vector width in number of elements. It also gives a good idea of the potential instruction count reduction factor. The speedups won't be so high for the following reasons:

- data need often to be reorganized to be processed efficiently with the SIMD instructions available. This overhead limits the speedup of all the programs that need data reorganization.
- The ILP that can be extracted from each algorithm is variable and often the theoretical speedup isn't reachable because of the instructions dependency graph that limits the ILP.

SIMD ISA provide generally specialized instructions that accelerate much the processing of most DSP and multimedia algorithms. These instructions, if they are only present in the SIMD extensions can raise the speedup of the SIMD version of the programs over the theoretical speedup. These specialized instructions are:

- meta-instructions: these instructions perform multiple operations at a time, the multiply accumulation is the most known example. The instruction that computes $\frac{1}{\sqrt{x}}$ is only found in the SIMD ISA and is used in vector normalization in the 3D geometry pipeline.
- *"vector if"* without branch: by using masking and selecting instructions the programmer can perform conditional tests on individual vector elements without any branch instruction.
- Type conversion, vector packing and unpacking. SIMD instruction sets provide float to int and int to float conversions and packing, unpacking instructions with saturated and unsaturated arithmetics. Saturated arithmetics and type conversions are generally high cost operations and are much used in multimedia algorithms that work on floats or 32-bit integers and that need the results to be converted into 8-bit integers to be displayed at screen.

The SIMD instruction sets use large register files with currently four times more space than conventional register files (same amount of registers, 4 times wider). This additional register space can be used in algorithms by maximizing the amount of data stored in registers and then exploit temporal locality at the register level. That reduces the first level cache overall number of miss and may raise significantly the performance of some algorithms.

Table 1. Datasets for the 9 benchmarks, number of elements per AltiVec vector (width) and instruction count reduction (ICR: executed instructions PPC/ AltiVec). Performance of the PPC and prefetch, AltiVec, AltiVec and prefetch versions relative to PPC version and prefetch impact on AltiVec version (PF=prefetch, AV=AltiVec

Benchmark	Dataset Size	Description	Width	ICR	PPC	AV	AV+pf (pf impact)
SOAD	1 MB	1 MPEG2 frame	16	16.3	1.05	2.71	3.44 (1.27)
RGB2YCbCr	9 MB	1 TVHD frame	16	9.8	1.00	4.34	5.95 (1.37)
IDCT	8 MB	8 MPEG2 frame	8	9.4	1.01	5.31	7.12 (1.34)
Img sparse	9 MB	1 TVHD frame	16	5.1	1.17	1.22	1.98 (1.62)
Img dense	9 MB	1 TVHD frame	16	18.4	1.01	2.18	3.63 (1.66)
FIR	10 MB	2400000 elts	4	3.5	1.00	3.02	3.20 (1.06)
DAXPY	8 MB	2000000 elts	4	4.0	1.90	1.12	1.93 (1.72)
Max	16 MB	4000000 elts	4	3.6	1.10	1.63	5.93 (3.65)
3D	10 MB	512000 vertices	4	4.3	1.07	2.18	2.98 (1.37)

5 Performance Evaluation

We have measured the execution time of the 9 micro-benchmarks on a PowerMac G4 450 with 1MByte of L2 cache. We have run each benchmark in its C version and AltiVec version with prefetch on and off. All the results are given as speedups against the C version without prefetch. We have used the datasets presented in Table 1. For all the benchmarks, the L1 misses are only cold misses because multimedia applications exploit mainly spatial locality via data streams. The speedups range from 1.8 to 4.9 for single precision floating-point kernels and from 1.9 to 7.1 for integer ones. The results are shown in table 1. Generally we have measured a speedup lower than the theoretical one. It is between 2.75 and 3.5 for floating point applications. FIR has the biggest instruction count reduction because there is no need for data reorganization because of the intra-iteration parallelization. Its speedup does not reach the theoretical one because the loop cannot be unrolled so the AltiVec functional units stay unoccupied most of the time. The 3D kernel that uses inter-iteration parallelization needs data reorganizations, that is an overhead in instruction count. The dependency graph between instructions is the same in AltiVec than in C (omitting the Permutations for reorganization) so the speedup is essentially limited by the overhead of the reorganization. AltiVec provides an independent permutation unit so a part of the reorganizations can be done in parallel with the computations. Max and DAXPY are more memory intensive than computation, so the speedup is limited by the memory hierarchy performance (cf. next section). For the integer benchmarks, IDCT is very computational and well parallelizable without any overhead, the number of executed instructions is reduced by a 9.4 factor (shown in table 1) and the speedup is 7.1. The sparse filter isn't much efficient because it performs many computations for nothing, just because the data structure is sparse. The AltiVec instruction count is near the one for the dense filter, versus a 4 times reduction for the PPC version. The two last benchmarks have an instruction reduction count of about 16. The 3D kernel uses some AltiVec specialized instructions as $\frac{1}{\sqrt{x}}$ in the normals transformation process. The clipping step uses intensively masking and selection instructions to perform "vector if". The phong lighting step uses vector packing, float to int conversions and saturated arithmetics. The part of the phong algorithm that uses these instructions has a speedup of 14, and the phong lighting step has a global speedup of 7.4. The functions we have implemented in our 3D kernels represent 85% of the time of the geometry transformations into the Mesa 3D graphic Library. The integration of our AltiVec functions into Mesa should give over a 100% increase in performance.

6 Latency Problems: Streaming Prefetch Impact

Our benchmarks are multimedia applications that have streaming data acess. We use blocked algorithm to avoid cache misses other than cold ones. In all our algorithms we have measured the impact of AltiVec streaming prefetch. We have chosen to launch streaming prefetch each 32Bytes of data. The impact on performance of enabling prefetch is shown in Figure ??. The impact of prefetch is much more important for AltiVec programs than PPC one but DAXPY.

DAXPY is memory bandwidth limited in both AltiVec and PPC version, and this limit is reached when activating prefetch (the performance are the same for PPC with prefetch than AltiVec with prefetch) so this explains why the speedup due to prefetch is lower for AltiVec version (the version without prefetch is faster in AltiVec).

Max in its PPC version is limited by the branch mispredictions that reduce the average number of instruction fetched each cycle. We see that the impact of prefetch is not very high because memory latency impact is much lower than branch mispredictions impact. Max has no mispredicted branches in its AltiVec version so the fetch does not limit the performance. The limiting factor becomes the memory latency. This explains the great impact of prefetch in the AltiVec version of this Kernel.

There are some kernels on which the activation of the streaming prefetch has a negative impact on the performance. The activation of prefetch generates a heavy load on the Load/store unit and on SOAD and the dense image filter (PPC) it has a negative impact on performance. On the other side, FIR performs many computations per data and it is not much dependent of the memory latency and the impact of prefetch on performance remains low for both versions.

For the PPC version the impact is greater in the sparse version of the image filter than for the dense version. In the dense version the first level cache hit rate is very high without prefetch (1 miss / 32 load), for the sparse version it is only 1/8 so the prefetch increases relatively more the L1 hit rate for the sparse filter. For the AltiVec version the acceleration due to prefetch are very similar because the data are accessed by 128 bit vectors even if they will not be processed (sparse filter). There are a little more computation in the sparse version (masking and selecting the element to be processed) so the impact of prefetch is reduced compared to the dense filter (memory access are less important).

For the rest of the kernels the impact of streaming prefetch for PPC versions is under 10% and between 27% and 66% for AltiVec ones. This is a great improvement in performance for AltiVec programs at a low programmer's effort cost.

7 Memory Bandwidth the Bottleneck of AltiVec Performance

We have seen that streaming prefetch has a great impact on AltiVec programs performance. AltiVec programs are much more sensible to memory latency than the PPC ones, but what impact has memory bandwidth? With streaming prefetch enabled is it the main factor limiting the performance of the AltiVec programs. We couldn't change the available memory bandwidth on our G4 platform, so we used Motorola G4 simulator with the same kernels to evaluate the impact of memory bandwidth on our micro-kernels. We have used pitsTT6 execution trace as input to the simulator. We have simulated the various memory bandwidth by changing the processor/memory ratio and the SDRAM timings because there was no other ways of modifying the relative memory bandwidth available. We have simulated a halved, doubled and quadrupled memory bandwidth. We have simulated a perfect memory hierarchy too (all data in L1 cache) to get a upper bound of the performance and see how far of this bound we stay.

All the results are in Figure 1. By looking to the speedup due to perfect memory hierarchy we can know if the kernel is memory bound or computation bound. SOAD, RGB2YCbCr and 3D are memory bound in their AltiVec version and DAXPY and Max both in PPC and AltiVec version. On most of the benchmark

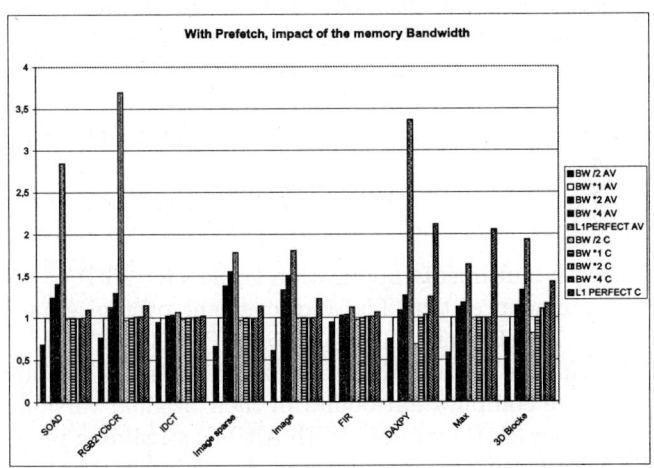

Fig. 1. Impact of the memory bandwidth for the 9 kernels, streaming prefetch on(BW=Memory Bandwidth, AV=AltiVec, L1PERFECT=All data preloaded in first level data cache)

memory bandwidth increase has much more impact on AltiVec performance than PPC. It is not a surprising result because the time spent in computations relatively to the memory accesses in AltiVec programs is much lower than in PPC due to SIMD processing. DAXPY and 3D kernel are sensible to memory bandwidth increase in both C and AltiVec version, but the impact is greater for AltiVec versions. SOAD, RGB2YCbCr, Image filters and Max are sensible to memory bandwidth increase only in their AltiVec versions when prefetch is activated. The two remaining programs IDCT and FIR are essentially computation bound, the impact of memory bandwidth is still greater in AltiVec than in PPC but it is quite negligeable.

The increase of main memory bandwidth has more impact when prefetch is activated for both C and AltiVec versions. When prefetch is used, memory access are more regular and optimized, the computations are accelerated because of the memory latency reduction, so the need for high bandwidth is more important.

With a quadrupled bandwidth the half of the programs have performance comparable to the performance with perfect memory hierarchy. SOAD, RGB2YCbCr, DAXPY, Max, 3D kernel have more requirements than a quadrupled memory bandwidth.

That shows that the main factor limiting the performance of multimedia, DSP and 3D applications with AltiVec is the main memory bus bandwidth. Currently the PowerPC G4 is limited by its 100MHz 64bit with SDRAM main memory bus on the studied applications. The only tested applications that have really no need for an increased memory bandwidth are applications that are only computation bound. The G4 bus is well designed for most of our applications when we don't use AltiVec but does not meet the requirements for the AltiVec versions. The memory technology that offer a doubled memory bandwidth are currently available with DDRSDRAM and RAMBUS. By using such memory technology some application performance would increase of up to 40% if the latency stays the same as the SDRAM (it is the case for DDRSDRAM).

8 Conclusion

We have optimized 9 multimedia application kernels for AltiVec SIMD instruction set and streaming prefetch. The improvement over original applications range from 1.9 to 7.1 with prefetch enabled on a PPC G4 450. The main factor limiting the performance of the SIMD media kernels is the memory hierarchy. Most applications are computation bound in their original version and become memory bound in their SIMD version. With AltiVec streaming prefetch enabled, the impact of memory latency is reduced and the main limiting factor for SIMD kernels becomes the memory bandwidth. We have shown that the memory bandwidth curently available on PowerPC G4 is sufficient for original kernels, but is the main bottleneck for 7 of our kernels. We show that a quadrupled memory bandwidth that can be achieved with current memory technology like DDRSDRAM or DRDRAM improves the performance of our kernels up to 55%.

References

1. R. Bhargava, L. John, B. Evans, and R. Radhakrishnan. Evaluating mmx technology using dsp and multimedia applications. In *Micro 31*, 1998.
2. Brian Case. 3dnow boosts non-intel 3d performance. *Microprocessor Report*, 12(7):18–21, juin 1998.
3. Barton Sano Chia-Lin Yang and Alvin R. Lebeck. Exploiting instruction level parallelism in geometry processing for three dimmensional graphics applications. In *Micro 31*, November 1998.
4. Jean-Luc Bechennec Julien Sebot and Nathalie Drach-Temam. A performance evaluation of multimedia kernels using altivec streaming simd extensions. *Third Workshop on Computer Architecture Evaluation Using Commercial Workloads (CAECW00) at HPCA-6*, january 2000.

5. Motorola. Mpc7400 risc microprocessor hardware sepcification. Technical report, Motorola, sept 1999.
6. H. Nguyen and L. K. John. Exploting simd parallelism in dsp and multimedia algorithm using altivec technology. In *ICS99*, 1999.
7. P. Ranganathan, S. Adve, and N. Jouppi. Performance of image processing with general purpose microprocessors and media isa extensions. In *ISCA 26*, may 1999.

Macro Extension for SIMD Processing

Patricio Bulić and Veselko Guštin

Faculty of Computer and Information Science, University of Ljubljana,
Tržaška cesta 25, 1000 Ljubljana, Slovenia
{Patricio.Bulic, Veselko.Gustin}@fri.uni-lj.si
http://lra-1.fri.uni-lj.si/index.html

Abstract. The need for multimedia applications has prompted the addition of a SIMD instruction set On the one hand we have modern multimedia execution hardware and on the other we have the software and the general compilers which are not able to automatically exploit the multimedia instruction set. Our solution to these problems is to find statement candidates in the program written in the language C/C++ (as we mainly use this language), and to employ the SIMD instruction set in the easiest possible way. We proposed the algorithm for identifying candidates for parallel processing (ICPP) which is based on the syntax and semantic cheching of statements. We define the macro library MacroVect.c as the substitution for the discovered statement candidates.

1 Introduction

The increasing need for multimedia applications has prompted the addition of a multimedia extension to most existing general-purpose microprocessors, based mostly on integer and floating point units [6]. These extensions introduce short single-instruction multiple data (SIMD) instructions to the microprocessor "scalar" instruction set. This instruction set is supported by special hardware which enables the execution of one instruction on multiple data sets. Such a vectorized instruction set is primarily used in multimedia applications, and it seems that it will grow rapidly over the next few years.

The short SIMD processing is exploited on larger words (from 64 to 128 bits) than usual. To store these words there are large register files inside the CPU, and also all the necessary logic, which enables the processing in parallel of 8 bytes, 4 word, 4 floating point value, etc.

We find three approaches targeting vector parallelism, first, use of an intrinsic instruction [7] second, library of function calls, and, third, use of vector compilers [1,7].

On the one hand we have modern multimedia execution [8,9] hardware, on the other we have the software and the general compilers which are not able to automatically exploit the multimedia instruction set. In addition, the compiler is not able to locate SIMD parallelism within a basic block. The only way to exploit the SIMD extension instruction set is by using intrinsics [5,7,8] or its primitive and unpopular version, the assembly language instruction set code.

Both methods require experienced programmers, who are able to use the machine code.

The task of exploiting parallelism from the program to employ the vectorization technique at least very hard and the trend is likely to continue in this direction [1]. The compiler needs some help in order to be able to extract the SIMD parallelism beyond vectorizable loops. We also believe that the development of C/C++ compilers will go in the direction of FORTRAN 90 performance, where an additional set of instructions for vectorizable processing is added. Our solution to these inconveniences is:

1. to find statement candidates in the program written in language C/C++ (as we mainly use this language), and
2. to employ the SIMD instruction set in the easiest possible way.

As we know that the compiler can not be user-changed or modified, we can only extend the functionality of the program (compiler) by the use of specialised library routines, or by macros. We prefer the latter.

2 Identifying Candidates for Parallel Processing (ICPP)

We based our ICPP algorithm on identifying the syntax and semantics of statements in C/C++ language, and extracting them from the "scalarized" compilation. We suppose that a statement which fulfils some syntax and semantic conditions can be transformed from singular word processing to vector (multi-word) parallel execution. the ICPP algorithm is composed of these steps:

1. Find innermost `for` statement.
2. Make list of array type variables, which were found in Step 1.
3. Analize syntax and semantic of statements inside the loop. Candidates for SIMD executeion are those statemnts which do some basic binary operations (this depends on the target processor) on the independent arrays. We can parallelize conditional execution, also. The basic idea is to convert a conditional execution into a conditional assignment [4].
4. Make dependency analysis.
5. If required make some loop fission. Parallelize those loops which fullfils all requirements for vectorization. Parallelization is done by replacing original statements with macros from our library.

The result of the algorithm is the list of candidate statements which can be executed in parallel by a technique we introduce with a macro library MacroVect.c. The ICPP algorithm was implemented as a LALR(1) sintax analizer which was extended with a set of semantic rules.

3 The Macro's Library of Vectorized Operations

As we see in Section 2 there are some approaches targeting vector parallelism, based on three main principles. Our approach is on the one hand connected to the usual compiler, and on the other to the use of a specific macro library as a result of one computation that can be used directly as a source in C/C++ computation.

By using the algorithm from Step 1 through Step 5 the program can use the macro as virtual function calls, at the same time it does not force us to use the assembly language. The macro library itself is written in assembly language, and can be downloaded from *http://lra-1.fri.uni-lj.si/vect/MacroVect.c*.

The library MacroVect.c is under development, and during its use we will be able to evaluate its pros and cons. From this perspective we have developed a general set of mostly usable macros. In the event that we did not fulfil some requirements we can add our own macro to the library.

4   Results

We measure the success of our ICPP algorithm on simple multimedia kernels. To test the performance of our ICPP algorithm in a real environment, we targeted our compilation system to the Intel MMX instruction set. Our preprocessor automatically replaces original C code with our macros where parallelization is successful. We then used a general C compiler to generate machine code. Table 1 and Figure 1 presents execution times for tested kernels compiled with our compiler and with Intel's C/C++ 5.0 vectorizing compiler.

Table 1. Execution times for tested kernels. These kernels are compiled with Intel vectorizing compiler and with our ICPP preprocessor. The used macros are implemented with MMX assembler code and with Intel's intrinsic calls

Kernel	Type of execution			
	Scalar	Intel vectorization	ICPP (asm)	ICPP (Intr)
Vector Assign (B)	152.0	70.0	128.0	---
Vector Assign (W)	341.0	242.0	305.0	---
Vector Assign (D)	586.0	565.0	612.0	---
Vector Addition (B)	238.0	124.0	235.0	194.0
Vector Addition (W)	428.0	340.0	467.0	399.0
Vector Addition (D)	801.0	781.0	932.0	799.0
Multiplication (W)	462.0	365.0	453.0	391.0
Cond. exec. (B)	160.0	---	140.0	123.0
Cond. exec. (W)	340.0	---	336.0	306.0
Vector add. (Multiple types)	904.0	---	816.0	573.0

5   Conclusion

We have developed a robust program based on the ICPP algorithm for detecting parallelism in 'for' statement loops. Detection is through a simple analysis in which independent simple statements were located within 'for' loops. We are

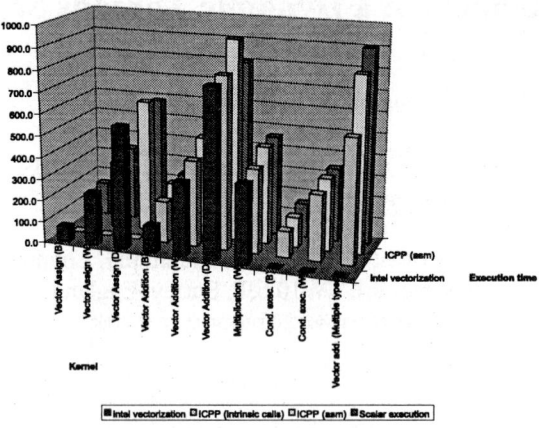

Fig. 1. Execution times

also able to translate vector parallelism into a SIMD instruction set. We obtained excellent performance for several application domains. Experiments on scientific and multimedia applications have yielded average performance improvements in some cases by even more than 100%.

Our program and macro library are still in their infancy. Although successful, we believe the effectiveness can be further improved.

References

1. S. Larsen, S. Amarasinghe. Exploiting Superword Level Parallelism with Multimedia Instruction Sets, Processing of the SIGPLAN'00 Conference on programming Language Design Implementation, Vancouver, B. C., June 2000.
2. R. Fisher. Compiling for SIMD within a register, In Processings of Workshop on Languages and Compilers for Parallel Processing, North Carolina, August 1998.
3. P. Artigas, M. Goupta, S. Mikiff. J. Moreira. Automatic Loop Transformation and Parallelization for Java, Parallel Processing Letters, Vol. 10 (2000), Nos. 2&3, pp. 153-165.
4. Millind Mitall, Alex Peleg, Uri Weiser. MMX Technology Architecture Overview, Intel Technology Journal, 1997.
5. Joe Wolf. Programming Methods for the Pentium(R) III processor's Streaming SIMD Extension Using the VTune(TM) Performance Enhancement Environment, http://developer.intel.com/technology/itj/Q21999/ARTICLES/art_6d.htm
6. -. Intel Architecture Software Developer's Manual Volume 1: Basic Architecture, http://download.intel.nl/design/pentiumii/manuals/24319002.pdf.
7. -, Intel Architecture Software Developer's Manual Volume 2: Instruction Set Reference, http://download.intel.nl/design/pentiumii/manuals/24319102.pdf.
8. -, Intel Architecture Software Developer's Manual Volume 3: System Programming, http://download.intel.nl/design/pentiumii/manuals/24319202.pdf.
9. -, Pentium (R) II Processor Application Notes, MMX (TM) Technology C Intrinsics, http://developer.intel.com/technology/collateral/pentiumii/907/907.htm.

Performances of a Dynamic Threads Scheduler

Smaïl Niar[1] and Mahamed Adda[2]

[1] Université de Valenciennes BP 311 LAMIH-ROI
Valenciennes 59304 cedex France,
niar@univ-valenciennes.fr
[2] American University of Richmond, London
Queens' Rd. TW10 6JP, Surrey, England
addam@richmond.ac.uk

Abstract. This paper presents the design and development of a dynamic scheduler of parallel threads in the Multithreaded multiProcessor Architecture (MPA). The scheduler relies on an on-chip associative memory whose management time is overlapped with the execution of ready threads. The scheduler efficiently assigns resources to threads, and permits them to communicate with great flexibility. The results achieved with small number of threads from programs with high degree of parallelism are very satisfactory, even under various degrees of cache misses.

1 Introduction

The next generations of processors provide a very high degree of integration. The challenges focus around embedding several units of processing inside the chip and offering them enough useful work to benefit from these technological advances. However, because these processors are gaining in processing speed, memory units and interconnection network can no longer follow their progression. Thread level parallelism is one of the techniques adopted by computer designers to bridge the speed gap between processors in one side, and memories and communication networks in the other side. There exists so far two ways of integrating the multithread mechanism:

1. *Simultaneous multithreading* (SMT)[1][2], which consists in using a super-scalar platform containing several issue slots. These slots are filled by instructions selected from several active threads.
2. *Single chip Multiprocessor* (CMP) [3], where several processors of simple structure are integrated on the same chip. These processors co-operate on the execution of a program containing several threads.

The MPA (Multithreading multiProcessing Architecture) project that we present in this paper, although different in concept, follows the second [4]. With respect to other multithreaded architectures, the following points characterize our MPA:

- The processor utilizes a hybrid execution model: Control-flow to execute a thread, data-flow to synchronize communicating threads, and instruction-flow to pass messages between threads.
- The thread scheduling is performed automatically with parallel threads detected at compilation time. This scheduling does not impose any burden on the processors
- Each processor of the MPA network executes simultaneously several instructions from different threads. Only one execution pipeline is embedded in the processor.
- The communication between threads uses a message passing mechanism (via shared registers) that reduces the overhead when threads are not actives.

In this paper, we describe the mechanisms used by the MPA processors to extract and schedule parallel threads from parallel loops to obtain high level of performance.

2 MPA Processor Structure

In the MPA, to each thread we associate a number of resources called *"Context"* (Figure 1.(a)). Each context represents the state of a thread and consists of data registers, a PC and status registers [4].

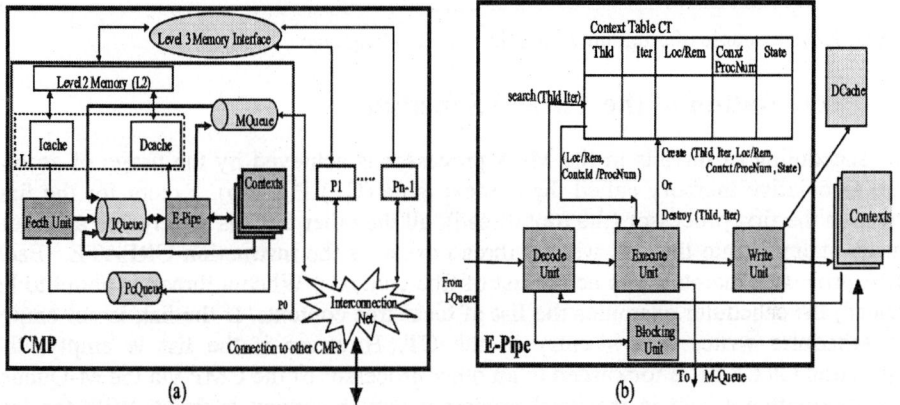

Fig. 1. (a) MPA processor internal structure in CMP environment and (b) its execution pipeline unit with the context table

The fetch unit continuously feeds the execution pipe (E-pipe) with ready instructions. The E-pipe consists of the decoding stage, followed either by the execution and the write stage or by the blocking stage fig 1.(b).

To maintain the synchronization between threads each data register is tagged with a presence bit **p** indicating the presence of an instruction or data. When an instruction, using a value sent by another thread, progresses through the E-pipe the availability of operands is checked before execution proceeds. If the operand is generated by another thread, it is written in the register. The arrival of an instruction requesting this data triggers the execution. When the operand is consumed, the register returns to the empty state. However, when the register is in an empty state, and an instruction requesting its data has entered the E-pipe, the **instruction** is suspended and **written into the register**. The arrival of data activates the instruction by sending it to the Instruction Queue (IQueue) and data is copied into the register in one clock cycle. In general, instructions may arrive from the remote threads, from the Pc-Queue, or from the pool of previously suspended instructions. This technique supports migration of instructions, and hence gives a common view on the execution of threads, regardless of their locations.

The program in figure 2 shows an example to create 10 parallel threads of a loop.

```
//Adding 1 to all the elements of a vector X of 10 elements starting from address 100 in memory
Main :              Add       #9, r0, r1                    //r1=9
NewTh:   Create     Increm, r1                              //Create a thread for executing
                                                            // the Increm loop for iteration r1
         Add        r1, r0, r1, Increm, r1                  //send r1 to th. Increm[r1]
         Sub        #1, r1, r1                              // r1=r1-1
         Jump       pz, NewTh                               //if (r1>=0) go to NewTh
         Destroy    main
/*********** Loop *********************************/
Increm :
?        Load       #100, r1, r2                            //receive r1 from main and load
                                                            // X[r1] in r2
         Add        #1, r2, r2                              // r2++
         Store      #100, r1, r2                            //store r2 in X[r1]
         Destroy    Increm
```

Fig. 2. An example of program written in the MPA language

3   Presentation of the Thread Scheduling

The scheduling of threads in the MPA processor is achieved by the usage of an on-chip associative memory called the context table (CT) Fig.1.(b). Except for the first thread in the first processor (the root thread), all the other threads are created and their entries stamped into the CT, when a thread executes the instruction CREATE. Each MPA processor maintains an active list of free contexts. When a thread is about to be created, the scheduler examines the list of local free contexts. If the list, is not empty the scheduler writes a new entry in the CT. However if the list is empty, the instruction CREATE is forwarded to an other processor of the CMP via the M-Queue, or is alternatively kept in the local processor until a context is freed. With the last approach we have examined several scenarios. When a CREATE instruction cannot be satisfied, the instruction is blocked in a special register or recycled in the I-Queue to be re-considered few cycles later. In the former, additional resources need be incorporated into the chip to hold instructions that cannot initiate a thread. In the latter, the instruction CREATE keeps circulating in the pipeline consuming useful cycles. The thread can carry on its execution even when there are insufficient resources (refereed to by CAF for "Continuation After Failure"). Another technique, consists of blocking the thread that initiated the unsatisfied CREATE. The instruction is written in the I-Queue and no subsequent instructions are fetched from this thread, until a context is freed (refereed to by SAF for "Stop After Failure").

The access to the CT is only needed when an instruction is transferring a value to another thread, and this is reported in the instruction. The access is performed during the execution phase and it is overlapped with the computations involved in the ALU. The search key is represented by the couple (thread starting address, iteration number). If the destination context is not local, the CT supplies the address of the remote processor. In the latter, the address of the destination processor and the result of the instruction is copied into the messages queue. The result is passed within a **"migrating instruction"**.

4 Experimental Results

In order to measure the performances of our MPA processor, we have designed an interactive graphical simulator. It enables the programmer to interactively change the parameters of the machine. In this paper, we expose the results attained from executing two programs on a single processor. Both programs are written in MPA language. In all the scenarios, we set the access time of the L1 caches to 1 clock cycle and the latencies of integer and floating functional units to 1 cycle.

4.1 Matrix Multiplication

Figure 3.(a) gives the execution time of the multiplication program of two matrices (C = A * B) function of the L2 memory latency in clock cycles. A, B and C are square matrices of 1600 (40*40) elements. The cache miss rate in L1 is fixed to 10% for all cases. Three versions of the matrix multiplication have been tested, corresponding to 1, 40, and 1600 threads extracted from the program. The first version (sequential) uses one thread and corresponds to the sequential program. In the second version (CAF40 and SAF40) the program calculates the matrix C in a line by line manner. As the processor has only 16 available contexts, a number of threads will be delayed until a context is freed. Before starting a new line of C, we ensure that all the previous threads have terminated their execution. Finally in the third version (CAF1600 and SAF1600), the program creates 1600 threads corresponding to 1600 points of the matrix C. We notice from figure 3.(a) that SAF method demonstrates higher performance over the CAF method. The later is very penalizing with large number of threads (1600). This is due to an increase in the number of recycling instructions.

In figure 3.(b), the latency of L2 is fixed to 10 cycles. Across all the spectrum of the cache misses, the method SAF remains the most significant over the method CAF and, in particular over the single threaded program (even with larger size L1 cache, miss = 0%). The single thread program pays a penalty of 2 clock cycles for every branch instruction. The SAF method on the other hand tends to fill these wasted cycles with some useful instructions from other threads.

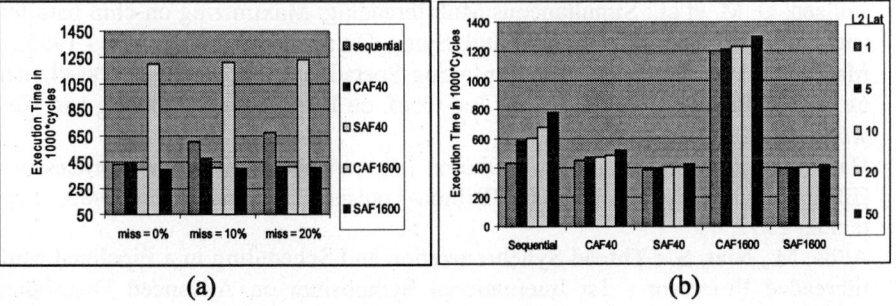

(a) (b)

Fig. 3. Experimental results for the matrix multiplication program

4.2 DNA Sequence Alignment

In the second program, we implement the code of aligning two DNA sequences using Smith Waterman algorithm. In our multithreaded program, each thread calculates the elements of one column of the matrix result. In this section we use the SAF method. The size of the 2 sequences to align has been fixed to 100. Fig.4.(a) shows that for a L1 miss rate of 5% and 10%, the execution time increases barely with the memory latency. Even for higher cache miss, the increase in execution time is not dramatic, considering the increase of the memory latency. In Fig.4.(b) we have fixed the L1 miss rate to 10%. For all memory latencies, the execution time diminishes as the number of thread increases. When the number of contexts, goes beyond 16, the execution pipe operates at its maximum throughput. We can also notice that because of the thread management overheads in a single threaded program, the sequential version of the algorithm performs better.

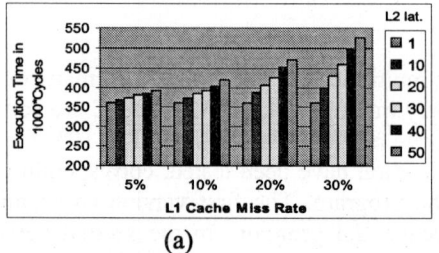
(a)

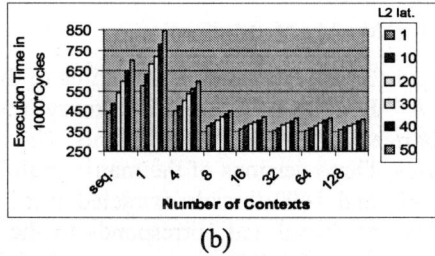
(b)

Fig. 4. Experimental results for the DNA sequence alignment program

5 Conclusions and Perspectives

In this paper we have presented the multithread scheduler for the MPA. The adopted approach is based on the utilization of an on-chip associative memory for stocking the information about the created threads. With a moderate number of parallel threads, it is possible to obtain higher performances in terms of execution time. The next stages of the project will be directed towards: the extension of the simulator to support multiple processors and to integrate speculative thread scheduling technique.

References

1. Tullsen, D. M. et al.: Simultaneous Multithreading: Maximizing on-chip parallelism. In Proc. Of the 22nd. annual. Intl. Symp. On computer architecture - 1995.
2. Marcuello, P., , González, A.: Exploiting Speculative Thread-Level Parallelism on a SMT Processor - Proc. of the Int. Conf. on High Perf. Computing and Networking - 1999.
3. Hammond, L., Nayfeh, B. A., Olukotun, K. : A Single-Chip Multiprocessor - IEEE Computer Special Issue on "Billion-Transistor Processors", p 79-85, September 1997.
4. Adda, M., Niar, S. : Thread Synchronization and Scheduling in a Pipelined Multithreaded Processor - 1st International Symposium on Advanced Distributed Systems - March 2000.

Topic 09
Distributed Systems and Algorithms

Bertil Folliot, Giovanni Chiola, Peter Druschel, and Anne-Marie Kermarrec

Topic Chairpersons

The wide acceptance of the internet standards and technologies makes it hard to imagine a situation in which it would be easier to argue about the importance of distributed systems and algorithms than it is today.

Topic 09 of Euro-Par intends to provide a forum for researchers from academia and industry interested in distributed systems and algorithms, including the areas of communications, mobile computing, distributed databases and operating systems, and security in distributed systems.

Out of the fourteen submissions to this track emanating from nine different countries, six papers, two regular and four short, have been accepted this year. One of the short papers was moved to Topic 06 for presentation. The remaining five papers (two regular and three short) are presented in one session.

The first paper presents a self-stabilizing probabilistic solution for the neighbourhood unique naming problem is uniform, anonymous networks. The paper considers the problem of assigning names to nodes in a graph so that no two nodes within a distance of two of each other have the same name. The second paper addresses the management of events in distributed simulations. This issue is of particular importance for performance of distributed simulators. Self-stabilization properties of distributed algorithms represents an interesting approach to fault-tolerant distributed systems. The presentation of three short papers will conclude this session: the first short paper presents a performance evaluation of plausible clocks, an alternative to vector clocks: the impact on the performance of several parameters such as the size of the system, the communication patterns, etc. are successively explored in this paper demonstrating the interest of plausible clocks. The second short paper discusses the construction of reliable servers based on TMR (Triple Modular Redundancy) scheme that prevents even Byzantine failures. The last paper proposes two improvements of the weighted reference counting distributed garbage collection algorithm based on expiration time and fractional weight that have been implemented on the Mozart platform.

We would like to thank the authors for their submissions, all the reviewers for their precious time and effort as well as the other members of the Euro-Par program committee for their valuable help in the entire selection process.

Self-stabilizing Neighborhood Unique Naming under Unfair Scheduler

Maria Gradinariu and Colette Johnen

Laboratoire de Recherche en Informatique, UMR CNRS 8623,
Université de Paris Sud, F91405 Orsay cedex, France
{mariag,colette}@lri.fr

Abstract. We propose a self-stabilizing probabilistic solution for the neighborhood unique naming problem in uniform, anonymous networks with arbitrary topology. This problem is important in the graph theory Our solution stabilizes under the unfair distributed scheduler. We prove that this solution needs in average only one trial per processor. We use our algorithm to transform the [6] maximal matching algorithm self-stabilizing to be able to cope up with a distributed scheduler.

1 Introduction

Self-stabilization. Self-stabilization introduced by Dijkstra, [2], provides an uniform approach to fault-tolerance, [9]. More precisely, this technique guarantees that, regardless of the initial state, the system will eventually converge to the intended behavior without the need for explicit exception handler of backward recovery. In this paper we are particular interested in uniform (every processor in the system executes the same algorithm) and anonymous systems (processors does not have a distinct identifier).

Neighborhood Unique Naming (NUN) problem. In [5] is defined the labeling graphs problem with conditions at distance 2. NUN problem, issued from this theoretical graph problem, ensures that in each neighborhood the vertex have distinct labels. In other words, there is no vertex with the same label as one of its neighbors and there is no vertex having neighbors named identically. This problem is a classical coloring problem with an additional restriction: the vertex at distance two have distinct labels. A practical application is the assigning radio frequencies to transmitters such that transmitters that are close (distance 1 or 2 apart) to each other use different frequencies.

Maximal Matching (MAM) problem. The MAM problem is issued from graph theory. A *matching* in a graph is a set of edges where no two edges are adjacent. The matching set M is called maximal if there is no other matching set M' such that $M \subset M'$. The main applications of this problem in distributed computing area are job assignment and task scheduling.

Related works. The classical vertex coloring problem is a restriction of the NUM problem. The vertex coloring was previously studied for planar and bipartite graphs (see [3,14,12,13]). Using a well-known result from graph theory, Gosh and Karaata [3] provide an elegant solution for coloring acyclic planar graphs with exactly six colors, along with an identifier based solution for acyclic orientation of planar graphs. This makes their solution limited to systems whose communication graph is planar and processors have unique identifiers. Sur and Srimani [14] vertex coloring algorithm is only valid for bipartite graphs. A paper by Shukla *et al.* (see [13]) provides a randomized self-stabilizing solution to the two coloring problem for several classes of bipartite graphs, namely complete odd-degree bipartite graphs and tree graphs. In [4] the authors presents three coloring algorithms for the arbitrary networks. Their solutions use $O(D)$ colors, where D is the maximal degree of the network.

Nevertheless, all the previous presented algorithms are not solutions for the NUN problem since it may be possible that vertex at distance 2 are labeled identically. The NUN has multiple applications such as: the acyclic orientation of general networks or finding the maximal matching sets. The first application is trivial, therefore we focus on the MAM problem. There are several works treating the MAM problem. The faster known sequential algorithm is a wave algorithm due to Micali and Vazirani, [7]. This solution is not self-stabilizing.

A deterministic self-stabilizing solution for the MAM problem was provided by Huang and Hsu in [6]. Their solution stabilizes only under a central scheduler.

Our contribution. We present the first self-stabilizing solution for the NUN problem. Our solution works on anonymous, uniform networks with any topology and it needs in average only one trial per processor under the distributed scheduler. (I.E. a processor randomly updates its local identifier one time on the average). This algorithm is used to transform the [6] MAM algorithm such that it stabilizes under a distributed scheduler. Note that in the transformed algorithm the randomization is used only for breaking the symmetry, once any processor of the network gets an unique local identifier, the NUN algorithm has no further influence (no action is performed), the MAM algorithm evolution is then deterministic. Our solution copes up with the most powerful scheduler — the distributed scheduler : only the processors with a locally maximal identifier can choose their match. Hence, we avoid the matching cycles generation (more details in Section 5).

2 Model

Distributed Systems. A distributed system is a set of state machines called processors. Each processor can communicate with some processors called neighbors. A processor p communicates to its neighbors via its variables that its neighbors can read but cannot update. We will use $\mathcal{N}_p$ to denote the set of neighbors of the processor p.

A processor p in a distributed system executes an algorithm which is a finite set of guarded actions where each guard is a boolean expression over its variables and the variables of its neighbors, and where each statement is a deterministic or probabilistic update of the local and variables of p.

The state of a processor p is the value of its variables. A *configuration* of a distributed system is an instance of the processor states. A processor is *enabled* in a given configuration if at least one of the guards of its algorithm is *true*. During a computation step, one or more enabled processors perform the statement of an enabled action. A *computation* of a distributed system DS is a *maximal* sequence of computations steps. *Maximality* means that the sequence is either infinite, or the terminal configuration is a deadlock.

A distributed system can be modeled by a transition system. A transition system is a three-tuple $S = (\mathcal{C}, \mathcal{T}, \mathcal{I})$ where $\mathcal{C}$ is the collection of all configurations, $\mathcal{I}$ is a subset of $\mathcal{C}$ called the set of initial configurations, and $\mathcal{T}$ is a function $\mathcal{T}$ from $\mathcal{C}$ to the set of $\mathcal{C}$ subsets. A $\mathcal{C}$ subset of $\mathcal{T}(c)$ is called a c transition. An element of a c transition t, is called an output of t. In a probabilistic system, there is a probabilistic law on the output of a transition; in a deterministic system, each transition has only one output.

Scheduler. In this model, a *scheduler* is a *predicate* over the system computations. In a computation, a transition (c_i, c_{i+1}) occurs due to the execution of a nonempty subset of the enabled processors in the configuration c_i. In every computation step, this subset is chosen by the scheduler : a *central* (resp. *distributed*) scheduler chooses one and only one enabled processor (resp. a subset of the enabled processors) to execute a statement action. A scheduler may be unfair.

A strategy is the set of computations that can be obtained under a specific scheduler choice. At the initial configuration, the scheduler "chooses" one set of enabled processors (it chooses a transition). For each output of the selected transition, the scheduler chooses a second transition, and so on. The strategy formal definition is based on the tree of computations. Let c be a system configuration. A *TS-tree* rooted in c, $\mathcal{T}ree(c)$, is the tree-representation of all computations beginning in c. Let n be a node in $\mathcal{T}ree(c)$ (i.e. a configuration), a *branch* rooted in n is the set of all $\mathcal{T}ree(c)$ computations starting in n with a computation step of the same n transition. The degree of n is the number of branches rooted in n. A *sub-TS-tree of degree* 1 rooted in c is a restriction of $\mathcal{T}ree(c)$ such that the degree of any $\mathcal{T}ree(c)$'s node (configuration) is at most 1. Let st be a strategy of the distributed system DS, an st-cone $\mathcal{C}_h$ is the set of all possible st-computations with the same prefix h (for more details see [10]). The last configuration of h is denoted $last(h)$. We have equipped a strategy with a probabilistic space (see [1] for more details). The measure of an st-cone $\mathcal{C}_h$ is the measure of the prefix h (i.e., the product of the probability of every computation step occurring in h).

Probabilistic self-stabilization. Let DS be a distributed system. A predicate P is closed for the computations of DS if and only if when P holds in a configuration c, P also holds in any configuration reachable from c. Let D be a scheduler and st be a strategy of DS under D. Let CP be the set of all system configurations satisfying a closed predicate P (formally $\forall c \in CP, c \vdash P$). The set of st-computations that reach configurations of CP is denoted by $\mathcal{EP}$ and its probability by $P_{st}(\mathcal{EP})$.

In this paper we study quasi-silent algorithms : those for which a legitimate configuration (i.e. it verifies the problem specification) is also a deadlock. A quasi-silent probabilistic self-stabilizing algorithm is not silent because it may have infinite executions (these executions do not converge). The measure of these executions is null, in any strategy.

Definition 1 (Probabilistic Stabilization of a quasi-silent algorithm).
A distributed system $\mathcal{DS}$ is self-stabilizing under a scheduler D for a specification $\mathcal{L}$ (a legitimacy predicate on configurations) such that in any strategy st of S under D, the following conditions hold :
- *The probability of the set of st-computations, that reach a configuration satisfying $\mathcal{L}$ is 1. Formally, $\forall st, P_{st}(\mathcal{EL}) = 1$.*
- *A configuration satisfies $\mathcal{L}$ iff it is a deadlock.*

Convergence of Probabilistic Stabilizing Systems. Building on previous works on probabilistic automata (see [11,15,10,8],), [1] presented a framework for proving self-stabilization of probabilistic distributed systems. In the following we recall a key property of the system called *local convergence* and denoted by LC. Let DS be a distributed system. Let st be a strategy of DS, $PR1$ and $PR2$ be two closed predicates on configurations of DS. Let $\mathcal{C}_h$ be a st-cone where $last(h) \vdash PR1$. In st, from $last(h)$, if the probability to reach a configuration that verifies $PR2$ in at most N computation steps is greater or equal than ϵ then we say that $\mathcal{C}_h$ satisfies $LC(PR1, PR2, \epsilon, N)$.
If in strategy st, there exist $\delta_{st} > 0$ and $N_{st} \geq 1$ such that any st-cone, $\mathcal{C}_h$ with $last(h) \vdash PR1$, satisfies $LC(PR1, PR2, \epsilon_{st}, N_{st})$, then the main theorem of [1] states that the probability of the set of st-computations reaching configurations satisfying $PR1 \wedge PR2$ is 1.

3 Impossibility Results

Unique Local Naming (ULN) problem is to ensure that neighbor processors have distinct identifiers but processors at distance 2 may have the same identifier.

Lemma 1. *There is no deterministic self-stabilizing algorithm solving the ULN or the NUM problem in uniform and anonymous networks under distributed scheduler.*

Proof. We will study a ring of n processors running such an algorithm. Let c_0 be a configuration where all processors are in the same state. c_0 is illegitimate : in c_0, at least one processor may execute an action. Thus, all processors are able to execute the same action. After the computation step where all processors have performed the same action, the obtained configuration is symmetrical : all processors are in the same state.

4 Self-stabilizing NUN under a Distributed Scheduler

In the current section, we present a self-stabilizing probabilistic solution for the NUN problem. Algorithm 4.1 idea is very simple. Each processor has a variable, referred in the algorithm as *lid*, which indicates its local identifier and a *flag* which signals the presence of at least two neighbors having the same *lid*. The space complexity for Algorithm 4.1 is $O(log(n))$ bits per processor. A processor which cannot execute $\mathcal{A}_2$, having at least two neighbors with the same local identifier, l, sets its $flag$ to l (Action $\mathcal{A}_1$). A processor having a neighbor with the same value of *lid* chooses randomly a new identifier from a bounded set of values (Action $\mathcal{A}_2$). The same action is executed by the processor, p, when it has a neighbor, q, which flag value is set to p's *lid*. In this case, the processor q has at least two neighbors (p and another one) with the same *lid*.

Algorithm 4.1 NUN algorithm on the processor i

Constant :
B : integer constant proven optimal for the value $2n^2$
Variable :
$flag.i$: a positive integer bounded by B
Actions :
$\mathcal{A}_1$: $(\forall j \in \mathcal{N}.i \ (lid.i \neq lid.j) \wedge (lid.i \neq flag.j)) \wedge$
   $(\exists (j,k) \in \mathcal{N}.i \ (lid.j = lid.k) \wedge (flag.i \neq lid.j)) \wedge$
   $(\not\exists (t,l) \in \mathcal{N}.i, \ (lid.t = lid.l = flag.i)) \longrightarrow flag.i = lid.j;$
$\mathcal{A}_2$: $\exists j \in \mathcal{N}.i \ (lid.i = lid.j) \vee (lid.i = flag.j) \longrightarrow lid.i = random(1, \dots, B);$

Definition 2. *Let p be a processor. $Correct\_lid(p)$ is the following predicate on configurations: (i) $\forall q$ neighbor of p, $lid.p \neq lid.q$; and $lid.p \neq flag.q$; (ii) $\forall r$ neighbor of a p's neighbor, $lid.p \neq lid.r$. Let c be a configuration. We name m_c the number of processors p which does not verify $Correct\_lid(p)$. c is legitimate iff c satisfies the predicate $\mathcal{LID} \equiv (m_c = 0)$.*

Observation 1 *In Algorithm 4.1, one may prove that a configuration is legitimate iff it is deadlock. In any computation from a configuration c there are at most $n - m_c$ consecutive computation steps in which Action $\mathcal{A}_2$ is not executed.*

Scena is the following scenario described informally by : "at each computation step, where at least one processor performs Action $\mathcal{A}_2$, (i) exactly one of these processors verifies the $Correct\_lid$ predicate after this computation step, (ii) the other processors keep their previous *lid* value". Let c be a configuration. On any computation following the scenario *Scena*, the predicate $Correct\_lid$ is closed : once a processor p verifies $Correct\_lid(p)$, no action of p, of p's neighbor, or of a neighbor of a p's neighbor will change that.

Lemma 2. *Let st be a strategy under a distributed scheduler on a system executing the Algorithm 4.1. There exist $\epsilon > 0$ and $N > 0$ such that all cone of st satisfy $LC\ (true, \mathcal{LID}, \epsilon, N)$.*

Proof. Let C_h be a cone of the strategy st such that $last(h) = c$ does not verify $\mathcal{LID}$. Assume that $m_c \neq 0$. After at most $n - m_c$ computation steps a processor executes Action $\mathcal{A}_2$. We study the scenario $Scena$
Let p be the processor which will change its lid value from the configuration c. Let d_p^1 and d_p^2 the numbers of neighbors at distance 1 and 2 of p and let $(lid_j)_{j=1,d_p^1+d_p^2}$ be their local identifiers and let $(flag_k)_{k=1,d_p^1}$ be the flag values for the neighbors at distance 1. The probability that p chooses a value equal to lid_j or $flag_k$ is $\frac{1}{B}$. The probability that the new chosen value be different of all lid values of its neighbors at distance 1 or 2 and of $flag$ values of its neighbors at distance 1 is $1 - (\sum_{j=1}^{j=d_p^1+d_p^2} P_{st}(lid_p = lid_j) + \sum_{j=1}^{j=d_p^1} P_{st}(lid_p = flag_j)) = 1 - \frac{2d_p^1+d_p^2}{B} \leq 1 - \frac{2(n-1)}{B}$.
The probability of the computation step that we have defined is greater than $\frac{1}{B}{}^{(m-1)}(1 - \frac{2(n-1)}{B})$ (The probability that a processor keeps its lid value, after $\mathcal{A}_2$ is $\frac{1}{B}$). m_c has decreased by 1, hence in at most $m - 1$ similar sequences of computation steps, a legitimate configuration is obtained. Thus in st, from C_h, the probability to reach a legitimate configuration in at most $N = n^2$ computation steps, is greater than $\epsilon = \left(\frac{1}{B}^{\frac{n}{2}}(1 - \frac{2n}{B})\right)^{n-1}$.

Theorem 1. *Algorithm 4.1 is self-stabilizing under a distributed scheduler for the NUN specification.*

Lemma 3. *When $B > 2n(n-1)$ where n is the system size, a processor performs in the average only one time the randomized Action $\mathcal{A}_2$.*

Proof. Let c be the initial configuration of Algorithm 4.1. The probability that after the action $\mathcal{A}_2$, a processor has an unique local name is $1 - \frac{2d_p^1+d_p^2}{B}$. Note that $2d_p^1 + d_p^2$ could be bounded by $2(n-1)$. In the average $m_c(1 - \frac{2(n-1)}{B})$ processors have an unique local identifier after all processors that do not verify $Correct\_lid$ have performed one time $\mathcal{A}_2$. $B > 2n(n-1)$ guarantees that in average, all processors have an unique local name after at most one Action $\mathcal{A}_2$.

5 Self-stabilizing MAM under a Distributed Scheduler

Definition 3 (Matched and Inactive processors). *A processor p is unmatched iff $match.p = 0$. Two neighbors (p, q) are matched iff $match.p = q$ and $match.q = p$. A processor p is inactive iff all its neighbors are matched and $match.p = 0$. A legitimate configuration satisfies the predicate $\mathcal{LID}$ and all processors are inactive or matched.*

Observation 2 *In a legitimate configuration, the states of match variables define a maximal matching. Let c be a deadlock configuration of Algorithm 5.1. In c, if $match.p \neq 0$ then the processor p is matched. Thus, the deadlock configurations are legitimate.*

Algorithm 5.1 MAM algorithm on the processor i

Constants :
  B : integer constant proven optimal for the value $2n^2$
Variables :
  $lid.i$: a positive and no-null integer bounded by B
  $match.i$: a positive integer bounded by B
Actions :
  $\mathcal{A}_1$: $(match.i = 0) \wedge (lid.i > max(lid.k, k \in \mathcal{N}.i \wedge match.k = 0) \wedge$
         $(\exists j \in \mathcal{N}.i,\ match.j = 0) \wedge (\forall k \in \mathcal{N}.i, match.k \neq lid.i) \longrightarrow match.i = lid.j$
  $\mathcal{A}_2$: $(match.i = 0) \wedge (\exists j \in \mathcal{N}.i,\ match.j = lid.i) \longrightarrow match.i = lid.j$
  $\mathcal{A}_3$: $(match.i = lid.j) \wedge (match.j \neq 0) \wedge (match.j \neq lid.i) \longrightarrow match.i = 0$
  $\mathcal{A}_4$: $(match.i \notin \{lid.j \mid j \in \mathcal{N}.i\} \bigcup \{0\}) \longrightarrow match.i = 0$

Theorem 2. *Any computation starting in a configuration satisfying the predicate $\mathcal{LID}$ is finite.*

Proof (outline). Let e be a computation starting in a configuration satisfying the predicate $\mathcal{LID}$. Assume that e is an infinite computation. e has an infinite suffix e' where no processor performs the action $\mathcal{A}_4$ or the action $\mathcal{A}_2$. Between two consecutive actions $\mathcal{A}_1$, a processor performs one and only one time the action $\mathcal{A}_3$. Let cs be a computation step along e' where a processor p performs the action $\mathcal{A}_1$ to choose the processor q as "match". Before the computation step, q is unmatched. During the computation step and after that q does not perform any action. Therefore, along e', a processor p performs at most one action $\mathcal{A}_1$ (one can prove that along e' no action $\mathcal{A}_1$ is performed).

6 Conclusion

We present the first algorithm for NUN problem, self-stabilizing on anonymous and uniform systems. Our solution copes up with distributed schedulers and is time optimal, more precisely we guarantee that the NUN is done in only one trial per processor in the average under any unfair scheduler. The presented solution is used as substratum in the modification of the [6] MAM algorithm such that the new algorithm stabilizes under any distributed scheduler.

References

1. Beauquier, J., Gradinariu, M., and Johnen, C.: Randomized self-stabilizing optimal leader election under arbitrary scheduler on rings. Technical Report 1225, Laboratoire de Recherche en Informatique (1999)
2. Dijkstra, E.: Self stabilizing systems in spite of distributed control. *Communications of the ACM*, vol. 17 (1974) 643-644
3. Ghosh, S., and Karaata, M. H.: A self-stabilizing algorithm for coloring planar graphs. *Distributed Computing*, 7 (1993) 55-59

4. Gradinariu, M., and Tixeuil, S.: Tight space uniform self-stabilizing l-mutual exclusion. Technical Report 1249, Laboratoire de Recherche en Informatique (2000)
5. Griggs, J. R., and Yeh., R. K.: Labeling graphs with a condition at distance two. *SIAM, Journal of Discrete Mathematics*, 5 (1992) 586-595
6. Hsu, S., and Huang, S.: A self-stabilizing algorithm for maximal matching. In *Information Processing Letters*, 43(2) (1992) 77-81
7. Micali, S., and Vazirani, V.: An algorithm for finding maximum matching in general graphs. In *21st IEEE Annual Symposium on Foundations of Computer Science* (1980)
8. Pogosyants, A., Segala, R., and Lynch N.: Verification of the randomized consensus algorithm of Aspen and Herlihy: a case study. In *Distributed Computing*, 13 (2000), 155-186
9. Schneider M.: Self-stabilization. *ACM Computing Surveys*, 25 (1993), 45-67
10. Segala, R.: *Modeling and Verification of Randomized Distributed Real-Time Systems*. PhD thesis, MIT, Dep. of Electrical EnG. and Comp. Science (1995)
11. Segala, R., and Lynch, N.: Probabilistic simulations for probabilistic processes. In LNCS, *CONCUR '94, Concurrency Theory, 5th International Conference*, Vol. 836 (1994)
12. Shukla, S., Rosenkrantz, D., and Ravi, S.: Developing self-stabilizing coloring algorithms via systematic randomization. In *Proc. of the Int. Workshop on Parallel Processing* (1994) 668-673
13. Shukla, S., Rosenkrantz, D., and Ravi, S.: Observations on self-stabilizing graph algorithms for anonymous networks. In *Proc. of the Second Workshop on Self-stabilizing Systems*, pages 7.1–7.15 (1995)
14. Sur S., and Srimani P. K.: A self-stabilizing algorithm for coloring bipartite graphs. *Information Sciences*, 69 (1993) 219-227
15. Wu, S. H., Smolka, S. A., and Stark, E. W.: Composition and behaviors of probabilistic i/o automata. In LNCS, *CONCUR '94, Concurrency Theory, 5th International Conference*, Vol. 836 (1994) 513-528

Event List Management in Distributed Simulation*

Jörgen Dahl[1], Malolan Chetlur[2]**, and Philip A. Wilsey[1]

[1] Experimental Computing Laboratory, Dept. of ECECS
PO Box 210030, Cincinnati, OH 45221–0030, philip.wilsey@ieee.org
[2] AT&T
Cincinnati, OH 45220, USA

Abstract. Efficient management of events lists is important in optimizing discrete event simulation performance. This is especially true in distributed simulation systems. The performance of simulators is directly dependent on the event list management operations such as insertion, deletion, and search. Several factors such as scheduling, checkpointing, and state management influence the organization of data structures to manage events efficiently in a distributed simulator. In this paper, we present a new organization for input event queues, called append-queues, for an optimistically synchronized parallel discrete-event simulator. Append-queues exploits the fact that events exchanged between the distributed simulators are generated in sequences with monotonically increasing time orders. A comparison of append-queues with an existing multi-list organization is developed that uses both analytical and experimental analysis to show the event management cost of different configurations. The comparison shows performance improvements ranging from 3% to 47% for the applications studied.

Keywords: Pending Event Sets, Event List Management, Distributed Simulation, Time Warp.

1 Introduction

In a discrete event simulation (DES), events are generated and exchanged by simulation objects. Events must be processed in nondecreasing timestamp order to preserve their causality relations [1]. In DES, the set of events that have not yet been processed is called the *pending event set* [6]. In a parallel and distributed discrete event simulation (PDES), the union of the set of already processed events and the pending event set is called an *input queue* [3].

In general, distributed simulations exchange timestamped event messages and as new messages arrive, a simulation object will merge incoming events into its (timestamp sorted) input queue. The Time Warp mechanism [3] is the most

---

* Support for this work was provided in part by the Defense Advanced Research Projects Agency under contract DABT63–96–C–0055.
** This work is done as part of author's research in University of Cincinnati

widely used optimistic synchronization strategy for distributed simulation [1]. It organizes the distributed simulation such that each simulation object maintains a local simulation clock and processes events in its input queue without explicit synchronization to other simulation objects. As messages arrive to a simulation object they are inserted into the input queue. If they arrive in the simulated past (called a *straggler* message), the simulation object recovers using a *rollback* mechanism to restore the causality relations of the straggler event. On rollback, a simulation object may have to retract output event messages that were prematurely sent when the events ahead of the straggler were processed. This occurs by the sending of *anti-messages*. Thus, in a Time Warp simulation, events are generated and communicated between simulation objects as sequences of events separated by one or more anti-messages.

This paper presents a new organization for input queues, called *append-queues*, that can be used in distributed simulators. Append-queues are designed primarily for optimistically synchronized simulations, but can be used with other distributed simulation synchronization mechanisms. The key advantage of append-queues is that they exploit the presence of the ordered sequences of events exchanged between the concurrently executing simulation objects. Instead of using the traditional method of merging each newly arrived event into the input queues [1], the append-queue operation appends events within a sequence with inter-sequence breaks triggering more complex operations. Append-queues require that the underlying communication subsystem provide reliable FIFO message delivery. In addition to presenting a detailed discussion of append-queues, we also present analytical and empirical comparisons between the append-queue and a multi-list technique that is used in the publically available Time Warp simulator called WARPED [5].

2 Pending Event Set Management

As described in the introduction, the temporal properties of events communicated between distributed simulation objects can be used as the basis for optimizing the organization of the pending event set. More precisely, let $t(e)$ be the timestamp of the event e, where a timestamp denotes the (simulation) time at which an event is to be processed. While processing the event e, several events might be sent to other simulation objects. Let $S(e)$ be the set of events generated while processing the event e and let $f(e)$ be the function that generates the timestamp of the events in $S(e)$. Since $S(e)$ can have a cardinality greater than one, $f(e)$ is a one-to-many function. In addition, let $T(S(e))$ be the set of timestamps of the events generated while processing event e. From Lamport's clock conditions [4], we can infer that the timestamps in the set $T(S(e))$ must be greater than $t(e)$. If $f(e)$ is an increasing function, then the set of messages received by a simulation object from a sending process is in increasing order of timestamps. This property is exploited by the receiving simulation object to order its input events.It can be seen that the insert operation needed to order the incoming events from each sender object is a simple append operation (provided that separate receive queues are maintained for each sender). This organization of pending events will hereafter be referred to as append-queues. Event list management is a well researched area. Many implementations and organizations of event sets and their data structures have been proposed [7,6,8].

3 Event List Management Analysis

The analysis of the pending event set management is based on the number of timestamp comparisons performed during insertion and scheduling of events. Events are inserted into an input queue when they are first sent to a simulation object. The scheduling of events is done to determine which event should be processed next in the simulation. An event may be inserted and scheduled more than once because of the occurrence of a rollback. An overview and analysis of the append-queue configuration is presented in the following sections, and followed by an overview and analysis of an existing input queue optimization, the multi-list [5].

3.1 Append-Queue Overview

The motivation behind the append-queues is to exploit the ordering of events already performed by the simulation objects that send messages to other simulation objects. In the append-queue configuration, the receiving simulation object maintains an individual queue for each simulation object that sends events to it. These queues are called *sender-queues*. The events from a particular sender object are appended to the sender-queue associated with its Id. The number of sender-queues can vary during simulation and is dependent on the characteristic of the simulation. Figure 1 provides an overview of the append-queue configuration. In this figure, there are k simulation objects that contribute a sender-queue in the simulation object, and there are a total of m simulation objects in the simulation. Each element in a sender-queue has a sender Id, a receiver Id, a send time, and a receive time. A list sorting the head element of each sender queue is maintained for scheduling. The events that have been scheduled and processed reside in a processed-queues. Any sender-queue i has events originating from simulation object i. Any event with receiver Id j will be put in processed-queue j when it has been scheduled and processed. The insertion of a new event in the individual sender-queue reduces to an append operation if the timestamp generating function $f(e)$ is a strictly increasing function. If $f(e)$ is not an increasing function, the insertion of a new event may not always be an append operation.

The events are to be processed in a nondecreasing time-stamp order to preserve the causality among the simulation objects in the simulation. In the append-queue configuration, the events from the same simulation object are already ordered in nondecreasing timestamp order. However, before any processing can be done, the ordering of the events among all the sender-queues has to performed. The ordering of events from all the sender queues is performed by a

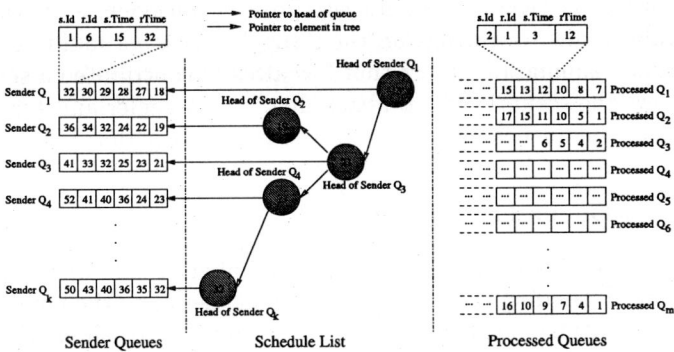

Fig. 1. Append-Queue Configuration

schedule-list that maintains a sorted order of the head of the individual sender-queues (see Figure 1). The schedule-list performs the function of a *Lowest Time Stamp First (LTSF) scheduler*. The event with the lowest time stamp in the schedule-list is the next event to be processed. The retrieval of the next event to process and insertion of a new event in the schedule-list can be optimized to logarithmic complexity using, for example, a heap or splay-tree implementation. On processing an event, the event is removed from the sender-queue and appended to a queue called the *processed-queue*. The receiver Id of all events in a processed-queue are the same, and thus the number of processed-queues is equal to the number of simulation objects in the simulation.

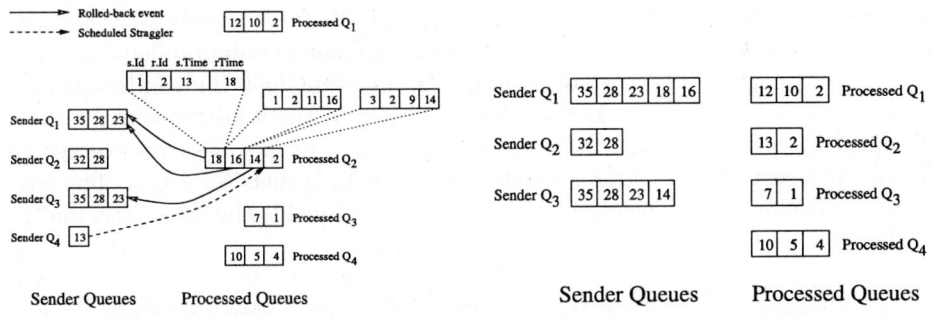

Fig. 2. A Rollback Due to a Straggler in the Append-Queue Configuration

Fig. 3. The Contents of the Queues After Rollback

The analysis of the append-queue configuration assumes that aggressive cancellation [1] mechanism is used in the simulation. On receiving an anti-message the events in the sender-queue with timestamps greater than the anti-message are flushed from the sender-queue. However, if the positive message equivalent of the anti-message is in the processed-queue of the simulation object, then the simulation object is rolled back and the positive message is canceled. In the case of a rollback due to a straggler, the straggler message could be from a new sender or from a simulation object that has already contributed a sender-queue. Figure 2 shows the scenario of a rollback due to a straggler and Figure 3 shows the contents of the queues after the rollback has been performed.

3.2 Append-Queue Cost Analysis

The cost in our analysis is measured by the number of timestamp comparisons performed during pending event list management. Let n_i be the number of events sent from an arbitrary simulation object i to some other simulation object in the simulation. Let m be the number of simulation objects in the simulation. Let k be the total number of simulation objects that send messages to any of the m simulation objects in the simulation. Since insertion of a new event into an individual sender-queue i is an append operation, the cost of inserting n_i events is simply n_i. The cost of finding the lowest time-stamped event from the schedule list of k sender-queues is $log_2 k$. The logarithmic complexity is due to inserting the next least time-stamped event from the currently scheduled event's sender-queue to the schedule-list. Therefore the cost of insertion and scheduling due to all k sender queues is:

$$C_{insert}^{append-queue} = N + N \times \log_2 k = N \times (1 + \log_2 k), \qquad (1)$$

where $N = \sum_{i=1}^{k} n_i$ is the total number of input events in the simulation.

On rollback, an event from the processed-queue is removed and added back into the corresponding sender-queue. This rolled-back event adds further cost during scheduling in addition to the cost involved in adding it back to the sender-queue. Let N_r be the total number of rolledback events in the simulation. Then, $N_r = \sum_{i=1}^{k} n_{r_i}$, where n_{r_i} is the number of events rolled-back into the sender-queue i. The cost of re-inserting an event into the sender-queue i is $\sum_{i=1}^{k} n_{r_i} \times l_{s_i}$, where l_{s_i} is the average length of the sender-queue i that is searched in order to insert the rolled-back event. Let $l_{s_{avg}}$ be the average of all l_{s_i}. The cost of reinserting all rolled-back events is then $N_r \times l_{avg}$. The cost of re-scheduling all N_r events is $N_r \times log_2 k$, which yields the total cost due to rollbacks:

$$C_{resched.}^{append-queue} = N_r \times l_{s_{avg}} + N_r \times \log_2 k = N_r \times (l_{s_{avg}} + \log_2 k). \qquad (2)$$

Thus, the total pending event set management cost for insertion and handling of rolledback events is:

$$C_{total}^{append-queue} = \underbrace{N}_{insertion} + \underbrace{N \times \log_2 k}_{scheduling} + \underbrace{N_r \times l_{s_{avg}}}_{re-insertion} + \underbrace{N_r \times \log_2 k}_{re-ched.}$$
$$= N \times (1 + \log_2 k) + N_r \times (l_{s_{avg}} + \log_2 k). \qquad (3)$$

3.3 Multi-List Overview

The publically available distributed simulation kernel called WARPED uses a multi-list configuration to manage the pending event lists [5]. The multi-list consists of individual input queues for the receiver objects called mini-lists that are abstracted into a single list called the main-list. This method of organizing the list of mini-lists is coined as the multi-list. Figures 4 and 5 illustrate the multi-list configuration. In the multi-list, the individual mini-lists are ordered on receive time of the events. In the main-list, the events are ordered on receive time and the receiver Id. It can be seen from the multi-list organization that every event must be inserted both in the main-list and its individual mini-list. However, the multi-list obviates the need for complex scheduling mechanism to determine the lowest time stamped event.

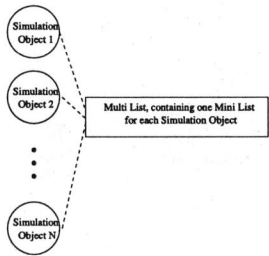

Fig. 4. Overview of Current Input Queue Configuration

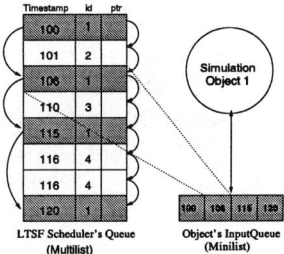

Fig. 5. Example of the Current Input Queue

3.4 Multi-List Cost Analysis

The input queue management cost consists of the insertion cost and the rollback cost. Let l_i be the average search length of mini-list i upon an insertion of an event. The average of the search lengths in all mini-lists is then $l_{avg} = \sum_{i=1}^{m} l_i/m$. Let n_i be the total number of events inserted in mini-list i. Thus, the total insertion and scheduling cost for all mini-lists is:

$$C_{insert}^{mini-list} = \sum_{i=1}^{m} n_i \times l_{avg} = l_{avg} \times \sum_{i=1}^{m} n_i = N \times l_{avg}, \qquad (4)$$

where $n_i \times l_{avg}$ is the average case total insertion cost of a particular mini-list.

Let L_i be the average length of the main-list that is searched when inserting an event into the main-list after inserting the event into mini-list i. The cost of main-list insertions contributed by receiver i is $n_i \times L_i$. Total insertion cost in the main list is the sum of the insertion cost of all receiver objects and is equal to $\sum_{i=1}^{m} n_i \times L_i$. Let L_{avg} be the average length of the main-list that is searched for all simulation objects, i.e. $L_{avg} = \sum_{i=1}^{m} L_i/m$. The expression for the main-list insertion cost is then reduced to:

$$C_{insert}^{main-list} = \sum_{i=1}^{m} n_i \times L_{avg} = L_{avg} \times \sum_{i=1}^{m} n_i = N \times L_{avg}. \qquad (5)$$

After a rollback, rolled back events must again be executed. The number of events that are re-executed are dependent on the rollback distance and the number of rollbacks. Therefore, rollback cost in receiver i is $\sum_{i=1}^{n_{r_i}} r_{d_i} = R_{D_i}$, where n_{r_i} is the number of rollbacks experienced by receiver object i and r_{d_i} is the ith rollback distance with respect to the number of rolled-back events experienced by the receiver object i. The total rollback cost in the simulation is the sum of the rollback costs in all the simulation objects and is equal to:

$$C_{rollback}^{multi-list} = \sum_{i=1}^{m} R_{D_i} = R_D. \qquad (6)$$

Thus, the total input queue management cost is equal to:

$$C_{total}^{multi-list} = \underbrace{N \times l_{avg}}_{mini-list\ insertion} + \underbrace{N \times L_{avg}}_{multi-list\ insertion} + \underbrace{R_D}_{rollback}$$
$$= N \times (l_{avg} + L_{avg}) + R_D. \qquad (7)$$

3.5 Comparative Review

For cost due to rollbacks, we can see that N_r and R_D must be equal (see Equations 2 and 6). The ratio between rollback costs for the append-queues and the multi-list is then

$$\frac{N_r \times (l_{s_{avg}} + \log_2 k)}{R_D} = \frac{l_{s_{avg}} + \log_2 k}{1}.$$

The cost will thus be higher for append-queues. We can also see that the difference in cost due to insertion and scheduling will be determined by the number of sending simulation objects versus how large l_{avg} and L_{avg} will grow.

4 Empirical Studies

The WARPED [5] simulation kernel was used to gather statistics for the multi-list and append-queue configurations. WARPED implements the multi-list and additional coding was added to the WARPED system to simulate the append-queue configuration. The results from these experiments were used to estimate the benefits of the append-queues. Three applications namely SMMP (a queuing model of a shared memory multiprocessor), RAID (simulation of a level 5 hardware RAID disk array) and PHOLD (simulation benchmark developed by Fujimoto [2] based upon the Hold model) were used during the experimentation.

In the applications used during experimentation, $l_{s_{avg}}$ was always 1.0, except in one PHOLD simulation where it was 1.2. Thus, the prediction that a re-insertion of a rolled-back event into a sender-queue can be considered to be a prepend operation was verified. In the performed simulations, k ranges between 9 and 100, and $log_2 k$ consequently ranges between 2.2 and 4.6. Therefore, the cost added by rollbacks was on the order of five times greater for the append-queue configuration than for the multi-list configuration.

The impact k, l_{avg} and L_{avg} have on the costs in Equations (3) and (7) is visualized in Tables 6 and 7. It can be seen that the insertion and scheduling cost $N + N \times log_2 k$ for the append-queue is considerably less than the insertion and scheduling cost $N \times l_{avg} + N \times L_{avg}$ for the multi-list. From the table we can see that $log_2 k$ grows much slower than L_{avg} as k and N increase. It can be inferred that applications of this size will generate more comparisons for the multi-list than for the append-queues.

N	k	$log_2 k$	l_{avg}	L_{avg}	$N(1+log_2 k)$	$N(l_{avg}+L_{avg})$
180793	13	2.6	3.2	2.1	644518	958203
350986	22	3.1	2.8	2.8	1435899	1965522
614336	40	3.7	2.6	4.9	2880547	4576803
815198	58	4.1	2.5	6.9	4125263	76628621
1059904	76	4.3	5.0	8.4	5650066	11552954

Fig. 6. Comparison of l_{avg}, L_{avg}, $N(1 + log_2 k)$, and $N(l_{avg} + L_{avg})$ for SMMP

N	k	$log_2 k$	l_{avg}	L_{avg}	$N(1+log_2 k)$	$N(l_{avg}+L_{avg})$
84813	9	2.2	24.3	1.9	271166	2222101
203185	10	2.3	18.8	2.6	671036	4348159
441219	12	2.5	13.1	3.7	1537607	7412479
741463	14	2.6	9.8	4.7	2698226	10751214
995760	16	2.8	8.6	5.6	3756593	14139792

Fig. 7. Comparison of l_{avg}, L_{avg}, $N(1 + log_2 k)$, and $N(l_{avg} + L_{avg})$ for RAID

As the simulation time and the number of input events (N) increase, the difference in number of comparisons performed between the append-queue configuration and the multi-list configuration increases, see Figures 8, 9 and 10. The largest difference can be seen for PHOLD where l_{avg} and L_{avg} tended to be large. The number of comparisons performed, on an average, in the multi-list configuration were 2.0 times that of the append-queue configuration for SMMP, 2.8 for RAID and 9.9 for PHOLD.

The `quantify` software from Rational Software was used to estimate how much performance impact the append-queues would have on total simulation time. The data from the `quantify` tests show that for the multi-list implementation an average of approximately 6% of the time is spent on event insertion

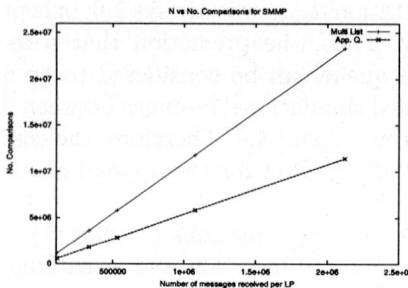

Fig. 8. Number of events received in an LP vs total number of comparisons for all events

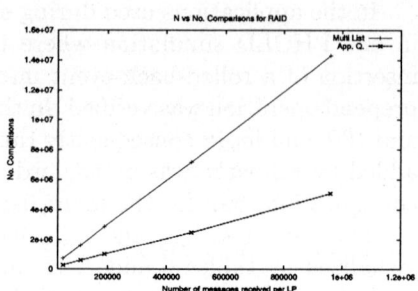

Fig. 9. Number of events received in an LP vs total number of comparisons for all events

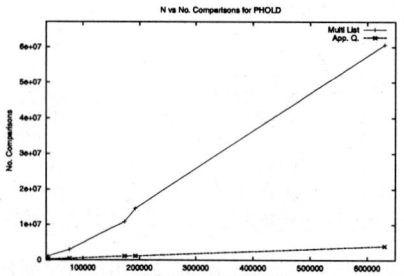

Fig. 10. Number of events received in an LP vs total number of comparisons for all events

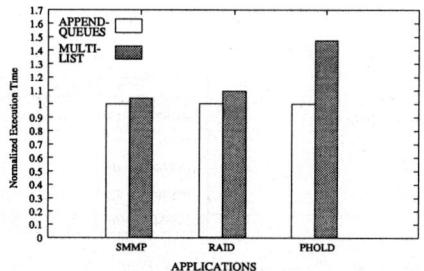

Fig. 11. Estimated performance of Append-Queues compared to performance of the Multi-List

for SMMP, 14% for RAID and 52% for PHOLD. Figure 11 was produced with the data from these tests and shows the estimated and normalized performance difference in terms of time between the append-queue configuration and the multi-list configuration. The performance improvements were estimated to be 3%, 9% and 47% for SMMP, RAID and PHOLD respectively.

5 Conclusion

The append-queue organization for pending event sets exploits the temporal properties of events generated by the concurrently executing simulation objects in a distributed simulation. The cost analysis of event management of a traditional pending event set data structure and the append-queue configuration was presented. Empirical studies show that the append-queue configuration may result in performance improvements, between 3% and 47%, over the traditional configuration.

References

1. FUJIMOTO, R. Parallel discrete event simulation. *Communications of the ACM 33*, 10 (Oct. 1990), 30–53.
2. FUJIMOTO, R. Performance of Time Warp under synthetic workloads. *Proceedings of the SCS Multiconference on Distributed Simulation 22*, 1 (Jan. 1990), 23–28.
3. JEFFERSON, D. Virtual time. *ACM Transactions on Programming Languages and Systems 7*, 3 (July 1985), 405–425.
4. LAMPORT, L. Time, clocks, and the ordering of events in a distributed system. *Communications of ACM 21*, 7 (July 1978), 558–565.
5. RADHAKRISHNAN, R., MARTIN, D. E., CHETLUR, M., RAO, D. M., AND WILSEY, P. A. An Object-Oriented Time Warp Simulation Kernel. In *Proceedings of the International Symposium on Computing in Object-Oriented Parallel Environments (ISCOPE'98)*, D. Caromel, R. R. Oldehoeft, and M. Tholburn, Eds., vol. LNCS 1505. Springer-Verlag, Dec. 1998, pp. 13–23.
6. RÖNNGREN, R., AND AYANI, R. A comparative study of parallel and sequential priority queue algorithms. *ACM Transactions on Modeling and Computer Simulation (TOMACS) 7*, 2 (Apr. 1997), 157–209.
7. RÖNNGREN, R., AYANI, R., FUJIMOTO, R. M., AND DAS, S. R. Efficient implementation of event sets in time warp. In *Proceedings of the 1993 workshop on Parallel and distributed simulation* (May 1993), pp. 101–108.
8. STEINMAN, J. Discrete-event simulation and the event horizon part 2: Event list management. In *Proceedings of the 10th Workshop on Parallel and Distributed Simulation (PADS96)* (1996), pp. 170–178.

Performance Evaluation of Plausible Clocks

Francisco J. Torres-Rojas
Centro de Investigaciones en Computación (CIC), Costa Rica Institute of Technology
Costa Rica
torres@ic-itcr.ac.cr

Abstract. Plausible Clocks do not *characterize* causality [6] but, under appropriate circumstances, their accuracy is close to vector clocks. This paper explores the effects that several factors have on the performance of these clocks.

1 Introduction

Vector clocks capture the causality relation between events in a distributed history H [2, 4]. However, these clocks require one entry for each one of the N sites of the system [1], which causes scalability problems [6, 7]. *Plausible clocks* are an scalable alternative to vector clocks that do not characterize causality but whose accuracy can be close to vector clocks under appropriate circumstances [8]. A detailed description of these clocks is presented in [7, 8]. This paper ponders the effects that several factors have on the performance of the plausible clock *Comb* [8] and identifies the conditions under which it performs better. The parameter ρ (proportion of cases whose causal relationship is incorrectly reported by *Comb*) is used as the response variable. Among other results, it was found that in client/server systems with high communication frequency, this clock can order more than 90% of the event pairs in the same way as vector clocks. Section 2 describes and analyzes a multifactorial experiment that considers the effects of several factors on the performance of *Comb*. Section 3 presents an experiment where the scalability of *Comb*, under conditions for best performance, is tested. Section 4 gives the conclusions of this paper.

2 Experiment 1: Multifactorial Design

We explore the effects that the following factors have on ρ: system size (20, 50 and 80 sites), clock size (6, 12 and 18 entries), communication pattern (random and client/server), local history size (10, 35 and 60 events), and message interval mean (exponential distribution with mean $1/\lambda$ = 3, 14 and 25 events). For each one of the 162 possible combinations of factor levels, 3 distributed histories are generated, i.e., there are 486 trials of the experiment. Each history is executed, sending and receiving messages and keeping the timestamps assigned to each event by *Comb*, together with vector clocks. Then, we determine the causal relationships between all the ordered pairs in the set $H \times H$ from the point of view of *Comb* [8], compare them with the actual causal relationships, and compute ρ. A total of 2,969,821,897 pairs of events were considered. The data set for this experiment can be found in [9]. The statistical procedure Analysis of Variance (ANOVA) checks k samples obtained from k populations, and determines if there is statistical evidence that some of them have different means [5]. The assumptions of ANOVA (random error normally and independently distributed with mean 0.0 and constant variance) are verified in [9] and, hence, its conclusions are statistically valid. Each one of the 162 combinations of factor levels defines a population characterized by a particular mean of ρ. We test if all these populations have the same mean, or if there is evidence that some of them have different means (i.e., that the investigated factors have significant effects on the behavior of *Comb*). Figure 1 shows the ANOVA output of the statistical package *Minitab* for this experiment. Each row corresponds to a possible source of variation in ρ. Column P presents the probability p of observing the analyzed set of samples when the particular source of variation has **no** significant effect on ρ. Usually, a factor whose value of p is greater than 0.01, is considered as not significant [5].

```
MTB > ANOVA 'RATE' = C1!C2!C3!C4!C5.

Factor       Type   Levels  Values
Sites        fixed     3      20     50    80
Clock        fixed     3       6     12    18
Pattern      fixed     2       0      1
Events       fixed     3      10     35    60
Mean         fixed     3       3     14    25

Analysis of Variance for RATE

Source                            DF         SS         MS         F        P
Sites                              2    0.495746   0.247873    388.71    0.000
Clock                              2    0.973416   0.486708    763.26    0.000
Pattern                            1    0.167167   0.167167    262.15    0.000
Events                             2    0.072725   0.036362     57.02    0.000
Mean                               2    0.210761   0.105381    165.26    0.000
Sites*Clock                        4    0.002875   0.000719      1.13    0.344
Sites*Pattern                      2    0.015301   0.007650     12.00    0.000
Sites*Events                       4    0.004351   0.001088      1.71    0.148
Sites*Mean                         4    0.003962   0.000990      1.55    0.187
Clock*Pattern                      2    0.147005   0.073503    115.27    0.000
Clock*Events                       4    0.001375   0.000344      0.54    0.707
Clock*Mean                         4    0.035201   0.008800     13.80    0.000
Pattern*Events                     2    0.308820   0.154410    242.15    0.000
Pattern*Mean                       2    0.713878   0.356939    559.75    0.000
Events*Mean                        4    0.933027   0.233257    365.79    0.000
Sites*Clock*Pattern                4    0.005532   0.001383      2.17    0.072
Sites*Clock*Events                 8    0.007138   0.000892      1.40    0.196
Sites*Clock*Mean                   8    0.003945   0.000493      0.77    0.627
Sites*Pattern*Events               4    0.064593   0.016148     25.32    0.000
Sites*Pattern*Mean                 4    0.079552   0.019888     31.19    0.000
Sites*Events*Mean                  8    0.010190   0.001274      2.00    0.046
Clock*Pattern*Events               4    0.011423   0.002856      4.48    0.002
Clock*Pattern*Mean                 4    0.019763   0.004941      7.75    0.000
Clock*Events*Mean                  8    0.082474   0.010309     16.17    0.000
Pattern*Events*Mean                4    0.227229   0.056807     89.09    0.000
Sites*Clock*Pattern*Events         8    0.029874   0.003734      5.86    0.000
Sites*Clock*Pattern*Mean           8    0.013133   0.001642      2.57    0.010
Sites*Clock*Events*Mean           16    0.013237   0.000827      1.30    0.196
Sites*Pattern*Events*Mean          8    0.056771   0.007096     11.13    0.000
Clock*Pattern*Events*Mean          8    0.048146   0.006018      9.44    0.000
Sites*Clock*Pattern*Events*Mean   16    0.017959   0.001122      1.76    0.035
Error                            324    0.206606   0.000638
Total                            485    4.983176
```

Figure 1. Analysis of Variance for Experiment 1 (*Minitab* Output).

All main factors are significant. The average effects are: ρ increases when the system is larger, ρ decreases when the clocks have more entries, and ρ is lower in client/server systems. There are 6 significant second level interactions, 4 of them include the communication pattern, while the system size is present in just one interaction. Figure 2 presents the average effect of the second level interactions. The value of ρ reduces when there are less sites in the system or when the clocks get larger (upper part of Figure 2). These effects tend to flatten after a certain point and, in client/server systems, this effect is not as noticeable. The performance of *Comb* improves when the local history grows and when the level of communications is higher (i.e., smaller values of 1/λ). There are 6 significant third level interactions, 5 of them include the communication pattern and the system size appears in 2 of the interaction. The interactions between system size, communication pattern and local history size can be analyzed with the plots presented in Figure 3. In general, when the system has fewer sites, the value of ρ is smaller. However, with a client/server system, an increment in the size of the local histories overrides or at least reduces the effects that the system size has on ρ. The average effects of the interactions between system size, communication pattern and $1/\lambda$ are plotted in Figure 4. The system size affects ρ, but, in a client/server system, a high level of communications reduces its influence. Figure 5 presents the interactions

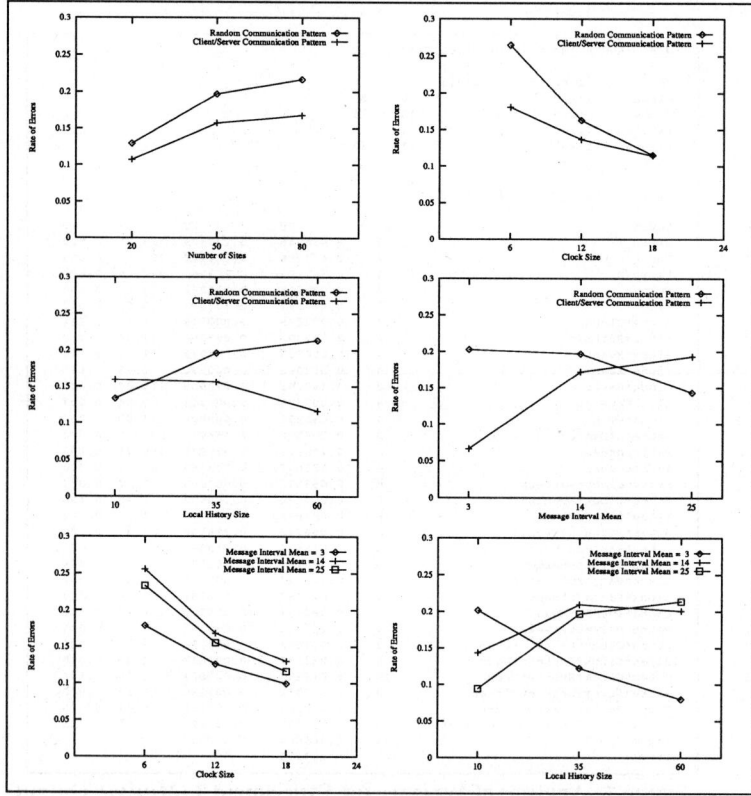

Figure 2. Average Effects of Second Level Interactions

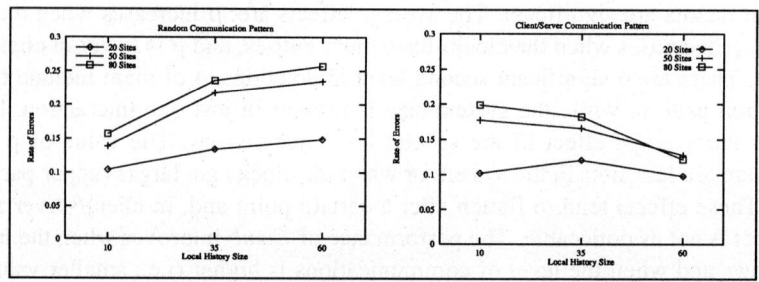

Figure 3. Interactions between Sites in the System, Communication Pattern and Local History Size

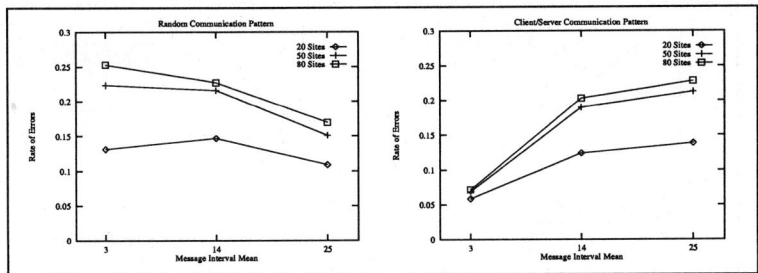

Figure 4. Interactions between Sites in the System, Communication Pattern and $1/\Lambda$

between clock size, communication pattern and local history size. Figure 6 presents the interactions between clock size, communication pattern and $1/\lambda$. In general, larger plausible clocks obtain better performance, but this effect is minimized in client/server systems when the local history size grows or when the level of communications increase. Figure 7 shows the interaction of clock size, local history size and $1/\lambda$. Larger logical clocks have better performance, and the values of ρ improve when the local histories are larger and the frequency of communications is higher. Figure 8 presents the interactions between communication pattern, local history size and $1/\lambda$. A client/server system has better results than a system with a random communication pattern. In particular, the minimum value of ρ is obtained by a client/server system, with a high rate of communications and large local histories.

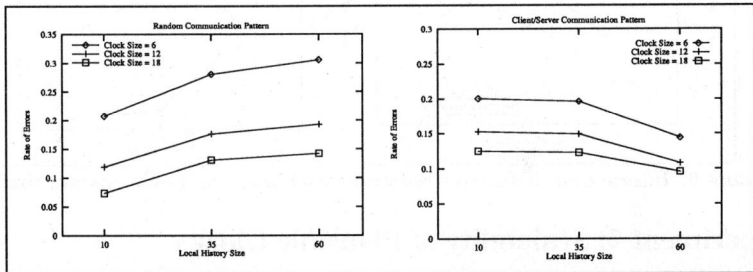

Figure 5. Interactions between Clock Size, Comm. Pattern and Local History Size

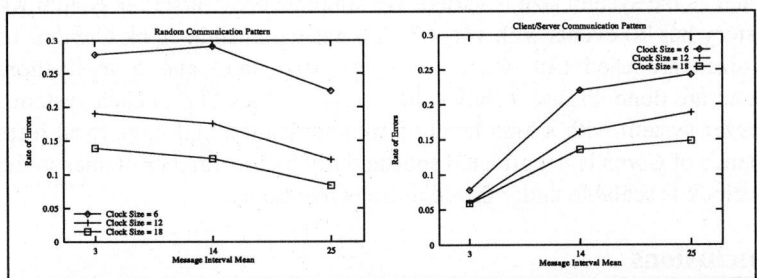

Figure 6. Interactions between Clock Size, Communication Pattern and $1/\Lambda$

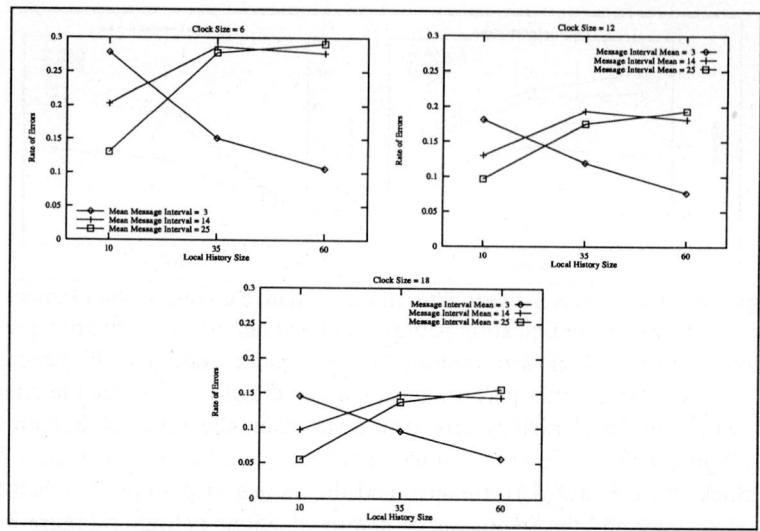

Figure 7. Interactions between Clock Size, Local History Size and $1/\Lambda$

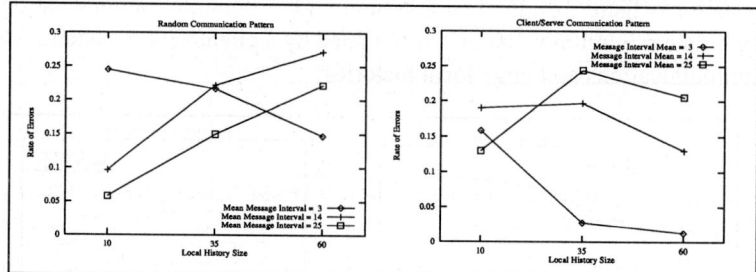

Figure 8. Interactions between Communication Pattern, Local History Size and $1/\Lambda$

3 Experiment 2: Scalability of Plausible Clocks

The conditions for optimal performance of *Comb* identified in Section 2 are maintained as the system size is varied. We simulate a client/server system where each local history has 70 events with $1/\lambda = 3$. A 6 entry plausible clock *Comb* is used. Five system sizes are used (20, 40, 60, 80 and 100 sites) and 5 replications of the experiment are done. Figure 9 shows the average values of ρ at each system size. In a client/server system with a high level of communication and large local histories, the performance of *Comb* is not affected substantially by the number of sites in the system, i.e., this clock is scalable under the conditions mentioned.

4 Conclusions

The effects that system size, logical clock size, communication pattern, local history size and $1/\lambda$ have on the performance of plausible clocks were explored using computer simulations. Experiment 1 proved that all the main factors have a statistically significant effect on ρ. There are 15 significant interactions of factors and 12 of them include the communication patterns studied, while only 5 include the

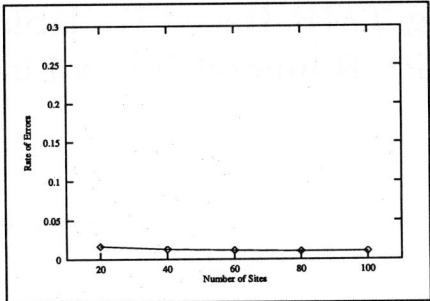

Figure 9. Scalability of Plausible Clocks under optimal conditions.

system size and in every case combined with the communication pattern. Based on the analysis of the second and third level interactions, we claim that even when the number of sites in the system and the size of the logical clock have a clear effect on the performance of plausible clocks, the interactions between the communication pattern and the other factors studied override their effects in many cases, especially with client/server systems. *Comb* performs better in client/server systems with high communications rates and large local histories. Experiment 2 shows that, under these conditions, the ability of *Comb* to accurately capture the causal relationships between a very high percentage (more than 98%) of the possible pairs of events is unaffected by the number of sites in the distributed system, even with a small number of entries.

References

1. B. Charron-Bost, "Concerning the size of logical clocks in Distributed Systems", Information Processing Letters 39, pp. 11-16. 1991.
2. C.J. Fidge, "Fundamentals of Distributed Systems Observation", IEEE Software, vol 13, No. 6, November 1996.
3. L. Lamport, "Time, clocks and the ordering of events in a Distributed System", Communications of the ACM, vol 21, pp. 558-564, July 1978.
4. F. Mattern, "Virtual Time and Global States in Distributed Systems", Conf. (Cosnard et al (eds)) Proc. Workshop on Parallel and Distributed Algorithms, Chateau de Bonas, Elsevier, North Holland, pp. 215-226. October 1988.
5. D. Montgomery, "Design and Analysis of Experiments", John Wiley and Sons, Fourth Edition. 1997.
6. R. Schwarz and F. Mattern, "Detecting causal relationships in distributed computations: in search of the holy grail", Distributed Computing, Vol. 7, 1994.
7. F. Torres-Rojas, "Scalable Approximations to Causality and Consistency of Distributed Objects", Ph.D. dissertation, College of Computing, Georgia Institute of Technology. July 1999.
8. F. Torres-Rojas and Mustaque Ahamad, "Plausible Clocks: Constant Size Logical Clocks for Distributed Systems", Distributed Computing, pp. 179-195, December 1999.
9. F. Torres-Rojas, "Performance Evaluation of Plausible Clocks", Technical Report, Computer Science Department, Costa Rica Institute of Technology, October 2000.

Building TMR-Based Reliable Servers Despite Bounded Input Lifetimes

Paul Ezhilchelvan[1], Jean-Michel Hélary[2], and Michel Raynal[2]

[1] Dept of Computing Science, University of Newcastle, NE1 7RU, UK
paul.ezhilchelvan@newcastle.ac.uk
[2] IRISA
Campus de Beaulieu, 35042 Rennes Cedex, France
{helary,raynal}@irisa.fr

1 Context

This paper comes from practical considerations [5]. It considers a client-server system made up of an arbitrary large number of clients that access a single server. To access the server, a client issues an input request and possibly waits for an answer. Then, the server processes the client input and sends back the result (if any) to the client.

The system is unreliable in the following way: clients can fail by crashing. This means a client behaves correctly until it possibly crashes. When a client fails, it stops its execution and never recovers. The implementation of the server relies on a TMR approach (Triple Modular Redundancy): it is made up of three server processes (in short *processes*). Each process processes every client input. Among the three processes, at most one of them can be faulty. Moreover, it can fail by exhibiting an arbitrary behavior. It is assumed that each process can sign the messages it sends, and authenticate the messages it receives from the other processes.

The system is synchronous in the following way. Local computations consume no time, and all communication delays are bounded. More precisely, D (resp. d) is an upper bound for the communication delays between any pair made up of a client and a correct process (resp. any pair of correct processes). Due to the geographic dispersion of clients and the locality of the processes implementing the server, we have $d << D$. Moreover, the clocks of the three processes implementing the TMR subsystem are assumed to be perfectly synchronized [6].

2 The Problem

The problem we address is the implementation of a correct TMR-based server. To this end, the correct processes (at least two) implementing the server must have mutually consistent copies of the state of the service they implement. This is obtained by requiring correct processes to order the client inputs in the same way before processing them according to this order [4]. This ordering is typically achieved by Atomic Broadcast protocols [1,3]. Moreover, every input has to be verified before processing, which involves accessing client-related data (such as authentication keys, input history, client privileges, credit limits, etc.). Owing to a large number of potential clients, this client-related data will be large and have to be stored in a disk. A process receiving input directly from a client must access this disk, and this can be time-consuming. A process receiving an input forwarded by a replica should also verify the input, since the forwarding process may be faulty: it may not have verified the input properly or, even worse, may be replaying an old input as a newly received one. To avoid other disk accesses, our approach verifies forwarded inputs through matching: the process waits for the ordered delivery of another identical input. So, if the forwarded input is replayed/invented or if it has been sent only to the forwarding process due to client crash, this input will remain unmatched but will not cause unwarranted verification. Let us also note that this approach requires a time bound so that waiting for the delivery of a matching input can be terminated even if no matching input occurs. Therefore, we introduce a duration bound (denoted Σ) as an essential requirement: every input (either directly received from a client or forwarded) is systematically discarded from a server process address space within at most Σ time units after it has been received. Note that, without this requirement, server processes should have an infinite memory: in fact, a faulty server process could invent infinitely many inputs and forward them to its peers. Such inputs would never match with another input and thus, without a time requirement, would never be discarded.

The novelty here comes from the fact that Atomic Broadcast has to be ensured despite the combined effects of the bounded lifetime Σ, the Byzantine server process, and the client crash failures. These constraints actually define a new problem that we call Σ-*constrained Atomic Broadcast*. A protocol solving the Σ-*constrained Atomic Broadcast* problem is called Σ-*ordering protocol*.

3 Results

The full paper [2] focuses on the family of Σ-ordering protocols. It presents two original results. First, a Σ-ordering protocol is presented; this protocol assumes $\Sigma > D + 3d$. Second, it is shown that it is impossible to design a Σ-ordering protocol when $\Sigma < D$.

3.1 Assumptions on Σ-Ordering Protocols

Let us first remark that, whatever the design of a Σ-ordering protocol, each input issued by a client is received by none, one, two or the three processes of the TMR subsystem (this depends on whether the client crashes or not when it issues the input). Then, the dissemination of copies of a client input among the processes depends on the protocol.

As far as the copies of a client input is concerned, a Σ-ordering protocol has the following three characteristics:

- A Σ-ordering protocol may force a process receiving an input (either directly from the client or from another process) to forward this input to none, one or the two other processes. This is the *forwarding policy* associated with the protocol. As a consequence of (1) this policy, (2) the client correctness, and (3) the correctness of the forwarding process, a process may have zero, one or more copies of an input, at the same time.
- When a Σ-ordering protocol requires a process to forward the client input it has received, it can permit some delay α (with $\alpha \leq \Sigma$) to elapse between the reception of an input and its forwarding. This is the *delay policy* of the protocol.
- A last feature of a Σ-ordering protocol lies in the number of input copies that a process must simultaneously have for ordering that input. This is the *decision policy* of the protocol.

3.2 Sketch of the Protocol

The proposed protocol uses an underlying Timed Atomic Broadcast protocol [1,3] (the timed atomic broadcast protocol described in [1] can be implemented in the TMR subsystem defined previously). Let TA-broadcast and TA-deliver be the two primitives defined by such a protocol. They ensure that all messages that are TA-broadcast by correct processes are TA-delivered to them. Moreover, the correct processes TA-deliver the same set of messages and these TA-deliveries occur in the same order. Finally, they satisfy the following timeliness property: a message that is TA-broadcast at time t is TA-delivered by every correct process before time $t + \Delta$. In the context of the TMR subsystem (with three processes, at most one faulty (Byzantine) process, message signatures, perfectly synchronized clocks, and an upper bound d on message transfer delays), we have $\Delta = 2d$.

The proposed Σ-ordering protocol is designed according to the following principles. When a server process p_i receives a *valid* input[1] directly from a client, it makes up a signed message m including this input, the current value of the clock and its identity. Then, it TA-broadcasts this message (forwarding policy) and does it immediately (delay policy $\alpha = 0$). A correct process orders a client input as soon as it has TA-delivered two messages including this input (decision policy). Note that, if a client is correct, each input μ of that client is received exactly once by each process. Since there are at least two correct processes, there will be at least two TA-broadcast invocations (by two different senders) with messages having μ as input field. So, each correct process will TA-deliver at least two messages containing μ as input field.

Due to the "Σ (bounded lifetime) constraint", every input stored in a process local memory is discarded Σ time units after it has been received. So, a crucial point in the design of the protocol is to ensure that, for each input μ from a correct client, at least two messages with an input field equal to μ will *simultaneously* be present in the local memory of at least two correct processes.

---

[1] i.e., an input verified by accessing the disk where client related data is stored.

This intuitively explains why those messages must not be removed too quickly due to the Σ bound, and why the protocol requires $\Sigma > D + \Delta + d = D + 3d$. The protocol ensures that two TA-broadcasts concerning the same input from a correct client, but issued by two different correct processes, will always have an "overlapping period" in the local memory.

The other important issue in the design of the protocol lies in ensuring that, despite the attempts from the faulty process to replay obsolete client inputs (or play false client inputs), any input ordered by correct processes is a client input and no client input is ordered more than once. The proposed protocol ensures this property by forcing processes to preventively discard messages (even before their lifetime Σ has elapsed) as soon as this discarding operation can be safely performed. The proof shows that no message is discarded too early (any input from a correct client is ordered at least once) or too late (any input is ordered at most once by a correct process). It also shows that the inputs from correct clients are actually ordered, and that the correct processes order the inputs in the same way.

3.3 The Impossibility Result

In the full paper [2], two lemmas are first proved. They show that, for every Σ-ordering protocol, only inputs received directly from clients may be forwarded (Lemma 1), and no process is allowed to order an input unless it simultaneously has at least two copies (from different sources) of this input (Lemma 2). Then, these Lemmas are used to construct a scenario showing no Σ-ordering protocol can be designed when $\Sigma < D$. The following theorem is proved by contradiction.

Theorem 1. *Let Σ be a constant. There is no Σ-ordering protocol if $\Sigma < D$.*

Proofs of the protocol and of the impossibility result can be found in [2].

References

1. Cristian F., Aghili H., Strong H. R. and Dolev D., Atomic Broadcast: From Simple Message Diffusion to Byzantine Agreement. *Proc. 15th Int. Symposium on Fault-Tolerant Computing*, Ann Arbor (MI), IEEE Computer Society Press, pp. 200-206, 1985.
2. Ezhilchelvan P., Hélary J.-M. and Raynal M., Building TMR-Based Reliable Servers with Arbitrary Large Number of Clients. *Research Report # 1398*, IRISA-IFSIC, Université de Rennes 1, May 2001.
http://www.irisa.fr/EXTERNE/bibli/pi/1398/1398.html.
3. Hadzilacos V. and Toueg S., Reliable Broadcast and Related Problems. In *Distributed Systems*, ACM Press (S. Mullender Ed.), New-York, pp. 97-145, 1993.
4. Schneider F. B., Implementing Fault-Tolerant Services Using the State Machine Approach: a Tutorial. *ACM Computing Surveys*, 22(4):299-319, 1990.
5. Shrivastava S., Ezhilchelvan P., Speirs N. A., Tao S. and Tully A., Principle Features of the Voltan Family of Reliable System Architectures for Distributed Systems. *IEEE Transactions on Computers*, 41(5):542-549, 1992.
6. Veríssimo P. and Raynal M., Time in Distributed Systems: Models and Algorithms. In *Advances in Distributed Systems*, Springer-Verlag, LNCS 1752, pp. 1-32, 2000.

Fractional Weighted Reference Counting

Erik Klintskog[1], Anna Neiderud[1], Per Brand[1], and Seif Haridi[2]

[1] Swedish Institute of Computer Science
Box 1263, SE-164 29 Kista, Sweden
http://www.sics.se/

[2] Royal Institute of Technology, Department of Teleinformatics, Electrum 204
S-164 40 Kista, Sweden
http://www.it.kth.se/

Abstract. We introduce a scheme for distributed garbage collection that is an extension of Weighted Reference Counting. This scheme represents weights as fractions. It solves the problem of limited weight, preserves the property of third-party independence, and does not induce extra messages for reference merging.

1 Introduction

When deciding on how to manage memory in a distributed application it is important to study how references to different objects or entities are spread and how long they are expected to live. Many traditional applications use a rather static client-server setup, where the client will have a few references to entities at the server during a session and then disconnect. For more novel applications following a dynamic peer-to-peer design pattern, a programming platform needs to provide faster means to collect garbage since many references will only live for a short period of time. In such applications references will also tend to spread more wildly over the network, and it is important that a garbage collection algorithm does not impose any third party dependencies. Allowing multiple instances of references to the same remote entity from one process is undesirable in a distributed programming platform since it complicates distributed entity-consistency protocols, and may require large amounts of memory. This puts demands on the garbage collection algorithm to handle merging of references.

As stated in numerous papers [4], Weighted Reference Counting (WRC) (presented independently by Watson and Watson [6] and Bevan [1]) is a distributed GC algorithm that efficiently and correctly collects garbage without requiring global synchronization. A problem with WRC is the weight underflow. Proposals for solving this problem exist but have some shortcomings. Piquer [3] creates indirection cells for weight extensions. Goldberg's [2] solution may lead to large tables at the distributed objects process. The algorithms have problems with reference merging. In a termination detection algorithm Mattern [5] proposed using rational numbers for the weight rather than integers. When a reference is shared the weight is divided by two, which gives unlimited weight, but requires a representation of the growing rational number. With long-lived and mergeable references the size of the numbers that must be stored will be unbounded.

We will present a version of WRC called Fractional Weight that solves the problem of weight underflow and is able to merge multiple instances of references. This is done in bounded memory without imposing any new third party dependencies. We will also show how Fractional Weight can be parameterized to handle different sharing patterns.

2 Fractional Weighted Reference Counting

All distributed entities have a home process. At the home process there exists an entry (stored in a table) that points to the entity. This is called the owner reference. At other processes there may exist one and only one remote reference pointing at the owner reference. As long as there exists at least one remote reference, the owner reference must not be reclaimed. A distributed garbage collector is responsible of maintaining the consistency of remote references to an entity.

2.1 Representing Fractions

In Fractional Weight, the total weight is defined to be one. All partial weights are represented as a fraction with a denominator D or a power of D, where D is a static integer. A fractional number is represented as a linked list of pairs, where the first value is the enumerator (1) and the second is the power of the denominator. The current weight of a reference can then be written as the sum of all its pairs (2).

$$D \geq N_k \geq 0 \tag{1}$$

$$W = \sum_{k=1}^{\infty} \frac{N_k}{D^k} \tag{2}$$

To avoid unnecessary calculations and large messages when sending fractions between different processes, sharing weight is taken from one single pair. This results in unit fractions representable as $1/D^k$. Sharing weight is done by giving out *GiveSize* such unit fractions. When an enumerator to be shared has reached the undivisable number one, it can be extended by equation (3) resulting in the creation of a new pair with the denominator $k+1$ and D smaller fractions.

$$\frac{1}{D^k} = \frac{D}{D^{k+1}} \tag{3}$$

When receiving a fraction pair with enumerator M and denominator power k it must be inserted into the linked list of pairs. If no pair exist with denominator power k a new pair is created with the received numbers. Otherwise, the enumerators of the received and the found pairs are added together. The property of (1) must still hold. In the case of overflow, N_k is set to $M + N_k - D$ and a new insert operation is performed with $1/D^{k-1}$.

By using a large denominator base D, we will have a large number of weight fractions of each denominator (each D^k) to share. How long these fractions will last before an extension must be performed, depends on how the reference is shared and on how many are shared each time.

This approach forces the Owner reference to be able to store an arbitrary number of pairs. A remote reference has the choice of how many pairs to store, and weight of other pairs can be returned. Returning weight minimizes memory usage but increases the network traffic to the owner reference. Therefore D, and *GiveSize* should be chosen carefully to minimize the traffic (see below).

2.2 Sharing Fractions

Wide sharing without extensions, as needed in client server applications with many clients, can be achieved by giving out only single unit fractions, and thus make the weight last long. Deep sharing without extensions can be achieved by giving all but a single unit fraction and may be needed in large peer-to-peer applications. In cases where the sharing pattern is random or not known to the programming platform, we define a default algorithm below for finding a *GiveSize* optimized for a combined sharing pattern. Instead of using fixed numbers, we use a fix divisor α, where $\alpha > 0$, to define how much of the available weight should be shared.

Recall that *GiveSize* is the number of unit fractions to give out. In order to have a system that strives towards larger fractions, we take unit fractions from the term of the sum (2) that has the smallest k where $N_k > 0$. If this $N_k = 1$, we start by extending it using equation (3). We then define *GiveSize* as:

$$GiveSize = \begin{cases} N_k \text{ div } \alpha , N_k > \alpha \\ 1 \qquad\qquad , N_k \leq \alpha \end{cases} \qquad (4)$$

Consider the maximum possible sharing of references without performing any merging or extending the range that is depicted in Figure 1 as a tree. A low α results in a skewed tree with a deep left leg. A slightly higher α changes the characteristics of the tree, the tree becomes wider and more shallow. There are three interesting properties of sharing: max width, max depth and average depth. Table 1 shows some sharing patterns for a set of different α. As can be seen, 'max depth' and 'max width' are inversely proportionally. A higher 'max depth' implies a lower 'max width'. The relation is not linear though, since $\alpha = 2$ has a 6 times higher max depth than $\alpha = 1000$, $\alpha = 1000$ has a 526 times higher max width than $\alpha = 2$. The 'average depth' shows an even smaller difference between the smallest and the greatest α. An application that needs a good depth as well as a good width can therefore use an α in the range of 10 - 50 and obtain a max depth four times lower than $\alpha = 2$, but have a max width ten times greater than what $\alpha = 2$ to gives. The loss in depth is even smaller when looking at the average depth, in this case the loss would only be a factor of three.

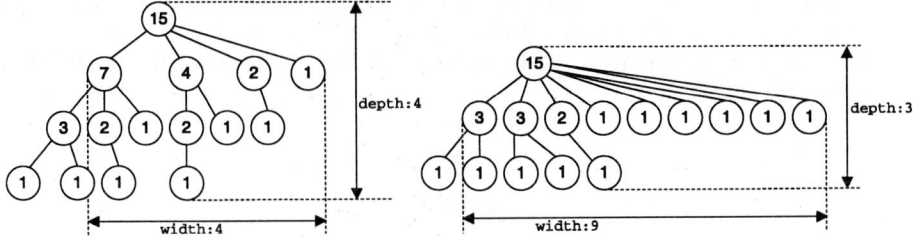

Fig. 1. The shape of the sharing tree using $D = 15$ and α 2 and 4. The top circle represents the owner reference and the rest represent remote references. The numbers denote the initial weight as number of fractions (N_1) at that node. Note that the number of nodes is always equal to D

Table 1. Shape of the tree for some different α with $D = 2^{32} - 1$. This value of D corresponds to using a 32-bit word for storing it

α	max depth	max width	average depth
2	32	32	18
3	21	55	13
4	17	77	11
8	12	161	9
10	11	203	8
50	7	981	6
100	6	1905	5
1000	5	16841	4

3 Conclusions

We have presented an extension to Weighted Reference Counting, called Fractional Weighted Reference Counting. The new algorithm solves the problem of limited weight by a fractional representation of weights. The algorithm preserves the property of third-party independence, and does not induce extra messages for reference merging.

We have also shown how the algorithm can be parameterized to adapt to different types of reference graphs in distributed applications including client-server and peer-to-peer.

References

1. D. I. Bevan. Distributed garbage collection using reference counting, 1987.
2. Benjamin Goldberg. Generational reference counting: A reduced-communication distributed storage reclamation scheme. In *Proceedings of the SIGPLAN '89 Conference on Programming language design and implementation*, Portland, OR (USA), June 1989.

3. José M. Piquer. Indirect reference counting: a distributed garbage collection algorithm. In *PARLE'91—Parallel Architectures and Languages Europe*, number 505 in Lecture Notes in Computer Science, pages 150–165, Eindhoven (the Netherlands), June 1991. Springer-Verlag.
4. David Plainfossé and Marc Shapiro. A survey of distributed garbage collection techniques. In *Proc. Int. Workshop on Memory Management*, Kinross, Scotland (UK), September 1995.
5. Gerard Tel. *Introduction to Distributed Algoritms*. Cambridge University Press, 1994.
6. Paul Watson and Ian Watson. An efficient garbage collection scheme for parallel computer architectures. In *PARLE Parallel Architectures and Languages Europe*, June 1987.

Topic 10
Parallel Programming: Models, Methods and Programming Languages

Scott B. Baden, Paul H. J. Kelly, Sergei Gorlatch, and Calvin Lin

Topic Chairpersons

The Field

This topic provides a forum for the presentation of the latest research results and practical experience in parallel programming. Advances in programming models, design methodologies, languages, interfaces, run-time libraries, implementation techniques, and performance models are needed for construction of correct, parallel software with portable performance on different parallel and distributed architectures.

The topic emphasises results which improve the process of developing high-performance programs. Of particular interest are novel techniques for assembling applications from reusable parallel components without compromising efficiency on heterogeneous hardware, and applications that employ such techniques. Related is the need for parallel software to adapt, both to available resources and to the problem being solved.

The Common Agenda

The discipline of parallel and distributed programming is characterised by its breadth – there is a strong tradition of work which combines

- Programming languages, their compilers and run-time systems
- Performance models and their integration into the design of efficient parallel algorithms and programs
- Architectural issues – both influencing parallel programming, and influenced by ideas from the area – including cost/performance modeling
- Software engineering for parallel and distributed systems

This research area has benefited particularly strongly from experience with applications. There is a very fruitful tension between, on the one hand, a *reductive approach*: develop tools to deal with program structures and behaviours as they arise, and on the other, a *constructive approach*: design software and hardware in such a way that the optimisation problems which arise are structured, and presumably, therefore, more tractable. To find the right balance, we need to develop theories, languages, cost models, and compilers - and we need to learn from practical experience building high-performance software on real computers.

It is interesting to reflect on the papers presented here, and observe that despite their diversity, this agenda really does underly them all.

The Selection Process

We would like to extend our thanks to the authors of the 19 submitted papers, and to the 50 external referees who kindly and diligently participated in the selection process.

Six papers are presented in full-length form. One of the strengths of Euro-Par is the tradition of accepting new and less mature work in the form of short papers. We were very pleased to select two submissions in this category. Brevity is a virtue, and the short papers propose interesting new approaches which we hope to see developed further in time for next year's conference.

The Papers

The 8 accepted papers have been assigned to three sessions based on their subject area.

Session 1: Thread-based models and concurrency

- "Accordion Clocks: Logical Clocks for Data Race Detection"
  Christiaens and De Bosschere introduce Accordion Clocks, a technique for managing the space occupied by vector clocks needed for race detection in multithreaded applications. Their results dramatically improve the practical usability of race detection in multithreaded Java applications.

- "Partial Evaluation of Concurrent Programs"
  Martel and Gengler present a prototype implementation of their theoretical work specializing a concurrent program to a particular context by partial evaluation. They show how messages can be automatically eliminated by propagating compile-time constants across process boundaries.

- "A Transparent Operating System Infrastructure for Embedding Adaptability to Thread-Based Programming Models"
  Venetis, Nikolopoulos, and Papatheodorou describe transparent, non-intrusive services, e.g. OS-level, to permit multiple threaded jobs to run efficiently together on a single machine. Individual parallel jobs are adaptable – they are able to exploit an additional idle CPU and to maintain efficiency when a CPU reallocated to another job.

Session 2: Parallel functional programming

- "Nepal – Nested Data Parallelism in Haskell"
  Chakravarty, Keller, Lechtchinsky, and Pfannenstiel present an extension to the Haskell language for nested parallel arrays, and demonstrate its usefulness with two case studies.

- "Introduction of Static Load Balancing in Incremental Parallel Programming"
  Goodman and O'Donnell describe an incremental development methodology with formal reasoning techniques that supports the introduction of static load-balancing in a functional model of a SPMD system. The potential benefits of the approach are a safe development framework and possible performance improvements.

Session 3: Cost models and their application in parallel programming

- "A Component Framework for HPC Applications"
  Furmento, Mayer, McGough, Newhouse, and Darlington present a component framework intended to provide optimal performance for the assembled component application. The framework offers an XML itemize schema, a run-time representation in Java, and a strategy for selecting component implementations.

- "Towards Formally Refining BSP *Barriers* into Explicit *Two-Sided* Communications"
  Stewart, Clint, Gabarró, and Serna describe a formal transformation scheme which translates BSP-style programs for execution on loosely coupled distributed systems employing asynchronous point-to-point communication.

- "Solving Bi-knapsack Problem Using Tiling Approach for Dynamic Programming"
  Sidi Boulenouar studies how to find the optimum tile size in solving the bi-knapsack problem, which interestingly has problem-dependent dependence distance vectors.

The common ground shared by the 8 papers presented here lies in understanding the goals and problems in parallel programming models and languages. What is also very striking is the diversity of approaches being taken!

Accordion Clocks: Logical Clocks for Data Race Detection

Mark Christiaens and Koen De Bosschere

Ghent University, Department ELIS
Sint-Pietersnieuwstraat 41, 9000 Gent, Belgium
{mchristi,kdb}@elis.rug.ac.be

Abstract. Events of a parallel program are no longer strictly ordered as in sequential programs but are partially ordered. Vector clocks can be used to model this partial order but have the major drawback that their size is proportional to the total number of threads running in the program. In this article, we present a new technique called 'accordion clocks' which replaces vector clocks for the specific application of data race detection. Accordion clocks have the ability to reflect only the partial order that is relevant to data race detection. We have implemented accordion clocks in a Java virtual machine and show through a set of benchmarks that their memory requirements are substantially lower than for vector clocks.

1 Introduction

Parallel systems have a notion of time which differs considerably from that of sequential programs. In sequential programs, all operations are ordered one after the other as they are executed. In parallel programs on the other hand, operations can be performed simultaneously. The total order of sequential programs is lost and replaced by a partial order.

To model this new notion of time, Lamport introduced the 'happened before' relation in [6]. Further investigations into this notion resulted in the definition of a data structure called 'vector clocks' [7,4,5]. Vector clocks exactly model the partial order of the events in a parallel system but have the major disadvantage that a vector timestamp (a 'moment' in vector time) consumes memory proportional to the number of concurrent threads in the system [1]. When dealing with systems with unbounded parallelism the modeling of the happened before relation can be a major problem since the vector clocks grow without limits.

Vector clocks are used in a large number of applications: distributed breakpoints, detection of global predicates, distributed shared memory, etc. In this article we will focus on another application: the detection of data races. A data race occurs when two threads modify a common variable without proper synchronisation. This results in non-deterministic behaviour and can be very hard to spot.

One method to detect data races maintains a set of vector clocks for every shared variable. Using these vector clocks, every access to the shared variables is checked. If the vector clocks show that a modification to a shared variable is not properly synchronized with previous or following accesses then a data race is detected. Since vector clocks are maintained for every shared variable, the problem of the size of the vector clocks cannot be ignored.

In this article we propose a refinement of vector clocks called 'accordion clocks'. An accordion clock can be used as a drop-in replacement for vector clocks. They have the additional property that when a new thread is created, they dynamically grow and when a thread 'dies', their size can sometimes be reduced. By taking into account that for data race detection, the full capability of a vector clock is not needed, an accordion clock has less strict requirements to reduce its size than traditional logical clocks. Accordion timestamps have a memory consumption proportional to the number of 'living' threads. Furthermore, accordion clocks have approximately constant execution time overhead.

We will give a short overview of the concept of vector clocks and more generally logical time and establish a formal framework in Section 2. In Section 3 we show how vector clocks are applied to detect data races and illustrate their inherent limitations. In Section 4 we will define accordion clocks. Finally, in Section 5 we present a number of measurements of a modified Java Virtual Machine which illustrate the performance of accordion clocks. In Section 6 we draw some conclusions.

2 Logical Time

Parallel systems consist of a set of threads, T, executing events from the event set, E. Events can be thought of as being processor instructions or could be a coarser type of operation. The subset of all events executed by thread, T_i : T, is $E_i \subset E$. Every event is executed on one thread so we can define $\forall e : E_i.T_{id}(e) = i$. It is clear that all events in E_i are sequentially ordered by the fact that operations are executed sequentially on a processor. We can therefore define a relation on the set E_i, $\stackrel{seq}{\to}$:

$$\forall (a,b) : E_i{}^2.(a \stackrel{seq}{\to} b \equiv \text{a is executed before b}) \tag{1}$$

Things are not so clear when dealing with events executed by different threads. Since there is usually no common clock to keep the two threads exactly synchronized, we cannot use 'real time' to order these events. Among different threads, the only order between events we can be sure of is between events that perform some sort of message exchange. Therefore we define a second relation on E:

$$\forall (a,b) : E^2.(a \stackrel{msg}{\to} b \equiv \text{a sends message to b}) \tag{2}$$

Using $\stackrel{seq}{\to}$ and $\stackrel{msg}{\to}$, we can build the 'happened before' relation (also called the 'causal relation'), $\stackrel{cau}{\to}$, as defined by Lamport in [6]:

$$\forall (a,b) : E^2.(a \stackrel{cau}{\to} b \equiv (a \stackrel{seq}{\to} b) \vee (a \stackrel{msg}{\to} b) \vee (\exists c : E.a \stackrel{cau}{\to} c \wedge c \stackrel{cau}{\to} b)) \tag{3}$$

Intuitively, it orders all events that *could* have influenced each other during the execution of the parallel system. It is also called the 'causal relation'. Two events are said to be parallel when they are not ordered by the causal relationship:

$$\forall (a,b) : E^2.(a \parallel b \equiv \neg(a \stackrel{cau}{\to} b \vee b \stackrel{cau}{\to} a)) \quad (4)$$

Many data structures have been constructed to detect part or whole of the causal relationship and are called 'logical clocks'. Logical clocks provide a mapping, $L : E \to D$, from events to 'timestamps', from set D, such that some or all properties of the causal relationship are carried over onto a relation of the timestamps, $<$.

One such mapping, V_c, is a vector clock [7,4]. A vector clock timestamp is an n-tuple of dimension equal to the number of threads in the parallel system, $\#T$. With $\Box n \equiv \{i : \mathbb{N} \mid i < n\}$ a subrange of the natural numbers, $I \equiv \Box(\#T)$ the set of all thread identifiers, $V \equiv I \to \mathbb{N}$ the set of all vector clock timestamps and $\delta_{i,j}$ the Kronecker symbol, the mapping, V_c, of events to vector clock timestamps becomes:

$$V_c : E \to V$$
$$\forall i,j : I^2.\forall a : E_i.V_c(a)[j] = \max(\{V_c(b)[j] \mid b : E.b \stackrel{cau}{\to} a\} \cup \{0\}) + \delta_{i,j} \quad (5)$$

A property of this mapping is that we can define a relation, $<$, on the resulting timestamps that reflects exactly the causal relation:

$$< \equiv (v_1, v_2) : V^2.(\forall i : I.v_1[i] \leq v_2[i]) \wedge v_1 \neq v_2 \quad (6)$$

i.e. one timestamp is 'smaller' than the other if all components are smaller or equal and the two timestamps are not identical.

The causal relationship is carried over exactly to the vector clock timestamps.

$$a \stackrel{cau}{\to} b \equiv V_c(a) < V_c(b) \quad (7)$$

If we know the threads, T_i and T_j, which executed the events, a and b, then this comparison can be optimized as follows.

$$\forall (a,b) : (E_i \times E_j).((i \neq j) \Rightarrow (a \stackrel{cau}{\to} b \equiv V_c(a)[i] \leq V_c(b)[i])) \quad (8)$$

It has been proven in [1] that the size of a vector clock timestamp for general programs must at least be equal to the number of parallel threads in the system. This poses some serious scalability issues in highly multi-threaded applications.

In what follows, we will describe a new technique, called 'accordion clocks', which alleviates the problem of the growing size of timestamps for the specific application of data race detection.

3 Data Race Detection

Using the happened before relation, we can define a datarace more formally. If we define $R(e)$ as the set all locations read during event e and similarly $W(e)$ as the set of all locations written to during event e then a data race between two events, e_1 and e_2, can be defined more formally as:

$$Race(e_1, e_2) \equiv \begin{cases} e_1 \parallel e_2 \\ (R(e_1) \cap W(e_2)) \cup (W(e_1) \cap R(e_2)) \cup (W(e_1) \cap W(e_2)) \neq \emptyset \end{cases} \tag{9}$$

Several approaches to detecting data races were described in [9,3,8,10]. The approach we will focus on consists of maintaining 'access histories' as described in [3]. An access history of a memory location consists of a list of previous read and write operations to this location. It contains all the most recent read operations that are not causally ordered with one another and the last write operation that occurred to this location.

Each time a new read or write operation is performed, this new operation is checked with the access history. If Condition 9 holds between the new read/write event and an event in the access history, a data race is reported. Afterwards, the read or write operation is recorded in the access history, possibly removing other events already present.

Since every access history can contain as many as $\#T + 1$ vector clock timestamps, there can be a very large number of vector timestamps present in the system. Each of these grows proportional to the number of threads. We can clearly conclude that this approach to data race detection does not scale well with an increasing number of threads.

4 Accordion Clocks

The basic idea for accordion clocks comes from the observation that usually not all threads are active at the same time. Consider the behaviour of a simple FTP-server as seen in Figure 1. We see that for each file request made to the server, a new slave thread is created. Depending on the size of the file to transfer, the bandwidth of the network connection to the client and many other factors, this slave thread can take a variable amount of time to finish. When the slave thread has finished transferring the file, it is destroyed.

Clearly, over a long period of time, only a small fraction of the slave threads will run concurrently. Still, the size of the vector clock will be equal to the total number of threads executed by the FTP-server. Indeed, if we would try to remove the information about the execution of thread T_2 when the thread has finished, we would run the risk of no longer detecting all data races.

Take for example event e_1 on thread T_2. Even when thread T_2 has finished execution, this event can still cause a race with another event e_2 on thread T_3. Indeed, if T_2 had run a little slower, e_2 would have been executed before e_1, which clearly constitutes a data race. The cause for this data race is that T_2 simply dies when it has finished its task without synchronizing with any other thread. Therefore, the risk for data races with event e_1 will continue to exist indefinitely.

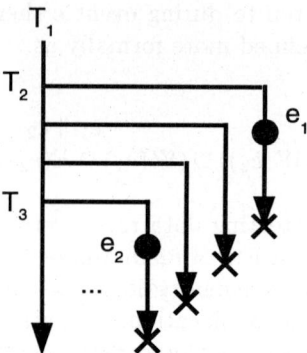

Fig. 1. A simple FTP-server spawning threads for each file request

Using vector clocks, we are stuck here. In general, we cannot reduce the size of a vector clock. The best we can do is increase the size of the vector clocks dynamically as new threads are created.

The Equation 8 shows us how to improve vector clocks. Suppose we have two events, e_i and e_j, from resp. threads, T_i and T_j. If we want to know whether these two events were executed in parallel then, according to Definition 4, we must verify that neither $e_i \stackrel{cau}{\to} e_j$ nor $e_j \stackrel{cau}{\to} e_i$ holds. To perform this check, Equation 8 tells us we only need the values of the vector clocks at indices i and j. Or, if we invert this reasoning, we can throw away all positions in the vector clocks corresponding to threads from which we have no events left that interest us when doing data race detection!

The events that still interest us are stored in the access histories of the shared variables. These events are gradually being removed by the following three mechanisms:

1. When a read operation occurs on a shared variable, its access history is updated. All the read operations that are causally ordered before the new read operation are removed. Then the new read operation is added. See [3].
2. When a data structure is destroyed and its memory is freed, there can no longer be data races on this data structure. There is therefore no more need for its access history. As a consequence, the access history can be destroyed.
3. Periodically, for example after every garbage collection, we can perform a 'cleanup' as follows. We take a consistent cut, c of the system from the set of consistent cuts CC, i.e. we stop the system in a consistent state. ($\mathcal{P}$ is the 'powerset', the set of all subsets of a set)

$$CC = \{c : \mathcal{P}(E) \mid \forall e_1 : c. \forall e_2 : E. e_2 \stackrel{cau}{\to} e_1 \Rightarrow e_2 \in c\} \quad (10)$$

For every thread, T_i, we look up the event it is currently executing, $cur(i, c)$, at the consistent cut, c. We combine the vector timestamps of each of these events to calculate the 'past' vector timestamp, $past : CC \to V$, of all these threads as follows.

$$\forall i: I.\forall c: CC.\text{past}(c)[i] \equiv \min\{V_c(\text{cur}(j,c))[i] \mid j \in I\} \quad (11)$$

All events present in the access history that have occurred before past(c) can no longer be parallel with any new events that will occur. This means that no race can occur between these old events and any new events. We can therefore safely remove these from the access history.

Due to the three mechanisms described above, the access histories at a consistent cut, $c: CC$, contain only a subset of all the events executed by the threads. If we let $S(c) \subset E$ be this set and if we let the predicate *running* indicate that a thread is currently running in the system then we can construct the set of active threads at a consistent cut, $T_{act}(c) \subset T$ as follows

$$\forall c: CC.T_{act}(c) \equiv \{t_i : T \mid \exists e: S(c).T_{id}(e) = i\} \cup \{t: T \mid running(t)\} \quad (12)$$

The threads that are not member of the active set have either not run yet or have run but all traces of their activities have disappeared from the access histories. If a thread has not run yet, no events performed by this thread can be involved in a data race yet so no room for it must yet be allocated in the timestamps of events. If a thread has run, but none of the events performed by it are stil 'remembered' in the access histories, again no room must remain allocated for it in the timestamps.

Either way, these threads can currently not be involved in a data race. We will not need to compare the vector timestamps of events from threads in this set with each other so there is no need to maintain the indices in the vector timestamps for these threads.

As threads enter and leave the active set, we can adjust the vector clocks accordingly. When a thread has not yet run, and is about to start, we can easily expand the existing vector clock timestamps to include a 0 at the index corresponding to the new thread. If a thread has finished its execution and none of its events are present in the access histories, then we can remove the corresponding index from all timestamps and vector clocks.

If we return to our example from Figure 1 we see that, although with vector clocks we can never remove or reuse the index corresponding to thread T_2 from the vector clocks because T_2 fails to synchronize at the end of its life, removing an index is possible with the above aproach. Suppose that event e_1 accessed a file descriptor that was used to read a file. When T_2 terminates, it frees the file descriptor (by itself or through a garbage collector). At this point, the access history of the file descriptor is also removed and e_1 is no longer of importance. If the other events performed by T_2 are also removed from the access history, then all knowledge of T_2 can be dropped from the timestamps.

Using this insight, we can define a logical clock which grows when threads are started and shrinks when all events of a thread are 'forgotten' by the other threads. We call this logical clock an 'accordion clock'.

An accordion clock, A_c, is a mapping from an event, $e: E$, to an accordion clock timestamp, $a: A$, at a consistent cut, $c: CC$, in the execution of the system. An accordion clock timestamp is a pair. The first component of the pair is denoted as a_s. It itself is a tuple of scalar values that indicate the local time, just like the values of the vector clock time stamp. The second component of the pair is a thread identifier, $a_{id} : I$, indicating the thread that performed the event for which this time stamp was generated.

$$A = T \times I$$
$$A_c : (E, CC) \to A \qquad (13)$$
$$\forall e : E. \forall c : CC. A_c(e,c) = (S_{ac}(e,c), T_{id}(e))$$

$$S_{ac} : (E, CC \ni c) \to T_{act}(c) \to \mathbb{N}$$
$$\forall c : CC, \forall e : E. \forall i : T_{act}(c). S_{ac}(e,c)[i] = V_c(e)[i] \qquad (14)$$

In essence, an accordion clock timestamp contains the same scalar values as the vector clock timestamp but only those we are still interested in at a certain point in the execution of the system. The timestamp therefor requires only $O(\#T_{act}(c))$ memory.

The comparison of accordion clock timestamp, $<_{ac}$, at a certain consistent cut, $c : CC$, becomes

$$<_{ac} \equiv (a_1, a_2) : A^2. a_{1,s}[a_{1,id}] \leq a_{2,s}[a_{1,id}] \qquad (15)$$

5 Implementation and Measurements

We have implemented accordion clocks in a race detection system called 'TRaDe' [2]. TRaDe is built on a Java virtual machine from Sun that is adapted to on-the-fly detect data races in multi-threaded Java programs that are being executed on the virtual machine. The definition of data races given in Formula 9 is used. The accordion clocks are used to avoid the size problem of vector clocks.

We have used Condition 14 to check whether an accordion clock's size could be reduced. We performed this check after every garbage collection of the JVM. Since the garbage collector requires that the JVM be halted temporarily, this seems an appropriate time to perform our analysis.

To test the performance of the accordion clocks we used the following set of benchmarks.

In Figure 5 we see the results of using vector clocks (on the left) vs. accordion clocks (on the right). In each of the graphs, we show the amount of memory consumed by the data structures needed for performing data race detection. We split the memory consumption into two parts. At the top of each graph we see the memory used to create resp. the vector clocks and accordion clocks in the system. At the bottom, we see the remaining memory used for storing, among others, the access histories. The memory used by the virtual machine itself is not shown. All other optimisations which reduce the size and number of the access histories are enabled during both executions. Only the improvement in memory consumption due to the use of accordion clocks is measured.

On the left of each of the figures, we see that in general the vector clocks continuously grow and tend to consume a large amount of memory after only a

Table 1. Description of the Java benchmarks used

Name	Description
SwingSet Demo	A highly multi-threaded demo, included with the JDK 1.2, of the Swing widget set. It demonstrates buttons, sliders, text areas, ... Every tab in the demo was clicked twice during our tests. Immediately thereafter it was shut down.
Java2D Demo	A highly multi-threaded demo, included with the JDK 1.2. It demonstrates the features of the Java 2D drawing libraries and is highly multithreaded. Every tab in the demo was clicked 5 times. Immediately thereafter it was shut down.
Forte for Java	A full-blown Java IDE with object browsers, visual construction of GUI code, ... To exercise the benchmark, we created a small dialog while doing race detection.

few minutes of performing data race detection. Clearly, this behaviour prohibits the use of vector clocks for doing data race detection for a long period of time.

On the right, we show the use of accordion clocks. For the Java2D and Forte benchmarks we see an almost ideal behaviour. Originally the vector clocks grew proportional with time. This memory consumption is reduced to a constant cost by using accordion clocks. What is more, we have succeeded in leveling off the memory consumption for data race detection since the other data structures apparently, after a startup period, also consume a constant amount of memory.

We have also added a figure of the memory consumption of the Swing benchmark. Again, we can see that the memory needed to maintaining accordion clocks is substantially smaller than for vector clocks. Here we do not yet succeed in reducing memory consumption for data race detection to a constant cost. Both the vector clocks and the access histories grow proportionally with time. Nevertheless, using accordion clocks, we at least succeed in reducing considerably the memory consumption for the clocks. The cause of the memory increase in this benchmark is not yet clear to us. Further research will be needed.

The time overhead of using accordion clocks is negligable. On the one hand, some overhead is incurred by reducing and increasing the size of the accordion clocks. On the other hand, since accordion clocks are usually substantially smaller than vector clocks, the cost of comparing, copying, etc. of their data structures is reduced. Time overhead of the accordion clocks is currently not a real concern since the time overhead incurred by performing the checks of read and write operations for data race detection is by far the predominant factor in the overhead.

6 Conclusions

In general, the maintenance of vector timestamps consumes memory proportional to the number of threads in a program. In this article, we have shown

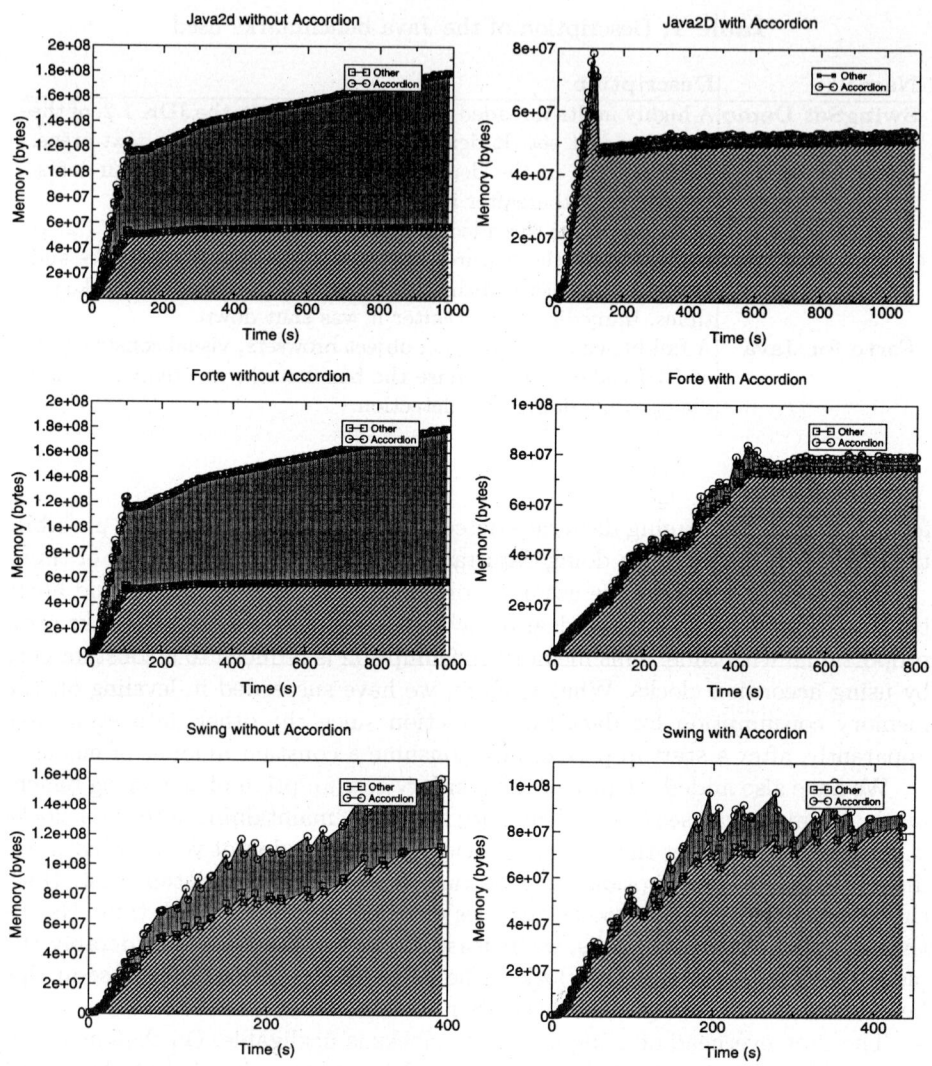

Fig. 2. Memory consumption of data structures for data race detection for the three benchmark programs used

that by taking into account what the vector timestamps will be used for, the size of timestamps can be reduced beyond the limit of the total number of threads running in the system. We have defined a new type of logical clock that has the ability to grow and shrink, called an accordion clock. An accordion clock has the same order of magnitude of execution time consumption as a vector clock. It has the potential to reduce the memory consumption considerably by adapting dynamically the size of the timestamps when it can be verified that no comparison between events of certain threads will be necessary in the future.

Acknowledgements

Mark Christiaens is supported by the IWT SEESCOA project (IWT/ADV/ 980.374). We are grateful to Michiel Ronsse for proofreading this article and his many stimulating remarks.

References

1. Bernadette Charron-Bost. Concerning the size of logical clocks in distributed systems. *Information Processing Letters*, 1(39):11–16, July 1991.
2. Mark Christiaens and Koen De Bosschere. Trade, a topological approach to on-the-fly race detection in java programs. In *Proceedings of the Java Virtual Machine Research and Technology Symposium 2001*, pages 105–116, Monetery, California, USA, April 2001. USENIX.
3. A. Dinning and E. Schonberg. An empirical comparison of monitoring algorithms for access anomaly detection. In *Second ACM SIGPLAN symposium on Principles & practice of parallel programming*, pages 1–10, March 1990.
4. C. J. Fidge. Partial orders for parallel debugging. In *Proceedings of the ACM SIGPLAN and SIGOPS Workshop on Parallel and distributed debugging*, pages 183–194, May 1988.
5. Dieter Haban and Wolfgang Weigel. Global events and global breakpoints in distributed systems. In *21st Annual Hawaii International Conference on System Sciences*, volume II, pages 166–175. IEEE Computer Society, January 1988.
6. Leslie Lamport. Time, clocks, and the ordering of events in a distributed system. *Communications of the ACM*, 21(7):558–565, July 1978.
7. Friedemann Mattern. Virtual time and global states of distributed systems. In *Proceedings of the Intl. Workshop on Parallel and Distributed Algorithms*, pages 215–226. Elsevier Science Publishers B. V., North-Holland, 1989.
8. Michiel Ronsse. *Racedetectie in Parallelle Programma's door Gecontroleerde Heruitvoering*. PhD thesis, Universiteit Gent, May 1999.
9. Michiel Ronsse and Koen De Bosschere. Recplay: A fully integrated practical record/replay system. *ACM Transactions on Computer Systems*, 17(2):133–152, May 1999.
10. Stefan Savage, Michael Burrows, Greg Nelson, Patrick Sobalvarro, and Thomas Anderson. Eraser: A dynamic data race detector for multi-threaded programs. In *Operating Systems Review*, volume 31, pages 27–37. ACM, October 1997.

Partial Evaluation of Concurrent Programs

Matthieu Martel[1] and Marc Gengler[2]

[1] CEA - Recherche Technologique
LIST-DTSI-SLA, 91191 Gif-sur-Yvette cedex, France
`mmartel@cea.fr`
[2] ESIL – Laboratoire d'Informatique de Marseille
163, avenue de Luminy, Case 925, 13288 Marseille cedex 9, France
`Marc.Gengler@esil.univ-mrs.fr`

Abstract. In this article, we introduce a partial evaluator for a concurrent functional language with synchronous communications over channels, dynamic process and channel creations, and the ability to communicate channel names. Partial evaluation executes at compile-time the communications of a program for which the emitter, the receptor and the message contents are statically known. The partial evaluator and the static analyses used to guide it were implemented and we show the results of the specialization of concurrent programs for particular execution contexts, corresponding to different assumptions on the network or on the messages.

Keywords: Partial Evaluation, Concurrent Languages, Binding-time Analysis, Control Flow Analysis.

1 Introduction

Partial evaluation is a technique used to execute a program for which only one part of the data is known [10]. The *static* instructions, depending on the known data, are executed, while the *dynamic* instructions, depending at least partly on unknown data, are frozen. We obtain a *residual* or *specialized* program, made of the pieces of code which could not be executed and of the results of those parts of the computation that could be executed. In order to determine the parts of a program which can be executed because they solely depend on known data, partial evaluators (PE) usually use the results of a static analysis called *binding-time analysis* (BTA) [3,10].

In this article, we are interested in partial evaluation of a concurrent language with synchronous communications over channels, dynamic process creation and the ability to communicate channel names and functions. Sequential parts of the programs are written in a functional style. For this kind of programs, partial evaluation allows the static execution of those communications for which the emitter, the receptor and the contents of the message are known [6,9,11]. We obtain a residual program with fewer communications than the original one. For instance, partial evaluation has been used to scale up a commercial version of the RPC protocol, yielding up to 3.75 times faster code [14]. However, since no specific techniques were used to specialize the communication primitives, the partial evaluation was done by means of run-time specialization techniques which could have been avoided by using an adequate method for partial evaluation of the communications.

We introduce a partial evaluator, denoted Pev which uses the result of a BTA and of a control flow analysis (CFA) [16,19] in two different ways. The analyses are used, first, to determine the functions possibly called at a given application point and, second, to determine the possible synchronizations of the program, i.e. the possible matching pairs of emitters and receptors. The CFA of [13], the BTA and the partial evaluator were implemented and we describe some experiments. We show how to specialize, by partial evaluation, concurrent programs with respect to particular execution contexts, considering for instance static knowledge on the topology of the network, or assumptions on the behavior of the network, or assumptions on the data transmitted. In all cases, we show that Pev reduces away all communications that rely only on the knowledge available and outputs residual programs with less communications than the original ones.

Even though partial evaluation techniques have been widely studied for sequential languages, partial evaluation of concurrent programs has received little attention. However, concurrency introduces new concepts in programming languages for which specific methods must be developed. Hosoya *et al.* have proposed an *on-line* PE for a concurrent language close to the one treated in this article [9]. On-line PE do not use the results of a BTA in order to improve their accuracy. Marinescu and Goldberg have proposed a PE for a CSP-like language with static channels [11]. The authors have proposed a PE for the π-calculus as well as sufficient conditions on the annotations to ensure the correctness of the residual program wrt. the original one [6,12]. Solberg *et al.* and Bodei *et al.* have proposed control flow analyses (CFA) which can be used to improve the precision of the BTA [2,20]. Improvements are proposed in [12,13].

This article is organized as follows. Section 2 gives the principles of the binding time analysis used to annotate the programs provided to the partial evaluator. Section 3 introduces the partial evaluator Pev and Section 4 presents and discusses the specialization obtained with Pev on some examples of concurrent programs.

2 Program Analysis

A partial evaluator uses the annotations attached to an input program p to determine how to specialize it. These annotations are the result of static analyses of p. Among these, a binding-time analysis of p determines which instructions depend on the static data and can be executed by the PE. For concurrent languages with explicit communications, the BTA has to determine which communications are static, i.e. occur on channels known at partial evaluation-time and transmit static data. Static communications are executed at partial evaluation-time while dynamic ones are left unchanged in the residual program output by the PE.

In order to produce a precise annotation of the program, the BTA itself uses the annotations given by an analysis of the topology of the communications which indicates the pairs of possibly matching emitters and receptors. In our implementation, the topology is computed by the control flow analysis described in [13]. This CFA builds a reduced product automaton, which is polynomial in size and describes an approximation of all possible interleavings of the program. This automaton is used to approximate the possible communications, independently of their relative ordering. Indeed, the exact position of a matching pair within the execution trace is not relevant in our context.

The BTA we use is formally defined in [12]. Concerning the sequential part of the language, it is a usual BTA based on the one introduced by Bondorf and Jorgensen [3], for instance. Concerning concurrency primitives, it uses the topological information provided by the CFA previously presented and discussed. In the following, we illustrate its specific features using some examples.

As indicated above, the precision of the BTA depends on the one of the topology provided by the CFA. Let us consider a program with two processes which realize first a static and next a dynamic communication on the same channel γ. The results produced by our BTA for this program are given in Equation (1), in which underlined operations are dynamic.

$$\texttt{let } p_1 = \texttt{fork} \begin{pmatrix} \texttt{let } s_1 = \texttt{send } \gamma \; S \texttt{ in} \\ \texttt{let } s_2 = \underline{\texttt{send}} \; \gamma \; D \texttt{ in} \\ ... \end{pmatrix} \texttt{ in} \begin{pmatrix} \texttt{let } r_1 = \texttt{receive } \gamma \texttt{ in} \\ \texttt{let } r_2 = \underline{\texttt{receive}} \; \gamma \texttt{ in} \\ ... \end{pmatrix} \quad (1)$$

We observe that only the second communication is annotated as being dynamic. This is due to the fact that the topological information allows, in this case, to determine the exact pairs of emitters and receptors [13]. A less precise BTA, for instance based on the topological information provided by the analysis used in [20], would annotate both communications as being dynamic since γ is at least once used to communicate a dynamic value.

A second aspect concerns the emission and reception primitives for which the channel and the contents of the message (for receptions) are static, but which cannot synchronize because there is no matching communication in the program. For instance, let us consider an emission send e_0 e_1 with e_0 and e_1 static. Such a communication point is annotated static by the analysis, leading the partial evaluator into a blocking state. This is however correct, since the original program would block in exactly the same way during a usual execution. This problem is in fact comparable to the problem of static infinite loops in partial evaluation of sequential programs.

Next, certain communications with static parameters must nevertheless be annotated as being dynamic, due to the context. This happens for instance in the program of Equation (2), in which a reception may synchronize with two different emissions, depending on a dynamic condition. In this case, the execution of the communication must be delayed, because the control is not known.

$$\texttt{let } p_1 = \texttt{fork} \begin{pmatrix} \texttt{if } \underline{cond} \texttt{ then } \underline{\texttt{send}} \; \gamma \; 0 \\ \underline{\texttt{else}} \; \underline{\texttt{send}} \; \gamma \; 1 \end{pmatrix} \texttt{ in } \underline{\texttt{receive}} \; \gamma \quad (2)$$

The creation of a new process is handled in a way similar to communications. A fork is static as long as it does not occur within a dynamic context (for example the conditional of Equation 2, or a dynamic loop). In this case, the process creation is frozen and all communications occurring in the code of the new process become dynamic.

3 Partial Evaluation

The language used by our PE is an untyped subset of Concurrent ML [1,18] based on the language λ_{cv} defined by Reppy in [17]. However, the technique described here does not depend on the functional nature of the language but only on the underlying model of communication that Concurrent ML supports. The choice of an untyped functional language is motivated by the fact that it makes self-application of the PE possible and allows to automatically generate, using the Futamura's projections [5], a compiler generator, as shown in [12]. λ_{cv} is a language with dynamic process and channel creations and synchronous communications over channels. Channel names created by the instruction channel() and functions are ground values which may be communicated. The basic syntax of Concurrent ML is defined by the first two lines of the grammar given in Equation (3). The third and fourth lines are introduced later.

$$\begin{aligned}
e ::= &\ c \mid x \mid \text{fun } x \Rightarrow e_0 \mid \text{rec } f\ x \Rightarrow e_0 \mid e_0 \ @\ e_1 \mid \text{if } e_0\ e_1\ e_2 \\
&\mid \text{channel()} \mid \text{fork } e_0 \mid \text{send } e_0\ e_1 \mid \text{receive } e_0 \\
&\mid \underline{c} \mid \underline{\text{fun } x \Rightarrow e_0} \mid \underline{\text{rec } f\ x \Rightarrow e_0} \mid \underline{e_0\ @\ e_1} \mid \underline{\text{if } e_0\ e_1\ e_2} \\
&\mid \underline{\text{channel()}} \mid \underline{\text{fork } e_0} \mid \underline{\text{send } e_0\ e_1} \mid \underline{\text{receive } e_0} \mid \text{lift } e
\end{aligned} \quad (3)$$

The language contains conditionals and the operator rec for recursive functions. channel() denotes a function call which creates and returns a new channel name k, different from all the existing ones. fork e_0 creates a new process which computes e_0. send $e_0\ e_1$ is the emission of the value of e_1 on the channel resulting from the evaluation of e_0. e_0 and e_1 respectively are the *subject* and the *object* of the communication. receive e_0 is the reception of a value on the channel name described by e_0 (the subject of the reception). Values are in the domains of basic types, channel names, or functions.

The input programs provided to the PE are annotated in order to indicate which expressions can be executed at partial evaluation-time. The annotations are computed by the BTA and extend the syntax of terms, yielding a *two-level language* [7,15] described by the full grammar of Equation (3). Underlined expressions are dynamic (of the second stage) while the other are static (of the first stage). lift c translates a first order static constant into a dynamic one.

The partial evaluation of a two-level expression e is defined by $\mathcal{P}[\![e]\!]\rho$ where ρ is an environment containing global variables (of first and higher order) shared by all the processes. When the PE, denoted CPev finds a free variable in the program being partially evaluated, it looks for its value in ρ, which can be seen as a global memory shared by all the processes and which is used to define all auxiliary functions called by CPev.

When CPev finds an instruction fork e in the program being treated, it creates a new process in which e is applied to a copy CPev' of CPev. The programs

$$\mathcal{P}[\![c]\!]\rho = c$$
$$\mathcal{P}[\![x]\!]\rho = \rho(x)$$
$$\mathcal{P}[\![\text{fun } x \Rightarrow e]\!]\rho = \lambda v.\mathcal{P}[\![e\{x \leftarrow v\}]\!]\rho$$
$$\mathcal{P}[\![\text{rec } f\ x \Rightarrow e]\!]\rho = \lambda v.\mathcal{P}[\![e\{x \leftarrow v\}\{f \leftarrow \text{rec } f\ x \Rightarrow e\}]\!]\rho$$
$$\mathcal{P}[\![(e_0\ @\ e_1)]\!]\rho = (\mathcal{P}[\![e_0]\!]\rho)\ (\mathcal{P}[\![e_1]\!]\rho)$$
$$\mathcal{P}[\![\text{if } e_0\ e_1\ e_2]\!]\rho = \text{IF}(\mathcal{P}[\![e_0]\!]\rho)(\mathcal{P}[\![e_1]\!]\rho)(\mathcal{P}[\![e_2]\!]\rho)$$
$$\mathcal{P}[\![\text{lift } c]\!]\rho = \text{BUILD-CONST}(c)$$
$$\mathcal{P}[\![\text{channel}()]\!]\rho = \text{CHANNEL}()$$
$$\mathcal{P}[\![\text{fork } e_0]\!]\rho = \text{FORK}\ (\mathcal{P}[\![e_0]\!]\rho)$$
$$\mathcal{P}[\![\text{receive } e_0]\!]\rho = \text{RECEIVE}\ (\mathcal{P}[\![e_0]\!]\rho)$$
$$\mathcal{P}[\![\text{send } e_0\ e_1]\!]\rho = \text{SEND}\ (\mathcal{P}[\![e_0]\!]\rho)\ (\mathcal{P}[\![e_1]\!]\rho)$$

$$\mathcal{P}[\![\underline{c}]\!]\rho = \text{BUILD-CONST}(c)$$
$$\mathcal{P}[\![\underline{\text{fun }} x \Rightarrow e]\!]\rho = \text{LET } nvar = \text{NEWVAR}()\text{ IN}$$
$$\text{BUILD-FUN}(nvar, \mathcal{P}[\![e\{x \leftarrow nvar\}]\!]\rho)$$
$$\mathcal{P}[\![\underline{\text{rec }} f\ x \Rightarrow e]\!]\rho = \text{BUILD-REC}(f, x, \mathcal{P}[\![e]\!]\rho)$$
$$\mathcal{P}[\![\underline{(e_0\ @\ e_1)}]\!]\rho = \text{BUILD-APP}(\mathcal{P}[\![e_0]\!]\rho, \mathcal{P}[\![e_1]\!]\rho)$$
$$\mathcal{P}[\![\underline{\text{if }} e_0\ e_1\ e_2]\!]\rho = \text{BUILD-IF}(\mathcal{P}[\![e_0]\!]\rho, \mathcal{P}[\![e_1]\!]\rho, \mathcal{P}[\![e_2]\!]\rho)$$
$$\mathcal{P}[\![\underline{\text{channel}()}]\!]\rho = \text{BUILD-CHAN}()$$
$$\mathcal{P}[\![\underline{\text{fork }} e_0]\!]\rho = \text{BUILD-FORK}(\mathcal{P}[\![e_0]\!]\rho)$$
$$\mathcal{P}[\![\underline{\text{receive }} e_0]\!]\rho = \text{BUILD-RCV}(\mathcal{P}[\![e_0]\!]\rho)$$
$$\mathcal{P}[\![\underline{\text{send }} e_0\ e_1]\!]\rho = \text{BUILD-SEND}(\mathcal{P}[\![e_0]\!]\rho, \mathcal{P}[\![e_1]\!]\rho)$$

Fig. 1. Evaluation rules of the partial evaluator

CPev and CPev' are the same and call the same auxiliary functions. On the contrary, when a function fun $x \Rightarrow e$ is applied, the effective parameter is directly substituted for x in e and ρ is left unchanged. This approach allows us to avoid the problems related to name clashes in different processes, as well as problems related to the closure of functions which have been communicated.

Note that we only define one kind of variables. In order to ensure that CPev behaves correctly when an unknown variable x is found, we extend the environment ρ by $\rho(x) = \llcorner x \lrcorner$, where $\llcorner x \lrcorner$ denotes the piece of code corresponding to the variable x. Doing so, CPev builds a residual piece of code for each variable for which the value is unknown at partial evaluation time.

In Figure 1, we describe the behavior of CPev. Functions written in small caps correspond to operations of the meta-language which are used to implement CPev. Actually, this language is the first-level language corresponding to the first two lines of the grammar of Equation (3). It enables self-application of the PE and makes CPev compatible with the Futamura's projections [5], as shown in [12]. The rules used to evaluate sequential expressions are usual, see for instance [8]. $\mathcal{P}[\![\text{channel}()]\!]\rho$ creates a new channel name. The evaluation of $\mathcal{P}[\![\text{fork } e]\!]\rho$ creates a new process which evaluates $\mathcal{P}[\![e]\!]\rho$ in ρ. When a reception $\mathcal{P}[\![\text{receive } e]\!]\rho$ is found, e is evaluated in ρ, yielding a result α and, next, the communication receive α is done. Similarly, for an emission $\llcorner \text{send } e_0\ e_1 \lrcorner$, the expressions e_0 and e_1 are evaluated and the results are used to realize the communication.

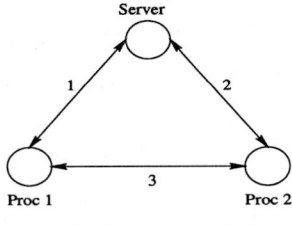

p_1 : let query = send γ_1 request$_1$ in
   let α_1 = receive γ_1 in
   send α_1 data

p_2 : let query = send γ_2 request$_2$ in
   let α_2 = receive γ_2 in
   receive α_2

server : let c_1 = receive γ_1 in
   let c_2 = receive γ_2 in
   let α = channel() in
   let foo = send γ_1 α
   in send γ_2 α

Fig. 2. Creation of a communication link between two processes, via a server

For second-level expressions, the sub-expressions are partially evaluated and a residual term is built. The functions of the form BUILD-FUN are auxiliary functions used to build the residual terms. They are defined in the environment ρ. In the next Section, we show how concurrent programs are partially evaluated by CPev.

4 Experimental Results

Partial evaluation of concurrent programs allows one to execute at compile-time the static communications of a distributed application. Here we describe some experiments realized with our implementation of CPev.

Our first example is given by the program of Figure 2, in which two processes p_1 and p_2 create a communication link between themselves by consulting a server called s. p_1 and p_2 are linked to the server by channels γ_1 and γ_2. The channel name used for the communications between p_1 and p_2 is provided by the server and is named α_1 in p_1 and α_2 in p_2.

We show how the specialization of this application for a particular network, i.e. in the case where the channels γ_1 and γ_2 are statically known and in which the server is able to know at compile-time the communication link that must be used for the communications between p_1 and p_2. The data exchanged between the processes p_1 and p_2 are assumed to be unknown at partial evaluation time.

We model this application by the program on the next page, in which the communication channels between the server s and the processes p_1 and p_2, as well as the contents of the message, are provided as input parameters.

Since the variable data is assumed dynamic, the actual communication between p_1 and p_2 cannot be achieved at partial evaluation-time. This is indicated in the above program by the symbol _ preceeding the related communication primitives. These annotations can be obtained by the BTA introduced in [12].

```
define p1-p2 = fun g1 g2 data ->
                let p1 = fork (let query = send g1 p2Id in
                               let a1 = receive g1 in
                               _send a1 data)
                in (* p2 *)    (let query = send g2 p1Id in
                               let a2 = receive g2 in
                               _receive a2) ;
```

We specialize this program in a context where the channels γ_1 and γ_2 are known and where the server is able to compute the communication link to be used for the communications between p_1 and p_2. So, γ_1 and γ_2 are known names and the program is encoded to be understood by the partial evaluator. In addition, we indicate that the variable data is unknown. Concurrently with the partial evaluation of the program describing the processes p_1 and p_2, we run the program corresponding to the server in order to allow the execution of the static communications. This corresponds to the following commands (rewritten for a better understanding).

```
> define ch1 = channel() ;
> define ch2 = channel() ;
> define p1-p2-encoded = encode p1-p2 with g1=ch1, g2=ch2, data=? ;
> run {let server = (fork (let c1 = receive ch1 in
                           let c2 = receive ch2 in
                           let p1p2Ch = channel() in
                           let foo1 = send ch1 p1p2Ch
                           in send ch2 p1p2Ch))
       in CPev @ p1-p2-encoded} ;
```

During specialization, the processes p_1 and p_2 are created and the communications with the server are executed. So, the effective channel name used as a communication link between p_1 and p_2, say #ch, is inserted in the code of these processes. We obtain the encoding of two residual processes, related to the specialized versions of p_1 and p_2 as shown hereafter.

{ send #ch data } | { receive #ch }

Our second example is given by the program of Figure 3, which describes a system composed of two processes exchanging a message sliced into packets. We assume the packets have a constant size and that their number depends on the size of the message. The process p_1 first sends to the process p_2 the size of the message (assumed, for the sake of simplicity, to be equal to the number of packets) and, next, builds and sends the packets. The process p_2 receives the size of the message, realizes as many packet receptions as needed, and rebuilds the message. We specialize this program for the particular case in which the size of the message is known at partial evaluation time, but not the contents of the message. For example, this happens in larger systems when the message is defined by a reference on a memory zone declared by a malloc-like primitive. The related annotations of the program are given in Figure 3 a). If we assume

a)
p_1 : let foo = send γ size
   in (rec f m s →
      if s=1 then
         send (lift γ) (head @ m)
      else
         let foo = send (lift γ)
                     (head @ m)
         in f @ (tail @ m) (s-1)
) @ msg size

p_2 : let size = receive γ
   in (rec g s →
      if s=1 then
         receive (lift γ)
      else
         let h= receive (lift γ)
         in append @ h (g @ (s-1))
) @ size

b)
p_1 : let symb$_1$ = send γ (head @ msg)
   in send γ (tail @ msg)

p_2 : let symb$_2$ = receive γ
   in append @ symb$_2$ (receive γ)

Fig. 3. Slicing of messages into packets of known size and unknown contents. a) Annotated version of the program. b) Residual program obtained by partial evaluation with size= 2

that the size of the message is 2, then Figure 3 b) shows the residual program produced by our partial evaluator. The first communication concerning the size of the message was executed and the loops were unrolled. Our last example is given by the program of Figure 4 a) which describes a system with two processes exchanging a message. When the message is received, a checksum is done. If the test fails, which corresponds to a transmission error, a message is sent to the emitter in order to indicate that the message must be sent again. Otherwise an acknowledgment is sent to the emitter. We specialize this system for a particular network which is assumed to be error free or to handle errors at some lower

a)
p_1 : rec emitter γ →
   let foo = send (lift γ) data in
   let ack = receive γ in
   if (error @ ack) then
      emitter @ γ
   else
      lift ()

p_2 : rec receiver γ →
   let msg = receive (lift γ) in
   let check = checksum @ msg in
   let foo = send γ check in
   if (error @ check) then
      receiver @ γ
   else
      lift ()

b)
p_1 : let symb$_1$ = send γ data
   in ()

p_2 : let symb$_2$ = receive γ
   in ()

Fig. 4. Partial evaluation of a communication protocol with error detection. a) Annotated version of the program. b) Residual program obtained assuming that the network is error free

layer of the transfer protocol. Thus, we assume that the `checksum` function always indicates that the received message is correct. As shown is Figure 4 b), we obtain by partial evaluation a new program in which the communications related to the acknowledgments are removed.

5 Conclusion

In this article, we introduced a partial evaluator for programs written in a concurrent functional language and we presented and discussed the results obtained for various small concurrent example programs.

The partial evaluator uses informations about the topology of the communications of the concurrent program. These informations are established using a sophisticated control flow analysis. The quality of the CFA is crucial, since its precision is directly related to the one of the BTA. The CFA we used is described in [13].

Partial evaluation of concurrent systems allows the specialization of applications for particular execution contexts, as shown in the examples of Section 3, i.e. assuming static knowledge of the network topology, or assuming some knowledge on the message sizes or contents. Concerning this latter example, we showed how to specialize a communication protocol by slicing messages into packets. The specialization was for a fixed size of message. This approach was first introduced by Muller et al. who used a partial evaluator to specialize the RPC protocol (Remote Procedure Call) w.r.t. the kind of data transmitted [14]. However, due to the fact that the partial evaluator used in [14] only reduced sequential programs, Muller et al. could not statically execute some communications and had to use run-time specialization techniques instead [4]. Partial evaluation of the communications, as proposed in this article, allows us to statically realize similar specializations without using any additional techniques or knowledge.

Finally, note that our partial evaluator is compatible with Futamura's projections [5] and automatic compiler generation by self-application of the partial evaluator. The compiler generator related to `Pev` was obtained in [12], where it is described in detail.

References

1. Dave Berry, Robin Milner, and David N. Turner. A Semantics for ML Concurrency Primitives. In *Proceedings of the ACM-SIGPLAN Symposium on Principles of Programming Languages POPL'92*. ACM, 1992.
2. Chiara Bodei, Pierpaolo Degano, Flemming Nielson, and Hanne Riis Nielson. Control Flow Analysis for the Pi-Calculus. In *Concur'98*, number 1466 in Lecture Notes in Computer Science, pages 84–98. Springer Verlag, 1998.
3. Anders Bondorf and Jesper Jorgensen. Efficient analyses for realistic off-line partial evaluation: Extended version. DIKU Research Report 93/4, University of Copenhagen, 1993.

4. Charles Consel and François Noöl. A General Approach for Run-time Specialisation and its Application to C. In *Proceedings of the ACM-SIGPLAN Symposium on Principles of Programming Languages, POPL'96*. ACM, 1996.
5. Yoshihito Futamura. Partial Evaluation of Computation Processes - an Approach to a Compiler-compiler. *Systems, Computers, Controls*, 2(5):49–50, 1971.
6. Marc Gengler and Matthieu Martel. Self-applicable Partial Evaluation for the Pi-Calculus. In *Proceedings of the ACM-SIGPLAN Symposium on Partial Evaluation and Semantics-based Program Manipulations, PEPM'97*, pages 36–46. ACM, 1997.
7. Marc Gengler and Matthieu Martel. Des étages en Concurrent ML. In *Rencontres Francophones du Parallélisme, Renpar10*, 1998.
8. Carsten K. Gomard and Neil D. Jones. A Partial Evaluator for the Untyped Lambda-Calculus. *Journal of Functional Programming*, 1(1):21–69, January 1991.
9. Haruo Hosoya, Naoki Kobayashi, and Akinori Yonezawa. Partial Evaluation Scheme for Concurrent Languages and its Correctness. In *Europar'96*, volume 1123 of *Lecture Notes in Computer Science*, pages 625–632. Springer Verlag, 1996.
10. Neil D. Jones, Carsten K. Gomard, and Peter Sestoft. *Partial Evaluation and Automatic Program Generation*. Prentice Hall International, International Series in Computer Science, 1993.
11. Mihnea Marinescu and Benjamin Goldberg. Partial Evaluation Techniques for Concurrent Programs. In *Proceedings of the ACM-SIGPLAN Symposium on Partial Evaluation and Semantics-based Program Manipulations, PEPM'97*, pages 47–62. ACM, 1997.
12. Matthieu Martel. *Analyse Statique et Evaluation Partielle de Systèmes de Processus Mobiles*. PhD thesis, Université de la Méditerranée, Marseille, France, 2000.
13. Matthieu Martel and Marc Gengler. Communication Topology Analysis for Concurrent Programs. In *SPIN'2000*, volume 1885 of *Lecture Notes in Computer Science*. Springer Verlag, 2000.
14. Gilles Muller, Eugen-Nicolae Volanschi, and Renaud Marlet. Scaling up Partial Evaluation for Optimizing the Sun Commercial RPC Protocol. In *Proceedings of the ACM-SIGPLAN Symposium on Partial Evaluation and Semantics-based Program Manipulations, PEPM'97*, pages 101–111. ACM, 1997.
15. Flemming Nielson and Hanne Riis Nielson. *Two-level Functional Languages*. Cambridge University Press, 1992.
16. Flemming Nielson, Hanne Riis Nielson, and Chris Hankin. *Principles of Program Analysis*. Springer Verlag, 1999.
17. John H. Reppy. An operational semantics of first-class synchronous operations. Technical Report TR-91-1232, Department of Computer Science, Cornell University, Ithaca, 1991.
18. John H. Reppy. *Concurrent Programming in ML*. Cambridge University Press, 1999.
19. Olin Shivers. *Control Flow Analysis of Higher Order Languages*. PhD thesis, Carnegie Mellon University, School of Computer Science, 1991. Technical Report CMU-CS-91-145.
20. Kirsten L. Solberg, Flemming Nielson, and Hanne Riis Nielson. Systematic Realisation of Control Flow Analyses for CML. In *Proceedings of the ACM-SIGPLAN International Conference on Functional Programming, ICFP'97*, pages 38–51. ACM, 1997.

A Transparent Operating System Infrastructure for Embedding Adaptability to Thread-Based Programming Models

Ioannis E. Venetis[1], Dimitrios S. Nikolopoulos[1,2]*, and
Theodore S. Papatheodorou[1]

[1] High Performance Information Systems Laboratory, Department of Computer Engineering and Informatics
University of Patras, Rion 26500, Greece
http://www.hpclab.ceid.upatras.gr

[2] Computer and Systems Research Laboratory, Department of Electrical and Computer Engineering
University of Illinois at Urbana-Champaign
1308 West Main Street, Urbana, IL, 61801
http://www.csrd.uiuc.edu

Abstract. Parallel programs executing on non-dedicated SMPs should be *adaptive*, that is, they should be able to execute on a dynamically varying environment without loss of efficiency. This paper defines a unified set of services, implemented at the operating system level, which can be used to embed adaptability in any thread-based programming paradigm. These services meet simultaneously three goals: they are highly efficient; they are orthogonal and transparent to the multithreading programming model and its API; and they are non-intrusive, that is, they do not compromise the native operating system's resource management policies. The paper presents an implementation and evaluation of these services in the Linux kernel, using two popular multithreading programming systems, namely OpenMP and Cilk. Our experiments show that using these services in a multiprogrammed SMP yields a throughput improvement of up to 41.2%.

1 Introduction

The advent of shared-memory multiprocessors (SMPs) and the broad spectrum of applications in which SMPs are employed have popularized thread-based parallel programming models. The multithreading paradigm is a convenient means for implementing concurrent tasks that communicate through a virtually or physically shared memory address space. A multitude of multithreading interfaces for parallel programming is in use, including standardized interfaces like POSIX threads [4] and experimental systems that serve as the backend of specific algorithmic (e.g. Cilk [2]) or compilation (e.g. Nanothreads [11]) frameworks.

---

* This work has been carried out while the second author was with the High Performance Information Systems Laboratory, University of Patras, Greece.

The metrics used so far as evaluation criteria of multithreading systems are primarily the overhead of thread management and the quality of the user-level thread scheduler in terms of response time. Recently, it has been recognized that the performance of applications and the overall throughput of the system in the presence of *multiprogramming* are becoming factors of increasing importance for the evaluation of multithreading systems. This stems from a shift from a dedicated to a non-dedicated mode of use of modern SMPs. In a non-dedicated mode of use, an SMP is shared among multiple programs and the workloads submitted to it often exceed the system's capacity, thus necessitating some form of resource multiplexing by the operating system.

From the perspective of a multithreading system, coping with multiprogramming and resource sharing requires a degree of *adaptability* embedded in the system. Each multithreading program should be capable of executing efficiently on a dynamically varying number of processors. The program should be able to both resume preempted computation, should it lose a processor and utilize a newly granted idle processor.

The literature provides a wealth of solutions for attacking the performance bottlenecks that arise from the interference between multiprocessing and multiprogramming [1,3,6]. However, little effort has been spent on the transparent integration of these solutions and multithreading programming models in a generic, model-independent manner. Existing frameworks for efficient multiprogrammed execution either pose stringent requirements on the multithreading model, or depend on the semantics of the multithreading model.

Some representative examples depict the situation. Process control and relevant frameworks [14] require that the multithreading system uses a task-queue execution paradigm. Hood [10], an extension of Cilk that encompasses a non-blocking user-level scheduler, works only under the assumption that the task queues are organized as stacks with complicated semantics and that the computation is expressed in a strict fork/join style, analogous to that of divide-and-conquer algorithms. The Nanothreads [11] architecture requires a compiler that parallelizes programs in multiple levels of task granularity and injects code to select the thread granularity that maximizes efficiency at runtime. It is rather unfortunate that despite the wealth of solutions, popular thread-based programming standards like POSIX threads and higher-level programming models based on thread-based systems, such as OpenMP [9], lack the required adaptability to ensure efficient parallel execution in the presence of multiprogramming.

This paper addresses the problem of embedding multiprogramming adaptability to thread-based systems in a totally transparent manner, that is, independently of the internals of the thread-system and without modifying its API. The ultimate purpose of our work is to improve the scalability of any thread-based system on a multiprogrammed SMP, regardless of the theoretical thread model that the system implements, or its implementation idiosyncrasies.

We present the design of a kernel-level infrastructure, which provides a minimal set of services for multiprogramming adaptability. These services can be used by any threads library and include a bidirectional communication channel between the operating system and multithreaded applications, a second-level scheduler that controls the execution of adaptive multithreaded applications and two mechanisms that enable applications to eliminate idling at synchronization points. These mechanisms are built on top of existing operating system components, however they do not alter the available resource management policies of the operating system. Furthermore, the services do not require changes in the source code or recompilation of multithreaded applications.

We implemented our services in the Linux kernel and modified the LinuxThreads library [7], which is an implementation of the POSIX 1003.1c threads standard for Linux-based systems. We used these modified versions to embed adaptability in two multithreading programming models with radically different characteristics, namely OpenMP and Cilk. Our results from multiprogrammed executions of programs written with both programming models show that our services achieve sizeable improvements in throughput (from 4.6% up to 41.2%) compared to the throughput of the native Linux kernel.

The remaining of this paper is organized as follows: Section 2 gives a general overview and Section 3 describes a prototype implementation of the proposed infrastructure in the kernel of Linux. Section 4 describes the additions required in threads libraries to use the kernel-level infrastructure and focuses on the modifications made in the LinuxThreads library. Section 5 provides experimental evidence on the value of our approach and Section 6 concludes the paper.

2 The Proposed System Software Architecture

The goal of the proposed system software architecture is to facilitate execution adaptability under multiprogramming. This implies that applications must be armed with mechanisms that enable them to adapt to a dynamically changing execution environment. The most valuable among these mechanisms are those that eliminate idling at synchronization points and minimize cache and memory interference by space sharing the processors of the system. It has been shown that adapting the number of threads of an application to the available number of processors and resuming threads that have been preempted while executing useful work in the critical path can improve significantly the performance of the operating system scheduler, in terms of execution time and throughput [8]. These services are orthogonal to both the programming model and the multithreading back-end used to express parallelism. As a consequence, the natural levels of implementation and exploitation of such services are the operating system and the run-time threads libraries respectively.

An implementation of these services should ideally satisfy three conflicting requirements. The first is efficiency; the overhead of the services must be kept at a minimum. The second is transparency. These services should be injected to any thread-based programming model or library, without having to change the native API. Non-intrusiveness, finally, implies that the services do not alter the fundamental resource management policies of the operating system, which

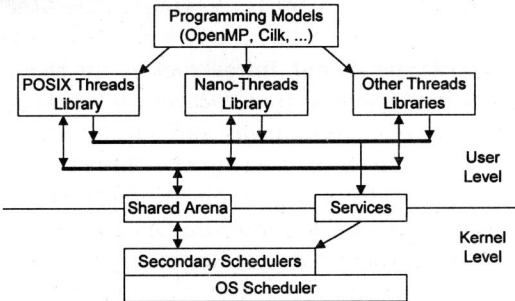

Fig. 1. The Proposed System Software Architecture

are always designed to satisfy a broader spectrum of criteria, rather than just executing efficiently multithreaded programs.

A schematic diagram of a kernel-level infrastructure designed to fulfill these requirements is depicted in Figure 1. There are three components that interact to provide the desired functionality. The first is a bidirectional communication channel between the operating system and each application. This channel allows applications to inform the kernel about their needs on resources and be informed about the scheduling decisions taken by the kernel. Since scheduling decisions are taken frequently, the communication channel has to be asynchronous and very efficient, in order to let applications access scheduling information with low overhead and only when required. A *shared arena* [11], i.e. a set of memory-resident pages mapped to both the user and the kernel address spaces can serve this purpose. Using the shared arena, applications exchange information with the kernel through loads and stores in shared memory.

The second component of our infrastructure is a non-intrusive scheduler, built on top of the native kernel scheduler. This scheduler controls only adaptive multithreading applications and its objectives are to distribute fairly CPU time among adaptive applications and apply suitable scheduling policies that enable applications to execute efficiently on a dynamically varying set of resources.

The last component of our infrastructure encompasses a set of services that let the applications effectively utilize idle processors. Most threads libraries overcome both the problem of eliminating idling at synchronization points and the implications introduced by inopportune preemptions of threads in an essentially similar way, i.e. by having idle threads yield their processors to other potentially non-idle threads. Exploiting this similarity makes it possible to provide a limited set of common services that can be used by most existing threads libraries.

Implementing such services in the operating system and exploiting them in threads libraries allows user applications to take advantage of these services in a totally transparent manner. There is no need to modify or recompile an application to use these services, provided that it is dynamically linked with a threads library. A new distribution of the library that uses the kernel-level infrastructure is sufficient to arm these applications with the desired adaptability.

3 Kernel Interface and Services Implementation

We implemented a prototype of our infrastructure in the Linux kernel. The shared arena has been implemented by allocating a resident memory page for each application that uses our mechanisms and sharing it between the threads library and the kernel. This page is used by the threads library to inform the kernel on the number of processors each application can effectively use. In addition, the kernel informs the threads library on the number of processors it has granted to each application, the number of its preempted threads and the states of its threads.

A new scheduler has been implemented, in order to apply the desired scheduling policies to the applications that use our infrastructure. For the purposes of this work we use a policy that mixes time- and space-sharing to equalize the CPU time allocated to each program in the long-term, while letting parallel programs utilize multiple processors [12]. Our scheduler ensures that all applications make progress at the same time and no application starves for CPU time. The decisions of our scheduler are taken into account by the native scheduler only at specific points. More specifically, the native operating system scheduler selects the next thread to run on a processor. If the chosen thread belongs to an application which is controlled by our scheduler we assign the processor to a thread of the same application selected by our scheduler. In this way, the native scheduler continues to share fairly CPU time between all applications running on the system, while our scheduler applies the desired policy to adaptive applications.

Two more services have been implemented to assist applications in effectively utilizing idle processors. The first one comprises a mechanism which a thread can use to voluntarily handoff a processor to another thread. This mechanism can be used at thread joining. Each thread that completes its assigned computation checks the shared arena to see if there are preempted threads of the same application. If this is the case, it hands off the processor to one of them. The second mechanism handles yielding of processors. A thread can yield its processor to the operating system if it decides that it cannot use that processor effectively. If such a thread belongs to an application that uses our infrastructure, *local scheduling* is initiated, which means that a new scheduling decision affecting only that processor will be taken. The second-level scheduler tries to assign the processor to another thread of the same application that has useful work to execute. If such a thread does not exist, the processor is assigned to a thread of another application [8]. Local scheduling is also performed if a thread controlled by our scheduler is dequeued from the run-queue of the native scheduler. Such a thread cannot use a processor until it is re-inserted in the run-queue.

4 Threads Library Modifications

Only minor modifications are required in threads libraries, in order to exploit the functionality of the kernel-level infrastructure described earlier. The threads library has to invoke a *registration* system call before it starts creating threads.

In practically all implementations of dynamic shared libraries, there exists a function that initializes the library, which is called at the beginning of execution of each application and can be used for this purpose. The second addition has to be made in the function that implements joining of threads. A check is performed in the shared arena to examine if the application, to which the joining thread belongs, has preempted threads. If this is the case, a second system call is used to handoff the processor to another thread in the application.

No modifications are required in the threads library in order to exploit the functionality offered for threads that yield their processor. The required functionality is embedded in the native system call that implements processor yielding and is activated in the case of registered applications.

As an example, we describe the modifications applied to the LinuxThreads library, which is a POSIX-like threads library for Linux based systems. In Linux, the GNU compiler and linker provide the option of *constructor* functions. These are functions that are executed on behalf of the application before the execution of main(). The LinuxThreads library uses such a function to initialize its internal data for each application that starts executing on the system. The invocation of the registration system call is added to that function.

The function that implements joining of threads in a POSIX compliant library is called pthread_join(). The check in the shared arena and the invocation of the handoff system call are added, in our case, in this function. The overall changes required in any threads library are minimal and in the case of the LinuxThreads library the additional code is only about 30 lines long.

The yielding functionality of our infrastructure is indirectly exploited by the pthread_mutex_lock() and pthread_cond_wait() functions. The first implements locks and yields its processor when a thread fails several times to grant a lock, while the second yields its processor when a thread reaches a barrier.

5   Performance Evaluation

To evaluate the efficiency of our approach we used a set of applications written with two different programming models, namely OpenMP and Cilk. These programming models differ in all aspects, including scheduling, synchronization, and most notably target application domain. OpenMP is nowadays the *de facto* standard for portable shared-memory parallel programming in FORTRAN, C and C++. Cilk is an algorithmic multithreaded language that achieves optimal scheduling bounds for a certain class of multithreaded computations, i.e. multithreaded computations expressed with recursive fork/join sequences and having unit-distance data-dependencies between their threads.

The first application used in our experiments is Heat, which is distributed as an example program together with the Cilk programming language. Heat uses a Jacobi-type iterative algorithm to solve parabolic partial differential equations using a finite-difference approximation that models the heat diffusion problem. As representatives of the OpenMP programming model, we have chosen four applications from the NAS Benchmark Suite [5]. The Embarrassingly Parallel (EP) benchmark generates pairs of Gaussian random deviates. The CG benchmark is an implementation of the Conjugate Gradient method, which performs unstructured grid computations and communications. MG uses a MultiGrid method to compute the solution of the 3-dimensional scalar Poisson equation. Finally, SP solves a 3-dimensional Scalar Pentadiagonal system. These applications were chosen because they mimic the data movement and computations of a wide range of real-world applications, with the exception of EP, which is used to determine the peak performance that a system can achieve.

We used version 5.3.1 of Cilk to compile Heat. For the applications selected from the NAS benchmarks suite we used the OmniMP [13] compiler, version 1.2s. Both environments convert programs written in the corresponding programming model into equivalent C programs that use POSIX threads. The executables are created from the intermediate code using the native C compiler of the system, which in our case is gcc 2.95.2.

The machine used for the evaluation is a Compaq Proliant 5500, equipped with 512 MBytes of physical memory and four Pentium-Pro processors, each one clocked at 200 MHz and incorporating 512 Kbytes of L2 cache. The operating system used is Linux 2.2.15 and the LinuxThreads library version is 2.1.3.

The first set of experiments consists of homogeneous workloads, i.e. workloads of concurrently running, identical copies of the same benchmark. Each benchmark creates four threads and the quantity of concurrently active benchmarks is equal to the degree of multiprogramming we want to achieve. We have experimented with multiprogramming degrees from 1 to 16 in powers of two. Each workload has been executed three times and the results reported are the averages of the three executions. We measure the average turnaround time of the benchmarks, which is a metric that characterizes the sustained throughput. The workloads used exceed the CPU capacity of the system by as much as a factor of four, which we consider as heavy load and representative for state-of-the-art SMP servers. We have used workloads with a total memory request less than the amount of memory available in the system, to isolate the impact of the schedulers on resident CPU-bound parallel jobs and factor out the adverse effects of paging.

The results are depicted in Figure 2. The absolute turnaround times of each benchmark have been normalized with respect to the absolute turnaround time of the same benchmark with 16-way multiprogramming and without using the kernel infrastructure. Table 1 lists the execution times used as normalization factors in each case. The maximum variation of run-times among the application instances within a workload is 2.96% for the modified and 2.4% for the unmodified kernel. The maximum variation of run-times among the repetitions of each experiment is 1.89% for the modified and 4.47% for the unmodified kernel. The differences are in both cases very small.

The execution times attained using the modified kernel and library are in most cases better and in the remaining few cases equal to the ones attained using the unmodified versions. A second observation is that embarrassingly parallel applications, like EP and SP, exhibit very good scalability in the presence

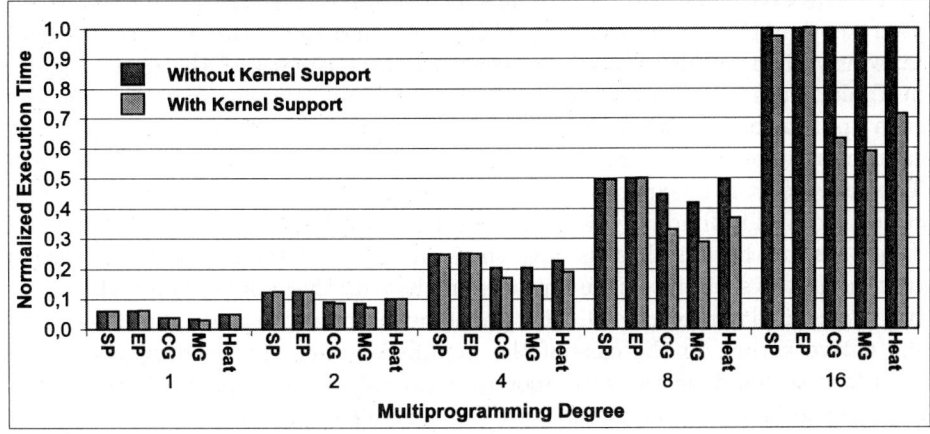

Fig. 2. Normalized turnaround times of the evaluation workloads

of multiprogramming, even without the modified versions of the kernel and the library. For such applications the execution times obtained by the modified versions are equal to the ones obtained by the standard versions. This indicates that the overhead of our infrastructure is negligible. The real value of our approach shows up in more complicated applications with irregular communication patterns and high synchronization requirements, like CG, MG and Heat. The system throughput improvement for these applications ranges from 4.6% to 41.2%. Moreover, using our services, the execution time increases linearly with respect to the increase of multiprogramming degree. This is not the case when the unmodified versions of the kernel and the library are used.

EP and SP have a coarse-grain barrier synchronization pattern, which facilitates fair allocation of CPU time among processes by the native scheduler. On the contrary, CG, MG and Heat synchronize more frequently. Under multiprogramming, the delay between the first and the last process arriving at a barrier is significantly increased. Our mechanisms reduce this delay by granting the processor to a process of the same application, whenever a yield occurs. The fairness of CPU time allocation among processes is preserved in the long term, via the native scheduler priority mechanism.

The second experiment consists of a mixed workload, which contains all five benchmarks. Each benchmark creates four threads and a copy of SP is the first

Table 1. Absolute turnaround times (in seconds) of all benchmarks with 16-way multiprogramming and without using the kernel infrastructure

SP	EP	CG	MG	HEAT
3392.61	570.64	351.90	274.61	306.87

that starts executing. After 15 seconds a copy of EP starts executing and finally, after another 15 seconds one copy of CG, MG and Heat start to execute simultaneously. The workload has been executed three times and the results, shown in Table 2, are the averages of the three executions. We measure the time that each application requires to complete its execution. The results show a significant improvement when the modified kernel is used, with the exception of Heat. This last result is unexpected, according to the execution time that each application requires individually. Further investigation showed that Heat never yields its processors, but its threads have the same probability with all other threads running in the system to take a processor that another application yields, when the unmodified kernel is used. This phenomenon raises an issue of unfairness for the native kernel. In the case of the modified kernel, the yielding system call tries first to hand off the processor to a thread of the same application. This reduces significantly the amount of CPU time allocated to the threads of Heat, thus improving the fairness of the system.

Table 2. Execution times (in seconds) of all benchmarks in the mixed workload

	CG	MG	HEAT	EP	SP
With kernel support	42.99	47.57	61.13	105.74	271.47
Without kernel support	95.42	77.93	54.12	121.39	289.51
Difference (%)	54.95	38.96	-12.96	12.89	6.23

6 Conclusions

We presented the design and implementation of a kernel-level infrastructure that provides a set of services to embed multiprogramming adaptability to thread-based systems in a totally transparent manner. The main advantages of this infrastructure are efficiency, transparency and non-intrusiveness. These services can be exploited by any threads library with limited modifications and applications benefit from our mechanisms and scheduling policies, without changing or recompiling their source code.

Our results have shown that applications conducting unstructured computations benefit greatly from the added functionality and that the performance gain increases when the multiprogramming degree is increased. Moreover, fully parallel applications that exhibit good scalability in the presence of multiprogramming without the modified versions of the kernel and the library, are not negatively affected by our mechanisms.

Currently, our implementation is focused on CPU bound applications. Our next step is to fine-tune the implemented services, in order to make them applicable to I/O bound applications. This will enable commercial applications with high I/O activity (e.g. databases, web servers etc.) to exploit our infrastructure.

Acknowledgments

This work has been supported by the Hellenic General Secretariat of Research and Technology (G.S.R.T.) research program 99$E\Delta$-566.

References

1. N. Arora, R. Blumofe, and G. Plaxton. Thread scheduling for Multiprogrammed Multiprocessors. In *Proc. of the 10th ACM Symposium on Parallel Algorithms and Architectures*, pages 119–129, Puerto Vallarta, Mexico, June 1998.
2. M. Frigo, C. Leiserson, and K. Randall. The Implementation of the Cilk-5 Multithreaded Language. In *Proc. of the 1998 ACM SIGPLAN Conference on Programming Language Design and Implementation*, Montreal, Canada, June 1998.
3. A. Gupta, A. Tucker, and S. Urushibara. The Impact of Operating System Scheduling Policies and Synchronization Methods on the Performance of Parallel Applications. In *Proc. of the 1991 ACM Conference on Measurement and Modeling of Computer Systems*, pages 120–132, San Diego, USA, May 1991.
4. IEEE. *Portable Operating System Interface (POSIX)-Part 1: System Application Program Interface (API) [C Language]*, 1996 edition, 1996.
5. H. Jin, M. Frumkin, and J. Yan. The OpenMP Implementation of NAS Parallel Benchmarks and its Performance. Technical report nas-99-011, NASA Ames Research Center, 1999.
6. L. Kontothanassis, R. Wisniewski, and M. Scott. Scheduler-Conscious Synchronization. *ACM Transactions on Computer Systems*, 15(1):3–40, February 1997.
7. X. Leroy. The LinuxThreads library home page. http://pauillac.inria.fr/~xleroy/linuxthreads/index.html.
8. D. Nikolopoulos, C. Antonopoulos, I. Venetis, P. Hadjidoukas, E. Polychronopoulos, and T. Papatheodorou. Achieving Multiprogramming Scalability on Intel SMP Platforms: Nanothreading in the Linux Kernel. In *Proc. of the 1999 Parallel Computing Conference*, pages 623–630, Delft, The Netherlands, August 1999.
9. OpenMP A. R. B. *OpenMP Fortran Application Program Interface, Version 2.0*, 2000 edition, November 2000.
10. D. Papadopoulos. Hood: A User-Level Thread Library for Multiprogrammed Multiprocessors. Master's thesis, Department of Computer Sciences, University of Texas at Austin, August 1998.
11. C. Polychronopoulos, N. Bitar, and S. Kleiman. Nanothreads: A User-Level Threads Architecture. Technical report 1297, CSRD, University of Illinois at Urbana-Champaign, 1993.
12. E. Polychronopoulos, D. Nikolopoulos, T. Papatheodorou, N. Navarro, and X. Martorell. An Efficient Kernel-Level Scheduling Methodology for Multiprogrammed Shared Memory Multiprocessors. In *Proc. of the 12th Int. Conference on Parallel and Distributed Computing Systems*, USA, August 1999.
13. M. Sato, S. Satoh, K. Kusano, and Y. Tanaka. Design of OpenMP Compiler for an SMP Cluster. In *Proc. of the 1st European Workshop on OpenMP*, pages 32–39, Lund, September 1999.
14. A. Tucker and A. Gupta. Process Control and Scheduling Issues for Multiprogrammed Shared-memory Multiprocessors. In *Proc. of the 12th ACM Symposium on Operating System Principles*, Litchfield Pk., USA, December 1989.

Nepal – Nested Data Parallelism in Haskell

Manuel M. T. Chakravarty[1], Gabriele Keller[2], Roman Lechtchinsky[3], and Wolf Pfannenstiel[4]

[1] University of New South Wales
[2] University of Technology, Sydney
[3] Technische Universität Berlin
[4] IT Service Omikron GmbH, Berlin

Abstract. This paper discusses an extension of Haskell by support for nested data-parallel programming in the style of the special-purpose language NESL. The extension consists of a parallel array type, array comprehensions, and primitive parallel array operations. This extension brings a hitherto unsupported style of parallel programming to Haskell. Moreover, nested data parallelism should receive wider attention when available in a standardised language like Haskell.

1 Introduction

Most extensions of Haskell aimed at parallel programming focus on *control parallelism* [1,7], where arbitrary independent subexpressions may be evaluated in parallel. These extensions vary in their selection strategy of parallel subexpressions and associated execution mechanisms, but generally maximise flexibility as completely unrelated expressions can be evaluated in parallel. As a result, most of them require multi-threaded implementations and/or sufficiently course-grained parallelism, and they make it hard for both the programmer and the compiler to predict communication patterns.

There are, however, also a few *data parallel* extensions of Haskell [14,12,11]. They restrict parallelism to the simultaneous application of a single function to all elements of collective structures, such as lists or arrays. This restriction might be regarded as a burden on the programmer, but it allows both the programmer as well as the compiler to better predict the parallel behaviour of a program, which ultimately allows for a finer granularity of parallelism and more radical compiler optimisations. Furthermore, the single-threaded programming model is closer to sequential programming, and thus, arguably easier to understand.

The programming model of *nested data parallelism (NDP)* [5] is an attempt at maximising flexibility while preserving as much static knowledge as possible. It extends *flat* data parallelism as present in languages like High Performance Fortran (HPF) [13] and Sisal [8] such that it can easily express computations over highly irregular structures, such as sparse matrices and adaptive grids. NDP has been popularised in the language NESL [4], which severely restricts the range of available data structures—in fact, NESL supports only tuples in addition to parallel arrays. In particular, neither user-defined recursive nor sum types are supported. This is largely due to a shortcoming in the most successful implementation technique for NDP—the *flattening* transformation [6,19], which maps nested to flat parallelism. Recently, we lifted these restrictions on flattening [16,10] and demonstrated that the combination of flattening with fusion techniques leads to good code for distributed-memory machines [15,17]. These results allow us to support NDP in Haskell and to apply flattening for its implementation. In the resulting system—which we call NEPAL (NEsted PArallel Language), for short—a wide range of important parallel algorithms (1) can be formulated elegantly and (2) can be compiled to efficient code on a range of parallel architectures.

Our extension is conservative in that it does not alter the semantics of existing Haskell constructs. We merely add a new data type, namely *parallel arrays*, parallel array comprehensions, and a set of parallel operations on these arrays. An interesting consequence of explicitly designating certain data structures as parallel and others as sequential is a type-based specification of data distributions. When compared to NESL, NDP in Haskell benefits from the standardised language, wider range of data types, more expressive type system, better support for higher-order functions, referential transparency, module system and separate compilation, and the clean I/O framework. In previous work [16,9], we have provided experimental data that supports the feasibility of our approach from a performance point of view.

This paper makes the following main contributions: First, we show how NESL's notion of nested data parallelism can be integrated into Haskell by adding parallel arrays. Second, we show how the combination of parallel and sequential types leads to a declarative specification of data distributions. Third, we demonstrate the feasibility of our approach by discussing well-known parallel algorithms.

2 Nested Data Parallelism Using Parallel Arrays

In this section, we briefly introduce the parallel programming model of nested data parallelism (NDP) together with our extension of Haskell by parallel arrays.

A *parallel array* is an ordered, homogeneous sequence of values that comes with a set of parallel collective operations. We require parallel arrays to be distributed across processing nodes if they occur in a program executed on a distributed memory machine. It is the responsibility of the execution mechanism to select a distribution that realises a good compromise between optimal load balance and minimal data re-distribution—see [15] for the corresponding implementation techniques. The type of a parallel array containing elements of type τ is denoted by $[:\tau:]$. This notation is similar to the list syntax and, in fact, parallel arrays enjoy the same level of syntactic support as lists where the brackets [: and :] denote array expressions. For instance, $[:a_1, \ldots, a_n:]$ constructs a parallel array with n elements. Furthermore, most list functions, such as *map* and *replicate*, have parallel counterparts distinguished by the suffix P, i.e., the standard prelude contains definitions for functions such as $mapP :: (\alpha \to \beta) \to [:\alpha:] \to [:\beta:]$

to map a function over a parallel array or *replicateP* :: $Int \to \alpha \to [:\alpha:]$ to create an array containing n copies of a value. The infix operators (!:) and (+:+) are used to denote indexing and concatenation of parallel arrays.

In contrast to sequential list operations, collective operations on parallel arrays execute in parallel. Thus, $mapP$ $(+1)[:1,2,3,4,5,6:]$ increments all numbers in the array in a single parallel step. The nesting level of parallel elementwise operations does not affect the degree of parallelism available in a computation so that if $xss = [:[:1,2:], [:3,4,5:], [::], [:6:]:]$, then $mapP\ (mapP\ (+1))\ xss$ executes in one parallel step as well. The same holds for expressions such as $[:sumP\ xs\ |\ xs \leftarrow xss:]$. Each application of $sumP$ uses parallel reduction *and* all of these applications are executed simultaneously. The standard function $sumP$ is described in section 3. The behaviour of array comprehensions corresponds to that of list comprehensions. The key property of nested data parallelism is that all parallelism can be exploited independent of the depth of nesting of data-parallel constructs.

2.1 Using Nested Data Parallelism

Consider the following definition of parallel quicksort:
$qsort :: Ord\ \alpha \Rightarrow [:\alpha:] \to [:\alpha:]$.

$$
\begin{aligned}
&qsort\ [::]\ =\ [::] \\
&qsort\ xs\ =\ \mathbf{let} \\
&\qquad m\quad\ \ =\ xs\ !:\ (lengthP\ xs\ `div`\ 2) \\
&\qquad ss\quad\ =\ [:s\ |\ s \leftarrow xs,\ s < m:] \\
&\qquad ms\quad =\ [:s\ |\ s \leftarrow xs,\ s == m:] \\
&\qquad gs\quad\ =\ [:s\ |\ s \leftarrow xs,\ s > m:] \\
&\qquad sorted\ =\ [:qsort\ xs'\ |\ xs' \leftarrow [:ss,\ gs:]:] \\
&\quad\mathbf{in} \\
&\quad (sorted\ !:\ 0)\ +:+\ ms\ +:+\ (sorted\ !:\ 1)
\end{aligned}
$$

The above NEPAL program looks strikingly similar to the sequential list-based implementation of this algorithm. This is not surprising since our approach seamlessly supports the usual functional programming style and integrates well into Haskell. This is mainly due to (1) the use of collection-based operations which are ubiquitous in sequential Haskell programs as well and (2) the absence of state in parallel computations. Note, however, that the recursive calls to *qsort* are performed in an array comprehension ranging over a nested array structure and are thus executed in parallel. This would *not* be the case if we wrote *qsort ss* +:+ *ms* +:+ *qsort gs*! The parallelism in *qsort* is obviously highly irregular and depends on the initial ordering of the array elements. Moreover, the nesting depth of parallelism is statically unbounded and depends on the input given to *qsort* at runtime. Despite these properties, the flattening transformation can rewrite the above definition of *qsort* into a flat data parallel program, while preserving all parallelism contained in the definition. Thus, it would be possible to achieve the same parallel behaviour in Fortran, too—it is, however, astonishingly tedious.

Hierarchical n-body codes, such as the Barnes-Hut algorithm [2], exhibit a similar parallel structure as qsort and there is considerable interest in their high-performance implementation. We showed that rose trees of the required form lend themselves to a particularly elegant nested data parallel implementation of the Barnes-Hut algorithm, which can be expressed elegantly in NEPAL and compiled into efficient code [15].

3 Parallel Arrays in Haskell

As we leave the semantics of standard Haskell programs entirely intact, we can make full use of existing source code, implementation techniques, and tools. We merely introduce a single new polymorphic type, denoted $[:\alpha:]$, which represents parallel arrays containing elements of type α.

Construction and Matching Construction of parallel arrays is defined analogous to the special bracket syntax supported in Haskell for lists. In particular, we have:

$[::]$	$:: [:\alpha:]$	– nullary array, i.e., an array with no elements
$[:e_1, \ldots, e_n:]$	$:: [:\tau:]$	– an array with n elements, where $e_i :: \tau$ for all i
$[:e_1..e_2:]$	$:: Enum\ \alpha \Rightarrow [:\alpha:]$	– enumerate the values between e_1 and e_2
$[:e_1, e_2..e_3:]$	$:: Enum\ \alpha \Rightarrow [:\alpha:]$	– enumerate from e_1 to e_3 with step $e_2 - e_1$

Moreover, we introduce $[:p_1, \ldots, p_n:]$ as a new form of patterns, which match arrays that (1) contain exactly n elements and (2) for which the ith element can be bound to the pattern p_i.

In contrast to lists, parallel arrays are not defined inductively, and thus, there is no constructor corresponding to $(:)$. From the user's point of view, parallel arrays are an abstract data type that can only be manipulated by array comprehensions and the primitive functions defined in the following. An inductive view upon parallel arrays, while technically possible, would encourage inefficient sequential processing of arrays. Usually, lists are a better choice for this task.

Evaluation Strategy To guarantee the full exposure of nested parallelism and to enable the compiler to accurately predict the distribution of parallel structures and the entailed communication requirements, we impose some requirements on the evaluation of expressions resulting in a parallel array. In essence, these requirements guarantee that we can employ the flattening transformation for the implementation of all nested data parallelism contained in a NEPAL program.

We require that the construction of a parallel array is strict in so far as all elements are evaluated to WHNF, i.e., $[:e_1, \ldots, e_{i-1}, \bot, e_{i+1}, \ldots, e_n:] = \bot$. Moreover, parallel arrays are always finite, i.e., an attempt to construct an infinite array like **let** $xs = [:1:] +:+ xs$ **in** xs diverges.

As a result, the execution mechanism can evaluate all elements of an array in parallel as soon as the array itself is demanded. Moreover, elements of primitive type (like Int) can always be stored unboxed in parallel arrays, so we can implement a value of type $[:Int:]$ as a flat collection of whatever binary representation the target machine supports for fixed-precision integral values. This is certainly much more efficient than having to heap-allocate each individual *Int* element, and thus, beneficial for most numerical applications. These properties of parallel arrays are what prevents us from using the *Array* type provided by Haskell's standard library for expressing NDP.

Array Comprehensions Experience with NESL suggests that array comprehensions are a central language construct for NDP programs. Parallel array comprehensions are similar to list comprehensions, but again use [: and :] as brackets. However, we extend the comprehension syntax with the new separator | that simplifies the elementwise lockstep processing of multiple arrays. For instance, the expression $[:x + y \mid x \leftarrow [:1,2,3:] \mid y \leftarrow [:4,5,6:]:]$ evaluates to $[:5,7,9:]$, and thus, is equivalent to $[:x + y \mid (x,y) \leftarrow zipP [:1,2,3:] [:4,5,6:]:]$. Therefore, the introduction of | is strictly speaking redundant. However, in contrast to the typical list processing usage of list comprehensions, experience with NDP code suggests that lockstep processing of two and more parallel arrays occurs rather frequently—moreover, the application of these comprehensions tends to be nested. For the sake of orthogonality, we also allow | to be used in list comprehensions. The semantics of array comprehensions is defined as follows (in correspondence to [18]):

$$
\begin{array}{ll}
[:e \mid :] & = [:e:] \\
[:e \mid b, Q:] & = \text{if } b \text{ then } [:e \mid Q:] \text{ else } [::] \\
[:e \mid p \leftarrow l, Q:] & = \text{let} \\
& \quad ok\ p = [:e \mid Q:] \\
& \quad ok\ \_ = [::] \\
& \quad \text{in} \\
& \quad concatMapP\ ok\ l \\
[:e \mid p_1 \leftarrow l_1 \mid & \\
\quad p_2 \leftarrow l_2 \mid Q_1, Q_2:] & = [:e \mid (p_1,p_2) \leftarrow zipP\ l_1\ l_2 \mid Q_1, Q_2:] \\
[:e \mid \text{let } decls, Q:] & = \text{let } decls \text{ in } [:e \mid Q:]
\end{array}
$$

As with list comprehensions, the above merely defines the declarative semantics of array comprehensions. An implementation is free to choose any optimising implementation that preserves this semantics.

Standard Operations on Parallel Arrays Besides supporting the entire Haskell prelude, NEPAL also provides a comprehensive set of functions for manipulating arrays. Most of these, such as *mapP*, *filterP*, *zipP*, and *concatMapP*, have sequential list-based counterparts with nearly identical denotational semantics. However, the definitions of some list functions, most notably of reductions and scans, preclude an efficient or even meaningful parallel implementation of their semantics. Consequently, no parallel versions of functions such as *foldr* are provided. Instead, the NEPAL prelude contains definitions of parallel reduction and scan functions, such as $foldP :: (\alpha \to \alpha \to \alpha) \to \alpha \to [:\alpha:] \to \alpha$ and $scanP :: (\alpha \to \alpha \to \alpha) \to \alpha \to [:\alpha:] \to [:\alpha:]$. The order in which individual array elements are processed is unspecified and the binary operation is required to be associative, thus permitting a tree-like evaluation strategy with logarithmic depth (cf. [3]). Other parallel reductions are defined in terms of these basic operations, e.g., $sumP :: Num\ \alpha \Rightarrow [:\alpha:] \to \alpha$ with $sumP = foldP\ (+)\ 0$. For these specialized reductions, the semantical differences between the parallel and the corresponding list-based versions, such as *sum*, are minimal and reflected in the definition of the more primitive operations (*foldP* in the above case).

3.1 Implementation of Nested Data Parallelism

We implement NEPAL by extending an existing Haskell system: the Glasgow Haskell Compiler (GHC), which is known to produce fast sequential code. The present paper only provides a sketch of each of the compiler phases and of the techniques involved. More details can be found in [15,17,9,10].

The first phase, the front end, simply converts Haskell code including parallel arrays into an intermediate language, i.e., syntactic sugar is removed. The second phase, the flattening transformation, maps all nested computations to flat parallel computations, preserving the degree of parallelism specified in the source program. As already mentioned, due to the presence of recursive data types in a parallel context, the type transformation, as well as the instantiation of polymorphic functions on arrays, requires special consideration—we present the complete transformation in a form suitable for the Haskell Kernel in [10]. In the third step, all the data parallel primitives are decomposed into their purely processor local and the communication components. In this unfolded representation, we apply GHC's simplifier, which has been extended with rules for array and communication fusion to optimise local computations and communication operations for the target architecture. This localises memory access, reduces synchronisation, and allows one to trade load balance for data re-distribution. Finally, the code-generation phase produces C or native code that uses our collective-communication library to maintain distributed data structures and to specify communication. The library internally maps all collective communication to a small set of one-sided communication operations, which makes it highly portable [9].

4 Solving Tridiagonal Systems of Linear Equations

In addition to the obvious uses of sum types, the extension of flattening to the full range of Haskell types allows a declarative type-based control of data distribution. Consider the operational implications for an array of arrays $[:[:Int:]:]$ versus an array of (sequential) lists $[:[Int]:]$. On a distributed memory machine, values of the former will be evenly distributed over the processing elements; in particular, if the subarrays vary substantially in size, they may be split up across processor boundaries to facilitate parallel operations over all elements of the nested array simultaneously. In contrast, arrays of lists are optimised for sequential operations over the sublists; although, the sequential processing of all the sublists is expected to proceed in parallel. One application where the distinction of parallel and sequential data-structures is useful is the parallel solution of tridiagonal systems of linear equations as proposed by Wang [21].

Tridiagonal systems of linear equations are a special form of sparse linear systems occuring in numerous scientific applications. Such system can be solved sequentially in linear time by first eliminating the elements of the lower diagonal by a top-down traversal, and then eliminating the upper diagonal by traversing the matrix from bottom to top. Unfortunately, in each step a pivot row is needed that is computed just in the step before, so the algorithm is completely sequential. In the parallel solution proposed by Wang, the matrix is subdivided into blocks of consecutive rows, which are then processed simultaneously. The algorithm runs in three phases. First, all rows of a block are traversed top-down and then bottom-up to eliminate the lower and upper diagonal, respectively. However, since the first row in each but the first block still contains the lower diagonal element, a vertical chain of fill-in elements appears in this column. As the matrix is symmetric, a chain of fill-ins also occurs on the right in all but the last block in the bottom-up traversal. The non-zero elements of the matrix after the first phase are shown in Fig. 1. To diagonalise the matrix, the left and right chains of fill-ins must be eliminated. The first block's last row contains non-zeros

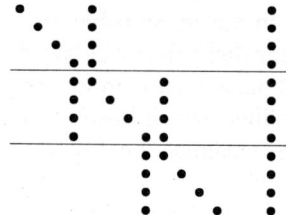

Fig. 1. Situation with 3 blocks after first parallel phase in Wang's algorithm

suitable for elimination of all left fill-ins in the second block. Once the left chain element of the second block's last row has been eliminated, this updated row can be used as a pivot for the elimination of the left fill-in chain in the third block etc. Thus, a pipelining phase is necessary over all blocks to propagate suitable pivot rows for the elimination of the left chains of fill-ins. Analogously, pivots can be propagated upwards starting with the last block to eliminate the right chains of extra non-zeros.

Elimination of the left chain can start only after the pivot row from the previous block is available, but this is the case only after the left fill-in of the previous block's last row has been eliminated already. Thus, it is important that during pipelining, only the first and last rows of each block are touched, because eliminating all fill-ins first before propagating pivots to the next block would mean a completely sequential traversal of the matrix.

After the pipelining phase, there are pivot rows for each block that can be used to eliminate both the left and the right chains of fill-ins. Like in the first phase, all blocks can be processed in parallel.

4.1 Encoding Wang's Algorithm in Nepal

In NEPAL, we model an equation with a tuple-type *TRow* containing the three diagonal elements, the two potential chain elements, and the right-hand side.

type *TRow* = (*Float, Float, Float, Float, Float, Float*)
— left, lower, main, upper, right, rhs

A row block is a list of rows, i.e., of type [*TRow*]. The whole matrix is a parallel array of row blocks of type [: [*TRow*] :]. The following encodes the top-level function of Wang's algorithm.

```
solve     :: [: [TRow] :] → [:[Float]:]
solve m =
  let
    res       = [:elimLowerUpper x | x ← m:]              — phase 1
    frv       = [:f | (_,f,_) ← res:]
    lrv       = [:l | (_,_,l) ← res:]
    rowv      = [:r | (r,_,_) ← res:]
    (fpl, lpl) = pipeline (pArrayToList frv) (pArrayToList lrv)   — phase 2
    (fpv, lpv) = (listTopArray fpl, listTopArray lpl)
    dm        = [:elimLR r fp lp | r ← rowv | fp ← fpv | lp ← lpv:]  — phase 3
  in
    mapP (map (λ (TRow _ _ maine _ _ rhs) → rhs/maine))
```

The functions *elimLowerUpper* and *elimLR* are normal, recursive list-traversals, eliminating elements on each row both in the descending and ascending phase of recursion—we omit the details of their definition here, as they do not use parallelism. However, these traversals are executed in parallel for all blocks. The function *elimLowerUpper* is of type [*TRow*] → ([*TRow*], *TRow*, *TRow*). It returns the updated row block plus the two rows needed for the pipelining phase. As the pipelining is sequential, lists are used and so the arrays with the first and last pivot rows are converted by the primitive *pArrayToList*. The function *pipeline* is again an ordinary list traversal, realizing the desired pivot generation and propagation. The lists of new pivot rows are transformed into parallel arrays using *listTopArray*, so that the third phase can work in parallel on all blocks to eliminate the fill-in values.

Controlling the degree of parallelism While it is possible to implement this algorithm in NESL, the trade-off between the computational depth of pipelining and the parallelism available in the other phases cannot be expressed cleanly in that language due to its lack of sequential types. Nepal's richer type system, on the other hand, allows us to make an explicit distinction between parallel and sequential computations. In the above example, we represent individual blocks by sequential lists which, in turn, are stored in a parallel array. Thus, the structure of the algorithm is reflected in the structure of the data it operates upon. This makes the code more readable and allows the compiler to optimize more aggressively since more static information is available.

5 Related Work

We can categorise the extensions of Haskell as either data or control parallel as well as either preserving Haskell's semantics or altering it.

The approach that is probably the one closest related to NEPAL is Jonathan Hill's data-parallel extension of Haskell [14]. The main difference between his and our approach is that he maintains the laziness of the collective type that is evaluated in parallel. The trade off here is, once more, one between flexibility and static information that can be used for optimisations. We chose to maximise the latter, he emphasised the former.

Two other approaches that do not alter the Haskell semantics and do, in fact, not extend the language at all are [12,11]. In both approaches, certain patterns in Haskell programs are recognised and treated specially—i.e., they are being given a parallel implementation. Both approaches choose to maximise static knowledge and are only applicable to regular parallelism, where the space-time mapping can be determined at compile time. This allows a maximum of optimisation by the compiler, but prevents the implementation of irregular parallelism.

Parallel Haskell (pH) [1] is an implicitly parallel approach that makes a fundamental change to Haskell's semantics: Instead of lazy evaluation, it requires *lenient* (non-strict, but eager) evaluation. Moreover, it introduces additional constructs that ultimately compromise referential transparency, but allow the programmer to maximise the available parallelism.

Glasgow Parallel Haskell (GPH) and the associated *evaluation strategies* [20] extend standard Haskell by a primitive **par** combinator that allows the programmer to designate pairs of expressions that may be evaluated in parallel. Based on this primitive, evaluation strategies allow to specify patterns of parallelism in the form of meaning-preserving annotations to sequential Haskell code.

6 Conclusion

We have presented NEPAL, a conservative extension of the standard functional language Haskell, which allows the expression of nested data-parallel programs. Parallel arrays are introduced as the sole parallel datatype together with data-parallel array comprehensions and parallel array combinators. In contrast to some other approaches, the parallel operational semantics of NEPAL does not compromise referential transparency.

Other than NESL, NEPAL supports the full range of both sequential and parallel data-types and computations, enlarging the class of algorithms suitable for a nested data-parallel programming style and allowing a declarative, type-based specification of data-distribution. In the context of NDP, NEPAL is the first flattening-based language that allows separate compilation in the presence of polymorphic functions on parallel arrays.

There are several hand-compiled examples such as the Barnes-Hut code or sparse-matrix vector multiplication delivering promising performance [16,9]. As we do not change Haskell as the sequential part of NEPAL, existing implementation techniques and compiler code for Haskell can be re-used.

References

1. S. Aditya, Arvind, L. Augustsson, J.-W. Maessen, and R. S. Nikhil. Semantics of pH: A parallel dialect of Haskell. In P. Hudak, editor, *Proc. Haskell Workshop, La Jolla, CA USA*, YALEU/DCS/RR-1075, pages 35–49, June 1995.
2. J. Barnes and P. Hut. A hierarchical $O(n \log n)$ force calculation algorithm. *Nature*, 324, December 1986.
3. G. E. Blelloch. Prefix sums and their applications. Technical Report CMU-CS-90-190, School of Computer Science, Carnegie Mellon University, Nov. 1990.
4. G. E. Blelloch. NESL: A nested data-parallel language. Technical Report CMU-CS-93-129, School of Computer Science, Carnegie Mellon University, 1993.
5. G. E. Blelloch. Programming parallel algorithms. *CACM*, 39(3):85–97, 1996.
6. G. E. Blelloch and G. W. Sabot. Compiling collection-oriented languages onto massively parallel computers. *Journ. o. Par. and Distr. Comp.*, 8:119–134, 1990.
7. S. Breitinger, U. Klusik, and R. Loogen. From (sequential) Haskell to (parallel) Eden: An implementation point of view. *LNCS*, 1490:318–328, 1998.
8. D. Cann. Retire fortran? A debate rekindled. *CACM*, 35(8):81, Aug. 1992.
9. M. M. T. Chakravarty and G. Keller. How portable is nested data parallelism? In *6th Australasian Conf. on Par. a. Real-Time Sys.*, pages 284–299. Springer, 1999.
10. M. M. T. Chakravarty and G. Keller. More types for nested data parallel programming. In P. Wadler, editor, *ACM SIGPLAN Conference on Functional Programming (ICFP '00)*, pages 94–105. ACM Press, 2000.
11. N. Ellmenreich, C. Lengauer, and M. Griebl. Application of the polytope model to functional programs. In J. Ferrante, editor, *Languages and Compilers for Parallel Computing*. Computer Science and Engineering Department, UC San Diego, 1999.
12. C. Herrmann and C. Lengauer. Parallelization of divide-and-conquer by translation to nested loops. *Journ. o. Functional Programming*, 9(3):279–310, May 1999.
13. High Performance Fortran Forum. High Performance Fortran language specification. Technical report, Rice University, 1993. Version 1.0.
14. J. M. D. Hill. *Data-parallel lazy functional programming*. PhD thesis, Department of Computer Science, Queen Mary and Westfield College, London, 1994.
15. G. Keller. *Transformation-based Implementation of Nested Data Parallelism for Distributed Memory Machines*. PhD thesis, Technische Universität Berlin, 1999.
16. G. Keller and M. M. T. Chakravarty. Flattening trees. In D. Pritchard and J. Reeve, editors, *Euro-Par'98*, number 1470 in LNCS, pages 709–719. Springer, 1998.
17. G. Keller and M. M. T. Chakravarty. On the distributed implementation of aggregate data structures by program transformation. In J. Rolim et al., editors, *Parallel and Distributed Processing, HIPS Workshop*, number 1586 in LNCS, pages 108–122. Springer, 1999.
18. Haskell 98: A non-strict, purely functional language. http://haskell.org/definition/, February 1999.

19. J. Prins and D. Palmer. Transforming high-level data-parallel programs into vector operations. In *Proceedings of the Fourth ACM SIGPLAN Symposium on Principles and Practice of Parallel Programming*, pages 119–128. ACM, 1993.
20. P. W. Trinder, K. Hammond, H.-W. Loidl, and S. L. Peyton Jones. Algorithm + strategy = parallelism. *Journal of Functional Programming*, 1998.
21. H. H. Wang. A parallel method for tridiagonal equations. *ACM Transactions on Mathematical Software*, 7(2):170–183, June 1981.

Introduction of Static Load Balancing in Incremental Parallel Programming

Joy Goodman and John O'Donnell

Glasgow University

Abstract. Formal program transformation in a functional language can be used to support incremental design of parallel programs. This paper illustrates the method with a detailed example: a program transformation that improves the static load balance of a simple data parallel program.

1 Introduction

Incremental design of programs allows the critical design decisions to be introduced one at a time, in a logical sequence. Sometimes this is simpler than writing the program directly in its final form, where all interconnected design decisions are made simultaneously. Incremental design is particularly useful for parallel programming [2,1], where there is a large space of decisions (eg. how to employ the available processors, how to distribute the data). One successful incremental methodology for parallel programming with a mixture of task and data parallelism is the TwoL model [4].

Incremental programming fits well with pure functional languages, such as Haskell, which provide a sound foundation for correctness-preserving program transformation [3]. Each step in the program derivation, which introduces additional low level detail about the implementation, can be proved equivalent to the preceding version of the program. There is also the potential for formal correctness proofs and support by automated tools.

This paper investigates the use of Haskell for incremental parallel programming based on formal transformations. In particular, we focus on one aspect of the design: the use of program transformations to improve the static load balance of a program, using a simple cost model to guide the transformation.

2 Expressing the Parallelism

The program is expressed using a *coordination language* that specifies how the computation may be performed using a sequence of *operations*, which may be abstract about the parallelism, or sequential or parallel. We use a superscript S or P to indicate that an operation is definitely sequential or parallel, and no superscript when this has not yet been decided.

The operations express computations over data structures called *finite sequences*, with types of the form $FinSeq\ \alpha$. Variants on this are $ParFinSeq\ \alpha$, whose elements are distributed, one per processor, and *SeqFinSeq* α, where all the elements reside in the same processor. A typical operation is

$$map :: (a \to b) \to FinSeq\ a \to FinSeq\ b,$$

which applies a function to each element of its argument. A sequential map, map^S, iterates the function over data stored in the memory of one processor, while a parallel map, map^P, can apply the function to multiple data elements simultaneously since they are stored in different processors.

In the remainder of this paper we will use as a running example the reduction of the columns of a lower triangular matrix X (Figure 1(a)), using an operator $\oplus$, which we assume to be a relatively expensive computation. The matrix contains a sequence of n columns $X_i = [x_{0,i}, \ldots, x_{n-1,i}]$ for $0 \leq i < n$, where column i contains $i + 1$ elements. The aim is to compute the vector of column sums: $s_i = \bigoplus_{j=0}^{n-1} x_{j,i}$ for $0 \leq i < n$.

				$x_{4,4}$					$x_{4,4}$					
			$x_{3,3}$	$x_{4,4}$				$x_{3,3}$	$x_{3,4}$					
		$x_{2,2}$	$x_{2,3}$	$x_{2,4}$			$x_{2,2}$	$x_{2,3}$	$x_{2,4}$	$x_{4,4}$	$x_{3,3}$	$x_{2,2}$	$x_{2,3}$	$x_{2,4}$
	$x_{1,1}$	$x_{1,2}$	$x_{1,3}$	$x_{1,4}$		$x_{1,1}$	$x_{1,2}$	$x_{1,3}$	$x_{1,4}$	$x_{3,4}$	$x_{1,1}$	$x_{1,2}$	$x_{1,3}$	$x_{1,4}$
$x_{0,0}$	$x_{0,1}$	$x_{0,2}$	$x_{0,3}$	$x_{0,4}$	$x_{0,0}$	$x_{0,1}$	$x_{0,2}$	$x_{0,3}$	$x_{0,4}$	$x_{0,0}$	$x_{0,1}$	$x_{0,2}$	$x_{0,3}$	$x_{0,4}$
(a)					(b)					(c)				

Fig. 1. (a) Original matrix; (b) partitioning; (c) load-balanced computations

This mathematical specification can be expressed in Haskell, with f in place of $\oplus$, by representing the matrix as a finite sequence of columns. Each column is a finite sequence of data values of type α. The columns are reduced using *foldl*, which takes an extra parameter, a, a unit of f. The unit parameter is not necessary at this point, but it simplifies the following presentation of the transformation. Each column of the matrix is reduced in a dedicated processor, so the map is parallel, but the reductions (folds) are performed sequentially. This is a more concrete version of the specification which would be written using *FinSeq* α.

$$maptri :: (\alpha \to \alpha \to \alpha) \to \alpha \to ParFinSeq\ (SeqFinSeq\ \alpha) \to ParFinSeq\ \alpha$$
$$maptri\ f\ a\ xss = map^P\ (foldl^S\ f\ a)\ xss$$

3 Generic Load Balancing

During the incremental derivation of a parallel program, we gradually transform it, in order to bring it closer to the low level executable code while improving its efficiency. One potential optimisation is *static load balancing*: reorganising the program so that the workload is spread evenly across the available processors. The *maptri* example is well suited for static load balancing, and this technique is useful for many realistic applications. Many problems, however, have irregular or dynamic processor loads that render static load balancing ineffective. In such cases, a better solution is *dynamic load balancing* supported by the runtime system.

The static load balancing is guided by a cost analysis that takes account of both the computation and communication costs. We illustrate the method by introducing a simple cost model. Let T_f be the time needed for a processor to apply f to an argument stored in the local memory, assuming that T_f does not depend on the value of the argument. Let $T_{com} = T_0 + k \cdot T_c$ be the time required by a total exchange operation, where k is the size of the largest message.

In the *maptri* program, processor i requires time $T\ (foldl^S\ f\ a\ [x_{0,i}, \ldots, x_{i,i}])$ $= i \cdot T_f$. This implies a poor load balance, since the processors' computation times vary from 0 to $(n-1) \cdot T_f$, and the time for the whole program depends on the maximum time required by a processor. By spreading the work evenly the computation time could be cut in half, although we must also consider the costs of the communications introduced to balance the load.

The first step in load balancing is to divide the tasks up into smaller pieces, and a natural idea is to split the folds over a long list into separate folds over shorter pieces (Figure 1(b)). The partial folds can then be rearranged so that each processor has about the same amount of work (Figure 1(c)). The following lemma permits the splitting of folds, provided that f is associative:

Lemma 1. *If* $f :: \alpha \rightarrow \alpha \rightarrow \alpha$ *is associative, and* $xs, ys :: SeqFinSeq\ \alpha$, *then* $foldl^S\ f\ a\ (xs \mathbin{+\!\!+} ys) = f\ (foldl^S\ f\ a\ xs)\ (foldl^S\ f\ a\ ys)$.

Now we have to divide up each of the columns. This can be done using the following lemma.

Lemma 2. $xs = take^S\ m\ xs \mathbin{+\!\!+} drop^S\ m\ xs$ *for* $xs :: SeqFinSeq\ \alpha,\ m \geq 0$.

Each processor splits its computation into two parts, $work1 = take^S\ m\ xs$ and $work2 = drop^S\ m\ xs$. The parameter m can be calculated so as to minimise the total time; by leaving m as a variable, we are describing a family of related algorithms.

The excess work $work2$ can be offloaded from processors with too much work. In other processors, $work2 = [\,]$. This is done using a communication operation $move^P$ with an inverse $move'^P$ that can be used later to return the partial fold results to the right processor.

Lemma 3. $map^P\ F = move'^P \circ (map^P\ F) \circ move^P$ *for any permutations* $move^P$ *and* $move'^P$ *such that* $move'^P \circ move^P = id$.

The following program moves the excess work, $work2$, to processors that have room for it. Each processor then computes two fold results, and sends the second, $res2$, back to its original processor, where it is combined with the first result, $res1$.

$$\begin{aligned}maptri\ f\ a\ xss\ =\ \textbf{let}\ work1\ &=\ map^P\ (take^S\ m)\ xss\\ work2\ &=\ map^P\ (drop^S\ m)\ xss\\ res1\ &=\ map^P\ (foldl^S\ f\ a)\ work1\\ res2\ &=\ move'^P(map^P\ (foldl^S\ f\ a)\ (move^P\ work2))\\ \textbf{in}&\\ zipWith^P\ f\ res1\ res2&\end{aligned}$$

4 Analysis and Transformation

The next step is to calculate values for m and $move^P$ so as to to minimise the total time. In general, the best performance may not result from an optimal load balance, since the communication time entailed by the load balancing must also be considered. If T_f is low compared to T_{com}, then the time taken to rearrange the data may be higher than the time saved by the improved load balance, so load balancing is not a good idea. On the other hand, if T_f is expensive, then the load balanced program is also the cost optimised one. In general, there are also cases between these two extremes, when moving a few elements can produce a sufficiently good load redistribution to improve the program, but achieving a perfect load balance would require a prohibitively large amount of communication.

There is not space here for a complete formal analysis, but the rest of this section shows the flavour of the calculation. p, the index permutation function of $move^P$, is used to calculate $move^P$, such that $(move^P\ xs)!!i\ =\ xs\ !!\ p\ i$. We assume that $T_f \gg T_{com}$ on the target architecture for all message sizes k, such that $0 \leq k \leq n+1$. Then the total cost is minimised by achieving a perfect load balance, subject to two sub-goals:

1. A processor's work load is proportional to the number of elements it holds. The total number of elements is $\frac{1}{2}n(n+1) \approx n\frac{n}{2}$, so each processor should have about $\frac{n}{2}$ elements.
2. Overloaded processors should only send data, under-loaded processors should only receive, and no processor should do both.

Now the parameters m and p must be calculated. In the original triangular matrix, processor i contains $i+1$ elements. Using this property and standard size lemmas, the number of elements remaining in processor i after load balancing is calculated as follows:

$$\begin{aligned}\text{task size }i\ &=\ \#((map^P(take^S\ m)xss)!!i) + \#((move^P(map^P(drop^S\ m)xss))!!i)\\ &=\ \min(m, i+1) + \max(0, p\ i + 1 - m)\end{aligned}$$

The first term in this expression corresponds to data kept and the second term to data received. The expression can be simplified further by considering the sending and receiving processors separately. Note that the sending processors receive no data, and receiving ones keep all their original data, ie. $i+1$ elements.

The simplified value of processor i's workload can now be equated with the mean workload $\frac{n}{2}$, allowing m and p to be calculated: $m = n`div`2 + 1$ and $p = n - i - 1 \Rightarrow move^P = reverse^P = move'^P$. All that remains is to substitute the chosen values for the variables:

$$
\begin{aligned}
maptri\ f\ a\ xss = \mathbf{let}\ & m = (length^P\ xss)`div`2 + 1 \\
& work1 = map^P\ (take^S\ m)\ xss \\
& work2 = map^P\ (drop^S\ m)\ xss \\
& res1 = map^P\ (foldl^S\ f\ a)\ work1 \\
& res2 = reverse^P\ (map^P\ (foldl^S\ f\ a)\ (reverse^P\ work2)) \\
\mathbf{in}\ & \\
& zipWith^P\ f\ res1\ res2
\end{aligned}
$$

However, this is not the end of the story. As indicated in the introduction, further transformations, which are not shown in this paper, convert the program into an imperative C+MPI program.

5 Conclusions

In this paper we have demonstrated how static load balancing can be introduced into a data parallel program, using formal program transformations based on a pure functional language. The transformation is introduced cleanly, without having to worry about other details involved in parallel programming. The programming methodology uses a library of suitable distributed types, parallel operations, collective communication operations, and lemmas.

Topics for future research include methods for introducing other optimisations, extensions to the library of combinators and their lemmas, and tools providing partially automated support for the programming process.

References

1. Joy Goodman. A methodology for the derivation of parallel programs. Workshop UMDITR03, Departamento de Informática, Universidade do Minho, September 1998.
2. Sergei Gorlatch. Stages and transformations in parallel programming. In *Abstract Machine Models for Parallel and Distributed Computing*, pages 147–162. IOS Press, 1996.
3. Kevin Hammond and Greg Michaelson, editors. *Research Directions in Parallel Functional Programming*. Springer, 1999.
4. Thomas Rauber and Gudula Rünger. The compiler TwoL for the design of parallel implementations. In *Proceedings of the 4th International Conference on Parallel Architecture and Compilation Techniques*, pages 292–301. IEEE Computer Society Press, 1996.

A Component Framework for HPC Applications[*]

Nathalie Furmento, Anthony Mayer, Stephen McGough,
Steven Newhouse, and John Darlington

Parallel Software Group, Department of Computing, Imperial College of Science,
Technology and Medicine
180 Queen's Gate, London SW7 2BZ, UK
icpc-sw@doc.ic.ac.uk
http://www-icpc.doc.ic.ac.uk/components/

Abstract. We describe a general component software framework designed for demanding grid environments that provides optimal performance for the assembled component application. This is achieved by separating the high level abstract description of the composition from the low level implementations. These implementations are chosen at run time by performance analysis of the composed application on the currently available resources. We show through the solution of a simple linear algebra problem that the framework introduces minimal overheads while always selecting the most effective implementation.

Keywords: Component Composition, Grid Computing, Performance Optimisation, High Level Abstraction.

1 Introduction

Within high performance and scientific computing there has been an increasing interest in component based design patterns. The high level of abstraction enables efficient end-user programming by the scientific community, while at the same time encapsulation encourages software development and reuse.

With the emergence of computational grids [1] it is increasingly likely that applications built from components will be deployed upon a wide range of heterogenous hardware resources. Component based design reveals both potential difficulties and opportunities within such a dynamic environment. Difficulties may arise where a component's performance is inhibited by the heterogenous nature of the environment. For example, an application consisting of tightly coupled components deployed across distant platforms will suffer performance penalties not present when executed locally. However the abstraction provided by the component methodology allows for a separation of concerns which enables specialisation and optimisation without reducing the flexibility of the high level design. Such resource and performance aware optimisation helps offset the difficulties of grid-based computation.

---

[*] Research supported by the EPSRC grant GR/N13371/01 on equipment provided by the HEFCE/JREI grants GR/L26100 and GR/M92455

Algorithmic skeletons [2] have illustrated how a high level abstraction can be married to an efficient low-level high performance code, utilising the knowledge of the abstraction to optimise the implementation composition. We propose a component architecture that exploits this meta-data to optimise performance.

In this paper we describe an implementation of this architecture, which consists of an abstract component description language incorporating composition and performance information and a run time framework, together with a simple example of a component application and its native implementations. We first consider an overview of the architecture, and then examine different aspects of the framework.

2 Overview of the Component Architecture

We present a layered component architecture consisting of a high level language (an XML schema [3]), an execution framework and a component repository containing the component implementations and meta-data [4]. The run time framework executes the application, selecting implementations from the repository according to the meta-data, resource availability and the application description. The design and deployment cycle using this component framework is determined by its layered abstraction.

1. **Component Construction** Component interfaces are designed and placed within the repository, together with any implementations which may be written in native code. The developer places meta-data describing the implementation and its performance characteristics in the component repository.
2. **Problem Definition** The end-user builds an application within a graphical problem solving environment (PSE). The PSE is connected to the component repository and is used to produce a high level XML representation of the problem. This representation is implementation independent, using only the component interface information.

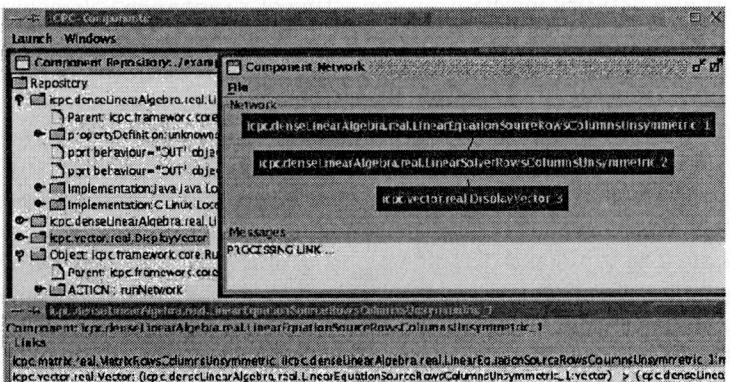

Fig. 1. GUI showing repository and composed application

3. **Run Time Representation** The XML representation is automatically converted into a set of executable Java objects, which act as the run time support for the application. This utilises the meta-data.
4. **Implementation Selection** The run time representation is deployed into an execution environment. Here available implementations are selected according to performance models and the available resources. High performance native code is loaded and executed by the run time representation. Implementation selection may occur more than once for a given component: changing circumstances, either through a changing resources or computation, may force the selection of a more efficient implementation.

3 XML Representation

The XML representation is the highest level of abstraction. The end-user composes the XML representation by means of an application builder tool. While we have provided a graphical user interface that enables rapid application development (see Figure 1), our Component XML (or CXML) provides a suitable target language for a number of possible end-user tools, without imposing constraints on their configuration.

```
<application>
  <network>
    <instance componentName="Source" componentPackage="icpc.LinearSource" id="1">
      <property name="degrees of freedom" value="100"/>  </instance>
    <instance componentName="Solver" componentPackage="icpc.LinearSolver" id="2"/>
    <instance componentName="DisplayVector" componentPackage="icpc.Matrix" id="3"/>
    <dataflow sinkComponent="2" sinkPort="matrix" sourceComponent="1" sourcePort="matrix"/>
    ...
  </network>
</application>
```

The application builder produces a CXML application description document, as shown in the example above. This consists of the `<network>` and `<repository>` information. The network represents a composition of component instances together with any user customisations. The composition is a simple typed port and network mechanism, consisting of `<instance>` elements together with `<dataflow>` connectors. The connectors are attached between source and sink ports according to the component type. The user may customise the component by specifying simple values that are recorded as `<property>` elements.

The choice of components within the builder tool is determined by those contained within the repository. The repository CXML data provides the interface information for the `<component>` types, specifying `<port>` and `<property>` elements. Thus ensuring that connections in a network correspond to a meaningful composition. The types and default properties specified in the repository CXML allow customisation where required. The repository component information also indicates component inheritance and package information.

The repository also contains information needed to create the run time representation, namely the meta-data for the methods in the component implementation. These are represented by `<implementation>` and `<action>` elements. The

`<action>` elements specify the bindings to ports and the location of corresponding performance data. The package and location information for the executables is stored alongside the implementation data in the repository. These are referred to with `<object>` elements.

```
<repository>
  <component package="icpc.LinearSource" name="Source" version="1">
    <propertyDefinition type="external" name="degrees of freedom" value="1000"/>
    <port behaviour="OUT" objectPackage="icpc.Matrix" objectName="DgeRC" portName="matrix"/>
    <port behaviour="OUT" objectPackage="icpc.Matrix" objectName="Vector" portName="vector"/>
    <implementation language="java" platform="java" url="file:.">
      <action portName="matrix">
        <binding method="getMatrix"> ... </binding>
        <classPerformanceModel type="initial" url="http:" />
      </action>
    </implementation>
    <implementation language="C" platform="Linux" url="file:.."> ... </implementation>
  </component>
  <object package="icpc.Matrix" name="DgeRC" version="1">
    <method name="getMatrix" type="action">
      <argument mode="out" typeName="DgeRC" typePackage="icpc.Matrix" />
    </method>
  </object>
</repository>
```

4 Run Time Representation

When deployed onto a resource the CXML application description is converted into a *run time representation*, consisting of a network of Java proxy objects (JPOs), corresponding to the component instances in the application description document. This abstraction of the component application enables the dynamic selection of implementations, cross-component optimisation and implementation independent management.

Each JPO provides a black box abstraction of the component's implementation and acts as the run time interface for the component. Any interaction between components occurs at the level of the JPO. This provides a means to trap method calls and select the appropriate implementation when required.

The network of JPOs is created and linked by means of automatic code generation. The complete application description, including the relevant repository

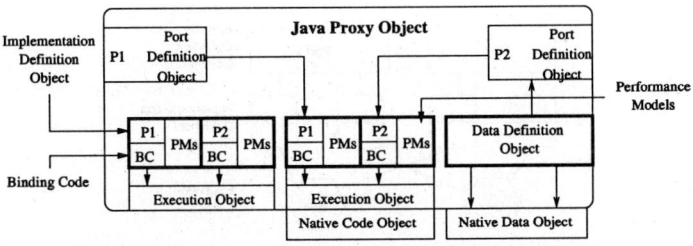

Fig. 2. A component's Java Proxy Object

data, is compiled from CXML into Java source code. The JPOs, together with the connections and property information, are represented by this 'glue code'.

The JPO contains Port Definition Objects, Implementation Definition Objects, Data Definition Objects and Execution Objects. See Figure 2.

Port Definition Objects (PDO) The CXML <port> element has an attribute 'type' that specifies whether it is an IN or OUT port. Each OUT <port> element has a corresponding PDO. Each IN <port> is represented by a reference to a PDO of the appropriate type. When the JPOs are created they are connected according to the application description by setting each IN port to refer to the appropriate PDO on the connected component. Each OUT <port> may offer many methods, which may then be called by any code within the component containing the corresponding IN port. It can be seen that this system provides a 'pull' model of computation.

During execution calls to a PDO are trapped, and an implementation is selected by examining the relevant IDOs.

Implementation Definition Objects (IDO) Each IDO is associated with a port. There are likely to be a number of different IDOs for each port, each representing a different implementation of the port's methods. The IDO contains the performance model meta-data for a given implementation, together with binding code that maps the ports methods to those of the actual implementation. When a method is called the PDO evaluates the relevant performance models and makes a decision as to which implementation to use. The binding code within the IDO maps the methods of the PDO to the actual implementation within the Execution Object.

Execution Objects (EO) Where an implementation is written in a native language (such as C), the execution object is a lightweight wrapper that makes use of the Java Native Interface [5]. This is responsible for the loading, unloading and execution of the native libraries. For pure Java implementations the EO acts as an intermediary between the actual implementation codes and the IDO. It should be noted that while there are possibly many IDOs for each port (corresponding to the different implementation options) there may also be many IDOs for a given EO. This is because a particular implementation may make use of shared objects and libraries appropriate for

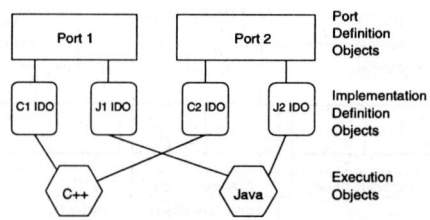

Fig. 3. Port, Implementation and Execution Objects

a number of different method calls from distinct ports. To maintain consistency a component will only select one EO at any given time. This is illustrated in Figure 3.

Data Definition Objects (DDO) To enable the migration of the component code between resources, and to allow the implementation selection to be altered during execution persistent data is stored outside the execution object. Thus the JPO needs to retain a reference to any data that may be used in subsequent method invocations. The format of the data clearly depends upon the implementation used to generate it. This reference together with mappings between the data format and Java are stored in a DDO.

Access to the persistent data is by method calls exposed in a PDO. By forcing calls to use the port mechanism, data access (often a significant part of a computation) is taken into account by the performance modelling and selection system. Where data is unavailable the PDO examines the respective IDOs as described above. Property values (which are stored as pure Java objects) are refered to by a DDO in the same way as any other data type. When the JPOs are created from the application description property values are assigned directly.

5 Implementation Selection

An application begins executing with an initial method call. The relevant PDO is responsible for the choice of implementation. By forwarding the relevant performance models from the IDOs to the framework a decision, based upon estimated running time, is made as to which implementation to use. The performance model usually refers to other calls the component needs to make. These calls are then forwarded to their respective PDOs, where they are trapped and the performance models returned. Thus a composite performance model for the application is built. The port mechanism exposes data movement between components allowing the data transfer time to be assessed and subsequently optimised to eliminate unecessary data copying. The technique is entirely deterministic, and results in a 'dry run' of the application. As each JPO may possess a number of possible implementations this procedure results in a call graph.

The performance model may also refer to data within the component, for example a property representing the number of entries in a matrix. As these

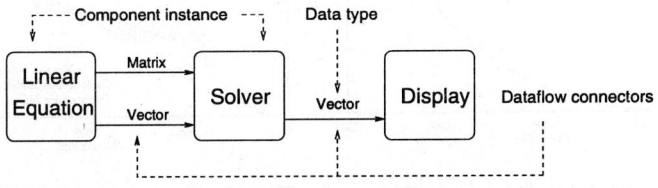

Fig. 4. Linear Equation Solver

properties may change during execution, or may not be known at start-up, the implementation decision can only take place during execution. The run time representation allows such a change of implementation with little overhead.

6 Example & Results

A composite application that solves a set of linear equations consists of three component instances; a simple linear equation generator, a solver, and a simple display component. See Figure 4. This example was used to provide the XML fragments already shown, and is now used to provide experimental results.

A set of real linear equations is generated from a component with a Java implementation. These equations are solved by one of two linear solvers written in C. The first is a direct solver using LU factorisation, whilst the second is an iterative Biconjugate Gradient method (BCG) [6]. These two algorithms have different time and memory requirements allowing the JPO to select the most appropriate implementation for the user-defined problem size. In this example the display component is only used to verify that the solutions are correct. All experiments were performed on a single 900MHz PC running Linux. The Java Native Interface [5] was used to allow access to the C implementations.

Figures 5 and 6 illustrate the performance models for the LU and BCG implementations. The performance models are generated by fitting curves to actual performance results. In both cases two curves are fitted to the data, each covering a range of problem sizes. Note that for the LU solver only the second curve is shown, as the first curve deals only with small matrix sizes and is not visible on the graph.

Figure 7 illustrates the execution time for the network, along with the solution times for a benchmark BCG and LU solver. For small matrix sizes the LU solution is more efficient, thus the JPO selects this implementation. It can be seen from the graph that both the network and LU execution times are close. For matrices of size 725 and larger the BCG method becomes more efficient and

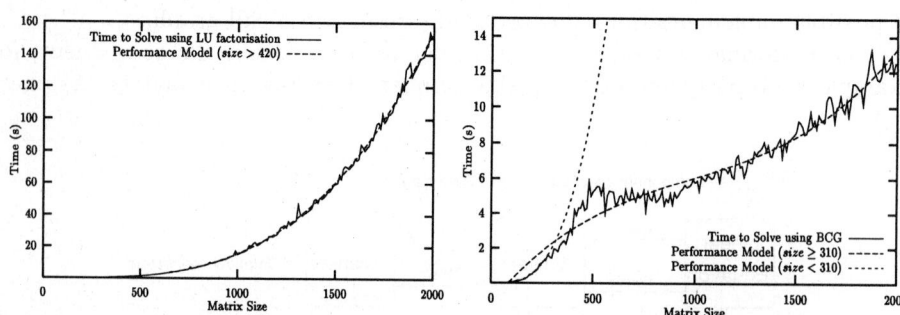

Fig. 5. Run time for LU solver   **Fig. 6.** Run time for BCG solver

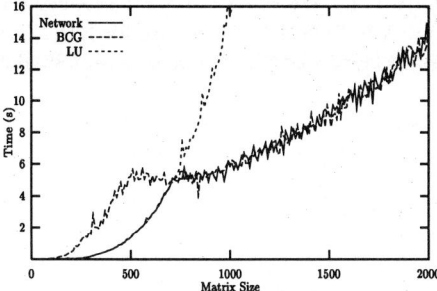 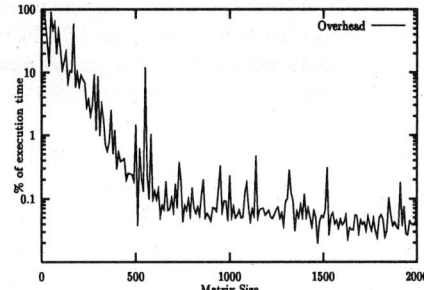

Fig. 7. Run time for the example system

Fig. 8. Overhead from component network

the JPO selects this approach. This is again visible on the graph as the network results follow the BCG solution.

The overhead incurred from the use of the network solution is shown in Figure 8. This is the proportion of execution time that is not spent in computation. It can be seen from this graph that initially the overheads are high, with the value decreasing to less than 0.1% as the matrix size increases. The large overheads, and variations in results, for small matrices are partly due to the inaccuracy in timings of the system. Fluctuations in the BCG solution times can be attributed to the variable number of iterations required which effects the relative proportion of the overhead.

7 Conclusion

We have shown that the solution of a problem described as a set of interacting components can be implemented successfully. Furthermore it has been shown that the cost of performing the computation through such a framework is negligible, in comparison to the overall execution, when the problem size is large. In this case, the overhead appears to be independent of the problem size. Hence it is clear that the separation of concerns together with layered abstraction provides flexibility without sacrificing the performance HPC applications demand.

The techniques developed here are not restricted to the example system, but are applicable to arbitrary component networks and application domains. We are continuing to develop this framework for distributed parallel components.

References

1. I. Foster and C. Kesselman, editors. *The Grid: Blueprint for a New Computing Infrastructure*. Morgan Kaufmann, 1999.
2. J. Darlington, P. Au, M. Ghanem, and Y. Guo. Co-ordinating heterogenous parallel computation. In *Proceedings of International Euro-Par Conference*, pages 601–614. Springer, August 1996. Distinguished Paper.

3. W3 Consortium. XML: eXtensible Markup Language. http://www.w3c.org/XML.
4. S. Newhouse, A. Mayer, and J. Darlington. A Software Architecture for HPC Grid Applications. In *Proceedings of International Euro-Par Conference*, pages 686–689. Springer, August/September 2000.
5. R. Gordon. *Essential JNI, Java Native Interface*. Prentice Hall, 1998.
6. William H. Press. *Numerical recipes in C : the art of scientific computing*. Cambridge University Press, 1988.

Towards Formally Refining BSP *Barrier*s into Explicit *Two − Sided* Communications*

Alan Stewart[1], Maurice Clint[1], Joquim Gabarró[2], and Maria J. Serna[2]

[1] School of Computer Science, The Queen's University of Belfast, N. Ireland
[2] Dep. LSI, Universitat Politècnica de Catalunya, Barcelona, Spain

Abstract. An experiment is conducted to assess the feasibility of transforming BSP computations into systems employing explicit asynchronous *two − sided* communications. The aim of the work is to show how a verified BSP program may be transformed into a guaranteed correct conventional message-passing implementation which may, in certain circumstances, avoid the expense of providing a synchronisation *barrier*.

1 Introduction

The construction of reliable distributed scientific software requires that complex correctness issues be addressed: for example, systems based on MPI [12] must be such that they are deadlock free and all execution interleavings produce correct outputs. Deadlock and non-deterministic execution patterns arise in the context of a *two − sided* point-to-point computation model [8]. In this paper it is proposed that a different (non-reactive) computation model, namely, BSP [15], be adopted for the *development* of scientific software. This model circumvents some of the semantic difficulties associated with conventional process algebras [9]. In particular, the advantages of a BSP design are:

- communication is asynchronous and *one − sided* - i.e. only one party specifies a communication rather than both sender and receiver (*two − sided*). One-sided asynchronous messages cannot be deadlocked.
- The basic computational unit in BSP is a *superstep*; a superstep involves initial and terminal synchronisations over all processes. A superstep can be treated semantically as a global state transformation [14]; this has the benefit of allowing a software developer to think about each parallel operation in a program in isolation rather than having to think about a composition of processes (threads). For example, a BSP-style implementation of a multigrid algorithm may involve relaxation, restriction and interpolation supersteps. The developer may address the correctness of each of these supersteps separately.

---

* Partially supported by (i) The British Council and Spanish Ministry of Education ACI HB1999-0093, (ii) Spanish CICYT under grants TIC1999-0754-C03-02 (Mallba) & TIC2000-1970-CE and (iii) the IST programme of EU under contract number IST-1999-14186 (ALCOM-FT).

– All of the asynchronous communications in a superstep are grouped together and delivered, conceptually, at a synchronisation *barrier*. A conventional, synchronous, $two-sided$ communication model involves a separate interaction point for each individual communication. The BSP approach has the advantage of greatly reducing the number of interference points and, consequently, simplifying correctness arguments.

One way of implementing a superstep *barrier* on a distributed architecture is to make a global round of communication in which every process informs every other process of the communications that it needs to perform. In this way it can be guaranteed that a process receives all incoming messages. However, for applications involving low levels of communications, this approach may be expensive. The aim of the work reported upon here is formally to devise an alternative way of implementing *barrier*; the set of communications within a superstep is transformed, by rewrite rules, to a collection of $two-sided$ communications which is guaranteed to be matching and deadlock free. In the transformed system a process without communication statements may "proceed through a *barrier* without delay". In less extreme circumstances a process may only need to interact with a small subset of the other superstep processes. Note, however, that the removal of synchronisation barriers means that the BSP cost calculus may no longer be used to predict execution times [15].

The idea of implementing global synchronisation (message passing) efficiently has been widely studied - for example, *synchronisers* [2] provide an efficient means of implementing synchronous algorithms on asynchronous hardware and KeLP [5] provides a range of high-level operations for distributing grids and managing associated communications. An alternative way of implementing *barrier* can be devised when the total number of messages to be received by each process within a superstep is known in advance [3,4,7,10]. The Paderborn BSP library (PUB) includes an alternative synchronisation primitive based on message counting.

The work reported in this paper does not use message counting as a way of implementing *barriers*. Rather, by explicitly rewriting superstep communications as series of $two-sided$ communications, it becomes possible to delimit the range of process interactions.

In §2 a semantic model of BSP [13,14] is summarised. An alternative semantic model - that of a system employing $two-sided$ asynchronous MPI-like communications - is given in §3. A transition system which maps BSP supersteps to a set of semantically equivalent $two-sided$ communications is defined in §4.

2 A Programming Model for BSP

In this section the basic properties of a BSP programming model are summarised. The notation used is based on the Unifying Theories of Programming [9]. Communications are treated as buffer updates and, as such, they obey assignment laws. Superstep composition can be expressed in terms of parallel independent composition and a *barrier* operation which delivers buffered messages to their destinations by means of a special form of simultaneous assignment. The proposed model is consistent with Valiant's original definition of BSP [15].

Let S, S_1 etc. denote superstep processes; $\alpha(S)$, $\alpha_R(S)$, $\alpha_W(S)$ denote, respectively, the set of free variables, the set of free read-only variables and the set of free read-write variables in S; x, y etc. denote simple variables; a, b etc. denote array variables; and $\|^{ss}$ denotes the superstep composition operator. The superstep $S_1 \|^{ss} S_2$ is valid provided that its constituent processes are disjoint:

$$disjoint(S_1, S_2) \;=_{df}\; (\alpha_W(S_1) \cap \alpha(S_2) = \{\}) \wedge (\alpha_W(S_2) \cap \alpha(S_1) = \{\}) \quad (1)$$

Thus, distinct superstep processes may have read only variables in common. For example, in the computation

$$\text{for } k := 1 \text{ to } n \text{ do } (S_1 \|^{ss} S_2)$$

we may have $\{k, n\} \subseteq \alpha_R(S_1) \cap \alpha_R(S_2)$. A superstep process is constructed using sequential programming operators and two asynchronous communication instructions *put* and *get*: these denote, respectively, a future assignment of the value of a local expression to a non-local destination and a request for non-local information.

The current state of ongoing communications is recorded by an auxiliary variable m, a relation from variable names (message destinations) either to values or (unevaluated) variable names (message content). The relation m is used to record all communications that are invoked in a superstep. Inside the composition $S_1 \|^{ss} S_2$, the data spaces of S_1 and S_2 are augmented by local message relations, $1.m$ and $2.m$ respectively. A message relation m may be modified by the execution of *get* and *put* instructions as follows:

$$put(x, e) \;=_{df}\; m := m \cup \{\text{``}x\text{''} \mapsto e\} \text{ with } \alpha(put(x, e)) = \alpha(e)$$
$$get(x, z) \;=_{df}\; m := m \cup \{\text{``}x\text{''} \mapsto \text{``}z\text{''}\} \text{ with } \alpha(get(x, z)) = \{x\}$$

where e denotes an expression and "z" denotes the syntactic string z rather than the value denoted by z. The definitions for *put* and *get* can be extended to realise conditional communications. For example:

$$put(x, e) \triangleleft b \triangleright \Pi \;=_{df}\; m := (m \cup \{\text{``}x\text{''} \mapsto e\}) \triangleleft b \triangleright m$$
$$get(x, z) \triangleleft b \triangleright \Pi \;=_{df}\; m := (m \cup \{\text{``}x\text{''} \mapsto \text{``}z\text{''}\}) \triangleleft b \triangleright m$$

where Π is the empty statement (SKIP) and the conditional statement $S_1 \triangleleft b \triangleright S_2$ satisfies $S_1 \triangleleft true \triangleright S_2 = S_1$ and $S_1 \triangleleft b \triangleright S_2 = S_2 \triangleleft \neg b \triangleright S_1$.

In many practical scientific applications, it is often necessary to communicate parts of arrays. Array based communication statements are more complex because they require the evaluation of index expressions. Consider the instruction $get(x, a[e])$. Here, $a[e]$ is assumed to be a non-local array reference (to be evaluated in a later state) whereas e is assumed to be a local index expression to be evaluated in the current state. Then,

$$put(a[e_1], e_2) \;=_{df}\; m := m \cup \{\text{``}a\text{''}[e_1] \mapsto e_2\}$$
$$get(z, a[e]) \;=_{df}\; m := m \cup \{\text{``}z\text{''} \mapsto \text{``}a\text{''}[e]\}$$
$$get(a_1[e_1], a_2[e_2]) \;=_{df}\; m := m \cup \{\text{``}a_1\text{''}[e_1] \mapsto \text{``}a_2\text{''}[e_2]\}$$

The characteristic feature of a superstep is the merging of individual process computations. Assume that processes S_1 and S_2 are such that all asynchronous communication statements (*puts* and *gets*) have been replaced by their definitions (updates of m). Then,

$$S_1 \parallel^{ss} S_2 \quad =_{df} \quad \text{var} \quad 1.m, 2.m := \{\mapsto\}, \{\mapsto\}$$
$$((S_1)_{1.m}^m \parallel^I (S_2)_{2.m}^m) \; ; \; barrier(1.m \cup 2.m)$$
$$\text{end} \quad 1.m, 2.m$$

Here, $S_{1.m}^m$ denotes S with all free occurrences of m replaced by $1.m$ (i.e. a local copy of m, $1.m$, is made within S_1), $\parallel^I$ denotes the independent parallel composition operator and $barrier(m)$ denotes a merge operation over the message space m. The merge operation *barrier* is defined as a multiple conditional assignment:

$$barrier(m) \quad =_{df} \quad \forall \text{``}z\text{''} \in dom(m). \; \text{``}z\text{''} := \sqcap m(z)$$

where $m = 1.m \cup 2.m$. Here, $\sqcap$ denotes non-deterministic selection.

Example. Given an array $a[0..N-1]$ such that $N = 2^l$ a prefix sum calculation computes the partial sums $prefix[r] = \sum_{0 \leq i \leq r} a[i]$ for $0 \leq r < N$. A superstep based program for prefix sum can be derived by modifiying a well known PRAM program [1]:

Prefix_Sum $\equiv$
    var $to\_add[0 \ldots N-1]$
    $\parallel_{0 \leq r < N}^I prefix[r] = a[r];$
    for $k := 0$ **to** $\log_2 N - 1$ **do**
        $\parallel_{0 \leq r < N}^{ss}(\quad put(to\_add[r + 2^k], prefix[r]) \triangleleft r < N - 2^k \triangleright \Pi \;);$
        $\parallel_{0 \leq r < N}^I \quad (\; prefix[r] := prefix[r] + to\_add[r] \triangleleft r \geq 2^k \triangleright \Pi \;)$
    end
    end to_add

where the alphabet of the rth superstep process is $\{prefix[r], to\_add[r], a[r]\}$.

3 Asynchronous *two − sided* Communications

An alternative to grouping together all messages in a superstep is explicitly to manage individual communications through matching pairs of *send* and *receive* instructions. Message passing may again be realised through buffered communications; each process, i, has a local buffer M_i which is used to receive incoming messages. In order to simplify the semantics of *two − sided* communications M_i is treated as a sequence of local buffers, $M_i = \cup_{0 \leq j < P} M_{i,j}$, where P is the number of processes in the system. The semantics of *send* is closely related to the definitions of *get* and *put* - relevant communication information is written to an appropriate buffer. The instruction $send(e, tag, i)$ denotes a communication identified by a unique tag, *tag*, which results in the value e being delivered to process i [1]. Let j denote the index of the sender process. Then:

$$send(e, tag, i) \quad =_{df} \quad M_{i,j} := M_{i,j} \cup \{tag \mapsto e\} \qquad (2)$$

where $tag \notin dom(M_{i,j})$. The instruction $receive(x, tag, j)$ retrieves a message identified by label *tag* from process j and stores the contents in variable x:

$$receive(x, tag, j) \quad =_{df} \quad \textbf{await } tag \in dom(M_{i,j}) \rightarrow \qquad (3)$$
$$x := M_{i,j}(tag);$$
$$M_{i,j} := \{tag\} \ominus M_{i,j}$$
$$\textbf{end}$$

where the **await** instruction is as given in Owicki & Gries [11]. The symbol $\ominus$ denotes domain deletion defined by:

$$\{a\} \ominus \{\mapsto\} = \{\mapsto\}$$
$$\{a\} \ominus (\{a \mapsto b\} \cup M) = \{a\} \ominus M$$
$$\{a\} \ominus (\{b \mapsto c\} \cup M) = \{b \mapsto c\} \cup (\{a\} \ominus M), \; a \neq b$$

The **await** clause excludes the possibility of interference since no two processes can have buffer write conflicts; the uniqueness of *tag* ensures that non-matching *send* and *receive* instructions cannot update the same buffer contents. A *send* instruction involves a remote assignment whereas a *receive* involves only local information. This execution model closely resembles the standard point-to-point communication of MPI [12].

Example. An informal transformation of *Prefix_Sum* into a semantically equivalent system employing point-to-point communications is performed below. The essence of the superstep transformation is the replacement of each *put* instruction (and the implicit delivery operation *barrier*) by a matching pair of *send* and *receive* communications. Thus the instruction:

$$put(to\_add[r + 2^k], prefix[r]) \lhd r < N - 2^k \rhd \Pi$$

within the rth superstep process is replaced by:

$$send(prefix[r], r, r + 2^k) \lhd r < N - 2^k \rhd \Pi$$

where r is assumed to be a unique identification label - see §4.4 for further details. In addition, a matching *receive* instruction is introduced to take the place of *barrier*:

$$receive(to\_add[r], r - 2^k, r - 2^k) \lhd r \geq 2^k \rhd \Pi$$

---

[1] Note: This definition requires that every process i has a set of local buffers $M_{i,j}$, one for each possible sender process. A single buffer implementation may be realised by prefixing a message identification tag with the sender's process number. The partitioned definition above is used in order to clarify interference issues.

The following computation results:

$Prefix\_Sum \equiv$
  $\textbf{var}\ to\_add[0 \ldots N-1]$
    $\|_{0 \le r < N}^{I}\ prefix[r] = a[r];$
    $\textbf{for}\ k := 0\ \textbf{to}\ \log_2 N - 1\ \textbf{do}$
      $\|_{0 \le r < N}\ (\textbf{var}\ M_{r,1} \ldots M_{r,N-1} := \{\mapsto\} \ldots \{\mapsto\};$
        $send(prefix[r], r, r + 2^k) \triangleleft r < N - 2^k \triangleright \Pi;$
        $receive(to\_add[r], r - 2^k, r - 2^k) \triangleleft r \ge 2^k \triangleright \Pi;$
      $\textbf{end}\ M_{r,1} \ldots M_{r,N-1});$
    $\|_{0 \le r < N}^{I}\ (prefix[r] := prefix[r] + to\_add[r] \triangleleft r \ge 2^k \triangleright \Pi\ )$
  $\textbf{end}$
$\textbf{end}\ to\_add$

Finally, the resulting sequential composition of parallel programs may be rewritten as a parallel composition of MPI-like threads [2]:

$Prefix\_Sum_r \equiv$
  $\textbf{var}\ r.k, M_{r,1}, \ldots, M_{r,N-1} := 0, \{\mapsto\}, \ldots, \{\mapsto\}\ ;$
  $prefix[r] := a[r]\ ;$
  $\textbf{for}\ r.k := 0\ \textbf{to}\ \log_2 N - 1\ \textbf{do}$
    $send(prefix[r], r, r + 2^{r.k}) \triangleleft r < N - 2^{r.k} \triangleright \Pi;$
    $receive(to\_add[r], r - 2^{r.k}, r - 2^{r.k}) \triangleleft r \ge 2^{r.k} \triangleright \Pi;$
    $prefix[r] := prefix[r] + to\_add[r] \triangleleft r \ge 2^{r.k} \triangleright \Pi;$
  $\textbf{end}$
  $\textbf{end}\ r.k, M_{r,1}, \ldots, M_{r,N-1}$

where $\|_{0 \le r < N}\ Prefix\_Sum_r$ denotes the composite system.

In the following sections semantics-preserving transformation rules for rewriting BSP programs as *two − sided* communications are developed and conditions under which the rewrite rules may usefully be employed are proposed.

4 From *barrier* to *two − sided* Communications

In this section a formal transformation method is developed that replaces BSP-style message generation instructions and the operation *barrier* with a set of explicit *two − sided* communications. Three sub-classes of parallel programs are considered: *straight line* processes (which serve to introduce the basic transformations), processes with *visible* communication guards (*visibility* defines conditions under which both parties involved in a communication can evaluate the guard) and *generic* processes.

---

[2] The generation of threads is not considered here - see [14] for details.

4.1 Straight Line Programs

A process is *straight line* if it contains only assignments (no conditional or iterative statements). Consider $S_1 \parallel^{ss} S_2$ where all S_i are straight line and where all communications are realised by *put* instructions. Note that, for straight line programs, *get* operations can always be rewritten as *put* instructions [14]:

$$((S_1 \, ; \, put(y,e)) \parallel^{ss} S_2) = (S_1 \parallel^{ss} (S_2 \, ; \, get(y,e)))$$

A transformation which replaces each BSP-style message by a corresponding pair of point-to-point communications is defined by means of a transition system. Let

$$[U_1, U_2 \mid \langle V_1 \rangle, \langle V_2 \rangle]$$

denote a partially transformed system; here U_1 and U_2 represent the partially transformed processes S_1 and S_2 where (some of) the *put* instructions have been replaced by *sends*; $\langle V_1 \rangle$ and $\langle V_2 \rangle$ comprise partially constructed collections of *receive* instructions corresponding to the *send* operations generated during the transformations of S_1 and S_2. $\langle V_1 \rangle$ and $\langle V_2 \rangle$ initially contain the empty statement, Π. After the transformation process $\langle V_1 \rangle$ (respectively, $\langle V_2 \rangle$) comprises the *receive* instructions corresponding to the *send* instructions resulting from the transformation of the *put* instructions in S_2 (respectively, S_1). Angle brackets $\langle \cdots \rangle$ are used to enclose atomic actions. Note that, since $\parallel^{ss}$ is commutative [14] (this follows from the commutitivity of $\parallel^I$), it follows that $[U_1, U_2 \mid \langle V_1 \rangle, \langle V_2 \rangle] = [U_2, U_1 \mid \langle V_2 \rangle, \langle V_1 \rangle]$.

1. *Initial state.* The initial state corresponding to $S_1 \parallel^{ss} S_2$ is: $[S_1, S_2 \mid \langle \Pi \rangle, \langle \Pi \rangle]$.
2. *Transformation.* A *put* operation is transformed into a *send-receive* pair as follows:

$$[U_{11}; put(x,e); U_{12} \, , \, U_2 \mid \langle V_1 \rangle \, , \, \langle V_2 \rangle] \quad \mapsto \quad (4)$$
$$[U_{11}; send(e, tag, 2); U_{12} \, , \, U_2 \mid \langle V_1 \rangle \, , \, \langle V_2 \parallel receive(x, tag, 1) \rangle]$$

where $x \in \alpha(U_2)$ and tag is a unique label.
3. *Termination.* Since all *receive* operations within $\langle V_1 \rangle$ and $\langle V_2 \rangle$ commute the transition system is confluent and has a unique final state:

$$[U_1 \, , \, U_2 \mid \langle V_1 \rangle \, , \, \langle V_2 \rangle] \quad \mapsto \quad (5)$$
$$(\text{var } M_{1,2} := \{\mapsto\}; U_1 \, ; \, V_1 \text{ end } M_{1,2})$$
$$\parallel$$
$$(\text{var } M_{2,1} := \{\mapsto\}; U_2 \, ; \, V_2 \text{ end } M_{2,1})$$

where U_1 and U_2 do not contain any *put* instructions. Here $V_1 \parallel V_2$ takes the place of the original *barrier* operation.

In a transformed program the receiving part of each process acts as a non-deterministic parallel assignment. For example, if the final state of $\langle V_1 \rangle$ is:

$$\langle receive(x, tag, 2) \parallel receive(x, tag', 2) \parallel receive(y, tag'', 2) \rangle$$

then, on execution, the following updates will take place:

$$x, y := \sqcap\{M_{1,2}(tag), M_{1,2}(tag')\}, M_{1,2}(tag'')$$

The correctness of the transition system is guaranteed iff the transformation from *puts* to *send-receive* pairs preserves the orginal semantics. Ignoring local variables and buffers we have:

Lemma 1. $(put(x, e) \parallel^{ss} \Pi) = (\ send(e, tag, 2)) \parallel (\ receive(x, tag, 1))$

4.2 Visible Conditional Communications

Consider a superstep process, S_i, with a conditional communication, $\gamma \triangleleft b \triangleright \Pi$, where γ is a simple BSP-type communication statement. Nested conditional communication statements can always be rewritten with a single guard [9]. The communication is *visible* iff it has a read only guard - that is, if $\alpha(b) \notin \alpha_W(S_i)$. Clearly $\alpha(b) \subseteq \alpha(S_i)$. Then, by superstep disjointness, $\alpha(b) \notin \alpha_W(S_j)$, for any superstep process, S_j, $i \neq j$. Thus, the boolean communication guard b is read-only over all processes and is *visible* to the entire system. *Visible* guards have the desirable property that they can be replicated in any other superstep process. Thus, the conditions under which the original BSP-type communication takes place can be expressed within the receiving processes. Many widely used algorithms can be expressed as supersteps with *visible* guards. Some examples are:

1. matrix multiplication (and many other BLAS operations) and Gauss-Seidel relaxation which employ unconditional communication schemes.
2. Gram-Schmidt orthogonalisation and Floyd's shortest path algorithm which employ *visible* communication guards in a generic process framework to define which process should broadcast data over the system.

The definition of *visibility* can be extended to cover non-local array references in BSP-type communication statements. An array communication $put(a[i], e)$ in process S_i has visible non-local indices iff $i \notin \alpha_W(S_i)$. Similarly, the instruction $get(a[e], b[j])$ in process S_j is *visible* iff $j \notin \alpha_W(S_i)$. A superstep with *visible* guards and non-local array indices may be transformed into a system with MPI-like $two-sided$ communications.

Transformation. An occurrence of a *visible* conditional BSP-type communication can be transformed into a *send-receive* pair as follows:

$$[U_{11}; (put(a[i], e) \triangleleft b \triangleright \Pi); U_{12}, U_2 \mid \langle V_1 \rangle, \langle V_2 \rangle] \mapsto \quad (6)$$
$$[U_{11}; (send(e, tag, 2) \triangleleft b \triangleright \Pi); U_{12}, U_2 \mid$$
$$\langle V_1 \rangle, \langle V_2 \parallel (receive(a[i], tag, 1) \triangleleft b \triangleright \Pi)\rangle]$$

Visible *get* instructions can always be rewritten as *put* operations. Let $visible(b) =_{df} b \in \alpha_R(S_1) \cap \alpha_R(S_2)$. If b is *visible* then:

$$((S_1; (put(y, e) \triangleleft b \triangleright \Pi)) \parallel^{ss} S_2) = (S_1 \parallel^{ss} (S_2; (get(y, e) \triangleleft b \triangleright \Pi))) \quad (7)$$

4.3 Generic Processes

In the examples in the previous sections a single BSP communication is transformed into a point-to-point communication. The situation is more complex for supersteps composed of generic processes; in these a single communication statement may be replicated across all processes giving rise to a set of communications.

Consider a superstep composed of generic processes, S_i, $0 \leq i < P$, in which S_i performs a communication $put(a[g(i)], e)$ where g is some *visible* index relation. The effect of executing this command is to route a set of messages over a communication transfer map h where

$$h : [0 \ldots P-1] \mapsto [0 \ldots P-1]$$

and $\forall i: 0 \leq i < P \Rightarrow a[g(i)] \in \alpha(S_{h(i)})$. In order to transform $\|_{0 \leq i < P} S_i$ into an MPI-like system it is necessary to generate transformed processes S'_i, $0 \leq i < P$, which both send and, possibly, receive messages. Clearly, $put(a[g(i)], e)$ can be transformed into a *send* instruction, $send(e, i.tag, h(i))$. Here i is prefixed to tag in order to distinguish distinct communications in the system. The corresponding set of receiving processes is $rng(h)$ where rng is a function which returns the range of its relation argument. Note that h may not be a function. A process S_i receives a message iff $i \in rng(h)$. However, a receiving process may have more than one message sent to it.

A transition system for a system composed of generic processes has the form: $[U_i, | \langle V_i \rangle]$ where U_i represents the partially transformed process S_i and $\langle V_i \rangle$ represents the partially constructed receiving part which will ultimately be appended to the first component. Let $a[g(i)] \in \alpha(S_{h(i)})$. The *transformation* phase of the transition system for *straight line* generic processes is:

$$[U1_i; put(a[g(i)], e); U2_i \mid \langle V_i \rangle] \mapsto \qquad (8)$$
$$[U1_i; send(e, i.tag, h(i)); U2_i \mid$$
$$\langle V_i \parallel ((\|_{r \in h^{-1}(i)} receive(a[g(i)], i.tag, r)) \triangleleft i \in rng(h) \triangleright \Pi) \rangle]$$

The transition system can be extended to include a *transformation* phase for generic processes with *visible* communication guards. Consider a superstep process S_i with a *visible* $b(i)$ and let h be a routing relation (as above). If h is bijective then the generated *receive* guard is $b(h^{-1}(i))$. More generally, it may be necessary to generate a *set* of receive guards for process S_i (as above). For each $r \in h^{-1}(i)$ a guard $b(r)$ is generated.

Example. A *visible* generic transformation system may be used to transform the BSP version of prefix sum into the MPI-like system. In particular, the communication guard of the rth process in the kth superstep, $r < N - 2^k$, is visible [3]. The kth superstep is associated with a communication transfer map, $h = \{r \mapsto r + 2^k | 0 \leq r < N - 2^k\}$. Each such map is a function with inverse: $h^{-1} = \{r \mapsto r - 2^k | 2^k \leq r < N\}$. The details of the remainder of the transformation are straightforward.

---

[3] Here it is assumed that the index of the ith superstep process, S_i, is such that $i \in \alpha_R(S_i)$.

5 Conclusions

The aim of the work reported here is to investigate the feasibility of employing a design framework for parallel programs which transforms a $one-sided$ communication model (BSP) into a $two-sided$ model. The first approach avoids problems of non-matching and deadlocked communications and allows global correctness assertions to be established [13,14].

For programs employing either unconditional or $visible$ conditional communications the proposed transformation technique produces systems employing $two-sided$ communications which are at least as efficient as the original computations - each $one-sided$ message has a corresponding direct $two-sided$ communication. However, the $two-sided$ model may avoid the expense of implementing a $barrier$ synchronisation operation.

Unfortunately, the transformation of systems employing $non-visible$ communication guards may result in a $loss$ of efficiency. For example, consider a conditional $one-sided$ communication, $put(x,e) \triangleleft b \triangleright \Pi$ which occurs in process S_i and where the guard b is $non-visible$. The communication can be transformed into the send/ receive commands:

$S_i \equiv$ $\qquad\qquad\qquad\qquad\qquad$ $S_p \equiv$
$\vdots$ $\qquad\qquad\qquad\qquad\qquad\qquad$ $\vdots$
$send(b, tag, p)$; $\qquad\qquad\qquad$ $receive(b', tag, i)$;
$send(e, tag, p) \triangleleft b \triangleright \Pi;$ $\qquad$ $receive(e, tag, i) \triangleleft b' \triangleleft \Pi;$

where b' is a fresh variable name and $x \in \alpha(S_p)$. Here, a $conditional$ communication is interpreted as an $unconditional$ communication. For computations in which communication guards are often false the transformation may result in unnecessary communications. Such situations often arise in practice - for example, a distributed version of Newton's root finding method in which each superstep process determines a local convergence condition and, only in the case of convergence, communicates a stop signal to the other processes.

There is some scope for applying the transformation rewrite rules automatically. However, one problem that arises is the $a\ priori$ determination of the process labels of both sender and receiver from a $one-sided$ communication statement. For example, the transformation of the communication $put(a[j], e)$, where j is an index expression, requires knowledge of the label of the process that stores datum $a[j]$ - in general, this cannot be determined statically. The problem may, to some extent, be circumvented by including information about the destination of a message in a $one-sided$ communication - for example, BSPlib routines for put and get include parameters for naming partner processes. An extended communication, $put'(a[j], e, i)$ where i is the label of the receiver process may be transformed to a $two-sided$ communication provided that the process label expression, i is $visible$. The problem of determing communication partners also arises in the construction of $communication\ transfer\ maps$ for communications within generic processes. Finally, the automatic calculation of inverse transfer maps may be possible for simple offset communications - as in the prefix sum example.

In the work reported a technique is proposed whereby a large sub-class of verified *one − sided* communication programs may be converted, at least semi-automatically, into potentially more efficient *two − sided* communication implementations. A transformed (*two − sided*) version of the prefix sum algorithm has been implemented in MPI and executed on a distributed (*grid*) environment comprising two clusters of PCs, one in Barcelona and the other in Canarias.

Acknowledgements

The authors are grateful to two anonymous referees for their constructive comments which have led to significant improvements in the paper.

References

1. Akl S. G.: The Design and Analysis of Parallel Algorithms, Prentice-Hall, 1989.
2. Awerbuch B.: Complexity of network synchronization, JACM, **32** (4) (1985), 804–823.
3. Bonorden O., Juurlink B., von Otto I., Rieping I.: The Paderborn University BSP (PUB) Library—Design, Implementation and Performance 13th International Parallel Processing Symposium & 10th Symposium on Parallel and Distributed Processing, (1999).
4. Fahmy A., Heddaya A., BSPk: Low overhead communication constructs and logical barriers for bulk synchronous parallel programming, Bulletin of the IEEE Technical Committee on Operating Systems and Application Environments (TCOS), **8**(2), (1996) 27–32.
5. Fink S. J., Baden S. B., Kohn S. R.,Efficient Run-Time Support for Irregular Block-Structured Applications, Journal Parallel and Distributed Computing, **50**(1-2), 1998, 61–82.
6. The Grid : blueprint for a new computing infrastructure, editor I. Foster, Morgan Kaufmann, 1999.
7. Gonzalez J. A., Leon C., Piccoli F., Printista M., Poda J. L., Rodriguez C., Sande, F.: Performance Prediction of Oblivious BSP Programs, EuroPar (2001).
8. Hoare C. A. R.: Communicating Sequential Processes, Prentice Hall, 1985.
9. Hoare C. A. R., Jefeng H.: Unifying Theories of Programming, Prentice Hall, 1998.
10. Kim J-S., Ha S., Jhon C. S., Relaxed barrier synchronization for the BSP model of computation on message-passing architectures Information Processing Letters, **66**(5), (1998) 247–253.
11. Owicki S., Gries D.: An axiomatic proof technique for parallel programs, Acta Informatica, **6** (1976) 319–340.
12. MPI: A Message-Passing Interface Standard. University of Tennessee, 1995.
13. Stewart A., Clint M.: BSP-style computation: a semantic investigation, Computer Journal (2001).
14. Stewart A., Clint M., Gabarró, J.: Algebraic rules for reasoning about BSP programs, Proceedings of Constructive Mathematics for Parallel Programming 2000 (2001).
15. Valiant L. G.: A bridging model for parallel computation, Comm. ACM, **33** (1990) 103–111.

Solving Bi-knapsack Problem Using Tiling Approach for Dynamic Programming

Benamar Sidi Boulenouar

LAMIH-ROI, UMR 8530,
ISTV - Le mont Houy -BP 311- 59304 Valenciennes Cedex- France
`sidi@univ-valenciennes`

Abstract. In this paper we present an efficient parallelization of the dynamic programming applied to bi-knapsack problem, in distributed memory machines(MMD). Our approach develops the tiling technique in order to control the grain parallelism and find the optimal granularity. Our proposed approach has been intensively validated on the Intel Paragon and IBM/SP2 using NX and MPI libraries. The experimental results show a linear acceleration, which enables to solve huge instances of the hardest known 0/1 bi-knapsack problems in a very reasonable time.

1 Introduction

For the knapsack problem, many parallel dynamic programming (DP) implementations are known [1,4,6,7]. This is not the case for bi-knapsack problem (BKP).

In this study, we discuss how to find optimal parallelism granularity on a distributed memory machine (DMM). The proposed approach is based on the tiling technique, which is a common method to improve the performance of loop programs on DMM. These techniques are developed very actively these last years around the automatic parallelization of the nest of loop [3,5,8].

Tiling consists in partitioning the iteration space into blocks called tile; each tile is executed by a single processor in an atomic way. Finding the optimal tiling parameters of the tile (shape and size) enables to minimize the execution time by reducing the extra cost of communications. The tiling technique is today well developed and widely used in case of Uniform Recurrent Equation(URE).

However, this technique cannot be applied directly to DP recurrences for the BKP because of the irregular nature of their dependencies, which vary with any problem instance.

We show here how the tiling technique can be extended and how it can be successively applied to a DMM DP implementation for the bi-knapsack problem.

2 Dynamic Programming for the Bi-knapsack

The bi-knapsack problem (BKP) is a classic NP-*hard* problem and can be formulated as follows: we are given a bi-knapsack of capacity c_1 and c_2, into which we may put m types of objects. Each object of type i has a *profit*, p_i, and two *weight*, (w_i, u_i), $(w_i, u_i, p_i, m, c_1$ and c_2 are all positive integers). Determine, for $i = 1 \ldots m$, the number x_i, of i-th type objects to be chosen so as to maximize the total profit without exceeding the capacity, i.e.,

$$\max \left\{ \sum_{i=1}^{m} p_i x_i \; : \; \sum_{i=1}^{m} w_i x_i \leq c_1, \; \sum_{i=1}^{m} u_i x_i \leq c_2 \; x_i \in \{0,1\}, \; i=1,2,\ldots,m \right\} \quad (1)$$

The dynamic programming method solves (*BKP*) following recurrences: let $\mathcal{D} = \{(i,j,k) : 0 \leq i \leq m \; ; \; 0 \leq j \leq c_1 \; ; \; 0 \leq k \leq c_2\}$ be the recurrence domain of iterations (2) ; for every couple (i,j,k) of $\mathcal{D}$, calculate.

$$f(i,j,k) = \begin{cases} f(i-1,j,k) & \text{if } i > 0 \text{ and } (j < w_k \text{ or } k < u_k) \\ \max(f(i-1,j,k), p_i + f(i-1,j-w_i, k-u_i)) & \text{if } i > 0 \text{ and } (j \geq w_i \text{ and } k \geq u_i) \end{cases} \quad (2)$$

The particularity of these dependencies that the values w_i and u_i vary in large interval with any index i and any instance of the problem. Figure 1 shows the dynamic characters of dependencies : the diagonal dependencies varies according to the values of w_i and u_i.

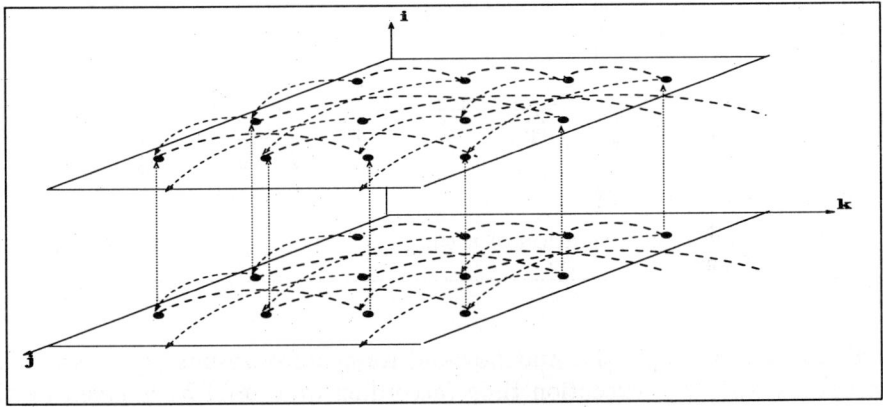

Fig. 1. Bi-knapsack dynamic dependencies

3 Tiling and Processors Allocation

The recurrences (2) are represented by three-dimensional nested loops. The associated iterations space is a cube of $(m \times c_1 \times c_2)$ size, in which the dependencies vectors are $(1,0,0)$ and $(1,w_i,u_i)$.

The particularity of these dependencies is that the values w_i and u_i vary in large interval with any index i and any instance of the problem. For these reasons, it is not possible to guaranty the local references and constant communications volume, when using tiling techniques on grid architecture.

In order to avoid that such dependencies involve no constant volume communications, the projection of the tile graph is made vertically on a p processors ring. In this case, by choosing an appropriate projection we can guaranty that the runtime dependencies require only local references.

The iteration space figure 2(a) is partitioned into rectangular parallelepipeds of size $x_1 \times x_2 \times x_3$. To compute each tile, the processor receive a message of $x_2 \times x_3$ elements from its left neighbor, and sends to its right neighbor message of the same size $x_2 \times x_3$. In this case, the important parameters to determine the optimal tile size are the values of x_1 and $x_2 \times x_3$. In order to simplify our model, we put $h = x_2 \times x_3$ and $W = m \times c_1 \times c_2$. Because the dependencies are orthogonal, we can easily demonstrate that 3D iteration space can be tiled which 2D tile [9]. By this transformation, we obtain a 2D iteration space tiled with rectangular surfaces as it is show in figure 2(b).

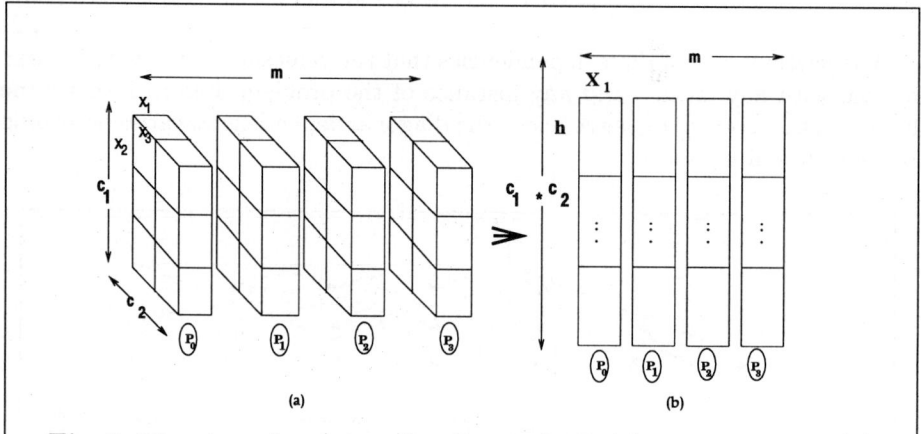

Fig. 2. Ring: transformation of a tile graph 3D (a) into a graph 2D(b)

Hence, we can apply the Andonov and Rajopadhye results [2] to determine the optimal tile. The execution time (according to x_1 and h) is given by the function:

$$T(x_1, h) = \frac{2W\beta}{px_1 h} + (p-1)\alpha x_1 h + (p-1)\tau h + (p-1)\beta + \frac{W\alpha}{p} \quad (3)$$

The optimal tile size is given by:

$$(h^*, x_1^*) = \begin{cases} \left[\sqrt{\frac{2pc_1 c_2 \beta}{(p-1)(m\alpha + p\tau)}}, \frac{m}{p}\right] & \text{if } \lambda_2 > 0 \text{ (no cyclic solution)} \\ \left[1, \sqrt{\frac{2W\beta}{(p-1)p\alpha}}\right] & \text{else (cyclic solution)} \end{cases} \quad (4)$$

with $\lambda_2 = 2pc_1 c_2 \beta - (p-1)m\alpha$

The constants β and τ respectively correspond to the time to establishing communication and to the transfer of data. α correspond to the execution time of a single instruction. In our case, λ_2 is always positive because $c_1 \times c_2 \gg m$ (BKP problem), $\beta > \alpha$ (Distributed Memory Machine) and $p \approx p - 1$). Therefore, in the rest of this paper, we consider the *no cyclic solution*.

4 Sensitivity of the Model

The same approach can be used in the case of dynamic dependencies of bi-knapsack type, only if the single instance computing is constant. This assumption is at the base of the previous results, but it is impossible to be considered here. The dynamic dependency (of w_i and u_i length) prevents the reference locality, the access time to data varies because the cache and pagination techniques. In this part, we propose a strategy assuring the stability of the result when α is not a constant. In order to simplify our study, we take a simple knapsack case with one constraint ($c_2 = 0$ and all $u_i = 0$).

The table 1 shows the computing times of a single instance obtained for different coefficient instances w_i generated randomly in a fixed interval. We can note that, the time for computing an instance increases with the coefficients value w_i, which confirms the memory effect.

Table 1. variation of α according to the values of coefficients w_i

w_i	$[1, 10]$	$[1, 5.10^2]$	$[10^3, 15.10^2]$	$[5.10^3, 10^4]$	$[10^4, 3.10^4]$
α(average)	$3\mu s$	$6\mu s$	$13\mu s$	$15\mu s$	$23\mu s$

Figure 3(c) shows the experimental curves which correspond to the total executing time, by varying the height of the tile (parameter h) for the w_i and coefficient values taken in the said interval. The size of the problem capacity ($c_1 = 20700$) and number of objects(m=1000) are kept fixed. We can notice that in a small interval the optimal value of h does not vary much, in spite of the important variation of the different values of α.

This observation led to consider the minimal value of α (obtained by fixing the w_i to 1) to calculate the optimal tile size. This strategy guarantees that the optimum calculated this way always stands on the right (hand) side of the real minimum. On this side, the time function has a weak slope, and the points in the neighborhood of the real minimum give a good approximation of the minimum value.

The following table describes a validation of this strategy. Each line represents a fixed instances of problem where the time value α is known (1st column). These values are taken into account to calculate h^* (using eq(4)) . The third column of the table shows the total executing time obtained for tile of h^* size. The fourth and the fifth columns show approximate values (h_{app}, T_{app}) obtained using the minimal value of α. $\triangle$ means $T_{opt} - T_{app}$. We can see in the last column, that the relative error does not exceed 3%.

α	$h^*(\alpha)$	T_{opt}(sec)	$h_{app}(\alpha=1\mu s)$	T_{app}(sec)	Δ	$\frac{\Delta}{T_{opt}}$
$1\mu s$	99	10.50	99	10.50	0.00	0.00
$3\mu s$	57	30.83	99	31.29	0.45	0.01
$6\mu s$	40	61.16	99	62.48	1.31	0.02
$13\mu s$	27	131.70	99	135.25	3.54	0.02
$15\mu s$	25	151.82	99	156.04	4.21	0.02
$23\mu s$	20	232.24	99	239.21	6.96	0.03

5 Experimental Results

We now describe some experimental results of our algorithm. The experiments were run on Intel Paragon at IRISA and IBM/SP2 at CINES, for bi-knapsack problems chosen randomly. The main characteristics of these machines are given in table 2.

Table 2. Technical characteristics of the Intel Paragon and the IBM SP2

	Intel Paragon	IBM SP2
number of processors	50	207
data cache per node	128KB	16KB
memory per processor	56MB	256MB
max peak processor speed	100Mflops	500Mflops
point to point bandwith	175MB/sec	35MB/sec
τ	$0.0015\mu s$	$0.0022\mu s$
β	$40\mu s$	$45.0\mu s$

Figure 3(a)(b)(d)(e) shows that the experimental curve is close to the theoretical curve; the optimum (h optimal) coincides with the estimate value. The experimental evaluation of the speed−up 3(f) allowed us to notice a linear speed-up, this being due to the memory effect. In fact, the size of the memory used by each processor is $(c_1 \times c_2 \times m/p)$, it decreases by increasing the number of processor (p), which in turn reduces the time access memory. If we choose the IBM/SP2, for big problems size, the choice of the optimal tiling is very important (Figure 3(e)).

6 Conclusion

This paper presents an efficient parallelization of the dynamic programming applied to bi-knapsack problem. The approach proposed develops the optimal tiling technique in order to have a best *computing/communication* ratio, for a particular case of dynamic dependencies. We analyze the sensitivity of the result for non-constant cycle times and we propose a strategy for this problem. Computational tests indicate that the strategy works well, giving linear speedup over

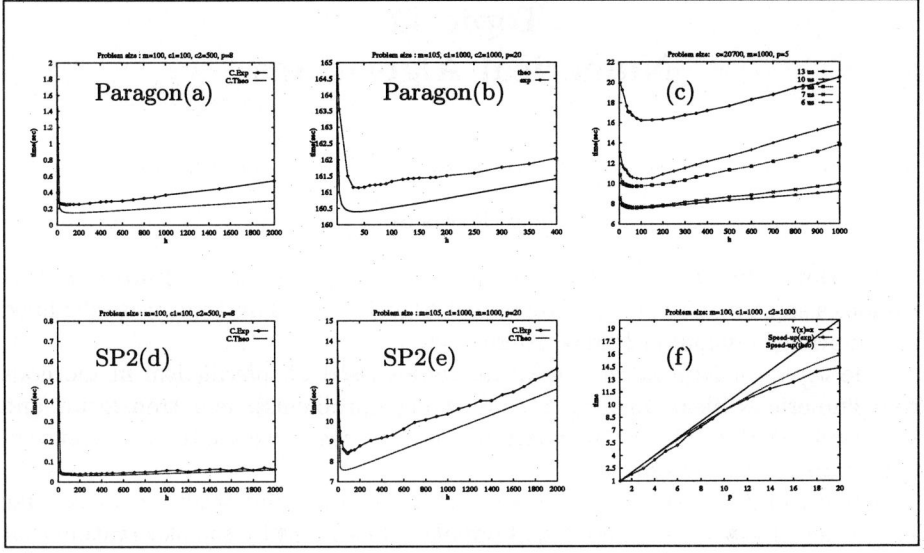

Fig. 3. Optimal tile size validation and acceleration obtained

a range of processor numbers and tracking theoretical performance predictions closely. According to our knowledge, it is the first parallel algorithm for the bi-knapsack problem.

References

1. R. Andonov and S. Rajopadhye. Knapsack on VLSI : from Algorithm to Optimal Circuit. *IEEE Transactions on Parallel and Distributed Systems*, 8(6):545–562, 1997.
2. R. Andonov and S. Rajopadhye. Optimal Orthogonal Tiling of 2-D Iterations. *Journal of Parallel and Distributed Computing*, 45:159–165, September 1997.
3. P. Boulet, A. Darte, T. Risset, and Y. Robert. (Pen)-Ultimate Tiling? *INTEGRATION, the VLSI journal*, 17:33–51, Nov 1994.
4. G. H. Chen, M. S. Chern, and J. H. Jang. Pipeline Architectures for Dynamic Programming Algorithms. *Parallel Computing*, 13:111–117, 1990.
5. F. Irigoin and R. Triolet. Supernode Partitioning. In *15th ACM Symposium on Principles of Programming Languages*, pages 319–328. ACM, Jan 1988.
6. J. Lee, E. Shragowitz, and S. Sahni. A Hypercube Algorithm for the 0/1 Knapsack Problems. *J. of Parallel and Distributed Computing*, 5:438–456, 1988.
7. J. Lin and J. A. Storer. Processor-Efficient Hypercube Algorithm for the Knapsack Problem. *J. of Parallel and Distributed Computing*, 13:332–337, 1991.
8. J. Ramanujam and P. Sadayappan. Tiling Multidimensional Iteration Spaces for Non Shared-Memory Machines. In *Supercomputing 91*, pages 111–120, 1991.
9. B. Sidi Boulenouar, H. Bourzoufi, and R. Andonov. Tiling and processors allocation for three dimensional iteration space. *In International Conference on Higt Performance Computing (HiPC), ACM/ IEEE*, pages 125–129, India, 1999.

Topic 11
Numerical Algorithms

Henk A. van der Vorst, Rob Bisseling, Iain S. Duff, and Bernard J. Philippe

Topic Chairpersons

Following the tradition of previous Euro-Par Conferences, Euro-Par 2001 includes a session on the topic "Numerical Algorithms". This topic was scheduled for a morning session on Friday, August 31.

The topic on Numerical Algorithms is focussed on parallelism in methods from numerical linear algebra (including eigenproblems), fast transforms and discretized partial differential equations. In most cases, we see the occurrence of large sparse linear systems.

Numerical Algorithms is an area with already a long tradition in parallel computing. It is still very active and popular, illustrated by the observation that we received 16 contributions. There is a vast literature on parallelizable algorithms and because of this we have decided to keep our yardstick relatively high. As a result we accepted only papers of high quality with really innovative parallel aspects. Essential, in our view, is that the parallel approaches are supported by performance analysis and/or actual performance statistics. In situations where variations on existing established algorithms are proposed, to the extent that the variants lead to numerically different results, we want to see some discussion on numerical stability. The above helps to explain why we have accepted only 5 contributions, but the effect is that these 5 contributions make it a must to attend our session for those interested in numerical computing.

The first paper in the session for Topic 11, by Sheung Hun Cheng and Nicholas Higham, discusses a parallelizable block algorithm for the matrix 1-norm estimation and can be used to efficiently calculate the 1-norm of the inverse. This is an essential ingredient for the computation of error bounds in computed solutions for various matrix problems, including linear systems and eigenvalue problems. In particular, such estimates lead to useful estimates of the 1-norm condition number. It is shown that the novel approach leads to better estimates than the ScaLAPACK alternative with similar execution time.

An estimate for the global eigenvalue distribution, rather than a few accurate isolated eigenvalues, is obtained by a variant of a lesser known algorithm by Lanczos, discussed in a paper by Ken Thomas *et al.* Similar to the more well-known Lanczos algorithm, the proposed method requires the matrix only as matrix-vector operations (either products or solves). The authors describe an interesting application to photonic crystal analysis.

Preconditioning plays an important role in the solution of many large sparse linear systems. In a paper by Liang, Weston, and Szularz, the authors consider polynomial preconditioning for symmetric indefinite linear systems with matrices that can be expressed as rank-one updates to diagonal matrices. Such matrices are reported to arise in the eigenvalue computation via divide-and-conquer methods. Results are given for a 16-processor system, indicating reasonable speed-ups.

Domain decomposition is still a hot topic in the parallel solution of PDEs. Peter Jimack and Sarfraz Nadeem describe, in their contribution, a novel weakly overlapping decomposition approach. Typically, the domains have levels of grid refinement and the overlap is largely occupied by the coarsest grids. In fact, each of the domains covers, through the coarsest grid, the entire domain. The method is specially attractive for convection-dominated problems.

In another contribution on PDEs, Sverker Holmgren and Dan Wallin discuss the parallelism in multi-dimensional FFTs for accurate PDE-solvers. Their study of the results obtained on a self-optimizing Sun WildFire system with 36 processors indicates almost perfect parallel scalability, when applied in the context of a generic PDE solver based on a pseudospectral method.

We believe that the sessions on Topic 11 contain a highly interesting mix of parallel numerical algorithms. We would like to thank all contributing authors for their work, which made it possible to realize the eventual representative programme. We also thank the Euro-Par Organizing Committee for selecting this topic.

Parallel Implementation of a Block Algorithm for Matrix 1-Norm Estimation*

Sheung Hun Cheng[1] and Nicholas J. Higham[2]

[1] Centre for Novel Computing, Department of Computer Science, University of Manchester
Manchester, M13 9PL, England
scheng@cs.man.ac.uk
http://www.cs.man.ac.uk/~scheng/

[2] Department of Mathematics, University of Manchester
Manchester, M13 9PL, England
higham@ma.man.ac.uk
http://www.ma.man.ac.uk/~higham/

Abstract. We describe a parallel Fortran 77 implementation, in ScaLA-PACK style, of a block matrix 1-norm estimator of Higham and Tisseur. This estimator differs from that underlying the existing ScaLAPACK code, PxLACON, in that it iterates with a matrix with t columns, where $t \geq 1$ is a parameter, rather than with a vector, and so the basic computational kernel is level 3 BLAS operations. Our experiments on an SGI Origin2000 show that with $t = 2$ or 4 the new code offers better estimates than PDLACON with a similar execution time. Moreover, with $t > 4$, estimates exact over 90% of the time are achieved with execution time growing much slower than t.

1 Introduction

Error bounds for computed solutions to linear systems, least squares and eigenvalue problems all involve condition numbers, which measure the sensitivity of the solution to perturbations in the data. Thus, condition numbers are an important tool for assessing the quality of the computed solutions. Typically, these condition numbers are as expensive to compute as the solution itself [6]. The LAPACK [1] and ScaLAPACK [2] condition numbers and error bounds are based on estimated condition numbers, using the method of Hager [3], which was subsequently improved by Higham [4]. Hager's method estimates $\|B\|_1$ given only the ability to compute matrix-vector products Bx and $B^T y$. If we take $B = A^{-1}$ and compute the required products by solving linear systems with A, we obtain an estimate of the 1-norm condition number $\kappa_1(A) = \|A\|_1 \|A^{-1}\|_1$.

In LAPACK and ScaLAPACK Higham's version of Hager's method is implemented in routines xLACON and PxLACON, respectively. Both routines have a

---

* This work was supported by Engineering and Physical Sciences Research Council grant GR/L94314. The work of the second author was also supported by a Royal Society Leverhulme Trust Senior Research Fellowship.

reverse communication interface. There are two advantages to having such an interface. First it provides flexibility, as the dependence on B and its associated matrix-vector operations is isolated from the computational routines xLACON and PxLACON, with the matrix-vector products provided by a "black box" [4]. By changing these black boxes, xLACON and PxLACON can be applied to different matrix functions for both dense and sparse matrices. Second, as the bulk of the computational effort is in matrix-vector operations, efficient implementation of these operations ensures good overall performance of xLACON and PxLACON, and thus a focus is provided for performance tuning.

The price to pay for using an estimate instead of the exact condition number is that it can sometimes be a poor estimate. Experiments in [4] show that the underestimation is rarely by more than a factor of 10 (the estimate is, in fact, a lower bound), which is acceptable in practice as it is the magnitude of the condition number that is of interest. However, counterexamples for which the condition numbers can be arbitrarily poor estimates exist [4], [5]. Moreover, when the accuracy of the estimates becomes important for certain applications [7], the method does not provide an obvious way to improve the estimate.

Higham and Tisseur [7] present a block generalization of the estimator of [3,4] that iterates with an $n \times t$ matrix, where $t \geq 1$ is a parameter, enabling the exploitation of matrix-matrix operations (level 3 BLAS) and thus promising greater efficiency and parallelism. The block algorithm also offers the potential of better estimates and a faster convergence rate, through providing more information on which to base decisions. Moreover, part of the starting matrix is randomly formed, which introduces a stochastic flavour and reduces the importance of counterexamples.

We have implemented this block algorithm using Fortran 77 in the ScaLA-PACK programming style and report performance on a 16 processor SGI Origin2000. The rest of the paper is organized as follows. We describe the block 1-norm estimator in Section 2. In Section 3 we present and explain details of our parallel implementation of the estimator. The performance of the implementation is evaluated in Section 4. Finally, we summarize our findings in Section 5.

2 Block 1-Norm Estimator

In this section we give pseudo-code for the block 1-norm estimator, which is basically a block power method for the matrix 1-norm. See [7] for a derivation and explanation of the algorithm. We use MATLAB array and indexing notation [8].

Algorithm 1 (block 1-norm estimator) *Given $A \in \mathbb{R}^{n \times n}$ and positive integers t and itmax ≥ 2, this algorithm computes a scalar* est *and vectors v and w such that* est $\leq \|A\|_1$, $w = Av$ *and* $\|w\|_1 =$ est$\|v\|_1$.

    Choose starting matrix $X \in \mathbb{R}^{n \times t}$ with columns of unit 1-norm.
    ind_hist = [ ] % Integer vector recording indices of used unit vectors e_j.
    est$_{\text{old}} = 0$, ind = zeros$(n, 1)$, $S =$ zeros(n, t)
    for $k = 1, 2, \ldots$

(1) $Y = AX$
              est = max$\{\,\|Y(:,j)\|_1 : j = 1\!:\!t\,\}$
              if est > est$_\text{old}$ or $k = 2$
                 ind_best = ind$_j$ where est = $\|Y(:,j)\|_1$, $w = Y(:,\text{ind\_best})$
              end
              if $k \geq 2$ and est $\leq$ est$_\text{old}$, est = est$_\text{old}$, goto (5), end
              est$_\text{old}$ = est, $S_\text{old} = S$
(2)   if $k >$ itmax, goto (5), end
              $S = \text{sign}(Y)$ % sign$(x) = 1$ if $x \geq 0$ else -1
              If every column of S is parallel to a column of S_old, goto (5), end
              if $t > 1$
(3)   Ensure that no column of S is parallel to another column of S
                 or to a column of S_old by replacing columns of S by rand$\{-1,1\}$.
              end
(4) $Z = A^T S$
              $h_i = \|Z(i,:)\|_\infty$, ind$_i = i$, $i = 1\!:\!n$
              if $k \geq 2$ and max$(h_i) = h_\text{ind\_best}$, goto (5), end
              Sort h so that $h_1 \geq \cdots \geq h_n$ and re-order ind correspondingly.
              if $t > 1$
                 If ind$(1\!:\!t)$ is contained in ind_hist, goto (5), end
                 Replace ind$(1\!:\!t)$ by the first t indices in ind$(1\!:\!n)$ that are
                 not in ind_hist.
              end
              $X(:,j) = e_{\text{ind}_j}$, $j = 1\!:\!t$
              ind_hist = [ind_hist ind$(1\!:\!t)$]
    end
(5) $v = e_\text{ind\_best}$

Statements (1) and (4) are the most expensive parts of the computation and are where a reverse communication interface is employed. It is easily seen that if statements (1) and (4) are replaced by "Solve $AY = X$ for Y" and "Solve Z for $A^T Z = S$ for Z", respectively, then Algorithm 1 estimates $\|A^{-1}\|_1$.

MATLAB 6 contains an implementation of Algorithm 1 in function normest1, which is used by the condition number estimation function condest.

3   Parallel Implementation

We have implemented Algorithm 1 in double precision using Fortran 77 in the ScaLAPACK programming style. For dense matrices, ScaLAPACK assumes the data to be distributed according to the *two-dimensional block-cyclic* data layout scheme; see Figure 1 for an example. Our code uses the highest level of BLAS and PBLAS whenever possible.

In PxLACON the vectors resulting from the matrix-vector operations are always stored in the first process column. In order to ensure all processes follow the same execution path, the resulting vectors are copied to every process column. We

$$\begin{array}{|ccccc|}\hline a_{11} & a_{12} & a_{13} & a_{14} & a_{15} \\ a_{21} & a_{22} & a_{23} & a_{24} & a_{25} \\ a_{31} & a_{32} & a_{33} & a_{34} & a_{35} \\ a_{41} & a_{42} & a_{43} & a_{44} & a_{45} \\ a_{51} & a_{52} & a_{53} & a_{54} & a_{55} \\ \hline\end{array}$$

Mapping $\Rightarrow$

		0			1	
0	a_{11}	a_{12}	a_{15}	a_{13}	a_{14}
	a_{21}	a_{22}	a_{25}	a_{23}	a_{24}
	a_{51}	a_{52}	a_{55}	a_{53}	a_{54}
1	a_{31}	a_{32}	a_{35}	a_{33}	a_{34}
	a_{41}	a_{42}	a_{45}	a_{43}	a_{44}

Fig. 1. A 5×5 matrix decomposed into 2×2 blocks mapped onto a 2×2 process grid using the two-dimensional block-cyclic data layout scheme

have adopted a similar approach in our implementation in that we assume all t search vectors are stored in the first process column. Consequently, the maximum value of t is equal to the column block size for partitioning the matrix. This restriction on t eliminates a large amount of communication between process columns, which in our experience is very costly. This restriction is not severe, as good norm estimates are obtained even with t relatively small compared with the column block size. Moreover, instead of copying the search vectors across process columns, which becomes increasingly expensive as t increases, the first process column performs all the computational work and then broadcasts two scalar variables (est in Algorithm 1 and an integer variable used in the reverse communication mechanism) across the process columns to ensure all processes follow the same execution path. This provides another large saving in communication cost. Furthermore, we arrange that S (the current sign matrix, whose elements are ± 1) and S_{old} (the previous sign matrix) share the same distribution scheme.

We set the maximum number of iterations itmax to 5, which is rarely reached. When this limit is reached we have, in fact, performed $5\frac{1}{2}$ iterations, as the test (2) in Algorithm 1 comes after the matrix product $Y = AX$. This allows us to make use of the new search direction generated at the end of the fifth iteration.

Most of Algorithm 1 is straightforwardly translated into Fortran code apart from statement (3), which deserves detailed explanation. Statement (3) is a novel feature of Algorithm 1 in which parallel columns within the current sign matrix S and between S and S_{old} are replaced by $\text{rand}\{-1, 1\}$, where $\text{rand}\{-1, 1\}$ denotes a random vector with entries -1 or 1. The replacement of parallel columns avoids redundant computation and may lead to a better estimate [7]. The detection of parallel columns is done by forming inner products between columns and looking for elements of magnitude n. Obviously, we should only check for parallel columns when $t > 1$. Using the notation of Algorithm 1, statement (3) is implemented as follows:

(A)
$$\begin{aligned}&\text{iter} = 0 \\ &\text{for } i = 1 : t \\ &\qquad \text{while iter} < n/t \\ &\qquad\qquad y = S_{\text{old}}^T S(:, i) \\ &\qquad\qquad \text{iter} = \text{iter} + 1\end{aligned}$$

(B)
$$\begin{aligned}&\text{if } \|y\|_\infty < n\\&\quad y = S(:,1\!:\!i-1)^T S(:,i)\\&\quad \text{iter} = \text{iter} + 1\\&\quad \text{if } \|y\|_\infty < n, \text{ goto } (\#), \text{ end}\\&\text{end}\\&S(:,i) = \text{rand}\{-1,1\}\end{aligned}$$
　　　　end
(#)　end

In the inner loop the number of matrix-vector products is limited to n/t. As the computational cost of Algorithm 1 is $O(n^2 t)$ flops and (A) and (B) both cost $O(nt)$ flops, this choice of limit ensures that the cost of replacing parallel columns does not dominate the overall cost.

The replacement of parallel columns involves the use of a random number generator and ScaLAPACK is intended to work in a heterogeneous environment. Our restriction that the first process column performs all the computations of random numbers ensures that the code works properly in a heterogeneous environment. Furthermore, by keeping a single copy of the search vectors, rather than multiple copies on each process column as in ScaLAPACK, we eliminate a potential performance-degrading communication overhead.

The new code is called PDLACON1. Its storage requirements are not significantly greater than those of PxLACON, unless t is large. Let m denote the number of process rows in the process grid. To be precise, PDLACON1 and PDLACON require $(2nt + n)/m + 4n + t$ and $3n/m$ storage space per process respectively.

Note that the replacement of parallel columns is not essential for Algorithm 1 to produce good estimates. The advantage of this feature in the distributed context is less clear than in the serial and shared-memory cases. We include this feature in our implementation so that it is consistent with our MATLAB and LAPACK-style versions.

4 Numerical Experiments

In this section, our aim is to examine the performance of PDLACON1. We have addressed the issues of accuracy and reliability of PDLACON1 by reproducing parts of the experimental results in Higham and Tisseur [7], thereby validating our code. Our main focus in this section is to measure the efficiency of our implementation. We investigate how the relation between accuracy and execution time varies with n and t.

We tested PDLACON1 on a SGI Origin2000. The compiler and library details are given in Table 1.

We use the same compiler flags as was used to compile the ScaLAPACK installation. This provides a basis for measuring and comparing the performance of our implementation with that of the ScaLAPACK routine PDLACON. All timing results were obtained on a shared machine with exclusive access to a set of consecutive CPUs and their memory using the IRIX command cpuset; see

Table 1. Characteristics of the SGI Origin2000, libraries and compiler options for the experiments

Compiler	Compiler Flags	SGI BLAS	Precision
MIPSpro Compilers: Version 7.3.1.2m (f77)	-O2 -64 -mips4 -r10000	-lblas (optimized)	double
ScaLAPACK version 1.6	MPI BLACS version1.1 + patch	PBLAS v2.0	SGI MPI -lmpi

Table 2. Parameters set in the configuration file of cpuset

Parameters
EXCLUSIVE, MEMORY_LOCAL, MEMORY_EXCLUSIVE, MEMORY_KERNEL_AVOID, MEMORY_MANDATORY, POLICY_KILL

Table 2 for the configuration of cpuset. Both row and column block sizes for partitioning the matrix were set to 64.

We estimate $\|A^{-1}\|_1$ for random matrices $A \in \mathbb{R}^{n \times n}$ with $1200 \le n \le 2700$. For each n, a total of 500 random matrices A are generated, variously from the uniform $(0,1)$, uniform $(-1,1)$ or normal $(0,1)$ distributions. The LU factorization with partial pivoting of A is supplied to the 1-norm estimators. The cost of this part of computation does not contribute to the overall timing result. This arrangement is reasonable as the LU factorization is usually readily available in practice, as when solving a linear system, for example. The inverse of A is computed explicitly to obtain the "exact" $\|A^{-1}\|_1$. For a given matrix A we first generated a starting matrix X_1 with 64 columns, where 64 is the largest value of t to be used, and then ran Algorithm 1 for $t = 1, 2, \ldots, 64$ using starting matrix $X_1(:,1:t)$. In this way we could see the effect of increasing t with fixed n. Each set of tests was repeated on 2, 4, 6, 8, 12 processors with different process grids. For example, we ran tests using 4 processors on 1×4, 2×2 and 4×1 process grids.

For each test matrix we recorded a variety of statistics in which the subscripts min, max and an overbar denote the minimum, maximum, and average of a particular measure respectively:

- α: the underestimation ratio $\alpha = \text{est}/\|A^{-1}\|_1 \le 1$, over each A for fixed t.
- %E: the percentage of estimates that are exact. An estimate is regarded as exact if the relative error $|\text{est} - \|A^{-1}\|_1|/\|A^{-1}\|_1$ is no larger than 10^{-14} (the unit roundoff is of order 10^{-16}).
- %I: for a given t, the percentage of estimates that are at least as large as the estimates for all smaller t.
- %A: For a given t, the percentage of the estimates that are at least as large as the estimates from PDLACON.

Table 3. Experimental results of 500 random matrices with dimensions $n = 1200$ and $n = 2700$ on a 2×2 process grid

t	$\alpha_{\min}$	$\overline{\alpha}$	%E	%I	%A	%T	$N_{\max}$	$\overline{N}$	$C_{\max}$	$\overline{C}$	$D_{\max}$	$\overline{D}$	$K_{\max}$	$\overline{K}$
	$n = 1200$													
1^a	0.29	0.98	84.8	–	–	–	–	–	1.00	0.71	23.26	20.25	9	5.4
1	0.29	0.98	84.8	–	100.0	0.0	0.94	0.83	7.85	5.15	29.40	28.25	8	4.4
2	0.59	0.99	90.8	98.6	98.6	1.6	1.37	0.88	5.38	5.07	28.65	27.40	6	4.1
4	0.67	1.00	96.0	98.8	99.4	83.2	1.62	1.02	5.41	4.83	25.94	24.91	6	4.0
8	0.97	1.00	98.4	99.8	100.0	97.6	1.80	1.37	5.45	4.50	22.45	21.19	4	4.0
16	0.94	1.00	98.6	99.6	100.0	100.0	2.89	2.20	5.54	4.08	21.02	19.42	4	4.0
32	1.00	1.00	99.0	100.0	100.0	100.0	4.81	3.67	6.01	4.38	18.25	16.36	4	4.0
64	1.00	1.00	99.0	100.0	100.0	100.0	8.97	6.81	6.97	4.85	16.62	14.39	4	4.0
	$n = 2700$													
1^a	0.67	0.99	80.2	–	–	–	–	–	0.37	0.32	13.64	11.99	11	5.4
1	0.67	0.99	80.2	–	100.0	0.0	0.94	0.83	3.37	2.97	17.58	16.88	10	4.4
2	0.76	1.00	86.0	98.4	98.4	2.2	1.29	0.83	3.14	3.07	17.90	17.22	8	4.1
4	0.89	1.00	91.0	99.4	99.6	0.8	1.48	0.94	3.08	2.99	16.67	16.06	6	4.0
8	0.94	1.00	92.0	99.2	99.6	83.0	1.97	1.25	2.90	2.72	14.07	13.63	6	4.0
16	0.96	1.00	92.6	99.8	100.0	99.8	2.10	1.97	2.65	2.44	13.20	12.72	4	4.0
32	1.00	1.00	92.8	100.0	100.0	100.0	3.58	3.36	2.97	2.53	11.82	11.26	4	4.0
64	1.00	1.00	92.8	100.0	100.0	100.0	6.96	6.53	3.35	2.77	10.90	10.21	4	4.0

[a] Data for PDLACON

- %T: the percentage of the cases for which our implementation took longer to complete than PDLACON.
- N: The execution time for PDLACON1 normalized against the time taken by PDLACON.
- C: the percentage of time spent in PDLACON1 for a given A on the leading process column.
- D: the percentage of time spent in PDLACON1 for a given A on non-leading process columns.
- K: the number of matrix-matrix operations for a given A.

We present a subset of experimental results that capture general characteristics of the performance of PDLACON1. In Table 3 we show detailed statistical results for a 2×2 process grid. In Figure 2 we compare the performance when running the experiments on the same number of processors but different process grids. We make the following comments.

- Increasing t usually improves the quality of the estimates. However, this is not always true as %I is not monotonic increasing. Nevertheless, estimates exact over 90% of the time can be computed with t relatively small compared with n. Fast convergence, which is not explained by the underlying theory, is recorded throughout the experiments. All these observations are consistent with those in [7].

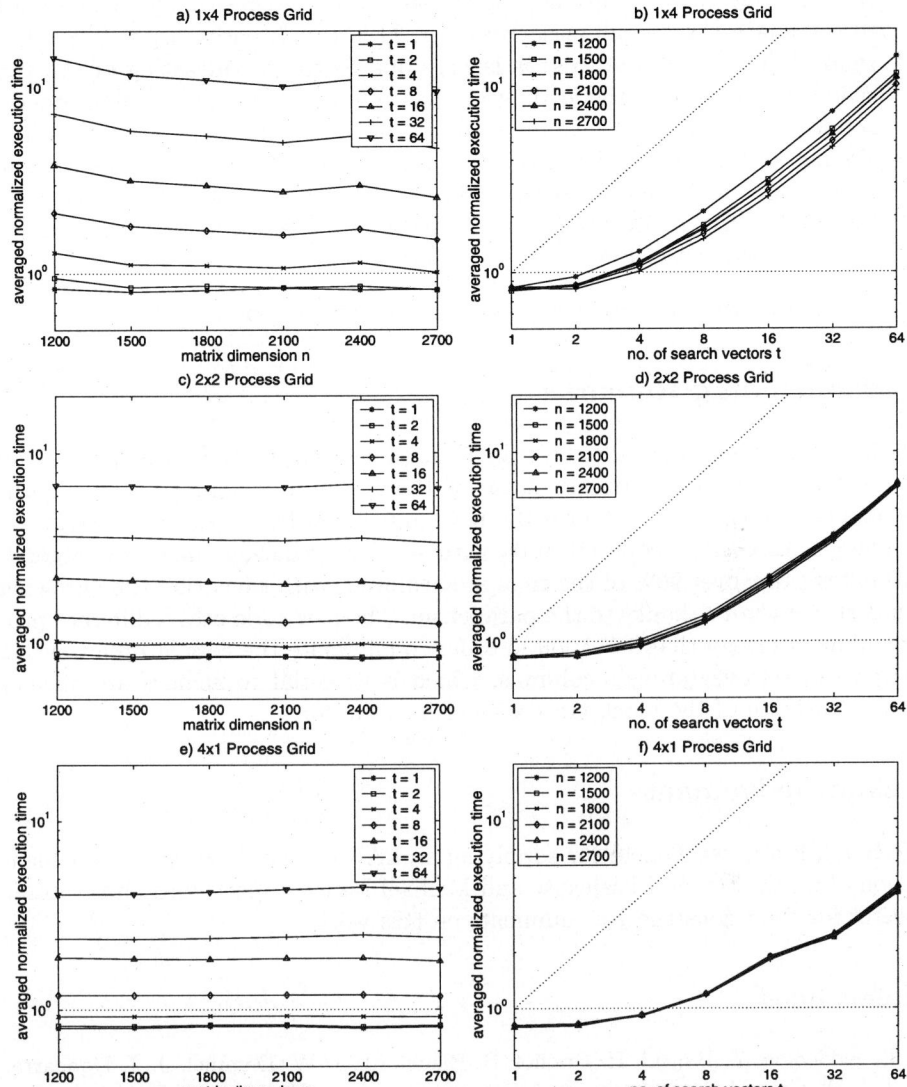

Fig. 2. Averaged execution time $\overline{N}$ of PDLACON1, normalized with respect to PDLACON, when experiments were run on 4 processors with 1×4, 2×2 and 4×1 process grids

- As t increases, the time taken for each iteration increases. However, using multiple search vectors ($t > 1$) also accelerates the rate of convergence. The results show that it is possible to obtain better estimates using less time on average compared with PDLACON. The cut-off is at $t = 2$ or $t = 4$ in our experiments, in which the matrix-matrix products in Algorithm 1 are evaluated by solving with LU factors.

- As n or t increases, $\overline{C}$ and $\overline{D}$ decrease as the matrix-matrix operations start to dominate the overall cost. However, D is consistently larger (5%–23%) than C. The additional cost is largely due to the broadcasting of the two scalar variables from the leading process column to the non-leading process columns at each reverse communication for PDLACON1. PDLACON suffers in a similar way as the search vector is broadcast at each reverse communication.
- In Figure 2, it is easy to see that PDLACON1 performs well compared with PDLACON and the execution time increases at a much slower rate than t, thanks to the use of level 3 BLAS and PBLAS.

For more processors all the above observations remain true.

5 Concluding Remarks

We have described a parallel Fortran 77 implementation in ScaLAPACK style of the block matrix 1-norm estimator of Higham and Tisseur [7]. Our experiments show that with $t = 2$ or 4 the new code offers better estimates than the existing ScaLAPACK code PDLACON with similar execution time. For larger t, estimates exact over 90% of the time are achieved, with execution time growing much slower than t thanks to the parallelism. The new code uses a different programming strategy than PDLACON in order to eliminate the cost of broadcasting search vectors over process columns, which is essential to achieve an efficient implementation of the block matrix 1-norm estimator.

Acknowledgements

We thank Françoise Tisseur for supplying an LAPACK-style Fortran implementation of quick sort, and Françoise and Michael Bane, Rupert Ford and Antoine Petitet for their constructive comments on this work.

References

1. E. Anderson, Z. Bai, C. H. Bischof, S. Blackford, J. W. Demmel, J. J. Dongarra, J. J. Du Croz, A. Greenbaum, S. J. Hammarling, A. McKenney, and D. C. Sorensen. *LAPACK Users' Guide*. Society for Industrial and Applied Mathematics, Philadelphia, PA, USA, third edition, 1999.
2. L. S. Blackford, J. Choi, A. Cleary, E. D'Azevedo, J. W. Demmel, I. Dhillon, J. J. Dongarra, S. Hammarling, G. Henry, A. Petitet, K. Stanley, D. Walker, and R. C. Whaley. *ScaLAPACK Users' Guide*. Society for Industrial and Applied Mathematics, Philadelphia, PA, USA, first edition, 1997.
3. W. W. Hager. Conditions estimates. *SIAM J. Sci. Stat. Comput.*, 5:311–316, 1984.
4. Nicholas J. Higham. FORTRAN codes for estimating the one-norm of a real or complex matrix, with applications to condition estimation (Algorithm 674). *ACM Trans. Math. Software*, 14(4):381–396, December 1988.
5. Nicholas J. Higham. Experience with a matrix norm estimator. *SIAM J. Sci. Stat. Comput.*, 11:804–809, 1990.

6. Nicholas J. Higham. *Accuracy and Stability of Numerical Algorithms*. Society for Industrial and Applied Mathematics, Philadelphia, PA, USA, 1996.
7. Nicholas J. Higham and Françoise Tisseur. A block algorithm for matrix 1-norm estimation, with an application to 1-norm pseudospectra. *SIAM J. Matrix Anal. Appl.*, 21(4):1185–1201, 2000.
8. *Using MATLAB*. The MathWorks, Inc., Natick, MA, USA. 2000. Online version.

Eigenvalue Spectrum Estimation and Photonic Crystals

Ken S. Thomas[1], Simon J. Cox[1], Duan H. Beckett[1], Ben P. Hiett[1], Jasek Generowicz[1], and Geoffrey J. Daniell[2]

[1] Department of Electronics and Computer Science, University of Southampton, SO17 1BJ
kst,sc,dhb99r,bph99r,jmg@ecs.soton.ac.uk
[2] Department of Physics and Astronomy, University of Southampton, SO17 1BJ
gjd@phys.soton.ac.uk

Abstract. We have developed an algorithm for the estimation of eigenvalue spectra and have applied it to the determination of the density of states in a photonic crystal, which requires the repeated solution of a generalized eigenvalue problem. We demonstrate that the algorithm offers significant advantages in time, memory, and ease of parallelization over conventional subspace iteration algorithms. In particular it is possible to obtain more than two orders of magnitude speedup in time over subspace methods for modestly sized matrices. For larger matrices the savings are even greater, whilst retaining accurate resolution of features of the eigenspectrum.

1 Introduction

Eigenvalue problems have wide applications in mathematical physics and numerical analysis. The method described in this paper is based on those described by [6, ch. 3] and [12], which estimate the spectrum of a matrix A by calculating a distribution from values of moments derived from matrix-vector products (or solves) starting from a number of randomly chosen initial vectors. The method remains applicable when the size of the matrix is large and this is the only operation that can be performed economically.

In this paper we discuss an application of the algorithm to the problem of determining the density of states in a Photonic Band Gap (PBG) system. PBG materials are periodic dielectric crystals that exhibit a "photonic band gap" similar to the electronic band gap present in semiconductors. Photons in the frequency range of the band gap are completely excluded so that atoms within such materials are unable to spontaneously absorb and re-emit light in this region. They have applications for optical processing, optical computing, and highly efficient narrow band (tunable) lasers [15]. An illustration is in Fig. 1

Fig. 1. Hexagonal arrangement of air rods in a dielectric medium with $\varepsilon = 12.25$ [3]. The rods are 260nm in diameter and the filling fraction is 50%. Finite Element mesh is shown (with 100 independent nodes): (left) unit cell for calculation, (right) the mesh is periodic- one repeat shown in all directions

It has been shown elsewhere that the problem of characterizing the band gap can be represented as a generalized eigenvalue problem [3,2,4,1],

$$\nabla \times \frac{1}{\varepsilon} \nabla \times H = \lambda H \tag{1}$$

$$\nabla \cdot H = 0, \tag{2}$$

where H is the magnetic field, ε is the position dependent dielectric constant, and λ are the permitted eigenmodes of propagation in the device. If the rods are considered to be infinitely long then we may reduce this to two independent Helmholtz eigenvalue problems and discretise using the finite element method giving a generalized eigenvalue problem,

$$A(k)x = \lambda Bx. \tag{3}$$

In (3), $A(k)$ is an Hermitian matrix dependent on the Bloch quasi momentum vector,

$$k \in \mathbb{R}^2, ||k||_\infty \leq \pi. \tag{4}$$

To characterise the PBG device it is necessary to solve (3) repeatedly over values of k chosen in the region of $\mathbb{R}^2$ to obtain the density of states, which is a union of the resulting eigenvalues.

This problem may be solved accurately using a Krylov subspace iterative method [8], [11]. However practical characterisation and optimisation of a PBG device [5] requires only an approximate estimate of the eigenvalue distribution, since we need to determine (i) whether there are eigenvalues in a given range, and (ii) how large the gap is between consecutive groups of eigenvalues. It may also not be known in advance how many eigenvalues must be found to locate the band gaps, only that for a finite element calculation with a given mesh, roughly the first third of the eigenvalues of the full system matrix should be regarded as representing accurate eigenmodes [11].

Our algorithm overcomes both of these problems. We introduce it in the next section, and then describe how it may be applied to a test problem. Finally we demonstrate that it is straightforward to parallelise, and does not require the expensive communication steps of Krylov subspace methods [9]

2 Method

We extend the previous work in this area [6],[12] and discuss the generalised $N \times N$ eigenvalue problem

$$Ax = \lambda Bx \tag{5}$$

where A is Hermitian and B is symmetric positive definite. We further assume that the matrices are scaled such that $\lambda \in (-1, 1)$. The method constructs a sequence of vectors $b_k, k = 0, \ldots, m$. The starting vector, b_0, has elements chosen from a normal distribution with mean zero and variance 1 and is scaled to unit length. The remaining values are generated from the Chebyshev recurrence formulae:

$$b_1 = L^{-1}A(L^{-1})^T b_0 \tag{6}$$
$$b_k = 2L^{-1}A(L^{-1})^T b_{k-1} - b_{k-2}, \ k = 2, \ldots, m. \tag{7}$$

where $B = L^T L$. From the vectors $b_k, k = 0, \ldots, m$, we can define $2m + 1$ real valued moments, μ_j:

$$\mu_{2j} = 2b_j^* b_j - b_0^* b_0 \tag{8}$$
$$\mu_{2j+1} = 2b_j^* b_{j+1} - b_0^* b_1 \tag{9}$$

The vectors b_j satisfy

$$b_j = T_j(L^{-1}A(L^{-1})^T)b_0, \tag{10}$$

where $T_j(t)$ is a Chebyshev polynomial of the first kind.

The size of the problem that is feasible in this instance is determined by the ability to calculate the Cholesky decomposition of B. If the Cholesky decomposition is not economic to compute, it may nevertheless be possible to solve $Bz = w$ by an iterative method such as preconditioned conjugate gradient. A recurrence formula similar to (9) can be constructed to produce the vectors b_j and the moments.

Fundamental to our method is the spectral theory of linear self-adjoint operators in Hilbert Spaces [14] that enables us to represent the moments as a Riemann-Stieltjes integral and so the data represent integrals over the eigenspectrum of the generalised eigenvalue problem:

$$\mu_j = \int_{-1}^{1} T_j(x) d\sigma(x), \tag{11}$$

where $\sigma(x)$ is the function defined by

$$\sigma(x) = \sum_{i=1}^{N} |\beta_i|^2 H(x - \lambda_i) \tag{12}$$

with H being the Heaviside step function, λ_i the eigenvalues and

$$\beta_l = z_l^* b_0. \tag{13}$$

z_l is the eigenvector corresponding to λ_l. Hence the derivative $d\sigma(x)$ can be expressed as a sum of delta functions and the purpose of the subsequent analysis is to recover $d\sigma(x)$, which gives the distribution of the eigenvalues.

By the change of variables $x = \cos(\theta)$ and $\rho(\theta) = 1 - \sigma(\cos\theta)$ in (11), we can show that

$$\mu_j = \int_0^\pi \cos(j\theta) d\rho(\theta). \tag{14}$$

We identify μ_j as cosine coefficients of $d\rho(\theta)$ and the reconstruction by Fourier analysis gives [6],

$$d\rho(\theta) \sim \frac{1}{\pi} + \frac{2}{\pi} \sum_{j=1}^{2m} \mu_j \cos(j\theta). \tag{15}$$

For efficiency a fast Fourier transform may be used. However the series in (15) does not converge pointwise and "ringing" is observed in reconstructions based on (15). The ringing can be reduced significantly by smoothing [7, p. 65] giving a smoothed reconstruction:

$$d\rho(\theta) \sim \frac{1}{\pi} + \frac{2}{\pi} \sum_{j=1}^{2m} \tau_j \mu_j \cos(j\theta) \tag{16}$$

where

$$\tau_j = \frac{2m}{j\pi} \sin(\frac{j\pi}{2m}). \tag{17}$$

An alternative method of reconstructing the spectrum is to use the Maximum Entropy method directly on (11). In this case we compute a distribution with the largest entropy subject to the constraint (11). Details of the method are found in [10],[5] [12]. The the approximate density has the form

$$d\sigma(t) \sim x_m(t) = \exp(\sum_{j=0}^{2m} c_j T_j(t)), \tag{18}$$

where the coefficients $c_j, j = 0, \ldots, 2m$ can be obtained by minimising the function

$$\Phi(c_0, \ldots, c_{2m}) = \int_{-1}^{1} \exp(\sum_{j=0}^{2m} c_j T_j(t)) dt - \sum_{j=0}^{2m} \mu_j c_j. \tag{19}$$

Quasi-newton methods are used for the reconstruction. This method can obtain very smooth and accurate reconstructions with significantly fewer moments than in the Fourier methods. There are drawbacks: the worst of these is the high condition number of the Hessian matrix associated with (19).

It is desirable to repeat the process for several (n_{seed}) starting vectors, b_0 and perform the analysis using the averaged moments $\overline{\mu_j}$. As is the case in Krylov subspace methods [11] we choose $(n_{seed} - 1)$ orthogonal starting vectors and the final vector at random. This reduces the chance of missing an eigenvalue, which can occur if the starting vector is almost orthogonal to any of the eigenvectors.

2.1 Algorithm

The pseudo-code algorithm is as follows

1. compute iterates using (7);
2. compute moments using (9) and average over different starting seeds;
3. compute smoothing coefficients using (17);
4. reconstruct spectrum using (16) or maximum entropy(19).

2.2 Application to Photonic Crystal Analysis

We set up the generalised eigenvalue problem from the finite element problem (3) and use n_k k-vectors chosen as in (4). This leads to a sequence of generalised eigenvalue problems. The density of states is then the solution for λ of the eigenvalue problem:

$$\begin{pmatrix} A(k^{(1)}) & 0 & 0 & 0 \\ 0 & A(k^{(2)}) & \ddots & 0 \\ \vdots & \ddots & \ddots & \vdots \\ 0 & \cdots & 0 & A(k^{(n_k)}) \end{pmatrix} x = \lambda \begin{pmatrix} B & 0 & 0 & 0 \\ 0 & B & \ddots & 0 \\ \vdots & \ddots & \ddots & \vdots \\ 0 & \cdots & 0 & B \end{pmatrix} x \qquad (20)$$

Clearly if this is tackled using a method which scales less favourably than $O(N)$ in the matrix size, N, it is much better to solve n_k separate smaller eigenproblems. For our algorithm it is straightforward to exploit the block structure in (20) and determine the vectors in (7) independently for each k, and then average the resulting moments, so that the Fourier (or Maximum Entropy) analysis of the moments immediately recovers the density of states.

3 Results

3.1 Ordinary Eigenvalue Problem

We firstly demonstrate that the method can perform extremely accurate eigenvalue spectrum estimation using relatively few iterates on a large matrix. We show results in Figure 2 for a 7000×7000 dense matrix, A, which has been given a predefined eigenspectrum. In this case we set B to be the identity matrix and solve a regular eigenvalue problem. The method resolves not only the general structure of the distribution, but also shows that there is a single eigenvalue at zero. This reconstruction is extremely accurate considering that it required *in total* only 250 matrix vector products to obtain information about the whole spectrum. An iterative method would require at least this many iterates to locate only the first few eigenvalues of a dense matrix [11].

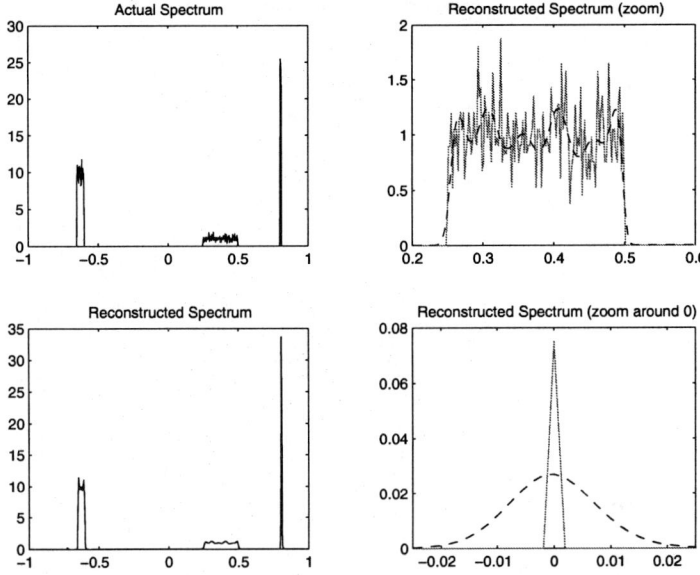

Fig. 2. Eigenvalue distribution of a 7000 square matrix reconstructed using the Maximum Entropy method with 50 iterates and 5 seed vectors. (Right) light line is actual spectrum, dashed is reconstruction

3.2 Generalised Eigenvalue Problem

We have set up and solved the eigenvalue problem in (20) for the photonic crystal in Figure 1 using 100 randomly chosen k-vectors to estimate the density of states. Two approaches may be adopted:

1. Solve 100 independent generalised eigenvalue problems of size 100. A Krylov subspace algorithm [11] was applied to the system to determine the true spectrum for comparison.
2. Solve a single 10 000 square generalised eigenvalue problem, but exploiting the block structure in (20) for any matrix-vector solves. The algorithm we describe was applied in this case.

We resolve the key features of the density of states shown in figure 3 which is in excellent agreement with those given in [15]. The eigenspectrum reconstructed using our estimation method matches precisely the form and position of the true band gaps. Furthermore our estimate was obtained nearly two orders of magnitude more quickly than the true solution, taking minutes rather than hours on a desktop machine! The results in figure 2 indicate that using the Maximum Entropy method to reconstruct the spectrum would reduce the total number of matrix-vector solves by a further factor of five.

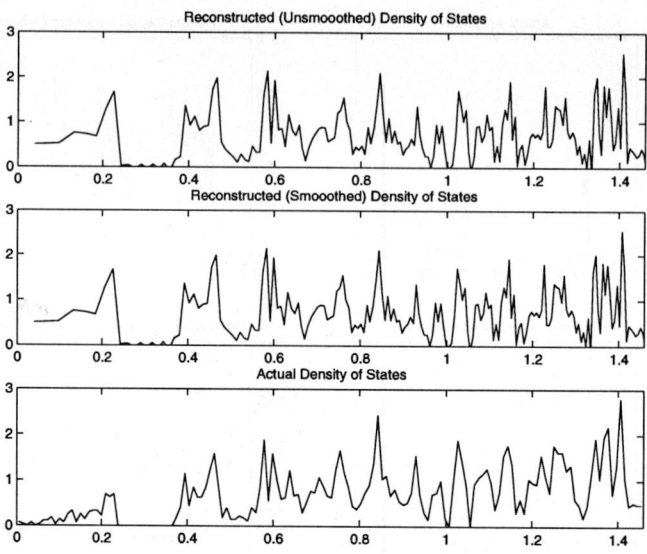

Fig. 3. Density of States for TE polarisation of a photonic crystal consisting of air rods ($\varepsilon = 1$) in a dielectric substrate ($\varepsilon = 12.25$). The Fourier reconstructed spectra used 256 matrix-vector solves and 5 starting seeds

3.3 Parallelism

The algorithm 2.1 proceeds in parallel in three ways for our application:

- It is possible to parallelise over the different k-vector samples in (3). This is also possible when a subspace iteration method is used. The efficiency of this 'natural' parallelism should not be dismissed, so long as the matrix and associated vectors can fit into the memory available on one processor. Our method, however, is considerably more memory efficient, since it is only necessary to store 2 vectors of length N to complete the iterations in (7). Subspace iteration methods require $\sim p$ full vectors where p is the number of eigenvalues required. For a sparse matrix it is this storage which can rapidly outweigh that required for the matrix and hence make it necessary to use multiple processors.
- In contrast to subspace iteration methods [11] a second level of parallelism is possible, since we can start the method with multiple random seeds in parallel on multiple processors. The resulting moments are averaged using a single global reduce step. We have implemented this in MPI, and find that it scales nearly linearly with the number of processors- this method too is 'naturally' parallel.
- If the matrix and two vectors of length N are too large to fit into memory on a single processor, then it is necessary to perform the steps in (7,9) in

parallel. We have implemented and described elsewhere an efficient parallel preconditioned conjugate gradient method for this, which scales linearly up to 16 nodes on a commodity cluster of Pentiums running Red Hat Linux 6.2, and also on a cluster of 21164 Compaq Alphas running Windows NT 4.0 [13].

4 Discussion and Conclusions

We have derived and implemented a new algorithm for estimating the eigenvalue spectrum of a generalised eigenvalue problem and have applied it to the calculation of the density of states of a photonic crystal. Our examples were a single large dense matrix and a sequence of small sparse generalised eigenvalue problems (equivalent to a single large block sparse problem). In each case we have demonstrated that a remarkably accurate estimation is possible using relatively few matrix-vector products offering significant advantages in time, memory, and ease of parallelisation over subspace iteration methods in the case when only information about the overall eigenspectrum is required.

References

1. W. AXMANN AND P. KUCHMENT, *An efficient finite element method for computing spectra of photonic and acoustic band-gap materials - I. scalar case*, Journal of Computational Physics, 150 (1999), pp. 468–481.
2. S. J. COX AND D. C. DOBSON, *Maximizing band gaps in two-dimensional photonic crystals*, SIAM Journal on Applied Mathematics, 59 (1999), pp. 2108–2120.
3. J. GENEROWICZ, B. HIETT, D. BECKETT, M. MOLINARI, M. CHARLTON, G. PARKER, AND S. COX, *Modelling photonic crystals using finite elements*, in NATO Advanced Study Institute: Photonic Crystals and Light Localization, Crete, 2000.
4. ———, *Modelling 3 dimensional photonic crystals using vector finite elements*, in Photonics 2000, Manchester, 2000.
5. E. JAYNES AND R. ROSENKRANTZ, *Papers on probability, statistics, and statistical physics*, Synthese library v. 158, D. Reidel, Dordrecht, Holland, 1983.
6. C. LANCZOS, *Applied analysis*, Isaac Pitman, London, 1957.
7. ———, *Discourse on fourier series*, Oliver and Boyd, London, 1966.
8. R. LEHOUCQ, D. SORENSEN, AND C. YANG, *ARPACK User's Guide*, SIAM Publications, 1998.
9. K. MASCHHOFF AND D. SORENSEN, *An efficient portable large scale eigenvalue package for distributed memory parallel architectures*, in Applied parallel computing in industrial problems and optimization, J. Wasniewski, J. Dongarra, K. Madsen, and D. Oleson, eds., vol. 1184 of LNCS, Springer Verlag, 1996.
10. L. R. MEAD AND N. PAPANICOLAOU, *Maximum-entropy in the problem of moments*, Journal of Mathematical Physics, 25 (1984), pp. 2404–2417.
11. N. SEHMI, *Large order structure eigenanalysis techniques algorithms for finite element systems*, Ellis Horwood, Chichester, 1989.
12. J. SKILLING, *The eigenvalues of mega-dimensional matrices*, in Maximum Entropy and Bayesian Methods, J. Skilling, ed., Kluver Academic, 1989, pp. 455–466.

13. A. TAKEDA, S. COX, AND A. PAYNE, *Numerical modelling of ice flow in antartica*, in International conference on parallel and distributed processing and techniques, 2000, pp. 335–342.
14. A. TAYLOR, *Introduction to functional analysis*, Wiley, New York, 1958.
15. P. R. VILLENEUVE AND M. PICHE, *Photonic bandgaps - what is the best numerical representation of periodic structures*, Journal of Modern Optics, 41 (1994), pp. 241–256.

Polynomial Preconditioning for Specially Structured Linear Systems of Equations

Y. Liang, J. Weston, and M. Szularz

School of Information and Software Engineering
University of Ulster at Coleraine, BT52 1SA, U.K.

Abstract. For the solution of the SID (Symmetric InDefinite) linear systems, the use of the GLS (Generalized Least-Squares) polynomial preconditioner can improve the execution efficiency of solvers, particularly for some specially structured systems. In this paper the suitability of GLS preconditioning for a class of specially structured linear system of equations is demonstrated. The algorithms are implemented using MPI in a highly parallel IBM SP2 environment and experimental results are presented. The performance of the GLS preconditioned FGMRES solver and the eigensolver based on it is critically assessed.

Keywords: polynomial preconditioner, FGMRES, specially structured, solution of linear systems, generalised least-squares.

1 Introduction

The interest in *polynomial preconditioners* [1] is motivated by the need for simple, yet efficient, methods for the speedup of iterative solvers [11] on vector and parallel processors. With respect to the SID (Symmetric InDefinite) linear systems, the use of the GLS (Generalized Least-Squares) polynomial preconditioner [1,9,10,12] is preferable to other polynomial preconditioning methods due to the ability to use a three-term recurrence relationship and the low implementation costs.

Two of the principal objectives of preconditioning may be considered to be the provision of efficient solution procedures for systems of linear equations and the improvement of the stability of such systems. Each of these objectives is addressed in this paper. Consider the polynomial preconditioned linear equations of form

$$P_m(A)Ax = P_m(A)b, \qquad (1)$$

where $P_m(A)$ is a polynomial in A with degree no more than m. It has been shown that, $P_m(\lambda)$ is constructed by solving the following generalised least-squares problem

$$\min_{P_m \in \wp_m[\Omega]} \|1 - \lambda P_m(\lambda)\|_w \quad (\lambda \in \Omega) \qquad (2)$$

where $\wp_m[\Omega]$ is the set of m-degree polynomials that is valid over Ω. Here $\Omega \supset \sigma(A)$ and $\sigma(A)$ is the spectrum of A. The accuracy of estimation of $\sigma(A)$, and hence that of Ω, determines the rate of convergence of the preconditioned system. In this paper only symmetric linear systems are discussed, consequently $\sigma(A) \subset \Re$ and is defined as

$$\Omega = \bigcup_{k=1}^{\mathcal{I}} [\ell_k, \hbar_k], \ 0 \notin \Omega \text{ and } \ell_1 < \hbar_1 \leq \ell_2 < \hbar_2 \leq \cdots \leq \ell_\mathcal{I} < \hbar_\mathcal{I}. \qquad (3)$$

In addition, $\|.\|_w$ represents the weighted quadratic norm which is induced by the innerproduct

$$<f,g>_w = \int_\Omega f(\lambda)g(\lambda)w(\lambda)d\lambda, \qquad (4)$$

$w(\lambda)$ is a non-negative *weight function* [9,10,12] over the interval Ω.

In this paper, GLS polynomial preconditioned FGMRES is applied in the solution of a class of specially structured linear systems

$$Ax \equiv (D + \rho tt^T)x = b \qquad (5)$$

where $D = diag(d_1, \cdots, d_\mathcal{N})$ ($d_1 < d_2 <, \cdots, < d_\mathcal{N}$), $\rho \neq 0$ and $t = [\tau_1, \cdots, \tau_\mathcal{N}]^T$ ($\tau_i \neq 0 \mid i = 1, \cdots, \mathcal{N}$). The algorithm is implemented using MPI in a highly parallel IBM SP2 environment and experimental results using specially structured linear systems were obtained.

2 GLS Polynomial Preconditioned FGMRES

In this paper a variant of GMRES (Generalized Minimal RESidual) [11] known as FGMRES (Flexible GMRES) [11] is used. This variant permits the construction of different preconditioners at selected stages in the iterative process.

It is known that a preconditioner is essential for the GMRES algorithm. The basic polynomial preconditioning operation consists of a series of matrix-vector products of the form

$$z = P_m(A)v, \qquad (6)$$

which can be computed using a *orthogonal polynomial sequence* $\{\lambda \phi_i(\lambda)\}_{i=0}^m$ [4,5,9,12] as a basis, i.e.,

$$P_m(A)v = \sum_{i=0}^m \mu_i \phi_i(A)v. \qquad (7)$$

Here

$$\mu_i = <1, \lambda\phi_i(\lambda)>_w, \qquad (8)$$

where w is a specified weight function which is defined in [5,9] and only valid over Ω which is expressed by (3). Observe also that the polynomial sequence $\{\phi_i(\lambda)\}_{i=0}^m$ may be constructed using a three-term recurrence relationship [9], thereby enabling efficient implementation.

In general, the order of the preconditioning polynomial $P_m(A)$ depends upon the perturbality of the preconditioning operation $P_m(A)v$ [8] and the resemblance of $\lambda P_m(\lambda)$ ($\lambda \in \Omega$) to 1. However, in the case of the specially structured linear systems considered in this paper, the order depends mainly upon the value of $\|1 - \lambda P_m(\lambda)\|_w$, which is computed through

$$\epsilon_{m+1} = [2\mathcal{I} - (\sum_{i=0}^{m} \mu_i^2)]^{\frac{1}{2}}, \qquad (9)$$

where $\epsilon_{m+1} = \|1 - \lambda P_m(\lambda)\|_w$ [10].

3 Solution of Specially Structured Linear Systems

In this paper, GLS preconditioned FGMRES is employed to solve specially structured linear systems (5), which belong to *rank-one modification* [2,6,7] problems. Such systems often appear in the solution of eigenvalue [2,6,7] and SVD (Singular Value Decomposition) [6] problems.

As a matter of fact, it follows from Shermann-Morrison's formula [6] that

$$(D + \rho t t^T)^{-1} = D^{-1} - \frac{\rho}{1 + \rho t^T D^{-1} t} D^{-1} t t^T D^{-1} \qquad (10)$$

and thus the solution of (5) can be directly achieved. However, in the case when D is of more relatively complicated structure such as tridiagonal, the direct method will not be the appropriate option.

When GMRES is chosen as a solver, the use of a preconditioner is essential. With respect to linear systems (5), the GLS polynomial preconditioner is preferable for two reasons:

1. Ω can be approximated by $\sigma(D)$. The smaller $\|\rho t t^T\|$ is, the closer $\sigma(D)$ is to Ω.
2. Matrix-vector products Av are transformed into vector operations since

$$Av \equiv (D + \rho t t^T)v \equiv Dv + \rho <v, t> t. \qquad (11)$$

Some other preconditioning methods such as *ILU* [11] and *SPAI* [11] are not appropriate because $D + \rho t t^T$ is fully dense.

4 Experimental Results

The generalized least-squares polynomial preconditioned FGMRES algorithm, henceforth referred to as FGMRES-GLS, was implemented using Fortran and MPI in a highly parallel IBM SP2 machine environment. The number of processors used ranged from 1 to 16. Named according to their dimension, four benchmark SID linear systems of the form $D + \rho t t^T$ [10], Dtt1K,Dtt2K,Dtt5K and Dtt50K, were generated. In all cases, $\rho = 0.01$, $t = [1, \cdots, 1]^T$, and D is of a segmently clustered spectrum.

Table 1 and 2 show the execution performance of the solution of linear equation where convergence was deemed to have occurred when $\frac{\|r_i\|_2}{\|r_0\|_2} \leq \mathbf{u}$ where $r_i = b - Ax_i$ and $\mathbf{u}(= 0.111 * 10^{-15})$ is the machine round-off unit. The results obtained using one processor are presented in Table 1 and the results obtained for Dtt50K using multiple processors are presented in Table 2.

Table 3 compares the performance of the *Rayleigh quotient iteration* (RQI) eigensolver [6] based on FGMRES with and without the GLS preconditioner with respect to Dtt50K. Here the convergence with regard to the eigenpair (v, λ) was deemed to have occurred when $\frac{\|r_i\|_2}{\|r_0\|_2} \leq \sqrt{\mathbf{u}}$ where $r_i = Av_i - \lambda v_i$. Deflation technique is excluded in our implementation. In Table 3, "p" is the number of participating processors and "m" is the degree of preconditioning polynomial.

Table 1. Iterations and CPU time(sec) of FGMRES-GLS(m)

Matrix	\multicolumn{10}{c}{m:degree of GLS Polynomial}									
	0		3		6		9		12	
	Its.	Time	Its.	Time	Its.	Time	Its.	Time	Its.	Time
Dtt1K	489	0.2239	244	0.1560	151	0.1269	42	0.0453	39	0.0495
Dtt2K	546	0.4885	237	0.2917	155	0.2475	47	0.0928	46	0.1083
Dtt5K	538	1.1983	269	0.9310	180	0.8521	48	0.2914	48	0.3516
Dtt50K	518	19.6394	321	19.1904	200	15.7250	85	8.3462	110	13.1218

Table 2. Dtt50K: Iterations, CPU Time(sec) and speedup of FGMRES-GLS(m)

p	\multicolumn{12}{c}{m: degree of GLS Polynomial}											
	0			3			6			9		
	Its.	Time	T_1/T_p	Its.	Time	T_1/T_p	Its.	Time	T_1/T_p	Its.	Time	T_1/T_p
1	518	19.6394	1.0000	321	19.1904	1.0000	201	15.7250	1.0000	85	8.3462	1.0000
2	546	10.6387	1.8460	221	6.6648	2.8794	199	8.0206	1.9606	86	4.3686	1.9105
4	546	5.5357	3.5478	271	4.1972	4.5722	177	3.7501	4.1932	84	2.2593	3.6942
8	400	1.5183	12.9351	358	2.2398	8.5679	156	1.5179	10.3597	84	0.9447	8.8348
16	546	1.3012	15.0933	342	2.0974	9.1496	170	0.9486	16.5771	75	0.5865	14.2305

Table 3. Dtt50K: CPU time(sec) for RQI eigensolver based on FGMRES-GLS(m)

	\multicolumn{5}{c}{$m = 0$}					\multicolumn{5}{c}{$m = 9$}				
	$p=1$	$p=2$	$p=4$	$p=8$	$p=16$	$p=1$	$p=2$	$p=4$	$p=8$	$p=16$
λ_{20K}	713.12	367.00	215.30	88.32	47.70	334.25	179.78	102.66	70.92	35.71
λ_{30K}	2941.64	65.83	756.40	257.60	153.00	1394.75	30.53	531.09	259.64	148.79
λ_{40K}	1098.53	630.72	640.51	193.36	130.06	604.19	348.98	324.52	152.98	96.11

5 Conclusions

The influence of the GLS preconditioning polynomial on the FGMRES solver in a one processor environment may be determined from the results presented in Table 1. They show that the number of iterations required for convergence was reduced in all, at the same time the time-cost was also reduced. Further, in many cases the reduction was significant. It should be observed that, the number of iterations required for convergence presented in Table 1 do not necessarily represent peak performance.

The parallel performance of FGMRES-GLS was also studied and a subset of the results obtained are presented in Table 2. The speedup obtained using FGMRES-GLS in the case of the largest system was very impressive. This would suggest that this algorithm is well suited to the computation of solutions of extremely large systems of the type under discussion.

Table 3 shows that the GLS preconditioners shortened the execution time of Rayleigh-quotient iterative eigensolver.

In conclusion, the solution of large specially structured linear systems of the type described in this paper may be efficiently computed using GLS polynomial preconditioning in either a uni-processor or a highly parallel multi-processor environment.

References

1. S. F. Ashby (1987), *Polynomial preconditioning for conjugate gradient methods*, Ph.D. thesis, Dept. of CS, Univ. of Illinois at Urbane-Champaign, Illinois.
2. J. R. Bunch, et al. (1978), *Rank-one modification of the symmetric eigenproblem*, Numer. Math., 31, 31-48.
3. J. J. M. Cuppen (1981), *A Divide and Conquer Method for Symmetric Tridiagonal Eigenproblem*. Numer. Math. 36, 177-195.
4. Bernd Fischer and Gene H. Golub (1991), *On Generating Polynomials Which are Orthogonal over Several Interval*, Mathematics of Computation, Vol.56, 711-730.
5. Bernd Fischer (1996), *Polynomial Based Iteration Methods for Symmetric Linear Systems*, Wiley-Teubner Series: Advances in Numerical Mathematics, 1996.
6. G. H. Golub and C. F. Van Loan (1993), *Matrix Computations, 2nd Edition*, The Johns Hopkins University Press, Baltimore and London.
7. Ming Gu and Stanley C. Eisenstat (1994), *A Stable and Efficient Algorithm for the Rank-One Modification of the Symmetric Eigenproblem*, SIAM J. on Matrix Analysis and Applications. 15(4), 1266-1276.
8. Y.Liang, J.Weston and M.Szularz (2000), *Stability of Polynomial Preconditioning*, Proceeding of ALGORITMY 2000 Conference on Scientific Computing, 264-272.
9. Y.Liang, J.Weston and M. Szularz (2001), *GLS Polynomial Preconditioner for the Solution of SID Linear Equations*, accepted by Parallel Computing.
10. Y.Liang (2001), *The Use of Parallel Polynomial Preconditioners in the Solution of Systems of Linear Equations*, Ph.D. thesis, University of Ulster, UK.
11. Yousef Saad (1996), *Iterative Methods for Sparse Linear Systems*, PWS Publishing.
12. Yousef Saad (1983), *Iterative Solution of Indefinite Symmetric Linear Systems by Methods Using Orthogonal Polynomial over Two Disjoint Interval*, SIAM J. Numer. Anal., Vol.20, 784-811.

Parallel Application of a Novel Domain Decomposition Preconditioner for the Stable Finite Element Solution of Three-Dimensional Convection-Dominated PDEs

Peter K. Jimack and Sarfraz A. Nadeem

Computational PDEs Unit, School of Computing
University of Leeds, Leeds, LS2 9JT, UK
{pkj,sarfraz}@comp.leeds.ac.uk
http://www.comp.leeds.ac.uk/pkj/

Abstract. We describe and analyze the parallel implementation of a novel domain decomposition preconditioner for the fast iterative solution of linear systems of algebraic equations arising from the discretization of elliptic partial differential equations (PDEs) in three dimensions. In previous theoretical work, [3], this preconditioner has been proved to be optimal for symmetric positive-definite (SPD) linear systems. In this paper we provide details of our 3-d parallel implementation and demonstrate that the technique may be generalized to the solution of non-symmetric algebraic systems, such as those arising when convection-diffusion problems are discretized using either Galerkin or stabilized finite element methods (FEMs), [9].

1 Introduction

Domain decomposition (DD) techniques for the solution of sparse linear algebraic systems arising from the discretization of PDEs have become extremely popular in recent years due to their obvious potential for parallel implementation. Typically, two main approaches have been followed: generating and solving systems of equations on the subdomain interfaces (e.g. [6,8], which each require exact subdomain solves at each iteration) or solving the complete system as a partitioned matrix (e.g. [5,7]). In this work we focus on a recently proposed method of the second type ([2,3]) which we refer to as a weakly overlapping additive Schwarz (AS) preconditioner.

Typical AS preconditioners (see, for example, [13]) require a fixed amount of overlap between subdomains in order to guarantee that the preconditioned linear systems which arise following discretization have a condition number which is independent of the mesh size h[1]. For practical applications therefore this optimality property is usually discarded in favour of keeping a fixed number of

---

[1] It is also necessary to add the solution of a restricted coarse grid problem at each iteration for such an optimal preconditioner (again see [13], or [5]).

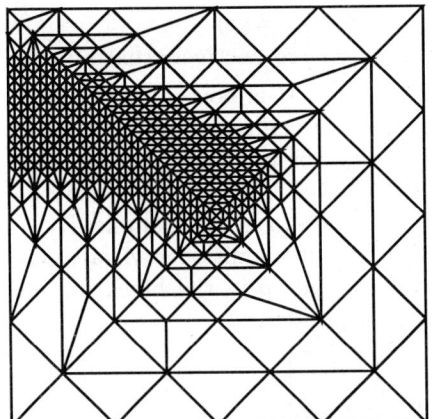 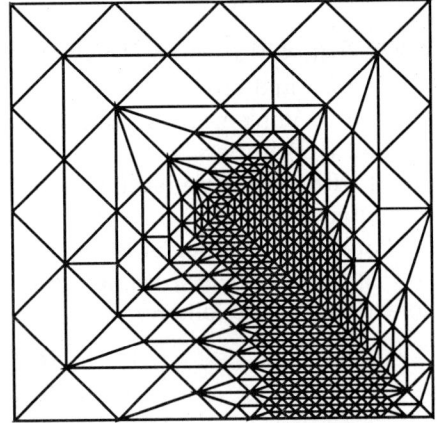

Fig. 1. An example (in 2-d for clarity) of two weakly overlapping finite element meshes generated from a coarse grid of 64 elements with three levels of hierarchical refinement

mesh layers in the overlap region (which, in three dimensions, therefore results in an overlap of $O(h^2)$ elements, as opposed to $O(h^3)$, as $h \to 0$). In [2] a hierarchical finite element technique is introduced which defines the solution space on each subdomain to consist of a global coarse grid plus a single layer of overlap at each level of refinement in the mesh hierarchy (see Fig. 1 for a two-dimensional illustration). It is then proved in [3] that for certain symmetric self-adjoint operators the resulting additive Schwarz preconditioner is still optimal, despite only having $O(h^2)$ elements in the overlap ($O(h)$ in 2-d).

To illustrate the technique algebraically consider solving a self-adjoint problem with just two subdomains (one on each of two processors say), as illustrated in 2-d in Fig. 1 (where the subdomains lie above and below diagonal from the bottom left to the top right of the domain). Following the usual parallel finite element approach (e.g. [8]), a distributed global stiffness matrix may be assembled in parallel on the two processors by permitting processor i to assemble contributions from those fine mesh elements inside subdomain i only. The corresponding linear system of finite element equations may then be represented in the following block matrix form:

$$\begin{bmatrix} A_1 & 0 & B_1 \\ 0 & A_2 & B_2 \\ B_1^T & B_2^T & A_s \end{bmatrix} \begin{bmatrix} \underline{u}_1 \\ \underline{u}_2 \\ \underline{u}_s \end{bmatrix} = \begin{bmatrix} \underline{f}_1 \\ \underline{f}_2 \\ \underline{f}_s \end{bmatrix}. \qquad (1)$$

Here $\underline{u}_i$ is the vector of unknown nodal values for nodes strictly inside subdomain i ($i = 1, 2$) and $\underline{u}_s$ is the vector of unknown nodal values for nodes on the interface between subdomains. Moreover, each block A_i, B_i and $\underline{f}_i$ may be computed (and stored) independently on processor i ($i = 1, 2$). Finally, we may express

$$A_s = A_{s(1)} + A_{s(2)} \quad \text{and} \quad \underline{f}_s = \underline{f}_{s(1)} + \underline{f}_{s(2)}, \tag{2}$$

where $A_{s(i)}$ and $\underline{f}_{s(i)}$ are the components of A_s and $\underline{f}_s$ respectively that may be calculated (and stored) independently on processor i. It is now quite straightforward to implement an iterative solver such as the conjugate gradient (CG) method ([1]) in parallel since distributed matrix-vector products may be computed with very little parallel overhead and distributed inner products may be computed with just a single global reduction operation (see, for example, [7]).

Parallel application of the weakly overlapping AS preconditioner, $\tilde{A}$ say, may now be described by considering the action of $\underline{z} = \tilde{A}^{-1}\underline{p}$ in the block matrix notation of (1) as follows. On processor 1 solve the system

$$\begin{bmatrix} A_1 & 0 & B_1 \\ 0 & \tilde{A}_2 & \tilde{B}_2 \\ B_1^T & \tilde{B}_2^T & A_s \end{bmatrix} \begin{bmatrix} \underline{z}_{1,1} \\ \underline{z}_{2,1} \\ \underline{z}_{s,1} \end{bmatrix} = \begin{bmatrix} \underline{p}_1 \\ M_2 \underline{p}_2 \\ \underline{p}_s \end{bmatrix} \tag{3}$$

and on processor 2 solve the system

$$\begin{bmatrix} \tilde{A}_1 & 0 & \tilde{B}_1 \\ 0 & A_2 & B_2 \\ \tilde{B}_1^T & B_2^T & A_s \end{bmatrix} \begin{bmatrix} \underline{z}_{1,2} \\ \underline{z}_{2,2} \\ \underline{z}_{s,2} \end{bmatrix} = \begin{bmatrix} M_1 \underline{p}_1 \\ \underline{p}_2 \\ \underline{p}_s \end{bmatrix}, \tag{4}$$

then set

$$\begin{bmatrix} \underline{z}_1 \\ \underline{z}_2 \\ \underline{z}_s \end{bmatrix} = \begin{bmatrix} \underline{z}_{1,1} + M_1^T \underline{z}_{1,2} \\ M_2^T \underline{z}_{2,1} + \underline{z}_{2,2} \\ \underline{z}_{s,1} + \underline{z}_{s,2} \end{bmatrix}. \tag{5}$$

In the above notation, the blocks $\tilde{A}_2$ and $\tilde{B}_2$ (resp. $\tilde{A}_1$ and $\tilde{B}_1$) are the assembled components of the stiffness matrix for the part of the mesh on processor 1 (resp. 2) that covers subdomain 2 (resp. 1). These may be computed and stored without communication. Moreover, because of the single layer of overlap in the refined regions of the meshes, A_s may be computed and stored on each processor without communication. Finally, the rectangular matrix M_1 (resp. M_2) represents the restriction operator from the fine mesh covering subdomain 1 (resp. 2) on processor 1 (resp. 2) to the coarser mesh covering subdomain 1 (resp. 2) on processor 2 (resp. 1). This is the usual hierarchical restriction operator that is used in most multigrid algorithms (see, for example, [11]) and requires the communication of data between the processors.

It is easy to verify that the above preconditioner is symmetric and may be generalized from 2 to p subdomains (see [2] or [3] for details). It should also be noted that each of the local problems ((3) and (4) in the two-subdomain example above) combines its own subspace solve with the coarse grid solve and so we are effectively repeating this coarse grid correction on each processor at each iteration. This is not a significant overhead however since the coarse grid is generally very much smaller than the refined grid so most parallel codes (e.g. [8]) solve this problem sequentially on a single processor anyway. Furthermore, as $h \to 0$, each of these local problems tends to exactly $\frac{1}{p}$ times the size of the full problem, even with the coarse grid included.

2 Solution of Convection-Diffusion Problems

Whilst the theoretical results of [3] demonstrate that the preconditioner given by (3) to (5) (when $p = 2$) is optimal for a class of linear self-adjoint PDEs (leading to SPD linear systems), it is clear that many important practical problems cannot be realistically modelled by such equations. One of the most important class of problem that comes into this category involves convection-diffusion equations of the form

$$-\varepsilon \nabla^2 u + \underline{b} \cdot \nabla u = f(\underline{x}) . \tag{6}$$

Provided $\varepsilon > 0$ this is an elliptic problem but, when $\underline{b} \neq \underline{0}$, it is not self-adjoint. When ε is small (relative to $\|\underline{b}\|$) the equation is said to be convection-dominated. Such problems arise frequently in fluid mechanics, heat and mass transfer, environmental modelling, etc. and, when discretized by the standard Galerkin FEM (see, for example, [9]), lead to a non-symmetric linear system.

When considering how to generalize the preconditioner introduced in the previous section to non-symmetric systems an important clue may be obtained from observations made in [2] and [4]. Both of these papers make the empirical observation that setting the M_i^T terms in (5) to zero (and scaling the interface terms accordingly) not only has the effect of reducing the communication cost of each iteration but, provided an appropriate solver is used, also leads to a reduction in the number of iterations required to converge[2]. In the case where $p = 2$ equation (5) therefore becomes

$$\begin{bmatrix} \underline{z}_1 \\ \underline{z}_2 \\ \underline{z}_s \end{bmatrix} = \begin{bmatrix} \underline{z}_{1,1} \\ \underline{z}_{2,2} \\ \frac{1}{2}(\underline{z}_{s,1} + \underline{z}_{s,2}) \end{bmatrix} , \tag{7}$$

which means that the preconditioner is no longer SPD. Hence, even for a self-adjoint differential operator, the CG algorithm can no longer be used and must be replaced by a more general alternative such as GMRES (again see [1], or [12] for details of a public domain implementation). Although the cost per iteration is greater for GMRES than CG, the reduced inter-processor communication at each iteration and the decrease in the number of iterations required always appear to more than make up for this (see [2] for specific comparisons in 2-d and [4] for corresponding remarks concerning conventional AS preconditioning).

With a parallel preconditioner for GMRES given by (3), (4) and (7) (we again focus on the special case $p = 2$ for simplicity) it is clear that our algorithm may easily generalize to non-symmetric problems such as that obtained from a finite element discretization of (6).

2.1 Parallel Implementation

Generalizing the above discussion to the solution of a non-symmetric linear system on p processors we may write the action ($\underline{z} = \tilde{A}^{-1}\underline{p}$) of the preconditioner in

---
[2] In [4] the observation is of course described for conventional AS preconditioning rather than the weakly overlapping modification being considered here.

terms of the computations required on each processor i (from 1 to p) as follows.
(i) Solve
$$\begin{bmatrix} A_i & 0 & B_i \\ 0 & \bar{A}_i & \bar{B}_i \\ C_i & \bar{C}_i & A_{i,s} \end{bmatrix} \begin{bmatrix} \underline{z}_i \\ \underline{\bar{z}}_i \\ \underline{z}_{i,s} \end{bmatrix} = \begin{bmatrix} \underline{p}_i \\ \bar{M}_i \underline{\bar{p}}_i \\ \underline{p}_{i,s} \end{bmatrix}. \qquad (8)$$

(ii) Average each entry of of $\underline{z}_{i,s}$ over all corresponding entries on neighbouring processors.

In (8) A_i, B_i and C_i are assembled components of the stiffness matrix for the elements of the mesh in subdomain i, $\bar{A}_i$, $\bar{B}_i$ and $\bar{C}_i$ are components for the elements of this mesh outside subdomain i and $A_{i,s}$ stores the components of the stiffness matrix where both the row and column correspond to nodes on the interface of subdomain i. A similar partition of the vector $\underline{p}$ is provided into components $\underline{p}_i$ inside subdomain i, $\underline{\bar{p}}_i$ outside subdomain i and $\underline{p}_{i,s}$ on its interface. $\bar{M}_i$ represents the hierarchical restriction operator from the fine mesh on each processor other than i to the coarser mesh outside of subdomain i on processor i (therefore requiring an all-to-one communication to compute its action for each i).

The main implementation issue that needs to be addressed is that of computing the action of each of the restriction operations $\bar{M}_i \underline{\bar{p}}_i$ efficiently at each iteration. Note that because the preconditioner is not symmetric we do not need to also evaluate the corresponding prolongation at the end of each preconditioning step. The evaluation of $\bar{M}_i \underline{\bar{p}}_i$ is completed in two phases: a set-up phase which occurs before the first iteration, and a communication phase which occurs at each iteration. All of our implementations have been in ANSI C using the MPI communication library, [10].

In the set-up phase each processor, i say, sends to each other processor, j say, a list of the nodes of mesh i which lie in, or on the boundary of, subdomain j. Processor i then receives from each other processor, j say, a list of all nodes of mesh j which lie in, or on the boundary of, subdomain i. For each of these lists processor i then matches each of the nodes in this list with the corresponding node on mesh i. This is achieved very efficiently by using the mesh hierarchy that is present on processor i (see [14] for a description of the hierarchical refinement of tetrahedral grids that is used on each processor).

At each iteration processor i then contributes to the restriction operation $\bar{M}_j \underline{\bar{p}}_j$ for each $j \neq i$. The part of the vector $\underline{p}$ which is stored on processor i ($\underline{p}_i$) corresponds to all nodes of mesh i in subdomain i or on its boundary. For each j this sub-vector, $\underline{p}_i$, may be restricted to the nodes of mesh j which lie in subdomain i or on its boundary (which are known from the set-up phase). This restriction uses the mesh hierarchy in the standard multilevel manner (as described in [11] for example). These restricted vectors may then each be sent to the corresponding processor, j. Following this, processor i should receive a list of its own restricted vectors from each of the other processors. These are then put together on processor i to produce the required vector $\bar{M}_i \underline{\bar{p}}_i$ before the solution to (8) is found locally. Note that in MPI ([10]) all of the above message passing may be implemented as a single all-to-all communication. Given the high cost of such a communication we again see the value of only requiring one of these per iteration (as opposed to two for the original symmetric preconditioner).

The final stage in computing the action of $\underline{z} = \tilde{A}^{-1}\underline{p}$ requires only neighbour-to-neighbour communication between processors sharing a subdomain boundary. This allows the $\underline{z}_{i,s}$ vectors to be updated on each processor i, as required for step (ii) above.

2.2 Numerical Results

In order to assess the performance of the proposed parallel preconditioner on typical convection-diffusion problems we consider here a specific test problem of the form (6). This equation is solved on the domain $\Omega = (0,2) \times (0,1) \times (0,1)$ with the parameters $\underline{b} = (1,0,0)^T$ and

$$f(\underline{x}) = 2\varepsilon \left(x - \frac{2(1 - e^{x/\varepsilon})}{(1 - e^{2/\varepsilon})} \right) (y(1-y) + z(1-z)) + y(1-y)z(1-z) ,$$

subject to the Dirichlet boundary condition $u|_{\partial\Omega} = u^*|_{\partial\Omega}$, where

$$u^* = \left(x - \frac{2(1 - e^{x/\varepsilon})}{(1 - e^{2/\varepsilon})} \right) y(1-y)z(1-z) \tag{9}$$

is the exact solution to this problem. It exhibits a steep layer of size $O(\varepsilon)$ near to the boundary $x = 2$ when $0 < \varepsilon \ll \|\underline{b}\| = 1$.

Table 1 shows the number of iterations required to solve the discrete finite element system to a moderately high level of accuracy using GMRES with our parallel implementation of the weakly overlapping DD preconditioner. Results are presented for a sequence of meshes which represent between one and four levels of refinement of a coarse tetrahedral mesh containing 768 elements. At each level of refinement each tetrahedron is subdivided into eight children, as described in [14]. It may be observed that, as the mesh is refined or the number of processors (subdomains) is increased, the total number of GMRES iterations increases only very slowly. It is not clear however whether this increase will be bounded as the mesh size tends to zero (as is proved in [3] for the symmetric version).

It is also evident from Table 1 that fewer iterations are required to solve the test problem when $\varepsilon = 10^{-2}$ than when $\varepsilon = 10^{-1}$. A similar observation is made when solving the problem sequentially using the package described in [12]. (This package is also used in the parallel preconditioner to solve the system (8) sequentially on each processor.) In this case a preconditioner based upon an incomplete LU (ILU) factorization of the finite element matrix is used, and this is able to exploit the weak coupling between neighbouring nodes with a common edge that is perpendicular to $\underline{b}$ when the problem is convection-dominated. Hence, although the discrete problem is more non-symmetric in this case, it turns out to be less complex to solve in practice. A discussion of the timings for these calculations follows in the next section.

Table 1. The performance of the proposed algorithm on the convection-diffusion test problem for two choices of ε: figures quoted represent the number of iterations required to reduce the initial residual by a factor of 10^5

Elements/Procs.	$\varepsilon = 10^{-1}$				$\varepsilon = 10^{-2}$			
	2	4	8	16	2	4	8	16
6144	3	3	4	5	3	3	4	4
49152	3	4	6	7	3	3	4	4
393216	4	6	7	8	3	4	4	5
3145728	4	7	9	10	4	5	6	6

3 Stabilized Finite Elements for Convection-Dominated Problems

The example of the previous section suggests that the proposed weakly overlapping parallel DD preconditioner works well in practice for three-dimensional convection-diffusion problems. When these become convection-dominated however (i.e. $0 < \varepsilon \ll \|\underline{b}\|$) it is well-known that the standard Galerkin FEM becomes oscillatory unless the size of the elements is sufficiently small. In this section we therefore extend our consideration to the solution of convection-dominated problems using a more stable finite element technique based upon streamline-diffusion (see [9], for example, for a full discussion of oscillations and stabilization using streamline-diffusion).

3.1 The Streamline-Diffusion Method

The standard FEM discretization of (6) on a domain Ω seeks an approximation u_h to u from a finite element space S_h such that

$$\varepsilon \int_\Omega \underline{\nabla} u_h \cdot \underline{\nabla} v \, d\underline{x} + \int_\Omega (\underline{b} \cdot \underline{\nabla} u_h) v \, d\underline{x} = \int_\Omega f(\underline{x}) v \, d\underline{x} \quad (10)$$

for all $v \in S_h$ (disregarding boundary conditions for simplicity). This in turn yields a non-symmetric linear algebraic system, $A\underline{u} = \underline{f}$, for which a typical entry in A is

$$\varepsilon \int_\Omega \underline{\nabla}\phi_i \cdot \underline{\nabla}\phi_j \, d\underline{x} + \int_\Omega \phi_i (\underline{b} \cdot \underline{\nabla}\phi_j) \, d\underline{x} \, , \quad (11)$$

where $\{\phi_i\}$ is the set of finite element basis functions for S_h.

The streamline-diffusion approach replaces v in (10) by $v + \alpha \underline{b} \cdot \underline{\nabla} v$ to yield

$$\varepsilon \int_\Omega \underline{\nabla} u_h \cdot \underline{\nabla}(v + \alpha \underline{b} \cdot \underline{\nabla} v) \, d\underline{x} + \int_\Omega (\underline{b} \cdot \underline{\nabla} u_h)(v + \alpha \underline{b} \cdot \underline{\nabla} v) \, d\underline{x} =$$
$$\int_\Omega f(\underline{x})(v + \alpha \underline{b} \cdot \underline{\nabla} v) \, d\underline{x} \quad (12)$$

for all $v \in S_h$.

Table 2. The infinity norm of the exact error in the two finite element approximations to (9), the solution of (6), when $\varepsilon = 10^{-2}$

Elements	Error 1 (Galerkin FEM)	Error 2 (stabilized FEM)	Error 2 / Error 1
6144	1.02×10^{-1}	2.41×10^{-2}	0.236
49152	1.01×10^{-1}	2.18×10^{-2}	0.216
393216	5.22×10^{-2}	1.74×10^{-2}	0.333
3145728	1.88×10^{-2}	8.10×10^{-3}	0.431

When $\alpha = 0$ the resulting linear system has a matrix with entries still given by (11) however α is usually chosen to be greater than zero and proportional to the mesh size h. This means that the linear system now being solved is even further from the SPD system analyzed in [3]. Nevertheless, it is possible to apply the same weakly overlapping domain decomposition preconditioning strategy to this stabilized problem. This requires only minor modifications to the code used to produce the results of the previous section (corresponding to the differences between (10) and (12)). The following results demonstrate that this extension also works well in practice.

3.2 Numerical Results

In Table 2 we illustrate the improved accuracy of the streamline-diffusion method when problem (6) is convection-dominated by considering the infinity norm of the exact error when solving the test problem considered in the previous section. As expected, we see that the stabilized FEM provides a less oscillatory solution with a smaller error, and that the relative improvement over the Galerkin FEM is greatest when the mesh is coarse.

Given that the stabilized method works best for small values of ε, in Table 3 we show iteration counts for the parallel preconditioned GMRES algorithm for the cases $\varepsilon = 10^{-2}$ and $\varepsilon = 10^{-3}$. The former permits comparison with the solution of the discrete Galerkin equations of Table 1 (there is little change in the iteration counts), whilst the latter demonstrates the effectiveness of the solver for even smaller ε. In each case the effectiveness of the preconditioner is again demonstrated in terms of the small numbers of iterations required (although exact iteration counts do depend upon the precise domain decomposition used).

3.3 Parallel Performance

The calculations described in Tables 1 to 3 were performed on a SG Origin 2000 computer which has a non-uniform memory access (NUMA) architecture. The non-uniform nature of the memory access means that timings of a given calculation may vary significantly between runs depending upon how memory has been allocated. For this reason the timings quoted in Table 4 (for solving the test problem in the case $\varepsilon = 10^{-2}$ using the finest mesh of 3145728 tetrahedral

Table 3. The performance of the proposed algorithm on the stabilized convection-diffusion test problem for two choices of ε: figures quoted represent the number of iterations required to reduce the initial residual by a factor of 10^5

Elements/Procs.	$\varepsilon = 10^{-2}$				$\varepsilon = 10^{-3}$			
	2	4	8	16	2	4	8	16
6144	2	3	3	3	2	3	3	3
49152	3	3	4	4	3	4	4	4
393216	3	4	4	5	3	4	4	4
3145728	4	5	6	6	3	4	4	4

Table 4. The performance of the parallel solver for both the Galerkin and stabilized FEM systems when solving the test problem with $\varepsilon = 10^{-2}$. The solution times are quoted in seconds and the speed-ups are relative to the best sequential solution time

	Galerkin FEM					Streamline-Diffusion FEM				
Processors	1	2	4	8	16	1	2	4	8	16
Solution Time	735.5	507.9	359.9	237.5	142.9	731.6	505.7	348.7	235.6	144.7
Speed-Up	—	1.45	2.04	3.10	5.15	—	1.46	2.10	3.11	5.06

elements) represent the best time that was achieved over numerous repetitions of the same computation. Furthermore, there are numerous parameters within the algorithm that affect the overall performance, such as the accuracy to which the systems (8) are solved on each processor at each iteration, or the drop tolerance that is used in the sequential ILU preconditioner ([12]) that is used for these systems. Our choices for these parameters, determined empirically, may well also contribute to some of the variation between the two sets of results.

Furthermore, there are additional reasons why it is not feasible to obtain efficiencies close to 100% for these calculations. Note that the preconditioner is algebraically different for each choice of p and that, when $p > 1$, the sequential solution time is not generally as good as that for the *best available* sequential algorithm (for which we use [12]). Also, the algorithm itself depends upon the domain decomposition that has been used and so far we have only applied simple variants of recursive coordinate bisection. This could well be improved significantly with further research, although it is unlikely that the efficiency will be such that the use of extremely large numbers of processors will be viable.

4 Conclusions

We have described the parallel implementation of a weakly overlapping domain decomposition preconditioner and successfully applied it to the finite element solution of convection-dominated PDEs in three dimensions. Provisional results show that the algorithm is fast and that the parallel implementation provides moderate speed-ups on up to sixteen processors. Extensions to a wider variety of convection directions to that considered here yield similar results and further improvements to the the mesh partitioning are likely to enhance the parallel performance. The work should also be extended to convection-dominated *systems*, which also arise frequently in scientific modeling.

Acknowledgments

SAN gratefully acknowledges the funding received from the Government of Pakistan in the form of a Quaid-e-Azam scholarship.

References

1. Ashby, S. F., Manteuffel, T. A., Taylor, P. E.: A Taxonomy for Conjugate Gradient Methods. SIAM J. on Numer. Anal. **27** (1990) 1542–1568.
2. Bank, R. E., Jimack, P. K.: A New Parallel Domain Decomposition Method for the Adaptive Finite Element Solution of Elliptic Partial Differential Equations. Concurrency and Computation: Practice and Experience **13** (2001) 327–350.
3. Bank, R. E., Jimack, P. K., Nadeem, S. A., Nepomnyaschikh, S. V.: A Weakly Overlapping Domain Decomposition for the Adaptive Finite Element Solution of Elliptic Partial Differential Equations. Submitted to SIAM J. on Sci. Comp. (2001).
4. Cai, X.-C., Sarkis, M.: A Restricted Additive Schwarz Preconditioner for General Sparse Linear Systems. SIAM J. on Sci. Comp. **21** (1999) 792–797.
5. Chan, T., Mathew, T.: Domain Decomposition Algorithms. Acta Numerica **3** (1994) 61–143.
6. Farhat, C., Mandel, J., Roux, F. X.: Optimal Convergence Properties of the FETI Domain Decomposition Method. Comp. Meth. for Appl. Mech. and Eng. **115** (1994) 365–385.
7. Gropp, W. D., Keyes, D. E.: Parallel Performance of Domain-Decomposed Preconditioned Krylov Methods for PDEs with Locally Uniform Refinement. SIAM J. on Sci. Comp. **13** (1992) 128–145.
8. Hodgson, D. C., Jimack, P. K.: A Domain Decomposition Preconditioner for a Parallel Finite Element Solver on Distributed Unstructured Grids. Parallel Computing **23** (1997) 1157–1181.
9. Johnson, C.: Numerical Solutions of Partial Differential Equations by the Finite Element Method. Cambridge University Press (1987).
10. Message Passing Interface Forum: MPI: A Message-Passing Interface Standard. Int. J. Supercomputer Appl. **8** (1994) no. 3/4.
11. Oswald, P.: Multilevel Finite Element Approximation: Theory and Applications. Teubner Skripten zur Numerik, B. G. Teubner (1994).
12. Saad, Y.: SPARSEKIT: A Basic Tool Kit for Sparse Matrix Computations, Version 2. Technical Report, Center for Supercomputing Research and Development, University of Illinois at Urbana-Champaign, Urbana, IL, USA (1994).
13. Smith, B., Bjorstad, P., Gropp, W.: Domain Decomposition: Parallel Multilevel Methods for Elliptic Partial Differential Equations. Cambridge University Press (1996).
14. Speares, W., Berzins, M.: A 3-D Unstructured Mesh Adaptation Algorithm for Time-Dependent Shock Dominated Problems. Int. J. for Numer. Meth. in Fluids **25** (1997) 81–104.

Performance of High-Accuracy PDE Solvers on a Self-Optimizing NUMA Architecture

Sverker Holmgren and Dan Wallin

Uppsala University, Information Technology, Department of Scientific Computing
P. O. Box 120, SE-751 04 Uppsala, Sweden
{Sverker.Holmgren,Dan.Wallin}@tdb.uu.se

Abstract. High-accuracy PDE solvers use multi-dimensional fast Fourier transforms. The FFTs exhibits a static and structured memory access pattern which results in a large amount of communication. Performance analysis of a non-trivial kernel representing a PDE solution algorithm has been carried out on a Sun WildFire computer. Here, different architecture, system and programming models can be studied. The WildFire system uses self-optimization techniques such as data migration and replication to change the placement of data at runtime. If the data placement is not optimal, the initial performance is degraded. However, after a few iterations the page migration daemon is able to modify the placement of data. The performance is improved, and equals what is achieved if the data is optimally placed at the start of the execution using hand tuning. The speedup for the PDE solution kernel is surprisingly good.

1 Introduction

The kernel in many important computational codes consists of multi-dimensional fast Fourier transforms, i.e. 2D, 3D, or higher-dimensional FFTs. One area where such computations arises is the numerical solution of partial differential equations (PDEs) using spectral or pseudospectral discretizations. Such methods are used in a wide spectrum of applications, e.g. computations of turbulent flows for optimization of aircraft performance, numerical weather prediction, and ab initio computations for predicting the outcome of chemical reactions.

When using discretization methods employing structured grids, the data is represented as large multi-dimensional arrays where the size is determined by the number of grid points. Using many grid points generally yields a more accurate solution. For multi-dimensional problems, the resolution is in practice often limited by the amount of main memory available. The major advantage of employing pseudospectral discretizations is that, for many problems, it gives the best possible accuracy for a given number of grid points.

The time-consuming part in a PDE solution algorithm consists of computing approximations of the derivatives. In a pseudospectral scheme, these computations are performed using multi-dimensional FFTs, which are *global* multi-stage grid operations. Each stage has a specific communication pattern involving a large amount of data, and every value in the solution array is updated using information originating from all other grid points. At a first glance, this is a very difficult situation for parallel computations. However, since the communication patterns are static and highly structured, efficient parallel implementations are possible. A number of quite efficient parallel implementations for multi-dimensional FFTs have been developed. For example, the FFTW package [3] includes both a multi-threaded (Pthreads) and a message passing (MPI) implementation.

We study a multi-threaded implementation of a kernel representing a PDE solver employing a pseudospectral discretization [10]. The aim is to examine the parallel performance of an important non-trivial algorithm with significant inherent communication on a cc-NUMA [6] system with SMP nodes. A similar investigation has earlier been performed for a finite difference solver kernel [9], which only involves local grid operations and very little communication. For our more realistic problem, we want to investigate the performance effects of self-optimizations such as page migration and replication. For a programmer, it is of interest to know how successful such techniques are. The result determines the importance of performing careful hand tuning, considering data allocation and thread scheduling policies.

The kernel algorithm is described in Section 2. The WildFire architecture and the different configurations used are presented in Section 3, and in Sections 4–7, a number of performance experiments are presented.

2 A Generic PDE Solver Using a Pseudospectral Method

The high-accuracy derivative approximation in a pseudospectral solver is performed by a convolution, i.e. a transform to frequency space, a local multiplication, and an inverse transform back again. For a uniform grid, the FFT and its inverse yield a very efficient tool for the transformations, resulting in $\mathcal{O}(n^2 \log_2 n)$ arithmetic complexity for computing the derivatives on a grid with n^2 grid points. Normally, the computation is performed within an iterative solver or a time-marching procedure. Hence, a representative kernel for a pseudospectral solver is an iteration where the loop body consists of convolution computations.

The standard implementation of a 2D FFT is to first perform 1D FFTs for all the columns in the data matrix, and then do the same for all the rows. In a convolution computation, this results in a five-stage scheme described in Figure 1. In general, it is sufficient to study 2D problems to get a picture of the performance also for multi-dimensional pseudospectral solvers, since the FFTs for the extra dimensions will be performed locally.

In Figure 1, each arrow represents a 1D FFT. For a vector of length n, this is a $\log_2 n$-stage computation involving a rather complex but structured communication pattern. There are a number of different FFT algorithms available, for a review see, e.g. [7]. In the experiments presented here, we use an in-place radix-2 Gentleman-Sande version of the FFT, and an radix-2 in-place Cooley-Tukey version for the inverse transforms. This allows for a convolution algorithm where no

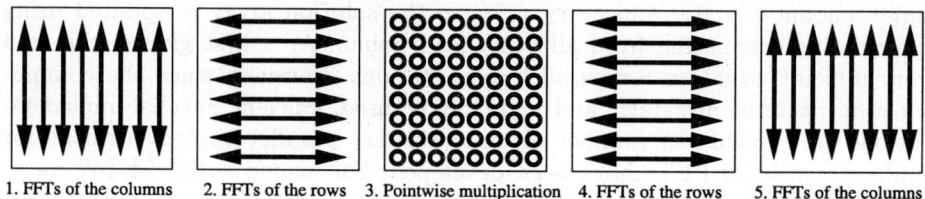

Fig. 1. A single convolution computation for a 2D problem

bit-reversal permutations are required. This is important, since the bit-reversal permutation introduces a lot of communication, and affects the performance significantly. Also, the FFTs should be performed in situ. If workspace is used, the maximal number of grid points is reduced, leading to a less resolved solution.

3 A Self-Optimizing cc-NUMA Architecture

The Sun WildFire system [5] is a prototype architecture developed to evaluate a scalable alternative to symmetric multiprocessors (SMPs). WildFire can be viewed as a cc-NUMA system with self-optimizing features, built from unusually large SMP nodes. Up to four nodes, each with up to 28 CPUs, can be directly connected by a point-to-point network between the WildFire Interfaces (WFI) in each node.

The experiments presented in this paper have been performed on the two-node WildFire system Albireo at the Department of Scientific Computing, Uppsala University. Each node has 16 processors (250 MHz UltraSPARC II with 4 Mbyte L2 cache) and 4 Gbyte memory. Logically, there is no difference between accessing local and remote memory, even though the access time varies: 310ns for local and 1700ns for remote memory. Coherence between all the 32 caches is maintained in hardware, which creates an illusion of a system with 8 Gbyte shared memory.

In order to ease the burden on the programmer, different forms of optimization are supported by the system. A software daemon detects pages which have been placed in the wrong node and migrates them to the other node. The daemon also detects pages used by threads in both nodes and replicates them. Wild-Fire's cache coherence protocol keeps the coherence between replicated memory pages with a cache line granularity. This is called *Coherent Memory Replication* (CMR), but the technique is also sometimes referred to as Simple COMA (S-COMA) [4]. The maximal number of replicated pages as well as other parameters in the page migration and CMR algorithms may be altered by modifying system parameters.

The codes were written in Fortran 90 using double precision complex (16 byte) data. The program was compiled and parallelized using the Sun Forte 6.1 compiler employing OpenMP-directives. In OpenMP, we use the default static scheduling. The experiments were performed on a lightly loaded system.

On WildFire, allocation of data uses a first-touch policy. The allocate statement reserves virtual address space, and the physical memory is allocated on the node where the thread first touching the data resides. The threads normally stay on the processor they are spawned at. The default WildFire scheduling policy is to, if possible, confine the threads to a single node. Only if the number of threads is larger than the number of processors in the first node, threads are spawned also on the other node. The compiler does not support memory placement directives. However, data distribution can be achieved by using a system call to bind the threads to a specific node and utilize the first-touch policy. Data placement should therefore be carried out within a parallel region to achieve a beneficial allocation.

If both page migration and CMR are disabled, the code will run in pure cc-NUMA mode. We have used the configurations listed below. Here, thread matched allocation means that the data is allocated such that the FFTs in phase 1 can be computed without introducing any remote accesses:

1. **Single node SMP** - Data is allocated on one node. The threads are bound to the same node. Migration and replication is turned off.
2. **Single node allocation WildFire** - Data is allocated on one node. The threads are not bound, and the WildFire default scheduling algorithm is used. Migration and replication is turned on.
3. **Thread-matched allocation WildFire** - Data is allocated using thread matching. The threads are not bound, and the WildFire default scheduling algorithm is used. Migration and replication is turned on.
4. **Single node allocation balanced WildFire** - Data is allocated on one node. The threads are evenly distributed between the two nodes and bound. Migration and replication is turned on.
5. **Thread-matched allocation balanced WildFire** - Data is allocated using thread matching. The threads are evenly distributed between the two nodes and bound. Migration and replication is turned on.
6. **Single node allocation balanced cc-NUMA** - Data is allocated on one node. The threads are evenly distributed between the nodes and bound. Migration and replication is turned off.
7. **Thread-matched allocation balanced cc-NUMA** - Data is allocated using thread matching. The threads are evenly distributed between the nodes and bound. Migration and replication is turned off.

4 Parallelization of the Pseudospectral Solver Kernel

As seen in Figure 1, the 1D FFTs in the convolution algorithm are first carried out for the columns of the data matrix, and then for the rows. For large number of grid points, experiments show that applying the FFTs directly to the matrix rows is not efficient. Using this type of implementation leads to extremely poor cache utilization, and the performance and speedup for large problems is not acceptable. If the threads reside in both nodes, optimizations like page migration and CMR are not able to detect and adapt to the changing access pattern fast enough, and in practice almost no migration/replication occurs. Hence, a large amount of remote accesses further degrades the performance.

To improve cache utilization and to allow for more efficient communication between the nodes, our experiments show that a better scheme is to explicitly transpose the data matrix, and again apply the FFTs to matrix columns. After applying the 1D FFTs in one direction, FFTs in the other direction should be computed. If the threads reside on more than one SMP node, some data will always be located on a remote node when the transpose is performed. On a two-node system with evenly distributed data, the lower left and the upper right matrix blocks will have to be exchanged between the nodes in the transpose operation, see Figure 2. Half of the data matrix will bounce back and forth

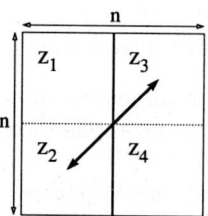

Fig. 2. The $n \times n$ matrix z consists of the blocks z_1, z_2, z_3 and z_4. If the data is evenly distributed between the two SMP nodes, the z_2 and z_3 block will travel across the WFI when the matrix transpose is applied

between the two nodes, still causing a large amount of communication over the WFI. In our implementation, the parallel transpose operation is performed using the ZTRANS routine in the Sun Performance Library.

5 Impact of Migration and Replication

The time per iteration for the PDE solver kernel for several configurations using 24 threads is shown in Figure 3(a).

The performance results for the finite difference algorithm presented in [9] are derived using the single node allocation WildFire configuration (2). Using the same setting, the results for the pseudospectral solver kernel are similar. There is a significant decrease of the time per iteration during the first 6-7 iterations, and then the curve levels out. The WildFire optimizations move/replicate data from the remote to the local node, and remote accesses become more and more rare. Hence, the time per iteration decreases to a steady-state. Further investigation shows that the amount of replicated pages is small. The number of pages migrated is large at the beginning but decreases over time. The same phenomena is also present for the single node allocation WildFire with balanced thread scheduling (4), but here the initial time per iteration is shorter. The reason could be that, when all processors on a single node are computing as in configuration

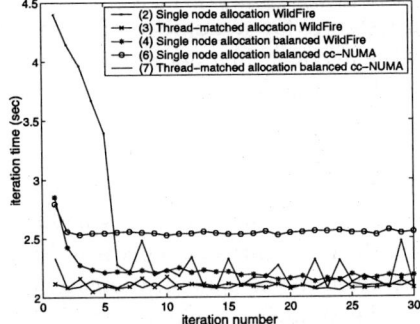 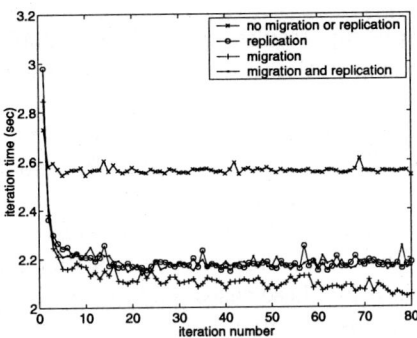

(a) Iteration times for the first iterations on different computer configurations.

(b) Iteration times for the single node allocation balanced configurations.

Fig. 3. Results for a 2048 × 2048 grid using 24 threads

(2), the bus is heavily loaded in this node, and the bandwidth available for page migration will be small. The page migration daemon will suffer from this, and the migrating pages will be unaccessable for a longer time.

Using all the threads in a single node for computations leads to large variation in iteration times, probably because activities of other users stall the computations. This is most apparent in the WildFire configurations with the default scheduling policy (2,3).

For the other configurations shown in Figure 3(a), the behavior is different. The first iteration takes longer time, but after this, a steady-state is immediately reached. Here, the relatively slow first iteration can be explained by cache effects. For the cc-NUMA configurations (6) and (7) the result is natural, since the adaptive optimizations are shut off. For the single node allocation balanced cc-NUMA configuration (6), one of the nodes perform exclusively remote accesses, leading to unbalanced execution times and a significantly larger time per iteration in steady-state.

The performance is almost the same for the thread-matched allocation WildFire (3) and cc-NUMA configurations (7). The memory is initially optimally placed for the first FFT, and in the matrix transpose a minimal amount of communication takes place. The WildFire optimizations are not activated, but it is also clear that they do not introduce any performance degradation.

Figure 3(b) shows an interesting, but not yet fully understood, result. Here, the single node allocation WildFire (4) configuration has been tested with different optimization strategies. With no migration and replication, the configuration is equivalent to the cc-NUMA case (6). The default setting is to enable both optimizations. Interestingly, the best results are achieved when only migration is enabled, and similar results have been observed also for a number of different problem sizes.

6 Speedup

Speedup results for a 2048 × 2048 grid are shown for a number of different configurations in Figure 4. The graphs show the average time per iteration when steady-state has been reached, c.f. Section 5. The results are normalized by the execution time of a single thread.

In general, the results are remarkably good. As mentioned before, the algorithm uses global operations, and involves heavy communication. The single node SMP (1) and the WildFire configurations using the standard scheduling policy (2,3) show very similar behavior up to about 14 threads. This is natural, since for these cases only one SMP node is involved in the computations. For 16 threads, the first SMP node is filled, and for the WildFire configurations (2,3), it is possible that one of the threads have been moved by the OS scheduler to the other (almost idle) SMP node. This is not possible for the SMP configuration (1), where the threads are bound to a single node. Again, the problem of computing on a filled SMP node results in a degradation of performance.

There is a short plateau in the speedup curve around 16 threads for the WildFire configurations (2,3). Here, the threads begin to be spawned on the other SMP node. For the balanced configurations (5,7), there is a more even growth in speedup as the number of threads is increased. The amount of communication causing remote accesses is constant, which should result in a smooth speedup curve. The communication results in that it is favorable to use the default thread scheduling, compared to spawning the threads in a balanced way on the two nodes.

The speedup is considerably smaller for the single node allocation cc-NUMA configuration (6) than for the other configurations. The reason is again that a large amount of remote accesses are being performed by threads in one of the nodes.

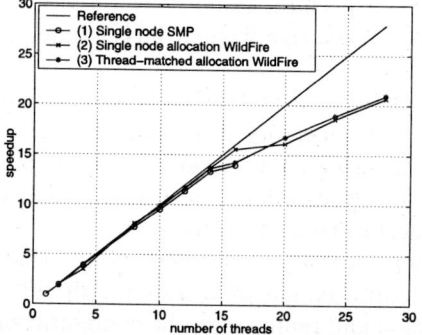 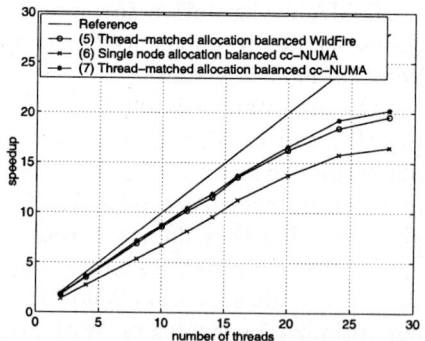

Fig. 4. The speedup for different configurations, compared to the execution time of a single thread. The grid size is 2048 × 2048

7 Impact of Problem Size

For the single node allocation WildFire configurations, we find that the number of iterations performed before steady-state is reached grows as the number of grid points is increased. This result is consistent with the results in [9].

As seen in Figure 5, there is no performance gain in using more than one SMP node for a small problem. However, as the problem size grows, the slope of the speedup curve once again approaches the ideal speedup ratio when the "WildFire-plateau" mentioned in Section 6 has been passed. For a very large grid, possibly more than two dimensions, the performance gain from using more than one SMP node will be large. Note that, for such problems, the memory of the additional SMP nodes will probably also be needed.

8 Conclusions

The pseudospectral solver kernel is an example of a non-trivial algorithm with heavy communication. The parallelization on the WildFire system is surprisingly successful; Using 28 OpenMP threads distributed over two SMP nodes, the speedup is approximately 21. For problems of interest in applications, the number of grid points will be even larger than used in the experiments, and the performance will probably be further improved.

The WildFire system will perform page migration if the initial distribution of data over the SMP nodes is not optimal. After some iterations, a steady-state is reached where no further migration occurs. For all configurations where the data is optimally distributed in steady-state, the difference in performance is very small. The WildFire migration optimization makes up for programming errors and/or deficiencies in the programming model, without introducing a performance loss when the data is optimally placed from the beginning. Note that, if the data is allocated on only one of the nodes and the optimizations are disabled, i.e. the code is executed in pure cc-NUMA mode (configuration 6), the performance is significantly reduced.

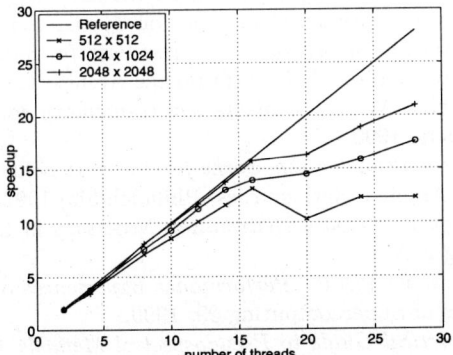

Fig. 5. Thread-matched WildFire configuration (3) speedups

The WildFire system using the default configuration exhibits a typical speed-up behavior for a problem involving communication, e.g. the pseudospectral solver kernel: Until the number of threads is almost equal to the number of processors in an SMP node, the performance is identical to that of the SMP. When the number of threads is further increased, there is a short plateau in the speedup curve before it starts to grow again. If the problem is large enough, the slope of the speedup curve will again be close to optimal.

The speedup curve becomes smoother using a balanced thread scheduling policy. For the pseudospectral solver this implies a small performance loss when the number of threads is small, because of the large amount of communication over the WFI. However, distributing the threads in a balanced way over the SMP nodes might yield improved performance for a memory bound algorithm with a small amount of communication.

Note that the initial distribution of data has a large effect on the execution time if the convolution in the pseudospectral solver is only performed a small number of times. The goal of algorithm improvements, e.g. preconditioning, is to reduce the number of iterations in the computational scheme. It is important to make sure that the data is optimally distributed from the beginning if only a few iterations are required. There is currently discussion whether directives for data distribution should be included in OpenMP [8,1]. Data placement can be achieved without such directives on the WildFire system using the first-touch scheduling policy. In certain cases, when data can not be accessed within a parallel region, e.g. file I/O, data distribution directives would be useful.

References

1. Bircsak J. et al., *Extending OpenMP for NUMA Machines*, Proceedings of Supercomputing 2000.
2. Falsafi M., Wood D. A., *Reactive NUMA: A Design for Unifying S-COMA with CC-NUMA*, Proceedings of ACM/IEEE International Symposium on Computer Architecture 1997.
3. Frigo M., Johnson S. G., *FFTW: An Adaptive Software Architecture for the FFT*, 1998 ICASSP proceedings (vol. 3, p. 1381).
4. Hagersten E., Saulsbury A., Landin A, *Simple COMA Node Implementations*, Proceedings of Hawaii International Conference on System Science, 1994.
5. Hagersten E., Koster M., *WildFire: A Scalable Path for SMPs*, Proceedings of 5th International Symposium on High-Performance Architecture, 1999.
6. Lenoski D. E., Weber W. D., *Scalable shared-memory multiprocessing*, Morgan Kaufmann publishers, 1995.
7. van Loan C., *Computational Frameworks for the Fast Fourier Transform*, Society for Industrial and Applied Mathematics, Philadelphia, 1992.
8. Nikolopoulo D. S. et al., *Is Data Distribution Necessary in OpenMP?*, Proceedings of Supercomputing 2000.
9. Noordergraaf L., van der Pas R., *Performance Experiences on Sun's WildFire Prototype*, Proceedings of Supercomputing 99, 1999.
10. Fornberg F., *A Practical Guide to Pseudospectral Methods*, Cambridge University Press, 1998.

Topic 12
Routing and Communication in Interconnection Networks

Ramón Beivide, Chris Jesshope, Antonio Robles, and Cruz Izu

Topic Chairpersons

We would like to welcome you to the Euro-Par 2001 topic on Routing and Communication in Interconnection Networks. The selected papers, the corresponding presentations as well as the interaction with other researchers promise to be both useful and enjoyable. We also hope that you enjoy your visit to Manchester.

The Routing and Communication in Interconnection Networks topic is devoted to research about interconnection subsystems for parallel computers and networks of workstations. All aspects of communication, including topologies, routing, flow control mechanisms, deadlock management, network packaging and implementation, performance evaluation and network modelling, among others, were considered by the Programme Committee of this topic.

This year 11 papers were submitted to this topic. All papers were reviewed by four referees. The quality and range of the submitted papers led to a high degree of competition in the reviewing process. Using the referees' reports as the basis of discussion, the programme committee picked five of the submitted papers for publication and presentation at the conference. Three of them were selected as regular papers and two more as short papers. All of them were scheduled for presentation in one session on Thursday, the 30th of August.

The first paper by S. Loucif and M. Ould-Khaoua describes an analytical model able to forecast the behaviour of hypercube networks using deterministic routing in presence of hot-spots. The model's predictions are very close to those obtained by standard simulation. Therefore, this model can be used to obtain performance results of large networks that are infeasible by simulation due to the excessive computational resources needed.

The paper by R. Alcover, V. Chirivella and J. Duato presents a model to evaluate the fault-tolerance capabilities of direct interconnection networks. Using a methodology based on Markov chains, the authors can accurately compute the network reliability behaviour. The model is applied to the popular 2-D mesh and takes into account the network size, the routing algorithm and the rates of failure and repair.

The paper by L. Fernández, J. M. García and R. Casado deals with dynamic reconfiguration techniques oriented to networks of workstations. Among the different alternatives, the authors evaluate the viability and performance of a methodology based on deadlock recovery. The paper shows that deadlocks may become very infrequent with few virtual channels and that misrouting can be used in order to reduce the number of lost messages.

The last two contributions of this session will be presented as short papers. The first one by A. Shahrabi, M. Ould-Khaoua and L. M. Mackenzie presents an analytical model for predicting latency of unicast and multicast communications in wormhole-routed tori. The second one, by A. Pietracaprina and G. Pucci, presents randomized and deterministic algorithms for many-to-one routing on two-dimensional meshes.

In closing, we would like to thank the authors who submitted a contribution, as well as the Euro-Par Organizing Committee, and the scores of referees, whose efforts have made this conference, and the Routing and Communication in Interconnection Networks track possible.

An Analytical Model of Deterministic Routing in the Presence of Hot-Spot Traffic

Samia Loucif and Mohamed Ould-Khaoua

Department of Computing Science, University of Glasgow, G12 8RZ, U.K.
{samia,Mohamed}@dcs.gla.ac.uk

Abstract. Analytical models of deterministic routing in common wormhole-routed networks have been widely reported in the literature. However, all these models have been discussed for the uniform traffic pattern. This paper presents the first analytical model of deterministic routing in the hypercube in the presence of hot-spot traffic. Simulation results confirm that the proposed model predicts message latency with a reasonable degree of accuracy under different traffic conditions.

1 Introduction

Existing multicomputers [5], [6] have adopted wormhole switching [2] (also known as wormhole routing) due to its low buffering requirement and its use of pipelined data transmission to reduce communication latency.

Deterministic routing [2] has been widely used in practice [5], [6] because it uses a simple algorithm to ensure deadlock-freedom with a minimal hardware requirement, leading to an efficient router implementation [4]. Analytical models of deterministic routing in common wormhole-routed networks have been widely reported in the past [1], [3], [7]. All these models have been based on the assumption that the traffic distribution is uniform. However, there are many real-world parallel applications that exhibit non-uniform traffic patterns such as, for example, hot-spots. Hot-spots arise when a number of nodes direct a fraction of their generated messages to a single destination node.

Although adaptive routing [4] has been suggested by the research community after deterministic routing, very recently the authors in [9], [11] have proposed analytical models for adaptive routing in the presence of hot-spot traffic. To our best knowledge, no similar model has yet been reported for deterministic routing. In an effort to fill this gap, we present a new analytical model of deterministic routing in the presence of hot-spot traffic. In this paper, we report on our initial modelling efforts by discussing the model for the hypercube network. The rest of the paper is organised as follows. Section 2 describes the new analytical model while section 3 validates it through simulation. Section 4 concludes this study.

2 The Analytical Model

The model is based on the following assumptions, which are commonly accepted in the literature [1], [3], [7], [9], [11]. (a) Each node generates messages with a probability h of being directed to the hot-spot node, and probability $(1-h)$ of being directed equally probably to the other network nodes [10]. Let us refer to these two types of messages as "hot-spot" and "regular" messages, respectively. (b) Nodes generate traffic independently of each other, and follow a Poisson process, with a mean rate of λ_g messages/cycle. (c) Message length is M flits, each of which requires one cycle transmission time across a channel. (d) The local queue in the source node has infinite capacity. Messages are transferred to the local node as soon as they arrive at their destinations. (e) Messages, both hot-spot and regular, are routed in the network according to deterministic routing [2]. Network dimensions are numbered in an increasing order from 0 to $n-1$, and crossed by messages in that order.

The mean message latency is the time to cross the network, L, and the mean waiting time, w_s. Therefore, we can write

$$\text{Latency} = L + w_s . \tag{1}$$

If L^r and L^h be the mean network latency of a regular and hot-spot message, respectively, the mean network latency, L, can be expressed as

$$L = (1-h)L^r + hL^h . \tag{2}$$

The average number of channels, $\bar{d}^r$, crossed by a regular message is given by [7]

$$\bar{d}^r = \sum_{i=1}^{n} i \times C_i^n \Big/ N-1 . \tag{3}$$

Due to the symmetry of the hypercube topology, the average number of channels crossed by a hot-spot message to reach the hot-spot node, $\bar{d}^h$, is equal to $\bar{d}^r$. Let $\alpha (=1/2)$ be the probability that a regular message is at the right coordinate along dimension i, and therefore it skips that dimension, the rate of regular messages, $\lambda_i^{L,r}$, entering the network through dimension i $(0 \le i < n)$ is given by

$$\lambda_i^{L,r} = (1-\alpha)\alpha^i \lambda_g (1-h) . \tag{4}$$

Among the 2^{n-1} channels of dimension i $(0 \le i < n)$ in the network, only 2^{n-i-1} channels are used by hot-spot messages to enter the network. So, the rate of hot-spot messages, $\lambda_i^{L,h}$, which enter the network through a channel of dimension i is

$$\lambda_i^{L,h} = 2^{n-i-1} \lambda_g h / 2^{n-1} = \lambda_g h / 2^i . \tag{5}$$

The probability that a regular message arrives, from dimension j, at dimension i and crosses on its next hop dimension i $(j < i < n)$ is $(1-\alpha)^2 \alpha^{i-j-1}$. So, the total rate of regular messages, $\lambda_i^{P,r}$, arriving from the previous dimensions and crossing dimension i can be written as

$$\lambda_i^{P,r} = \begin{cases} 0 & i = 0 \\ \sum_{j=0}^{i-1}(1-\alpha)^2 \alpha^{i-j-1} \lambda_g (1-h) & 0 < i < n \end{cases} \qquad (6)$$

Hot-spot messages, which are at dimension i $(0 \le i < n)$, can arrive from any of the j $(0 \le j < i)$ previous dimensions. The total rate of hot-spot messages, $\lambda_i^{P,h}$, arriving at dimension i from the previous dimensions is found to be

$$\lambda_i^{P,h} = \begin{cases} 0 & i = 0 \\ \dfrac{\lambda_g h}{2^{n-i-1}} \sum_{j=0}^{i-1}\left[C_j^i \sum_{k=0}^{n-i-1} C_k^{n-i-1} \right] & 0 < i < n \end{cases} \qquad (7)$$

A regular message entering the network through dimension i $(0 \le i < n)$ sees a network latency S_i^r to reach its destination, and a mean service time T_i^r after exiting that dimension. Moreover, S_i^r is T_i^r increased by the mean blocking delay, B_i^r, experienced by the regular message at dimension i. Similarly for a hot-spot message, S_i^h is T_i^h, increased by B_i^h. Therefore, S_i^r and S_i^h are given by

$$S_i^r = T_i^r + B_i^r . \qquad (8)$$

$$S_i^h = T_i^h + B_i^h . \qquad (9)$$

Once a regular message exits dimension i $(0 \le i < n)$, it either terminates with the probability $P_{t_i}^r$ $(= \alpha^{n-i-1})$, or it crosses subsequent dimensions j $(i < j < n)$ with the probability $(1 - P_{t_i}^r)$. In the former case, the mean service time is only the consumption time at the ejection channel. In the latter case, however, the mean service time is the sum of the blocking delays at the subsequent dimensions j $(i < j < n)$, increased by the consumption time at the destination. So, T_i^r is

$$T_i^r = \begin{cases} M & i = n-1 \\ P_{t_i}^r M + (1 - P_{t_i}^r) \sum_{j=i+1}^{n-1} P_{j/i}^r (W_j^r + T_j^r) & 0 \le i < n-1 \end{cases} \qquad (10)$$

Let $P_{j/i}^r$ and W_j^r be the probability that a regular message passes dimension j after exiting dimension i, and the mean blocking delay experienced by the regular message when crossing dimension j, respectively. A regular message passes dimension j after exiting dimension i with a probability $P_{j/i}^r (=(1-\alpha)\alpha^{j-i-1})$. When a regular message arrives to dimension j $(i<j<n)$, it competes with regular and hot-spot messages crossing that dimension. To compute the mean waiting time, W_j^r, in the event of blocking, a physical channel is treated as an M/G/1 queue [8], and with the variance of the service time distribution approximated by $(S-M)^2$ (S being the mean service time of a given physical channel) [3]. W_j^r can be written as

$$W_j^r = \frac{\left[\lambda_j^{L,r} + \sum_{k=0,k\neq i}^{j-1}\lambda_k^{P,r}\right](T_j^r)^2\left[1+\frac{(T_j^r-M)^2}{(T_j^r)^2}\right]}{2\left[1-\left(\lambda_j^{L,r}+\sum_{k=0,k\neq i}^{j-1}\lambda_k^{P,r}\right)T_j^r\right]} + \frac{\left[\lambda_j^{L,h} + \sum_{k=0}^{j-1}\lambda_k^{P,h}\right](T_j^h)^2\left[1+\frac{(T_j^h-M)^2}{(T_j^h)^2}\right]}{2\left[1-\left(\lambda_j^{L,h}+\sum_{k=0}^{j-1}\lambda_k^{P,h}\right)T_j^h\right]} \quad (11)$$

Using a similar argument used above for the determination of T_i^r, the mean service time, T_i^h, seen by a hot-spot message when exiting dimension i, is given by

$$T_i^h = \begin{cases} M & i = n-1 \\ P_{t_i}^h M + (1-P_{t_i}^h)\sum_{j=i+1}^{n-1} P_{j/i}^h (W_j^h + T_j^h) & 0 \leq i < n-1 \end{cases}. \quad (12)$$

The probability that a hot-spot message terminates after crossing dimension i, $P_{t_i}^h$, is $1/2^{n-i-1}$, since only one channel among the 2^{n-i-1} channels of dimension i is directly connected to the hot-spot node. The total number of nodes that can generate or forward hot-spot messages on channels of dimension i is 2^{n-i-1}. When these messages exit dimension i, only 2^{n-j-1} nodes forward these messages on dimension j. Therefore, the probability that a hot-spot message crosses dimension j after exiting dimension i is $P_{j/i}^h (=2^{i-j})$.

A hot-spot message crossing dimension j, and arriving from dimension i, competes with regular and hot-spot messages crossing that dimension. We can therefore write W_j^h as

$$W_j^h = \frac{\left[\lambda_j^{L,r} + \sum_{k=0}^{j-1}\lambda_k^{P,r}\right](T_j^r)^2\left[1+\frac{(T_j^r-M)^2}{(T_j^r)^2}\right]}{2\left[1-\left(\lambda_j^{L,r}+\sum_{k=0}^{j-1}\lambda_k^{P,r}\right)T_j^r\right]} + \frac{\left[\lambda_j^{L,h} + \sum_{k=0,k\neq i}^{j-1}\lambda_k^{P,h}\right](T_j^h)^2\left[1+\frac{(T_j^h-M)^2}{(T_j^h)^2}\right]}{2\left[1-\left(\lambda_j^{L,h}+\sum_{k=0,k\neq i}^{j-1}\lambda_k^{P,h}\right)T_j^h\right]} \quad (13)$$

The mean blocking delay, B_i^r, experienced by a regular message entering dimension i is found to be

$$B_i^r = \frac{\sum_{j=0}^{i-1}\lambda_j^{P,r}(T_i^r)^2\left[1+\frac{(T_i^r-M)^2}{(T_i^r)^2}\right]}{2\left[1-\sum_{j=0}^{i-1}\lambda_j^{P,r}T_i^r\right]} + \frac{\left[\lambda_i^{L,h}+\sum_{j=0}^{i-1}\lambda_j^{P,h}\right](T_i^h)^2\left[1+\frac{(T_i^h-M)^2}{(T_i^h)^2}\right]}{2\left[1-\left(\lambda_i^{L,h}+\sum_{j=0}^{i-1}\lambda_j^{P,h}\right)T_i^h\right]}. \quad (14)$$

Similarly, the mean blocking delay, B_i^h, experienced by a hot-spot message entering dimension i is found to be

$$B_i^h = \frac{\left[\lambda_i^{L,r}+\sum_{j=0}^{i-1}\lambda_j^{P,r}\right](T_i^r)^2\left[1+\frac{(T_i^r-M)^2}{(T_i^r)^2}\right]}{2\left[1-\left(\lambda_i^{L,r}+\sum_{j=0}^{i-1}\lambda_j^{P,r}\right)T_i^r\right]} + \frac{\sum_{j=0}^{i-1}\lambda_j^{P,h}(T_i^h)^2\left[1+\frac{(T_i^h-M)^2}{(T_i^h)^2}\right]}{2\left[1-\sum_{j=0}^{i-1}\lambda_j^{P,h}T_i^h\right]}. \quad (15)$$

A regular message enters the network through dimension i ($0 \leq i < n$) with the probability p_i^r ($=(1-\alpha)\alpha^i$). Taking into account all possible ways that a regular message can enter the network, L^r is given by

$$L^r = \overline{d}^r + \sum_{i=0}^{n-1} p_i^r S_i^r. \quad (16)$$

Similarly, a hot-spot message enters the network through dimension i with the probability p_i^h ($= 2^{n-i-1}/(N-1)$). So, L^h can be written as

$$L^h = \overline{d}^h + \sum_{i=0}^{n-1} p_i^h S_i^h. \quad (17)$$

Finally, the mean waiting time seen by a message (regular or hot-spot) at the source is expressed as

$$w_s = \lambda_g L^2\left(1+\frac{(L-M)^2}{L^2}\right)\Big/[2(1-\lambda_g L)]. \quad (18)$$

3 Validation of the Model

The above model has been validated through a discrete-event simulator that mimics the behavior of deterministic routing in the network at the flit level. For the sake of specific illustration and due to space limitation, we provide results for the following cases only: network size is $N=2^8$ nodes, message length is $M=32$ and 100 flits reflecting the cases of short and moderately long messages, respectively; fraction of hot-spot traffic is set to $h = 0.08$, 0.15, and 0.30.

Fig. 1 and Fig. 2 reveal that the analytical model predicts the mean message latency with a close degree of accuracy when the network is in the steady state regions. However, there are discrepancies in the results provided by the model and simulation when the network is under heavy traffic. This is due to the approximations that have been made in the analysis to ease the model development like, for instance, the approximation used for computing the variance of the service time at a given channel. Such an approximation allows us to avoid computing the exact distribution of the message service time, and which is not a straightforward task due to the interdependencies between service times at successive channels. Nonetheless, given that most evaluation studies focus on network performance in the steady state regions, we can conclude that the proposed model can be a practical evaluation tool that can help network designers to gain an insight into the dynamic behavior of deterministic routing in the presence of hot-spot traffic.

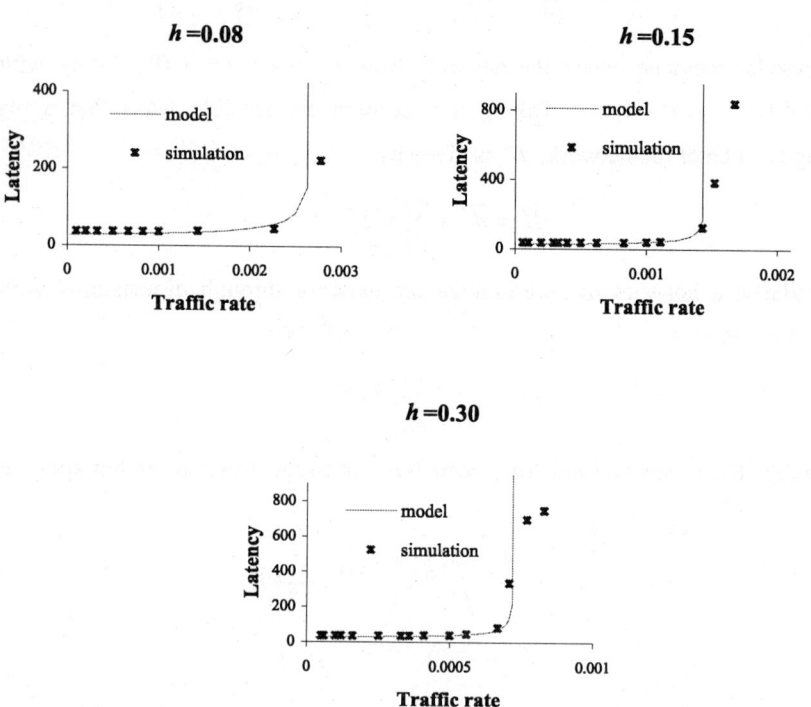

Fig. 1. Latency predicted by the model against simulation in the 2^8 hypercube, $M=32$ flits

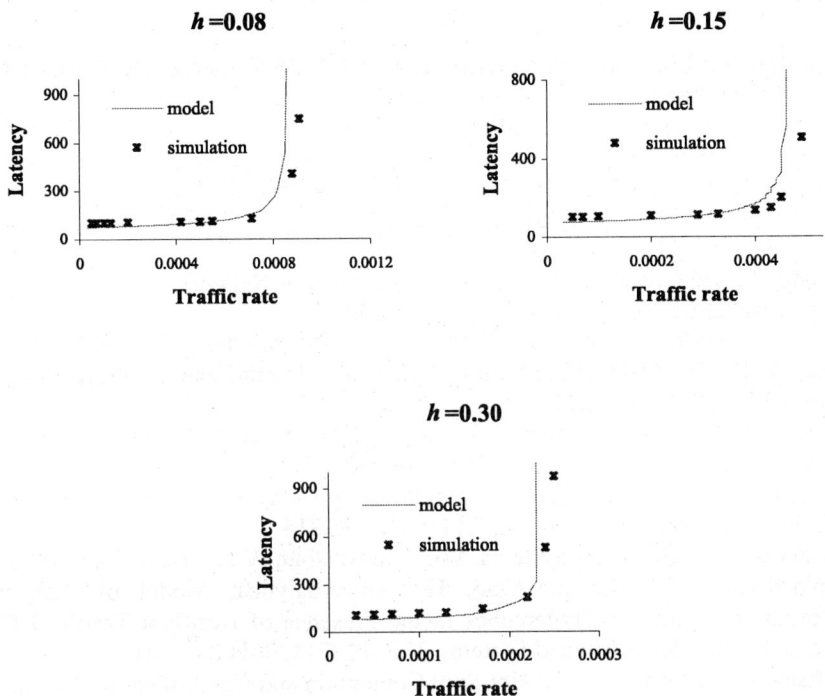

Fig. 2. Latency predicted by the model against simulation in the 2^8 hypercube, $M=100$ flits

4 Conclusion

Several analytical models of deterministic routing have been proposed for wormhole-routed networks under the uniform traffic pattern. However, there are many real-world parallel applications which generate non-uniform traffic patterns, e.g. hot-spots, in the network. This paper has presented the first analytical model to compute the mean message latency in wormhole-routed hypercubes with deterministic routing in the presence of hot-spot traffic. Simulation experiments have revealed that the analytical model produces latency results which are in a good agreement with those produced by simulation. Our next objective is to extend the above model to k-ary n-cubes, and to develop new and simple analytical models of deterministic routing under other important non-uniform traffic patterns.

References

1. Agrawal, A.: Limits on Interconnection Network Performance. IEEE Parallel & Distributed Systems, Vol. 2 (1991) 398-412
2. Dally, W. J., Seitz, C.: Deadlock-Free Message Routing in Multiprocessor Interconnection Networks. IEEE Trans. Computers, Vol. 36 (5) (1987) 547-553
3. Draper, J. T., Ghosh, J.: A Comprehensive Analytical Model for Wormhole Routing in Multicomputer Systems. J. Parallel & Distributed Computing, Vol. 23 (1994) 202-214
4. Duato, J., Yalamanchili, S., Ni, L.: Interconnection Networks: An Engineering Approach. IEEE Computer Society Press (1997)
5. Fillo, M., Keckler, S. W., Dally, W. J., Carter, N. P., Chang, A., Gurevich, Y., Lee, W. S.: The M-Machine Multicomputer. Int. Journal Parallel Programming, Vol. 25 (3) (1997) 183-212
6. Kessler, R. E., Swarszmeier, J .L.: Cray T3D: A New Dimension for Cray Research. in Compcon, Spring (1993) 176-182
7. Kim, J., Das, C. R.: Hypercube Communication Delay with Wormhole Routing. IEEE Trans. Computers, Vol. 43 (7) (1994) 806-814
8. Kleinrock, L.: Queueing Systems. Vol. 1 (eds): John Wiley, New York (1975)
9. Ould-Khaoua, M., Sarbazi-Azad, H.: An Analytical Model of Adaptive Wormhole Routing in Hypercubes In the Presence of Hot-Spot Traffic. IEEE Trans. Parallel & Distributed Systems, Vol. 12 (3) (2001) 283-288
10. Pfister, G. J., Norton, V. A.: Hot-Spot Contention and Combining in Multistage Interconnection Networks. IEEE Trans. Computers, Vol. 34 (10) (1985) 943-948
11. Sarbazi-Azad, H., Mackenzie, L., Ould-Khaoua, M.: An Analytical Model of Fully-Adaptive Wormhole-Routed k-ary n-cubes in the Presence of Hot-Spot Traffic. Proc. Proc. 14th Int. Parallel & Distributed Processing Symposium (IPDPS'2000), IEEE Computer Society (2000) 605-610

Improving the Accuracy of Reliability Models for Direct Interconnection Networks*

Rosa Alcover[1], Vicente Chirivella[1], and José Duato[2]

[1]Department of Statistics and Operation Research,
{ralcover,vchirive}@eio.upv.es
[2] Department of Information Systems and Computer Architecture
Polytechnic University of Valencia,
Camino de Vera s/n, 46020 Valencia, Spain
jduato@gap.upv.es

Abstract. Fault-tolerance in multicomputer interconnection networks has been traditionally studied by determining the worst possible combination of faulty components that causes a network failure and then assuming that this will occur. But, the worst possible combination may occur with low probability and the routing algorithm may allow the network to work, even when there is a large number of faults. Thus, the network dependability parameters computed according to this approach will be underestimated. In a previous paper [3], we have proposed a new methodology, based on Markov chains, for evaluating interconnection network dependability. Using this methodology, we can accurately compute the network reliability behavior. In this paper we apply it to evaluate dependability parameters in a 2-D mesh, taking into account network size, routing algorithm, failure and repair rates of nodes and coverage. Finally, we compare the computed results under traditional and our approach.

1 Introduction

Day by day, many scientific disciplines demand more computing power. These demands should be satisfied by new generations of multicomputers constructed with larger number of processors. As the number of elements in the interconnection networks increases with the number of processing units, the probability of component failures increases too. Therefore, the network fault-tolerance properties are a key issue in determining the overall performance of these machines. Dependability [2] analysis of multicomputers is essential to evaluate their effectiveness for critical and real time applications.

The objective is to design an interconnection network that works in the presence of faulty components. Fault-tolerant routing algorithms allow to achieve this objective

---

* This work was supported by the Polytechnic University of Valencia under Grant 6645.

[5], [7] because they bypass faulty components, taking advantage of the alternative paths existing in the network. However, the maximum number of faults supported by these algorithms is bounded [5].

On the other hand, although many fault-tolerant routing algorithms have been proposed, hardly any one has been implemented in commercial machines. Nevertheless, some commercial machines implement simple fault-tolerant routing algorithms, for instance, the Cray T3E [8]. When fault-tolerant routing algorithms are defined, the authors determine the maximum number of failures that the algorithms can support. This number corresponds to the worst possible combination of failure positions that leads to the network failure [7]. Of course, this number is bounded by the interconnection network topology. For these cases, very few papers analyze the behavior of the network when the number of faults goes beyond the limits imposed by topology. The only studies we know about this have been performed from an experimental point of view, by randomly generating sets of faulty components [4], [7], [9]. As a consequence, there is not a clear idea about the system reliability based on those routing algorithms. This is the traditional approach. However, the worst possible combination does not always occur, and the routing algorithm is usually able to route in the presence of a larger number of failures. This fact has not been considered in previous papers and is the focus of our research.

In a previous paper [3] we proposed an analytical methodology for reliability and availability prediction of interconnection networks based on *continuous-parameter Markov chains* [2]. This methodology takes into account the topology, network size and the routing algorithm used, and allow us to measure the effect of the routing algorithm in the interconnection network reliability.

In this paper, we apply this methodology to evaluate dependability parameters in a mesh. Also, we measure the differences between the traditional approach and a more accurate one, in connection with these parameters. We summarize this methodology in section 2. Then, in section 3 we apply it to compute the reliability function and the mean time to failure for an interconnection network with mesh topology, wormhole switching and Duato's Double East Last West Last (DELWL) fault tolerant routing algorithm [5].Also, we propose a model to compute the reliability function and the mean time to failure for an interconnection network, and we compare the obtained results with both approaches. We show that network reliability parameters obtained with the traditional approach are always underestimated. Finally, in section 4 some conclusions are drawn in connection with our previous paper.

2 A Basic Dependability Methodology Based on Markov Chains

In our previous paper [3] we proposed the basic dependability methodology. It can be briefly summarized in the following steps:

1- Define the Interconnection Network Fault Model.
2 - Select the network dependability parameters.
3 - Define the network states and the transition rates.
4 - Compute the values of the network reliability parameters.
5 - Analyze the results.

3 Applying the Dependability Methodology

In this section we apply the analytical methodology summarized in section 2. We also propose two models to compute the reliability function ($R(t)$) and the mean time to failure ($MTTF$) for a network with mesh topology. One model is proposed from the traditional point of view and the other under our approach.

Step 1. The interconnection network fault model includes the network selection and the establishment of the assumed hypothesis about its operation.

As in our previous paper, the interconnection network selected is a mesh, with wormhole switching as flow control mechanism, and the DELWL fault-tolerant routing algorithm. Unlike our previous paper, channels are reliable and only the node failures are studied in this paper.

Concerning to the hypothesis assumed in the network fault model, we suppose that a network fails when a node cannot communicate with another one, either because there are no physical links between them, or because the routing algorithm cannot select a route to reach the destination node. We also assume that if there is a selectable path between two nodes, the path will be selected. Some faulty node positions combination may disconnect the network. If the network is disconnected, the network fails. A failed node simply ceases to work, and the channels connected to a malfunctioning node are not selected by the routing algorithm.

Fault-tolerant routing algorithms automatically recover the system from the occurrence of some node failures during normal operation. The recovery consists on the detection of the fault, the identification of the faulty node, the correction of the errors induced by the fault, and notification to the neighboring nodes that there is a faulty node in the network. However, fault detection mechanisms can fail with a certain probability. The probability of system recovery when a fault occurs is called coverage, C [6]. This probability is assumed to be constant. Finally, the network is repairable, either after a complete failure, or after the partial failure of some nodes.

The modeling of network operation has been based on continuous-parameter Markov chains. We have considered exponential distribution with λ parameter for the nodes failure times, with μ parameter for the nodes reparation times, and a uniform distribution of message destinations. The mean time to node failure is measured in months, its typical value being between 1 and 6 months. The lowest value corresponds to machines mounted in rooms and wired externally, while the highest one corresponds to multicomputers assembled in cabinets. The mean time to node repair is measured in hours. We have considered 3, 6, 12, 24, 48 and 72 hours. The lowest value corresponds to military applications, while the highest values correspond to non-critical applications. Finally, the chosen values for C are 0'95, 0'99 and 0'999.

Step 2. In this step, we must select the parameters that will quantify the dependability characteristics that we want to study. For the sake of clarity, in this paper we have selected the reliability function $R(t)$, and the mean time to failure $MTTF$ [1].

Step 3. Now, we define the Markov chains used for modeling the two approaches proposed in this paper. For this, we must specify the states that represent the network operation and establish the transitions between them. First, we define the model from the traditional approach. Then, we will do the same with our approach, and will pay special attention to the expressions of the transition rates between states.

A Markov chain consists of a set of states and a set of labeled transitions between the states. In our paper, we define the states taking into account the *MTTF* and according to the number of faulty nodes in the network. Thus, we have considered the following states in the models: *Correct State*, when there is no faulty node; *Degraded State*, when there is a faulty node, but the fault detection mechanisms have detected the fault and the routing algorithm can transmit messages between any pair of nodes; and *Failed State*, when the failure of the network occurs, whatever its cause is.

After a sojourn in a state, the network state will make a transition to another state, with a certain probability, according to its functioning. Transition rates are the change with time of the probability of transit from one state to another state. With the previous states, we propose two models (shown in Figure 1) to compute the network reliability function. The model on the left corresponds to the traditional approach, while the other one fits to our approach. The traditional approach to fault-tolerant routing on a 2-D mesh assumes that the routing algorithm can support a single failure; that is, the network fails with the failure of the second node (worst combination). Thus, the transition rates among states depend on the size of the mesh, but not on the algorithm used for routing. As it is considered that the algorithm cannot route after the second failure, there are no differences among fault-tolerant routing algorithms proposed by different authors.

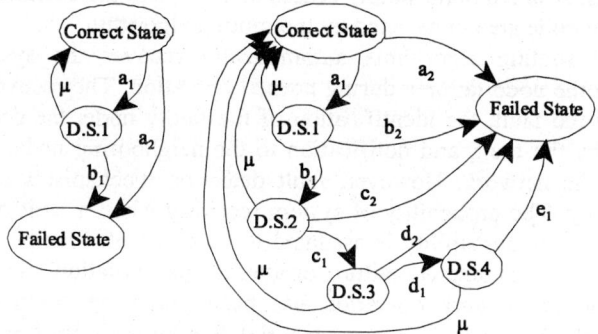

Fig. 1. Reliability models. Traditional (left) and new approach (right)

The model on the left in Figure 1 allows us to obtain $R(t)$. From the *Correct State*, the network changes to the *Degraded State*, D.S.1 (transition rate $a1$) if a failure occurs and the fault is covered, or to the *Failed State* ($a2$) if the fault is uncovered. In the *D.S.1*, the network changes to the *Correct State* if repaired (μ) or to the *Failed State* when the next failure occurs ($b1$). For example, in a 16x16 mesh, the transition rate $a1$ is the product of the number of nodes (256), the coverage and the node failure rate ($a1=256C\lambda$); $a2$ is the product of the number of nodes, the failure probability in the fault detection mechanism and the node failure rate ($a2=256(1-C)\lambda$); $b1$ is the product of the number of remaining non-faulty nodes and the node failure rate ($b1=255\lambda$).

As the algorithm can route messages if certain combinations of failure locations occur, the transition probabilities will depend on the fault-tolerant routing algorithm chosen and on the mesh size. The state diagram on the right in Figure1, shows the model when our approach is used. The network starts in the *Correct State* and evolves to the *Degraded State* when a fault occurs if the failure is covered and, the routing algorithm can still establish communication between any pair of nodes. The network changes to the *Failed State* if at least one of the two conditions fails. The difference with the previous model is that from a *Degraded State*, the network can reach another *Degraded State*. The transition rate between the two states depends on the ability of the routing algorithm to maintain communication after a new failure. We consider that after the fifth faulty node, the network performance are too low. Thus, after the *D.S.4* the network evolves to the *Failed State*.

The evolution of the network state could be explained as follows. The network initial state is the *Correct State*. As failures occur, the network state evolves into the final *Degraded States*, if the faults are covered, or to the *Failed State* if the fault is not covered. When λ is small, the network spends most of the time in the *Correct State* and the initial *Degraded States*, specially when C is high. This is due to the long time to network failure and the high repair rate. If the network is repaired quickly, the network will usually be in the *Correct State*, and it will move away from this state as time to repair increases. If C is high, the network will tend to move to the degraded states and there will be more opportunities to repair the network. The failure of the network usually occurs when a failure is not covered rather than when many connections have failed. As the node failure rate increases, the network state evolves to intermediate degraded states. The network can be repaired and its more frequent states are the *Correct State* and the intermediate *Degraded States*, although now the *Failed State* is reached more frequently. As C increases, the network tends to continue working because it has more opportunities to be repaired. The failure of the network occurs more frequently when the number of node failures reaches the maximum number of failed nodes allowed. When the node failure rate is high, the network quickly evolves to the *Failed State*. A high value of μ allows the network to work. Otherwise the network will be repaired only in a very few occasions.

Given a topology, a routing algorithm and a number of faulty nodes, it is necessary to study the combinations of faulty locations that cause the network to fail. Then, the transition rates can be computed. In our model, the expression of the transition rate $q_{i,i+1}$ from the *Degraded State i* ($i \geq 0$) to the next *Degraded State i+1* is given by

$$q_{i,i+1} = (N-i)rp_{i+1}C\lambda, \tag{1}$$

and the transition rate from the *Degraded State i* to the *Failed State* is given by

$$q_{i,F.S.} = (N-i)(1-rp_{i+1}C)\lambda, \tag{2}$$

with

$$rp_{i+1} = nfc_{i+1}/(ncf_i(N-i))$$

where N is the number of nodes; rp_{i+1} is the probability of network working when a new failure takes place, knowing that i failures have already taken place in an operational network; and nfc_{i+1} is the number of combinations of $i+1$ faulty nodes that do not cause the network failure, knowing that such combinations are obtained from the combinations of i faulty nodes that did not cause the network failure, with the positions of a new faulty node. For example, taking into account the network size (16x16) and the routing algorithm, the transition rate *b1* from *D.S.1* to *D.S.2*, computed with equation (1), is now the product of the number of remaining non faulty nodes, the probability of routing after the occurrence of two given failures, the fault coverage and the failure rate of a node. So, the expressions of $b1$ and $b2$ are $b1 = 253'9C\delta$, and from equation (2), $b2 = (255-253'9C)\ \delta$. Table 1 shows the transition rates computed according both approaches and the routing algorithm DELWL.

Step 4. Now, the values of the selected dependability parameters must be obtained. So, we must solve the system of differential equations that govern the state probabilities [2]. The expressions of this parameters can be easily obtained. Thus, $R(t)$ for the traditional approach is the sum of the probabilities of being in the *Correct State*, or in the *Degraded State*, while in our approach, it is the sum of the probabilities of being in the *Degraded States*, numbered from 1 to 4, or in the *Correct State*. With the values of λ, μ, and C, the *MTTF* has been computed and the results have allowed us to obtain the plots shown in the next section.

Table 1. Transition rates for both approaches in 5x5 and 16x16 meshes

	Traditional approach		
5x5 Mesh	$a1 = 25\ \delta C$	$a2 = 25\ \delta (1-C)$	$b1 = 24\ \delta$
16x16 Mesh	$a1 = 256\ C\ \delta$	$a2 = 256\ (1-C)\ \delta$	$b1 = 255\ \delta$
	New approach		
5x5 Mesh	$a1 = 25\ \delta C$	$b2 = (24 - 21'6\ C)\ \delta$	$d1 = 11'84\ \delta C$
	$a2 = 25\ \delta (1-C)$	$c1 = 16'18\ \delta C$	$d2 = (22 - 11'84\ C)\ \delta$
	$b1 = 21'6\ C\ \delta$	$c2 = (23 - 16'18\ C)\ \delta$	$e1 = 21\ \delta$
16x16 Mesh	$a1 = 256\ C\ \delta$	$b2 = (255 - 253'9\ C)\ \delta$	$d1 = 249'5\ C\ \delta$
	$a2 = 256\ (1-C)\ \delta$	$c1 = 251'19\ C\ \delta$	$d2 = (253 - 249'5\ C)\ \delta$
	$b1 = 253'9\ C\ \delta$	$c2 = (254 - 251'19\ C)\ \delta$	$e1 = 252\ \delta$

4 Results

Step 5. To compare the *MTTF* between both approaches, we have used the ratio of the *MTTF* obtained with our approach and the *MTTF* obtained with the traditional one. The results appear in Figure 2, represented as a function of λ, μ, and C.

As shown in the plots, the *MTTF* ratio is always larger than one. The ratio is in the range 1'2 to 60, that is, the network *MTTF* obtained with our approach can be up to 60 times larger than the value obtained with the traditional approach. As our model is much more accurate than the traditional one to evaluate dependability parameters, the *MTTF* obtained with the traditional approach is always largely underestimated.

The differences between both approaches increase with failure coverage. This can be observed in the sequence formed by Figures 2a, 2b, and 2c, and by Figures 2d, 2e, and 2f, which are ordered according to growing C values. The previous fact occurs because the network tends to transit to a *Degraded State* instead of to the *Failed State*, and then there are more opportunities to network repair. The difference between both approaches also increases when δ diminishes and μ, C increase. The effects of C and network repair diminish as δ increases. This occurs because the network state evolves quickly to the *Failed State*, and the importance of the possibility of network repair diminishes. Only when C is high and the repair time is low, the *Degraded States* are important and they mark the difference between both approaches.

Therefore, the differences between both approaches grow as the size of the network increases. We can see this fact by comparing Figures 2a and 2d, 2b and 2e, and 2c and 2f. As the size of the mesh increases, it also increases the number of network nodes that could fail. Since the network state evolves quickly to the *Failed State*, the importance of the possibility of network repair diminishes. The difference between both approaches increases when δ diminishes and μ, C increase. Once more, only when C is high and the repair time is low, the *Degraded State*s mark the difference between both approaches.

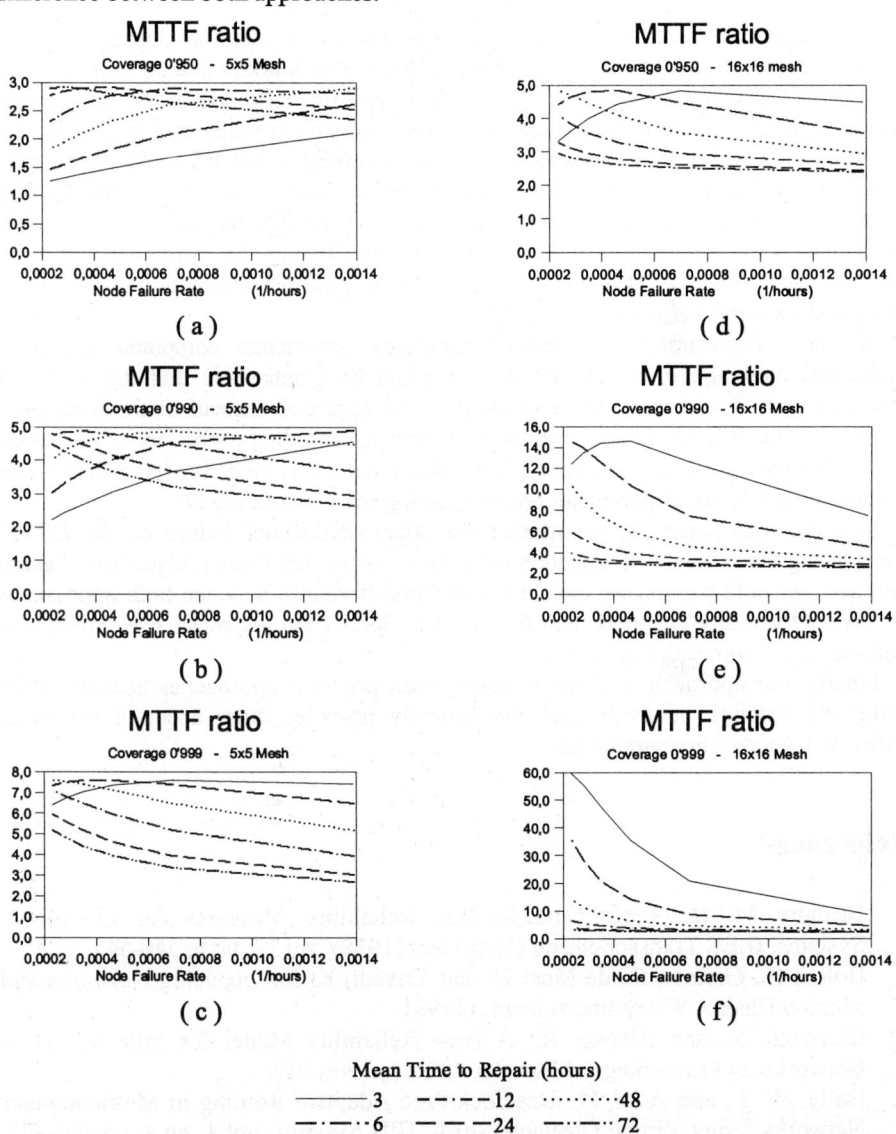

Fig. 2. MTTF ratio as a function of mesh size, coverage and node failure and repair rate

Finally, we can see in the Figure 2 that sometimes the *MTTF* ratio presents a maximum. This is due to the combination of the effects of the new operational states, *Degraded States*, and the values of δ and μ. The importance of these effects can be incremented or diminished by particular values and combination of values of δ and μ.

5 Conclusions

In this paper we have used a new methodology for computing dependability in interconnection networks based on Markov chains. The Markov chains have allowed us to model the effects of the routing algorithm and the node failure locations in the network. State transitions in Markov chain have been determined by considering the topology (5x5 and 16x16 meshes), the routing algorithm (DELWL) and the number and locations of faulty nodes. This study has taken into account that networks may work even when the number of faulty nodes is larger than the number of faulty nodes supported by the routing algorithm in the worst case. Indeed the main contribution of the proposed model is that they consider all the possible combinations of faults, analyzing their probability and their effects.

We have determined that network reliability parameters computed using the traditional method are too conservative. It must be emphasized that the *MTTF* is always larger if it is computed according to our approach instead of the traditional approach. The differences are up to 60 times larger, according to the size of the mesh. The differences grow as *C* increases, $1/\mu$ is short and $1/\delta$ is long. We have shown that *C* is the most important parameter on determining the network *MTTF*.

In a previous paper [3] we studied the effect of channel failure on the *MTTF*, considering the same interconnection network topology and routing algorithm. Taking into account both papers, we conclude that the differences between both approaches are larger for faulty channels than for faulty nodes. When the mesh size grows, this relationship becomes the opposite.

Finally, our approach is closer to reality than previous approaches because it fits better the network behavior, and consequently provides more accurate values of network dependability parameters.

References

1. Beaudry M. D.: Performance-Related Reliability Measures for Computing Systems, IEEE Transactions on Computers (1978), vol.27, no.6, 540-547.
2. Bolch, G., Greiner, S., de Meer H. and Trivedi, K. S.: Queueing Networks and Markov Chains, Wiley-Interscience, (1998).
3. Chirivella V. and Alcover R.: A New Reliability Model for Interconnection Networks, in Proceedings of EuroPar 2000, pp. 909-917.
4. Dally, W. J., and Aoki, H., Deadlock-Free Adaptive Routing in Multicomputer Networks Using Virtual Channels, IEEE TPD Systems, vol.4, no.4, pp.466-477, April 1993.

5. Duato, J.: A Theory of Fault Tolerant Routing in Wormhole Networks, IEEE TPD Systems (1997), vol.8, no.8, 790-802.
6. Dugan, J.B. and Trivedi, K. S.: Coverage Modeling for Dependability Analysis of Fault-Tolerant Systems, IEEE Transactions on Computers (1989), vol.38, no.6, 775-787.
7. Gaughan P. T. and Yalamanchili S.: A Family of Fault-Tolerant Routing Protocols for Direct Multiprocessor Networks, IEEE TPD Systems (1995), vol.6, no.5, 482-497.
8. Scott, S. L. and Thorson, G.: The Cray 3TE Networks: Adaptive Routing on High Performance 3D Torus, in Proc. of Hots Interconnects IV, August 1996.
9. Vaidya, A. S., Das, R. C. and Sivasubramaniam A.: A Testbed for the Evaluation of Fault- Tolerant Routing in Multiprocessor Interconnection Networks, IEEE TPD Systems (1999), vol.10, no.10, 1052-1081.

On Deadlock Frequency during Dynamic Reconfiguration in NOWs*

Lorenzo Fernández[1], José M. García[1], and Rafael Casado[2]

[1] Universidad de Murcia
Murcia, Spain 30071
{lfmaimo,jmgarcia}@ditec.um.es
[2] Universidad de Castilla-La Mancha
Albacete, Spain 02071
rcasado@info-ab.uclm.es

Abstract. NOWs executing multimedia and real-time applications need to handle dynamic changes in their irregular topologies. This may be carried out in two ways: statically and dynamically. In the former, user traffic is stopped, causing latencies to increase dramatically. In the latter, user traffic is not stopped but deadlocks may appear in the transition phase between the old and the new routing function. To solve this problem, dynamic reconfiguration methods based on deadlock avoidance have been proposed. However, another possibility not studied yet, is to use dynamic reconfiguration allowing deadlock formation with an efficient detection/recovery mechanism. It is necessary to know deadlock frequency during the reconfiguration process in order to assess the viability of this alternative proposal. In this paper, we show that deadlocks may become very infrequent with few virtual channels and the lost message problem can be reduced by using a simple misrouting technique.

1 Introduction

High performance networks of workstations (NOWs) have become a low-cost alternative to parallel computers, not only for high-performance scientific computing but mostly as a platform for high-end servers. A high performance NOW is built by interconnecting workstations by means of point-to-point links and switches. NOWs may suffer topological updates due to link failures, switches/ hosts being turned on/off, link remapping, hot expansion, etc. Usually, the network itself detects the change and starts a reconfiguration process in order to obtain the new topology. The main problem in reconfigurable networks is to guarantee deadlock-free routing during the reconfiguration process. Another related problem is the number of lost messages during this process.

A simple way to avoid deadlocks while the reconfiguration process is being executed is *static reconfiguration*. In this approach, deadlock-free routing is

---

* This work has been supported in part by the spanish Ministry of Ciencia y Tecnología under project TIC2000-1151-C07-03

guaranteed by stopping user traffic until reconfiguration finishes. In this case, there is no risk of deadlocks, but user messages have to wait for the reconfiguration to end, dramatically increasing their latency and making it inappropiate for multimedia and real-time applications with strict traffic requirements.

On the other hand, in *dynamic reconfiguration*, user messages can flow during the reconfiguration in a normal way. During the reconfiguration process deadlocks may appear, even when a deadlock-free routing function is being used. This is due to the coexistence in the network of at least two versions of the routing tables (the old ones and the new ones). To solve this important problem, there are two strategies: dynamic reconfiguration based on either a deadlock detection/recovery mechanism, or on a deadlock avoidance mechanism.

Deadlock-avoidance mechanisms are more dificult to implement and possibly, they may need more network resources than deadlock detection/recovery ones. However, the former are more efficient. To develop an alternative efficient deadlock detection/recovery mechanism during the dynamic reconfiguration process, it is necessary to guarantee that deadlocks are very infrequent. In this paper, our main objective is to estimate deadlock frequency and the amount of lost messages. We have found that deadlocks are not very frequent for irregular networks with a low number of virtual channels (for 64 switches, the ratio deadlocked/delivered messages are below 2%). Moreover, the ratio lost/delivered messages is also maintained at a very low level (for 64 switches, below 0.2%).

This paper is organized as follows. In Sect. 2, we provide some background on high-performance networks, including static and dynamic reconfiguration. Section 3 shows the importance of choosing a good mechanism for detecting deadlocks and how often both deadlocks and lost messages occur during the reconfiguration process, even when misrouting is allowed. Section 4 depicts the evaluation results and finally, we end the paper by showing some conclusions as well as future work.

2 Background

Current high-speed LANs (Autonet [14], Myrinet [3], ServerNet [6] and Infini-Band [9]) may change their topology due to switches and host being turned on/off, link remapping, and component failures. A very important issue in these high-speed LANs is the deadlock problem. It is known that deadlocks occur more frequently when irregular networks are used [15]. There are two main strategies for deadlock handling: deadlock avoidance and deadlock recovery. Deadlock avoidance prevents deadlocks by restricting routing so that there may not be cyclic dependencies between channels [5]. Autonet implements up*/down* routing tables for this purpose. Myrinet implements a deterministic version of up*/down* based on source routing. Deadlock avoidance can be also achieved by providing some virtual channels and escape paths [7].

Deadlock recovery requires both deadlock detection and recovery mechanisms. The classic method for deadlock detection has been the timeout-based mechanism, that measures the inactivity time of blocked messages, leading to a high probability of false deadlock detection and a high dependency on message length. ICT (Inactive Channels Time) [12] and a very efficient improvement of ICT [10] can be found in literature as two alternative methods. ICT measures the time that channels requested by messages are inactive due to the fact that the current messages occupying them remain blocked. A message is presumed to be deadlocked only if all of the alternative virtual output channels requested by that message contain blocked messages and have been inactive for a given period of time.

Recovery may be carried out in either a progressive or a regressive way. This depends on whether some resources are deallocated from a non-deadlocked message and reassigned to a deadlocked one for quick delivery [1,8], or some resources are deallocated from deadlocked messages, usually discarding them.

2.1 Reconfiguration Mechanisms

Reconfiguration mechanisms in current high-speed LANs are based on static reconfiguration techniques. When a change in the topology occurs, a three-phases reconfiguration process (propagation, collection and distribution) is triggered. The node which detects the change cleans its buffers, stops accepting user messages and becomes the root node of the new topology. Then, it sends control messages to every neighbour announcing that a reconfiguration has started and including information about the new spanning tree that is beginning to be built. A node that receives such a control message must also join the spanning tree at its best position, clean its buffers, stop accepting user messages and propagate the reconfiguration process to its neighbours. The spanning tree built in this way is called *Propagation-Order Spanning Tree* (POST) and it may not be a minimal spanning tree. The collection phase begins when every node has joined the spanning tree. Then, each node sends the topological information about its sub-tree to its parent. When this information reaches the root node, it is known that the second phase has ended. At this point, the root knows the whole network topology. The last phase distributes the new topology through the spanning tree until all switches are aware of it. Next, user messages are allowed again.

A first proposal of dynamic reconfiguration based on deadlock avoidance, called PPR (Partial Progressive Reconfiguration) was presented in [4]. In this approach, routing tables are gradually asynchronously updated, in a controlled way, so that they remain deadlock-free after each partial update. User messages are not stopped, and this technique is valid for both regular and irregular topologies. Recently, other similar approaches [2,11,13] has been proposed in this context.

3 Deadlock Formation in Dynamic Reconfiguration

Our research work is focused on estimating the deadlock frequency during dynamic reconfiguration. The underlying dynamic reconfiguration method is a dynamic version of the static one implemented in Autonet. Deadlocks produced by routing table interaction may occur during dynamic reconfiguration. Messages that cross switches using only old routing tables, only new ones or a mixture of both can be found. Thus, although both old routing tables and new ones are deadlock-free, a "mix-routed" message may break the restrictions, forming a cycle in the channel dependency graph.

Warnakulasuriya [15] showed that deadlock formation likelihood decreases as the number of virtual channels increases in a network. If enough virtual channels are provided, it is expected the number of deadlocks to remain low also in the course of the reconfiguration. Therefore, an appropiate number of virtual channels has to be selected in order to obtain a low number for deadlocks.

In order to implement deadlock recovery, it is necessary to detect deadlock formation. We are interested in distributed deadlock detection mechanisms that use only local information and few hardware resources. These mechanisms find every true deadlock, but they also detect false ones. ICT has been the mechanism selected because it detects much fewer false deadlocks than timeout and it is very easy to implement.

A regressive deadlock recovery technique has been used. When a deadlock is detected, the message responsible for the triggering is discarded and its buffer resources are released so that the rest of the messages can advance towards their destinations. The discarded message is supposed to be injected again into the network by an upper-level protocol.

3.1 Lost Messages

Deadlocks are not the only problem faced during network reconfiguration. The loss of messages is another important question. When a switch is deactivated, crossing messages get lost.

For the purpose of this work, user traffic is not stopped; thus, in dynamic reconfiguration there are three categories of lost messages: (a) those messages addressed to a non-existent switch in the network, which will be dropped when meeting their destination; (b) those messages traveling towards an existent switch but following a deadlock-free path that crosses a deactivated switch; and (c) those messages that are routed using contradictory information that breaks the up*/down* rules. These messages cannot continue on their way satisfying the restrictions on routing tables for remaining deadlock-free, so they are discarded. Lost messages can be managed by a higher-level protocol, and then, resent, discarded or even reinjected by means of in-transit buffers [8], but, in any case, it is desirable to reduce their number.

3.2 Reducing the Number of Deadlocked and Lost Messages

A first approach for reducing the deadlock frequency, is to re-route a deadlocked message using any free channel with enough free buffer space, in order to avoid discarding it. In small networks, such a misrouted message will probably soon be involved in another deadlock. However, as network size grows it is expected that the likelihood of a new deadlock being formed will decrease. In addition, the

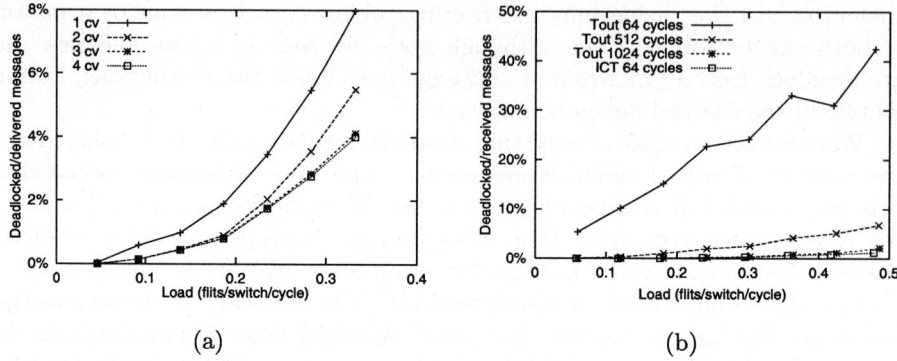

Fig. 1. (a) Deadlocked/delivered messages vs. accepted traffic when varying the number of adaptive virtual channels used. (b) Comparing ICT vs. timeout. Network with 32 switches and packet length of 512 bytes

greater adaptivity provided by virtual channels is expected to help avoid new deadlocks. If there are no free channels, the message is discarded as mentioned above. This misrouting is only used during the reconfiguration process because there is no possibility of a deadlock occurring after it finishes. Livelock cannot occur because reconfiguration always ends.

On the other hand, this technique could be also useful for reducing the number of lost messages. When a message is about to be lost, it can be applied misrouting to avoid losing it. Probably, this could also increase the number of deadlocked messages because a misrouted message augments its probability of involvement in a deadlock configuration. Therefore, it is interesting to obtain some experimental results about the use of misrouting in this contex.

4 Evaluation

Our network simulator has the characteristics described in Sect. 3, i.e. dynamic version of the reconfiguration method of Autonet, ICT with message discarding as deadlock recovery policy and misrouting. Our switch architecture implements virtual cut-through and virtual channels, with a partially multiplexed crossbar. There is just one escape channel and the rest are adaptive ones. Several irregular topologies have been randomly generated containing 16, 24, 32 and 64 switches, with one host per switch. Packet length is 512 bytes, destination distribution is uniform and deadlock detection mechanism is ICT.

One by one, each switch is deactivated while the rest remain activated. This triggers as many one-deactivation reconfigurations as switches the network has. For 64-switch network, it was deactivated only a random subset of switches instead of the whole set. Simulations were made progressively increasing the applied load until the network saturation was achieved. The measures were taken from the time the reconfiguration begins, until the time the last switch finishes

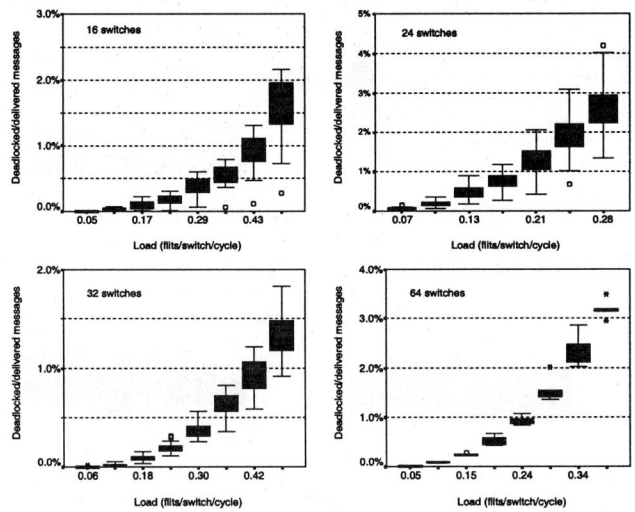

Fig. 2. Deadlock frequency versus delivered traffic

its reconfiguration process. Inserting a new node behaves in the same way than a deactivation, but with much few lost packets.

Firstly, an evaluation of the number of virtual channels needed to maintain the deadlock frequency low will be carried out. Figure 1(a) shows that three adaptive virtual channels are enough to maintain low the number of deadlocked messages, thus, we choose to use three adaptive channels plus an escape one.

Concerning deadlock detection, timeout and ICT were tested. This is depicted in Fig. 1(b). It can be noted that ICT needs a lower threshold than timeout. Moreover, due to this, ICT detects deadlocks before timeout does. Thus, ICT was chosen as the deadlock detection mechanism for the rest of our evaluations.

In Fig. 2 deadlocked/delivered messages ratio versus accepted traffic is depicted for networks of 16, 24, 32 and 64 switches. In order to obtain a comprehensive view of the deadlock behaviour, a box-and-whiskers [1] graph of the mean latencies was used.

When the network has a light traffic load, deadlock frequency remains low in all tested networks (e.g. below 1%-2%). The closer to saturation the network is, the more frequent deadlocks become. In addition, we have found that the ratio of deadlocked/delivered messages does not depend on deactivating a particular node. However, there are some particular cases, such as disconnecting a leaf node, which results in an almost up*/down* graph inversion. In those cases, deadlocks are more frequent because there is a large amount of conflicting routing information between old and new routing tables. Conversely, when a node near

---

[1] This statistical graph draws a box containing 50% of the sample, marking the median with a line. The whiskers that stick out of the box represent the rest of the sample. Rare cases are shown by means of small circles and asterisks.

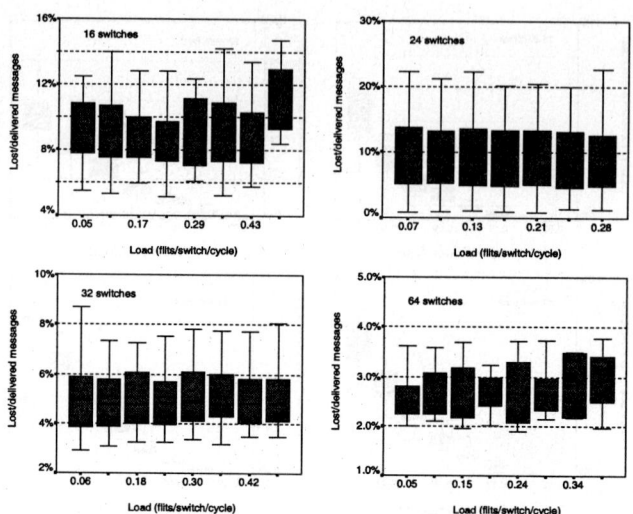

Fig. 3. Lost message frequency versus delivered traffic

the root is deactivated, the new routing table has much common information with the old one, producing much fewer deadlocks.

With respect to lost messages, the ratio lost/received messages strongly depends on the particular disconnected switch whereas it does not depend on the load. A set of Box-and-whiskers graphs summarize lost message frequency when every switch, each in turn, is deactivated and the traffic is increased until network saturation. The parameters of the network are the same as Fig. 2 and it is shown in Fig. 3.

For leaf nodes, there are few up*/down* paths that use it. Thus, few messages will get lost. However, when the switch that disappears is close to the root node, a great number of messages will probably try to cross it. As a result, many messages will get lost. Figure 4 shows the results of simulating the misrouting mechanism with the same networks as early experiments. With low load, deadlock frequency is higher than it was without misrouting, but this frequency is aproximately the same when the network is close to saturation. A misrouted message stays into the network longer than a well-routed one, thus augmenting both load and deadlock frequency. As far as lost messages are concerned, Fig. 4 shows that the ratio lost/delivered messages considerably decreases for every network size. The larger the size, the greater the enhancement; for example, a 32-switch network reduces this ratio from a maximum of approximately 9% to 2%. Indeed, in 64-switch network the frequency drops from a maximum of 3.75% to 0.3% approximately.

5 Conclusions and Future Work

In this paper, we have shown that using a low number of virtual channels (only four), deadlocks during the dynamic reconfiguration become infrequent in high

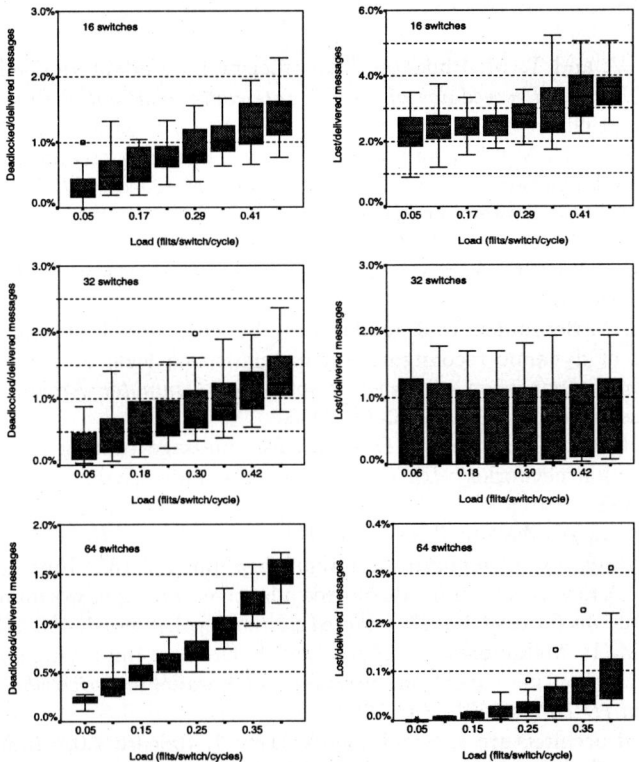

Fig. 4. Deadlock frequency and lost/delivered message ratio when misrouting is allowed

speed local area networks (NOWs). In order to obtain both lower and upper boundaries we have carried out several evaluations for each switch being deactivated one by one, while the rest remain activated. This fact, in addition to the relatively short duration of the reconfiguration process, could lead us to consider a deadlock detection/recovery approach as a suitable proposal. But the percentage of lost messages become an important problem. It only depends on the particular switch that is disconnected and does not depend on the traffic load. However, it has been shown that a simple misrouting technique provides good results in both the ratio of deadlocked and lost messages.

Future work include to carry out a deeper analysis of deadlock frequency, and to make a comparison between dynamic reconfiguration methods with deadlock avoidance and the one developed in this paper, based on deadlock detection/recovery.

Acknowledgements

The authors would like to thank Jose Duato, Juan Peinador and Francisco Alfaro for providing insightful comments that greatly improved this paper.

References

1. Anjan K. V. and T. M. Pinkston, "An efficient fully adaptive deadlock recovery scheme: DISHA," *Proceedings of the 9th International Parallel Processing Symposium*, April 1995.
2. D. R. Avresky, N. Natchev and V. Shubarnov, "Dynamic reconfiguration in high-speed computer networks." *IEEE Workshop on Embedded Fault Tolerant Systems*, Washington D.C., September 21-22, 2000.
3. N. J. Boden, D. Cohen, R. E. Felderman, A. E. Kulawik, C. L. Seitz, J. Seizovic and W. Su, "Myrinet - A gigabit per second local area network," *IEEE Micro*, pp. 29-36, February 1995.
4. R. Casado, A. Bermúdez, F. J. Quiles, J. L. Sánchez, and J. Duato, "Performance evaluation of dynamic reconfiguration in high-speed local area networks." *Sixth International Symposium on High Performance Computer Architecture (HPCA-6)*, Toulouse, France. January 10-12, 2000.
5. W. J. Dally and C. L. Seitz, "Deadlock-free message routing in multiprocessor interconnection networks," *IEEE Trans. on Computers*, vol. C-36, no. 5, pp.547-553, May 1987.
6. D. García and W. Watson. "ServerNet II," *Proceedings of the 1997 Parallel Computer, Routing, and Communication Workshop*, pp. 119-135, June 1997.
7. J. Duato, "A new theory of deadlock-free adaptive routing in wormhole networks," *IEEE Trans. on Parallel and Distributed Systems*, vol. 4, no. 4, 466-475, April 1993.
8. J. Flich, M. P. Malumbres, P. López and J. Duato, "Improving routing performance in Myrinet networks," in *International Parallel and Distributed Processing Symposium (IPDPS 2000)*, May 2000.
9. "InfiniBand architecture specification. Volume 1. Release 1.0," Infiniband Trade Association, October 2000. http://www.infinibandta.org
10. P. López, J. M. Martínez and J. Duato, "A very efficient distributed deadlock detection mechanism for wormhole networks," *Proceedings of the Fourth International Symposium on High-Performance Computer Architecture (HPCA-4)*, IEEE Computer Society Press (1998) 57-66.
11. O. Lysne and J. Duato, "Fast dynamic reconfiguration in irregular networks," *International Conference on Parallel Processing (ICPP 2000)*, August 2000.
12. J. M. Martínez, P. López, J. Duato and T. M. Pinkston, "Software-based deadlock recovery technique for true fully adaptive routing in wormhole networks," *Proceedings of the 1997 International Conference on Parallel Processing (ICPP'97)*, IEEE Computer Society Press (1997) 182-189.
13. R. Pang, T. Pinkston and J.Duato, "The double scheme: Deadlock-free dynamic reconfiguration of cut-through networks," *International Conference on Parallel Processing (ICPP 2000)*, August 2000.
14. M. D. Schroeder et al, "Autonet: a high-speed, self-configuring local area network using point-to-point links," *IEEE Journal on Selected Areas in Communications*, 9(8):1318-1335, October 1991.
15. S. Warnakulasuriya and T. M. Pinkston, "Characterization of deadlocks in interconnection networks," *Proc. of the 11th International Parallel Processing Symposium (IPPS'97)*, April 1997.

Analysis of Broadcast Communication in 2D Tori

A. Shahrabi, M. Ould-Khaoua, and L. M. Mackenzie

Department of Computing Science, University of Glasgow
Glasgow G12 8QQ, U.K.
{alireza,mohamed,lewis}@dcs.gla.ac.uk

Abstract. This paper presents an analytical model for predicting latency of broadcast messages in adaptive wormhole-routed Tori. Results obtained through simulation experiments show that the model exhibits a good degree of accuracy in predicting message latency.

1 Introduction

Previous research studies of collective communication have focused primarily on the design of efficient algorithms for wormhole-routed networks and there has been comparatively little activity in the area of analytical modelling of these algorithms. As a result, most such studies have relied solely on software simulation to evaluate the performance merits of collective communication. This paper presents an analytical model to compute the broadcast latency in the wormhole-routed bi-directional torus. All messages are routed according to Duato's routing algorithm [5]. Moreover, the broadcast algorithm considered in this study is based on the algorithm proposed by Bose et al [2] for the multiple-port k-ary n-cube.

2 The Proposed Analytical Model

Details of the router structure and broadcast algorithm used in the analysis can be found in [8]. The proposed model is based on the following assumptions which are commonly accepted in the literature [1], [4], [7].

a) When a message is generated in a given source node, it has a finite probability β of being a broadcast message and probability $(1-\beta)$ of being unicast. A broadcast message is delivered to every node using the broadcast algorithm. A unicast message is sent to other nodes in the network with equal probability.
b) Nodes generate traffic independently of each other, via a Poisson process with a mean rate of λ_g messages/cycle.
c) All messages experience a start-up latency of Δ cycles.
d) Message length is M flits, each of which is transmitted in one cycle across the physical channel.
e) A local queue in a given source node has infinite capacity. Moreover, messages are transferred to the local PE as soon as they arrive at their destinations.

f) V (V>2) virtual channels are used per physical channel. According to Duato's adaptive routing algorithm [5], class a contains V-2 virtual channels, which are crossed adaptively, and class b contains two virtual channel, which are crossed deterministically.

Examining the structure of the broadcast tree reveals that the broadcast latency is the time needed for a broadcast message to reach the most remote node from its source node in the broadcast tree. As a result, the broadcast latency is the delay in traversing the longest branch of the broadcast tree, composed of $2\lfloor k/2 \rfloor$ latencies, each the time needed to send a broadcast message one step down the tree. Let us refer to the broadcast message that makes only one hop in the network as "one-step broadcast message" and let $\overline{L}_b$ be the mean latency seen by this message. Then, the mean broadcast latency can be written as

$$Latency = 2\lfloor k/2 \rfloor (\overline{L}_b + \Delta) \qquad (1)$$

where Δ denotes the start-up latency. The mean latency of a one-step broadcast message, $\overline{L}_b$, is the sum of the mean network latency, $\overline{S}_b$, i.e. the time required to make one hop in the network, and the mean waiting time, $\overline{W}_s$, seen by the message at the source node before entering the network. However, to model the effects of virtual channel multiplexing message latency has to be scaled by a factor, $\overline{V}$, representing the average degree of virtual channels multiplexing that takes place at a given physical channel. Therefore, we can write $\overline{L}_b$ as

$$\overline{L}_b = (\overline{S}_b + \overline{W}_s)\overline{V} \qquad (2)$$

Before describing how to determine the quantities $\overline{S}_b$, $\overline{W}_s$, and $\overline{V}$, we determine first the traffic rate on a given network channel, λ_c. Adaptive routing distributes traffic evenly across network channels as it enables messages to use channels in any order that bring them closer to their destinations. Moreover, given that the destinations for unicast messages are uniformly distributed and the broadcast traffic is balanced across the network channels result in channels having an equal traffic rate. In the broadcast algorithm, a broadcast message is replicated at various stages in the broadcast tree. A replicated message is copied into the local queue of the node to be injected later across the required output channels. So, a source node generates three different type of messages: unicast messages with a rate of $\lambda_{s_u} = (1-\beta)\lambda_g$, one-step broadcast messages with a rate of $\lambda_{s_b} = \beta\lambda_g$, and replicated messages with a rate of λ_{s_r}, which is determined as follows. Given that a source node has generated a broadcast message, the probability that a particular node in the network replicates the broadcast message and delivers copies to its neighbouring nodes is $\sum_{i=0}^{2n-1} N_r^i / (k^2 - 1)$.

N_r^i is the number of nodes in the broadcast tree of a torus of radix k that replicate the broadcast message i times and is given by [8]

$$N_r^i = \begin{cases} 2k & i=0 \\ k^2 - 3k & i=1 \\ 2 & i=2 \\ k-3 & i=3 \end{cases} \tag{3}$$

Since there are $(k^2 - 1)$ other nodes in the network and the generation rate of broadcast messages is $\lambda_{s_b} = \beta \lambda_g$, the rate of replicated messages originating from a given node is given by

$$\lambda_{s_r} = \sum_{i=0}^{2n-1} N_r^i \lambda_{s_b} = \sum_{i=0}^{2n-1} N_r^i \beta \lambda_g \tag{4}$$

Consider now an output channel. The traffic rate, λ_c, on the channel consists of the rates due to unicast, λ_{c_u}, broadcast, λ_{c_b}, and replicated messages, λ_{c_r}. Thus,

$$\lambda_c = \lambda_{c_u} + \lambda_{c_b} + \lambda_{c_r} \tag{5}$$

In a bi-directional torus, the average numbers of hops that a message makes along a given dimension and across the network, $\bar{k}$ and $\bar{d}$, are given by

$$\bar{k} = \begin{cases} k/4 & k \text{ is even} \\ (k - 1/k)/4 & k \text{ is odd} \end{cases} \tag{6}$$

$$\bar{d} = n\bar{k} \tag{7}$$

Since a router in the torus has $2n$ output channels and a node generates, on average, $\lambda_{s_u} = (1-\beta)\lambda_g$ unicast messages in a cycle, the traffic rate of unicast messages, λ_{c_u}, received by each channel in the network is simply

$$\lambda_{c_u} = (1-\beta)\lambda_g \bar{d}/2n \tag{8}$$

A source node generates broadcast messages with a rate $\lambda_{s_b} = \beta \lambda_g$. Since a copy of the broadcast message has to be sent to the all neighbouring nodes through the output channels, the rate of one-step broadcast traffic on a given channel can be expressed as

$$\lambda_{c_b} = \beta \lambda_g \tag{9}$$

In order to compute the traffic rate due to replicated broadcast messages we need to know the mean number of replications that a given node performs in a given broadcast operation. The number of replication varies from one node to another depending on the node position in the broadcast tree. The probability that a broadcast message is replicated i times when it reaches an intermediate node is given by

$$P_{r_i} = N_r^i / k^2 - 1 \qquad (0 \le i \le 3) \tag{10}$$

Hence, the mean number of replication of a broadcast message in a given node can be expressed as

$$\bar{\omega} = \sum_{i=0}^{2n-1} i\, P_{r_i} = \sum_{i=0}^{2n-1} i\, N_r^i / (k^2 - 1) \tag{11}$$

Given that a replicated message can be sent over one of the output channels with equal probability, the traffic rate of replicated messages on each channel is given by

$$\lambda_{c_r} = \frac{\bar{\omega}}{2n} \lambda_{s_r} = \frac{\bar{\omega}}{4} \sum_{i=0}^{2n-1} N_r^i \beta \lambda_g \tag{12}$$

Since a one-step broadcast message makes one hop to reach the next destination node, the mean network latency can be written as

$$\overline{S}_b = M + B_b \tag{13}$$

where B_b is the mean blocking tiem seen by the message as it crosses an output channels. Since there is a balance traffic on network channels, the message sees the same mean waiting time, $\overline{W}_c$, to acquire a virtual channel at an output channel, regardless of its position in the network. Let P_v denote the probability the v virtual channels at a physical channel are busy (P_v is calculated below). Given that a one-step broadcast message is blocked when all the V virtual channel at the required output channel are busy, the mean blocking time, B_b, can be written as

$$B_b = P_V \overline{W}_c \tag{14}$$

To determine the mean waiting time to acquire a channel in the event of blocking, a physical channel is treated as an M/G/1 queue [6]. To compute the variance of the service time, we follow a suggestion of Draper [4] and approximate the variance of the service time distribution by $(\overline{S} - M)^2$. As a result the mean waiting time becomes

$$\overline{W}_c = \lambda_c \overline{S}^2 (1 + ((\overline{S} - M)^2 / \overline{S}^2)) / 2(1 - \lambda_c \overline{S}) \tag{15}$$

where $\overline{S}$ is the mean service time. The mean service time seen by a message considering broadcast and unicast messages with thier appropriate weights is given by

$$\overline{S} = ((\lambda_{c_b} + \lambda_{c_r}) / \lambda_c) \overline{S}_b + (\lambda_{c_u} / \lambda_c) \overline{S}_u \tag{16}$$

The mean network latency of a uniacst message is determined in a similar manner to the case of one-step broadcast message. Let B_j be the mean blocking time seen by a unicast message at the j-th hop channel ($1 \le j \le \overline{d}$) along its network path. Given that a message makes, on average, $\overline{d}$ hops to reach its destination, $\overline{S}_u$ can be written as

$$\overline{S}_u = M + \overline{d} + \sum_{j=1}^{\overline{d}} B_j \tag{17}$$

The mean blocking time can be written as [8]

$$B_j = P_{b_j} \overline{W}_c \tag{18}$$

where P_{b_j} are given by [8]

$$P_{b_j} = \begin{cases} P_a P_d & 1 \le j \le \overline{k} \\ (1 - P_{c_j}) P_a P_d + P_{c_j} P_d & \overline{k} + 1 \le j \le \overline{d} \end{cases} \tag{19}$$

$$P_{c_j} = 2/(\overline{d} - j + 2) \tag{20}$$

By modelling the injection channel in the source node as an M/G/1 queue, the mean arrival rate and mean service time are given by the following equations

$$\lambda_s = (\lambda_{S_u} / n) + \lambda_{S_b} + (\overline{\omega} \lambda_{S_r} / n) \tag{21}$$

$$\overline{S}_s = (\lambda_{s_b} + \lambda_{s_r}) / (\lambda_{s_u} + \lambda_{s_b} + \lambda_{s_r}) \overline{S}_b + (\lambda_{s_u} / (\lambda_{s_u} + \lambda_{s_b} + \lambda_{s_r})) \overline{S}_u \tag{22}$$

Approximating the variance of the service time distribution by $(\overline{S}_s - M)^2$ yields a mean waiting time at the source as

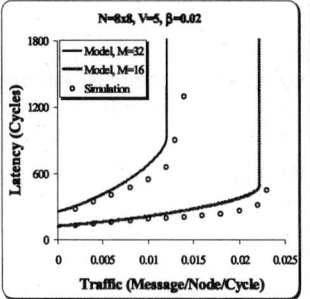 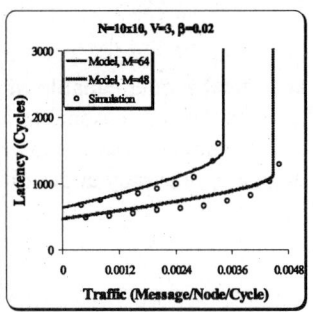 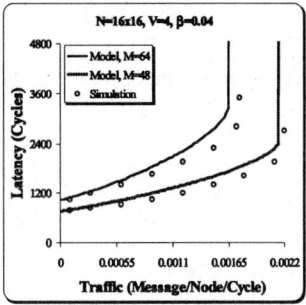

Fig. 1 Validation of the broadcast latency predicted by the model against simulation

$$\overline{W}_s = \lambda_s \overline{S}_s^2 \, (\overline{S}_s^2 + (\overline{S}_s - M)^2) / 2\overline{S}_s^2 (1 - \lambda_s \overline{S}_s) \tag{23}$$

The average degree of multiplexing of virtual channels, which takes place at a given physical channel, is given by [3]

$$\overline{V} = \sum_{i=1}^{V} i^2 P_i \Big/ \sum_{i=1}^{V} i P_i \tag{24}$$

where P_v are found to be [8]

$$P_v = \begin{cases} 1/\sum_{j=0}^{V} q_j & v = 0 \\ P_0 q_v & 1 \le v \le V \end{cases} \tag{25}$$

$$q_v = \begin{cases} (\lambda_c \overline{S})^v & 0 \le v < V \\ (\lambda_c \overline{S})^v / (1 - \lambda_c \overline{S}) & v = V \end{cases} \tag{26}$$

3 Simulation Experiments

The above model has been validated using a discrete-event simulator. Extensive validation experiments have been performed for several combinations of network sizes, message lengths, different fractions of broadcast messages and virtual channels. Figure 1 depicts results from the mean broadcast message latency predicted by the above analytical model plotted against those provided by the simulator as a function of traffic injection. The figure reveal that the simulation results closely match those predicted by the analytical model in the steady state regions (i.e. under light and moderate traffic) and even when the network starts to approach saturation. Therefore, we can conclude that the model produces accurate results in the steady state regions, and its simplicity makes it a practical evaluation tool that can be used to gain insight into the behaviour of torus in the presence of broadcast communication.

4 Conclusion

This paper has presented an analytical model capable of computing broadcast latency in wormhole-routed tori under a number of reasonable assumptions, widely accepted in the literature. Simulation experiments have shown that the analytical model predicts latency with a good degree of accuracy under different traffic conditions.

References

1. S. Abraham, K. Padmanabhan, Performance of the direct binary n-cube network for multiprocessors, *IEEE Trans. Computers* 38(7) (1989) 1001-1011.
2. B. Bose, et al, Lee distance and Topological Properties of k-ary n-cubes, *IEEE Trans. Computers* 44(8) (1995) 1021-1030.
3. W. J. Dally, Virtual channel flow control, *IEEE Trans. Parallel & Distributed Systems* 3(2) (1992) 194-205.
4. J.T. Draper, J. Ghosh, A comprehensive analytical model for wormhole routing in multicomputer systems, *J. Parallel & Distributed Computing* (32) (1994) 202-214.
5. J. Duato, A new theory of deadlock-free adaptive routing in wormhole routing networks, *IEEE Trans. Parallel & Distributed Systems* 4(12) (1993) 320-1331.
6. L. Kleinrock, Queueing Systems (1), John Wiley, 1975.
7. M. Ould-Khaoua, A performance model for Duato's fully-adaptive routing algorithm in k-ary n-cubes, *IEEE Trans. Computers* 42(12) (1999) 1-8.
8. Shahrabi, M. Ould-Khaoua, L. M. Mackenzie, "Analytical Modeling of Broafdcast in Torus Networks", Tech. Report, Dep. of Computing Science, Glasgow University, 2001.

Optimal Many-to-One Routing on the Mesh with Constant Queues*
(Extended Abstract)

Andrea Pietracaprina and Geppino Pucci

Dipartimento di Elettronica e Informatica, Università di Padova
Padova, Italy {andrea,geppo}@artemide.dei.unipd.it

Abstract. We present randomized and deterministic algorithms for many-to-one routing on an n-node two-dimensional mesh under the store-and-forward model. We consider a general instance of the problem, where each node is source (resp., destination) of ℓ (resp., k) packets, for arbitrary values of ℓ and k. All our algorithms run in optimal $O\left(\sqrt{\ell k n}\right)$ time and use queues of only constant size at each node to store packets in transit. The randomized algorithms, however, are simpler to implement. Our result closes a gap in the literature, where time-optimal algorithms using constant-size queues were known only for the special cases $\ell = 1$ and $\ell = k$.

1 Introduction

In this paper we study the routing of *many-to-one* message-sets on the mesh, where each node is the source and the destination of several messages [Lei92]. When the maximum number of messages originating at (resp., destined to) a node is ℓ (resp., k) the corresponding many-to-one routing instance is known in the literature as (ℓ, k)-*routing*. We will develop randomized and deterministic algorithms for (ℓ, k)-routing on an n-node square mesh. The performance of a store-and-forward algorithm is typically given by two key quantities: completion time, defined as the maximum delivery time of any packet to its destination, and maximum queue size (usually measured in packet units) needed at a node to store packets in transit. Our mesh algorithms turn out to be optimal with respect to both these metrics.

Routing under the store-and-forward model has been intensively studied over the last two decades [GH+98]. The first result on routing many-to-one message sets on an n-node square mesh is due to Makedon and Symovnis [MS93], who devised an optimal deterministic $O\left(\sqrt{kn}\right)$-time algorithm with constant queues for the special case of $(1, k)$-routing, where each node is the source of at most one packet. Subsequently, in [SK94], Sibeyn and Kaufmann proved an $\Omega\left(\sqrt{\ell k n}\right)$

---

* This work was supported, in part, by CNR and MURST of Italy under projects *Multicast Techniques with Applications to Robotics and Packet Routing* and *Algorithms for Large Data Sets: Science and Engineering*.

lower bound for general (ℓ, k)-routing (which holds for both randomized and deterministic algorithms) and obtained the first general, time-optimal deterministic algorithm, which however requires large queues of size $O(k)$. They also obtained a time-optimal randomized algorithm with constant queues and a more complex deterministic algorithm with similar performance for the case $\ell = k$. Their deterministic algorithm, however, works under the assumption that messages can be temporarily swapped out of the queues to be stored within the processors' internal memories, at the cost of a time penalty proportional to the length of the packet to be swapped out.

In this paper, we close the gap left open by the previous literature by devising time-optimal randomized and deterministic algorithms with constant queues for general (ℓ, k)-routing on the mesh. Both the algorithms implement a variant of the well-established idea of splitting the original message set into subsets of lower congestion that can then be routed independently within smaller submeshes [SK94]. However, the splitting is rather simple to achieve using randomization, while it requires a more complex and careful protocol to be accomplished deterministically.

2 Preliminaries

We make the reasonable assumption that messages departing from the same node have distinct destinations, which implies $\ell, k \leq n$. Every message is encapsulated into a distinct *packet* that consists of a header, containing the destination address, and a payload, containing the message itself. Each mesh node is provided with a *working queue* and an *internal queue*. The working queue is used during the routing to maintain packets in transit through the node, while the internal queue is used exclusively to hold the packets originating at or destined to the node. Hence, internal queues cannot be used for buffering purposes during the routing. The *queue size* of an algorithm is the maximum number of packets that any working queue must hold at any fixed time.

The mesh is synchronous and in one *step*, regarded as a unit of time, a node can perform a constant amount of local computation or one packet exchange along each of its four adjacent links. Also, extraction/injection of a packet from/into any internal queue takes constant time.

In our algorithms, we will make use of tessellations of the mesh into square submeshes of equal size. When the mesh is tessellated into s square submeshes of n/s nodes each, we call each such submesh an *s-tile*. Furthermore, we number the mesh nodes from 0 to $n-1$, according to the natural row-major indexing, and the s-tiles from 0 to $s-1$ according to a *hamiltonian indexing* so that s-tile i is adjacent to s-tile $(i+1) \bmod s$, for every $0 \leq i < s$.

In what follows, all proofs are omitted for lack of space. Details will be provided in the full version of this abstract.

3 Randomized Algorithm

In this section we present a randomized algorithm for (ℓ, k)-routing on the mesh which attains optimal performance using constant queue size. Our algorithm builds upon the ideas employed in the (k, k)-routing algorithm developed by Sibeyn and Kaufmann [SK94], and extends their result to the general case of (ℓ, k)-routing with $\ell \neq k$. We assume that at the beginning of the routing the mesh nodes know the values ℓ and k. (This assumption can be easily removed by means of standard techniques [HPP01].)

For ease of presentation, we distinguish among the cases $\ell \leq k$ and $\ell > k$. Interestingly, the strategies in these two cases are somehow one the "mirror image" of the other.

3.1 (ℓ, k)-Routing with $\ell \leq k$

As in [SK94] the algorithm exploits an initial random ℓ-coloring of the packets, and delivers the packets of each color class in a separate stage. However, unlike the case $\ell = k$, the coloring does not reduce the problem to easily routable subproblems, and more sophisticated techniques are needed to deal with these subproblems.

The algorithm performs the following sequence of steps. Define $s = \sqrt{nk/\ell}$ and note that, since both ℓ and k are not larger than n, we have $s \geq k/\ell$.

1. Within each node, assign a *distinct* random *color* in $\{1, \ldots, \ell\}$ to each packet in the internal queue. Use the term *j-packet* to refer to a packet of color j. (Note that there are at most n j-packets, for each $j \in \{1, \ldots, \ell\}$.)
2. For each color j, $1 \leq j \leq \ell$, do the following:
   (a) Sort the j-packets in lexicographic order (destination s-tile, destination).
   (b) Reshuffle the j-packets so that a packet of rank r in the sorted sequence is sent to the node of index r **div** (k/ℓ) in the (k/ℓ)-tile of index r **mod** (k/ℓ).
   (c) Repeat k/ℓ times in each (k/ℓ)-tile:
      i. Route all j-packets with destinations within the (k/ℓ)-tile to their destination s-tile, so that each node of an s-tile receives roughly the same number of packets. (Note that s-tiles are contained within (k/ℓ)-tiles.)
      ii. Within each s-tile move the j-packets along a hamiltonian cycle of the tile's nodes, thus letting each packet reach its destination.
      iii. Perform a blockwise shift of all unrouted j-packets to bring them to the same position within the next (k/ℓ)-tile in the hamiltonian indexing of the (k/ℓ)-tiles.

The analysis of the algorithm relies on the following lemma and theorem.

Lemma 1. *The coloring performed in Step 1 guarantees that for every $j \in \{1, \ldots, \ell\}$ the number of j-packets destined to the same s-tile is $O\left((n/s)(k/\ell)\right)$, with high probability.*

Theorem 1. *For any $\ell \leq k$, the above algorithm performs (ℓ, k)-routing in optimal $O\left(\sqrt{\ell k n}\right)$ time using constant queue size, with high probability.*

3.2 (ℓ, k)-Routing with $\ell > k$

As mentioned before, the algorithm for the case $\ell > k$ can somehow be seen as a backward run of the previous algorithm. However, some slight modifications are needed. The algorithm consists of the following sequence of steps. Define $s = \sqrt{n\ell/k} \geq \ell/k$ and $s' = \sqrt{nk/\ell}$.

1. Within each node, assign a random *color* in $\{1, \ldots, k\}$ to each packet in the internal queue. Use the term *j-packet* to refer to a packet of color j. (Note that, since $k \leq \ell$, more than one packet in a node may be assigned the same color.)
2. For each color j, $1 \leq j \leq k$, do the following:
   (a) Rank all j-packets so that the ranks assigned to the j-packets originating from the same s-tile form an interval of consecutive integers.
   (b) For $0 \leq i < \ell/k$ do the following within each (ℓ/k)-tile T:
      i. Let T be the (ℓ/k)-tile of index u in the hamiltonian indexing of the (ℓ/k)-tiles. From each s-tile contained in T, inject all j-packets whose rank r is such that $(u-r) \bmod (\ell/k) = i$, and distribute such packets among the nodes of the s-tile. The injection is accomplished by viewing each s-tile as a linear array of n/s nodes and applying a straightforward balancing algorithm [Lei92].
      ii. Reshuffle all j-packets currently residing in the working queues of the nodes of T, so that they are evenly distributed among such queues.
      iii. Perform a blockwise shift of all j-packets to bring them to the same position within the next (ℓ/k)-tile in the hamiltonian indexing of the (ℓ/k)-tiles.
   (c) Route all j-packets to their destination s'-tile so that each node of an s'-tile receives roughly the same number of packets.
   (d) Within each s'-tile move the packets along a hamiltonian cycle of the nodes of the tile, thus letting each packet reach its destination.

The analysis of the algorithm relies on the following lemma and theorem.

Lemma 2. *The coloring performed in Step 1 guarantees that, with high probability, for every color $j \in \{1, \ldots, k\}$, every s-tile U, and every s'-tile U', the following properties hold: (i) The total number of j-packets is $O(n)$; (ii) The number of j-packets with sources in U is $O((n/s)(\ell/k))$; (iii) The number of j-packets with destinations in U' is $O(n/s')$.*

Theorem 2. *For any $\ell > k$, the above algorithm performs (ℓ, k)-routing in optimal $O\left(\sqrt{\ell k n}\right)$ time using constant queue size, with high probability.*

4   Deterministic Algorithm

In the algorithms presented in the previous section, randomization is employed exclusively to assign colors to the packets, so to partition them into subsets characterized by lower congestion at source or destination tiles of suitable size. Therefore, in order to obtain a deterministic algorithm we must adopt a (more sophisticated) coloring strategy that provides similar guarantees in the worst case. The required modifications to the algorithms are described below.

Let us first consider the case $\ell \leq k$. The coloring performed in Step 1 of the randomized algorithm for this case can be substituted with the following computation. Let $s = \sqrt{nk/\ell}$.

1. In parallel for each s-tile T, rank the packets destined to T with consecutive integers ensuring that packets whose sources are in consecutive nodes of the mesh receive consecutive ranks. Assign color j to every packet whose rank r is such that $r \bmod \ell = j$, with $0 \leq j < \ell$. Call j-packets the packets of color j.

Step 1 can be accomplished in $O(s + \sqrt{n})$ time by running s pipelined prefix operations on the entire mesh, where each prefix ranks the packets destined to a distinct s-tile.

It is easy to see that, for every j, there are $O((n/s)(k/\ell))$ j-packets with destination in the same s-tile, and there are $O(s)$ j-packets originating at the nodes of any stripe of $\lceil s/\sqrt{n} \rceil$ rows of the mesh. However, the coloring does not guarantee that a node has only $O(1)$ j-packets. Therefore, the sorting step (Step 2.(a)) of the randomized algorithm must be modified as follows.

2.(a).i Evenly distribute the j-packets within each stripe of $\lceil s/\sqrt{n} \rceil$ consecutive rows.
2.(a).ii Sort the j-packets in lexicographic order (destination s-tile, destination).

Step 2.(a).i can be accomplished as a balancing of $O(s)$ packets in a linear array of $O(s)$ nodes in $O(s)$ time [Lei92]. The rest of the algorithm is identical to the randomized one.

Consider now the case $\ell > k$. We modify the randomized algorithm for this case by substituting the coloring performed in Step 1 with the following computation. Let $s = \sqrt{n\ell/k} \geq \ell/k$ and $s' = \sqrt{nk/\ell}$.

1. In parallel for each s'-tile T, rank the packets destined to T with consecutive integers ensuring that packets whose sources are in the same s-tile receive consecutive ranks. Assign color j to every packet whose rank r is such that $r \bmod k = j$, with $0 \leq j < k$. Call j-packets the packets of color j.

It is easy the see that the above coloring, which can be performed with techniques aking to those used for the case $\ell \leq k$, guarantees that the three properties stated in Lemma 2 hold in the worst case.

Theorem 3. *Any instance of (ℓ, k)-routing can be performed in optimal $O\left(\sqrt{\ell k n}\right)$ time in the worst case using constant queue size.*

References

FRU96. S. Felperin, P. Raghavan, and E. Upfal. A theory of wormhole routing in parallel computers. *IEEE Trans. on Computers*, C-45(6):704–713, June 1996.

GH+98. M. D. Grammatikakis, D. F. Hsu, , M. Kraetzel, and J. F. Sibeyn. Packet routing in fixed-connection networks: A survey. *Journal of Parallel and Distributed Computing*, 54(2):77–132, November 1998.

HR90. T. Hagerup and C. Rüb. A guided tour of Chernoff bounds. *Information Processing Letters*, 33(6):305–308, February 1990.

HPP01. K. T. Herley, A. Pietracaprina, and G. Pucci. One-to-many routing on the mesh. In *Proc. of the 13th Symp. on Parallel Algorithms and Architectures*, June 2001. To appear.

KK79. P. Kermani and L. Kleinrock. Virtual cut through: a new computer communication switching technique. *Computer Networks*, 3(4):267–286, April 1979.

Lei92. F. T. Leighton. *Introduction to Parallel Algorithms and Architectures: Arrays • Trees • Hypercubes*. Morgan Kaufmann, San Mateo, CA, 1992.

MS93. F. Makedon and A. Symvonis. Optimal algorithms for the many-to-one routing problem on two-dimensional meshes. *Microprocessors and Microsystems*, 17:361–367, 1993.

NS95. I. Newman and A. Schuster. Hot-potato worm routing via store-and-forward packet routing. *Journal of Parallel and Distributed Computing*, 30(1):76–84, January 1995.

SK94. J. F. Sibeyn and M. Kaufmann. Deterministic 1-k routing on meshes, with application to hot-potato worm-hole routing. In *Proc. of the 11th Symp. on Theoretical Aspects of Computer Science*, pages 237–248, March 1994.

Topic 15+20
Multimedia and Embedded Systems

Stamatis Vassiliadis, Francky Catthoor, Mateo Valero, and Sorin Cotofana

Topic Chairpersons

This combined topic embraces two broad themes: *multimedia* and *embedded systems*. Multimedia has become an important technological innovation and plays an important role in our daily activities. It is defined as the combination of the following forms of information: text, graphics, video, and audio – referred to as multimedia formats. Traditionally, the multimedia formats were being represented in an analog form, but nowadays we are observing a migration from the analog representation to the digital representation. The digital representation of the multimedia formats proved to have certain advantages, for example easier editability and improved error resilience. However, the digital representation presented the scientific community and the industry with a sizeable problem which is the enormous size of the digital representation/information and extreme computational requirements.

The second theme covered relates to embedded systems. A technology turning point that made embedded systems an everyday reality has to be the advent of microprocessors. The technological developments that allowed single chip processors (microprocessors) made the embedded systems inexpensive and flexible. Consequently, microprocessor based embedded systems have been introduced into many new application areas. Currently, embedded programmable microprocessors in one form or another, from 8-bit micro-controllers to 32-bit digital signal processors and 64-bit RISC processors, are everywhere, in consumer electronic devices, home appliances, automobiles, network equipment, industrial control systems, etc.

Some of the driving forces behind the fast expansion of the embedded systems market relates to the proliferation of computing technologies to traditionally non-computing domains, e.g., medical instrumentation, automotive industry, the fast advances in VLSI technologies, and the tendency to replace analog signal processing with digital signal processing.

From the papers submitted to both the original topics, six papers were accepted for presentation.

The first paper, by F. Seinstra, D. Koelma, and J.-M. Geusebroek, describes a software architecture that allows image processing researchers to develop parallel applications in a transparent manner. The architecture's main component is an extensive library of low level image processing operations that can be run on distributed memory MIMD-style parallel hardware.

In the second paper, by U. Assarsson and P. Stenström, a comparative performance evaluation of a number of load distribution strategies is conducted. It is shown that several strategies suffer from a too high an orchestration overhead to provide any meaningful speedup. However, it is also indicated that by applying some straightforward tricks to get rid of most of the locking needed, it is possible to achieve interesting speedups.

The third paper, by R. Kutil, deals with a fast and efficient coding algorithm using the wavelet transform. It investigates a new algorithm with a simple and spacially oriented coefficient scan order which is suitable for parallelization.

The fourth paper, by D. Tcheressiz, B. Juurlink, S. Vassiliadis and H. Wijshoff, presents performance evaluations for the Complex Streamed Instruction architecture on a set of important image processing kernels. The Complex Streamed Instruction (CSI) set is an architectural paradigm designed to accelerate multimedia applications. These applications are characterized by streaming operations on small-width data elements such as 8-bit pixels or 16-bit audio samples. CSI instructions operate on two-dimensional data streams in a SIMD fashion and are able to process streams of arbitrary length. When evaluating the performance of the CSI architecture on a set of important image processing kernels simulation results indicate that CSI provides a speedup by a factor of up to 3.98 (2.60 on average) when compared to Sun's media ISA extension VIS. Moreover CSI scales much better than VIS with increasing bandwidth.

The fifth paper, by A. El-Mahdy and I. Watson, presents a novel vector instruction set that combines the benefits of sub-word parallelism and traditional vector processing. The proposed hardware support is meant for multimedia processing on a general purpose processor and comprises a vector based instruction set with a submatrix addressing mode that utilizes subword vectors. The authors propose also a cache prefetch optimization that exploit the two dimensional access pattern of multimedia MPEG2 video applications. Detailed simulation results suggesting that the optimized cache removes 75% of the misses are also presented.

The final paper, authored by V. Kianzad and S. S. Bhattacharyya, addresses the embedded system design issue by proposing novel partitioning and scheduling techniques that aggressively streamline interprocessor communication. The paper evaluates the benefit of using Genetic Algorithms for automatic clustering of parallel embedded applications. The two key trends in the synthesis of implementations for embedded processors are addressed: the increasing importance of managing interprocessor communication in an efficient manner and the acceptance of significantly longer compilation time by embedded system designers.

In closing, we would like to thank the authors who submitted a contribution, as well as the Euro-Par Organizing Committee, and the scores of referees, whose efforts have made this conference, and the Multimedia and Embedded Systems topics possible.

A Software Architecture for User Transparent Parallel Image Processing on MIMD Computers

Frank Seinstra, Dennis Koelma, and Jan-Mark Geusebroek

Faculty of Science, University of Amsterdam
Kruislaan 403, 1098 SJ Amsterdam, The Netherlands
{fjseins,koelma,geusebroek}@science.uva.nl

Abstract. This paper describes a software architecture that allows image processing researchers to develop parallel applications in a transparent manner. The architecture's main component is an extensive library of low level image processing operations that can be run on distributed memory MIMD-style parallel hardware. Since the library has an application programming interface identical to that of an existing sequential image library, all parallelism is completely hidden from the user.
In this paper we give an overview of all architecture components, and show how issues related to automatic parallelization and optimization are dealt with by the application of domain specific performance models. Results obtained for a realistic application indicate that model-based optimization of a wide range of imaging software indeed is possible.

1 Introduction

Although many image processing applications are ideally suited for parallel implementation, most researchers in imaging do not benefit from high performance computing on a daily basis. Essentially, this is due to the fact that the image processing community considers most parallel solutions 'too cumbersome' to apply. As it is unrealistic to expect image processing researchers to be experts in parallel computing, tools must be provided to allow them to develop high performance applications in a highly familiar manner.

The ideal solution would be a fully automatic parallelizing compiler. Unfortunately, the fundamental issue of automatic and optimal problem partitioning remains unsolved. Another possibility is to design a parallel programming language, either general purpose [10] or aimed at image processing specifically [1]. However, in accordance with the remarks made in [6], we feel that a parallel language is not the preferred solution. Even a few simple language annotations are often considered cumbersome, and thus should be avoided.

A more practical approach is to design a software library containing parallel versions of operations commonly used in image processing. Due to the relative ease of implementation, many such libraries have been described (for example, see [3], [4]). Often, efficiency of execution on a range of machines is obtained by hard-coding a number of different implementations, one for each platform. We feel that this solution to *intra-operation optimization* requires too much implementation effort, and is impossible to maintain on the long term. Also, the important aspect of *inter-operation optimization* (or optimization across library calls) is often not dealt with. For these reasons, we take a different approach.

In our research we aim at creating a parallel image processing architecture that brings the benefits of high-performance computing to the image processing community in a transparent manner (i.e., hidden from the user). The core of the architecture is a library containing a set of abstract data types and associated pixel level operations executing in data parallel fashion. The most distinctive aspect of our work is that we apply domain specific performance models as a basis for automatic optimization of applications implemented using our library.

This paper is organized as follows. Section 2 discusses all architecture components. Section 3 introduces a high-level abstract machine for parallel image processing (APIPM). In Section 4 APIPM-based performance models are introduced. In Section 5 model predictions are compared with results obtained on a machine from the class of target platforms. Conclusions are given in Section 6.

2 Architecture Overview

The software architecture consists of eight logical components (see Figure 1):

C1. Sequential Image Processing Operations. The first component contains a large set of sequential operations typically used by image processing researchers. As recognized in, for example, Image Algebra [7], a small set of *operation classes* can be identified that covers the bulk of all commonly applied image operations. We have implemented each operation class as a *generic algorithm*, using the C++ *function template mechanism*. Each operation that maps onto the functionality as provided by a generic algorithm is implemented by instantiating the generic algorithm with the proper parameters, including the function to be applied to the individual data elements (e.g., pixels).

In our current library the following set of generic algorithms is implemented: (1) unary pixel operation, (2) binary pixel operation, (3) global reduction, (4)

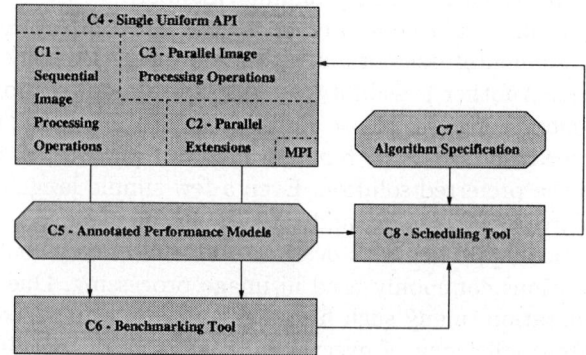

Fig. 1. Architecture overview

neighborhood operation, (5) generalized convolution, and (6) geometric transformation. In the future additional generic algorithms will be added, e.g. iterative and recursive neighborhood operations, and queue based algorithms.

C2. Parallel Extensions. Three classes of routines are implemented (using MPI 1.1) that introduce the parallelism into the library: (1) data *partitioning* routines, to indicate which data parts should be processed by each processing unit, (2) *distribution* and *redistribution* routines, to scatter, gather, broadcast, and redistribute data structures, and (3) *overlap communication* routines, to exchange *shadow regions*, such as image borders in neighborhood operations.

C3. Parallel Image Processing Operations. Much of the source code for the sequential generic algorithms in C1 is reused in the implementation of their respective parallel counterparts. To that end, for each generic algorithm we have defined a so-called *parallelizable pattern*. Each pattern constitutes the maximum amount of work in a sequential generic algorithm that can be performed both sequentially and in parallel - in the latter case without having to communicate to obtain non-local data. This topic is discussed in detail in [9].

Implementation of a sequential generic algorithm is obtained by concatenating basic memory operations and a single parallelizable pattern. Parallel implementations of generic algorithms are obtained by inserting communication operations (from C2) in the concatenation of sequential library routines.

C4. Single Uniform API. The library is provided with an application programming interface identical to that of an existing sequential library (Horus [5]). As such, all parallelism has been made fully transparent to the user.

C5. Annotated Performance Models. In the library we provide only one parallel implementation of each generic algorithm. To ensure efficiency of execution on all target platforms, the parallel operations are implemented such that they are capable of adapting to the performance characteristics of a specific parallel machine. To make these characteristics explicit, each library operation is annotated with a performance model. An overview is given in Section 4.

C6. Benchmarking Tool. For a specific machine, performance values for the model parameters are obtained by running a set of *benchmarking* operations. Based on the models and the benchmarking results, intra-operation optimization can be performed automatically, fully transparent to the user.

C7. Algorithm Specification. Besides intra-operation optimization, optimization across library calls can be performed if information is available on the order in which library operations are applied in a given application. Essentially, this information is obtainable from the original program code. As implementation of a complete parser is not an essential part of this research, we assume that an algorithm specification is provided in addition to the program itself.

C8. Scheduling Tool. Once the benchmarking results and the algorithm specification are available, a scheduling component is applied to find an optimal solution for the application at hand. In the implementation of each parallel generic algorithm, requests for scheduling results are performed to determine which parallelization strategy is required. Whether scheduling results are static only, or should be generated at run-time is still an open future research issue.

3 Abstract Parallel Image Processing Machine

The design of the annotated performance models is based on the definition of an abstract parallel image processing machine (or APIPM, see Figure 2(a)). An APIPM consists of one or more abstract sequential image processing machines (ASIPMs), each consisting of four related components: (1) a *sequential image processing unit* (SIPU), capable of executing APIPM instructions, one at a time, (2) a *memory unit*, capable of storing (image) data, (3) an *I/O unit*, for transporting data between the memory unit and external sensing or storage devices, and (4) *data channels*, the means by which data is transported between ASIPM units and external devices. In a complete APIPM the memory unit of each ASIPM is connected with those of all other ASIPMs.

The APIPM instruction set (Figure 2(b)) consists of four classes of operations: (1) *generic image instructions*, i.e. the specialized parallelizable patterns of Section 2, (2) *memory instructions*, for allocation and copying of (image) data, (3) *I/O instructions*, for transporting data between memory and external devices, and (4) *communication instructions*, for exchanging data among ASIPM units. For simplicity, in Figure 2(b) the operands for each opcode are left out.

The description of the APIPM reflects a state-of-the-art distributed memory MIMD-style parallel machine. It differs from a general purpose machine in that each SIPU is designed for imaging tasks only. Although a fully connected network is often not present, we still have included one in the APIPM. This is because in most multicomputer systems communication is based on circuit-switched message routing, which makes a network *virtually* fully connected.

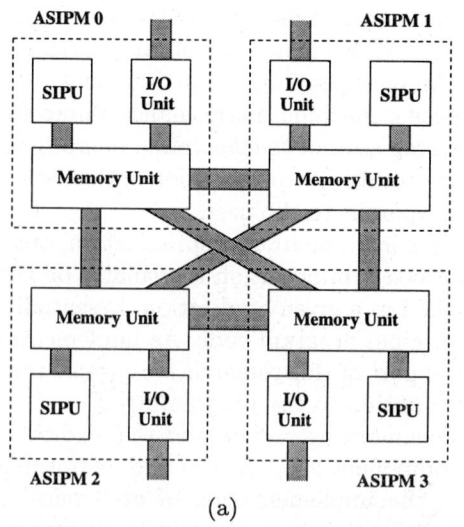

opcode	generic image instructions
UPOP	unary pixel operation
BPOPV	binary pixel operation (arg: vector)
BPOPI	binary pixel operation (arg: image)
REDUCOP	global reduction operation
NEIGHOP	neighborhood operation
GCONVOP	generalized convolution
GEOMAT	geom. transform (arg: matrix)
GEOROI	geom. transform (region of interest)
opcode	**memory instructions**
CREATE	allocate data block in memory unit
MEMCPY	copy data in memory unit
DELETE	free up data block in memory unit
opcode	**I/O instructions**
IMPORT	import data from external device
EXPORT	export data to external device
opcode	**communication instructions**
SEND	send data to other ASIPM
RECV	receive data from other ASIPM

Fig. 2. APIPM comprising of four ASIPMS, and related instruction set

4 Performance Models

Here, we assume all library operations to be implemented by concatenation of APIPM instructions only. Also, we assume that the execution time of each library operation can be partitioned into *independent* time intervals, each corresponding to the cost of a single APIPM instruction. The performance of a library operation is obtained by adding the execution times of all APIPM instructions used.

This is formalized as follows. Let $\mathbf{I} = \{I_1, I_2, \cdots, I_n\}$ be the APIPM instruction set. Let $\mathbf{P} = \{P_{I_1}, P_{I_2}, \cdots, P_{I_n}\}$ be the set of *performance values* for all n instructions in $\mathbf{I}$. We assume that, for any given system capable of running APIPM instructions, and for each instruction in $\mathbf{I}$, P_{I_i} can be obtained by benchmarking. Also, let $\mathbf{L} = \{\mathbf{L}_1, \mathbf{L}_2, \cdots, \mathbf{L}_m\}$ be the set of all m operations implemented using instructions in $\mathbf{I}$ only. For all library operations $\mathbf{L}_x$ ($x \in \{1, \cdots, m\}$) we define $\mathbf{L}_x = \{I_1, I_2, \cdots, I_n\}$, in combination with the total number of occurrences (or *count*) of each APIPM instruction in $\mathbf{L}_x$: $\mathbf{C}_x = \{C_{I_1,x}, C_{I_2,x}, \cdots, C_{I_n,x}\}$. The expected total execution time of operation $\mathbf{L}_x$ is obtained by $T_{\mathbf{L}_x} = \sum_{i=1}^{n} C_{I_i,x} P_{I_i}$.

A problem with the simplistic model formalized here is that most APIPM instructions are not single static entities. This is because the execution of an instruction often depends on the values of its operands. Therefore, a static entity for each possible operand combination must be incorporated in our model. To avoid an explosion of the number of static entities we allow each instruction I_i and each value P_{I_i} to be *parameterized*. As we have not discussed the operands of the APIPM instructions we will not give a detailed overview of the model parameterization. To give an example, however, in almost all instructions a 'datatype' parameter is incorporated (e.g., giving $I_i('int')$ and $I_i('float')$). Also, a 'data-input-size' parameter is required for most performance values in $\mathbf{P}$ (e.g., giving $P_{I_i(datatype)}(size)$). For a complete overview we refer to [8].

5 Measurements and Validation

In this section we show how a realistic image processing application, implemented using our library, is executed in parallel. The application is highly relevant as it incorporates all generic image instructions as referred to in Section 3. First, a description is given of the underlying algorithm. Next, both a straightforward sequential implementation as well as the related parallel implementation are discussed. Finally, measured results are compared with APIPM model predictions.

5.1 Detection of Curvilinear Structures in Images

As discussed in [2], the problem of detecting (curved) lines in images is solved by considering the second order directional derivative in the gradient direction, for each possible line direction. This is achieved by applying anisotropic Gaussian filters, parameterized by orientation θ, smoothing scale σ_v in the line direction, and differentiation scale σ_w perpendicular to the line, given by

$$r''(x, y, \sigma_v, \sigma_w, \theta) = \sigma_v \sigma_w \left| f_{ww}^{\sigma_v, \sigma_w, \theta} \right| \frac{1}{b^{\sigma_v, \sigma_w, \theta}}. \tag{1}$$

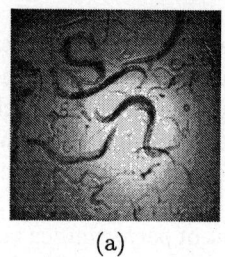 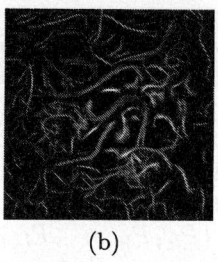

(a)   (b)

Fig. 3. Left: typical input image, courtesy of Janssen Pharmaceuticals, Beerse, Belgium. Right: result image obtained after application of the directional filtering program

When the filter is correctly aligned with a line in the image, and σ_v, σ_w are optimally tuned to capture the line, filter response is maximal. Hence, the per pixel maximum line contrast over the filter parameters yields line detection:

$$R(x,y) = \arg \max_{\sigma_v, \sigma_w, \theta} r''(x, y, \sigma_v, \sigma_w, \theta). \tag{2}$$

This directional filtering problem can be implemented sequentially in several ways. Here, we have implemented the operation by rotating the image data, whilst keeping the orientation of the filters fixed. We have chosen this implementation as we expect it to be the solution preferred by most image processing researchers. We do not claim, however, that this implementation provides optimal performance when executed either sequentially or in parallel.

Figure 3(a) gives a typical example of an image used as input to the program. The result obtained for a reasonably large subspace of $(\sigma_v, \sigma_w, \theta)$ is shown in Figure 3(b). Sequentially, the program may take from a few minutes up to several hours to complete, depending on the size of the image and the extent of the parameter subspace. Consequently, parallel execution is highly desired.

The main body of the sequential implementation is presented in pseudo code in Listing 1. The program starts by rotating the original input image for a given orientation θ. In addition, for all (σ_v, σ_w) combinations the filtering is performed

```
FOR all orientations θ
    Rotated_IM = GeometricOp(Original_IM, "rotate", θ);
    FOR all smoothing scales σ_v
        FOR all differentiation scales σ_w
            Filtered1_IM = GenConvOp(Rotated_IM, "gaus", σ_w, σ_v, 2, 0);
            Filtered2_IM = GenConvOp(Rotated_IM, "gaus", σ_w, σ_v, 0, 0);
            Detected_IM = BinPixImArgOp(Filtered1_IM, "absdiv", Filtered2_IM);
            Detected_IM = BinPixCnstArgOp(Detected_IM, "mul", σ_v * σ_w);
            BackRotated_IM = GeometricOp(Detected_IM, "rotate", -θ);
            Contrast_IM = BinPixImArgOp(Contrast_IM, "max", BackRotated_IM);
```

Listing 1: Directional filtering pseudo code

by six operations executed in sequence. First, $f_{ww}^{\sigma_v,\sigma_w,\theta}$ and $b^{\sigma_v,\sigma_w,\theta}$ are produced by two generalized convolution operations, each with the appropriate parameters. Next, the result of Equation (1) is obtained by executing two binary pixel operations. Finally, the result image is rotated back to match the orientation of the original input image, and the maximum response image is obtained.

5.2 Parallel Execution

As all parallelization issues are shielded from the user, the pseudo code of Listing 1 directly constitutes a parallel program as well. Optimization of the efficiency of the program is to be taken care of by the architecture's scheduling component. As a fully functional scheduling tool is not yet available in the current version of our architecture, we have created two different schedules for the program by hand. In the first schedule *all* library operations run in parallel, using all available processing units. The second schedule differs from the first in that the last two operations in the inner loop are run on one node only.

In both schedules the Original_IM structure is broadcast to all nodes. This is because the structure is applied in the initial rotation operation. This broadcast needs to be performed only once, as Original_IM is not updated in subsequent operations. Also, in both schedules the first four operations in the inner loop are executed locally on partial image data structures. The only need for communication is in the exchange of shadow regions in the Gaussian convolutions.

In the first schedule the last two operations in the innermost loop are run in parallel as well. This requires the distributed image Detected_IM to be available in full at each node. This can be achieved by executing a gather-to-all operation, which is logically equivalent to a gather followed by a broadcast. Finally, a partial maximum response image Contrast_IM is calculated on each node, which requires a final gather operation to be executed just before termination of the program. In the second schedule, the intermediate image Detected_IM is gathered to the single node that produces the back-rotated image, as well as the final maximum response image.

As stated before, the scheduling tool should pick the optimal solution out of such competing schedules. Next, we will show that the models as used in our architecture are powerful enough to allow such decisions to be made correctly.

5.3 Performance Evaluation

To initialize our performance models we have performed a small set of benchmarking operations. For each instruction in the directional filtering program not more than two measurements were performed, i.e. for input (image) sizes of 200^2 and 1000^2 elements. Based on the measurements, predictions for each instruction and for each required input size were obtained as indicated in Section 4. A model for the complete program was obtained by adding the measured performance values for all APIPM instructions executed by the program in sequence.

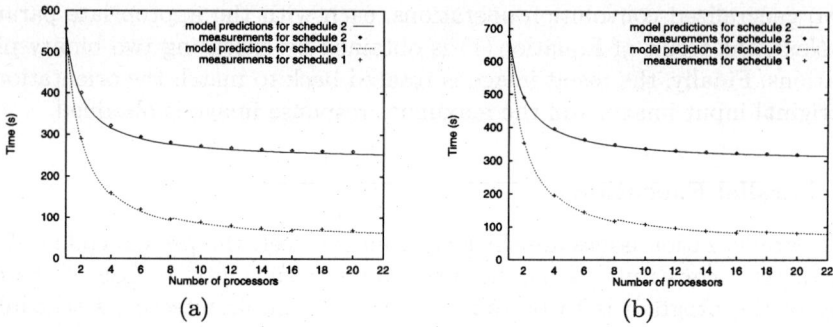

Fig. 4. Comparison of predictions and measurements for the two program schedules. Left: results for input image of size 1098^2, and for a parameter subspace including 12 orientations and 4 (σ_v, σ_w) combinations. Right: results for input image of size 707^2, and for a parameter subspace including 36 orientations and 4 (σ_v, σ_w) combinations

The benchmarking operations, as well as the directional filtering program were executed on the 20-node homogeneous DAS-cluster located at the University of Amsterdam. All nodes in the cluster contain a 200 Mhz Pentium Pro with 64 MByte of EDO-RAM, and are connected by a 1.2 Gbit/sec full-duplex Myrinet SAN network. The nodes run the RedHat Linux 6.2 operating system.

Based on our performance models we are able to decide which schedule is optimal. As shown in Figure 4(a) (depicting the *complete* execution time of both schedules), our models indicate that the first schedule is always preferred - for any number of processing units. Clearly, broadcasting a full-sized image structure is not as expensive as performing the complete image rotation sequentially on one node. The 'hops' in the graph of schedule 1 are explained by the fact that the broadcast operation is implemented using a spanning binomial tree (SBT), which has a cost related to $logN$.

To test the accuracy of our performance models we have executed the directional filtering program for both schedules. The resulting mean execution times for each run are included in Figure 4(a) as well. In most situations measured lower and upper bounds are within 0.5 seconds of the mean execution times. The presented results indicate that the model predictions for both schedules are highly accurate - for any number of processors. Even worst case predictions are within 5.5% of the measured values. It is noteworthy, however, that our models are slightly optimistic in all situations. This is explained by the fact that the performance measured in a benchmarking process tends to be somewhat higher than what is actually obtained in a real application. Similar results for a smaller input image, but for a larger parameter subspace are shown in Figure 4(b).

For schedule 1, our models predict that maximum speedup (10.16) is obtained on 64 nodes; adding more nodes is counterproductive. The efficiency of the program drops dramatically from 96.5%, 88.2%, and 72.9% for 2, 4, and 8 nodes respectively, to 15.9% for 64 nodes. This is due to the large impact of communication, and especially the repeated broadcast. If the image processing researcher would have produced a sequential implementation with rotating filters instead of a rotating image, parallel performance may have been significantly better.

6 Conclusions and Future Work

In this paper we have described a software architecture that allows an image processing researcher to develop parallel applications in a transparent manner. The architecture's core is formed by an extensive parallel image processing library that has a programming interface identical to that of an existing sequential library. Application of the library is not expected to be considered 'cumbersome', as it fully adheres to the image processing researcher's frame of reference.

We have shown that, by applying domain-specific performance models, optimization is performed automatically. Experiments show that, for a realistic application, the models are highly accurate. Given these results we are confident in that the architecture's core forms powerful basis for automatic parallelization and optimization of a wide range of image processing applications.

It should be noted that, although all parallelism is hidden inside the library, much of the efficiency of parallel execution is still in the hands of the library user. As shown in the previous section, if a sequential implementation is provided that requires expensive communication operations when run in parallel, program efficiency may be disappointing. Therefore, the library user should be aware that certain operations are expensive, and should be avoided as much as possible.

In the near future we will start creating a fully functional scheduling component. Also, we will extend the set of generic algorithms described in Section 2. Finally, we will continue investigating the implications of parallelization of typical (example) applications, especially in the area of real-time image processing.

References

1. J. Brown and D. Crookes. A High Level Language for Parallel Image Processing. *Image and Vision Computing*, 12(2):67–79, March 1994.
2. J. M. Geusebroek. *Color and Geometrical Structure in Images*. PhD thesis, Faculty of Science, University of Amsterdam The Netherlands, November 2000.
3. L. H. Jamieson, E. J. Delp, and C.-C. Wang. A Software Environment for Parallel Computer Vision. *IEEE Computer*, 25(2):73–75, February 1992.
4. Z. Juhasz and D. Crookes. A PVM Implementation of a Portable Parallel Image Processing Library. In *EuroPVM'96*, pages 188–196, Munich, Germany, 1996.
5. D. Koelma, E. Poll, and F. Seinstra. Horus (Release 0.9.2). Technical report, Faculty of Science, University of Amsterdam, The Netherlands, February 2000.
6. C. M. Pancake and D. Bergmark. Do Parallel Languages Respond to the Needs of Scientific Programmers. *IEEE Computer*, 23(12):13–23, December 1990.
7. G. X. Ritter and J. N. Wilson. *Handbook of Computer Vision Algorithms in Image Algebra*. CRC Press, Inc, 1996.

8. F. J. Seinstra and D. Koelma. Accurate Performance Models of Parallel Low Level Image Processing Operations Based on a Simple Abstract Machine. ISIS internal report, Faculty of Science, University of Amsterdam, The Netherlands, Sept. 2000.
9. F. J. Seinstra and D. Koelma. The Lazy Programmer's Approach to Building a Parallel Image Processing Library. In *Proc. of the 15th International Parallel & Distributed Processing Symposium (IPDPS 2001)*, San Francisco, USA, April 2001.
10. G. V. Wilson and P. Lu. *Parallel Programming Using C++*. Scientific and Engineering Computation Series. The MIT Press, 1996.

A Case Study of Load Distribution in Parallel View Frustum Culling and Collision Detection

Ulf Assarsson[1] and Per Stenström[2]

[1] ABB Robotics
Drakegatan 6, SE-412 50 Göteborg, Sweden
uffe@ce.chalmers.se
[2] Department of Computer Engineering Chalmers University of Technology
SE-412 96, Göteborg, Sweden
pers@ce.chalmers.se

Abstract. When parallelizing hierarchical view frustum culling and collision detection, the low computation cost per node and the fact that the traversal path through the tree structure is not known à priori make the classical load-balance versus communication tradeoff very challenging. In this paper, a comparative performance evaluation of a number of load distribution strategies is conducted. We show that several strategies suffer from a too high an orchestration overhead to provide any meaningful speedup. However, by applying some straightforward tricks to get rid of most of the locking needed, it is possible to achieve interesting speedups. For our industrially related test scenes, we get about a four-fold speedup on eight processors for view frustum culling and three times speedup for collision detection.

1 Introduction

View frustum culling (VFC) and collision detection (CD) are two common components of real time computer graphics applications. VFC aims at reducing the computational complexity of a succeeding rendering pass by extracting the graphics objects that are in the view frustum. For hierarchical VFC, a hierarchy is built up as a tree structure from the bounding volume of each object. Each node in the tree has a bounding volume enclosing a part of the scene. The tree is traversed from the root in a depth-first manner, and if a bounding volume is found to be outside the frustum during the traversal, the contents of that subtree can be culled from rendering. While some research has been devoted to improving performance of VFC and CD (see e.g. [1,6,7,5]), parallel implementations of them are to the best of our knowledge not reported in the open literature, except for some preliminary experiments [17]. As rendering performance is constantly improving, the bottleneck may eventually end up in VFC and CD which is the main motivation behind this work. Note that while rendering is typically performed by graphics engines, VFC and CD are typically run on general-purpose processors. In the tree-search algorithms inherent in both these applications, the typically low computation cost of each node in comparison with the node distribution cost makes the load distribution in a parallel implementation extremely challenging.

In this paper we evaluate the effectiveness of a set of load distribution strategies on parallel implementations of hierarchical view frustum culling with scenes from an industrial application. We also examine the capability of the most promising scheme applied on collision detection. For VFC we use axis aligned bounding box (AABB) trees [11], while for collision detection we use both AABB- and oriented bounding box (OBB) trees [5].

The load distribution schemes we select are a global task queue, and a number of distributed task queue schemes well-known from the literature. We evaluate the speedup of the parallel implementations using these strategies on a 13-node Sun Enterprise shared-memory multiprocessor and on a dual Pentium-III 500 MHz personal computer.

We find that while some of the schemes were expected to provide a reasonable speedup, they performed inferior owing to the high communication and synchronization cost. Our results show that due to the low computation cost per node compared to the distribution cost, only the more sophisticated lock-free scheme provides interesting speedup numbers. By considering a number of optimizations – especially by getting rid of the synchronizations – we managed to get promising results, even for the highly unbalanced trees resulting from the industrial scenes we use. For our scenes, we achieve a speedup of around four on eight processors for view frustum culling and about three on seven processors for collision detection with real test cases from an industrial case study.

2 Experimental Set-Up

The code for testing a bounding volume against the view frustum is the one of a previously proposed optimized algorithm [1]. This implements many optimizations such as caching of previous computations, implying little computation cost per node in many cases. Other optimizations include plane-coherency, octant, and translation and rotation coherency tests (see [1] for details).

We use three trees that are the hierarchical scene graph representations of three 3D models - all of real environments and all used in industrial applications. The three highly unbalanced trees used in the tests are: a car factory shop floor with 3,932 graph nodes, a factory shop floor with 1,137 graph nodes and a factory cell with 254 graph nodes. We refer to them as the *large model*, the *medium model*, and the *small model*, respectively.

The camera–or view frustum–used in the view frustum culling computations is moved along one specific path for each model, each sampled from a user walk through in the model. The presented traversal times and speedups are the average times and average speedups of all traversals during the walk through.

The experiments are carried out on a Sun Enterprise 4000 shared-memory multiprocessor. This machine is equipped with 14 UltraSPARC-II CPUs running at 248 MHz. Each CPU is attached to a 16-Kbyte L1 data cache and a 1-Mbyte L2 cache, both using a line size of 32 bytes. The locks used have been implemented using the SPARC-instruction ldstub which loads a byte followed by a store that sets all bits in that byte atomically. We only show results for up to 13 processors. One processor is left for the operating system to avoid the perturbation it would cause when it is invoked every millisecond.

3 Evaluation of Load-Distribution Schemes

In this section, we consider the effectiveness of load distribution strategies that seem adequate for the dynamic behavior of our workload. As a reference, we use the classical global task queue scheme which we consider first.

3.1 Global Task Queue

In this approach, each processor removes and add tasks (tree-nodes) using a global task queue. The virtue is good load balance while the overhead associated with orchestrating the global task queue is known to be high.

Results from the experiments of parallel VFC are presented in Figure 1. Figure 1.a-1.c show the average speedup and Figure 1.e-1.f show the average execution time for VFC of one frame.

For the global task queue, the maximum number of processors that can provide speedup before the global task queue becomes the bottle-neck, is limited to the total time for processing a node divided by the time for accessing the global queue (*node_cost/ access_cost*). We see that we get a maximum speedup of only 1.5, with only three processors on the small model. Moreover, when we increase the number of processors, the speedup goes down owing to serialization effects, as expected.

3.2 The Global Counter Scheme

A more scalable strategy is to associate a local task queue with each processor. Each processor adds tasks to the local queue pointed to by a global counter that is incremented after each insertion by any processor and protected by a lock[1] according to [14]. In this way the load will be nearly optimally balanced if all processors can process nodes equally fast. The serialization of accesses to one single queue is replaced by the serialization of reading and incrementing the global counter, which is usually faster. However, the lock mechanism around the counter can potentially become a new bottleneck when we increase the number of processors. In addition, the locks that synchronize the accesses to the queue attached to each processor is another potential bottleneck.

As can be seen in Figure 1a, compared to the global task queue algorithm, the stagnation in speed-up which peaks at about 1.9, comes later – at more

---

[1] For some processors it is possible to atomically read and increment a variable with just one or two assembler instructions instead of using a lock.

than eight processors instead of three, which is expected since incrementing a counter is quicker than inserting or removing a task (which in our implementation basically consists of changing an array index and reading the contents of the array element, i.e about twice the cost). The stagnation comes from the global lock which gives a high cost and introduces serialization.

3.3 The Hybrid Scheme

To further reduce the orchestration overhead and contention due to locking and shared memory access, we considered two optimizations of the global counter scheme. The resulting scheme is referred to as *hybrid*.

The skip-pointer tree optimization A common optimization in ray tracing is to represent the tree in depth-first order in an array [19], with a skip index for each node that points out the next element to access if the underlying subgraph should be skipped during the traversal. Then a full tree traversal can be performed by simply accessing the array sequentially from start to end. Every subtree will be represented in the array as a consecutive chunk of elements, so instead of distributing a node (subtree), we send the start-index and the stop-index of the array. While it provides good cache-locality in the sequential single processor case, it can also give better locality in the parallel case.

Trading off larger tasks for less load balance This straightforward optimization uses the observation that at a certain depth, when the underlying subtree only contains a few nodes, it will be faster to process the nodes rather than distributing them, if the computation-cost is smaller than the distribution-cost

Since the size of each subtree is not known beforehand, the heuristic we have tried is to distribute tasks at the node-level until a certain level after which the rest of the subtrees are considered as tasks. The first phase uses the global counter scheme according to Section 3.2, whereas the second phase serially executes the tree traversal algorithm with no further balancing of the load. Both phases use the skip pointer optimization and thus will enjoy the increased locality it provides. A counter keeps track of how many nodes that so far have been processed by the distribution algorithm. If a threshold number is exceeded, all processors finish the computations and distribution of children for the node it is currently working on, and enter the serial phase. We found empirically that a threshold of six times the number of processors gave the best performance for our models with a difference in load of less than 2% for the large model.

The skip-pointer tree optimization contributed with an overall speedup of 15 − 40% compared to the global counter scheme. Despite the possibility to also trade off load balance for larger tasks, the total speedup for both optimizations together peaks at only 2.2 times (for 10 processors).

We also made measurements showing that if the cost of the VFC computations at each node were virtually zero, we would get a huge slowdown using more than one processor. The reason is the high distribution cost compared to the cost of the serial traversal of the skip-pointer tree. Skipping the distribution phase, resulting in a serial single processor algorithm, would actually have been optimal for this case.

The schemes used so far suffer from too much overhead, especially concering lock accesses. This motivated us to seek for a lock-free approach which we study in the next section.

4 A Lock-Free Scheme

The Lock-Free scheme distributes the load without requiring locks or any synchronization. The way we adapted the original scheme to avoid locking is as follows.

Each processor has one local-queue and some in-queues. A processor removes tasks from its local-queue and its in-queues, and adds new tasks to its local queue and dedicated in-queues of neighboring processors. The in-queues are created such that one processor can insert tasks at one end of the queue and another processor can remove tasks from the other end of the queue, without any need for synchronization between the two. There is one dedicated in-queue for each sender/receiver pair. We use a ring buffer with two indices to point out the start and the end of the buffer.

The insert() method only needs to affect the start-index, and the remove() method only needs to affect the end-index. It is easy to assure that the insert() and remove() operations never can access the same memory location simultaneously.

The remove() operation needs to check if the queue is empty before allowing removal of a task, and because the insert() operation always inserts a task into the array before incrementing the end-index, computing end - start will always give a safe result. The same safe situation holds for the insert() method, when checking if the queue has room for more elements before inserting a task. The array simulates a ring and the indices will wrap around to the first element after passing the last element of the array, but this is easy to adjust for.

Since we want to avoid locks completely, we only allow a processor to either insert or remove jobs from an in-queue - not both. The opposite could be interesting to try, since there are ways to implement this such that the locks, with a high probability, seldom will be used [4].

4.1 Topology

In order to easily change the number of processor connections in the topology, we first order the processors virtually in a ring, where each processor distributes tasks to its successor's in-queue. When increasing the connectivity and wanting every processor to send tasks to n receivers, with p processors in the ring, we add connections to every $(\frac{p}{n} + 1)$:th successor. When inserting a connection between two processors, we assign an in-queue for the receiver and let the sender send tasks to this queue. Figure 1.h) shows an example of 6 processors, each distributing to 3 receivers.

Load Balancing For Adaptive Contracting within neighborhood (ACWN), the least loaded nearest neighbor is always selected as the receiver of a newly generated job. It is known that local averaging strategies generally outperforms methods such as the randomized allocation and the ACWN algorithm significantly in large scale system [22]. Since our shared memory system is a so called one-port communication system (i.e at most one neighbor can receive a message in a communication step) with one central data bus, we use the Local Averaging Dimension Exchange (LADE) policy. Generally it is better than the diffusion method (LADF) on such a system [23]. In LADF, load balancing is done with all neighbors, while in LADE load balancing is only done with one of the neighbors, or one at a time with the new load-balance successively considered.

Our approach is to use a sender-induced rather than a receiver-induced load distribution strategy. An advantage of the receiver-induced approach is that tasks are only distributed on demand which potentially reduces the overall cost of distribution. A disadvantage, however, is that processors may sit idle to wait for tasks to be available which may waste computing cycles. We briefly tried some receiver-induced approaches for the lock-based schemes, but they were inferior to the sender-induced, and thus we decided to try the sender-induced policy first for the lock-free schemes. Cilk-5 [4] is a parallel development system that uses the other approach (see Section 6).

A high degree of connections between processors in the virtual topology enables better load-balancing. Since the communication is the bottle-neck and the computation cost at each node in the tree is low, we need a simple/fast load-balancing scheme. Only sending newly generated jobs to each receiver and to the local queue in a round-robin fashion, was found to be insufficient to maintain good load-balance. We needed to consider the load difference between processors, which costs computation and communication. If a processor has more jobs than the receiver, it sends half the difference of the load. However, empirically we found that it was enough to even out the load balance this way with only one of the receivers and send blindly to the rest, to get similar load balance as the global task queue. We chose to consider the load balance difference only with the successor in the main ring. If n jobs are transferred in this step, we wait at least n traversed nodes before trying to load-balance carefully again, since load balancing is expensive and the successor probably will have work to do at least the corresponding time. In the final algorithm, after every processed node we distribute the newly generated jobs to the local-queue and the receiving processors in a round-robin fashion. If $n = 0$, where n is a variable set to the number of tasks sent to the successor last time and decreased after every traversed node, we also do the extra load-balancing with the successor. Every time we distribute jobs to the successor we may increment n.

If we have a topology with many connections for each processor, we potentially risk lowering cache-locality when we spread the jobs over many queues.

In the shared memory system, the jobs are physically sent when the receiving processor reads its in-queues and the corresponding cache-blocks are transferred from the sending processor to the receiving. In order to minimize the number of cache-block reads, the receiving processor selects one in-queue for reading until it is empty, before selecting a new in-queue. We could also avoid using an in-queue for reading that does not fill up an entire cache-block, if there are others that do, but we did not implement this.

In general, a high number of connections between processors in the virtual topology seemed to be preferred (see tables at the side of Figure 1.a-1.c).

4.2 Experimental Results

For this scheme, the speedup is substantially better for the large and medium model, with 4.3 and 3.1 times respectively. For the small model it is only 1.7, but this model provides poor speedup for all the schemes. Load balance is similar to that of the other schemes.

It was found that the time for just traversing the trees in parallel, not doing any VFC-computations, was fairly constant independently of the number of processors used. This means that we can decompose the total execution time as:

$$time_{total} = time_{traversal} + time_{VFC} \qquad (1)$$

where $time_{VFC}$ is the only term that enjoys speedup from the parallelism in VFC. This speedup, however, is basically optimal with respect to the possible parallelism provided by the traversed paths.

Depending on which parts of the scene-graph that are visible in a frame, the maximum of possible parallelism can vary, since there is a limited amount of parallel paths in the traversed graph. We found that if the whole tree is traversed, with each child selected for continued traversal disregarding the result of the VFC computations, the speedup peaks at 5.1, which is slightly higher than the average speedup. This indicates that the speedup is limited by the appearance of the scene graph. Since it represents a bounding box hierarchy, we cannot rearrange the graph without caution.

We also tested the Lock-Free scheme on a 2-processor PentiumIII 500MHz, with 256 Mb RAM, with a simpler load distribution policy that just keeps every 2:nd child and distributes the other to the other processor. The topology is a virtual ring of 2 nodes. With this approach we got 1.7, 1.5 and 1.3 times speedup for the large-, medium- and small model respectively. The load balance was practically perfect.

5 Collision Detection

Since the lock-free scheme was pretty successful in parallelizing VFC we tested it on hierarchical collision detection to see how it performs on this similar type of problem. We kept the same load balancing strategy. Collision detection is known as non-trivial to parallelize [17,2].

To find collision between two objects, their bounding box hierarchies are tested against each other for overlap. If any of the leaves between the two trees intersect, the objects are considered colliding. The algorithm starts with the root boxes of both trees. If intersection occurs, the algorithm continues recursively by testing the smallest of the two boxes (or the one that is not a leaf) against the children of the larger box respectively. If both boxes are leaves, a collision is found and the algorithm terminates. In this way a virtual graph is traversed.

A hierarchical AABB-tree of a small industry-robot with 102 nodes and a tree-depth of 11, was tested for intersection against the large model (a car factory). The robot was spatially placed such that the algorithm is forced to traverse deep down in both trees to verify that collision (in this case) does not occur.

Testing two AABBs against each other for overlap is extremely fast and basically consists of just 6 comparisons, while testing two arbitrarily oriented bounding boxes (OBBs) costs about 200 flops in average [5]. OBBs, however, can be more tight fitting and are thus often preferred. We wanted to test both cases. In the OBB-case, for simplicity, the AABBs were treated as OBBs in the overlap-computation with the orientation incidentally coinciding with the x,y,x-axes.

We found that for collision detection as well as for VFC, the traversal time without collision computations was nearly independent of the number of processors used. Consequently, since AABBs are very fast to test for overlap, we only got very limited speedup - 30% with 4 processors. For OBBs, however, the speedup peaks at 3.2 as can be seen in Figure 1.d).

6 Related Work and Discussion

Several older parallel branch-and-bound techniques [3,8,10,12,13,24] and depth-first search algorithms like backtracking [14,15,16] seem at a first glance to be applicable to the applications we have at hand. Our results indicate, however, that the load distribution strategies in these algorithms do not apply very well to tree traversals found in VFC and collision detection because of the low computation cost per node compared to the distribution cost.

In this paper we have focused on sender-induced schemes since this seemed most promising for the lock-based approaches. However, Cilk-5, which has been available for a short time, uses task-stealing in a way that looks promising. It requires the use of locks, but there are convincing arguments that they seldom will cause contention or significantly increased communication. Two of the main features of Cilk-5 is 1) that it compiles two versions of the code: one serial and one parallel, and can switch in run-time when load-balancing requests are issued, and 2) that load-balancing can occur efficiently through queues similar to those we use in our lock-free schemes.

Other related work that aims at reducing the orchestration overhead in tree traversals includes using prefetching techniques to tolerate communication latencies in the system. Karlsson et al. [9] studied how annotation of prefetch instructions can speed up tree traversals to tolerate the latency of cache misses.

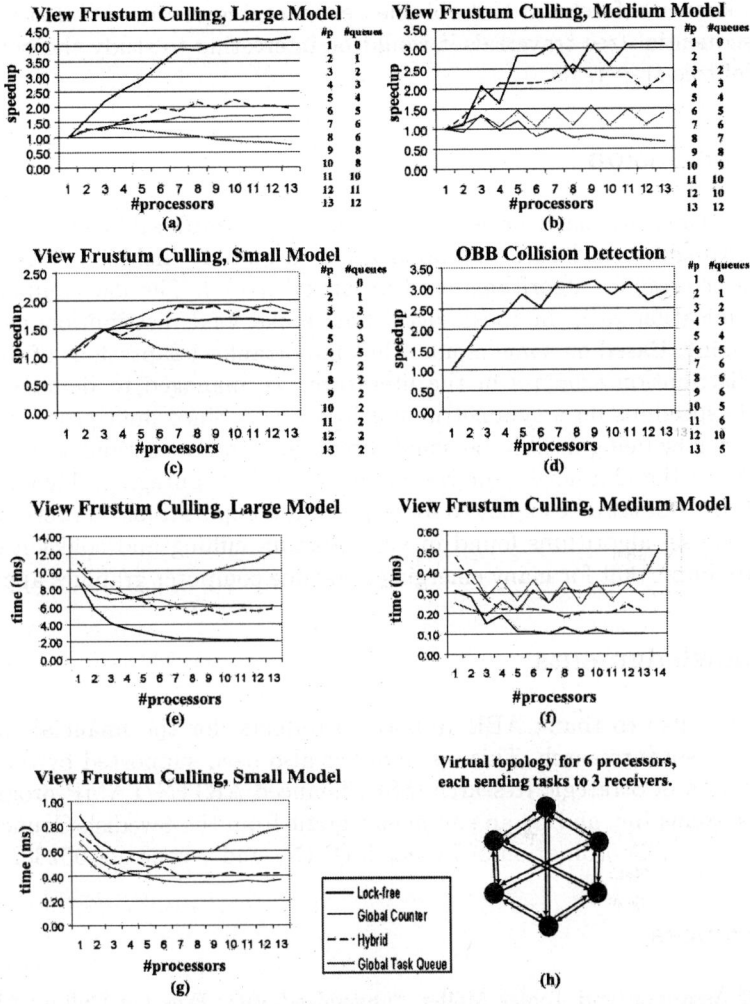

Fig. 1. (a-c) Speedup with 1 to 13 processors for the large, medium and small model. For the lock-free scheme, the figures are for the best topology, with the number of connections (in-queues) per processor marked at the side. (d) Speedup for collision detection with an OBB-algorithm with the lock-free scheme. The jaggedness comes from the difference in topology and number of optimal connections. (e-g) Corresponding execution time for the algorithms. (h) Virtual topology for 6 processors where each processor distributes load to 3 other processors. Note that depending on the camera position, a larger tree can be faster to traverse than a smaller. This is the case for the small vs. medium model, where the small offers more immerse navigation

They especially considered the class of tree traversals where the traversal path is not known beforehand and obtained encouraging results. While they studied only sequential tree traversals it would be interesting to study the potential for parallel tree traversals.

7 Conclusion

In this paper we have presented a comparative evaluation of load distribution strategies based on a real application case study including two important computer graphics algorithms used in virtual reality. The low computation-to-communication ratio in these algorithms make load distribution particularly challenging. Based on some minor – but important – adaptations of well-known load distribution schemes in the literature, we managed to demonstrate reasonable speedups on a symmetric multiprocessor. Since multiprocessors of this scale are now being used in personal computers, and are seriously considered to migrate to the chip-level, our results are indeed encouraging. They show that multiprocessors can be exploited for important computational kernels such as the tree-traversal algorithms found in view frustum culling and collision detection that are important for many emerging real-time computer graphics applications.

Acknowledgments

We would like to thank ABB Robotics Products, for the financial support of Ulf Assarsson's research. This research has also been supported by the Swedish Foundation of Strategic Research (SSF) financed ARTES/PAMP program, Sun Microsystems Inc, and by an equipment grant from the Swedish Council for the Planning and Coordination of Research (FRN) under contract 96238.

References

1. Ulf Assarsson and Tomas Möller, "Optimized View Frustum Culling Algorithms for Bounding Boxes", Journal of Graphics Tools, 5(1), Pages 9-22, 2000.
2. L. Boxer and R. Miller, "Dynamic computational geometry on parallel computers", Proceedings of the third conference on Hypercube concurrent computers and applications (Vol. 2), Pages 1212 - 1219, 1988.
3. E. W. Felten, "Best-first Branch-and Bound on a Hypercube", Proceedings of the Third Conference on Hypercube Concurrent Computers and Applications, (Vol. 2), Pages 1500-1504, 1988.
4. Matteo Frigo, Charles E. Leiserson, and Keith H. Randall, "The Implementation of the Cilk-5 Multithreaded Language", ACM SIGPLAN Conference on Programming Language, 1998.
5. S. Gottschalk, M.C Lin, and D. Manocha, "OBBTree: A Hierarchical Structure for Rapid Interference Detection", Proc. of ACM Siggraph, Pages 171-180, 1996.
6. Taosong He, "Fast collision detection using QuOSPO trees", Proceedings of the 1999 symposium on Interactive 3D graphics, Pages 55 - 62, 1999.

7. Martin Held, James T. Klosowski, Joseph S. B. Mitchell, "Collision Detection for Fly-Throughs in Virtual Environments", Symposium on Computational Geometry, V-13-V-14, 1996
8. V. K. Janakiram, D. P. Agrawal, and R. Mehrotra, "A Randomized Parallel Branch-and-Bound Algorithm", in Proc. Int. Conf. Parallel Process., Pages 69-75., Aug. 1988.
9. M. Karlsson, F. Dahlgren, and P. Stenström, "A Prefetching Technique for Irregular Accesses to Linked Data Structures", Proc. of 6th Int. Symp. on High Performance Computer Architecture, Pages 206-217, Jan. 2000.
10. Richard M. Karp, Yanjun Zhang, "Randomized Parallel Algorithms for Backtrack Search and Branch-and-Bound Computation", Journal of the ACM, Volume 40, Pages 765-789, Issue 3, 1993.
11. Tomas Möller and Eric Haines, "Real-Time Rendering", A. K. Peters Ltd, ISBN 1-56881-101-2, 1999.
12. Roy P. Pargas and E. Daniels Wooster, "Branch-and-Bound Algorithms on a Hypercube", Proceedings of the Third Conference on Hypercube Concurrent Computers and Applications, (Vol. 2), Pages 1514 - 1519, 1988.
13. Michael J. Quinn, "Analysis and Implementation of Branch-and-Bound Algorithms on a Hypercube Multicomputer", IEEE Transactions on Computers, vol. C-39, Pages 384-387, no. 3, March, 1990.
14. V. Nageshwara Rao and Vipin Kumar, "Parallel Depth-First Search on Multiprocessors — Part I: Implementation; and Part II—analysis", International Journal of Parallel Programming, vol. 16, no. 6, 1987.
15. V. Nageshwara Rao, Vipin Kumar, "On the Efficiency of Parallel Backtracking", IEEE Transactions on Parallel and Distributed Systems, vol 4, no. 4, Pages 427–437, April, 1993.
16. A. Reinefeld, V. Schnecke, "Work-Load Balancing in Highly Parallel Depth-First Search", Proc. Scalable High Performance Computing Conf. SHPCC'94, IEEE Comp. Sc. Press, Pages 773-780, 1994.
17. Peter Rundberg, "An Optimized Collision Detection Algorithm", http://www.ce.chalmers.se/staff/biff/exjobb, 1998.
18. A. Saulsbury, F. Pong, and A. Novatzyk, "Missing the Memory Wall: The Case for Processor/Memory Integration" Proc. of 23rd Int. Symp. on Computer Architecture, Pages 90-101, June, 1996.
19. Brian Smits, "Efficiency Issues for Ray Tracing", A K Peters, Ltd, Journal of Graphics Tools, vol 3, no 2, Pages 1-14, 1999.
20. Seth Teller, John Alex, "Frustum Casting for Progressive, Interactive Rendering," MIT LCS Technical Report 740, January, 1998.
21. Maurice van der Zwaan, Erik Reinhard, Frederik W. Jansen, "Pyramid Clipping for Efficient Ray Traversal", in Hanrahan, P. M. and Purgathofer, W., eds., Rendering Techniques '95', Springer-Verlag Wien, pp 1-10, 1995.
22. C. Xu, S. Tschoke, and B. Monien, "Performance Evaluation of Load Distribution Strategies in Parallel Branch and bound Computations", Proc. of the 7th IEEE Symposium of Parallel and Distributed Processing (SPDP95), Oct. 1995.
23. C. Xu and R. Lüling and B. Monien and F. Lau, "An analytical comparison of nearest neighbor algorithms for load balancing in parallel computers", Proceedings of 9th International Parallel Processing Symposium, 1995.
24. Myung K. Yang, Chita R. Das, "Evaluation of a Parallel Branch-and-Bound Algorithm on a Class of Multiprocessors", IEEE Transactions on Parallel and Distributed Systems, vol. 5, no. 1, January, 1994.

Parallelisable Zero-Tree Image Coding with Significance Maps

Rade Kutil[*]

Salzburg University
Jakob Haringer-Str. 2, A-5020 Salzburg, Austria
rkutil@cosy.sbg.ac.at
http://www.cosy.sbg.ac.at/sc/staff/rade.kutil.html

Abstract. The wavelet transform is more and more widely used in image and video compression. As today the parallelisation of the wavelet transform is sufficiently investigated this work deals with the compression algorithm (SPIHT) itself as a next step. A derived algorithm with a simpler and spacially oriented coefficient scan order is presented, which is more suitable for parallelisation.

1 Introduction

Algorithms like SPIHT [6] and the JPEG-2000 standard [1] prove the superiority of wavelet methods in still image coding. Likewise, rate-distortion efficient 3-D algorithms for video coding exist (as e.g. [3]). A significant amount of work has already been done on parallel wavelet transform algorithms. This work concentrates on the parallelisation of the coding algorithm as the next step. A 3-D variant [3] of the SPIHT algorithm [6] was chosen for this purpose.

In [2] two approaches to parallelise the EZW algorithm (predecessor of SPIHT) are proposed: One is a straight-forward parallelisation with local algorithm execution on each processor element (PE) for distinct blocks. A similar approach was applied to SPIHT in [7]. This results in a loss of rate-distortion performance and bitstreams that are incompatible to the sequential algorithm. Therefore, the second approach reorders the encoded symbols after collection of the PE-local results. This approach was adopted to SPIHT in [4]. Unfortunately, it reveals some drawbacks as e.g. complicated bit-stream handling, additional communication and sequential code parts.

Here we will follow another approach, that is to modify the algorithm itself. The basic idea is to substitute the lists of coefficient positions involved in the algorithm by bitmaps to facilitate the parallelisation of the coefficient scan.

---

[*] The author wants to thank the EPCC (Edinburgh Parallel Computing Centre) and the TRACS programme (Training and Research on Advanced Computing Systems) for providing equipment, infrastructure and support for parallel computing (especially on Cray T3E). The author was also supported by the Austrian Science Fund FWF, project no. P13903.

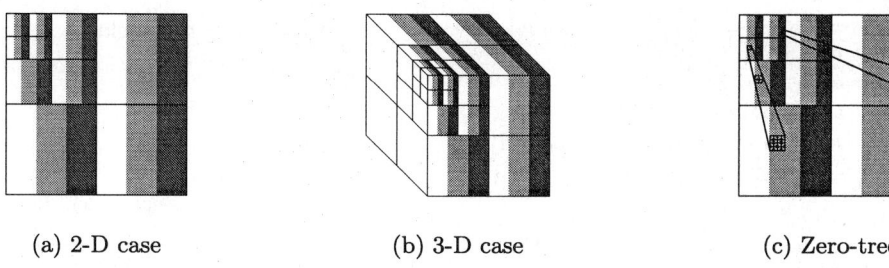

(a) 2-D case   (b) 3-D case   (c) Zero-tree

Fig. 1. Distribution of coefficients. Different colours indicate different PEs

2 Wavelet Transform and Zero-Trees

In contrast to the parallelisation of the wavelet transform as presented in [5] the parallel wavelet transform used here dispenses with video data distribution as well as collection of transformed data. Parallelisation is data driven by distributing data in slices. After parallel decomposition data are distributed as shown in Fig. 1. Note that the speedups reported in this work do not include I/O operations as I/O is not viewed as a part of the algorithm.

Zero-tree based algorithms arrange the coefficients of a wavelet transform in a tree-like manner, i.e. each coefficient has a certain number of child coefficients in another sub-band (mostly 4 in the 2-D, 8 in the 3-D case). Here the following notations are used: off(p) is the direct offspring of a coefficient p, i.e. all coefficients whose parent coefficient is p. desc(p) are all descendants of a coefficient p. This includes off(p), off(off(p)) and so on. parent(p) is the parent coefficient of p. $p \in$ off(parent(p)).

Furthermore, a zero-tree is a sub-tree which entirely consists of insignificant coefficients. The significance of a coefficient is relative to a threshold: sig$(c) \Leftrightarrow |c| \geq$ threshold. The statistical properties of transformed image or video data (self-similarity) ensure the existence of many zero-trees. Zero-trees can be viewed as a collection of coefficients with approximately equal spacial position. While this fact implies that the coefficients significances are statistically related which is exploited by the SPIHT algorithm, this also means that zero-trees are local objects corresponding to the data distribution produced by the parallel wavelet transform (see Fig. 1(c)). This can be exploited by the parallelisation of the SPIHT algorithm (see Section 4).

3 The Modified Zero-Tree Compression Algorithm

To substitute the lists of coefficients used in SPIHT by bitmaps we have to rewrite the whole algorithm. In the following we will use three logical predicates $A(p)$, $B(p)$ and $C(p)$ as defined in Fig. 2. Corresponding to these predicates we will use the mappings a, b and c which essentially represent the same as A, B

```
ProcessAll :=
    threshold ← max_{p∈allcoefficients} | p |
    set a, b and c to all false
    for each refinement step
        threshold ← threshold /2
        for p in approximation-subband
            ProcessCoeff(p, true)

ProcessCoeff(p, ĉ) :=
    if a_p then Refine(p) else a_p ← A(p)
    if ¬b_p ∧ ĉ then b_p ← B(p)
    if b_p ∧ ¬c_p then c_p ← C(p)
    if b_p then
        for q in off(p)
            ProcessCoeff(q, c_p)
```

$$A(p) \Leftrightarrow |p| \geq \text{threshold}$$

$$B(p) \Leftrightarrow \bigvee_{q \in \text{desc}(p)} A(q)$$

$$C(p) \Leftrightarrow \bigvee_{q \in \text{off}(p)} B(q)$$

Fig. 2. Zero-tree coding algorithm

and C. The difference is that A, B and C implicitly depend on threshold (implemented as a function) while a, b and c have to be updated explicitly (implemented as array of boolean values). We call a, b and c "significance maps".

The algorithm is responsible for the equality of a, b, c and A, B, C respectively while the threshold is successively decreased by a factor of $\frac{1}{2}$. The evaluation of A, B and C should be avoided as far as possible because – following the idea of SPIHT – the result of each evaluation will be coded into the bit-stream as one bit to allow the decoder to reproduce the algorithms decisions. The algorithm that obeys these rules is shown in Fig. 2. It encodes the same information as SPIHT. Only, the order of the bits within a refinement step is different. Unfortunately, this causes a loss of rate-distortion efficiency in the middle of the refinement steps of up to 1 dB. There exists an approach to overcome this problem.

4 Parallelisation Results

In contrast to [4] the parallelisation of our modified algorithm is easy. All we have to do is to parallelise the inner loop in the procedure ProcessAll (which reads "for p in approximation-subband") according to the data distribution of the approximation sub-band (see Fig. 1). Each PE produces one continuous part of the bit-stream for each refinement step. At the end these parts have to be collected by a single PE and assembled properly (i.e. in an alternating way).

Experimental results were conducted on a Cray T3E-900/LC at the Edinburgh Parallel Computing Centre. Video data size is always 864 frames with 88 by 72 pixels. The video sequence used here is the U-part of "grandma". The wavelet transform is performed up to a level of 3.

Experiments show that the sequential algorithm outperforms SPIHT for higher bitrates by a factor of up to 1.6. Fig. 3 shows speedups of the modi-

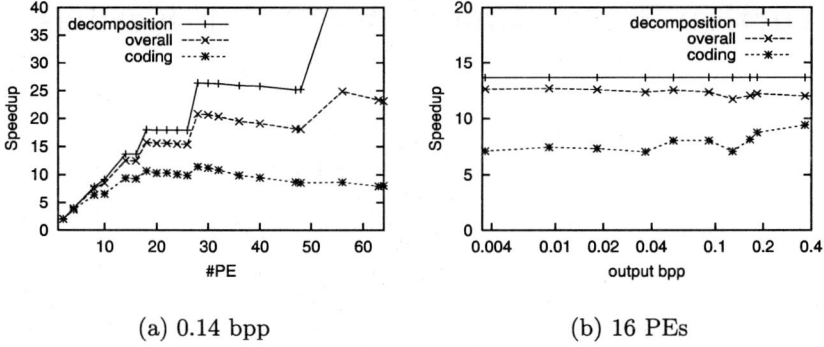

(a) 0.14 bpp (b) 16 PEs

Fig. 3. Speedup of decomposition, zero-tree coding and overall speedup for varying #PE (a) and varying bitrate (b)

fied algorithm for both varying #PE and varying bitrate. For higher numbers of PEs the assembly of the bit-streams takes more execution time and thus limits the speedups. Note that although the speedup of the coding part increases with the bitrate the overall speedup remains almost constant because the share in execution time of the coding part increases with the bitrate.

References

1. ISO/IEC JPEG committee. JPEG 2000 image coding system, March 2000. Final Committee Draft.
2. C. D. Creusere. Image coding using parallel implementations of the embedded zerotree wavelet algorithm. In B. Vasudev, S. Frans, and S. Panchanathan, editors, *Digital Video Compression: Algorithms and Technologies 1996*, volume 2668 of *SPIE Proceedings*, pages 82–92, 1996.
3. B. J. Kim and W. A. Pearlman. An embedded wavelet video coder using three-dimensional set partitioning in hierarchical trees (SPIHT). In *Proceedings Data Compression Conference (DCC'97)*, pages 251–259. IEEE Computer Society Press, March 1997.
4. R. Kutil. Zerotree based video coding on mimd architectures. In S. Panchanathan, V. Bove, and S. I. Sudharsanan, editors, *Media Processors 2001*, volume 4313 of *SPIE Proceedings*, pages 61–68, January 2001.
5. R. Kutil and A. Uhl. Hardware and software aspects for 3-D wavelet decomposition on shared memory MIMD computers. In P. Zinterhof, M. Vajtersic, and A. Uhl, editors, *Parallel Computation. Proceedings of ACPC'99*, volume 1557 of *Lecture Notes on Computer Science*, pages 347–356. Springer-Verlag, 1999.
6. A. Said and W. A. Pearlman. A new, fast, and efficient image codec based on set partitioning in hierarchical trees. *IEEE Transactions on Circuits and Systems for Video Technology*, 6(3):243–249, 1996.
7. F. W. Wheeler and W. A. Pearlman. Low-memory packetized SPIHT image compression. In *Proceedings of the Asilomar Conference on Signals, Systems, and Computers*, October 1999.

Performance of the Complex Streamed Instruction Set on Image Processing Kernels

Dmitri Tcheressiz[1], Ben Juurlink[2], Stamatis Vassiliadis[2], and Harry Wijshoff[1]

[1] LIACS, Leiden University, The Netherlands
[2] Computer Engineering Laboratory, Electrical Engineering Department
Delft University of Technology, The Netherlands

Abstract. The Complex Streamed Instruction (CSI) set is an architectural paradigm designed to accelerate multimedia applications. These applications are characterized by streaming operations on small-width data elements such as 8-bit pixels or 16-bit audio samples. CSI instructions operate on two-dimensional data streams in a SIMD fashion and are able to process streams of arbitrary length. In this paper we evaluate the performance of the CSI architecture on a set of important image processing kernels. These kernels are characterized by little data reuse which results in poor cache performance. Simulation results show that CSI provides a speedup by a factor of up to 3.98 (2.60 on average) compared to Sun's media ISA extension VIS. We also analyze the scalability of VIS and CSI with respect to memory bandwidth. The results show that CSI scales much better than VIS with increasing bandwidth.

1 Introduction

Multimedia applications have begun to play an important role in our lives and are expected to do so even more in the future [4,12]. In reaction to this trend, many vendors have extended their instruction set architecture (ISA) with instructions targeted to multimedia applications. Examples are MMX [16], VIS [18], and MDMX [13]. These instructions exploit SIMD parallelism at the subword level, i.e., they operate concurrently on, e.g., 8 bytes packed in one 64-bit register.

It has been shown that these multimedia ISA extensions can improve the performance of many multimedia codes (see, e.g., [1,17]). Nevertheless, they have several limitations which can be summarized as follows:

- The multimedia register size is architecturally visible and fixed. So, in order to exploit more data parallelism, there are two options. One is to add more multimedia functional units and increase the issue width. However, it is generally accepted that this requires a substantial amount of hardware and may negatively affect the cycle time [7,15]. A second option is to increase the multimedia register size, thereby changing the ISA. However, this implies that existing codes have to be recompiled or rewritten.
- Another drawback of increasing the multimedia register size is that it may not be beneficial, because multimedia kernels often operate on sub-matrices and the vector length in both directions is rather small.

- Codes employing SIMD-like instructions typically incur a lot of overhead for converting between different packed data types and alignment-related instructions.

Previously, we proposed the *Complex Streamed Instruction* set that avoids these limitations [19,10]. However, the considered benchmarks exhibited very high cache hit rates (98-99%) and were compute-bound. The purpose of this paper is to evaluate the performance of the CSI extension on memory-bound benchmarks. In particular, we are interested in the scalability of the CSI architecture when the memory bandwidth improves while the latency does not. This interest is motivated by the observation that new memory chip generations such as SDRAM [9] and RAMBUS [5] yield higher bandwidths but not much shorter access latencies. To evaluate the efficiency of CSI in such systems, we selected several image processing kernels that exhibit low hit rates, and simulated their execution on a superscalar processor, on the same processor extended with VIS [18], and on the same processor augmented with CSI.

This paper is organized as follows. In Section 2 the CSI architecture is briefly described. Section 3 describes the benchmarks, the modeled processors and presents the experimental results. Related work is discussed in Section 4, and conclusions and topics for future research are given in Section 5.

2 The CSI Architecture

In this section we briefly describe the CSI multimedia ISA extension and list some of its benefits. More details can be found in [10].

CSI is a memory-to-memory architecture for two-dimensional streams. Most CSI instructions load two data input streams from memory, operate on them element-wise, and store the resulting stream back to memory. The streams can be of any length and follow a matrix access pattern. A stream is specified by a *stream control register set* (SCR-set) that signifies the base address, the stream length, the horizontal and vertical strides, and the number of stream elements in a row. Each SCR-set also contains a control register that specifies the size and sign of the stream elements, if saturation or modular arithmetic should be performed, and the position of the binary point in fixed-point calculations.

The main advantages of the CSI instruction set can be listed as follows:

- It increases the amount of data-level parallelism that can be exploited. This cannot be achieved by enlarging the multimedia registers, since the vector length in both directions is typically 8 or 16 bytes.
- Since streams can be of any length, the number of elements that are processed in parallel (the *section size*) does not appear explicitly in the code. Instead, the hardware is responsible for dividing streams into sections. This implies that existing codes do not have to be recompiled or rewritten when the width of the SIMD datapath is increased.
- Conversion between different packed data types (if required) is performed internally in hardware.

– It eliminates loop control and address generation overheads, since one CSI instruction can replace two embedded loops.

3 Experimental Evaluation

To evaluate the performance of CSI on image processing kernels, we simulated their execution on three different processors: a 4-way superscalar processor, the same processor extended with VIS, and the same processor augmented with CSI. The following benchmarks taken from the VIS Software Development Kit (VSDK) were selected: add8 (adding two images using mean of corresponding pixels), blend8 (alpha-blending of two images), scale8 (linear scaling) and convolve3x3 (convolution with a 3x3 kernel). As input, we used 332x345 images in Sun rasterfile format with 3 color components. These benchmarks are characterized by little data reuse which results in poor cache performance (the average L1 hit rate is 79%). The memory bandwidth, therefore, is a decisive factor for overall system performance.

3.1 Simulation Methodology and Tools

We used the sim-outorder simulator of the SimpleScalar toolset (version 2.0) [2]. This execution-driven simulator emulates an out-of-order superscalar processor. Its architecture (Portable ISA or PISA) is derived from the MIPS-IV ISA. CSI and VIS instructions were synthesized by using annotations to instructions in the assembly files.

Three different executables of each kernel were created: a baseline PISA version, a VIS version, and a CSI version. The baseline PISA versions were obtained by compiling the C code taken from the VSDK using the gcc compiler with option -O4. For VIS and CSI we manually rewrote the assembly files, using for VIS a 1-1 translation of the VIS codes provided in the VSDK.

Since VIS instructions are register-to-register and operate on the floating-point register file, they do not interfere with the existing processor pipeline. CSI instructions are memory-to-memory and require extra care: one must ensure that the execution of a CSI instruction does not overlap with scalar memory instructions. We, therefore, took the following conservative approach. When a CSI instruction is detected, the pipeline is stalled. The processor then waits until all memory instructions have committed, after which it issues the CSI instruction. Fetching and decoding resumes after the CSI instruction has finished.

3.2 Modeled Processors

The base system is a 4-way superscalar processor with out-of-order issue and execution running at 500 MHz. Its main parameters are listed in Table 1.

The VIS-enhanced processor is modeled after the UltraSPARC [18], except that we assumed two 64-bit VIS multipliers whereas the UltraSPARC has only

Table 1. Processor parameters

Clock frequency	500 MHz		
Issue width	4-way	*FU latency/recovery (cycles)*	
Reorder buffer size	16	Integer ALU	1/1
Load-store queue size	8	Integer MUL	
Branch Prediction		multiply	3/1
Bimodal predictor size	2K	divide	20/19
Branch target buffer size	2K	Cache port	1/1
Return-address stack size	8	FP ALU	2/2
Functional unit type and number		FP MUL	
Integer ALU	4	FP multiply	4/1
Integer MULT	1	FP divide	12/12
Cache ports	2	sqrt	24/24
Floating-point ALU	4	VIS adder	1/1
Floating-point MULT	1	VIS multiplier	
VIS adder	2	multiply and pdist	3/1
VIS multiplier	2	other	1/1

Table 2. Memory parameters

Instruction cache	ideal
Data caches	
L1 line size	32 bytes
L1 associativity	direct-mapped
L1 size	32 KB
L1 hit time	1 cycle
L2 line size	128 bytes
L2 associativity	2-way
L2 size	128 KB
L2 replacement	LRU
L2 hit time	6 cycles

Main memory	
type	page-mode
page size	4 KB
first page access	30 cycles
next page access	10 cycle
bus clock frequency	100 MHz
bus width	8/16/32 bytes

one. We chose this configuration because CSI instructions are assumed to process two 128-bit packed data types in parallel. Any speedup of CSI over VIS, therefore, does *not* result from exploiting more data-level parallelism.

The cache and memory parameters are summarized in Table 2. The memory latencies are expressed in CPU clock cycles. Converted to absolute time, they correspond to access latencies of 20-60ns, which is close to those of contemporary DRAM chips. The frontside memory bus (between the L2 cache and the memory controller) is clocked at 100 MHz as in current PCs [9]. In order to study the effect of memory bandwidth on the performance of the modeled processors, we vary the bus width from 8 bytes (current PC standard) to 16 and 32 bytes, which corresponds to bandwidths ranging from 0.8 to 3.2 GB/sec. Contemporary PCs have a memory bandwidth of 0.8 GB/s using a 64-bit wide bus and *DDR SDRAM* [14] and *Direct Rambus* [5] already provide 1.6 GB/s of bandwidth.

3.3 Experimental Results

In this section the performance improvements attained by the CSI and VIS extensions are presented and discussed. We also analyze the different components of the execution time in order to identify the bottlenecks.

Figure 1 depicts the execution times of the baseline, VIS-enhanced and CSI-enhanced processor on each benchmark. The bars labeled '8b', '16b', '32b' depict the execution time when the bus width is 8 bytes, 16 bytes, or 32 bytes, respectively. The execution time is normalized w.r.t. the time taken by the baseline superscalar system with an 8-byte wide bus.

Figure 1 shows that the baseline system is compute-bound and hardly benefits from higher memory bandwidths. This is evidenced by the fact that the add8 kernel (which requires a small amount of computation per pixel) scales better than convolve3x3 (which is computationally more expensive). The VIS ISA extension significantly improves performance across all benchmarks. Nevertheless, the processor core becomes the bottleneck when the bandwidth is increased from 1.6 GB/s to 3.2 GB/s, since the performance improvements are smaller than when going from 0.8 GB/s to 1.6 GB/s. The CSI-enhanced processor provides additional performance gains ranging from a factor of 1.2 to 3.9. This can be seen more clearly from Figure 2, which depicts the speedups of CSI over VIS. Observe that the speedup increases with the bus width.

In order to further identify the performance bottlenecks, we analyze the different components of the execution time. Every cycle is classified either as *non-*

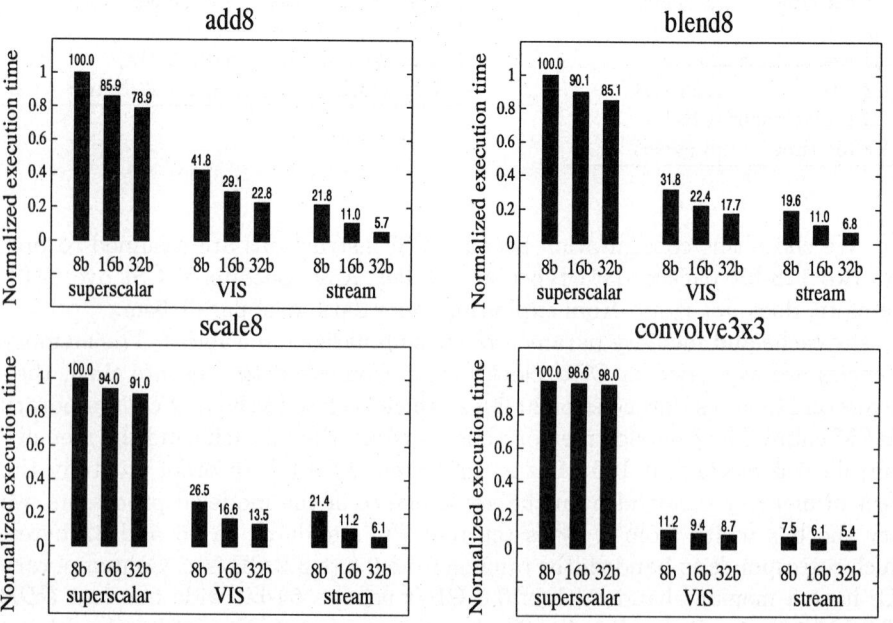

Fig. 1. Normalized execution time of the image processing kernels

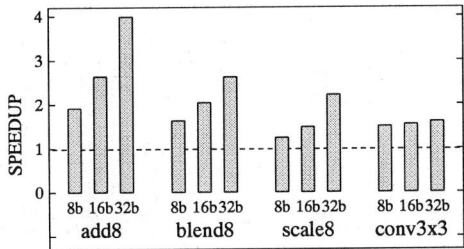

Fig. 2. Speedup of CSI over VIS

stall, *cpu stall* or *memory stall*. A cycle is classified as non-stall if the number of instructions retired that cycle is equal to the issue rate (4). If not, we look at the first instruction that could not retire. If it is a memory access instruction, it is classified as memory stall. Otherwise, it is classified as cpu stall. Since instructions retire in order, the first instruction that cannot retire stalls all instructions behind it. We used this metric instead of busy time used in [17] because it clarifies why less than the maximum number of instructions retired.

For the CSI architecture, a cycle is classified as non-stall if a SIMD operation was initiated at that cycle. Otherwise, it is classified as memory stall, meaning that data has not yet been delivered by the memory. The CSI-enhanced processor does not experience cpu stall cycles because there are no dependencies between stream elements, and there are enough resources to initiate a SIMD operation every cycle.

Figure 3 breaks down the execution times in non-stall, cpu stall and memory stall cycles. It shows that neither the superscalar nor the VIS-enhanced processor can fully utilize the increased memory bandwidth. The superscalar system gets saturated already when the bus width is 8 bytes, since the CPU component of the execution time (non-stall plus cpu stall) increases only marginally. The VIS-enhanced system utilizes the available bandwidth much better, but the growth of its CPU component is mostly due to the cpu stall component. Increasing the memory bandwidth of the CSI-enhanced system, on the other hand, leads to a significant reduction in memory stall cycles and a corresponding increase in non-stall cycles.

We remark that some execution may occur during cpu stall cycles. The fact that a given cycle is cpu stall means that a certain instruction was not able to retire (i.e., its result was not ready) although it was allowed. There can be multiple reasons why an instruction did not finish, the main being the following. Either the instruction was issued and started execution too late because no functional unit was available, or the instruction was decoded and placed in the reorder buffer too late because there were no free entries.

These observations suggest that the performance of the superscalar and VIS-enhanced processors may be improved by increasing the number of functional units and/or by increasing the size of the reorder buffer. We conducted experiments using these techniques. Adding 2 VIS adders and 2 VIS multipliers pro-

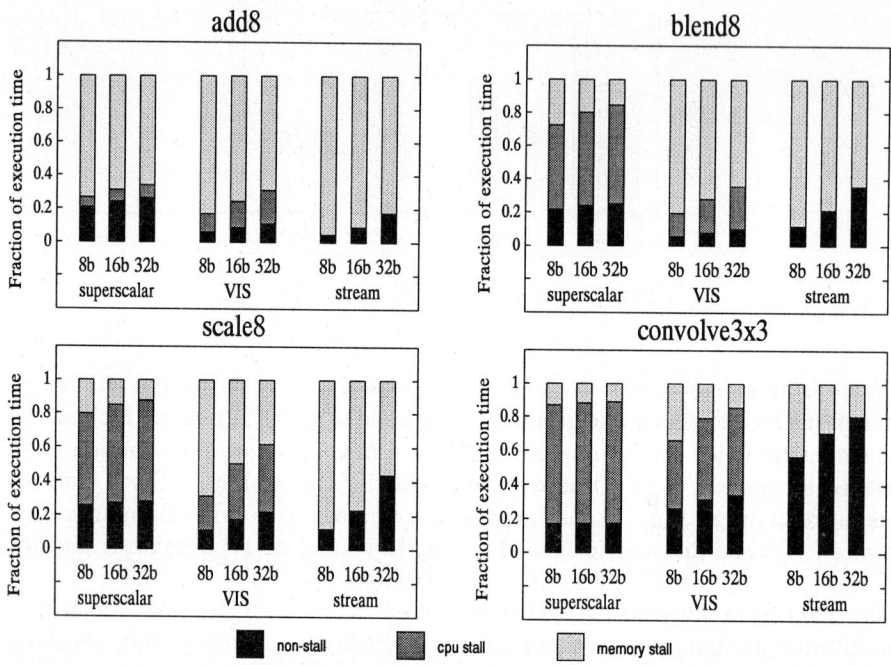

Fig. 3. Execution time partitioned in non-stall, cpu stall and memory stall cycles

duced no effect. Doubling the size of the reorder buffer and the load/store queue indeed improved performance (for the VIS-enhanced system by a factor of up to 1.20). However, this improvement is still significantly less than that achieved by CSI (cf. Figure 2). This shows that the performance of the superscalar and VIS architectures is limited by the execution engine and cannot be improved much by low-cost techniques such as resource duplication. So, it seems that to improve performance one has to pack more parallel operations in a single instruction, but this may result in binary incompatibility.

4 Related Work

The CSI architectural paradigm was introduced in [19]. A detailed description of the CSI instruction set, its implementation and performance on video and image codecs can be found in [10]. Here we extend that work by studying a new application domain with different memory behavior and by evaluating the effect of memory bandwidth.

CSI is a memory-to-memory architecture for two-dimensional streams. Early vector architectures such as the TI ASC and the Star-100 [8] were also memory-to-memory and could also process vectors of arbitrary length. However, these architectures suffered from long startup times, which was mainly due to overhead instructions needed for setting up the parameters and to long memory latency. Since CSI is implemented next to a superscalar core, the overhead needed for setting the parameters is small. Furthermore, because the streams are two-dimensional, they are longer than one-dimensional vectors, allowing the memory latency to be overlapped with execution.

The performance of image processing benchmarks on superscalar processors with and without the VIS extension was also studied by Ranganathan et al. [17]. They studied the effect of varying the L1 and L2 cache size and of prefetching, but not the effect of memory bandwidth.

A related proposal aimed at exploiting more data-level parallelism in multimedia applications is the Matrix Oriented Multimedia (MOM) extension [3]. MOM instructions can be seen as vector versions of current SIMD media extensions. Two main differences between MOM and CSI are that MOM has architectured registers (and, hence, sectioning) and requires explicit data conversion instructions.

Another related proposal is the Imagine processor [11], which has a load/store architecture for one-dimensional streams of data records. It is centered around a large, 128KB stream register file, and consists of 48 functional units grouped in 8 arithmetic clusters. Each cluster must execute the same VLIW operation and is controlled by a microcoded controller. Imagine is suited for applications performing many arithmetic operations on each element of a long, one-dimensional stream. It seems less suited when only a few operations on each record are performed and when the vector length is small.

5 Conclusions

In this paper we have evaluated the performance of the CSI multimedia ISA extension on a set of image processing kernels characterized by little data reuse. We have also studied the scalability of the proposed architecture with respect to the memory bandwidth. The results show:

- On the high-bandwidth system (3.2 GB/s), the CSI extension improves performance by a factor of 1.6 to 3.9 (2.6 on average) compared to the VIS-enhanced processor.
- On the low-bandwidth system (0.8 GB/s), the speedups range from 1.2 to 1.9 with an average of 1.56.
- Neither the superscalar nor the VIS-enhanced processors are able to fully utilize the high memory bandwidth provided by current high-performance and future generations DRAM architectures. We identified the CPU core as the bottleneck and observed that increasing the size of the reorder buffer and the number of functional units does not alleviate the problem.

We plan to continue our investigation of CSI in the following directions. First, we want to further improve the memory system performance for CSI instructions by exploiting the information available in the stream control registers. This information could be communicated to an intelligent DRAM controller such as proposed in [6]. Second, we would like to apply our approach to another important application domain characterized by abundant data-level parallelism and high computational demands, namely 3D graphics.

References

1. R. Bhargava, L. K. John, B. L. Evans, and R. Radhakrishnan. Evaluating MMX Technology Using DSP and Multimedia Applications. In *MICRO 31*, 1998.
2. D. Burger and T. M. Austin. The SimpleScalar Tool Set, Version 2.0. Technical Report 1342, Univ. of Wisconsin-Madison, Comp. Sci. Dept., 1997.
3. J. Corbal, M. Valero, and R. Espasa. Exploiting a New Level of DLP in Multimedia Applications. In *MICRO 32*, 1999.
4. K. Diefendorff and P. K. Dubey. How Multimedia Workloads Will Change Processor Design. *IEEE Computer*, 30(9):43–45, September 1997.
5. Direct RDRAM 64/72-Mbit data sheet. Document available via http://www.rambus.com/docs/64dDDS.pdf, 1998.
6. S.McKee et al. Design and Evaluation of Dynamic Access Ordering Hardware. In *Proc. of the 10th ICS*, 1996.
7. J. L. Hennessy and D. A. Patterson. *Computer Architecture - A Quantitative Approach*. Morgan Kaufmann, second edition, 1996.
8. K. Hwang and F. A. Briggs. *Computer Architecture and Parallel Processing*. McGraw-Hill, second edition, 1984.
9. PC SDRAM Specification,Rev 1.7. Intel Corp., November 1999.
10. B. Juurlink, D. Tcheressiz, S. Vassiliadis, and H. Wijshoff. Implementation and Evaluation of the Complex Streamed Instruction Set. In *PACT-2001*, 2001. To appear.
11. B. Khailany, W. J. Dally, U. J. Kapasi, P. Mattson, J. Namkoong, J. D. Owens, B. Towles, A. Chang, and S. Rixner. Imagine: Media Processing With Streams. *IEEE Micro*, 21(2):35–47, March/April 2001.
12. R. B. Lee and M. D. Smith. Media Processing: A New Design Target. *IEEE Micro*, 16(4):6–9, August 1996.
13. MIPS Extension for Digital Media with 3D. Document available via http://www.mips.com/Documentation/isa5_tech_brf.pdf, 1996.
14. 256Mbit DDR SDRAM part specification. Document available via http://samsungelectronics.com/semiconductors/DRAM/DDR_SDRAM/256M_bit/K4H560438B/256mB_R03.PDF, 2000.
15. S. Palacharla, N. P. Jouppi, and J. E. Smith. Complexity-Effective Superscalar Processors. In *ISCA 24*, 1997.
16. A. Peleg, S. Wilkie, and U. Weiser. Intel MMX for Multimedia PCs. *Comm. of the ACM*, 40(1):24–38, January 1997.
17. P. Ranganathan, S. Adve, and N. P. Jouppi. Performance of Image and Video Processing with General-Purpose Processors and Media ISA Extensions. In *ISCA 26*, 1999.
18. M. Tremblay, J. Michael O'Conner, V. Narayanan, and L. He. VIS Speeds New Media Processing. *IEEE Micro*, 16(4):10–20, August 1996.
19. S. Vassiliadis, B. Juurlink, and E. Hakkennes. Complex Streamed Instructions: Introduction and Initial Evaluation. In *EUROMICRO 26*, pages 400–408, 2000.

A Two Dimensional Vector Architecture for Multimedia

Ahmed El-Mahdy and Ian Watson

Computer Science Department, University of Manchester
Manchester M13 9PL, UK,
{aelmahdy,watson}@cs.man.ac.uk

Abstract. Vector processing is gaining attention for supporting multimedia workloads, particularly small subword vectors. In this paper we propose a novel vector instruction set combining the benefits of subword parallelism and traditional vector processing. We also develop a simple cache prefetching optimisation that exploits the two dimensional data access pattern of multimedia MPEG2 video applications. The architecture parameter space is explored by a simple analytical study. The analysis is complemented by detailed simulation of the actual system where it is shown that the optimised cache removes 75% of the misses and the instruction set performance is equivalent to a subword instruction with double the word size on the average.

1 Introduction

There is currently a convergence between general-purpose processors and multimedia processors [2]. Major microprocessor manufacturers have extended their instruction sets with multimedia specific instructions. These include Intel x86's MMX, PowerPC's AltiVec, UltraSPARC's VIS, and PA-RISC's MAX-2. However, more radical architecture changes are sought for meeting the increasing high performance requirement of multimedia applications [5,9].

Microprocessor technology is progressing very fast. It is expected that by the year 2010 it will be possible to build billion-transistor microprocessors with clock speeds approaching 10 GHz [1]. However, there are two main issues; memory and global clocking. Memory is not progressing at the same rate and thus the memory processor gap is increasing. With a billion transistors on a chip, wire delays will dominate and the global clocking of large synchronous systems will become a problem. Single-chip multiprocessors may be a way to overcome these problems.

In this paper we develop a *two dimensional* vector architecture for supporting multimedia on the Jamaica processor. Jamaica [12] is a proposal for a single-chip multithreaded multiprocessor targeting Java. The architecture combines the benefits of traditional vector processing and subword parallelism found in current general-purpose processors. The instruction set architecture is described in section 2 together with related work. We have observed 2D spatial locality in MPEG2 video data accesses and developed a simple cache optimisation to exploit that locality. This is described in section 3 together with related work. To explore the wide ranging parameter space, we have developed a simple analytical model. In section 4 we describe the model and use it to analyse MPEG2 encode and decode applications (mpeg2encode and mpeg2decode). Initial simulation results are presented in section 5.

2 The 2d-Vector Instruction Set

Multimedia workloads are inherently data-parallel which makes a vector architecture a suitable candidate. The vector instruction set has the benefit of decreasing address generation and loop control overheads. Our *2d-vector* instruction set combines the benefits of a traditional vector instruction set and the subword parallelism used in current microprocessor multimedia extensions.

We propose the use of 8 vector registers, each containing a maximum of 8 32-bit elements. The vector length is specified in a 'vl' register. Each element can be viewed as a simple vector of 8-bit or 16-bit subword data types. Thus a vector register is a vector of simple subword vectors, effectively a two dimensional vector.

The main memory is addressed in a *submatrix* addressing mode. The vector load instruction 'vld', is specified as follows:

```
vld vi, Xm, Ystride
```

Where, 'vi' is the destination vector register, 'Xm' is the number of stride-1 memory accesses, and 'Ystride' is a variable stride. The X and Y characters refer to row and column matrix access respectively. 'Xm' memory words (32-bits) are loaded with stride-1 from a base address (specified in a control register), then 'Ystride' is added to the base address, and the process is repeated until 'vl' words have been loaded. Another addressing mode is called the transpose mode. In this mode, 'Xm' words are accessed with the 'Ystride', the base address is then incremented by one and the process is repeated as above. A similar instruction is defined for vector store operations.

Loads and stores are word aligned. Two other instructions are specified for unaligned access. An extra memory access is required for every row access even if the address is aligned. This makes the instruction simpler to implement and it is a compiler/programmer decision instead.

The other instructions are similar to the PowerPC's AltiVec multimedia extensions. It is worth noting that pack and unpack instructions are modified so that they take advantage of the variable vector length. Packing and unpacking halves and doubles 'vl' respectively.

The following is an example code for the metric operation A=B+C. Where A, B, and C are 16×16 byte submatrices. Assuming that each instruction takes one cycle, the scalar code takes $16 \times (16 \times 9 + 1 + 5) = 2400$ cycles while the *2d-vector* takes $8 \times (4 \times 8 + 2) = 279$ cycles (assuming 32-bit word size).

```
Scalar instruction set                    2d-vector instruction set
...                                       ...
mov r1, 16                                mov r1, 8
loop1: mov r2, 16                         loop:      !two rows added
loop2:                                               !each loop iteration
ld   r3, 0(r4); add r4, 1, r4             vld  v1, 4, r9
ld   r5, 0(r6); add r6, 1, r6             vld  v2, 4, r9
add  r3, r5, r7                           vadd v1, v2, v3
st   r7, 0(r8); add r8, 1, r8             vst  v3, 4, r9
sub  r2, 1, r2; jnz r2, loop2;
add  r4, r9, r4;
add  r6, r9, r6; add r6, r9, r8;
sub  r1, 1, r1; jnz r1, loop1             sub  r1, r, r1; jnz r1, loop
```

2.1 Related Work

There are two classes for vector addressing modes; regular and sparse addressing [8]. Regular addressing is used for dense data that are organised in regular structures (fixed stride), whereas sparse addressing is used for other sparse structures. The former is more suited to multimedia applications.

Within the regular class, there are three main addressing varieties; the first is *sequential* addressing where data are stored in stride-1 organisation. Current general-purpose processors' multimedia extensions [10] implement this addressing mode. They exploit the wide data paths in microprocessors and small data types in multimedia applications and implement small subword vectors in wide registers (64- and 128-bit). However this implementation restricts matrix access and misalignment is introduced. Most implementations have permutation instructions to overcome the addressing restrictions.

An alternative addressing method is *nonsequential* addressing where data are stored with a stride-n organisation. The MOM instruction set architecture [3] implements this technique and also has a small subword vector in each vector element. This technique subsumes sequential addressing and adds extra flexibility, however, the row size is limited by the word size and misalignment problems still exist.

Our *submatrix* addressing method is closest to the MOM instruction set. The main differences are that row size is not limited by word size and the effect of misalignment is decreased for large row sizes, and column accesses are enhanced.

3   The 2D Cache

Conventional caches exploit spatial and temporal locality. Multimedia applications process massive amounts of data and temporal locality is not very abundant. Spatial locality for conventional caches occurs in one dimension; on a cache miss a line is fetched, effectively fetching nearby data. Multimedia video applications operate on small blocks of data (16 × 16). The operations range from regular scanning of all the blocks on a frame, to searching for a matching block.

Such searches are used, for example, in motion estimation and data access is unpredictable. However, once a block is determined all other rows are predictable. Data access has thus a two dimensional locality.

Our 2D cache works as follows: on a cache miss, $b + 1$ lines are loaded from memory. The first line fetched is the miss line, and the other b lines are prefetched with a specified stride. We assume that the data being accessed is within a big fixed matrix (e.g. a large image). The stride represents the row size of the matrix. Thus, a submatrix is effectively prefetched on a cache miss. The stride information is conveyed by vector load and store instructions. Also, a control register is used to specify stride information for scalar load and store instructions.

3.1 Related Work

The existence of 2D spatial locality in multimedia video applications was observed by Kuroda and Nishitani [10], though no design was suggested. Cucchiara et al. [4] proposed a 2D cache architecture similar to our technique where lines are prefetched on a cache miss. However, they maintain the stride information for every address referring to a 2D data structure, in a hardware table. Our technique uses instructions instead to control the 2D access; specifying current stride and possibly turning prefetching off.

Another relevant prefetch technique, though not intended to cache 2D locality, was developed by Fu et al. [6]. They developed a vector cache for vector processors. On a cache miss, either consecutive lines or stride-n lines are prefetched depending on the stride of the vector instruction. The prefetch in the latter case is similar to the one we propose. However, in our technique stride-n prefetching can also be initiated on scalar misses. A different technique is software prefetching where a prefetch is initiated by a prefetch instruction. A main drawback is the complexity of scheduling the prefetches especially for motion prediction kernels where data access is not predictable.

4 Analytical Study

The *2d-vector* instruction set has the potential to remove address generation, missalignment, and loop overheads. In addition, the subword parallelism decreases the instruction execution cycles. However the relative memory latency will increase, limiting further improvements. In the next subsection, we develop a simple analytical model that relates the overall speedup to the instruction set and cache components and gives performance bounds.

4.1 Analytical Performance Model

The performance can be decomposed into instruction execution cycles and memory access cycles. Fig. 1-a shows this situation. On average every h execution cycles a cache miss occurs and instruction execution is stalled for $T1$ cycles while memory is accessed.

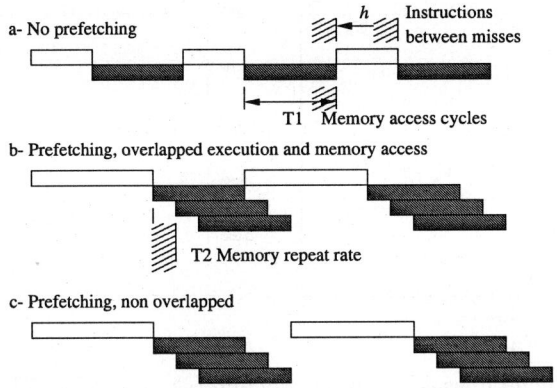

Fig. 1. Performance model

The effect of the 2D cache is that $b + 1$ memory access cycles happen on every cache miss but h should be increased (h'). Multiple memory accesses can be pipelined with a new memory access cycle starting every $T2$ cycles. The best case performance occurs with maximum overlap between execution and prefetching. This is depicted in Fig. 1-b. The worst case occurs when there is no overlap, as shown in Fig. 1-c.

The minimum and maximum execution cycles (t_{min}, t_{max} respectively.) are given by:

$$t_{\min} = misses \cdot \max(h' + T1, b \cdot T2 + T1) \tag{1}$$

$$t_{\max} = misses \cdot (h' + T1 + b \cdot T2) \tag{2}$$

Where $misses$ is the total number of misses.

4.2 Cache Misses

Data cache misses are relatively independent of the instruction set and machine word size. They are highly dependent on the cache and memory access patterns (application dependent). With prefetching, the number of misses will be affected by the number of lines loaded into the cache on a miss.

We have developed a cache simulation using the shade tools [11] and modelled the 2D cache using a 16Kb, 4-way set associative organisation with 32 byte line size. The benchmark programs, written in C, were run on an UltraSPARC-II processor. Our high level language target is Java, however both C and Java versions have the same data access pattern and we thus opted to use C for this exercise (the same C program is manually converted into Java). This enabled us to achieve much higher simulation speed as the program runs in native mode.

Fig. 2-a and Fig. 2-b show the number of misses for the 2D cache against the number of lines loaded on a cache miss for mpeg2encode and mpeg2decode applications [7] processing two 720 × 480 frames. 'Actual' is the misses obtained

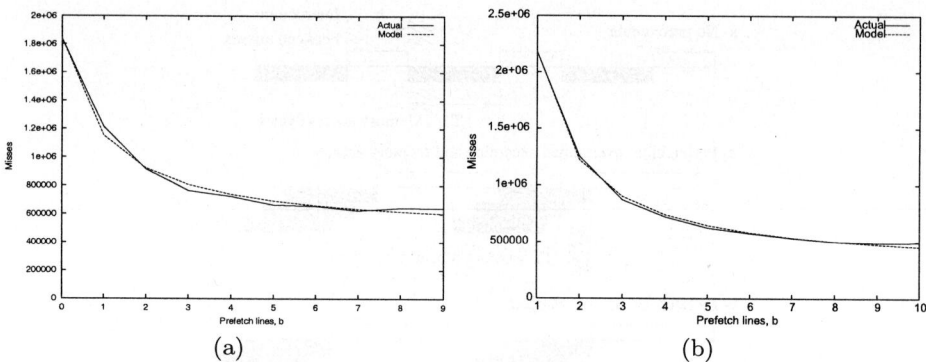

Fig. 2. Cache misses for mpeg2encode (a), and mpeg2decode (b)

by cache simulation and show that, as the number of lines is increased, up to 75% and 88% of the misses can be removed for the mpeg2encode and mpeg2decode respectively.

'Model' is the misses obtained by formulating the behaviour of the cache by the following equation:

$$misses(b) = misses(0)/(b+1) \cdot \alpha + misses(0) \cdot (1-\alpha) \qquad (3)$$

Where $misses(0)$ is the initial misses (without prefetching), and α is the ratio of the initial misses that have 2D spatial locality. Since on a cache miss, $b+1$ lines are loaded, b misses can be removed and thus misses are decreased by $b+1$. Fitting Equation 3 to the asymptotic simulation results, we get α equal to 0.75 and 0.88 for mpeg2encode and mpeg2decode respectively. A close fit can then be observed over the range of b.

We have carried out experiments with different cache sizes. However, the working data set (3 frames, each of 338Kb) is sufficiently large that it will not be contained in realistic first level cache sizes and the effects are therefore small. It is worth noting that prefetching did not increase the number of misses in any kernel for mpeg2encode. For mpeg2decode some kernels had their misses doubled. However, these misses are less than 0.5% of the initial misses.

4.3 Instruction Execution Cycles

Fig. 3 shows the speedup of the instruction execution cycles for the vectorised kernels of the mpeg2encode and mpeg2decode benchmarks for various multimedia instruction set proposals relative to a scalar one. The programs have been manually translated into Java then compiled and assembled using the Jamaica tools. The *2d-vector* instructions can be generated directly, the others have been hand generated. The cycles are calculated assuming zero memory latency and no register spills for the scalar model (to isolate the submatrix addressing benefit). The instruction types (address generation, loop control, memory, ALU)

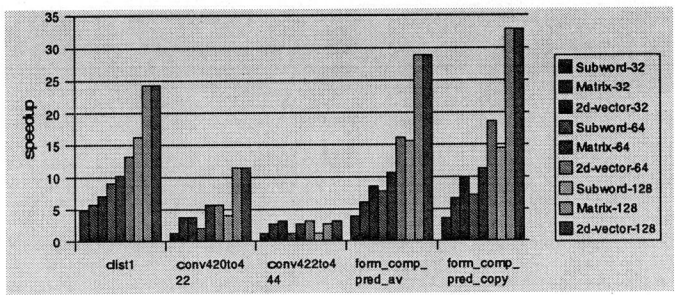

Fig. 3. Instruction execution cycles for various instruction set models

are scaled to reflect a subword based instruction set (*subword*), a subword non-sequential access instruction set (*matrix*) which is similar to MOM, and our proposed instruction set (*2d-vector*).

The *2d-vector* outperforms *subword* for all the kernels, with double the speedup on average. This is mainly due to the removal of address generation, misalignment and loop overhead. For smaller word sizes, *2d-vector* is generally faster than *matrix* (average of 25% for 32-bit word size). We have not used *subword* permute instructions nor matrix transpose instruction for the *subword* and *matrix* models in order to isolate the effect of the submatrix addressing. Using these instructions would improve the performance of all the models especially for the 'conv422to444' kernel (data parallelism is in the vertical direction).

4.4 Overall Performance

Fig. 4-a and Fig. 4-b show the speedup bounds (speedup over the scalar case with no prefetching) for mpeg2encode and mpeg2decode respectively against the memory latency. The bounds are shown for the *2d-vector* architecture with 32-, 64-, and 128-bit word sizes. Three simulations were done: two to obtain the instruction cycle speedup of the *2d-vector* over the scalar instruction set with zero memory latency (used to adjust the analytical kernel speedups to account of detailed factors and to have a better estimate of actual speedups), and the other to obtain h for the scalar instruction set. These data are used in Equations 1, 2, and 3 together with kernel speedups (section 4.3) to plot the bounds. The number of lines prefetched on a cache miss (b, prefetch count) is calculated so that it gives a near optimal (95%) upper bound. These are shown in Fig. 1-c and Fig. 1-d. Specifying the optimal upper bound will result in large values to b without having a significant improvement on the bound.

The memory repeat rate $T2$ is set to $T1/3.5$ which is a typical value. A memory access time $T1$ of 70 cycles is typical for current technology assuming 1 GHz CPU speed, we might expect $T1$ to be about 220 cycles (10 GHz CPU) in 10 years time.

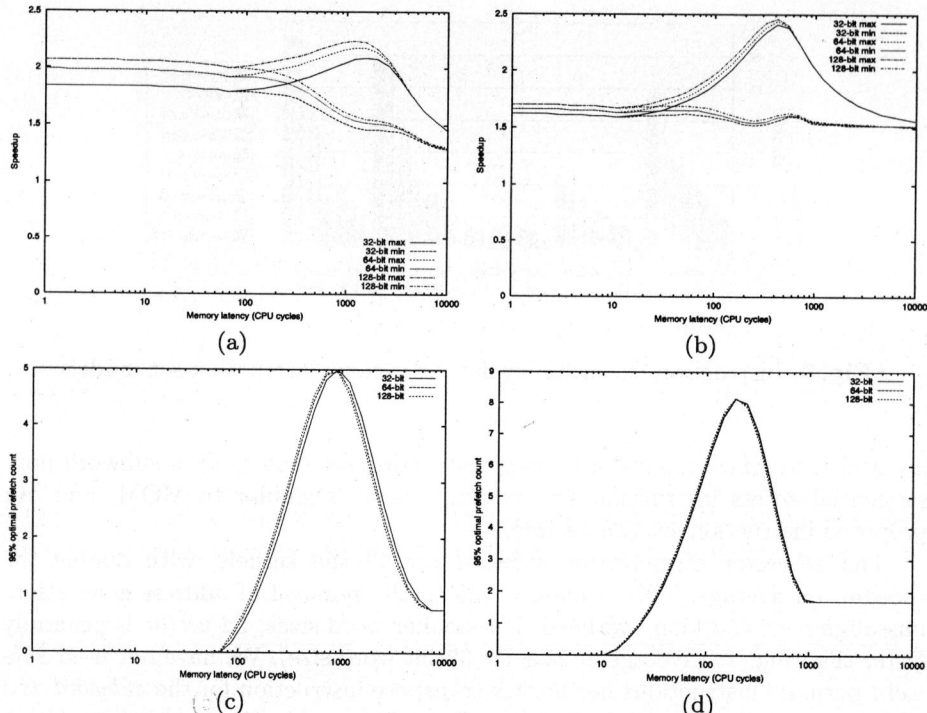

Fig. 4. Performance near optimal (95%) bounds for mpeg2encode (a), and mpeg2decode (b) and corresponding prefetch count curves (c) and (d)

For fast memory, the upper and lower bounds coincide as there is hardly any memory latency to hide and thus no prefetching is necessary. For the mpeg2-encode, as memory latency increases from 70 cycles (Fig. 4-a), the positive effect of prefetching increases, peaking in the region 400-3000 cycle. As memory latency increases further, the optimal b is limited by the relative speeds of memory access and repeat rate and cache efficiency parameter α and thus b stays constant.

The mpeg2decode is more memory bound than mpeg2encode ($h \approx 1980$ for mpeg2encode and $h \approx 335$ for mpeg2decode). The prefetching has a much more significant effect and the bounds are shifted to the right accordingly (peaking in the region 200-700). It is interesting to note that the lower bound does not decrease significantly while the upper bound peaks.

5 Simulation Study

We have carried out an initial simulation study to assess how far real results are from the theoretical bounds presented earlier on. We assume a slow memory configuration to account for the fact that the memory is shared by other processors in our multiprocessor configuration and thus is likely to emphasise the effect of the 2D cache.

The base architecture is the Jamaica processor. Jamaica is a single-chip multiprocessor with multithreading. We have extended the Jamaica simulator [12] with the multimedia extensions. The architecture, modelled by simulation, is bus based using shared memory with private 16Kb, 4-way set associative L1 caches with a 32 byte cache line. The processors share a pipelined, split transaction bus. The memory is four channel Rambus with a bus speed of 400 MHz. The processor speed is 10 GHz. We developed a Java translator tool that supports the *2d-vector* instruction set. Mpeg2encode and mpeg2decode applications are simulated, processing 2 video frames (720 × 480).

Fig. 5 shows the speedup obtained over the scalar case with no prefetching. The x-axis represents the number of lines prefetched on a cache miss. The simulation results are shown for mpeg2encode and mpeg2decode together with the upper bound assuming perfect prefetch ($\alpha = 1$). For the mpeg2encode, 86% of the maximum is achieved. The *2d-vector* contributes 59% speedup and the 2D cache contributes 18%. For the mpeg2decode, about 88% of the maximum is achieved. The *2d-vector* contributes 50% speedup and the 2D cache contributes 25%.

It is also interesting to compare the results with the bounds presented in section 4.4. From the simulation, we can obtain an effective memory access time. Due to the L2 cache and the bus protocol this is application dependent. For the mpeg2encode, we get $T1 \approx 455$ cycles which gives a speedup bound of 1.93 compared to the 1.79 achieved in simulation (within 7%) for 3 prefetched lines. For mpeg2decode, $T1 \approx 108$ cycles, which gives a speedup bound of 1.91 against 1.84 obtained in simulation for 7 prefetched lines (within 4%). The mpeg2decode is closer to the bound as the vectorised 'Conv420to420' kernel has a better spatial locality than the original scalar kernel.

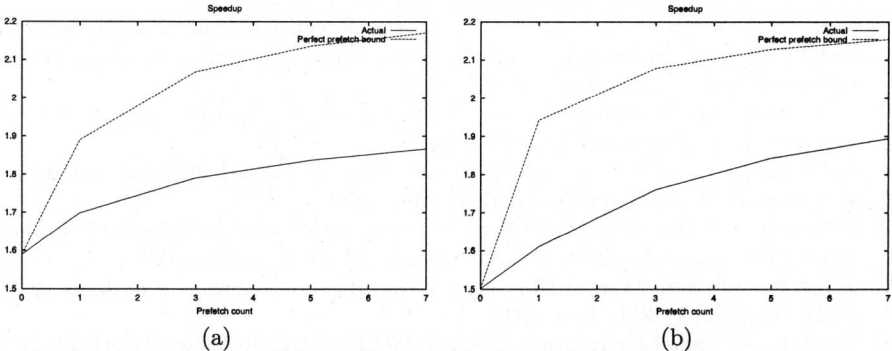

Fig. 5. Simulation results for mpeg2encode (a), and mpeg2decode (b)

6 Conclusions

In this paper we have proposed hardware support mechanisms for multimedia processing in a general purpose processor. The support comprises a vector-based instruction set with a submatrix addressing mode which utilises subword vectors. Examining mpeg2encode and decode kernels, the *2d-vector* shows a distinct performance advantages over other instruction sets.

The other hardware support is a simple cache prefetch technique that exploits the two dimensional data access patterns in MPEG2 encode and decode video applications. The technique gives a significant reduction in memory latency.

An initial detailed simulation of the system is presented demonstrating the benefits of the approach. However, an exhaustive simulation study is a subject for future work, together with examining other multimedia kernels. Future work is also needed to consider the effect of multithreading and real-time scheduling. On the software side, just-in-time vectorisation for Java programs needs to be pursued.

References

1. Doug Burger and James R. Goodman. Billion-transistor architectures. *IEEE Computer*, 30(9):46–49, September 1997.
2. Thomas M. Conte, Pradeep K. Dubey, Matthew D. Jennings, Ruby B. Lee, Alex Peleg, Salliah Rathnam, Mike Schlansker, Peter Song, and Andrew Wolfe. Challenges to combining general-purpose and multimedia processors. *IEEE Computer*, 30(12):33–37, December 1997.
3. J. Corbal, R. Espasa, and M. Valero. MOM: a matrix SIMD instruction set architecture for multimedia applications. In *SC'99 "Supercomputing Conference"*, Oregon, 1999.
4. R. Cucchiara, M. Piccardi, and A. Prati. Exploiting cache in multimedia. In *International Conference on Computing and Systems*, Florance, Italy, 1999. IEEE.
5. Keith Diefendorff and Pradeep K. Dubey. How multimedia workload will change processor design. *IEEE Computer*, 30(9):43–45, September 1997.
6. John W. C. Fu and James H. Patel. Data prefetching in multiprocessing vector cache memories. In *Proceedings of the 18th Annual International Symposium on Computer Architecture*, pages 54–63. ACM, 1991.
7. MPEG Software Simulation Group. *MPEG-2 Encoder/Decoder, version 1.2 July 19, 1996*. http://www.mpeg.org/MSSG.
8. P. M. Kogge. *The Architecture of Pipelined Computers*. Hemisphere Publishing Corporation, Washington New York London, 1981.
9. Christoforos E. Kozyrakis and David A. Patterson. A new direction for computer architecture research. *IEEE Computer*, pages 24–32, November 1998.
10. Ichiro Kuroda and Takao Nishitani. Multimedia processors. *Proceedings of the IEEE*, 86(6):1203–1221, June 1998.
11. Sun Microsystems Laboratories. *Shade V5.33A*. Mountain View, CA 94043, June 1997.
12. G. M. Wright. *A single-chip multiprocessor architecture with hardware thread support*. PhD thesis, Dept. of Computer Science, University of Manchester, January 2001.

Multiprocessor Clustering for Embedded Systems[1]

Vida Kianzad and Shuvra S. Bhattacharyya
University of Maryland at College Park
{vida, ssb}@eng.umd.edu

Abstract. In this paper, we address two key trends in the synthesis of implementations for embedded multiprocessors — (1) the increasing importance of managing interprocessor communication (IPC) in an efficient manner, and (2) the acceptance of significantly longer compilation time by embedded system designers. The former aspect is evident in the increasing interest among embedded system architects in innovative communication architectures, such as those involving optical interconnection technologies, and hybrid electro-optical structures [7]. The latter aspect results because embedded multiprocessor systems are typically designed as final implementations for dedicated functions. While multiprocessor mapping strategies for general-purpose systems are usually designed with low to moderate complexity as a constraint, embedded system design tools are allowed to employ more thorough and time-consuming optimization techniques.

1. Introduction

In this paper, we develop novel partitioning and scheduling techniques that aggressively streamline interprocessor communication. We address the increasing importance of managing interprocessor communication in an efficient manner. This importance is due to the increasing interest among embedded system architects in innovative communication architectures, such as those involving optical interconnection technologies, and hybrid electro-optical structures [7]. Effective experimentation with unconventional architectures requires adequate design tools that can exploit such architectures. We also address the increased compile time tolerance in embedded system design. This results because embedded multiprocessor systems are typically designed as final implementations for *dedicated* functions; modifications to embedded system implementations are rare, and this allows embedded system design tools to employ more thorough, time-consuming optimization techniques. In contrast, multiprocessor mapping strategies for general purpose systems are typically designed with low to moderate complexity as a constraint.

Our work builds on the two-phased decomposition of multiprocessor scheduling that was introduced by Sarkar [5], and explored subsequently by other researchers such as Yang and Gerasoulis [10]. In this decomposition, the application graph is first mapped to a *fully-connected* multiprocessor architecture that has an unbounded number of processors. The goal of mapping here is to minimize the net execution time. In the second phase of Sarkar's two-phase process, called *merging*, the derived schedule is mapped onto the given resource-constrained architecture. Our use of Sarkar's decomposition scheme and the associated breakdown of scheduling into different phases is motivated by the idea of

---

1. This research was sponsored by the Defense Advanced Research Projects Agency, and the U. S. National Science Foundation.

introducing modularity, and hence more flexibility, in allocating compile-time resources throughout the optimization process. In this paper, we focus on the first phase (*clustering*) of this decomposed problem. Algorithms to address second phase have been discussed in [8].

2. Background and Previous Work

In the context of embedded system implementation, one limitation shared by many scheduling algorithms is that they have been designed for general purpose computation. In the general-purpose domain, there are many applications for which short compile time is of major concern. In such scenarios, it is highly desirable to ensure that an application can be mapped to an architecture within a matter of seconds. Sarkar's internalization algorithm (SIA) and the dominant sequence clustering algorithm (DSC)[10] provide such low complexity algorithms.

However, being deterministic in nature, neither SIA nor DSC can exploit the increased compile time tolerance in embedded system implementation. There has been some probabilistic search implementation of scheduling heuristics in the literature, such as genetic algorithms (GAs), that exploit this increased compile time tolerance. Hou et al. [2], Wang and Korfhage [9], Kwok and Ahmad [4], Zomaya et al. [12], and Correa et al. [1] have proposed different genetic algorithms in the scheduling context. Hou and Correa use similar integer string representations of solutions. Wang and Korfhage use a two-dimensional matrix scheme to encode the solution. Kwok and Ahmad also use integer string representations, and Zomaya et al. use a matrix of integer substrings. All of these algorithms have relatively complex solution representations in the underlying GA formulation. We show that in the context of the clustering/merging decomposition, we can avoid these complications in the clustering phase, and use more streamlined solution encodings for clustering.

We have explored a number of approaches for exploiting the increased compile-time tolerance in embedded multiprocessor implementation, the first of which applies the concept of GAs to develop a novel approach for multiprocessor clustering and scheduling. We represent the applications that are to be mapped into parallel implementations in terms of the widely-used *task graph model*. A task graph is a directed acyclic graph (DAG) $G = (V, E)$, where

- V is the set of task nodes, which are in one-to-one correspondence with the computational tasks in the application (($V = \{v_1, v_2, ..., v_{|V|}\}$)).
- E is the set of communication edges (each member is an ordered pair of tasks).
- $t : V \rightarrow \aleph$ denotes a function that assigns an execution time to each member of V.
- $C : V \times V \rightarrow \aleph$ denotes a function that gives the cost (latency) of each communication edge. That is, $C(v, v) \equiv 0$ for all V; $C(v_1, v_2) = C(v_2, v_1)$ for all v_1, v_2; and $C(v_1, v_2)$ is the cost of transferring data between v_1 and v_2 if they are assigned to different processors.

The **net execution time** is defined by the following expression:

$$\tau_N = max(tlevel(v_x) + blevel(v_x) | v_x \in V), \qquad (1)$$

where $tlevel(v_x)$ ($blevel(v_x)$) is the length of the longest path between node v_x and the source (sink) node in the *scheduled graph*, including all of the communication and computation costs in that path, but excluding $t(v_x)$ from $tlevel(v_x)$. Here, by the scheduled graph, we mean the task graph with all known information about clustering and task execution ordering modeled using additional zero-cost edges. In particular, if v_1 and v_2 are clustered together, and v_2 is scheduled to execute immediately after v_1, then the edge (v_1, v_2) is inserted in the scheduled graph.

3. Solution Representation

We propose a new framework for applying GAs to scheduling problems. Our solution representation encodes scheduling-related information as a single subset of graph edges β, with no notion of an ordering among the elements of β. This representation can be used with a wide variety of scheduling and clustering problems. It exploits the view of a clustering as a subset of edges in the task graph. Gerasoulis and Yang have suggested this view of clustering in their characterization of certain clustering algorithms as being *edge-zeroing* algorithms [10]. One of our contributions in this paper is to apply this subset-based view of clustering to develop a natural, efficient genetic algorithm formulation. For the purpose of a genetic algorithm, the representation of graph clusterings as subsets of edges is attractive since *subsets have natural and efficient mappings into the framework of genetic algorithms.*

Derived from the *schema* theory (a schema denotes a similarity template that represents a subset of $\{0, 1\}^n$), canonical GAs (which use binary representations of solution spaces) provide near-optimal sampling strategies. Furthermore, binary encodings in which the semantic interpretations of different bit positions exhibit high symmetry (e.g., in our case, each bit corresponds to the existence or absence of an edge within a cluster) allow us to leverage extensive prior research on genetic operators for symmetric encodings rather than forcing us to develop specialized, less-thoroughly-tested operators to handle the underlying non symmetric representation. Accordingly, our binary encoding scheme is favored both by schema theory, and significant prior work on genetic operators. Furthermore, by providing no constraints on genetic operators, our encoding scheme preserves the natural behavior of GAs.

Our approach to encoding clustering solutions is based on the following definition.
Definition 1: Suppose that β is a subset of task graph edges. Then $f_\beta : E \to \{0, 1\}$ denotes the **clusterization function** associated with β. This function is defined by:

$$f(e_i) = \begin{cases} 0 \text{ if } (e_i \in \beta) \\ 1 \text{ otherwise} \end{cases} \qquad (2)$$

When using a clusterization function to represent a clustering solution, the edge subset β is taken to be the set of edges that are contained in clusters. An illustration is shown in Figure 1. Because it is based on using clusterization functions to represent candidate solutions, we refer to our GA approach as the *clusterization function algorithm* (CFA).

In the CFA, the initial population is initialized with a random selection of clusterization functions (mappings from E into $\{0, 1\}$) and its fitness is evaluated from the net execution time τ_N (from (1)). To compute τ_N, we have applied a modified version of list scheduling that abandons the restrictions imposed by a global scheduling clock, as proposed in [6]. More details on our implementation can be found in [3].

4. Performance Evaluation and Comparison

In this section, we present an experimental comparison of DSC, SIA and CFA. To be fair in comparison of these algorithms (DSC and SIA are deterministic heuristics, while our GA is a guided probabilistic search method), we have implemented randomized versions of DSC and SIA — each such randomized algorithm, like CFA, can exploit increases in additional computational resources to explore larger segments of the solution space.

We have incorporated randomization into to the edge selection process when deriving randomized versions of DSC (RDSC) and SIA (RSIA). In the randomized versions, the

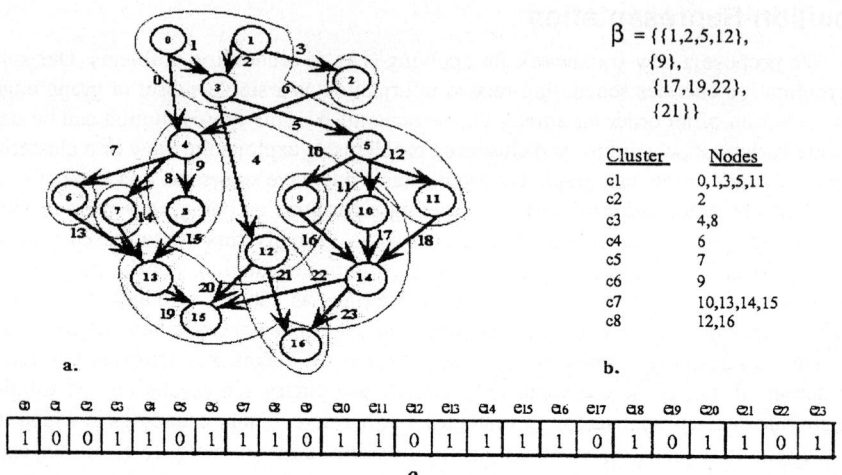

Figure 1. (a) A clustering of an application graph; (b) the corresponding subset β of "zeroed" edges; (c) the corresponding clusterization function f_β.

first element of the sorted edge list — the candidate to be zeroed — is selected with probability p, (we call p the *randomization parameter*); if this element is not chosen, the second element is selected with probability p; and so on, until some element is chosen, or no element is returned after considering all the elements in the list. In this last case (no element is chosen), a random number is chosen from a uniform distribution over $\{0, 1, ..., |T| - 1\}$ (where T is the set of edges that have not yet been clustered). Further details on this general approach to incorporating randomization into greedy, priority-based algorithms can be found in [11], which explores randomization techniques in the context of DSP memory management.

Each randomized algorithm begins by first applying the underlying (original) deterministic algorithm, and then repeatedly computing additional solutions with a "degree of randomness" determined by p. The best solution computed within the allotted compile-time tolerance (e.g., 10 min., 1 hr., etc.) is returned. The allotted running time for each input graph to RDSC or RSIA was determined from the CFA running time on the same graphs for 3000 iterations, which allows comparison under equal amounts of running time.

All the heuristics have been tested with two sets of input graphs, DSP-related task graphs and random graphs (with 50 to 1000 nodes). We have also varied the *communication to computation cost ratio* (CCR), between 0.1 to 10 when experimenting with each task graph. The net execution times of random graphs for all algorithms are shown in Figure 2 (more

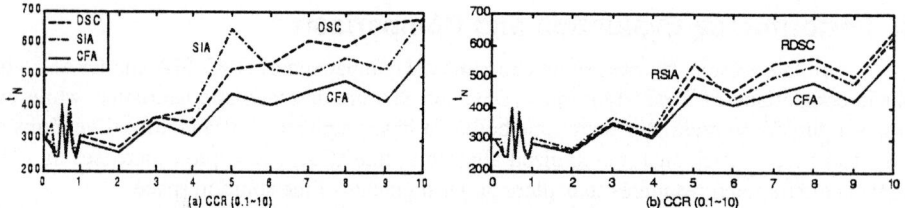

Figure 2. τ_N of different heuristic and randomized algorithms for random graphs.

results, including those on the DSP-related graphs, can be found in [3]). It can be seen from the figure that CFA consistently performs significantly better than the other approaches, and the benefit of the CFA approach increases with increasing CCR values. Overall, for both random and application-related graphs, our experimental results [3] show that CFA is preferable for compile time tolerances that accommodate the underlying GA configuration (less than 1 min. to 10 hrs for the graphs that we considered in our experiments).

5. Summary and Conclusions

This paper has explored multiprocessor clustering techniques to exploit the increased compile time tolerance of the embedded systems domain, and achieve efficient mapping of applications onto multiprocessor architectures. We have developed a novel and natural genetic algorithm formulation, called CFA, for multiprocessor clustering, as well as randomized versions, called RDSC and RSIA, of two well-known deterministic algorithms, DSC [10] and SIA [5], respectively. RDSC and RSIA perform at least as well as DSC and SIA, but are able to exploit arbitrary increases in compile time tolerance due to their incorporation of probabilistic selection. Based on these developments, we have performed an extensive experimental study that compares the alternative strategies under equal amounts of running time (compile time tolerance). Our experiments have demonstrated that the CFA algorithm significantly outperforms RDSC and RSIA, and that the improvement offered by CFA increases with increasing communication costs in the application relative to the amount of computation. Thus, CFA is especially useful when managing communication costs is important. Presently, we are developing further experiments to quantify these distinctions. Another useful direction for further work is exploring the integration of merging algorithms into the CFA framework (e.g., in the fitness evaluation phase).

References

1. R.C. Correa, A. Ferreira, P. Rebreyend, "Scheduling Multiprocessor Tasks with Genetic Algorithms," *IEEE Trans. on Parallel and Distributed Sys.*, Vol. 0, 825-837, 1999.
2. E.S. H. Hou, N. Ansari, H. Ren, "A Genetic Algorithm for Multiprocessor Scheduling," *IEEE Trans. on Parallel and Distributed Systems*, Vol. 5, 113-120, 1994.
3. V. Kianzad, S. S. Bhattacharyya, Multiprocessor clustering for embedded system implementation. Tech. report, Inst. for Advanced Computer Studies, UMCP June 2001.
4. Y. Kwok, I. Ahmad, "Efficient Scheduling of Arbitrary Task Graphs to Multiprocessors Using A Parallel Genetic Algorithm," *Journal of Parallel and Distributed Computing*, 1997.
5. V. Sarkar. *Partitioning and Scheduling Parallel Programs for Multiprocessors*. MIT Press, 1989.
6. G. C. Sih, E. Lee, "A compile-time scheduling heuristic for interconnection-constrained heterogeneous processor architectures." *IEEE Trans. on Parallel and Dist. Sys.*, Vol. 4, No. 2, 1993.
7. D. Spencer, J. Kepner, D. Martinez, "Evaluation of advanced optoelectronic interconnect technology," MIT Lincoln Laboratory August 1999.
8. T.Yang, A. Gerasoulis, "PYRROS: States scheduling and code generation for message passing multiprocessors," *Proc. of 6th ACM Int. Conf. on Supercomputing*, 1992.
9. P. Wang, W. Korfhage, "Process Scheduling Using Genetic Algorithms," *IEEE Symp. on Parallel and Distributed Processing*, 638-641, 1995.
10. T.Yang, A.Gerasoulis, "DSC: scheduling parallel tasks on an unbounded number of processors," *IEEE Trans. on Parallel and Distributed Sys.*, Vol. 5, 951-967, 1994.
11. E. Zitzler, J. Teich, S. S. Bhattacharyya. Optimized software synthesis for DSP using randomization techniques. Tech. report, Swiss Federal Institute of Technology, Zurich, July 1999.
12. A.Y. Zomaya, C. Ward, B. Macey, "Genetic scheduling for parallel processor systems: comparative studies and performance issues," *IEEE Trans. on Parallel and Dist. Sys.*, Vol. 10, 795-812, 1999.

Topic 16
Cluster Computing

Mark Baker, John Brooke, Ken Hawick, and Rajkumar Buyya

Topic Chairpersons

We would like to welcome readers to the Cluster Computing topic of Euro-Par 2001 that was held in the British city of Manchester in the summer of 2001.

Without doubt clusters are now the platform of choice for most scientific, engineering, commercial and industrial applications. In addition, as evidence from a casual browse through these proceedings of Euro-Par 2001 reveals, clusters, of one form or another, are being used for research and development by most of the topics within the conference.

The popularity of Clusters is due to a number of reasons; the foremost of these are price/performance, availability of packaged hardware and software components, ease of installation, configuration and customization, as well as the take-up of standard practices and a growing user community. This is not to say that all the problems with the use of Clusters have been solved. For example, areas like comprehensive managements tools, dealing with heterogeneity, and the availability of application development tools and utilities are matters that are still far from mature and under active research. In addition, issues brought up by the papers in this topic highlight some of the areas that are considered of current interest.

Topic 16 received a very high quality paper submission this year, with fifteen papers being submitted and twelve papers accepted. The papers were reviewed by a topic programme committee of some world experts in the field of cluster computing. All papers were reviewed by four, and sometimes by five reviewers. This is a quite exceptional rate of acceptance and we hope that the topic programme reflects this excellence.

Session 1 includes an invited talk (not available in these proceedings), one regular and two short paper presentations. The invited talk by Kenji Takeda of the University of Southampton reports on their recent experiences in purchasing and installing a large Cluster. The paper by Jørgen S. Hansen and Eric Jul then discusses their work on providing a means of improving the stability and reducing the latency of network event handling in clusters. Wolfgang Schreiner, Gabor Kusper, and Karoly Bosa, in their paper, talk about an extended version of distributed Maple. The final paper in this session, by Eric Renault and Pierre David, describes PAPI, a system that has been designed to provide multiple levels of security for remote writes.

Session 2 consists of three regular papers. The first paper by Yariv Aridor, Michael Factor and Avi Teperman discusses a Java-based virtual machine, which executes on a cluster and presents a single system image to its users. Francesc Solsona, Francesc Giné, Porfidio Hernández and Emilio Luque, in their paper, describe an implementation of a predictive co-scheduling technique for a Linux cluster. The final paper of the session is by Elisa Heymann, Miquel A. Senar, Emilio Luque and Miron Livny. They present their experiences with a self-adaptive scheduling strategy that can dynamically adjust the number of resources used by an application.

Session 3 also consists of three regular papers. Anne-Marie Kermarrec and Christine Morin talk about their work on the integration of a backward error recovery high-availability support mechanism for a parallel single level store system used in clusters. Next, Ligang He, Hai Jin, Ying Chen and Zongfen Han in their paper discuss an algorithm for scheduling aperiodic jobs on a cluster. Finally, in this session, the paper by Francesc D. Muñoz-Escoí, Óscar Gomis, Pablo Galdámez and José M. Bernabéu-Aubán provides details about the Hidra Membership Monitor, a distributed service that maintains the current set of active nodes in a cluster and handles the detection of nodes that join and fail.

Session 4 was composed of an invited talk, two regular papers and a short paper. The invited talk (not available in these proceedings), by Tim Mattson of Intel, presents the work be undertaken on OSCAR — a software package for configuring and managing high performance clusters. Next, César A. F. De Rose and Hans-Ulrich Heiss in their paper report on an investigation into a distributed approach to the processor allocation problem in large mesh-connected multicomputers. The paper by Andres Ibañez, Valentin Puente, Jose Angel Gregorio and Ramón Beivide discusses their work on an adaptive routing algorithm for irregular networks, which avoids the deadlocks often encountered in regular networks. The final paper in this session is by Michael Kalantar and Jun Fong who present a new Web farm-hosting model in which hardware resources are dynamically allocated based on observed request streams.

In closing, we would like to thank all those authors who submitted papers to this topic, the topic programme committee for their help in providing high quality reviews of all the papers and finally the Euro-Par Organizing Committee for including this topic within the conference.

Prioritizing Network Event Handling in Clusters of Workstations

Jørgen S. Hansen[1,*] and Eric Jul[2]

[1] SIRAC Project
INRIA Rhône-Alpes, France
jorgen.hansen@inrialpes.fr
[2] Department of Computer Science, University of Copenhagen, Denmark
eric@diku.dk

1 Introduction

The use of modern system area networking technologies [9,3] to construct tightly integrated clusters of workstations exposes two weaknesses of current operating systems. First, the low latency of current networks is often hidden from the application due to the high cost of interrupt handling. Second, network event handling during high load may result in serious performance degradation because all processor time is used for network event handling resulting in application starvation. This paper concerns the problems related to providing efficient and stable network event handling for clusters of workstations and network servers. By stable we mean that the throughput and response time of the system does not suffer when the workload offered to the system is increased beyond the maximum capacity of the system.

Our approach is based on assigning each network device a priority in the regular process priority range and allow events from the device to enter the system based on this priority. The handling of events from the device does not preempt processes with equal or higher priority, but will preempt lower priority processes. This integrates the processing of the stream of events from the device with the scheduling of regular processes thereby allowing for a natural batch processing of the events from the network adapter, and eliminating the risk of livelock. Making the devices visible to the operating system scheduler also allows us to eliminate the overhead of interrupts when the system is idle. When the scheduler detects that no process is runnable, it continuously poll the devices.

The rest of this paper is organized as follows. Section 2 explains our event handling approach in detail. Section 3 describes a prototype implementation in the Linux operating system, it's measured overhead, and the effects on a stream protocol for a system area network based on Scalable Coherent Interface (SCI). Related work is covered in Section 4, and our conclusions are drawn in Section 5.

---

* The main part of this work was carried out as a Ph.D. student at the Department of Computer Science, University of Copenhagen

2 Integrating Device Priorities with Scheduling

In this section, we present our device event handling based on device priorities and describe how it can be used to increase the stability of systems processing large amounts of network related events and to decrease network communication latency. We base our discussion on a priority-based scheduler using preemptive round robin scheduling of processes with the same priority. We first describe how our approach can be applied to uniprocessor systems, and then we look at the additional complexities of supporting multiprocessors.

2.1 Integrating Event Handling with Process Scheduling

In present day operating systems, the handling of events from a device usually has higher priority than any other task in the operating system. This can lead to degraded system performance when events arrive at a high rate [13,4] as time is spent on performing processing of arriving events instead of allowing applications or operating system to react to earlier events.

Instead of having a static high priority for device event handling, we propose viewing device event handling as a task whose scheduling is controlled by the operating system scheduler. In a priority based scheduler, this is done by assigning the device (or actually the device event handling) a priority in the priority range available for the scheduler. Thus, when events with a given priority are ready, one of the following three cases will occur: 1) processes with higher priority than the device are runnable, and the processing of events should be postponed, 2) processes with a priority equal to the device are runnable, and the processing of events should share the processor resources with these processes, and 3) no process with priority equal to or higher than the device is runnable, and the processing of events should take place immediately. From this, it is clear that when events are available for processing, a thread with the device priority dedicated to handling events by polling the device will behave as described in the three cases, and we therefore base our event handling on such polling threads.

2.2 Event Notification Using a Mix of Polling and Interrupts

Allowing the device polling thread to remain runnable even when there is no event to be processed obviously wastes processor resources. This problem can be avoided by having the thread block when there is no event available, and then using interrupts to schedule the process [13] when the first event occurs after a period of inactivity. However, the interrupt overhead is still incurred and the total latency experienced by the event will typically be higher. Instead, we use a combination of polling integrated with the operating system scheduler and interrupts to wake up a blocked thread. When there are runnable threads and they all have a priority lower than the device, we use interrupts to activate the polling thread, and in all other cases we rely on the operating system scheduler to poll the device. When there exists runnable processes, the scheduler polls all devices with priority equal to or lower than the highest priority runnable process at the time when it needs to make a scheduling decision. Lower priority devices are polled to represent their polling threads in ready queues, if there are events to be processed. Thus, techniques such as aging can be used to prevent device starvation. When there are no runnable threads, we let the scheduler (or the idle thread) poll all devices continuously to allow the system to react quickly to new events. If processor power consumption is a concern, the processor can be halted (and interrupts enabled) after a certain period of time, e.g., a couple of minutes.

Polling I/O adapters across an I/O bus can be time consuming (relative to CPU-speeds) and should be avoided, if possible. Instead, we base our polling on event flags placed in physical memory. A network adapter that needs attention must raise its associated event flag to request kernel processing. On each scheduling decision, the scheduler checks these flags to detect pending events. This limitation on the signalling of events might seem restrictive, but most current high-speed networking technologies [3,6] include the necessary support for such event signalling. Conventional network designs could be supported through alternative polling handlers at a cost but having interrupts schedule the polling thread is likely to be more efficient.

One possible problem with postponing network adapter servicing is that the postponement may cause overflow of on-board buffers. If the network adapter supports the generation of high water mark interrupts, buffer overflow can be avoided by having these interrupts schedule a high-priority event handling thread. If, on the other hand, polling is used to increase stability, buffer overflow is how the increased stability during high load situations is obtained, i.e., by shedding network load as early as possible.

2.3 Priority-Based Event Handling on Multiprocessor Systems

Multiprocessor systems provide further opportunities for decreasing network latency through polling on idle processors because the many processors increase the probability of an idle processor. Additionally, compared to the limited form of prioritized distribution of interrupts supported in modern interrupt controllers [10], the use of polling threads allows a strict enforcement of the scheduling policy of the operating system. However, such interrupt controllers can be used to reduce the number of interruptions of high priority processes.

To review the added cost (in terms of additional processor synchronization) of priority-based event handling on multiprocessors, we revisit our two additions to process scheduling: polling of event flags and disabling and enabling of interrupts on priority changes. The polling of event flags need not be implemented as a critical region, as the worst case is that several idle threads activate the same polling thread. Enabling and disabling interrupts requires more careful handling than for single processors. The interrupts for a device should be enabled only when at least one processor is executing a thread with priority lower than the device and neither the device polling thread nor an idle thread is executing. If the scheduler uses a single run queue, the necessary global state is already maintained by the scheduler, but if a local run queue on each processor is used priority-based event handling adds synchronization to the scheduling loop.

3 An Example of Priority-Based Event Handling

We have implemented a prototype of the priority-based event handling for Linux 2.0 and 2.2. As the Linux scheduler implements a variation of priority based FIFO scheduling, the approach described in the previous section can be directly applied. The prototype has been used for the communication in a cluster of workstations connected by Dolphin's SCI cluster adapters [6]. These adapters provide hardware support for low overhead remote memory access through regular processor load and store operations as well as DMA. In the cluster, communication across the SCI network was handled by SciStream [8]—a TCP compatible stream protocol for SCI, and all nodes used 450MHz Pentium II processors.

In this section, we present an evaluation of the overhead added to the Linux scheduler and of the effects of priority-based event handling on SciStream communication latency and SciStream stability during high network load.

3.1 Added Scheduler Overhead

The overhead added to the Linux scheduler by (1) polling event flags and (2) changing interrupt status for devices was measured by augmenting the scheduler with measurements using the Pentium processor cycle counters. We implemented a kernel module that registers event flags as a real device would. The action taken by the module, when an event flag is raised, is simply to find the event flag handle in an array and reenable the event flag. Changing interrupt status increments a counter, and thus reflects only the cost of invoking such a function. We used three configurations, where each configuration used from 0 to 16 allocated event flags with a size of four bytes each. In the **No Activity** configuration event flags are allocated but never raised. In the **Heavy Activity** configuration event flags are allocated and continuously raised. Finally, the **Interrupt** configuration forces a change in interrupt status on each scheduling decision.

We measured the overhead of the different configurations on a single processor system using Linux version 2.0. For **No Activity** the overhead amounts to 67 ns, and each additional flag adds an overhead of 25 ns. This is a bit more expensive than the cost of single memory reference suggested in Section 2.2, but our current implementation includes additional functionality such as partial masking of event flags. In the **Heavy Activity** case, the overhead is 135 ns for a single flag, and 91 ns are added for each flag. Finally, for **Interrupt** the overhead is 56 ns in the case with no allocated flags, and for a single allocated flag the overhead is 180 ns. Here each additional flag adds 39 ns of overhead. On multiprocessors, the priority-based event handling mechanism increases the overhead of each scheduling decision with the cost of taking and releasing a spin-lock.

We measured the cost of a context switch in Linux to be 4.2 microseconds. Thus, priority-based event handling adds between 1.6% and 11% overhead to the process scheduling in the case of no activity. The scheduling of low priority processes may suffer further due to the cost of changing the interrupt status. In most cases, the number of network devices in a single node will be small, and the overhead of supporting priority-based event handling will hardly be noticeable.

3.2 Latency of Event Handling

The priority-based event handling in SciStream is implemented using the remote memory access and remote interrupt facilities of the SCI cluster adapters. In the current implementation, raising the event flag is done by performing a remote fetch and increment, and throwing an interrupt (when interrupts are enabled) adds to this the triggering of a remote interrupt.

To establish the benefits of avoiding interrupts and the cost of using kernel threads for processing events, we compare the performance the priority-based event handling (**PriThread**) with interrupts (**Interrupt**) and application polling (**AppPol**) where the SciStream receive operation continuously check a single connection for incoming data. The effects of low priority compute-intensive jobs is determined through a **XXHog** version for **PriThread** and **Interrupt**, where an application, that only yields the processor when preempted, is present.

We evaluated the configurations by measuring the average one-way latency of 10,000 request-response exchanges of a one byte packet on a uniprocessor system. **AppPol** results in a latency of 10.1 microseconds. **PriThread** adds 20.0 microseconds to this overhead due to the remote event notification, context switch, and selecting the proper process for execution. The two stage process of generating the remote interrupt in **PriThreadHog** adds another 32.6 microseconds to the latency. The newer versions of the SCI driver software allow this to be performed in a single remote operation resulting in a latency equivalent to **Interrupt**. Both **Interrupt** and **InterruptHog** are 20.1 microseconds more expensive than **PriThread**. Thus, using priority-based event handling results in a latency reduction to $\frac{20.0+10.1}{40.1+10.1} = 60\%$ when compared to interrupts. We achieve similar performance gains on a dual processor system.

In summary, we see that allowing an idle workstation to continuously poll it's network adapters can significantly decrease network communication latency.

3.3 High Load Behavior of a Web Server

The high load behavior of SciStream was examined using the Apache web server and the tool httperf [14]. Using httperf, we determined the maximum sustainable load for each configuration through a series of experiments where we gradually increased the offered fixed request rate. For all test cases, we were able to exceed the maximum sustainable load. We let the web server supply two different documents: a small document with a size of 1,622 bytes (**SD**), and a large document with a size of 56,257 bytes (**BD**). For both **SD** and **BD** we used the **PriThread** configuration described in Section 3.2 and **PriImm** that performs event handling immediately when an event flag is raised and therefore resembles the static high priority of interrupts. In the experiments, we issued one request per connection and the device and web server threads had the same priority.

The resulting reply rates (replies/s) for the Apache web server are shown in Figure 1. The **PriImm** configuration is able to provide the highest reply rate (471 replies/s for **BD** and 1,150 replies/s for **SD** as opposed to 466 replies/s and 1,066 replies/s respectively for **PriThread**) for both document types. This

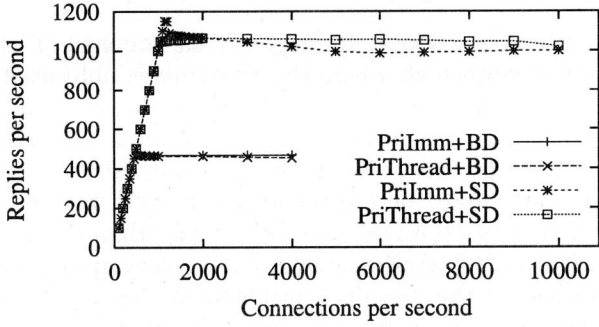

Fig. 1. Apache Reply Rates under High Load

is a result of the overhead of scheduling a polling thread in the **PriThread** configuration. Surprisingly, the **PriImm** configuration is able to sustain a rather high reply rate beyond the maximum sustainable load. This is the result of how a full connection request queue in the web server is handled in SciStream (see also Banga et al. [1]). While the queue is full, the client program will get a "connection refused" error for any connection attempts. However, as shown by the average connection times in Figure 2 the full queues delay the processing of all incoming requests considerably. Our Apache web server used 255 concurrent processes to service requests, and the scheduling of these concurrent threads also increase the average connection time of the **PriThread** configurations as the offered load is increased.

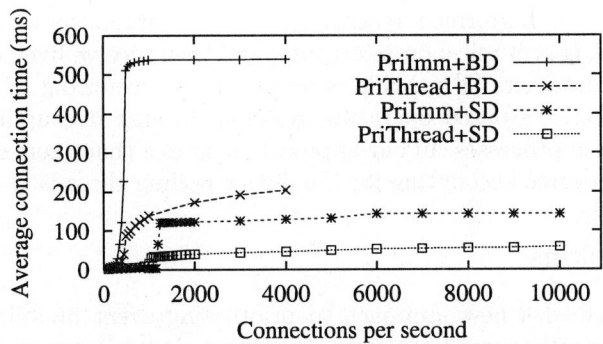

Fig. 2. Average Connection Time for Apache under High Load

Overall, we find that using priority-based event handling increases the stability (in the sense that the average response times are much lower during high network load) of the web server in the experimental setup.

4 Related Work

The work on eliminating livelock [13] explores the problem of livelock in great detail. A solution is suggested, where the interrupt is only used to schedule a polling kernel thread. The approach uses a kernel thread with higher priority than any user thread and can therefore result in thread starvation problems.

Polling and interrupts have been integrated with the thread management in a user-level thread library by Langendoen et.al. [11], but in contrast to our approach, they statically prioritize interrupts higher than thread processing.

Polling Watchdogs [12] consider polling network adapters when scheduling decisions are made, but they do not consider reducing the polling penalty by using flags in physical memory. Special purpose hardware is needed to keep the system responsive and to avoid network hardware buffer overflow.

Ensuring responsiveness when a network API does not support interrupts has been investigated by Perkovic et al. [15]. They perform low overhead network polling using event flags similar to ours but they mainly consider inserting this polling code into applications through source-code manipulation.

In scientific parallel programs, it might be beneficial to poll the network for a limited time before blocking, e.g., when a computation is followed by a data exchange. Damianakis et al. [5] successfully use fixed busy-wait thresholds before blocking on receive operations to reducing communication overhead.

Lazy receiver processing [7] makes each process perform most of the processing of its own network communication. This makes it easier to account for the time spent by each process on network communication. Preferably, the network hardware performs the packet demultiplexing onto the communication endpoints but if this is not possible a kernel thread handles the demultiplexing.

In signaled receiver processing [4], the protocol processing is also performed by the application, but the applications themselves can control whether the processing shall be performed synchronously, asynchronously or be suspended. Packet processing still relies on interrupts, and thus receive livelock may occur.

Resource containers [2] provide more accurate accounting of resource consumption for process-based operating systems through decoupling accounting information from processes. In our approach, resource containers can be used to improve the resource accounting for the device polling threads.

5 Conclusions

We have described a new approach to prioritizing event handling of network devices in a general operating system. A network device is assigned priorities in the scheduler priority range and by confining network event handling to a polling thread using this device priority, the processing of network events is integrated with the operating system process scheduling. The scheme relies on modifying the scheduler to perform part of the device polling. Our results show that this priority-based event handling increases the stability of network servers under high load, and, in addition, the scheme may reduce latency for lightly loaded systems.

Acknowledgements

Kåre Løchsen and Hugo Kohmann from Dolphin Interconnect (Norway) granted us access to the source codes for the PCI-SCI adapter and answered all of our questions. Povl Koch, Nokia and Emmanuel Cecchet, Simon Nieuviarts and Xavier Rousset de Pina, SIRAC project, provided us with valuable support for the SciOS prototype.

References

1. G. Banga and P. Druschel. Measuring the capacity of a Web server. In *USENIX Symposium on Internet Technologies and Systems Proceedings*, pages 61–71, 1997.
2. G. Banga, P. Druschel, and J. C. Mogul. Resource containers: A new facility for resource management in server systems. In *Proceedings of the Third Symposium on Operating Systems Design and Implementation*, pages 45–58, February 1999.
3. N. J. Boden, D. Cohen, R. E. Felderman, A. E. Kulawik, C. L. Seitz, J. N. Seizovic, and Wen-King Su. Myrinet: A gigabit-per-second Local Area Network. *IEEE Micro*, 15(1):29–36, February 1995.
4. J. C. Brustoloni, E. Gabber, A. Silberschatz, and A. Singh. Signaled receiver processing. In *Proceedings of the 2000 USENIX Annual Technical Conference*, 2000.
5. S. Damianakis, Y. Chen, and E. Felten. Reducing waiting costs in user-level communication. In *Proceedings of the 11th International Parallel Processing Symposium (IPPS-97)*, pages 381–387. IEEE Computer Society Press, April 1–5 1997.
6. Dolphin Interconnect Solutions. PCI-SCI cluster adapter specification, May 1996. Version 1.2. See also http://www.dolphinics.no.
7. P. Druschel and G. Banga. Lazy receiver processing (LRP): A network subsystem architecture for server systems. In *The Second Symposium on Operating Systems Design and Implementation Proceedings*, pages 261–276, October 1996.
8. J. S. Hansen, P. T. Koch, and E. Jul. A stream protocol implementation for an SCI-based cluster of workstations. In *Proceedings of the 1999 Workshop on Cluster-Based Computing*, pages 16–20, Rhodes, Greece, June 1999. ACM.
9. IEEE. *IEEE Standard for Scalable Coherent Interface (SCI)*. IEEE, 1992. Standard 1596-1992.
10. Intel Corporation. *Pentium Pro Family Developer's Manual. Volume 3: Operating Systems Writer's Guide*. Order Number 242691.
11. K. G. Langendoen, J. Romein, R. A. F. Bhoedjang, and H. E. Bal. Integrating polling, interrupts, and thread management. In *Proceedings of the 6th Symposium on the Frontiers of Massively Parallel Computation*, pages 13–22. IEEE, 1996.
12. O. Maquelin, G. R. Gao, H. H. J. Hum, K. Theobald, and X. Tian. Polling watchdog : Combining polling and interrupts for efficient message handling. In *Proceedings of the 23rd Annual International Symposium on Computer Architecure*, pages 179–190, 1996.
13. J. C. Mogul and K. K. Ramakrishnan. Eliminating Receive Livelock in an Interrupt-Driven Kernel. *ACM Transactions on Computer Systems*, 15(3):217–252, August 1997.
14. D. M. Mosberger and T. Jin. httperf—a tool for measuring web server performance. In *Proceedings of the 1998 Workshop on Internet Server Performance*. ACM, 1998.
15. D. Perkovic and P. J. Keleher. Responsiveness without interrupts. In *Proceedings of the 1999 International Conference on Supercomputing*, June 1999.

Fault Tolerance for Cluster Computing Based on Functional Tasks*

Wolfgang Schreiner, Gabor Kusper, and Karoly Bosa

Research Institute for Symbolic Computation (RISC-Linz)
Johannes Kepler University, Linz, Austria
FirstName.LastName@risc.uni-linz.ac.at
http://www.risc.uni-linz.ac.at

Abstract. We have extended the parallel computer algebra system Distributed Maple by fault tolerance mechanisms such that computations are not any more limited by the meantime between failures. This is complicated by the fact that task arguments and results may embed task handles and that the system's scheduling layer has only a little information about the computing layer. Nevertheless, the mostly functional parallel programming model makes it possible with relatively simple means.

1 Introduction

Distributed Maple is a portable system for implementing parallel computer algebra algorithms [5]. We have used it for parallelizing various applications in algebraic geometry [6] and executed them in numerous distributed environments. However, as we began to attack larger and larger problems, the meantime between failures became a limiting factor in the applicability of the system.

Most parallel programming environments pursue fault tolerance by *checkpointing* [1,2]. These approaches are complex because they deal with general parallel computations; for special problems much simpler solutions exist [3]. However, also parallel programming models that are more abstract than message passing allow to deal with fault tolerance in a simpler way. In particular, the *functional* programming model has this potential [4].

Distributed Maple runs programs in the imperative language of Maple, but its *parallel* programming model is essentially functional: it provides the ability to spawn function applications as concurrent tasks and to wait for their results (extended by a non-deterministic synchronization facility and single assignment shared data objects). Our primary goal is to extend the scheduling layer of Distributed Maple to provide fault-tolerance in a way that is *transparent* to the application. However, computation layer and scheduling layer are clearly separated by a communication protocol such that the scheduling layer is completely unaware of the actual nature of the computation. Our secondary goal is to preserve this distinction such that the use of the scheduling layer for different kinds of computing engines is not compromised. We thus have to deal with the *limited information* that the scheduling layer has about the computation.

---

* Supported by grant SFB F013/F1304 of the Austrian Science Foundation (FWF).

2 System and Execution Model

A session comprises a set of *nodes* each of which holds a pair of processes: a *kernel* which performs the actual computation, and a *scheduler* which coordinates the created tasks. The scheduler communicates with the kernel on the same node and with the schedulers on other nodes. The *root* is that node from which the session was established. Initially, a single task runs on the root kernel; this task may create new tasks which are distributed to other kernels and may in turn create new tasks. A kernel emits messages task:$\langle t, d \rangle$ where t identifies the task and d describes it. The task needs to be forwarded to some idle kernel which eventually returns a message result:$\langle t, r \rangle$ where r represents the computed result. When a kernel emits wait:$\langle t \rangle$, this task is blocked until the scheduler responds with the result of t. Thus, if this result not yet available, the scheduler may submit to the now idle kernel another task; when this task has returned its result, the kernel may receive the result waited for or yet another task.

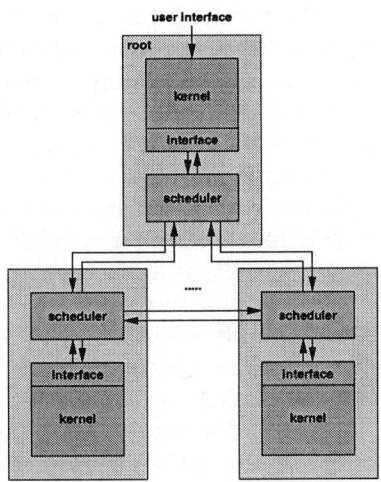

Fig. 1. System Model

A task identifier t encodes a pair $\langle n, i \rangle$ where n identifies the node on which the task was created and i is a running index. The node n thus serves as the rendezvous point between node n' computing the result of t and node n'' requesting this result. When the scheduler on n receives a task:$\langle t, d \rangle$ from its kernel, it thus allocates a result descriptor that will eventually hold the result r; the task itself is scheduled for execution on some node n'. When a kernel on some node n'' issues a wait:$\langle t \rangle$, the scheduler on n'' forwards a request:$\langle t, n'' \rangle$ to n. If r is not yet available on n, this request is queued in the result descriptor. When the kernel on n' eventually returns the result:$\langle t, r \rangle$, the scheduler on n' forwards this message to n, which constructs a reply:$\langle t, r \rangle$ and sends it to n''.

3 Logging Results: First-Order Tasks

Our first step towards fault tolerance is to log task results on stable storage. If the session fails, we can thus re-run the session and read the logged results without re-executing the corresponding tasks. Our only assumption is that the root has access to a writable file system; this file system implements the stable storage and the root becomes in charge of maintaining the log. We now restrict our consideration to programs whose tasks are *first order*: no task description d and no task result r contains any task identifier t, i.e., task identifiers are not passed as parts of task arguments and or parts of task results. The logging mechanism utilizes the fact that the root is in charge of task distribution: every new task:$\langle t, d \rangle$ is forwarded to the root which eventually assigns it to some node for execution. The result logging and failure recovery operations are as follows:

Logging When the root receives a task:$\langle t, d \rangle$, it computes a hash code $h(d)$ and appends to file taskid.$h(d)$ the task identifier t. Then the root starts an asynchronous thread to write the task description d into a new file descr.t. When a node sends a result:$\langle t, r \rangle$ to some node n different from the root, it forwards a copy to the root. When the root receives this result, it creates an asynchronous thread to write the task result r into a new file result.t. All data are written in a format that enables a reader to recognize incomplete writes. At any time, taskid.$h(d)$ holds a sequence of task identifiers t for which there may exist description files descr.t and/or result files result.t. When the session terminates without failure, the files are discarded.

Recovery When a session is re-started after a failure, the root may receive from a node n a task:$\langle t, d \rangle$ such that a file taskid.$h(d)$ exists. If for some complete task identifier t' in this file there exist file descr.t' with a complete description identical to d and file result.t' with a complete result r, the root need not schedule the task but may immediately return result:$\langle t, r \rangle$ to n. The comparison of task descriptions is required because task identifiers are not valid across sessions; since the result r of a task only depends on its description d, the identity of descriptions ensures the identity of results.

4 Logging Results: Higher-Order Tasks

Assume that a task t creates another task and embeds its identifier t' in result r. If r is logged and the session fails, in the recovery session this result may be read from the log such that task identifier t' is re-created. A task may subsequently issue a wait:$\langle t' \rangle$ referring to a no more existing task or, even worse, to a task that computes a different result than in the failed session. Similar situations may occur if t' is passed as an argument to another task.

To support such *higher-order tasks*, we introduce a *session identifier* which distinguishes task identifiers from different sessions. In an original session, the session identifier is initialized to 0 and a file session is written with content 0. In a recovery session, the previous identifier s is read from session, the new identifier is taken as $s+1$ and overwrites session. If the recovery session also fails, a new recovery session may be initiated. A *task identifier* now encodes a triple $\langle s, n, i\rangle$ that embeds the number s of the session in which the corresponding task was created. We generalize the mechanism of the previous section as follows:

Logging As long as the description of a task t created on node n is not completely logged, the root does not schedule the task for execution and does not start the logging of any other task created on n. As long as n has not received the confirmation that the description has been logged, it does not return the result of t to any other task. In this way, we make sure that the identifier of a task is not propagated across tasks before its description has been logged such that a later recovery session can restart the task.

Recovery The root is in charge of tasks whose identifiers refer to previous sessions. If a kernel on node n issues a wait:$\langle t\rangle$ where t refers to a previous session, the scheduler on n sends a request:$\langle t, n\rangle$ to the root. If the root receives this request, it looks up whether it holds a result descriptor for t; if yes, it responds with the result or, if this is not yet available, queues the request in the descriptor. If the root does not hold a result descriptor for t, it creates one and queues the request there. It then looks up file result.t for the result of t. If this file exists and holds a complete result r, the scheduler writes r into the descriptor and responds with reply:$\langle t, r\rangle$. Otherwise, the scheduler looks up descr.t for the description d of t. The scheduler creates a new task:$\langle t, d\rangle$ which is handled as usual. When a kernel issues a result:$\langle t, r\rangle$ for a task t of a previous session, the scheduler forwards it to the root.

5 Tolerating Node Failures

We have also introduced a mechanism that enables a session to cope with faults *without* aborting. We restrict our attention to the scenario where a non-root node becomes unreachable (stop failure) and the root continues operation with the remaining nodes (if the root fails, the session also fails). A necessary condition to detect this failure is that the root cannot contact a node for a certain period of time. We thus let the root periodically check whether a message has been recently received from every node and, if not, send a ping message that has to be acknowledged. If no acknowledgement arrives within a certain time bound, this node is considered as *dead*. However, we must assume that an allegedly dead node may still send messages to the root or to any other node. Thus, when the root designates a node as dead, it informs all other nodes correspondingly: every node closes the connection to the dead node and ignores any buffered messages from this node.

There are two main problem that the root now has to deal with:

1. the management of all result descriptors that have been stored on the dead node, and
2. the rescheduling of all tasks that were executing on the node at the time of its alleged death.

Since the root is in charge of task scheduling, the root sees every task created in the session. Furthermore, by the logging mechanism discussed in the previous sections, the root sees every result computed in the session. For every node n, the root can therefore maintain two sets T_n and S_n:

1. T_n denotes all tasks scheduled on n; for a subset T_n^r the results are available (in the logging files). All tasks in $T_n - T_n^r$ have to be executed again; the root puts them back into the pool of tasks to be scheduled for execution.
2. S_n denotes all tasks whose descriptors are stored on n; for a subset S_n^r the results are available (in the logging files). The root becomes the owner of elements in S_n; it allocates the corresponding result descriptors and, for all elements of S_n^r, fills them with results.

Subsequently, every node will send requests for a result in S_n to the root. However, there may be still outstanding requests sent to n but not yet answered at the time of its death. Every node n' therefore holds a table R_n of all request:$\langle t, n' \rangle$ messages sent to node n but not yet answered by a reply:$\langle t, r \rangle$. When n is marked dead, the node re-sends all messages in R_n to the root which will eventually answer them.

Thus all tasks scheduled on an eventually dead node n are executed (possibly on a different node n') and every descriptor originally housed by n finds a new home on the root to which all open and all future requests are redirected.

More details on the fault tolerance mechanisms can be found in the long version of this paper on http://www.risc.uni-linz.ac.at/software/distmaple.

References

1. A. Clematis and V. Gianuzzi. CPVM — Extending PVM for Consistent Checkpointing. In *4th Euromicro Workshop on Parallel and Distributed Processinge (PDP'96)*, pages 67–76, Braga, Portugal, January 24–26, 1996. IEEE CS Press.
2. G. E. Fagg and J. J. Dongarra. FT-MPI: Fault Tolerant MPI, Supporting Dynamic Applications in a Dynamic World. In *Recent Advances in Parallel Virtual Machine and Message Passing Interface, Proceedings of the 7th European PVM/MPI Users' Group Meeting*, volume 1908 of *Lecture Notes in Computer Science*, pages 346–353, Balatonfüred, Hungary, September 10–13, 2000. Springer.
3. A. Iamnitchi and I. Foster. A Problem Specific Fault Tolerance Mechanism for Asynchronous, Distributed Systems. In *29th International Conference on Parallel Processing (ICPP)*, Toronto, Canada, August 21–24, 2000. Ohio State University.
4. R. Jagannathan and E. A. Ashcroft. Fault Tolerance in Parallel Implementations of Functional Languages. In *21st International Symposium on Fault-Tolerant Computing*, pages 256–263, Montreal, Canada, June, June 1991. IEEE CS Press.
5. W. Schreiner. Distributed Maple — User and Reference Manual. Technical Report 98-05, RISC-Linz, Johannes Kepler University, Linz, Austria, May 1998. http://www.risc.uni-linz.ac.at/software/distmaple.
6. W. Schreiner, C. Mittermaier, and F. Winkler. On Solving a Problem in Algebraic Geometry by Cluster Computing. In *Euro-Par 2000, 6th International Euro-Par Conference*, volume 1900 of *Lecture Notes in Computer Science*, pages 1196–1200, Munich, Germany, August 29 - September 1, 2000. Springer, Berlin.

PAPI Message Passing Library: Comparison of Performance in User and Kernel Level Messaging

Eric Renault and Pierre David

Laboratoire PRiSM, Université de Versailles – Saint-Quentin-en-Yvelines
78 035 Versailles Cedex, France
`Eric.Renault@prism.uvsq.fr`
`Pierre.David@crc.u-strasbg.fr`

Abstract. Most of the recent message passing libraries are built to provide users the best raw performance. Unfortunately, security is often sacrified. PAPI (for PCI-DDC Application Programming Interface) was designed with the goal of providing administrators of clusters implementing the remote-write protocol a single programming interface with different possible levels of security. In this article, we discuss the results obtained on our plateform for both user and kernel level messaging.

1 Introduction

The aim of the Multi-PC project is to get high performance clusters at an affordable price. In order to achieve the best performance, hardware and software were developed implementing the remote-write protocol. In this article, we present the results we got in both user and kernel level messaging demonstrating that our interface is as good as the best interfaces in user level messaging and measuring the cost of the overhead in kernel level messaging.

This article is divided in three parts. The first one is a brief description of the Multi-PC machine and the PCI-DDC Application Programming Interface; the second one deals with raw performance in user-level messaging; then, we present the integration of the PAPI message-passing library in the kernel of the operating system and the induced overhead.

2 Description

The Multi-PC project started in 1995 as a collaborative endeavour between the LIP6 and PRiSM laboratories. Its goal is the development of low cost clusters implementing the remote-write protocol, i.e. a protocol in which the sender of a message specifies all the information needed for the transaction to be performed (essentially both sender and receiver physical start addresses and the size of the message). In this section, we present the different hardware elements and the programming interface we developed.

A Multi-PC machine is composed of nodes, each one with one or more processors and 1 Gb/s HSL (for High Speed Link) links (IEEE 1355 [1]). On each node, a Fast-HSL card (a 32-bit 33-MHz PCI card) includes a RCube (for Rapid Reconfigurable Router) component [2] (a $8 times 8$ crossbar) which provides a low latency of 150 ns per hop and a maximum user bandwidth of 83 MB/s (64 MB/s on our plateform), and a PCI-DDC (for PCI-Direct Deposit Component) component [3] connected to the PCI bus (where it can act as a master) and sends/receives messages to/from the RCube component without processor intervention, using Direct Memory Access.

In order to enable users to take benefits of the HSL network performance, we developed PAPI [4] (for PCI-DDC Application Programming Interface). The programming model is the remote write. After both virtual (to read and write data) and physical (to send messages) addresses are returned to the user, the receiver physical address must be transmitted to the sender using, for example, a short message (a message which requires no physical address and is limited to eight bytes). Then, the sender specifies both local and remote physical addresses and the size of the message to perform the transmission. Once a physical address is known from a remote node, it may be used at any moment. This highlights that the programming model of PAPI matches exactly the one of the Multi-PC machine.

3 Raw Performance

The program used to determine the performance of the Multi-PC machine is the classical ping-pong program. It sends and receives one million messages between two nodes (one message can be sent once the message from the remote node has been received). Then, the elapsed time is divided by two million in order to determine the total average time to send one message from one node to another one (this time is also called "one-way latency"). The effective user bandwidth is performed by dividing the size of messages by the latency (throughout this section, we will refer to the effective user bandwidth as bandwidth).

At PRiSM laboratory, our Multi-PC machine is composed of four nodes linked by a daisy chain. Each node is composed of two 233-MHz Pentium II processors with 32 MB of memory. Another network (a 10-Mb/s Ethernet TCP/IP network) is used for control operations, such as program launching. The operating system is FreeBSD 3.2.

These results can be compared with Myrinet [5] message-passing libraries, especially BIP [6] (for Basic Interface for Parallelism) and Fast Messages [7]. The Myrinet architecture is similar to that of the Multi-PC project and is part of the fastest available. Performance results for the other message-passing libraries are taken from literature [8][9] with similar hardware configuration.

Figure 1 shows the time required to send a message from one node to another for different message-passing libraries. PAPI is the only interface which can send messages not aligned to a frontier of word and with a size which is not a multiple of the size of a word. For less than 64 byte messages, the latency is quite the

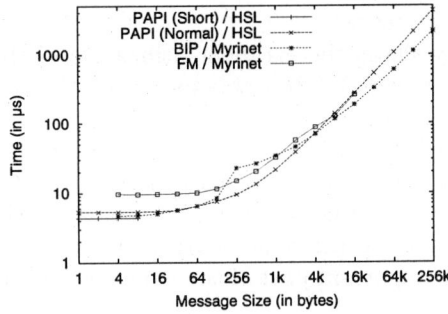

Fig. 1. Latency for various message passing libraries

same for the three interfaces. For message size between 64 bytes and 4 kB, PAPI has a better latency.

The knee in the BIP curve above 128 bytes is due to the short message concept of BIP. The boundary is software-dependent, and reflects the threshold where messages are sent directly from the host memory rather than copied in the adapter memory. The PCI-DDC concept of short messages is quite different: short message data are copied in the LMI of the receiving node and are restricted to eight bytes. Thus, the boundary is hardware dependent and both short and normal messages may be used for message size between one and eight bytes.

For message size greater or equal to 4 kB, PAPI performance are very good even if those for BIP are better. This is due to the bandwidth available in both networks. The first graph on figure 2 shows the bandwidth for the three message passing libraries.

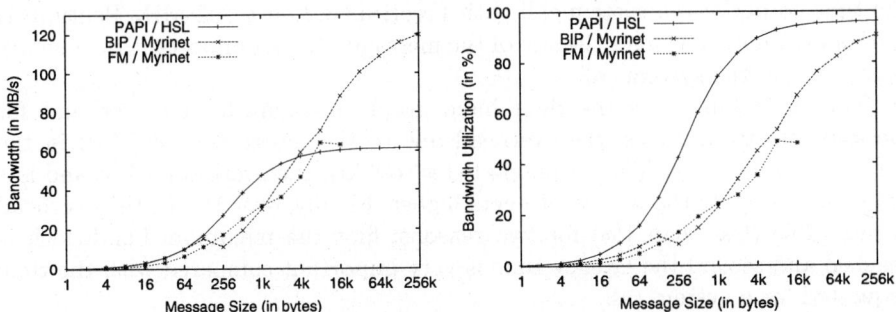

Fig. 2. Bandwidth for various message passing libraries

Moreover, these networks differ by the maximum user bandwidth they provide: 160 MB/s (1.28 Gb/s) restricted to 132 MB/s by the PCI bus for Myrinet and 64 MB/s for HSL. Thus, in order to compare these interfaces in a fair basis, the second graph on figure 2 shows the rate of user bandwidth effectively used, wiping out network differences.

This graph clearly shows the excellent utilization of the available network, especially for small messages: PAPI is able to use 50% of the available bandwidth with only 321-byte messages.

As a conclusion about PAPI performance, the most important point is that both latency and user bandwidth are very interesting. Obviously, due to its minimalist design, PAPI is able to provide the best performance on any high speed network implementing the remote-write protocol. In particular, it allows applications to use an important part of the bandwidth even for small messages.

4 Integration in the Kernel

PAPI is divided in modules; each one can be integrated in the kernel or left in user space. Even if there are dependencies between modules, many configurations can be generated. We demonstrated in [10] that only two are really interesting: the user level and the kernel level configurations. In the first case, every module is placed in user space and no system call is performed except at initialization; in the second case, every module is placed in kernel space and one system call is performed each time a function of our API is called. In any intermediate case, at least one system call must be performed for critical operations (like sending or receiving a message) and less security is provided: the "all in kernel" solution is a better choice.

The left hand graph on figure 3 shows the time requested to send messages with various sizes. The lowest curve recalls the performance of the previous section. This corresponds to the user level configuration. The upper curve shows the results for the kernel configuration. As a logarithmic representation is used for the y-axis, the curves are joining for large messages. However, the distance between them remains the same whatever the size of messages: 1.74 μs, i.e. the time to perform a system call with FreeBSD 3.2 on a 233-MHz Pentium II processor. Thus, the larger the size of the message, the less important the penalty induced from the system call.

This is presented on the right hand graph on figure 3. It shows that for messages up to 32 bytes, the overhead due to the integration of PAPI in the kernel is close to 25%. Then, from 64 bytes to 8 kB, the overhead is less and less important because the bandwidth gets higher. Finally, over 16 kB, the overhead is negligible (less than 1%) for two reasons: first the maximum bandwidth is reached and second the latency time is very important compared with the time requested for a system call.

5 Conclusion

The PAPI message passing library allows the administrator of a cluster to choose the best solution between security and performance. In this article we presented first the maximum performance (i.e. in user space) for our interface and showed

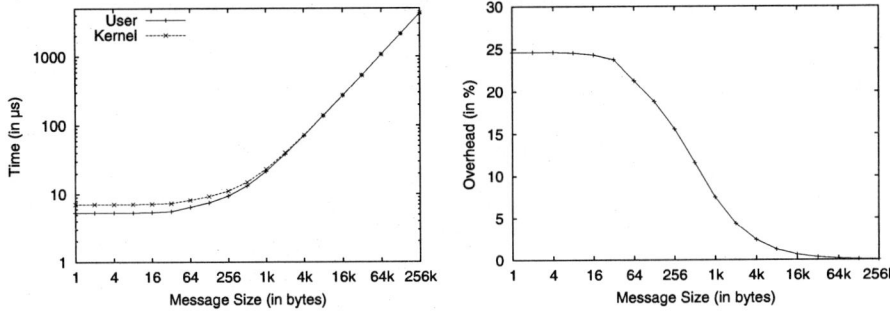

Fig. 3. Introduction of PAPI in the Kernel

it can be compared to the best actual ones. Second, we provided the performance for the same interface in kernel space and showed that the overhead only consists in the cost of a system call.

The overhead is very high for small messages, making the kernel mode not tolerable for the majority of scientific applications which exchange little quantity of data. Thus, methods giving security to user mode applications become interesting in system area networks.

References

1. C. Whitby-Strevens and al. IEEE Draft Std P1355 — Standard for Heterogeneous Interconnect — Low Cost Low Latency Scalable Serial Interconnect for Parallel System Construction, 1993.
2. V. Reibaldi. *RCube Specifications*. Laboratoire Informatique de Paris VI, Université Pierre et Marie Curie, February 1997. Version 1.7.
3. J. J. Lecler, F. Potter, A. Greiner, J. L. Desbarbieux, and F. Wajsburt. *PCI-DDC Specifications*. Laboratoire Informatique de Paris VI, Université Pierre et Marie Curie, April 1996. Revision 1.1.
4. É. Renault. Pci-ddc Application Programming Interface User Manual. Technical Report RR2000/9, Laboratoire PRiSM, Université de Versailles – Saint-Quentin, France, May 2000.
5. N. J. Boden, D. Cohen, R. E. Flederman, A. E. Kulawik, C. L. Seitz, J. N. Selzovic, and W.-K. Su. Myrinet – A Gigabit-per-Second Local-Area Network. In *IEEE-Micro*, volume 15, pages 29–36, 1995.
6. *BIP Messages User Manual for BIP 0.94*. Université de Lyon, July 1998.
7. S. Pakin, V. Karamcheti, and A. Chien. Fast Message (FM): Efficient, Portable Communication for Workstation Clusters and Massively-Parallel Processors. January 1997.
8. Concurrent Systems Architecture Group. University of California at San Diego. Fast Messages Performance. http://www-csag.ucsd.edu/projects/fm.html.
9. Réseaux haut-débit et Supports d'Applications Multimédia. Raw bip performance on myrinet. http://rhdac.univ-lyon1.fr/Resultats/perfs.html, August 1997.
10. É. Renault. Progressive Introduction of the PAPI Message Passing Library in the Kernel of the FreeBSD Operating System. Technical Report RR2001/6, Laboratoire PRiSM, Université de Versailles – Saint-Quentin, France, January 2001.

Implementing Java on Clusters

Yariv Aridor, Michael Factor, and Avi Teperman

IBM Research Laboratory in Haifa
MATAM, Advanced Technology Center, Haifa 31905, Israel
phone: +972-4-8296350, fax: +972-4-8296114
{yariv,factor,teperman}@il.ibm.com

Abstract. We have implemented a virtual machine (VM) for Java which executes on a cluster. Our cluster VM completely hides the cluster from the application, presenting a single system image (SSI) (i.e., the application sees a traditional virtual machine). At the same time it leverages the cluster to achieve improved performance for a range of applications. We show how the flexibility and constraints of the Java Virtual Machine (JVM) Specification [7] impacted the design of our cluster VM. We describe issues related to class loading and distribution-aware implementations of the bytecodes. We also point out the limits on providing a solution for completely transparent distribution of multi-threaded Java applications if one does not modify the VM or the core classes.

1 Introduction

The Java Virtual Machine (JVM) Specification [7] is both abstract (i.e, the implementation is not constrained) and complete (i.e., all externally visible effects are totally specified). We have taken advantage of these two properties in implementing a virtual machine (VM) for Java which executes on a cluster. Our cluster VM hides the cluster from the application, presenting a single system image (SSI) (i.e., the application sees a traditional virtual machine); at the same time it leverages the cluster to improve performance for a range of applications.

By implementing a single system image of a VM on a cluster, we have learned a great deal about the limits of solutions for distribution that do not change the VM. Specifically, a solution that allows *arbitrary* multi-threaded, legacy applications to *transparently* leverage a cluster can be mostly built on top of an existing JVM; however, certain critical changes must be made to the JVM and the core classes to achieve complete SSI and to achieve acceptable performance.

We previously have introduced our cluster virtual machine (VM) for Java[1] and presented detailed performance results [2]. Here, we put particular emphasis on class loading because it is difficult to ensure SSI for class loading on a cluster. In this context we show why SSI cannot be achieved without VM modifications. We also discuss the get and put bytecodes as an examples of the bytecodes which need cluster-aware implementations. A longer version of the paper discusses the remaining bytecodes [1].

---

[1] Previously known as "cJVM".

This work is interesting not only in its own right but also for what it tells us about the JVM specification. Our observations include: 1) without modifying the VM, one cannot provide SSI for class loading in a distributed VM implementation, 2) the flexibility inherent in opaque object references makes it easy to hide the cluster from an application and 3) symbolic evaluation, which is made possible by the complete specification of the behavior of the bytecodes, is useful for eliminating the overhead of distribution and not only for verification and traditional compiler optimizations.

The next section summarizes the architecture of our cluster VM. We discuss class loading in Section 3 and the byecodes in Section 4. We give performance results and describe the state of our prototype in Section 5. After discussing related work in Section 6, we present our conclusions and discuss future work.

2 Architecture

Our cluster virtual machine runs on a collection of independent computers connected by a fast interconnect. A cluster VM process resides on each computer. Each process contains a subset of the application's threads and objects. When taken as a whole, the set of processes constitutes the VM.

Figure 1 shows the basic architecture of our system. The top half of the figure shows the application's perspective; from this point of view, the cluster is completely hidden and we present a complete single system image (SSI). The lower half of the figure shows the implementation of our virtual machine. The implementation is aware of the cluster.

The implementation distributes objects and threads. To allow access to an object located on another node we use proxies. This applies to all objects including class objects and threads. The *master* is the object's authoritative copy and

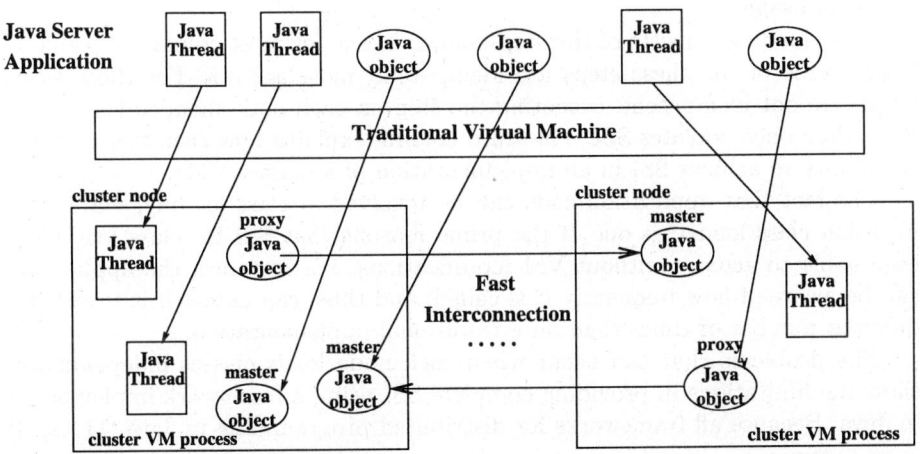

Fig. 1. Architecture of our cluster VM for Java

in general exists where the object was initially created - the *master node*. Note, the location of the master of an instance object is independent of the master node for the instance's class.

Every object has one master and possibly multiple proxies. We have developed *smart proxies* [2] which enable us to hide the master-proxy distinction from the application. Smart proxies also support caching and other behaviors beyond simply remoting an access to the master. Smart proxies work by allowing multiple implementations of a method to be associated with a single class.

Object placement is determined at run time on a per-instance basis and is driven by actual run-time usage. In addition to placing individual objects, we also replicate both objects and individual fields (see [2]).

We distribute computation using two mechanisms. First, when a thread is created, we decide, based upon a pluggable load balancing function, where the thread should be created. Second, our default means of accessing a remote object is *method shipping*, whereby we bring the thread to the master of the object it is accessing. Note, as we describe in [2], we do not always use method shipping.

3 Class Loading

Class loading[2] is complicated in a cluster-aware implementation of a virtual machine. On the one hand, in a shared-nothing distributed implementation, such as ours, for performance reasons the code for a given class needs to be locally available on all nodes where it will be executed; remotely accessing the code would add too great overhead. Replicating the code requires replicating the internal data structures of the class such as method blocks, run-time constant pool, etc. On the other hand, as we elaborate below, it violates SSI, and thus is incorrect, to allow each node to independently load each class it needs to execute. Our focus for class loading is on functional correctness, i.e., SSI, and not performance; we assume that the cost will be amortized over a significant period of usage.

Class loading consists of the steps shown in the leftmost column of Table 1. While some of the these steps are idempotent, most are not. For those steps which are not idempotent, executing the step on each node independently, i.e., more than once, violates SSI. The third column explains how each step impacts the ability to achieve SSI in an implementation of a cluster VM.

The fact that application code can be involved in class loading, via an application class loader, is one of the prime reasons that SSI for class loading is impossible to achieve without VM modifications. For instance, the application can be aware of how frequently it is called, and thus, can detect if it is called a different number of times than on a traditional implementation.

The problems that can occur when each node loads classes independently show the limitations in providing complete SSI using a framework implemented in Java. Because all frameworks for distributed programming in Java [11,12,14]

---

[2] We use the phrase "class loading" generically to refer to the three steps of loading, linking and initializing.

Table 1. Phases of class loading and their impact on SSI

Step	Impact	Explanation
find external representation (loading)	not idempotent	Since the external representation may change over time, loading it independently on multiple nodes can lead to different representations being loaded which would violate SSI. In addition, since this function is performed by the method loadClass which can be overridden by the application, the application can be aware of how many times the external representation is requested.
create internal representation (loading)	idempotent	The internal representation depends only upon the external representation. While this function is performed by ClassLoader.defineClass which an application class loader can override, the internal representation is created by the (native) implementation provided by the VM as part of java.lang.ClassLoader; thus, the application need not be aware how many times an internal representation is created.
create Class object (loading)	not idempotent	There must be a single master copy of the class object on one node, with other nodes having proxies. The VM-provided implementation of ClassLoader.resolveClass performs this function.
verify (linking)	idempotent	Verification depends only upon the internal representation. The VM-provided implementation of ClassLoader.resolveClass performs this function.
prepare (linking)	not idempotent	Executing this step more than once could allow an application to see the default value on one node after the application initialized the class and wrote a value on another node. The VM-provided implementation of ClassLoader.resolveClass provides this function.
resolve (linking)	idempotent	Given the same internal representations two nodes will reach the same conclusion in resolving a symbolic constant pool entry.
initialize	not idempotent	Executing <clinit> more than once violates SSI. It can break memory coherence (e.g., an application seeing the result of the class initialization on one node after it wrote a value on another node), and the application can count how many times the class initializer executed.

independently load a class on every node where it is used, they are inherently limited in how close they can come to achieving a single system image.

If one is willing to work at the VM level, there are several ways to support SSI for class loading. The approach we took is to use the mechanisms as implemented in a JVM for a traditional platform, modifying the way these mechanisms are invoked to address the issues from Table 1. One alternative is to completely load the class on one node and then transfer the internal representation to the other nodes. While we experimented with this alternative, it has two difficulties. The first, purely technical issue, is that due to the complicated graph structures and inter-class references, it is hard to cleanly determine which data needs to be replicated and how to copy this data. The second is that given the lazy nature of some of the steps of class loading it is unclear when the class should be replicated.

The master node for a class C is the node which is the master for the class loader L_C which is to be used to load C; for system classes we use an arbitrary fixed node as the master. In our approach, the master executes those aspects of class loading which are not idempotent. All nodes that use the class execute those aspects which are idempotent. Other than the master, a node loads a class when it first needs the class, e.g., to create an instance (either master or proxy); the master loads the class the first time it is needed by any node in the cluster. The master is also the authoritative source for values of static fields; although, we do make extensive use of caching (see [2]).

When the master node loads a class, it follows the same flow as a traditional JVM implementation. The interesting scenario is when a node n_p, which will have a proxy of class C needs to load C. In this case, n_p sends a message to node n_m, the master node for L_C. n_m will be the master for C. The message requests that, unless the class is already loaded, n_m call loadClass on L_C to load the class. This eventually leads to a call to defineClass on java.lang.ClassLoader; defineClass is passed the binary image of the external representation for the class. Node n_m completes the processing of the message by returning the binary image to n_p.[3] Node n_p then calls the implementation of the defineClass from java.lang.ClassLoader to create the internal representation on n_p.

We also modify defineClass to analyze the method's bytecodes; this analysis is used to construct the smart proxy implementations. We perform this analysis on each node in our implementation; although depending upon the tradeoffs between computation and communication, we could perform this analysis only on the master and send the results to the proxies.

Once the internal representation is created, the class needs to be linked, i.e., verified, prepared and possibly resolved. The class's master executes the normal flow to verify the class. On a node containing a proxy, we have two options depending upon relative costs. We can either verify the class (which is correct but expensive) or send a message to the master requesting that it link (and verify) the class. We are currently experimenting with local verification.

To support caching, we allocate memory in proxies of Class objects as well as in the master.[4] Thus, we prepare the static fields on all nodes. Preparation, however, is not idempotent; we address this problem by being careful in how we read and write static fields. In particular, a proxy node prior to reading a local copy of static field will pull the value of the field from the master, after either verifying that the master has been initialized or initializing the master if necessary. Any writes to the static field are always performed at the master and invalidate any cached copies of that field.

---

[3] To allow returning the external representation even if the class was already loaded, we persistently associate the external representation with the class object.

[4] To be precise, to support caching we allocate memory in all proxies.

We ensure that classes are initialized at most once by only running class initializers on the class's master node. We mark a proxy as initialized only after its master has been initialized.

Resolution in our implementation occurs on-demand and not during the linkage phase. Resolution is idempotent, since all nodes see a consistent view of the internal representation of classes and since classes are initialized at most once.

Since all classes loaded by a given class loader have the same master node, we have a potential bottleneck which can have two embodiments: accesses to static fields and static method invocations. By default we ship accesses to a proxy's fields and invocations of its methods to the master; however, we avoid these bottlenecks by providing heavy caching of static fields and executing static methods directly on the proxy.

4 Bytecodes

In building a cluster virtual machine – a virtual machine which looks to the application like a traditional JVM – a critical aspect is determining which bytecodes need to have a cluster-aware implementation. For lack of space this section looks only at put/get bytecodes showing how they are made cluster-aware and how they can be optimized for performance. The interested reader is refered to [1] for full discussion on other bytecodes such as object creation, method invocation, exception throwing and handling and synchronization.

4.1 Accessibility

Our master-proxy model provides accessibility to objects independent of their physical location. In more detail, the implementation of all gets and puts contains a *barrier* which determines if the operation is being performed on a master or a proxy as shown:

```
ObjectRef o = popStack();
if (cJVM_isMaster(o))     // barrier
   <do normal flow>
else
   <perform Remote Bytecode (RBC) >
```

As shown, if the operation is being performed on the master, the operation proceeds as in a traditional implementation of the JVM. To handle operations performed on a proxy, we have implemented a remote bytecode (RBC) mechanism to send a message to the master node for the target object; a server thread, which is part of our cluster VM implementation, handles this message.

4.2 Performance

The reason we changed the VM to support get and put operations on a cluster was performance. As we described above, to support remote accesses, we need to determine if an instance is a master or a proxy. We cannot make this determination by using different classes for the master and proxy, or by adding a field to flag the object as proxy, as the introspection APIs would make this visible to the application, violating SSI. In our VM, we made this determination by modifying the implementation of the handle, the mechanism used by the JVM to reference the object. If we modify neither the VM nor the core classes, we will need to access an auxiliary data structure to determine if the object is a master or a proxy. It is fairly obvious that such overhead would be completely unacceptable.

Furthermore, simply modifying the VM is insufficient to achieve good performance. The algorithms described above have three performance aspects that require further consideration. First, we need to ensure that execution of a remote bytecode is rare. Second, we need to ensure that we do not pay too great overhead for the barriers.[5] Third, we need to reduce the cost of a RBC.

Given our use of method shipping, we only access a field of a proxy if an application makes an unencapsulated access. Method shipping ensures that encapsulated accesses are executed against the master. Thus, well-structured code should have only a small number of remote gets and puts.

To reduce the number of remote accesses further, we employ several caching mechanisms. First, we cache all final fields. We also cache all static fields based upon the empirical observation that these fields are rarely modified [2]. Finally, we replicate fields which we heuristically determine to be effectively read-only, i.e., we believe they will not be written in the given run of the program.

The use of barriers can be greatly reduced, at least for getfield and putfield, given the observation that most accesses are encapsulated; [5] made a similar observation. The target object of an encapsulated access is the this reference which is specified to be stored in the zeroth local variable. Therefore, for code executed against masters, if we prove that the access is targeted against the zeroth local variable, we can eliminate the barrier.[6]

Proving that the target of getfield is this is fairly easy. Assuming no prior astore_0, the target of the getfield is this in the following code snippets:

```
aload_0
getfield
```

or

```
aload_0
dup
getfield
```

These and other very simple pattern-based, static analyses account for anywhere from 64% to 80% of the occurrences of getfield as measured for our

---

[5] As was observed in the field of garbage collection [6], read barriers can be prohibitively expensive.

[6] In implementation terms, one way to eliminate barriers is in a JIT which generates different code depending upon whether a barrier is needed.

Table 2. Description of Benchmarks

Program	Description
pBOB	A business logic kernel. Creates m threads which generate transactions concurrently. $m = 4$ is used for measurements.
N-Body	Simulates the motion of n particles due to gravitational forces, over ts number of simulation time steps, using m threads. $n = 640$, $m = 4$ and $ts = 10$ are used for measurements
TSP	Find, in parallel, the shortest route among n cities using m threads. $n = 14$ and $m = 4$ are used for measurements

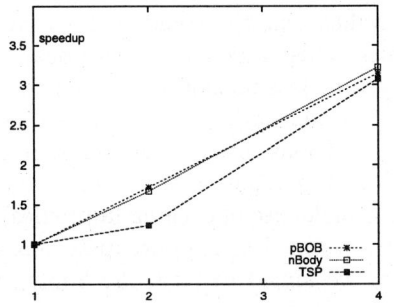 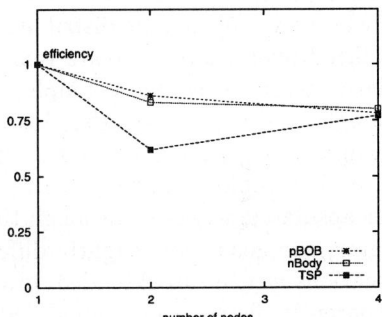

Fig. 2. Speedup and Efficiency

benchmark applications (set Table 2) and around 75% of the `getfield`s in the Spec98JVM benchmarks [13]. Based upon dynamic data collected from an instrumented JVM, roughly 85% of the uses of getfield are for the `this` pointer.

5 Status

Our cluster VM for Java prototype runs on a cluster of IntelliStations running Windows NT and connected via a Myrinet fast switch [10]. In our prototype we have modified the interpreter loop of the Sun reference implementation of JDK 1.2; we have implemented all of the features we described except for some aspects of class loading and `this` elimination. Even though our prototype runs on Windows NT, our code is not NT specific and can easily be ported to other operating systems.

We have run several benchmarks as shown in Table 2.[7] Figure 2 shows the speedup and the efficiency for each of these benchmarks.

---

[7] Detailed description of the benchmarks can be found in [2]

6 Related Work

The tools and infrastructure supporting Java applications on a cluster range from completely explicit solutions to implicit solutions similar to our VM. Explicit approaches [14,12,11,3] assume multiple JVMs, handling remote objects and threads at the level of the Java frameworks. To varying degrees, these frameworks do not support SSI, e.g., the reflection APIs can detect proxies, local and remote method invocations have slightly different semantics, class loading does not present a single system image, etc.

In contrast with the aforementioned frameworks, are approaches based upon modified VMs. Those that we are aware of (other than ours) either build upon underlying support to hide the cluster and/or extend the semantics of Java.

Hicks, et al., [5] support distributed Java applications by extending Java with specialized operations to create remote objects. This work has a great deal of similarity to our work. For example, they only run class initializers on one node (although it is unclear how they load classes on other nodes); they use method shipping and avoid barriers prior to method invocations through the use of multiple method tables; and they use barriers prior to get/put instructions except for encapsulated accesses (although they do not make use of caching in proxies). However, our goals were slightly different – they aimed to support distributed applications written in extended Java whereas we aimed to push the limits of transparently distributing unmodified, multi-threaded Java applications.

JESSICA [8] is a modified JVM focusing on thread migration for purposes of load balancing. While it leveragess the semantics of the language to achieve a single system image, performance in JESSICA is obtained from a low-level, usage-neutral DSM system and not by leveraging the JVM semantics.

Hyperion [9] is an implementation of a JVM on top of an object-based, distributed shared memory. It is based on an object shipping model in which a copy of a remote object is brought to the accessing node. The accessing node uses this local cached copy which is written back to the origin at synchronization points. It should be contrasted to our use of method shipping enhanced by caching provided by smart proxies.

7 Conclusion and Future Work

This paper has described how we have leveraged the flexibility of the JVM specification to provide an efficient implementation of a VM on a cluster e.g., by the use of opaque object references as opposed to memory addresses and the use of symbolic evaluation to eliminate barriers.

We have also described the extent to which it is required to modify the VM or core classes to provide a solution for distributing an application with 100% transparency. Our analysis showed that primarily due to the presence of application class loaders, without modifying the VM, one cannot provide a SSI for class loading. We described our approach for class loading based upon leveraging the mechanisms from a non-distributed JVM implementation, but changing the way these mechanisms are used to avoid problems of non-idempotence.

Our approach to implementing a cluster VM for Java was invasive, changing the implementation of the bytecodes and classloading. While such an approach promises maximum performance (e.g., take advangate of semantics) it has downsides in terms of a propriety implementation of an entire VM, poor portability, and the necessity for multiple implementations for both an interpreter loop and a JIT. In this context, we are now considering an alternative approach that will replace the implementation of bytecode with techniqes such as aggressive code rewriting (e.g., as in JavaParty [11]), a Java utility class with native support to access the cluster (e.g., as in [3,4]) or a compiler-based approach to access the cluster directly (e.g., as in JaguarVIA [15]).

References

1. Yariv Aridor, Michael Factor, and Avi Teperman. Implementing Java on Clusters. Technical report, IBM Research Laboratory in Haifa, 2001.
2. Yariv Aridor, Michael Factor, Avi Teperman, Tamar Eilam, and Assaf Schuster. Transparently obtaining scalability for Java applications on a cluster. *Journal of Parallel and Distributed Computing*, 60(10):1159–1193, October 2000.
3. Denis Caromel and Julien Vayssiere. A Java framework for seamless sequential, multi-threaded, and distributed programming. In *ACM 1998 Workshop on Java for High-Performance Network Computing*, Palo Alto, CA, February 1998. ACM.
4. Vladimir Getov, Susan Flynn-Hummel, and Sava Mintchev. High-performance parallel programming in Java: Exploiting native libraries. In *ACM 1998 Workshop on Java for High-Performance Network Computing*, Palo Alto, CA, February 1998. ACM.
5. Michael Hicks, Suresh Jagannathan, Richard Kelsey, Jonathan T. Moore, and Cristian Ungureanu. Transparent communication for distributed objects in Java. In *Proceedings of the ACM 1999 Conference on Java Grande*, pages 160–170, Palo Alto, CA, 1999. ACM.
6. Richard Jones and Rafael Lins. *Garbage Collection: Algorithms for Automatic Dynamic Memory Management*. John Wiley & Sons, Chichester, England, 1996.
7. Tim Lindholm and Frank Yellin. *The Java Virtual Machine Specification*. Addison-Wesley, second edition, 1999.
8. Matchy J. M. Ma, Cho-Li Wang, Francis C. M. Lau, and Zhiwei Xu. JESSICA: Java-enabled single-system-image computing architecture. In *Proceedings of 1999 International Conference on Parallel and Distributed Processing Techniques and Applications (PDPTA'99)*, volume VI, pages 2781–2787, Las Vegas, NV, June 1999.
9. Mark W. MacBeth, Keith A. McGuigan, and Philip J. Hatcher. Executing Java threads in parallel in a distributed-memory environment. In *Proceedings of the IBM Centre for Advanced Studies Conference*, Toronto, Canada, 1998.
10. http://www.myri.com/.
11. Michael Philippsen and Matthias Zenger. JavaParty: Transparent remote objects in Java. *Concurrency: Practice and Experience*, 9(11):1225–1242, November 1997.
12. http://java.sun.com/products/jdk/rmi/index.html.
13. http://www.spec.org/osg/jvm98.
14. http://www.objectspace.com/products/voyager/.
15. Matt Welsh and David Culler. Jaguar: Enabling efficient communication and I/O in Java. *Concurrency: Practice and Experience*, 12:519–538, December 1999. Special Issue on Java for High-Performance Applications.

Predictive Coscheduling Implementation in a Non-dedicated Linux Cluster*

Francesc Solsona[1], Francesc Giné[1], Porfidio Hernández[2], and Emilio Luque[2]

[1] Departamento de Informática e Ingeniería Industrial, Universitat de Lleida, Spain
{francesc,sisco}@eup.udl.es
[2] Departamento de Informática, Universitat Autònoma de Barcelona, Spain
{p.hernandez,e.luque}@cc.uab.es

Abstract. Our research is focussed on keeping both local and parallel jobs together in a non-dedicated cluster or NOW (Network Of Workstations) and efficiently scheduling them by means of coscheduling mechanisms.
A real implementation of a predictive coscheduling technique in a Linux cluster is presented in this article and its performance analyzed and compared with other coscheduling algorithms in the literature.

1 Introduction

The studies in [1] indicate that the workstations in a non-dedicated cluster or NOW are normally underloaded. There are basically two methods of making use of these CPU idle cycles, namely task migration [3] and job scheduling [5,8]. In a NOW, in accordance with the research carried out by Arpaci [6], task migration overheads and the unpredictable behavior of local users may lower the effectiveness of this method.

A large number of scheduling schemes have been proposed for parallel machines. One of these is gang scheduling [2], successfully implemented in the Connection Machine CM-5, SGI workstations and so on. In gang scheduling, all the threads in a job are scheduled and de-scheduled at the same time, so threads making up jobs should be known in advance. In distributed systems like clusters or NOWs, this information is very difficult to obtain. The alternative is to identify them during execution [4]. Thus, only a sub-set of the processes are scheduled together, leading to coscheduling rather than gang scheduling.

Coscheduling deals with minimizing synchronization/communication waiting time between remote processes. Thus, coscheduling may be applied to reduce message waiting time and to make good use of the idle CPU cycles by executing distributed applications in a cluster or NOW system. Some of the relevant coscheduling work is explained below, attention being focussed on real implementations.

Explicit coscheduling [5] ensures that a simultaneous global context switch is performed in all the processors. In [12], a real explicit coscheduling algorithm was implemented in a Linux cluster. Despite the speedup achieved in

---

* This work was supported by the CICYT under contract TIC98-0433

intensive message-passing distributed applications, the response time of the local workload slowed down significantly. Consequently, a mechanism to detect high-communicating distributed applications was incorporated into the original explicit coscheduling technique. This added more overhead in managing the overall system and detecting advantageous situations where this technique can be applied. Due to the centralized nature of this technique, fault tolerance is a problem: the possibility of master crashes or abnormal behavior of the explicit scheme should be taken into account.

In [9], implicit coscheduling ([6,7,8,9]) was implemented in an MPI environment, achieving performance for various coarse-grain message-passing distributed applications. In implicit coscheduling, a process waiting for messages spins for a determined time before blocking. In [13], a variation of implicit coscheduling was also implemented and evaluated in a Linux cluster. Even for low spin values, the spinning gain in blocked receives due to context switch reduction was exceeded by the overhead introduced in active waiting for messages. Also, the penalty in both return and response time added in local tasks generally yields poor performance. The conclusion is that active waiting for an event to occur (in our case blocking receive) is not a good solution in time sharing systems.

Demand-Based (divided between dynamic and predictive) coscheduling was first introduced in [10]. In contrast to implicit coscheduling, dynamic coscheduling deals with all message arrivals (not just those directed to blocked tasks). It is based on increasing the receiving task priority, even causing CPU preemption of the task being executed inside. It also provides a mechanism for avoiding local task starvation. In [11], despite the good behavior of this technique in a real system, only the execution of one distributed application was evaluated. Predictive coscheduling is based on scheduling the correspondents -the most recent communicated- processes in the overall system at the same time. Apart from this definition, there is no other predictive coscheduling work in the literature. It thus remains an open question.

The implementation of a predictive coscheduling algorithm in a non-dedicated cluster (the main aim of this article) implies that the sets of corresponding processes must be known in advance to schedule each of them at the same time. However, in such systems, this information is very difficult to obtain. The selection of the corresponding processes in each node is proposed, taking into account both high message communicating frequency and low penalty introduction into the delayed processes. An implicit and distributed nature is thus provided for this method and no centralized extra work need be done in managing or controlling the system, as in explicit techniques [5,12].

Furthermore, the obtaining of the communicating frequency is based on both message sending and receiving, not only on message receiving as in implicit and dynamic techniques [6,7,8,9,10,11]. There is perhaps no need to coschedule those processes only performing receiving messages. This is also true for sending processes. We think that processes performing both sending and receiving have a higher potential need for coscheduling than those performing only sending or receiving. This way, an approximation to predictive coscheduling is performed.

2   The Linux Scheduler and Design Decisions

In this section, the Linux scheduler behavior is explained. Based on this, some predictive coscheduling design decisions are also commented on.

In Linux, the Ready to run task Queue (RQ) is implemented by a double linked list of *task_struct* structures, the Linux PCB's (Process Control Block). The fields used in implementing predictive coscheduling are:

- *policy*: scheduling policy. There are four scheduling policies in Linux. The "normal" tasks policy and three "real-time" scheduling policies (with more scheduling priority than the normal ones).
- *rt_priority*: scheduling priority between real-time tasks.
- *priority* -"*static*" priority-: scheduling priority between normal tasks. This ranges from 1 (low priority) to 40 (high priority). Default value = 20.
- *counter*: "*dynamic*" normal tasks priority. The initial value is set to the *priority* one. When the task is executing, each tick[1], *counter* is decremented towards 0 in one unit, then the CPU is yielded. Thus, the maximum *time slice* for a normal task with a default static priority is 210 ms.
- *files*: open files structure. This saves information about the task open files.
- *freq*: sending and receiving message frequency. Added field to the structure and used later for implementing predictive coscheduling (see sec. 3). The initial value is 0.

There are other fields like *pid* (process identifier), *state* and so on, but these have no influence on our coscheduling scheme and so there are no more comments about them (see [16] or the Linux source for more information).

Tasks making up distributed applications are normally executed in a cluster as local (owner or interactive) ones, so no explicit information is supposed in advance for differentiating between both kinds of task. This way, all these tasks will have a "normal" scheduling policy. In Linux, the normal tasks have a Round Robin scheduling policy, with a variable time slice. Real-time tasks must acquire this condition explicitly, so we are not interested in, for example, promoting distributed tasks to real-time. Field *rt_priority* will have no influence on our coscheduling implementation and only one policy (the normal one) will be taken into account. However, a means to promote distributed tasks must be provided to implement predictive coscheduling in the normal task queue. As will be seen below, field *priority* and *counter* for "normal" tasks (in field *policy*) jointly with a new one (*freq*), will be used to do so.

In normal task creation, the field *counter* is set equal to the field *priority* and then it is appended to the RQ. The Linux scheduler picks up the next process to be executed (*current*) by means of the internal function *goodness*

---
[1] 1 tick $\simeq$ 10 ms

Algorithm 1 Linux scheduler algorithm

Step 1: While (RQ is empty) do skip // the CPU is idle
Step 2: Lock RQ   // the scheduling must be performed in an exclusive manner
Step 3: Schedule *current* ≡ task with the highest *goodness* in the RQ
Step 4: Unlock RQ   // exclusive access (to the RQ) deactivation
Step 5: Dispatch *current*   // execution in the CPU
Step 6: Do *current* accounting // the accounting fields are updated accordingly
Step 7: Goto Step 1

(Algorithm 1, Step 3), which depends on the *counter* and *priority* values for normal tasks and field *rt_priority* for real-time tasks. Higher values indicate higher priority of execution, that is, the task with the highest returned value from the *goodness* function is scheduled. If all the returned RQ tasks values are 0, the field *counter* of every normal task is reset to be equal to *priority* and the scheduling process begins again. Note that to implement predictive coscheduling in an implicit manner, it is only necessary to increase the *goodness* value for the normal tasks proportionally to both receiving and sending communicating frequency (as mentioned earlier in section 1).

The socket packet-buffering queues, in the Linux system layer, have been chosen to collect message sending/receiving frequency information. Accordingly, packets would be a more accurate terminology for messages. The reason for doing so in the kernel space is that, coscheduling can thus be applied to any distributed application. For example, PVM ([17]) uses the sockets. If coscheduling were implemented in the user space, in the PVM sending or receiving libraries, no means for promoting the correspondents would be possible inside PVM (in the user space) when potential coscheduling was met. A new daemon or system call should be added, leading to extra overhead that could reduce coscheduling performance. Implementing coscheduling in the kernel space provides transparency to the overall system and allows the application of coscheduling independently of the message passing environment (PVM, MPI, etc ...). The drawback is in portability. A patch must be introduced into each cluster node in the Linux source. However, the Linux modifications are minimum.

3 Implementing a Predictive Coscheduling Algorithm

The proposed predictive algorithm (Algorithm 2) is based on the assumption that high receive-send message frequencies imply that potential coscheduling with remote processes is met and an accurate selection of the correspondents in each node can be made. Thus, a predictive coscheduling technique could be implemented by increasing the priority of the correspondents. The algorithm is based on the task frequency ($freq$) in sending and receiving messages, defined as:

$$freq = P * freq + (1 - P) * cur\_freq, \tag{1}$$

where P is the percentage assigned to the past frequency ($freq$) and $(1-P)$ is the current frequency percentage (cur_freq), which is also defined as:

$$cur\_freq = rq + sq, \qquad (2)$$

where rq (sq) is the number of packets in the receive (send) socket packet-buffering queue.

Algorithm 2 Predictive algorithm. Inside function *goodness(task)*
---
1 if (task->policy != "normal") weight = task->rt_priority + 1000;
2 else {
3   weight = task->counter;
4   if (! weight) {
5   weight += task->priority;
6   task->freq = $freq()$; // $freq() = P * task$->$freq + (1 - P) * cur\_freq$
7   weight += task->freq; }}
8 return weight;

In Algorithm 1, Step 3, the task with the highest *goodness* is scheduled. Algorithm 2 shows how the *goodness* value (*weight*) for a task is obtained. In line 1, the *weight* for a real-time task is obtained with the help of the *policy* and *rt_priority* task fields. The returned value for the normal tasks is *weight = counter + priority* (lines 3 to 5).

To implement predictive coscheduling, only lines 6 and 7 are added to the original goodness algorithm. The implemented function "$freq()$" returns the communicating frequency computed as in formulas (1) and (2), and is used to increase the priority of distributed tasks. The frequency value obtained is saved in the PCB *freq* field to compute the following values for the frequency as past frequency. The current frequency (*cur_freq*) is obtained by the function *number_packets* (explained below). Initially, the first four values for task->*freq* are the mean of the obtained *cur_freq* values. This way a more approximated initial value for the communicating frequency is obtained.

Starvation of local tasks is avoided because when the *counter* field of any normal task reaches 0, it can not be executed while there are other tasks with non zero values in their respective *counter* fields.

Finally, it only remains to explain how the current frequency is obtained. To do so, the send and receiving socket packet-buffering queues must be accessed. The implemented function *number_packets(task)* (Algorithm 3) returns the number of received/transmitted packets by a task and used as *cur_freq* in line 6, Algorithm 2.

In Unix (Linux), the sockets are treated as files. Thus, it will first be necessary to identify the open files that correspond to sockets. To do so, the structure that represents each file in Linux (the *inode*) must be accessed. As Fig. 1 shows, it will be necessary to descend through the following structures in this order:

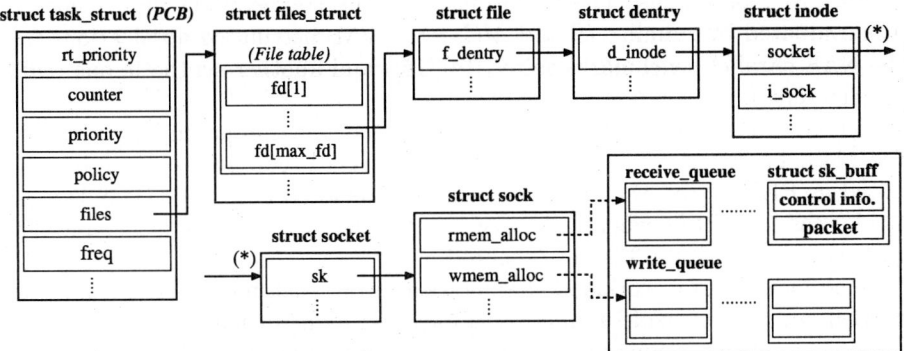

Fig. 1. Main used Linux structures (and its fields)

Algorithm 3 Function number_packets(task)
---

1 rq=rs=0;
2 **if** (task-¿files) {
3   **for** (fd = 0; fd ¡ task-¿files-¿max_fds; fd++) {
4   file = task-¿files-¿fd[fd];
5   **if** (file) {
6   inode = file-¿f_dentry-¿d_inode;
7   **if** (inode && inode-¿i_sock && (socket = socki_lookup(inode))) {
8   rq += ⌈ socket-¿sk-¿rmem_alloc.counter / 4096 ⌉;
9   sq += ⌈ socket-¿sk-¿wmem_alloc.counter / 4096 ⌉; }}}}
10 **return** (rq + sq);

---

task_struct, *files_struct*, *file*, *dentry*, and finally *inode*. Then, if the inode corresponds to a socket (condition "inode-¿i_sock" of the Algorithm 3) it will be necessary to access the socket related structures *(socket* and *sock)* by means of the obtained pointer to the socket, socket = *socki_lookup*(inode), where *socki_lookup* is an internal Linux function.

The *sock* structure points to two lists of *sk_buf* structures, which buffer packets (the socket transmission unit, = 4096 Bytes or 4KB). One such list, called the *receive_queue*, buffers receiving packets, and the other, called the *write_queue*, buffers packets to be transmitted. The *rmem_alloc* sock field saves the number of bytes in *receive_queue*, and the *wmem_alloc* field saves the number of bytes in the *write_queue*. The returned value for this function is then assigned to the current frequency (*cur_freq*).

4 Experimentation

The experimental environment used in this study was composed of four 350MHz Pentium II with 128MB of memory and 512KB of cache. They were all connected through a 100Mbps bandwidth Ethernet network and a minimal latency in the order of 0.1 ms. The performance of the coscheduling implementation was evaluated by running *IS* and *MG*, two PVM distributed applications from the NAS parallel benchmarks suite ([14],[15]) and another synthetic one (called *master-slave*).

Three different environments were evaluated and compared between them, the plain Linux scheduler, (denoted as LINUX), Predictive coscheduling (denoted as PRED) and Dynamic coscheduling (denoted as DYN). DYN is a particular case of PRED, where only receiving frequency is taken into account. That is, line 9 in Algorithm 3 is not executed.

The local or user workload characterization in each node of the cluster was carried out by means of running an application (called *calcula*) which performs floating point operations indefinitely (or a variable number of times when the local task overhead is measured). This loading is not typical in real clusters (normally, more interactive, I/O-bound and with more unpredictable behavior). In the other hand, it is more helpful in obtaining and comparing performance of the different environments.

4.1 Predictive Coscheduling Performance

Fig. 2 shows the execution time of both NAS benchmarks when the number of local tasks (instances of *calcula*) is increased. As in the rest of the Figures of this experimentation, one of the low axis (local tasks) indicates the number of local tasks in the ready queue and the other one the different models and P values for DYN and PRED. The value P=0 and P=1 represents values for P close to 0 and 1 (i.e. $P \simeq 0$ and $P \simeq 1$) respectively.

In general, the performance of both coscheduling models was better than the LINUX one as the multiprogramming level increased (except for the case DYN and $P \simeq 1$). In both benchmarks, the best results were obtained with the predictive model (and more precisely when $P \simeq 1$). This difference was due to predictive coscheduling takes both the sending and receiving messages into account, whereas dynamic only considers the receiving ones, so the opportunity for promoting through the ready queue is greater in the predictive case. The necessity for coscheduling and the communicating pattern is more closely approximated to by such a model.

The NAS benchmarks were executed simultaneously to evaluate performance in executing various distributed applications (see Fig. 3). It is important to mention that both benchmarks fit in the main memory together with the local workload. If not, the page faulting mechanism (one or two orders of magnitude slower than the network latency) would corrupt the performance results. In this case, and for the memory fitting requirement explained above, IS is class A and MG is class T (with 600 iterations). In all the rest of the experimentation, both IS and MG are class A. The difference between the different classes is that class A of every benchmark is scaled with respect to the same one in class T.

In general, better IS results were even obtained for the PRED case. It confirms the good behavior of the predictive model with respect to LINUX and DYN. The MG results are very similar because class T is not as message-passing

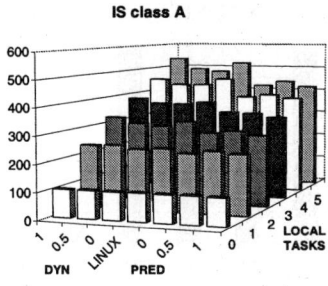 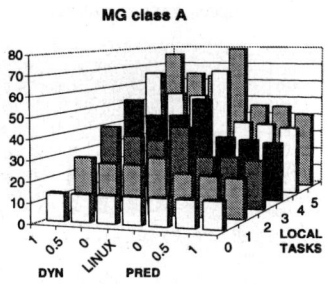

Fig. 2. NAS bench. execution times (in seconds): (left) IS, (right) MG

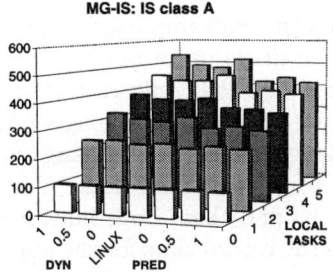 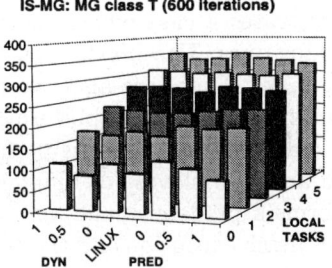

Fig. 3. Simultaneously IS and MG execution times (in seconds): (left) IS, (right) MG

intensive as class A or even as IS class A, and consequently synchronization measures provided by DYN and PRED models have fewer opportunities to improve performance.

4.2 Local Tasks Overhead and P Tuning

Fig. 4(left) shows the overhead introduced by the coscheduling models in the execution of *calcula* together with IS, MG, and both IS (class A) and MG (class T, 600 iterations).

It can be seen that the results are very similar in the three cases (with a slightly better result obtained for the LINUX model, as the communicating frequency is not taken into account). This means that this coscheduling implementation avoids the starvation of the local tasks. The reason is that the local tasks are executed when all the PCB *counter* fields of the distributed applications reach the value 0 (they have consumed their time slices). Thus, an opportunity arises for the execution of local tasks. The coscheduling methods advance the execution of distributed tasks (because it is necessary for them to be coscheduled with their correspondents) without delaying the local ones excessively.

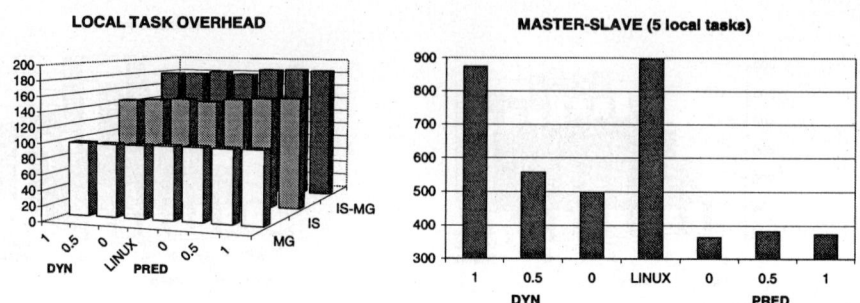

Fig. 4. Execution times (in seconds): (left) *calcula*, (right) *master-slave*

Finally, a synthetic distributed application (*master-slave*) was developed. It illustrates a case where the P parameter has more importance than in the previous ones. The *master-slave* application is made up of one master and six slave tasks. There are also two kinds of slaves, one that only receives messages (*r_slave*) and other that performs both receiving and sending messages (*rs_slave*). The mapping in 4 nodes is performed as follows: the master is assigned to one node and two slaves (of different kinds) to each remaining node. The master performs a predetermined number of iterations and then, both master and the slaves finish execution and the master reports the return time for the application. In each iteration, the master sends a message to all the slaves. All the slaves, after receiving the message, perform a simple floating-point computation. In addition, the *rs_slaves* reply to the master with the computation result. After receiving all the *rs_slave* messages, the master repeats the process again.

Fig. 4(right) shows the good performance of the predictive model in the execution of the synthetic application with a workload of five local tasks in each node. As was expected, PRED promoted the *rs_slave* tasks earlier than DYN and LINUX, so the round-trip time of each iteration decreased. Moreover, P$\simeq$0 obtained the best results because taking the current receiving frequency into account, a closer approximation to the message pattern was obtained. However, any mean between the current and past receiving frequency caused a drop in performance. Note as P has more influence in the DYN case: performance decreases strongly by increasing P.

5 Conclusions and Future Work

A predictive coscheduling technique with reasonable performance was implemented in a Linux cluster and discussed and compared with dynamic coscheduling and the plain Linux scheduler. The experimental results obtained corroborated the importance of applying a coscheduling technique over a non-dedicated cluster and the predictive model in particular.

Future work is directed towards proposing more coscheduling techniques taking into account network latency, paging faults, context switch costs, etc... Moreover, as was shown, the coscheduling performance may vary depending on P, the message pattern of distributed applications and their relationship. Consequently, a more accurate analysis based on this should be performed.

The future trend is to determine metrics for evaluating the effects of coscheduling techniques on execution time. They should be employed this way in tuning parameters while the distributed tasks are executing and not in later executions. The traditional ones (speedup, efficiency, etc...) only serve for performance evaluation at execution end.

References

1. Anderson, T., Culler, D., Patterson, D. and the Now team: A case for NOW (Networks of Workstations). IEEE Micro. 1995.
2. Ousterhout, J. K.: Scheduling Techniques for Concurrent Systems. 3rd International Conference on Distributed Computing Systems. 1982.
3. Litzkow, M., Livny, M. and Mutka, M.: Condor - A Hunter of Idle Workstations. 8th Int'l Conference of Distributed Computing Systems. 1988.
4. Feitelson, D. G. and Rudolph, L.: Coscheduling Based on Runtime Identification of Activity Working Sets. International J. Parallel Programming 23 (2). 1995.
5. Crovella, M. et al.: Multiprogramming on Multiprocessors. 3rd IEEE Symposium on Parallel and Distributed Processing. 1994.
6. Arpaci, R. H., Dusseau, A. C., Vahdat, A. M., Liu, L. T., Anderson, T. E. and Patterson, D. A.: The Interaction of Parallel and Sequential Workloads on a Network of Workstations. ACM SIGMETRICS'95. 1995.
7. Arpaci, R. H., Dusseau, A. C., Culler, D. E. and Mainwaring, A. M.: Scheduling with Implicit Information in Distributed Systems. ACM SIGMETRICS'98. 1998.
8. Dusseau, A. C., Arpaci, R. H. and Culler, D. E.: Effective Distributed Scheduling of Parallel Workloads. ACM SIGMETRICS'96. 1996.
9. Wong, F. C., Arpaci-Dusseau, A. C. and Culler, D. E.: Building MPI for Multiprogramming Systems Using Implicit Information. 6th European PVM/MPI User's Group Meeting. LNCS. 1999.
10. Sobalvarro, P. G. and Weihl, W. E..: Demand-based Coscheduling of Parallel Jobs on Multiprogrammed Multiprocessors. IPPS'95 Workshop on Job Scheduling Strategies for Parallel Processing. 1995.
11. Sobalvarro, P. G., Pakin, S., Weihl, W. E. and Chien, A. A.: Dynamic Coscheduling on Workstation Clusters. IPPS'98 Workshop on Job Scheduling Strategies for Parallel Processing. 1998.
12. Solsona, F., Giné, F., Molina, F., Hernández, P. and Luque, E.: Implementing and Analysing an Effective Explicit Coscheduling Algorithm on a NOW. VECPAR'2000. LNCS vol. 1981. 2001.
13. Solsona, F., Giné, F., Hernández, P. and Luque, E.: Implementing Explicit and Implicit Coscheduling in a PVM Environment. Europar'2000. LNCS vol. 1900. 2000.
14. Bailey, D. et al.: The NAS parallel benchmarks. International Journal of Supercomputer Applications 5 (3). 1991.
15. Parkbench Committe: Parkbench 2.0. http://www.netlib.org/parkbench. 1996.
16. Beck, M., et al.: LINUX Kernel Internals. Addison-Wesley. 1996.
17. Geist, A., Beguelin, A., Dongarra, J., Jiang, W., Manchek, R. and Sunderam, V.: PVM: Parallel Virtual Machine - A User's Guide and Tutorial for Networked Parallel Computing. MIT Press. 1994.

Self-Adjusting Scheduling of Master-Worker Applications on Distributed Clusters*

Elisa Heymann[1], Miquel A. Senar[1], Emilio Luque[1] and Miron Livny[2]

[1] Unitat d'Arquitectura d'Ordinadors i Sistemes Operatius,
Universitat Autònoma de Barcelona, Barcelona, Spain
{e.heymann,m.a.senar,e.luque}@cc.uab.es
[2] Department of Computer Sciences,
University of Wisconsin– Madison, Wisconsin, USA
miron@cs.wisc.edu

Abstract: Strategies for scheduling parallel applications on a distributed system must trade-off processor application speed-up and resource efficiency. Most existing strategies focus mainly on achieving high application speed-up without taking into account the efficiency factor. This paper presents our experiences with a self-adaptive scheduling strategy that dynamically adjusts the number of resources used by an application based on performance measures gathered during its execution. The strategy seeks to maximize resource efficiency while minimizing the impact in loss of speedup. It also uses the measured times to decide how to assign tasks to resources. This work has been carried out in the context of opportunistic clusters of machines and we report the results achieved by our strategy when it was applied to an image thinning application run on a Condor pool.

Keywords: Scheduling, resource management, cluster computing, Master-Worker applications.

1 Introduction

Scheduling of parallel tasks is one of the crucial issues that must be solved in order to achieve efficient execution in large-scale clusters of machines. Researchers have focused on the development of heuristic methods to solve the scheduling problem. In some cases, task scheduling is done prior to execution and is done only once –called static scheduling-. This static scheduling can be quite effective for computations for which a precise knowledge of their run-time behavior is available. However, this information is not usually available a priori for most applications. For these cases, it might be better to perform the scheduling periodically during run-time, as the problem's variable behavior more closely matches available computational resources. These techniques are usually referred to as dynamic scheduling.

---

* This work was supported by the CICYT (contract TIC98-0433), by the Commission for Cultural, Educational and Scientific Exchange between the USA and Spain (project 99186) and partially supported by the Generalitat de Catalunya (Grup de Recerca consolidat 1999SGR86).

Dynamic scheduling techniques lend themselves well to many parallel programming paradigms (like Master-Worker, Divide and Conquer, or Speculative Parallelism [11]) which exhibit a dynamic behaviour that precludes the use of static scheduling techniques. From the previously mentioned paradigms, the Master-Worker paradigm is especially attractive because, as has been shown by empirical evidence [9], tasks executed by workers in successive iterations tend to behave similarly, so that the measurements taken at run-time may be good predictors of near future behavior. We focus on the dynamic scheduling of master-worker applications.

We propose an approach for increasing system utilization in a cluster environment by using application-level agents which negotiate with a resource manager for an appropriate level of resource allocation. Agents try to allocate and schedule the tasks of a given master-worker application by following five main criteria: 1) dynamically measure application performance and task execution times 2) predict the resource requirements from measured history, 3) schedule tasks on the resources according to that prediction in order to minimize the completion time of the application, 4) voluntary relinquish resources when they are not plentifully utilized by the application, and 5) allocate more resources whenever a significant loss in speedup is detected.

We have designed and tested a scheduling agent for iterative master-worker applications that allows adaptive and reliable management and scheduling of the application running in a cluster environment. We have experimentally evaluated the effectiveness of our scheduling strategy using an image thinning application.

The rest of the paper is organized as follows. In section 2 we present the background and the parameters considered in our problem. Section 3 outlines our adaptive scheduling strategy for master-worker applications. In section 4 we show some experimental data obtained when the proposed scheduling strategy was applied to a thinning application. In section 5 we survey some related work and section 6 summarises the main conclusions of this work.

2 Problem Motivation and Background

We focused on the study of dynamic scheduling strategies for parallel applications that fit the iterative Master-Worker paradigm running onto a distributed cluster of machines. This model has been used to solve a significant number of problems such as Monte Carlo simulations [2] or material science simulations [9]. A Master-Worker application consists of two entities: a master and multiple workers. The master is responsible for decomposing the problem into small tasks (and distributes these tasks among a farm of worker processes), as well as for gathering the partial results in order to produce the final result of the computation. The worker processes receive a message from the master with the next task, process the task, and send back the result to the master. The master process may carry out some computations while tasks of a given batch are being completed. After that, a new batch of tasks is assigned to the master and this process is repeated several times until completion of the problem (after K cycles or *iterations*).

When a Master-Worker application is running on a distributed cluster of machines, one of the machines will be occupied by the master process and one worker process will be running in each one of the other available machines. This means that using as many workers as possible is a natural way to reduce the computation times of a given Master-Worker application. With this allocation scheme we would expect that the larger the number of workers assigned to the application, the better the speedup achieved (speedup is defined, for each number of processors N, as the ratio of the execution time when executing a program on a single processor to the execution time when N processors are used). However, most applications exhibit a temporal pattern in their individual tasks that implies that not all the allocated workers can be kept usefully busy. As a consequence, efficiency, defined as the ratio of the time that N processors spent doing useful work to the time those processors would be able to do work, will be low. For these applications, it is important to choose a processor allocation carefully so that under-utilized processors are released back to the system.

Releasing under-utilized processors could be beneficial both for the whole system and for the particular user. From the system perspective, released processors could be allocated to other users which, in turn, will improve the overall throughput of the cluster. A particular user will also benefit because cluster job managers normally make use of priority and aging mechanisms in their allocation policies. Every user has a priority and the job manager uses that priority to directly decide how many resources are going to be allocated to him. The better the priority, the more resources the user will get. The aging mechanism assigns a lower priority to a user when he has already been allocated resources for a long time. This mechanism will ensure that the resources will be fairly allocated to all users through time. Therefore, the priority of a user for allocating resources will be more negatively affected when his applications are running on a set of under-utilized resources.

In a previous work, we evaluated several scheduling policies for applications that followed the Master-Worker programming model mentioned above [6]. All the strategies assigned tasks to machines in decreasing order of execution time. The evaluated strategies differ in the amount of precise knowledge that they have about the expected execution time of the tasks.

We evaluated the scheduling policies using different workload distributions and, in general, our results showed that for any given workload distribution, a similar scenario is found. We observed that for any application there is an interval in the number of machines that corresponds to the situation in which the application is using an *ideal* number of workers. Efficiency is high and speedup is also high. All the workers are doing useful work and the application is close to its maximum parallelism utilization. The use of a number of machines belonging to the *ideal interval* guarantees that the largest tasks of the batch are executed alone in a single machine each (or together with some small tasks), and small tasks are executed together sharing some other machines. Using a number of machines belonging to this interval guarantees, in general, a good ratio between execution time and efficiency.

3 Self-Adjusting Scheduling Strategy

The facts mentioned above were used in [7] to design an early version of a self-adjusting algorithm that was responsible for both assigning tasks to workers and determining the number of workers to be allocated. Tasks were sorted in decreasing order of average execution time. This sorting criterion succeeded in obtaining good performance even if task execution times exhibit significant variations from one iteration to another. At each iteration, they were assigned to workers according to the sorted list. The number of allocated workers was adjusted dynamically at run-time by analysing the particular workload of a given application and determining the appropriate number of workers according to an empirical table. This table categorized applications according to the distribution of task execution times, and provided the number of machines that should be allocated to them. There were two main drawbacks with that strategy. First, the computation cost incurred at runtime to evaluate the workload distribution exhibited by an application in order to determine the appropriate table entry. Second, the sensitivity of the method to small variations in task execution times in successive iterations. This problem resulted in scenarios in which some machines were released and immediately reclaimed back because the workload of the application was oscillating between two table entries.

Our new strategy, presented in next subsection, tries to overcome the problems related to the allocation of workers by, on the one hand, being more conservative in releasing machines and, on the other hand, trying to approach the "ideal" number of processors in a more gentle way once the application runs with a number of machines close to the upper limit of the ideal interval. The assignment of tasks to workers has not changed from our previous work.

3.1 Description of the Self-Adjusting Scheduling Algorithm

Initially as many workers as tasks per iteration (N) are allocated for the application. Later, at the end of each iteration, the Self-Adjusting algorithm (shown in figure 3.1) computes the number of workers (*Nworkers*) that should be allocated to the application using two main criteria:

1. First the *AdjustBySpeedup* function computes *Nworkers* by evaluating *asp* (achievable speedup), defined as the ratio between the execution time of the whole application (by adding all the time tasks) and the execution time of the largest task (*ItMaxTaskExecTime*) obtained in the last iteration. From our theoretical studies we know that the upper limit of the ideal number of machines is *asp*. Therefore, the number of workers (*Nworkers*) is set to $\lceil asp \rceil + 1$. This procedure is always used when the application has not allocated all the machines requested in a previous iteration. It is possible that the requirement of workers has changed from one iteration to the next one. Therefore, *asp* is recomputed to check whether the previous requirement of workers is still valid or not.

2. When the application is running with the number of workers previously computed in *Nworkers*, the adjusting criterion to update *Nworkers* is based on two metrics: the execution time (*ItExecutionTime*) and efficiency (*ItEfficiency*) obtained in the last iteration. If the execution time is greater than the execution time of the largest task plus a given threshold, then one more worker is allocated. We have fixed the threshold as being the maximum between the time of the smallest tasks (*ItMinTaskExecTime*) and 15% of the largest tasks. This threshold was fixed empirically as it proved able to detect most of the situations in which the application is not exploiting all its parallelism due to lack of workers, and it does

not yield unstable situations in which workers are claimed and released too frequently. When the second metric is applied, a machine is released when efficiency is smaller than 0.8.

It is important to point out that the criteria described in point 2 above are applied only when the application runs during a whole iteration with a stable number of machines. In this way we do not consider metrics obtained under unstable situations, in which a new machine that was requested previously is allocated in the middle of an iteration and used for executing pending tasks. This situation may produce a temporarily contradictory result in the efficiency or in the execution time metrics. This refinement is not shown in figure 3.1 for the sake of simplicity.

In our experimental system the number of machines is handled cumulatively. This means that when *Nworkers* machines are requested and the application already has allocated *CurrentNworkers* machines, if (*Nworkers* > *CurrentNworkers*), only *Nworkers* - *CurrentNworkers* machines will be added to the application. Otherwise, *CurrentNworkers* - *Nworkers* machines will be released.

---

1. In the first iteration *Nworkers* = *Ntasks*

For next iterations (While convergence condition is not met) {

2. Compute *ItEfficiency*, *ItExecutionTime*, *ItMinTaskExecTime*, *ItMaxTaskExecTime*, *CurrentNworkers*.

3. if (*CurrentNworkers* < *Nworkers*) // We have not got the number of workers needed
       Nworkers = *AdjustBySpeedup()*
     else
       if (*ItExecutionTime* > (*ItMaxTaskExecTime* +
                         MAX (*ItMinTaskExecTime*, 15%(*ItMaxTaskExecTime*))))
         Nworkers = *Nworkers* + 1
       else
         if (*ItEfficiency* < 0.8)
           Nworkers = *Nworkers* – 1
}

Figure 3.1. Algorithm to determine *Nworkers*

Our self-adjusting algorithm is based on two main assumptions: application parallelism will not exhibit drastic increases over time, and the value of asp obtained after the first iteration will not change significantly in the near future. None of these assumptions were violated in our experiments. However, there are simple extensions that can be included in our basic algorithm to deal with scenarios in which the above-mentioned assumptions were not valid.

3.2 Implementation

We have included our adaptive algorithm into the MW [4] middleware library to experimentally evaluate its performance. MW is a runtime library that allows quick and easy development of master-worker computations on a distributed cluster of machines. It handles the communication between master and workers using PVM, and performs processor allocation and fault-detection through the services provided by a Condor job manager [8]. An application in MW has three base components: a Driver that is the master and manages a set of user-defined tasks and a pool of workers; and the Workers that execute the Tasks. We have extended MW to support both the iterative master-worker paradigm and the self-adjusting scheduling algorithm.

4 Experimental Study

In this section, we report the results obtained with the aim of testing the effectiveness of the proposed adaptive scheduling algorithm. We have executed an image thinning application. We run the applications on a distributed cluster and we have evaluated the ability of our scheduling strategy to dynamically adapt the number of workers without any *a priori* knowledge about the behavior of the application.

4.1 Thinning Application

Our thinning algorithm for binary images was adapted from the AFP3 (Fully Parallel Algorithm) described in [5]. The application works in the following way. Initially the image is divided into *M* horizontal parts. Each part contains the pixels of a piece of the image, plus border pixels from neighboring parts. One task is created to compute the thinning operation of one part, which basically consists of deleting pixels. At the end of each iteration, workers send the image back to the master, which updates the border pixels. If there are no more pixels to delete, the part achieves the local convergence criterion and finishes. When all the parts have finished then the global convergence criterion is met, the skeleton image is reconstructed combining the parts in order, and the application finishes. Figure 4.1 shows an original image and the result obtained by the thinning algorithm.

Figure 4.1. Reference image *Boy&Ball* and its thinning result

This application exhibits two characteristics that make its use attractive for evaluating a self-adjusting strategy. First, tasks corresponding to different parts of the application usually exhibit different execution times. Tasks that are assigned complex part of the image spend more time than tasks that deal with simple parts of the image. Therefore, a self-adjusting strategy must be able to schedule together short tasks to the same worker and relinquish spare workers. Secondly, the execution time of each task gradually decreases as the image thinning approaches convergence. Again, the self-adjusting strategy must also be able to reduce the number of workers as the execution time of converging tasks is close to zero.

4.2 Experimental Results

We conducted experiments using a distributed cluster platform consisting of a Condor pool of machines at the University of Wisconsin. The total number of available machines was around 700 although we restricted our experiments to machines with Linux architecture. The execution of our application was carried out with a set of processors that do not exhibit significant differences in performance, so that the platform could be considered to be homogeneous.

We ran the thinning application with 3 images: *Figures*, *Letters* and *Boy&Ball*. Images were initially divided into 8, 16 and 32 parts, which corresponded to the initial set of tasks created at the initial iteration. The number of iterations until thinning convergence was 92, 105 and 97 for the three images, respectively. We enlarged the size of the images so that the execution time of the largest task was initially in the range of 50 seconds when images were divided into 8 parts.

Different runs of the same programs generally produced slightly different final execution and efficiency results due to the changing conditions in the opportunistic environment. Hence, average-case results are reported for sets of three runs.

Results of efficiency and execution time (in seconds) are shown in table 4.1 when the thinning application was run both using our self-adjusting strategy (Self-Adjusting column) and without using it (No Self-Adjusting column). When no adaptive scheduling was used, the initial number of requested workers was equal to the initial number of tasks. Once a task met the convergence criterion, the corresponding worker was released. In contrast, in the self-adjusting case, workers were released only according to our strategy and no workers were released automatically on task completion. Tasks were assigned to workers in decreasing order of average execution time in both Self- and Non Self-Adjusting cases. Therefore, our results reflect mainly the effectiveness of our strategy to dynamically adjust the number of resources.

In addition to the results obtained for both strategies using an initial number of tasks of 8, 16 and 32, we also include the execution time of a sequential thinning application (column *InitialTasks* = 1) for comparison purposes. In the *NworkersAvg* rows the average of the number of workers used are shown.

As can be seen in table 4.1, self-adjusting obtains efficiency values above 0.8 in all cases, while no self-adjusting obtains efficiency values that are significantly smaller (between 0.4 and 0.65 in most cases). The execution time results indicate that the self-adapting strategy results in a penalty that in most cases is less than 15% compared to the non self-adjusting case. Only for the *Letters* example with 16 and 32 tasks, was the difference in execution time 17% and 19%, respectively. In general, the execution time of the application does not decrease linearly as the image is decomposed in more parts because the maximum parallelism is only achievable at the initial iterations of the algorithm. Later, as different parts of the image converge, parallelism decays and consists only of the tasks that compute the most complex parts of the images.

Table 4.1. Results of the master-worker thinning application

InitialTasks			Non Self-Adjusting			Self-Adjusting		
		1	8	16	32	8	16	32
Nworkers Avg.	Figures	1	5,5	9,12	12,85	2,45	4,17	7,37
	Letters	1	5,3	10,36	21,11	3,89	6,55	9,41
	Boy&Ball	1	5,57	7,02	11,34	2,85	4,01	8,92
Efficiency	Figures	1	0,41	0,41	0,48	0,88	0,89	0,86
	Letters	1	0,64	0,59	0,399	0,8	0,82	0,83
	Boy&Ball	1	0,59	0,64	0,7	0,88	0,86	0,87
Exec. Time (in seconds)	Figures	12746	4141	2634	1533	4473	2648	1703
	Letters	12803	3179	1562	1204	3230	1833	1399
	Boy&Ball	10080	2948	1678	1001	3094	1732	1002
Exec.Time/ Efficiency Ratio	Figures	12746	10100	6424,39	3193,75	5082,95	2975,28	1980,23
	Letters	12803	4967,18	2647,45	3010	4037,5	2234,36	1685,54
	Boy&Ball	10080	4996,61	2621,87	1430	3515,9	2013,95	1151,72

As a global index of performance, the last three rows of table 4.1 show the index between execution time and efficiency corresponding to both strategies. The lower the index, the better the use of resources achieved by a given strategy. This means that our strategy achieves a better trade-off between efficiency and execution time.

Although 8, 16 and 32 workers were claimed initially by both strategies, a smaller number of workers were effectively allocated throughout the computation. The Non Self-Adjusting strategy simply relinquished workers as tasks were completed. Our Self-Adjusting strategy further reduced the number of allocated workers, as can be seen in the *Nworkers Avg.* row which contains the average number of workers used from the beginning to the end of the computation. In general, our strategy saved between 20% to 55% of workers compared to the Non Self-Adjusting case.

Figure 4.2 shows a detailed example of one execution of the thinning application applied to the *Figures* image divided initially into 32 parts. This example is a representative illustration of the general behavior and the performance achieved by both the Self-Adjusting and the Non Self-Adjusting algorithms. We show the information related to number of workers, efficiency and execution time after iterations 1, 5, 10, 15, and so on. Execution times are shown in a logarithmic scale.

As can be seen, the allocation of resources is not serviced immediately after request. This implies, for instance, that the Non Self-Adjusting algorithm achieves a maximum number of 23 workers in iteration 15. At this time, some of the tasks have already finished (those corresponding to image borders) and, therefore, the application does not need the whole set of 32 workers requested at the beginning. In general, the Self-Adjusting algorithm is able to tune the number of workers from the initial iterations, fixing the maximum number of workers to 15 after iteration 10. Significant differences in the number of workers (and, consequently, in efficiency) are mainly observed at the central iterations of the computation (from iteration 15 to 75). In these stages, the execution time of each iteration is slightly better for the Non Self-Adjusting algorithm at the expense of sometimes using twice the number of workers that the Self-Adapting strategy uses. Later, the application is close to the end and the number of workers is very small in both cases, so efficiency and execution time are very similar for both strategies.

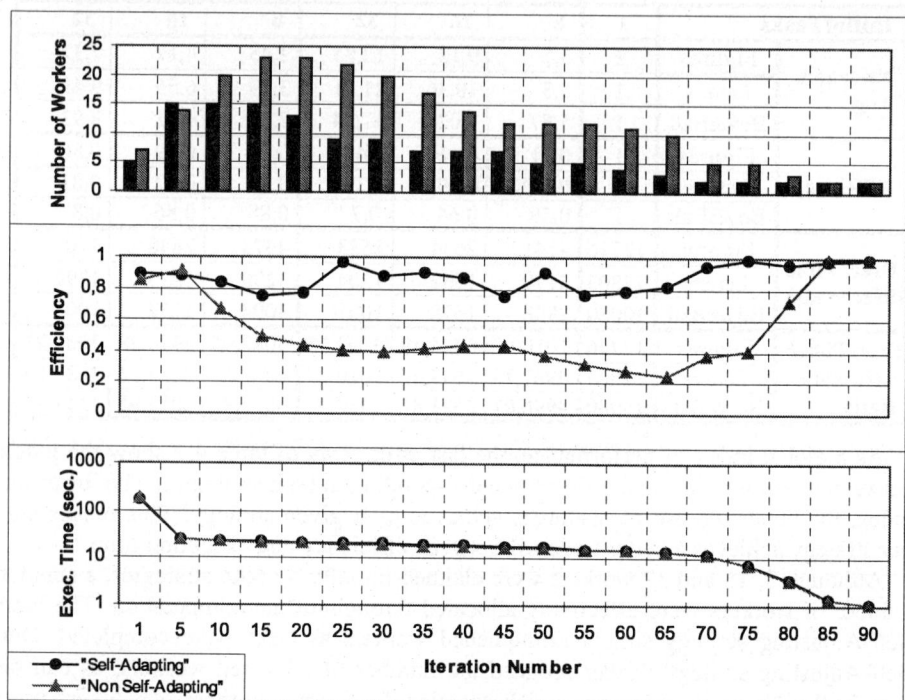

Figure 4.2. Number of workers, efficiency and execution time obtained with the *Figures* image divided in 32 parts

5 Related Work

The problem of self-adaptive scheduling has been investigated recently in different frameworks. There are several middleware environments that allow the development of adaptive parallel applications running on distributed clusters. They include NetSolve [3], Nimrod [1] and AppLeS [10]. NetSolve and Nimrod provide API for creating task farms that can only be decomposed by a single bag of tasks. Therefore, no historical data can be used to allocate workers, and their adaptive algorithms rely on different metrics to the ones adopted here. In AppLeS, the application programmer is supplied information about the computing environment and is given a library to allow them to react to changes in available resources.

6 Conclusions

In this paper we have discussed the problem of scheduling master-worker applications on distributed cluster environments. We have presented a self-adjusting strategy that takes into account runtime information about the application. This information is used to allocate and schedule the minimum number of processors that guarantees good speedup by keeping the processors as busy as possible and avoiding situations in which processors sit idle, waiting for work to be done. The strategy is rather straightforward at the moment and is not guaranteed to adjust the number of workers to the optimal in all cases. However, our early experimental results with a thinning application running in a homogeneous cluster of machines are encouraging, as they have shown that our algorithm worked well in practice. In general, our adaptive strategy achieved an efficiency higher than 80% in the use of processors, while the execution time was only slightly worse than the execution time achieved with a significantly larger number of processors.

References

1. D. Abramson, R. Sosic, J. Giddy and B. Hall, "Nimrod: a tool for performing parameterised simulations using distributed workstations", Symposium on High Performance Distributed Computing, Virginia,
2. J. Basney, B. Raman and M. Livny, "High throughput Monte Carlo", Proceedings of the Ninth SIAM Conf. on Par. Proc. for Scientific Computing, San Antonio Texas, 1999.
3. H. Casanova, M. Kim, J. S. Plank and J. Dongarra, "Adaptive scheduling for task farming with Grid middleware", International Journal of Supercomputer Applications and High-Performance Computing, pp. 231-240, Volume 13, Number 3, Fall 1999.
4. J.-P. Goux, S. Kulkarni, J. Linderoth, M. Yoder, "An enabling framework for master-worker applications on the computational grid", Proceedings of the Ninth IEEE Symposium on High Performance Distributed Computing (HPDC9), pp. 43-50, 2000.
5. Z. Guo and R. Hall. "Fast Fully Parallel Thinning Algorithms". CVGIP: Image Understanding. Vol. 55, No. 3, pp. 317-328, May 1992.
6. E. Heymann, M. A. Senar, E. Luque and M. Livny, "Evaluation of an Adaptive Scheduling Strategy for Master-Worker Applications on Clusters of Workstations", Proc. of 7th Int. Conf. in High Perf Comp. (HiPC 2000), LNCS series, Vol. 1970, pp. 310-319, 2000.
7. E. Heymann, M. A. Senar, E. Luque and M. Livny, "Adaptive Scheduling for Master-Worker Applications on the Computational Grid", Proc. of 2000 Int. Workshop on Grid Computing (GRID'2000), LNCS series, Vol. 1971, pp. 214-227, 2000.
8. M. Livny, J. Basney, R. Raman and T. Tannenbaum, "Mechanisms for high throughput computing", SPEEDUP, 11, 1997.
9. J. Pruyne and M. Livny, "Interfacing Condor and PVM to harness the cycles of workstation clusters", Journal on Future Generations of Computer Systems, Vol. 12, 1996.
10. G. Shao, R. Wolski and F. Berman, "Performance effects of scheduling strategies for Master/Slave distributed applications", Tech. Rep. TR-CS98-598, University of California, San Diego, September 1998.
11. L. M. Silva and R. Buyya, "Parallel programming models and paradigms", in R. Buyya (ed.), "High Performance Cluster Computing: Architectures and Systems: Volume 2", Prentice Hall PTR, NJ, USA, 1999.

Smooth and Efficient Integration of High-Availability in a Parallel Single Level Store System

Anne-Marie Kermarrec[1] and Christine Morin[2]

[1] Microsoft Research
St George House, 1 Guildhall StreetCambridge CB2 3NH, UK
Tel: +44 1223 724 823, Fax: +44 1223744 777
annemk@microsoft.com

[2] Irisa/Université de Rennes 1
Campus Universitaire de Beaulieu 35042 Rennes Cedex, France
Tel: +33 2 99 84 72 90, Fax: +33 2 99 84 71 71
cmorin@irisa.fr

Abstract. A parallel single level store (PSLS) system integrates a shared virtual memory and a parallel file system representing an attractive support for long running parallel applications in a cluster. In this paper we present the smooth integration of a backward error recovery high-availability support into a PSLS system. Our highly-available PSLS system relies on a high degree of integration and re-usability between high-availability and standard supports. We focus on the parallel file system management at checkpointing and recovery time. A prototype has been implemented and we show some performance results.

1 Introduction

Clusters of SMPs represent an attractive support for the execution of long-running parallel scientific applications. Targeted applications for clusters such as large-scale numerical simulations usually rely on the simple shared memory programming model and need to perform large input/output operations as well. To cope with this twofold requirement, namely the shared memory abstraction and a large and efficient file system, parallel single level store systems (PSLS) [5], which integrate a shared virtual memory (SVM) [1] and a parallel file system (PFS) [12] are very well-suited for the execution of high performance applications in a cluster.

To provide both disk capacity of a PFS and the natural way of programming of an SVM, our system relies on a single level of addressing: a global shared virtual address space manages both memory and file data. A mapping interface enables disk data to be mapped in the SVM system such as all operations, including PFS ones, are made using standard memory reads and writes. Concurrent accesses to the same file data are automatically handled by the SVM coherence protocol.

Tolerating failures in a PSLS system becomes more and more important as the size and execution time of applications increase. In this paper we present a highly-available PSLS which smoothly integrates the high-availability support into the standard functioning of a PSLS without requiring any specific hardware. This integration enables to combine fault-tolerance and efficiency in failure-free executions which are two statements often considered as contradictory. First the high-availability support takes benefit of the standard features thus decreasing the additional cost and complexity traditionally inherent to any high-availability mechanism. Second, high-availability features are exploited to improve the standard functioning during failure-free executions. The remainder of the paper is organized as follows: we present the design guidelines of our highly available PSLS in Section 2 and the system itself in failure-free executions (Section 3) and at rollback (Section 4). Section 5 concludes. Results are depicted along the paper.

2 Smooth Integration of Standard and High-Availability Features

2.1 Fault-Tolerance Assumptions

Our system is able to tolerate *(i)* multiple transient failures, which do not involve the loss of memory contents, *(ii)* a single permanent node failure involving the loss of both the memory contents and the disk contents including the PFS part managed by the faulty node and *(iii)* power failures that might affect the whole cluster. We consider a system of failure-independent fail-silent nodes connected by a reliable interconnection network. Our system relies on backward error recovery (BER) [6]: a consistent system state, a checkpoint, is periodically snapshot and stored on stable storage and restored upon detection of a failure. The coherence of the checkpoint is ensured by an incremental global coordinated checkpointing policy where all nodes save simultaneously a checkpoint. A two-phase commit protocol guarantees the atomic update of a checkpoint.

2.2 Design Guidelines

In our highly available PSLS, no specific hardware is required to ensure the persistence of recovery data and this keeps the fault-tolerance mechanism to a reasonable cost. We exploit the fact that nodes are failure-independent to implement a stable storage in standard support storage both at memory and disk levels by replicating every checkpointed page in two distinct nodes.

Despite the fact that efficiency and high-availability are somewhat contradictory, they rely on the same mechanism namely *replication*: replication is used in SVM systems to exploit data locality and distribute the load between nodes and is intrinsic to any high-availability mechanism. We widely exploit this commonality in our system. At the memory level, already existing replication, implemented by the SVM is exploited at checkpointing time to avoid replication of recovery data and data transfers across the network and conversely, created recovery data can be used afterwards to anticipate page faults in failure-free executions. Likewise, at the PFS level, page mirroring, required to tolerate the lost of a disk, is used during failure free executions to increase the probability of local accesses. Each page stored in the PFS exists in two copies in two distinct nodes: the **primary** and the **mirror** copies. Both copies can be used to serve files accesses.

To ensure as much efficiency as possible, the SVM part of the PSLS implements a software injection mechanism to delay as long as possible expensive disk write operations. Instead, data selected to be evicted from a local memory is preferably injected in the memory of a remote node rather than being written back onto disk. Likewise this injection mechanism implemented for efficiency in our standard PSLS is also used to handle replacement of readable recovery data.

Our SVM in based on a statically distributed directory [7]. For each page, an SVM *manager* is statically defined by using a simple modulo function. The SVM manager of a page is always able to locate a copy. The primary PFS manager of a page is also the node storing the primary copy of a page. The same modulo function is used to distribute the primary copies of the PFS on different nodes. We have proposed another function, used in coordination with the modulo function *(i)* to reconfigure the SVM management upon detection of a permanent failure, *(ii)* to choose the location of the mirror PFS pages and to access them afterwards, and *(iii)* to reconfigure the PFS storage and management in the event of a permanent failure.

3 Failure-Free Execution

3.1 Data Management in a PSLS

Our PSLS system defines a single global address space which includes both the memory and PFS pages. **Volatile** pages are allocated in the SVM memory only, their life time is the duration of the computation. Such pages do not have any counterpart in the PFS disks. They may be swapped on disk when evicted from memory. **Mapped** pages are mapped in the SVM from a parallel file. Such pages have corresponding disk copies in the PFS disks. A page is **clean** if its copies in memory are identical to the disk copy and **dirty** if the disk copy of a page is not up-to-date, Data replication in an SVM leads to the presence of several copies of a page in different memories. A sequential consistency model [2] implemented with a write-invalidate protocol managing both mapped and volatile pages is implemented in order to ensure the consistency of multiple copies.

Each node is equipped with two disks: *(1)* The **pfs disk** is used to store user files and is managed by the PFS part of the PSLS system; *(2)* The **system disk** is viewed as an extension of the local memory and is composed of two distinct areas: *(i)* The **checkpoint area** consists itself of two zones: the **memory area** is used to store pure recovery copies of (volatile or mapped) pages that belong to the current checkpoint; the **permanent area** is used to store permanent recovery copies of volatile pages (see Section 3.2). The checkpoint area is never checked on a page reference during failure-free execution; *(ii)* The **swap area** is used to swap active[1] or readable recovery[2] copies of volatile pages. Pages belonging to a mapped file are not swapped in the *system* disk when they are evicted from memory but copied to their disk counterpart in the PFS disks. The swap area is checked upon a page reference.

The interface between the SVM and the PFS is file mapping which makes disk accesses transparent to the programmer. Files are not accessed using standard and complex input/output operations but by direct read and write operations in virtual memory. A memory area, called mapping area, is allocated to store file data. The PFS primary manager of a page stores the primary copy in its PFS disk and is in charge to serve requests regarding this page. When a processor first references a data in the mapping area, a page fault occurs and the corresponding data is automatically loaded from disk. Disks writes only occur in the event of a modified page replacement or at the end of the application. A memory page granularity is used by the PFS to access disks. In the SVM, the nodes memories are used as large caches. Pages in an SVM are transparently replicated in the node memory of the processor which references them. The owner of a page owns a page copy in its memory. Figure 1 represents the architecture of a 2-nodes PSLS.

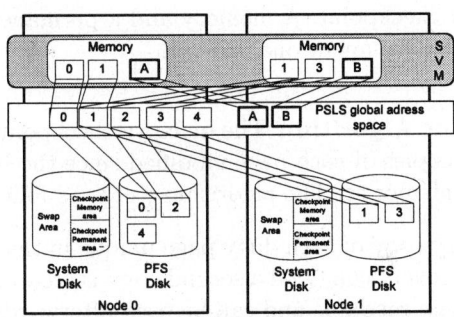

Pages A,B : volatiles pages ; Pages 1,2...: mapped pages

Fig. 1. Example of a PSLS system

The considered mechanisms are illustrated along this paper with performance results obtained from an implementation of our PSLS. Our prototype has been implemented on a 4-nodes cluster of dual-processors running Linux based on the Scalable Coherent Interface (SCI) [3] interconnection technology. Nodes are based on Intel Pentium II (450 MHz) and have a 256 M-byte local memory. The SCI network has a latency of about 5 microseconds and a throughput of about 60 M-bytes per second.

The coherence management unit size in the SVM and the PFS striping unit size is equal to the size of the memory page (4KB). Performance results have

---
[1] Active data is data used for computation and does not belong to a checkpoint
[2] Readable recovery data represents recovery data not modified since the last checkpoint, it remains readable and can be used for standard execution as long as it is not modified.

been obtained from the execution of two applications: Modified Gram Schmidt (MGS) and matrix multiplication algorithms. The MGS algorithm produces from a set of vectors an orthonormal basis of the space generated by these vectors. We consider a base of 1024 vectors of 1024 double floats elements. The matrices used in the matrix multiplication algorithm contains 1024 x1024 double float elements. The SVM size for all the experiments is 64 M-bytes.

3.2 Checkpointing

Two types of checkpoints are considered in the system. A **memory checkpoint** consists in establishing a checkpoint in memories only. Saving as long as possible checkpoints in memory without any disk access, we keep the cost of a checkpoint reasonable. Nevertheless, this efficient implementation of a checkpoint is not sufficient to handle power failures. To this end, we define a **permanent checkpoint** where pages are checkpointed on disk.

For efficiency reasons, permanent checkpoints are much less frequent than memory ones. Several memory checkpoints may occur between two permanent checkpoints. Upon detection of a failure, the last checkpoint is restored, whether it is a permanent or a memory one. Note that a permanent checkpoint invalidates the previous memory checkpoint. A memory and a permanent checkpoints may cohabit as long as the permanent one is older.

Memory Checkpoint Algorithm The memory checkpoint algorithm consists in ensuring that two copies of each page modified since the last checkpoint exist in two distinct node memories. The algorithm works as follows:

- The single memory copy of each dirty page unique in the SVM is transformed into a readable recovery copy and a second copy is created in a distinct node. These copies remain readable and can be used afterwards during failure-free executions. Upon the first write access to a readable recovery copy, the two recovery copies are transformed into pure recovery copies no longer usable during failure-free execution. These copies are restored in the event of a failure.
- Two already existing copies of each dirty shared and already replicated page are transformed into readable recovery copies, thus avoiding page creation and transfer at checkpointing.

On one hand, this algorithm takes benefit of the replication inherent to the SVM by using data already replicated to avoid the need to create additional page copies to store recovery data. On the other hand, recovery data remains readable between two checkpoints as long as the corresponding page has not been modified since the last checkpoint. They can be used for anticipating page faults during failure-free executions. A complete description of the memory checkpoint algorithm can be found in [9]. In our experiments of the MGS algorithm, between 55% and 83% of recovery pages comes from existing page copies.

Since it is not worthwhile keeping pure recovery copies in memory since they are useless for failure-free executions, they can be moved into the checkpoint memory area. A memory checkpoint is thus composed of *(1)* Volatile and mapped recovery page copies in memory, *(2)* Volatile readable recovery page copies in the swap area of the system disks, *(3)* Volatile and mapped pure recovery copies in the checkpoint memory area of the system disks and, *(4)* Mapped pages on the PFS which do not have corresponding recovery data of previous type (1) and (3) in memory.

Permanent Checkpoint Algorithm A permanent checkpoint algorithm consists in ensuring that two copies of every page are present on two disks. The checkpointing algorithm follows a two-phase commit algorithm, thus ensuring the atomic update of the primary and the mirror copies of a page. The algorithm is presented in Algorithm 1 and works as follows: *(i)* recovery data associated to volatile pages are created in the checkpoint permanent area of two system disks since they do not have counterpart on the PFS disks, and *(ii)* recovery data corresponding to mapped pages are mirrored on the PFS disks.

Volatile pages are replicated onto different system disks using the injection mechanism (request to inject onto disk rather than onto memory). Each mapped page has to be replicated in two different PFS disks. A permanent checkpoint is composed of the volatile page recovery copies stored in the permanent zone of the checkpoint area, and of all pages stored on the PFS. This is actually in order to stick to this checkpoint composition that dirty mapped pages are injected rather than being written back onto disk.

---

1 Permanent checkpoint (two-phase commit algorithm) performed on each node

for each volatile active page p in memory or in swap area do
    write_back(p,   local   permanent_checkpoint_area);   injection_disk(p,   remote   permanent_checkpoint_area);
    {*The remote system disk is on the same node as the one which would have been chosen for memory checkpoint (neighbor node in the implementation)*}
end for
for each page copy p in checkpoint memory area do
    invalidation(p);
end for
for each readable recovery copy of volatile page p in memory or in swap area do
    write_back(p, local permanent_checkpoint_area);
end for
for each dirty mapped page p in memory and each mapped page p having readable recovery copies in memory do
    write_back(p, PFS_Primary_Manager(p)); write_back(p, PFS_Mirror_Manager(p));
end for
{*The memory contents is not modified at all. This enables the application to carry on in the same configuration, no access pattern is lost due to the checkpoint*}

The memory checkpoint algorithm is much more efficient than the permanent checkpoint algorithm (approximatively 6 times less overhead). This difference is due to the remote disk accesses performed during a permanent checkpoint.

Mirror Function Our goal while defining a PFS mirror manager is twofold: *(i)* being able to easily locate from a page number the mirror node of a page in order to send the request either to the primary manager or to the mirror manager and *(ii)* not attributing the same mirror manager for all the pages having the same primary manager in order to distribute the load if this initial manager fails permanently.

We use a function, called *PFS_Mirror_Manager*, to distribute uniformly the replication of pages previously managed by a faulty node. When a page p is referenced and needs to be loaded in memory, the node originating the request can easily find the primary manager of the page by using a simple modulo function considering a system with N nodes, numbered from 0 to $N - 1$: $PFS\_Primary\_Manager(p) = p \bmod N$ as well as its mirror manager using the following function:

$$PFS\_Mirror\_Manager(p) =$$
$$[k \bmod (N - 1) + PFS\_Primary\_Manager(p) + 1] \bmod N$$

where $p = M(p) + kN$, is the address of the considered page, $M(p) \in \{0, ..., N-1\}$ is the primary manager of p, and $k = \frac{M(p)}{N}$ is the ordering number of the considered page in the page list initially managed by $PFS\_Primary\_Manager(p)$. This function ensures a uniform mirroring of pages managed by a node between the remaining nodes. The proof can be found in [4]. Figure 2 depicts the example of a 4-nodes system and 15 pages.

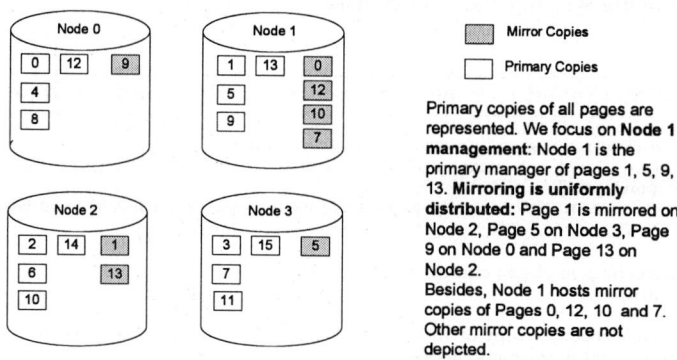

Fig. 2. Example of Node 1 mirroring management

3.3 Using Mirrored Copies for PFS Efficiency

When a node initiates a request on a page p, it computes simultaneously the primary and the mirror managers of the page and sends the request to either one. If the node is itself one of the two nodes, the request is served locally. Enabling mirrored copies to be used to serve requests as well as primary copies increases by two the probability that a request is served locally. The impact of

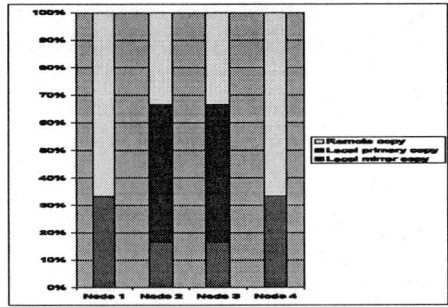 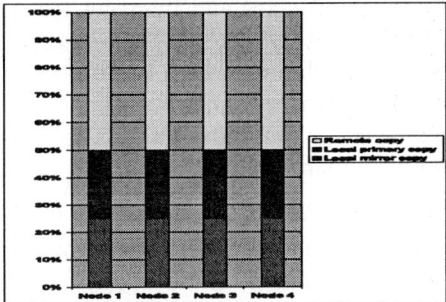

Fig. 3. Utilization of local primary and mirror disk page copies in MGS and matrix multiplication

this optimization clearly depends on the access patterns of the application as regards to the PFS pages distribution among nodes.

Figure 3 depicts the proportion of local accesses to the PFS, distinguishing between primary and mirror copies versus the number of remote accesses. These plots show that the use of mirroring, implemented for high-availability purpose increases significantly the number of local disk accesses. 50 % in average of disk accesses are performed locally both for MGS and matrix multiplication.

4 Rollback Recovery

Handling Transient Failures When a transient failure occurs, the last checkpoint must be restored. If it is a memory checkpoint, pure recovery copies are restored in readable recovery pages. All active copies are discarded, except clean copies of mapped pages that are still valid.

If a permanent checkpoint is restored, memories are emptied except for clean active mapped pages, checkpoint memory and swap areas are emptied, volatile page copies in the permanent area are copied back to memory where they are transformed into readable recovery copies.

Reconfiguration after a Permanent Failure Once a permanent failure has been detected, the previous checkpoint must be restored the same way as in the case of a transient failure. However, the contents of the memory and disks of the faulty node have been lost. Thus the PSLS must be reconfigured as in order to be able to tolerate right away another failure. We assume a crash-stop model where a node permanently crashed and never recovers. At the end of the rollback, each page should have two readable recovery copies. The aim of the reconfiguration is to duplicate lost data which was located on the faulty node so that the persistence property is satisfied again. Algorithms 2 and 3 present the whole reconfiguration process.

SVM Reconfiguration In the SVM, each node is the *manager* of a statically defined set of pages and manages for each page a directory entry containing the identity of its owner and the replicas location. A new recovery copy must be created for each page which had one of its two recovery copies located in the faulty node. Moreover, a spare SVM manager has to be defined for pages previously managed by the faulty node. The same function as the *PFS_Mirror_Manager* is used to define a spare manager.

PFS Reconfiguration From the PFS point of view, the faulty node acted as a primary manager and a mirror manager for two different sets of pages. A new function has to be applied to define a *PFS_mirror^2*. At reconfiguration time, each node checks if it stores on its PFS disk a page for which either the *PFS_Primary_Manager* or the *PFS_Mirror_Manager* is the faulty node. To define a *PFS_mirror^2* we iterate on the *PFS_Mirror_Manager* function.

PFS_mirror^2_Manager The *PFS_mirror^2* function must have the ability for a given page to avoid both the faulty node and the node holding the other disk copy of the page.

Consider the following situation where z becomes faulty, all the pages present on the PFS disk of each node y must be considered, namely:

- the pages p for which the *PFS_Primary_Manager* is z and y is the *PFS_Mirror_Manager*: $p = kN + z$ and $PFS\_Mirror\_Manager(p) = y$
- the pages p for which z is the *PFS_Mirror_Manager* and y is the *PFS_Primary_Manager* : $p = kN + y$ and $PFS\_Mirror\_Manager(p) = z$

The same *PFS_Mirror_Manager* function is applied to find a spare (primary or mirror) manager but since two nodes must be ignored (the node itself y and the faulty node z), the applied modulo is $(N - 2)$.

The function to define PFS_Mirror^2 is the following:

$$PFS\_Mirror^2 y, z(p) = PFS\_Mirror^2 z(p) + 1_{y,(z-2)}[PFS\_Mirror^2 z(p)]$$

where $PFS\_Mirror^2 z = [k \bmod (N-2)+z+1]$ and $1_{y,(z-2)}[PFS\_Mirror^2 z(k) = 1$ if $PFS\_Mirror^2 z(k) \in \{y...(z-2)\}$ else 0.

Power Failure Recovery after a power failure is performed from last permanent checkpoint. The memory is emptied and filled from the permanent checkpoint area of the system disk for volatile pages and from the PFS regarding mapped pages. It is assumed that the private state of each process of the application has been checkpointed atomically with PSLS checkpoint.

5 Conclusion and Related Work

Very few other work has been done on file mapping in SVM with a PFS. [8] is one such system but it is not designed to tolerate node failures. Several recoverable

2 Memory and disk reconfiguration after a permanent failure applied locally on node n

```
{Memory reconfiguration}
if (last_checkpoint == memory_checkpoint) then
   for each page p in memory do
      if (p== pure_recovery_page) then
         p = readable_recovery
      else
         if ((p != recovery_page) && (p != clean mapped page)) then
            invalidation(p)
         end if
      end if
   end for
   for each volatile page p in swap area do
      if (p== readable_recovery_page) then
         Copy back p to memory
         invalidation(p);
      end if
   end for
   for each page p in the checkpoint memory area do
      p = readable_recovery_page;
      copy back p to memory
   end for
end if
```

shared virtual memory systems have been proposed [11]. However, to our knowledge, all these memory management systems do not consider issues related to the interactions between the memory management system and a file system.

XFS [13] is a highly available parallel file system which implements cooperative caching. In contrast to our system, memory and disk management is not fully integrated resulting in a worse usage of the cluster memory resource. Moreover, XFS provides a standard read/write interface and implements RAID-5 rather than mirroring to ensure the high availability of files. To efficiently implement a distributed RAID-5 mechanism, complex mechanisms are needed.

Our highly-available PSLS tolerates multiple transient, unique permanent and power cut failures without requiring any specific hardware. Every single feature in this system is based on re-usability and integration. We implement a two-level checkpointing algorithm: a memory checkpoint is established very efficiently and a permanent checkpoint is established on a much lower frequency basis but enables to tolerate permanent cut failures. Moreover a permanent checkpoint can also be used when memories are saturated to clean the memories [10]. Another contribution is the use of a function, used in conjunction with the modulo function which ensures a well-balanced PFS mirroring mechanism. It is also possible to iterate this function to reconfigure the PFS in the event of a permanent failure. We have implemented a prototype of our highly-available PSLS and results show that the integration of standard and high availability supports results in a very efficient system.

3 Memory and disk reconfiguration in case of permanent failure (continued)

```
if (last_checkpoint == permanent_checkpoint) then
  for each page p in memory do
    if (p!= clean mapped page) then
      invalidation(p);
    end if
  end for
  for each volatile page p in swap area do
    invalidation(p);
  end for
  for each page p in the checkpoint memory area do
    invalidation(p);
  end for
  for each page p in the checkpoint permanent area do
    copy_back_into_memory(p);
  end for
end if
{SVM reconfiguration (replication of lost pages and spare manager )}
for each page p (mapped or volatile) do
  if (recovery-replica belongs to f) then
    replication(p, remote memory);
  end if
  if ((manager(p) == f) && (n == p.owner)) then
    new_manager = spare_manager(p);
  end if
  update_Manager(p.owner, new_manager);
  {Update the new manager of the page with owner information}
end for
{PFS reconfiguration}
for each page p on the PFS disk do
  if ((PFS_Primary_Manager(p)== f) or (PFS_Mirror_Manager(p)==f)) then
    PFS_Mirror$^2$_Manager == PFS_Mirror$^2$_Manager(p);
    Mirror (p, PFS_Mirror$^2$_Manager);
  end if
end for
```

References

1. C. Amza, A. L. Cox, S. Dwarkadas, P. Keleher, H. Lu, R. Rajamony, W. Yu, and W. Zwaenepoel. TreadMarks: Shared Memory Computing on Networks of Workstations. *Computer*, pages 18–28, February 1996.
2. M. Dubois, C. Scheurich, and F. A. Briggs. Synchronization, coherence and event ordering in multiprocessors. *IEEE Computer Survey, Tutorial Series*, February 1988.
3. D. B. Gustavson. The Scalable Coherent Interface and Related Standards Projects. *IEEE Micro*, pages 10–21, February 1992.
4. A.-M. Kermarrec, C. Morin, and M. Banâtre. Design, implementation and evaluation of icare: an efficient recoverable dsm. *Software Practice & Experience*, 28(9), July 1998.
5. P. J. Leach, P. H. Levine, B. P. Douros, J. A. Hamilton, D. L. Nelson, and B. L. Stumpf. The architecture of an integrated local network. *IEEE Journal on Selected Areas in Communications*, 1(5):842–857, November 1983.
6. P. A. Lee and T. Anderson. Dependable computing and fault-tolerant systems, vol. 3. In J. C. Laprie A. Avizienis, H. Kopetz, editor, *Fault Tolerance : Principles and Practice*. Springer Verlag, New York, 1990.
7. K. Li and P. Hudak. Memory coherence in shared virtual memory systems. *ACM Transactions on Computer Systems*, 7(4):321–359, November 1989.

8. Qun Li, Jie Jing, and Li Xie. BFXM: A parallel file system model based on the mechanism of distributed shared memory. *ACM Operating Systems Review*, 31(4):30–40, October 1997.
9. C. Morin, A.-M. Kermarrec, M. Banâtre, and A. Gefflaut. An efficient and scalable approach for implementing fault tolerance architectures. *IEEE Transactions on Computers*, 49(5):414–430, May 2000.
10. C. Morin, R. Lottiaux, and A.-M. Kermarrec. High-availability of the memory hierarchy in a cluster. In *19th IEEE Symposium on reliable Distributed Systems*, pages 134–143, Nurnberg, Germany, October 2000.
11. C. Morin and I. Puaut. A survey of recoverable distributed shared memory systems. *IEEE Transactions on Parallel and Distributed Systems*, 8(9), September 1997.
12. N. Nieuwejaar and D. Kotz. The Galley parallel file system. In *Proceedings of the 10th International Conference on Supercomputing*, pages 374–381, August 1996.
13. T. Anderson M. Dahlin J. Neefe D. Patterson D. Roselli R. Wang. Serverless network file systems. In *proc. of 15th ACM Symposium on Operating Systems Principles*, December 1995.

Optimal Scheduling of Aperiodic Jobs on Cluster

Ligang He, Hai Jin, Ying Chen, and Zongfen Han

Huazhong University of Science and Technology, Wuhan, 430074, China
hjin@hust.edu.cn

Abstract. This paper presents an algorithm to schedule aperiodic jobs on a cluster system. A cluster consists of one dispatcher and multiple schedulers. The algorithm is optimal for the response time of each aperiodic job. Aperiodic jobs are partitioned into phases and assigned deadlines by the dispatcher. With the deadline, the aperiodic jobs can be scheduled uniformly under EDF (Earliest Deadline First) together with periodic jobs. With rigorous theoretical analysis and proof, we have that even if the dispatcher has no scheduling information, the algorithm can still dispatch the aperiodic jobs onto the proper scheduler to achieve optimal response time and also guarantee the deadline requirements of periodic jobs.

1. Introduction

A cluster system [4] is a multiple stand-alone computers connected with high-speed network. Cluster system has gained its popularity due to its cost-effectiveness, scalability and high availability. The main topic of this paper is the mixed scheduling of periodic and aperiodic jobs in a cluster.

Many scheduling algorithms for periodic jobs [1][2][8][9] or aperiodic jobs [3][7][10][11][13] have been proposed. An optimal fixed priority scheduling algorithm and an optimal dynamic priority scheduling one for periodic jobs were presented in [9]. These algorithms have been extended to resolve more complicated problems, which is necessary to the actual system. A new scheduling approach for servicing soft aperiodic requests and hard periodic jobs was presented in [3]. The mixed job-scheduling problem has also been considered in some papers, such as the Deferrable Server[12], slack stealing policy[7] and Total Bandwidth Server[5].

Lehoczky et al. [7] presented an optimal algorithm for scheduling soft-aperiodic tasks in fixed-priority preemptive systems. The scheduler counts different time expenses in the scheduling to get the optimal assignment. For multicomputer, it is difficult for a node to have the detailed scheduling information on the other nodes. Although some periodic job scheduling algorithms on multiprocessor have been proposed in[2][6][9], but none of them considered the scheduling of aperiodic jobs.

Our algorithm proposed in this paper has two major contributions compared with [7]. It can schedule both aperiodic and periodic jobs on a cluster system simultaneously. The scheduling is based on EDF (Earliest Deadline First), not fixed-priority. The cluster system consists of one dispatch node, called dispatcher, and multiple schedule nodes, called schedulers. The dispatcher partitions the aperiodic job into some phases and assigns a reasonable deadline to each one. The schedulers schedule them using uniform policy according to the deadlines together with periodic jobs. Under the theoretical analysis and proof, we have that even if the dispatcher has no scheduling information, the algorithm can still dispatch the aperiodic jobs onto the proper scheduler node to achieve optimal response time for every aperiodic job under the condition of guaranteeing the deadline requirements of the periodic jobs.

2. System Modeling and Notation

A job set includes both periodic and aperiodic jobs. A periodic job J_i is denoted as (C_i, T_i), where C_i is the execution time of J_i, T_i is the constant interval at which J_i arrives. Both of them are known deterministic quantities. An arrival of a periodic job is called a job instance and the j-th arrival is called the j-th instance of the job, denoted as J_{ij}. The first instance of all periodic jobs arrives at time 0. For J_{ij}, it arrives at (j-1)*T_i and has to be complete before the time j* T_i, at which $J_{i,\,(j+1)}$ arrives. So J_{ij} has two parameters: R_{ij} (Ready-time of J_{ij}) and D_{ij} (Deadline of J_{ij}). R_{ij} equals (j-1)* T_i and D_{ij} equals j* T_i (We assume that a job instance is ready when it arrives).

An aperiodic job AJ is denoted as (R_i, C_i), where R_i is the arriving time of an aperiodic job AJ_i and C_i is its execution time. R_i is unknown beforehand.

In this paper, *w* time units of workload means *w* time units of work to be executed. All aperiodic jobs have no deadline requirements. We call an aperiodic workload in a given time period [a, b] is *full* if the aperiodic workload equals to the largest amount of time units that a processor can provide in [a, b] while keeping the deadline requirements of all periodic jobs. The response time of an aperiodic job is defined as the time at which the aperiodic job finishes. The optimal response time means the least one at which an aperiodic job finishes while keeping all periodic jobs schedulable.

We make following assumptions in our scheduling system:
- Compared to job execution time, the communication time between the dispatch node and the schedule nodes is ignored.
- All jobs can be instantly preempted under EDF (Earliest Deadline First).
- Any time in following analysis is the multiple of one time unit.

3. Dispatch of Aperiodic Jobs

The following functions are defined in [8]:

$S_i(t) = S_{ij, max}$ ($t_{ij-1, max} \leq t < t_{ij, max}$, $1 \leq i \leq n$, $j \geq 0$) $S(t) = min\{S_i(t) / 1 \leq i \leq n\}$

where $S_{ij,max}$ is the largest amount of time units that the processor can provide for aperiodic workload under the condition of guaranteeing the periodic job instance J_{ij} to meet its deadline. n is the number of periodic jobs. $t_{ij,max}$ is the finishing time of J_{ij} when $S_{ij,max}$ time units for the aperiodic workload is provided by a processor.

A jump point t_{ikjk} (k>0) is the finishing time of a job instance J_{ikjk}. We call ($t_{i0j0}, t_{i1j1}, t_{i2j2}, \cdots, t_{ikjk}, \cdots, t_{irjr}$) a jump point sequence in S(t). t_{i0j0} is set to be 0. The function S(t) represents the number of time units a processor can provide during the period [0, t_{ikjk}] (0<k≤r) for the aperiodic workload while keeping the periodic job set J = {$J_1, J_2, \ldots, J_i, \ldots, J_n$} still schedulable. The largest number of time units provided for aperiodic workload in [0, t_{ikjk}] equals to S(t_{ikjk} -1)

Figure 1 illustrates an example of a periodic job set J consisting of two periodic jobs, J_1 and J_2. The maximum time units J_1 and J_2 can provide for the aperiodic workload is $S_1(t)$ and $S_2(t)$. S(t) is constructed by getting the minimal value of $S_1(t)$ and $S_2(t)$, shown in Figure1.b. (4, 6, 9,...) is the jump point sequence in S(t).

Figure1.c shows the schedule of J_1, J_2 and an aperiodic job with 4 time units of workload arriving at time 0. We can see that the aperiodic workload is full in [0, 10]. If no aperiodic job arrives in [0, 5] and an aperiodic job with 3 time units of workload arrives at time 5, the schedule is shown in Figure1.d.

For the above example, we explain how to assign time units to aperiodic jobs arriving at random time t while keeping all periodic jobs meet their deadlines. We determine how many time units a processor can provide for the aperiodic jobs between 5 and the consequent jump points, that is, [5, 6], [5, 9],... S(5) and S(8) represent the time units a processor can provide for the aperiodic workload in [0, 6], [0, 9]. They are 3 and 4 respectively. Since there is no aperiodic workload in [0, 5], those time units for aperiodic workload are wasted. When we compute the time units for the aperiodic workload in [5, 6], we first deducted these wasted time units from S(5), whose result is 0. When the aperiodic workload is full, J_{22} is executed in [5, 6]. If there is no aperiodic workload in [0, 5], J_{22} is executed in [3, 4] in advance, shown in Figure1.d. So the time unit [5, 6] can be used for aperiodic workload. We add the value to the result gotten in the first step. Therefore the final number of time units for the aperiodic job in [5, 6] is 1.

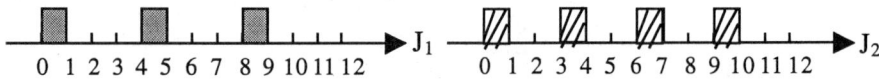

(a) Two periodic jobs J_1, J_2 with the period of 4 and 3, respectively

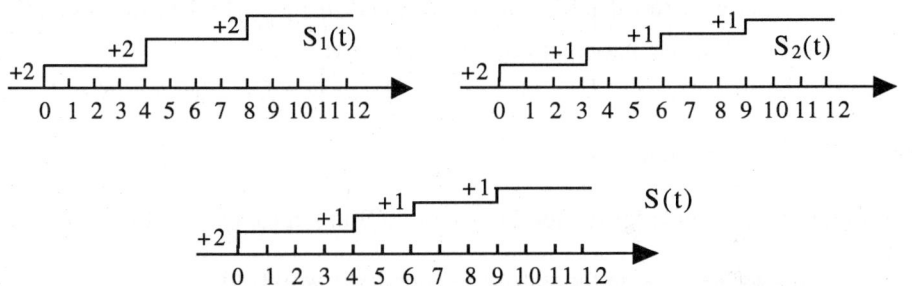

(b) The maximum time units for aperiodic workload provided by J_1, J_2, and J

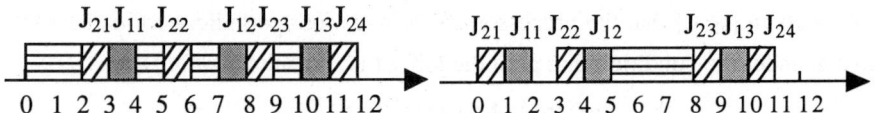

(c) Scheduling of J_1, J_2 and an aperiodic job with full workload

(d) Schedule of J_1, J_2 and an aperiodic job with 3 time units of workload arriving at time 5

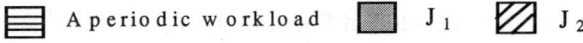

Fig. 1. An example of periodic job set J consisting of J_1 and J_2

Similarly, the time units for the aperiodic job in [5, 9] is S(8)-3+2=3. The remaining part of the paper finds the general methods to compute these two kinds of time units.

Let an aperiodic job arrive at t_0. Define $CJ(t_0)$ as a set of job instances arriving before t_0 with deadlines greater than t_0, $PJ(t_0)$ as a set of job instances must be finished before t_0 under EDF, whose deadlines are less than t_0.

$$CJ(t_0)=\{J_{ij} \mid R_{ij} <t_0<D_{ij}\} \qquad PJ(t_0)=\{J_{ij}\mid D_{ij} \leq t_0\} \qquad (1)$$

Others in all job instances will not execute in $[0, t_0]$, since their Ready-time are no less than t_0.

Let $I(t_0)$ be idle time units in $[0, t_0]$, $P(t_0)$ be total time units for those periodic job instances in $PJ(t_0)$, $L(t_0)$ be the total time units for the job instances in $CJ(t_0)$ in $[0, t_0]$.

$$P(t_0) = \sum_{i=1}^{n} \lfloor t_0/T_i \rfloor * C_i \qquad (2)$$

Let $t_1,\ldots, t_k, \ldots t_r$ be the jump points after t_0 in $S(t)$. t_1 is the nearest jump point to t_0. t_k is the finishing time of J_{ikjk}.

Define $CJ_k(t_0)$ as a set of job instances executed in $[t_{k-1}, t_k]$ when the aperiodic workload is full. The calculation of $CJ_k(t_0)$ is as follow:

$$CJ_k(t_0)=\{ J_{ij}|R_{ij} <t_0<D_{ij} \text{ and } (D_{i(k-1)j(k-1)} <D_{ij}< D_{ikjk} \text{ or } D_{ij}= D_{ikjk}, \text{ but } R_{ij}< R_{ikjk})\} \qquad (3)$$

where, D_{ikjk} is the deadline of J_{ikjk}.

$L_k(t_0)$ is the time units for the job instances in $CJ_k(t_0)$ in $[0, t_0]$. $L_1^f (t_0)$ is the time units for the jobs in $CJ_1(t_0)$ in the state of *full* aperiodic workload.

Theorem 3.1 Let the periodic job set J schedulable and aperiodic jobs with total workload of A have been finished in $[0, t_0]$. $S(t_0, t_k)$ is denoted as the largest amount of time units in $[t_0, t_k]$ that the processor can provide for aperiodic workload arriving at time t_0 under the condition that periodic job set is still schedulable. Then,

$$S(t_0, t_k)=S(t_k-1)-I(t_0)-L(t_0)-A+\sum_{j=1}^{k} L_j(t_0) \qquad (4)$$

(The proofs of all theorems in this paper are omitted due to space imitation.)

Since the deadlines of job instances in $CJ(t_0)$ are less than those in $PJ(t_0)$, they can only occupy the time units left in $PJ(t_0)$. In order to compute the finished work in $[0, t_0]$, we need to know how many time units left by the job instances in $PJ(t_0)$.

Theorem 3.2 Let $I_P(t_0)$ be the total idle time units in $[0, t_0]$ left after executing the job instances in $PJ(t_0)$ in the case of no aperiodic jobs in $[0, t_0]$. If aperiodic jobs with total workload of A time units are complete in [0, t_0], then the remaining idle time units are $I_P(t_0)-A$.

Let the k-th aperiodic job arrive at time t_0. a_i and f_i are the arriving and finishing time of the i-th aperiodic job AJ_i, respectively($i<k$). A_i is the execution time of the i-th aperiodic job. If a job instance in $CJ(t_0)$ finishes part of its work before [0, a_{k-1}], it has been computed when the former k-1 aperiodic jobs arrive. So we only need to compute how much workload of job instances in $CJ(t_0)$ should be done in [f_{k-1}, t_0].

Theorem 3.3 Let $I_{P,A}^{t}(a,b)$ be the total idle time units in [a, b] ($0 \leq a, b \leq t$), which are left after executing both job instances in PJ(t) and aperiodic jobs. Let the k-th aperiodic job arrive at time t_0, then

$$I_{P,A}^{t0}(f_{k-1},t_0) = I_P(t_0) - \sum_{i=1}^{k-1} A_i - \sum_{i=1}^{k-1} I_{P,A}^{t0}(f_{i-1},a_i) \quad (5)$$

For $0 \leq a, b \leq t_0$, let I(a, b) be the idle time units in [a, b] left after executing the aperiodic and periodic jobs, L(a, b) be the sum of finished work of job instances in $CJ(t_0)$ in [a, b], then

$$I_{P,A}^{t0}(f_{i-1},a_i) = I(f_{i-1},a_i) + L(f_{i-1},a_i) \quad (6)$$

Besides the amount of time units in [f_{k-1}, t_0], we need to know the distribution of these time units to compute workload of job instances in $CJ(t_0)$ finished in [f_{k-1}, t_0].

Theorem 3.4 Let $I_P^{t0}(a,b)$ be the idle time units in [a, b] ($0 \leq a, b \leq t_0$), which are left after executing the job instances in $PJ(t_0)$ when there are no aperiodic jobs. Let an aperiodic job finishes at time f, then $\exists t_s \in [f, t_0]$, such that:

1> there is no idle time unit in [f, t_s],

2> the idle time units in [t_s, t_0] equals to $I_P^{t0}(f,t_0)$,

3> the distribution of these idle time units in [t_s, t_0] is the same as that in the case of no aperiodic job,

4> Let the aperiodic job be the k-th aperiodic job. t_s can be determined by:

$$I_P(t_0) - I_P^{t0}(0,t_s) = I_{P,A}^{t0}(f_{k-1},t_0) \quad (7)$$

In order to get the value of t_s by using Equ.(7), we first compute the value of $I_{P,A}^{t0}(f_{k-1},t_0)$ by using Equ.(5), and then get such a time point by binary searching in the time period of [f_{k-1}, t_0] as to satisfy Equ(7). The time point is t_s. As $I_P(t)$ is the function of idle time units left by the job instances in $PJ(t_0)$, which can be computed off-line, $I_p^{t_0}(a,b)$ ($0 \le a$, $b \le t_0$) is also available. Now, we can compute the workload of job instances in job instance set $CJ(t_0)$ finished in period of $[t_s, t_0]$. It is based on the idea that in $[a, b]$, if the job instance with higher priority hasn't finished, one with lower priority can't start to execute. At any time t, all job instances in $CJ(t)$ can be ordered by their deadlines off-line.

The following algorithm partitions an aperiodic workload into phases, designates proper deadline to each phase and determinates the response time of the aperiodic workload.

Algorithm Partition the aperiodic job AJ, which is the k-th one arriving at t_0.

1. get all job instances in $CJ(t_0)$ and determine t_s using Equ.(5) and Equ.(7);
2. for each job instance in $CJ(t_0)$, compute the amount of finished workload in $[t_s, t_0]$ and $\bigcup_{i=1}^{k-1}[f_{i-1}, a_i]$
3. assign a-remain = a; $k = 1$;
4. while (a-remain>0) { k++;
   a) get t_k in the function $S(t)$;
   b) compute the sum of finished work, which is $\sum_{j=1}^{k} L_j(t_0)$, of job instances in $\bigcup_{j=1}^{k} CJ_j$ in $[t_s, t_0]$;
   c) compute $S(t_0, t_k)$ according to Equ. (4);
   d) if (a-remain>$S(t_0, t_k)$−$S(t_0, t_{k-1})$) {
      i.   set the aperiodic workload of $S(t_0, t_k)$−$S(t_0, t_{k-1})$ as a phase and designate t_{k-1}+ $S(t_0, t_k)$−$S(t_0, t_{k-1})$ as its deadline;
      ii. a-remain = a-remain− $(S(t_0, t_k)$−$S(t_0, t_{k-1}))$}
   e) else {
      i.   set the aperiodic workload of a-remain as a phase and designate t_{k-1}+a-remain as its deadline;
      ii. the response time of the aperiodic job AJ is t_{k-1}+a-remain}}
6. compute $I(f_{k-1}, t_0)$ using Equ. (6)

Theorem 3.5 Let J be a periodic job set and J is schedulable. AJ is an aperiodic job arriving at time t_0. If AJ is partitioned according to the above algorithm, then J is still schedulable and the response time of AJ is optimal for the periodic job set.

Under EDF, the sufficient and necessary condition to have a periodic job set schedulable is that for any m periodic jobs in single processor, $\sum_{i=1}^{m} C_i/T_i \leq 1$ [8]. In our algorithm, the dispatcher dispatches a periodic job set by assigning every periodic job to a schedule with minimal $\sum C_i/T_i$.

Since the parameters of periodic jobs are known beforehand, we can take advantage of off-line operations to partition the periodic job set and construct the functions $S(t)$ and $I_P(t)$ for the periodic job set on each schedule node. The dispatcher uses Algorithm 3.2 on-line for each schedule when an aperiodic job arrives. By running Algorithm 3.2, the dispatcher determines the schedule node that can provide the optimal response time for an aperiodic job. The dispatcher then assigns the job and deadlines of all phases to that node. The schedulers in the schedule nodes schedule the aperiodic and periodic job uniformly as EDF.

Theorem 3.5 specifies the feasibility of partitioning an aperiodic job according to the above algorithm, and proves the response time of the aperiodic job is optimal.

4. Conclusions

In this paper, we present an algorithm to dispatch and schedule aperiodic jobs in a cluster system while keeping the schedulability of periodic job set. For an aperiodic job arriving at random time, the dispatcher partitions it into multiple phases and assigns proper deadline to each phase by the current workload on each schedule node. By running algorithm proposed in this paper, the dispatcher determines the schedule node that can provide the optimal response time for the aperiodic job. The dispatcher then assigns the job and its deadlines of all phases to that node. The schedulers schedule the aperiodic and periodic jobs uniformly by EDF.

References

[1] T. P. Baker, "Stack-Based Scheduling of Real-Time Processes", *The Journal of Real-Time System*, 3(1), 1991, pp.67-100.

[2] A. Burchard, J. Liebeherr, Y. Oh, and S. H. Son, "New Strategies for Assigning Real-time Tasks to Multiprocessor Systems", *IEEE Trans. on Computers*, 44(12): 1429-1442, 1995.

[3] G. C. Buttazzo and F. Sensini, "Optimal Deadline Assignment for Scheduling Soft Aperiodic Tasks in Hard Real-time Environment", *Proc. of the 3rd IEEE International Conference on Engineering of Complex Computer Systems*, September 1997, pp.39-48.

[4] R. Buyya (Ed.), *High Performance Cluster Computing*, Prentice Hall, 1999.

[5] M. Caccamo, G. Lipari, and G. Buttazzo, "Sharing Resources with the TB* Server", *Technical Report TR 04-99, Retis Lab*, Scuola Superiore S.Anna, April 1999.

[6] M. Colajanni, P. S. Yu, and D. M. Dias, "Scheduling Algorithms for Distributed Web Servers," *Proceedings of ICDCS'97*, 1997.

[7] J. P. Lehoczky and S. Ramos-Thuel, "An Optimal Algorithm for Scheduling Soft-Aperiodic Tasks in Fixed-Priority Preemptive Systems", *Proc. of Real-Time Systems Symposium*, 1992, pp.110-123.

[8] C. L. Liu and J. W. Layland, "Scheduling Algorithms for Multiprogramming in a Hard-Real-Time Environment", *JACM*, 20(1): 46-61, 1973.

[9] Y. Oh and S. Son, "Allocating Fixed-Priority Periodic Tasks on Multiprocessor Systems", *The Real-Time Systems Journal*, 9:207-239, 1995.

[10] M. Spuri and G. C. Buttazzo, "Efficient Aperiodic Service under Earliest Deadline Scheduling", *Proc. of the IEEE Real-Time Systems Symposium*, December 1994.

[11] M. Spuri and G. C. Buttazzo, "Scheduling Aperiodic Tasks in Dynamic Priority Systems", *The Journal of Real-Time Systems*, 10(2), 1996.

[12] J. K. Strosnider, J. P. Lehoczky, and L. Sha, "The Deferrable Server Algorithm for Enhanced Aperiodic Responsiveness in Hard Real-Time Environments," *IEEE Transactions on Computers*, 44(1), January 1995.

[13] T. S. Tia, J. W. S. Liu, and M. Shankar, "Algorithm and Optimality of Scheduling Aperiodic Requests in Fixed-Priority Preemptive Systems", *The Journal of Real-Time Systems*, 1995.

HMM: A Cluster Membership Service*

Francesc D. Muñoz-Escoí, Óscar Gomis, Pablo Galdámez, and José M. Bernabéu-Aubán

Instituto Tecnológico de Informática, Universidad Politécnica de Valencia
Camino de Vera, s/n, 46071 Valencia, Spain
{fmunyoz,ogomis,pgaldam,josep}@iti.upv.es

Abstract. The *Hidra Membership Monitor* (HMM) is a distributed service that maintains the current set of active nodes in a cluster of machines. This protocol allows the detection of multiple machine joins or failures in a unique reconfiguration, using a low amount of messages (with a cost that is linear on the number of nodes). These membership services are needed to detect cluster changes as soon as possible, initiating then the reconfiguration of the cluster state, where support for replicated objects has been included.
The HMM also manages and synchronises the reconfiguration steps needed by the kernel and Hidra components of each node, ensuring that all of them take the same steps at once. Thus, our system does not need an atomic multicast protocol to deliver the messages in these reconfiguration steps. All these services provide the basis to develop reliable intracluster transport protocols and to reduce the reconfiguration time of replicated objects and services.

1 Introduction

Hidra [3,8] is an architecture that provides high availability support in a distributed environment based on a cluster of machines interconnected by a private network. This architecture uses a low-level ORB [9] placed in the kernel of each node which includes the support needed for replicated objects. Thus, replicated objects can be used either in user-level applications or in kernel components needed to provide a single-system image.

Our ORB is not completely CORBA-compliant, since it extends some of the support that such an ORB must provide. Particularly, support for replicated objects and reference counting has not been considered in CORBA as a service of the ORB core, but they have been included in ours [6,4]. Both reference counting and replication support need a membership service to know which are the current active machines in the cluster and to reconfigure their state when a new machine joins or a previously active node fails.

In general, a distributed system with high availability support needs a membership service. This service must be placed in the lowest layers of the system

---

* This work was partially supported by the CICYT (Comisión Interministerial de Ciencia y Tecnología) under project TIC99-0280-C02.

architecture to assist in the development of other fault tolerant services, and to drive the reconfiguration protocols of these components, either in case of failures or in case of new machines joining the system.

In our Hidra architecture, the reconfiguration protocols that must be executed when a node fails or joins the cluster, need be synchronised, i.e., a reconfiguration step has to be started only when all the active nodes have concluded its previous step. Thus, the reconfiguration protocols know that the results of other previous protocols are ready in all system nodes. This characteristic has been used to recompute the reference counts of the ORB, which needs several reconfiguration steps, and the state of the main serialiser object [7], whose reconfiguration must be done afterwards.

HMM provides this kind of synchronisation in its *Steps* stage. Thus, our protocol manages in parallel the notification steps, their sinchronisation and the periodic interchange of messages among live nodes. As a result, only a few messages are needed to develop all these tasks.

The rest of the paper is structured as follows. Section 2 describes the system model. Section 3 describes the entire protocol. Section 4 compares HMM with other membership protocols and, finally, Sect. 5 provides the conclusions.

2 System Model

HMM is aimed to provide membership monitoring in a dynamic cluster with a preconfigured maximum number of machines interconnected by a private network. This scope determines the behaviour of the system and the assumptions made by our protocol. Thus, cluster nodes have static identifiers, but these identifiers are complemented with a node sequence number that is increased each time the node is restarted and allows us to use a fail-stop failure mode (since each time a node is restarted, it joins the cluster with a different identifier).

No clock synchronisation is needed, but a maximum message delivery time must exist. This allows us to decide when a message is lost, either due to a network failure, a sender failure or lack of available buffers to receive it.

We also assume that the private network being used presents a kind of interconnection that prevents the appearance of network partitions. This assumption is valid for a small cluster and some network topologies.

HMM uses the services of an unreliable transport layer which is assumed to provide broadcast, multicast and point-to-point transmissions. It does not check the delivery of such messages nor waits for any acknowledgement.

On top of the HMM, our ORB core uses the HMM notification services. To this end, the HMM object provides a set of operations in its interface that allow the registration of any Hidra component that wants to be notified when a given reconfiguration sequence step number has been initiated. These steps constitute the core of the ORB and associated components reconfiguration tasks and are driven by the HMM.

3 Protocol

HMM has to deal with either unique or multiple joins and failures in a single reconfiguration of the cluster membership. This objective has been attained with a sequence of stages (see Fig. 1) that manage the detection of a membership change and its reconfiguration steps. Moreover, cluster nodes have a role that can change in each stage.

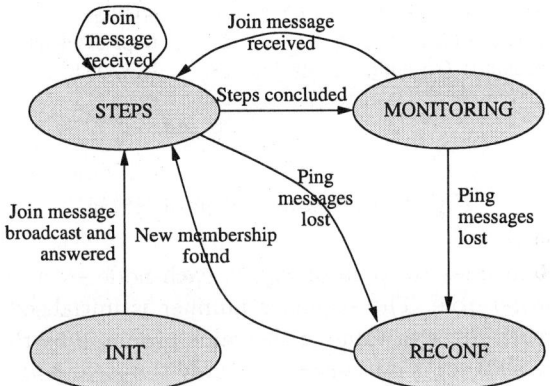

Fig. 1. HMM stages and transitions

3.1 Member Roles

A node that uses the HMM may play one of the following roles:

- *Master.* The basic role of the *master* node is to drive the reconfiguration steps and to accept join messages when new members arrive.
- *Slave.* Once a stable membership set has been found and the first step in the *Steps* stage has been started, the *slaves* must receive the *master*'s messages, notify the registered packages about them and reply to the master.
- *Beginner.* This role applies to the node that detects a given number of ping message losses. Once this situation arises, the sender of these messages is assumed faulty, and the *beginner* node enters the *Reconf* stage.
- *Unknown.* When the *Reconf* stage is entered, all members that are not *beginners* are marked as *unknown*.

3.2 Algorithm

The main algorithm is implemented as an automaton that uses the global variables shown in lines 8 to 14 of Fig. 2. There are several timers not shown in the algorithm. They detect missed step, ends and endp messages. Thus, the sender of the missed message can send it again.

```
1: algorithm hmm;                                  16:    stage := INIT;
2: type                                            17:    masterid := thisid;
3:   stage_t = ( INIT, STEPS,                      18:    seqnum := -1;
4:             MONITORING, RECONF );               19:    step := 0;
5:   role_t = ( MASTER, SLAVE,                     20:    while true do
6:             BEGINNER, UNKNOWN );                21:      case stage of
7: var                                             22:        INIT:         set := emptySet;
8:   stage : stage_t;   (* Current stage. *)       23:                      addMember( set, thisid );
9:   thisid : node_t;   (* Local node ID. *)       24:                      role := MASTER;
10:  step : integer;    (* Step number. *)         25:                      stInit;
11:  masterid : node_t; (* Current master ID. *)   26:        STEPS:                    stSteps;
12:  set : nodeset_t;   (* Membership. *)          27:        MONITORING:               stMonitoring;
13:  seqnum : seqnum_t; (* Config number. *)       28:        RECONF:                   stReconf;
14:  role : role_t;     (* Role of this node. *)   29:      esac;
15: begin                                          30: end;
```

Fig. 2. Main automaton of HMM

As we can see in lines 16 to 25 of Fig. 2, each node starts in the *Init* stage and plays the *master* role. The sequence number is initialised to -1 to ensure that it will start with the zero value or the value proposed by the elected *master* node. The membership set is initialised with only the local node. Once this node joins the cluster, it receives the complete membership set.

```
1: algorithm stInit;                       17:      stage := STEPS;
2: var                                     18:      requeueMessage;
3:   theMsg : msg; elapsed : boolean;      19:      elapsed := TRUE;
4: begin                                   20:    end else if theMsg.kind = JOIN
5:   elapsed := FALSE;                     21:    then if theMsg.sender ≠ thisid
6:   theMsg.kind = JOIN;                   22:      then begin
7:   bcast( theMsg );                      23:        stage := STEPS;
8:   installTimer( joinTime );             24:        addMember(set, theMsg.sender);
9:   while not elapsed do begin            25:      end else begin
10:    waitFor event;                      26:        stage := INIT;
11:    case event of                       27:        elapsed := TRUE;
12:    recv( theMsg ):                     28:      end;
13:      if theMsg.kind = NEWMEM           29:    joinTimeout: elapsed := TRUE;
14:      then begin                        30:    esac;
15:        role := SLAVE;                  31:  end;
16:        masterid := theMsg.sender;      32: end;
```

Fig. 3. Algorithm of the *Init* stage

All the protocol stages are described in the following paragraphs.

Init Stage: Figure 3 shows the *Init* stage. The local node builds a join message and broadcasts it (lines 6 and 7). Later, it installs a timer (line 8) that raises a timeout when joinTime has elapsed.

An event is later expected. It can be the reception of a message (line 12) or the timeout signal (line 29). In the first case, HMM checks if the join message has been answered by a *master* node using a newmem message. If so, the role is changed to *slave* and the stage is changed to *Steps* where this message will be processed (lines 15 to 19).

If a join message is received in this stage, the sender static identifier is checked. If it is greater than the local identifier, the sender is added to the current membership set (lines 23 to 24) and the stage is marked as *Steps*, but no transition is made until the join timeout is signaled. Thus, multiple nodes can be added simultaneously when all nodes are powered on at once. If the sender identifier is lower than the local one, this stage is reinitiated immediately.

Steps Stage: The algorithm of the *Steps* stage appears in Fig. 4. Once a node has entered this stage, it enables the sending and reception of ping messages in line 5. In this and the *Monitoring* stages the nodes are arranged in a logical ring, using an increasing order of their static node identifiers. Thus, each node periodically sends a ping message to its neighbour with greater static identifier, except for the last node of the ring, which sends it to the first node in this order.

Lines 7 to 39 contain the code that has to be executed by the *master* node. In each one of the steps, the master has to send a message to all current members. This task is done using the multicast procedure provided by the unreliable transport. Lines 8 to 18 give the message contents, depending on the step being processed. When step 0 is initiated, the cluster sequence number is increased.

The notifyStep in line 19 is a procedure that invokes all registered Hidra components that are interested in the current step number.

Once all these tasks have been completed, the *master* waits for an event (line 20). If all members have answered with ends or endp messages, the allAnswersReceived case is taken. If so, the step number is increased and the *Steps* stage is entered again. When all members have sent their final endp message (line 24), the *Steps* stage is left and the *Monitoring* stage is entered. If a join message is received, its sender is added to the membership set, and the step number is reset to zero. As a result, the *Steps* stage is reinitiated. When some ping messages have been lost, a pingTimeout arises (lines 31 to 34), the role is changed to *beginner* and the stage becomes a *Reconf*. Finally, when some change message arrives, the role is changed to *unknown* and the stage to *Reconf* (lines 35 to 38).

On the other hand, if the node has a *slave* role, its tasks are shown in lines 41 to 67 of Fig. 4. To begin with, once it has entered this stage it waits immediately for an event. The usual case is the reception of a message, either a newmem (lines 43 to 48) or a step one (lines 49 to 52). In both cases, the registered clients are informed about the beginning of the step, using the notifyStep procedure described above. Once this has concluded, an answer is returned to the *master* node. Finally, the step is increased in both cases. If the received message was a

```
 1: algorithm stSteps;
 2: var
 3:    theMsg : msg;
 4: begin
 5:    enablePings;
 6:    if role = MASTER
 7:    then begin
 8:       if step = 0
 9:       then begin
10:          theMsg.kind = NEWMEM;
11:          theMsg.contents = set;
12:          seqnum := seqnum + 1;
13:       end else begin
14:          theMsg.kind = STEP;
15:          theMsg.contents = step;
16:       end;
17:       theMsg.seqnum = seqnum;
18:       multicast( theMsg );
19:       notifyStep;
20:       waitFor event;
21:       case event of
22:       allAnswersReceived:
23:          step := step + 1;
24:       allStepsConcluded:
25:          step := 0;
26:          stage := MONITORING;
27:       joinReceived:
28:          addMember( set,
29:             sender );
30:          step := 0;
31:       pingTimeout:
32:          step := 0;
33:          role := BEGINNER;
34:          stage := RECONF;
35:       changeReceived:
36:          step := 0;
37:          role := UNKNOWN;
38:          stage := RECONF;
39:       end;
40:    end else begin (* Role is SLAVE. *)
41:       waitFor event;
42:       case event of
43:       newmemReceived:
44:          setMembership( receivedMsg,
45:             set, seqnum );
46:          notifyStep;
47:          sendEndsOrEndp;
48:          step := step + 1;
49:       stepReceived:
50:          notifyStep;
51:          sendEndsOrEndp;
52:          step := step + 1;
53:       joinReceived:(* Ignore JOINs *);
54:       pingTimeout:
55:          step := 0;
56:          role := BEGINNER;
57:          stage := RECONF;
58:       changeReceived:
59:          step := 0;
60:          role := UNKNOWN;
61:          stage := RECONF;
62:       end;
63:       if stepsConcluded then begin
64:          step := 0;
65:          stage := MONITORING;
66:       end;
67:    end;
68: end;
```

Fig. 4. Algorithm of the *Steps* stage

newmem one, the membership set and the configuration number of the node are updated according to the message contents.

Another possibility is the reception of a join message, but this type of message cannot be managed by a *slave* node and it is ignored. The last two cases are managed the same way as the *master* node did.

Monitoring Stage: This stage is shown in Fig. 5. Take into account that the procedure enablePings shown at the *Steps* stage, created a thread that periodically sends ping messages to its neighbour. This thread still runs in this stage.

In lines 3 to 24 there is a loop that only terminates when the stage is changed. In this loop an event is waited for. Lines 7 to 9 deal with a newmem message, leading to the *Steps* stage where this message will be processed. Lines 10 to 12 process a ping timeout, i.e., when several ping messages have been lost. In

```
 1: algorithm stMonitoring;           14:      if role = MASTER
 2: begin                             15:      then begin
 3:   while stage = MONITORING do     16:         addMember( set,
 4:   begin                           17:                    sender );
 5:     waitFor event;                18:         stage := STEPS;
 6:     case event of                 19:      end;
 7:     newmemReceived:                20:    changeReceived:
 8:       stage := STEPS;             21:      step := 0;
 9:       requeueMessage;             22:      role := UNKNOWN;
10:     pingTimeout:                  23:      stage := RECONF;
11:       role := BEGINNER;           24:    esac;
12:       stage := RECONF;            25:  end;
13:     joinReceived:                 26: end;
```

Fig. 5. Algorithm of the *Monitoring* stage

that case, the stage is changed to *Reconf* and the role of the detector becomes *beginner*. On the other hand, lines 13 to 19 maintain the actions to be taken when a join message is received. If the receiver node is the *master*, it adds the new node to the membership set, and changes the stage to *Steps*, otherwise the message has to be ignored. Finally, when a change message is received (lines 20 to 23), the behaviour is the same shown in the previous stage.

Reconf Stage: Figure 6 shows the *Reconf* stage. While the nodes are in this stage, ping messages are not sent nor expected. To this end, the disablePings procedure is used in line 3.

The rest of the code depends on the role the local node plays. If it is a *beginner*, it executes the instructions in lines 6 to 29, otherwise, it executes that contained in lines 31 to 47. Note that several simultaneous failures may arise, and several *beginners* may exist.

In case of a *beginner* node, it starts broadcasting a change message (line 7). Next, the local node is added to the membership set and a reconfiguration timer is set in line 9. When this time expires, all nodes that have replied with an alive message form the next membership set. Later, an event is waited for. Thus, if an alive message is received, its sender is included in the membership set being built; if a change message is received, an alive message is replied to its sender. This answer is needed because several simultaneous failures may arise, and all *beginners* must behave as the rest of the nodes when a change message arrives. When the reconfiguration timer is out, a new master is chosen among all live nodes using the getMaster function, (line 18) and a setmem message is sent to it. Finally, if a setmem message is received the node becomes *master* or if the message is a newmem one, it becomes *slave* and in both cases a transition is initiated to the *Steps* stage. These messages are generated by other *beginner* nodes that have concluded this stage of the protocol before the local one. Additionally, if a setmem message has been received, its message contents are used to build the new membership set.

```
 1: algorithm stReconf;                         25:       role := SLAVE;
 2: begin                                       26:       stage := STEPS;
 3:   disablePings;                             27:       requeueMessage;
 4:   set := emptySet;                          28:     esac;
 5:   if role = BEGINNER                        29:   until stage     RECONF;
 6:   then begin                                30: end else begin
 7:     broadcastChange;                        31:   replyAlive;
 8:     addMember( set, thisid );               32:   repeat
 9:     installTimer( reconfTime );             33:     waitFor event;
10:     repeat                                  34:     case event of
11:       waitFor event;                        35:       changeReceived:
12:       case event of                         36:         replyAlive;
13:         aliveReceived:                      37:       setmemReceived:
14:           addMember( set, sender );         38:         role := MASTER;
15:         changeReceived:                     39:         stage := STEPS;
16:           replyAlive;                       40:         setMembers(set, msgContents);
17:         reconfTimeout:                      41:       newmemReceived:
18:           masterid := getMaster( set );     42:         role := SLAVE;
19:           send( masterid, setmemMsg );      43:         stage := STEPS;
20:         setmemReceived:                     44:         requeueMessage;
21:           role := MASTER;                   45:     esac;
22:           stage := STEPS;                   46:   until stage     RECONF;
23:           setMembers(set, msgContents);     47: end;
24:         newmemReceived:                     48: end;
```

Fig. 6. Algorithm of the *Reconf* stage

On the other hand, if the node plays the *unknown* role, it replies immediately to its known *beginner* and later it waits for a message. Several messages are accepted in this case, but they are treated as they had been in the other role.

4 Related Work

In [2] three membership algorithms are described and an environment with bound delivery time is assumed. Its members are machines and no network partition management is considered, as in our algorithm. However, it assumes atomic multicasts that require an additional –and costly– protocol to implement them. Its first algorithm is called *periodic broadcast*. In it, each member broadcasts periodically a message indicating that it is present and that it belongs to the group. To join a group, the new node has to broadcast a different message. It is also able to detect multiple failures and joins, but requires a lot of messages to do so.

The second and third algorithms of [2] are quite similar and we only describe the third one (*neighbour surveillance*). It reduces the amount of messages needed to check the stability of the membership set. The members are arranged in a logical ring and they only send a message to one of their neighbours. However, when a failure is detected all live members have to initiate a round of atomic broadcasts to rebuild the set. Our algorithm requires a lower amount of messages to do so. Like our algorithm, these protocols are able to detect multiple joins and failures.

In [5], a redundant broadcast channel interconnects all cluster nodes. It is in a real-time system, and a *time-division multiple-access* (TDMA) schema is used to gain access to the network. So, each node has an access period (or sending slot) to the network in each TDMA round. In this environment, a node is considered faulty if it has not sent anything in a given number of TDMA rounds, and all nodes are aware of that fault. When a node restarts, it joins the cluster simply sending a message in its sending slot for the current TDMA round (but it has to wait until that sending slot arrives). Its main disadvantage is that it requires that all nodes share the same clock or that they have highly synchronised clocks. This requirement is not needed by our algorithm and it is difficult to achieve in general-purpose systems. As an advantage, multiple failures and joins are detected immediately without any extra messages.

In the *strong group membership protocol* of [10], a solution quite close to ours is described. It uses a similar algorithm to join a new member and a logical ring with a master once the membership set is stable. Once the ring is built, a member sends heart-beat messages to its both neighbours. However, in case of failure, the master is searched for initiating the reconfiguration. Their solution does not work with multiple failures, since they depend on its master or in a submaster, but if both fail, all nodes have to be restarted and they have to initiate again all the protocol. They also use a two-phase commit protocol to commit the changes, driven by the master. This solution requires more messages than ours in case of join detection and in case of multiple failures or joins.

The following table summarises the worst-case costs (expressed in transmitted messages) of several membership algorithms, assuming that no broadcast service is available and that the number of nodes in the cluster is "N". The "join" and "failure" columns describe the amount of messages needed when a join or failure arises, respectively. The last column gives how many messages are needed in each of the monitoring rounds.

Protocol	Amount of messages		
	Join	Failure	Monitoring
Periodic broadcast [2]	$N^2 - N$	$N^2 - N$	$N^2 - N$
Neighbour surveillance [2]	$N^2 - N$	$N^2 - N$	N
Delta-4 [12]	$4N - 4$	$4N - 4$	$2N - 2$
Totem [1]	$2N^2 + 2N$	$6N$	N
Strong [10]	$3N - 2$	$3N - 2$	$2N$
Isis [11]	$3N - 2$	$5N - 5$	unknown
TTP [5]	$N^2 - N$	$N^2 - N$	N
HMM	$2N - 1$	$4N - 2$	N

5 Conclusions

We have presented a membership protocol for a multi-computer cluster with machine granularity, integrated failure detectors, management of step-synchronous reconfiguration protocols and a low amount of messages needed to accomplish its tasks. It does not need clock synchronisation among the nodes that participate in the protocol, although the distributed system where it runs cannot be considered totally asynchronous.

References

1. Y. Amir, L. E. Moser, P. M. Melliar-Smith, D. A. Agarwal, and P. Ciarfella. Fast message ordering and membership using a logical token-passing ring. In *Proc. of the 13th International Conference on Distributed Computing Systems*, pages 551–560, Pittsburgh, PA, EE.UU., May 1993. IEEE-CS Press.
2. F. Cristian. Reaching agreement on processor-group membership in synchronous distributed systems. *Distributed Computing*, 6(4):175–187, 1991.
3. P. Galdámez, F. D. Muñoz-Escoí, and J. M. Bernabéu-Aubán. High availability support in CORBA environments. In F. Plášil and K. G. Jeffery, editors, *24th Seminar on Current Trends in Theory and Practice of Informatics, Milovy, Czech Republic*, volume 1338 of *LNCS*, pages 407–414. Springer Verlag, November 1997.
4. P. Galdámez, F. D. Muñoz-Escoí, and J. M. Bernabéu-Aubán. Garbage collection for mobile and replicated objects. In J. Pavelka, G. Tel, and M. Bartosek, editors, *26th Seminar on Current Trends in Theory and Practice of Informatics, Milovy, Czech Republic*, volume 1725 of *LNCS*, pages 373–380. Springer Verlag, November 1999.
5. H. Kopetz and G. Grünsteidl. TTP - A protocol for fault-tolerant real-time systems. *IEEE Computer*, pages 14–23, January 1994.
6. F. D. Muñoz-Escoí, P. Galdámez, and J. M. Bernabéu-Aubán. ROI: An invocation mechanism for replicated objects. In *Proc. of the 17th IEEE Symposium on Reliable Distributed Systems, Purdue Univ., West Lafayette, IN, USA*, pages 29–35, October 1998.
7. F. D. Muñoz-Escoí, P. Galdámez, and J. M. Bernabéu-Aubán. A synchronisation mechanism for replicated objects. In B. Rovan, editor, *Proc. of the 25th Conference on Current Trends in Theory and Practice of Informatics, Jasná, Slovakia*, volume 1521 of *LNCS*, pages 389–398. Springer Verlag, November 1998.
8. F. D. Muñoz-Escoí, P. Galdámez, and J. M. Bernabéu-Aubán. The NanOS cluster operating system. In R. Buyya, editor, *High Performance Cluster Computing*, volume 1, chapter 29, pages 682–702. Prentice-Hall PTR, Upper Saddle River, NJ, USA, 1999.
9. OMG. *The Common Object Request Broker: Architecture and Specification*. Object Management Group, July 1999. Revision 2.3.
10. R. Rajkumar, S. Fakhouri, and F. Jahanian. Processor group membership protocols: Specification, design and implementation. In *Proc. of the 12th IEEE Symposium on Reliable Distributed Systems, Princeton, NJ*, pages 2–11, October 1993.
11. A. Ricciardi and K. P. Birman. Consistent process membership in asynchronous environments. In K. P. Birman and R. van Renesse, editors, *Reliable Distributed Computing with the Isis Toolkit*, chapter 13, pages 237–262. IEEE Computer Society Press, Los Alamitos, CA, USA, 1994.
12. L. Rodrigues, P. Veríssimo, and J. Rufino. A low-level processor group membership protocol for LANs. In *Proc. of the 13th International Conference on Distributed Computing Systems*, pages 541–550, May 1993.

Dynamic Processor Allocation in Large Mesh-Connected Multicomputers*

César A. F. De Rose[1] and Hans-Ulrich Heiss[2]

[1] Catholic University of Rio Grande do Sul, Computer Science Department
90619-900 Porto Alegre, Brazil
derose@inf.pucrs.br
[2] University of Paderborn, Department of Computer Science
33098 Paderborn, Germany
heiss@upd.de

Abstract. Current processor allocation techniques for highly parallel systems are based on centralized front-end based algorithms. As a result, the applied strategies are restricted to static allocation, low parallelism and weak fault tolerance. To lift these restrictions we are investigating a distributed approach to the processor allocation problem in large mesh-connected multicomputers. A noncontiguous version of a distributed dynamic processor allocation strategy is proposed and studied in this paper as an alternative for parallel programming models that allow dynamic creation and deletion of tasks. Simulations compare the performance of the proposed dynamic strategy with the static counterpart and also with well-known centralized algorithms in such an environment with growing and shrinking processor demands. We also present the results of experiments on a Siemens hpcLine Primergy Server with 96 nodes that show dynamic allocation is feasible with current technologies.

1 Introduction

Parallel machines with distributed memory, such as massively parallel processing systems (MPP) or cluster computers are called *multicomputers*. Their processing nodes consist of a processor and private memory and are connected by some kind of network to exchange messages. Despite some specific applications where a program is running permanently on a dedicated machine, it is almost inevitable in large systems with hundreds or thousands of nodes, to allow *multiprogramming*, i.e. many parallel programs share the machine in space in order to achieve high machine utilization. We assume that upon arrival, each program requests a specific number of processing nodes. Such a request is usually satisfied by allocating a sufficiently large *partition* of the processors to the program. *Processor allocation* involves the selection of a partition for a given parallel job, with the goal of maximizing throughput over a stream of many jobs. A resource management scheme for processor allocation has to meet several partly contradicting goals:

---

* This research was supported in part by HP-Brazil and Fapergs.

High utilization It should maximize the utilization of the resources, i.e. it has to avoid any kind of fragmentation so that all processors can be used.

Appropriate shapes It should support low execution times of the parallel programs. The execution time will be affected by the allocation scheme with regard of the communication bandwidth and latencies within the partition (in a 2D-mesh, a partition that forms a square would better serve an arbitrary program than a partition shaped as a narrow and long stripe).

Low overhead Since all requests are processed at run-time, the resource allocation algorithms have to be fast and should cause only low overhead.

Scalability The algorithms should be able to support systems of thousands of nodes without becoming a bottleneck.

In the following, we constrict our work to multicomputers connected by a two-dimensional mesh since most of the currently existing MPPs and also cluster computers connected with SCI boards [3] are based on 2D- or 3D-meshes (the extension of our 2D-algorithm to the 3D-case is rather straightforward).

2 Processor Allocation Policies

Because allocation operations need to be fast, usual allocation techniques restrict the feasible shapes of partitions to achieve some regularity, which facilitates their management. A partitioning scheme can be called *structure preserving* if it generates partitions that are of the same topological graph family as the entire processor graph. In our case of 2D-meshes it means that always rectangular submeshes are allocated. In addition, most systems also require that the allocated processors are constrained to be physically adjacent (*contiguous* allocation). So each request will be served by exactly one rectangular partition of sufficient size. When using rectangles, however, a 100% utilization of the processor resource is impossible due to two types of *fragmentation*: internal fragmentation, when processors are allocated, but not used, and external fragmentation, when there are free processor partitions that cannot be allocated since they are too small.

Another important point is the dynamic behavior of parallel programs. Previously presented schemes have assumed that the processor demand of a program is constant through its execution time. This is an idealized or simplified assumption. Many parallel programming models and their corresponding language constructs allow dynamic creation and deletion of tasks, resulting in growing and shrinking demands. A partitioning scheme where partitions can "breathe" will result in better utilization. Dynamic partitions will minimize the internal fragmentation, since the size of the partition closely follows the number of processors actually needed. This is difficult to achieve when we stick to rectangular partitions because we only could add or remove some boundary rows or columns which again would result in some internal fragmentation. To completely avoid internal fragmentation, free-form partitions have to be used which can be of arbitrary shape. However, even with free-form partitions, there will be still a considerable amount of external fragmentation, since there will be "holes" between the partitions. Holes in general are not completely bad, since they represent free space that allows the partitions to breathe. If a partition wants to grow and there is no adjacent free space available, the request for more processors has to be denied. A solution to this problem could be to resort to noncontiguous allocation, i.e. the request of an application will be served by more than one contiguous partition.

Several approaches to deal with the processor allocation problem can be found in the literature [9,4,5,1,2]. In spite of the fact that they apply different policies in the resource management, all the schemes have one in common: the control of allocated resources is done with a global data structure localized mostly in a host machine. This is easy to implement and may be the natural approach. There are, however some problems associated with such a centralized management which may become important for large systems: (i) lack of scalability, (ii) the incompatibility with adaptive processor allocation schemes [6] (dynamic allocation), and (iii) it's weak fault tolerance. The scalability problem is caused by the utilization of centralized structures in the management. By increasing the number of processors to be managed, the global data structure grows, increasing its processing time and reducing the performance to a level that may not be acceptable for a procedure done at execution time. In a centralized model, a *dynamic behavior* as described above would result in frequent updates to the global data leading to an overhead in communication between host and parallel machine. The host eventually becomes a bottleneck of both I/O and computation of the parallel machine. Regarding the fault tolerance problem, since all allocation operations have to go through the host, a host failure may stop all processing in the system.

Most of the previous policies cause also a high machine fragmentation. This is a direct consequence of the simplifications made by the allocation schemes concerning the shape of the partitions (rectangles) and the restriction to contiguity. These simplifications reduce the processing time of an allocation operation but increase both types of fragmentation, compromising the overall machine utilization. To summarize, there are several alternatives when considering a processor allocation scheme: static vs. dynamic, rectangular vs. free-form, contiguous vs. noncontiguous and centralized vs. distributed.

In [8] we have already presented a distributed model for processor allocation with some initial results for a structure preserving and a free-form distributed allocation scheme. We also analyzed the impact of noncontiguous allocation in a distributed scheme. In this paper, we analyze the feasibility of the dynamic allocation model in large PC clusters. We propose and study an enhanced noncontiguous version of one of our algorithms, called *Leak* as an alternative for parallel programming models that allow dynamic creation and deletion of tasks. We consider the use of a distributed implementation as rather natural for this type of environment, however, centralized implementations are also possible.

3 Distributed Processor Allocation

Figure 1 shows a global view of the distributed allocation model [8] and the distributed *Processor Managers* involved in the allocation operation. The main differences to the centralized management are (i) the absence of a central data structure with information about the state of all processors, and (ii) the execution of allocation operations directly in the processor mesh in a distributed way, and not in a data structure localized in the host. The host machine is now only responsible for queuing the incoming requests and forwarding them to the processor mesh. Each node in the mesh has a local Processor Manager (PM) responsible for the processor allocation. The PM's cooperate to solve the allocation problem in a distributed way.

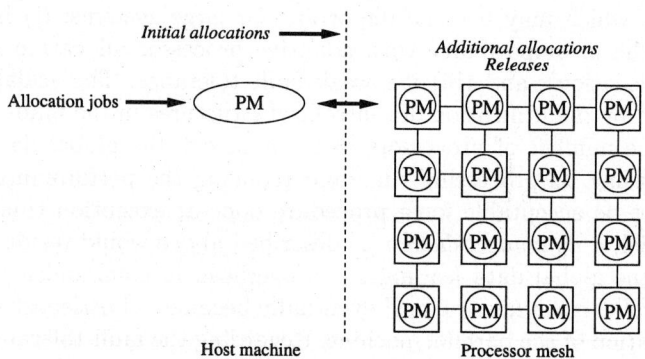

Fig. 1. Distributed allocation

Processor Allocation Operations To match the distributed characteristics of this new allocation model the basic allocation operations are adapted and new dynamic allocation operations are implemented in the distributed processor manager. This results in allocation operations being divided in two groups: static (initial allocation and final release) and dynamic (partial allocation and partial realease). The initial allocation is the most costly operation in the distributed environment. It originates in the host computer and initiates a search wave in the mesh for the desired partition. Since all the mesh nodes are possible candidates, and we are considering large machines with many nodes, the search scope is very large. The first-fit strategy is used in the search and different initial nodes are used each time as mesh entry-points to increase the probability of finding free nodes in early stages of the search wave. In contrast to centralized list-based algorithms (released processors may have to be concatenated to an free partition or will concatenate multiple free partitions in one), the release operation is trivial in a distributed management. Starting in one of the partition nodes, a wave is used to change the state of the involved processes to *free*.

The dynamic operations allow a running parallel application to allocate additional processors and to adapt the partition in use dynamically to a new processor demand (breath). To start this operation, the application sends a local allocation request to the PM of one of its nodes. A search wave for free processors will be originated in this node and will search for possible candidates around this partition in the case of a partial allocation or, in the case of a partial release, for specific nodes to be liberated. Both operations generates much fewer messages than the static operations due to the smaller search scope.

Distributed Allocation Algorithm The implemented PM from section 3 uses an enhanced version of the Leak algorithm [8]. This algorithm is based on the principle of leaking water. From an origin point, an amount of water leaks and flows to the directions where no resistance is encountered. The algorithm has two phases. In the first phase a suitable origin point is searched with a sequential search wave (in the used mesh topology the nodes are searched from left to right in each row until all rows are traversed). In the second phase all the direct neighbors of the origin point are tested in parallel if they are free. Each free neighbor becomes part of the load and the second phase continues recursively and in parallel until no more load is available. All nodes found free are tried as origin point until a free partition of suitable size is found or no more nodes are available to try and the allocation is denied. Figure 2 exemplifies the execution of a 4-processor request. After a feasible origin point is found with a search wave (Figure 2a), the possible flowing directions are determined and the remaining load is distributed (Figure 2b-c). This procedure is repeated recursively until all processors are allocated.

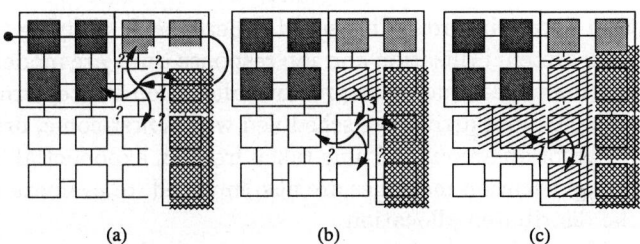

Fig. 2. Contiguous Leak algorithm

The essential feature of the algorithm is its free-form allocation strategy, i.e. partitions are no longer restricted to rectangles, but may have an arbitrary shape. This gives the processor management more flexibility to find a partition of suitable size, and results in less fragmentation. Due to the recursive nature of the algorithm and its distributed execution in the machine, it is also important to notice that different flowing directions allocate processors in parallel, resulting in a reduced allocation time. The parallel potential of an allocation operation increases with the size of the requested partition.

Current communication technologies like wormhole routing [7] enable us to consider noncontiguous allocation schemes, since the number of hops between nodes is not the dominant factor determining message latency [5]. The idea is to try to serve a request with contiguous allocation, and to look for noncontiguous additions only on demand. Under our noncontiguous scheme, a partial allocation is sustained, and the search wave continues only looking for the additional processors.

4 Performance Analysis

In order to investigate the potential and the feasibility of the proposed dynamic allocation in large PC clusters we conducted (i) fragmentation experiments and (ii) allocation overhead experiments. For (i) we used the Siemens hpcLine Primergy High Scalable Compute Sever at the Paderborn Center for Parallel Computing (PC^2). The Primergy Server is a distributed memory multicomputer with 96 compute nodes (two Intel Pentium II with 450 MHz and 512 megabyte DRAM) connected by a 500 megabyte per second unidirectional two dimensional SCI mesh [3], with wormhole XY routing. Programs were written in a special MPI version for the SCI hardware (ScaMPI) that run over the Solaris operating system. Our discrete event simulator is a multicomputer simulator supporting experimentation with distributed allocation strategies on architectures with mesh- connected network topologies. The simulator evaluates the effects of system fragmentation and the generated allocation messages. It was used in (ii) to study the effects of fragmentation for the proposed strategies in bigger machines (up to 1024 nodes).

Fragmentation Experiments This set of experiments, studying the effects of fragmentation on system utilization and job response time, are modeled after the simulation experiments conducted in previous allocation strategy research [5,9]. In these experiments, jobs arrive, are scheduled with a first-come, first-serve policy (FCFS), delay for an amount of time taken from an exponential distribution, and then depart. Allocation messages are also modeled, to evaluate the message overhead in the distributed allocation.

The strategies simulated in these experiments are a dynamic and a static version of the distributed noncontiguous free-form Leak algorithm, a static contiguous version of Leak and the contiguous structure preserving Frame Sliding [5]. Frame sliding examines the first candidate "frame" from the lowest leftmost available processor and slides the candidate frame horizontally or vertically by the stride of width or height of the requested submesh, respectively, until an available frame is found, or all candidate frames are checked. The independent variable in these experiments was the system load, defined as the ratio of the mean service time to mean interarrival time of jobs. Higher system loads reflect the greater demands when jobs arrive faster than they can be processed. Jobs only delay for an exponentially distributed service time with mean of 10.0 time units. For example, under a system load of 1.0, jobs arrive as fast as they are serviced, on the average, and under a system load of 2.0, jobs arrive twice as fast as they can be serviced. Job request size is randomly generated from one of two different distributions, uniform and exponential. In the uniform distribution the size of each job is uniformly distributed over the range U[a, b], with a = 1 and b having four times the side length of the entire mesh. In the exponential distribution, job size is exponentially distributed with a mean of twice the side length of the entire mesh. In this case, there are many small jobs and fewer large ones. To simulate the dynamic behavior of parallel programs four processor profiles are randomly generated for each job: constant, increasing, decreasing and triangular. In the constant profile the processor demand do not vary during execution. By the increasing and decreasing profiles the processor demand varies from 1 to job size and from job size to 1 respectively during execution. The triangular profile simulates divide-and-conquer algorithms, with the processor demand increasing from 1 to job size in the first half of the execution time and then decreasing to 1 again in the second half. For each job size distribution in these experiments, we measure: *Finish Time (Ft)*: the time required for completion of all the jobs, *Job Response Time (Jrt)*: the time from when a job arrives in the waiting queue until the time it completes, *System Utilization (Su)*: the percentage of processors that are utilized over time and *Messages per allocation (Mpa)*: the total number of generated messages by the processor management to allocate the incoming requests divided by the number of generated requests.

All simulations model a 32×32 mesh and run until 1,000 jobs have been completed. Results reported for the fragmentation experiments represent the statistical mean after 10 simulation runs with identical parameters, and given 95 percent confidence level, mean results have less than five percent error. Table 1 shows how well the three algorithms handle a system saturated by job requests with job sizes taken from each distribution. Simulation results for a heavy system load of 10.0 are presented. At this load, the system waiting queue is filled very early in the simulation (full load), allowing each allocation strategy to reach its upper limits of performance.

Table 1. Fragmentation experiments for a heavy system load (10.0)

Algorithms	Distribution	Ft	Jrt	Su	Mpa
Dynamic Leak	Uniform	185	57.73	96.85%	750.3
	Exponential	157	32.75	97%	507
Static Leak	Uniform	266	99.07	60.49%	5949
	Exponential	180	43.82	63.72%	2184
Frame Sliding	Uniform	357	152.85	47.82%	1083
	Exponential	243	72.53	50.45%	849

As expected, we can see that the dynamic strategy achieved the highest system utilization since it is the only strategy that can cope with the dynamic processor requests. Static strategies have to allocate fixed partitions with the highest number of needed processors increasing the internal fragmentation. It is important to notice that this not always results in the highest throughput and lowest job response time. Especially with high load, the optimistic approach of the dynamic allocation (no reservation are made for possible future increases in the number of processors) may result in partitions that are allocated but do not have space to grow. The processing time of these partitions have to be extended, increasing the response time and reducing throughput. The dynamic strategy also profits from allocating free-form noncontiguous partitions. Bigger partitions are difficult to find in contiguous schemes resulting in long search waves and a lot of tries, each of them increasing the number of messages and time. In a noncontiguous scheme, allocations are cumulative resulting in shorter search waves and no waste of messages and time. The difficulties of structure-preserving contiguous allocation can be verified with the frame sliding strategy and the resulting poor system utilization.

Figure 3 (left) show the average job response times for the uniform job size distributions at varying system loads. For the uniform distribution, the system cannot maintain stability with the contiguous FS strategy past a system load of about 1.5. At this point, the job response times for this algorithm begin to increase very sharply. However, for the noncontiguous strategies, represented by Leak, with the uniform distribution, the system remains stable until a system load of about 2.5, where job response times begin to increase significantly, though not as dramatically as with the other strategies. Notice that the curves in these graphs begin to reach a plateau at high average response times. This is due to the fact that the simulated job stream is finite in length, and all response times are bounded by the overall finish time of the simulation. For an infinite job stream, the response time curves would continue to increase exponentially, resulting in near-infinite response times at high system loads. Figure 3 (right) graph the system utilization for these same algorithms and job size distribution at varying system loads. Notice that peak utilization is reached just after the same load where the system was seen to become unstable in its response time graph. All three strategies attained their peak utilization at system loads of about 3.0. The dynamic noncontiguous Leak reached up to 97 percent utilization, whereas the contiguous Leak reached only 65 percent because of the fixed partitions. The structure preserving contiguous leak was only able to reach 51 percent because of the high internal and external fragmentation.

The results measured in these experiments are all consistent with those reported by Zhu in [9] for the contiguous Frame Sliding strategy and by Lo [5] for the noncontiguous strategies. These fragmentation experiments indicate that dynamic noncontiguous allocation is superior to static noncontiguous allocation and far superior to contiguous allocation in terms of its ability to utilize the processors. Because noncontiguous allocation can always allocate a job if there are enough processors available, eliminating external fragmentation, it is shown to achieve higher system utilization. Thus, noncontiguous allocation allows for greater job throughput. However, these results ignore the increased communication contention that may be introduced as a result of noncontiguous allocation. This is not significant in machines with little contention like our Primergy Server or with switched machines like Myrinet clusters with no contention at all, but should be evaluated in machines where message contention could become a problem.

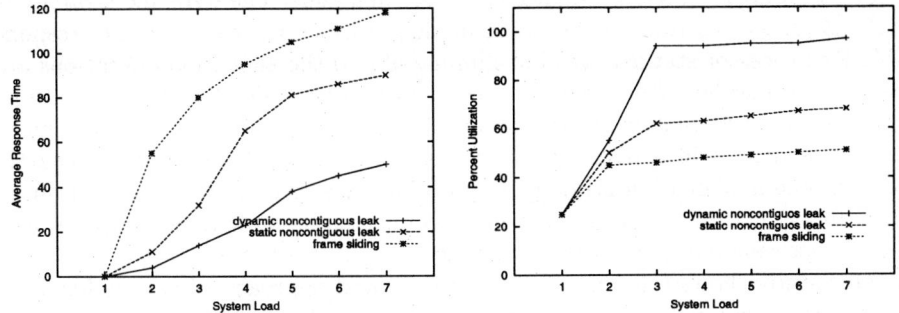

Fig. 3. Average job response time vs. system load and system utilization vs. system load for the uniform distribution of job sizes

Allocation Overhead As a first step in evaluating the feasibility of the dynamic allocation with current technologies we implemented the processor managers in the Primergy server and simulated incoming requests (the same load generation module of the simulator was used). Only 64 nodes were used for this experiments connected as an 8x8 torus. The incoming parallel jobs were not actually loaded in the machine and the allocated partitions are only reserved during the job duration and only global allocations are generated. In our preliminary performance test for a medium system load (5.0) we obtained allocation times around 0.03s for dynamic allocation and 0.162s for static allocation. Due to the small search scope of the partial allocation operation in the dynamic version of the algorithm we observed that the number of generated messages per allocation is much smaller then in the static version. This results also in a reduction in the average time for an allocation. Altough, since in our test for each static allocation 10 dynamic operations are realized in mean (partition duration has a mean of 10) the total time needed for the dynamic allocation of all jobs is around twice as slow then the static allocation.

Table 2. Allocation time in the Primergy multicomputer

Algorithm	Mean allocation time (s)	Generated messages per allocation
Dynamic Noncontiguous Leak	0.03	23
Static Noncontiguous Leak	0.162	128

5 Conclusions

This paper proposes a dynamic distributed processor allocation strategy for parallel programming models that allow dynamic creation and deletion of tasks, resulting in growing and shrinking processor demands. The dynamic strategy is built up on our distributed allocation model, in which the central entity responsible for processor status control is eliminated and the allocation operations are executed in parallel in the processor mesh itself. The basic allocation operations were redefined to match the characteristics of this new dynamic environment and implemented in a distributed processor manager. A distributed dynamic noncontiguous allocation strategy was evaluated and compared to static freeform and structure preserving in a mesh-connected 96-node multicomputer and results were simulated for bigger machines.

Our study shows that the dynamic distributed approach is feasible for large cluster machines with current communication technologies and permitted a greater parallelization of the allocation operations, eliminated the bottlenecks of the centralized model, and achieved a much better utilization of the processors. As a result, system utilization for the noncontiguous version of our dynamic algorithm reaches as high as 97 percent.

We conclude that distributed dynamic allocation provides a new approach that will help highly parallel systems to achieve better price/performance ratios in high demand, multi-user environments.

References

1. G.-M. Chiu and S. Kung Chen. An efficient submesh allocation scheme fot two-dimensional meshes with little overhead. *IEEE Transactions on Parallel and Distributed Systems*, pages 471–486, 1999.
2. H. Choo, S.-M. Yoo, and H. Y. Youn. Processor scheduling and allocation for 3d torus multicomputer systems. *IEEE Transactions on Parallel and Distributed Systems*, pages 475–484, 2000.
3. IEEE. Ieee standard for scalable coherent interface (sci). *IEEE 1596-1992*, 1992.
4. G. Kim and H. Yoon. On submesh allocation for mesh-connected multicomputers: A best-fit allocation and a virtual submesh allocation for fautly meshes. *IEEE Transactions on Parallel and Distributed Systems*, 9(2), feb 1998.
5. V. Lo and et al. Noncontiguous processor allocation algorithms for mesh-connected multicomputers. *IEEE Transactions on Parallel and Distributed Systems*, 8(7):712–726, July 1997.
6. V. K. Naik, S. K. Setia, and M. S. Squilante. Performance analysis of job scheduling policies in parallel supercomputing environments. In *Supercomputing 1993*, pages 824–833, 1993.
7. L. M. Ni and P. K. McKinley. A survey of wormhole routing techniques in direct networks. *IEEE Transactions on Computers*, 1993.
8. C. A. F. D. Rose, H.-U. Heiss, and P. Navaux. Distributed processor allocation for large pc clusters. In *9th International Symposium on High Performance Distributed Computing*, 2000.
9. Y. Zhu. Fast processor allocation and dynamic scheduling for mesh multicomputers. *International Journal of Computer Systems Science and Engineering*, 2(11):99–107, 1996.

A New Communication Mechanism for Cluster Computing*

Andres Ibañez, Valentin Puente, Jose Angel Gregorio, and Ramón Beivide

Computer Architecture Group, Universidad de Cantabria
39005 Santander, Spain
{andres,vpuente,jagm,mon}@atc.unican.es

Abstract. A new fully adaptive routing algorithm for irregular networks is proposed in this paper. When compared to the most relevant routing proposals for networks of workstations with irregular topology, our routing algorithm has the characteristic of avoiding the existence of packet deadlock without using virtual channels. For a 256-node network, uniform traffic, and virtual cut-through flow control, our mechanism can outperform the classic up*/down* algorithm by a factor of 10. In fact, for medium size networks, the new technique can obtain better performance than its virtual channel-based counterparts even though it has a lower hardware complexity.

Keywords: irregular networks, routers, routing algorithm, deadlock, virtual channels, bubble method.

1 Introduction

Networks of workstations (NOWs) or other forms of cluster computing currently appear to be good alternatives for parallel computing due to their competitive cost/performance ratio. They are normally organized as switched-networks with irregular topology. It is precisely that irregularity which makes the packet routing and deadlock avoidance mechanisms more complex than in regular networks. Classical solutions impose some artificial order on the network nodes, normally forming a "tree", and route the packets by using non-minimal paths. In this way, the routing algorithms are simpler and the possible cyclic dependencies, responsible for packet deadlock, are eliminated [2]. However, these techniques have the drawbacks of the increase of packet latencies and waste of resources.

With the aim to avoid these limitations, in this paper we propose a new fully adaptive routing algorithm for irregular networks based on a solution, first proposed for multiprocessor systems [4], which avoids deadlock in regular networks. To achieve this, the new routing proposal selects a subset of physical links forming a Pseudo-Hamiltonian (PH) cycle, i.e., a cycle made up of those links and nodes which could generate cyclic dependencies in the network. Subsequently, the so-called "bubble flow control method" is applied, thus avoiding the exhaustion of the storage resources belonging to the PH-cycle. Without modifying

---

* This work has been supported by Spanish CICYT, project TIC98-1162-C02-01.

the current routers[1], this new method outperforms other standard techniques, obtaining a notably higher performance for network sizes over 64 nodes.

The rest of the paper is organized as follows. In Section 2, the main characteristics of the irregular networks and the router model used in this work are shown. Section 3 reviews classical and newer routing proposals for irregular networks. The new routing mechanism is presented in Section 4. The simulation environment is described in Section 5 and comparative results are shown in Section 6. Finally, we present the main conclusions in Section 7.

2 Irregular Networks

NOWs are normally organized as switched networks with irregular topology. Each switch or router is shared among several workstations connected to it through its ports. The rest of the switch ports are used for connecting the switch with other switches, facilitating network connectivity. Network switches or routers are connected by means of physical channels, generally bidirectional point-to-point links. The messages interchanged among nodes cross the network following paths that fulfill the rules of a routing algorithm. The specific route a packet will follow can be determined either in the emitting workstation or in the intermediate routers. The first method, known as source routing, includes in the packet header enough information to get to the destination. On the contrary, in distributed routing, each router has information (usually as a look-up table) for selecting the most profitable output channel for each incoming packet. In both cases, before the network is prepared to receive traffic, the routing tables have to be initialized with the appropriate information, depending on the selected routing algorithm.

With respect to the switching methodology, the router can implement one of the following three techniques: store-and-forward (SF), virtual cut-through (CT) and wormhole (WH). However, for high-performance networks, only virtual cut through and wormhole are good candidates. Both techniques have pros and cons and the selection is an important decision due to the consequences for the whole network. A comparison between the two techniques can be found, for example, in [2].

2.1 Router Structures

The basic router model used is shown in Figure 1.a. It consists of an internal crossbar able to switch every input link to every output link, allowing multiple messages to cross the router simultaneously without interference. The number of input and output ports is generally the same, and for simplicity, the temporary storage (buffers) are located at the input links. However, the results of this work are not affected by buffer location.

---

[1] Throughout this work, we will use the terms *router* or *switch* indistinctly.

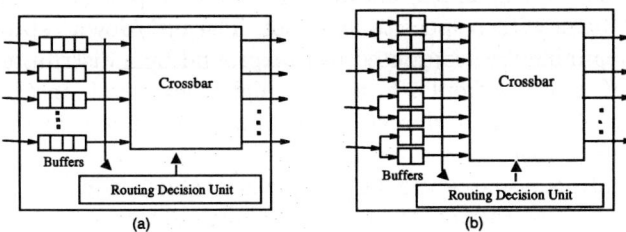

Fig. 1. Router models with input buffers, (a)without virtual channels (b)with two virtual channels per link

The switch has a Routing Decision Unit (RDU) responsible for routing each incoming packet toward its destination and selecting the most convenient output link. This profitable link is selected from a local look-up table (distributed routing) addressed by the input port and the final packet destination, taking also into account the neighboring router status.

In order to compare the results of our technique, another router structure based on virtual channels, such as the one in Figure 1.b, has also been used. This router allows several packets to share the same physical link in a multiplexed way. The virtual channels are implemented using separated buffers for each virtual channel. This scheme facilitates the design of deadlock-free routing algorithms and improves throughput significantly. Nevertheless, it requires additional hardware, because the RDU is more complex and the crossbar either has more inputs to arbitrate or these inputs must be multiplexed.

3 Classical Routing Algorithms for Irregular Networks

Routing algorithms can be deterministic or adaptive. The first type always provides the same path for any packet traveling between the same pair of nodes. On the contrary, adaptive routing algorithms determine the packet route depending not only on the source-destination pair but also on the network status. In any case, deadlock-free routing must be provided by every practical algorithm. A deadlock refers to a situation in which a set of packets is blocked forever because each packet of the set holds some resources (links or buffers) that are also needed by another packet. Next, we will focus on two deadlock-free minimal routing algorithms for irregular networks with different adaptability degrees.

3.1 Up*/Down* Algorithm

The up*/down* algorithm was proposed for Autonet networks [5]. It is a distributed deadlock-free routing scheme that provides partial adaptability in irregular networks. Its general strategy is based on routing packets in a tree, where the routes go up the tree on leaving the source and then, come back down at the destination. One of the nodes is chosen as the root of the tree (usually, the one closest to the rest of the nodes) and all links of the topology are designated as up* or down* links with respect to this root. The up*/down* state of a link is relative to a spanning tree computed in background by a distributed algorithm. A link is up* if it points from a lower to a higher-level node in the tree (i.e. to a node closer to the root). Otherwise, it is down*. For nodes at the same level, nodes IDs break the tie.

The routing from a source to a destination is established in such a fashion that zero or more up* links (towards the root) are traversed before zero or more down* links are traversed (away from the root) in order to reach the destination. This prevents cyclic dependencies among packets and thus, the routing is deadlock-free.

The advantage of this approach is that each node's hardware and software are simple and it provides some adaptability. The drawbacks are that the selected paths are generally not the shortest paths and that links near the root get congested and become bottlenecks that lead to low throughput. Moreover, these problems become critical when the network size increases.

3.2 Adaptive Up*/Down* Algorithm

Recently, a general methodology for the design of adaptive routing algorithms for networks with irregular topology has been proposed in [6]. This methodology attempts not only to provide minimal routing between every pair of nodes, but also to increase the adaptability. To summarize, this methodology starts from a deadlock-free routing algorithm for a given interconnection network, and shares physical links in the network by two virtual channels: escape and adaptive channels. The latter are used for fully adaptive routing, while escape channels are used in the same way as in the original routing function. A packet arriving at an intermediate router first tries to reserve an adaptive channel. If all the suitable outgoing adaptive channels are busy, then an escape channel is selected. If none of these provides a minimal path to the packet destination, the shortest path is chosen. The routing algorithms designed with this methodology are deadlock-free provided that the original routing algorithm is deadlock-free [1].

4 Bubble Routing

In this section, a new fully adaptive minimal routing algorithm is proposed for irregular virtual cut-through networks. The algorithm called "Bubble Routing" (BR), makes use of flow control for avoiding storage exhaustion in all those physical channels which could generate cyclic dependencies among packets and, therefore, produce deadlock. The aim of the BR mechanism is to obtain full adaptability allowing packets to follow minimal routes without any restriction, provided it is always possible that, in case of blocking, packets are routed to their destination through some deadlock-free route.

To achieve this goal, BR selects a subset of physical links forming a Pseudo-Hamiltonian (PH) cycle, i.e., a cycle made up of those links and nodes that could generate cyclic dependencies in the network. Figure 2.a shows an example of an irregular network where a PH cycle has been defined. Note that those nodes forming open branches in the network, such as node number 7, do not belong to the Pseudo-Hamiltonian cycle. Messages stored in such nodes can never generate deadlock because their links can not form cyclic dependencies with other links.

Once a PH cycle is defined including all nodes and links that could generate cyclic dependencies, it is possible to achieve full adaptability. A PH cycle can always be obtained. In the worst case, a path traversing all the network nodes could be used. Links belonging to the PH cycle might be used as an adaptive option to follow minimal paths or as an escape route if there are no more choices. It is necessary that deadlock never occurs in this cycle so packets can never be indefinitely blocked. To achieve this goal, Bubble Routing is applied to avoid packet deadlock in links belonging to the PH cycle. A condition must be fulfilled to allow any packet to enter in this cycle. There must be room for at least two packets, one for the packet itself and another one to establish a "bubble". This "Bubble Condition" guarantees that the storage resources of the PH cycle are never exhausted and therefore packets inside the cycle can always advance. Once a packet is in the PH cycle, for advancing it to the next router, space is only necessary for the packet itself, i.e. using classical flow control techniques. It can be noted that the Bubble Condition can be verified at any storing resource (buffer) belonging to the PH cycle. In particular, the condition can be tested locally, in the same router where the routing decision is taking place [4].

It should be remarked that it is possible to achieve fully adaptive routing avoiding deadlocks without using virtual channels. The routing algorithm is deadlock-free as long as a deadlock-free PH cycle is always offered as an escape route. As with the adaptive up*/down* algorithm, packets can switch between escape channels and adaptive ones and vice versa (obviously, for entering the escape channels, the Bubble Condition must always be fulfilled). This packet movement freedom can give rise to livelock[2]. However, the Bubble Routing algorithm gives preference to minimal paths over non-minimal ones. This guarantees that as time tends to infinity, the livelock probability tends to zero. A similar strategy was used in [3] to prove that the Chaos routing algorithm, which allows packets to follow non-minimal paths when all the minimal paths are busy, was livelock-free. Next, we are going to describe the simulation environment used for comparing the different strategies against our new proposal.

5 Simulation Framework

For comparison purposes, simulation techniques have been used to evaluate the performance achieved by different routing algorithms. A general-purpose interconnection network simulator, named NOWSIM (Network of Workstations Simulator), has been implemented as an extension of the network simulator NETSIM [7], developed at Rice University in the YACSIM environment [7].

---

[2] Packets traveling in the network that never reach their destination nodes.

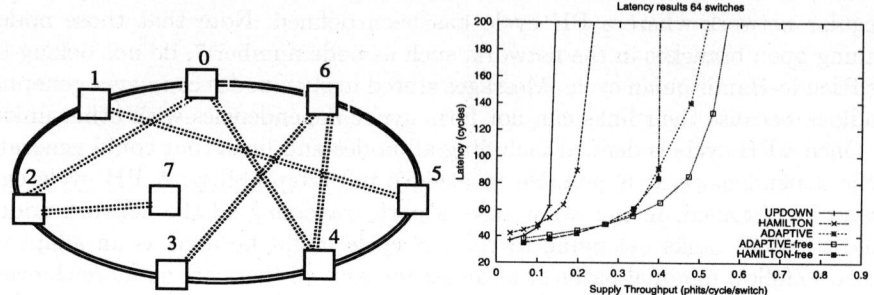

Fig. 2. (a) Pseudo-Hamiltonian (PH) cycle in an irregular network. (b) Average packet latency versus applied traffic for a 64-nodes

Network topology is completely irregular and randomly generated. However, for the sake of simplicity, three restrictions to possible topologies are imposed. First, it is assumed that all the routers have a structure such as that of Figure 1, with the same size, 5 input and 5 output ports. Also, there is one processor connected to each router, thus leaving 4 ports available to connect to other routers. Finally, two neighboring routers are connected by means of a single link. The analyzed routing algorithms being partially or fully adaptive, all of them offer several routing choices. Therefore, all the algorithms require accessing a routing table, selecting among several options, and determining the most suitable output channel. Thus, it is assumed that it takes one clock cycle to compute the routing algorithm in all cases. Also, two cycles are needed to transmit one phit across both the crossbar and the buffer. And, finally, another cycle is spent in travelling between routers.

A virtual cut-through switching technique is assumed in the simulations. Messages are one-packet sized divided into 16 phits and we assume that each one can be transferred across a physical link per cycle. Buffers can store 8 packets. When multiplexing physical links between two virtual channels, buffers can only store 4 packets in order to maintain constant the buffer capacity per physical link.

6 Comparative Results

In this section, a performance comparison of the routing algorithms described in Section 3 against Bubble Routing has been carried out. Irregular networks of different sizes (just 64 and 256 nodes are shown) have been simulated. Under the same evaluation methodology and simulation environment, results for the different routing algorithms have been obtained.

However, in order to clearly identify the performance range, we have considered two extreme situations for packet adaptability. On one hand, complete freedom for routing packets to their destinations following any minimal route and, on the other hand, to enforce any packet to follow the safe path determined by the deadlock-free algorithm though this is not minimal. Figure 2.b shows the average packet latency versus the applied load for 64 switches under uniform traffic. This Figure shows results of the up*/down* algorithm (UPDOWN), the two virtual channel adaptive algorithm with and without freedom for routing the packets (ADAPTIVE-free and ADAPTIVE), and the new fully adaptive proposal also with and without freedom (HAMILTON-free and HAMILTON). In these cases, the maximum number of hops necessary for a packet to reach its destination will always be the corresponding to the safe route (up*/down*-path for ADAPTIVE and Hamilton-path for HAMILTON). While in the ADAPTIVE-free and in the HAMILTON-free cases, that number of hops will usually be lower but only statistically limited.

As shown in Figure 2.b, for a 64-switches network, HAMILTON-free outperforms the throughput achieved by the classical strategy UPDOWN in a factor of 3.5. In fact, for this network size, the BR performance is close to that obtained by the ADAPTIVE-free, though for this case the router complexity is greater because it is necessary to implement two virtual channels per link. Even without doing misrouting respect to the safe routes, both algorithms behave better than UPDOWN because packets do not concentrate around the root. The cost is a little increase on base latency. However, the new proposal presents the more amazing results when network size is larger. Figure 3 shows the average packet latency and throughput for a 256-nodes network under uniform traffic. HAMILTON-free outperforms UPDOWN in a factor greater than 9, and surprisingly, it duplicates the performance of the more costly ADAPTIVE-free strategy.

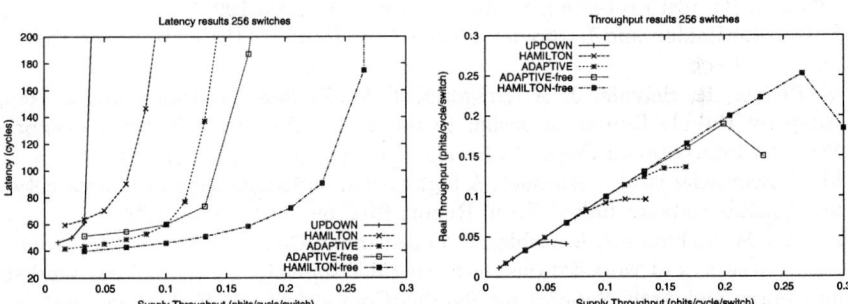

Fig. 3. Average packet latency and throughput versus applied traffic for a 256-nodes network

Obviously, the saturation points correspond to those in which the slope of the latency curves goes to infinite. But beyond these points, Figure 3 shows the misrouting effect on the HAMILTON-free and on the ADAPTIVE-free algorithms. If we try to inject more packets than the network is able to handle, the performance of these algorithms will drop bellow the maximum achievable throughput. HAMILTON and ADAPTIVE algorithms eliminates this throughput decreasing by limiting the adaptability and by selecting non-minimal routes, therefore diminishing the maximum achievable throughput. However, it is possible to control the decay effect limiting the number of times a packet can leave the safe route (up*/down* or Hamilton). Depending on this limit, the maximum achievable performance will be greater, but the misrouting effect will also has more impact beyond the saturation point.

7 Conclusions

Bubble Routing for irregular networks means an important improvement over the classical up*/down* algorithm at, practically no extra cost. Avoiding the concentration of packets around the root node, the performance improvement can be as high as 10 times for a 256-node network under random traffic.

Bubble Routing even outperforms the adaptive up*/down* algorithm in spite of the fact that in our case it is not necessary to implement virtual channels in the router. The Bubble condition can be tested locally in the routers with a practically negligible hardware cost [4].

References

1. J. Duato, "A necessary and sufficient condition for deadlock-free routing in cut-through and store-and-forward networks". IEEE Transactions on Parallel and Distributed Systems, vol. 7, no. 8, pp. 841-854, August 1996.
2. J. Duato, A. Robles, F. Silla and R. Beivide, "A comparison of router architectures for virtual cut-through and wormhole switching in a NOW environment", Proc. of 13th Int. Parallel Processing Symp., pp. 240-247, April 1998.
3. S. Konstantinidou and L. Snyder, "The Chaos Router", IEEE Trans. on Computers, Dec. 1994.
4. V. Puente, R. Beivide, J. A. Gregorio, J. M. Prellezo, J. Duato and C. Izu, " Adaptive Bubble Router: a design to improve performance in torus networks", Proc. Of International Conf. On Parallel Processing, Japan, Sep. 1999.
5. M. D. Schroeder et al., "Autonet: A high-speed, self-configuring local area network using point- to-point links," Tech. Report SRC 59, DEC, April 1990.
6. F. Silla, M. Malumbres, A. Robles, P. López and J. Duato, "Efficient adaptive routing in networks of workstations with irregular topology", Proc. of the Workshop on Comm. and Arch. Support for Parallel Computing, pp. 46-60, Feb. 1997.
7. J. R. Jump, "YACSIM (Ver.2.1), NETSIM(Ver.1.0) Reference Manuals", Electrical & Computer Engineering Department, RICE University, March 1993.

Isolated Dynamic Clusters for Web Hosting

Michael Kalantar and Jun Fong

T.J. Watson IBM Research Center
P.O. Box 704, Yorktown Heights, NY 10598
{kalantar,fong}@us.ibm.com

Abstract. In a web farm, a collection of hardware and software resources is used to host a number of distinct sites. In general, resources are permanently assigned to a single customer site. Because peak loads are an order of magnitude greater than average loads [8], site availability is guaranteed by allocating excess resources, that are largely unused, to each site. Océano [1] proposes a new hosting model in which availability is guaranteed by rapid dynamic allocation of hardware resources based on observed request streams. Resources are quickly assigned when load increases and may be reassigned when load decreases. This paper describes how Océano uses the underlying network infrastructure to dynamically reassign nodes between customer site and how it provides site isolation.

Keywords: dynamic clusters, web hosting, private VLAN

1 Introduction

A web hosting infrastructure, or web farm, is composed of many servers that are dedicated to serving web applications for a number of different web sites. These may include, for example, routers, request dispatchers (load balancers), cache servers, web servers, application servers, file servers, video servers, and database servers. For explanatory purposes we will assume, in this paper, that a web site is composed of "front end" web and application servers and of "back end" database servers. To enable server allocation on an as needed basis, the underlying network infrastructure must contain mechanisms that allow automation and can provide site isolation.

2 Infrastructure Requirements

We assume that web sites in a server farm may share network bandwidth and some network hardware such as routers and request dispatchers, but do not share other servers. The servers within a site cluster must be able to freely, and efficiently, communicate with each other. Servers in other clusters, however, should not be able to communicate directly with them; their only means to communicate should be through the Internet. That is, a site cluster should be isolated from other site clusters.

To support dynamic de/allocation, it must be possible to assign a server to a cluster without physically rewiring it. To enable efficient communication between resources within a single site cluster, it is desirable that they be on the same physical network.

However, it is not possible to have all servers (from all clusters) on the same physical local area network as this would violate the requirement for isolation. A mechanism that allows a random group of servers to be assigned to a single network without rewiring and to isolate this network from other, similar, networks is needed.

3 Supporting Switch Technologies

Océano achieves isolation using *virtual local area networks* (VLANs). VLANs are now supported by many switches. A VLAN is a group of networked devices in the same broadcast domain. That is, it is a group of devices that can communicate as if they were on a common LAN. However, the devices in a VLAN need not be located on the same physical LAN segment. Further, the devices in a VLAN are restricted from communicating with other devices that are not in the same VLAN, except through a network layer router.

In addition to providing a mechanism for grouping devices into broadcast domains, the VLAN abstraction provides MAC layer isolation of the domains. Further, VLANs improve the manageability of the network by allowing for more centralized configuration: at the switches. Manageability can be further centralized to a single point of control; central configuration software that uses SNMP MIBs can be used to configure all of the switches.

In addition to VLANs the Cisco Catalyst 6500 series of switches also support *private VLANs*. A private VLAN is a VLAN specified by a group of switch ports in which there are distinctions in membership status. Some ports are *promiscuous*, they can send and receive from all other VLAN members. Others are *isolated* or *community* ports. An isolated port has complete MAC layer separation from the other VLAN members except from the promiscuous ports. Devices attached to community ports can intercommunicate with each other and the promiscuous ports. There can be several distinct groups of community ports in a single private VLAN. Figure 1 shows an example of a private VLAN. It contains a router and the devices in 3 site clusters. Only the router is connected to a promiscuous port. It can therefore send and receive data from all the devices in the VLAN. Each of the devices in the clusters is connected to community (for clusters 1 and 3) or an isolated port (for cluster 2). The devices in each cluster can therefore send layer 2 packets to each other and to the router. They are unable to send layer 2 packets to devices in other clusters. Private

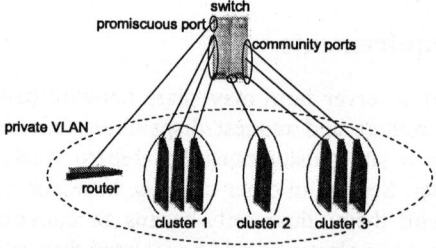

Fig. 1. An example of a private VLAN. The router, connected through the promiscuous port, can communicate with the all members of the private VLAN. However, the devices in each cluster can only communicate with the router and the other members of its community VLAN

VLANs, in essence, provide a second layer of hardware implemented access control by subdividing a VLAN into smaller units.

4 Océano Network Infrastructure

Océano is designed to dynamically allocate server resources and provide isolation using VLANs and distributed control software. The servers are connected to Cisco Catalyst 6509 switches. Each server has three network adapters. One connects the server to the *administrative VLAN*, one to the *front end VLAN*, and one to the *back end VLAN*. These VLANs are designed as follows. The administrative VLAN is a private VLAN that connects administrative servers, running the Océano system software, to all other servers. The servers in a single site cluster are connected in a secondary VLAN. The front end VLAN is one or more primary VLANs. It connects request dispatchers to several site clusters. Here the request dispatchers are to be configured with promiscuous ports while the servers of a single site form secondary VLANs. Finally, the back end VLANs may be either plain VLANs that connect the servers in a site together or they may be a private VLAN that would allow servers to share a common back end resource such as a storage area network. This design allows the servers in a site cluster to directly communicate with all of the other servers in their site and with the devices connected to the promiscuous ports (administrative nodes, request dispatchers, and back end SAN), but not with servers in other site clusters. The network infrastructure provides the isolation properties sought.

Membership of the VLANs, and hence of the site clusters, is dynamically altered by Océano control software which reconfigures the switches. Such reconfiguration can be done at any time without stopping the flow of packets through the switch. When allocating a server, Océano would first configure the switches to place the server in a special build cluster. Here the server is primed with an operating system, the site applications and site data. Océano can then reconfigure the switches to "move" the server into the appropriate VLANs supporting its site cluster. Programmatic reconfiguration can be accomplished either by directly programming the switch console or through the use of SNMP.

5 Summary and Current Status

This paper outlined the design and main features of the network infrastructure used in Océano. The infrastructure provides Océano with isolated site clusters. The approach used enhances site availability allowing Océano to demonstrate a computing utility infrastructure that provides dynamically carved site clusters.

An Océano prototype has been developed and runs on testbed containing 55 Linux and AIX nodes. These are interconnected using 100 Mbps switched Ethernet. We have demonstrated server allocation in between 10 and 12 minutes depending on the size of the data to be installed. All except 8 to 12 seconds of this time is spent installing the operating system, applications and data. The 8 to 12 seconds includes, but is not exclusively, time spent reconfiguring the switch. The software dynamically establishes VLAN membership using SNMP. The current prototype implementation does not yet use private VLANs because the switch software does not yet provide the necessary SNMP MIBs. Use of private VLANs is not expected to add significant overhead to the cost of server allocation.

6 Related Work

A number of other approaches to sharing resources in web hosting server farms [2,3,5,6,7] focus on sharing the CPU cycles of single servers. In contrast, Océano focuses on sequential sharing at the granularity of whole servers, and the management of a whole farm of servers. Approaches that do sequentially allocate whole servers allow only static server allocation. These approaches, unlike Océano, make no attempt to modify the computing environment to satisfy the allocation (for example, by installing an operating system or by changing the network configuration). Rather, they allocate the server as is. A matchmaking algorithm [4] must ensure that the environment is suitable. In general, these approaches create virtual domains without providing network isolation. IcorpMaker [6] does provide isolation via virtual private networks; Océano does so via virtual LANs.

References

1. Appleby, K., Fakhouri, S., Fong, L., Goldszmidt, G., Kalantar, M., Krishnakumar, S., Pazel, D. P., Pershing, J., and Rochwerger B., "Océano – SLA Based Management of a Computing Utility", To appear in Proceedings of the 7th IFIP/IEEE International Symposium on Integrated Network Management (IM 2001), 2001.
2. Bruno, J., Gabber, E., Ozden B., and Silberschatz A. "The Eclipse Operating System: Providing Quality of Service via Reservation Domains", Proceedings of the 1998 USENIX Annual Technical Conference., pp. 117-130, June 1998.
3. Ensim Corp., "ServerXchange" (White Paper), http://www.ensim/com. Moutain View, California.
4. Raman, R., Livny, M., and Solomon, M. "Matchmaking: An extensible framework for distributed resource management", Cluster: Journal of Software, Networks and Applications, 2(2), 1999.
5. Reumann, J., Mehra, A., Shin, K. G., and Kandlur, D. "Virtual Services: A New Abstraction for Server Consolidation", Proceedings of the 2000 USENIX Annual Technical Conference, pp. 117-130, June 2000.
6. Rooney, S. "The IcorpMaker: A Dynamic Framework for Application-Service Providers", Proceedings of the IEEE Workshop on IP-oriented Operations and Management, Cracow, Poland, Sept 4-6, 2000.
7. Sun Microsystems Inc., "Sun Enterprise 10000 Server: Dynamic System Domains" (White Paper), Palo Alto, California.
8. Squillante, M. S., Yao, D. D., and Zhang L., "Web Traffic Modeling and Web Server Performance Analysis," Proceedings of the 39th IEEE Conference on Decision and Control, December 1999.

Topic 17
Metacomputing and Grid Computing

Alexander Reinefeld, Omer F. Rana, Jarek Nabrzyski, and David W. Walker

Topic Chairpersons

The growing number of computers accessible through a network, such as the Internet, has meant that these computers can be collectively employed to solve complex problems. Since the networks that connect such machines are distributed, many attempts have been made to create an infrastructure for distributing large scale applications across regional and national boundaries, to enable nation-scale or continent-scale computing to be realized. The components within such an infrastructure can also range in complexity from workstation clusters to dedicated parallel machines and data repositories.

New paradigms have been introduced to support the programming and deployment of such computational resources, generally as extensions to existing parallel computing models (such as SPMD) and distributed computing techniques based on distributed object technologies. The primary objective in many such systems is to achieve uniformity in programming and use, whilst supporting heterogeneity and transparency in architectures, operating systems and environments. The use of Web technologies, such as HTML, Perl/CGI and various scripting languages, have provided useful middleware tools for integrating information resources to support such large scale applications. These tools have limitations, and are often hard to extend beyond a given application. Java and CORBA have also played an important role in such developments, providing an infrastructure which facilitates integration across platform and programming language boundaries – albeit at a performance cost.

Emerging network applications in areas such as multi-disciplinary information analysis, distributed collaborative environments, post-genomics, and distributed visualization, require the coordinated use of geographically distributed resources. The development of such applications can be significantly simplified if specialized operations were supported in the infrastructure – such as the provision of caching, authentication, resource discovery, resource scheduling, albeit for heterogeneous environments.

A Grid can be thought of as a collection of resources, and infrastructure services, supporting the development, deployment and operational support for applications that are multi-disciplinary and require complex management. The Euro-Par Topic "Metacomputing and Grid Computing" explores such infrastructure technologies which can be successfully employed in the context of heterogeneous, distributed computing, to enable integration and management of application across organizational and national boundaries.

The first session focuses on the experiences made with existing Grid testbeds. The first two papers discuss the use of the Cactus Grid environment which is in daily use in the astrophysics community. Cactus is a representative for a whole class of scientific applications with the following characteristics: tightly coupled, regular space decomposition, huge memory and processor time requirements. The first paper, written by Matei Ripeanu, Adriana Iamnitchi, and Ian Foster, presents performance predictions of Cactus running on several thousand nodes in the Internet, while the second paper, authored by Gabrielle Allen *et al.*, presents useful tools for remote steering, remote monitoring and remote visualization that have been developed around the Cactus code. Also the third paper, written by Dietmar Erwin and David Snelling, describes a practical Grid testbed, the UNICORE environment. The paper gives an overview on the UNICORE architecture, including the data model, the abstract job objects and the security model.

The second session starts with two papers on the use of CORBA in distributed environments. Alexandre Denis, Christian Pérez, and Thierry Priol describe a parallel CORBA model for interconnecting different MPI code modules without degradation in performance. Thereafter, Diego Sevilla, José García and Antonio Gómez present a lightweight CORBA components model named CORBA-LC which allows to build distributed applications by assembling independent binary components. The third paper in this session by Nathalie Furmento, Steven Newhouse and John Darlington presents a framework on building computational communities with Java and Jini by federating resources from different organizations.

The third session starts with a paper of Karan Bhatia, Keith Marzullo, and Lorenzo Alvisi on causal message logging protocols which employ a hierarchy of shared logging sites (proxies) to improve the fault tolerance and availability in grid environments. Thereafter, Zoltán Balaton, Péter Kacsuk, Norbert Podhorszki, and Ferenc Vajda propose to adapt the GRM and PROVE tools of the P-GRADE graphical program development environment so that they can be used in the monitoring subsystem of the EU Datagrid project. Finally, Junwei Cao, Darren Kerbyson, and Graham Nudd present an agent-based hierarchical model for resource management in grid environments.

Cactus Application:
Performance Predictions in Grid Environments

Matei Ripeanu[1], Adriana Iamnitchi[1], and Ian Foster[1,2]

[1] Departmet of Computer Science, The University of Chicago
1100 E. 58th Street, Chicago, IL 60637, USA
{matei,anda,foster}@cs.uchicago.edu

[2] Mathematics and Computer Science Division, Argonne National Laboratory
Argonne, IL 60439, USA

Abstract. The Cactus software is representative for a whole class of scientific applications; typically those that are tightly coupled, have regular space decomposition, and huge memory and processor time requirements. Cactus proved to be a valuable tool for astrophysicists, who first initiated its development. However, today's fastest supercomputers are not powerful enough to perform realistically large astrophysics simulations with Cactus. The emergence of innovative resource environments like Grids satisfies this need for computational power. Our paper addresses issues related to the execution of applications like Cactus in Grid environments. We focus on two types of Grids: a set of geographically distributed supercomputers and a collection of the scale of one million Internet-connected workstations. We study the application performance on traditional systems, validate the theoretical results against experimental data, and predict performance in the two new environments.

1 Introduction

Historically, large scientific simulations have been performed exclusively on dedicated supercomputer systems. In many cases, a single supercomputer is not capable of simulating a real size problem in reasonable time. A solution to this huge need for resources is provided by Grid computing [10], a new field that is distinguished from conventional distributed computing by its focus on large-scale sharing of Internet-connected resources. Computational Grids are collections of shared resources customized to the needs of their users: they may be collections of resources for data intensive applications, or collections of powerful supercomputers, or simply opportunistic collections of idle workstations. In addition, to facilitate access to a potentially very large number of resources, computational Grids provide the necessary tools for resource discovery, resource allocation, security and system monitoring.

Experiments on large pools of Internet-connected resources have been successful. For example, [4] demonstrated the potential efficiency of these environments by solving an optimization problem (stated in 1968 and unsolved since then) on a pool of 1000 computers distributed across the US and Europe. However, because of the characteristics of this new environment, not all applications seem, at first sight, to be capable of exploiting it fully. One such example is the class of tightly coupled, synchronous applications, which are sensitive to communication characteristics.

We evaluate the performance of a tightly coupled scientific application, a classic 5-point stencil computation, on two Grids: a pool of geographically distributed supercomputers (like those presented in [5]) and a pool of one million workstations [8]. Our goals are to determine what factors limit performance, to analyze the benefits of different algorithm tunings, and to design a performance prediction model.

Cactus [1] was originally developed as a framework for finding numerical solutions to Einstein's equations and has since evolved into a general-purpose, open source, problem solving environment that provides a unified, modular, and parallel computational framework for scientists and engineers. Its name comes from the application design: a central core (*flesh*) connects to application modules (*thorns*) through an extensible interface. Thorns can implement custom developed scientific or engineering applications, or standard computational tools, such as parallel I/O, data distribution, or checkpointing. We analyze an application that simulates the collision of two black holes.

A basic module (thorn) implements unigrid domain decomposition. It decomposes the global domain over processors and places an overlap region (referred to as *ghost-zone*) on each processor. This reduces the number of messages (and hence the communication latency costs) while the total amount of data exchanged remains constant. We shall see later the costs and benefits of this approach on different architectures.

To better understand our test application, we study its sequential behavior and build and validate the performance model for two different supercomputer architectures (Section 2). This performance model is later adapted to a pool of supercomputers (Section 3.1). We predict the application efficiency in this environment and study the factors that limit performance. In Section 3.2 we move our application performance discussion to Internet computing.

2 Application Execution on Traditional Architectures

We analyzed the sequential and parallel execution of our application on two supercomputers: a shared memory machine (Silicon Graphics Origin 2000) and a message passing based supercomputer (IBM SP). We built a performance model for the parallel execution, validated it against real data, and used it in the next section to predict performance in the two computational Grids considered: a pool of Internet-connected supercomputers and one million of Internet-connected workstations.

Details on the analysis of the sequential execution are presented in [12]. Relevant for our problem are memory usage and execution time per grid point. We learned that, for avoiding memory penalties, the problem space allocated on a processor with a RAM MB of associated memory should be $10^6 \times \frac{RAM-16}{512}$ grid points. We determined the time to process one grid-point is $t_c = 17\mu s$ on a RISC 10000 processor and $t_c = 24\mu s$ on a Power3 processor. In addition, we learned how to avoid cache conflicts (also presented in [12]) that strongly degrade performance.

Communication among processors is what differentiates the parallel algorithm. The use of ghost-zones decreases the number of messages exchanged but only at the cost of replicated work: the grid points within a ghost-zone are computed twice, on different processors. In the rest of this section we analyze communication costs and execution time. We present the efficiency of the parallel algorithm as per experiments and explain the differences from our theoretical model. We also observe that on the architectures considered increasing the size of the ghost-zones does not improve performance.

Communication Costs The values corresponding to each grid point in the problem space are updated with each iteration based on values of the neighboring grid points. To reduce the number of messages exchanged, larger chunks of data can be sent at once. A ghost-zone of depth $g \geq 1$ decreases the frequency of messages from 1 message per iteration to 1 message every g iterations. We consider $g_x = g_y = g_z = g$.

For brevity, we analyze only the 3D problem decomposition on a 3D processor topology: each processor is allocated a volume of grid points and has neighbors on all the 3 axis. Moreover, we observe that the speed of the whole computation is the speed of the slowest processor, and model only interior processors, e.g., those processors that have 6 neighbors.

We consider a simple latency/bandwidth communication cost model: the cost of sending a message of length L between any two processors is:

$$t_{msg} = t_s + L \times t_w \qquad (1)$$

where t_s is the message start-up time and t_w is the cost for sending one byte of data. This model does not account for the complex interconnection network that modern supercomputers use, but we chose it for its simplicity. We shall discuss later the implications of this choice.

During the execution of I iterations, each processor sends and receives $\frac{6I}{g}$ messages. For a ghost-zone size of g, δ bytes sent per grid point, and assuming the link connecting any two neighboring processors is not shared, the total time spent communicating is: $T_{comm} = \frac{6I}{g} t_s + 4I t_w (yz + xz + xy)\delta$

Execution Time Each processor spends its time on *useful* work, communicating, and on *redundant* work. We ignore idle time due to synchronization, assuming perfect load balance (identical processors and identical work load per processor).

Redundant work is the work done on the grid points of the ghost-zones. In every iteration $i \leq I$ replicated work is done on (i modulo g) lines of the ghost-zone. Therefore, in each of the $\frac{I}{g}$ phases replicated work is done for $\sum_{j=1}^{g-1} j(xy+$

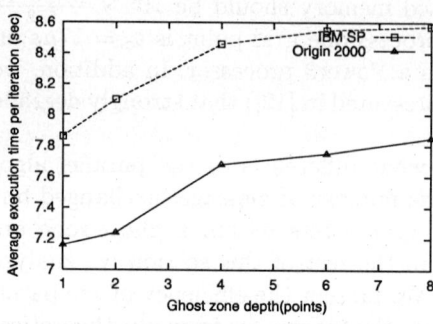
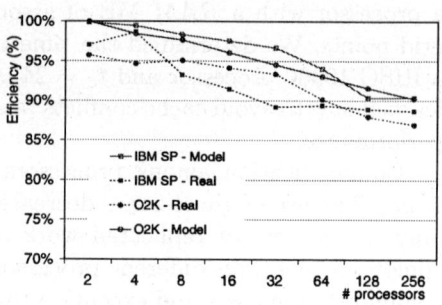

Fig. 1. Average time per iteration as a function of ghost-zone size

Fig. 2. Efficiency measured when problem size per processor is constant

$yz+xz) = \frac{g(g-1)}{2}(xy+yz+xz)$ grid points. For 3D decomposition, because each processor has 2 ghost-zones on each direction, the time spent on replicated work over I iterations is: $T_r = It_c(g-1)(xy+yz+xz)$.

For $x = y = z$ and a regular 3D decomposition, the total overhead time is:

$$T_{overhead} = T_{comm} + T_r = 6\frac{I}{g}t_s + 12It_w x^2 \delta + 3It_c(g-1)x^2 \qquad (2)$$

Optimal Ghost-Zone Size We determine the optimal ghost-zone size for which the overhead introduced by parallelism is minimum. $T_{overhead}$ (2) is minimum when $g_{min} = \frac{1}{x}\sqrt{\frac{2t_s}{t_c}}$. However, if $g \geq 1$ then $x \leq \frac{2t_s}{t_c}$. For a realistic problem size (x in the range 50 to 100 grid points, limited by the available memory) and for t_s, t_c of the two supercomputers considered, this condition is not met. Therefore the execution time increases with the ghost-zone size.

We have validated this theoretical conclusion by measuring the execution time on 8 processors on Origin2000 and IBM SP with different ghost-zone sizes. The experimental data (Figure 1) confirms our result: execution time grows with ghost-zone size on both supercomputers.

The intuition behind this result is that latency related costs are smaller than redundant computation costs. The use of larger ghost-zones to increase performance is justifiable on architectures where $\frac{t_s}{t_c} > 5000$. Since t_c is always in the order of tens of μs, ghost-zones with $g > 1$ make sense only in environments with very large (more than $100ms$) latency.

Efficiency We used efficiency values to validate our performance models. For $g = 1$, P processors, and a problem space of x^3 grid points per processor, maximum efficiency is:

$$E_{max} = \frac{T_{seq}}{P \times T_{par}} = \frac{1}{1 + \frac{6t_s}{x^3 t_c} + \frac{12t_w \delta}{xt_c}} \qquad (3)$$

Equation 3, in which predicted efficiency is independent of the number of processors and therefore of the number of data flows, shows the limitations of the simplified communication model used: the model ignores the fact that links within a supercomputer's interconnection network are shared and assumes that interconnections switches scale linearly. For a more accurate prediction, we use a competition for bandwidth model [7] adapted to the interconnection characteristics of the two supercomputers: we identify shared hardware components, compute the number of competing flows, and use manufacturer's performance specifications. For these experiments we use a memory constrained model: the problem size per processor remains constant while the number of processors increases up to 256. Figure 2 compares experimental results with our predictions. Although our communication models are simplistic, the test results match the predictions within a 10% range. Other models, like hyperbolic [16], could lead to more accurate predictions.

3 Predicted Performance in Grid Environments

We consider two different computational Grids. The first is a collection of supercomputers connected by a Grid middleware infrastructure like the Globus toolkit [9]. This computational Grid already exists and we used it to validate our approach on performance predictions. The second Grid environment we analyze is a very large collection of workstations likely to be used in the near future.

3.1 Performance on a Pool of Supercomputers

We predict the application efficiency on a collection of Internet-connected supercomputers and study the application and environment characteristics that limit performance. We also investigate ways to increase performance by tuning application parameters and improving the code. For example, we evaluate the benefits of using larger ghost-zone size for inter-supercomputer communication to offset latency costs, while maintaining minimal ghost-zone size for intra-supercomputer communication.

We make the following assumptions and notations:

- Greek letters describe functions/values at supercomputer level while the corresponding English alphabet letters describe values at processor level. For example, Θ_{comm} is the communication time between supercomputers, while T_{comm} is the communication time between processors.
- Supercomputers are identical. This assumption is realistic since a set of heterogeneous machines can behave in a 1D decomposition as a set of identical processors if loaded proportionally to their computational powers.
- The problem space is decomposed using a 1D decomposition among supercomputers and a 3D decomposition among the processors of each supercomputer. 1D decomposition among supercomputers is realistic since a relatively

small number of supercomputers (maybe hundreds) is likely to be simultaneously available to a group in the near future. However, it is straightforward to extend the model to a 2D or 3D decomposition.
- Supercomputers are connected through identical network links to the Internet. We use the same linear model (1) for communication costs. In addition, we assume the communication cost of transferring data over a link is independent of the number of concurrent TCP connections.
- Each supercomputer is assigned a grid space of size $X \times Y \times Z$. Since we assume a 3D regular partition at supercomputer level, each processor will be assigned a grid space of size $\frac{X}{\sqrt[3]{P}} \times \frac{Y}{\sqrt[3]{P}} \times \frac{Z}{\sqrt[3]{P}}$ (which is $x \times y \times z$). We assume S supercomputers, each having P processors. We assume ghost-zone depth G for inter-supercomputer communication and ghost-zone depth g for intra-supercomputer communication.

To build the performance model for the architecture described above, we consider each supercomputer a computational entity that obeys the performance model described in Section 2. Hence, we model a supercomputer as a 'faster' processor with a 'big' associated memory. This *super*processor will be characterized by the time θ_c needed to update one grid point (the equivalent of t_c presented in Section 2).

Execution Time. Using the model described in Section 2, the time spent for useful work on a problem of size $X \times Y \times Z$ on a supercomputer with P processors is: $\Theta_{seq} = \theta_c XYZ$. The same amount of time is spent by each processor solving its part of the problem $\frac{X}{\sqrt[3]{P}} \times \frac{Y}{\sqrt[3]{P}} \times \frac{Z}{\sqrt[3]{P}}$ but working in parallel with efficiency E: $\Theta_{seq} = \frac{t_c}{E} \times \frac{X}{\sqrt[3]{P}} \frac{Y}{\sqrt[3]{P}} \frac{Z}{\sqrt[3]{P}}$ We can now compute θ_c the time it takes to process a grid-point: $\theta_c = \frac{t_c}{EP}$.

Consider that each processor has ghost-zones of depth g and each supercomputer has ghost-zones of depth G. This is meant to accommodate the variation in communication costs (inter-supercomputer vs. intra-supercomputer). Since replicated time on the processor ghost-zones (of size g) is already included in the model through the efficiency value E, the time spent by each supercomputer on doing replicated work is a function of $(G-g)$. In each iteration replicated work is done on $(G-g)XY$ grid points. Each supercomputer has at most two ghost-zones. The total time spent doing replicated work over I iterations is therefore $\Theta_r = 2I\theta_c(G-g)XY$.

For S identical supercomputers with P processors each and a problem space of $SX \times Y \times Z$ grid points, each supercomputer has to solve a $X \times Y \times Z$ grid point problem. Total execution time for I iterations is:

$$\Theta_{par} = \Theta_{seq} + \Theta_{comm} + \Theta_r = I\theta_c XYZ + \frac{2\theta_s I}{G} + 4I\theta_w XY\delta + 2\theta_c I(G-g)XY \quad (4)$$

Communication Costs. For each message sent from a supercomputer to another, communication time is: $\Theta_{msg} = \theta_s + \theta_w L$. Over I iterations there are

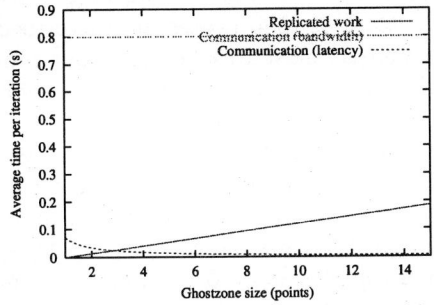

Fig. 3. Components of parallel overhead time. Gigabit links are assumed

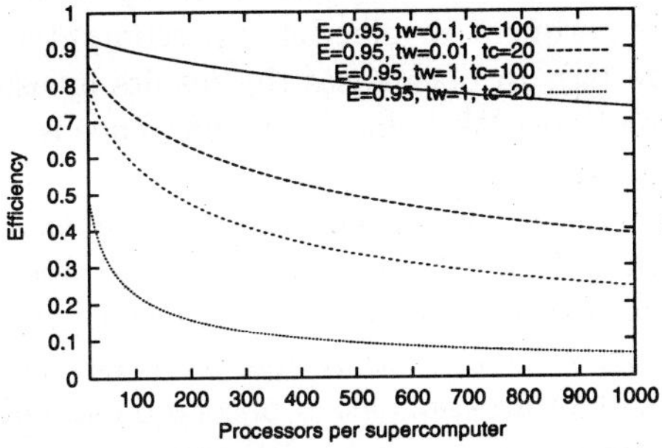

Fig. 4. Achievable efficiency on a pool of supercomputers with in-place networks

$\frac{I}{G}$ communication phases, in which each supercomputer sends two messages of $L = GXY\delta$ bytes each. Incoming and outgoing messages share the communication link. Therefore, the time spent communicating is:

$$\Theta_{comm} = \frac{I}{G} \times 2(\theta_s + 2\theta_w GXY\delta) = \frac{2I\theta_s}{G} + 4I\theta_w XY\delta \quad (5)$$

Optimal Ghost-Zone Size. From (4) maximum efficiency E' is obtained for

$$G_{opt} = \frac{1}{x\sqrt[3]{P}}\sqrt{\frac{\theta_s}{\theta_c}} \quad (6)$$

This validates our intuition that larger inter-supercomputer communication latency requires larger ghost-zones while slower processors or larger problems would require smaller ghost-zones. For $\theta_s = 35ms$ (usual value for coast-to-coast links), supercomputer efficiency $E = 90\%$, $t_c \simeq 20\mu s$, $P = 1024$ and 60^3 gridpoints per processor, the maximum overall efficiency is obtained for $G_{opt} = 2$.

These results suggest that using different ghost-zones sizes for supercomputer communication does increase overall efficiency. However, Figure 3 shows that more than 95% overhead is due to limited network bandwidth even in the optimistic scenario when each supercomputer has a Gigabit connection to the outside world. We need one order of magnitude faster links to obtain significant savings due to deeper ghost-zones.

Predicted Efficiency. In our model the overall efficiency is the product of the efficiency of a single supercomputer and the efficiency of the collection of supercomputers. For $G = g = 1$, we have:

$$E_{overall} = E\varepsilon = E\frac{\Theta_{seq}}{S \times \Theta_{par}} = \frac{1}{\frac{1}{E} + \frac{2\theta_s}{xyzt_c} + \frac{4\theta_w\delta\sqrt[3]{P^2}}{zt_c}} \quad (7)$$

We validated (7) with two experiments executed on supercomputers across the US. The experimental setup, including details on the middleware infrastructure used (Globus and MPICH-G2), is presented in [3]. The first experiment used 2 supercomputers with up to 64 processors each. The second, large-scale experiment involved 4 supercomputers of a total of 1500 processors (described in [2]). In both cases the results measured were at most 15% less than our predictions. We believe this difference is mostly due to the highly variable behavior of the wide area network.

In Figure 4 we consider the existing network infrastructure in our testbed ($\theta_s = 35ms$ and $\theta_w = 1\mu s$) and show the variation of the predicted efficiency $E_{overall}$ with the number of processors. We also plot efficiency for an application configuration that is 5 times more computationally intensive ($t_c = 100\mu s$) and for an application-observed bandwidth of 10MB/s ($\theta_w = 0.1\mu s$). Although in our test we have not benefitted from 10MB/s application-observed bandwidth, this is easily achievable with currently deployed networks. It is interesting to note that efficiency as high as 83% could be obtained if all supercomputers were connected to Internet using Gigabit links.

From equation (7) and from Figure 4, we observe that overall efficiency $E_{overall}$ increases with the sequential execution time per grid point and with the decrease in communication costs. Even with new, more computationally demanding numerical algorithms, since the processors are increasingly powerful, we believe that a real improvement in efficiency is possible only through efficient use of 'fatter' network pipes.

3.2 Internet Computing

There are over 400 million PCs around the world, many as powerful as early 1990s supercomputers. Every large institution has hundreds or thousands of such systems. Internet Computing [8] is motivated by the observation that at any moment millions of these computers are idle. With this assumption, using computer cycles and data storage on these computers becomes virtually free provided satisfactory (1) middleware infrastructure and (2) network connectivity.

Computational grids provide the middleware infrastructure: dependable, consistent, and pervasive access to underlying resources. The continuous growth of the Internet is going to provide the necessary connectivity. Internet demand has been doubling each year for more than a decade now. This has caused backbone network capacity to grow of an even faster rate [15]. Moreover, it is estimated that in the near future we will witness an explosion in network capacity [6]. Optical technologies that are driving this transition will also transform the physical structure of the Internet from one based on backbone networks carrying thousands of (virtual) network flows through dozens of large pipes to one based on backbone "clouds" consisting of thousands of possible optical paths, each with the capacity to carry multi-Gb/s traffic.

The available middleware infrastructure and the soon-to-be-available network connectivity bring the vision of a general-purpose 1 million-processor system (*megacomputer*) closer to reality. Megacomputers might be the world's first Peta-op (10^{15} FLOPS) computing systems. However, for applications like Cactus, increased computational power may be less significant than the aggregated memory of millions of computers which will allow solving problems of unprecedented scale and resolution.

We consider the processor space divided in 'clusters': groups of computers on the same Gigabit local area or campus network. They might also be PCs using DSL (ADSL, HDSL) or cable modem technologies within the same geographical area (and thus probably using the same provider's POP). We assume that communication within a cluster is low delay, high bandwidth. A shared hub allows communication with other clusters. We imagine a cluster to have 100s to 1000s machines. To minimize communication, we use a 3D decomposition among clusters. Even with this problem decomposition aimed at minimizing inter-cluster communication (and thus the number of flows that traverse cluster boundaries), the networking infrastructure will have to deal with an enormous number of flows. For a cluster of size P there will be $6\sqrt[3]{P^2}$ communication flows going out. Given TCP's limited ability to fairly and efficiently deal with large number of simultaneous flows ([14]) some mending is needed at the network transport level. Possible solutions are: use TCP concentrator nodes for inter-cluster communication, use an improved TCP protocol (along the lines of RFC2140), or simply replace TCP with a future transport protocol.

We analyzed the performance of a megacomputer using the same model as in previous sections. Instead of describing the whole process in detail, we just summarize our conclusions. Efficiency of 15-20% can be obtained even without modifying Cactus' tightly coupled computational pattern. This might seem low, but considering the huge aggregated computational power of this environment, the result is more than one order of magnitude larger than the fastest supercomputer available today. We assumed 1000 clusters with 1000 machines each. We considered a 2-level hierarchy of Gigabit LANs within a cluster and non-shared OC48 links among clusters. We picked rather conservative values for application's uniprocessor execution rates (100MFLOPS) and grid-point processing time ($20\mu s$). We note that the application is extremely sensitive to communication costs. This means that simple improvements like overlapping computation and communication will bring up to 100% improvements in efficiency.

To conclude, we estimate that Cactus could run at an execution rate of 20 TFLOPS on a megacomputer. This about 30 times faster than the best execution rate achievable now [13] on a supercomputer. Based on Moore's Law (which, judging by the power of the fastest supercomputer worldwide as per the annual Gordon Bell awards, still holds), it will take 6 years to have a supercomputer as powerful as the megacomputer we imagined. Certainly, the assumptions we made about network connectivity and the omnipresence of Grid environments will become reality well before then.

4 Summary

We provided a detailed performance model of a scientific application—a typical stencil computation code—and validated it on two architectures. We adapted our performance model for two computational Grids: an Internet-connected collection of supercomputers and a megacomputer. We investigated the benefits of increasing ghost-zone depth for increasing performance and we determined that these are insignificant because of the high bandwidth-related communication costs. We also determined that the limiting factor for efficiency is network bandwidth, which is going to improve dramatically over the next few years.

Our prediction model shows that with better network connectivity than in place today and using computational Grids, scientists will shortly have a powerful computational platform at a low cost.

References

1. G. Allen, W. Benger, C. Hege, J. Massó, A. Merzky, T. Radke, E. Seidel, J. Shalf, *Solving Einstein's Equations on Supercomputers*, IEEE Computer 32(12), 1999.
2. G. Allen, T. Dramlitsch, I. Foster, N. Karonis, M. Ripeanu, E. Seidel, B. Toonen. *Supporting efficient execution in heterogeneous distributed computing environments with Cactus and Globus*. Submitted to Supercomputing, 2001.
3. G. Allen, T. Dramlitsch, I. Foster, T. Goodale, N. Karonis, M. Ripeanu, E. Seidel, B. Toonen. *Cactus-G toolkit: Supporting efficient execution in heterogeneous distributed computing environments*, In Proceedings of 4th Globus Retreat, July 2000.
4. K. Anstreicher, N. Brixius, J. P. Goux, J. Linderoth, *Solving Large Quadratic Assignment Problems on Computational Grids*, 17th International Symposium on Mathematical Programming, Atlanta, GA, August 2000.
5. W. Benger, I. Foster, J. Novotny, E. Seidel, J. Shalf, W. Smith, P. Walker, *Numerical Relativity in a Distributed Environment*, Proceedings of the Ninth SIAM Conference on Parallel Processing for Scientific Computing, March 1999.
6. C. Catlett, I. Foster, *The network meets the computer: Architectural implications of unlimited bandwidth*, 2001, to appear.
7. I. Foster, *Designing and Building Parallel Programs*, Addison-Wesley, 1995.
8. I. Foster, *Internet Computing and the Emerging Grid*, Nature 408(6815), 2000.
9. I. Foster, C. Kesselman, *Globus: A Metacomputing Infrastructure Toolkit*, International Journal of Supercomputing Applications, 11(2), 1997.
10. I. Foster, C. Kesselman, *The Grid: Blueprint for a New Computing Infrastructure*, Morgan Kaufmann, San Francisco, CA, 1999.
11. IBM, *IBM SP POWER3 SMP node system architecture*, Technical report, IBM.
12. M. Ripeanu, A. Iamnitchi, *Performance Predictions for a Numerical Relativity Package in Grid Environments*, Technical Report TR-2001-23, U. of Chicago, 2001.
13. J. Makino, T. Fukushige, M. Koga, *A 1.349 TFLOPS simulation of black holes in a galactic center in GRAPE-6*, In Supercomputing 2000.
14. R. Morris, *TCP behavior with many flows*, IEEE International Conference on Network Protocols, Atlanta, Georgia, October, 1997.
15. A. Odlyzko, *Internet growth: Myth and reality, use and abuse*, Information Impacts Magazine, November, 2000.
16. I. Stoica, F. Sultan, D. Keyes. *A hyperbolic model for communications in layered parallel processing environments*, Journal of Parallel and Distributed Computing, 39(1):29–45, 1996.

Cactus Grid Computing: Review of Current Development

Gabrielle Allen[1], Werner Benger[1,2], Thomas Dramlitsch[1], Tom Goodale[1], Hans-Christian Hege[2], Gerd Lanfermann[1], André Merzky[2], Thomas Radke[1], and Edward Seidel[1,3]

[1] Max-Planck-Institut für Gravitationsphysik, Albert-Einstein-Institut, Golm (AEI)
[2] Konrad-Zuse-Zentrum für Informationstechnik, Berlin (ZIB)
[3] National Center for Supercomputing Applications, Champaign, IL, (NCSA)

Abstract. Cactus is an open source problem solving environment designed for scientists and engineers. Its modular structure facilitates parallel computation across different architectures and collaborative code development between different groups. Here we detail some of the various Grid Tools which have been developed around Cactus, and describe Grid experiments which have been performed to test their application.

1 Introduction

Cactus [1], [2] is an open source problem solving environment designed to provide a unified modular, parallel, portable and collaborative computational framework for physicists and engineers.

The modularity and flexibility in Cactus is achieved by its design of a central core (or *flesh*) which connects to application or computational infrastructure modules (or *thorns*) through an extensible interface. Thorns provide all the functionality, from parallel drivers, I/O and checkpointing to physics applications such as black hole evolvers. Cactus is distributed with a Computational Toolkit containing thorns which provide, for example, coordinate systems, boundary conditions, parallel interpolation and reduction operations, elliptic solvers, and various parallel output methods using different data formats. Cactus contains a sophisticated and flexible make system, and is supported on a wide range of HPC architectures, including Origin 2000, Cray T3E, IBM SP, Hitachi SR8000, Compaq AlphaServer, as well as IA32/IA64 clusters running Windows or Linux.

2 Grid Computing with Cactus

Cactus, and the physics codes from which it evolved, have been used as a Grid computing software laboratory since 1993. Simulations of Einstein's equations, with live 3D visualizations shown in a CAVE, were distributed across multiple machines (CM-5's and SGI Power Challenges) at SC'93 and SIGGRAPH 94. Large scale distributed computing across the vBNS was demonstrated at Supercomputing 1995 (SC'95), with a direct ancestor of Cactus using the Cornell

Fig. 1. Sites of the EGrid testbed set up by the *applications working group* of the European Grid Consortium [8] for the development of Grid infrastructure and applications. The *Cactus Worm*, a new dynamic grid application, was demonstrated running across all testbed sites during Supercomputing 2000 [6]

SP-2 and Power Challenges at Cornell and SDSC to run a simulation and visualization of gravitational waves [3]. This was one of the experiments leading to the development of the grid infrastructure Globus [4], [5].

Cactus was used to perform intercontinental distributed simulation-visualization scenarios at SC'97, and at SC'98, a simulation of colliding neutron stars across the two continents was shown, distributing the computational grid across three T3E's in Garching, Berlin and SDSC. Distributed demonstrations were also shown at SC'99 and 2000, with emphasis more on sophisticated and robust interactive visualization, monitoring and steering, dynamic scenarios, exploitation of networks and the development of user portals and testbeds [6].

We learned many things from this collection of experiments, particularly about the need for a well developed infrastructure, not only to support the Grid *but also the applications themselves*. The Cactus Toolkit was designed from the outset such that any application making use of the framework could easily make use of the Grid. In order to perform distributed Cactus simulations, the standard MPI driver thorn PUGH can be simply linked against the Grid-enabled MPICH-G [9] implementation of MPI which is available with the Globus toolkit. Thus, preparing a Grid-enabled version of Cactus using Globus is a compilation choice. Using the Globus job submission tools, users can then start their Cactus runs in a Grid environment just as easily as they do on a single machine.

It is important to emphasize that although all of our large scale distributed experiments to-date have been performed using Globus, Cactus is in no way tied to this software. Smaller distributed runs have been performed across collections of workstations on a LAN using the standard MPI driver thorn with just MPICH, and other Grid infrastructures could be used and tested, possibly required the development of new driver thorns.

The thorn architecture and design of Cactus is such that the computational infrastructure layer providing eg. the driver layer, I/O, interpolation or reduction operators is hidden from application programmers by a fixed API. This makes it possible for any chosen thorn to implement the functionality, providing it satisfies the appropriate interface with the flesh and other thorns. This means that as soon as new techniques, eg. for more efficient use of the Grid, are implemented as thorns, they become immediately available to the whole Cactus User community, without requiring changes to physics application code.

3 Current Grid Development

The typical user working practice with remote supercomputers is something like: (i) search for username/password/hostname for remote machine; (ii) login, copy code and compile an executable; (iii) search for details of remote queuing system and submit job to queue; (iv) check queue everyday; and finally (v) when simulation is complete transfer data back to local machine and perform analysis.

A major aim of Grid computing is to use infrastructure, such as the Globus Toolkit [4], together with Grid aware applications, such as Cactus, to simplify each of these points, making a user's remote resources as easy-to-use and accessible as their local resources. But Grid computing has the potential to be much more than "remote-computing-made-easy". Indeed, we expect Grid applications ultimately to be fully aware of the global Grid environment, with the ability to adapt themselves as both their computational needs and available resources change in time, migrating from site to site, spawning off remote processes, and in so doing enabling both faster throughput and larger scale simulations, with a complexity never before attainable.

Grid capabilities are being developed in connection with Cactus through several projects [10], [11], [8], [17]. Here we describe briefly the areas of research and development most closely related to the Cactus Project.

Remote File Access

Large-scale computer simulations generate large-scale data sets, with single simulations generating files containing of order a TByte of data. Conventional analysis and visualization then becomes prohibitively resource-intensive when remote simulation data must be moved to a local machine for processing. Further, in many cases, *eg.* for initial analysis, only a small fraction of the overall data is really needed, for example the data just for one grid variable, or a downsampled subset of high-resolution data.

To enable such access to remote data, we have enhanced the *Hierarchical Data Format* HDF5 I/O library [12] *Virtual File Driver* VFD layer with a driver that builds on top of the Data Grid software components [13] from the Globus toolkit. This allows existing I/O layers to operate directly on any remote HDF5 file. These files are uniquely addressed by their URL, and all read/write operations are then performed, transparently to the application, as network transactions on the Grid.

Data selection capabilities of HDF5 allow hyperslabbing and downsampling of the remote files before the data is transferred.

Remote Visualization

Remote visualization is the capability to visualize data from a resource at a remote site using a client on a local machine. This data could either be located on a remote file system, or it could be contained in a *virtual file*, streamed live from a running simulation via socket connections.

Such visualization is important for effective use of remote resources, as it prevents the need to shift enormous amounts of data between machines, and coupled with techniques such as downsampling and hyperslabbing allows users with only modest local resources to be able to quickly and easily analyze data from their simulations wherever they take place.

Cactus provides several different implementations of data streaming. The most generic approach, for arbitrary data of any type, is based on the HDF5 I/O library and its VFD layer. We have developed a *Stream* driver which holds the HDF5 data to be streamed out of the Cactus simulation as an in-memory file, which can then be sent through a socket to a connected client. The client application uses the same driver to reconstruct the in-memory file which then can be accessed to read the HDF5 datasets. The design means that applications can use their existing HDF5 file-based I/O methods immediately for online remote data access without changing I/O interfaces.

Such live streaming data from Cactus simulations can be viewed using many different visualization tools, including Amira [14], IBM Data Explorer [15] (see Figure 2), and LCA Vision [16].

Remote Monitoring

Computer scientists working with applications which run using large scale computing resources at remote sites have to learn to deal with multiple accounts, variable networks, different operating systems, and unpredictable queuing systems. This can make even the simple task of checking if a run has started yet, or finding how far it has reached, time consuming. The Cactus Computational Toolkit contains a thorn, HTTPD, which provides remote monitoring capabilities, alleviating many of these problems. Thorn HTTPD can be trivially added to any Cactus application to provide the simulation with its own webserver, which can then be accessed from any remote web browser by simply accessing the URL of the host machine, along with the chosen port number.

The main page of thorn HTTPD is shown in Figure 3, from this page users can access information about the simulation, such as the time it started, the current iteration number, the code version, as well as information about the thorn set used, and full information about the values of parameters and variables used in the simulation. As described in the following section the web interface also provides access to a secure method of steering the simulation.

Remote Steering

Application steering means changing the behavior of a simulation externally during its execution, for example by changing simulation parameters or variables.

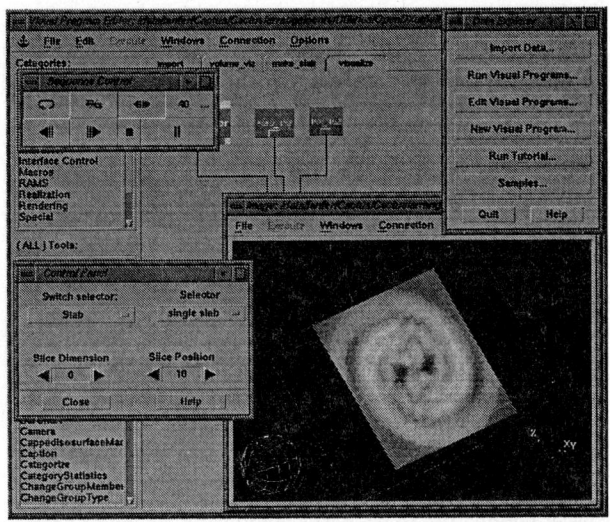

Fig. 2. Streaming data from a remotely running Cactus application is read into the visualization client IBM Data Explorer [15], where it can be locally manipulated

Good applications of steering which can save many hours of supercomputer allocation time include changing I/O parameters to add the output of variables which were missed from the initial parameter file, changing an output directory to prevent an overfull disk crashing a simulation, or switching on analysis tasks such as black hole horizon finding.

Cactus provides an interface for steering applications by providing functions to change the values of parameters which are designated steerable. Cactus already provides one thorn HTTPD which implements a password protected steering interface accessible from web browsers. Thorn HTTPD also has a control interface, from which users can pause, single-step, or terminate the simulation. This interface will be further enhanced to include debugging and other features.

Dynamic Grid Computing

The Grid is inherently dynamic: machine loads and availability, and network latencies and bandwidths, change continually. The resources available to a user can be dramatically different from one hour to the next. It is essential that any simulation and remote visualization technology that utilizes the Grid must be able to adapt to its dynamically changing environment.

Just as importantly, applications are now becoming increasing dynamic. Techniques such as adaptive mesh refinement, interactive steering and the real-time addition of code modules change the resources required for a simulation.

We plan to develop core capabilities for simulation and visualization codes to be aware of the Grid environment, and to be able to adapt and exploit it. These capabilities, implemented in a *Grid Application Toolkit* will allow fundamentally

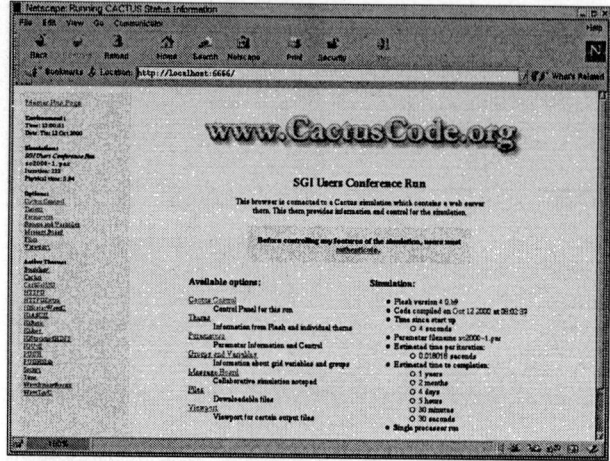

Fig. 3. Web browser connecting to a Cactus simulation, showing details about the simulation, and providing interfaces for steering parameters and controlling the simulation from any remote location

new uses of the computational resources of the global Grid, for example the automatic migration of a simulation to a larger, faster, or cheaper machine, or the spawning of independent subtasks to new resources. A prototype example of such a dynamic Grid-enabled application, the *Cactus Worm*, was demonstrated running on a new European testbed (Figure 1) at Supercomputing 2000 [6].

Distributed Computing

Distributing a single simulation across two or more resources connected by a network provides two benefits. Firstly, it provides a way to run simulations too large to fit on a single machine. For example, the Numerical Relativity Group at the Albert Einstein Institute would like to be able to run black hole simulations with grid resolutions of over 1000^3, which require more than a TeraByte of core memory. The largest machine to which they have access has 928GB, however if they could run a single simulation across all their resources, they could use over 2TB. In this case, the efficiency of the simulation takes second place to the ability to perform such a simulation at all. Secondly, queues on supercomputers mean that researchers must sometimes wait weeks for even a medium-sized simulation. The same simulation could be run quicker, if not immediately, distributed over a pool of resources, even including a large network of local workstations. While efficiency may be lower, turn-around time can be increased dramatically.

Cactus applications have been used for several years to demonstrate the feasibility of distributing large simulations across a pool of computer resources, using the Globus grid infrastructure [4] for authentication and the Globus enhanced implementation of MPI, MPICH-G [9] for communications. The applications used for these experiments have all been from the field of Numerical Relativ-

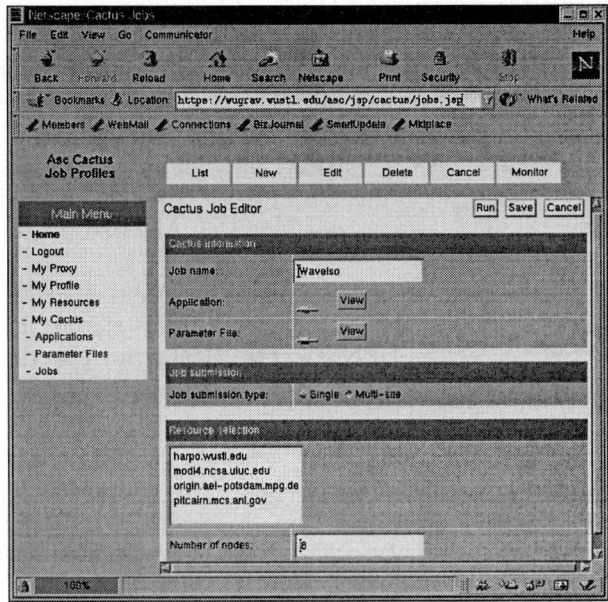

Fig. 4. The ASC Portal provides a secure web-based user interface for managing and running Cactus simulations on remote machines. This page shows job submission to a chosen machine, or, for a distributed runs, to a set of machines. The portal automatically locates machines for which a user has access using Globus tools

ity, whose relativity high computation to communication ratio make them well suited for developing distributed computing techniques for closely coupled codes.

Currently, development is focussed on understanding how the communication structure of applications can be instrumented and enhanced to make best use of network properties such as latency and bandwidth, and to understand and automatically determine, which applications are best suited for running in a distributed environment. In addition, we are developing techniques, such as a user portal, to improve accessibility and ease-of-use for distributed computing.

User Accessibility to the Grid

The Grid is a confusion of wildly different machines, with their associated operating systems, security practices, schedulers and local policies. One direction for more transparent access is to develop *Users Portals*, perhaps customized to a particular application, giving a unified and consistent window to the Grid.

The ASC Portal [17],[7], currently undergoing testing, has been designed to provide a easy-to-use interface for using Cactus in both a local and Grid environment, providing code assembly, resource finding and authentication, executable staging, and simulation monitoring and steering. Figure 4 shows the portal interface for job submission. Users select a Cactus executable and parameter file, and then start an, optionally distributed, simulation on a set of remote resources.

4 Acknowledgements

The development of the Cactus Code is a highly collaborative effort, and we are indebted to a great many experts at different institutions for their advice, visions and support. It is a pleasure for us to thank our many colleagues who continue to contribute to this work, especially Dave Angulo, Ian Foster, Nick Karonis, Matei Ripeanu, Michael Russell, John Shalf, and Brian Toonen. Computing resources and technical support have been provided by AEI, ANL, NCSA, Rechenzentrum Garching/Germany, and ZIB.

We greatly acknowledge financial support for André Merzky and Thomas Radke as well as provision of a gigabit network infrastructure in the course of the TIKSL research project by DFN (German Research Network).

References

1. Cactus Code: http://www.cactuscode.org
2. G. Allen, T. Goodale, G. Lanfermann, E. Seidel, W. Benger, H.-C. Hege, A. Merzky, J. Massó, T. Radke and J. Shalf, *"Solving Einstein's Equation on Supercomputers."* IEEE Computer, p.52-59, December, 1999.
   http://www.computer.org/computer/articles/einstein_1299_1.htm
3. R. Gjertsen, J. Massó, M. Nardulli, E. Seidel, J. Shalf, and D. Weber. "Distributing Spacetime: Computing and Visualizing Einstein's Gravitational Waves across the Metacenter". *Forefronts*, 11(3), 1996. Cornell Theory Center.
4. Globus Metacomputing Toolkit: http://www.globus.org
5. Supercomputing '95 distributed computing experiments:
   http://jean-luc.aei.mpg.de/Projects/SC95/
6. G. Allen et. al, *Early experiences with the Egrid testbed*, in IEEE International Symposium on Cluster Computing and the Grid, 2001.
7. M. Russell, G. Allen, G. Daues, I. Foster, T. Goodale, E. Seidel, J. Novotny, J. Shalf, W. M. Suen and G. Von Laszewski *"The Astrophysics Simulation Collaboratory: A Science Portal Enabling Community Software Development"*, Proceedings of Tenth IEEE International Symposium on High Performance Distributed Computing, HPDC-10, San Francisco.
8. The European Grid-Forum: http://www.egrid.org
9. Grid-enabled MPICH Implementation: http://www.globus.org/mpi
10. DFN Gigabit Project *"Tele-Immersion: Collision of Black Holes"*:
    http://www.zib.de/Visual/projects/TIKSL/
11. Grid Adaptive Development Software (GrADS): http://www.isi.edu/grads/
12. Hierarchical Data Format Version 5: http://hdf.ncsa.uiuc.edu/HDF5
13. A. Chervenak, I. Foster, C. Kesselman, C. Salisbury, S. Tuecke, *"The Data Grid: Towards an Architecture for the Distributed Management and Analysis of Large Scientific Datasets."* (1999), submitted to NetStore '99
14. *Amira - Users Guide and Reference Manual* and *AmiraDev - Programmers Guide*, Konrad-Zuse-Zentrum für Informationstechnik Berlin (ZIB) and Indeed - Visual Concepts, Berlin, http://amira.zib.de
15. IBM Data Explorer: http://www.research.ibm.com/dx
16. LCA Vision: http://zeus.ncsa.uiuc.edu/~miksa/LCAVision.html
17. Astrophysics Simulation Collaboratory: http://www.ascportal.org/ASC

UNICORE: A Grid Computing Environment

Dietmar W. Erwin and David F. Snelling

Forschungszentrum Jülich GmbH, ZAM
D.Erwin@fz-juelich.de
Fujitsu European Centre for Information Technology
snelling@fecit.co.uk

Abstract. This paper describes the result of the UNICORE (BMBF grant 01 IR 703) project, the goals and the initial results of the follow-on project UNICORE Plus (BMBF grant 01 IR 001). It outlines the original goals of the German funded project to provide a seamless batch interface for German HPC centers and its evolution toward a Grid Computing Environment. The focus is on technical results, like abstraction to achieve seamlessness and use of certificates for authentication and security. The rationale behind technical decisions will be provided and the future role of UNICORE will be presented.

1 Introduction

Grid Computing is an extremely valuable concept and a convincing and compelling computing paradigm. It is easily understood. Directives, from the European heads of state at the June 2000 summit in Lisbon to the European Commission to take appropriate actions, affirm it. Grid Computing has it roots in may developments (references can be found in [2]) that preceded the ground-breaking book by Ian Foster and Carl Kesselmann [1]. By this token, UNICORE is a is a true grid project, although it originated as a project about seamless access to remote resources. The acronym 'Uniform Interface to Computing Resources' indicates this, and it is still well characterized in these terms.

As terminology changes, new concepts are used as buzzwords by the media, politicians, and even insiders, and therefore expectations change. This paper will present both the research and development results of the UNICORE projects and the technical, and sometimes non-technical context, in which the work took place.

2 A Brief History of UNICORE

UNICORE was conceived in 1997 to produce a solution to a real problem: Make the German HPC resources, located for example in Berlin, Munich, Stuttgart and Jülich, accessible to users in a seamless, secure and intuitive way over the Internet. This was what the directors of the German HPC centers demanded [5], and this was fully consistent with the recommendations of the German science council [4]. After reviewing related work, especially in Europe and the US, a project proposal was developed and submitted by the prospective project partners to the BMFT (Federal

Ministry for Research and Technology), later renamed to BMBF (Federal Ministry for Education and Research).

The project partners decided to combine existing and emerging technologies with new ideas to build a software infrastructure for remote access without relying on the successful and timely completion of other related projects. It was also a major challenge to include European partners – even without funding – into a project funded by a German agency. The challenge was further magnified by the inclusion of US and Japanese vendors of HPC systems, which were critical to the success of UNICORE. The project was fortunate to manage this, and the complete list of partners can be found in [6].

The original goals of UNICORE can be summarized as follows:

- Development of a seamless interface to allow creation, manipulation, and control of complex batch jobs to be executed at heterogeneous systems at different remote sites including automatic data staging.
- Use of existing and emerging technologies, components, and standards where ever possible.
- Minimal intrusion into existing computing center practices and policies, especially in the areas of security and administration.
- Modular design that allows replacement of components whenever new solutions are mature enough.

The implementation was based on Java and Java applets; it used the Jigsaw Web Server (see [3]) with Security extension from IAIK Graz and Codine from Genias. It relied on X.509 certificates.

In retrospect, the project was launched at the right time. Traditional HPCN funding declined and novel ideas could prosper and eventually evolve into new strategic directions, even in the absence of accepted terminology. The UNICORE project started in August 1997 for a duration of two years initially, with a target to develop a prototype within this time frame. The result was successfully demonstrated in an international symposium on 'Metacomputing and Distributed Computing' [7] in Jülich, Germany in September of 1999.

During the course of the project it became obvious that some components used for building the first UNICORE system were themselves early implementations of emerging technologies. They made it possible to demonstrate the concept in a very short time but the total solution lacked the necessary robustness to permit its deployment at partner centers in day-to-day operation. The results of UNICORE secured funding for a follow-on project – obviously named UNICORE Plus – for a three year period from January 2000 to December 2002. This project's overall objectives are:

- Re-implement the UNICORE software to create a robust and extensible system for use at partner installations and in additional projects.
- Extend the capabilities of UNICORE in selected areas that had been omitted from the first prototype.
- Add functions to allow maintenance and administration of the UNICORE environment.

- To take the UNICORE software from a research tool to a viable, production quality tool for a research environment.
- Ensure the commercial exploitation of UNICORE after the end of the project.

The final point is one of the formal requirements of BMBF funding and will be fulfilled by Pallas GmbH, which intends to market and support UNICORE software and services.

Since UNICORE Plus, like its predecessor, is a fixed budget project, its scope has to be restricted to meet the objectives stated in the proposal. It is expected that other projects will add functions to extend UNICORE and that UNICORE's design allows interoperation and integration with other Grid solutions. This is indeed already happening.

3 R&D Results of UNICORE

3.1 The UNICORE Architecture

The functions of UNICORE and its implementation have been described in [8] and [6]. In short, UNICORE, as implemented in the first production prototype, creates a three-tier architecture.

The UNICORE client supports the creation, manipulation, and control of complex batch jobs, which may require multiple systems at one or more UNICORE sites to complete. The jobs and actions the user defines are represented as *Abstract Job Objects,* effectively Java classes, which are serialized and signed when transferred between the components of UNICORE. The server level of UNICORE consists of a Gateway, the secure entry point into a UNICORE site, which authenticates requests from UNICORE clients based on X.509 certificates and passes them to a *Network Job Supervisor (NJS)* for further processing. The NJS maps the abstract request, as represented by the AJO, into concrete jobs or actions to be performed by the target system, if the target system is part of the local UNICORE site. This process is called incarnation. Sub-jobs that have to be run at a different site are transferred to this site's gateway for subsequent processing by the peer NJS (see Fig. 1.). Additional functions of NJS are: Synchronization of jobs to honor the dependencies specified by the user, automatic transfer of data between UNICORE sites as required for the job execution, collection of results from jobs, especially *stdout* and *stderr*, import and export of data between the UNICORE space and target system, and client workstation.

The third tier of the architecture is the target host which executes the incarnated user jobs. A small daemon, called the *Target System Interface (TSI)* resides on the host to interface with the local batch system on behalf of the user. A stateless protocol is used to communicate between NJS and TSI. Multiple TSIs may be started on a host to increase performance.

3.2 The UNICORE Job and Data Model

Sometimes the question is asked why an old-fashioned concept like batch processing is supported at all by UNICORE. The answer is pragmatic and threefold:

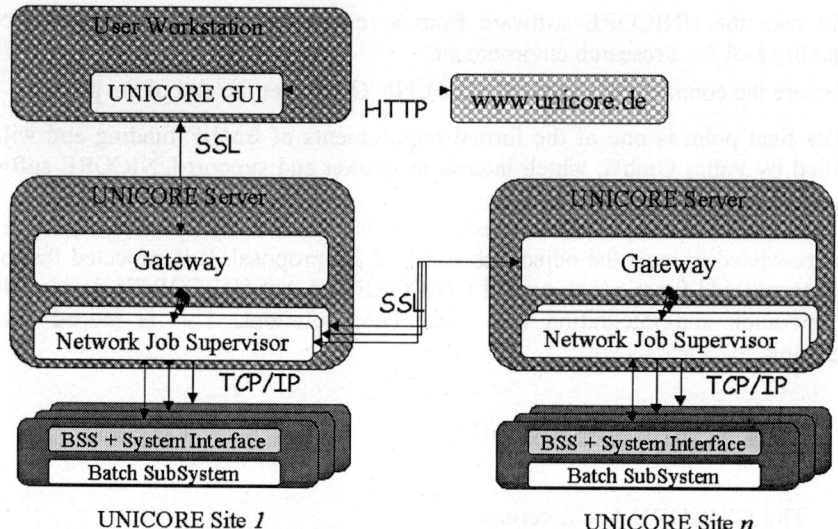

Fig. 1. Multisite UNICORE systems

- Up to 80 percent of the cycles in the German HPC centers are still consumed in batch mode (even scientists sleep some times) and the production environments of HPC centers are UNICORE's primary target.
- Automatic data transfer between sites can be slow over the Internet, but for batch applications the associated latencies can be hidden.
- The need for interactive access to remote systems using the full security and functions of UNICORE are recognized. This however, will be implemented in other UNCIORE based projects, like EUROGRID.

UNICORE defines two important terms: Task and Job Group. A task is the atomic entity that is eventually incarnated into a real batch job for the target system. This fact is not an architectural requirement, but depicts the present implementation. A Job Group is recursively defined to consist of Job Groups and Tasks. The top level Job Group is called a UNICORE job. It is the entity that represents the complete computational solution to the user's problem. The UNICORE job is submitted as a whole to UNICORE.

For the duration of a UNICORE job, the NJS creates a temporary UNICORE space (*Uspace*) using installation specified disk space. The Uspace holds temporary files created by NJS, for example the incarnated jobs, consolidated stdout and stderr, files transmitted from the client to the target, or data created by the executing jobs. UNICORE provides functions to transfer files between Uspaces and to import or export data from or to a permanent file space to which the user has access.

3.3 The Abstract Job Object

When UNICORE was designed to address seamless computing, it became obvious that this goal could realistically be realized only through abstraction. The operations that are to be performed on behalf of the user on a target system are specified by the user in a system independent way using UNICORE's graphical client. Examples are: perform a Fortran compilation, produce highly optimized code, transfer data between two systems, or to show the status of a job. The actions are likewise represented in a system independent way as Abstract Job Objects, which the client creates. These abstract descriptions are translated into system specific actions during the incarnation process. This approach has several advantages:

- The user need not concern herself with system specific conventions and can execute jobs at a foreign installation without having to learn their local conventions.
- The installation can make changes without having to re-train all users.
- The installation can add new systems and have them used in the best known way by all users, not only those who take the time to learn the intricate features.

The Abstract Job Object (AJO) is the basis for the platform and site neutral specification of requests for computational and data resources. The AJO is a conceptual representation of a "Job" as a collection of possibly interdependent operations to be carried out on various computational and data services at collaborating sites. The object-oriented structure and syntax of the AJO are intended to support a specification largely independent of hardware architecture, system software interfaces, and site-specific operational rules. In this way, seamless descriptions of user's work can be created without interfering with site autonomy.

As with the platform-independence realised in the Java virtual machine, complete uniformity of the AJO may in some cases conflict with performance goals. There may, for instance, be architectural features of HPC platforms for which it is not possible to construct an abstraction that maps uniformly to all HPC platforms. When the detailed control of such features is necessary to achieve the maximum performance of the architecture, a performance versus seamlessness trade-off may result. For example the AJO class CompileTask, which includes parameters strongly affecting machine performance, defines uniform concepts such as optimisation levels, to which machine-specific parameters can be assigned. More work will be required in this area. However, the UNICORE consortium have agreed that the following abstract notion of an abstract job is rich enough to describe most of the functions necessary in a batch oriented supercomputing environment. It is not, however, intended to replace the operating system or its batch subsystem, but to inter-operate with them.

Although the complete definition is beyond the scope of this paper, the following summary should illuminate its structure. The AJO is composed of Java Object Classes, as follows:

- **AbstractAction** is an Abstract Class; the superclass JobGroup and AbstractTask.
  - A **JobGroup** is a directed acyclic graph (DAG) of AbstractActions. The DAG structure is the mechanism for specifying dependencies among its actions.

An **AbstractJob** is a specialized JobGroup that provides security services. It acts as the container for the top level UNICORE Job and for sub jobs to be run at remote sites.

- **AbstractTask** is an Abstract Class; the superclass of all task classes.

ExecuteTask is an Abstract Class representing a program execution.
  - **CompileTask:** A class of object which performs a compilation.
  - **LinkTask:** A class of object which executes a linker.
  - **UserTask:** A class of object which executes a user's program.

FileTransfer is an Abstract Class representing transfer of files.
  - **ImportTask:** A class of object which transfers a file from a storage server, which the user is authorised to access, into the temporary UNICORE space (Uspace) in which ExecuteTasks will run.
  - **ExportTask:** A class of object which transfers a file from the Uspace to an external storage server.

Note that this basic AJO object structure is both hierarchical and recursive. Since a JobGroup contains a DAG of AbstractActions and is also a subtype of AbstractAction, an AJO may itself contain AJOs, called sub-AJOs, which may execute at the same or different site.

In addition to this basic structure, the AJO model is supported by an architecture of object hierarchies for representing such things as users, files, priorities, projects, administration parameters, security specifications, and resource requirements. For example, a CompileTask includes a set of resource requirements, a priority, source files, object files, and uniform notions specifying levels for optimisation and compiler output. All these are translated to system/site-specific representations by the NJS at the target site.

Given the diversity of HPC systems, the variety of site administrative policies, and the breath of user requirements, the AJO architecture models the process of job submission and control remarkably well. The aspect of the AJO that makes this both a challenge and ensures its success is that the AJO aims to model the problem domain rather than provide a language to describe all possible situations. In this way, the AJO is more like the CORBA infrastructure of precisely defined services than the resource description language RSL of Globus [1].

The choice of a Java Class Library to represent AJOs has many advantages, not the least being that it was directly usable by the implementation language Java, practically a must for project in 1997. This has also allowed the easy extension of services and abstractions without disrupting the rest of the UNICORE architecture. In the UNICORE Plus project, with its emphasis on deployment of frequently used applications, application specific services are being developed. The AJO has been extended to support these developments with the addition of a new sub-class of AbstractJobObject, called Idiomatic. This subclass provides a collection of frequently used job templates. This allows the development of application specific clients, without the need for a detailed understanding of the complexities required to construct recursive UNICORE jobs.

The AJO architecture and the Unicore Protocol Layer are open interfaces to which implementers are welcome to develop alternative or specialized implementations. The source and documentation are under the control of the UNICORE Forum and can be found at www.unicore.de.

3.4 The UNICORE Client

Graphical user interfaces are important to allow end-users to access Grid resources in a seamless fashion. Batch submission through web interfaces has been developed in several projects, for example Websubmit [9]. The client development in UNICORE focuses on functionality, consistency, and portability. The primary role of the client is to guide the user to create complex jobs consisting of tasks that may execute on multiple systems and/or at different remote sites. The user can combine previously created tasks or job groups to build new jobs, incorporate legacy scripts, specify temporal and data dependencies between tasks, and instruct UNICORE to transfer data. A client component, called the *Job Preparation Agent (JPA)*, creates an Abstract Job Object which can be submitted to a UNICORE gateway once the Job is syntactically correct.

The latter is an important design objective; the client prevents submission of obviously incorrect jobs, thus avoiding the all too familiar pitfall of batch processing - a user waiting many hours for the completion of a job only to find out that the job could not be run because the specified resource limits exceeded the those allowed at the target system. This consistency check occurs, for example, when the user changes the destination. The JPA verifies the values and gives the user the option to adjust the resource requirements. In addition to these client side checks, the NJS supports an extensive framework of defaults, which further increase the chances of successful execution.

A second component of the client is the *Job Monitor Controller (JMC)*, which allows the user to monitor the progress of submitted jobs. An intuitive color scheme indicates the status of the job. Icons representing the job groups and tasks are marked in green (completed successfully), red (failed), yellow (executing), or blue (queued). The user may drill down to the individual task to obtain its status, retrieve stdout or stderr or data created by the job. In addition, the user may terminate executing and remove or hold queued jobs.

Consistency of the graphical interface is achieved by adhering to the JAVA Look and Feel Design Guide [10] and by sharing components developed by the partners. This approach was selected over of trying to present a Windows look-and-feel to PC users and a Unix desktop to Unix users.

When the first UNICORE project was started in 1997 there was great hope that the promise of Java 'Write once, run anywhere' would be fulfilled soon. The client was implemented as a signed applet which allowed rapid deployment of functions to end-users. However, the developers learned the hard way that subtle differences exist between Java implementations on different platforms and some not so subtle differences between browsers. At one time X.509 certificates would either be recognized Netscape or Internet Explorer, but not by both. This forced the project to restrict client support to Netscape, because it is available on Windows and Unix. Based on this experience, the UNICORE Plus project decided to implement the client as a Java application for higher stability, portability, and performance. The results are very promising. There is of course a small price to pay: a tool has to be included into the UNICORE distribution to automate the installation of new client versions as much as possible.

3.5 Application Support in UNICORE

UNICORE's key features, seamless access to remote resources and transparent data transfer, can be exploited by many applications. It would, however, be impractical to create a full new client for each potential application. The project develops mechanisms to generate graphical interfaces for new applications and to integrate applications with existing GUIs into UNICORE. The latter is prototyped for codes like Fluent and STARCD. To support new applications, a wizard has been designed with input from a scientist performing simulations using the Car-Parinello Molecular Dynamics code (CPMD). The wizard guides the user through the process of specifying the relevant parameters for the simulation. Although CPMD is primarily used as an example to demonstrate the technique, it is a worthwhile endeavor in itself. In addition, the researchers can exploit UNICORE to run the CPMD simulation as part of a more complex job including visualization at the workstation or post-processing on a different system. The final project result will be a toolkit to ease integration of existing and new applications into UNICORE.

3.6 System Integration and Security

New software, especially if it is still under development, is accepted in production environments only if it provides substantial additional value and if it requires almost no changes to existing practices or procedures. This might not be true outside Germany. Nevertheless only exposure and usage in production will demonstrate the viability of a new software. Therefore, one of the key objectives of UNICORE is to coexist with exiting administration and security policies.

The task of combining two independently administered, multi-user Unix systems, possibly at different sites is not a challenge, it is a nightmare. The necessary changes to external user names and internal Unix uids and gids creates work and frustration for both the user and the administrator. To require that installations agree on global user names and Unix identification would have certainly prevented deployment. Therefore, UNICORE decided from the beginning to rely on the newly standardized X.509V3 certificates for grid-wide user identification and for authentication of users, systems, and software. An X.509 certificate issued by an accepted Certificate Authority (CA) is a mandatory requirement to access UNICORE resources at participating installations. The NJS maps the user's certificate to a login name for the target system controlled by the NJS. This means that installation need not change their naming conventions, and users need not bother with different identities at different systems.

Hereby, installations retain full autonomy over their resources at two levels: only users that are registered in the login data base may submit jobs at all, and at the second level, the system dependent regulations and limits, like user or project quotas for a particular machine, may be used unchanged. UNICORE explicitly assumes that grid resources have to be accounted for and that the responsibility and accountability remains with the installation.

X.509 certificates are also used to encrypt the communication between UNICORE components, for example a client and a gateway or an NJS and its peer at a different site. Gateways coexist with firewalls. AJOs in transit are signed with the user's private key to protect against tampering. UNICORE implements end-to-end security and privacy.

The decision to use certificates has proved to be excellent one. The expectation, however, that e-commerce would proliferate certificates during the lifetime of the project, to such an extend that everybody would use certificates and that the necessary Public Key Infrastructure (PKI) would be well established, did not come true. As a consequence the project had to establish its own CA under the umbrella of the DFN-PCA [11].

3.7 New Functions

The first UNICORE project restricted itself to demonstrating the basic set of functions. It included a simple, static – but never the less sufficient – resource model. The UNICORE Plus project extends this to a flexible and extensible resource model, which allows the addition of new resource categories in a non-disruptive way and which supports dynamic resource information, such as system load. The interface will enable UNICORE to exploit resource brokers; their implementation, however, will occur as part of the EUROGRID project.

UNICORE's data management is being extended to support specialized servers to move data between different sites and in and out of archives, like HPSS or ADSM, using the full UNICORE security model. Initially, these servers will be run parallel to the context of job submission, be tested independently, and then be evaluated prior to full integration into UNICORE.

There are many scientific applications which require repetitive or conditional execution of jobs with different parameter sets to run computational experiments. To support these scenarios the AJO is enhanced to handle extended control of tasks; graphical support will be provided in the UNICORE client to let the user formulate loops, if-then-else constructs, case statements, and specialized error handling.

4 The EUROGRID Project

The UNICORE project restricted its goals to meet budget and resources limitations, expecting that additional funding could be secured for further development. As one of the first European Grid projects the European Commission decided to fund EUROGRID (EC contract IST 20247) for a period of three years, to demonstrate grid technology based on UNICORE using the existing European network infrastructure. The functions to be added include interactive access, resource brokering, and application services. The project is to demonstrate a European Bio-Grid, a Meteo-Grid, and a CAE-Grid, with the results being commercialized by Pallas GmbH.

5 Globus and UNICORE

Among the international Grid projects, Globus has a well established position. Its goals and functions are described for example in [12]. When the UNICORE project was proposed to BMBF in 1997 it decided not to repeat the development of Globus, but to create a software infrastructure focusing on the practical needs of users of HPC Centers. Today, the strength of Globus is clearly in providing layers of grid services, that enable developers to build additional layers on top of Globus. UNICORE and Globus complement each other. To demonstrate this, a project was started between Argonne National Laboratory and Forschungszentrum Jülich, to develop an interface between Globus and UNICORE, leaving the core components of the two environments unchanged. UNICORE will serve a batch submission portal to Globus resources. A Globus Grid, or part thereof, would in turn assume the role of a UNICORE site making Globus services available to UNICORE clients. Once this has been demonstrated and the respective similarities and differences are fully understood at the technical level, optimized technical solutions can be developed.

6 Summary

UNICORE is demonstrating that Grid computing can be used to solve real problems in day-to-day production. Its particular strength is the seamless, secure and intuitive access to remote heterogeneous resources over the Internet. UNICORE's key achievements, the Abstract Job Object – an open specification – as well as security and authentication based on the X.509 standard, make it a viable implementation of a Grid computing environment.

References

1. Foster and C. Kesselmann, (Ed.) The Grid: Blueprint for a New Computing Infrastructure. Morgan Kaufman Publishers, 1998
2. http://dast.nlanr.net/Clearinghouse
3. http://www.w3c.org/Jigsaw/Doc
4. Wissenschaftsrat: Empfehlung zur Versorgung von Wissenschaft und Forschung mit Höchstleistungsrechenkapazität, Wissenschaftsrat, Drs. 2104/95, 7.7.1995
5. F. Hoßfeld, et. al. Verbund der Supercomputer-Zentren in Deutschland – eine Machbarkeitsanalyse Jülich, 1997
6. D. Erwin, (Ed.) UNICORE – Uniformes Interface für Computing Ressourcen (Final report – in German) http://www.unicore.org, 2000
7. http://www.fz-juelich.de/mcdc
8. Romberg, M. The UNICORE Architecture–Seamless Access to Distributed Ressources
Proceedings of the Eight IEEE International Symposium on High Performance Computing, Redondo Beach, CA, USA, August 1999, Pages 287-293
9. http://www.itl.nist.gov/div895/sasg/websubmit/websubmit.html
10. http://java.sun.com/products/jlf
11. http://www.cert.dfn.de/dfnpca/
12. http://www.globus.org

Portable Parallel CORBA Objects:
An Approach to Combine Parallel and Distributed Programming for Grid Computing

Alexandre Denis[1], Christian Pérez[2], and Thierry Priol[2]

[1] IRISA/IFSIC,
[2] IRISA/INRIA,
Campus de Beaulieu – 35042 Rennes Cedex, France
{Alexandre.Denis,Christian.Perez,Thierry.Priol}@irisa.fr

Abstract. With the availability of Computational Grids, new kinds of applications that will soon emerge will raise the problem of how to program them on such computing systems. In this paper, we advocate a programming model that is based on a combination of parallel and distributed programming models. Compared to previous approaches, this work aims at bringing SPMD programming into CORBA. For example, we want to interconnect two MPI codes by CORBA without modifying MPI or CORBA. We show that such an approach does not entail any loss of performance compared to previous approaches that required modification to the CORBA standard.

1 Introduction

With the availability of high-performance networking technologies, it is nowadays feasible to couple several computing resources together to offer a new kind of computing infrastructure that is called a Computational Grid [3,4]. A Computational Grid acts as a high-performance virtual computer to users to perform various applications such as for scientific computing or for data management. This idea has already been addressed since a Computational Grid can be seen as a kind of distributed and parallel system. Some years ago, A. Tanenbaum[14] gave a definition for such system: "A distributed system is a collection of independent computers that appear to the users of the system as a single computer". Therefore, building Computational Grids raises the same design issues as for distributed systems: transparency (location of resources is transparent to the user), interoperability (to hide the heterogeneity of computing and networking resources) and reliability (the system has to survive the unavailability of computing and networking resources). It also shares the same design issues as for parallel systems: performance (best use of both computing and networking resources) and scalability (efficient management of a huge number of resources).

Software infrastructures, such as Globus[3] or Legion[5], aim at providing runtime systems to allow the execution of applications on Computational Grids. However, Globus was mainly designed to allow the execution of parallel applications. Such approach makes senses since there are already a huge number of existing parallel applications that should benefit from Computational Grids. However, the availability of Computational Grids will give rise to new kind of applications for which parallel programming, based on the use of message-passing libraries, is not suitable. Coupled simulations are an example of such new kinds of application. It aims at coupling several parallel codes to simulate complex systems that require a multi-physics approach. Therefore, one important question arises when using a grid system: what is the most appropriate approach to program a Computational Grid, or said differently, what programming models have to be provided to Grid application designers ? On that matter, there is no consensus mainly due to the wide nature of applications that could benefit from Computational Grids. Since such systems are a combination of parallel and distributed systems, it is very tempting to extend programming models that were associated to parallel systems (message passing libraries, shared memory) so that they can be used for distributed programming. Similarly, programming models for distributed systems (remote procedure call, distributed objects) can be adapted to program parallel systems. Neither of these two approaches can be seen as viable solutions for the future of Grid Computing. It is thus important to try to combine the two different worlds into a single coherent one. Such a programming model will have to give an answer to the design issues already mentioned: transparency, interoperability, reliability, scalability and performance.

This paper aims at showing how two combine parallel and distributed programming technologies. More precisely, it gives a method that combines SPMD (Single Program Multiple Data) with CORBA (Common Object Request Broker Architecture) without modification.

The remainder of this paper is structured as follows. Section 2 gives an overview of different approaches to perform parallel computations with CORBA. Section 3 presents an approach that allows SPMD computation to be performed with standard CORBA. Section 4 provides some experimental results. Finally, we conclude in section 5 by laying the grounds for future works.

2 Parallel Computing with CORBA

Among a large set of distributed programming technologies, CORBA is probably the most promising one due to its object oriented approach and its independence from operating systems and languages. CORBA is a specification from the OMG (Object Management Group) to support distributed object-oriented applications. CORBA acts as a *middleware* that provides a set of services allowing the distribution of objects among a set of computing resources connected to a common network. Transparent remote method invocations are handled by an Object Request Broker (ORB) which provides a communication infrastructure independent of the underlying network. An object interface is specified using the Interface Definition Language (IDL) that gives a list of allowed operations on a particular object. As a distributed programming technology, CORBA can be used as a "glue" to couple several high-performance simulation codes that are executed on different computing resources connected to the Internet. However, CORBA lacks of supporting efficiently the encapsulation of parallel codes. To overcome this problem, several attempts have already been made to extend CORBA in such a way that an object implementation can rely on a SPMD model.

The PARDIS CORBA-based environment [7,8] is one of the first attempts to allow data parallel programming within a CORBA object. PARDIS designers propose a new kind of object they call SPMD object which is an extension of a CORBA object. To support data distribution among different threads associated with a SPMD objects, PARDIS provides a generalization of the CORBA sequence called *distributed sequence*. This new argument type requires the modification of the IDL compiler. PARDIS provides a mechanism to invoke operations on objects asynchronously based on the *future* concept. A *future* is the basic mechanism to get the results of services activated asynchronously.

The PaCO CORBA-based environment [11,13,6] is another attempt for parallel programming in CORBA. We introduced the concept of parallel CORBA object as a collection of identical CORBA objects. It aims at encapsulating a MPI code into CORBA objects so that a MPI code can be fully integrated into a CORBA-based application. Execution of parallel CORBA objects is based on the SPMD execution model. Data distribution between the objects belonging to a collection is entirely handled by the system. However, to let the system carry out parallel execution and data distribution between the objects of the collection, some specifications have been added to the object interface. A parallel object interface is thus described by an extended version of IDL, called Extended–IDL. It is a set of new keywords, added to the IDL syntax[1], to specify the number of objects in the collection, the shape of the virtual node array where objects of the collection will be mapped, the data distribution modes associated with parameters and the collective operations applied to parameters of scalar types.

More recently, the OMG has issued an RFP[10] (Request For Proposal) that solicits proposals to extend CORBA functionality to conveniently and efficiently support parallel processing applications. A response[9] was submitted by a consortium of several industrial companies and a supporting organization. The proposed approach shares some similarities with previous works ([7,11]). However, specification of behaviors of parallel objects (data and request distributions) is not performed thanks to IDL extensions. Instead, it is included in a POA (Portable Object Adapter) policy associated with a Parallel Part Adapter (PPA) that is an extension of the POA. This approach requires a specific ORB (parallel ORB) to manage parallel objects. Calling an operation to a parallel object from a standard ORB requires the use of a proxy object that aims at performing a bridge between the two different ORBs.

In the previous three approaches, adding support for parallel processing within CORBA requires some modifications to the actual standard. These extensions concern either the IDL language or the ORB itself. There are serious doubts that such extensions will be provided by numerous existing CORBA implementations. Our current work is aiming at incorporating SPMD programming

---

[1] A more complete description of these extensions is given in [11,13]

```
#include "Matrix.idl"

interface IExample {
    void send_data(Matrix m);
}
```

Fig. 1. IDL interface of the parallel object

```
void f(long* A, int size) {
    IExample obj("Servant");
    Matrix<long> data(1);         // create a Matrix of 1 dimension
    data->setBounds(0,1,size);    // bounds [1,size[ for dimension 0
    data->setData(A);             // initialize data pointer (no data copy)
    obj->send_data(data);         // remote invocation
}
```

Fig. 2. Motivating Example: a sequential client calls a parallel method.

within CORBA without modifying the standard. It does not entail a lost of performance compared to those approaches that require modifications to CORBA and it has to be easy to use.

3 Portable Parallel CORBA Objects

Parallel CORBA objects are defined as a collection of identical CORBA objects. They aim at providing parallelism support to CORBA. Obviously, CORBA objects of a collection are assumed to work together. They are expected to communicate thanks to an external mechanism, like for example MPI. This work targets parallel CORBA objects on top of compliant CORBA ORBs without involving whatsoever modification of the CORBA specifications. We call such objects portable parallel CORBA objects. Throughout this section, we discuss with respect to a motivating example.

3.1 Motivating Example

Figure 1 presents the user level IDL interface of the motivating example presented in Figure 2. A sequential client wants to send an array A to a method void send_data(Matrix m) of the interface IExample. The client knows that this service is implemented by an object of named Servant. But, the client does not know – and does not want to know – that the implementation is in fact parallel. To connect to the object, the client instantiates a local object obj of type IExample with the name of the remote object as argument. Then, once the Matrix view of its local array A is built, the method is invoked.

3.2 Achieving Portable Parallel CORBA Objects

To implement this kind of example on top of a compliant CORBA ORB, we need to introduce a layer between the user code and the ORB, as depicted in

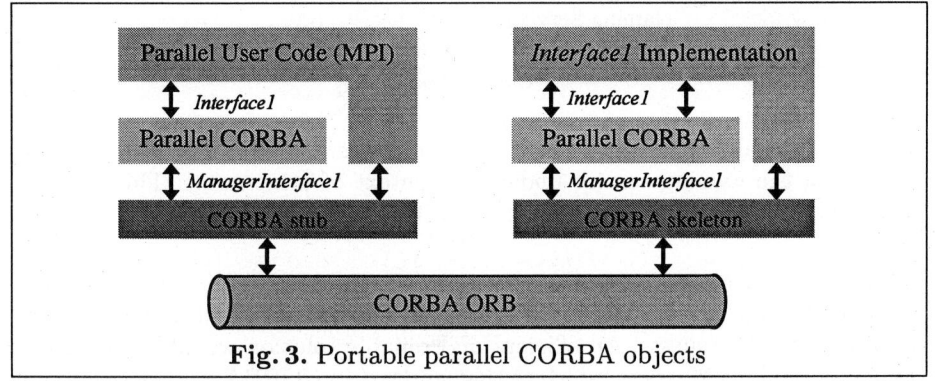

Fig. 3. Portable parallel CORBA objects

Figure 3. This layer embeds the complexity of connection and data distribution management. Its main role is to map an user-level interface – IExample in the example – to an IDL interface, that is called ManagerIExample. This latest interface contains the methods define by the user as well as private methods. The private methods provide services like the localization of all remote objects being part of the implementation of IExample and the retrieval of the data distribution of arguments of user-level methods.

The client and server side methods of the parallel CORBA object layer are analog to the stub and the skeleton of ORB requests. But, while stubs and skeletons of ORB requests deal with peer-to-peer issues (like data marshaling), the stub and skeletons of the parallel CORBA object layer concentrate on data distribution issues. Finally, the stubs and the skeletons of the parallel CORBA layer should be generated from an IDL level description of the user services. However, they are currently hand-written.

The rest of this section reviews different aspects of the internals.

Connection Management. A parallel object is defined by a name (string). This name in fact represents a context in the Naming Service that contains two kind of entries: the IOR of the service manager and all the IOR of the objects that belongs to the parallel objects, as illustrated in Figure 4. The constructor of IExample retrieves information like the number of objects thanks to the Manager object. Then, it can collect their respective IOR from the Naming Service.

Method Invocation. When the client invokes the send_data method, it in fact calls the corresponding method of the ManagerIExample interface, locally implemented into the parallel CORBA layer. This method builds CORBA requests according to the data distributions expected by the parallel objects. Such information is available thanks to methods belonging to the ManagerIExample Interface. Then, it sends the CORBA requests to the ManagerIExample objects. The role of the server side method is to gather data coming from different clients (when the client is parallel) before calling the server side implementation of the send_data method. Similarly, it scatters the out arguments.

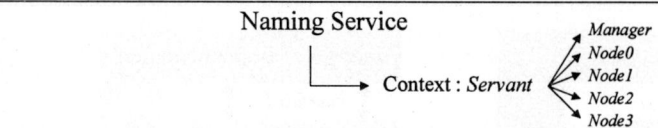

Fig. 4. A parallel CORBA object of name *Servant* registers all its CORBA objects in the naming service under the context of same name. This context also contains the IOR of the manager and the IOR of all objects.

When a client invokes a method of a parallel object, it potentially has to send several CORBA requests. An efficient and reliable solution would be the use of the Asynchronous Message Interface that appears in CORBA 2.4. As we are not aware of open source ORB that supports this feature, we implement a temporary solution based on *oneway* requests. This solution has severe limits. First, it is not a reliable solution as such kind of requests are not reliable according to the CORBA specifications. But, as we used TCP to transport CORBA requests, all *oneway* requests are delivered. Second, we have to build a system to detect the termination of the request.

Data Distribution Management. The core of parallel objects is the data distribution management. From our experience, mainly derived from PaCO and High Performance FORTRAN[2], we believe its important to have a high level of transparency: our choice is to separate the data distribution from the interface. By decoupling the data distribution from the interface, we obtain four major benefits. A first benefit is there is no need to modify the CORBA IDL. The second benefit is that argument data distribution is transparent to the user, as distribution does not appear in the interface. A third benefit is that a parallel object can dynamically change the distribution pattern it is awaiting. This may happen for example if some objects are removed (due to node failure for example) or some objects are added. This feature implies some interesting issues. For example, how is the client informed? A solution would be to use a listener design pattern. A second issue is: what does a parallel object do with incoming requests that have an argument with an old distribution? If all the data has correctly been received, a redistribution may be performed. However, whenever some data is missing (node failure) or the parallel object does not implement the redistribution feature, a CORBA exception is returned to the client. The fourth benefit is the ease of the introduction of new data distribution patterns as only clients and parallel objects that use non standard data distributions have to know about these.

Intermediate Matrix Type. Applications are expected to be written with their own data distribution scheme. So, we face the problem of embedding user data into a standard IDL representation so as to provide interoperability. We achieve data distribution interoperability thanks to a `Matrix` interface, sketched in Figure 5. It provides a logical API to manipulate an internal IDL representation

```
interface  Matrix {

  struct dim't { long  size,   low,   high; };

  struct  matrix {
    dis_t              dis;    // current distribution
    long               ndim;   // number of dimension
    sequence<dim_t>    rdim;   // global view of the array
    sequence<dim_t>    ddim;   // local  view of the array
    data_t             data;   // data
  };
};
```

Fig. 5. IDL distributed array representation

```
Matrix<float> data(2);          // matrix with 2 dimension

data.setBounds(0,0,size1);      // Set bounds for dimension 0
data.setBounds(1,0,size2);      // Set bounds for dimension 1
Distribution d0(Matrix::BLOCK, procid, nbproc);
Distribution d1(Matrix::SEQ);
data.setDistribution(0, d0);    // Set distribution for dimension 0
data.setDistribution(1, d1);    // Set distribution for dimension 1
data.allocateData();            // Allocate memory

for( int i0 = data.low(0); i0 < data.high(0); i0++ )
  for( int i1 = data.low(1); i1 < data.high(1); i1++ )
    data(i0, i1) = ...
```

Fig. 6. C++ server side example: initialization of a 2D distributed array of floats which has a block-distributed dimension. i0 and i1 are global indexes

of data distributions. This API should be straightforward for client (like in the example of Figure 2) and should provide functionalities for implementers. Internally, the Matrix interface manages an IDL structure that contains distribution information as well user data. That's this structure which is sent through the ORB.

Currently, we only implement the Matrix interface as a C++ class whose API provides methods that manages a C++ representation of the IDL Matrix structure. While Figure 2 has provided a client side example, Figure 6 presents a server side example that illustrates the initialization of a 2D distributed array.

4 Preliminary Experiments

The goal of this section if to evaluate the performance of the portable parallel CORBA objects on basic situations: a client connected to a parallel object. First, we use a sequential client connected to a parallel object. Then, we connect a parallel client to a parallel object. All CORBA objects belonging to a parallel CORBA object are located on different machines. For most experiments, we limit the parallelism to two nodes. We concentrate on the overhead generated on a node as we know that aggregated performance is possible [6]. However, we finish this section by presenting experiments involving two clusters of height nodes connected by VTHD, a gigabit wide-area network.

Table 1. Performances of Mico and OmniORB ORBs for a sequential client connected to a parallel CORBA object (2 objects) over Fast Ethernet

	Version 1 - Explicit data copy			Version 2 - No explicit data copy		
	Mico	Mico patch	OmniORB	Mico	Mico patch	OmniORB
Building (ms)	267	250	284	103	2.80	2.93
Sending (ms)	1020	1003	861	986	1005	863
Total (ms)	1288	1253	1156	1090	1008	866
Sending (MB/s)	9.80	9.97	11.61	10.14	9.95	11.59
Total (MB/s)	7.76	7.98	8.65	9.17	9.92	11.55

4.1 Basic Experiments

We perform experiments for two version of the portable parallel CORBA object layer. Version 1 does explicit data copy when creating CORBA requests while Version 2 uses sequence data constructor.

An important goal is to have *portability*. So, we experiment two different ORBs: Mico 2.3.4 [12] and OmniORB 3 [1]. As Mico 2.3.4 performs a copy when used with sequence data constructor, we remove this (unnecessary) copy by patching the unbounded sequence C++ template of Mico 2.3.4. We reference this patched Mico version as "Mico patch". We do not modify OmniORB 3 as it does not copy data in sequence data constructors. The ORBs have been compiled for speed as well as the test programs. The compilers are gcc/g++ 2.95.2. The test platform is a PC cluster. The nodes are dual-processor Pentium II 450 Mhz with 256 MB memory. The network is a standard Fast Ethernet (100 Mb) and the communication protocol is TCP/IP. The operating system is Linux 2.2.13.

The experiments presented in Table 1 are for a sequential client transferring an array to a parallel object. The performances are presented for the portable parallel CORBA objects with Mico 2.3.4, Mico 2.3.4 patch and OmniORB 3. The first row of the table represents the building time (computing part), the second row the sending time and the third row the whole time of the operation, which is very close of the building time plus the sending time. The fourth and the fifth rows present the data bandwidth of the sending row and the total row.

As shown in Table 1, the building time leads to a huge overhead when there are data copies. The use of sequence data constructor improve performances. But, the use of a zero-copy sequence data constructor allow a more important decrease of the building time (divided by 100). The consequence is an bandwidth improvement of 24 % for Mico patch and of 33 % for OmniORB.

The experiments presented in Table 2 are for a parallel client invoking a method on a parallel object. We observe that a strategy based on sequence data constructor leads to better performance. The use of zero-copy data constructor leads again to better performances. The reason why the overhead is so small is we really re-use the buffer of the incoming request (forward) and so there are no creation of new sequences. The building time in Version 2 is negligible with respect to the communication time.

Table 2. Performances of Mico and OmniORB ORBs for a parallel client (2 objects) connected to a parallel object (2 objects) over Fast Ethernet. No data redistribution

	Version 1 - Explicit data copy			Version 2 - No explicit data copy		
	Mico	Mico patch	OmniORB	Mico	Mico patch	OmniORB
Building (ms)	129	117	141	50	0.27	0.25
Sending (ms)	547	508	432	544	518.6	431.5
Total (ms)	676	625	574	593	519.2	432.1
Sending (MB/s)	9.14	9.84	11.57	9.19	9.64	11.59
Total (MB/s)	7.39	8.00	8.71	8.43	9.63	11.57

4.2 VTHD Experiments

Very recently, we had access to the VTHD network. It's an experimental network of 2.5 Gb/s that in particular interconnects two INRIA laboratories, which are about one thousand kilometers apart. In a peer-to-peer situation using OmniORB we measure a throughput of 11 MB/s; the Ethernet 100 Mb/s card being the limiting factor. For experiments with an 8-node parallel client and an 8-node parallel object, we measure an aggregated bandwidth of 85.7 MB/s, which represents a point-to-point bandwidth of 10.7 MB/s. Portable CORBA parallel objects prove to efficiently aggregate bandwidth.

4.3 Comparison with PaCO Performance

With PaCO, we perform experiments similar to those of section 4.1. We used the last available version which is based on Mico 2.3.3. We obtain 8.77 MB/s for the sequential client and 8.51 MB/s for the parallel client. When compared to Table 1 and Table 2, one can see that performances are similar and depend mostly on the performance of the underlying ORB. So, the portable parallel CORBA objects are as efficient as parallel CORBA objects of PaCO.

5 Conclusion

Thanks to the continuous improvement of networks, Computational Grids are becoming more and more popular. Some Grid Architectures, like Globus, provide a parallel programming model, which does not appear well suited for certain applications, for example coupled simulations. For such applications, we advocate a programming model based on a combination of parallel and distributed programming models.

CORBA has proved to be an interesting technology. However, as it does not handle parallelism, there is a clear need of parallel CORBA objects when interconnecting for example two MPI parallel codes. Previous works on parallel CORBA objects [7,11] have required modifications of CORBA specifications. In this paper, we have shown that it is feasible to define parallel CORBA objects on top of CORBA compliant ORB without modification of the IDL. As we do not modify CORBA specifications, we need to introduce a layer between the user code and the ORB to handle data distribution issues. Thanks to this layer, we can achieve data distribution transparency at the client side while allowing parallel objects to dynamically change the expected data distribution of their method arguments. Experiments show that the overhead of this layer is very small. Efficiency relies on the no-copy sequence data constructor and on the efficiency of the communications of the ORB. Also, contrary to a belief, the numbers show that current CORBA implementation can be very efficient on Ethernet networks.

Future work will concern the definition of interfaces related to parallel objects that we have just sketched in this paper. A second direction is to further study issue with dynamic modification of data distribution. Note that distributions are always decided by the server side application.

References

1. AT&T Laboratories Cambridge. OmniORB Home Page. http://www.omniorb.og.
2. High Performance Fortran Forum. *High Performance Fortran Language Specification.* Rice University, Houston, Texas, October 1996. Version 2.0.
3. I. Foster and C. Kesselman. Globus: A metacomputing infrastructure toolkit. *The International Journal of Supercomputer Applications and High Performance Computing*, 11(2):115–128, Summer 1997.
4. I. Foster and C. Kesselman, editors. *The Grid: Blueprint for a New Computing Infracstructure.* Morgan Kaufmann Publishers, Inc, 1998.
5. A. S. Grimshaw, W. A. Wulf, and the Legion team. The Legion Vision of a Worldwide Virtual Computer. *Communications of the ACM*, 1(40):39–45, January 1997.
6. T. Kamachi, T. Priol, and C. René. Data distribution for parallel corba objects. In *EuroPar'00 conference*, August 2000.
7. K. Keahey and D. Gannon. PARDIS: A Parallel Approach to CORBA. In *Supercomputing'97*. ACM/IEEE, November 1997.
8. K. Keahey and D. Gannon. Developing and Evaluating Abstractions for Distributed Supercomputing. *Cluster Computing*, 1(1):69–79, May 1998.
9. Mercury Computer Systems, Inc. and Objective Interface Systems, Inc. and MPI Software Technology, Inc. and Los Alamos National Laboratory. Data Parallel CORBA - Initial Submission, August 2000.
10. Object Management Group. Request For Proposal: Data Parallel Application Support for CORBA, March 2000.
11. T. Priol and C. René. COBRA: A CORBA-compliant Programming Environment for High-Performance Computing. In *Euro-Par'98*, pages 1114–1122, September 1998.
12. A. Puder. The MICO CORBA Compliant System. *Dr Dobb's Journal*, 23(11):44–51, November 1998.
13. C. René and T. Priol. MPI code encapsulating using parallel CORBA object. In *Proceedings of the Eighth IEEE International Symposium on High Performance Distributed Computing*, pages 3–10, August 1999.
14. A. Tanenbaum. *Distributed Operating System.* Prentice Hall, 1994.

CORBA *Lightweight Components*: A Model for Distributed Component-Based Heterogeneous Computation*

Diego Sevilla[1], José M. García[1], and Antonio Gómez[2]

[1] Department of Computer Engineering
{dsevilla,jmgarcia}@ditec.um.es
[2] Department of Information and Communications Engineering
University of Murcia, Spain
skarmeta@dif.um.es

Abstract. In this article we present CORBA *Lightweight Components*, CORBA–$\mathcal{LC}$, a new network-centered reflective component model which allows building distributed applications assembling binary independent components spread on the network. It provides a *peer* network view in which the component dependencies are managed automatically to perform an intelligent application run-time deployment, leading to better utilization of resources. We show the validity of the CORBA–$\mathcal{LC}$ approach in dealing with CSCW and Grid Computing applications.

1 Introduction

Component-Based Development[21] has emerged as the natural successor of the Object-Oriented paradigm. Components allow (1) to develop independent binary units that can be packaged and distributed independently, and (2) to build modular applications based on the assembly of those binary units. Binary interchangeability leads to the maximum reuse as components can be added to (and removed from) a system even without the need of recompiling, provided that the components state what they require and what they offer to the system.

When component technology is applied to distributed applications, programmers can develop independent components that can interact transparently with other components residing in remote machines. However, while programmers would expect the component infrastructure to utilize all the computing power and resources available for running their components, traditional component models force programmers deciding the hosts in which their components are going to be run and build a "static" description of the application (*assembly*).

This article describes CORBA *Lightweight Components* (CORBA–$\mathcal{LC}$), a new component model based on CORBA[13]. CORBA–$\mathcal{LC}$ offers the traditional component models advantages (modular applications development connecting binary interchangeable units) allowing automatic placement of components in network

---

* Partially supported by Spanish SENECA Foundation, Grant PB/13/FS/99.

nodes, intelligent component migration and load balancing, leading to maximum network resource utilization. Thus, it introduces a more *peer* network-centered model in which all node resources, computing power and components can be used at run-time to automatically satisfy applications dependencies.

This paper is organized as follows. Section 2 describes the CORBA-$\mathcal{LC}$ Component Model. Section 3 outlines other distributed component models and how CORBA-$\mathcal{LC}$ is related to them. Section 4 describes the principal application domains we are targeting in this research: Computer-Supported Cooperative Work (CSCW) and Grid Computing. Finally, Section 5 presents the conclusions, current development status and future work.

2 CORBA *Lightweight Components*

CORBA-$\mathcal{LC}$ is a lightweight component model based on CORBA, sharing many features with the CORBA Component Model (CCM)[12].

2.1 Components

Components are the most important abstraction in CORBA-$\mathcal{LC}$. They can be seen, at least, under two different dimensions:

1. **Binary package**: Components are independent binary units that can be used to compose applications. Thus, components include information which allow them (a) to be installed, (b) to be managed as a binary package, (c) to be dynamically (un)loaded as a Dynamic Link Library (DLL), and (d) to be instantiated. This information includes static hardware and software (such as Operating System, *Object Request Broker*) dependencies (***Static*** dimension).
2. **Component Type**: Component instances are run-time incarnations of the behavior stored in a component. Thus, components are also a description of run-time properties and requirements of their instances (***dynamic*** dimension). These properties and requirements can be either internal or external.

Internal properties describe requirements and properties that instances expose to the framework in which they are immerse. This framework is described in the following subsections.

External properties are those that component instances expose to their clients (other components or applications). These external communication points are collectively called "ports". Ports allow components to be connected together to accomplish the required task. A set of IDL and XML files is used to establish the *minimal* set of ports a component needs from and offers to other components. Those files are included within the component binary package (§2.3).

CORBA-$\mathcal{LC}$ does not limit the different port kinds that a component can expose. However, there are two basic kinds of ports: interfaces and events.

A component can indicate that its instances (***provide***) or ***use*** some interfaces[1] for their internal work. Interfaces represent agreed synchronous communication points between components.

Events can be used as asynchronous communication means for components. They can also specify that they produce or consume some kind of event in a publish/subscribe fashion. For each event kind produced by a component, the framework opens a push event channel. Components can subscribe to this channel to express its interest in the event kind produced by the component.

The set of external properties of a component is not fixed and may change at run-time. This is supported by the **Reflection Architecture** described in §2.4.

Finally, factory interfaces[5] are needed in CORBA-$\mathcal{LC}$ to manage the set of instances of a component. Clients can search for a factory of the required component and ask it for the creation of a component instance. Factory code can be automatically generated depending on component requirements.

2.2 Containers and Component Framework

Component instances are run within a run-time environment called **container**. Containers become the instances view of the world. Instances ask the container for the required services and it in turn informs the instance of its environment (its *context*). As in CCM and Enterprise Java Beans (EJB)[20], the component/container dialog is based on agreed local interfaces, thus conforming a component framework. Containers leverage the component implementation of dealing with the non-functional aspects of the component[3], such as instance activation/de-activation, resource discovery and allocation, component migration and replication, load balancing[14] and fault tolerance among others. Containers also act as component instance representatives into the network, performing distributed resource queries in behalf of their managed component instances.

2.3 Packaging Model

The packaging allows to build self-contained binary units which can be installed and used independently. Components are packaged in ".ZIP" files containing the component itself and its description as IDL and XML files. This is similar to the CCM Packaging Model[12]. This information can be used by each node in the system to know how to install and instantiate the component. The packaging allows storing different binaries of the same component to match different Hardware/Operating System/ORB.

2.4 Deployment and Network Model

The deployment model describes the rules a set of components must follow to be installed and run in a set of network-interconnected machines in order to cooperate to perform a task. CORBA-$\mathcal{LC}$ deployment model is supported by

---
[1] We use "interface" here in the same sense that it is used in CORBA.

a set of main concepts: **nodes**, the **reflection architecture**, the **network model**, the **distributed registry** and **applications**.

Nodes The CORBA–$\mathcal{LC}$ network model can be effectively represented as a set of nodes that collaborate in computations. *Nodes* are the entities maintaining the logical network behavior. Each host participating must have running a server implementing the *Node* service. Nodes maintain the logical network connection, encapsulate physical host information and constitute the external view of the internal properties of the host they are running on. Concretely, they offer (Fig. 1):

- A way of obtaining both node static characteristics (such as CPU and Operating System Type, ORB) and dynamic system information (such as CPU and memory load, available resources, etc.): *Resource Manager* interface.
- A way of obtaining the external view of the local services: the *Component Registry* interface reflects the internal *Component Repository* and allows performing distributed queries.
- Hooks for accepting new components at run-time for local installation, instantiation and running[10] (*Component Acceptor* interface).
- Operations supporting the protocol for logical *Network Cohesion*.

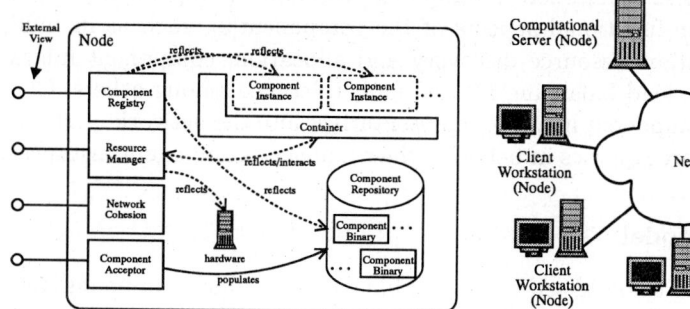
Fig. 1. Logical Node Structure

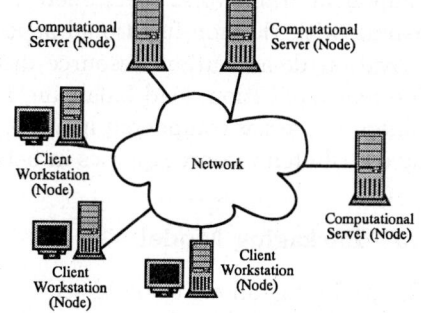
Fig. 2. Network-centered architecture

The Reflection Architecture The **Reflection Architecture** is composed of the meta-data given by the different node services and is used at various stages in CORBA–$\mathcal{LC}$ (Fig. 1):

- The *Component Registry* provides information about (a) the set of installed components, (b) the set of component instances running in the node and the properties of each, and (c) how those instances are connected via ports (assemblies)[15]. This information is used when components, applications or visual builder tools need to obtain information about components.

– The **Resource Manager** in the node collaborates with the **Container** implementing initial placement of instances, migration/load balancing at run-time. Resource Manager also reflects the hardware static characteristics and dynamic resource usage and availability.

With the help of the reflection architecture, new components (or new version of existing components) can be aggregated to the system at any time, and become instantly available to be used by other components.

In contrast to CCM, the set of external properties of a component is not fixed and may change at run-time. Thus, component instances can adapt to the changing environment requesting new services or offering new ones. CORBA-$\mathcal{LC}$ offers operations which allow modifying the set of ports a component exposes[17].

Network Model and The Distributed Registry The CORBA-$\mathcal{LC}$ deployment model is a network-centered model (Fig. 2): The complete network is considered as a repository for resolving component requirements.

Each host (node) in the system maintain a set of installed components in its **Component Repository**, which become available to the whole network. When component instances require other components, the network issues the corresponding distributed queries to each node's **ComponentRegistry** in order to find the component which match better with the stated QoS requirements. Once selected, the network can decide either to fetch the component to be locally installed, instantiated and run or to use it remotely (a component decoding a MPEG video stream would work much faster if installed locally).

This network behavior is implemented by the **Distributed Registry**. It stores information covering the resources available in the network as a whole, and is responsible of managing these. Component Registries, Resource Managers and the Network Cohesion interface of each node support the Distributed Registry behavior. Component Registries collaborate to resolve distributed component queries and reflect the internal Component Repository of each node.

Applications and Assembly In CORBA-$\mathcal{LC}$, *applications* are just special components. They are special because (1) they encapsulate the explicit rules to connect together certain components and their instances, and (2) they are created by users with the help of visual building tools.

With the given definition, applications can be considered as *bootstrap* components: when applications start running, they expose their explicit dependencies, requiring instances of other components and connecting them following the user stated pattern for that particular application. This is similar to what in CCM is called an *assembly*. Conversely, in CORBA-$\mathcal{LC}$ the matching between component required instances and network-running instances is performed at run-time: the exact node in which every instance is going to be run is decided when the application requests it, and this decision may change to reflect changes in the load of either the nodes or the network. The deployment of the application, instead of being fixed at deployment-design time, is intelligently performed at run-time, which allows intelligent run-time scheduling, migration and load balancing schemes. Fixed *versus* run-time deployment can be compared with static *versus* dynamic linking of Operating Systems libraries, but augmented to the distributed heterogeneous case.

3 Related Work

To date, several component models have been developed. Although CORBA-$\mathcal{LC}$ shares some features with them, it also has some key differences.

Java Beans[19] is a framework for implementing Java-based desktop applications. It is limited to both Java and the client side of the application. In contrast, CORBA-$\mathcal{LC}$ is not limited to Java and allows components to be distributed among different hosts, still allowing seamless integration of local GUI components.

Microsoft's Component Object Model (COM)[11] offers a component model in which all desktop applications are integrated. Its main disadvantages are that, (1) it does not fit well the distributed case (DCOM), and (2) its support is rather limited to Windows. Moreover, COM components do not expose their requirements (other required components)[15,8]. CORBA-$\mathcal{LC}$ inherits from CORBA its Operating System, programming language and location transparency, thus effectively adapting to heterogeneous environments. Moreover, it is designed from the beginning to automatically exploit the computing power and components installed in the network using its Reflection Architecture.

In the server side, SUN's Enterprise Java Beans[20] and the new Object Management Group's CORBA Component Model (CCM)[12,18] offer a server programming framework in which server components can be installed, instantiated and run. These models are fairly similar, but EJB is a Java-only system, and CCM continues the CORBA heterogeneous philosophy. Both models are designed towards supporting enterprise applications, thus offering a container architecture with convenient support for transactions, persistence, security, etc.[17] They also offer the notion of components as binary units which can be installed and executed (following a fixed assembly) in Application Servers.

Although CORBA-$\mathcal{LC}$ shares many features with them, it presents a more dynamic model in which the deployment is performed at run-time using the dynamic system data offered by the Reflection Architecture. It also allows adding new components and modifying component instances properties and connections at run-time and reflecting those changes to visual building tools. It is a *lightweight* model: the main goal is the optimal network resource utilization instead of supporting the overhead of enterprise-oriented services. This complexity is one of the main reasons why the CCM specification is still not finished.

In general, component models have been designed to be either client-side *or* server-side. This forces programmers to follow different models for different layers of applications. CORBA-$\mathcal{LC}$ offers a more *peer* approach in which applications can utilize all the computing power available, including the more and more powerful user workstations and high-end servers. Application components can be developed using a single component model and spread into the network. They will be intelligently migrated into the required hosts. Thus, a *homogeneous* component model can be used to develop all the tiers (GUI, application logic) of distributed multi-tiered applications.

In[8], a dynamic configuration management system is described. This work provides us with valuable ideas for our research. However, it is centered in the process of automatic component configuration and does not offer a complete component model.

4 Application Domains

The CORBA–*LC* model represents a very convenient infrastructure for developing applications in a wide range of domains. It can be seen as a general purpose infrastructure. However, we are specially interested in dealing with Computer-Supported Cooperative Work (CSCW) and Grid Computing.

4.1 Computer Supported Cooperative Work (CSCW) Domain

Collaborative work applications allow a group of users to share and manipulate a set of data (usually multi-media) in a synchronous or asynchronous way regardless of user location[22]. We are interested in the development and deployment of *synchronous* CSCW applications, including video-conferencing, shared whiteboard and workspaces, workflow and co-authoring systems. CORBA–*LC* represents an optimal environment for various reasons:

- It offers a peer distributed model, which matches the inherently peer distributed nature of these applications.
- GUI components can be considered within the whole application design, allowing the presentation layer to evolve smoothly.
- It allows bandwidth-limited, multimedia components (such as video stream decoding) to be migrated and installed locally to minimize network load.
- It allows Personal Digital Assistants (PDAs) to be used as normal nodes with limited capabilities: they can use all components remotely.

Figure 3 depicts the relationships between a CSCW application and other components, including GUI ones. The latter can be either local or remote, painting in their portion of the window using the local *Display* component which provides painting functions. Applications can change how the data is shown by replacing the GUI components at run-time. Can be all remote, enabling thin clients such as PDA.

4.2 Grid Computing Domain

Our view of Grid Computation targets scalable and intelligent resource and CPU usage within a distributed system, using techniques such as *IDLE*

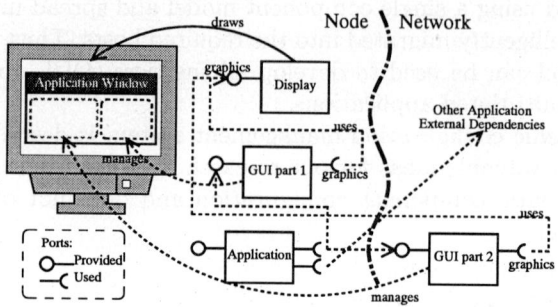

Fig.3. CSCW application model

computation[6] and *volunteer computing*[16]. These techniques fit seamlessly within the CORBA-$\mathcal{LC}$ model to suit Grid Computation needs.

Other component-based alternatives such as the Common Component Architecture (CCA)[1] have appeared in the High-Performance Computing (HPC) community. These models introduce components kinds which reflect the special characteristics of the field (for example, components whose instances must be split to perform a highly-parallel task). While we find this approach very interesting, those models usually become only a minimum wrapper[9] for reusing legacy scientific code and do not offer a complete component model. A similar approach was presented also by Walker *et al.*[23]. Their interest is in Problem-Solving Environments (PSEs) using an XML-based component model to wrap legacy scientific components.

FOCALE[2] offers a component model for grid computation. It uses CORBA and Java (although it supports legacy applications). It provides a system view at different levels: federation, server, factories, instances and connections.

Developments in the Grid Computing field include Globus[4] and Legion[7]. They are systems which offer services for applications to access to the computational grid. However, they are huge systems, difficult to manage and configure, somewhat failing in its primary intentions. Moreover, they do not address very well the interoperability and code reuse through component technology.

5 Conclusions and Future Work

In this article we have described the CORBA-$\mathcal{LC}$ Component Model. Also, we have stated the validity of the design to target the CSCW and Grid Computing domains. Current CORBA-$\mathcal{LC}$ implementation allows building components with the stated external characteristics and packaging. However, the implementation is still incomplete, so we have some future work to do: Explore strategies to maintain the described Reflection Architecture and the network-awareness of both nodes and the Distributed Registry[8], also introducing fault-tolerance techniques; Implement visual building tools allowing users to build applications based on all available network components; Further identify CSCW and Grid-based application needs enhancing CORBA-$\mathcal{LC}$ to better support them; And study the integration of this model with future CCM implementations.

Finally, we plan to continue enhancing CORBA-$\mathcal{LC}$ as a general computing platform, to offer programmers both the advantages of the Component-Based Development and Distributed Computing.

References

1. R. Bramley, K. Chiu, S. Diwan, D. Gannon, M. Govindaraju, N. Mukhi, B. Temko, and M. Yechuri. A Component Based Services Architecture for Building Distributed Applications. In *Proceedings of the High Performance Distributed Computing Conference*, 2000.
2. G. S. di Apollonia, C. Gransart, and J-M. Geib. FOCALE: Towards a Grid View of Large-Scale Computation Components. In *Grid'2000 Workshop, 7th Int. Conf. on High Performance Computing*, Bangalore, India, Dec. 2000.
3. J. Fabry. Distribution as a set of Cooperating Aspects. In *ECOOP'2000 Workshop on Distributed Objects Programming Paradigms*, June 2000.
4. I. Foster and C. Kesselman, editors. *The Grid: Blueprint for a New Computing Infrastructure*. Morgan Kaufmann Publishing, 1999.
5. E. Gamma, R. Helm, R. Johnson, and J. Vlissides. *Design Patterns: Elements of Reusable Object-Oriented Software*. Addison-Wesley, Reading, MA, 1995.
6. D. Gelernter and D. Kaminsky. Supercomputing out of Recycled Garbage: Preliminary Experience with Piranha. In *Sixth ACM International Conference on Supercomputing*, pages 417–427, July 1992.
7. A. S. Grimshaw and Wm. A. Wulf. The Legion Vision of a Worldwide Virtual Computer. *Communications of the ACM*, 40(1), January 1997.
8. F. Kon, T. Yamane, C. Hess, R. Campbell, and M.D. Mickunas. Dynamic Resource Management and Automatic Configuration of Distributed Component Systems. In *Proceedings of the 6th USENIX Conference on Object-Oriented Technologies and Systems (COOTS'2001)*, San Antonio, Texas, February 2001.
9. M. Li, O. F. Rana, M. S. Shields, and D. W. Walker. A Wrapper Generator for Wrapping High Performance Legacy Codes as Java/CORBA Components. In *Supercomputing'2000 Conference*, Dallas, TX, November 2000.
10. R. Marvie, P. Merle, and J-M. Geib. A Dynamic Platform for CORBA Component Based Applications. In *First Intl. Conf. on Software Engineering Applied to Networking and Parallel/Distributed Computing (SNPD'00)*, France, May 2000.
11. Microsoft. *Component Object Model (COM)*, 1995. http://www.microsoft.com/com.
12. Object Management Group. *CORBA Component Model*, 1999. OMG Document ptc/99-10-04.
13. Object Management Group. *CORBA: Common Object Request Broker Architecture Specification, revision 2.4.1*, 2000. OMG Document formal/00-11-03.
14. O. Othman, C. O'Ryan, and D. Schmidt. The Design and Performance of an Adaptative CORBA Load Balancing Service. *Distributed Systems Engineering Journal*, 2001.
15. N. Parlavantzas, G. Coulson, M. Clarke, and G. Blair. Towards a Reflective Component-based Middleware Architecture. In *ECOOP'2000 Workshop on Reflection and Metalevel Architectures*, 2000.
16. L. F. G. Sarmenta. Bayanihan: Web-Based Volunteer Computing Using Java. In *2nd International Conference on World-Wide Computing and its Applications (WWCA'98)*, March 1998.

17. D. Sevilla. CORBA & Components. Technical Report TR-12/2000, University of Extremadura, Spain, 2000.
18. D. Sevilla. *The CORBA & CORBA Component Model (CCM) Page*, 2001. http://www.ditec.um.es/~dsevilla/ccm/, visited April, 2001.
19. SUN Microsystems. *Java Beans specification*, 1.0.1 edition, July 1997. http://java.sun.com/beans.
20. SUN Microsystems. *Enterprise Java Beans specification*, 1.1 edition, December 1999. http://java.sun.com/products/ejb/index.html.
21. C. Szyperski. *Component Software: Beyond Object-Oriented Programming.* ACM Press, 1998.
22. G. Henri ter Hofte. *Working Apart Toguether. Foundation for Component Groupware.* PhD thesis, Telematica Institut, The Netherlands, 1998.
23. D. Walker, O. F. Rana, M. Li, M. S. Shields, and Y. Huang. The Software Architecture of a Distributed Problem-Solving Environment. *Concurrency: Practice & Experience*, 12(15):1455–1480, December 2000.

Building Computational Communities from Federated Resources*

Nathalie Furmento, Steven Newhouse, and John Darlington

Parallel Software Group, Department of Computing, Imperial College of Science,
Technology and Medicine
180 Queen's Gate, London SW7 2BZ, UK
icpc-sw@doc.ic.ac.uk
http://www-icpc.doc.ic.ac.uk/components/

Abstract. We describe the design and the implementation in Java and Jini of a *Computational Community*, which supports the federation of resources from different organisations. Resources from the local *Administrative Domain* are published in a Jini space to form a *Computational Community*. Different access control policies can be applied to the same resource in different *Computational Communities*. We show how this architecture can be extended through the addition of an *Application Mapper* and *Resource Broker* to build a computational economy.

Keywords: Computational Community, Computational Economy, Grid Computing, Distributed Systems.

1 Introduction

The accelerating proliferation of computing resources together with the rapid expansion of high speed connection networks has increased the interest of users in computational grids. A computational grid is defined as a combination of geographically distributed heterogeneous hardware and software resources that provide a ubiquitous computation environment [1]. The motivation behind computational grids is to deliver computational power to a user's application in a similar way the electrical power is delivered to an electrical appliance. This can only be achieved through integration between the resources and the application.

As no single organisation is able to provide all the resources in such an infrastructure, it is inevitable that the grid will be composed of federated resources. However, organisations will only be willing to contribute their resources to the grid if they retain ultimate control of how and when they are used. Therefore, any grid middleware must not only provide strong authentication mechanisms suitable for a distributed computing environment, but must also support sophisticated access control policies capable of differing between individuals, groups and

---

* Research supported by the EPSRC grant GR/N13371/01 on equipment provided by the HEFCE/JREI grants GR/L26100 and GR/M92455

organisations. Resource federation is more likely to take place between organisations if there is mutual self interest or a natural inter-organisational grouping, e.g. to build a *Computational Community* of particle physics users.

Ensuring effective utilisation of these distributed federated resources is a challenge to both users and resource providers. It is essential that any *Computational Community* is able to balance the computational demand and supply of its users and resource providers. We will show how our *Computational Community*, built from federated resources, can be extended through market mechanisms to a computational economy where resources are traded between providers and consumers to ensure effective resource utilisation.

Roadmap. This paper will present our vision of a *Computational Community* and how it can be extended to form a computational economy. Section 2 gives a global overview of the *Computational Community* middleware as well as related work. Sections 3 and 4 give further details of the abstractions in the middleware. Before concluding, we describe in Section 5 how the *Computational Community* can be extended through higher level services.

2 Building a Computational Community

2.1 Concepts

Our middleware (see Fig. 1) consists of: (1) a private *Administrative Domain* that allows the local administrator to manage the resources of their organisation (see §3), (2) a *Domain Manager* that acts as a conduit between the private and public areas of the infrastructure. It annotates publishable resources in the private *Administrative Domain* with access control information, and authenticates and authorises incoming requests to use these local resources (see §4), and (3) a public *Computational Community* where the information about the resources and how they can be used are made available to the users (see §5).

The *Computational Community* is built from potentially diverse computational, storage and software resources that have both static and dynamic attributes. These resources are managed through the local *Administrative Domain*. The *Domain Manager* is used by the local administrator to publish the resources from the *Administrative Domain* in any number of public *Computational Communities*. The *Identity Manager* is trusted by the *Domain Manager* to authenticate the identity of the users wishing to access the local resources and is administered by the local administrator.

Three management tools – the *Resource Manager*, the *Policy Manager* and the *Resource Browser* – allow both users and administrators to interact with the framework through a graphical interface.

2.2 Prototype

A prototype of this architecture has been completed using a Java and Jini environment. We exploit the cross-platform portability of Java [2] with its diverse class libraries to simplify many of the development tasks. Jini [3] is used as the primary service infrastructure of the architecture as it has several desirable features for a wide-area grid environment. It supports dynamic registration, lookup and connection between the Java objects which represent our grid resources. We use a Jini lookup server to implement the public *Computational Communities* and the private *Administrative Domains* defined in our architecture.

Our middleware could be implemented using technologies other than Java and Jini. For example, the private domain could use a LDAP server to maintain a register of the available resources [4].

2.3 Related Work

Our approach is a combination and a logical extension of two major grid infrastructure projects: (1) Globus which provides a toolkit of services (information management, security, communication etc.) to integrate heterogeneous computational resources into a single infrastructure [5], and (2) Legion which uses a uniform object model for both applications and resources allowing users and administrators to subclass generic interfaces to their specific local needs [6].

Our initial implementation indicates that the Java/Jini combination is capable of providing an extensible fault tolerant distributed infrastructure for grid computing. Other projects have also demonstrated the effectiveness of Jini in providing a grid middleware [7] and the use of Java to provide a homogeneous distributed computing environment across heterogeneous resources [8].

3 Local Resources

3.1 Overview

Resources within an organisation are managed by a local administrator. Once started, the *Administrative Domain* (a Jini space) maintains a list of the cur-

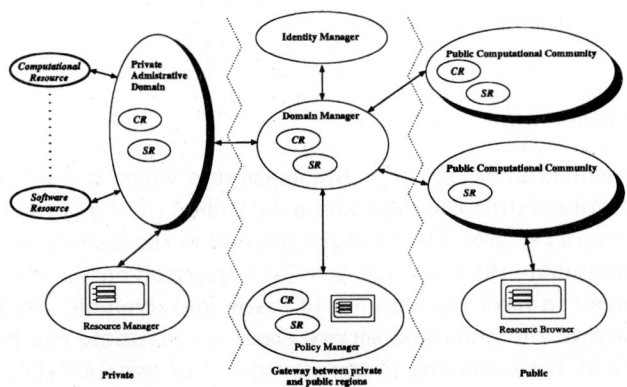

Fig. 1. Building a *Computational Community* through Federated Resources

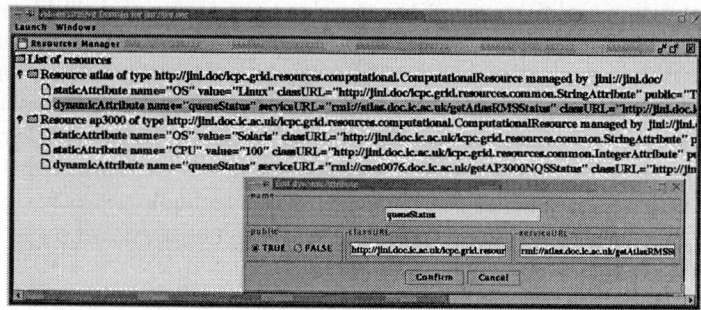

Fig. 2. The *Resource Manager*

rently available resources. These resources are monitored by the *Resource Manager* (see Fig. 2), which is notified when a resource enters or leaves the Jini space. The *Resource Manager* allows the administrator to alter the resources' configuration by adding, modifying or removing attributes. An XML scheme and configuration file (maintained on disc to ensure persistence) describes the resources (see §3.2).

We are currently concentrating on three different resources types:

- **Computational Resources.** We access our own local computational hardware through a batch scheduler abstraction with implementations for NQS, PBS [9] and Condor [10]. Each computational resource executes its own segment of an XML defined execution plan passed to it by the *Domain Manager*.
- **Storage Resources.** The user must be able to access their storage space from any resource. This allows input and output files to be transferred to the execution location. Read and write access policies are defined to allow authenticated individuals, groups or organisations to use their file space.
- **Software Resources.** Our current implementation only represents unlimited-use software libraries but the execution of a licensed library or application has to be scheduled in the same manner as a computational resource to ensure that a licence is available.

3.2 Implementation

A resource is defined by its *name*, a Jini space into which it *publishes* its availability (the *Administrative Domain*) and a Java class (its *type*) that extends the appropriate `Resource` class. The `execute` method in the `Resource` class accepts an XML file describing the task that is to be performed on the resource.

The resource can have any number of static and dynamic attributes which are encapsulated in the published service class. An attribute can be static (i.e. initialised once at the beginning of the execution) or dynamic (i.e. periodically updated during the execution). A static attribute is defined by its name, a value, and the location of the defining Java class. A dynamic attribute is defined by its name, the URL of the service used to update the attribute (e.g. Remote Method Invocation), and the location of the defining Java class. A *public* attribute is visible to the whole *Computational Community*, while a *non-public* (i.e. private) attribute is only visible to the *Administrative Domain* and the *Domain Manager*.

Example. The XML configuration file defining a computational resource (the AP3000) is shown below and in Fig. 2. It has two static attributes (only one of which is public) and a dynamic attribute updated through a RMI service.

```
<resource name="ap3000" publish="jini://jini.doc/"
    type="http://jini.doc/icpc.grid. ... .ComputationalResource">
  <staticAttribute name="OS" value="Solaris" public="TRUE" classURL="http://jini.doc..."/>
  <staticAttribute name="CPU" value="100" public="FALSE" classURL="http://jini.doc..."/>
  <dynamicAttribute name="queueStatus" public="TRUE" classURL="http://jini.doc..."
    serviceURL="rmi://cnet0076.doc/getAP3000NQSStatus"/>
</resource>
```

4 Resource Federation

4.1 Overview

The *Domain Manager* is the sole route between the private *Administrative Domain* containing the local resources of an organisation and the *Computational Community* in which the resource is published. Its role is to enforce the access control policies defined by the administrator for users in each of the *Computational Communities*. It is also able to restrict the published information in order to hide a specific resource, an attribute of a specific resource (the resource itself can decide which attributes are publicly visible), or the details of the access policy from a particular *Computational Community*.

When a new resource becomes available in the *Administrative Domain*, it is automatically published in the appropriate *Computational Community* if the *Domain Manager* already has an entry for it in its configuration file (see below). If there is no record in the configuration file of the resource for a specific *Computational Community*, then the administrator can use the *Policy Manager* to define where the resource should be published.

```
<domainManager manage="jini://jini.doc/" name="icpc">
  <promote domain="jini://trident.doc">
    <!-- the list of resources                                                -->
    <resource name="condor"/>
    <!-- this resource ap3000 got some specific access permission             -->
    <resource name="ap3000">
      <deny stopDay="monday"> <entity type="person" name="nfurSigned"/> </deny>
    </resource>
    <!-- default access control policies for the domain                       -->
    <deny startDay="saturday" stopDay="sunday"> <entity type="group" name="ra"/> </deny>
    <allow startDay="tuesday"> <entity type="organization" name="ICPC"/> </allow>
  </promote>
  <promote domain="jini://ariane.doc"> ... </promote>
</domainManager>
```

4.2 Access Control

Access to individual resources is controlled through conventional access control lists based on the following entities: individuals, groups and organisations. An organisation is composed of any number of groups, each containing any number of individuals. The *Domain Manager* is able to implement fine-grained access control policies relating to the resources in the local *Administrative Domain*.

The access control policy is qualified through a time interval, defined by a start time (by default, Monday at 00:00) and a stop time (by default, Sunday at 23:59). The access policies of an organisation are also applied to all the groups inside the organisation. Similarly, the access policies of a group are applied to all the individuals inside the group.

The *Domain Manager* configuration file allows an administrator to define the default access control policies for a *Computational Community*, which will be used for all the resources published within this community. Additional access policies can also be defined for specific resources as they are required.

4.3 The Management Tools

The *Policy Manager* allows an organisation's administrator to define the behaviour of the *Domain Manager* and therefore how the organisation's resources are contributed into the *Computational Communities* (see Fig. 3). It shows the available resources and the communities in which they are published. For each resource promoted in a specific community, it is possible to modify the access control policies, every modification will be propagated from the *Domain Manager* to the corresponding *Computational Community*.

Example. In Fig. 3, the AP3000 is published in the *Computational Community* hosted by jini://trident.doc. The default access policies of the community

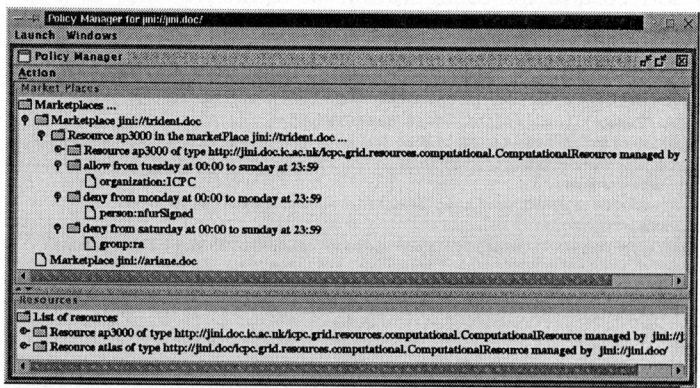

Fig. 3. The *Policy Manager*

are extended by a resource specific access policy. Note, that the non-public resource attribute, the CPU, is no longer visible. The *Domain Manager* retains knowledge of this attribute but it is not available outside the private domain.

The *Identity Manager* contains the X.509 certificates [11] (used by our public key authentication infrastructure) of the trusted organisations and their associated groups. An organisation acts as a certification authority for the individuals that are members of that organisation. All individuals using a resource within a domain have to belong to one of the trusted organisations. Global access control policies can also be defined within the *Identity Manager*. For instance, a particular user or group of users could be barred from all of the resources in an *Administrative Domain*.

5 The Computational Community

The *Resource Browser* (see Fig. 4) allows the users to examine the usage policies and the attributes of the accessible resources in a particular *Computational Community*. Dynamic attributes are updated periodically or on request.

Example. The *Computational Community* shown in Fig. 4 is hosted by jini://trident.doc and currently contains a computational resource, the AP-3000. The access control policies and attributes match those defined by the *Policy Manager* and *Resource Manager* respectively. Fig. 4 also shows the current status of the batch queuing system on the AP3000.

The *Computational Community* can be used to provide information to high level services, e.g. to improve job turnaround and increase resource utilisation. We will enhance the usability of the *Computational Community* to provide automatic or semi-automatic resource selection by using meta-data relating to both the performance of the application on different resources and the user's requirements.

A related project within our group is to define an application as a composition of software components annotated with implementation and performance information [12,13]. This meta-data, together with the user's requirement, will

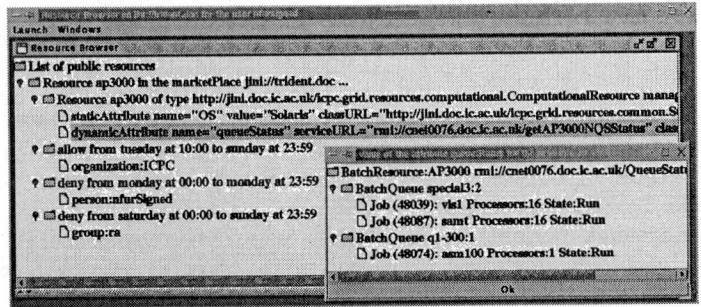

Fig. 4. The *Resource Browser*

be used by: (1) an *Application Mapper* to select the most effective implementations by utilising the application's knowledge, and (2) a *Resource Broker* to optimise the global job mix through computational economics [14,15].

6 Conclusion

Computational communities will eventually, like the Internet, change the way we work. However, to effectively exploit the computational potential of the grid, we need to balance the needs of the users, their applications and the resource providers, in order to deploy an application to a resource that will satisfy the stated requirements of both the user and the resource provider.

As we have shown, our *Computational Community* can make an efficient use of this information to enable us to build application mappers to effectively match applications to resources and brokers to make the best economic use of the available resources. We are therefore able to address some of the weaknesses in current grid infrastructures.

Acknowledgements

We would like to thank Keith Sephton, the Imperial College Parallel Computing Centre's Systems Manager, for his help with this work.

References

1. I. Foster and C. Kesselman, editors. *The Grid: Blueprint for a New Computing Infrastructure*. Morgan Kaufmann, 1998.
2. K. Arnold, J. Gosling, and D. Holmes. *The Java Programming Language*. Addison-Wesley, 3rd edition, 2000.
3. Sun Microsystems. Jini(tm) Network Technology. http://www.sun.com/jini/.
4. S. Fitzgerald and I. Foster et al. A Directory Service for Configuring High-Performance Distributed Computations. In *6th IEEE Symp. on High-Performance Distributed Computing*, pages 365–375, 1997.
5. I. Foster and C. Kesselman. Globus: A Metacomputing Infrastructure Toolkit. *The International Journal of Supercomputer Applications and High Performance Computing*, 11(2):115–128, 1997.
6. A. S. Grimshaw and W. A. Wulf et al. The Legion Vision of a Worldwide Virtual Computer. *Communications of the ACM*, 40(1):39–45, 1997.
7. Z. Juhasz and L. Kesmarki. A Jini-Based Prototype Metacomputing Framework. In *Euro-Par 2000*, volume 1900 of *LNCS*, pages 1171–1174, 2000.
8. M. O. Neary, B. O. Christiansen, P. Cappello, and K. E. Schauser. Javelin: Parallel Computing on the Internet. In *Future Generation Computer Systems*, volume 15, pages 659–674. Elsevier Science, 1999.
9. Veridian Systems. Portable Batch Systems. http://www.openpbs.org.
10. Condor Team. Condor Project Homepage. http://www.cs.wisc.edu/condor.
11. Sun Microsystems. X.509 certificates. http://java.sun.com/products/jdk/1.2/docs/guide/security/cert3.html, 1998.

12. S. Newhouse, A. Mayer, and J. Darlington. A Software Architecture for HPC Grid Applications. In *Euro-Par 2000*, volume 1900 of *LNCS*, pages 686–689, 2000.
13. N. Furmento, A. Mayer, S. McGough, S. Newhouse, and J. Darlington. A Component Framework for HPC Applications. Accepted for Euro-Par 2001.
14. C. A. Walspurger and T. Hogg *et al.* Spawn: A Distributed Computational Economy. *IEEE Transactions on Software Engineering*, 18(2):103–117, 1992.
15. R. Buyya and S. Chapin. Architectural Models for Resource Management in the Grid. In *Grid 2000*, volume 1971 of *LNCS*, 2000.

Scalable Causal Message Logging for Wide-Area Environments

Karan Bhatia[1], Keith Marzullo[2], and Lorenzo Alvisi[3]

[1] Advanced Technology Group, Entropia Inc.
San Diego, CA 92121
karan@entropia.com
http://www.entropia.com/

[2] University of California, San Diego,
Department of Computer Science and Engineering
marzullo@cs.ucsd.edu
http://www-cs.ucsd.edu/users/marzullo/

[3] Department of Computer Sciences
The University of Texas at Austin
lorenzo@cs.utexas.edu
http://www.cs.utexas.edu/~lorenzo

Abstract. Causal message logging spread recovery information around the network in which the processes execute. This is an attractive property for wide area networks: it can be used to replicate processes that are otherwise inaccessible due to network partitions. However, current causal message logging protocols do not scale to thousands of processes. We describe the Hierarchical Causal Logging Protocol (HCML) that is scalable. It uses a hierarchy of *proxies* to reduce the amount of information a process needs to maintain. Proxies also act as caches for recovery information and reduce the overall message overhead by as much as 50%. HCML also leverages differences in bandwidth between processes that reduces overall message latency by as much as 97%.

1 Introduction

Large scale computational grids are gaining popularity as infrastructure for running large scientific applications. Examples of such grids exist in the academic world (SETI@Home [5], Globus [9], and Nile [13]) as well as in the commercial sector (Entropia and Parabon among others). A primary goal of all these grids is to leverage the increased computational power of desktop personal computers and workstations that are linked by high speed communication protocols to provide a virtual supercomputer with the aggragate computational power that is many times that of current supercomputers. For example, the largest current grid is the SETI@Home grid that includes over two million desktop personal computers. The aggragate computing power of this grid exceeds that of all the top 500 supercomputers [12].

Before applications can leverage this virtual supercomputer, many problems inherent to large-scale systems must be solved. One of the key challenges is fault tolerance. In any system of thousands or millions of computers, the likelihood of multiple failures is high. Many of the current applications that utilize these grids are decomposed into independent pieces where each piece is assigned to a particular host machine. For such applications, failures can be dealt with by re-running a failed computation on a different host. Consistency is not an issue since each piece of computation is independent of all other pieces. Such is the case for the Seti@Home application.

However, for many other applications, the application can not be divided into independent pieces. Each piece has dependencies on other pieces of the application, and it is not sufficient to simply restart a failed piece of the computation on another host. The system must ensure that the restarted computation maintains consistency with the other parts of the application. Examples of such applications include Jacobi grid and other relaxation style algorithms. Such applications are typically written using a communication library where each piece of the computation communicates with other pieces by sending and receiving messages. The messages define the dependencies between the sender process and the receiver process. The transitive closure of the message dependencies define the overall application dependencies. Restarted processes must respect the application dependencies.

Simple checkpointing mechanisms will not suffice for fault tolerance in these environments. The host machines are geographically widely distributed. Network partitions can make checkpoint files ubavailable when needed. The checkpointed state needs to be cached at various places in the network.

One class of protocols, called Causal Message Logging protocols [4,8], cache recovery information in an appropriate manner. They operate by logging the recovery information in the volatile memory of the application processes and by dispersing the recovery information by piggybacking it on to application messages. The dispersed recovery information can then be used to generate replicas that are *causally consistent* [1] with the rest of the application. Causal message logging protocols also have a low overhead during failure-free executions and send no extra messages to distribute the recovery information.

While causal message logging protocols have been used successfully in local-area-networks, they are not suitable for use in large wide-area environments. These protocols maintain data structures that grow quadratically in the number n of processes in the system. For large n the memory needed to maintain these data structures can easily become unmanageable. In addition, the higher latency and decreased bandwidth of wide area computing can lead to a large increase in the amount of data that these protocols piggyback on the ambient message traffic.

This paper presents an implementation of causal message logging that is designed for use in large scale, wide-area grid infrastructures. An expanded version of the paper is available as [6]. Hierarchical Causal Message Logging (HCML) utilizes a network of *proxies* situated throughout the network that cache recovery information while routing application messages. Using proxies exponentially reduces the size of the data structures needed to track causality. We have also found that using proxies reduces significantly the bandwidth overhead of distributing recovery information throughout the network.

2 System Model

We assume a system with a set $\mathcal{P}$ of n processes, whose execution is represented by a *run*, which is an irreflexive partial ordering $\rightarrow$ of the *send* events, *receive* events and *local* events based on potential causality [11]. Processes can communicate only by sending and receiving messages; communication is FIFO and reliable. The system is asynchronous: there exists no bound on the relative speeds of processes, no bound on message transmission delays, and no global time source. A deliver event is a local event that represents the delivery of a received message to the application or applications running in that process. For any message m from process p to process q, q delivers m only if it has received m, and q delivers m no more than once.

We assume that processes are *piecewise deterministic* [7,14], *i.e.* that it is possible to identify all the non-deterministic events executed by each process and to log for each such event a *determinant* [4] that contains all the information necessary to replay the event during recovery. In particular, we assume that the order in which messages are delivered is non deterministic, and that the corresponding deliver events are the only non-deterministic events that a process executes. The determinant $\#m$ for the deliver event of a message m includes a unique identifier for m as well as m's position in the delivery order at its destination. The contents of the message need not be saved because it can be regenerated when needed [4].

Given a message m sent from process p to process q, we define $Dep(m)$ to be the set of processes that have executed an event e such that $receive_q(m,p) \rightarrow e$. Informally, this is the set of processes that causally depend on the delivery of message m (including q) once it has delivered m. We also define the set $Log(m)$ as the set of processes that have stored a copy of $\#m$ in their volatile memory.

Definition 1 (Causal Logging Property). *The causal logging specification defined in [2] requires that $Dep(m) \subseteq Log(m)$ when any subset of processes can crash.*

We define a *locality hierarchy* as a rooted tree $\mathcal{H}$ with the processes in $\mathcal{P}$ as the leaves of the tree. Each interior nodes of the tree represent a *locale*, such as a specific processor, local-area network, or a stub domain. Given $\mathcal{H}$, we denote with $\mathcal{C}(x,y)$ the least common ancestory or x and y and $\hat{x}$ to be the parent of x.

Each locale in $\mathcal{H}$ has associated with it a characteristic that defines the available bandwidth for communication among the locale's children. If two application processes s and t have the same parent p in $\mathcal{H}$, then the communication cost of a message m from process s to process t depends on the bandwidth characteristics of their parent p. If s and t do not have the same parent, then the communication cost of message m depends on the bandwidth characteristics of the locale $\mathcal{C}(p,q)$. We assume that all locales at the same height i have the same bandwidth BW_i (measured in MB/sec).

The overhead of a message m, denoted as $|m|$, is the size in bytes of the fault tolerance information piggybacked on m. The transmission overhead of m is a the time it takes to transmit $|m|$ from its sender to its destination $m.dest$ (based on the slowest locale in the path). The *total message overhead* of a run is the sum of the message overhead for all the messages sent in the run. The message overhead at depth i of the hierarchy is the sum of the message overhead of messages that traverse locales at height i. The *total transmission overhead* is the sum of the transmission overheads for all messages in the run.

3 Hierarchical Design

In this section we first review a simple causal message logging protocol that we call SCML. It is equivalent to the protocol Π_{det} with $f = n$ described in [3] and to Manetho [8]. We then discuss its limitations with respect to scaling, and present a hierarchical and scalable causal message logging protocol.

3.1 Review of SCML

Like other message logging protocols, causal message logging is built using a *recovery unit* abstraction [14]. The recovery unit acts like a filter between the application and the transport layer. When an application sends a message, the recovery unit records fault tolerance information on the message and hands it off to the transport layer. Similarly, on the receiving end, the recovery unit reads the fault tolerance information on the message and updates its in-memory data structures before passing the contents of the message to the application layer.

The recovery unit for causal message logging maintains a *determinant array* $\mathbf{H}_s$ at each process s. For every process t, $\mathbf{H}_s[t]$ contains the determinant of every message delivered by t in the causal past of s. $\mathbf{H}_s[t]$ is ordered by the order of message delivery at t. We denote with $\mathbf{H}_s[t,i]$ the ith determinant in $\mathbf{H}_s[t]$.

A simplistic way to maintain $\mathbf{H}_s$ is as follows. When a process s sends a message m to t, it piggybacks on m all determinants in $\mathbf{H}_s$. When process t receives m, it extracts these piggybacked determinants, incorporates them into $\mathbf{H}_t$, generates the determinant for m, and appends $\#m$ to $\mathbf{H}_t[t]$. By doing so, when process t delivers m it has all the determinants for messages that were delivered causally before and including the delivery of m and therefore satisfies the causal logging property. This method of maintaining $\mathbf{H}$, however, needlessly piggybacks many determinants. To reduce the number, each process s maintains a *dependency matrix* $\mathbf{D}_s$. This is a matrix clock where the value $\mathbf{D}_s[t,u]$ is an index into $\mathbf{H}_s[u]$. If $\mathbf{D}_s[t,u] = j$, then process s knows that all of the determinants in $\mathbf{H}_s[u]$ up through $\mathbf{H}_s[u,j]$ have been sent to t.

This protocol does not scale well with n because the size of $\mathbf{D}$ is $O(n^2)$, and grid computation middleware is being designed for systems in which n in the thousands or millions. Even if n were the relatively small value of 10,000, then each process would need to maintain a dependency matrix whose size would be measured in gigabytes.

3.2 Proxy Hierarchy

HCML addresses the scalability problems of causal message logging through hierarchy. Each process tracks only a small subset of the processes, thereby effectively reducing n for each process. Doing so also reduces the number of times a process is affected by another process joining or leaving the system; a process is affected only when the joining or leaving process is in the subset of processes it tracks. The hierarchy we use is based on the locality hierarchy $\mathcal{H}$ discussed in Section 2. The leaves in the HCML hierarchy are the application processes, and the internal nodes (corresponding to locales in $\mathcal{H}$) are HCML proxy processes called simply *proxies*. There is no proxy corresponding to the root of $\mathcal{H}$. In the degenerate case of a single locale, the only processes are the application processes, and HCML degenerates to SCML.

An application process can directly send messages to other application processes within its immediate locale and to the one proxy associated with that locale which acts as a surrogate for all of the other application processes outside of the locale. Proxies operates similarly to other processes: each proxy has a set of sibling processes with which it can communicate directly. To communicate with any non-sibling, the proxy forwards a message to *its* proxy.

The routing of messages is done automatically by the communication layer and is invisible to the application. This can be done efficiently when the locales are defined in terms of IP subnets.

3.3 Peers and Proxies

Each proxy in the system simultaneously runs two causal message logging protocols: one with its siblings and parent in the role of a *peer*, and one with its children in the role of a *proxy*. Since application processes are at the leaves of the hierarchy and have no children, they only run one causal message logging protocol with their siblings and parent in the role of a peer. Hence, for a hierarchy containing i internal nodes, there are i distinct protocols running at any time. We call this basic causal message logging protocol CML, and we associate a CML protocol with each proxy in the system. Thus proxy x runs both $\text{CML}^{\hat{x}}$ with its siblings and parent and CML^x with its children. Application process s only runs $\text{CML}^{\hat{s}}$.

CML is SCML with two differences: proxies have access to the determinants that are piggybacked on messages and proxies do not generate determinants. The first difference is needed for coupling instances of CML; as for the second, it is not necessary for proxies to generate determinants because their state can be safely reconstructed even if their messages are delivered in another order during recovery.

To satisfy the Causal Logging property, a proxy x couples CML^x and $\text{CML}^{\hat{x}}$. Process x acts as a proxy to all of its children for all processes outside of its locale. Therefore, all determinants stored in $\mathbf{H}_x^{\hat{x}}$ (that is, the determinant array of process x associated with protocol $\mathrm{CML}^{\hat{x}}$) and assigned to remote processes are also stored in $\mathbf{H}_x^x$ (the determinant array of process x associated with protocol CMLx and assigned to process x: it is always the case that

$$\forall r, d : (d \in \mathbf{H}_x^{\hat{x}}[r] \Rightarrow d \in \mathbf{H}_x^x[x]). \tag{1}$$

Process x also acts as a proxy to the processes in its peer group for its child processes. Therefore, determinants stored in $\mathbf{H}_x^x$ are also stored in $\mathbf{H}_x^{\hat{x}}$: it is always the case that

$$\forall r, d : (d \in \mathbf{H}_x^x[s] \Rightarrow d \in \mathbf{H}_x^{\hat{x}}[x]). \tag{2}$$

We call the conjunction of Equations 1 and 2 the *Coupling invariant*.

It is easy to see that the Coupling invariant combined with CML satisfies the Causal Logging property. Consider a message m sent from application process a to application process b. Let $T = \langle t_1, t_2, \ldots, t_k \rangle$ be the sequence of proxies that lead from a to b via $\mathcal{C}(a,b)$; thus, $t_1 = \hat{a}$, $t_k = \hat{b}$, and $t_{k/2+1} = \mathcal{C}(a,b)$. Due to the routing of messages through the proxies, m is forwarded via $\mathrm{CML}^{t_1}, \mathrm{CML}^{t_2}, \ldots \mathrm{CML}^{t_k}$. For the protocols $\mathrm{CML}^{t_1}, \mathrm{CML}^{t_2}, \ldots \mathrm{CML}^{t_{k/2+1}}$ Equation 2 ensures that the determinants needed to satisfy the Causal Logging property are available and forwarded appropriately. For the remaining protocols $\mathrm{CML}^{t_{k/2+2}}, \mathrm{CML}^{t_{k/2+3}}, \ldots \mathrm{CML}^{t_k}$ Equation 1 ensures that the determinants needed to satisfy the Causal Logging property are forwarded.

3.4 Recovery

When a process crashes, a new process must be created as a replacement for the failed process. In order to maintain consistency, causal message logging protocols gather the relavent recovery information from the set of processes (or proxies) and use it to ensure that the recovered process is consistent. Existing recovery protocols (see [3]) can be easily adapted for HCML.

HCML, however, has additional processes to maintain over those of standard causal message logging protocols, namely the proxy processes. Fortunately, a crashed proxy can simply be restarted and its neighbors in the heirarchy need to be informed. The proxies state includes only the cached recovery information, and subsequent messages will simply refill the cache after recovery.

4 Performance

Using the proxy hierarchy ensures that no process needs to track the causality of a large number of processes. This technique provides an exponential space reduction as compared to tracking the full causality. For example, assume that the locality hierarchy has depth of five and the fanout is 10 at each node. Such an architecture can accommodate 100,000 application processes, yet each process only tracks either six or twelve processes (depending on whether it is an application process or a proxy respectively). With SCML, on the other hand, each application process would maintain a dependency matrix with $10^5 \times 10^5 = 10^{10}$ entries.

However, the tradeoff is that HCML will over-estimate the causality as compared to SCML and and more often needlessly piggyback determinants to processes that are not dependent on them. In addition, HCML will send more messages than SCML because all non-local messages are relayed through the proxy hierarchy. This, however, is offset by the fact that the proxies act as local caches for determinants. This caching of determinants reduces the overall message overhead by over 50% percent. More importantly, HCML reduces the message overhead over slower communication channels and reduces the effective message communication latency.

In this section, we first describe our application, the proxy hierarchy, and the scheduling of processes within the hierarchy. We then discuss the performance results.

4.1 Effect of the Hierarchy

In order to gauge the effect of the hierarchy on both the message overhead and the message cost for HCML and SCML, we analyzed the performance of an application of 256 processes where, on average, each process communicates with four other processes selected randomly. The application proceeds in rounds. At each round, each process sends a message to its neighbors and delivers the messages sent in the previous round. The run ends after approximately 5,000 messages have been delivered.

An execution completely defines a run, but the performance of the run using HCML depends on the structure of the hierarchy and on how the processes are scheduled in the hierarchy. We then considered proxy hierarchies of different depths:

1. A depth-one hierarchy consisting of one locale containing all 256 application processes and no proxies. As stated earlier, this is identical to SCML.
2. A depth-two hierarchy with four locales (hence four proxies), each containing 64 application processes.
3. A depth-three hierarchy with sixteen application processes per lowest level locale. Their proxies have three siblings each, and so there are 20 proxies total.
4. A depth-four hierarchy that divides each of the application process locales of the previous hierarchy by four. Thus, there are four application processes per lowest level locale, and there are 84 proxies total.

The application processes are placed into locales independently of the communication patterns that they exhibit.

We used the Network Weather Service [16] to measure the available bandwidth for processes communicating in different locales. The values we measured ranged from over 200 MB/s for communication within the locale of a simple workstation to less than 0.4 MB/s for the wide area locale containing San Diego and western Europe. Thus, we set $BW_1 = 1MB/s$ (intercontinental communications), $BW_2 = 10MB/s$ (intra-stub domain communications), $BW_3 = 100MB/s$ (local area network communications), and $BW_4 = 1,000MB/s$ (intra-high performance multiprocessor communications). [1] Figure 1 shows the total message size for the run using both HCML and SCML as a function of depth. Because SCML does not take advantage of the locale hierarchy, its performance is constant with respect to the depth. HCML, on the other hand, relays non-local messages through the hierarchy and therefore sends more messages overall. Hence, one might expect that HCML would have a higher total message overhead. As the figure shows, the caching of the determinants actually improves the message overhead of HCML over SCML by as much as 50%. As the hierarchy gets deeper, the net effect of the caches is reduced. For a depth of four, for example, the locales at depth 3 have only four processes in them each and so the opportunity to benefit from caching is low.

To see how the caches reduce the communication costs, consider the example from the last section once again. After m_2 is finally delivered to process u, the determinant for message m_1 is stored at the intermediate nodes p and r as well as the application process u. Consider what happens if a third message m_3 is sent from process t to process v. In SCML t simply piggybacks $\#m_1$ on m_3 which gets sent from the locale of p to the locale of r. Using HCML, however, m_3 is redirected to node p which knows that r already has a copy of $\#m_1$. Therefore p does not need to piggybacked $\#m_1$ again. Process r does not know whether v has stored $\#m_1$, and hence piggybacks the determinant to v.

A secondary effect of the proxies is that more of the communication occurs lower in the hierarchy, where there is more bandwidth available. Figure 1 also shows the total transit overhead for SCML and HCML. In the case of depth 3 hierarchy, HCML reduces the total transit overhead by 97%. It should be noted that this metric does not include any added latency arising from the processing time of proxies.

We have found similar results for different application with different communication properties. In most cases, HCML is able to leverage the locality and produce a net reduction in both the total message overhead and the total message transit time. In addition, HCML performs better when the communication pattern the application processes use biases communication to be mostly within the higher bandwidth locales. Hence, we believe that HCML can only benefit from the the careful scheduling of grid-based applications.

---

[1] For hierarchies of depth less than three, we assigned bandwidths starting with BW_1. While doing so is unrealistic—for example, one would not expect a program to consist of 256 processes, each running in its own stub domain—it is at least well defined and no less arbitrary than any other choice. Furthermore, doing so does not affect the relative total transmission overheads for a fixed depth.

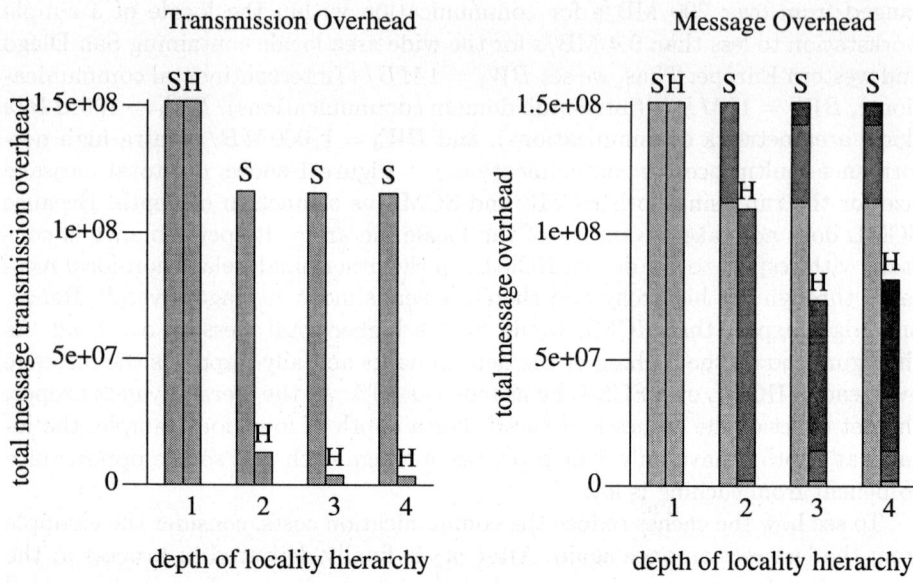

Fig. 1. HCML (H) and SCML (S) performance. Darker areas represent bandwidth overhead sent between locales lower in the hierarchy, and hence locales with greater available bandwidth

5 Conclusions

We have developed a scalable version of causal message logging. Our preliminary measurements indicate that it can easily scale to the largest grid-based computing environments that are being envisioned. Not only are the data structures that are maintained by each application process reduced by an exponential amount, but a caching effect reduces the message overhead as well when compared to traditional causal message logging. To attain these benefits, one sets up a hierarchy of proxies, each serving both as a router of causal message logging communication and as a cache of recovery information. Indeed, an interesting open question is if the routing of fault-tolerant information could be implemented as part of the underlying network routing function.

The protocol as described here is very simple, and appears to be amenable to refinement. For example, each proxy p manages an instance $CML^{\hat{p}}$ of a causal message logging protocol. It seems straightforward to allow $CML^{\hat{p}}$ to be replaced with a pessimistic message logging protocol to limit the spread of recovery information to be below p in the locale hierarchy. Another refinement we are developing would allow one to give specific failure model information about locales, thereby allowing one to replicate recovery information more prudently.

One spreads recovery information for the purpose of recovery, which is not discussed in any detail in this paper. In fact, we have designed HCML to allow us to experiment with recovery in the face of partitions. HCML does not appear to be hard to extend to support dynamic replication of a process (or an object) when a partition makes it inaccessible to a set of clients that require its service. The approach we are developing has some similarities with other dynamic replication services and with wide-area group programming techniques [10,15].

References

1. M. Ahamad, G. Neiger, J. Burns, P. Kohli, and P. Hutto. Causal memory: Definitions, implementation, and programming. *Distributed Computing*, 9(1):37–49, 1995.
2. L. Alvisi, B. Hoppe, and K. Marzullo. Nonblocking and orphan-free message logging protocols. In *Proceedings of the 23rd Fault Tolerant Computing Symposium*, pages 145–154, June 1993.
3. L. Alvisi and K. Marzullo. Trade-offs in implementing causal message logging protocols. In *Proceedings of the 15th ACM Annual Symposium on the Priciples of Distributed Computing*, pages 58–67, Jan 1996.
4. L. Alvisi and K. Marzullo. Message logging: pessimistic, optimistic, causal, and optimal. *IEEE Transactions on Software Engineering*, 24(2):149–159, Feb. 1998.
5. D. Anderson and D. Werthimer. The seti@home project. http://setiathome.ssl.berkeley.edu/.
6. K. Bhatia, K. Marzullo, and L. Alvisi. Scalable causal message logging for wide-area environments. Technical Report CS2001-0671, University of California–San Diego, May 2001.
7. E. Elnozahy, L. Alvisi, Y. Wang, and D. Johnson. A survey of rollback recovery protocols in message passing systems. Technical Report CMU-CS-99-148, CMU, June 1999.
8. E. Elnozahy and W. Zwaenepoel. Manetho: transparent roll back-recovery with low overhead, limited rollback, and fast output commit. *IEEE Transactions on Computers*, 41(5):526–531, May 1992.
9. I. Foster and C. Kesselman. The Globus project: a status report. In *Proceedings Seventh Heterogeneous Computing Workshop (HCW'98)*, pages 4–18, 1998.
10. R. Ladin, B. Liskov, L. Shrira, and S. Ghemawat. Providing high availability using lazy replication. *ACM Transactions on Computer Systems*, 10(4):360–391, Nov. 1992.
11. L. Lamport. Time, clocks, and the ordering of events in a distributed system. *Communications of the ACM*, 21(7):558–565, July 1978.
12. H. Meuer, E. Strohmaier, J. Dongarra, and H. Simon. The top 500 supercomputers list. http://www.top500.org/.
13. F. Previato, M. Ogg, and A. Ricciardi. Experience with distributed replicated objects: the Nile project. *Theory and Practice of Object Systems*, 4(2):107–115, 1998.
14. R. E. Strom, D. F. Bacon, and S. A. Yemini. Volatile logging in n-fault-tolerant distributed systems. In *Proceedings of the Eighteenth Annual International Symposium on Fault-Tolerant Computing*, pages 44–49, June 1988.
15. D. B. Terry, M. M. Theimer, K. Petersen, A. J. Demers, et al. Managing update conflicts in Bayou, a weakly connected replicated storage system. In *Proceedings of the Fifteenth ACM Symposium on Operating System Principles*, pages 172–183, Dec. 1995.
16. R. Wolski, N. Spring, and J. Hayes. The Network Weather Service: a distributed resource performance forecasting service for metacomputing. *Future Generation Computer Systems*, 15(5-6):757–768, Oct. 1999.

From Cluster Monitoring to Grid Monitoring Based on GRM[*]

Zoltán Balaton, Péter Kacsuk, Norbert Podhorszki, and Ferenc Vajda

MTA SZTAKI
H-1518 Budapest, P.O.Box 63. Hungary
{balaton,kacsuk,pnorbert,vajda}@sztaki.hu

Abstract. GRM was originally designed and implemented as part of the *P-GRADE* graphical parallel program development environment running on supercomputers and clusters. In the framework of the biggest European Grid project, the DataGrid we investigated the possibility of transforming GRM to a grid application monitoring infrastructure. This paper presents the architectural redesign of GRM to become a standalone grid monitoring tool.

Keywords: grid monitoring, message passing, grid monitoring architecture.

1 Introduction

With the emergence of computational grids it became very important to support grid-based applications with dynamic performance monitoring infrastructure. GRM 1 and PROVE were and still are available as parts of the *P-GRADE* graphical parallel program development environment 2. *GRM* is a "semi-on-line monitor" that collects information about an application running in a distributed heterogeneous system and delivers the collected information to the *PROVE* visualisation tool. The information can be either event trace data or statistical information of the application behaviour. "Semi-on-line" monitoring means, that any time during execution all available trace data can be requested by the user, and the monitor is able to gather them in a reasonable amount of time. PROVE has been developed for performance visualisation of Tape/PVM 3 trace files. It supports the presentation of detailed event traces as well as statistical information of applications. It can work both off-line and semi-on-line, and it can be used for observation of long-running distributed applications.

P-GRADE is a graphical programming environment integrating several tools to support the whole life cycle of building parallel applications. It provides an easy-to-use, integrated set of programming tools for development of general message passing applications to be run in heterogeneous computing environments. Its main benefits are the visual interface to define all parallel activities in the application, the syntax independent graphical definition of message passing instructions, full support of compilation and execution in a heterogeneous environment and the integrated use of

---

[*] This work was supported by a grant of the Hungarian Scientific Research Fund (OTKA) no. T032226

the debugger and the performance visualisation tool. For detailed overview of the tools in P-GRADE, see 4 while further information, tutorial and papers about P-GRADE can be found at 2.

In this paper we present four possible architectural designs and related issues of the GRM monitor for semi-on-line general application monitoring in a grid environment. In the next Section, the original design goals and the structure of GRM are shortly presented. In Section 3 the problems with GRM in a grid environment is discussed and four architectures designed for grid monitoring are presented.

2 Original Design Goals and Structure of GRM

The monitoring in GRM is *event-driven*, both *trace collection* and *counting* are supported. The measurement method is *software tracing* and the instrumentation method is *direct source code instrumentation*. For a classification of monitoring techniques, see 5. Direct source code instrumentation is the easiest way of instrumentation. Since P-GRADE controls the whole cycle of application building, and source code instrumentation is supported by graphics, the chosen one was a natural option. The precompiler inserts instrumentation function calls into the source code and the application process generates the trace events.

The main goals in the original design of GRM have been strongly related to the P-GRADE environment. The monitor and the visualisation tool are parts of an *integrated* development environment and they support monitoring and visualisation of P-GRADE applications at source level. The monitor is portable among different UNIX operating systems (Irix, Solaris, Linux, Tru64 UNIX, etc.) which is achieved by using only standard UNIX programming solutions in the implementation. GRM is a semi-on-line monitor, that is, the user can let GRM to collect the actual trace data or statistical information about the application any time during the execution. Semi-on-line monitoring is very useful for the evaluation of long-running programs and for supporting debugging with execution visualisation. Both trace collection and statistics are supported by the same monitor and by the same instrumentation of the application. Trace collection is needed to pass data to PROVE for execution visualisation. Statistics mode has less intrusion to the execution by generating fixed amount of data and it supports initial evaluation of long-running applications.

For trace storage *shared-memory segments* have been used on each host, since semi-on-line monitoring requires direct access to all trace data any time during the execution. The monitor can read the shared buffer independently from the application process, when the user asks to collect trace data. Moreover, if a process aborts its trace data can be saved and analysed to the point of failure.

GRM consists of the following three main components (see its structure in Fig. 1):

> **Client Library**
> The application is instrumented with functions of the client. Both trace events and statistics can be generated by the same instrumentation. The trace event types support the monitoring and visualisation of P-GRADE programs. An instrumented application process does not communicate outside of the host it is running on. It places trace event records or increments counters in a shared memory buffer provided by the Local Monitor.

Local Monitor

A Local Monitor (LM) is running on each host where application processes are executed. It is responsible for handling trace events from processes on the same host. It creates a shared memory buffer where processes place event records directly. Thus even if the process terminates abnormally, all trace events are available for the user up to the point of failure. In statistics collection mode, the shared memory buffer is used to store the counters and LM is responsible for generating the final statistics data in an appropriate form.

Main Monitor

The Main Monitor (MM) is co-ordinating the work of the Local Monitors. It collects trace data from them when the user asks or a trace buffer on a local host becomes full. The trace is written into a text file in Tape/PVM format (see 3), which is a record based format for trace events in ASCII representation. The Main Monitor also performs clock synchronisation among the hosts.

PROVE collects trace data for execution visualisation. PROVE communicates with MM and asks for trace collection periodically. It can work remotely from the Main Monitor process. With the ability of reading new volumes of data and removing any portion of data from its memory, PROVE can observe applications for arbitrary long time.

The integration of GRM into a development environment made it possible to put several functionalities of a stand-alone monitoring tool into other components of P-GRADE. Instrumentation is done in the GRED 4 graphical editor of P-GRADE. Trace events of different

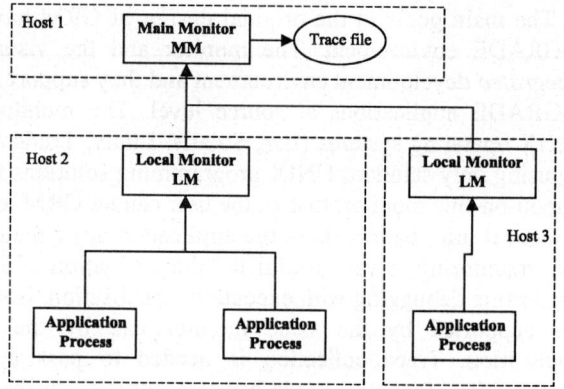

Fig. 1. Structure of GRM

processes are not sorted into time order since the pre-processing phase in PROVE does not need a globally sorted trace file. The monitor is started and stopped by GRED and GRM does no bookkeeping of processes. Local Monitors are started on the hosts defined by the environment.

3 Required Modifications of GRM in a Grid Environment

Monitoring of applications in a grid environment brings new requirements for a monitoring tool. The monitor should be scalable to a large number of resources and events. The start-up of the monitor and collection of data from remote sites are more complex and difficult than in a single cluster. Measurements must have accurate cross-site timestamps. Moreover, original design goals of GRM must be reviewed. In particular, two goals must be changed. First, general application monitoring should be supported, not only P-GRADE-based. This also requires user defined event data types. Second, GRM and PROVE should be standalone monitoring and visualisation tools, that is, not part of an integrated development environment. Other design goals (see Section 2) are unchanged. Portability remains very important, since a grid consists of heterogeneous resources. Semi-on-line monitoring must be supported, because a grid is a changing environment, where off-line monitoring does not help. Both statistics and event trace collection is needed to monitor large and long running applications that are typical in a grid. Getting trace data to the point of failure is very important, since errors are more frequent in a grid.

The start-up of the monitoring system becomes difficult because Local Monitors cannot be started on a host explicitly, since it is the competence of the local job-manager on a grid resource to decide where jobs will run. This local policy cannot be influenced. Because of this, the Main Monitor cannot start the Local Monitors as in GRM. Instead, it should be prepared to accept connections from them.

The clock synchronisation in GRM is done through the sockets connecting Local Monitors with the Main Monitor, see details in 1. MM performs the synchronisation with each LM. This technique works well on clusters of workstations connected by a LAN. In a grid environment the resources (e.g. clusters) are usually connected by WAN links that have higher latency than the LAN used inside the resource. GRM determines the clock offsets of each LM (running on a host at the remote grid resource) relative to the host of the MM but the accuracy of this measurement is limited by the latency of the WAN link. Because of this, the error of the clock-offset measurement can be comparable to or bigger than the time intervals between events generated at the remote resource (e.g. the start and end of a communication on the LAN). Since there are several tools (e.g. NTP) that can be used to synchronise clocks, this problem can be solved independently from monitoring. For this reason, GRM does not support clock synchronisation in grid environments, instead it assumes that the clocks are already synchronised.

There are a number of performance measurement and resource control systems used in grid (e.g. Network Weather Service, Autopilot, NetLogger, etc.). For their comparison see 6.

In the following subsections four different architectures of GRM are examined that can be used in a grid environment for application monitoring.

3.1 Simple Architecture

In the simplest monitoring architecture (see Fig. 2) Local Monitors are omitted and application processes send trace events immediately to the Main Monitor which is waiting for trace data in a remote site. The application process can store trace records temporarily in its local memory. However, with this architecture we loose the following advantages of GRM.

Local buffering of trace data in GRM is done independently from the monitored application, so the Main Monitor can collect it any time. In the simple architecture data should be sent immediately to the remote collector process or can be buffered locally by the application process but in this case the visualisation tool must wait until the block of trace data have arrived. In GRM the visualisation tool can request for trace data any time and the monitor collects data from the Local Monitor processes.

With local buffering in a shared memory segment, application processes and sensors can give trace events to the monitoring tool quickly so they can have very low intrusiveness. Thus, the application can run almost as efficiently as without instrumentation. In the simple architecture, the application process is blocked while it sends trace events to the collecting process over wide-area network.

The simple architecture is not as scalable as GRM using Local Monitors. Moreover, with trace buffering in the local memory of the process we loose trace events when a process aborts. Thus, the visualisation tool cannot show all events until the point of failure.

The start-up of the monitor is simple. Application processes should be started with the Main Monitor address as parameter and should connect to the Main Monitor. Since Local Monitors are excluded, both the Main Monitor code and the instrumentation library should be modified for the new functionality. However, one problem remains. The use of firewalls in the different computing sites can prohibit the direct connection

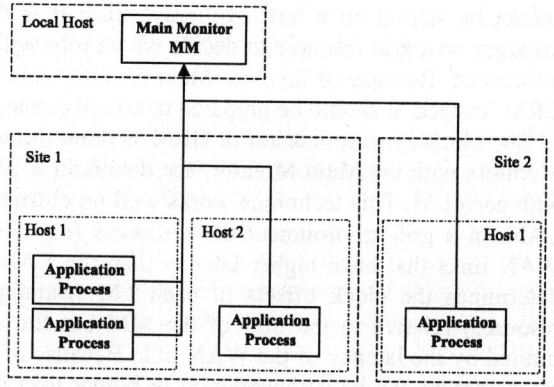

Fig. 2. Simple monitoring architecture

of the application processes to the Main Monitor. Either firewalls should enable this connections (which cannot be expected from the administrators) or some proxy-like solutions should be introduced for indirect connections.

3.2 Local Monitors as Site Monitors

If we want to use Local Monitors to keep the benefits of GRM, Local Monitors can be used in two different ways. The first one is to use one Local Monitor for each computing site. This option is discussed in this subsection. The second one is to use Local Monitors in each machine, using them the same way as in the original GRM. This solution is discussed in the next subsection.

In this architecture (see Fig. 3) a Local Monitor collects all trace data in a computing site (cluster or supercomputer) and sends data to the remote Main Monitor. Data is sent over the wide-area network only when the Main Monitor requests for it. With this solution, the remote connection of the application processes can be avoided. A process should send trace events to the Local Monitor, which is on the same site as the process. This architecture is more scalable and less intrusive than the simple architecture. However, the start-up of the monitor becomes much more complex. The Local Monitor should be started remotely in a site where an application process is to be started. The Main Monitor and the user have no exact information at launch time about where the application will be executed. Moreover, the Main Monitor cannot start a process in a remote site freely. The grid management software itself should be prepared to launch a Local Monitor on a site where an application process is started.

The problem of the firewalls can be solved if the Local Monitor is started on the server machine of the site, which has connections to the external world. Administrators should enable only one connection between the Main Monitor and the server machine instead of enabling connections from any machines in their domain.

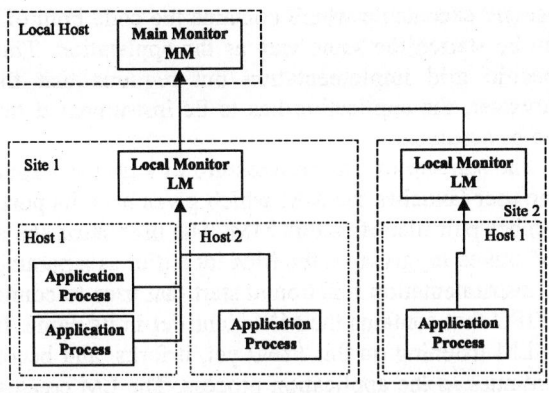

Fig. 3. Local Monitors at each site

The code of the Local Monitor and the instrumentation library should be modified because shared memory cannot be used between two machines. Data exchange between the Local Monitor and the application processes should be performed now through sockets instead of shared memory.

3.3 Local Monitors with Their Original Functionality

The Local Monitor, Main Monitor and the instrumentation library of GRM can be used without modification if Local Monitors are started on all single machines where processes of the application are started. The structure and the logical work of this solution (see Fig 4) is the same as the original GRM (Fig 1). The only difference is that a Local Monitor and the Main Monitor should communicate through a WAN and not in a LAN. Thus, we can use shared memory buffering of trace data, less intrusive monitoring of the processes and more efficient transfer of data.

The problem of this architecture is the start-up of the Local Monitor. The executable of the Local Monitor should be transferred to the grid resource where the application is run. The easiest way to do this is to link the LM executable to the process as a library. This way we have

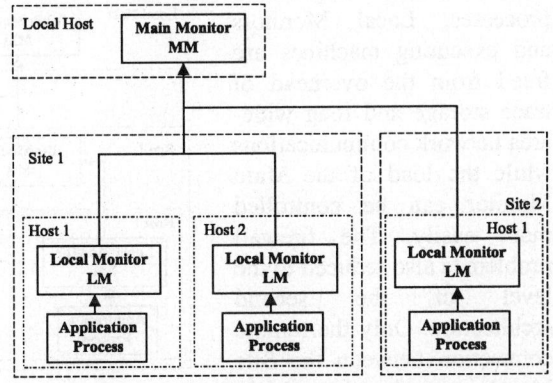

Fig. 4. Local Monitors on each machine

a single executable which contains the code both of the application and the LM, and can be started the same way as the application. This solution is independent of any specific grid implementation but requires that the application can be relinked. However, the application has to be instrumented for monitoring with GRM, so this can be assumed.

The start-up of this architecture in a grid environment goes in the following way. The user launches the MM which gives back its port number. The hostname and port number pair identifies this MM. The user starts the application that also contains the LM linked in, giving it the MM identifier as a parameter. An application process calls an instrumentation function at start that tries to connect to the Local Monitor through a FIFO that contains the MM identifier in its name. If the process detects that there is no LM listening on this FIFO yet, it forks, and becomes the Local Monitor. Its child continues as the application process. The LM creates the shared buffer and the FIFO through which processes can now connect to it. When an LM is created, the application process connects to it and the LM connects to the MM. After successfully connecting to the Main Monitor, the LM notifies the process. From this point, the process can start generating trace events. The problem of firewalls is the same as at the simple architecture. Here Local Monitors in the machines should be able to connect to the remote Main Monitor.

This architecture is examined in detail in 7.

3.4 Local Monitors and Site Monitors

A fourth possible architecture (see Fig. 5) is the combination of the previous two ones. Local Monitors are used as in the original GRM and Site Monitors are introduced as intermediate monitoring processes between the Main Monitor and the Local Monitors. Site Monitors are used to forward data from Local Monitors to the Main Monitor avoiding the problems of the firewall. With this solution, Local Monitors are exactly the same as the Local Monitors of the original GRM, communicating with a higher-level monitoring process in the local area network.

This architecture is the most scalable for a grid. Site Monitors can store trace data of the site. Application processes, Local Monitors and executing machines are freed from the overhead of trace storage and long wide-area network communications while the load of the Main Monitor can be controlled more easily. The firewall problem is also reduced to the level of the second architecture. Only the remote connection between the Site Monitor and the Main Monitor should be enabled. However, the start-up

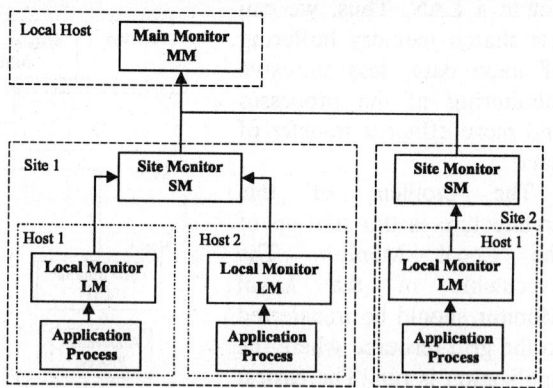

Fig. 5. Combination of Local and Site Monitors

problem is raised to the level of the second architecture. The start-up of the Site Monitor should be supported by the grid management software.

4 Conclusions

A grid environment brings new requirements for monitoring. The GRM monitoring tool of the P-GRADE graphical parallel programming environment is a good candidate to be a standalone grid-application monitoring tool. We examined its features and monitoring mechanisms and compared them to the requirements of a grid. With architectural redesign and code modifications GRM can collect traces from large distributed applications in a grid that can be analysed. In the architectural design of GRM, scalability and problematic start-up issues in grid were considered. Since the third structure keeps the original structure of GRM and the functionality of the elements we have chosen this architecture to implement the first version of the grid application monitor.

References

1. N. Podhorszki, P. Kacsuk: "Design and Implementation of a Distributed Monitor for Semi-on-line Monitoring of VisualMP Applications", Proceedings. DAPSYS'2000 Distributed and Parallel Systems, From Instruction Parallelism to Cluster Computing, Balatonfüred, Hungary, pp. 23-32, 2000.
2. P-GRADE Graphical Parallel Program Development Environment:
   http://www.lpds.sztaki.hu/projects/p-grade
3. É. Maillet: "Tape/PVM: An Efficient Performance Monitor for PVM Applications. User's guide", LMC-IMAG, Grenoble, France, 1995. Available at http://www-apache.imag.fr/software/tape/manual-tape.ps.gz
4. P. Kacsuk, G. Dózsa, T. Fadgyas, and R. Lovas: "The GRED graphical editor for the GRADE parallel programming environment", FGCS journal, Special Issue on High-Performance Computing and Networking, Vol. 15 (1999), No. 3, April 1999, pp. 443-452.
5. J. Chassin de Kergommeaux, É. Maillet and J-M. Vincent: "Monitoring Parallel Programs for Performance Tuning in Cluster Environments", In "Parallel Program Development for Cluster Computing: Methodology, Tools and Integrated Environments" book, P.Kacsuk and J.C.Cunha eds, Chapter 6., Nova Science, 2000.
6. Z. Balaton, P. Kacsuk, N. Podhorszki and F. Vajda: "Comparison of Representative Grid Monitoring Tools", Reports of the Laboratory of Parallel and Distributed Systems (SZTAKI), LPDS-2/2000, 2000. Available at:
   ftp://ftp.lpds.sztaki.hu/pub/lpds/publications/reports/lpds-2-2000.pdf
7. Z. Balaton, P. Kacsuk, N. Podhorszki: "Application Monitoring in the Grid with GRM and PROVE ", Proceedings of the ICCS'2001 (Intl. Conf. on Computational Science), San Francisco, CA, May 28-31, 2001.

Use of Agent-Based Service Discovery for Resource Management in Metacomputing Environment

Junwei Cao, Darren J. Kerbyson, and Graham R. Nudd

High Performance Systems Laboratory, Department of Computer Science
University of Warwick, U.K.
{junwei,djke,grn}@dcs.warwick.ac.uk

Abstract. A new methodology is presented in this paper for resource management in a metacomputing environment using a hierarchy of homogeneous agents that has the capability of service discovery. The PACE [6] tools are used to provide quantitative data concerning the performance of sophisticated applications running on local high performance resources. At metacomputing level, an agent hierarchy is used to model the resource management system, and the implementation of resource management, scheduling, and allocation can be abstracted to the processes of service advertisement and service discovery. Different optimisation strategies can be used to improve the performance of the agent system.

1 Introduction

The overall aim of the resource management in the metacomputing environment is to efficiently schedule applications that need to utilize the available resources [5]. Such goals within the high performance community will rely on accurate performance prediction capabilities.

Our previous works on PACE [2] can be used to provide quantitative data concerning the performance of sophisticated applications running on local high performance resources. While extremely well-suited for managing a locally distributed multi-computer, the PACE functions do not map well onto wide-area environments, where heterogeneity, multiple administrative domains, and communication irregularities dramatically complicate the job of resource management. There are two key challenges that must be addressed.

Scalability. A given component of the grid will have it's own functions, resources, and environment. These are not necessarily geared to work together in the overall grid. They may be physically located in different organizations and may not be aware of each other.

Adaptability. A grid is a dynamic environment where the location, type, and performance of the components are constantly changing. For example, a component resource may be added to, or removed from, the grid at any time. These resources may not be entirely dedicated to the grid; hence their computational capabilities will vary over time.

In this work, an agent-based service discovery model for resource management in metacomputing environment is introduced to address above challenges. An agent is a local computing resource manager equipped with PACE functions. These homogeneous agents are organised into a hierarchy, which can be used to address the problem of the scalability. An agent is considered to be both a service provider and a service requestor. We use service here to describe the details of a resource within the grid. Resource management, scheduling, and allocation can be abstracted to the processes of service *advertisement* and service *discovery*. Performance issues arise when service is advertised and discovered in the agent system. Different optimisation strategies can be used to improve the system performance.

2 PACE Toolset

Our previous works on PACE toolset provide the base of the implementation of resource management for metacomputing.

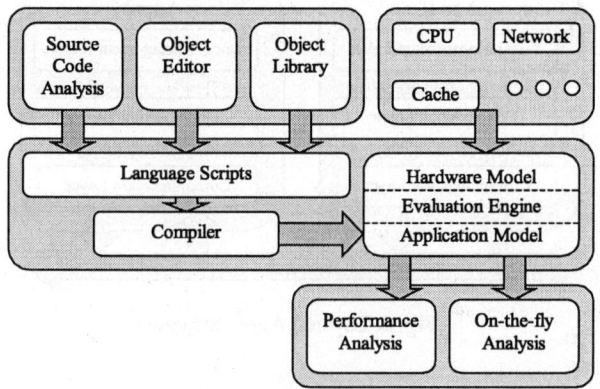

Fig. 1. The PACE Toolset

The main components of the PACE toolset are shown in Fig. 1. A core component of PACE is a performance language, CHIP^{3}S, which describes the performance aspects of an application and its parallelisation. The evaluation engine combines the workload information with component hardware models to produce time estimates, or trace information of the expected application behaviour. An important application of prediction data is that of dynamic multi-processor scheduling, which can be applied for efficient local resource management.

The key features of PACE performance prediction capabilities include: a reasonable prediction accuracy; a rapid evaluation time and easy performance comparison across different computational systems [1]. These enable the prediction data to be used for resource management in a highly dynamic environment.

3 Agent-Based Service Discovery for Resource Management

In this section, a hierarchy of homogenous agents with service discovery capabilities is used for resource management in metacomputing environment. The introduction below includes four parts: agent structure, agent hierarchy, service model and service discovery.

3.1 Agent Structure

There is a single type of the component, the agent, which is used to compose the whole resource management system. Each agent has the same set of functions and acts as a manager of local high performance resources. However, at a meta-level, an agent must also take part in the cooperation with other agents, which differentiate an agent from a current PACE system. A layered agent structure is shown in Fig. 2 and described in detail below.

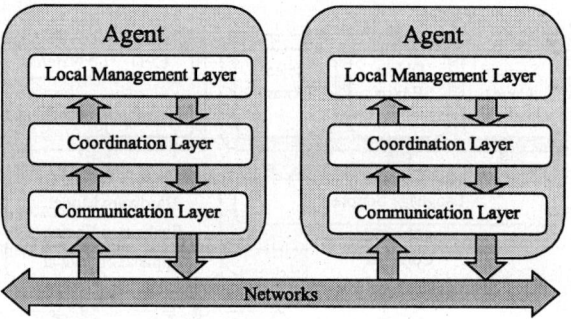

Fig. 2. Layered Agent Structure

Communication Layer – Agents in the system must be able to communicate with each other using common data models and communication protocols.

Coordination Layer – The data an agent receives at the communication layer should be explained and submitted to the coordination layer, which decides how the agent should act on the data according to its own knowledge. The work described in this paper mainly focus on the implementation of this layer, and the service discovery model used to achieve the agent coordination will be described in sections later.

Local Management Layer – This uses existing PACE tools for the management of the locally distributed computing resources. The local manager can also provide information needed by the coordination layer to make decisions.

3.2 Agent Hierarchy

Different agents cannot work together without some base organisation. In this section, a hierarchical model is introduced, which is an extension of our previous work [3].

When a new resource is added into the grid, a new agent is created. The new agent can register with one of existing agents, and hence join the agent hierarchy. An agent can only have one connection to an agent higher in the hierarchy to register with, but be registered with many lower level agents. An agent in the hierarchy has only the identities of its upper agent and lower agents and can communicate with them at the beginning. However, after joining the system, agent can learn more information about other agents and communicate with more agents gradually. Then the agent can benefit from the other agents' capabilities, cooperate with each other, and manage all of the computing resources in the metacomputing environment. An agent can also leave the hierarchy at any time, which means the resources it manages are not available to the grid any more. In this situation, its lower agents must be informed to register with a new agent to keep the relations with the hierarchy.

The agent-based hierarchical model is used to address the problem of the scalability. The key feature that enables the scalability of this model is the homogeneity of agents. There is no agent with more special functions than any other. The broker does not have any privileges compared to coordinators and agents.

3.3 Service Model

An agent is considered to be both a service provider and a service requestor. Every agent can also act as a router between a request and a service. A service model is used to describe the details of local high performance resources within the grid. An initial implementation of a service model is a simple data structure, including an agent identity, corresponding resource information, and some optimisation options.

The main part of a service model is the resource information. This should include all of the information needed for performance prediction of corresponding resources, from hardware statistics to application states. When a request arrives, it should be able to turn into useful performance information of corresponding resources using the PACE evaluation engine. These predictions can be used for agents to make decision whether the corresponding resources can meet the performance requirements from the request at the coordination layer.

An agent can use several kinds of Agent Capability Tables (ACTs) for maintenance of service models from other agents. The resource performance can vary over time, thus the service offered by the agent will change over time. When this occurs, the resource information in corresponding service model needs also to be updated. The dynamics of this system increases the difficulty of resource management and allocation. The essential issue is how an agent advertises its services and also coordinates with other agents to discover the required services in the most efficient way.

3.4 Service Discovery

Resource management, scheduling, and allocation at the meta-level are abstracted to the processes of service advertisement and service discovery in this work. These are performed at the coordination layer in each agent in the system.

Service Advertisement. The service model of an agent can be advertised in the hierarchy (both up and down).

Service Discovery. When an agent receives a request, it will first check its own knowledge to see if it is already aware of an available service, which can meet the performance requirements of the request. If it is, it will contact the target agent directly. Otherwise it may contact other (e.g. its upper or lower) agents until the available service is found.

Different strategies can be used to decide when, and how, to advertise or discover a service but with different performances. These include use of cache, using local and global knowledge, limit service lifetime, limit scope. The performance issues are discussed in greater detail in [4].

4   Conclusions

The resource management system in the grid computing environment will be a large-scale distributed software system with high dynamics. In this work, we have developed a homogeneous agent-based hierarchical model to meet the requirements of the scalability. We also abstract the resource management, scheduling and allocation into the processes of the service advertisement and discovery.

Ongoing works include the implementation of an agent communication language and a service description language. Future implementation will also integrate a new version of PACE toolset, which is specially lightened up for remote performance evaluation.

References

1. J. Cao, D. J. Kerbyson, E. Papaefstathiou, and G. R. Nudd, "Modeling of ASCI High Performance Applications Using PACE", in Proc. of 15th Annual UK Performance Engineering Workshop, Bristol, UK, pp. 413-424, 1999.
2. J. Cao, D. J. Kerbyson, E. Papaefstathiou, and G. R. Nudd, "Performance Modeling of Parallel and Distributed Computing Using PACE", in Proc. of 19th IEEE Int. Performance, Computing and Communication Conf., Phoenix, USA, pp. 485-492, 2000.
3. J. Cao, D. J. Kerbyson, and G. R. Nudd, "Dynamic Application Integration Using Agent-Based Operational Administration", in Proc. of 5th Int. Conf. on Practical Application of Intelligent Agents and Multi-Agent Technology, Manchester, UK, pp. 393-396, 2000.
4. J. Cao, D. J. Kerbyson, and G. R. Nudd, "Performance Evaluation of an Agent-Based Resource Management Infrastructure for Grid Computing", in Proc. of 1st IEEE Int. Symp. on Cluster Computing and the Grid (CCGrid'01), Brisbane, Australia, pp. 311-318, 2001.
5. I. Foster, and C. Kesselman, "The Grid: Blueprint for a New Computing Infrastructure", Morgan-Kaufmann, 1998.
6. G. R. Nudd, D. J. Kerbyson, E. Papaefstathiou, S. C. Perry, J. S. Harper, and D. V. Wilcox, "PACE – A Toolset for the Performance Prediction of Parallel and Distributed Systems", Int. J. of High Performance Computing Applications, Special Issues on Performance Modelling – Part I, Sage Science Press, 14(3), pp. 228-251, Fall 2000.

Topic 18
Parallel I/O and Storage Technology

Peter Brezany, Marianne Winslett, Denis A. Nicole, and Toni Cortes

Topic Chairpersons

Introduction

Input and output (I/O) is a major performance bottleneck for large-scale scientific applications running on parallel platforms. For example, it is not uncommon that performance of carefully tuned parallel programs can slow dramatically when they read or write files. This is because many parallel applications need to access large amounts of data, and although great advances have been made in the CPU and communication performance of parallel machines, similar advances have not been made in their I/O performance. The densities and capacities of disks have increased significantly, but improvement in performance of individual disks has not followed the same pace. For parallel computers to be truly usable for solving real, large-scale problems, the I/O performance must be scalable and balanced with respect to the CPU and communication performance of the system. Parallel I/O techniques can help to solve this problem by creating multiple data paths between memory and disks. However, simply adding disk drives to an I/O system without considering the overall software design will improve performance only marginally.

The parallel I/O and storage research community is pursuing solutions in several different areas in order to solve the problem. Active areas of research include disk arrays, network-attached storage, parallel and distributed file systems, theory and algorithms, compiler and language support for I/O, runtime libraries, reliability and fault tolerance, large-scale scientific data management, database and multimedia I/O, real-time I/O, and tertiary storage. The MPI-IO interface, defined by the MPI Forum as part of the MPI-2 standard, aims to provide a standard, portable API that enables implementations to deliver high I/O performance to parallel applications.

The Parallel I/O Archive at Dartmouth, http://www.cs.dartmouth.edu/pario is an excellent resource for further information on the subject. It has a comprehensive bibliography and links to various I/O projects.

Papers in this Track

This year nine papers, from three continents and five countries, were submitted. All papers were reviewed by three or more referees. Using the referees' reports guidelines, the program committee picked three papers for publication and presentation at the conference. These were presented in one session.

The first paper, by Hakan Ferhatosmanoglu, Divyakant Agrawal and Amr El Abbadi, explores optimal partitioning techniques for data stored in large spatial databases for different types of queries, and develops multi-disk allocation techniques that maximize the degree of I/O parallelism obtained during the retrieval. The authors show that hexagonal partitioning has optimal I/O cost for circular queries compared to all possible non-overlapping partitioning techniques that use convex regions. The second paper, by Xavier Molero, Federico Silla, Vicente Santonja and José Duato, proposes several strategies for dealing with short control messages and analyzes their impact on the performance of storage area networks. This analysis is carried out for a fully adaptive routing algorithm in the context of different network topology environments. The third paper, by Jonathan Ilroy, Cyrille Randriamaro and Gil Utard, deals with improving the performance of the MPI-IO implementation running on top of the Parallel Virtual File System (PVFS). Their optimization mainly focuses on the collective I/O functionality of MPI-IO.

Optimal Partitioning for Efficient I/O in Spatial Databases*

Hakan Ferhatosmanoglu, Divyakant Agrawal, and Amr El Abbadi

Computer Science Department, University of California at Santa Barbara
{hakan,agrawal,amr}@cs.ucsb.edu

Abstract. It is desirable to design partitioning techniques that minimize the I/O time incurred during query execution in spatial databases. In this paper, we explore optimal partitioning techniques for spatial data for different types of queries, and develop multi-disk allocation techniques that maximize the degree of I/O parallelism obtained during the retrieval. We show that hexagonal partitioning has optimal I/O cost for circular queries compared to all possible non-overlapping partitioning techniques that use convex regions. For rectangular queries, we show that although for the special case when queries are rectilinear, rectangular grid partitioning gives superior performance, hexagonal partitioning has overall better I/O cost for a general class of range queries. We then discuss parallel storage and retrieval techniques for hexagonal partitioning using current techniques for rectangular grid partitioning.

1 Introduction

Spatial databases and Geographical Information Systems(GIS) have gained in importance by the recent developments in information technology. In these applications, the data objects are represented as two-dimensional feature vectors, and the similarity between objects are defined by a distance function between corresponding feature vectors. Several index structures have been proposed for retrieval of spatial data [4,8]. Most of these approaches are based on data partitioning with a rectangular organization. Grid based file structures have been effectively used to index spatial data, and there have been several approaches based on the grid partitioning. Because of their simplicity in hashing and mapping to physical storage, *regular* equi-sized partitioning are widely used for retrieval and storage of spatial data. A common example of such techniques is the regular grid partitioning. One very important application of regular grid partitioning is multi-disk *declustering* of spatial data. First, the data space is partitioned into disjoint regular rectangular partitions. Then the data partitions or buckets are allocated to multiple I/O devices such that neighboring partitions are allocated to different disks. Performance improvements for queries occur when the buckets involved in query processing are stored on different disks, and hence can

---

* This work was partially supported by NSF grant EIA98-18320, IIS98-17432 and IIS99-70700.

be retrieved in parallel. Numerous declustering methods using *non-overlapping* rectangular partitioning have been proposed [1,7]. Another successful application of rectangular partitioning is the vector approximation (VA) based indexing for multi-dimensional data [9]. The VA-file approach divides the data space into rectangular partitions, and each data point is represented by the bit representation of the corresponding partition. In several similar applications, it is desirable to design partitioning techniques that tile the data space without holes and overlaps. These techniques have simple hashing schemes, and they don't have the problems caused by high number of overlaps between partitions which result severe degradation in the query performance.

Minimizing the number of I/O operations in query processing is crucial for fast response times. This cost can be reduced by reducing the expected number of page retrievals during the execution of queries. In a range query, the pages that may have the query result need to be retrieved from secondary storage. As we will establish, the expected number of page retrievals directly depends on the underlying technique that is used to organize the data set, i.e., partitioning of the data [2]. It is therefore very important to develop partitioning techniques which minimize the expected number of partitions retrieved by a query and hence the number of disk accesses. It is well known that rectangles are effective for non-overlapping partitioning. An important question to ask is whether rectangular grid based partitioning is the optimal approach for non-overlapping partitioning to minimize the I/O cost?

In this paper, we explore optimal partitioning techniques for different types of queries. In particular, we show that hexagonal partitioning has optimal I/O cost for circular queries compared to all possible non-overlapping partitioning techniques that use convex regions. For rectangular queries, we show that although for the special case when queries are rectilinear rectangular grid partitioning gives superior performance, hexagonal partitioning has overall better I/O cost for a general class of range queries. We also develop simple techniques for the storage and retrieval of hexagonal partitioning by applying the techniques developed for rectangular grid partitioning. The techniques developed in this paper considers the objectives that are crucial for multi-disk searching: i) minimizing the number of page accesses during the execution of the query, ii) maximizing the I/O parallelism, iii) minimizing the disk-arm movement (seek time).

In Section 2 we discuss the importance of data organization on minimizing the I/O cost of spatial queries and summarize alternative partitioning techniques. In Section 3, we analyze the partitioning techniques with respect to the I/O cost of spatial queries and show the optimal partitioning technique for each query type. Section 4 discusses techniques for storage and retrieval of hexagonal partitioning using current techniques for rectangular grid. Section 5 includes the final discussion and conclusions.

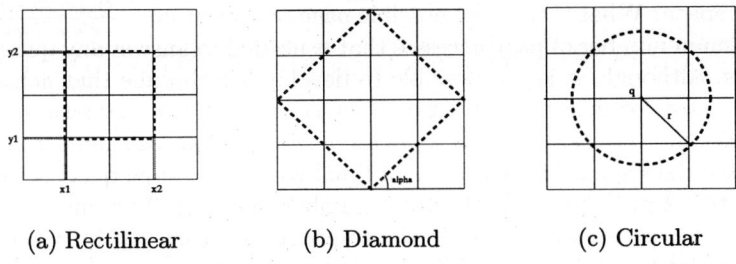

(a) Rectilinear (b) Diamond (c) Circular

Fig. 1. Range queries intersecting all partitions

2 Data Organization for Efficient Spatial Queries

The two most common spatial queries are range queries and similarity queries. In a range query, the user specifies an area of interest and all data points in this area are retrieved. In a similarity query, the query point is specified and all points "similar" to the query point are retrieved. A popular related query is k-nearest neighbor query. The k-nearest neighbor, $k - NN$, problem is defined as finding the k nearest points to the query point q. Traditional range queries have been specified using rectilinear queries, i.e., rectangular with sides parallel to axes. A rectilinear range query $Q_r = ([a_1, b_1], [a_2, b_2])$ specifies a range of values for each dimension. The result of the query is the set of all data objects that have values within the specified range in each dimension. More generally, a rectangular query can be defined as a rectilinear rectangle with a rotation angle of α with respect to the x−axis. For example, a rectilinear square range query with a rotation of $\pi/4$ gives us a diamond query (see Figure 1(b)). A commonly used query is the circular range query which is also called as ϵ-similarity query. It specifies a query point q and and a radius r, $Q_c = (q, r)$, which defines the acceptable region of similarity. All data objects that fall into the circle defined by the pair (q, r) are in the answer set. It is interesting to note that range queries of different shapes correspond to different types of similarity queries using different metrics. For example, the circular range query corresponds to similarity in L_2 metric, the rectilinear rectangular range query corresponds to similarity in the L_∞ metric and the diamond range query corresponds to similarity in the L_1 metric.

In both range and similarity queries, the pages that have the possibility to contain a portion of the query result are retrieved as a result of the query. As mentioned before, the spatial data objects are grouped according to their spatial locations and they are stored as pages in physical storage. Each page represents a spatial location in the data space. Therefore, in range queries the pages that are intersected by a query are retrieved as a result of the query. Similarly, $k - NN$ queries have to retrieve all pages that intersect the circle with the query point as the center and the distance between the query point and the $k - NN$ point as the radius. Even if there is a small portion of intersection of a page with the query region, the page needs to be retrieved since it may contain relevant data.

Is it possible to reduce this I/O cost by changing the initial page organization of the data space? What is the best possible page organization? $\lceil \frac{QueryResultSize}{PageCapacity} \rceil$ is the minimum number of page accesses that is needed to answer any query on any data sets. Although, it is not possible to develop a technique that achieves this minimum cost for every possible range query, a careful investigation is needed to reduce the I/O cost as much as possible. In general, assuming a uniformly distributed data space of area 1, the optimal cost for a range query with area A is equal to $\lceil A.p \rceil$, where p is the total number of pages. The number of pages accessed plays an important role in the response time incurred by range queries. The key point to minimize the I/O cost for queries depends on how data points are organized into pages. If a query is executed in two differently organized copies of the same data set, different numbers of pages will be retrieved depending on the way the data-space is initially organized. For efficient queries, the underlying organization of the data must be designed to reduce the expected number of pages retrieved by the queries. An organization of a database is *I/O optimal* if and only if it minimizes the expected number of page accesses incurred by the queries.

Regular equi-sized partitioning are widely used for organization of spatial data. They provide very efficient functions for hashing and mapping the partitions to pages in storage. The general approach is first to tile the data space into disjoint regular rectangular partitions and then to map each partition to a physical page in the storage. Are there any alternative techniques that tile the data space with non-overlapping partitions of identical shapes? It is known that it is not possible to tile the space with regular non-overlapping identical convex polygons with edges of more than 6 and there are only three basic tile shapes (triangles, rectangles, and hexagons) for regular partitioning [3]. We will consider these three basic shapes and compare their behavior under various conditions. Equilateral triangle, square, and regular hexagon are considered for triangle, rectangle, and hexagon respectively. They all have simple hashing properties that can be used to map the partitions to physical storage easily. We note that, although we consider these possible partitionings for our analysis, the optimality results in this paper are not restricted to these shapes.

3 I/O Cost for Various Query Types

Given a query, we explore different partitioning techniques that minimize the expected number of pages retrieved. The partitions that have to be accessed are the ones that intersect the range query region. Therefore, we will compute the expected number of partitions that intersect a range query region by using the methodology of Minkowski sum, $MSum$ [9]. In general, the Minkowski sum of two closed regions can be considered as expanding one region by the other. To compute the expected number of partitions that intersect a query, first the region of a partition, which also corresponds to a page region, is enlarged by considering the shape of the query. Suppose the partitions, which also correspond to the pages, are square shapes of side length c and the queries are circular.

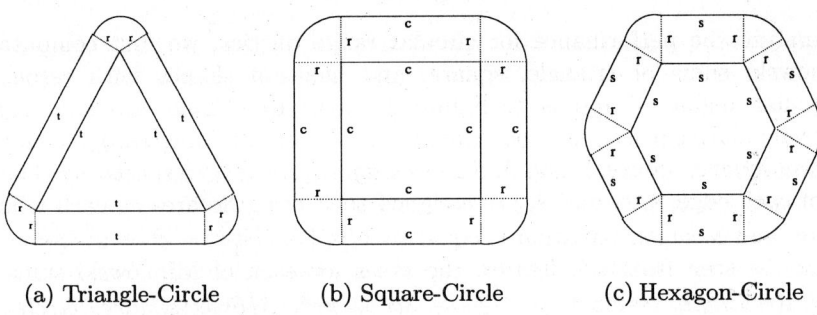

(a) Triangle-Circle (b) Square-Circle (c) Hexagon-Circle

Fig. 2. Minkowski Sums w.r.t. Circles

The Minkowski sum methodology is used to compute the expected number of partitions that intersect the circular query region as follows. The Minkowski sum of a square page of side length c, with respect to a circular region with a radius of r, is the enlarged object with area $MSum(square_c, circle_r)$. The enlarged object is created by moving the center of the circular query over the surface of the square (Figure 2(b)). Therefore, it consists of all points that are either in the square page or have a distance to the surface of the page less than r. The points within this enlarged object correspond to the center of all possible circular queries that intersect this page. Assuming uniform distribution, the fraction of the area of the enlarged object to the area of the data space is the probability that the corresponding page is being accessed, $P(page)$. Considering the unit data space, i.e., $[0,1]^2$, or simply normalizing the areas with respect to the total area, the area of the enlarged object gives the probability of the page to be accessed. Note that, the regions that are created by the Minkowski sum of the partitions in the border of the two-dimensional data space are negligible when compared to the total amount of regions created by Minkowski sums of all partitions. The expected number of pages which are intersected by a query q is $E(q)$ and it is the sum of the probabilities of the pages intersected by the query. If we have regular equi-sized partitioning, i.e., p partitions of identical shape, then the expected number of intersected partitions by the query is p times the probability of a page being accessed, i.e., $E(q) = p \cdot P(page)$. Therefore, for a partitioning scheme that tiles the space with pages of shape s, the expected numbers of intersected partitions for a query q of any shape is $E_s(q) = p \cdot MSum(s, q)$, where p is the number of partitions. For example, for a square partitioning this equation is simply $E_{square}(q) = p \cdot MSum(square_c, q)$. In this section, we analyze the I/O cost performance of the partitioning techniques for range queries. We will investigate the optimal partitioning, assuming uniform distribution, that must be used for different conditions to minimize the I/O cost.

3.1 I/O Cost for Circular Range Queries

To analyze the performance for circular range queries, we first compute the Minkowski sums of triangle, square, and hexagon shapes with respect to a circular region of radius r. Figure 2 shows the Minkowski sum regions for triangular, square, and hexagonal pages, i.e., $MSum(triangle_t, circle_r)$, $MSum(square_c, circle_r)$, and $MSum(hexagon_s, circle_r)$, respectively. The values of each edge, t, c, and s, are assigned such that the area of each triangle, square, and hexagon partition is equal to $1/p$, i.e., $\frac{t^2\sqrt{3}}{4} = c^2 = s^2\frac{3\sqrt{3}}{2} = 1/p$. As can be seen from the figures, the areas for each of Minkowski sums are: $MSum(triangle_t, circle_r) = \frac{t^2\sqrt{3}}{4} + 3tr + \pi r^2$, $MSum(square_c, circle_r) = c^2 + 4cr + \pi r^2$, and $MSum(hexagon_s, circle_r) = s^2\frac{3\sqrt{3}}{2} + 6sr + \pi r^2$. After substitutions we find $MSum(triangle_t, circle_r) \approx s^2\frac{3\sqrt{3}}{2} + 7.35sr + \pi r^2$, and $MSum(square_c, circle_r) \approx s^2\frac{3\sqrt{3}}{2} + 6.45sr + \pi r^2$. Comparing all three equations, we find $MSum(hexagon_s, circle_r) < MSum(square_c, circle_r) < MSum(triangle_t, circle_r)$. This result means that for circular regions the Minkowski sum of a hexagon is always less than the Minkowski sum of a square and the Minkowski sum of a triangle. Substituting this result into the equation for $E_s(q)$, we finally find $E_{hexagon}(circle_r) < E_{square}(circle_r) < E_{triangle}(circle_r)$. The expected number of partitions intersected by a circular query in a hexagonal grid is always less than the one in a square grid and a triangular grid. This result simply tells us that if the sole or dominant types of the queries in a spatial database have circular shapes, then hexagonal partitioning of the data space will give better results in terms of the number of the page accesses, i.e., I/O operations, occurred during query.

Indeed, we will now generalize the superiority of hexagonal partitioning over other possible approaches and prove that hexagonal partitioning is optimal, among all non-overlapping partitioning techniques of equal area convex regions, with respect to the number partitions retrieved as a result of a circular query of any size.

Lemma 1. *For a convex polygon with a perimeter of length M, the Minkowski Sum with respect to circular regions of radius r is:*

$$MSum(polygon, circle_r) = area(polygon) + M \cdot r + \pi r^2 \quad (1)$$

Proof. For a convex polygon of n sides, the $MSum$ region with respect to a circle of radius r contains the polygon itself, plus n rectangles with sides r and the corresponding side of the polygon, plus n pies with an angle of Γ_i, for $1 \leq i \leq n$. The area of the n rectangles sum up to $M \cdot r$, where M is the perimeter of the polygon. Each Γ_i is equal to $180 - \Theta_i$ degrees, where Θ_i is the corresponding angle in the polygon. Since the summation of all these n angles of pies is 360 degrees, $\sum_1^n (180 - \Theta_i) = 180n - 180(n-2) = 360$, they sum up to a full circle.

Lemma 2. *Minimizing the perimeter of the shape that is used for partitioning also minimizes the expected number of partitions intersecting the circular query.*

Proof. In Equation 1, since r does not change with partitioning and $area(polygon) = 1/p$, the only value that makes a difference is the perimeter M that is used in the pages. This is true for all possible r values that a circular query can take.

Minimizing the perimeter of each partition minimizes the total boundary length of the partitioning. The total boundary of the partitions is defined as the length of the boundaries that are used to divide the data-space into partitions [3]. If each non-overlapping partition uses smaller perimeters to cover larger areas, the total lengths of boundaries of these partitions are also minimized [3]. What is the optimal way of minimizing the perimeter and the total boundary? Recently, it has been proved that any partitioning of the plane into regions of equal area has perimeter at least that of the regular hexagonal honeycomb tiling [5]. This has been known as the classical honeycomb observation and has been the motivation for numerous interesting applications. The surprising geometry of the beehives is the best that could be done for their major purpose. In 1743, Colin Mac Laurin summarizes the nice property of the beehives as follows: "The geometry of the beehive supports *least wax* for containing *the same quantity of honey*, and which has at the same time a very remarkable regularity and beauty, connected of necessity with its frugality" [6].

By Lemma 1 and 2 we conclude that a partitioning that minimizes the total boundary also minimizes the expected number of partitions retrieved as a result of a circular query. Since hexagon partitioning minimizes the total boundary compared to all possible equal area partitioning techniques, it also minimizes the expected number of partitions retrieved as a result of a circular query. Hence, we have the following theorem.

Theorem 1. *Hexagonal partitioning is I/O optimal for circular queries (among all non-overlapping partitioning techniques using equal area convex regions).*

3.2 I/O Cost for Square Range Queries

In this section, we analyze the I/O cost for square range queries. We start with rectilinear square query analysis on the three basic partitioning discussed in this paper. Then, we analyze a more general class of square range queries where the sides of the range query do not have to be parallel to the axes. We establish that hexagonal partitioning has better average performance than square grid for the general class of square range queries.

Rectilinear Square Range Queries For the analysis of rectilinear square range queries, we first compute the Minkowski sums of three shapes and a rectilinear square region. Similar to the previous analysis we find the Minkowski

Sum values for each shape as [3]:

$$MSum(square_c, rectilinear_a) = \frac{3\sqrt{3}}{2}s^2 + 2\sqrt{\frac{3\sqrt{3}}{2}}as + a^2,$$

$$MSum(hexagon_s, rectilinear_a) = \frac{3\sqrt{3}}{2}s^2 + (2+\sqrt{3})as + a^2,$$

$$MSum(triangle_t, rectilinear_a) = \frac{3\sqrt{3}}{2}s^2 + (\frac{3\sqrt{2}}{2} + \sqrt{6})as + a^2.$$

Comparing these three equations, we find $MSum(square_c, rectilinear_a) < MSum(hexagon_s, rectilinear_a) < MSum(triangle_t, rectilinear_a)$, and therefore,
$E_{square}(rectilinear_a) < E_{hexagon}(rectilinear_a) < E_{triangle}(rectilinear_a)$. We conclude that for rectilinear square queries, the expected number of intersected partitions in a square grid is less than the one in a hexagonal grid and a triangular grid. The technical report of this paper contains a detailed analysis of this case and also a similar analysis of the rectilinear rectangular range queries [3].

General Square Range Queries In the previous section, we focused on *rectilinear* square range queries, but queries can take any orientation and are not restricted to have sides parallel to the axes, e.g., as in diamond queries. In this section, we analyze *general* square queries with any *orientation*. We will compare the hexagonal and square partitioning by starting to compute the Minkowski Sums for square and hexagon tiles and general square region. The square region has an angle α with the $x - axis$. The examples of special cases include the diamond query, i.e., $\alpha = \pi/4$, and the rectilinear square query, i.e., $\alpha = 0$. In this section, for simplicity in $MSum$, we assume that the area of each partition is 1, i.e., $c^2 = s^2 \frac{3\sqrt{3}}{2} = 1$. Figure 3 illustrates the case when $\alpha = \pi/4$. Because of the symmetric property of $MSum$, i.e., $MSum(hexagon_s, square_a) = MSum(square_a, hexagon_s)$, for simplicity we illustrate $MSum(square_a, hexagon_s)$ in Figure 3.

The $MSum$ of a square page with respect to a square query with an angle of α with the x−axis is:

$$MSum(square_1, square_a) = 1 + a^2 + 2\sqrt{2}a \cdot sin(\pi/4 + \alpha) \qquad (2)$$

where $0 \leq \alpha \leq \frac{\pi}{4}$. Similarly, the $MSum$ of a hexagon with respect to a square with a rotation angle of α, is computed as $MSum(hexagon, square_a) = a^2 + 1 + 2(S_1 + S_2)$, where $S_1 = as \cdot sin(\frac{\pi}{3} + \alpha)$ and $S_2 = as \cdot sin(\frac{\pi}{2} - \alpha)$. Therefore,

$$MSum(hexagon, square_a) = a^2 + 1 + 2as(sin[\frac{\pi}{3} + \alpha] + sin[\frac{\pi}{2} - \alpha]) \qquad (3)$$

where $0 \leq \alpha \leq \frac{\pi}{6}$.

The reason that the rotation angle α varies between 0 and $\pi/6$ in the hexagon and between 0 and $\pi/4$ in the square is that the symmetry is captured within

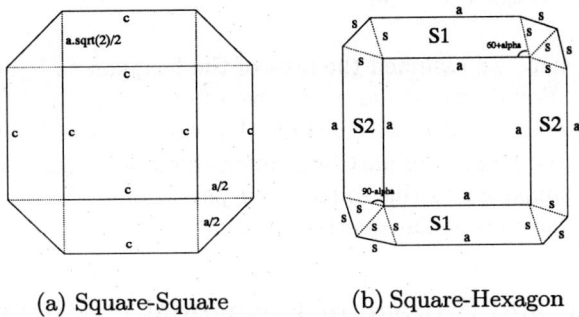

Fig. 3. Minkowski Sums w.r.t. Squares (with any orientation α)

these angles. There is no need to compute the other angles, because rotating an angle of β not in this range gives the same result as rotating with an angle of $\alpha = \beta \bmod \pi/6$ for a hexagon and $\alpha = \beta \bmod \pi/4$ for a square. For majority of the angles which correspond to different query types, including the diamond query which represents similarity in L_1 metric, hexagonal partitioning achieves better performance results by requiring fewer I/O accesses. The technical report [3] has more discussion of the performance behavior of both partitioning under various angles.

Since we have the general formula for the square query specified with a center and an angle, we can compute the expected number of partitions intersected by such queries for both square and hexagonal grid. By integrating all such possible queries and computing the expected number by taking the uniform average, we can compute the expected $MSum$, E_{MSum}, of each technique. As shown before, the comparison of $MSums$ will give the comparison of techniques with respect to the expected number of partitions intersected by a random square query. Integrating Equations 2 and 3 for all possible values of α, we compute the expected $MSum$ for each partition as. For the case of square,

$$E_{MSum_{square}}(square_a) = \frac{4}{\pi} \int_{\pi/4}^{\pi/2} (MSum(square_1, square_a)$$

$$= a^2 + 1 + \frac{8\sqrt{2}a}{\pi} \int_{\pi/4}^{\pi/2} sin\alpha d\alpha,$$

$$E_{MSum_{square}}(square_a) = 1 + a^2 + \frac{8a}{\pi}. \qquad (4)$$

Similarly, for hexagon,

$$E_{MSum_{hexagon}}(square_a) = 1 + a^2 + \frac{2as \cdot 6}{\pi} \int_0^{\pi/6} [sin(\pi/3+\alpha) + sin(\pi/4-\alpha)]d\alpha.$$

$$E_{MSum_{hexagon}}(square_a) = 1 + a^2 + \frac{12as}{\pi} \approx 1 + a^2 + \frac{7.44a}{\pi} \tag{5}$$

where $s \approx 0.62$ since we assumed the area of the hexagon as 1, i.e., $s^2 \frac{3\sqrt{3}}{2} = 1$.

Comparing Equations 4 and 5, we find $E_{MSum_{hexagon}}(square_a) < E_{MSum_{square}}(square_a)$. Hence, we conclude that the hexagonal partitioning minimizes the expected number of partitions intersected by a square query with any orientation α, compared to the square grid partitioning. The analysis can be easily extended for rectangular queries.

4 Retrieval and Storage of Hexagonal Partitioning

We have shown that the hexagonal partitioning is effective for range queries, and hence can be used as an effective alternative for regular grid partitioning. Traditional retrieval methods developed for single disk and single processor environments may be ineffective for the storage and retrieval of spatial data in multiprocessor and multiple disk environments. It is essential to develop techniques that are optimized for such environments. In this section, we discuss multi-disk organization for hexagonal partitioning, i.e., declustering of buckets to multiple disks and clustering each bucket within each disk. For lack of space, here we just describe how to develop a simple hash function for regular hexagonal partitioning, and we refer the technical report of this paper for a complete discussion of declustering and clustering functions. In particular, it discusses how techniques for rectangular grid partitioning can be adapted for hexagonal partitioning. It also proves that the number of devices needed for optimal declustering of hexagonal partitions is less than the rectangular grid partitions [3].

The hashing function finds the corresponding hexagonal partition of a given data point and is needed for both declustering and clustering purposes. Hash functions for rectangular partitioning are very simple and well-known. We will use rectangular hashing in the development of the hexagonal hashing. We divide the data space logically into a regular grid of rectangles with sides (s, h), where s is the side length of the hexagonal partitions and $h = \frac{s\sqrt{3}}{2}$ (See Figure 4). A hexagonal partition is defined by $H(i,j)$, where i is the row number and j is the column number of the partition. Similarly, a (logical) rectangular cell is defined by $G(i,j)$. Obviously, the number of rectangular cells is more than the number of hexagonal cells. Depending on the location, some of the cells in this regular grid fall entirely into a single hexagonal partition, and some fall into two hexagonal partitions. For example, in Figure 4, $G(0,0)$ is entirely in $H(0,0)$. Therefore, if a point is found to be in $G(0,0)$, it is also in $H(0,0)$. On the other hand $G(1,1)$ falls mostly in $H(1,1)$ but also in $H(0,0)$. Each grid cell can be mapped to one or two hexagonal partitions. Therefore, given a data point we can hash the point using hashing on regular grid and find the corresponding hexagon(s). If there are two hexagons an additional simple check (whether the point is in the first hexagon) is needed to identify the hexagon where the point is located. The different cases for mapping of rectangular grid cells to hexagonal partitions are

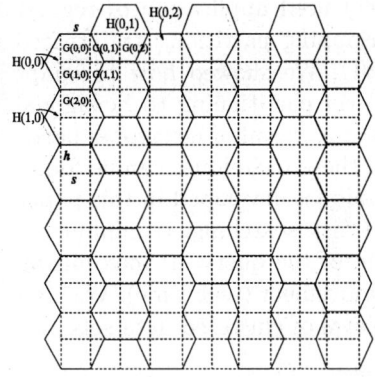

Fig. 4. Hexagonal hashing using grid

$$G(2m, 3n) \subseteq H(m, 2n)$$
$$G(2m, 3n + 1) \subseteq H(m, 2n) \cup H(m, 2n + 1)$$
$$G(2m, 3n + 2) \subseteq H(m, 2n + 1) \cup H(m, 2n + 2)$$
$$G(2m + 1, 3n) \subseteq H(m, 2n)$$
$$G(2m + 1, 3n + 1) \subseteq H(m, 2n) \cup H(m + 1, 2n + 1)$$
$$G(2m + 1, 3n + 2) \subseteq H(m + 1, 2n + 1) \cup H(m, 2n + 2)$$

Fig. 5. Mapping of rectangular grid cells to hexagonal partitions

shown in Figure 5. A grid cell $G(i, j)$ is mapped to hexagonal partitions with a simple analysis on the value of (i mod 2) and (j mod 3). For example, grid cell $G(2m, 3n)$, i.e., i mod $2 = 0$ and j mod $3 = 0$, is mapped to $H(m, 2n)$. Given a point in $G(2m, 3n)$, e.g., $m = 2$ and $n = 1$ so $G(4, 3)$, it is located only in $H(m, 2n)$ (see Figure 5), e.g., $H(2, 2)$.

5 Discussion

In this paper, we explored optimal partitioning techniques for different types of queries on spatial data sets. We focused on partitioning techniques that tile the data space without holes and overlaps, and therefore have simple hashing schemes. We discussed the possible cases and computed the expected number of pages retrieved for circular and rectangular queries. We showed that hexagonal partitioning has optimal I/O cost for circular queries over all possible non-overlapping partitioning techniques that use convex regions. We also show that hexagonal partitioning has less I/O cost than the traditional grid for the general class of square queries. It is, however, interesting to note that for the special case of rectilinear queries, the traditional grid partitioning provides superior performance. This could be explained due to the symmetric relationship between the rectilinear square query and the rectilinear square page. This may also indicate why for traditional relational database applications only rectangular grid partitioning were considered [1,7]. In a relational database, a select operation specifies a range in each dimension or attribute which corresponds to a rectilinear rectangle. Novel spatial applications need more general query structures with queries of any orientations. Our results indicate that for such applications, a hexagonal partitioning of the space should be used. The hexagonal partitioning is shown to be effective for circular and rectangular queries. It can be used as an effective alternative for regular grid partitioning with no major changes on the existing algorithms. For instance, a widely used application of regular grid partitioning is declustering where non-overlapping partitions are created and distributed to multiple disks for efficient I/O. We showed how to adapt the techniques that were developed for regular grid partitioning to hexagonal partitioning and develop techniques for storage and retrieval of hexagonal partitioning in multi-disk environments. The details of these techniques can be found in the technical report of this paper [3]. The techniques developed in this paper consider the objectives that are crucial for multi-disk searching: i) minimizing the number of page accesses during the execution of the query, ii) maximizing the I/O parallelism, iii) minimizing the disk-arm movement (seek time). We plan to extend our techniques to support efficient retrieval of clustered data sets also in the presence of frequent updates.

References

1. H. C. Du and J. S. Sobolewski. Disk allocation for cartesian product files on multiple-disk systems. *ACM Transactions of Database Systems*, 7(1):82–101, March 1982.
2. H. Ferhatosmanoglu, D. Agrawal, and A. El Abbadi. Concentric hyperspaces and disk allocation for fast parallel range searching. In *Proc. Int. Conf. Data Engineering*, pages 608–615, Sydney, Australia, March 1999.
3. H. Ferhatosmanoglu, D. Agrawal, and A. El Abbadi. Optimal partitioning for spatial data. Technical report, Comp. Sci. Dept., UC, Santa Barbara, December 2000.
4. V. Gaede and O. Gunther. Multidimensional access methods. *ACM Computing Surveys*, 30:170–231, 1998.
5. Thomas C. Hales. The honeycomb conjecture.
available at http://xxx.lanl.gov/abs/math.MG/9906042, June 1999.
6. Thomas C. Hales. Historical background on hexagonal honeycomb. http://www.math.lsa.umich.edu/ hales/countdown/honey/hexagonHistory.html, March 2000.
7. S. Prabhakar, K. Abdel-Ghaffar, D. Agrawal, and A. El Abbadi. Cyclic allocation of two-dimensional data. In *International Conference on Data Engineering*, pages 94–101, Orlando, Florida, Feb 1998.
8. H. Samet. *The Design and Analysis of Spatial Structures*. Addison Wesley Publishing Company, Inc., Massachusetts, 1989.
9. R. Weber, H.-J. Schek, and S. Blott. A quantitative analysis and performance study for similarity-search methods in high-dimensional spaces. In *Proceedings of the Int. Conf. on Very Large Data Bases*, pages 194–205, New York City, New York, August 1998.

Improving Network Performance by Efficiently Dealing with Short Control Messages in Fibre Channel SANs[*]

Xavier Molero, Federico Silla, Vicente Santonja, and José Duato

Departament d'Informàtica de Sistemes i Computadors,
Universitat Politècnica de València, Camí de Vera, 14. 46022 València, Spain
jmolero@disca.upv.es

Abstract. Traffic in a Storage Area Networks is bimodal, composed of long messages carrying several KBytes of data, and short messages containing control information (I/O commands). From the network point of view, latency of control messages is highly affected by the transmission of data messages, due to their length. As a consequence, it is necessary to establish management policies that benefit the transmission of short control messages, thus reducing the overall response time for I/O operations and increasing network throughput.
In this paper we propose several strategies for dealing with short control messages and analyze their impact on the performance of storage area networks. This analysis is carried out for a fully adaptive routing algorithm in the context of two different network topology environments: buildings and departments. Simulation results show that both I/O response time and network throughput may be improved when efficiently managing control messages.

1 Introduction and Motivation

I/O technology has been traditionally based on the server-storage architecture, where each storage device is connected to a single server, usually by means of a SCSI bus. However, this approach is now facing several problems such as unavailability of data due to server down times, bandwidth saturation during backups, and also a great number of limitations when implementing large configurations.

An emerging alternative to the traditional I/O architecture is based on the concept of SAN (*Storage Area Network*) [4,11]. A SAN is a high-speed network, similar to a LAN, that makes possible to connect servers to storage devices (see Figure 1). Thus, in the same way that LANs allow clients easy access to many servers, SANs provide access to storage devices from many servers. SANs allow storage to be shared among many servers without impacting LAN performance, which is improved because now it is free from the high overhead associated with

---

[*] This work was supported by the Spanish CICYT under grants TIC2000-1151-C07 and TIC2000-0472-C03-03

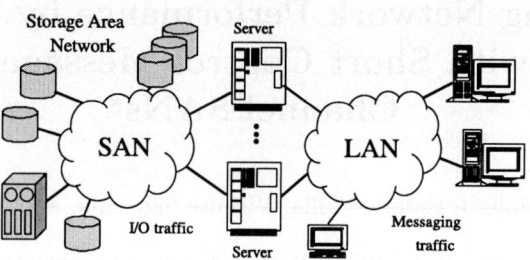

Fig. 1. A typical SAN environment

file retrieval, storage, and data backing up tasks. Moreover, data access is enhanced because file read/write and data migration are more effectively handled by a network that can be optimized for the demands of storage operations (e.g., high throughput and large packet data transfers). Most of current SANs are implemented using Fibre Channel technology [2,4] due to its suitability for storage networking.

Servers initiate the communication with disks by issuing a read or a write I/O operation. In both cases each I/O operation implies the transmission of two messages: a request and a response. In the case for read operations, the server first sends to the selected disk a request message containing the number of sectors to read, and the initial location of the data. Once the device has processed the request, it sends back the data to the server. Regarding write operations, servers initiate them by sending to the selected disk the data and the location where they must be stored. Once the data have been stored, the device returns an acknowledgment message to the server.

Thus, messages exchanged between servers and storage devices can be classified into two different types: short control messages (read requests or write acknowledgments) and long data messages. Usually, control messages are not longer than a few bytes, while typical data messages are a few KBytes long. Therefore, traffic in a storage area network becomes bimodal, being composed of long and short messages in the same percentage. From the network point of view, latency of control messages is highly affected by the transmission of data messages, which tend to monopolize physical links due to their length, making control messages to experience long queueing times, thus increasing the overall I/O response time. On the other hand, when a control message arrives at a switch it reserves an entire input buffer, which is usually large enough to store a whole data message or, at least, part of it. Due to the short length of control messages, reserving a whole buffer means wasting most of the buffering capacity, leading to a decrement in network throughput, and thus increasing the overall I/O response time.

In [6], Kim and Chien discusses different techniques to deal with bimodal traffic in the context of wormhole-routed networks. In this paper we propose several ways of managing control messages and analyze their effect on the performance of Fibre Channel storage area networks.

The remainder of this paper is organized as follows. Section 2 presents our model of SANs. The different strategies proposed for dealing with control messages are described in Section 3. Section 4 describes the evaluation methodology. The effect of each strategy is evaluated in Section 5. Finally, Section 6 summarizes the conclusions from our study.

2 System Model

The basic switch architecture we have considered is shown in Figure 2. Each input port has an associated pool of buffers to store incoming messages. When a message arrives at a port, it starts being read into one of those buffers. The routing unit iteratively polls input ports, in a round-robin scheduling policy, for new messages that need to be routed. This unit can start routing a message as soon as the header information has arrived. If it finds new messages in a port, the router selects the first one and reads the header information, which contains the destination address. If the requested output link is busy, then the incoming message remains in the input buffer until it is successfully routed. An internal crossbar with as many input ports as input buffers allows multiple messages to be simultaneously forwarded without interference.

Fibre Channel uses the virtual cut-through switching mechanism [5]. In this case, when a message finds the output port busy, it is blocked in place, being completely stored at the input buffer of the current switch. Thus, message length is bounded by the input buffer size. This limitation can be easily overcome by splitting messages into packets. The flow control mechanism used in Fibre Channel to manage the transfer of data between two adjacent switches is based on credits.

Network topologies used in a SAN environment can be classified into two different categories: those that map an entire building and those intended to be used in a single room (laboratory, data center, computing site, etc.). Topologies in the first group can easily map to a multi-floor installation [9]. In these topologies most connections are between switches and devices in each floor. The

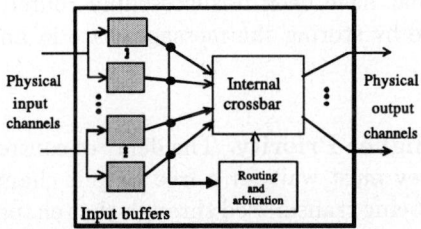

Fig. 2. Switch architecture

structure at each floor consists of a star configuration with center switches and arm switches. This structure is replicated as many times as floors are included in the SAN. Center switches are specifically devoted for connecting switches at different floors. Servers and storage devices are attached to the SAN by means of arm switches. We have used the tree topology as an example of toplogies used in departmental environments. Servers and disks are connected to the leaf switches. The rest of switches are devoted to communication between devices attached at different leaves.

Fibre Channel uses distributed routing, leaving routing decisions to each of the switches in the path from source to destination. In our study, we have considered the minimal adaptive routing algorithm [10].

3 Strategies for Managing Control Messages

In this section we present several strategies for managing short control messages. The main purpose of these policies is to improve response time of I/O operations by reducing network latency of control messages, at the same time network throughput is increased due to a better management of input buffers.

Routing with Higher Priority. Incoming messages are managed by the routing and arbitration unit, which polls input ports for messages to be routed in a round robin fashion. While control messages are waiting to be routed, output channels may be assigned to data messages located ahead in the polling path, thus diminishing the choices that control messages will have when being routed later, and increasing their queueing time. Therefore, if control messages were routed with a higher priority, they would be able to leave the switch sooner, decreasing I/O response time.

When routing depends on message priority, the routing and arbitration unit also polls input ports in a round robin scheme, but the scheduling policy is modified so that control messages arriving at a switch have higher priority. They will be routed before than the rest of messages at the switch. In each round, a maximum of one new control message per port can be routed. If a high priority control message has not been successfully routed, then it will be assigned a regular priority in following rounds. This will prevent starvation. In order to implement this scheme, the routing unit must be able to distinguish newly arrived control messages from those that have been unsuccessfully routed in previous rounds. This can be easily done by storing the message state in an one-bit register per input buffer.

Transmission with Higher Priority. The delay of control messages is mainly due to the fact that they must wait for a free output channel before being forwarded. If the message being transmitted through that channel is a data message, then the control message should wait for long. Control message queueing delay may be avoided if control messages were assigned the required output channel once they have been routed, preempting the transmission of the data message owing the output link. Once the control message has been transmitted, then the switch can continue the transmission of the stopped data message. The transmission of a control message cannot be preempted by another control message.

In order to implement this scheme, the receiving switch must be able to correctly identify and extract the control messages that have been inserted into the data stream of a data message, so that they are stored in the proper buffers. This is easily overcome by using the header and the tail information associated with each message. When a control message preempts the transmission of a data message, the header of the control message helps the receiving switch to store the incoming message in a different buffer. At the same time, it would record the preemption, so that when the tail of the control message arrives, the receiving switch may continue storing the rest of the data message in the proper buffer.

Separating Input Buffers. Buffers at input ports may be divided into two disjoint sets: one for storing data messages and another one for control messages. As a consequence, the network would behave as divided into two independent subnetworks, one for data messages and another one for control messages. However, both kinds of messages still share the same physical links, routing units, and internal crossbars. Thus, long data messages can already interfere with control messages. Nevertheless, this solution avoids wasting input buffer capacity because buffers intended for control messages may be considerably reduced in size.

Message Packetization. When using message packetization, messages are decomposed into several packets of fixed length, which travel through the network independently from each other. Each packet carries its own routing information at its header.

From the network point of view, transmitting packets instead of longer messages avoids the monopolization of physical channels, allowing short control messages to advance to their destination faster. However, some disadvantages arise when using message packetization. One of them is the overhead introduced in the amount of information transmitted. It may also increase the amount of credit messages transmitted because of the flow control protocol. Also, the network must independently route each of the packets at the switches they traverse, thus highly increasing the number of cycles wasted in the routing process. The implementation of this strategy only needs modifying the software at the sender and the receiver ends: the sender must split the message into smaller packets, and the receiver must reassemble the received packets in order to get the original message.

4 Evaluation Methodology

In order to accurately model the SAN, we have used byte level simulation. Our simulator [7] has been implemented using the CSIM language [3]. Simulations were run for a number of cycles high enough to obtain steady values of I/O response times. An initial transient period corresponding to the completion of 500 I/O operations has been considered. Then, simulations were run for a number of cycles high enough to obtain steady values of I/O operation times.

We have used synthetic traffic, considering that interarrival time for the generation of I/O operations is exponentially distributed and it is the same for all the servers attached to the storage network. Moreover, we have assumed that the destination disk of each I/O operation initiated by a server is randomly chosen among all the disks in the network. We have also assumed that the number of I/O read operations is similar to the number of I/O write operations.

Disk access time has been shown to be the dominant factor in the total I/O response time [8], thus becoming the bottleneck of the entire storage system. In order to stress the network, we have assumed that disks access data fast enough to avoid becoming a bottleneck.

Due to the lack of information about current Fibre Channel implementations, switch parameters have been taken similar to those in high-speed Myrinet networks [1]. In Myrinet networks, the time needed to route and forward the first byte of a message is 150 ns. Following bytes take 6.25 ns to traverse the switch. We have considered that each switch has eight 2048-byte buffers per input port devoted to store data messages.

Current Fibre Channel switches use full duplex serial links at 100 MBytes/s. However, higher bandwidths are under development nowadays. Thus in this study we have considered that links transfer data at 160 MBytes/s. Link length may range from a few meters until several kilometers when optical fiber is used. We have considered both 3 and 30 meter links.

Our case study for the analysis of the floors topologies is a 5-floor topology where each floor has 2 center switches ("floors+" topology). Four arm switches provide connectivity at each floor between the vertical backbone on one hand and servers and disks on the other. Each of the arm switches are connected to a single server and 5 disks. Thus, our storage area network is composed by 20 servers and 100 disks. Links connecting servers or disks to the corresponding arm switch are 3 meters long, while links in the backbone are 30 meters long.

In the case for departmental topologies ("tree" topology), our storage area network is composed of 10 servers and 50 disks. All links in the network are 3 meters long.

5 Performance Analysis

This section analyzes the effect of the strategies proposed in Section 3 on network performance, which is measured by means of the response time of I/O operations and the delivered traffic.

Figure 3 displays the simulation results for the first management policy where incoming control messages are assigned a higher priority in order to be routed first. These results, referred to as "routing", are compared with the performance achieved by the basic switch architecture in Figure 2 and referred as "basic".

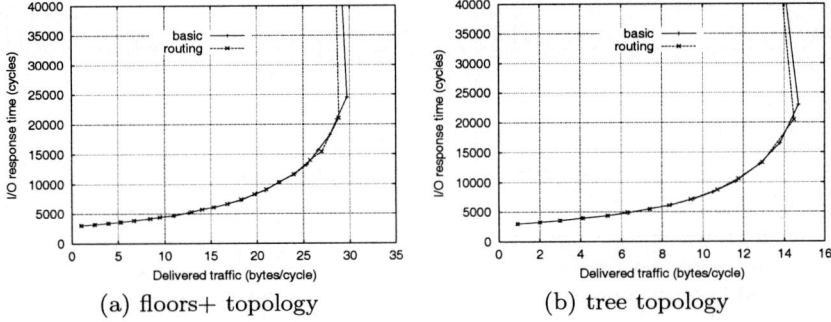

Fig. 3. Effect of routing control messages with higher priority

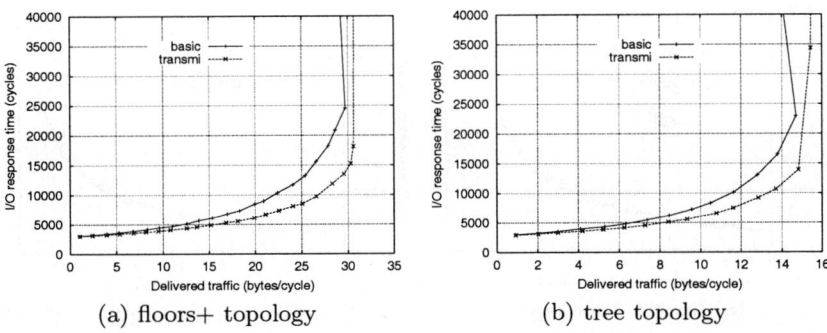

Fig. 4. Effect of transmitting control messages with higher priority

As can be seen, the effect on performance of this strategy is negligible. The reason is that routing incoming control messages first has no advantage if the required output channel is busy. In this case, once the newly arrived control message has been unsuccessfully routed, its priority is reduced, and therefore, it is handled as a regular message in following routing cycles. Note that only when a control message arrives at a switch and the required output link is available, this policy would provide some benefit. Unfortunately, these circumstances are not common.

The effect on network performance of the second management strategy is shown in Figure 4. This policy allows preempting the transmission of data messages in order to transmit control messages once they are routed. Results for this management scheme are referred to as "transmi". As can be seen, the average I/O response time is improved In the case for the floors+ topology, an improvement in I/O response time near 40% is achieved when the network is near saturation. For tree, the improvement is about 30%.

Improvement in I/O response time is due to an important reduction in the latency of control messages, which do not have to wait until the completion of the transmission of data messages. However, improving the transmission of

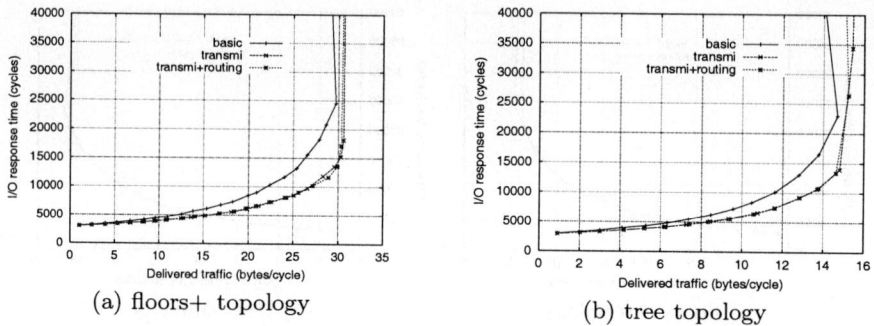

Fig. 5. Combined effects of both transmission and routing with higher priority

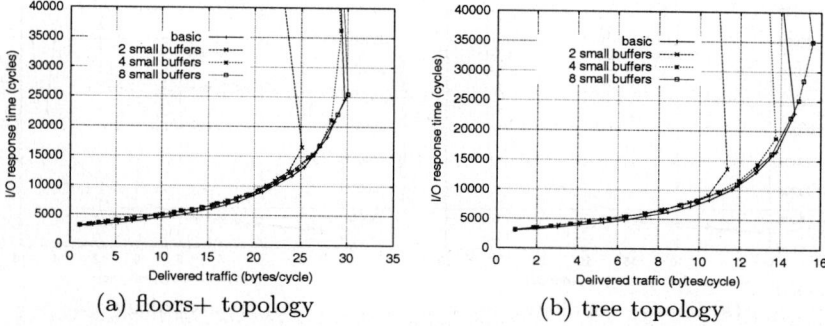

Fig. 6. Effect of separating input buffers for both data and control messages

short control messages has a negative effect on the transmission of long data messages, whose latency is increased. This makes that network throughput is not noticeably increased, because the contribution of data messages to the overall network throughput is much more important than the contribution of control messages, due to their smaller size. Therefore, the main effect of transmitting control messages with a higher priority is a reduction in I/O response time.

When control messages are allowed to preempt the transmission of data messages, the network latency achieved by the former is the minimum one if we do not consider the delay introduced by the routing unit due to its round-robin scheduling policy. This delay may be avoided if this management strategy is combined with the first one. In this case, when a control message arrives at a switch, it would be immediately routed and then it would preempt, if necessary, the transmission of the data message being forwarded through the selected output channel. We have analyzed the effect on performance of this new strategy. Figure 5 shows results for the topologies under study. As can be seen, for high loads, the combination of both strategies reports a slight benefit, mainly near network saturation.

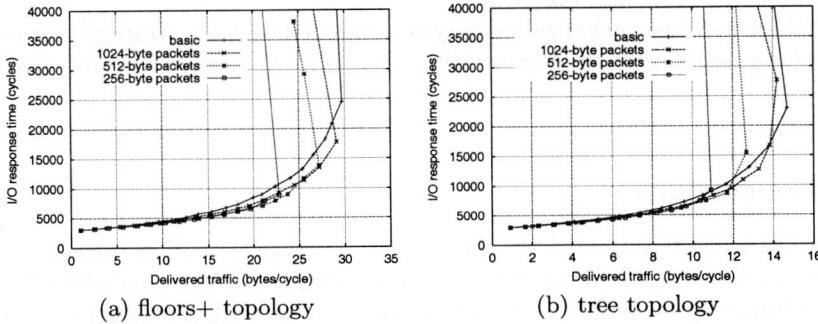

Fig. 7. Effect of message packetization

Regarding the implementation of the third strategy for managing control messages, switch buffering capacity should be kept similar for all the configurations analyzed. This would provide a fear comparison of the results. The basic 8-port architecture has a storage capacity of eight 2048-byte buffers per port, providing an overall capacity of 128 KBytes. Therefore, the switch architecture implementing this scheme should provide a similar capacity. More concretely, we have assumed eight buffers devoted to data messages, and a variable number of small buffers intended to store control messages, ranging from two to eight buffers. This will result only in an additional maximum buffering capacity of 1% for the larger configuration.

Figure 6 shows the I/O response time versus delivered traffic when 2, 4, and 8 additional buffers are considered, as well as results for the basic switch architecture. As can be seen, when the number of input buffers intended for storing control messages is very low, network throughput is reduced. The reason for this is that the maximum amount of control messages present in the network is limited by the amount of small input buffers. Thus, I/O response time is increased because control messages must wait for a free small buffer before entering the network.

As the number of additional small buffers is increased, control messages reduce their queueing time, and therefore network throughput is improved. When eight additional buffers are intended for control messages, network throughput is slightly increased with respect to the basic switch architecture because of the larger overall buffering capacity available in the network. As more additional small buffers are attached to each input port, the improvement in performance becomes smaller. Finally, it must be taken into account that increasing the number of small buffers will increase the size of the internal crossbar, thus leading to a much more complex design of the switch architecture.

Figure 7 shows the effect of using packetization. Results when messages are split into 256, 512, and 1024-byte packets are plotted, as well as results for the initial architecture. As can be seen, a reduction in the I/O response time is achieved when messages are packetized, independently of the analyzed topology. However, network performance is also reduced, being the reduction more noticeable as packet size diminishes.

Finally, message packetization may be combined with the strategy that routes control messages with higher priority, in order to forward control messages sooner. We perform some simulations for such a combination, and conclude that routing control messages with higher priority provides no additional benefit.

6 Conclusions

The main insights provided by our analysis show that SAN performance may be improved if control messages are efficiently handled. More concretely, I/O response time may be lowered at the same time that network throughput is slightly increased when control messages are allowed to preempt the transmission of data messages. In the case for I/O response time, the actual improvement factor depends on network topology, ranging from 10% to 40%. Maximum throughput increment is about 5%.

Regarding the rest of management policies analyzed: routing control messages with higher priority, additional buffers intended for storing control messages, and packetizing data messages, they provide no noticeable benefit, despite of the fact that some of them are costly, as is the case for additional input buffers devoted for control messages.

References

1. N. J. Boden, D. Cohen, R. E. Felderman, A. E. Kulawik, C. L. Seitz, J. N. Seizovic and W. Su, Myrinet - A gigabit per second local area network, *IEEE Micro*, pp. 29–36, February 1995.
2. T. Clark, *Designing storage area networks: a practical reference for implementing fibre channel SANs*, Addison Wesley, 1999.
3. *User's guide: CSIM18 Simulation Engine (C version)*, Mesquite Software, Inc.
4. M. Farley, *Building storage area networks*, McGraw-Hill, 2000.
5. P. Kermani and L. Kleinrock, Virtual cut-through: a new computer communication switching technique, *Computer Networks*, vol. 3, pp. 267–286, 1979.
6. J. H. Kim and A. A. Chien, Network Performance Under Bimodal Traffic Loads, *Journal of Parallel and Distributed Computing*, vol. 28, no. 1, pp. 43–64, 1995.
7. X. Molero, F. Silla, V. Santonja and J. Duato. Modeling and simulation of storage area networks, *Proceedings of the 8th International Symposium on Modeling, Analysis, and Simulation of Computer and Telecommunication Systems*. IEEE Computer Society, August 2000.
8. X. Molero, F. Silla, V. Santonja and J. Duato. Performance analysis of storage area networks using high-speed LAN interconnects, *Proceedings of the 8th International Conference on Networks*. IEEE Computer Society, September 2000.
9. S. S. Owicki and A. R. Karlin. Factors in the performance of the AN1 computer network, Digital SRC research report 88, June 1992.
10. F. Silla and J. Duato, High-performance routing in networks of workstations with irregular topology, *IEEE Transactions on Parallel and Distributed Systems*, vol. 11, no. 7, pp. 699–719, July 2000.
11. D. Tang, *Storage area networking: the network behind the server*, Gadzoox Microsystems Inc., 1997.

Improving MPI-I/O Performance on PVFS*

Jonathan Ilroy[2], Cyrille Randriamaro[1], and Gil Utard[1]

[1] LaRIA, Université de Picardie Jules Verne, 80000 Amiens, France
[2] Université de Mons-Hainaut, 7000 Mons, Belgique

Abstract. Since the definition of the MPI-IO, a standard interface for parallel IO, some implementations are available for cluster of workstations. In this paper we focus on the ROMIO implementation (from Argonne Laboratory), running on PVFS. PVFS [5] is a Parallel Virtual File System developed at Clemson University. This file system uses local file systems of I/O nodes in a cluster to store data on disks. Data is striped among disks with a stripe parameter. The ROMIO implementation is not aware of the particular data-distribution of PVFS. We show how to improve performances of collective I/O of MPI-IO on such a parallel and distributed file system: the optimization avoids the data-redistribution induced by the PVFS file system. We show performance results on typical file access schemes found in data-parallel applications, and compare to the performances of the original PVFS port.

1 Introduction

Many scientific and engineering problems can involve data sets that are too large to fit in main memory. This kind of application are referred to as "parallel *out-of-core*" applications. To solve parallel *out-of-core* problems, there is a crucial need of high performance parallel IO library. The MPI Forum has defined a standard application programming interface for parallel IO called MPI-IO. MPI-IO is part of the MPI-2 specification and should be widely used by the community. There are two main implementations of MPI-IO: PMPIO from NAS and ROMIO [6] from Argone National Laboratory. These implementations are available for several file systems such that the intel PFS or the IBM PIOFS.

There are new parallel file systems for commodity cluster such that BPFS [1], PPFS, ViPIOS, GFS and PVFS [5]. Such file systems distribute file across several disks in the cluster, and provide better IO bandwidth and throughput than conventional UFS or NFS. ROMIO is running on the PVFS file system.

In [4], we presented preliminary performance results of ROMIO on PVFS. In this paper, we show how to improve performances of collective I/O of MPI-IO on such a parallel and distributed file system: the optimization avoids the data-redistribution induced by the PVFS file system. We show new performance results on a typical file access scheme found in data-parallel applications, and compare to the performances of the original PVFS port.

---

* This work is supported by a grant from "Pôle de Modélisation de la Région Picardie"

The rest of the paper is organized as follows. In section 2, we present the MPI-IO standard and the ROMIO implementation. In Section 3, we present the PVFS file system and ROMIO port. We describe how to improve performances for collective IO in Section 4. We draw overall conclusions in Section 5.

2 The MPI-IO Standard and the ROMIO Implementation

The application programming interface MPI-IO is part of the new MPI-2 definition [3]. To optimize parallel accesses to a shared file (e.g.requests coordination, cooperative caching), information about access pattern and synchronization are crucial. MPI-IO is a comprehensive extension of MPI which allows programmer to put these information at the interface level: MPI-IO inherits of *MPI derived data type* to describe access patterns and it also introduces new collective IO operations.

It is one key feature of MPI-IO to allow user to access several noncontiguous data in one call by the use of derived datatype. ROMIO is an MPI-IO implementation of Argone National Laboratory [7]. It is also part of the MPICH implementation since the version 1.1.1. ROMIO run on several parallel platforms (SGI Origin 2000, IBM SP, HP/Convex Exemplar, ...) with the following parallel file systems: IBM PIOFS, Intel PFS, and SGI XFS. ROMIO run also on network and cluster of workstations with the UFS file system (for multiprocessor) and the NFS file system. ROMIO was built on an intermediate interface called ADIO (Abstract Device Interface) for easy ports to other file systems.

3 ROMIO on PVFS

The IO performances are directly dependent of the file system. ROMIO was ported on PVFS to improve parallel IO performances on workstation cluster. In this Section we present the PVFS file system and ROMIO port.

PVFS (Parallel Virtual File System) was developed at Clemson University [5]. It is a parallel file system which distribute file across the local disk of each node in the cluster. Like RAID, the file is partitioned into *stripe unit*, and the stripes are distributed along disks in a round-robin fashion. The main advantage of such an organization is the aggregation of the disk space and disk bandwidth.

ROMIO is built on top of ADIO (Abstract Device Interface for IO). ADIO is a mechanism specifically designed for implementing parallel-IO API's portably on multiple file systems. ADIO consists of a small set of basic functions for parallel IO: open and close, collective read and write, strided access, asynchronous IO, file control. So porting ROMIO on PVFS is mainly porting ADIO on PVFS.

For performances, ROMIO implements two main optimizations related to the use of derived data type and collective IO: the *data sieving* and the *two phase collective IO*. We focus on the later.

Two phase collective IO is used to optimize collective non contiguous access to the file. When the programmer uses derived data type to describe a collective access to non contiguous data in the file, it is possible to determine the *extend* for the whole data access (mainly the first and last byte offset in the file). This extend is partitioned along processor according a *conforming distribution*: the distribution which provides the best throughput when all processors collectively access data. For a read operation, the processors first access data according this conforming distribution. In a second phase, processors redistribute data according the final distribution.

4 Optimization of Collective IO on PVFS

PVFS port of ROMIO inherits of the generic two phases collective IO optimization. Unfortunately, the confirming distribution used in ROMIO is a block distribution of the extend of the data access on processor: each one read a contiguous chunk of data in the distributed file. This algorithm can lead to inefficient data access. The two main problems are :

1. Processes will generally access data on remote disks. This can lead to poor performance compared to data access on a local disk. Besides, there will generally be concurrent accesses to disks. The problem here is that ROMIO makes the assumption that consecutive data on a file will be *physically* stored in a contiguous way on disks, which is not the case in PVFS.
2. Requested data by I/O flows through the network 2 times : the first time when PVFS nodes access data on remote disks and the second time when processes perform the redistribution phase.

A way to improve ROMIO collective accesses to PVFS data is to use the PVFS API which allows the user to use *strided* data access in one function call. If we modify the ROMIO data access policy in a way that processes only access data on their local disk, we will improve performance. This can be done by using a strided access with a stride equal to $n_d * S$ where n_d is the number of disks on which data is striped across and S is the PVFS stripe parameter. Note that modifying the data access implies a different redistribution.

We integrated this optimization in the current ROMIO port on PVFS. We measured the performances of our optimization and the performance of the original ROMIO on PVFS. To validate our optimizations, we chose to test collective two phase IO performances for cyclic distributions of arrays (of integer) which are are typically found in data parallel applications.

After reading, the array must be distributed by block cyclic of size k in each dimension, like the DISTRIBUTE A(CYCLIC(k),CYCLIC(k)) HPF directive or the distribution found in ScaLAPACK.The array is stored in row order in the file. Each process reads all its block(s) according to the distribution. We measure the time for the read operation.

For the experiment, we used a cluster of four DEC Alpha 21140 at 533 MHz. Each node has 128 MB of RAM and one SCSI disk of 9 GB at 10,000 RPM (IBM Ultrastar). The OS is Linux and nodes are interconnected by a fast Ethernet switch. PVFS (version 1.1.3) was installed with an IO daemon on each node.

Experimental results proved that PVFS collective read is much more efficient with a local disk access than with a distant disk access. The present results show the impact of such an optimization for the global ROMIO collective read operation.

In Figure 1, for different matrix orders there is a plot which gives results for the read operation of both algorithms: the current data access distributed in ROMIO package and the modified data access where PVFS routine read from local disks only. Each plot shows the data throughput (in MB/s) depending on the block size in the cyclic distribution resulted from the collective read.

We observe the gain obtained with the modified data access for small block sized (almost 1/3). For such a configuration, the redistributions for both algorithms provided by MPI routines are equivalents: the same amount of data is exchanged to the same processors. So the lake of redistribution inside PVFS routine explains that performance gain.

Nevertheless, when the block size becomes big compared to the matrix order, we observe a loss of gain up to no gain for full block distribution. This comes from the pathologic case of full block distribution: the way ROMIO divides the file is close to the final distribution. Hence while data are read from distant disks, they are directly stored on their target processor, there is no need to redistribute them again. The number of I/O accesses and redistributions for both algorithms are the same, so the collective read performances are almost the same. ROMIO data access is a little beat much faster that the modified algorithm for full block distribution, it means that PVFS redistribution is faster. Actually, PVFS redistribution is pipelined with data accesses.

5 Conclusion and Future Work

In this paper we presented an optimization of collective IO accesses for an MPI-IO implementation (ROMIO) on a parallel file system for cluster (PVFS). The original generic algorithm used in collective I/O assumes that performances for reading any contiguous piece of data is independent of its position in the file. On a parallel distributed file system, like PVFS, there is better performance when data acceded is the corresponding stripe unit is in the current node: Accessing a file on a local disk is more efficient than reading a file on a remote disk. In our optimization, we are aware of the data distribution in the cluster and the disk access is local for each node. The optimization avoid the redistribution phase introduced by the parallel file system. The gain of the first performance results is mainly the cost of one redistribution.

We are now studying the problem of the redistribution used in collective IO. Currently the ROMIO implementation use a basic all to all algorithm. We plan to develop a structured data exchange as described in [2].

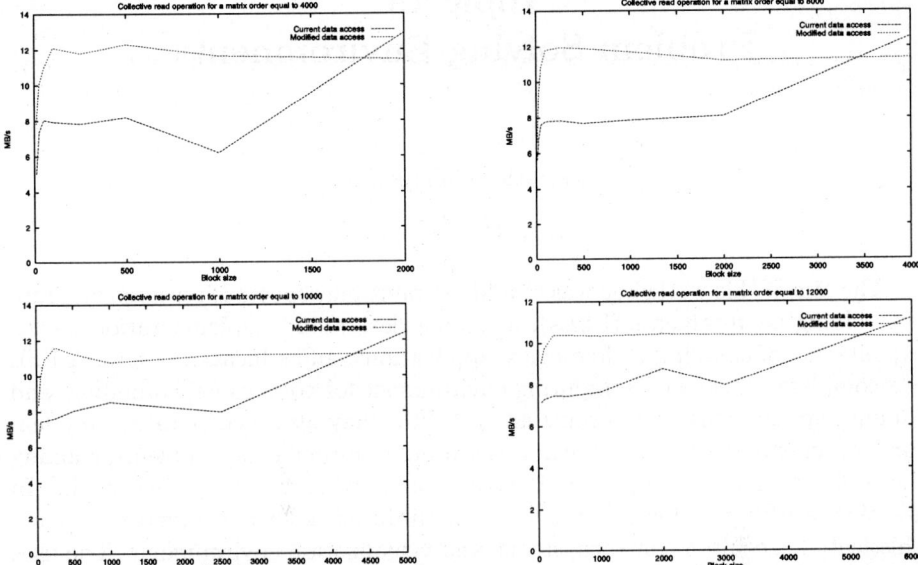

Fig. 1. Collective read operation measurement for the current version of ROMIO and for the modified data access algorithm

References

1. Alexis Agahi, Robert D. Russel, and Gil Utard. A High Performance Modular File System. In *Proc. of High Performance Computing and Networking Europe'98*, volume 1401 of *LNCS*, Amsterdam, April 1998. Springer.
2. Frédéric Desprez, Jack Dongarra, Antoine Petitet, Cyril Randriamaro, and Yves Robert. Scheduling block-cyclic array redistribution. *IEEE Trans. Parallel Distributed Systems*, 9(2):192–205, February 1998.
3. Message Passing Interface Forum. Mpi-2: Extensions to the message-passing interface, July 1997. Available at http://www.mpi-forum.org.
4. Taki Hakan and Gil Utard. MPI-IO on a Parallel File System for Cluster of Workstations. In *IWCC'99, International Workshop on Cluster Computing*, Melbourne, Australia, December 1999. IEEE Press.
5. W. B. Ligon III and R. B. Ross. An Overview of the Parallel Virtual File System. In *Proc. of the 1999 Extreme Linux Workshop*, June 1999.
6. R. Thakur, W. Gropp, and E. Lusk. On implementing MPI-IO Portably and with High Performance. In *Proc. of the Sixth Workshop on IO in Paraleel and Distributed Systems*, May 1999.
7. Rajeev Thakur, William Gropp, and Erwing Lusk. User's guide for ROMIO: A High-Performance, Portable MPI-IO Implementation. Technical Report ANL,MCS-TM-234, Argonne National Laboratory, 1998.

Topic 19
Problem Solving Environments

David W. Walker, Ken Hawick, Domenico Laforenza, and
Efstratios Gallopoulos

Topic Chairpersons

The aim of this workshop was to address multiple aspects of research on problem solving environments (PSEs), including design and implementation issues, exploitation of enabling technologies, applications, and education issues. A PSE is a complete, integrated computing environment for composing, compiling, and running applications in a specific area. A PSE may also incorporate many features of an expert system and can assist users in formulating problems, running the problem on an appropriate platform, and viewing and analyzing results. In addition, a PSE may have access to virtual libraries, knowledge repositories, sophisticated execution control systems, and visualization environments. The uses of PSEs include modeling and simulation, decision support, design optimization, and industrial process management.

The main motivation for developing PSEs is that they make available advanced hardware resources, software tools, and expert assistance in a user-friendly environment, allowing more rapid prototyping of ideas and higher research productivity. The user formulates and solves problems through the use of abstractions that are specific to a particular problem domain, and which in general provide transparent access to heterogeneous distributed hardware and software resources. These abstractions are often implemented by means of software components. By relieving the end-user of the burdens associated with the inessential details of specific hardware and software systems, the PSE leaves him/her free to concentrate on the problem itself.

PSEs have generated much interest in recent years, and there are now several fully developed PSEs in several areas such as the automotive and aerospace industries. In addition PSEs are being investigated in many academic projects. Modern PSEs increasingly depend on the effective integration of diverse heterogeneous components, such as parallel and distributed problem solvers, tools for data processing, advanced visualization and computational steering, and access to large databases and scientific instruments.

However, more research is needed to realise the full potential of PSE systems, and to exploit several emerging technologies, such as Grid computing, component-based software engineering, advanced interactive visualization, intelligent knowledge processing and discovery, and large-scale distributed computing. Such technologies are enabling the handling of more complex simulation models, higher degrees of human-computer interaction, and larger volumes of input or generated data. They will also enable more effective cooperation among multiple users in distributed collaborative problem solving environments.

The three papers presented in the workshop demonstrate quite clearly the scope of PSEs in their use in different application domains. The first paper in the workshop, by Erik Engquist (Royal Institute of Technology, Sweden), is concerned with the remote visualization of electro-magnetic simulations. Here we see the importance of immersive visualization in the exploration, navigation, and analysis of the large data sets produced by realistic three-dimensional time-dependent simulations. In common with many other PSEs, much of the software infrastructure is generic. In this case the PSE is based on the Globus toolkit. The second paper by Dana Petcu (Western University of Timisoara, Romania) addresses the research issues raised in the distributed solution of large-scale systems of ordinary differential equations using the Parallel Virtual Maple (PVMaple) software. This work is of particular interest as it shows how a commercial product, Maple, can be extended for use in a distributed environment. The importance of being able to use commercial and third-party software products in PSEs is also evident in the final paper by F. Oliver Bunnin *et al.* (Imperial College, UK) who make use of Mathematica, and the SPRNG and ScaLAPACK parallel software libraries, in their PSE for valuing industrial investment projects.

Finally, we would like to thank all the contributors and referees for the excellent work they have performed in helping to make the workshop a success.

Remote Visualization of Distributed Electro-Magnetic Simulations

Erik Engquist[1,2]

[1] Department of Numerical Analysis and Computer Science,
Royal Institute of Technology, Stockholm, Sweden
erike@pdc.kth.se
[2] San Diego Supercomputer Center,
University of California, San Diego, USA

Abstract. GEMSviz is a framework for visualization of distributed computations. It has been extended to handle remote monitoring and steering, as well as tele-immersive collaboration. The computational core consists of a code for 3D finite difference time domain (FDTD) approximation of Maxwell's equations written as part of the General Electro-Magnetic Solvers (GEMS) project. Large parts of the remote visualization software is general but details in the choice of control variables and visualization is specialized to the electro-magnetics code. Implementation challenges stem from the large computational requirements of both simulation and visualization as well as the communication demands of distributed computing and computational steering. The framework builds on the Globus toolkit for communication, data handling, and resource coallocation and the Visualization Toolkit for data filtering and the generation of visualization elements. The software has been used between sites in Europe, Japan, and the US.

1 Introduction

General Electro-Magnetic Solvers (GEMS) is a project for producing a parallelized software suite for solving the Maxwell equations. As an extension to this project, a framework for steering and visualization was developed. Typical applications are in electro-magnetic compatibility, radar cross section analysis, and antenna design.

To enable visualization and interaction in a 3D immersive environment, the code made use of the Visualization Toolkit (VTK) [9] in combination with OpenGL Performer [3] and pfCAVELib [7]. This code has been run on immersive VR platforms, among them the six wall VR-Cube at the Center for Parallel Computers (PDC), Stockholm, Sweden.

The Globus toolkit allows the computational code to communicate with the visualization client. Most communication is handled by the Nexus [5] communication library. As Nexus is a multi-threaded communication library it is especially well suited to the event driven nature of user interaction.

A user interface was also created as part of the project. Interaction is carried out through the use of a tracked wand and floating menu buttons. The user may choose to display different features of the computed solution. Examples of such features include surface currents, electric or magnetic fields in cutting planes, and electric or magnetic field strength iso surfaces, see Fig. 1.

The computational code has been edited to communicate with the visualization code as well as be interactively controlled by the user. Data transfer and translation routines have been written for the exchange of information between separate processes. Synchronization structures and routines have been created to allow multi-threaded communication. A visualization code was written which handles both geometric and volume data with multiple methods of presentation. The displayed information can be manipulated in an immersive environment using a wand and menu interface.

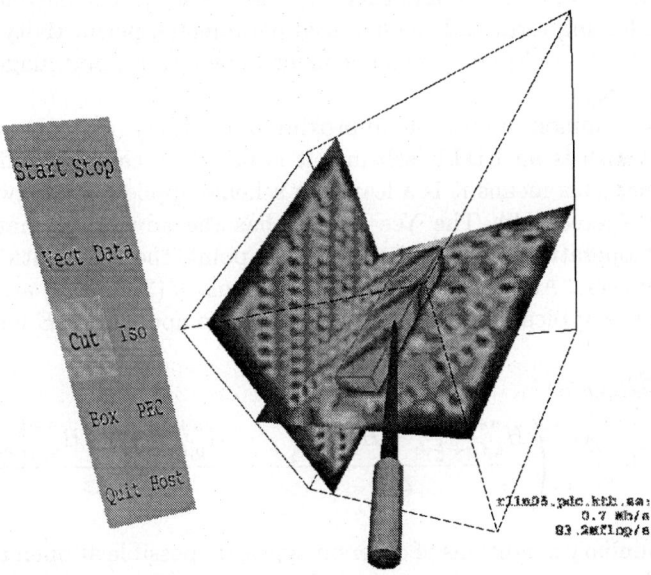

Fig. 1. Example of session in progress, field strength can be seen on the cutting planes, and the induced current is shown on the object

2 The Electro-Magnetic Application

For our implementation of a steering and visualization package we began with an existing computational package. Since the code is a part of a larger project, we needed to minimize changes to the numerical simulation code.

2.1 The Mathematical and Numerical Models

The electro-magnetic calculations are based on Maxwell's equations,

$$\frac{\partial E}{\partial t} = \frac{1}{\varepsilon} \nabla \times H - J \quad (1)$$

$$\frac{\partial H}{\partial t} = -\frac{1}{\mu} \nabla \times E \quad (2)$$

$$\nabla \cdot E = 0 \quad (3)$$

$$\nabla \cdot H = 0 \quad (4)$$

The three dimensional electric, $E(x,t)$, and magnetic, $H(x,t)$, fields are defined as functions of space, $(x \in \Omega)$, and time, (t), $(\mathbb{R}^4 \to \mathbb{R}^6)$. The current $J(x,t)$ is regarded as a forcing term and the material parameters, permittivity, $\varepsilon(x)$, and permeability, $\mu(x)$, could be space dependent. The electric and magnetic fields are divergence free.

The most common numerical approximation of (1) and (2) is the Yee scheme [11], which is an FDTD scheme. It is based on centered differences in space and time. This means it is a leap-frog scheme applied to Maxwell's equations on a staggered grid. The Yee scheme has the advantage that very few floating point operations are required per grid point, the E evolution depends on H and vice versa. Additionally, the discrete forms of (3) and (4) are preserved by the scheme. A typical difference step for the x-component of E looks like,

$$E^{n+1}_{x,i,j,k} = E^n_{x,i,j,k} + \frac{\Delta t}{\varepsilon_{i,j,k}} \left(\frac{H^{n+\frac{1}{2}}_{z,i,j+\frac{1}{2},k} - H^{n+\frac{1}{2}}_{z,i,j-\frac{1}{2},k}}{\Delta y} - \frac{H^{n+\frac{1}{2}}_{y,i,j,k+\frac{1}{2}} - H^{n+\frac{1}{2}}_{y,i,j,k-\frac{1}{2}}}{\Delta z} \right) \quad (5)$$

Absorbing boundary conditions of different types are possible at open boundaries which limit the computational domain [10].

2.2 The FDTD Code

This code is a part of the Large Scale FDTD project, GEMS [2]. The programming language is FORTRAN90 with MPI message passing. Domain decomposition is used as a basis for parallelization. The input to the code consists of an initialization file which gives simulation parameters and defines the names of files which describe geometry, sources, and output. The output files contain the electro-magnetic fields and surface currents. Modifications to the code have mainly been limited to rewriting the initialization and output routines. A goal of the project was to require minimal changes to the computational code in order to simplify its integration into existing projects.

The core solver originally consisted of almost 5,000 lines of code, the changes amounted to the removal of a initialization file read in function and result write out commands. These were replaced by calls to corresponding data I/O routines in the communication code. Inside the main computational loop we also added a call to a state update function in the communication code.

The number of FLOPs required each time-step of the computational code is approximately $N_x \times N_y \times N_z \times 36$ for each field, where N_x, N_y, and N_z are the number of grid points in each dimension of the computational domain. Unfortunately, (5) shows that there are six unknowns for each component update. On scalar architecture machines, this will mean a high memory access to computation ratio which results in memory bound performance.

The domain decomposition strategy means boundary updates are necessary between the distributed compute nodes. In the current code there is a one level overlap in each dimension. On a 3D staggered grid this means a node will send E-field values in three directions and H-field values in the three opposite directions. Efficient interleaving of the inter-node communication is critical to performance, depending on the speed and latency of the interconnects, one can also adjust the width of the update boundaries. For a further discussion see [1].

The performance of this code on a dual 350PII Linux cluster was around 80-90 MFLOP/s per node, as seen in Fig. 2. On the four way 333MHz Power-PC 604e SMP nodes on the SP, performance rose to 220-240 MFLOP/s per node, while the Power2 nodes performed at 180-190 MFLOP/s. The code has also been ported to parallel vector machines with performance around 1.2 GFLOP/s per node an a Fujitsu VX/2 and 100 MFLOP/s on a Cray J932. This type of information is useful for gauging the feasibility of interacting with a particular computation. One can look at the performance requirements of a particular case and then demand the necessary hardware. More likely, one can see the limits a given hardware sets and scale the size of the computation appropriately.

Nodes	MFLOP/s			
	PC MPI-SM	PC SMP	SP Power2	SP SMP
1	85	89	190	240
2	164	167	373	467
4	301	323	737	906
8	639	631	1455	1749

Fig. 2. Performance of FDTD code on PC cluster using MPI with shared memory (PC MPI-SM), threaded code (PC SMP), on IBM Power2 nodes (SP Power2), and IBM SMP nodes (SP SMP)

Compared to the results in [1] the performance effect of adding communication hooks to to the solver is negligible. The basic performance requirements show the necessity of distributed computing for this case. Since the visualization machine is burdened by transforming the field data and generating geometric elements, it cannot simultaneously support large scale numerical computations.

3 Implementation

In our program we make use of a wide range of specialized software tools. These tools are freely available and quite portable, which simplified the integration process and also adds to the extensibility of the final code.

3.1 Program Structure

The choice of different tools for each aspect of the project resulted in the need to program in several different languages. As one can see in Fig. 3 there are three main parts of the code, calculation, visualization, and communication, as well as three respective languages FORTRAN90, C++, and C. The function calling interface between C and C++ is similar for most compilers, once one takes steps to avoid C++ name mangling. Unfortunately this is not the case with C and FORTRAN, the few compilers we tested each used different naming conventions.

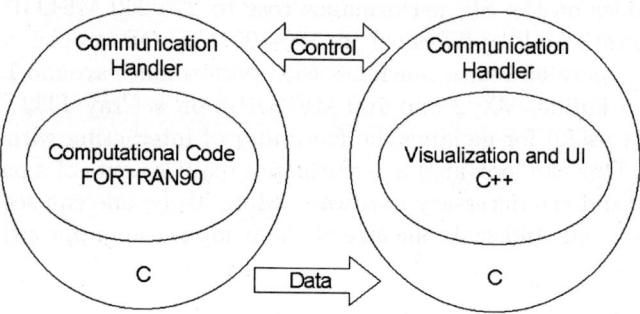

Fig. 3. Program structure

When assembling requirements for our software, we identified a visualization hierarchy, ranging from concurrent computation and visualization to pure visualization of a static data set. We begin by describing fully interactive computation and visualization. At this level the control data, consisting of user input and information about the state of the computational code is exchanged between the visualization and computation hardware. This data is asynchronous and low bandwidth. The computed data consists of much more information and moves only from the calculating machine to the visualization machine.

The other end of this visualization hierarchy is simply post processing data visualization. After a computational run has been completed, the results are saved to disk and visualization work can begin on the data set. In this case the user does not have interactive control of the computation, but the calculations may be so demanding that interactivity would not be reasonable.

3.2 Visualization

The data flow structure of our visualization code is shown in Fig. 4. We are only making use of the data processing capabilities of VTK. The product of our VTK pipeline, vtkActors, are translated into Performer pfGeodes by the vtkActorToPF [8] code. These VTK generated structures are loaded into a Performer scene graph. Performer uses a scene graph structure to track the relative transformations and other connections of geometric objects. By traversing this graph, Performer can find collisions, cull invisible objects, and gather other information valuable to the final rendering of a scene. A description of the graphics core is found in [4].

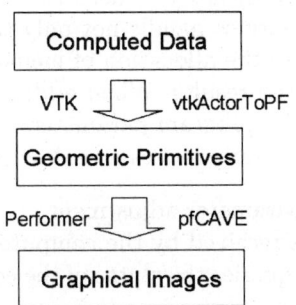

Fig. 4. Visualization structure

3.3 Communication

The communication between processors in the computational code is via MPI. The information exchange between the computation and visualization code seen in Fig. 3 uses the Nexus communication library. Both of these APIs support shared memory communication as well as external interconnects. Keeping the communication processes close to the computational processes on hybrid machines such as the IBM SMP nodes reduced interruptions to computation. Shared memory communication could be used in the first stage of data transfer from computational client to the communication server.

The thread interface routines are used to query the state of communicated information. After each time step, the computational code checks state information to see if it should continue. When initializing, the code checks what control information is dirty and needs to be updated. There are also flags which inform the visualization process to update itself with new data. On the visualization side the code can access the state information directly, which removes the need for any such interface routines.

In the FDTD code. On initialization, the FDTD code starts a small server process before beginning computation. This process publishes connection information to the local grid information servers. At this point the server listens for connections from visualization clients. Only when a connection is made does the server process attempt to control the computation. If no steering client connects the run will complete as submitted.

When dealing with parallel code, one has to deal with the problem of synchronization. In this project there are not only separate processes running on different machines, but also separate threads running within some processors. This situation is further complicated by the different programming languages involved, FORTRAN90 for example does not have a standard threading interface. Threading exists in FORTRAN through the use of APIs or compiler directives such as OpenMP which is used on the SMP machines described in Sect. 2.2. The threading interface for the computational code consists of small C functions wrapped around the shared memory structures.

The communication routines handle not only the exchange of data between different processes, but also the allocation of memory when setting up the computation and presenting the results. When adding interactivity to the computational code, control of the program parameters was moved to the UI process. Adjusting computational parameters can be described as follows:

1. The user commits a parameter adjustment
2. The new parameter is received by the compute process and dirty flag is set
3. The FORTRAN code queries the states of the communication flags and halts on the dirty parameter
4. Adjustments are made to the compute process and calculation can resume

For the FDTD code, the computation is usually restarted after a parameter change, especially when changing computational domains or parallel data distribution.

In the visualization code. The integration of the message handlers and the C++ visualization code was more straightforward. The UI was built with the unpredictable behavior of the user in mind, so special synchronization routines were not necessary to exchange control information. The VTK routines were able to handle externally allocated memory which simplified receiving the computational data, but we had to coordinate the arrival of new data with the drawing processes.

The visualization client is given machine and port information which points to the same grid information server with which the FDTD program is communicating. Information which the client collects includes further machine and port lists of currently running computations. Through the host button on the menu, a user can connect and to a server and take control of the computation.

To avoid illegal memory accesses, the computational result arrays were protected by locks. This way, the communication handler threads and visualization processes could safely share the primary data with a minimum of duplication. Once the VTK and Performer pipelines are reinitialized with new data such precautions are not needed since there are facilities for internal updates of data. The steps taken in the visualization process when data is being received is to halt any data processing tasks, receive the data array, and update the visualization pipeline. Interaction with the old data representation is maintained until the pipeline is fully updated.

4 Conclusion

A framework for visualization and computational steering of numerical software has been developed. We have applied it to a FDTD code for the simulation of electro-magnetic fields. The computational code scales well with increasing processor counts for several different architectures. The communication software in the visualization and steering system integrates with existing grid infrastructure. The application has been tested between multiple international sites.

Acknowledgments

I would like to thank my advisors and colleagues at KTH for their help and guidance, Per Öster, Jesper Oppelstrup, Ulf Andersson and Gunnar Ledfelt. Also, I extend my gratitude to PDC and its staff for support, ideas and facilities.

References

1. U. Andersson. Time-Domain Methods for the Maxwell Equations. phD Thesis, Royal Institute of Technology, Stockholm, Sweden, to appear.
2. U. Andersson and G. Ledfelt. Large Scale FD-TD–A Billion Cells. *15th Annual Review of Progress in Applied Computational Electromagnetics*, volume 1, pages 572-577, Monterey, CA, March 1999.
3. G. Eckel and K. Jones *OpenGL Performer Programmer's Guide*. SGI, 2000.
4. E. Engquist. Steering and Visualization of Electromagnetic Simulations Using Globus. *Simulation and Visualization on the Grid*. Springer, pages 82-97, 1999
5. I. Foster, C. Kesselman, R. Olson, and S. Tuecke, *Nexus: An Interoperability toolkit for parallel and distributed computer systems*. Mathematics and Computer Science Division, Argonne National Laboratory, 1993.
6. I. Foster and N. Karonis. A Grid-Enabled MPI: Message Passing in Heterogeneous Distributed Computing Systems. In *Proceedings of SC'98*. ACM Press, 1998.
7. D. Pape. *pfCAVE CAVE/Performer Library (CAVELib Version 2.6)*. Electronic Visualization Laboratory, University of Illinois at Chicago, March 1997.
8. P. Rajlich, R. Stein and R. Heiland. vtkActorToPF.
http://brighton.ncsa.uiuc.edu/~{}prajlich/vtkActorToPF/
9. W. Schroeder, K. Martin, and B. Lorensen. *The Visualization Toolkit: An Object-Oriented Approach To 3D Graphics*. Prentice Hall, 1997.
10. A. Taflove. *Computational Electromagnetics: The Finite Difference Time-Domain Metod*. Artech House, 1995.
11. K. S. Yee. Numerical Solution of Initial Boundary Value Problems Involving Maxwell's Equations in Isotropic Media. *IEEE Trans. Antennas Propagat.*, 14(3):302-307, March 1966.

Solving Initial Value Problems with Parallel Maple Processes

Dana Petcu

Western University of Timişoara, B-dul V.Pârvan 4, 1900 Timişoara, Romania,
petcu@info.uvt.ro,
http://www.info.uvt.ro/~petcu

Abstract. The recently developed PVMaple (Parallel Virtual Maple) provides a message-passing programming environment to solve complex problems, like large systems of ordinary differential equations (ODEs), on network of workstations. The computing facilities proposed by PVMaple are briefly presented. Numerical tests concerning the approximate solutions of some particular ODEs are reported and discussed.

1 Introduction

Computer algebra systems, like Maple or Mathematica, can be used with success in prototyping sequential algorithms for symbolic or numeric solution of mathematical problems. Constructing prototypes and libraries of parallel algorithms in such currently used systems is an actual challenging problem.

Several successful attempts have been made to combine Maple with parallel or distributed computation features (see for example [15] or [17]). We shortly present in Section 2 a prototype system, Parallel Virtual Maple, shortly PVMaple, which interconnects PVM (Parallel Virtual Machine) and Maple. PVMaple package has been developed in the idea to allow several independent Maple kernels on various machines connected by a network to participate in computation, hopefully leading to faster results. More details about can be found in [11].

The aim of this paper is to investigate in what extent the theoretical parallelization of special iterative methods can be achieved in practice using PVMaple. In particular, we solve large initial value problems (IVPs) for ordinary differential equations (ODEs), problems of the form $y'(t) = f(t, y(t))$, $y(t_0) = y_0$, where $t \in [t_0, t_0+T]$, $y_0 \in R^n$ and $f : [t_0, t_0+T] \times R^n \to R^n$, and y is the unknown function. For the simulation of many problems of practical importance, such as large scale integrated circuits (VLSI), the dimension n may be extremely large. Standard techniques have been shown to be adequate for solving moderately sized systems, but they may be inappropriate for systems consisting of many thousands of equations. As a consequence, substantial effort has been focused towards the development of numerical methods which are capable of solving very large systems of ODEs. With the advent of parallel technologies, it is natural to desire to take advantage of the increasing computing power available. Section 3 discuss some implementation issues of parallel ODE solving methods. Previously proposed parallel methods are examined from the perspective of computation graph distribution and PVMaple facilities. Section 4 presents and interprets the results of some numerical tests which have been run in a PC network. We show that an ODE solver for large problems can significantly benefit from the distributed computing environment provided by PVMaple. We consider the resulting Maple code for ODEs as a first step in the direction of designing and testing a more extensive library in Maple for parallel algorithms.

2 PVMaple

Parallel Virtual Maple is a prototype system allowing to study the issue of interconnecting PVM and Maple. Its design principles are very similar to that of Distributed Maple [15], a portable system for writing parallel programs in Maple and for network environments where Maple and Java are available. Other systems combining Maple with parallel or distributed computation features are ||Maple|| [17] (built as an interface between the parallel declarative programming language Strand and the sequential CAS Maple), Sugarbush [2] (combines the parallelism of C/Linda with the Maple kernel), or FoxBox [3] (a client/server style interface to Maple which provides an MPI-compliant distribution mechanism allowing for parallel execution of FoxBox programs). The PVMaple functionality is described by Figure 1. Combining Maple with parallel computation factors is done in PVMaple wrapping Maple by an external system which takes care of the parallel execution of tasks. PVM active daemons (PVMDs) ensure the interprocessor communications. In order to start PVMaple, a workstation user must have access to a functional Maple V version and it must have the possibility to create a parallel virtual machine with PVM. Each node connected to a PVMaple session comprises three main components: command messenger, Maple interface

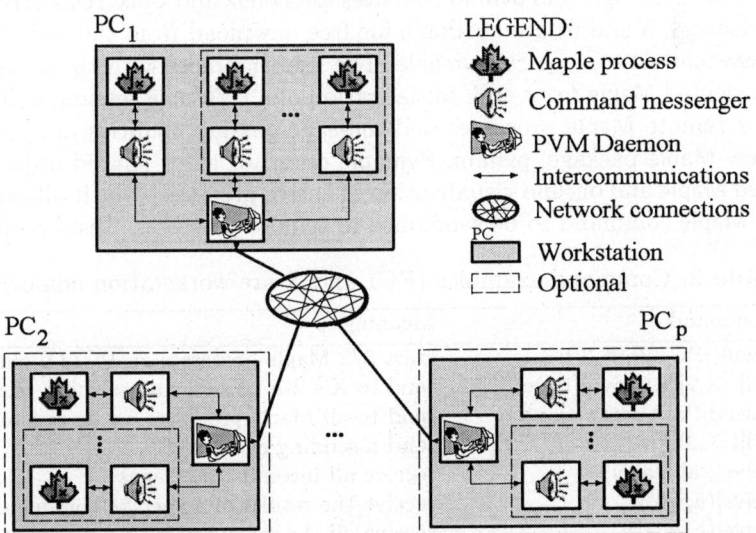

Fig. 1. Active processes and intercommunication routes

Table 1. Package pvm.m

Function	Meaning	Equivalence with Distributed Maple
spawn	create local or remote Maple processes	initialize
send	send commands to Maple processes	start
receive	receive results from Maple processes	wait
settime	start a chronometer	trace (post-processing)
exit	stop PVMaple	terminate
time	post-processing time diagram in Maple	visualise (on line)
ProcID	process identifier on one machine	-
MachID, TaskID	station/process identifier into PVMaple	-

and PVMD daemon. The special binary named command-messenger is responsible for the message exchanges between the Maple processes (into the PVM machine), coordinates the interaction between Maple kernels via PVM daemons, and schedules tasks among nodes. The Maple file pvm.m implements the interface between the Maple kernel and command-messenger. Each Maple process has its own command-messenger (his pair) which receives Maple commands from other Maple processes (local or remote), sends its results in Maple format to other processes, activates or destroy other Maple processes. At least two Maple processes must be activated to apply PVMaple functions. The command-messenger must be placed on the workstation which will start the virtual machine. This binary reads a special file with the paths of the Maple and PVM binaries. The remote Maple processes and their pairs, command-messengers, are activated using the PVM facilities of dynamically hosts and processes adding. Table 1 shows the current available functions of this package and the equivalence with Distributed Maple functions. Table 2 presents some suggestive examples of function synopsis.

Command-messenger and pvm.m (binaries for Win9x and Unix, respectively for Maple Release 4, 5 and 6) are available for free download from the web address http://www.info.uvt.ro/~petcu/pvmaple. The user interacts with the system via the text oriented Maple front-end: initialization of a PVMaple session, activation of local or remote Maple processes and message-passing facilities are provided by the new Maple package, pvm.m. Pvmaple does not allow shared objects like Distributed Maple and on-line visualization of active processes, but it allows more than one Maple command to be send once to remote processes. Tests performed

Table 2. Command examples (PC1 and X are workstation names)

Maple command	Meaning
pvm[spawn]([PC1,3],[X,2]);	start 3/2 Maple processes on PC1/X machine
pvm[send]([X,2],'x:=pvm[ProcId]');	send to X's 2th process an assigning comm.
a:=pvm[send]('all','int(y^ x,x)');	send to all Maple processes an int comm.
pvm[send]([X,2],'pvm[send]([X,1],"...	send a sending command
pvm[receive]('all','all');	receive all incoming messages
pvm[receive](a,'all');	receive the results of a specific command
pvm[receive](a,[X,1]);	receive all the messages from a workstation

on Unix networks where both applications are available have not reveal significant differences in application execution times [14].

A facility for post-execution analysis of the dynamic behaviour of a session is provided by the time function. In [11] is presented the graphical result of a pvm[time] call in the case of a distributed square matrix-vector multiplication (of hundred order of magnitude). Another example is presented in Section 4.

3 Implementation Issues of Parallel Methods for ODEs

Finding methods and strategies for solving an IVP on parallel computers has been the matter of several researches in the last thirty years (see [5] for a more complete overview). Such methods have been classified in different classes, according to the way they explore the potentialities of a parallel machine. A general way of devising parallel ODE solvers is that of considering methods whose work per time-step can be split over certain number of processors. The so-called solvers with parallelism across the method are then obtained. Other options are parallelism across system and parallelism across steps. Parallelism across system can be applied if the current IVP can be split into independent subsystems. Parallelism across steps is encouraged when a linear IVP is solved.

Concerning the Runge-Kutta methods a special scheme was proposed in [7] to distinguish their degree of parallelism: the digraph method. We have extended this method to the case of an arbitrary difference method for IVP [9] and we have implemented it in an ODE solving environment [10]. So, we have propose in [9] the following form for a difference method for ODEs:

$$Y^{(n+1)} = AY^{(n)} + h_n \Phi(t_n, Y^{(n)}, Y^{(n+1)}, h_n), \ Y^{(0)} = \Psi(h), \ e^{(n)} = Y^{(n)} - Z(t_n, h_n)$$

where Ψ is a starting procedure, and A is a problem independent matrix. The first equation is an advance formula, $e^{(n)}$ is a global error estimation for the approximate solution, and $Z(t_n, Y)$ is a procedure for approximate solution validation. Ψ is a problem-dependent function, $h_n = t_{n+1} - t_n$ is the step-size used to the current iteration step, and Y_n is a vector representing numerical values of the dependent variable y at different values of the independent variable t or numerical values of f at different values of y and t.

Consider the set S of all values of the dependent variable y which appear in the above iterative formulae of a method. The computation necessary to advance the solution from one step to another can be expressed by some relationships between the values from S. These relationships can be expressed by a graph. Execution of a graph means computing the output values of a computation node when all of the input values to that node have been computed. When there are cycles in the graph, computation is not possible until the graph has been modified to break the cycles (by predictor-corrector schemes). Examples of such graphs are presented in [9].

Distributed execution of a computation graph consists in assigning each node in the graph to a process. All processes can operate simultaneously only if every process has nodes which are ready to be evaluated at all times. A method is a said to be a *s*-value *q*-level *p*-process if q is the smallest integer for which the s new dependent variable values can be evaluated in q time-steps and p is the smallest number of processes for which this value of q can be attained. For an explicit IVP method each time-step is equal to the time required by some function evaluations plus the time for some vector operations, while for an implicit IVP method, each time-step is equal to the time required to solve some implicit equations plus the time for some vector operations. For load balancing, formulas with $s \approx pq$ are preferred.

4 Numerical Experiments

We present the results obtained by using PVMaple prototype and implementing the procedure from Table 3 (sketches the main parts of a PVMaple procedure for a parallel method using p processors). We have selected some large IVPs and known parallel methods. Numerical tests have been performed on a network composed by four identical PCs Pentium at 450 MHz with 64 MB of RAM running Windows'98 and connected by Ethernet links.

Three test problems are referred here. The first one, a linear problem, is denoted by $T(n)$ and it is was described in [16] (a partial differential equation solved with the method of lines):

$$y_i' = \pi^{-2}(n+1)^2(y_{i+1} - 2y_i + y_{i-1}), \ y_{-1} = y_{n+1} = 0, i = 1,\ldots,n$$

on the interval $[0, 2.5]$, with the initial values $y_i(0) = \sin(\pi i(n+1)^{-1})$, $i = 1,\ldots,n$. The second one (denoted by $V(n)$) is a nonlinear problem [1]:

$$y_i' = (y_{i-1}y_{i+2} - y_{i+1}y_i)^2 - 0.1 i y_i, \ i = 2,\ldots,n-2, \ y_i' = -0.1 i y_i, \ i = 1, n-1, n$$

on the interval $[0, 1]$, with the initial values $y_i(t) = 1$, $i = 1,\ldots,n$ and the exact solution $y_i(t) = e^{-0.1it}$. The third one is a mathematical model of the movement of a rectangular plate under the load of a car passing across it (plate problem denoted by $P(n)$, from [8]):

$$u_{tt} + \omega u_t + \sigma \Delta\Delta u = f(x,y,t), \ u|_{\partial\Omega} = 0, \ \Delta u|_{\partial\Omega} = 0, \ u_t(x,y,0) = 0$$

on the interval $[0, 7]$, with $\Omega = [0,1]^2$, $\omega = 1000$, $\sigma = 100$ and f being the sum of two Gaussian curves with four wheels which move in the x-direction. Applying

Table 3. Implementation of a *s*-value *q*-level *p*-process iterative scheme (the procedures sys_solve, update, P, and the iterative equation equ, specific for each particular method, must be defined outside the discussed procedure)

```
one_step_paral_scheme:=proc(Y, h)
  for j from 1 to q do comm:='eqs:={ }; ukn:={ };
    for i in P(pvm[TaskId],j) do eqs:=eqs union equ[i]; ukn:=ukn union {uk[i]}; od;
    sys_solve(eqs, ukn);'; S:=pvm[send]('all',cat('Y:=',Y,'; h:=',h,';',comm));
    K1:=execute(comm); K2:=pvm[receive](S,'all'); od;
  update(y, K1, K2); end;
```

the method of lines, the partial derivatives in x and y directions are replaced with approximation evaluated at different spatial grid points. The procedure lead to an ODE system with independent variable t. The number of spatial grid points depends on the accuracy required in the PDE solution. As the accuracy requirement increases, the spatial grid needs to be refined and this leads to a larger ODE system. Obtaining the solutions of such problems like the above ones can be a time and space expensive process. For example, using a simple method like Euler's implicit rule for the discretized plate problem with 180 ODEs, the time necessary to complete the integration with EpODE [10], with the highest step allowed by the problem stiffness is around 45 hours. One solution to this inconvenient situation is to apply a parallel method which can solve faster the above problems.

Four parallel methods are discussed here. The first one, denoted by PC is the second-order explicit block predictor-corrector scheme proposed in [6] (in our definition, a 4-value 1-level 4-process method):

$$y^P_{2n+2} = y^C_{2n-2} + 4hf^P_{2n}, \quad y^P_{2n+1} = y^C_{2n-2} + 3h(f^P_{2n} + f^P_{2n-1})/2$$
$$y^C_{2n} = y^C_{2n-3} - h(3f^P_{2n} - 9f^P_{2n-1})/2, \quad y^C_{2n-1} = y^C_{2n-3} + 2hf^C_{2n-2}.$$

The second one, DIRK method, is the fourth-order L-stable block diagonally implicit Runge-Kutta method from [7] (a 5-value 2-level 2-process method):

$$y_{n+1} = y_n + h[a(k_1 + k_2) + (d-a)(k_3 + k_4)],$$
$$k_1 = f(v_n, y_n + h(ck_1 + (f-c)k_2)), \quad k_2 = f(u_n, y_n + h((e-c)k_1 + ck_2)),$$
$$k_3 = f(v_n, y_n + h(dk_3 - bk_4)), \quad k_4 = f(u_n, y_n + h(bk_3 + dk_4)),$$

$a = \frac{3}{2}, b = \frac{\sqrt{3}}{6}, c = \frac{5}{12}, d = \frac{1}{2}, e = d+b, f = d-b, u_n = t_n + eh, v_n = t_n + fh.$
The third one is a PDIRK method, a third-order L-stable parallel diagonally implicitly iterated Runge-Kutta method [5] (a 7-value 4-level 2-process method):

$$y_{n+1} = y_n + hb^T f(t_n e + hc, Y^{(m)}), \quad Y^{(0)} = y_n e, \quad e = (1, \ldots, 1)^T,$$
$$Y^{(j)} - hDf(t_n + hc, Y^{(j)}) = y_n e + h(A-D)f(t_n e + hc, Y^{(j-1)}),$$

with $m = 3$, $D = 0.4358665\,I$, $A = \dfrac{1}{12}\begin{pmatrix} 5 & -1 \\ 9 & 3 \end{pmatrix}$, $b = \dfrac{1}{4}\begin{pmatrix} 3 \\ 1 \end{pmatrix}$, $c = \dfrac{1}{3}\begin{pmatrix} 1 \\ 3 \end{pmatrix}$

The last one is a 9-stages, 3-processor, 4th-order, A-stable parallel singly diagonally iterated Runge-Kutta method (PSDIRK) presented in [4] and [12] (a 10-value 4-level 3-process method, with a too big iterative representation to be reproduced here). Between the first method and the other three is a big difference in time requirements to fulfill an integration step. The first method is explicit and do not need supplementary procedures in order to solve some implicit equations at each integration step. Unfortunately, large IVPs are almost all stiff, i.e. cannot be integrated by explicit methods since then time step-sizes are restricted to very small values due to method stability conditions. Moreover, if we think to implement a parallel method we must take into account that an exchange information between two processors is a time-expensive operation. For

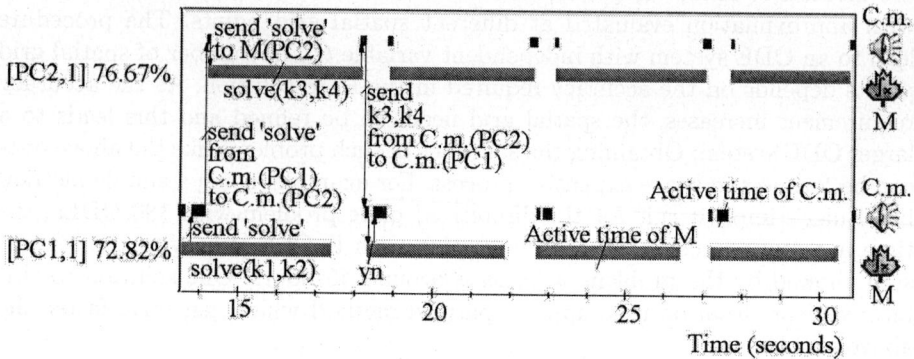

Fig. 2. Time diagram of 4 steps of DIRK applied to $T(30)$. The active periods of Maple processes and command messengers are indicated by horizontal lines. The total active time (between a settime and an exit) of a Maple process is expressed in %, so that the user can easily estimates the load balance of parallel algorithm and the delays sources

example, the time necessary to send a n-dimensional vector between two PCs via PVM environment is $10^4/2$ times greater than the time of a function evaluation and 10 times greater than the time of a Newton iteration in the case of solving with DIRK method the discretized plate problem with 80 ODEs.

We solve the advance equations corresponding to each level of the above mentioned methods on different processors (like in Table 3). If we use the Maple implicit equation solver, fsolve, as sys_solve procedure, most of the time is spent in solving stage equations. The reported execution times of problem solving sessions, provided by pvm[time] procedure, demonstrate this assumption. A concrete example is presented in Figure 2.

Table 4. Efficiency results $E_p = T_s/(pT_p)$. T_s is the sequential time reported by Maple as problem solving time using one of the above described methods; T_p is registered by PVMaple in solving same problem with same method but using p kernels on p machines

Pro-	No.	Methods			
blem	ODEs	PC	DIRK	PDIRK	PSDIRK
	eqs.	$p = s = 4, q = 1$	$p = q = 2, s = 5$	$p = 2, q = 4, s = 7$	$p = 3, q = 4$
$T(n)$	10	1%	35%	14%	10%
	20	3%	63%	29%	23%
	60	5%	88%	77%	68%
$V(n)$	5	1%	63%	28%	24%
	10	4%	92%	51%	52%
	20	8%	99%	97%	99%
$P(n)$	32	8%	96%	94%	93%

The efficiency measurements of the distributed implementation of the selected methods are presented in Table 4 and, shortly, in [13]. We conclude that small linear IVPs cannot be integrated in a distributed computational environment faster than using a sequential computer, since the distributed computation tasks are small (in time sense) relative to the communication tasks. In the case of nonlinear problems of similar dimensions, almost all computation time is spent by a Runge-Kutta type method on computing stage solutions. The time overhead introduced by distributing the computational effort to different Maple kernels is not significant when we deal with large IVPs. We cannot expect to obtain similar efficiency results when we use explicit methods, since one integration step involves only a small number of function evaluations and vector operations (see first column of Table 4). The efficiency results are similar to those reported by D-NODE [12] which is based also on Distributed Maple and PVM on a cluster of SGI Octanes (T_p's reported on such Unix stations using PVMaple and Distributed Maple are approximately identical). Comparative to the results obtained using EpODE [9], a specialized numerical software for ODEs, in our case an acceptable efficiency level can be obtained for smaller problems due to the fact that T_s and T_p are greater in the case of using a CAS. The limit on problem dimension which can be solved is unfortunately much lower. On other side, solving exactly the stage equations of a Runge-Kutta type method can lead to more accurate solution and an easier error control mechanism.

References

1. Bruder, J., Numerical results for a parallel linearly-implicit Runge-Kutta method, *Computing* **59**, 1997, 139-151.
2. Char, B. W., Progress report on a system for general-purpose parallel symbolic algebraic computation, *ISSAC '90*, ACM Press, New York, 1990, 96-103.
3. Diaz, A., Kartofen, E., FoxBox: a system for manipulating symbolic objects in black box representation, *ISSAC '98*, ACM Press, New York (1998), 30-37.
4. Franco, J. M., Gomez, I., Two three-parallel and three-processor SDIRK methods for stiff initial-value problems, *J. Comput. Appl. Math.* **87** (1997), 119-134.
5. Houwen, P. J., Parallel step-by-step methods, *Appl. Num. Math.* **11** (1993), 68-81.
6. Hutchinson, D., Khalaf, B. M. S., Parallel algorithms for solving initial value problems: front broadening and embedded parallelism, *Paral.Comp.* **17** (1991), 957-968.
7. Iserles A., Nørsett, S. P., On the theory of parallel Runge-Kutta methods, *IMA J. Num. Anal.* **10** (1990), 463-488.
8. Lioen, W. M., de Swart, J. J. B., van der Veen, W. A., Test set for IVP solvers, Report NM-R9615, CWI, 1996, available at http://www.cwi.nl/cwi/projects/IVPtest.
9. Petcu, D., Solving initial value problems with a multiprocessor code, *LNCS* **1662**, Springer (1999), 452-466.
10. Petcu, D., Drăgan, M., Designing an ODE solving environment, *LNCSE* **10**, Springer (2000), 319-338.
11. Petcu, D., PVMaple: a distributed approach to cooperative work of Maple processes, *LNCS* **1908**, Springer (2000), 216-224.
12. Petcu, D., Numerical solution of ODEs with Distributed Maple, *LNCS* **1988**, Springer (2001), 666-674.

13. Petcu, D., Experiments with PVMaple and Parallel Methods for ODEs, *Cluster 2000*, IEEE Computer Society (2000), 393-394.
14. Petcu D., Working with multiple Maple kernels connected by Distributed Maple or PVMaple, Technical Report RISC Series No. 01-18, March 2001.
15. Schreiner, W., Developing a distributed system for algebraic geometry, *EuroCM-Par'99*, Civil-Comp. Press, Edinburgh (1999), 137-146.
16. Shampine L. F., Reichelt, M. W., The Matlab ODE suite, *SIAM J. Sci. Comput.* **18**, No. 1 (1997), 1-22.
17. Siegl, K., Parallelizing algorithms for symbolic computation using ||Maple||, *4th ACM SIGPLAN*, ACM Press, San Diego (1993), 179-186.

Design of Problem-Solving Environment for Contingent Claim Valuation

F. Oliver Bunnin, Yike Guo, and John Darlington

Department of Computing, Imperial College
London, SW7 2BZ, England

Abstract. We present the design and initial implementation of a problem-solving environment that values industrial investment projects. We use the contingent claim, or real option, valuation method, which views a project as a claim to future cash flows which are dependent on underlying stochastic factors, such as the market price of a produced commodity. The problem-solving environment enables the user to use domain and mathematical level constructs to specify the nature of the project and the stochastic behaviour of underlying factors. Meaning preserving symbolic rewrite rules transform these specifications into problem representations that are suitable for numerical solution. The transformed problem representations are then combined with components implementing parallel algorithms in order to compute solutions.

The aim of this approach is to benefit strategic industrial decision-making by enabling high-level and flexible problem formulation and by using high performance computational resources.

1 Introduction

Contingent claim modelling, or the Real Option method, is the use of methods from stochastic mathematics to value contracts or investments whose value is contingent on the uncertain future state of the world. It is regarded as one of the most general and sophisticated investment valuation methods applicable to a broad class of industrial investment projects. These methods were pioneered in the financial field, for the valuation and risk management of financial derivatives, but are now becoming popular in a wide range of other industrial contexts [1,10]. Prime examples are investment decision making for oil and gas wells and for the development and testing of new medicines in the pharmaceutical industry [10].

The basic method is to model the system on which the claim is contingent as a stochastic process and then find a functional relationship between the value of the claim and the state of the underlying system throughout a given period of time. This involves the use of stochastic and partial differential equations, dynamic programming and optimal stopping theory. Suitable numerical methods to solve these problems are finite differences, lattice methods and Monte Carlo simulation [11]. There exists a vast literature on these techniques, both mathematical and numerical, yet generating an efficient method for a particular problem, on a particular architecture, remains a serious challenge, due to the computational and software complexity.

There are significant technical and practical challenges to the computer implementation of this methodology. The algorithms required for contingent modelling are computationally intensive, involving the solution of high dimensional partial differential equations and/or stochastic simulations. Efficient algorithms must be selected and implemented, on a problem by problem basis. The cost of employing expert mathematicians with first class programming skills for model implementation is very high and increases software development costs. Auditing and validation of contingent claims systems are mandatory, but notoriously difficult when programs are hand-coded and dynamically updated.

Therefore the overall objective is to facilitate rapid development of transparent and theoretically sound investment project valuation programs delivering real time results using advanced hardware, algorithms and software techniques. This is achieved by allowing users to specify models naturally and easily at the mathematical level and by using symbolic rewrite rules and component technology to automatically construct solution code.

2 Overview of Environment

In order to simplify and structure the generation of solution code from specifications we generate components representing views of the problem at different levels of abstraction: the domain level, the mathematical level and the numerical level. Such views are often used in PSEs: for example see Gallopoulos [2]. At the domain level the user specifies the project in terms of its contingent cash flows. These define the profit rate function $\Pi(t, d, X)$ which is a function of t, time, d, the decision variables of the project management, and X the random underlying factors. Components of d may be the capacity of machinery employed, whether or not to suspend production and so on. Components of X may be the market price of output or input factors, or macroeconomic variables that influence market prices.

We assume the project has a finite horizon, T. The objective of the management is then to maximise the expected profit, discounted over time, of the project over its lifetime:

$$\max_{d \in D} E[\int_0^T e^{-rs} \Pi(s, d, X) ds] \tag{1}$$

where D is the space of allowable decisions, r is an appropriate continuously compounded interest rate and expectation is taken using a risk-neutral probability measure. Alternative utility based formulations are possible when the cash flows of the project cannot be replicated by trading in market instruments, i.e. when the market is incomplete (see Henderson and Hobson [3]). This is a stochastic control problem, and its relation to the non-linear Hamilton-Jacobi-Bellman PDE is discussed in Oksendal [9]. The mathematical treatment of various formulations of contingent claim problems are discussed in Lund and Oksendal [8].

We construct a C++ component to represent the project, which has as its data members the specified decision variables d, the random underlying factors X and as a member function the profit function Π. Note that at this point we have not yet defined the stochastic behaviour of X. This is because often the user may wish to try out various different stochastic models, and over time may change his or her view of which model is most appropriate. The domain level C++ component is independent of model, and thus need not change when the model or its numerical implementation changes.

A stochastic model for X is specified using stochastic differential equations (SDEs). For this we have defined notation in Mathematica. Once the SDE is represented in this way we can apply symbolic transformations that we have written in Mathematica. The symbolic transformations encode results from stochastic analysis, such as the Ito formula and Girsanov's theorem [9], and results from contingent claim modelling theory. Thus we automatically formulate the stochastic control problem defined in equation (1) with the project defined profit function and model defined SDEs substituted appropriately. A second set of symbolic rewrite rules are used to approximate the problem for numerical solution. For example the continuous time SDEs may be discretised in order to be used in a Monte Carlo simulation.

The symbolic transformations applied to the SDE model result in a C++ model component. This is combined with the C++ project component and with predefined parallel algorithm components to form a computational component solving the specific problem. The algorithm components are designed to abstract common patterns of parallel behaviour in stochastic modelling, such as time stepping over a distributed spatial grid, updating discretely sampled variables across processors, combining results from independent paths of a stochastic variable calculated on separate processors. As such they support a wide class of algorithms when combined with sequential algorithms, such as linear system solvers and random number generators. This facilitates the rapid construction of new algorithms, such as the Pseudospectral method, by re-using existing components. The code formed by composing algorithm components and solvers is re-usable in other applications. Note that the re-use of financial algorithmic code is widespread in practise: perhaps the best example is the use of sophisticated methods for constructing discount factor curves from liquid traded instruments, which are used in almost every derivative valuation.

3 Conclusion

Contingent claim valuation is an important commercial area that presents computationally intensive and mathematically interesting problems. It is an area that is eminently suitable for a problem-solving environment which generates software that utilises high performance computers and allows end-users to compute solutions from high level specifications. Related work by Kant et al. [6,7] and Pantazopoulos and Houstis [5] has concentrated on financial contingent claims and finite difference methods. We build on such research, focussing on the more general and more complicated area of industrial project valuation, and utilising a wider range of solution techniques. This paper presents an overview of our design and initial implementation and indicates the direction of further research.

We have implemented a set of symbolic transformations and using these have constructed several stochastic model components. Components for parallel simulation and sequential finite difference and pseudospectral algorithms have also been built. We have demonstrated the effectiveness of the design through the construction of computational components for exotic financial contingent claims and are presently working on extension to more complex industrial project valuation problems. For more material on this research please see http://www.doc.ic.ac.uk/~fob1/project.html.

Acknowledgments

This work is supported by the EPSRC grant GR N14675.

References

1. Dixit, Avinash K., and Robert S. Pindyck, Investment under Uncertainty. Princeton University Press, 1994
2. Gallopoulos E., E. Houstis, J. Rice, Computer as Thinker/Doer: Problem-Solving Environments for Computational Science, IEEE Computational Science and Engineering vol. 1 no. 2 (1994)
3. Henderson, V. and Hobson, D. Real Options with Constant Relative Risk Aversion, preprint, University of Warwick
4. Hughston, Lane P., Zervos, Mihail, Martingale Approach to Real Options, preprint King's College London 2000
5. Pantazopoulos K. N., Houstis E. N., Modern software techniques in computational finance, in Modern Software Tools for Scientific Computing, Birkhauser, 1997
6. Kant E., Synthesis of Mathematical Modelling Software, IEEE Software 1993
7. Kant E., C. Randall, A. Chhabra, Using Program Synthesis to Price Derivatives, Journal of Computational Finance vol. 1 no. 2 (Winter 1997/98) 97-129
8. Lund D. and Oksendal B. (eds), Stochastic models and option values : applications to resources, environment and investment problems (Amsterdam ; Oxford : North-Holland, 1991)
9. Oksendal B., Stochastic Differential Equations, (Springer, 1998)
10. Trigeorgis L., Real Options: Managerial Flexibility and Strategy in Resource Allocation, MIT Press 1996
11. Wilmott, P., Dewynne, J., Howison, S., Option Pricing. Mathematical Models and Computation, Oxford Financial Press 1993

Author Index

Abbadi, Amr El 889
Adda, Mahamed 452
Agrawal, Divyakant 889
Ahmad, Ishfaq 154
Alcover, Rosa 621
Allen, Gabrielle 817
Allsopp, Nicholas K. 380
Almeida, Francisco 117
Alvisi, Lorenzo 864
Aridor, Yariv 722
Arita, Itsujiro 428
Arlia, Domenica 326
Assarsson, Ulf 663
Ayguadé, Eduard 385

Baden, Scott B. 491
Bahi, Jacques M. 175
Baker, Mark 132, 702
Balaton, Zoltán 874
Bange, Martin 142
Barli, Niko Demus 413
Beckett, Duan H. 578
Beivide, Ramón 611, 793
Benger, Werner 817
Bernabéu-Aubán, José M. 773
Bhatia, Karan 864
Bhattacharyya, Shuvra S. 697
Bilardi, Gianfranco 332
Bisseling, Rob 566
Błażewicz, J. 191
Boeres, Cristina 156
Boncz, Peter 6
Booth, Stephen 80
Bosa, Karoly 712
Bosschere, Koen De 494
Boukerche, Azzedine 301
Boulenouar, Benamar Sidi 560
Bramley, Randall 358
Brand, Per 486
Brezany, Peter 887

Broberg, Magnus 57
Brooke, John 198, 702
Brunie, Lionel 278
Brunst, Holger 148
Bulić, Patricio 448
Bull, Mark 84
Bunnin, F. Oliver 935
Buyya, Rajkumar 702

Cao, Junwei 882
Cardinale, Yudith 75
Casado, Rafael 630
Casanova, Henri 154
Catthoor, Francky 651
Cengiz, İlker 321
César, Eduardo 36
Chakravarty, Manuel M. T. 524
Chandra, Punit 352
Chandra, Sumir 171
Chavarría-Miranda, Daniel 241
Chen, Ying 764
Cheng, Sheung Hun 568
Chetlur, Malolan 466
Cheung, Lap-Sun 183
Cheung, W. L. 371
Chiola, Giovanni 457
Chirivella, Vicente 621
Christiaens, Mark 494
Chu, Yul 394
Clauss, Philippe 262
Clint, Maurice 549
Coppola, Massimo 326
Cortes, Toni 887
Costen, Fumie 198
Cotofana, Sorin 651
Cox, Simon J. 578
Cunha, Gerson N. da 156

Dahl, Jörgen 466
Dahlgren, Fredrik 385
Daniell, Geoffrey J. 578

Author Index

Darlington, John 540, 855, 935
David, Pierre 717
Debray, Saumya 221
Denis, Alexandre 835
DeRose, Luiz A. 122
Dongarra, Jack 33
Drach-Temam, Nathalie 439
Dramlitsch, Thomas 817
Druschel, Peter 457
Duato, José 621, 901
Duff, Iain S. 566

Eisenbeis, Christine 385
El-Mahdy, Ahmed 687
Engelen, Robert van 235
Engquist, Erik 918
Ercan, M.F. 371
Ertl, M. Anton 403
Erwin, Dietmar W. 825
Espasa, Roger 221, 385
Ezhilchelvan, Paul 482

Faber, Peter 230
Factor, Michael 722
Farrell, Paul A. 132
Feldmann, Rainer 332
Ferhatosmanoglu, Hakan 889
Fernández, Lorenzo 630
Fernández, Manel 221
Fink, Stephen 273
Folliot, Bertil 457
Fong, Jun 801
Ford, Rupert 154
Foster, Ian 1, 807
Frankenfeld, U. 375
Fung, Y. F. 371
Furmento, Nathalie 540, 855

Gabarró, Joaquim 549
Gaber, Jaafar 175
Galdámez, Pablo 773
Gallivan, Kyle 254
Gallopoulos, Efstratios 916
Gannon, Dennis 5

Gao, Guang R. 385
García, José M. 630, 845
Garg, Nivea 310
Gautama, Hasyim 106
Gemund, Arjan J. C. van 106
Generowicz, Jasek 578
Gengler, Marc 504
Gerndt, Michael 34
Geusebroek, Jan-Mark 653
Ghose, Kanad 86
Giné, Francesc 732
Gómez, Antonio 845
Gomis, Óscar 773
González, Daniel 117
González, Jesús A. 96
Goodale, Tom 817
Goodman, Joy 535
Gorlatch, Sergei 491
Gradinariu, Maria 458
Grahn, Håkan 57
Gregg, David 403
Gregorio, Jose Angel 793
Griebl, Martin 230
Guo, Yike 935
Gupta, Manish 204
Gupta, Rajiv 418
Guralnik, Valerie 310
Guštin, Veselko 448
Gürsoy, Attila 321

Hague, John F. 380
Hameurlain, Abdelkader 278
Han, Zongfen 764
Hansen, Jørgen S. 704
Haridi, Seif 486
Hawick, Ken 702, 916
He, Ligang 764
Hege, Hans-Christian 817
Heiss, Hans-Ulrich 783
Hélary, Jean-Michel 482
Helstrup, H. 375
Herley, Kieran 332
Hernández, Emilio 75
Hernández, Porfidio 732
Heymann, Elisa 742

Hiett, Ben P. 578
Higham, Nicholas J. 568
Ho, T.K. 371
Holmgren, Sverker 602
Hoppe, Hans-Christian 148

Iamnitchi, Adriana 807
Ibañez, Andres 793
Ilroy, Jonathan 911
Ito, M. R. 394
Iwama, Chitaka 413
Izu, Cruz 611

Jesshope, Chris 611
Jimack, Peter K. 592
Jin, Hai 764
Johnen, Colette 458
Jul, Eric 704
Juurlink, Ben 678

Kacsuk, Péter 874
Kalantar, Michael 801
Karypis, George 310
Keller, Gabriele 524
Keller, Jörg 333
Kelly, Paul H. J. 491
Kerbyson, Darren J. 882
Kermarrec, Anne-Marie ... 457, 752
Kersten, Martin 6
Kianzad, Vida 697
Kisuki, Toru 254
Klintskog, Erik 486
Knijnenburg, Peter M. W. 254
Knoop, Jens 204
Koelma, Dennis 653
Kosch, Harald 278
Kshemkalyani, Ajay 352
Kusper, Gabor 712
Kutil, Rade 674
Kwok, Yu-Kwong 183

Laforenza, Domenico 916
Lanfermann, Gerd 817
Larriba-Pey, Josep L. 386

León, Coromoto 96
Lechtchinsky, Roman 524
Lengauer, Christian 230
Liang, Y. 587
Liebrich, Alex 62
Lien, J. 375
Lin, Calvin 491
Lindenstruth, V. 375
Livny, Miron 742
Lodha, Sandeep 352
Loechner, Vincent 262
Loucif, Samia 613
Löwe, Welf 62
Lundberg, Lars 57
Luque, Emilio 36, 732, 742

Machowiak, M. 191
Mackenzie, L. M. 639
Maggs, Bruce 332
Malony, Allen D. 84
Manegold, Stefan 6
Margalef, Tomàs 36, 84
Martel, Matthieu 504
Märtens, Holger 291
Marzullo, Keith 864
Mayer, Anthony 540
McGough, Stephen 540
Meister, Benoît 262
Mellor-Crummey, John 241
Merzky, André 817
Meyer, Ulrich 343
Mohr, Bernd 84
Molero, Xavier 901
Morajko, Anna 36
Moreno, Luz Marina 117
Morin, Christine 752
Mounié, G. 191
Muller, Henk 385
Muñoz-Escoí, Francesc D. 773
Mueller, Frank 207
Muralidhar, Rajeev 67
Muraoka, Yoichi 358

Nabrzyski, Jarek 805
Nadeem, Sarfraz A. 592

Nagel, Wolfgang E. 148
Neiderud, Anna 486
Nes, Niels 6
Newhouse, Steven 540, 855
Niar, Smaïl 452
Nicole, Denis A. 887
Nikolopoulos, Dimitrios S. 514
Nudd, Graham R. 882

O'Boyle, Michael F. P. 204
O'Donnell, John 535
Ong, Hong 132
Önder, Soner 418
Ould-Khaoua, Mohamed .. 613, 639

Papatheodorou, Theodore S. ... 514
Parashar, Manish 67, 171
Paton, Norman W. 280
Pérez, Christian 835
Petcu, Dana 926
Pfannenstiel, Wolf 524
Philippe, Bernard J. 566
Piccoli, Fabiana 96
Pietracaprina, Andrea 645
Pingali, Keshav K. 204
Podhorszki, Norbert 874
Ponomarev, Dmitry 86
Printista, Marcela 96
Priol, Thierry 835
Prost, Jean-Pierre 380
Pucci, Geppino 645
Puente, Valentin 793

Qasem, Apan 235

Radke, Thomas 817
Ramirez, Alex 386
Rana, Omer F. 805
Randriamaro, Cyrille 911
Rawat, Mayank 352
Raynal, Michel 482
Rebello, Vinod E. F. 156
Reinefeld, Alexander 805
Renault, Eric 717

Riley, Graham D. 84
Ripeanu, Matei 807
Robert, Yves 154
Robles, Antonio 611
Roda, José L. 96
Rodríguez, Casiano 96, 117
Röhrich, D. 375
Rose, César A. F. De 783

Sakai, Shuichi 413
Sakellariou, Rizos 385
Saksonov, Eugeny 86
Sampaio, Pedro R. Falcone 278
Sampaio, Sandra de F. Mendes 280
Sande, Francisco de 96
Santonja, Vicente 901
Sarang, Trushar 241
Sarkar, Vivek 273
Sato, Toshinori 428
Schimmler, Manfred 360
Schmidt, Bertil 360
Schreiner, Wolfgang 712
Schröder, Heiko 360
Schulz, M. 375
Scott, Stephen L 132
Sebot, Julien 439
Seidel, Edward 817
Seinstra, Frank 653
Senar, Miquel A. 742
Serna, Maria J. 549
Sevilla, Diego 845
Seznec, André 385
Shahrabi, A. 639
Sibeyn, Jop F. 333
Silla, Federico 901
Sinnen, Oliver 166
Skaali, B. 375
Smith, Jim 280
Snelling, David F. 358, 825
Solsona, Francesc 732
Sorribes, Joan 36
Sousa, Leonel 166
Steinbeck, T. 375
Stenström, Per 663
Sterling, Thomas 16

Stewart, Alan 549
Strey, Alfred 142
Szularz, M. 587

Tanaka, Hidehiko 413
Taylor, David J. 46
Tcheressiz, Dmitri 678
Teperman, Avi 722
Thomas, Ken S. 578
Torres-Rojas, Francisco J. 476
Trystram, D. 191
Tuck, Terry 301

Ullaland, K. 375
Unger, Sebastian 207
Utard, Gil 911

Vajda, Ferenc 874
Valero, Mateo 386, 651

Vassiliadis, Stamatis 651, 678
van der Vorst, Henk A. 566
Venetis, Ioannis E. 514
Vestbø, A. 375

Walker, David W. 805, 916
Wallin, Dan 602
Ward, Paul A.S. 46
Watson, Ian 687
Watson, Paul 280
Weston, J. 587
Whalley, David 235
Wiebalck, A. 375, 678
Wijshoff, Harry 358, 678
Wilsey, Philip A. 466
Winslett, Marianne 887

Yuan, Xin 235

Lecture Notes in Computer Science

For information about Vols. 1–2048
please contact your bookseller or Springer-Verlag

Vol. 1982: S. Näher, D. Wagner (Eds.), Algorithm Engineering. Proceedings, 2000. VIII, 243 pages. 2001.

Vol. 1996: P.L. Lanzi, W. Stolzmann, S.W. Wilson (Eds.), Advances in Learning Classifier Systems. Proceedings, 2000. VIII, 273 pages. 2001. (Subseries LNAI).

Vol. 2049: G. Paliouras, V. Karkaletsis, C.D. Spyropoulos (Eds.), Machine Learning and Its Applications. VIII, 325 pages. 2001. (Subseries LNAI).

Vol. 2060: T. Böhme, H. Unger (Eds.), Innovative Internet Computing Systems. Proceedings, 2001. VIII, 183 pages. 2001.

Vol. 2062: A. Nareyek, Constraint-Based Agents. XIV, 178 pages. 2001. (Subseries LNAI).

Vol. 2064: J. Blanck, V. Brattka, P. Hertling (Eds.), Computability and Complexity in Analysis. Proceedings, 2000. VIII, 395 pages. 2001.

Vol. 2065: H. Balster, B. de Brock, S. Conrad (Eds.), Database Schema Evolution and Meta-Modeling. Proceedings, 2000. X, 245 pages. 2001.

Vol. 2066: O. Gascuel, M.-F. Sagot (Eds.), Computational Biology. Proceedings, 2000. X, 165 pages. 2001.

Vol. 2068: K.R. Dittrich, A. Geppert, M.C. Norrie (Eds.), Advanced Information Systems Engineering. Proceedings, 2001. XII, 484 pages. 2001.

Vol. 2069: C. Peters (Ed.), Cross-Language Information Retrieval and Evaluation. Proceedings, 2000. IX, 389 pages. 2001.

Vol. 2070: L. Monostori, J. Váncza, M. Ali (Eds.), Engineering of Intelligent Systems. Proceedings, 2001. XVIII, 951 pages. 2001. (Subseries LNAI).

Vol. 2071: R. Harper (Ed.), Types in Compilation. Proceedings, 2000. IX, 207 pages. 2001.

Vol. 2072: J. Lindskov Knudsen (Ed.), ECOOP 2001 – Object-Oriented Programming. Proceedings, 2001. XIII, 429 pages. 2001.

Vol. 2073: V.N. Alexandrov, J.J. Dongarra, B.A. Juliano, R.S. Renner, C.J.K. Tan (Eds.), Computational Science – ICCS 2001. Part I. Proceedings, 2001. XXVIII, 1306 pages. 2001.

Vol. 2074: V.N. Alexandrov, J.J. Dongarra, B.A. Juliano, R.S. Renner, C.J.K. Tan (Eds.), Computational Science – ICCS 2001. Part II. Proceedings, 2001. XXVIII, 1076 pages. 2001.

Vol. 2075: J.-M. Colom, M. Koutny (Eds.), Applications and Theory of Petri Nets 2001. Proceedings, 2001. XII, 403 pages. 2001.

Vol. 2076: F. Orejas, P.G. Spirakis, J. van Leeuwen (Eds.), Automata, Languages and Programming. Proceedings, 2001. XIV, 1083 pages. 2001.

Vol. 2077: V. Ambriola (Ed.), Software Process Technology. Proceedings, 2001. VIII, 247 pages. 2001.

Vol. 2078: R. Reed, J. Reed (Eds.), SDL 2001: Meeting UML. Proceedings, 2001. XI, 439 pages. 2001.

Vol. 2079: E. Burke, W. Erben (Eds.), Practice and Theory of Automated Timetabling III. Proceedings, 2001. XII, 359 pages. 2001.

Vol. 2080: D.W. Aha, I. Watson (Eds.), Case-Based Reasoning Research and Development. Proceedings, 2001. XII, 758 pages. 2001. (Subseries LNAI).

Vol. 2081: K. Aardal, B. Gerards (Eds.), Integer Programming and Combinatorial Optimization. Proceedings, 2001. XI, 423 pages. 2001.

Vol. 2082: M.F. Insana, R.M. Leahy (Eds.), Information Processing in Medical Imaging. Proceedings, 2001. XVI, 537 pages. 2001.

Vol. 2083: R. Goré, A. Leitsch, T. Nipkow (Eds.), Automated Reasoning. Proceedings, 2001. XV, 708 pages. 2001. (Subseries LNAI).

Vol. 2084: J. Mira, A. Prieto (Eds.), Connectionist Models of Neurons, Learning Processes, and Artificial Intelligence. Proceedings, 2001. Part I. XXVII, 836 pages. 2001.

Vol. 2085: J. Mira, A. Prieto (Eds.), Bio-Inspired Applications of Connectionism. Proceedings, 2001. Part II. XXVII, 848 pages. 2001.

Vol. 2086: M. Luck, V. Mařík, O. Stěpánková, R. Trappl (Eds.), Multi-Agent Systems and Applications. Proceedings, 2001. X, 437 pages. 2001. (Subseries LNAI).

Vol. 2087: G. Kern-Isberner, Conditionals in Nonmonotonic Reasoning and Belief Revision. X, 190 pages. 2001. (Subseries LNAI).

Vol. 2088: S. Yu, A. Păun (Eds.), Implementation and Application of Automata. Proceedings, 2000. XI, 343 pages. 2001.

Vol. 2089: A. Amir, G.M. Landau (Eds.), Combinatorial Pattern Matching. Proceedings, 2001. VIII, 273 pages. 2001.

Vol. 2090: E. Brinksma, H. Hermanns, J.-P. Katoen (Eds.), Lectures on Formal Methods and Performance Analysis. Proceedings, 2000. VII, 431 pages. 2001.

Vol. 2091: J. Bigun, F. Smeraldi (Eds.), Audio- and Video-Based Biometric Person Authentication. Proceedings, 2001. XIII, 374 pages. 2001.

Vol. 2092: L. Wolf, D. Hutchison, R. Steinmetz (Eds.), Quality of Service – IWQoS 2001. Proceedings, 2001. XII, 435 pages. 2001.

Vol. 2093: P. Lorenz (Ed.), Networking – ICN 2001. Proceedings, 2001. Part I. XXV, 843 pages. 2001.

Vol. 2094: P. Lorenz (Ed.), Networking – ICN 2001. Proceedings, 2001. Part II. XXV, 899 pages. 2001.

Vol. 2095: B. Schiele, G. Sagerer (Eds.), Computer Vision Systems. Proceedings, 2001. X, 313 pages. 2001.

Vol. 2096: J. Kittler, F. Roli (Eds.), Multiple Classifier Systems. Proceedings, 2001. XII, 456 pages. 2001.

Vol. 2097: B. Read (Ed.), Advances in Databases. Proceedings, 2001. X, 219 pages. 2001.

Vol. 2098: J. Akiyama, M. Kano, M. Urabe (Eds.), Discrete and Computational Geometry. Proceedings, 2000. XI, 381 pages. 2001.

Vol. 2099: P. de Groote, G. Morrill, C. Retoré (Eds.), Logical Aspects of Computational Linguistics. Proceedings, 2001. VIII, 311 pages. 2001. (Subseries LNAI).

Vol. 2100: R. Küsters, Non-Standard Inferences in Description Logocs. X, 250 pages. 2001. (Subseries LNAI).

Vol. 2101: S. Quaglini, P. Barahona, S. Andreassen (Eds.), Artificial Intelligence in Medicine. Proceedings, 2001. XIV, 469 pages. 2001. (Subseries LNAI).

Vol. 2102: G. Berry, H. Comon, A. Finkel (Eds.), Computer-Aided Verification. Proceedings, 2001. XIII, 520 pages. 2001.

Vol. 2103: M. Hannebauer, J. Wendler, E. Pagello (Eds.), Balancing Reactivity and Social Deliberation in Multi-Agent Systems. VIII, 237 pages. 2001. (Subseries LNAI).

Vol. 2104: R. Eigenmann, M.J. Voss (Eds.), OpenMP Shared Memory Parallel Programming. Proceedings, 2001. X, 185 pages. 2001.

Vol. 2105: W. Kim, T.-W. Ling, Y-J. Lee, S.-S. Park (Eds.), The Human Society and the Internet. Proceedings, 2001. XVI, 470 pages. 2001.

Vol. 2106: M. Kerckhove (Ed.), Scale-Space and Morphology in Computer Vision. Proceedings, 2001. XI, 435 pages. 2001.

Vol. 2107: F.T. Chong, C. Kozyrakis, M. Oskin (Eds.), Intelligent Memory Systems. Proceedings, 2000. VIII, 193 pages. 2001.

Vol. 2108: J. Wang (Ed.), Computing and Combinatorics. Proceedings, 2001. XIII, 602 pages. 2001.

Vol. 2109: M. Bauer, P.J. Gymtrasiewicz, J. Vassileva (Eds.), User Modelind 2001. Proceedings, 2001. XIII, 318 pages. 2001. (Subseries LNAI).

Vol. 2110: B. Hertzberger, A. Hoekstra, R. Williams (Eds.), High-Performance Computing and Networking. Proceedings, 2001. XVII, 733 pages. 2001.

Vol. 2111: D. Helmbold, B. Williamson (Eds.), Computational Learning Theory. Proceedings, 2001. IX, 631 pages. 2001. (Subseries LNAI).

Vol. 2116: V. Akman, P. Bouquet, R. Thomason, R.A. Young (Eds.), Modeling and Using Context. Proceedings, 2001. XII, 472 pages. 2001. (Subseries LNAI).

Vol. 2117: M. Beynon, C.L. Nehaniv, K. Dautenhahn (Eds.), Cognitive Technology: Instruments of Mind. Proceedings, 2001. XV, 522 pages. 2001. (Subseries LNAI).

Vol. 2118: X.S. Wang, G. Yu, H. Lu (Eds.), Advances in Web-Age Information Management. Proceedings, 2001. XV, 418 pages. 2001.

Vol. 2119: V. Varadharajan, Y. Mu (Eds.), Information Security and Privacy. Proceedings, 2001. XI, 522 pages. 2001.

Vol. 2120: H.S. Delugach, G. Stumme (Eds.), Conceptual Structures: Broadening the Base. Proceedings, 2001. X, 377 pages. 2001. (Subseries LNAI).

Vol. 2121: C.S. Jensen, M. Schneider, B. Seeger, V.J. Tsotras (Eds.), Advances in Spatial and Temporal Databases. Proceedings, 2001. XI, 543 pages. 2001.

Vol. 2123: P. Perner (Ed.), Machine Learning and Data Mining in Pattern Recognition. Proceedings, 2001. XI, 363 pages. 2001. (Subseries LNAI).

Vol. 2124: W. Skarbek (Ed.), Computer Analysis of Images and Patterns. Proceedings, 2001. XV, 743 pages. 2001.

Vol. 2125: F. Dehne, J.-R. Sack, R. Tamassia (Eds.), Algorithms and Data Structures. Proceedings, 2001. XII, 484 pages. 2001.

Vol. 2126: P. Cousot (Ed.), Static Analysis. Proceedings, 2001. XI, 439 pages. 2001.

Vol. 2129: M. Goemans, K. Jansen, J.D.P. Rolim, L. Trevisan (Eds.), Approximation, Randomization, and Combinatorial Optimization. Proceedings, 2001. IX, 297 pages. 2001.

Vol. 2130: G. Dorffner, H. Bischof, K. Hornik (Eds.), Artificial Neural Networks – ICANN 2001. Proceedings, 2001. XXII, 1259 pages. 2001.

Vol. 2132: S.-T. Yuan, M. Yokoo (Eds.), Intelligent Agents. Specification. Modeling, and Application. Proceedings, 2001. X, 237 pages. 2001. (Subseries LNAI).

Vol. 2136: J. Sgall, A. Pultr, P. Kolman (Eds.), Mathematical Foundations of Computer Science 2001. Proceedings, 2001. XII, 716 pages. 2001.

Vol. 2138: R. Freivalds (Ed.), Fundamentals of Computation Theory. Proceedings, 2001. XIII, 542 pages. 2001.

Vol. 2139: J. Kilian (Ed.), Advances in Cryptology – CRYPTO 2001. Proceedings, 2001. XI, 599 pages. 2001.

Vol. 2141: G.S. Brodal, D. Frigioni, A. Marchetti-Spaccamela (Eds.), Algorithm Engineering. Proceedings, 2001. X, 199 pages. 2001.

Vol. 2143: S. Benferhat, P. Besnard (Eds.), Symbolic and Quantitative Approaches to Reasoning with Uncertainty. Proceedings, 2001. XIV, 818 pages. 2001. (Subseries LNAI).

Vol. 2146: J.H. Silverman (Eds.), Cryptography and Lattices. Proceedings, 2001. VII, 219 pages. 2001.

Vol. 2147: G. Brebner, R. Woods (Eds.), Field-Programmable Logic and Applications. Proceedings, 2001. XV, 665 pages. 2001.

Vol. 2149: O. Gascuel, B.M.E. Moret (Eds.), Algorithms in Bioinformatics. Proceedings, 2001. X, 307 pages. 2001.

Vol. 2150: R. Sakellariou, J. Keane, J. Gurd, L. Freeman (Eds.), Euro-Par 2001 Parallel Processing. Proceedings, 2001. XXX, 943 pages. 2001.

Vol. 2154: K.G. Larsen, M. Nielsen (Eds.), CONCUR 2001 – Concurrency Theory. Proceedings, 2001. XI, 583 pages. 2001.

Vol. 2161: F. Meyer auf der Heide (Ed.), Algorithms – ESA 2001. Proceedings, 2001. XII, 538 pages. 2001.

Vol. 2164: S. Pierre, R. Glitho (Eds.), Mobile Agents for Telecommunication Applications. Proceedings, 2001. XI, 292 pages. 2001.